# MIDDLE EAST CONFLICTS FROM ANCIENT EGYPT TO THE 21ST CENTURY

# MIDDLE EAST CONFLICTS FROM ANCIENT EGYPT TO THE 21ST CENTURY

An Encyclopedia and Document Collection

VOLUME 3: O–Z

Dr. Spencer C. Tucker

Editor

ABC-CLIO®

An Imprint of ABC-CLIO, LLC
Santa Barbara, California • Denver, Colorado

Copyright © 2019 by ABC-CLIO, LLC

All rights reserved. No part of this publication may be reproduced, stored in a retrieval system, or transmitted, in any form or by any means, electronic, mechanical, photocopying, recording, or otherwise, except for the inclusion of brief quotations in a review, without prior permission in writing from the publisher.

Every reasonable effort has been made to trace the owners of copyright materials in this book, but in some instances this has proven impossible. The editors and publishers will be glad to receive information leading to more complete acknowledgments in subsequent printings of the book and in the meantime extend their apologies for any omissions.

**Library of Congress Cataloging-in-Publication Data**

Names: Tucker, Spencer, 1937– editor.
Title: Middle East conflicts from Ancient Egypt to the 21st century : an encyclopedia and document collection / Spencer C. Tucker, Editor.
Description: Santa Barbara, CA : ABC-CLIO, [2019] | Includes bibliographical references and index. |
Identifiers: LCCN 2019020655 (print) | LCCN 2019021604 (ebook) | ISBN 9781440853531 (ebook) | ISBN 9781440853524 (set : alk. paper)
 | ISBN 9781440853548 (volume 1 : alk. paper) | ISBN 9781440853555 (volume 2 : alk. paper) | ISBN 9781440853562 (volume 3 : alk. paper) | ISBN 9781440853579 (volume 4 : alk. paper)
Subjects: LCSH: Middle East—History, Military. | Arab countries—History, Military. | Middle East—History, Military—Encyclopedias. | Arab countries—History, Military—Encyclopedias.
Classification: LCC DS63.15 (ebook) | LCC DS63.15 .M53 2019 (print) | DDC 355.020956/03—dc23
LC record available at https://lccn.loc.gov/2019020655

ISBN: 978-1-4408-5352-4 (set)
 978-1-4408-5354-8 (vol. 1)
 978-1-4408-5355-5 (vol. 2)
 978-1-4408-5356-2 (vol. 3)
 978-1-4408-5357-9 (vol. 4)
 978-1-4408-5353-1 (ebook)

23 22 21 20 19    1 2 3 4 5

This book is also available as an eBook.

ABC-CLIO
An Imprint of ABC-CLIO, LLC

ABC-CLIO, LLC
147 Castilian Drive
Santa Barbara, California 93117
www.abc-clio.com

This book is printed on acid-free paper ∞
Manufactured in the United States of America

*To Laurent Boetsch:*
*Gentleman scholar, linguist, university president,*
*leader in international education, and esteemed friend.*

# About the Editors

**Spencer C. Tucker**, PhD, has been senior fellow in military history at ABC-CLIO since 2003. He is the author or editor of 66 books and encyclopedias, many of which have won prestigious awards. Tucker's last academic position before his retirement from teaching was the John Biggs Chair in Military History at the Virginia Military Institute. He has been a Fulbright scholar, a visiting research associate at the Smithsonian Institution, and, as a U.S. Army captain, an intelligence analyst in the Pentagon. His recently published works include *World War I: The Definitive Encyclopedia and Document Collection, Wars That Changed History: 50 of the World's Greatest Conflicts,* and *Enduring Controversies in Military History: Critical Analyses and Context,* all published by ABC-CLIO.

**Priscilla Roberts**, PhD, is an associate professor of business at the City University of Macau and codirector of the university's Asia-Pacific Business Research Centre. With Spencer C. Tucker and others, she has coedited and contributed the documents volumes to 11 ABC-CLIO encyclopedias on the Korean War, World War I, World War II, the Cold War, the Arab-Israeli conflict, and Middle East wars. Roberts is the editor of *Cuban Missile Crisis: The Essential Reference Guide, World War II: The Essential Reference Guide, Voices of World War II: Contemporary Accounts of Daily Life, Arab-Israeli Conflict: The Essential Reference Guide, Arab-Israeli Conflict: A Documentary and Reference Guide,* and *The Cold War: Interpreting Conflict through Primary Documents.* In addition, she is the author of numerous other books and articles in international history. Roberts spent 2003 at George Washington University as a Fulbright scholar and has received numerous other academic awards for research in the United States, Great Britain, Australia, Canada, Hong Kong, and Macao. She earned her PhD at King's College, Cambridge, England, and specializes in 20th-century diplomatic and international history.

# Contents

### Volume 1: A–F
List of Entries   ix
List of Maps   xxiii
Preface   xxv
Introduction   xxvii
General Maps   xxxv
Entries   1

### Volume II: G–N
List of Entries   ix
List of Maps   xxiii
General Maps   xxv
Entries   441

### Volume III: O–Z
List of Entries   ix
List of Maps   xxiii
General Maps   xxv
Entries   901
Chronology   1383
Glossary   1389
Selective Bibliography   1391
Editors and Contributors   1397

### Volume IV: Documents
List of Documents   ix
Documents   1405
Index   1775

# List of Entries

Abadi, Haider al- (1952–)
Abbas, Abu (1948–2004)
Abbas, Mahmoud (1935–)
Abbasid Caliphate (750–1258, 1261–1517)
Abbasid Revolution (747–751)
Abbas Mirza (1789–1833)
Abbas I the Great (1571–1629)
Abd Allah ibn al-Zubair (624–692)
Abdel-Rahman, Omar (1938–2017)
Abdulhamid II (1842–1918)
Abdullah I (1882–1951)
Abdullah II (1962–)
Abizaid, John Philip (1951–)
Aboukir, First Battle of (July 25, 1799)
Aboukir, Second Battle of (March 8, 1801)
Aboukir Bay, Battle of (August 1, 1798)
Abu Abbas (1948–2004)
Abu Ghraib
Abulustayn, Battle of (April 15, 1277)
Abu Muslim Khorasani (718?–755)
Abu Nidal (1937–2002)
Achaemenid Empire (550–330 BCE)
Acre, Battle of (November 3, 1840)
Acre, 1189 Siege of (August 28, 1189–July 12, 1191)
Acre, 1291 Siege of (April 6–May 28, 1291)
Acre, 1799 Siege of (March 17–May 20, 1799)
Actium, Battle of (September 2, 31 BCE)
Adan, Avraham "Bren" (1926–2012)

Adana Massacre (April 1909)
Aden Emergency (1963–1967)
Adrianople, Battle of (August 9, 378)
Adrianople, Crusades Battle of (April 14–15, 1205)
Adrianople, 1444 Treaty of (June 12, 1444)
Adrianople, 1713 Treaty of (June 24, 1713)
Adrianople, 1829 Treaty of (September 14, 1829)
Aegospotami, Battle of (405 BCE)
Ager Sanguinis, Battle of (June 28, 1119)
Agha Muhammad Khan Qajar (1742–1797)
Agranat Commission (November 18, 1973–January 30, 1975)
Ajnadain, Battle of (July 30? 634)
Akkad
Akroinon, Battle of (740)
Al-Adil (1145–1218)
Al-Afdal (?–1122)
Alam el Halfa, Battle of (August 31–September 7, 1942)
Al-Amin, Muhammad (787–813)
Al-Anfal Campaign (1987–1988)
al-Aqsa Martyrs Brigades
Al-Aqsa Mosque Massacre (October 8, 1990)
al-Atrash, Sultan (1891–1982)
Alawites
Aleppo, Battle for (July 19, 2012–December 22, 2016)
Alexander I Balas (ca. 173–145 BCE)
Alexander III the Great (356–323 BCE)
Alexander III's Invasion of the Persian Empire (334–323 BCE)

Alexander Severus, Roman Emperor (ca. 208–235)
Alexandria, Bombardment of (July 11, 1882)
Alexandria, Sack of (October 9–12. 1365)
Alexandropol, Treaty of (December 2, 1920)
Alexios I Komnenos (1048–1118)
Alexios III Angelos (ca. 1153–1211)
Alexios V Doukas Mourtzouphlos (1140–1204)
Algiers Agreement (March 6, 1975)
Algiers Declaration (November 15, 1988)
Ali, Ahmad Ismail (1917–1974)
Ali Bey al-Kabir (1728–1773)
Ali ibn Abi Talib (ca. 600–661)
Aliya Bet
Allawi, Ayad (1944–)
Allenby, Sir Edmund Henry Hynman (1861–1936)
Allon, Yigal (1918–1980)
Allon Plan (July 26, 1967)
Al-Mamun, Abd Allah (786–833)
Al-Nusra Front
Alp Arslan (ca. 1030–1072)
Al Qaeda
Al Qaeda in Iraq
Al Qaeda in the Arabian Peninsula
Al-Sabah, Jaber al-Ahmad (1926–2006)
al-Sannabra, Battle of (June 28, 1113)
*Altalena* Incident (June 23, 1948)
Amalric of Jerusalem (1136–1174)
Amara, Battle of (June 3, 1915)
Amasya, Treaty of (May 29, 1555)
Ambush Alley
Amer, Abdel Hakim (December 11, 1919–September 14, 1967)
Amiriyah Shelter Bombing (February 13, 1991)
Amman Campaign (March 21–September 25, 1918)
Amr ibn al-As (ca. 585–664)
Anbar Awakening Movement
Anglo-American Committee of Inquiry (1946)
Anglo-Egyptian Treaty (August 26, 1936)
Anglo-Egyptian War (1882)
Anglo-Iranian Oil Crisis (1951–1953)
Anglo-Iraqi Treaties of 1922 and 1930
Anglo-Jordanian Defense Treaty (March 15, 1948)
Anglo-Ottoman Treaty (1838)
Anglo-Ottoman War (1807–1809)
Anglo-Persian War (1856–1857)
Anglo-Sudan War (1883–1899)
Ankara, Battle of (July 20, 1402)
Ankara, Pact of (October 19, 1939)

Ansar al-Islam
Anti-Arab Attitudes and Discrimination
Antigonus I Monophthalmus (382–301 BCE)
Antioch, Principality of
Antioch, Sieges of (1097–1098)
Antioch on the Meander, Battle of (1211)
Antiochus I Soter (ca. 324–261 BCE)
Antiochus III Megas (ca. 241–187 BCE)
Antiochus IV Epiphanes (ca. 215–164 BCE)
Antiochus VII Sidetes (ca. 159–129 BCE)
Antiochus Hierax (ca. 260–226 BCE)
Anti-Semitism
Aoun, Michel (1935–)
Aqaba, Capture of (July 6, 1917)
Aqaba, Gulf of
Arab Economic Boycott of Israel
Arabi, Ahmed (1841–1911)
Arabia, Roman
Arab-Jewish Communal War (November 30, 1947–May 14, 1948)
Arab League
Arab Legion
Arab Liberation Army
Arab Nationalism
Arab Oil Embargo (October 17, 1973–March 18, 1974)
Arab Revolt in Palestine (1936–1939)
Arab Revolt of World War I (June 5, 1916–October 31, 1918)
Arab Riots, Jerusalem (April 4–8, 1920)
Arab Spring (December 17, 2010–Mid-2012)
Arafat, Yasser (1929–2004)
Ardashir I (180–240)
Arif, Abd al-Salam (1921–1966)
Armenians and the Armenian Genocide
Army of Islam
ARROWHEAD RIPPER, Operation (June 19–August 19, 2007)
Arsuf, Battle of (September 7, 1191)
Artah, Battle of (August 11, 1164)
Artaxerxes I (?–424 BCE)
Artaxerxes II (435 or 445–358)
Artaxerxes III (359–338 BCE)
Artemisia I (5th Century BCE)
Artuqid Dynasty (1101–1408)
*Asabiyya*
Ascalon, Battle of (August 12, 1099)
Ashkenazic Judaism
Ashurbanipal (ca. 693–627 BCE)
Assad, Bashar al- (1965–)

Assad, Hafez al- (1930–2000)
Assassins
Assyrian Empire
Ataturk, Mustafa Kemal (1881–1938)
Auchinleck, Sir Claude John Eyre (1884–1981)
Aurelian, Emperor (214–275)
Auspicious Incident (June 15, 1826)
AUTUMN CLOUDS, Operation (November 1–8, 2006)
Ayn Jalut, Battle of (September 3, 1260)
Ayyubid Dynasty

Baath Party
Babylon, Siege of (539–538 BCE)
Babylonian Empire, Neo- (626–539 BCE)
Babylonian Empire, Old (ca. 1894–911 BCE)
Badr, Battle of (March 15, 624)
Badr al-Jamali (1015–1094)
Baghavard, First Battle of (June 14, 1735)
Baghavard, Second Battle of (August 9, 1745)
Baghdad, Capture of (March 11, 1917)
Baghdad, 812–813 Siege of (August 812–September 813)
Baghdad, 1258 Siege of
Baghdad, 1401 Siege of
Baghdad, 1638 Siege of
Baghdad, 1733 Battle of (July 19, 1733)
Baghdad, 2003 Battle of (April 5–10, 2003)
Baghdadi, Abu Bakr al- (1971–)
Baghdad Pact (February 4, 1955)
Bahrain
Bakhchisarai, Treaty of (January 3, 1681)
Bakr, Ahmad Hassan al- (1914–1982)
Balak ibn Bahram ibn Ortok (?–1124)
Baldat al-Shaykh Massacre (January 31, 1947)
Baldwin I of Constantinople (1171–1206)
Baldwin I of Jerusalem (ca. 1061–1118)
Baldwin II of Constantinople (1217–1273)
Baldwin II of Jerusalem (1060–1131)
Baldwin III of Jerusalem (1130–1163)
Baldwin IV of Jerusalem (1161–1185)
Balfour Declaration (November 2, 1917)
Balkans, Ottoman Conquest of the (1350s–1593)
Balkan Wars (1912–1913)
Balta Liman, Convention of (May 1, 1849)
Baltim, Battle of (October 12–13, 1973)
Bapheus, Battle of (July 27, 1301)
Barak, Ehud (1942–)
Barkiyaruq (1079/1080–1105)
Bar Kochba Revolt (132–135)

Bar-Lev Line
Basian, Battle of (1203)
Basil II Bulgaroctonos (958–1025)
Basra, Battle for (March 23–April 7, 2003)
Bassorah, Battle of (November 7, 656)
Baybars I (1223–1277)
Bayezid I (1360–1403)
Bayezid II (1447–1512)
Bedouins
Beersheba, Battle of (October 31, 1917)
Begin, Menachem (1913–1992)
Belisarius (ca. 505–565)
Ben-Gurion, David (1886–1973)
Bernadotte, Folke (1895–1948)
Beth-Horon, Battle of (October 66 CE)
Bible
Bin Laden, Osama (1957–2011)
Bithynia
Black September (September 6, 1970–July 1971)
Black September Organization
Bohemund I of Antioch (ca. 1054–1111)
Bohemund VI of Antioch-Tripoli (ca. 1237–1275)
Bohemund VII of Antioch-Tripoli (1261–1287)
Bonaparte, Napoleon (1769–1821)
Boniface I of Montferrat (ca. 1150–1207)
Border War (1949–1956)
Bremer, Lewis Paul, III (1941–)
Bubiyan Island, Battle of (January 29–30, 1991)
Burqan, Battle of (February 25, 1991)
Bush Doctrine
Byzantine Empire (330–1453)
Byzantine Empire Civil War (1341–1347)
Byzantine-Muslim Wars (629–1035)
Byzantine-Ottoman Wars (1280–1479)
Byzantine-Sassanid War (602–628)
Byzantine-Seljuk Wars (1048–1308)

Caesar, Gaius Julius (100–44 BCE)
Caesar's Campaign in Egypt (48–47 BCE)
Cairo Accord (May 4, 1994)
Cairo Agreement (November 3, 1969)
Cairo Declaration, Palestine Liberation Organization (November 7, 1985)
Cambyses II (?–522 BCE)
Camp David Accords (September 17, 1978)
Camp Speicher Massacre (June 12, 2014)
Carrhae, Battle of (June 9, 53 BCE)
Carter Doctrine (January 23, 1980)

Caucasus Front, World War I
Cezayirli Gazi Hasan Pasha (1713–1790)
Chaldiran, Battle of (August 23, 1514)
Chamoun, Camille (1900–1987)
Chancellor, Sir John Robert (1870–1952)
Chemical Weapons and Warfare
Chesma, Battle of (July 5–7, 1770)
Chinese Farm, Battle of the (October 14–18, 1973)
Cleopatra VII (69–30 BCE)
Clermont, Council of (1095)
Climate of the Middle East
Cold War in the Middle East
Cole, USS, Attack on (October 12, 2000)
Conrad III, King of Germany (1093–1152)
Constantine I (ca. 277–286–337)
Constantine XI Palaiologos (1405–1453)
Constantinople, Crusader Siege and Capture of (April 8–13, 1204)
Constantinople, Latin Empire of (1204–1261)
Constantinople, Muslim Siege of (August 15, 717–August 15, 718)
Constantinople, 1590 Treaty of (May 21, 1590)
Constantinople, 1700 Treaty of (July 3, 1700)
Constantinople, 1720 Treaty of (November 16, 1720)
Constantinople, 1832 Treaty of (July 21, 1832)
Constantinople, 1913 Treaty of (September 29, 1913)
Constantinople, Ottoman Siege of (April 6–May 29, 1453)
Constantius II, Emperor (317–361)
Copts
Corupedium, Battle of (281 BCE)
Crassus, Marcus Licinius (ca. 115–53 BCE)
Cresson, Battle of (May 1, 1187)
Croesus of Lydia (ca. 595–547 BCE)
Crusades in the Holy Land, Christian (1096–1291)
Ctesiphon, 363 Battle of (May 29, 363)
Ctesiphon, 1915 Battle of (November 22–25, 1915)
Cunaxa, Battle of (401 BCE)
Cunningham, Sir Alan Gordon (1887–1983)
Cyprus
Cyprus, Athenian Expedition to (450–449 BCE)
Cyprus, Ottoman Conquest of (1570–1571)
Cyrus II the Great (ca. 601/590–530 BCE)
Cyrus the Younger (ca. 423–401 BCE)

Damascus, Allied Capture of (October 1, 1918)
Damascus, Siege of (634–635)
Damascus Agreement (December 28, 1985)

Damietta
Danishmendid Dynasty (1071–1178)
Daoud, Abu (1937–2010)
Dar al-Islam and Dar al-Harb
Dardanelles Campaign (February–March 1915)
Darius I (ca. 549–486 BCE)
Darius II (?–404 BCE)
Darius III (ca. 380–330 BCE)
Dawud Pasha (1767–1851)
Dayan, Moshe (1915–1981)
Debecka Pass, Battle of (April 6, 2003)
DEFENSIVE SHIELD, Operation (April 3–May 10, 2002)
Definitive Treaty (March 14, 1812)
Degania, Battle of (May 20, 1948)
Deir Yassin Massacre (April 9–11, 1948)
Demetrius I Poliorcetes (336–282 BCE)
Demetrius II Nicator (ca. 160–125 BCE)
DESERT FOX, Operation (December 16–19, 1998)
DESERT THUNDER I, Operation (1998)
DESERT THUNDER II, Operation (1998)
Devshirme System
Dhahran, Scud Missile Attack on (February 25, 1991)
Dhofar Rebellion (1962–1976)
Diadochi, Wars of the (323–275 BCE)
Diaspora
Djemal Pasha, Ahmed (1872–1922)
Doha Agreement (May 21, 2008)
Donkey Island, Battle of (June 30–July 1, 2007)
Dorylaion, Battle of (July 1, 1097)
Druze-Ottoman Wars
Druzes

EARNEST WILL, Operation (1987–1989)
Edessa, County of
Edward I, King of England (1239–1307)
Egypt
Egypt, Ancient
Egypt, Arab Conquest of (640–642)
Egypt, Athenian Intervention in (460–454 BCE)
Egypt, British Invasion of (1807)
Egypt, French Invasion and Occupation of (1798–1801)
Egypt, Ptolemaic and Roman Periods
Egyptian-Arab Wars (1811–1840)
Egyptian-Ottoman Wars (1831–1833 and 1838–1841)
Egyptian Revolution of 2011
Egyptian-Soviet Arms Deal (Summer 1955)
Egypt under British Rule (1882–1936)
Eilat, Israel

*Eilat,* Sinking of (October 21, 1967)
Eisenhower Doctrine (1957)
Eitan, Rafael (1929–2004)
El Alamein, First Battle of (July 1–27, 1942)
El Alamein, Second Battle of (October 23–November 11, 1942)
Elazar, David (1925–1976)
Entebbe Hostage Rescue (July 3–4, 1976)
Enver Pasha (1881–1922)
Erdoğan, Recep Tayyip (1954–)
Erzincan, 1230 Battle of (August 10–12, 1230)
Erzincan, 1916 Battle of (July 25–26, 1916)
Erzurum, First Treaty of (July 28, 1823)
Erzurum, Second Treaty of (May 31, 1847)
Erzurum Offensive (January 10–March 25, 1916)
Eshkol, Levi (1895–1969)
Eumenes of Cardia (ca. 361–316 BCE)
Eumenes I of Pergamum (r. 263–241 BCE)
Eumenes II of Pergamum (r. 197–159 BCE)
Euphrates River
Eurymedon, Battle of (ca. 468–466 BCE)
Eustace III of Boulogne (ca. 1058–1125)
Evagoras I (ca. 435–374 BCE)
*Exodus* Incident (July 11–August 22, 1947)
Expellees and Refugees, Palestinian

Fahd, ibn Abd al-Aziz al-Saud (1922–2005)
Faisal I, King of Iraq (1885–1933)
Faisal II, King of Iraq (1935–1958)
Fallujah, First Battle of (April 4–May 1, 2004)
Fallujah, Second Battle of (November 7–December 23, 2004)
Fallujah, Third Battle of (May 23–June 28, 2016)
Fao Peninsula
Farouk I, King of Egypt (1920–1965)
Fatah, al-
Fatimid Dynasty (909–1171)
Fatwa
Fedayeen
Finckenstein, Treaty of (May 4, 1807)
Forbie, Battle of (October 17, 1244)
Franco-Lebanese Treaty (November 13, 1936)
Franco-Syrian Treaty (September 9, 1936)
Franco-Turkish War (1920)
Franks, Tommy (1945–)
Frederick I or Frederick Barbarossa (1122–1190)
Frederick II, Holy Roman Emperor (1194–1250)
Frederick V, Duke of Swabia (1167–1191)

Gabiene, Battle of (316 BCE)
Galerius, Roman Emperor (ca. 250s–311)
Galilee
Gallipoli Campaign (April 25, 1915–January 9, 1916)
Gamaat Islamiya
Ganja, Treaty of (March 10, 1735)
Gaugamela, Battle of (October 1, 331 BCE)
Gaza, Battle of (November 13, 1239)
Gaza, First Battle of (March 26–27, 1917)
Gaza, Second Battle of (April 17–19, 1917)
Gaza, Third Battle of (October 31–November 7, 1917)
Gaza Raid (February 28, 1955)
Gaza Strip
Gaza Strip Disengagement (August 15–September 12, 2005)
Gaza War of 2006 (June 27–November 26, 2006)
Gaza War of 2008–2009 (December 27, 2008–January 18, 2009)
Gaza War of 2012 (November 14–22, 2012)
Gaza War of 2014 (July 8–August 26, 2014)
General Treaty of Peace (1820)
Geneva Accord (December 1, 2003)
Geneva Peace Conference (December 21, 1973–January 9, 1974)
Geography of the Middle East
Georgian-Seljuk Wars (11th–13th centuries)
*Ghazi*
*Ghulams*
Giddi Pass
Glubb, Sir John Bagot (1897–1986)
Godfrey of Bouillon (ca. 1060–1100)
Gog and Magog
Golan Heights
Golden Horde–Ilkhanid Wars (1261–1323)
Goltz, Wilhelm Leopold Colmar von der (1843–1916)
Gordian III, Emperor (225–244)
Gouraud, Henri Joseph Eugène (1867–1946)
Granicus, Battle of the (May 334 BCE)
Greco-Persian Wars (499–479 BCE)
Greco-Turkish War (1919–1922)
Green Line
Green Zone, Iraq
Grivas, Georgios (1898–1974)
Gulf Cooperation Council
Gulistan, Treaty of (October 24, 1813)
Gulnabad, Battle of (March 8, 1772)
Guy of Lusignan (ca. 1150–1194)

## List of Entries

Haditha, Battle of (August 1–4, 2005)
Hadrian, Emperor (76–138)
Haganah
Haifa Street, Battle of (January 6–9, 2007)
Hama Massacre (February 3–28, 1982)
Hamas
Hammurabi (ca. 1810–1750 BCE)
*Hanit,* Attack on the (July 21, 2006)
HARD SURFACE, Operation (June 12, 1963–January 1964)
Haredim
Harim, Battle of (August 12, 1164)
Hariri, Rafik (1944–2005)
Harran, Battle of (May 7, 1104)
Harun al-Rashid (763–809)
Hashemites
Hashomer
Hasidic Judaism
Hasmonean Tunnel Incident (September 23–28, 1996)
Hattin, Battle of (July 3–4, 1187)
*Havlaga*
Hayreddin Barbarossa (ca. 1483–1546)
Hebron Massacre (August 23–24, 1929)
Hebron Mosque Massacre (February 25, 1994)
Hejaz Railroad, Attacks on (1916–1918)
Hellespont
Hellespont Campaign (411–410 BCE)
Henry of Constantinople (ca. 1178–1216)
Henry VI of Germany (1165–1197)
Heraclius (ca. 575–641)
Herzl, Theodor (1860–1904)
Hezbollah
Holocaust (1941–1945)
Homs, First Battle of (December 11, 1260)
Homs, Second Battle of (October 29, 1281)
Homs, Third Battle of (December 23, 1299)
Hormuz, Strait of
Houthi, Hussein Badr al-Din al- (?–2004)
Houthis
Hrawi, Elias (1925–2006)
Hulegu (1218–1265)
Hunkar Iskelesi, Treaty of (July 8, 1833)
Husaybah, Battle of (April 17, 2004)
Hussein, Saddam (1937–2006)
Husseini, Haj Amin al- (1895–1974)
Hussein ibn Ali ibn Mohammed (1856–1931)
Hussein ibn Talal, King of Jordan (1935–1999)
Hyksos

Ibelin, Battle of (May 29, 1123)
Ibn Saud, King (1875–1953)
Ibrahim Pasha (1789–1848)
Ikhwan
Ilghazi ibn Artuq, Najm al-Din (ca. 1062–1122)
Ilkhan Dynasty (ca. 1261–1353)
IMMINENT THUNDER, Operation (November 15–21, 1990)
Improvised Explosive Devices
Inab, Battle of (June 29, 1149)
INHERENT RESOLVE, Operation (August 8, 2014–)
İnönü, İsmet (1884–1973)
Intifada, First (1987–1993)
Intifada, Second (2000–2004)
Ionian Revolt (499–493 BCE)
Ipsus, Battle of (Spring, 301 BCE)
Iran
Iran, Islamic Revolution in (1978–1979)
Iran Air Flight 655, Downing of (July 3, 1988)
Iran Hostage Crisis (November 4, 1979–January 20, 1981)
Iran Hostage Rescue Mission (Operation EAGLE CLAW, April 25, 1980)
Iran-Iraq War (1980–1988)
Iran Nuclear Deal (July 14, 2015)
Iraq
Iraq, Sanctions on
Iraq Insurgency (2003–)
Iraq No-Fly Zones
Iraq War (March 19, 2003–December 15, 2011)
Irgun Tsvai Leumi
Isfahan, Siege of (March–October 23, 1722)
Islamic Army of Aden
Islamic Civil War, First (656–661)
Islamic Civil War, Second (680–692)
Islamic Radicalism in the 20th and 21st Centuries
Islamic State of Iraq and Syria
Ismail, Khedive (1830–1895)
Ismail Ali, Ahmad (1917–1974)
Ismail I, Shah (1487–1524)
Ismailis
Israel
Israel-Egypt Peace Treaty (March 26, 1979)
Israeli Air Strikes Beginning the Six-Day War (June 5, 1967)
Israeli Air Strike on Presumed Syrian Nuclear Facility (September 6, 2007)
Israeli Security Fence
Israeli War of Independence (1948–1949)

Israeli War of Independence, Truce Agreements (February 24, 1949–July 20, 1949)
Israel-Jordan Peace Treaty (October 26, 1994)
Issus, Battle of (November 333 BCE)
Italo-Ottoman War (1911–1912)
IVORY JUSTICE, Operation (July 24–August 1990)
Izz ad-Din al-Qassam Brigades

Jabotinsky, Vladimir Yevgenyevich (1880–1940)
Jadid, Salah al- (1926–1993)
Jaffa, Battle of (August 5, 1192)
Jaffa, Treaty of (September 2, 1192)
Jam, Battle of (September 24, 1528)
Janissaries
Jarring Mission (December 9, 1967–October 1973)
Jassy, Treaty of (January 9, 1792)
Jawhar (?–992)
Jeddah, Siege of (February 10–December 17, 1925)
Jenin, Battle of (April 3–11, 2002)
Jericho Conference (December 1, 1948)
Jerusalem, Capture of (December 9, 1917)
Jerusalem, Crusader Siege of (June 7–July 15, 1099)
Jerusalem, Latin Kingdom of
Jerusalem, Roman Siege of (70 CE)
Jewish Brigade
Jewish Legion
Jewish-Roman War, First (66–73 CE)
Jihad
John of Brienne (ca. 1170–1237)
Jordan
Jordan River
Joscelin I of Edessa (?–1131)
Jovian (331–364)
Judaea
Judas Maccabeus (ca. 190–130 BCE)
Julian, Emperor (331–363)
Justinian I the Great, Emperor (483–565)

Kabakchi Incident (May 25, 1807)
Kadesh, Battle of (1274 BCE)
Kafr Qasim Massacre (October 29, 1956)
Kafur, Abu al-Misk (905–968)
Kapikulu Corps
Karameh, Battle of (March 21, 1968)
Karbala, Battle of (October 10, 680)
Karbala, First Battle of (March 31–April 6, 2003)
Karbala, Second Battle of (August 27–29, 2007)

Karbala Gap
Karbugha (d. 1102)
Karim Khan Zand, Muhammad (ca. 1705–1779)
Karlowitz, Treaty of (January 26, 1699)
Kars, Battle of (August 9–19, 1745)
Kars, Treaty of (October 13, 1921)
Kassites
Khadairi Bend, Battle of (December 13, 1916–January 29, 1917)
Khafji, Battle of (January 29–February 1, 1991)
Khalid bin Sultan, Prince (1949–)
Khalid ibn al-Walid (ca. 592–642)
Khanaqin, Battle of (June 3, 1916)
Khandaq, Battle of the (January–February 627)
Khan Yunis
Kharijites
Khartoum Resolution (September 1, 1967)
Khirokitia, Battle of (July 7, 1426)
Khobar Towers Bombing (June 25, 1996)
Khomeini, Ruhollah (1900–1989)
Khosrow I Anushiravan (496?–579)
Kirkuk
Kobanî, Siege of (September 27, 2014–January 26, 2015)
Kobanî Massacre (June 25–26, 2015)
Konya, Battle of (December 21, 1832)
Köprülü Abdullah Pasha (1694–1735)
Köprülü Fazil Ahmed Pasha (1635–1676)
Köprülü Mehmed Pasha (1583?–1661)
Köse Dağ, Battle of (June 26, 1243)
Kress von Kressenstein, Friedrich Sigismund Georg (1870–1948)
Kuchuk Kainardji, Treaty of (July 21, 1774)
Kurdan, Treaty of (September 4, 1746)
Kurds
Kurds, Massacres of
Kutahya Convention (May 4, 1833)
Kut al-Amara, Siege of (December 7, 1915–April 29, 1916)
Kuwait
Kuwait, Iraqi Invasion of (August 2, 1990)
Kuwait, Iraqi Occupation of (August 2, 1990–February 27, 1991)
Kuwait, Liberation of (February 27, 1991)

Lahoud, Émile Jamil (1936–)
Latakia, Battle of (October 6, 1973)
Latrun, Battles of (May 25–July 18, 1948)
Lausanne, First Treaty of (October 18, 1912)

Lausanne, Second Treaty of (July 24, 1923)
Lavon Affair (July–December 11, 1954)
Lawrence, Thomas Edward (1888–1935)
League of Nations Covenant Article 22
Lebanon
Lebanon, First U.S. Intervention in (July 15–October 25, 1958)
Lebanon, Israeli Operations against (July 13–August 14, 2006)
Lebanon, Israeli Security Zone in
Lebanon, Second U.S. Intervention in (August 24, 1982–February 26, 1984)
Lebanon Civil War (April 13, 1975–August 1990)
Lebanon-Israeli War (June 6–September 1982)
Leilan, Battle of (November 9, 1733)
Leo III the Isaurian (ca. 680–741)
Leopold V of Austria (1157–1194)
Lepanto, Battle of (October 7, 1571)
*Liberty* Incident (June 8, 1967)
Libyan-Egyptian War (July 21–24, 1977)
Liman von Sanders, Otto (1855–1929)
LITANI, Operation (March 14–21, 1978)
Lod Airport Massacre (May 30, 1972)
Lohamei Herut Israel
London, 1840 Treaty of (July 15, 1840)
London, 1913 Treaty of (May 30, 1913)
London Round Table Conference (February 7–March 17, 1939)
London Straits Convention (July 13, 1841)
Long Campaign in Hungary (1443–1444)
Long War in Hungary (1593–1606)
Louis VII, King of France (1120–1180)
Louis IX, King of France (1214–1270)
Lucius Verus (130–169)
Lydia
Lysimachus (ca. 355–281 BCE)

Ma'an, Siege of (April 17–September 28, 1918)
Maccabean Revolt (167–160 BCE)
MacMichael, Sir Harold (1882–1969)
Madrid Conference (October 30–November 1, 1991)
Magnesia, Battle of (December 190 BCE)
Mahmud, Muhammad Sidqi (1923–)
Mahmud II, Sultan (1785–1839)
Majid al-Tikriti, Ali Hassan al- (1941–2010)
Makarios III, Archbishop (1913–1977)
Maliki, Nuri Muhammed Kamil al- (1950–)
Malik Shah I (1055–1092)

Mamluk-Ilkhanid Wars (1260–1323)
Mamluk-Ottoman Wars (1485–1491 and 1516–1517)
Mamluk Sultanate (1250–1517)
Mandates, League of Nations
Mansurah, Battle of (February 8–11, 1250)
Manuel I Komnenos, Emperor (1118–1180)
Manuel II Palaiologos, Emperor (1350–1425)
Manzikert, Battle of (August 26, 1071)
Marcus, David (1901–1948)
Marcus Aurelius, Emperor (121–180)
Marj Dabiq, Battle of (August 24, 1516)
Maronites
Marsh Arabs
Martyrdom
Masada
Mashal, Khaled (1956–)
Massacre at the Citadel (March 1, 1811)
Maududi, Abul A'Ala (1903–1979)
Mawdud (?–1113)
Maysalun, Battle of (July 24, 1920)
McMahon-Hussein Correspondence
Medina, Siege of (1916–1919)
Medina Ridge, Battle of (February 27, 1991)
Megiddo, Ancient Battle of (1479 BCE)
Megiddo, Battle of (September 19–21, 1918)
Mehmed Ali (1769–1849)
Mehmed II, Sultan (1432–1481)
Meir, Golda Mabovitch (1898–1978)
Mersa Matruh, First Battle of (June 26, 1942)
Mersa Matruh, Second Battle of (November 7, 1942)
Mesopotamia
Mesopotamian Theater, World War I
Michael VIII Palaiologos (1223–1282)
Miletus, Battle of (411 BCE)
Mithridates VI Eupator Dionysius (ca. 134–63 BCE)
Mithridatic Wars (89–84, 83–81, and 73–63 BCE)
Mitla Pass
Mizrahi Judaism
Mongol Invasion of the Middle East (1256–1280)
Montenegrin-Ottoman Wars (1852–1913)
Mont Giscard, Battle of (November 25, 1177)
Montgomery, Bernard Law (1887–1976)
Morrison-Grady Plan (July 31, 1946)
Morsi, Mohamed (1951–2019)
Mosul, First Battle of (November 8–16, 2004)
Mosul, Second Battle of (October 17, 2016–July 9, 2017)
"Mother of All Battles"

Moudros, Armistice of (October 30, 1918)
Mount Lebanon Civil War (1860)
Muawiyah I (602–680)
Mubarak, Hosni (1928–)
Müezzinzade Ali Pasha (?–1571)
Mughal-Safavid Wars (1622–1623 and 1648–1653)
Muhammad, Campaigns of the Prophet (622–632)
Muhammad, Prophet of Islam (ca. 569–632)
Multinational Force and Observers in the Sinai
Multi-National Force–Iraq (2004–2009)
Murad II, Sultan (1404–1451)
Murray, Sir Archibald James (1860–1945)
Muslim Brotherhood
Muslim Wars of Expansion (623–732)
Mutla Ridge (February 25–27, 1991)
Mwawi, Ahmad Ali al- (1897–ca. 1979)
Mycale, Battle of (479)
Myriokephalon, Battle of (September 17, 1176)

NACHSHON, Operation (April 5–20, 1948)
Nadir Shah (1688–1747)
Naguib, Mohammad (1901–1984)
Nahr al-Bared Refugee Camp, Siege of (May 20–September 2, 2007)
Najaf, First Battle of (August 5–27, 2004)
Najaf, Second Battle of (January 28, 2007)
Nasar, Mustafa bin Abd al-Qadir Setmariam (1958–)
Nasiriyah, Battle of (March 23–29, 2003)
Nasser, Gamal Abdel (1918–1970)
Nasuh Pasha, Treaty of (1612)
Nebuchadnezzar II (ca. 634–562 BCE)
Nelson, Horatio (1758–1805)
NEMESIS, Operation (1920–1922)
Netanyahu, Benjamin (1949–)
Nicaea, Empire of (1204–1261)
Nika Uprising (January 13–18, 532)
Nikopolis, Crusade in (1396)
Nile River
NIMBLE ARCHER, Operation (October 19, 1987)
Nineveh, Battle of (December 12, 627)
Nisibis, Battle of (217)
Nissa, Treaty of (October 3, 1739)
Nixon, Sir John Eccles (1857–1921)
Nixon Doctrine (November 3, 1969)
Nizip, Battle of (June 24, 1839)
Norfolk, Battle of (February 26–27, 1991)
NORTHERN WATCH Operation (January 1, 1997–March 17, 2003)

Nur al-Din (1118–1174)
Nuri al-Said (1888–July 15, 1958)

O'Connor, Richard Nugent (1889–1981)
Odenathus (ca. 220–268)
Olmert, Ehud (1945–)
Oman
Organization of Petroleum Exporting Countries
Osiraq Raid (June 7, 1981)
Oslo Accords (September 13, 1993)
Osman I (ca. 1254–1324/1326)
Osman Nuri Pasha (1832–1900)
Otlukbeli, Battle of (August 11, 1473)
Ottoman Empire (1299–1922)
Ottoman Empire, Entry into World War I
Ottoman Empire, Post–World War I Revolution in
Ottoman-Habsburg Wars (1529–1791)
Ottoman-Hungarian Wars (1437–1526)
Ottoman-Persian Wars of the 18th and 19th Centuries
Ottoman-Polish Wars of the 17th Century
Ottoman-Safavid Wars (1526–1639)
Outremer

Palestine, British Mandate for (1922–1948)
Palestine, Partition of
Palestine, Pre-1918 History of
Palestine and Syria Campaign, World War I (1915–1918)
Palestine Liberation Army
Palestine Liberation Front
Palestine Liberation Organization
Palestinian Islamic Jihad
Palestinian National Authority
Palmach
Palmyra
Pan-Arab Congress (September 8, 1937)
Pan-Arabism and Pan-Arabist Thought
Paraetacene, Battle of (317 BCE)
Parthian Empire (247 BCE–224 CE)
Passarowitz, Treaty of (July 21, 1718)
*Patria*, Destruction of (November 25, 1940)
Patrona Halil Revolt (September 28, 1730)
Peel Commission (August 1936–July 7, 1937)
Pelagius of Albano (ca. 1165–1230)
Pelekanon, Battle of (June 10–11, 1329)
Pelusium, Battle of (525 BCE)
Perdiccas (365–321 BCE)
Pergamum
Persia, Arab Conquest of (642–671)

## List of Entries

Persia, 18th-Century Wars of Succession
Persian Cossack Brigade
Persian Front, World War I
Persian Gulf
Persian Gulf War, Air Campaign (January 17–February 28, 1991)
Persian Gulf War, Cease-Fire Agreement (April 6, 1991)
Persian Gulf War, Ground Campaign (February 24–28, 1991)
Persian Gulf War, Naval Operations (January 17–February 28, 1991)
Persian Gulf War, Overview (January 17–February 28, 1991)
Peshmerga
Peter the Hermit (1050?–1115)
Petraeus, David Howell (1952–)
PHANTOM STRIKE, Operation (August 15, 2007–January 2008)
PHANTOM THUNDER, Operation (June 16–August 14, 2007)
Pharnabazus (?–ca. 370 BCE)
Phase Line Bullet, Battle of (February 26, 1991)
Philippe II, King (1165–1223)
Philomelion, Battle of (1116)
Phoenicia
Pompeius Magnus, Gnaeus (106–48 BCE)
Pontus (281 BCE–62 CE)
Popular Front for the Liberation of Palestine
Popular Front for the Liberation of Palestine–General Command
Popular Front for the Liberation of the Occupied Arabian Gulf
Portuguese Colonial Wars in Arabia (1507–1650)
PRAYING MANTIS, Operation (April 18, 1988)
PRIME CHANCE, Operation (1987–1989)
PROVIDE COMFORT, Operation (1991)
Pruth, Treaty of (July 23, 1711)
Ptolemaic Kingdom (305–30 BCE)
Ptolemy Ceraunus (ca. 320–279 BCE)
Ptolemy I Soter (367–282 BCE)
Ptolemy II Philadelphus (308–246 BCE)
Ptolemy III Euergetes (r. 246–221 BCE)
Ptolemy IV Philopator (ca. 244–205 BCE)
Ptolemy V Epiphanes (ca. 210–180)
Ptolemy VI Philometor (ca. 186–145 BCE)
Pyramids, Battle of the (July 21, 1798)

Qaboos bin Said al-Said (1940–)
Qadisiyya, Battle of (November 16–19, 636)
Qalawun (ca. 1222–1290)
Qarmatians
Qasim, Abdul Karim (1914–1963)
Qassam, Izz ad-Din al- (1882–1935)
Qatar
Qawuqji, Fawzi al- (1890–1976)
Qibya Massacre (October 14, 1953)
Qilij Arslan I of Rum (1079–1107)
Qilij Arslan II of Rum (ca. 1115–1192)
Quran
Qurna, Battle of (December 4–9, 1915)
Qutb, Sayyid Ibrahim Husayn Shadhili (1906–1966)
Quwatli, Shukri al- (1891–1967)

Rabat Summit (October 26–29, 1974)
Rabin, Yitzhak (1922–1995)
Rafah Tunnels
Ramadi, Fall of (November 21, 2014–May 17, 2015)
Ramadi, First Battle of (April 6–10, 2004)
Ramadi, Recapture of (November 25, 2015–February 9, 2016)
Ramadi, Second Battle of (June 17–November 15, 2006)
Ramesses II the Great (ca. 1303–1213 BCE)
Ramla, First Battle of (September 7, 1101)
Ramla, Second Battle of (May 17, 1102)
Ramla, Third Battle of (August 27, 1105)
Raphia, Battle of (June 22, 217 BCE)
Reagan Plan (September 1, 1982)
Red Sea
Reform Judaism and Zionism
Regime Change, Iraq War
Religious Sites in the Middle East, Christian
Religious Sites in the Middle East, Jewish
Religious Sites in the Middle East, Muslim
Republican Guard, Iraq
Resht, Treaty of (February 1, 1732)
Revisionist Zionism
Reza Shah Pahlavi (1878–1944)
Rhodes, Demetrius's Siege of (305–304 BCE)
Rhodes, Suleiman's Siege of (July 28–December 21, 1522)
Richard I, King (1157–1199)
Richard of Cornwall (1209–1272)
Ridda Wars (632–633)
Right of Return, Palestinian
Rogers Plan (December 9, 1969)
Rognvald Kali Kolsson (ca. 1099–1158)
Romani, Battle of (August 4–5, 1916)
Roman-Parthian Wars (53 BCE–215 CE)

Roman-Sassanid Wars (232–440)
Rommel, Erwin Johannes Eugen (1891–1944)
Rum, Sultanate of (1080–1307)
Russo-Ottoman Wars (1676–1911)
Russo-Persian Wars (1722–1911)

Saadabad Pact (July 8, 1937)
Sabra and Shatila Massacre (September 16–18, 1982)
Sadat, Anwar (1918–1981)
Saddam Line, Persian Gulf War
Sadeh, Yitzhak (1890–1952)
Sadr, Muqtada al- (1973–)
Sadr City, Battle of (March 26–May 11, 2008)
Safavid Dynasty (1501–1722 and 1729–1736)
Saif al-Dawla (926–967)
Sakarya, Battle of the (August 23–September 13, 1921)
Saladin (1138–1193)
Salafism
Saleh, Ali Abdullah (1942–2017)
Samawah, Battle of (March 30–April 4, 2003)
Samita Incident (December 1972–April 1973)
Samu Raid, West Bank (November 13, 1966)
Sanchez, Ricardo S. (1951–)
San Remo Conference (April 19–26, 1920)
San Stefano, Treaty of (March 3, 1878)
Saracen
Sargon of Akkad (ca. 2350–2279 BCE)
Sarikamish, Battle of (December 22, 1914–January 17, 1915) in pages.
Sassanid Empire (224–651)
Saudi Arabia
Saudi-Hashemite War (1919–1925)
Saudi King as Custodian of the Two Holy Mosques
Saudi-Kuwaiti War (1921–1922)
Saudi-Ottoman War (1911–1913)
Saudi-Rashidi Wars (1887–1921)
Saudi-Yemeni War (1934)
SCATHE MEAN, Operation (January 17, 1991)
Schwarzkopf, H. Norman, Jr. (1934–2012)
SCORPION, Operation
Seleucid Empire (312–63 BCE)
Seleucus I Nicator (ca. 358–281 BCE)
Selim I, Sultan (1470–1520)
Selim III, Sultan (1761–1808)
Seljuk Dynasty (1016–1153)
Seljuk War of Succession (1092–1105)
Sennacherib (?–681 BCE)
Sephardic Judaism

September 11, 2001, Attacks on the United States
Septimius Severus, Emperor (ca. 145–211)
Serbian-Ottoman War (1876)
Settlements, Israeli
73 Easting, Battle of (February 26, 1991)
Sèvres, Treaty of (August 10, 1920)
Shakur, Yusuf bin Raghib (1928–)
Shallah, Ramadan Abdullah Mohammad (1958–)
Shamir, Yitzhak (1915–2012)
Shapur I the Great (ca. 215–270)
Shapur II the Great (309–379)
Sharia
Sharm El Sheikh
Sharon, Ariel (1928–2014)
Shatt al-Arab Waterway
Shaw Commission (August 1929–March 31, 1930)
Shazly, Saad el- (1922–2011)
Shia Islam
Shiqaqi, Fathi (1951–1995)
Shishakli, Adib al- (1909–1964)
Shomron, Dan (1937–2008)
Shultz Plan (March 4, 1988)
Siffin, Battle of (July 26–28, 657)
Sinai Campaign of 1916–1917 (March 1916–January 1917)
Sinai Campaign of 1956 (October 29–November 6, 1956)
Sinai I and Sinai II Agreements (January 19 and September 4, 1974)
Sinai Peninsula
Siniura, Fuad (1943–)
Sinope, Battle of (November 30, 1853)
Sisi, Abdel Fattah el- (1954–)
Sistani, Sayyid Ali Hisayn al- (1930–)
Six-Day War (June 5–10, 1967)
Smyrna Crusade (1344–1348)
SOUTHERN WATCH, Operation (1992–2003)
South Lebanon Army
South Yemen Civil War (January 13–24, 1986)
Special Night Squads
Special Republican Guards
*Stark* Incident (May 17, 1987)
STEEL CURTAIN, Operation (November 5–22, 2005)
Stern, Avraham (1907–1942)
St. Petersburg, Treaty of (September 12, 1723)
Strait of Tiran Crisis (1956–1967)
St. Sabas, War of (1256–1270)
Suez Canal

Suez Canal, World War I Ottoman Operations against
Suez Canal and Egypt, World War II Campaigns for Control of (1940–1942)
Suez Crisis (July 26, 1956–March 6, 1957)
Suicide Bombings
Suleiman I (1494–1566)
Sumer
Sunni Islam
Sunni Triangle
Sykes-Picot Agreement (May 16, 1916)
Syria
Syria and Lebanon Campaign (June 8–July 14, 1941)
Syrian Civil War (March 25, 2011–)
Syrian-Egyptian Wars (274–168 BCE)
Syrian-Roman War (192–188 BCE)

Taalat Pasha, Mehmed (1874–1921)
Tahmasp I, Shah (1514–1576)
Taif Accords (October 22, 1989)
Taji Bunkers, Attacks on (January 17–February 27, 1991)
Talmud
Tamerlane (1336–1405)
Tammuz I Reactor
Tancred (ca. 1076–1112)
Tanzimat
Task Force Normandy (January 17, 1991)
Tehran Treaty (November 25, 1814)
Tel el-Kebir, Battle of (September 13, 1882)
Ten Thousand, March of the (401–399 BCE)
Terrorism
Thani, Khalifa bin Hamad al- (1932–2016)
Theodore I Laskaris (ca. 1174–1221)
Thutmose III, Pharaoh (ca. 1504–1425 BCE)
Thymbra, Battle of (546 BCE)
Tiglath-Pileser I (?–1077 BCE)
Tiglath-Pileser III (?–727 BCE)
Tigris and Euphrates Valley
Tigris River
Titus, Emperor (39–81)
Townshend, Sir Charles Vere Ferrers (1861–1924)
Trajan (53–117)
Transjordan Campaign (1918)
Trebizond, Empire of (1204–1461)
Tripartite Declaration (May 25, 1950)
Tripoli, County of
Troop Surge, U.S., Iraq War

Troy, Siege of (1194–1184 BCE)
Turan Shah (?–1250)
Turcopoles
Turkey
Turki ibn Abdullah, Campaigns of (1823–1833)
Turkish-Armenian War (1920)
Tutush I (1066–1095)
Tuwaitha Nuclear Facility
Tyre and Gaza, Sieges of (332 BCE)

Umayyad Caliphate (661–750)
Umm Qasr, Battle of (March 21–23, 2003)
United Arab Emirates
United Arab Republic (1958–1961)
United Nations Palestine Partition Plan (November 29, 1947)
United Nations Special Commission on Palestine (May 13–August 31, 1947)
Uzun Hasan (1425–1478)

Valens, Emperor (ca. 328–378 CE)
Valerian, Emperor (ca. 193–260/264)
Valley of Tears, Battle of the (October 6–9, 1973)
Varna Crusade (1444)
Vasvár, Treaty of (August 10, 1664)
Venetian-Ottoman Wars (1416–1718)
Vespasian, Emperor (9–79)
VIGILANT WARRIOR, Operation (October 8, 1994–December 8, 1994)
VIKING HAMMER, Operation (March 28–30, 2003)

Wadi al-Batin, Battle of (February 26, 1991)
Wahhabism
War of Attrition (July 1969–August 1970)
Wauchope, Sir Arthur Grenfell (1874–1947)
West Bank
White Paper of 1922 (June 3, 1922)
White Paper of 1930 (October 31, 1930)
White Paper of 1939 (May 17, 1939)
Wingate, Orde Charles (1903–1944)
Woodhead Report (November 9, 1938)
World War I, Impact on the Middle East
World War II, Impact on the Middle East
Wye River Agreement (October 23, 1998)

Xenophon (ca. 431–ca. 354 BCE)
Xerxes I (519–465 BCE)

Yarmouk River, Battle of (August 15–20, 636)
Yazidis
Yemen
Yemen, Civil War in the North (1962–1970)
Yemen, Civil War in the South (May 4–July 7, 1994)
Yemen Civil War (2015–Present)
Yemen Hotel Bombings (December 29, 1992)
Yemenite War (February 24–March 19, 1979)
Yom Kippur War (October 6–25, 1973)
Young Turks
Yudenich, Nikolai Nikolaevich (1862–1933)

Zab, Battle of (February 26, 750)
Zangi, Imad ad-Din (1084/1085–1146)
Zanj Slave Revolts
Zarqawi, Abu Musab al- (1966–2006)
Zayed bin Sultan Al Nahyan (1918–2004)
Zenobia (240–274?)
Zionism
Zoroastrianism
Zsitvatorok, Peace of (November 11, 1606)
Zuhab, Treaty of (May 17, 1639)
Zuravno, Treaty of (October 16, 1676)

# List of Maps

**General Maps**
Ancient Near East, ca. 1400 BCE
The East, ca. 600 BCE
Middle East, 1945–1990

**Entry Maps**
Battle of the Nile, August 1, 1798
Naval Battle of Actium, September 2, 31 BCE
The Empire of Alexander the Great
Drive on Baghdad, March 20–April 12, 2003
Bahrain
Byzantine Empire, 1355
Siege of Constantinople, April 6–May 29, 1453
The Crusades
Cyprus
Egypt
Ancient Egypt
Gallipoli Campaign, April 25, 1915–January 9, 1916
Persian Empire, ca. 500 BCE
Greece during the Persian Wars

Iran
Iraq
Israel
Israeli War of Independence, 1948–1949
Jordan
Kuwait
Lebanon
Expansion of Islam, 814
Oman
Expansion of the Ottoman Empire, 1361–1571
Asia Minor in 189 BCE
Israel and Phoenicia, 860 BCE
Qatar
Saudi Arabia
Balance of Forces, May 14–24, 1967
Syria
Battle of Tel el-Kebir, September 13, 1882
Turkey
United Arab Emirates
Yemen

# General Maps

# Ancient Near East, ca. 1400 BCE

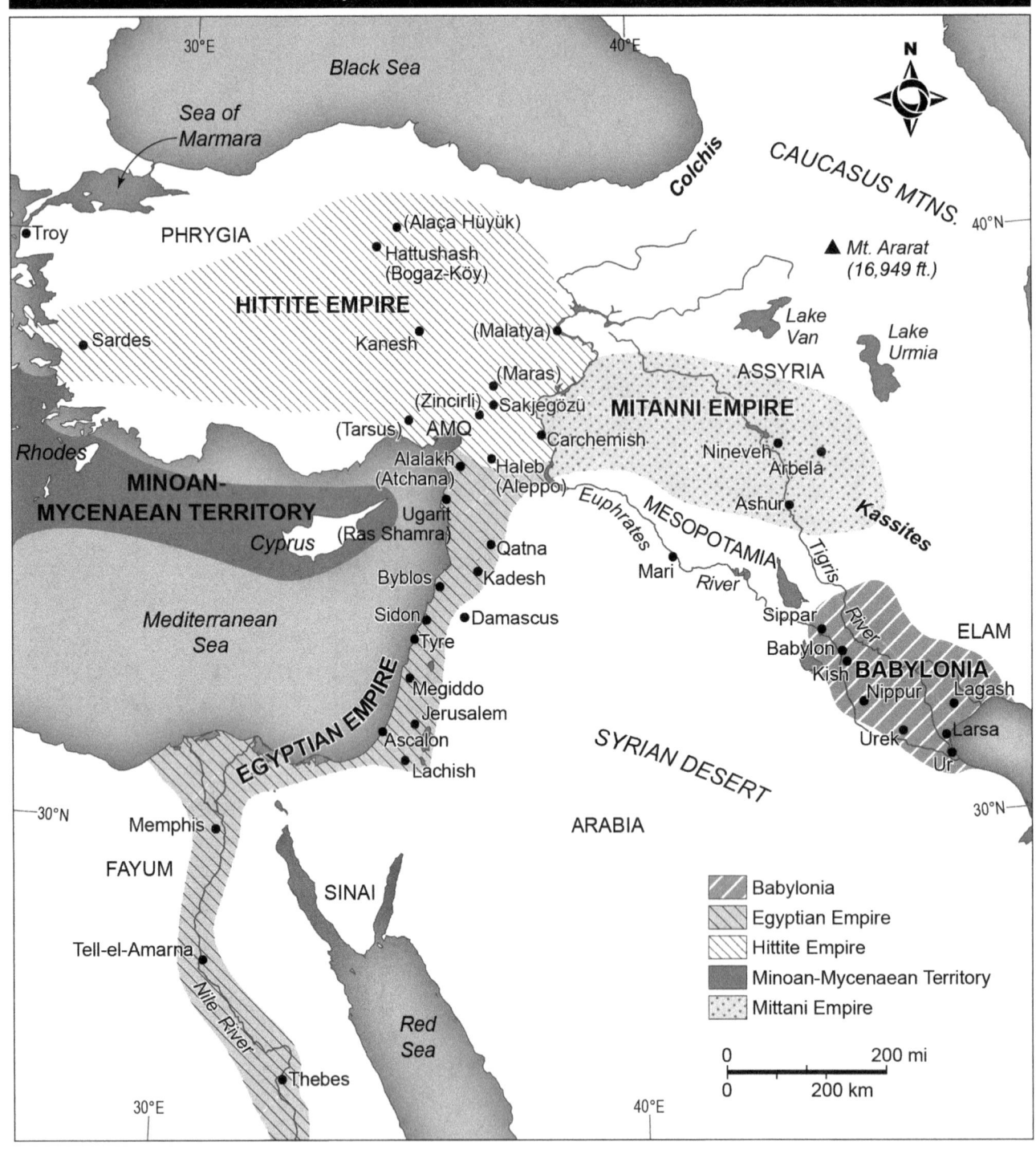

# The East, ca. 600 BCE

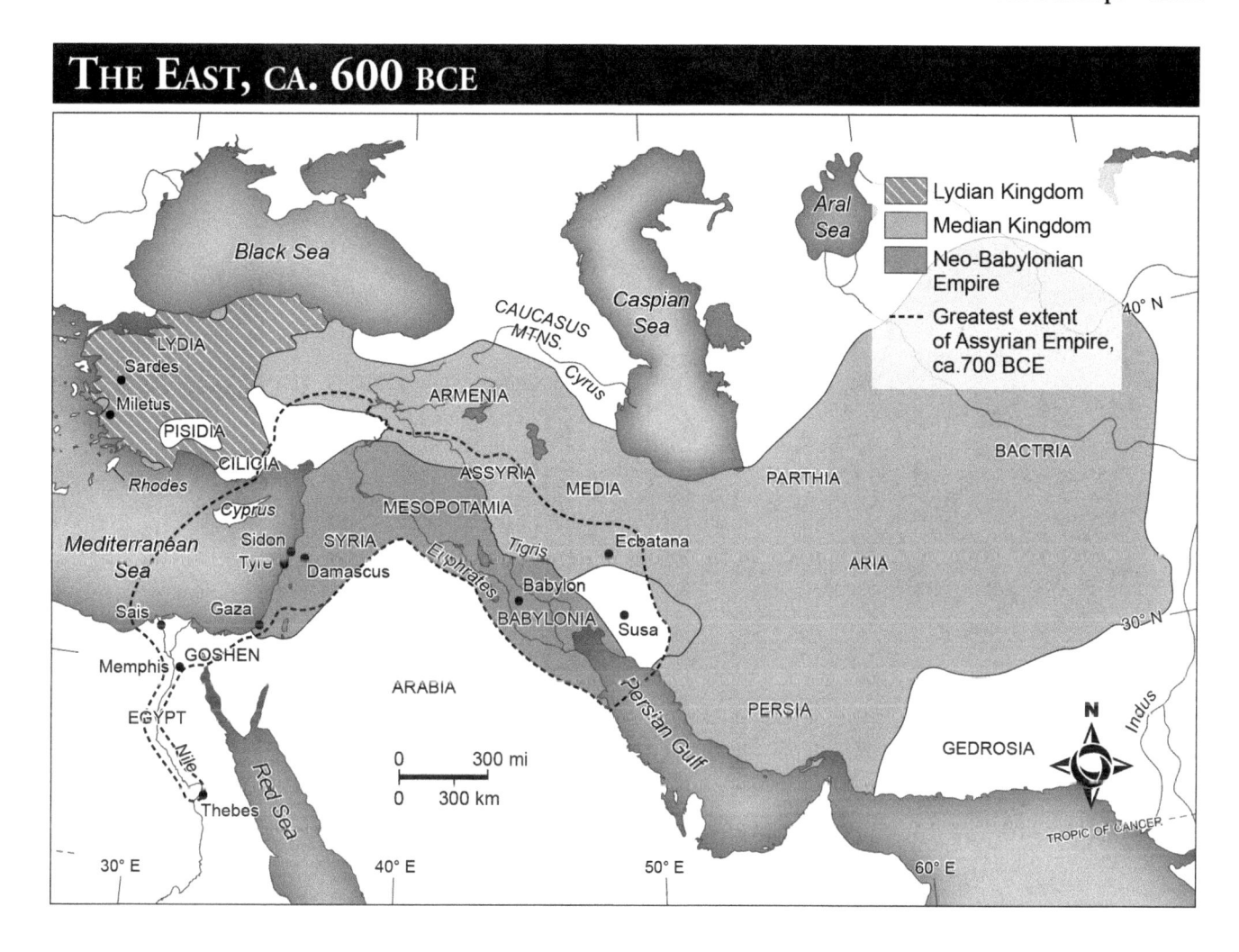

xxviii General Maps

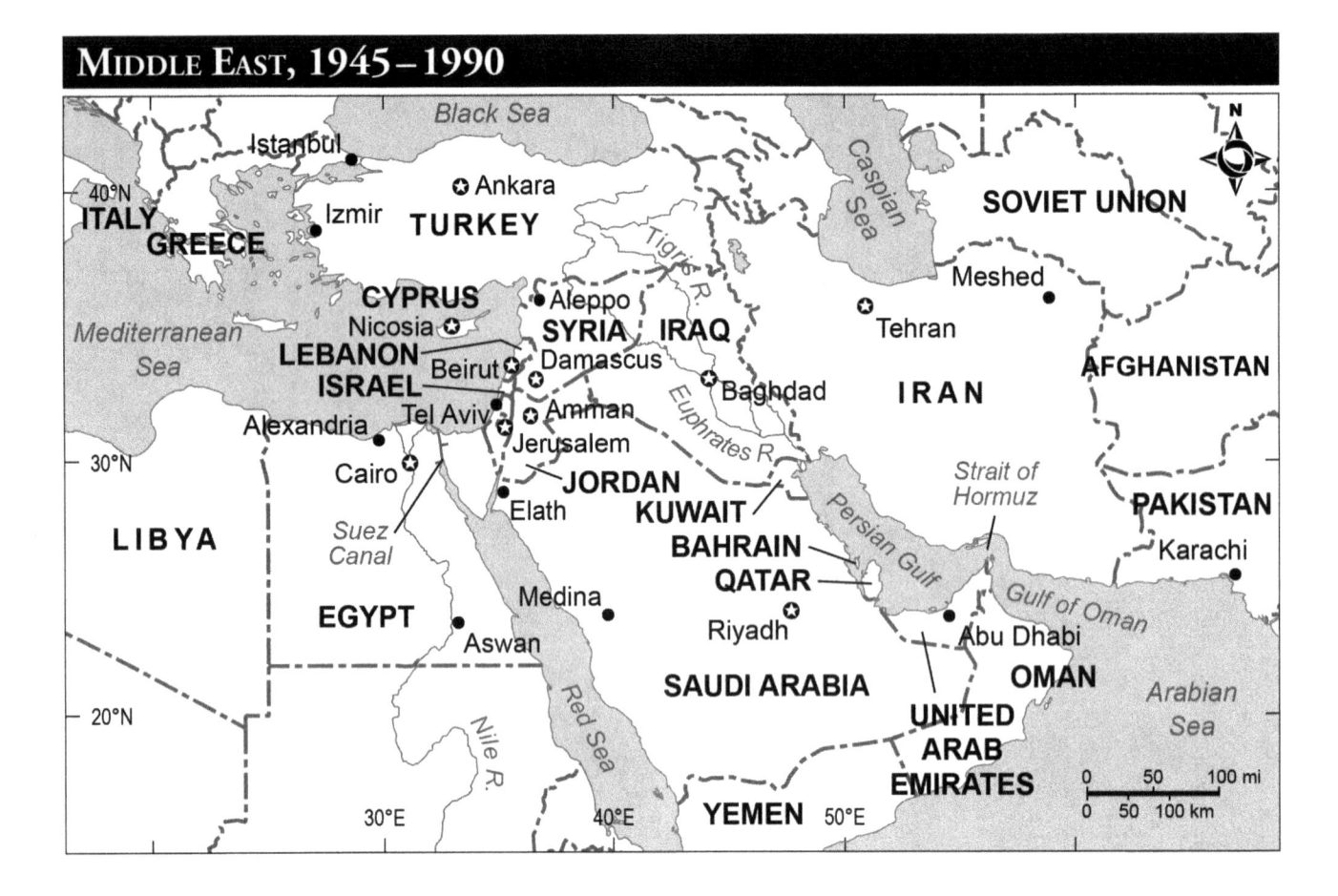

## Middle East, 1945–1990

# O

## O'Connor, Richard Nugent (1889–1981)

British Army general. Born in Sringar, Kashmir (his father was a major in the Royal Irish Fusiliers), on August 21, 1889, Richard Nugent O'Connor was educated at the Royal Military College, Sandhurst, and commissioned in the Scottish Rifles in 1909. In World War I, he was posted to the 7th Division on the Western Front. In June 1917, O'Connor assumed command of a battalion as a temporary lieutenant colonel, but he reverted to captain at the end of the war. Postwar service included attendance and an instructor assignment at the Staff College, Camberley. In 1936, he was again promoted to lieutenant colonel and commanded the 1st Cameronians.

Promoted to brigadier general, O'Connor then commanded the Peshawar Brigade on the northwest frontier in India. After two years there, he was promoted to major general and took charge of the 7th Division in Palestine, a position that also made him the military governor of Jerusalem.

In June 1940, O'Connor moved his division to Egypt, and as a lieutenant general, he took command of the small Western Desert Force in Egypt. When Italian forces invaded Egypt from Libya that September, O'Connor skillfully led his vastly outnumbered troops in Operation COMPASS (December 7, 1940–February 7, 1941). His forces destroyed an Italian army; captured prisoners, equipment, and supplies; and secured the port of Tobruk on January 21–22, 1941. In 10 weeks at a cost to his own forces of fewer than 2,000 casualties, Connor's troops inflicted 12,000 killed or missing and took 138,000 prisoners, including 5 generals, and also secured 400 tanks and 850 guns.

Following the arrival of the German Afrika Korps in North Africa in February 1941, Lieutenant General Erwin Rommel launched a counterattack in March that enjoyed success in large part because much of the Western Desert Force had been sent to fight in Greece. O'Connor was then commanding British troops in Egypt, and he was ordered to the front to serve as adviser to his successor, Lieutenant General Philip Neame. Both O'Connor and Neame were captured by a German patrol on April 6. Held as prisoners of war in Italy for the next two and a half years, both men managed to escape in September 1943 and return to Britain.

O'Connor returned to duty in January 1944 and commanded the VIII Corps beginning in June but was posted to India in November to head first the eastern and then northwestern commands. He was promoted to full general in April 1945. He later served as adjutant general to the forces in 1946 and 1947. O'Connor retired in September 1947 and died in London on June 17, 1981.

BRITTON W. MACDONALD

**See also**
Egypt; World War II, Impact on the Middle East

**References**
Baynes, John. *The Forgotten Victor: General Sir Richard O'Connor KT, GCB, DSO, MC.* London: Brassey's, 1989.
Pitt, Barrie. "O'Connor." In *Churchill's Generals*, ed. John Keegan, 183–199. New York: Grove Weidenfeld, 1991.

## October War

*See* Yom Kippur War

## Odenathus (ca. 220–268)

Septimius Odenathus or Odaenathus was a Palmyrene aristocrat who became ruler of Palmyra and Roman commander in chief and de facto vice emperor in the Near East during the reign of Gallienus (260–268). Born around 220 in Palmyra in present-day Syria, Odenathus ruled a multicultural city, for Palmyra was a depot for the Silk Road trade and had been settled by Semites, Greeks, and Persians. His family had been given Roman citizenship by Emperor Septimius Severus (r. 193–211). In native (Aramaic) inscriptions, Odenathus bore the title "Ruler of Tadmor," the Aramaic name for Palmyra.

Needing a buffer state to deter the aggressive Sassanid Persian Empire, Gallienus conferred on Odenathus the title *corrector totius Orientis* (regent of the East), giving him commander in chief authority over all Roman forces in the Near East. Odenathus also received the title *dux Romanorum* (commander of the Roman forces).

Odenathus successfully campaigned against the Persians, detaching northern Mesopotamia from the Persian Empire and capturing Nisibis. By 263, Odenathus in effect had control of the Levant, Mesopotamia, and Anatolia's eastern region. He then launched an offensive farther into the Persian Empire, reaching Ctesiphon and laying siege to the Persian capital in 264. Although the city withstood the siege and Odenathus was obliged to withdraw, he had retaken all the Roman territory in the east occupied by the Persians since 252.

Odenathus celebrated his victories and was saluted as imperator by his troops, a rank that he was not authorized to use and that made him a usurper, but Gallienus was not in a position to suppress him. Odenathus declared himself king of kings, crowning his son Hairan I as coruler.

Odenathus was married to Septimia Zenobia (b. ca. 240). They had at least two children, both sons, Septimius Herodianus and Septimius Vaballathus. When Odenathus was assassinated under mysterious circumstances in 268, he was succeeded by his younger son Vaballathus and by Zenobia, who governed for her son. Herodianus was dead by this time. Vaballathus and Zenobia began to aggressively extend Palmyrene power in the Near East, conquering Roman Arabia, Egypt, and Syria and extending into Asia Minor. Aurelian, now Roman emperor (r. 270–275), could not tolerate this threat and made war upon the Palmyrene Empire, reconquering it and capturing Zenobia, whom he displayed in his triumph in 274.

Sara E. Phang

### See also
Aurelian, Emperor; Roman-Sassanid Wars; Zenobia

### References
Potter, David S. *The Roman Empire at Bay, AD 180–395*. New York: Routledge, 2004.

Southern, Pat. *Empress Zenobia: Palmyra's Queen*. New York: Continuum, 2008.

Watson, Alaric. *Aurelian and the Third Century*. New York: Routledge, 1999.

## Olmert, Ehud (1945–)

Israeli politician and prime minister (2006–2009). Born in Binyamina in the British Mandate for Palestine on September 30, 1945, Ehud Olmert graduated from Hebrew University of Jerusalem in 1968 with a degree in psychology and philosophy. In 1973 he earned a law degree. Olmert then began his mandatory military service with the Israel Defense Force (IDF), which he completed in 1971 as a military correspondent for the IDF journal *Bamachance*.

In 1973 Olmert was elected to the Knesset (Israeli parliament), making him the youngest member at the time. From 1993 to 2003 as mayor of Jerusalem, he became a national figure as the first member of the Likud Party to hold the position. While in office, he spearheaded the development of the light rail system in Jerusalem, improved education, augmented infrastructure, and supported controversial housing developments reserved exclusively for Jews on the Mount of Olives and Ras al-Amud.

In January 2003 Olmert was again elected to the Knesset. Following the elections, he assumed the posts of deputy prime minister and minister of industry, trade, and labor. In August 2005 he became acting finance minister, taking over for Benjamin Netanyahu, who resigned in protest against Prime Minister Ariel Sharon's Gaza disengagement plan. Olmert had initially opposed withdrawing from land captured in the 1967 Six-Day War and had voted against the 1978 Camp David Accords. But he actively supported the Gaza pullout and championed Sharon's efforts to pave the way for a comprehensive settlement of the Palestinian problem.

As deputy prime minister in Sharon's second term, Olmert became the prime minister's most important ally during the September 2005 unilateral disengagement plan, which met with howls of protest from many in the Likud

Party. When Sharon bolted from Likud in November 2005 and formed a new party, Kadima, Olmert became one of the first to join him.

On January 4, 2006, after Sharon suffered a catastrophic brain hemorrhage that permanently incapacitated him, Olmert became acting prime minister and acting chairman of Kadima. In office, he continued many of Sharon's policies, including construction of the highly controversial security fence with the stated aim of protecting Israeli civilians from Palestinian bombers along the border of Israel and the West Bank. On January 24, 2006, however, Olmert formally announced at the Herzliya Conference that he backed the creation of a Palestinian state and asserted that Israel would have to relinquish parts of the West Bank to maintain its Jewish majority.

On April 14, 2006, Olmert officially became prime minister. He continued to be challenged by the Palestinian land issue controversy and the erection of the security fence. In June 2006 he signaled his willingness to meet with Palestinian Authority (PA) president Mahmoud Abbas to fulfill the prescriptions of the so-called Road Map to Peace and create the way for the establishment of a Palestinian state. In the meantime, Olmert stated that Israel would continue to abide by the unilateral disengagement plan first introduced by his predecessor.

The brief but damaging Israeli invasion of southern Lebanon during June–July 2006 brought sharp criticism from both the Left and the Right because of Olmert's handling of the crisis. The Right accused him of not going far enough to break the back of the Hezbollah fighters, while the Left rebuked him for ordering attacks that devastated Lebanon's infrastructure and killed scores of innocent civilians. His administration was also roundly criticized in the international community for its actions during the brief conflict. At the end of the war his approval rating stood at just 22 percent, and the subsequent Winograd Commission interim report was sharply critical of his handling of the crisis. In September 2006 his chief of staff resigned, another signal of eroding support.

Olmert approved Operation ORCHARD, the September 6, 2007, Israeli air strike against a suspected nuclear reactor in Syria, allegedly being built with North Korean and Iranian assistance. In May 2008, however, the Omert government opened indirect peace talks with Syria, brokered by the Turkish government. Syria broke off the talks several months later in response to the Israeli invasion of Gaza.

With southern Israel having come under rocket attacks from the Gaza Strip, Olmert threatened invasion. When the rocket attacks did not stop, on December 27, 2008, Israeli aircraft and warships attacked Gaza in Operation CAST LEAD. Ground forces followed on January 3. The fighting lasted 22 days until a cease-fire was agreed to. Israel forces subsequently withdrew from Gaza.

In July 2008 amid growing charges of corruption, Olmert had announced that he would not stand for reelection as party leader. On March 31, 2009, he was succeeded as premier by Benjamin Netanyahu. In August 2009 an Israeli court indicted Olmert on five criminal counts, most of which involved fraud and corruption. Found guilty of bribery, in May 2014 Omert received a sentence of six years in prison. One of the principal charges against him was later thrown out on appeal. Olmert entered prison in February 2016 and was relased in July 2017 after serving only 16 months of a 27-month sentence for fraud and bribery.

LaVonne Jackson Leslie and Paul G. Pierpaoli Jr.

### See also
Abbas, Mahmoud; Camp David Accords; Gaza Strip Disengagement; Israeli Air Strike on Presumed Syrian Nuclear Facility; Israeli Security Fence; Netanyahu, Benjamin; Sharon, Ariel

### References
Ben-Ami, Shlomo. *Scars of War, Wounds of Peace: The Israeli-Arab Tragedy.* New York: Oxford University Press, 2006.

Gorenberg, Gershom. *The Accidental Empire: Israel and the Birth of the Settlements, 1967–1977.* New York: Times Books, 2006.

Slater, Elinor, and Robert Slater. *Great Jewish Men.* Middle Village, NY: Jonathan David Publishers, 1996.

## Oman

The Sultanate of Oman is an Arab nation located along the southeastern coast of the Arabian Peninsula and strategically situated at the mouth of the Persian Gulf. Oman is 119,498 square miles in area. It is bordered by Yemen to the southwest, Saudi Arabia to the west, the United Arab Emirates (UAE) to the northwest, the Arabian Sea to the southeast, and the Gulf of Oman to the northeast. Oman also shares marine borders with Iran and Pakistan. The two Omani territorial exclaves Madha and Musandam are surrounded by the UAE on their land sides, with the Strait of Hormuz and the Gulf of Oman forming Musandam's coastal boundaries.

Oman had a 2018 population of some 4.75 million. Its capital and largest city is Muscat. Islam is practiced by some 95 percent of the population and is the state religion. There are no governmental statistics on religious affiliation, but nearly half the Muslims, including the sultan, are of the Ibadi School of Islam, which resulted from one of the first

# Oman

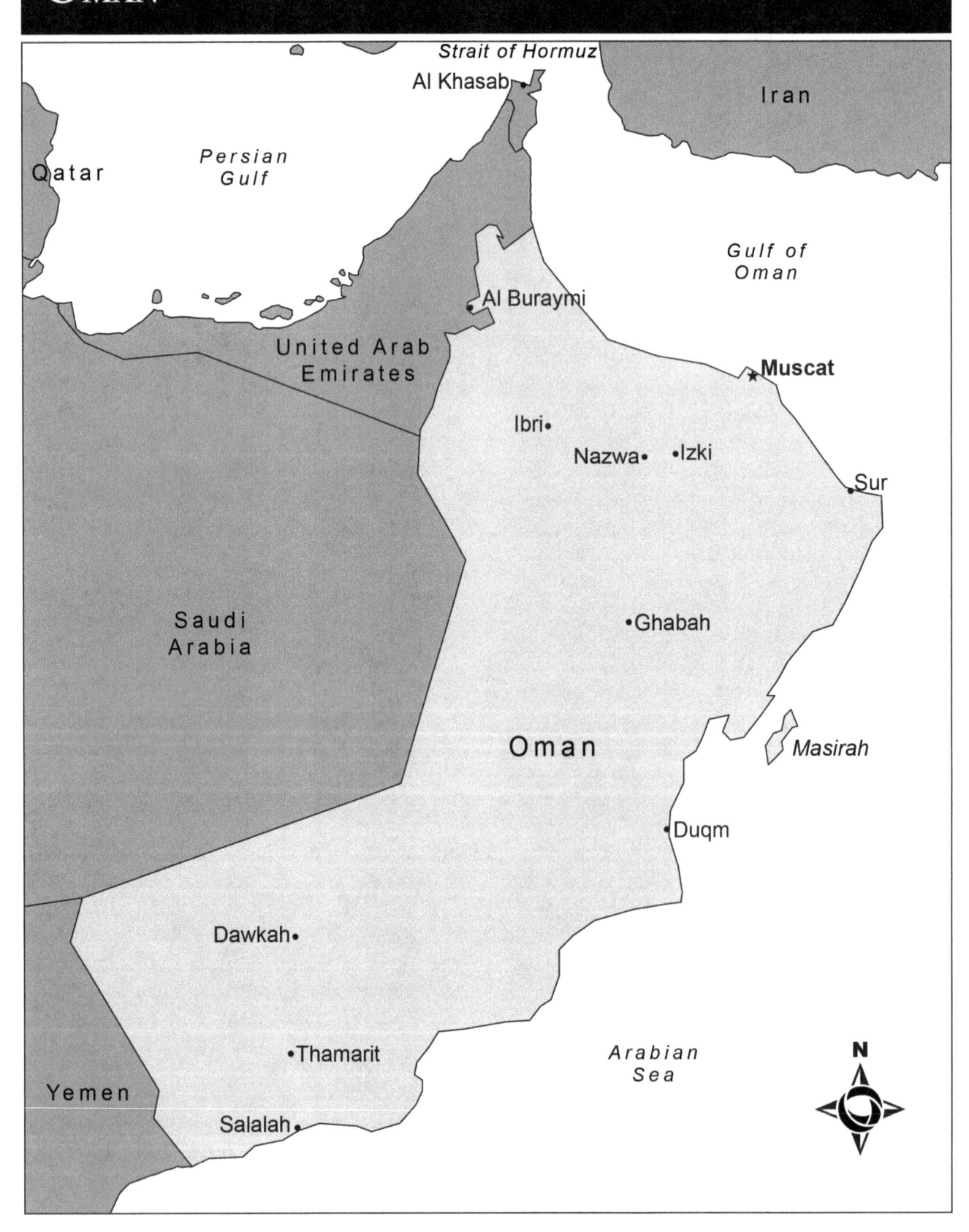

schisms in Islam and is close to mainstream Islam. Another 20 percent are Sunni Muslims. The remainder are Shiites, who generally live in coastal communities. Virtually all the non-Muslims in Oman are foreign workers. In religion they include Jains, Buddhists, Zoroastrians, Sikhs, Baha'is, Hindus and Christians.

Oman enjoys a relatively high standard of living primarily as a consequence of its petroleum revenues, ranking 25th globally. Oil was discovered in 1964, and production began in 1967. In sharp contrast to most of its neighboring states, which rely heavily on oil exports, much of Oman's economy is based on trade and tourism.

Oman is an absolute hereditary monarchy based on male primogeniture. Sultan Qaboos bin Said al-Said is the longest-serving ruler of any country in the Middle East, having ascended the Omani throne in 1970. Although the sultan has enacted some political reforms, he retains much control over the government and has sole control over the armed forces. There are no political parties, and there is no official opposition to the sitting government. Sharia law is the source of all legislation.

Arabs came to dominate Oman and introduced Islam in the late 600s. In 1507 the Portuguese attacked and sacked the port of Muscat and captured much of the Omani coast. They were not driven out until 1650. From the late 17th century, however, the Omani Sultanate was a powerful empire with considerable influence in the Persian Gulf and Indian Ocean regions. Indeed, Muscat was the principal trading port of the Persian Gulf region. The height of Omani influence came in the 19th century, when it included parts of the Indian subcontinent and reached as far south as Zanzibar (now part of Tanzania) and Mombasa. The Persians invaded Oman in 1737 but were driven out in 1749. Ahmad bin Said al-Busaidi became sultan on June 10, 1749, beginning the al-Said dynasty that continues to rule Oman to the present.

In 1913 the interior of Oman came under the control of Ibadite imams, restricting the power of the sultan to the coastal areas. Under a British-brokered agreement in 1920, the sultan recognized the autonomy of the interior. On February 10, 1932, Said bin Taimur became sultan. He took a feudal and isolationist approach. In 1954, however, fighting resumed between the imamate forces who sought an independent state and those of the sultan.

In July 1957 Imam Ghalib bin Ali, who had conspired against the sultan in 1955 and been exiled, received the support of Egypt and Saudi Arabia and led a new revolt. After major fighting near Nizwa on July 15, 1957, the sultan requested British military assistance. This aid, consisting mostly of air support, enabled the sultan's forces to crush the revolt in mid-August. An effort by Arab states in the United Nations to censure the British for their intervention failed to win approval, and by 1959 the sultan's forces had regained control of the interior.

During 1962–1976 the government had to contend with a rebellion in the southern dependency of Dhofar in which leftist forces were pitted against government troops. Said bin Taimur had attempted to outlaw most aspects of 20th-century life, and he had subjected Dhofar to greater restrictions and economic exploitation than in the rest of Oman. The rebellion was led by tribal leader Mussalim bin Nafl, who formed the Dhofar Liberation Front (DLF). Saudi Arabia, which had already attempted to gain control of the Buraimi Oasis, provided arms and equipment to the insurgents. Ghalib bin Ali, the exiled imam of Oman, also supported the revolt.

Fighting commenced in December 1962, with hit-and-run raids against the British air base at Salalah. This intensified in 1964 with hit-and-run attacks against government installations and oil industry facilities. Following a failed assassination attempt in April 1966, Sultan Said bin Taimur retired to his palace and was never again seen in public. His forces, however, launched major search-and-destroy missions in Dhofar in which villages were attacked and laid waste and wells were destroyed.

Egypt and leftist movements in Yemen and Aden furnished aid to the rebels. With the establishment of the People's Democratic Republic of Yemen in 1967, the rebels secured a steady stream of arms, but this also led to a split, with some of the rebels breaking off to form the Popular Front for the Liberation of the Occupied Arabian Gulf (PFLOAG) with the aim of establishing a Marxist-Leninist state. It received the support of South Yemen and the People's Republic of China.

By 1969, the DLF and the PFLOAG controlled large stretches of Dhofar. The sultan's forces were outnumbered, with only some 1,000 men in the rebel province. The British were then forced to deploy small military detachments to protect the airfield at Salalah. Meanwhile, another guerrilla organization appeared in northern Oman in the National Democratic Front for the Liberation of Oman and the Arabian Gulf (NDFLOAG).

With it now clear that the insurgency could not be ended without new leadership, on July 23, 1970, Said bin Taimur was deposed in a coup led by his son, Qaboos bin Said al-Said, who then commenced a liberalization and modernization program, pledging to use Oman's wealth to benefit its people. Assisted by the British Special Air Service, he launched a comprehensive counterinsurgency program that included a "hearts and minds" component and amnesty for the rebels. At the same time, government forces assisted by the British endeavored to cut off rebel resupply. Aircraft proved to be a major assist, as did training personnel and military assistance provided by the shah of Iran. Indeed, on February 2, 1975, Oman signed a defense pact with Iran whereby that country pledged to support Oman in the event of an attack. The Kingdom of Jordan also sent aid. Government forces now made steady gains, and the rebellion was declared at an end in January 1976, although isolated incidents continued into 1983.

Under Sultan Qaboos, Oman's foreign and economic policies have generally favored the West. In an agreement concluded on June 4, 1980, the United States secured rights to certain air and naval bases in Oman in return for military and economic assistance. Oman also regularly participated in regional multinational military exercises involving the United States, Egypt, and other nations.

On June 6, 1982, Oman joined Saudi Arabia, Bahrain, Kuwait, Qatar, and the United Arab Emirates in establishing a joint military command structure and integrated air defense system. This was prompted by the perceived threats of the Islamic Republic of Iran, the ongoing Iran-Iraq War (1980–1988), and the Soviet-Afghan War (1979–1989).

In the years leading up to the Persian Gulf War of 1991, Sultan Qaboos steadily increased the size and effectiveness of Oman's armed forces, especially in the Iran-Iraq War during which al-Said deployed an infantry battalion to serve in the Peninsula Shield force, a military arm of the Gulf Cooperation Council (GCC) meant to deter aggression from either Iraq or Iran. Meanwhile, the British Royal Air Force continued to use an air base on Masirah Island off Oman's southern coast.

After Iraq invaded and occupied Kuwait in August 1990, Oman became a strong supporter of the international military coalition that drove Iraqi forces from Kuwait. Coalition forces used several of Oman's air bases as key staging areas for the conflict. The country also contributed 6,300 ground troops, who were deployed to Saudi Arabia. On the second day of the ground war in February 1991, Omani troops, along with the Saudi 10th Mechanized Brigade, entered Kuwait, helping to effect its liberation by February 28.

In 1999, Oman and the UAE signed a border agreement delineating most of their disputed common frontier. In October 2001, large-scale British-Omani military exercises in the Omani desert coincided with the launch of strikes against the Taliban in Afghanistan prompted by the terror attacks on the United States on September 11.

Sultan Qaboos meanwhile continued his liberalization program. In 1997 he decreed that women could vote and stand for election to the Majlis al-Shura, or Consultative Council. Two women were duly elected. In November 2002 he extended voting rights to all citizens over the age of 21, the voters having previously been chosen from among tribal leaders, intellectuals, and businessmen. The first elections under universal suffrage occurred in October 2003.

In January 2005, nearly 100 suspected Islamists were arrested in Oman. Thirty-one were subsequently convicted of trying to overthrow the government, but they were pardoned in June. In late February 2011 as part of the so-called Arab Spring, protests erupted, with demonstrators demanding jobs and political reform. One demonstrator was shot dead by the police. Sultan Qaboos sought to tamp down the protests with a pledge of more jobs and improved benefits. On March 5 he also replaced three of his top government officials, and late that year he granted the newly elected Majlis al-Shura greater powers. There was a limit to criticism allowed, however, for in September 2012 trials occurred of activists who had criticized the government online. Six were given jail terms of 12–18 months, but the next March Qaboos pardoned a number of those convicted.

Oman's military consists of an army, a navy, and an air force. Its military establishment is well equipped with modern hardware and weapons systems purchased chiefly from Great Britain, the United States, and France. Sultan Qaboos has long worried about potential incursions from rival Arab nations and remains particularly concerned about Iran's foreign and military policies. As such, the nation spends a huge portion of its gross domestic product (GDP) on defense expenditures, which are currently estimated at about $2.1 billion a year, or 11.5 percent of GDP. Active military personnel number some 44,000. The ground forces are equipped with some 117 main battle tanks and 37 light tanks. The air force has approximately three dozen combat aircraft.

Although Oman's armed forces did not actively participate in the subsequent Afghan War or Iraq War, Oman cooperated with coalition forces by permitting overflights of its air space and allowing coalition forces to utilize some of its bases as staging areas. In the summer of 2018 the U.S. Congress was considering an aid package for Oman, which would help bolster the country's border defenses and keep the chaos in neighboring Yemen from spilling over into Oman.

PAUL G. PIERPAOLI JR. AND SPENCER C. TUCKER

See also

Dhofar Rebellion; Gulf Cooperation Council; Persian Gulf War, Overview; Qaboos bin Said al-Said; United Arab Emirates

**References**

Jones, Jeremy, and Nicholas Ridout. *A History of Modern Oman.* Cambridge: Cambridge University Press, 2015.

Kechichian, Joseph A. *Oman and the World: The Emergence of an Independent Foreign Policy.* Santa Monica, CA: Rand Corporation, 1995.

Owtram, Francis. *A Modern History of Oman: Formation of the State since 1920.* London: I. B. Tauris, 2004.

Valeri, Marc. *Oman: Politics and Society in the Qaboos State.* Oxford: Oxford University Press, 2015.

## OPERA, Operation

*See* Osiraq Raid

## Organization of Petroleum Exporting Countries

Oil cartel founded on September 14, 1960, during the Baghdad Conference to give oil-exporting countries leverage in negotiations with foreign oil companies that, at the time, controlled production and dictated prices and the share of profits going to producing nations. In the late 1960s and early 1970s, the Arab member nations of the Organization of Petroleum Exporting Countries (OPEC) enacted embargoes against supporters of Israel during the 1967 Six-Day War and the 1973 Yom Kippur (Ramadan) War in an effort to influence Middle East policy. Since the 1980s OPEC has acted largely apolitically, seeking to stabilize oil production and prices to maximize members' profits while guaranteeing a reliable oil supply to the world economy.

As early as 1945, oil-producing nations recognized that a unified stance on pricing and output would improve their effectiveness in bargaining with the major oil companies. In 1959 the U.S. government established a mandatory quota on all imported oil to the United States in an attempt to give preferential treatment to oil producers in Canada and Mexico. In so doing, the world's largest oil consumer had effectively imposed a partial boycott on Middle East oil. The net result was depressed prices for Persian Gulf crude. To make matters worse, the oil companies enacted a series of unilateral price cuts in 1959 and 1960 that caused oil prices to fall even lower.

The severe impact that these policies had on Middle East oil provided the impetus for the world's five largest oil exporters—Saudi Arabia, Iran, Iraq, Kuwait, and Venezuela—to band together with the express purpose of reversing these price cuts. Over its first two decades of operations, OPEC expanded its membership to include Qatar, Indonesia, Libya, the United Arab Emirates, Algeria, Nigeria, Ecuador, and Gabon. During its first decade of operations, OPEC enjoyed little success. Prices continued to float lower well into 1971. In 1958 oil sold for $10.85 per barrel (in 1990 dollars). In 1971 it sold for just $7.46 per barrel. The cartel doggedly negotiated with oil companies but with little success in eroding the oil companies' power to set prices. Beginning in 1973, however, OPEC finally succeeded in wresting pricing power from the oil companies, which were increasingly vulnerable to political decisions made in the oil-producing states that housed their operations. On October 16, 1973, in reaction to the Yom Kippur War, OPEC cut production, which ultimately quadrupled the price of oil, beginning a series of price hikes that effectively ended the companies' control over all but the technical side of oil production.

As Arab nations' production made up an increasing share of the world oil market, they began to use their power politically, applying oil embargoes against Britain and France during the 1956 Suez Crisis and against the United States, Britain, and West Germany during the 1967 Six-Day War. These embargoes failed, however, in large part because of U.S. willingness to make up the oil shortfalls to its allies. Also, because oil is a worldwide commodity, limited embargoes have little effect, as nations targeted by an embargo will usually find other ways to purchase petroleum.

Arab oil producers' attempts to use the oil weapon to influence the Arab-Israeli conflict enjoyed great success in October 1973 during the Yom Kippur (Ramadan) War, precipitated by Egypt and Syria's surprise attack on Israel. On October 17, one day after OPEC initiated its production cuts that spiked sharp price increases, the Organization of Arab Petroleum Exporting Countries (OAPEC) decreased overall oil production and initiated a five-month oil embargo against the United States and the Netherlands to protest their support for Israel. The oil price shock together with worldwide production cuts and the embargo caused severe economic disruptions in much of the world. The impact on the United States was particularly severe. The nation's economy, which was already groaning under inflation, relatively high unemployment, low growth, and budget deficits, tilted into a serious recession. Government efforts to cap prices and control supplies only worsened the situation, as shortages and even limited rationing of gasoline became widespread. From 1973 to 1974, the price of oil catapulted from about $8 per barrel to more than $27 (1990 dollars). The American economy remained in a virtual recession into the mid-1980s.

The Soviet Union, an oil exporter, had little to lose from the Arab states' use of oil as a weapon. As such, it encouraged the oil embargo because it weakened the West economically and resulted in increased oil revenues for itself. At the same time, the Soviet Union took advantage of decreased Arab production and higher prices, significantly increasing its oil exports to the United States during the embargo, a fact that neither nation publicized at the time.

The oil embargo caught Americans largely unprepared. As a result, the U.S. government instituted gasoline rationing that resulted in long lines at gasoline stations and national anxiety over energy supplies. In response to the price increases and the embargo, the United States sought to establish a cartel of oil-consuming nations to confront OPEC directly, but the major importers' diverse oil needs and political positions on the Arab-Israeli conflict stymied this plan. In 1975 the U.S. Congress did pass legislation to establish a Strategic Petroleum Reserve (SPR) to protect against future supply disruptions. Since then, the government has stored millions of barrels of oil in massive underground salt caverns along the Gulf of Mexico coast. The SPR may exist more for psychological reasons than anything else, however. The reserve would run out very quickly in the event of a partial or complete oil supply shutdown, and there is not enough oil in the caverns to affect the worldwide price of oil.

Although the Arab states ended the oil embargo soon after hostilities ceased and without securing the desired Israeli withdrawal from territories occupied in 1967, this unprecedented attempt transformed the position of oil-producing states, gave OPEC major clout, and fueled Arab nationalism. Since 1973, both the United States and the Soviet Union have devoted increasing attention to the Middle East as a strategic battleground. The Arab world meanwhile has endeavored to exercise political influence independent of the superpowers.

OPEC's achievement of higher oil prices in 1973 and 1974 ultimately damaged the oil producers' economies by the late 1970s, when the resulting worldwide recession produced inflation and falling demand for oil. Two major crises in the Middle East during 1979–1980 resulted in yet another oil price spike. As a result of the 1979 Iranian Revolution, which saw the ousting of Mohammad Reza Shah Pahlavi, the imposition of an anti-Western Islamic fundamentalist government in his stead, and the taking of American embassy personnel by radical Iranian students, oil prices shot up from $24.46 per barrel (1990 dollars) to $49.52 by mid-1980. The effects on the world's economy were stunning. In the United States, inflation peaked at more than 13 percent, while interest rates approached 20 percent. The 1979–1980 oil shock was not part of OPEC's strategy, although it did benefit handsomely from it in the immediate term. Clearly, the markets were reacting to great regional instability in the Middle East, which began with the Iranian Revolution and was exacerbated by the start of the Iran-Iraq War (1980–1988).

Since the 1980s, OPEC has pursued a policy of relatively prudent price control, ensuring substantial profits without adversely affecting the world economy. Beginning in the mid-1980s, the price of oil dropped and continued to drop until the Iraqi invasion of Kuwait in August 1990 precipitated more jolting price hikes. After mid-1991, however, when an international coalition reversed the Iraqi invasion and soundly defeated Iraqi dictator Saddam Hussein's army, oil prices fell again. They would continue to drift downward, reaching new inflation-adjusted lows by the late 1990s. After 2002, however, OPEC again began to reap record revenues, as war and unrest in the Middle East and simple greed drove oil prices to record highs. This situation was reversed at the end of 2008 with the onset of the world economic crisis when oil plunged to $38 a barrel, more than $100 less than it had been trading six months before. During late 2017 and into the summer of 2018, oil prices again began to rise, increasing to about $70 per barrel. This prompted large producers such as Saudi Arabia to pledge more output and prompted U.S. president Donald Trump to complain publicly in July 2018 that OPEC's policies were the chief source of the price increases.

OPEC currently has 14 member states. Indonesia resigned at the end of 2008, having become a net importer of oil and being unable to meet its production quotas, while Qatar resigned on January 1, 2019.

Elun Gabriel

**See also**
Iran; Iraq; Kuwait; Persian Gulf War, Overview; Saudi Arabia

**References**
Ahrari, Mohammed E. *OPEC: The Failing Giant*. Lexington: University Press of Kentucky, 1986.
Al-Sowayegh, Abdulaziz. *Arab Petro-Politics*. New York: St. Martin's, 1984.
Klinghoffer, Arthur Jay. *The Soviet Union & International Oil Politics*. New York: Columbia University Press, 1977.
Rustow, Dankwart A. *Oil and Turmoil: America Faces OPEC and the Middle East*. New York: Norton, 1982.
Skeet, Ian. *OPEC: Twenty-Five Years of Prices and Politics*. Cambridge: Cambridge University Press, 1988.

# Osiraq Raid (June 7, 1981)

Israeli air strike, also known as Operation OPERA, on Iraq's nuclear power facility on June 7, 1981. The slowly developing Iraqi nuclear program, begun in the 1960s, received French assistance in the late 1970s through a light-water reactor at the al-Tuwaytha Nuclear Center, located some 11 miles southeast of Baghdad. The type of French reactor was known as Osiris, and it was named Osiraq (Osirak in French) for the reactor and Iraq. The Iraqis named it Tammuz I for the month in the Babylonian calendar when the Baath Party took power in Iraq in 1968.

Although the 40-megawatt light-water nuclear reactor was ostensibly for peaceful purposes, there were widespread concerns that Iraqi dictator Saddam Hussein would instead use it as part of his plan to secure nuclear weapons. The International Atomic Energy Agency monitored the handling of fuel at the new facility, but there was general agreement that its oversight was not adequate.

On September 30, 1980, at the beginning of the Iran-Iraq War (1980–1988), two Iranian McDonnell-Douglas F-4 Phantom aircraft bombed the reactor as part of a larger strike on a nearby power facility. Damage was only minor, and the program was not seriously impeded.

Israel meanwhile greatly feared nuclear weapons in the hands of any Arab nation. Intelligence estimates about the Iraqi capability to develop an atomic bomb ranged from a few months to as long as 10 years. The government of Prime Minister Menachem Begin rejected Iraqi explanations that the Osiraq reactor was only for electricity generation. Nor was Begin prepared to wait to take action until after the Iraqis had actually built a nuclear bomb. But within Israeli political and even military circles, there was strong opposition to a preemptive strike against the facility. Some, such as Labor Party leader Shimon Peres, feared that such a raid would ostracize Israel within the international community or that the Arab-Israeli peace process would be derailed. Others fretted that a retaliatory Arab air strike would be launched against the Israeli nuclear facility at Dimona. Attempts on the part of Israeli foreign minister Yitzhak Shamir to enlist French and American assistance in halting Iraqi nuclear development failed. France was unwilling to end its assistance to Iraq. Iraq was a major purchaser of French arms, and the relationship ensured France access to oil.

With Knesset elections looming in 1981, Begin feared that he might be voted out of office and that a new government might not have the resolve to stop Iraq's nuclear ambitions. By mid-1980, intelligence reports indicated that the French would soon deliver uranium fuel rods to the Iraqis. Once these were installed, any attack on the facility would lead to the dispersion of radiation. If a preemptive strike was to occur, it would have to be mounted soon.

In October 1980, convinced that the Osiraq nuclear reactor would soon allow Iraq to achieve nuclear status, Begin ordered Lieutenant General Rafael Eitan, chief of staff of the Israel Defense Force (IDF), to begin planning for an Israeli Air Force (IAF) preemptive strike to destroy the plant no later than June 1981, when the reactor was expected to become operational. In the meantime, new Israeli foreign minister Moshe Dayan conducted talks with French, Italian, and U.S. officials, all without meaningful result.

Attacking the Iraqi nuclear facility presented the IAF with great challenges. Israeli planes would have to travel a greater distance than any other Israeli air sortie up to that time (a round trip of about 1,350 miles), and the flight would violate the air space of several Arab countries. Recently acquired American-made F-16 fighter-bombers gave the IAF the capability of flying that distance without refueling while carrying the necessary ordnance. Ironically, the F-16s that Israel purchased had originally been earmarked for sale to Iran, a deal that was cancelled after the overthrow of Mohammad Reza Shah Pahlavi in 1979.

In May 1981 Begin learned that enriched uranium was about to be shipped to the Osiraq facility. Israeli pilots had been carrying out practice attack sorties, and eight IAF pilots from the 116th and 117th Squadrons were then selected for the dangerous mission. Six F-15 fighter aircraft provided air escort for the eight attack F-16s, while an additional two F-15s provided communications support.

Operation COBRA was launched beginning at 3:05 p.m. on June 7, 1981, from Etzion Air Force Base in the Negev. Colonel Zeev Raz commanded the mission. Also flying on the mission were Yiftah Spector, Israel's second-highest-scoring ace, and Ilan Ramon, who would become Israel's first astronaut and die in the *Columbia* space shuttle disaster of February 1, 2002. Each of the F-16s carried two 2,000-pound bombs fused for delayed detonation in order to ensure adequate penetration. In their flight to the Iraqi facility, Israeli aircraft violated the air space of both Jordan and Saudi Arabia.

Flying at extremely low altitudes to avoid detection by radar, the F-16s arrived in the vicinity of the facility at 5:35 p.m. local time. The F-16 pilots individually ascended to attack altitude and then dove toward the reactor. Iraqi antiaircraft and surface-to-air missile fire was poorly coordinated and had no effect on the outcome of the raid. The raid lasted less than two minutes. The raiders scored at least 10 direct hits, and the reactor lay in ruins. The attack was on a

Sunday when the workers had the day off, and there were no civilian casualties. All IAF planes returned safely to base.

International condemnation of Israel immediately followed. Even the normally pro-Israeli United States voted in favor of the United Nations Security Council resolution formally condemning the attack. But there was also secret support for the successful mission. Other nations, notably Iran, had harbored fears of a Hussein-led nuclear-armed Iraq bullying its way to regional hegemony. Indeed, had Iraq achieved nuclear status, the regime there would have held the upper hand over Iran in the Iran-Iraq War.

After the attack, France at first agreed to rebuild Osiraq but then found excuses not to do so. Nevertheless, throughout the 1980s Iraq continued to seek nuclear weapons programs. During the 1991 Persian Gulf War air campaign, coalition raids decimated the Osiraq nuclear facility and ended the possibility of near-term success for Hussein's nuclear program.

Thomas D. Veve and Spencer C. Tucker

### See also
Begin, Menachem; Eitan, Rafael; Hussein, Saddam; Iran-Iraq War

### References
Claire, Rodger W. *Raid on the Sun: Inside Israel's Secret Campaign That Denied Saddam the Bomb.* New York: Broadway, 2004.

Federation of American Scientists. *Israel's Strike against the Iraqi Nuclear Reactor, 7 June 1981.* Jerusalem: Menachem Begin Heritage Center, 2003.

Feldman, Shai. *The Raid on Osiraq: A Preliminary Assessment.* Tel Aviv: Center for Strategic Studies, 1981.

McCormack, Timothy L. H. *Self-Defense in International Law: The Israeli Raid on the Iraqi Nuclear Reactor.* New York: St. Martin's, 1996.

Perlmutter, Amos, Michael Handel, and Uri Bar-Joseph. *Two Minutes over Baghdad.* 2nd ed. London: Frank Cass, 2003.

Vandenbroucke, Lucien S. *The Israeli Strike against Osiraq: The Dynamics of Fear and Proliferation in the Middle East.* Washington, DC: U.S. Government Printing Office, 1984.

## Oslo Accords (September 13, 1993)

The agreement commonly called the Oslo Accords and formally known as the Declaration of Principles on Interim Self-Government Arrangements was signed on September 13, 1993, in Washington, D.C., by Israeli prime minister Yitzhak Rabin, Palestine Liberation Organization (PLO) chairman Yasser Arafat, and U.S. president Bill Clinton. In the Oslo Accords, the PLO, the Palestinians' major representative party and de facto government-in-exile, formally recognized Israel's right to exist and Israel's sovereignty over 78 percent of historic Palestine and pledged to end military actions against Israel. Israel, while failing to recognize Palestinian statehood, did recognize Palestinian nationhood, including the right of self-determination, and the PLO's role as the Palestinians' legitimate representative body.

The document spelled out ways in which the Palestinians could achieve a degree of autonomy in parts of the West Bank and the Gaza Strip, which had been occupied by Israeli forces since the June 1967 Six-Day War. The hope was that by the PLO's demonstration of competent self-governance and control over anti-Israel violence, the Israelis would gain the confidence needed to make a phased withdrawal from the occupied territories and grant the Palestinians an independent state alongside Israel. Similarly, it was hoped that the removal of foreign occupation forces from certain areas, increasing levels of self-government, and the prospects of a viable independent state would give the Palestinian population the incentive to end the violence against Israelis. The interim peace period was to be completed by 1998, at which time a permanent peace agreement would be signed.

Although the U.S. government became the guarantor of the Oslo Accords, Washington had little to do with the agreement itself. Soon after the election of a more moderate Israeli government in 1992, direct talks began in secret between representatives of Israel and the PLO. They were first facilitated by Norwegian nongovernmental organizations and later with the assistance of the foreign ministry. This apparently took place without the knowledge of American officials, who still took the position that the PLO should not be allowed to take part in the peace process, excluding it from the stalled peace talks then going on in Washington. As the secret negotiations in Norway progressed during the summer of 1993, the Clinton administration put forward what it called a compromise proposal for Palestinian autonomy. This compromise was actually less favorable to the Palestinians than what was then being put forward by the Israelis.

The U.S. role in the Oslo process began with a historic signing ceremony on the White House lawn on September 13, 1993. The agreement had been finalized in Oslo on August 20. Given the ambiguities in the agreement, both parties agreed that the United States should be its guarantor. Indeed, the Israelis saw the U.S. government as the entity most likely to support its positions on outstanding issues, and the Palestinians saw the U.S. government as the only entity capable of forcing Israel to live up to its commitments and able to move the occupying power to compromise.

U.S. president Bill Clinton watches as Israeli prime minister Yitzhak Rabin and Palestine Liberation Organization leader Yasser Arafat shake hands at the signing of the historic Israeli-Palestinian Declaration of Principles (also known as the Oslo Accords), September 13, 1993. (William J. Clinton Presidential Library)

Peace talks resumed in Washington in the fall of 1993 within the Oslo framework. Over the next seven years, the United States brokered a series of Israeli-Palestinian agreements that led to the withdrawal of Israeli forces from most of the Gaza Strip and parts of the West Bank. By the end of the decade, about 40 percent of the West Bank and the Gaza Strip, including most of its towns and cities, had been placed under the rule of the new Palestinian Authority (PA), headed by Arafat, and divided into dozens of noncontiguous zones wherein the Palestinians could for the first time exercise some limited autonomy within their sphere of control.

During this period, the Israeli government severely limited the mobility of Palestinians within and between the West Bank and the Gaza Strip, dramatically expanded its expropriation of land in the occupied territories for colonization by Jewish settlers, and refused to withdraw from as much territory as promised in the U.S.-brokered disengagement agreements. In addition, the United States tended to side with the Israelis on most issues during talks regarding the disengagement process, even after a right-wing coalition that had opposed the Oslo Accords came to power in Israel in 1996. This served to alienate many Palestinians who had been initially hopeful about the peace process and hardened anti-Israeli attitudes.

Meanwhile, much of the PA proved itself to be rather inept, corrupt, and autocratic in its governance of those parts of the occupied territories under its control. The corruption alienated much of the Palestinian population, and the PA's lack of control made it difficult to suppress the growth of radical Islamic groups. On more than two dozen occasions between 1994 and 2000, Islamic extremists from the occupied Palestinian territories engaged in terrorist attacks inside Israel, killing scores of Israeli civilians and thereby hardening anti-Palestinian attitudes.

The Palestinians had hoped that the United States would broker the negotiations based on international law that forbids the expansion of any country's territory by military force and prohibits occupying powers from transferring their civilian population into occupied land. The Palestinians also hoped that American officials would support a series of specific United Nations (UN) Security Council resolutions demanding that Israel honor these principles. From the Palestinians' perspective—as well as that of the UN, most U.S. allies, and most international legal experts—the onus of the burden was on Israel, as the occupying power, to make most of the compromises for peace. The Clinton administration, however, argued that the UN resolutions were no longer relevant and saw the West Bank and the Gaza Strip simply as disputed territories, thereby requiring both sides to compromise. This gave the Israelis a clear advantage in the peace process.

In signing the Oslo Accords, the Palestinians operated on the assumption that the agreement would result in concrete improvements in the lives of those in the occupied territories. They hoped that the interim period would be no more than five years and that the permanent settlement would be based on UN Security Council Resolutions 242 and 338, which called upon Israel to withdraw from the territories seized in the 1967 war. For their part, the Israelis had hoped that the Oslo Accords would lead to the emergence of a responsible Palestinian leadership and greater security. None of these wishes, however, came to pass.

Stephen Zunes

**See also**
Arafat, Yasser; Palestine Liberation Organization; Palestinian National Authority; Rabin, Yitzhak

**References**
Brown, Nathan J. *Palestinian Politics after the Oslo Accords: Resuming Arab Palestine.* Berkeley: University of California Press, 2003.
Freedman, Robert Owen, ed. *The Middle East and the Peace Process: The Impact of the Oslo Accords.* Gainesville: University Press of Florida, 1998.
Peres, Shimon. *The New Middle East.* New York: Henry Holt, 1993.
Weinberger, Peter. *Co-opting the PLO: A Critical Reconstruction of the Oslo Accords, 1993–1995.* New York: Rowman and Littlefield, 2006.

# Osman I (ca. 1254–1324/1326)

Founder of the Ottoman dynasty. Born circa 1254, Osman I was descended from the Kayi branch of Oguz Turkmen. His father, Ertugrul, had established a small state centered at Söğüt, a town in the present-day district of Bilecik Province in the Marmara region of Turkey. Söğüt is located just to the southeast of the Sea of Marmara. Osman I became the bey (ruler) of this beylik or emirate circa 1280 to 1299 until 1324 or 1326. Some scholars have suggested that his name was actually Atman or Ataman but this was only later changed to the Arabic Osman.

Very little is known of Osman's life, with no written record of his lifetime surviving. Indeed, the earliest writing about him dates from the 15th century. Controlling the territory around Söğüt, Osman and his men began a steady campaign against the Byzantine Empire, which sought to retain territories it held on the Asiatic shore opposite Constantinople (now Istanbul). Osman's territory was ideally located for operations against the Byzantines as it was just to the southeast of the Sea of Marmara, and he gradually extended his control over several former Byzantine fortresses, including Yenisehir, which provided the Ottomans with a strong base to lay siege to Bursa and Nicaea (now Iznik), in northwestern Anatolia.

Osman was succeeded by his son Orhan, who captured Bursa on April 6, 1326. Ottoman tradition holds that Osman died just after this event, but others suggest that this came in 1324, the year of Orhan's accession. While Osman I ruled only a small state in Anatolia in his lifetime, he set in motion the expansion of this territory into what would become the world power of the Ottoman Empire that lasted until 1923 and the proclamation of the Republic of Turkey or the abolition of the caliphate in 1924.

Spencer C. Tucker

**See also**
Byzantine Empire; Ottoman Empire

**References**
Finkel, Caroline. *Osman's Dream: The Story of the Ottoman Empire, 1300–1923.* New York: Basic Books, 2005.
Fleet, Kate. "The Rise of the Ottomans." In *The New Cambridge History of Islam,* Vol. 2, ed. Maribel Fierro, 313–331. Cambridge: Cambridge University Press, 2010.
Imber, Colin. *The Ottoman Empire, 1300–1650: The Structure of Power.* 2nd ed. New York: Palgrave Macmillan, 2009.
Kafadar, Cemal. *Between Two Worlds: The Construction of the Ottoman State.* Berkeley: University of California Press, 1995.
Zachariadou, Elizabeth, ed. *The Ottoman Emirate (1300–1389).* Rethymnon: Crete University Press, 1991.

# Osman Nuri Pasha (1832–1900)

Prominent Ottoman military commander. Born in Tokat in Asia Minor in 1832, Osman Nuri moved with his family to Istanbul, where he attended military high school. He entered the Istanbul Military Academy in 1850 and graduated at the top of his class. Shortly afterward he fought in the Crimean War (1853–1856) as a cavalry lieutenant, distinguishing himself at the Battle of Eupadoria (February 17, 1855). Rapid promotion followed, and he became a general by 1870. During the 1876 insurrection in Serbia, Osman was awarded the rank of *mushir* (field marshal) for a string of victories.

It was the Russo-Ottoman War of 1877–1878 and specifically the Siege of Plevna (July 20–December 10, 1877), the most important battle of the war, that made Osman famous. His skillful defense of Plevna, despite the crushing numerical advantage enjoyed by his adversaries, earned him the title of *ghazi* (victor for Islam). Osman Pasha had wanted to withdraw and preserve his army while it was yet possible but was denied permission until it was too late.

Wounded and captured during a desperate final attempt to break out, Osman Pasha was treated with great respect by the Russians. Returning to Istanbul a hero, he later served as minister of war, in which capacity he instituted major military reforms, and was made a marshal of the palace. Osman Pasha died in Istanbul on April 5, 1900.

NICHOLAS MURRAY

**See also**
Russo-Ottoman Wars

**References**
Herbert, Frederick William von. *The Chronicles of a Virgin Fortress*. London: Osgood, McIlvane, 1896.
Greene, Francis Vinton. *Report of the Russian Army and Its Campaigns in Turkey in 1877–1878*. Nashville: Battery Press, 1996.
Pasha, Osman. *Défense de Plevna*. Paris: Librarie Militaire de L. Baudoin et Co., 1889.

## Otlukbeli, Battle of (August 11, 1473)

A major military engagement, the Battle of Otlukbeli, also known as the Battle of Otuk Beli and the Battle of Bashkent, was fought in Erzincan between forces of the Ottoman Empire and those of the Aq-Qoyunlu Confederation on August 11, 1473. By the mid-15th century, the rising Ottoman state had successfully expanded into former Byzantine territory, but in the east it faced a major threat where the powerful Turkoman Aq-Qoyunly Confederation, led by the maverick Uzun Hasan, challenged Ottoman authority over Anatolia. In his struggle against Ottoman sultan Mehmed II, Uzun Hasan formed an alliance with Venice but was unable to prevent the Ottoman invasion.

The Ottoman and Aq-Qoyunly armies met near the village of Bashkent on the Otlukbeli River in Erzincan on August 11, 1473. Uzun Hasan's army was divided into five corps and occupied high ground above the Ottoman camp that was partially surrounded by a wagon laager. Unlike the traditional cavalry-dominated army of Uzun Hasan, Mehmed's troops incorporated firearms and artillery. Deployed behind a barrier of wagons chained together, the Ottomans exploited their superiority in firearms to repel a charge by the Turcomen cavalry. As the Aq-Qoyunlu units began to fall back in panic, the Ottoman cavalry charged from the camp, pursuing the confused enemy and inflicting heavy losses. The battle lasted about eight hours and ended with the near total destruction of the Turkoman army.

This victory opened eastern Anatolia to the Ottoman expansion because Uzun Hasan had to accept the Euhprates River as the western frontier of his realm.

ALEXANDER MIKABERIDZE

**See also**
Mehmed II, Sultan; Uzun Hasan

**References**
Jackson, Peter, and Lawrence Lockhart, eds. *The Cambridge History of Iran: The Timurid and Safavid Periods*, Vol. 6. Cambridge: Cambridge University Press, 1986.
Uyar, Mesut, and Edward J. Erikcson. *A Military History of the Ottomans: From Osman to Ataturk*. Wesport, CT: Greenwood, 2009.

## Ottoman Empire (1299–1922)

Until the beginning of the 20th century, the Ottoman Empire was the dominant political, economic, and military power in the Middle East. Established in 1299 and centered in Anatolia, the empire saw centuries of considerable expansion, reaching the zenith of its power and territorial control during the 16th and 17th centuries. It then controlled a vast swath of the Mediterranean basin, including portions of Southern Europe, Asia Minor, North Africa, and the Middle East. The empire gradually declined, became subject to outside forces, and lost significant amounts of territory. The decision of its leaders to side with the Central Powers in World War I led to the defeat and occupation of the empire and its end in 1922.

The earliest neolithic sanctuaries date from about 10000 BCE at Göbekli Tepe in southern Turkey, and Anatolia was home to many ancient civilizations, including the Assyrians, Armenians, Greeks, and Thracians. It was then part of the western reaches of the Persian Empire, which in 334 BCE was conquered by King Alexander III the Great of Macedon.

# Expansion of the Ottoman Empire, 1361–1571

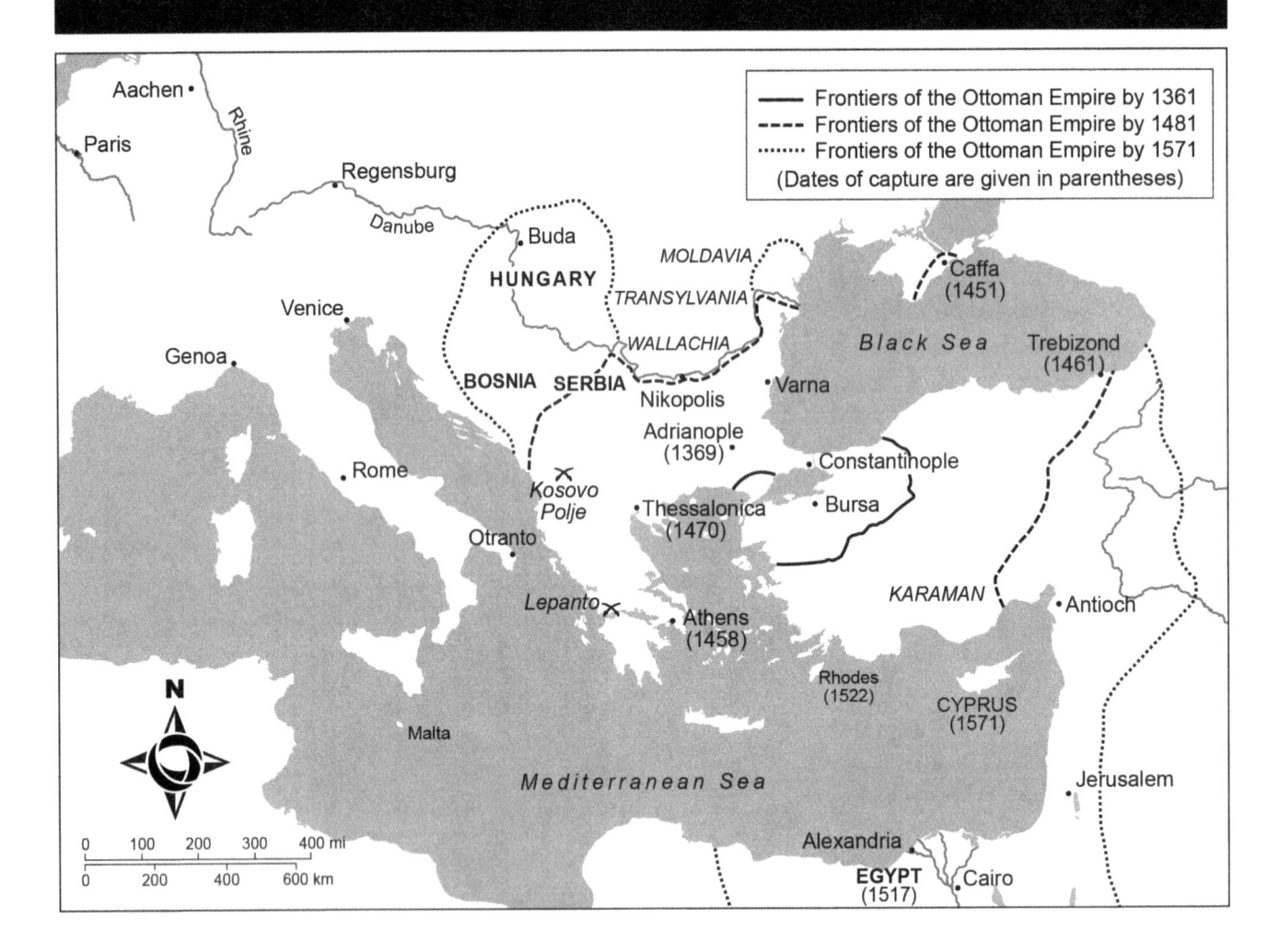

His successors, the Diadochi, fought over what remained. Although Anatolia was subsequently part of the Roman Empire, Greek language and culture predominated.

In 324 CE, Emperor Constantine I designated Byzantium on the Bosporus as the new capital of the Roman Empire. In 395, however, the Roman Empire was formally divided into the Western Roman Empire and the Eastern Roman Empire. The latter became known as Byzantium or the Byzantine Empire, although its capital city was popularly known as Constantinople.

Between the 3rd and 7th centuries, the Byzantine Empire engaged in frequent warfare with the Persian Sassanid Empire to the east, with the result that both were weakened to the extent that they fell prey to Muslim conquest in the 7th century. The Seljuk Turks became a major threat in the 11th century, and on August 26, 1071, they defeated the Byzantines in the important Battle of Manzikert.

With the demise of the Seljuk Sultanate of Rum around 1300, Anatolia became a patchwork of independent states, the so-called Anatolian Beyliks, with the weakened Byzantine Empire losing most of its Anatolian territory to these Turkish principalities. One of the beyliks was led by Osman I (r. ca. 1280–1323/1324), from whose name Ottoman is derived. The state established by Osman in 1299 was centered on Eskişehir in western Anatolia.

In the century following the death of Osman I, his successors extended their control over the eastern Mediterranean and the Balkans. In 1326 Osman's son Orhan (r. 1326–1362) captured Bursa from the Byzantines and made it the new capital of the Ottoman state. This marked the end of Byzantine control of northwestern Anatolia. Under Murad I (r. 1362–1389) the Ottomans captured Edirne (Adrianople) in eastern Thrace and made it their new capital in 1363. In 1387 the Ottomans took the important city of Thessaloniki from the Venetians. Then in 1389 the Ottomans won the important Battle of Kosovo. This marked the end of Serbian power in the Balkans, brought most of the region under Ottoman rule, and opened the way for Ottoman expansion into Europe.

Christian Europe's efforts to halt the expansion of Islam failed in the Battle of Nikopolis in 1396 in what is widely seen as the last large-scale crusade of the Middle Ages. With their territory now extending into the Balkans and in control of almost all the former Byzantine lands surrounding the city, the Ottomans made a major effort to capture Constantinople. The Byzantines secured a respite in this regard when Tamerlane (Timur) invaded Anatolia and, in the Battle of Ankara in 1402, took sultan Bayezid I (r. 1389–1402) prisoner. This brought civil war during 1402–1413, as Bayezid's sons fought over the succession. The interregnum ended when Mehmed I (r. 1413–1421) became sultan.

Some Ottoman holdings in the Balkans were lost after 1402, but these were recovered by Sultan Murad II (r. 1421–1444). Then on November 10, 1444, Murad II defeated a coalition of Hungarians, Poles, and Walacians in the Battle of Varna, the final battle of the Crusade of Varna. Murad was again victorious in the Second Battle of Kosovo in 1448.

Murad II's son Mehmed II the Conqueror (r. 1451–1481) reorganized both the Ottoman state and military, and he demonstrated his martial prowess at only age 21 by capturing Constantinople on May 29, 1453. This feat confirmed the Ottoman Empire as the preeminent power in Southeastern Europe and the eastern Mediterranean.

The Ottoman Empire prospered under a line of committed and effective sultans. Sultan Selim I (r. 1512–1520) dramatically expanded Ottoman territory by defeating Shah Ismail I of Safavid Persia in the Battle of Chaldiran (August 23, 1514). Selim also brought Egypt under Ottoman control, and he established a naval presence in the Red Sea. He and his successor, Suleiman I the Magnificent (r. 1520–1566), made the Ottomans a major Mediterranean naval power. The Ottoman Navy significantly aided this expansion and secured key seagoing trade routes in competition with the Italian city-states in the Black, Aegean, and Mediterranean Seas as well as with the Portuguese in the Red Sea and the Indian Ocean. At the same time, the state benefited economically from its control of the major overland trade routes between Europe and Asia.

Suleiman captured Belgrade in 1521. Also victorious over the Hungarians in the Battle of Mohács in 1526, Suleiman established Ottoman control over all Hungary except for the western part. He laid siege to Vienna in 1529, but the onset of winter forced a withdrawal. In 1532, he mounted another effort to take Vienna but was repulsed in the Siege of Güns, some 60 miles south of the city. Under Suleiman, Transylvania, Wallachia, and intermittently Moldavia became tributary principalities of the Ottoman Empire. In the east in 1535 the Ottomans took Baghdad from the Persians, giving them control of Mesopotamia and naval access to the Persian Gulf.

Suleiman's naval commander Barbarossa Hayreddin Pasha won important victories over the Christian navies leading to the conquest of Algiers (in 1516 and 1529), Tunis (in 1534 and 1574), and the Balearic Islands (1558) from Spain; Rhodes (1522) and Tripoli (1551) from the Knights of St. John; Nice (1543) from the Holy Roman Empire; Corsica (1553) from Genoa; and Aden (1548), Muscat (1552), and Aceh (1565–1567) from Portugal.

Suleiman's effort to completely dominate the Mediterranean basin ended when an Ottoman force of some 50,000 men was rebuffed in the Siege of Malta in 1565. Their defeat in the Battle of Lepanto in 1571, brought on by the Ottoman conquest of Venetian-controlled Cyprus in 1570, was a major psychological blow but only a temporary military setback, as the Ottomans quickly rebuilt their fleet. This led the Venetians to come to terms in 1573, and the Ottomans recovered Tunisia from Spain the next year.

During this period the Ottomans received substantial military and financial aid from Catholic France, with the two states sharing a common enemy in the Habsburgs. The Ottomans also forged alliances with the English and the Dutch Republic against Habsburg Spain and Austria, and the Italian states. Despite these alliances, the Ottoman Empire was severely strained by the logistical challenges of ongoing and widely separated military struggles with Austria and the Safavid Persian Empire.

Because the Ottomans controlled the traditional trading routes by sea and land with Asia, the European states, especially Portugal and Spain, took to the seas in an effort to discover new routes to Asia. The Ottomans soon found themselves at war with the Portuguese in the Indian Ocean. At the same time, Muscovite Russia began making inroads in the Volga and Caspian region at the expense of the Tatar khanates, regarded by the Ottomans as their buffer with Russia.

The 17th century saw considerable change in the empire, particularly in the Köprülü era (1656–1703), named for a series of grand viziers from this family. The Köprülüs were capable administrators credited with reviving the empire's fortunes in projecting military might and state power while restoring financial stability. The Ottomans reestablished control of

Transylvania, conquered Crete in 1669, and extended their authority into Polish southern Ukraine in 1676.

This territorial expansion proved short-lived, however. In May 1683 Grand Vizier Kara Mustafa Pasha led a huge army northward in yet another attempt to take Vienna during the Great Turkish War (1683–1699). Ottoman forces suffered a crushing and unsuspected retreat by an allied force of Habsburg, German, and Polish forces under king of Poland and grand duke of Lithuania John III Sobieski, who then went on to campaign in Hungary.

Sultan Murad IV (r. 1612–1640) recaptured from Safavid Persia both Yerevan (1635) and Baghdad (1639), while Mustafa II (r. 1695–1703) led the Ottoman counteroffensive of 1695–1696 against the Habsburgs in Hungary, only to suffer a disastrous defeat at the hands of Prince Eugene of Savoy in the Battle of Zenta in 1697. The Treaty of Karlowitz (January 26, 1699) ended the war, with the Ottomans surrendering substantial territory, including Ottoman Hungary. This failed war saw the end of an expansionist Ottoman Empire and the beginning of a protracted period of Ottoman decline, during which the empire would become known as "the Sick Man of Europe."

By the 18th century the Ottomans faced not only the Habsburgs but also a more pressing new threat in the Russians, now led by Tsar Peter I the Great. Also, Egypt and Algeria became independent of the empire in all but name. At the same time, the empire's central authority was eroded by increasing provincial autonomy.

With Russian expansion a major threat, Sultan Ahmed III (r. 1703–1730) declared war, with the Ottomans enjoying success in the Pruth River Campaign of 1710–1711. The Treaty of Passarowitz of 1718 brought a period of peace but also signaled that the empire was now on the defensive, as was seen in Ottoman construction of fortresses in the Balkans.

Russian tsarina Catherine II joined with Austria in renewing warfare against the Ottomans during 1735–1739. The Treaty of Belgrade ending this war saw the Ottomans regain Belgrade and other territories from Austria but lose Azov to the Russians. The empire then enjoyed a respite when Russia and Austria turned their attention against the rising Kingdom of Prussia. The Ottomans were unable to capitalize on this protracted period of peace, however. Although some advances were registered in education and technology, conservatives were able to block important military, fiscal, and administrative reforms.

Three decades of peace ended in 1768 when Russia again sought southern expansionism in the Russo-Ottoman War of 1768–1774. In the Treaty of Kuchuk Kainardji ending this conflict, Sultan Abdul Hamid I (r. 1773–1789) recognized the independence of the Crimean Khanate, which Russia annexed nine years later—the first time that an Ottoman ruler surrendered a largely Muslim populated territory. The Ottomans also surrendered major fortresses that gave Russia a strong presence in the northern Caucasus and the Black Sea. The Ottoman Empire retained Moldavia and Walacia but recognized Russia's special position in the region. The Ottomans also had to pay a heavy indemnity and, perhaps most important, were forced to grant Russia special privileges within the empire itself.

Sultan Selim III (r. 1789–1807) began the effort to modernize the Ottoman Army. This encountered immediate opposition from the clergy but also from the moribund Janissary Corps. Indeed, a Janissary revolt cost Selim his throne and his life.

The reign of Selim's successor Mahmud II (r. 1808–1839) saw the beginning of the end of Ottoman rule in the Balkans and the rise of what came to be called "the Balkan question." War with Russia, which had continued despite a truce in 1807, ended in the Treaty of Bucharest in 1812 with the Ottomans ceding Bessarabia to Russia. Serbia revolted in 1804. This lasted 11 years, but in 1815 Serbia was recognized as autonomous, and in 1867 it achieved de facto independence.

In 1821 a revolt began in Greece, causing Mahmud II to call on his vassal Mehmed Ali Pasha, governor of Egypt, who sent an army under his son Ibrahim Pasha. After considerable bloodshed, Ottoman rule had been partly restored in Greece when other powers intervened. Combined British, French, and Russian squadrons destroyed the Ottoman-Egyptian ships in the Battle of Navarino Bay (October 20, 1827). Mahmud then declared war against Russia, leading to another Ottoman defeat in the Russo-Ottoman War of 1828–1829. Greece meanwhile achieved independence in 1830.

Falling out with Mahmud II regarding terms of compensation for his Greek effort, Mehmed Ali launched a nine-year struggle against the Ottoman Empire during 1831–1840, sending Egyptian forces into Syria under Ibrahim, who captured Damascus and Aleppo and routed the Ottoman army at Konya in 1832 before advancing on Istanbul. Mahmud sought British aid, but with France supporting Egypt, the British refused, and Mahmud turned to Russia, which sent a fleet to the Bosporus and signed a mutual defense treaty with the Ottomans in July 1833. Mahmud dispatched forces to Syria, only to see them defeated by the Egyptians at Nizip (June 24, 1839).

Mahmud was well aware of his nation's military backwardness. On June 15, 1826, he destroyed the Janissary

Corps, killing some 10,000 of them in the so-called Auspicious Incident. This paved the way for the establishment of a new military force under the direct control of the sultan and with German instructors. Such changes came too late to affect the military outcome, however. Serbia, Walacia, Moldavia, and Montenegro all secured de jure independence during the 1860s and 1870s. Ottoman leaders, painfully aware of the empire's weaknesses, sought alliances with other European powers while endeavoring to carry out internal reform.

Russian efforts to secure control of the Bosporus and gain access to the Mediterranean brought the Crimean War of 1853–1856. Britain and France supported the Ottomans. Most of the fighting occurred in the Crimean Peninsula, with the major military operation being the siege of the Russian Black Sea port and naval base of Sevastopol (October 17, 1854–September 9, 1855). The allies, joined by the Kingdom of Sardinia (Sardinia-Piedmont), at last secured Sevastopol and victory in the war. The subsequent Treaty of Paris (1856) secured Ottoman control over the Balkan Peninsula and the Black Sea basin.

A major reform effort, known as the Tanzimat (Organization) Period, occurred during 1839–1876. It saw the Ottoman government institute a series of reform measures, resulting in a reorganized, modern, conscripted army; a central bank with a modern banking and financial system; educational reforms to include the first modern universities; replacement of religious law with secular law; a new civil and criminal code; abolition of slavery; major railroad construction; introduction of the telegraph (and later the telephone); a modern postal system; a modern factory system to replace that of the guilds; and new tax codes supported by regular collection.

The reforms culminated in the promulgation in 1876 of a constitution. Known as the Basic Law, it was written by reformers known as the Young Ottomans, most of whom had been educated in Western universities. It provided for freedom of religion and equality of all citizens before the law.

Through a military coup in 1876, the reformers forced Sultan Abdulaziz (r. 1861–1876) to abdicate in favor of Murad V, who was mentally ill and was deposed within a few months. The new sultan, Abdul Hamid II (r. 1876–1909), assumed the throne on the condition that he would declare a constitutional monarchy, which he did on November 23, 1876, beginning what is known as the First Constitutional Era. A representative parliament was put into place, but two years later the sultan suspended both the constitution and parliament.

The Tanzimat reforms failed to halt the rise of nationalism in the Danubian Principalities. Nor did the outcome of the Crimean War end Russian territorial aspirations at Ottoman expense. In 1875 Serbia and Montenegro, joined by the United Principalities of Walacia and Moldavia (the future Romania), declared their independence. They were assisted by Russia, which sought to secure both client states and Mediterranean access. The ensuing Russo-Turkish War of 1877–1878 saw considerable bloodshed and the great Siege of Plevna (July 20–December 10, 1877). The Ottomans were defeated.

Worried about substantial Russian gains, German chancellor Otto von Bismarck invited representatives of the Great Powers and the Ottoman Empire to Berlin in an effort to settle Balkan matters. The ensuing Congress of Berlin (June 13–July 13, 1878) was an effort to curtail Russian influence and stabilize the situation in the Balkans (Bismarck allegedly predicted that "some damned foolish thing in the Balkans" would bring a general European war).

The congress established Bulgaria as an independent principality inside the Ottoman Empire, but Bulgaria lost Eastern Rumelia, which was restored to the Turks under a special administration, while Macedonia was returned outright to them. Romania achieved full independence but had to cede part of Bessarabia to Russia. Serbia and Montenegro gained complete independence. Serbia, Montenegro, and Greece all made territorial gains but less than won on the battlefield.

In 1878, Austria-Hungary unilaterally occupied the Ottoman provinces of Bosnia and Herzegovina. The Ottoman government contested this move and maintained troops in both provinces. The stalemate lasted until 1908, when the Dual Monarchy took advantage of the political turmoil of the Young Turk Revolution to annex Bosnia-Herzegovina outright, nearly resulting in war with Russia.

In gratitude for their assistance in the Congress of Berlin, the Ottomans in 1878 gave the British administration of Cyprus. In 1882, on the pretext of helping the Ottoman government to put down a revolt there, the British sent troops to Egypt. Control of Egypt was immensely important to Britain, for trade with India now passed by way of the Suez Canal, opened in 1869. Britain formally annexed the still nominally Ottoman territories of Cyprus and Egypt in November 1914, when the Ottoman Empire entered World War I on the side of the Central Powers. France, on its part, occupied Tunisia in 1881, and Italy took Libya and the Dodecanese Islands as a consequence of the Italo-Ottoman War of 1911–1912.

Turkish nationalism had been on the rise, and the Committee of Union and Progress (CUP), part of the Young Turk movement, convinced Sultan Abdul Hamid II to restore the parliament on July 14, 1908, beginning the Second

Constitutional Era. Following an attempted monarchist counterrevolution in favor of Abdul Hamid the next year, the CUP deposed Abdul Hamid and replaced him with his younger brother, Mehmed V (r. 1909–1918). The Young Turks, however, split into two parties: the procentralization CUP and the prodecentralization Freedom and Accord Party.

The return to the Ottoman Empire by the Congress of Berlin of territories taken by the Balkan states from the Ottoman Empire in 1877 led to a strong revanchist movement among them, most notably in Bulgaria with the loss of Macedonia. This led to the First Balkan War of 1912–1913 in which the Turks were defeated and lost nearly all their territory in Europe. These losses greatly discredited Mehmed V, and on January 23, 1913, in the Raid on the Sublime Port, the CUP seized power in a coup d'état. A triumvirate of leaders dominated: Ismail Enver Pasha as minister of war, Mehmed Taalat Pasha as minister of the interior, and Ahmed Djemal Pasha as minister of marine.

In the crisis that followed the June 28, 1914, assassination of Austrian archduke Franz Ferdinand, both sides courted the Ottoman Empire. The Austrian decision to go to war with Serbia brought World War I in August. Two months later on November 14, Mehmed V sided with Germany and Austria and proclaimed a holy war against the Entente powers.

Ottoman participation in the war had immense consequences, for despite its diminished territory (in 1914 it included all of modern-day Turkey, Mesopotamia, Syria, and Palestine, with a population of some 21 million), the empire controlled land and sea routes to three continents. The closure of the Dardanelles was a great blow to the Entente as it isolated Russia economically and strategically and severely weakened its ability to wage war. Great Britain was also forced to shift major resources to protect the Suez Canal. Soon the Ottoman Empire was fighting in Egypt, Mesopotamia, and Caucasia as well as in Europe at the Dardanelles.

Domestically, the Ottoman government instituted numerous reforms. It reorganized the administration and attempted to introduce a merit system into the state bureaucracy. It also restructured and updated the taxation system, including introduction of an income tax. The government poured money into infrastructure, improving and expanding transportation and communication systems and laying sewage, electric, and water lines in major urban areas.

The government also challenged the power of the traditionally influential Islamic clerics by placing Islam more under its own control. The government completely secularized the religious courts and schools, and Muslim judges (*kadis*) were appointed and overseen by the secular Ministry of Justice. In 1917 the government took control of family law.

The government also brought about major reforms concerning the emancipation of women, equalizing their legal rights concerning marriage and inheritance. It created opportunities for girls and women in all levels of education, vocational training, and employment. In urban areas, women began to assume greater economic responsibility outside of the home, particularly once mobilization necessitated workforce replacements. More women adopted European-style clothing and discarded the traditional veil. However, complete emancipation did not occur until after the war.

The leaders of the Ottoman Empire believed that the war would be over quickly. Consequently, the government did not institute planning to secure sufficient food and civilian supplies for an extended war. By 1915 a grain shortage existed in Constantinople and many other major cities. Famine became widespread because of the lack of agricultural laborers, who had been conscripted into the military; a prolonged drought; and the monopolization of railroads by the military. War refugees fled into major urban areas, bringing instability and a further drain on resources and also spreading typhus. Inflation skyrocketed, reaching perhaps 400 percent in the first year of the war alone.

The internal stability of the Ottoman Empire was badly weakened during World War I. Two groups in particular rebelled against Ottoman rule: the Armenian Christians in eastern Anatolia and the Arabs in the Hejaz. The Armenians, who sought independence, forced the Ottomans to divert troops there from major campaigns against the Russians. In order to stabilize the situation, the government forcibly relocated the Armenian population to the Syrian desert, an area remote from potential collusion with the Russians. Forced to march through the desert with inadequate water, food, clothing, and medical supplies, as many as 1.2 million died in what has been called the Armenian Massacre or Armenian Genocide, for which the Turkish government has never assumed responsibility. The other major source of revolt was the Arab community of the Hejaz. Its push for independence began in June 1916 with strong British support.

Although the Ottomans registered some successes against the British and French in the Dardanelles and Gallipoli Campaigns, in Mesopotamia against British Empire troops, and late in the war against the Russians, the Allies defeated the Ottomans in Mesopotamia and in Palestine and forced the empire from the war. The armistice of Mudros on October 30, 1918, ended Ottoman participation in the war, and Allied troops occupied much of the empire. The government at Istanbul disintegrated, and its leaders fled.

The Ottoman Empire unofficially ended on November 15 when Sultan Mehmed VI, who had succeeded to the throne only the month before on the death of Mehmed V, established a new government under the control of Greek and British troops.

The punitive Allied terms of the 1919 Paris Peace Conference, whereby the Allies divided much of the territory of the former Ottoman Empire among themselves, spurred Turkish nationalism and led to a revolution under Mustafa Kemal. Under the terms of the punitive Treaty of Sèvres in 1920, the empire was largely restricted to Anatolia, and its economy was controlled by the Entente powers. After fighting for three years and defeating the Armenians in the east and Greek forces in western Anatolia in the Greco-Turkish War (Turkish War of Independence) during 1919–1922, the Turks secured Anatolia. The sultanate was officially abolished on November 1, 1922, and the last sultan, Mehmed V, abdicated and left the country later that same month. The new independent Grand National Assembly of Turkey (GNA) was internationally recognized with the Treaty of Lausanne on July 24, 1923, and the GNA officially declared the Republic of Turkey on October 29, 1923. The caliphate was constitutionally abolished on March 3, 1924.

Spencer C. Tucker

**See also**

Adrianople, Battle of; Alexander III the Great; Armenians and the Armenian Genocide; Ataturk, Mustafa Kemal; Balkan Wars; Bayezid I; Chaldiran, Battle of; Constantine I; Constantinople, Muslim Siege of; Constantinople, Ottoman Siege of; Diadochi, Wars of the; Djemal Pasha, Ahmed; Enver Pasha; Greco-Turkish War; Ismail I, Shah; Karlowitz, Treaty of; Konya, Battle of; Köprülü Abdullah Pasha; Köprülü Fazil Ahmed Pasha; Köprülü Mehmed Pasha; Kuchuk Kainardji, Treaty of; Lausanne, Second Treaty of; Lepanto, Battle of; Manzikert, Battle of; Mehmed Ali; Murad II, Sultan; Nikopolis, Crusade in; Nizip, Battle of; Osman I; Ottoman Empire, Entry into World War I; Ottoman Empire, Post–World War I Revolution in; Ottoman-Habsburg Wars; Ottoman-Hungarian Wars; Ottoman-Persian Wars of the 18th and 19th Centuries; Ottoman-Polish Wars of the 17th Century; Ottoman-Safavid Wars; Russo-Ottoman Wars; Sassanid Empire; Seljuk Dynasty; Sèvres, Treaty of; Suleiman I; Taalat Pasha, Mehmed; Tamerlane; Turkey; Turkish-Armenian War; Varna Crusade; World War I, Impact on the Middle East

**References**

Ágoston, Gábor. *Guns for the Sultan: Military Power and the Weapons Industry in the Ottoman Empire.* Cambridge: Cambridge University Press, 2005.

Aksan, Virginia H. *Ottoman Wars: An Empire Besieged.* London: Routledge, 2014.

Butler, Daniel Allen. *Shadow of the Sultan's Realm: The Destruction of the Ottoman Empire and the Creation of the Modern Middle East.* Dulles, VA: Potomac Books, 2011.

Finkel, Caroline. *Osman's Dream: The History of the Ottoman Empire.* New York: Basic Books, 2007.

Fromkin, David. *A Peace to End All Peace: The Fall of the Ottoman Empire and the Creation of the Modern Middle East.* Lakewood, WA: Owl Books, 2001.

Imber, Colin. *The Ottoman Empire, 1300–1650: The Structure of Power.* New York: Palgrave Macmillan, 2009.

Lewis, Bernard. *The Emergence of Modern Turkey.* 3rd ed. New York: Oxford University Press, 2002.

McCarthy, Justin. *The Ottoman Turks* London: Longman, 1997.

Palmer, Alan. *The Decline and Fall of the Ottoman Empire.* London: Murray, 1992.

Quataert, Donald. *The Ottoman Empire, 1700–1922.* Cambridge: Cambridge University Press, 2013.

## Ottoman Empire, Entry into World War I

In one of the major turning points of World War I, in November 1914 the Ottoman Empire entered the war on the German side. When war began in Europe in early August 1914, Ottoman leaders were torn over the appropriate response for their country: continued neutrality or entering the war on the side of Germany or the Entente.

Both the German and British governments had worked hard to win Ottoman goodwill in the years before the war. The British had long sought to uphold the Ottoman Empire's territorial integrity against Russian encroachments and desire for a Mediterranean port, but efforts by the Ottoman government in the years immediately before World War I to secure an alliance with Britain had been rebuffed, largely because London feared alienating its new ally, Russia. The British had, however, sent a naval mission to help train the Ottoman Navy, and the Ottomans had ordered warships from Britain. On the other side, Kaiser Wilhelm II had traveled to the Ottoman Empire and had pushed development of a railroad (the Berlin-to-Baghdad railway project) there to exploit Ottoman resources. In 1913 Berlin had also dispatched an advisory group under Generalleutnant Otto Liman von Sanders to Istanbul to help train the Ottoman Army.

A decision by the British government may have tipped the balance in favor of the Ottomans joining the war on the German side. On the eve of British entry into the war, First

Lord of the Admiralty Winston Churchill had, on August 1, ordered sequestered two powerful battleships being built in British yards that had already been paid for by popular Ottoman Empire subscription. These were the *Sultan Osman I* (renamed *Agincourt*) and the *Reshadieh* (renamed *Erin*). This decision greatly angered the Ottoman public and turned it against the Entente. The Germans also sought to capitalize on the traditional animosity between the Ottoman and Russian Empires.

Still, the Ottoman leadership was undecided and on August 3 declared Ottoman neutrality in the war. While the government in Istanbul vacillated, German vice admiral Wilhelm Souchon's German Mediterranean Squadron of the new battle cruiser *Goeben* (the most formidable warship in the entire Mediterranean) and light cruiser *Breslau* changed the course of the war. Although British and French naval units heavily outnumbered his own squadron, Souchon succeeded in escaping to the Dardanelles and then on to Istanbul, where he arrived on August 11. The presence of these two warships off the Turkish capital was of immense benefit to the pro-German faction.

Then, without Berlin's concurrence, on August 18 Souchon arranged to "sell" both warships to the Ottomans as replacements for the two dreadnoughts sequestered by Britain. Renamed, the two warships nonetheless retained their German crews, and Souchon became commander of the Ottoman Navy while retaining his position in the German Navy. The Ottoman public was elated over the news of the acquisition of the two ships.

Then with the secret support of Ottoman minister of war Enver Pasha, the leading supporter of the German alliance, Souchon used his warships to provoke war between Russia and Turkey. On October 27, he set sail from Constantinople under the guise of a training exercise in the Black Sea. Early on October 29 he bombarded Russian bases at Odessa and Novorossiysk and laid mines. The Ottoman cabinet was not informed in advance, and Souchon falsely reported that the Russians had attacked him first.

On November 4, 1914, Russia formally declared war on the Ottoman Empire. Despite the resignation of four members of the Turkish cabinet in protest against what Enver and Souchon had engineered, the Ottomans remained in the war on the side of the Central Powers. This decision resulted in a new theater of war in the Middle East and caused the Western Allies to divert important resources to the Ottoman theaters of war, perhaps enabling Germany to prolong the war. Having the Ottoman Empire as an active military opponent also cut off Russia from easy access to the West and imposed heavy economic burdens on that country, forcing it to divert military resources from the fight against Germany and Austria-Hungary. This added immensely to Russia's internal difficulties, and this helped bring about the revolutions in that country three years later.

Dino E. Buenviaje and Spencer C. Tucker

**See also**
Enver Pasha; Liman von Sanders, Otto; Ottoman Empire

**References**
Hale, William. *Turkish Foreign Policy, 1774–2000*. London: Cass, 2003.
Hamilton, Richard F., and Holger H. Herwig, eds. *The Origins of World War I*. Cambridge: Cambridge University Press, 2003.
Palmer, Alan. *The Decline and Fall of the Ottoman Empire*. London: Murray, 1992.
Van der Vat, Dan. *The Ship That Changed the World: The Escape of the Goeben to the Dardanelles in 1914*. Bethesda, MD: Adler and Adler, 1986.
Weber, Frank G. *Eagles on the Crescent: Germany, Austria, and the Diplomacy of the Turkish Alliance, 1914–1918*. Ithaca, NY: Cornell University Press, 1970.

# Ottoman Empire, Post–World War I Revolution in

In October 1918 the Ottoman Empire lay in ruins. Allied troops controlled the Middle East and much of the Balkans and even threatened Constantinople itself. Under these pressures, Sultan Mehmed VI agreed to the Armistice of Mudros of October 30, 1918. The armistice terms opened the straits, demobilized the Ottoman armed forces, and placed all remaining Ottoman territory at the disposal of the Allies.

In the chaos following the armistice, significant Allied forces moved into Ottoman territory, beginning with a naval force arriving at Istanbul (Constantinople) and British troops pushing into the Caucasus. During the next six months the British, French, and Italian governments established a three-power administration of Istanbul, garrisoned the Alexandretta-Smyrna-Istanbul railway, and encouraged the creation of independent Georgian and Armenian armies. By the summer of 1919 more Allied troops entered the country, with Italian troops in southwest Anatolia, French troops in the southeast, and a large Greek army at Smyrna.

Nationalist resistance to these events developed in eastern Anatolia, particularly under Ottoman generals Mustafa Kemal in Samsun and Kazim Karabekir at Erzurum. In September 1919 the nationalists issued the Declaration of Sivas, affirming the unity of Ottoman territory and denying the Allies occupation rights. The nationalists—Karabekir in particular—also turned to the Bolsheviks of Russia for military aid, concluding an agreement with them the following spring. Contacts with Bolshevik officials served two purposes: they tapped a possible source of funds and provided a bargaining chip to use against the anticommunist British.

During the winter of 1919–1920, Turkish nationalist troops skirmished with Allied detachments along the railroad and near Constantinople. On March 16, 1920, British troops seized government buildings in Istanbul and set up a pro-Allied cabinet, preparatory to forcing the Ottoman government to sign the Treaty of Sèvres worked out by the Paris Peace Conference. Agreed upon by the British, French, and Italians in April, the treaty made the Kingdom of Hejaz independent, gave Smyrna and many Aegean islands to Greece, ceded the Dodecanese Islands to Italy, internationalized the straits, and made Armenia an independent state. In addition, Syria, Palestine, and Mesopotamia were established as independent states under French and British mandates. The latter two powers also signed the San Remo oil agreement, delimiting their oil interests in Persia, Mesopotamia, and the Caucasus.

These demands were presented to the sultan and the pro-Allied cabinet on June 10. Twelve days later, about 60,000 Greek troops advanced from Smyrna to help enforce these terms. Fighting also began in the Caucasus. Turkish nationalist forces were unprepared for this advance, and Greek military columns soon seized the major cities in western Anatolia and took Adrianople in Thrace. In the east an Armenian attack collapsed near Erzurum, and the Turkish counterattack forced the Armenians to sue for peace. The ensuing peace treaty reduced Armenia to the province of Erivan. On March 16, 1921, Turkish nationalists signed a treaty with Soviet Russia, delimiting the border in the east and securing more military aid.

On March 23, the Greeks opened a new offensive toward Ankara. Although initially stalled, the Greeks regrouped and advanced again in July. The Turks withdrew across the Sakarya River and stood on the defensive. Between August 23 and September 13, they fought a successful series of engagements over a 120-mile front known as the Battle of the Sakarya. At this point the French (as with the Italians earlier in the summer) agreed to withdraw from Anatolia in return for economic concessions.

During the winter of 1921–1922 the British attempted to negotiate an end to the war through a partial revision of the Treaty of Sèvres. The nationalists in Ankara refused, and the Turks took the offensive on August 18, 1922. In the ensuing war of maneuver, superior Turkish cavalry forced the Greeks back. The Greek retreat then turned into a rout, with their forces fleeing in confusion to the coast.

Responding to the Turkish advance toward Istanbul, a British force landed to protect the straits. Armistice negotiations began shortly thereafter. The opposing sides opened negotiations in November and agreed to the Treaty of Lausanne on July 24, 1923. Although Turkey agreed to relinquish all prewar non-Turkish territory in the Middle East and lost almost all the offshore islands in the Aegean and Mediterranean, its success in the fighting against the Greeks saw them depart Anatolia. There were also no reparations, and no legal restrictions remained on the Turkish government. During this same period, the sultanate was abolished. The last British troops evacuated Istanbul on October 2, and the Turkish Republic was formally established on October 29, 1923.

Timothy L. Francis

**See also**
Ataturk, Mustafa Kemal; Franco-Turkish War; Greco-Turkish War; Lausanne, Second Treaty of; Sèvres, Treaty of; Turkish-Armenian War

**References**
Kent, Marian, ed. *The Great Powers and the End of the Ottoman Empire.* London: Allen and Unwin, 1984.
Kinross, Lord. *Atatürk: Biography of Mustapha Kemal, Father of Modern Turkey.* New York: William Morrow, 1965.
Macfie, A. L. *The End of the Ottoman Empire, 1918–1923.* London: Longman, 1998.
Metz, Helen Chapin. *Turkey: A Country Study.* Washington, DC: Federal Research Division, Library of Congress, U.S. Government Printing Office, 1996.
Palmer, Alan. *The Decline and Fall of the Ottoman Empire.* London: Murray, 1992.
Shaw, Stanford J., and Ezel Kural Shaw. *History of the Ottoman Empire and Modern Turkey.* 2 vols. Cambridge: Cambridge University Press, 1977.

## Ottoman-Habsburg Wars (1529–1791)

The Habsburg (later Austrian) and Ottoman Empires had a long history of rivalry and conflict. Ottoman expansion into Serbia and Hungary in the 15th century led to Ottoman raids into Habsburg territory and prolonged fighting that shaped the history of both empires.

### Early Conflicts
Initial Ottoman raids occurred in the southern regions of the Habsburg realm between 1408 and 1426, but subsequent decades saw more serious attacks. Sultan Suleyman's

successful invasion of Hungary, which resulted in the destruction of the Hungarian Army in the Battle of Mohacs in 1526, opened the way for subsequent systematic Ottoman attacks. The Ottoman threat facilitated the Habsburgs' unification of the crowns of Austria, Hungary, and Bohemia. In 1515 a treaty of alliance, concluded between Holy Roman emperor Maximilian I and King Vladislaus II Jagiello of Hungary and Bohemia, specified that if one dynasty died out, the other would inherit its holdings. The death of King Louis II Jagiello in the Battle of Mohacs allowed Archduke Ferdinand of Austria, Maximilian's grandson, to become king of Hungary and Bohemia, eventually inheriting the Austrian crown as well.

**The Ottoman-Habsburg War of 1529–1533**
Ferdinand's succession, however, brought local resistance, notably from János Szapolyai (John Zápolya), who claimed the crown of Hungary. Ferdinand successfully campaigned in Hungary, capturing several major fortresses, including Buda. He occupied Györ, Komárom, Esztergom, Buda, and Székesfehérvár and defeated Szapolyai in several battles. However, Ferdinand was unable to unseat his rival, who sought Ottoman help and recognized Sultan Suleyman's suzerainty.

In 1529, Ottoman forces under Petry Rareş, *voivod* of Moldavia and Suleyman's vassal, defeated Ferdinand at Feldioara in southern Transylvania. Furthermore, to protect his vassal, Suleyman launched a major invasion of Austria proper in 1529. The Ottoman siege of Vienna (September 27–October 14, 1529) ended after the Ottoman forces compelled Süleyman to withdraw but had a profound effect on the Austrians, who offered to yield the whole of Hungary to Szapolyai on the condition that at his death it should revert to Ferdinand.

After peace negotiations failed, hostilities resumed in 1530. In the absence of the Ottoman Army, the Austrians captured several cities in Hungary. But Suleyman returned in 1532, leading some 200,000 men from Istanbul (Constantinople) at the end of April. Holy Roman emperor Charles mobilized his army and sought support from other European states. Fortunately for the Habsburgs, the Ottoman Army did not reach Vienna but became bogged down at Güns (Koszeg), where a Habsburg garrison heroically defended the fortress for three weeks in August.

Sultan Suleyman showed his great admiration for his adversary, inviting the Habsburg commander to his camp, where he was cordially received and awarded a robe of honor. The dogged Habsburg defense of Güns convinced Suleyman

Depiction of Ottoman troops laying siege to Vienna in 1529 in a miniature from *Hunername hazine* (1524), in the Topkapi Museum Library, Istanbul. (De Agostini/Getty Images)

to give up on besieging Vienna, which was much more heavily fortified. After campaigning in Syria and parts of Lower Austria, he returned back to Istanbul in early November.

The Habsburgs were more successful at sea. There Andrea Doria, Emperor Charles's admiral, successfully operated against the Ottoman fleet and captured Coron, one of the strongest Ottoman coast fortresses in the Morea, as well as Patras and a few others forts.

Fearing another Ottoman invasion, the Habsburgs sought to compromise while Suleyman, concerned about rising Persian power in the east, was quite willing to negotiate. In early 1533 a truce was concluded, with Suleyman demanding the keys of Gran in token of Austrian submission and homage; he later generously returned these without insisting on the surrender of the fortress. The formal Treaty of Constantinople was negotiated in June 1533. Ferdinand gave up his claims on and status quo in Hungary, which meant that Szapolyai retained his crown under

Ottoman suzerainty. The Habsburgs also agreed to pay an annual tribute of 30,000 guldens.

The treaty survived for seven years, although it was violated on several occasions, since neither Szapolyai nor Ferdinand were fully satisfied with it. In 1537, a Habsburg attempt to capture the Ottoman fortress at Essek (Osijek) resulted in a disastrous defeat at Đakovo. The new Treaty of Nagyvárad (February 1538) confirmed Szapolyai's rule in Hungary, while Ferdinand was recognized as heir to the Hungarian throne if Szapolyai died childless.

### The Ottoman-Habsburg War of 1540–1547

Szapolyai died in 1540, but shortly before his death his wife bore him a son, John II Sigismund Szapolyai. Although Suleyman recognized the succession, Ferdinand refused and laid siege to the Hungarian capital city of Buda. Yet, he soon faced an Ottoman invasion, as Sultan Suleyman sought to strengthen his authority in Hungary. The Ottomans defeated the Habsburgs at Buda and occupied central Hungary. In the Treaty of Gyula (December 29, 1541), the Habsburgs and Ottomans agreed to partition Hungary. The Habsburgs secured the western and northern regions, while the Ottomans received central Hungary, and the eastern regions of the principality of Transylvania ruled by John Sigismund became an Ottoman client state.

Hostilities soon resumed, however. The Habsburgs attempted to avenge their defeat by seizing Algiers and Tunis, leading to another disastrous failure. In 1543 Suleyman captured all fortresses on the way to Buda, including Grau and Stuhlweissenberg, the largest in the area. Distracted by a new war against Safavid Persia in the east, however, the sultan entrusted the Hungarian theater to his lieutenants, who carried out successful campaigns in Styria, Carinthia, and Croatia in 1544. The hard-pressed Habsburgs sued for a truce in 1545, but hostilities continued until 1547, when the Treaty of Edirne (Adrianople) was signed. It confirmed provisions of the Treaty of Gyula.

### The Ottoman-Habsburg War of 1551–1553

The Peace of Edirne was supposed to extend for five years but lasted only three. By 1550 George Martinuzzi, who acted as regent for John Sigismund, concluded an alliance with the Habsburgs to drive the Ottomans from Hungary. Although the allies gained some success and defeated the Ottomans at Deva, relations soon soured, and Ferdinand had Martinuzzi assassinated in 1551.

An Ottoman counteroffensive soon reclaimed lost ground as the Ottomans captured major Hungarian fortresses, including Temesvar and Szolnok, but they failed to overcome determined Habsburg resistance at Erlau (Eger) in 1552. Hostilities were ended by an armistice in 1553, but a formal peace treaty came only 10 years later and simply confirmed the terms of the 1547 accord, keeping Hungary divided into Austrian (Royal) Hungary, Ottoman-held Central Hungary, and Transylvania.

### The Ottoman-Habsburg War of 1566

Following a failed Ottoman siege of Malta (1565), the 72-year-old Sultan Süleyman turned to Hungary, where he wanted to offset his failure at Malta and also punish Holy Roman emperor Ferdinand I, who refused to pay tribute required by treaty. In 1566, the sultan's army invaded southwestern Hungary and besieged Szigetvár, whose Croatian commander Miklos Zrinyi led a valiant defense that brought the destruction of most of the fortress and its garrison but inflicted heavy losses on the Ottoman attackers. Süleymen died during the siege on September 6, but his death was concealed from the army until the fortress was stormed and taken on September 8. Informed of the sultan's death, the Ottoman Army returned to Istanbul with Süleyman's embalmed body for burial.

### The Ottoman-Habsburg War of 1591–1606

The so-called Long War of 1591–1606 was caused by intermittent border strife between Austria and Ottoman Hungary that intensified in 1591. Two years later, Croatian forces inflicted a major defeat on the Bosnian Ottoman army at Sissek (Sisak) that provoked a wider conflict. In 1594–1595, with Pope Clement VIII's help, the Habsburgs established an alliance with Transylvania, Moldavia, and Walacia. In 1595 the Habsburgs reclaimed Győr, Esztergom, and Visegrád, while Michael the Brave of Walacia successfully campaigned on the Lower Danube, seizing Giurgiu, Silistra, Nicopolis, and Chilia. In late August 1595, Michael celebrated one of the most important Romanian victories over the Ottomans at Calugareni, but he was unable to exploit it owing to a lack of support from his allies. The Ottomans still managed to occupy Bucharest and Târgoviște, but they suffered a series of defeats at the hands of Transylvanian-Walacian forces at Târgoviște, Bucharest, and Giurgiu.

Alarmed by these setbacks, Ottoman sultan Mehmet III arrived in Hungary to lead his troops in person. In 1596 he captured Erlau (Eger), and in October he snatched victory from the jaws of defeat at Mezokeresztes, for with his troops fleeing en masse, Muhammad personally led a desperate charge with the remaining forces, turning the tide of battle.

For the next five years, the war became a battle of fortresses in which the Habsburgs gradually gained key fortresses in central Austria, although its attack on Buda failed in 1598. In 1599, the sultan rejected Habsburg peace overtures. His new offensive led to the capture of Kanizsa in 1600 but also to a defeat at Stuhlweissenberg (1601). In Transylvania, the situation favored the Ottomans after tensions among the allies led to the splitting of the coalition. In 1599 Michael the Brave invaded Transylvania and was victorious at Şelimbăr, causing the defection of Sigismund Báthory of Transylvania to the Ottoman side.

Threatened by Walacian success, Habsburg forces under Giorgio Basta invaded Transylvania and defeated the Walacian army at Mirăslău (September 1600), with Michael later assassinated on Basta's orders. In August 1601 Habsburg forces defeated Sigismund Báthory at Guruslău and later scored another victory over the Transylvanians at Braşov (1603). After a Habsburg defeat at Buda in 1605, the Ottomans seized Esztergom, Visigrad, Veszperm, and Palota, thus regaining much of the land lost since 1595.

In Transylvania, István Bocskay launched an anti-Habsburg uprising in 1604, recognizing Ottoman sovereignty in exchange for military aid. The Long War ended with the Treaty of Zsitva-Torok of 1606, which marked the first major check of Ottoman expansion and stabilized the Habsburg-Ottoman frontier for half a century.

**The Ottoman-Habsburg War of 1663–1664**
The new conflict between Austria and the Porte broke out following the 1658 invasion of Poland by Prince György Rákóczi II of Transylvania, an Ottoman vassal who, however, acted without the sultan's permission. To reign in his unruly vassal, Grand Vizier Köprülü Mehmet Pasha conducted a successful campaign in Transylvania in 1660 that claimed Rákóczi's life and annexed the region to the Porte. Rákóczi's successor, Transylvanian prince János Kemény, fled to Vienna seeking Habsburg support against the Turks. Holy Roman emperor Leopold I, desiring to bring Transylvania under his influence and prevent the spread of Ottoman authority, pledged his support. In 1663 following Habsburg rejection of the Ottoman demands to evacuate Transylvania, Fazıl Ahmad led some 100,000 Ottoman troops into Hungary and besieged the strategically important fortress of Nové Zámky (Neuhäusel, in Slovakia). The small Habsburg army under Count Raimondo Montecúccoli was too weak to attack the Ottomans and sought protection on the fortified island of Schutt that protected the eastern frontier of Austria. The fortress of Nové Zámky offered a determined resistance to the Ottomans, who captured it only at the end of September. With winter now fast approaching, Köprülü Fazıl Ahmad decided to winter in Serbia and resume the offensive in the spring.

The threat of a major Ottoman invasion, the first since the time of Suleiman the Magnificent, of Austria proper prompted Leopold I to seek a wider alliance with European states. The Imperial Diet voted a levy of money and troops from the Holy Roman Empire, while King Louis XIV of France, a traditional enemy of the Habsburgs, chose to set aside his grievances and dispatched some 4,000 men under Jean de Coligny to assist the imperial army under Montecúccoli.

Köprülü Fazıl Ahmad resumed the offensive in the spring of 1664 but conducted it very slowly. To avoid devastation of their territory, the Habsburgs chose to reach a peaceful settlement with the Porte, and negotiations began at Vasvar (Eisenburg) in late July. However, while these were in progress the imperial and Ottoman armies continued to fight. As the Ottomans advanced, Montecúccoli chose to wait for them behind the Raab River in western Hungary, shadowing their march along the right bank of the river.

On August 1, Köprülü Fazıl Ahmad found a convenient place near Szentgotthárd (St. Gotthard) Abbey to cross the Raab. But while this was in progress, his army was surprised by Montecúccoli, who exploited the fact that the Ottomans could only move across river in small detachments that could be defeated in detail. Although the Ottomans fought fiercely, they were driven back across the river, abandoning most of their artillery and suffering heavy losses.

Simultaneously another Habsburg army, operating in northern Hungary, won a series of smaller victories against Kutschuk Mehmet Pasha, most notably at Levice. Despite these victories, Emperor Leopold chose to accept the Treaty of Vasvar with the Ottomans.

**The Ottoman-Habsburg War of 1683–1699**
The Treaty of Vasvar lasted for 20 years before it was broken by another war. The so-called Great Turkish War, however, was not limited to an Ottoman-Habsburg conflict but instead involved other European states in an anti-Ottoman coalition. Relations between the Habsburgs and the Ottoman Empire remained tense. The Habsburg position in Royal Hungary was tenuous, facing resistance from the Kuruc movement led by Imre Thököly.

In 1682 Thököly recognized Ottoman sovereignty, and the subsequent Habsburg attempt to subdue him prompted an Ottoman military response. The Ottoman invasion of Austria in 1683 almost succeeded in capturing Vienna before Habsburg-Polish forces under King John III Sobieski of Poland scored a major victory at Vienna (September 1683) and then drove the Ottomans from northwestern Hungary.

Pope Innocent XI assisted in the creation of the Holy League of the Holy Roman Empire, Venice, and Poland (Russia joined in 1686). The Poles conducted campaigns in Moldavia in 1686 and 1691, while Venetians attacked Ottoman interests in Dalmatia, Morea (southern Greece), and the eastern Mediterranean. The Ottomans repelled Russian invasions of the Crimea (Ottoman vassal) in 1687 and 1689 as well as attacks on the Ottoman fort of Azov in 1695–1696. Yet, the fate of the war was decided in Hungary, where the Ottomans suffered defeats at Gran (Esztergom) and Neuhäusel (1685), Buda (1686), and Mount Harsan (near Mohacs, 1687). By the end of 1687, southern Hungary and much of Transylvania came under Habsburg control, with Habsburg military operations extending into Serbia, where Habsburg forces were victorious at Belgrade (1688) and Nis (1689). Ottoman sultan Süleyman II's counterattack into Transylvania and Serbia was at first successful and led to the conquest of Belgrade in 1690. The Ottomans then suffered defeats at Slankamen (1691) and Grosswardein (Oradea, 1692).

The Habsburgs then were distracted by the War of the Grand Alliance (War of the League of Augsburg, 1689–1697) against France and turned away from the Ottoman front for almost five years. In 1697 as Ottoman forces marched from Belgrade toward Hungary, an Austrian army under Prince Eugene of Savoy routed it at the Battle of Zenta on September 11. This crushing defeat compelled the sultan to accept peace negotiations, which resulted in the Treaty of Karlowitz on January 26, 1699. The Ottoman Empire, while retaining Serbia, accepted Habsburg control of all of Hungary (except the Banat of Temesvar), Transylvania, Croatia, and Slavonia and recognized Venice's influence in Morea and Dalmatia and Poland's presence in Podolia.

### The Ottoman-Habsburg War of 1716–1718

The Treaty of Karlowitz maintained peace between the Habsburg and Ottoman Empires for 15 years. Both empires waged wars on other fronts, however, with Sultan Ahmad III concentrating his efforts on reclaiming lands in Greece, which resulted in the start of the Venetian-Ottoman War in 1714. The Habsburgs accused the Ottomans of breaking the Treaty of Karlowitz by endangering Venetian interests and concluded a defensive alliance with Venice in 1716.

Habsburg forces, led by the brilliant commander Prince Eugene of Savoy, routed the Ottomans in the Battle of Peterwardein on the Danube River (August 5, 1716) and then secured the Banat of Temesvar, the only remaining Ottoman region in Hungary. The following year Habsburg forces invaded Serbia, defeating Ottoman forces and capturing Belgrade in August 1717. With the Habsburgs controlling much of Serbia and western Walacia, the Ottomans sued for peace. the Treaty of Passarowitz in 1718 confirmed the Habsburg gains in Hungary, Serbia, and Walacia.

### The Ottoman-Habsburg War of 1737–1739

In 1735, Russia and the Ottoman Empire became embroiled in a war that two years later involved the Habsburgs as well. A Russian ally since the late 1720s, the Habsburgs watched closely the Russian campaigns in Crimea in 1736–1737. Following a series of Russian victories and alarmed by Russia's ambitions, the Habsburgs joined the war in July 1737. The Ottoman Army, however, proved to be much better prepared and inflicted several major defeats on the Habsburgs, most notably at Banja Luka (1737) and Grocka (1739), forcing them to sue for peace. The Treaty of Belgrade, signed in 1739, proved to be a sweet revenge for the Ottomans, for the Habsburgs were forced to surrender Belgrade and parts of Walacia.

### The Ottoman-Habsburg War of 1787–1791

Until the end of the 18th century, Ottoman-Habsburg relations remained relatively peaceful and focused on commercial and diplomatic contacts. The Russo-Ottoman War of 1787–1792 changed that, however. Empress Catherine II of Russia shared her "Greek Project" of partitioning the Ottoman Empire with Holy Roman emperor Joseph II (r. 1765–1790) and convinced him to join Russia in war against the Porte.

In 1783 the Habsburgs supported Russian annexation of the Crimea, an Ottoman vassal state, which greatly strained Ottoman-Habsburg relations. When the Porte declared war on Russia in August 1787, Austria joined as Russia's ally, hoping to reverse territorial losses suffered in 1739. Yet, early on Austrians suffered a major defeat at Karánsebes (September 1788), allowing the Ottomans to launch devastating raids deep into the Banat of Temesvar. Although the Habsburgs later recovered and even captured Belgrade, unrest in the Netherlands and Hungary, compounded by Prussian hostility, compelled Vienna to end the war. The Treaty of Svishtov (Sistova), reestablished the prewar situation, with only minor Habsburg territorial gains in Croatia.

### Later Relations

The Ottoman-Habsburg War of 1787–1791 was the last major conflict between these two states. Occupied by events in Europe, the Habsburgs abandoned their expansionist policy in the Balkans for decades to come, while the Ottoman Empire became embroiled in a prolonged conflict with Russia. The Habsburgs remained neutral during the Crimean War (1853–1856), which proved to be beneficial for the Ottoman Empire. The Russian expansionism in the Balkans and the spread of Pan-Slavism as well as nationalism among the Slav peoples brought the Ottoman Empire and the Habsburgs closer as Vienna sought to restrain Russia's influence in the region. The Habsburgs, while interested in the partition of the Ottoman Empire, perceived it as undesirable, since it would greatly strengthen Russia and create difficulties with Slav peoples in the Balkans. In 1878 following Russia's military triumph over the Ottomans, the Austrian Empire (proclaimed during the Napoleonic Wars in 1804) succeeded in containing Russian gains in the region and even secured permission to occupy Bosnia and Herzegovina, which remained under nominal Ottoman rule. This proved to be fateful for both empires. In 1908 Austria annexed Bosnia and Herzegovina, provoking a confrontation with Serbia that eventually contributed to the start of World War I. Austria and the Ottoman Empire fought as allies in the war, and both perished as a result of it.

ALEXANDER MIKABERIDZE

### See also
Köprülü Fazil Ahmed Pasha; Suleiman I; Vasvár, Treaty of

### References
Aksan, Virginia. *Ottoman Wars 1700–1870: An Empire Besieged.* Harlow, UK: Longman, 2007.

Fleet, Kate, Suraiya Faroqhi, and Reşat Kasaba, eds. *The Cambridge History of Turkey.* 3 vols. Cambridge: Cambridge University Press, 2006–2008.

Hochendlinger, Michael. *Austria's Wars of Emergence: War, State and Society in the Habsburg Monarchy, 1683–1797.* London: Longman, 2003.

Inalchik, Halil, and Cemal Kafadar, eds. *Suleyman the Second and His Time.* Istanbul: Isis, 1993.

Murphey, Rhoads. *Ottoman Warfare.* New Brunswick, NJ: Rutgers University Press, 1999.

Parvev, Ivan. *Habsburgs and Ottomans between Vienna and Belgrade, 1683–1739.* Boulder, CO: East European Monographs, 1995.

# Ottoman-Hungarian Wars (1437–1526)

Series of wars between the Ottoman Empire and the Kingdom of Hungary and the Ottoman Empire, beginning with the Ottoman occupation of Serbia (1438–1439) and ending with the collapse of Hungary in the Hungarian Civil Wars (1526–1547).

### Ottoman-Hungarian War of 1437–1438

The failure of European crusading efforts against the Ottomans introduced a new phase of Ottoman expansion in the Balkans, which were now waged up to and across the borders of Hungary. In 1437 The Ottomans besieged the city of Belgrade and, moving along the Danube River to the south, also laid siege to Semendria (Smederevo) fortress. Hungarian forces led by John Hunyadi defeated the Ottomans and relieved the fortress in 1437. As a consequence, King Albert II (r. 1437–1439) appointed Hunyadi military governor (*bán*) of Severin in Walacia (part of Romania), where he became even more deeply involved with the Ottomans.

### Ottoman-Hungarian War of 1441–1444

In retaliation for Hungary's support for the pretender Mustafa Çelebi and his claim to the Ottoman sultanate, Ottoman sultan Murad II (1421–51) attacked Hungary in 1440. Hunyadi's forces, however, secured victories at Semendria (Smederevo) in 1441 and at Herrmannstadt in 1442. To support deposed Serbian despot George Brankovic, Hunyadi counterattacked into Walacia in 1442 and Bulgaria in 1443. He soundly defeated the Ottomans at Nish (in Serbia) and then captured Sofia. Joining the forces of King Vladislaus I (r. 1440–1444) of Hungary and Croatia, Hunyadi defeated Murad's army at the Battle of Snaim (Kustinitza) in 1443, thus destroying Ottoman power in the Balkan region. Fearful of possible future losses, Murad entered into peace negotiations at Szeged, Hungary, which led to a 10-year truce with Hungary on July 12, 1444. The sultan ceded to Hungary control over Serbia and Walacia.

### Ottoman-Hungarian War of 1444–1456

Assured by Pope Eugenius IV (1383–1447) that promises made to infidels need not be honored, Hungarian king Vladislaus I broke the peace and launched another crusade in 1444. The crusading army was destroyed by Murad in the Battle of Varna (November 10, 1444), where Vladislaus was killed. Hunyadi escaped but was defeated by the Ottomans again at Kosovo Polje in 1448. After securing Constantinople in 1453, Murad's son and successor as sultan, Muhammad II (1430–1481), began new attacks on the Hungarians. Hunyadi led a successful expedition against the Ottomans in Serbia in 1454, forcing the Ottomans to retreat from Semendria (Smederevo) to Krusevac.

The Ottomans besieged the city of Belgrade for three weeks in July 1456, until Hunyadi's troops breached the siege, defeated the Ottomans, and freed the city. Muhammad then withdrew to Istanbul (Constantinople). On August 11, 1456, Hunyadi died from an epidemic. Although Hunyadi's campaigns against the Ottomans ultimately failed to recover territory, they did revitalize and provide leadership for the resistance of the Balkan peoples fighting against Ottoman rule, encouraging Skander Beg (George Kastriota) to renounce Ottoman suzerainty and launch the Albanian-Ottoman wars for independence.

### Ottoman-Hungarian War of 1463–1483

In 1463 Sultan Mehmet II invaded and occupied Bosnia, prompting a winter counterattack by Hunyadi's son, Matthias Corvinus, king of Hungary (r. 1458–1490), who recaptured several strategic fortresses and drove back the Ottomans. In the spring of 1464 Sultan Muhammad II "the Conqueror" besieged the Bosnian fortress of Jajce, but Hungarian forces managed to defend it and northern Bosnia; the rest of the territory fell to the Ottomans by 1483. A large raid by Ali Beg of Smederevo in 1479 was followed by a campaign by Matthias into Walacia, Serbia, and eastern Bosnia in 1480, capturing Srebrenica and briefly restoring the frontier defenses. Subsequently, Matthias focused on strengthening the line of fortresses established by King Sigismund along the southern borders of Transylvania and Slavonia through Bosnia to the Adriatic while the Ottomans consolidated their Balkan conquests.

### Ottoman-Hungarian War of 1492–1494

In 1492, Ottoman sultan Bayezid II (1481–1512) launched a surprise attack on Belgrade but was unable to take the city from the Hungarians. The same year, Holy Roman emperor Maximilian I (1486–1519) defeated the Ottomans at Villach in Carinthia (southern Austria). But by the first decades of the 16th century Ottoman raiders were penetrating deeper into the frontier zone and inflicting defeats on Hungarian counterattacks inside Croatia and Hungary, notably at Sinj (1508), Knin (1511), and Dubica (1520). The recurrent raids devastated the frontier regions, leaving the fortresses isolated and unsupported in the deserted land. The Ottomans recaptured Srebrenica in 1512, completing their conquest of Bosnia.

### Ottoman-Hungarian War of 1521–1526

The last major Ottoman expansion into Hungary occurred during the reign of Ottoman sultan Suleiman I "the Magnificent" (1520–1566), who demanded tribute from King Louis II (1506–26) of Hungary. Louis's refusal, accompanied by an insult to the Ottoman ambassador, led to the Ottoman invasion of Hungary in 1521. The Hungarian fortress of Sabac and Belgrade were captured in 1521, while Orsova and Knin fell in 1522. Hungary countered the Ottoman threat by concluding an alliance with Safavid Persia and the Holy Roman Empire, but the Ottomans secured the support of French king Francis I (1515–1547).

Advancing up the Danube River, Sultan Suleiman led a massive Ottoman army to the plain of Mohacs in present-day southern Hungary, where King Louis assembled his army. There on August 29, 1526, the two sides fought a decisive battle in which the Hungarians were crushed and Louis drowned in the disorganized flight. The Battle of Mohacs marked the end of the Hungarian kingdom, as Hungary was now partitioned between the Ottoman Empire, the Habsburg Monarchy, and the Principality of Transylvania.

ALEXANDER MIKABERIDZE

**See also**
Bayezid II; Mehmed II, Sultan; Murad II, Sultan; Ottoman Empire; Suleiman I

**References**
Sugar, Peter. *Southeastern Europe under Ottoman Rule, 1389–1814.* Seattle: University of Washington Press, 1977.
Szakály, Ferenc. "Phases of Turco-Hungarian Warfare before the Battle of Mohács." *Acta Orientalia Academiae Scientiarum Hungaricae* 33 (1979): 65–111.

## Ottoman-Montenegrin Wars

*See* Montenegrin-Ottoman Wars

## Ottoman-Persian Wars of the 18th and 19th Centuries

The Ottoman Empire and Persia underwent a long history of rivalry and conflict that escalated in the 17th century with the rise of a powerful Safavid state in Peria. However, in 1722 the Safavid dynasty was overthrown as a result of an Afghan invasion and Ottoman exploitation of Persian weakness to claim considerable territories in present-day Iraq and the Caucasus.

### Ottoman-Persian War of 1730–1736

Persia remained in a state of internal anarchy for almost a decade as various claimants vied for power. By the early 1730s, however, maverick Persian commander Nadir Khan had emerged victorious, announced the Safavid restoration, and demanded that the Ottomans withdraw from the Iranian territory they had occupied since 1722. The Ottomans agreed to restore Kimanshah, Tabriz, Hamadan, Ardalan, and all of Luristan in exchange for Persian recognition of Ottoman authority in eastern Georgia and Shirvan. While accepting this arrangement, Shah Tahmasp and Nadir Khan wanted greater territorial concession from the Porte and were encouraged by the news of popular turmoil in Istanbul.

In the spring of 1730 Nadir Khan captured Farahan and Yazdikhwast and crushed Ottoman forces under Kopruluzadeh Abdallah near Tabriz, which he seized in July. Sultan Ahmed III (r. 1703–1730) responded by imprisoning the Persian ambassador and ordering Ottoman forces in the Caucasus and eastern Anatolia to invade western Persia and confront Nadir. Yet the Patrona Revolt of 1730 shook the Ottoman capital, causing the downfall of Ahmed III and the rise of Sultan Mahmud I (r. 1730–1754).

This turmoil delayed the Ottoman military response and allowed the Persians to invade Ottoman-controlled Armenia. However, a revolt by the Abdali tribesmen in Afghanistan forced Nadir to march against them, leaving the inexperienced Shah Tahmasp to deal with the Ottomans. In Nadir's absence, Ottoman forces under Hakimoglu Ali Pasha recaptured Urmiya in November 1730 and Tabriz that December. Mahmud I then granted Hakimoglu the title of *ghazi*.

At the same time, Ottoman forces in Mesopotamia, led by governor of Baghdad Ahmad Pasha, reclaimed Kirmanshah and Hamadan, then routed Shah Tahmasp himself at Kurijan on September 15, 1731. The shah agreed to a peace treaty with Ahmad Pasha that surrendered substantial territory (Erivan, Ganja, eastern Georgia, Dagestan, and Shirvan) to the Porte while retaining Hamadan, Tabriz, Kirmanshah, Luristan, and Ardalan. The sultan was upset by Ahmad's concession of Tabriz, while Nadir Khan was infuriated by the shah's cession of so much territory. Nadir Khan used the peace treaty as the justification for replacing Tahmasp with his eight-month-old son Abbas III while retaining real power himself.

Nadir Khan then resumed war against the Ottomans in western Iran and Iraq. He repelled Ottoman attacks in Shahrazur and Derne and laid siege to Baghdad. However, the Ottoman army under Topal Osman Pasha scored a major victory against Nadir near Baghdad on July 20, 1733, protecting the Anatolian heartland, relieving Baghdad, and reclaiming Kirkuk and Derne.

Despite this defeat, Nadir quickly regrouped his forces and counterattacked later the same year. On November 30 he routed Topal Osman Pasha at Lailan, capturing the entire Ottoman camp and killing the Ottoman commander in chief himself. Following up on this success, Nadir reclaimed Kirkuk, Derne, and Shahrazur. He also besieged Baghdad in January 1734 but again failed to capture it. After his peace proposals were twice rejected, Nadir resumed his campaign by attacking Ottoman interests in the Caucasus. He captured Shirvan (August 1734) and eastern Georgia before Kopruluzadeh Abdallah stopped him at Kars and pushed Nadir back beyond the Arpa Chay River (January–May 1735).

A Persian counterattack proved decisive, however. On June 19, 1735, Nadir crushed the Ottomans in a battle at Baghavard that claimed the life of Kopruluzadeh Abdallah. This decisive victory allowed the Iranians to capture Ganja (July 9), Tbilisi (August 12), and Erivan (October 3). These victories extended Persian authority to much of Armenia and eastern Georgia. They also prompted a power struggle in Istanbul where two grand viziers were dismissed within six months. The Porte agreed to an armistice and opened diplomatic negotiations on a peace treaty signed in Constantinople (Istanbul) in late 1736.

Preoccupied with his wars against the Habsburgs and Russia, Mahmud I was compelled to recognize Nadir as shah of Persia and accept Persian control of the disputed territories in the Caucasus and Mesopotamia.

### Ottoman-Persian War of 1742–1746

The Treaty of Constantinople of 1736 proved contentious, since Persia insisted that a small Shiite sect, the Jafari, be declared orthodox. Disagreements regarding this religious issue led to the Ottoman proclamation of war on April 30, 1742. Mahmud made preparations to invade the Caucasus and western Persia, while Nadir Shah raided Baghdad and unsuccessfully besieged Mosul (September 1743). The Persian offensive resumed in early 1744 as Nadir Shah marched west from Hamadan, besieging Kars (July 1744) and then quelling a revolt in Dagestan incited by the Ottomans. He returned in time to rout the Ottoman army, led by Yegen Mehmet Pasha, at Kars (August 9–19, 1745).

The Persian victory at Kars compelled the sultan to accept the peace treaty signed in September 1746 in Kordan, northwest of Tehran. The sultan again recognized Nadir as shah and agreed to the restoration of Persia's frontiers as set by the 1639 Treaty of Zuhab (Qasr-e-Shirin). The treaty recognized present-day Iraq (including Baghdad and the Shatt al-Arab), western Caucasia, and Kurdish territories as part of the Ottoman Empire; Persia secured southwestern Caucasia.

## Ottoman-Persian War of 1776–1779

The death of Nadir Shah in 1747 plunged Persia into civil anarchy and provided the Porte with a long period of peace. Sultans Mahmud, Osman (r. 1754–1757), and Mustafa (r. 1757–1774) were preoccupied with struggles against European powers and resisted the temptation to exploit Persian weakness. Furthermore, Ottoman authorities imprisoned any fugitive Persian leader who threatened to upset the 1746 peace accords. By 1770s, however, civil strife in Persia ended with the victory of Karim Khan, who then pursued an aggressive policy toward the Ottomans and intervened in Ottoman affairs in Mesopotamia.

In 1775 Karim Khan attacked and captured the Ottoman town of Basra, prompting a declaration of war by Sultan Abdul al-Hamid's (r. 1774–1789) in June 1776. Ottoman armies then raided Persian territory from Baghdad and Mosul but internal power struggles between Ottoman commanders and local governors allowed Karim Khan to repel these attacks and retain Basra. He made plans for a joint Persian-Russian invasion of the Ottoman Empire, but his death in March 1779 put an end to this undertaking and restored an uneasy peace between the two empires.

## Ottoman-Persian War of 1820–1823

Relations between Persia and the Ottoman Empire now entered a more peaceful stage that lasted almost five decades. Following defeats in the Russo-Ottoman Wars of 1787–1791 and 1806–1812, Ottoman authorities sought to compensate for their territorial losses in Europe by acquiring new territory in the east. This was particularly enticing in light of the poor Persian performance in the Russo-Persian War of 1804–1813. At the same time, territorial losses to Russia in the Caucasus encouraged the ruling Persian Qajar dynasty to seek to offset these with acquisitions at the expense of the Ottomans. The Russian victories also compelled Fath Ali Shah (r. 1797–1834) to embark on military reforms supervised by his son Crown Prince Abbas Mirza, who employed European officers and military techniques to train the Persian Army.

Exploiting Sultan Mahmud II's preoccupation with European affairs, Fath Ali Shah interfered in the territory of present-day Iraq, where he supported local mamluk rulers and raided the vicinity of Baghdad and Shahrazur in early 1812. By 1817–1818 Persian forces raided all the way to Van, inciting local Kurdish tribes to rebel against the Ottomans. In October 1820, Sultan Mahmud II declared war on Persia and dispatched Khusrau Pasha, the governor of Erzurum, to command the Ottoman army in northern Iraq; however, the Ottomans' war effort was halfhearted, since their best forces were then engaged in Greece. In late 1821 Persian forces under Muhammad Ali Mirza attacked in the direction of Baghdad, but a cholera epidemic that also took its commander's life forced the army to withdraw. Abbas Mirza, however, enjoyed success in Armenia, capturing Bayazid, Toprak Qala, Diyarbakir, and Bitlis in the fall of 1821. However, he was soon forced to withdraw into winter quarters, which allowed the Ottomans under new commander Muhammad Amin Rauf Pasha to regroup. In the spring, fighting in the Lake Urmiya area culminated in the Persian victory at Khuy (May 1822), where Abbas Mirza routed a superior Ottoman force. But the Persians were unable to exploit their success owing to a cholera epidemic that devastated their army and forced a withdrawal.

On July 28, 1823, Persia and the Porte signed an agreement at Erzerum that restored the border as determined by the Treaty of Zuhab (Qasr-e Shirin) in 1639 and the Treaty of Kuran in 1746. The 1823 treaty recognized Iraq (including Baghdad and the Shatt al-Arab), western Caucasia, and Kurdish territories as part of the Ottoman Empire but granted southeastern Caucasia to Persia.

This was the last major war between the Ottoman Empire and Persia. Facing unrelenting Russian expansion in the Caucasus, both powers were either unwilling or too weak to continue their rivalry in Iraq and eastern Anatolia, although minor cross-border skirmishes did continue.

ALEXANDER MIKABERIDZE

### See also
Abbas Mirza; Karim Khan Zand, Muhammad; Nadir Shah; Ottoman-Safavid Wars; Zuhab, Treaty of

### References
Aksan, Virginia. *Ottoman Wars: An Empire Besieged, 1700–1870.* London: Longman, 2007.

Avery, Peter, Gavin Hambly, and Charles Melville, eds. *The Cambridge History of Iran: From Nadir Shah to the Islamic Republic,* Vol. 7. Cambridge: Cambridge University Press, 1991.

Axworthy, Michael. *Nader Shah: From Tribal Warrior to Conquering Tyrant.* New York: I. B. Tauris, 2006.

Faroqhi, Suraiya, ed. *The Cambridge History of Turkey: The Later Ottoman Empire, 1603–1839,* Vol. 3. Cambridge: Cambridge University Press, 2006.

Olson, Robert W. *The Siege of Mosul and Ottoman-Persian Relations, 1718–1743.* Bloomington: University of Indiana Press, 1975.

Shaw, Stanford J. *History of the Ottoman Empire and Modern Turkey.* 2 vols. Cambridge: Cambridge University Press, 1976–1977.

Ward, Steven. *Immortal: A Military History of Iran and Its Armed Forces.* Washington, DC: Georgetown University Press, 2009.

# Ottoman-Polish Wars of the 17th Century

By the 16th century after consolidating their Balkan victories, Ottoman armies pushed closer to Central Europe. Genoese Black Sea trading posts the like Kaffa (Caffa) fell under Ottoman control in the 1470s–1480s, while Moldavia submitted to Ottoman domination in 1495. These developments drew the attention of Austria, Hungary, and the Commonwealth of Poland and Lithuania. Diplomacy and royal marriages often connected these Christian nations in efforts to halt Muslim Ottoman territorial expansion. The Nikopolis (1396) and Varna (1444) crusades are early examples, albeit disastrous defeats for the allies. These actions exacerbated already poor relations between the Ottomans and the Commonwealth. Despite a 1533 treaty that pledged "perpetual friendship and alliance," Ottoman advances saw the sultan's armies closer to Poland-Lithuania, while regional politics drew both countries toward war.

Moldavia, desired for its resources and trade routes by both the Commonwealth and the Ottomans, played a part in this. When not directly battling each other, as in 1620–1621, both nations sponsored outside forces to conduct proxy wars—the Crimean Tatars for the Ottomans and the Ukranian Cossacks for the Commonwealth. The Cossacks, headquartered in the "Wild Lands," a sparsely settled frontier zone of southern Ukraine and Moldavia, were a collection of adventurers, bandits, pirates, and mercenaries. Seldom unified under one leader, Cossack factions maintained fortified outposts, such as the Zaparozhskaya Sich, located on an island in the Dnieper River.

Fearless and contemptuous of authority, the Cossacks prized their independence above all else. Although a problem for all their neighbors, they were most often at odds with the Ottomans and Tatars. Both Moscow and Poland-Lithuania employed Cossacks as border guards, mainly to protect the Wild Lands and beyond from Tatar raiders. These Muslim descendants of the Mongols maintained a predatory state based in the Crimea. Every year, Tchambouls, large parties of Tatar horsemen that could number as many as 20,000 men, moved north seeking loot and slaves.

These raids were but one part of a complex series of rebellions, invasions, and general chaos that racked Moldavia and Ukraine between 1648 and 1667. Cossacks aligned for and then against both the Commonwealth and Moscow. Finally, the new leader of the Tatars, Khan Adil Ghiray, forged an alliance with Piotr Doroszenko, a Cossack faction leader, for a grand raid into Polish territories.

In the late summer of 1667 a combined Tatar-Cossack army of nearly 30,000 men crossed the frontier. Noted for their horsemanship and raiding skills, Tatars and Cossacks were excellent light cavalry, but they lacked artillery and were easily disrupted by massed musket fire. The leaders of the Commonwealth knew this and, refusing to believe that Orthodox Christian Cossacks would make common cause with Muslim Tatars, denied funds for building a counterforce.

Poland-Lithuania's local commander, Jan Sobieski, combining his personal retinue with local troops, had but 8,000 men. Moving into the Polish sector of the Wild Lands placed the Ottoman invaders in Podolia, a land of plains, hills, swamps, and sparse forests dominated by the Dniester and Southern Bug Rivers. The former is navigable for its entire length, while the latter is interrupted by swamps and rapids. Podolia also boasted Kamieniec Podolski (Kamianets-Podilskyi), a powerful fortress and arms depot. Brilliant tactics allowed Sobieski to defeat the Tatar-Cossack alliance. Using Kamieniec Podolski, strategically placed earthworks, and mobile wagon forts, Sobieski divided his army into small mutually supporting units. These held river crossings, smashed enemy raiders, and fell back on fortified positions when faced by superior numbers.

Taking 3,000 of his best men, Sobieski constructed a fortified camp at Podhajce, which allowed him to cut the invaders' main supply line. A large Tatar-Cossack force moved against his position but was routed by a Polish assault on the night of October 1667. Sobieski then secured a truce, but he also requested reinforcements. Parsimonious magnates who dominated Poland-Lithuania's Sejm (parliament) refused to fund this request, arguing that Sobieski was capable of dealing with any contingency. Their focus was not on military affairs but rather the election of a new monarch, as Jan Kazimierz had died on August 16, 1668.

After considerable politicking Michal Wisniowiecki, leader of a Ruthenian magnate family greatly disliked by the Cossacks, became king on September 29, 1669. An inept ruler, he would only make enemies and encourage dissension within his semianarchic government. Doroszenko positioned himself to benefit from this by aligning his Cossacks with the Ottomans. Thus encouraged, Sultan Mehmet IV declared himself "the protector of the Cossacks" and sent an Ottoman army northward while calling up his Tatar vassals.

Poland-Lithuania now faced a severe challenge, as the Ottoman-Tatar forces had a significant advantage in numbers, and the Ottomans possessed a first-rate army.

Numbering some 80,000 men, it moved into Podolia during August 1672. On August 29 after a siege of only seven days, Kamieniec Podolski surrendered. This powerful fortress was symbolic of the weakened state of Polish-Lithuanian armies, for despite its more than 200 cannon, its garrison numbered only 250 men—all but 4 of them incapable of serving as artillerymen.

Sobieski responded with a 150-mile raid into Tatar/Cossack-controlled Ukraine, destroying forts, arms depots, and villages. During October 5–14 he smashed smaller Tatar forces, killing, capturing, or dispersing nearly 22,000 of the enemy. Although a brilliant raid showing that Sobieski could out-Tatar the Tatars, it did not prevent Polish diplomats from recognizing Podolia as an Ottoman fief administered by Doroszenko and pledging a yearly tribute of 22,500 gold ducats to the sultan. Unwilling to ratify this humiliating document, the Sejm instead voted to raise a 40,000-man army for a war of revenge. Sobieski began this campaign with additional defeats of Tatar raiders at Niemirów and Komarno. Dispersed by Sobieski's superior generalship, the Tatars were hunted down by enraged peasants and killed.

These setbacks sent the Tatars reeling back to the Crimea and deprived the Ottoman Army of valuable scouts. Some 30,000 Ottomans were entrenched at Chocim, on the Dniester, under the command of Grand Vizier Hussein. Sobieski, now reinforced and commanding a force of similar size, managed to surprise the enemy on November 11, 1673. Routed, the Ottomans attempted to flee over a single bridge, which quickly collapsed under their combined weight. The Ottoman force was annihilated, with the Poles capturing 120 guns, hundreds of standards, and substantial loot.

Sobieski followed up his victory with an offensive into Ottoman-dominated Moldavia, forcing the Ottoman garrison at Jassam to flee southward. In addition, he detached a force to regain Kamieniec Podolski. Neither action was completed before news arrived of the death of King Michal on November 10. In the Commonwealth there was no right of inheritance, and kings were elected. Voting was the prerogative of all aristocrats and a chance to enrich themselves at the expense of candidates. Combined with Poland-Lithuania's perennial lack of funds for the military, there was little chance to keep the army in Moldavia. Instead, it disintegrated.

Sobieski himself returned to Warsaw, where his victories over the Cossacks, Tatars, and Ottomans made him a candidate for the throne. After some debate, this hero of Chocim was chosen king of Poland-Lithuania on May 19, 1674.

In addition, the Sejm authorized funding for a new army to fight the Ottomans. It was organized just in time, as a new force of more than 100,000 Ottoman soldiers had crossed the Dniester and was advancing on Lwow.

Sobieski again used his hit-and-run tactics backed by mobile wagon forts and earthworks. On August 24, 1675, in the Battle of Lwow, he demolished a Tatar army of 20,000 men. Reconcentrating his forces, Sobieski drove the Ottomans back into Moldavia. The final battle of the war took place at Zurawno during September 25–October 14, 1676. Sobieski again employed earthworks and wagon forts to protect his 20,000 troops from the 100,000 Ottoman and Tatar soldiers under Ibrahim Pasha. Spirited Ottoman assaults only produced heavy losses for the attackers, while Sobieski steadily advanced his redoubts to within musket range of the principal Ottoman camp. At this point Ibrahim suggested negotiations, and the Ottoman-Polish Wars concluded with the Treaty of Zorawno on October 16. The treaty required the Commonwealth to surrender part of Podolia but eliminated any tribute.

John P. Dunn

**See also**
Ottoman-Habsburg Wars; Ottoman-Hungarian Wars; Russo-Ottoman Wars

**References**
Pasek, Jan Chryzostom. *Memoirs of the Polish Baroque.* Ed. and trans. by Catherine Leach. Berkeley: University of California Press, 1976.
Turk ve Islam, Eserleri Muzesi. *War and Peace: Ottoman-Polish Relations in the 15th–19th Centuries.* Istanbul: n.p., 1999.

## Ottoman-Safavid Wars (1526–1639)

A series of conflicts between the Ottoman Empire and Safavid Persia in the 16th and 17th centuries. In the early 16th century Ismail, a Safavid leader who claimed descent from Prophet Muhammad and Ali, succeeded in establishing a theocratic state in western Persia. In 1501–1503 Shah Ismail gained control of central and southern Persia, and by 1508 he was campaigning in southwest Persia and Iraq. Growing Safavid power soon threatened Ottoman interests in the region. In 1509–1512, Ismail played an active role in a civil war fought between the sons of Sultan Bayezid II, supporting Prince Ahmed against Selim.

After seizing the Ottoman throne in 1512, Sultan Selim I prepared for a campaign against the Safavids. Aside from political considerations, religious differences (Sunni Ottomans vs. Shii Safavids) played an important role in provoking this conflict. In 1514, Selim began the long march from Adrianople to Azerbaijan. After initially practicing a scorched-earth policy, Ismail then engaged the Ottomans in a decisive battle. Lacking artillery and trained infantry, the Safavid army suffered a decisive defeat in the Battle of Chaldiran in August 1514.

Selim then plundered the Safavid capital of Tabriz and returned to Anatolia. In the next year's campaign, the Ottomans captured the fortress of Kamakh and established control over Kurdistan and parts of Syria (Albistan). However, Ottoman inroads in Syria led to the Mamluk-Ottoman War in 1516–1517, which diverted Ottoman attention from the Safavids and allowed Ismail to regroup, although he never seriously threatened the Ottoman domain.

### Ottoman-Safavid War of 1526–1555

With the death of Shah Ismail in 1524, the Safavid crown went to Shah Tahmasp, who exploited Ottoman preoccupation in Europe, where Sultan Suleiman I (Suleiman the Magnificent) conducted major campaigns in Serbia and Hungary, to stir up rebellion in eastern provinces of the Ottoman Empire. Tahmasp also opened diplomatic negotiations with the Habsburgs regarding creation of a Habsburg-Safavid alliance against the Ottomans. In response, Suleiman provoked the Uzbeks in Transoxania to attack Persia from the east.

The war between Suleiman and Tahmasp began in earnest in 1526. Ottoman forces, led by Grand Vizier Ibrahim Pasha and later joined by Suleiman himself, invaded Iraq and during the course of the next eight years captured Baghdad, Bitlis, and Tabriz. Tahmasp avoided pitched battles and practiced a scorched-earth strategy. Tabriz, recaptured by Tahmasp in early 1535, was sacked later that year by Suleiman. Minor skirmishes and border fighting persisted for almost a decade.

The Safavid capture of Tabriz and Van provoked a second campaign by Suleiman in 1548. Yet again, Tahmasp adopted a scorched-earth policy against the Ottoman offensive, laying waste to the Armenian highlands. In the fighting the Ottomans reclaimed both Tabriz and Van as well as additional fortresses in Armenia and Georgia.

Following a three-year hiatus, the war resumed in earnest. A Safavid attack on Erzurum in 1552 led to a counterattack by Suleiman, who reclaimed Erzurum and invaded western Persia in 1553–1554. Unable to defeat the Ottomans, Tahmasp chose to negotiate and signed the Treaty of Amasya in 1555. Under its terms, the two powers determined their spheres of influence, with Persia receiving Azerbaijan, eastern Armenia, eastern Kurdistan, and eastern Georgian kingdoms while the Ottomans claimed all of western Georgia, Arabia, Iraq, and western Armenia and Kurdistan. Kars was declared neutral, and its fortress was destroyed.

### Ottoman-Safavid War of 1578–1590

The Peace of Amasya lasted until an Ottoman offensive in 1578 sought to take advantage of a period of Persia's weakness under Shah Muhammad Khudabanda (r. 1578–1587). The death of Shah Tahmasp I in 1576 resulted in a two-year-long civil war regarding the succession that weakened the Safavid state and led the Ottoman Turks to believe that Persia could at last be conquered. In 1578 Mustafa Pasha, known as Lala Pasha, defeated the Persian forces on Lake Childir and invaded Georgia and Shirvan.

The Ottoman expansion into eastern Caucasia forced Shah Muhammad to release King Simon I of Kartli (eastern Georgia) to fight the common enemy. Simon achieved considerable success in eastern Georgia, where he reclaimed the key fortresses of Lori and Gori before besieging Tbilisi in 1579. In 1580 he repulsed the Ottoman expeditions in Kartli, and in 1582 he routed a major Ottoman army on the Mukhrani Field. The Ottomans meanwhile conducted operations in Dagestan and Azerbaijan and gained considerable success at Ganna and Karabagh in 1588. With Uzbek attacks intensifying in eastern Persia and the Ottomans capturing Tabriz in 1590, Shah Abbas I, who had succeeded Shah Muhammad two years earlier, chose to enter into peace talks. The Treaty of Constantinople (also known as the Treaty of Ferhat Pasha, who commanded the Ottoman forces), signed in May 1590, ended the war. It gave the Ottomans control of Azerbaijan, Georgia, Armenia, most of Qarabagh (except for Ardabil), most of Persian Kurdistan, Luristan, and Dagestan.

### Ottoman-Safavid War of 1603–1612

The Safavids refused to accept the loss of their vast Caucasus territories. After subduing the Uzbeks, Abbas exploited Ottoman problems in Hungary to launch an offensive from the east. A surprise attack by the Safavids led to the capture of Tabriz in late 1603. While Abbas commanded the main offensive in the northwest against Ottomans forces led by Chighalah Pasha, smaller Safavid forces raided Iraq and southern Caucasia. Ottoman sultan Ahmed I led a large army against Abbas but was defeated near Lake Urmia in

1604. Following up on his success, Abbas captured Baghdad, Mosul, and Diarbekh by 1608, thus reclaiming almost all the territory lost by the Safavids in the previous decade. In 1612, a new Treaty of Constantinople confirmed the Ottoman-Safavid frontier on the line established by Selim I and Ismail almost 100 years earlier; in return, the shah pledged to deliver 200 pack loads of fine silk annually to the Sublime Porte.

### Ottoman-Safavid War of 1616–1618

The Safavid failure to deliver the silk served as a pretext for the resumption of hostilities in 1616. An Ottoman army besieged Erivan (Yerevan) in 1616 but was repulsed and forced to withdraw. In 1618 the Ottomans attacked toward Tabriz but were defeated at Soltaniyeh. Afterward peace negotiations began, resulting in the Treaty of Sarab (1618) that confirmed the terms of the last peace treaty.

### Ottoman-Safavid War of 1623–1639

The war of 1623–1639 was the last major conflict between the Safavids and Ottomans. It began as a result of a power struggle involving local officials in the eastern Ottoman provinces. Abaza Mehmed Pasha, governor of Erzurum, rose in rebellion. Since 1621, Baghdad had been in the hands of the Janissary Subashi Bakr and his followers. Bakr futilely appealed to Sultan Murad IV for recognition as the new pasha. When the sultan ordered Hafiz Ahmed Pasha, the governor of Diyarbakir, to restore order in Baghdad, Bakr turned to Abbas, who sent troops to assist him.

In order to prevent the Safavid capture of Baghdad, Hafiz Ahmed chose to negotiate with Bakr and convinced him to recognize the sultan's authority. Nonetheless, Safavid forces besieged Baghdad and captured it in January 1624. Abbas's troops then went on to seize control of most of Iraq, including Kirkuk, Mosul, Najaf, and Karbala, the last two cities being holy to the Shiites.

To recover these territories, the sultan dispatched Hafiz Ahmed Pasha, who was appointed the grand vizier. The Ottomans organized several campaigns in 1625–1639. In the first of these, the Ottomans captured Mosul in northern Iraq but unsuccessfully besieged Baghdad in 1625–1626. Shah Abbas died in January 1629 as Grand Vizier Gazi Ekrem Khusrev Pasha led another campaign into Iraq. Although he was victorious at Mihriban (near Kermanshah) in May and sacked Hamadan in June, the grand vizier failed to capture Baghdad in November and was forced to return to withdraw owing to winter weather. The Safavids reclaimed parts of Iraq, their efforts facilitated by the events in the Ottoman Empire of the Janissary revolt and the murder of the grand vizier in February 1632.

Sultan Murad spent almost five years subduing internal revolts before he was able to turn his attention to Iraq. In March 1635 the sultan opened his campaign against Erivan, capturing it that August. One month later the Ottomans occupied Tabriz, but their campaign then stalled. Shah Sefi organized a Safavid counterattack that reclaimed Erivan in April 1636 and defeated the Ottomans at Ardalan (central Persia) in October. Sultan Murad delayed the start of a new campaign until 1638, when his army marched to Baghdad. Led personally by Murad, the Ottomans captured Baghdad in December 1638 and effectively restored their authority in Iraq. Peace negotiations soon began resulting in the Treaty of Zuhab (Treaty of Qasr-e-Shirin) of May 1639, which established a boundary between the two empires that remained virtually unchanged into modern times. The treaty recognized Iraq (including Baghdad and the Shatt al-Arab), western Caucasia, and Kurdish territories as part of the Ottoman Empire but granted southwestern Caucasia to Persia.

In 1722, the Safavid dynasty collapsed following the Afghan invasion. As Persia descended into political chaos, the Ottomans regarded it as an opportunity to expand their territory in Azerbaijan and western Persia, but their efforts failed owing to local resistance as well as the rise of Nadir Shah (1730–1747) of the Afshar dynasty.

Alexander Mikaberidze

**See also**
Abbas I the Great; Amasya, Treaty of; Chaldiran, Battle of; Ismail I, Shah; Nadir Shah; Selim I, Sultan; Suleiman I; Tahmasp I, Shah; Zuhab, Treaty of

**References**
Fisher, William Bayne, Peter Jackson, and Laurence Lockhart, eds. *The Cambridge History of Iran: The Timurid and Safavid Periods,* Vol. 6. Cambridge: Cambridge University Press, 1986.

Imber, Colin. *The Ottoman Empire 1300–1650: The Structure of Power.* Basingstoke, UK: Palgrave Macmillan, 2002.

İnalcik, Halil. *The Ottoman Empire: The Classical Age, 1300–1600.* London: Weidenfeld and Nicolson, 1973.

Newman, Andrew J. *Safavid Iran: Rebirth of a Persian Empire.* London: I. B. Tauris, 2009.

Savory, Roger M. *Iran under the Safavids.* Cambridge: Cambridge University Press, 1980.

## Ottoman-Wahhabi War

*See* Egyptian-Arab Wars

# Outremer

Outremer is the name used in medieval sources and in modern scholarship as a collective term for the four Frankish states established in Syria and Palestine by the First Crusade (1096–1099): the county of Edessa (1098–1150), the principality of Antioch (1098–1287), the Kingdom of Jerusalem (1099–1291), and the county of Tripoli (1102–1289). The Kingdom of Jerusalem extended over the southern parts of Outremer, in the area historically known as Palestine (modern-day Israel, the West Bank, the Gaza Strip, and adjacent regions); the other three states were situated in the north, in areas known historically as Syria and Upper Mesopotamia (roughly modern-day Syria, southeastern Turkey, and Lebanon). During its relatively short existence, the county of Edessa extended much farther to the east than the other Frankish states, well beyond the Euphrates River.

The word "Outremer" derives from the Old French expression *ou(l)tremer,* meaning "[the land] beyond the sea," that is, the lands on the far side of the Mediterranean Sea, seen from the perspective of Western Christians. Similar formulations are found in other languages: Spanish, Ultramar; Italian, Oltremare; and Middle High German, *daz lant über mer.* An alternative name for the four Frankish principalities in modern historical writing is the "Crusader States." Although common, this term is less accurate, since after around 1130 extremely few of their Frankish inhabitants were actually crusaders, in the sense of people who had taken a vow to go on crusade. In the Middle Ages the Frankish states were also often collectively known as Syria (Latin, Syria; French, Syrie).

The geography of Outremer and its neighboring lands to the east can be conceived in broad terms as a series of elongated bands or zones running north-south; viewed from west to east, these can be visualized as having distinct physical characteristics. Adjoining the Mediterranean Sea is a relatively fertile coastal plain, narrower in the north and central areas but quite broad in the south. This plain rises, quite dramatically in the north but more gradually in the south, to a spine. In the north and center, the spine consists of high mountains: the Amanus, Nusairi, and Lebanon ranges. These are fairly impenetrable and impeded communications, but they are broken by larger gaps in places, notably the Syrian Gates and the lower reaches of the Orontes River (in the principality of Antioch) and the Buqaia (in the county of Tripoli). In the south the spine is formed by the highlands of Judaea, Samaria, and Galilee, with the settlements of Jerusalem, Nablus, and Nazareth. The spine descends to a long valley formed by a series of rivers and lakes: the Orontes and Litani in the north and center and the Jordan River, together with Lake Tiberias and the Dead Sea, in the south. To the east of the valley, the country rises again to a wide, mostly fertile zone that is higher in the center (the Anti-Lebanon range and Mount Hermon). Its northern section, including the cities of Aleppo and Damascus, is very fertile, but its fertility decreases to the south of the area known as the Hauran. While the Franks were able to penetrate and partially control this zone in the 12th century, they were never able to capture the major Muslim cities of Aleppo, Hama, Homs, and Damascus. The conquests of Saladin in the late 12th century and of the Mamluk Sultanate in the 13th century successively pushed Frankish-held territory farther back toward the west until it was reduced to a series of unconnected coastal strips by the 1280s.

Water was relatively scarce in the time of the crusades, as in modern times, and irrigation was common in agriculture. The relative availability of water supplies not only restricted communications but was also a significant factor in determining where armies could go. The main staple crop was wheat, and other important products were olives, citrus fruits, and sugarcane. Muslim prohibitions on wine had restricted the cultivation of vines; wine production gained new impetus under the Franks, who required it for everyday drinking as well as liturgical purposes. Because of water shortages, much of the land was not cultivated and was given over to pasture, mainly grazed by sheep and goats. There was little suitable pasture for cattle or horses, and it was necessary to import horses for military purposes.

Frankish-held territory comprised several important cities, particularly on the coast. Acre (modern-day Akko, Israel) and to a lesser extent Tyre (modern-day Soûr, Lebanon), Tripoli (modern-day Trâblous, Lebanon), and Beirut connected with major trade routes from the east and served as entrepôts for luxury products such as spices and textiles as well as local and regional products. These cities also had important industries, as did Antioch (modern-day Antakya, Turkey) and other major towns. The coastal cities attracted settlers from the Italian republics of Genoa, Venice, and Pisa, who received legal and financial privileges and in some places were able to establish their own autonomous quarters. The inland city of Jerusalem, by contrast, had no large-scale industry or trade; its main economic role was to service the royal and ecclesiastical administrations and cater to the important pilgrim traffic from the West.

The Franks constituted a privileged minority in all four states of Outremer, the only ethnic group in possession of all legal rights. The majority of the Frankish population lived in urban centers or as garrisons and support personnel in castles. During the initial phase of conquest the Muslim and Jewish urban populations were largely either massacred or expelled, although the native Christians were allowed to remain and Jews were later allowed to return. The city of Jerusalem remained barred (at least in theory) to non-Christians. Most rural settlement was in villages, known in Latin as *casalia* (sing. *casale*), while there were many deserted or seasonally occupied settlements (*gastinae*, sing. *gastina*).

The native rural population consisted largely of Muslims (known to the Franks as Saracens) and native Christians of various denominations. There were also smaller rural minorities of Jews and Samaritans in Galilee and Druzes in the mountains of Lebanon. In some cases Franks settled in newly founded villages, such as Magna Mahomeria (modern-day al-Bira, West Bank) near Jericho. In some cases these new settlements were exclusively meant for Franks, but other settlements had mixed communities of Franks and native Christians.

Most of the native population, whether Christian, Muslim, or Jewish, used Arabic as their everyday language, although there were also significant numbers who used Syriac, Armenian (notably in the county of Edessa), and Greek (notably in the cities of Antioch and Laodikeia in Syria). The Frankish settlers and their descendants spoke French and wrote Latin, while Italian dialects were also found in the coastal cities where Venetians, Genoese, and Pisans resided, and many other languages were heard from the numerous pilgrims who visited the Holy Land under Frankish rule. However, few Franks seem to have learned Arabic, and such knowledge was often remarked on (and, by implication, regarded as unusual) in both Western and Arabic sources.

ALAN V. MURRAY

**See also**

Antioch, Principality of; Edessa, County of; Jerusalem, Latin Kingdom of; Tripoli, County of

**References**

Boas, Adrian. *Le comté de Tripoli sous la dynastie toulousaine (1102–1187)*. 2nd ed. Paris: Geuthner, 2000.

Cahen, Claude. *La Syrie du Nord à l'époque des croisades et la principauté franque d'Antioche*. Paris: Geuthner, 1940.

Edbury, Peter. "The Crusader States." In *The New Cambridge Medieval History*, Vol. 5, c. 1198–c. 1300, ed. David Abulafia, 590–606. Cambridge: Cambridge University Press, 1999.

Jotischky, Andrew. *Crusading and the Crusader States*. Harlow, UK: Pearson Longman, 2004.

Le Strange, Guy. *Palestine under the Moslems: A Description of Syria and the Holy Land from A.D. 650 to 1500*. London: Palestine Exploration Fund, 1890.

Prawer, Joshua. *The Latin Kingdom of Jerusalem: European Colonialism in the Middle Ages*. London: Weidenfeld and Nicolson, 1972.

Richard, Jean. *The Latin Kingdom of Jerusalem*, 2 vols. Amsterdam: North-Holland, 1979.

Setton, Kenneth M., et al. *A History of the Crusades*. 2nd ed., 6 vols. Madison: University of Wisconsin Press, 1969–1989.

## Palestine, British Mandate for (1922–1948)

The political entity controlled by Britain during 1922–1948 under the authority of the League of Nations. Palestine had been part of the Ottoman (or Turkish) Empire until the end of 1917. Beginning in the 1920s, Palestine became increasingly subject to violent clashes between Arabs and Jews, as both groups claimed the territory as their homeland. Complicating matters was the fact that both groups believed that Britain had promised Palestine to them.

During World War I, the British government sought the supports of world Jewry for the Allied war effort. In November 1917, British foreign secretary Arthur Balfour declared that London favored "the establishment in Palestine of a National Home for the Jewish people." At the same time, Britain also sought Arab support against the Ottoman Empire, pledging support for an Arab Middle Eastern kingdom following an Allied victory if the Arabs would take up arms against the Ottomans. This became the Arab Revolt of 1916–1918. Also in 1916, Britain and France concluded the Sykes-Picot Agreement that would establish French hegemony over Syria and Lebanon and British hegemony over what became Palestine and Iraq. This agreement ultimately became the basis of four mandates under the authority of the new League of Nations. The European powers pledged to grant these nascent states independence when they were deemed ready for self-government.

Palestine passed under British control as a mandate as a consequence of the San Remo Conference in April 1920, defined for the first time to consist of the present-day countries of Israel and Jordan. The British then divided Palestine and turned the territory east of the Jordan River into the state of Transjordan and announced that the Balfour Declaration did not apply to Jordan. This is why some Jews claim that present-day Jordan is part of Palestine, or the homeland of the Palestinian Arabs.

The Arab elites of Palestine were intensely opposed to the Jewish pursuit of a state in Palestine, which the British government certainly understood by 1918. The Arabs believed that the creation of a Jewish homeland in Palestine would eventually turn them into a marginalized minority among a majority Jewish population. Thus, the 500,000 inhabitants of the Arab community of Palestine, approximately 85–90 percent of the total population, was unwilling to compromise with either the British or the Jews.

The British mandate government in Palestine during 1922–1948 failed to keep the peace between the Arabs and the Jews. The escalating violence between the two sides was the result of the British policy that sought to achieve mutually exclusive goals: implementing the Balfour Declaration while safeguarding the interests and rights of the majority Arab population. Much of the tension arose over the numbers of Jewish immigrants admitted to the country. In response to Arab violence and riots, the British attempted

British and Arab troops stand guard at a checkpoint in Jerusalem following the Arab Riots that occurred in the city in April 1920. (Library of Congress)

the suspension of Jewish settlements and Jewish land purchases in Palestine, which were often from wealthy absentee Arab landowners but then led to the eviction of Arab peasants. But London relented in the face of strong Jewish opposition.

In 1920 Palestinian Arabs began sporadically attacking Jewish settlements, and in response in 1921 the Jews formed a clandestine defense organization known as Haganah. To encourage cooperation between Arabs and Jews, the British in 1922 and 1923 attempted to create a legislative council, but the Arabs refused to participate. They were suspicious of British manipulation and Jewish favoritism but also believed that their participation would signal their acceptance of the British mandate and recognition of the Balfour Declaration.

Violence between Arabs and Jews throughout 1929 led the British to halt all Jewish settlement in Palestine. But in the face of outcries by Jews in Palestine and Zionists in London, the British government soon reversed its policy. By 1936 the Jewish population of Palestine was approximately 400,000, or 30 percent of the total population. That same year the British resurrected the idea of a legislative council, but this time both Arabs and Jews rejected the idea. Also in 1936, a full-fledged Arab uprising known as the Arab Revolt began. It lasted until 1939. This forced Britain to dispatch 20,000 troops to Palestine and led to temporary collaboration between the British and Jews against Arabs to suppress the rebellion.

In 1937 the British recommended partitioning Palestine into separate Arab and Jewish states, but a year later they rejected partition as not feasible. By the end of the Arab Revolt in 1939, some 5,000 Arabs had been killed and thousands more wounded or arrested. That same year, the British announced that Palestine would become an independent state within 10 years. They also seemingly repudiated the Balfour Declaration by severely limiting future Jewish immigration and restricting the land sales to Jews.

By 1939 with the threat of a new world war looming, Britain sought to secure its Middle East interests by placating the Arabs. Jews found themselves marginalized and ignored by the British. As a result, some Jews began taking up arms against the British administration in Palestine. There was a temporary lull in fighting between Arabs and Jews owing to the Axis threat in the Middle East, but by the end of 1942 and the looming defeat of the Axis in North Africa, Arabs and Jews resumed fighting. At the same time, Jewish groups stepped up their attacks against the British.

News of the Holocaust carried out by the Nazis in Europe led to demands for additional Jewish settlement in Palestine but also the creation of a Jewish state there that would protect Jews in the future. At the same time, some Jewish groups such as Lohamei Herut Israel (also known as Lehi and the Stern Gang) and the Irgun Tsvai Leumi (National Military Organization) resorting to increased violence against the British authorities.

As for the Arabs, they took the view that as they were not responsible for the Holocaust, they should not be forced to sacrifice for it in the creation of a Jewish state in Arab territory. Still, for much of the world the Holocaust became the legitimizing force behind creation of the State of Israel.

At the end of World War II, European governments struggled with what to do with more than 250,000 displaced Jews, survivors of the Holocaust. Britain resisted Zionist demands that they be allowed to settle in Palestine, especially while experiencing mounting terrorist violence there perpetrated by Jewish groups. This included the bombing by Irgun of the British military headquarters at the King David Hotel in Jerusalem on July 22, 1946, which killed some 90 people. Between November 1945 and July 1946 Jewish terrorism increased, with some 40 British soldiers and police killed by Irgun and Lehi along with the sabotage of infrastructure. As it had during the war, Britain continued its practice of turning back ships carrying Jewish refugees from Europe to Palestine. The terrorist violence only reinforced Britain's uncompromising position.

Efforts to resolve the situation diplomatically failed when the British government refused to accept the recommendation of the Anglo-American Committee of Inquiry to admit 100,000 Jewish refugees into Palestine. On February 14, 1947, seeking to extricate itself from Palestine, Britain turned the matter of the future of Palestine over to the newly created United Nations (UN).

On August 31, 1947, the UN Special Commission on Palestine (UNSCOP) recommended the termination of the British Mandate for Palestine and the granting of Palestinian independence. A majority of UNSCOP members agreed to partition Palestine into both Arab and Jewish states, with Jerusalem remaining an international city. Although the Arab population was 1.2 million and the Jewish population was just 600,000, the Arab state would have constituted only 43 percent of the land of Palestine. The Jewish state would take up 56 percent.

The Jews generally supported the partition plan, but the Arabs did not. The newly created Arab League threatened war if the UN approved and implemented the partition plan. Desperate to quit Palestine, the British government announced that it would accept the UN recommendation and declared in September 1947 that the British Mandate for Palestine would terminate on May 14, 1948. By announcing the end of the British mandate before the UN had approved the UNSCOP proposal and by refusing to enforce whatever decision the UN made, Britain undermined the UN effort to solve the Palestine problem.

On November 29, 1947, the UN officially approved the partition of Palestine according to the UNSCOP report by a vote of 31 to 13 with 10 abstentions. This ensured the establishment of a Jewish state in Palestine. In January 1948 the Arab Liberation Army (ALA) invaded Palestinian territory and initially enjoyed considerable success in isolating rural Jewish settlements from Jews living in the major cities such as Haifa, Jerusalem, and Tel Aviv. But in April 1948 following the arrival of arms shipments from abroad, the Jews took the offensive and seized much territory, including Haifa and Jaffa. Arabs evacuated or were attacked and fled their villages and towns as Jews advanced during the spring 1948 offensive. The cause for this mass exodus remains controversial and disputed. Arabs had believed that the Jews would be swiftly defeated. Survivors also reported that in the chaos and invasions or hurried exits of their homes, they had no idea that they would be forbidden from returning. During this time, both Arabs and Jews resorted to terrorism with little regard for noncombatants. By May 2, 1948, Jews had militarily occupied a state roughly the equivalent of that approved by the UN.

On May 14, 1948, Jewish leaders in Palestine proclaimed the establishment of the State of Israel. Both the United States and the Soviet Union immediately recognized the new state, but the next day the Arab armies of Egypt, Lebanon, Jordan, Syria, and Iraq invaded Palestine, beginning the Israeli War of Independence (1948–1949).

STEFAN BROOKS

**See also**
Arab Liberation Army; Arab Revolt in Palestine; Arab Revolt of World War I; Balfour Declaration; Haganah; Holocaust; Irgun Tsvai Leumi; Israel; Israeli War of Independence; Lohamei

Herut Israel; Sykes-Picot Agreement; United Nations Special Commission on Palestine; Zionism

**References**

Bickerton, Ian J., and Carla L. Klausner. *A Concise History of the Arab-Israeli Conflict.* 4th ed. Upper Saddle River, NJ: Prentice Hall, 2004.

Dowty, Alan. *Israel/Palestine.* Malden, MA: Polity, 2005.

Sachar, Howard M. *A History of Israel: From the Rise of Zionism to Our Time.* 3rd ed. New York: Knopf, 2007.

Shepherd, Naomi. *Ploughing Sand: British Rule in Palestine, 1917–1948.* New Brunswick, NJ: Rutgers University Press, 1999.

Yapp, M. E. *The Making of the Modern Near East, 1792–1923.* London: Longman, 1987.

# Palestine, Partition of

The idea of partitioning Palestine into Jewish and Arab political entities emerged early in Zionist thought. In his negotiations with the Ottoman government in 1902, Zionist leader Theodor Herzl suggested that a charter be granted for a Zionist entity that would run from Haifa by the Jezreel Valley to Lake Kinneret (the Sea of Galilee) and include all of Galilee to the Litani River. Zionist leader and organizer of agricultural settlements in Palestine Arthur Rupin planned to concentrate Jewish settlements in Judaea and around Lake Kinneret in an effort to achieve a sufficient population mass to achieve Jewish autonomy in these areas.

Zionists were active during the Paris Peace Conference following World War I, proposing the creation of a large Palestinian state under the assumption that rapid Jewish migration would soon allow them to constitute the majority of its population. This found a sympathetic ear in the British delegation if only because a large Palestine would ipso facto extend British influence in the region. Strong French opposition, however, excluded from the 1920 Palestinian mandate areas of western Galilee to the Litani River and the Golan Heights to the Yarmuk River. Then, in 1922 the lands east of the Jordan River were placed under the rule of Emir Abdullah.

Following increasing violence in Palestine between Arabs and Jews and especially the Arab riots of 1929, in 1932 Victor Jacobson, World Zionist Organization (WZO) representative to the League of Nations, suggested to the League of Nations the possibility of Palestinian partition. He proposed that the Jewish area include the coastal plain and the relatively thinly populated valleys. With the beginning of the Arab Revolt of 1936–1939, calls for partition became more frequent and widespread and were even mentioned in the press. The British Peel Commission of 1936–1937 supported the partition of Palestine, with the Jews having an area of the country in which they would be the majority of the population. It also reached the rather erroneous conclusion that partition could end Jewish-Arab conflict. Zionists were divided on the issue, but the majority was inclined to accept partition as a means of rescuing Europe's Jews, then under increased persecution in both Germany and Poland. The British government was inclined to accept partition whereby there would be two separate states in Palestine, both of which would be tied to Britain.

Arab leaders adamantly opposed partition, the notable exception being Abdullah. Faced with the strong opposition by the Arabs and German and Italian support for this, the British government reconsidered its stance. Indeed, the subsequent Woodhead Commission, charged with recommending ways of implementing partition, devised a plan that was disadvantageous to the Jews. The British government white paper of 1939 and regulations the next year sharply restricting Arab land sales to Jews were strongly detrimental to the Jewish position. British policies were at this point in large part conditioned by London's desire to win Arab support for the war against the Axis. Meanwhile, the Zionist Biltmore Program of 1942 called for Jewish rule over all Palestine and extensive Jewish immigration there.

In late 1943 a British ministerial committee appointed by Prime Minister Winston Churchill proposed a partition plan in which there would be Arab and Jewish states and a British-mandated area that would include Jerusalem. The two states carved from Palestine would be part of a larger federation of states under the protection of Britain, France, and the United States. The Labor government that came to power in July 1945 did not initially favor partition or the granting of independence. Rather, it supported autonomous districts with ultimate authority to remain in British hands. The British government tended to be anti-Zionist, while the U.S. government was pro-Zionist. For a number of reasons, London was forced to follow Washington's position. The Anglo-American Committee of Inquiry of 1946, created under U.S. pressure, recommended creation of a single Arab-Jewish state, under the trusteeship of the United Nations (UN), and the admission of 100,000 Jewish refugees to Palestine. In the summer of 1946, Zionist leaders informed U.S. president Harry S. Truman that they were withdrawing their demands for a Jewish state that would encompass the whole of Palestine and were prepared to accept a Jewish state in part of the country.

Unable itself to resolve the Palestinian issue and under increasing financial pressures, the British government was determined to divest itself of Palestine. In February

1947 British foreign secretary Ernest Bevin announced that Britain was referring the matter to the UN, which in turn appointed the UN Special Commission on Palestine (UNSCOP) to come up with a recommendation. The two alternatives before the committee were the partition of Palestine into two separate sovereign states or one state in which there would be a federated state with an Arab majority and autonomy for a Jewish minority. A majority of the committee members favored partition. The UNSCOP plan called for Jerusalem to be internationalized. The original plan also called for the Jewish state to receive the Negev area for future immigration, but in negotiations with the General Assembly, the Negev was restored to the Arab state. While the Jews were willing to accept the UN plan, the Arabs firmly rejected it. Indeed, approval of the plan by the UN on November 29, 1947, led to the beginning of the Arab-Jewish Communal War. On May 14, 1948, the Jews announced the independence of the State of Israel, and this immediately led to an Arab invasion and the Israeli War of Independence (1948–1949). Israel won that war and at the conclusion of the armistice agreements of early 1949 ended up with three-quarters of the territory of the Palestine mandate.

Spencer C. Tucker

**See also**
Abdullah I; Anglo-American Committee of Inquiry; Arab Revolt in Palestine; Herzl, Theodor; Peel Commission; White Paper of 1939; Woodhead Report; Zionism

**References**
Sachar, Howard M. *A History of Israel: From the Rise of Zionism to Our Time*. 3rd ed. New York: Knopf, 2007.
Shepherd, Naomi. *Ploughing Sand: British Rule in Palestine, 1917–1948*. New Brunswick, NJ: Rutgers University Press, 1999.

## Palestine, Pre-1918 History of

Palestine is a geographical area of the eastern Mediterranean coast bounded by the Jordan Valley to the east, the Negev Desert to the south, and Lebanon to the north. Its territorial extent has varied over time, but because it occupied an important transportation route between larger empires, it was destined for a stormy existence and has been fought over and disputed since ancient times. The current dispute is primarily between Palestinian Arab nationalists and the State of Israel but on a larger scale involves Islam, Judaism, Christianity, the United States, Europe, and the predominantly Muslim countries of the Middle East.

The Bible introduces the geographical region as Canaan. The Old Testament book of Numbers first names the area as Eretz Israel (the Land of Israel) in Chapter 34 and there clearly delineates Israel's boundaries that include portions of present-day Jordan. Palestine has been settled, disputed, conquered, and ruled by the Canaanites, Philistines, Samaritans, Nabataeans, Greeks, Romans, Byzantines, Ottomans, British, Jews, Muslims, and Christians.

The ownership of Palestine is disputed. As is true of most things in the Middle East, perspective is everything. For the Muslims the inheritance of the land revolves around the story in Genesis, the first book of the Bible, of a man named Abraham who had a special relationship with God. The major character in Genesis is Abraham, and many groups both present and past, such as the Edomites, the Arab peoples, and the Jews, trace their origins to Abraham. The Arabs assert that the story of Genesis accepted by Jews and Christians is fiction, a reconstructed story created by the Jews to establish Jewish ownership of the land. The Arab and Muslim perspective is that God's promise to make of Abraham a great nation and to give Abraham's offspring the land now disputed as Palestine or Israel was actually a promise to Ishmael, Abraham's son by his Egyptian wife Hagar, and to Ishmael's descendants through Ishmael's 12 sons. Muslims assert that the story was rewritten to make the promise to Isaac, Abraham's son by his wife Sarah. Isaac's first son, Esau, was the progenitor of the Edomites, who returned as enemies of Jacob's descendants later in biblical history.

The origin of the name "Palestine" is also subject to dispute. Israelis and Palestinians have different perspectives on this as well. Israeli prime minister Golda Meir asserted that the name was unknown until the British revived it after the demise of the Ottoman Empire at the end of World War I. The Palestinians and Arab peoples assert that "Palestine" is the ancient name for the region, while both worldwide Jewry and Israel assert that "Israel" is the ancient name.

As early as the fifth century BCE, the Greek historian Herodotus used the Greek-language equivalent of the English "Philistine Syria" to designate the eastern coast of the Mediterranean Sea. This designation was used six centuries later when the Bar Kokhba Revolt so angered Roman emperor Hadrian that he wanted to erase from history the name "Provencia Judaea," the Latin name for the region. Hadrian renamed the area "Provincia Syria Palaestina," the Latin version of the name used by Herodotus. The name was later shortened to "Palaestina," the Latin name from which the English "Palestine" is derived.

The Romans divided the region into three parts in the fourth century and named them First Palestine, Second Palestine, and Third Palestine. This division remained until the Romans lost control of the region to the Persians in 614 CE. Palestine continued as the general name of the region until the end of the crusader kingdom in 1291 and thereafter as a colloquial term for the areas east and west of the Jordan River in the province of Damascus until the demise of the Istanbul-based non-Arab Muslim Ottoman Empire (1517–1917) following World War I.

## BCE History of Palestine

Ancient Canaan was a loose confederation of city-states paying tribute to Egypt's pharaohs until it was conquered by the Hebrews at the end of their 40-year wilderness wandering led by Moses, believed in Jewish tradition to have been during 1240–1200 BCE, although some scholars assert a date as early as 1500–1460 BCE and others as late as 1140–1100 BCE. The Edomites also resided in the area south of the Dead Sea during this time. The lands west of the Jordan River were divided among 11 of the 12 tribes of Israel, and the lands east of the Jordan River were divided among the 2 tribes descended from the 12th tribe of Joseph.

There is general agreement that Saul became the first king of united Israel around 1025 after periods of oppression from neighboring peoples during the time of the Judges that followed Joshua's incomplete conquest. This left pockets of Canaanites throughout the land. David eventually became king after the death of Saul, and David's reign is generally dated by his conquest around 1000 of the Jebusite city of Jerusalem. David's son Solomon (Suleiman) became king during 970–962 and built the First Temple during 960–950 on land chosen by his father.

There was a brief period of unity after Solomon died around 928 BCE, but during 930–920 the United Kingdom (Israel) split into the Northern Kingdom and the Southern Kingdom. The Northern Kingdom, known also as Israel and later as Samaria after its capital, consisted primarily of the ancestral lands of the descendants of the 10 northern tribes. The Southern Kingdom, known also as Judah, had Jerusalem as its capital and was constituted primarily of the ancestral lands of the descendants of the tribes of Judah and Benjamin.

The Northern Kingdom was destroyed in 722 after Assyrian king Sennacherib laid siege to Samaria. Sennacherib resettled the 10 northern tribes into other parts of his empire and forced them to integrate culturally, religiously, and linguistically, thereby reducing the opportunity for the conquered people to organize and support a rebellion. This forced integration, and the ensuing loss of ethnic and religious identity was why these tribes were referred to as "lost." Sennacherib then moved another conquered people into the area vacated by the northern tribes and forced them to integrate into what remained of the culture and religion of the 10 lost tribes. These outsiders became the Samaritans, referred to in the New Testament. One reason they were hated by the Jews of the first century is that these outsiders were not the people of the promise given to Abraham. Although Sennacherib was unsuccessful in his siege of Jerusalem in 701, the Assyrians maintained control of the region until they were conquered by the Babylonians.

A series of three confrontations between Babylonians under Nebuchadnezzar and Judah beginning in 608 and ending with the siege and surrender of Jerusalem in 597 sent three waves of captives to exile in Babylon. Their departure left only a small remnant of the descendants of Abraham, Isaac, and Jacob in the land to which they claimed divine promise. Unlike the Assyrians, however, the Babylonians allowed the exiles from Judah to maintain their ethnicity, language, and religion, although they no longer had the First Temple, Solomon's Temple. As these exiles congregated, they became known as the people from Judah, or Jews. Because they could not sacrifice to make themselves right with their God, they began to codify the law contained in the Torah, the first five books of the Bible, believing that if they could not atone for their sins through sacrifice, they might avoid sin by following the minutiae of the Torah law.

This period was known as the Babylonian Captivity. Many of the inhabitants of Judah fled to or were taken as slaves to Egypt, Syria, Mesopotamia, and Persia. The forced movement of the inhabitants of Judah into Babylon and throughout the Middle East is called the First Dispersion, or Diaspora, of the Jews.

Cyrus the Great became king of Persia in 559 and conquered Babylon in 539, allowing a group of the Jews led by Sheshbazzar and Zerubbabel to return to resettle on their ancestral land and rebuild Jerusalem. Darius I, also known as Darius the Great, became the king of Persia in 521 BCE, and in 520–515 BCE he allowed the construction of the Second Temple in Jerusalem under the prophets Haggai and Zechariah. Nehemiah, a cupbearer to Darius's successor Artaxerxes I (ruled 465–424 BCE), was allowed to go to the region in 446 BCE, 11 years after Ezra returned to restore true temple worship. Nehemiah rebuilt the walls of Jerusalem, and Ezra instituted synagogues similar to those that had developed in Babylonia to study the Torah law during the Babylonian

Captivity. He also publicly reintroduced the Torah to the people in a general assembly. The Samaritans built their temple on Mount Gerizim in 428 BCE and began to worship the God of the region in a manner not in agreement with the Jewish understanding of the Torah law or of God's nature.

The region remained a province of Persia until 333 BCE, when Alexander the Great of Macedonia conquered Persia and brought the region under Greek rule. The control of the region was disputed and alternately ruled by the dynasties of the generals, the Ptolemies in Egypt, and the Seleucids in Syria, who fought for control of Alexander's empire upon his death in 323 BCE. During this period, the Nabataeans and other Arab tribes from the Arabian Peninsula began to encroach into the region and eventually occupied the area between Syria and Arabia bounded on the east by the Euphrates River and on the west by the Jordan River, the Dead Sea, and the Red Sea. The Nabataeans occupied Petra in 312 BCE and made it their capital, although overall control remained with the Greek dynasties.

Seleucid ruler Antiochus IV, known also as Antiochus Epiphanes (ruled 175–163 BCE), attempted to Hellenize the Jews under his governance. When they resisted, he occupied Jerusalem, profaned the Temple with swine's blood in 168 BCE, and in 167 BCE outlawed Jewish religious practices. The Jews, led by a Hasmonean Jewish priest named Mattathias and then by his son Judas Maccabeus, rebelled during 167–160 BCE and in 165 BCE regained the Temple.

The cleansing and rededication of the Temple was remembered annually in the Jewish festival of Hanukkah (Chanukah). The Essenes established their religious community at Qumran (Qumrun, Qumron) around 160 BCE. Even though the environs of Jerusalem and Judaea became semiautonomous following the Maccabean Revolt, the first fully autonomous Jewish state since the Babylonian conquest was not established until the Hasmonean dynasty was founded by Simon Maccabaeus in 142–140 BCE.

The Hasmonean Empire expanded to encompass Transjordan, Samaria, Galilee, and Idumea, reaching its zenith under John Hyrcanus (134–104 BCE). Hyrcanus forced many of the peoples in these incorporated territories to convert to Judaism, a practice that Hasmonean king Alexander Jannaeus (103–76 BCE) continued in his burgeoning rivalry with the Nabataeans, who had previously allied themselves with the Maccabees against the Seleucids.

In 63 BCE Roman consul Pompey the Great invaded Judah, sacked Jerusalem, brought the Hasmoneans under Roman control, and called the area Judaea. In 57–55 BCE the Roman proconsul of Syria, Aulus Gabinius, divided the Hasmonean Kingdom into Galilee, Samaria, and Judaea. The Idumean Herod the Great, appointed the king of the Jews in 74 BCE by the Roman Senate, made Jerusalem his capital in 37 BCE and began restoring the Second Temple in 20 BCE. Herod Antipas, the son of Herod the Great, was made tetrarch (ruler of the quarter) of Galilee and Perea under the rule of the Roman procurators at about the time of the births of Jesus and John the Baptist (6 BC–0). At the same time Herod Archelaus (23 BCE–18 CE), the brother of Herod Antipas, became ethnarch (a leader of an ethnic group within a designated area) of Judaea (4 BCE–6 CE).

**CE History of Palestine**
Jewish antipathy and Zealotian resistance to the Romans swelled after Jerusalem was made part of the Roman province of Judaea in CE 6, when Caesar Augustus removed Herod Archelaus as ethnarch and brought Samaria, Judaea, and Idumea under direct Roman rule as part of the province of Iudaea (Judaea). Augustus made Caesarea on the Mediterranean coast the capital of the province and placed the province under the control of Quirinius, the legate (governor) of Syria. Pontius Pilate served as the governor (procurator) of the province of Judaea (26–36) at the time of the crucifixion of Jesus (30–33).

Roman emperor Claudius first appointed Herod Agrippa I king of the Jews (r. 41–44) and then appointed Herod Agrippa II king of the Jews, the seventh and last Herodian king, giving him control of the Temple in 48. Agrippa I ordered James the Great, leader of the Christians in Jerusalem, killed in 44, but this only served to disperse the Christians and spread their religion.

The Christian leadership endorsed the apostle Paul's evangelism and inclusion of gentiles in the religion at the Council of Jerusalem around 50. In 59–60 Paul was brought before Herod Agrippa II, who then sent him on to Rome when Paul exercised his right as a Roman citizen to have his case heard before Caesar. Both Peter and Paul died around 64–69 during Nero's persecution of the Christians.

Herod Agrippa II fled Jerusalem to Galilee and the safety of the Romans when the First Jewish Revolt (66–73), also known as the Great Revolt and the First Jewish-Roman War, began. The Romans under Vespasian destroyed Jerusalem and the Second Temple in 70 after a 134-day siege. This destruction of the Second Temple during the reign of Emperor Titus marked the end of a Jewish state and the beginning of the Second Diaspora of the Jews.

It was during the Great Revolt that a small band of Zealots (meaning "the zealous ones") under the command of

The ruins of a Roman aqueduct leading to Caesarea in northern Israel. (iStockphoto.com)

Eleazar ben Ya'ir fled to the Masada fortress built by Herod the Great on a rock mesa overlooking the Dead Sea in the eastern Judaean Desert near Ein Gedi. As the Romans prepared to surmount the redoubt after a lengthy siege, Eleazar exhorted the Zealot defenders and their families to a final act of defiance. The defenders and their families burned their personal belongings and selected by lot 10 defenders to kill the general population. These 10 then killed each other in turn, leaving only the final defender to commit suicide.

The Nabataean Empire was incorporated into the Roman Empire in 102. There were then two Jewish revolts against the Romans: the Second Jewish-Roman War, also known as the Kitos War (115–117), and the Third Jewish-Roman War (132–135), also known as the Bar Kokhba Revolt and the Third Jewish Revolt. Jericho and Bethlehem were destroyed in the Bar Kokhba Revolt. Roman emperor Hadrian retaliated by barring the Jews from Jerusalem, razing the city, building a pagan city named Aelia Capitolina over the ruins, and changing the name of the region to Palaestina from which the contemporary name "Palestine" is derived. Many Jews were killed or sold into slavery. Although many of the Jews who survived fled the region in the Third Diaspora of the Jews, a remnant remained.

Byzantine emperor Constantine, after adopting Christianity in 312, sought to rebuild Jerusalem after it came under Byzantine rule in 324. Although Constantine removed some of the restrictions that had been placed on the Jews following the Bar Kokhba Revolt and even permitted them to mourn annually the destruction of the city and the Temple, he continued to bar Jews from residing in the city. In 326 Constantine's mother Helena, a Christian, made a pilgrimage to the region and initiated construction of the Church of the Holy Sepulchre in Jerusalem and the Church of the Nativity in Bethlehem. In 362 Byzantine emperor Flavius Claudius Iulianus (361–363), also known as Julian the Apostate, allowed Jews to resettle in Jerusalem.

Jerusalem fell to the Persians in 614 but was retaken by the Byzantines in 629, only to be lost again in 638 to the Arab Muslim caliph Omar Ben Hatav, also known as Omar ibn al-Khattaab. The Arab Muslims adopted the Greco-Roman name "Palastina," pronouncing it as "Falastin." Control of Palestine (661–750) passed to the Damascus-based Umayyad caliphate—an Islamic government that governed and applied sharia (Islamic law) to all Muslims—under the leadership of Caliph Abdal-Malik (685–705).

Abdal-Malik, also known as Abdul Malik ibn Marwan, built the Dome of the Rock (Mosque of Omar) in 690. The Dome of the Rock is the oldest holy building in Islam and surrounds the large rock from which Islamic tradition believes Prophet Muhammad ascended (621) on his horse Al-Buraq to Heaven at the end of his Night Journey. This rock is also considered to be the place that Abraham was to sacrifice his son. Jews and Christians assert that the potential sacrifice was Isaac, and Muslims assert that it was Ishmael. The Dome of the Rock was erected near what the Jews believe was the site of the Temple of Solomon and the Second Temple. The only remaining physical remnant, the Western Wall (Wailing Wall), was a retaining wall built at the base of the Temple Mount during Herod the Great's reconstruction of the Second Temple about 19 BCE. Muslims today generally dispute any connection between the Western Wall and any previous Jewish religious site.

Abdal-Malik also planned the building on the same site of the al-Aqsa Mosque, which was completed in 710 CE by his son al-Walid (705–715). The al-Aqsa Mosque complex became a center of Islamic learning and worship when law schools were established there.

Palestine came under control of the Baghdad-based Abbasid caliphate in 750 and remained under its administration until the North African (Egyptian) Fatimid dynasty and caliphate took Palestine by force in the ninth century. The Fatimid caliph al-Hakim (996–1021) persecuted the Christians and Jews residing in Palestine and commanded the destruction of many of the region's churches and synagogues. The Turkic Muslim Seljuks took control of Jerusalem and a portion of Palestine in 1071, bringing the administration of these areas again under the Abbasid caliphate.

European crusaders invaded the region in 1099 seeking to regain the Holy Land for Christendom. The crusaders captured Jaffa and Jerusalem and began referring to the region as Palestine. The crusader Latin Kingdom of Jerusalem, ruled by Godfrey of Bouillon, was responsible for the deaths of so many Jews and Muslims that a papal bull was issued in 1119 directing that the Jews no longer be killed. The papal bull reiterated St. Augustine's 427 entreaty that the Jews should be made to wander Earth as evidence that they rejected Jesus, the true God. Crusader control of Palestine ended in 1187 when the (half-Kurdish) Muslim Saladin (Salah al-Din al-Ayyubi) defeated a large crusader force at the Battle of Hattin, captured Jerusalem, and made Palestine part of the Province of Syria. English king Richard I the Lionheart tried to recapture Palestine and Jerusalem in 1192 during the Third Crusade but was unsuccessful.

Three hundred French and English rabbis were allowed to settle in Jerusalem in 1212, but Jerusalem was despoiled by the Tartars in 1244 and then by the Mongols in 1259–1260. The Mamluks, dynasties of professional soldier-slaves and then rulers of Egypt, ousted the Mongols from Palestine in 1260 and administered the region from Cairo. The Mamluks eradicated the last crusader states in Palestine, Acre (Akka) and Qaysariyya, in 1291. Although Jews from Spain and other parts of the Mediterranean began to resettle in Palestine during the 1300s, the poor administration of the Mamluks and Palestine's 1351 Black Death epidemic contributed to a decrease in the population of Palestine to just over 200,000 people by 1500.

The Ottoman Turkish Muslims began just over 400 years of rule over Palestine when Sultan Selim I (1457–1520), ruler of the Ottoman Empire during 1512–1520, defeated the Mamluks in Syria in 1516, captured Jerusalem, and seized Gaza. Mamluk Egypt was incorporated into the Ottoman Empire in 1517. Suleiman I (1494–1566), known also as Suleiman the Magnificent and Suleiman the Lawgiver, reconstructed Jerusalem during 1535–1538, and in 1541 he sealed the Golden Gate through which Jewish tradition holds that the Messiah would enter the city. The importance of Palestine as an overland trade crossroads diminished as sea routes were discovered to the east. There is little change to the area, and there were no conflicts during the 18th century and the first quarter of the 19th century. In 1705 the Ottomans restricted Jewish immigration after Judah the Pious and 1,000 followers took up residence in Jerusalem. In 1831 a new personal tax on Muslim subjects caused a revolt in Damascus and the murder of the Ottoman governor and other officials.

In 1831 Muhammad Ali Pasha, the khedive (viceroy) of Egypt from 1805 to 1849, ostensibly an administrator for Ottoman sultan Mahmud II (ruled 1808–1839), conquered and occupied Syria under troops led by his son Ibrahim. Muhammad Ali had previously demanded that the sultan place Syria under his governorship in exchange for his military assistance in quelling a Greek revolt against the empire. The Egyptian administration raised taxes, and increased the size of the bureaucracy and the army, and encouraged cash crops. In 1839 Mahmud II lost his army and his naval fleet in an attempt to regain Syria. A coalition of European nations together with a popular uprising finally drove out Muhammad Ali's government in 1840. Palestine, like other parts of the Ottoman Empire with the exception of Egypt under

Muhammad Ali, suffered from lowered export tariffs, meaning that early industrial development, mainly textiles, could not compete with imports.

Meanwhile, oppression and persecution of the Jews in Eastern Europe in the latter part of the 19th century gave impetus to the Zionist emigration for Palestine and led to the establishment of Petach Tikva, the first agricultural community (i.e., Zionist settlement) in Palestine a year after the first Ottoman parliament (1876–1877). Jews accounted for 24,000 of the 400,000 residents of Palestine in 1880, but that number more than doubled after the initial wave of immigration (the First Aliya) of East European Zionists. These immigrants settled on small farms throughout Palestine and at first employed Arab labor. By 1895 Jews accounted for 47,000 of the 500,000 residents of Palestine and owned 0.5 percent of the land. The Jewish Colonization Association began aiding Zionist settlements in Palestine in 1896.

In 1897 Austrian Jewish journalist Theodor Herzl convened the First Zionist Congress in Basel, Switzerland, in response to increasing European anti-Semitism following the Dreyfus Affair in France in 1894 and his call for a Jewish state in his influential short book *Der Judenstaat* (The Jewish State), published in 1896. The First Zionist Congress created the World Zionist Organization (WZO), elected Herzl as the first WZO president, authorized the WZO to establish branches in all countries with consequential Jewish populations, and determined Zionism's goal to be the creation of a legal (guaranteed) Jewish homeland in Palestine (Israel). The WZO was formed to unite the Jewish people politically so that Judaism acting as one organic whole might exert more power in addressing the plight of world Jewry and in creating a homeland in Israel (Palestine) for Jews.

At the First Zionist Congress, the political Zionism of the Jews of Western Europe merged with the settlement activities in Turkish Palestine, promoted and successfully engaged in by the East European Hovevei Tsion. The WZO created companies and institutions designed to accomplish its policies, the most prominent among many being the Jewish Colonial Trust, established in 1899; the Jewish National Fund (Keren Keyemeth), established in 1901; the Anglo-Palestine Bank, the Jewish Colonial Trust's subsidiary, established in 1902; and Keren Hayesod, established in 1920. The Jewish National Fund was created to acquire land in Palestine. Keren Hayesod funded Zionist and Yishuv (Jewish communities in Palestine) activities and created companies such as the Palestine Electric Company, the Palestine Potash Company, and the Anglo-Palestine Bank.

The WZO's actions promoted and facilitated the Second Aliya (1904–1914), which brought primarily secular Jews (including socialists) into Palestine and raised the Jewish population to 6 percent of the Palestinian total. The many farms and factories bought or built by the Baron Edmond de Rothschild Foundation were insufficient to employ this number of people, so many participants in the Second Aliya eventually left Palestine.

Fearing that the publication in 1904 of Najib Azury's *The Awakening of the Arab Nation in Turkish Asia,* which publicly warned the Arabs of the Zionist plan for Palestine, would hamper its plans, the 1904 Fourth Zionist Congress determined that there was a need for an alternative Jewish national homeland in Argentina. However, the 1906 Fifth Zionist Congress reaffirmed Palestine as the future Jewish national homeland. The Arabic-language newspaper *Al-Karmil* was founded in 1908 in Haifa with the express purpose of opposing Zionist colonization, but this did not prevent the 1909 establishment of the first Zionist kibbutz (collective) farm. By 1910, Arabic-language newspapers in Beirut and Damascus sounded the alarm over Zionist land acquisitions and the growing Jewish population, and in 1911 the Arab newspaper *Filastin* began calling Arabs living in Palestine "Palestinians." One of the earliest books in Arabic, Najib Nassar's *Zionism: Its History, Objectives and Importance,* was also published in 1911. The Jews accounted for 85,000 (12 percent) of the 700,000 total population of Palestine by 1913, the same year that the First Arab Nationalist Congress met in Paris.

During World War I the British government, eager to secure the support of both Arabs and Jews, made promises to the Arabs and the Zionists that Britain never kept in whole for either side. Britain promised independence for Arab lands under Ottoman rule while at the same time courting world Jewry. By 1915 the Anglo-Jewish politician and diplomat Herbert Samuel (1870–1963), eventually to be the first high commissioner of the British Mandate for Palestine in 1920, secretly proposed that Britain annex Palestine and populate it with 3 million to 4 million European Jews. The Arabs, on the other hand, were opposed to plans that would divest them of their land and property. Many understood the 1916 talks and correspondence between Hussein ibn Ali, sharif of Mecca and later king of the Hejaz, and Sir Henry McMahon, British high commissioner in Egypt, as ensuring their rights in Palestine as part of a postwar Arab nation.

On May 16, 1916, the British and French secretly concluded the Sykes-Picot Agreement that specified their respective interests in the Arab provinces of the Ottoman

Empire, dividing them into postwar areas directly or indirectly administered by the French and British. Later in 1916, uninformed of British participation in the Sykes-Picot Agreement and acting on his correspondence with McMahon, Sharif Hussein declared independence from the Ottoman Empire and began an Arab revolt against its control.

The British government issued the Balfour Declaration on November 2, 1917, expressing official British support for a Jewish homeland in Palestine. In December 1917, Ottoman forces in Jerusalem surrendered to British lieutenant general Sir Edmund Allenby. Allenby's allied forces then occupied all of Palestine by September 1918. World War I and the Ottoman Empire's rule of Palestine ended in October 1918, paving the way for a British mandate over the area that would endure until 1948.

RICHARD M. EDWARDS

**See also**

Abbasid Caliphate; Al-Aqsa Mosque Massacre; Alexander III the Great; Allenby, Sir Edmund Henry Hynman; Antiochus IV Epiphanes; Artaxerxes I; Balfour Declaration; Bar Kochba Revolt; Caesar, Gaius Julius; Constantine I; Cyrus II the Great; Darius I; Diaspora; Fatimid Dynasty; Hussein ibn Ali ibn Mohammed; Jerusalem, Crusader Siege of; Jerusalem, Roman Siege of; Jewish-Roman War, First; Mamluk Sultanate; Masada; McMahon-Hussein Correspondence; Muhammad, Prophet of Islam; Nebuchadnezzar II; Ottoman Empire; Palestine, British Mandate for; Richard I, King; Seleucid Empire; Selim I, Sultan; Sennacherib; Sykes-Picot Agreement; Umayyad Caliphate; Vespasian, Emperor; Zionism

**References**

Ahlstrom, Gosta W. *The History of Ancient Palestine.* Minneapolis: Augsburg, 1993.

Avi-Yonah, Michael. *The Jews of Palestine: A Political History of Palestine from the Bar Kokhba War to the Arab Conquest.* New York: Schocken, 1984.

Biale, David. *Cultures of the Jews: A New History.* New York: Schocken, 2002.

Bright, John. *A History of Israel.* 4th ed. Louisville, KY: Westminster John Knox, 2000.

Coogan, Michael D. *The Oxford History of the Biblical World.* New York: Oxford University Press, 2001.

Dimont, Max. *Jews, God and History.* New York: Simon and Schuster, 1962.

Farsoum, Samih K., and Naseer H. Aruri. *Palestine and the Palestinians: A Social and Political History.* 2nd ed. Jackson, TN: Westview, 2006.

Pappe, Ilan. *A History of Modern Palestine: One Land, Two Peoples.* Cambridge: Cambridge University Press, 2003.

Parkes, James. *A History of Palestine from 135 AD to Modern Times.* Elibron Classics Replica Edition. Brighton, MA: Adamant Media Corporation, 2005.

Provan, Iain W., et al. *A Biblical History of Israel.* Louisville, KY: Westminster John Knox, 2003.

Russell, Michael. *Palestine or the Holy Land from the Earliest Period to the Present Time.* Kila, MT: Kessinger, 2004.

Thompson, Thomas L. *Early History of the Israelite People: From the Written & Archaeological Sources.* Leiden: Brill Academic, 2000.

## Palestine and Syria Campaign, World War I (1915–1918)

British World War I land campaign aimed at liberating Jerusalem and forcing the Ottoman Empire to surrender. In January 1915 the British War Cabinet discussed a plan for a Palestine campaign. This envisioned an attack on Syria combined with an advance north from Basra to Baghdad. The plan was shelved, however, in favor of a landing on the Gallipoli Peninsula (the Gallipoli Campaign of April 25, 1915–January 9, 1916).

In February 1915 Ottoman forces, urged on by their German ally, mounted an effort to seize the Suez Canal. The British Egyptian Expeditionary Force (EEF) and Royal Navy ships easily defeated this effort by Djemal Pasha's Second Army. In July 1916 they also turned back another Ottoman effort against the canal, led by German lieutenant colonel Friedrich Kress von Kressenstein. Stymied by the immense manpower demands of the Western Front, troops in the EEF mostly remained on the defensive until 1917. During 1916 the EEF, led by Lieutenant General Archibald Murray, began construction of a road, a railroad, and a water line across Sinai. These would be crucial in any British campaign in Palestine and Syria.

New British prime minister David Lloyd George was appalled by the great wastage of manpower on the Western Front and sought military victories they could achieve at far less human cost in the Middle East. He urged Murray to take Gaza and then move up the coast to Jerusalem.

The British Palestine offensive began in December 1916 with the capture of El Arish, 25 miles south of the Palestinian border. However, southern Palestine between Gaza and Beersheba was heavily fortified. The Ottoman troops in Palerstine were led by German general der infanterie Erich von Falkenhayn.

With offensive preparations complete, Murray attacked Gaza on March 26, 1917. Lieutenant General Sir Charles Dobell led a cavalry attack from the east in combination with an infantry attack from the south. Just as the battle turned to British advantage, Dobell, who was hampered by poor communications, ordered his troops to withdraw. This failure produced more than 3,000 British casualties. A second attempt to take Gaza, beginning on April 17, also failed, this time with more than 5,000 casualties. Murray was then replaced by Lieutenant General Sir Edmund Allenby, a cavalryman and veteran of fighting in South Africa and on the Western Front.

Allenby arrived in Egypt at the end of June 1917. After taking stock of the situation, he requested reinforcements and supplies to extend the railroad and water lines. He then reorganized his forces into three corps: the XX Corps under Lieutenant General Philip Chetwode, the XXI Corps under Lieutenant General Edward S. Bulfin, and the Desert Mounted Corps under Lieutenant General Henry Chauvel. Allenby also moved his headquarters from Cairo to the front. Lloyd George saw to it that Allenby's requests were met, and Allenby received two infantry divisions from Europe and one infantry division from Salonika, in addition to artillery and Royal Flying Corps support.

Allenby decided to strike at Beersheba but with a deception to convince the Ottomans that he was massing troops to attack at Gaza. For the attack, he would have four infantry divisions and three cavalry divisions (80,000 men and 218 guns, supported by 5 tanks). The Ottomans defended the 30-mile line between Gaza and Beersheba with five infantry divisions and one cavalry division (35,000 men and 200 guns).

Allenby prepared meticulously for the attack. He ordered the construction of new roads, commissioned updated maps, and studied campaigns in the area, including both the Christian crusades and Napoleon Bonaparte's invasion. He also organized 30,000 camels to supply water. Colonel Richard Meinertzhagen, Allenby's chief of intelligence, played an important role. Meinertzhagen established a wireless receiving station and used it to intercept Ottoman radio transmissions. He also brought about the death of one of the principal Arab spies by sending him a letter thanking him for service to the British with payment for said services. He then arranged for the letter to be intercepted by the Ottomans, and the spy was executed.

Meinertzhagen also arranged a deception, making it widely known that Allenby would be in Cairo during October 29–November 4. Finally, he devised a plan whereby a staff officer would arrange to be pursued by Ottoman forces and drop a haversack filled with papers that described an impending attack on Gaza rather than at Beersheba. The first two attempts at the latter failed, until Meinertzhagen took on the task himself and succeeded.

On October 31, 1917, the offensive opened with a massive artillery attack against the Ottoman positions at Gaza, which was well fortified by barbed wire and a formidable trench system. But the artillery attack was a feint. A full-scale attack was then launched against Beersheba. The Desert Mounted Corps (4th Brigade Australian Light Horse) executed a dangerous long ride across the Judaean Desert, then charged the Ottoman left flank and seized control of the water wells before they could be destroyed.

Following the capture of Beersheba, Allenby turned his attention to Gaza, which he secured in four days. The XX Corps (10th, 60th and 74th Divisions) steadily pushed back the Ottomans. Allenby sent the XXI Corps up the coast into Palestine, and the Ottomans retreated to the Judaean Hills 20 miles south of Jerusalem.

Allenby did not want to allow Ottoman forces time to establish a defensive line south of Jerusalem and so refused to permit a halt to let his men and their animals rest. Although his supply and communication lines were stretched, Allenby pushed his forces toward Jerusalem. On November 16, 1917, his forces took Jaffa on the coast.

Allenby sought to minimize fighting within the holy city of Jerusalem and devised a plan of encirclement. The British brought 18,000 infantry, 8,000 cavalry, and 172 guns to this battle; the Ottomans had 15,000 infantry, 800 cavalry, and 120 guns. Following fierce fighting on the city's outskirts, on December 8 the XXI Corps, supported by artillery fire, broke through from the west. Ottoman forces then evacuated Jerusalem, which surrendered on December 9, 1917, ending 401 years of Ottoman control. In anticipation of an advance across the Jordan River, Allenby set a defensive line from the Mediterranean shore east to the Jordan River Valley, approximately 10 miles north of Jerusalem.

Allenby wanted to push northward quickly to Damascus, but with the start of the Ludendorff Offensives (March 21–July 18, 1918) on the Western Front, the British government recalled two of his divisions to meet critical manpower needs in France. Allenby received reinforcements from Mesopotamia, but these required reorganization and training. He was able to take advantage of internal Arab unrest within the Ottoman Empire. Control by the Ottomans had been weakened by the Arab Revolt led by Hussein (Husayn) ibn Ali, beginning in June 1916. As grand sharif of Mecca, Hussein's family controlled the Hejaz, which contained the holy cities of Mecca and Medina. Hussein's third son, Prince Faisal, became an important Arab military leader and, along with British captain (later major) Thomas E. Lawrence, scored important victories against Ottoman forces in 1916 and 1917, including the seizures of Aqaba and Wejh. Allenby integrated Faisal's actions into his own plans and sent the Arabs additional supplies to support Faisal's Arab Army of the North in its raids on Ottoman outposts and railroad lines.

On the other side of the battle lines, dramatic changes in personnel occurred. General der Kavallerie Otto Liman von Sanders replaced Falkenhayn in March 1918; Liman replaced almost all the German staff officers with Ottomans. Within the Ottoman Empire, the death of Sultan Mehmed V brought his brother, Mehmed VI, to the throne. Mehmed VI appointed General Mustafa Kemal as commander of the Seventh Army in Syria.

By the summer of 1918 three Ottoman armies were positioned across the Jaffa-Jerusalem line. The Seventh and Eighth Armies were between the coast and the Jordan River; the Third Army lay east of the river. The Ottomans, however, had been fighting for six months without relief and lacked reserves. Ottoman forces consisted of 26,000 infantry, 3,000 cavalry, and 370 guns. An additional 6,000 troops guarded the Hejaz railroad to the east. Allenby enjoyed a two-to-one advantage in manpower as well as a tremendous edge in cavalry and airpower. The British had 57,000 infantry, 12,000 cavalry, and 540 guns.

Allenby's goal was to capture Damascus, but he first needed to gain control over the Jordan Plain. After two failed attempts to take Amman, Allenby regrouped and devised a plan to advance northward by which he would outflank Ottoman forces to the east while depending on the Arab forces to cut the railroad line between Déraa (50 miles south of Damascus) and Haifa.

Early on the morning of September 19, 1918, in the Battle of Megiddo, Allenby's forces struck the Ottoman right flank. A simultaneous Royal Air Force bombing raid on Nazareth destroyed the Ottoman communications center there, hampering Ottoman troop redeployment. In a few hours the Ottoman defensive line had been pierced, and soon the 9,000-man British 4th Cavalry Division had advanced 10 miles north and then 30 miles east to Jenin and Megiddo. By nightfall the British had taken 2,500 prisoners and almost captured General Liman von Sanders. Déraa fell on September 27.

To the north and east the offensive continued. On September 23 the 23rd Cavalry Regiment captured Haifa, Acre, and Es Salt. On September 25 it took Amman, giving the British control over the Hejaz railroad. On September 30, British troops entered Damascus with little opposition. On October 2 the city formally surrendered, and 75,000 Ottomans became prisoners of war. British forces sustained only 5,600 casualties in the capture of Damascus. In the entire campaign, Allenby's forces suffered some 50,000 casualties, the majority of them from disease. The other wing of the British forces took Beirut on October 8.

In the meantime Kemal, whose Seventh Army remained intact, was ordered to retreat toward Damascus. When he arrived there in late September, the city was in disarray. Kemal was ordered to hand over his troops to commander of the Fourth Army General Djemal Pasha and proceed to Rayak to gather scattered units. Upon arrival at Rayak, Kemal realized that there were insufficient troops to halt the British offensive. He then took matters into his own hands and ordered all his troops to reassemble at Aleppo, 200 miles north of Damascus in the extreme northwest corner of Syria. When the British called on Kemal to surrender and then attacked on October 25, he withdrew to the northwest outskirts of the city in defense of the southern border of the Ottoman Empire rather than Aleppo.

Kemal's forces attacked repeatedly, forcing the British, outnumbered six to one, to call for reinforcements from Damascus. Reinforced, the British took Aleppo on October 26. The Ottoman Empire surrendered on October 30, and Liman von Sanders officially handed over his command to Mustafa Kemal.

Laura J. Hilton

**See also**

Allenby, Sir Edmund Henry Hynman; Arab Revolt of World War I; Ataturk, Mustafa Kemal; Beersheba, Battle of; Damascus, Allied Capture of; Djemal Pasha, Ahmed; Faisal I, King of Iraq; Gallipoli Campaign; Gaza, First Battle of; Gaza, Second Battle of; Gaza, Third Battle of; Hussein ibn Ali ibn Mohammed; Jerusalem, Capture of; Kress von Kressenstein, Friedrich Sigismund Georg; Lawrence, Thomas Edward; Liman von Sanders, Otto; Megiddo, Battle of; Mesopotamian Theater, World War I; Murray, Sir Archibald James; Suez Canal

**References**

Bruce, Anthony P. C. *The Last Crusade: The Palestine Campaign in the First World War.* London: Murray, 2002.

Bullock, David L. *Allenby's War: The Palestinian-Arabian Campaigns, 1916–1918.* London: Blandford, 1988.

Butler, Daniel Allen. *Shadow of the Sultan's Realm: The Destruction of the Ottoman Empire and the Creation of the Modern Middle East.* Dulles, VA: Potomac Books, 2011.

Erickson, Edward J. *Ordered to Die: A History of the Ottoman Army in the First World War.* Westport, CT: Greenwood, 2000.

Falls, Cyril. *Armageddon, 1918: The Final Palestinian Campaign of World War I.* Philadelphia: University of Pennsylvania Press, 2003.

Gardner, Brian. *Allenby of Arabia: Lawrence's General.* New York: Coward-McCann, 1966.

Hankey, Lord Maurice P. A. *The Supreme Command, 1914–1918.* 2 vols. London: Allen and Unwin, 1961.

Kinross, Lord. *Atatürk: Biography of Mustapha Kemal, Father of Modern Turkey.* New York: William Morrow, 1965.

MacMunn, George, and Cyril Falls. *Official History of the Great War: Military Operations, Egypt and Palestine, from the Outbreak of the War with Germany to June 1917.* London: HMSO, 1928.

Mortlock, Michael J. *The Egyptian Expeditionary Force in World War I: A History of the British-Led Campaigns in Egypt, Palestine, and Syria.* Jefferson, NC: McFarland, 2011.

Preston, R. M. P. *The Desert Mounted Corps.* Boston: Houghton Mifflin, 1922.

Woodward, David R. *Hell in the Holy Land: World War I in the Middle East.* Lexington: University Press of Kentucky, 2006.

## Palestine Liberation Army

Military organization established by the first Palestinian National Congress in 1964. Proposed by Ahmad Shukeiri, the first chairman of the Palestine Liberation Organization (PLO), the Palestine Liberation Army (PLA) was created to serve as the conventional military arm of the PLO. The PLO was originally a forum for traditional, influential Palestinian notables. Its leadership did not consider guerrilla or commando activities at that time. Instead, PLO leaders established the PLA as a force of three brigades, totaling some 20,000–30,000 men, that would be hosted and trained in Egypt, Iraq, and Syria and would fight alongside these Arab armies under their command.

Although nominally under PLO direction, in practice the PLA has always been firmly under the control of its host nations, and PLA units have been incorporated into their military establishments. Thus, the Ayn Jalut Brigade in Gaza came under Egyptian Army control, the Hittin Brigade came under Syrian control, and the Qadisiyya Brigade came under Iraqi control. In Jordan where much larger numbers of Palestinians resided, Shukeiri had to promise King Hussein that Palestinians would not arm or organize Palestinians. Later, however, the Yarmuk Brigade formed with defectors from the Jordanian Army. The presence of Palestinian troops has proved to be a convenient circumstance on a number of occasions particularly for Syria, which utilized PLA troops during its armed actions in Jordan and Lebanon.

The 1967 Six-Day War made it impossible for the Egyptian government to oppose commando activities. Hence, Egyptian president Gamal Abdel Nasser met with Fatah leaders and arranged to help arm and train them. Shukeiri was ousted as PLO leader and replaced first by Yahya Hammuda in 1967 and then by Yasser Arafat in 1969. This period saw a displacement of the PLO leaders who had emphasized politics and diplomacy for those who wanted more independent Palestinian military activities. Arafat, who had opposed the creation of the PLA out of concern that it would be dominated by its host nations, argued that the PLA hurt the recruitment of Palestinian fighters. This lack of unity demonstrated the inherent weakness of the PLO, which had never maintained even rudimentary control over its military wing. In 1970 Arafat was named head of the PLA at the Seventh Palestinian National Council, but the commander of the PLA, Uthman Haddad, refused to recognize Arafat's supremacy and remained in power. In a face-saving gesture, Haddad was renamed the PLA's chief of staff, and in this position he continued his policy of maintaining PLA autonomy from Arafat's control. Haddad maintained close ties with the Syrian Army and effectively continued the policy of subordinating the PLA to the Syrians.

In 1970 both Syria and Jordan deployed PLA troops to Jordan during the events of Black September. More than 5,000 PLA troops remained in Jordanian territory until the threat of foreign intervention compelled their withdrawal. Syria also used PLA units in Lebanon. However, some of these refused to fight other Palestinians. The Yarmuk and Hittin Brigades comprised a major part of the Syrian assault on Lebanese sovereignty. In 1976 Egypt deployed the PLA's Ayn Jalut Brigade to fight alongside Fatah forces resisting the Syrian advance, with the result that PLA units were ordered to fight one another. The PLA presence in Lebanon was virtually destroyed in 1982 when Israel invaded the southern portion of the country. However, the PLA quickly recruited new members from Palestinian refugee populations in Syria, Egypt, Iraq, and Jordan. By the mid-1980s, the PLA had grown to a peak strength of approximately 14,000 permanent forces divided into eight brigades.

After the signing of the Declaration of Principles and the Cairo Agreement on May 4, 1994, some of the PLA was redeployed into the autonomous area to serve as the police force of the Palestinian Authority (PA).

The Syrian brigade, in principle autonomous as it is staffed entirely by drafted Palestinian refugees, is in fact completely controlled by Syria. In 1970 Syria sent hastily repainted Syrian Army tanks under PLA command into Jordan to aid the PLO fighters engaging the Jordanian Army during so-called Black September. They were soon beating a hastily withdrawal, however, an embarrassment that proved to be a major factor in the Syrian coup d'état by Hafez al-Assad. Syria again made use of the PLA as a proxy force during the Lebanese Civil War (1975–1990). The Syrian PLA was largely destroyed as a fighting force during the 1982 Lebanon-Israeli War. Those who remained left Lebanon with the PLO when it departed Beirut for Tunis under the cease-fire agreement. Units of the Egyptian PLA were also deployed in Lebanon in 1976. After the 1993 Oslo Accords, portions of the Egyptian and Jordanian PLA brigades became the core of the Palestinian Authority's National Guard.

The Syrian PLA remains in operation. Composed entirely of Palestinians and said to number some 4,500 soldiers, it is nonetheless completely controlled by the Syrian Army and has sustained casualties in the Syrian Civil War (2011–present). The PLA has been fighting alongside Syria's progovernment forces.

Paul J. Springer, Spencer C. Tucker, and Sherifa Zuhur

**See also**
Arafat, Yasser; Assad, Hafez al-; Black September; Fatah, al-; Lebanon Civil War; Lebanon-Israeli War; Oslo Accords; Palestine Liberation Organization; Palestinian National Authority; Syrian Civil War

**References**
Amos, John W., II. *Arab-Israeli Military/Political Relations: Arab Perceptions and the Politics of Escalation.* New York: Pergamon, 1979.
Brand, Laurie. *Palestinians in the Arab World: Institution Building and the Search for State.* New York: Columbia University Press, 1988.
Khouri, Fred J. *The Arab-Israeli Dilemma.* 3rd ed. Syracuse, NY: Syracuse University Press, 1985.
Norton, Augustus Richard, and Martin H. Greenberg, eds. *The International Relations of the Palestine Liberation Organization.* Carbondale: Southern Illinois University Press, 1989.

## Palestine Liberation Front

Militant Palestinian group that was characterized by the United States and some European nations as a terrorist organization. The Palestine Liberation Front (PLF) was founded in 1959 by Ahmed Jibril with Syrian backing. In 1967 it merged with two other organizations, the Heroes of the Return and the Youth of the Revenge Group, to form the Popular Front for the Liberation of Palestine (PFLP), led by George Habash. In 1968, however, Jibril split off part of the membership to form the Popular Front for the Liberation of Palestine–General Command (PFLP-GC) that supported Syria in doing battle with the Palestine Liberation Organization (PLO) in 1976 during the Lebanese Civil War.

The PFLP-GC action led to the reestablishment of the PLF in April 1977 under Abu Abbas (Muhammad Zaidan) and Talat Yaqub. PLF leaders were angry that the PFLP-GC did not oppose Syrian support for the Phalangists against the PLO in Lebanon. Some fighting occurred thereafter between the PLF and the PFLP-GC, including the bombing of the PLF headquarters in August 1977 in which some 200 people died.

In 1983 following the Israeli invasion of Lebanon, the PLF split into three factions. The two principal groups were a pro-Syrian faction led by Yaqub and a larger pro-Iraq group led by Abbas. Both kept the same name and claimed to represent the original organization. Yaqub died in November 1988, and only then did his group rejoin that led by Abbas.

Reportedly receiving some Libyan funding, the PLF believed strongly in armed struggle against Israel in the form of terrorist attacks, most of them mounted along Israel's northern border from Lebanon. The most notorious of its terrorist actions was the hijacking of the Italian cruise ship *Achille Lauro* on October 7, 1985. It also mounted an unsuccessful attack on Nizamim Beach near Tel Aviv on May 30, 1990. The attack was to kill both Israelis and tourists in the hopes of torpedoing any move toward peace talks between the PLO and Israel. Abbas came under heavy criticism from within the PLO leadership for this and was forced to resign from the PLO Executive Committee. Following the 1993 Oslo Accords, the PLF accepted the PLO policy of halting terrorist activity against Israel. The PLF campaigned in the 2006 Palestinian elections under the name of Martyr Abu Abbas but failed to win any seats.

Spencer C. Tucker

**See also**
Abbas, Abu; Lebanon Civil War; Lebanon-Israeli War; Syria

**References**
Alexander, Yonah. *Palestinian Secular Terrorism.* Ardsley, NY: Transnational Publishers, 2003.
Bohn, Michael K. *The Achille Lauro Hijacking: Lessons in the Politics and Prejudice of Terrorism.* Dulles, VA: Potomac Books, 2004.
Cassese, Antonio. *Terrorism, Politics and Law: The Achille Lauro Affair.* Princeton, NJ: Princeton University Press, 1989.
Nassar, Jamal R. *The Palestine Liberation Organization: From Armed Struggle to the Declaration of Independence.* New York: Praeger, 1991.

## Palestine Liberation Organization

A political and military organization founded in 1964 and dedicated to protecting the human and legal rights of Palestinians and creating an independent state for Palestinian Arabs in Palestine. Since the 1960s, the Munazzamat al-Tahrir Filastiniyyah (Palestine Liberation Organization,

PLO) has functioned as the official mouthpiece for the Palestinian people. There are numerous factions and organizations that loosely fall under the PLO's umbrella. In addition to Fatah, which is the largest of these groups, the PLO has also encompassed the Popular Front for the Liberation of Palestine (PFLP), the Democratic Front for the Liberation of Palestine (DFLP), the Palestinian People's Party, the Palestine Liberation Front (PLF), the Arab Liberation Front, al-Saiqa (Syrian Baathists), the Palestine Democratic Union, the Palestinian Popular Front Struggle, and the Palestinian Arab Front. Two groups no longer associated with the PLO include the Popular Front for the Liberation of Palestine-General Command (PFLP-GC) and the Fatah Uprising.

The PLO is composed of centrist-nationalist groups (such as Fatah), rightist groups, leftist groups (including communists), militant groups, and nonmilitant groups. It has purposely eschewed embracing any one political philosophy so as to be as inclusive as possible in its membership. The PLO has been enormously successful in attracting funding over the years. Indeed, a 1993 survey estimated the PLO's total assets at between $8 billion and $10 billion and its average yearly income at $1.5 billion to $2 billion.

The PLO was founded in 1964 by the Arab League and Egypt. Its first president was Ahmad Shukeiri. The stated purpose of the PLO was the liberation of Palestine, condemnation of Zionist imperialism, and the dissolution of Israel through the use of armed force. Throughout its existence, the PLO has often used violence to express its viewpoints and gain international attention. This has earned it the reputation of being a terrorist organization, although Palestinians and many international observers dispute that characterization. In 1988, PLO chairman Yasser Arafat—who led the organization from 1969 to 2004—renounced violence as a means to achieve Palestinian goals, but a number of PLO groups did not follow this decree and have continued to mount terrorist attacks in Israel and elsewhere.

Although the PLO has been reorganized many times since its inception, its leading governing bodies have been the Palestinian National Council (PNC), the Central Council, and the Executive Committee. The PNC has 300 members and functions as a nominal legislature. The Executive Committee has 15 members elected by the PNC and holds the PLO's real political and executive power. The Palestinian Revolutionary Forces are the PLO's military arm. (The Palestine Liberation Army, or PLA, a military group in Syria during the 1970s, was never part of the PLO.)

The PLO has always had a variety of viewpoints represented, some more radical and prone to violence than others,

General Wagih el Madany, commander of the Palestine Liberation Organization (PLO) army, and Ahmad Shukeiri, first chairman of the PLO, in Cairo during a meeting of the Arab Defence Council, December 7, 1955. (AFP/Getty Images)

and Egyptians dominated the organization in its first years. As the 1960s wore on, fedayeen organizations, groups that existed expressly to take up the armed struggle against the Israelis, became more powerful. These groups used guerrilla and paramilitary tactics to resist the encroachment of Israelis on what they considered Palestinian territory.

In 1968 Fatah took control of the PLO's activities after Arafat appeared on the cover of *Time* magazine as the chairman of the Palestinian movement. On February 3, 1969, the PNC in Cairo officially appointed Arafat chairman of the PLO. Over the next four years, Arafat had become the commander in chief of the PLO's military branch, the Palestinian Revolutionary Forces, and the political leader of the organization. He based the PLO in Jordan.

In 1968 and 1969, the PLO functioned as a well-organized unofficial state within Jordan, with its uniformed soldiers acting as a police force and collecting their own taxes. In 1968 King Hussein of Jordan and the PLO signed an agreement by which the PLO agreed that its members would stop patrolling in uniform with guns, stop searching civilian vehicles, and act as Jordanian civilian citizens. The PLO did not comply with this agreement, however, and attacks on civilians and clashes between Palestinians and Jordanian soldiers increased. By 1970 Hussein decided that the Palestinians threatened national security and ordered his army to evict them. This led to several months of violence, during which Syria aided the Palestinians and the United States aided Jordan. The events of Black September (including an attempt on Hussein's life), several airliner hijackings by the PFLP, and a declaration of martial law in Jordan culminated with the PLO agreeing to a cease-fire on September 24 and promising to leave the country.

Arafat then relocated the PLO to Beirut, Lebanon. There Palestinians moved into existing refugee settlements. The Lebanese government tried to restrict the PLO's movements, which led to tensions, but the Palestinians used their position to launch periodic attacks across the Israeli border. Lebanese Muslims and members of Kamal Jumblatt's progressive coalition supported the Palestinian cause, seeing the Palestinians as allies in their struggle against certain Christian factions who dominated the government and the Lebanese Forces (Maronite militias). The latter disliked the PLO presence and wanted to drive the Palestinians out by force.

During the early 1970s, Arafat and the various groups that comprised the PLO often came into conflict over the proper means of achieving the organization's goals. Although Arafat agreed that a certain amount of violence against Israel was necessary to accomplish the PLO's purposes, he believed that diplomacy and compromise were also key to gaining international support. After 1968 the more politically radical groups, such as the PFLP, the DFLP, and other smaller factions, strongly disagreed because it seemed apparent that the Arab countries could not defeat Israel militarily. Such groups gained notoriety for their airplane hijackings in the late 1960s and early 1970s, carried out in Europe and the Middle East. These attacks were intended to further efforts to destroy Israel and create a socialist secular Arab society in its stead. Arafat himself condemned overseas attacks because he believed that they hurt the PLO's international image.

When the radical Black September organization killed several Israeli athletes at the Olympic Games in Munich in 1972, Arafat promptly stated that the PLO was not responsible for the attacks. Arafat closed down the Black September organization in 1973, and in 1974 he ordered the PLO to restrict its violent attacks to Israel, the Gaza Strip, and the West Bank.

In 1974 the Arab Summit recognized the PLO as the sole representative of the Palestinian people. Arafat then appeared before the United Nations (UN) that same year as the official representative of the Palestinians. Speaking before the UN General Assembly, he condemned Zionism and said that the PLO would continue to operate as freedom fighters but also said that he wanted peace. This was the first time the international community had heard directly from the PLO, and many international observers praised Arafat and came to support the Palestinian cause. The UN granted the PLO observer status on November 22, 1974.

Also in 1974, the leaders of Fatah, in the guise of the PNC, created the Ten-Point Program that set forth the PLO's goals. This program called for a secular state in Israel and Palestine that would welcome both Jews and Arabs and provide all citizens equal rights regardless of religion, race, or gender. It also called for the creation of a Palestinian Authority (PA) on free Palestinian territory. Israel rejected the Ten-Point Program. Meanwhile, the radical guerrilla groups the PFLP and the PFLP-GC, which had earlier split from the PFLP, departed from the PLO in protest of its attempt to negotiate with Israel.

In 1975 the Lebanese Civil War began. Israel pursued a strategy of support of the Lebanese Forces, the Maronite militias who opposed the Palestinians. The PLO and Fatah joined forces with the National Front, a more left-wing coalition of Muslims, Druzes, and Christians. Syria intervened at first on behalf of Muslim forces but later came to the aid of the Maronites and in the 1980s also supported the Shia militias.

On January 12, 1976, the UN Security Council voted to grant the PLO the right to participate in Security Council debates. The PLO became a full member of the Arab League that same year.

During the late 1970s, PLO members continued to enter Lebanon and maintain positions in Beirut, from which they exchanged attacks with Israel. On July 24, 1981, the PLO and Israel agreed to a cease-fire within Lebanon and on the border between Lebanon and Israel. Arafat interpreted the cease-fire agreement literally and continued to allow the PLO to attack Israel from Jordan and the West Bank. The Israelis violated the cease-fire numerous times, bombing PLO targets in Beirut. That autumn, Israeli prime minister Menachem Begin and Defense Minister Ariel Sharon planned an invasion into Lebanon to occupy southern Lebanon and territory all the way up to Beirut, where they planned to destroy the PLO. Israeli troops invaded, occupied much of southern Lebanon, and rounded up much of the male population of the area. The UN passed one resolution demanding that Israel withdraw its troops, but the United States vetoed another resolution repeating this demand. The United States demanded that the PLO withdraw from Lebanon. Sharon ordered the bombing of West Beirut beginning on June 15. The UN once again demanded that Israel withdraw, but the United States again vetoed the resolution.

On August 12, 1982, the two sides agreed to another cease-fire in which both the PLO and Israel would leave Lebanon. As a result, about 15,000 Palestinian militants left Lebanon by September 1. The Israelis, however, claimed that PLO members were still hiding in Beirut and returned to the city on September 16, killing several hundred Palestinians, none of whom were known to be PLO members. Sharon resigned as defense minister after the Sabra and Shatila massacres, which were carried out by Lebanese Christian militias with Israeli foreknowledge and approval.

Arafat and many surviving PLO members spent most of the 1980s in Tunisia rebuilding the organization, which had been severely damaged by the fighting in Beirut. During this time, Iraq and Saudi Arabia donated substantial sums of money to the organization. But relations between the PLO and Israel remained intractably bad. The Israel Defense Force (IDF) bombed the PLO headquarters in Tunis in 1985, an attack that killed 73 people.

In December 1987 the First Intifada began spontaneously in the West Bank and Gaza, surprising Israelis with its intensity. On November 15, 1988, the PLO officially declared the formation of the State of Palestine. The PLO claimed all of Palestine as defined by the former British mandate. However, the PLO had decided to seek a two-state solution. That December Arafat spoke before the UN, promising to end terrorism and to recognize Israel in exchange for the Israeli withdrawal from the occupied territories, according to UN Security Council Resolution 242. This was a distinct change from the PLO's previous position of insisting on the destruction of Israel. The PNC symbolically elected Arafat president of the new Palestinian state on April 2, 1989.

Arafat and the Israelis began conducting peace negotiations at the Madrid Conference in 1991. Although the talks were temporarily set back when Arafat and the PLO supported Iraq in the 1991 Persian Gulf War, over the next two years the two parties held a number of secret discussions. These negotiations led to the 1993 Oslo Accords in which Israel agreed to Palestinian self-rule in the Gaza Strip and the West Bank and Arafat officially recognized the existence of the State of Israel. Despite the condemnation of many Palestinian nationalists, the peace process appeared to be progressing apace. Israeli troops withdrew from the Gaza Strip and Jericho in May 1994.

In 1994 the PLO established the Negotiations Affairs Department (NAD) in Gaza to implement the interim agreement. Mahmoud Abbas, then secretary-general of the PLO Executive Committee, headed NAD until April 2003, when the Palestinian Legislative Council chose him as the first prime minister of the PA. He was replaced by Saeb Erakat. The Gaza office of NAD handled Israeli affairs, agreements between Israel and Palestine, colonization, and refugees. It also kept careful track of Israeli expansion into Palestinian territory. NAD also opened an office in Ramallah to handle the implementation of the interim agreement and prepare the Palestinian position for negotiations toward permanent status. The government of the United Kingdom began assisting NAD with its preparation for permanent status talks in 1998.

In 1996 the PNC agreed to remove from the PLO charter all language calling for armed violence aimed at destroying Israel, and Arafat sent U.S. president Bill Clinton a letter listing language to be removed, although the PLO has dragged its feet on this. The organization claimed that it was waiting for the establishment of the Palestinian state, when it would replace the charter with a constitution.

Arafat was elected leader of the new PA in January 1996. The peace process began unraveling later that year, however, after rightist hard-liner Benjamin Netanyahu was elected prime minister of Israel. Netanyahu distrusted Arafat and condemned the PLO as a terrorist organization responsible for numerous suicide bombings on Israeli citizens. The accord collapsed completely in 2000 after Arafat and Israeli prime minister Ehud Barak failed to come to an agreement at a Camp David meeting facilitated by Clinton. After that, the Second (al-Aqsa) Intifada began when Palestinians, already experiencing the intractability of the Israeli government, saw Ariel Sharon lead security forces onto the Haram al-Sharif. During that period, suicide bombings increased. These attacks were in some instances claimed by Islamic Jihad of Palestine, Hamas sympathizers, and other groups. Arafat and the PLO disavowed any support for such attacks. But whether right or wrong, the Israeli media continued to state or suggest that Arafat clandestinely supported the work of the terrorists.

Arafat died on November 11, 2004. There was much dissension over the succession, but Abbas eventually came to represent the PLO's largest faction, Fatah. In December 2004 he called for an end to the violence associated with the Second Intifada that began in September 2000. In January 2005 he was elected president of the PA but has struggled to keep the PLO together and Fatah from losing its political and financial clout. In the January 2006 PA parliamentary elections, Abbas and Fatah were dealt a serious blow when

Hamas captured a significant majority of seats. An even greater blow came in June 2007 when Hamas seized control of Gaza. Since Hamas seized the Gaza Strip, it has been involved in numerous military confrontations with Israel, most notably in 2008–2009, 2012, and 2014.

The Fatah-Hamas break was not substantially mended until early June 2014, when Abbas announced the formation of a unity government. However, unlike the short-lived 2007 unity government, this one did not include any Hamas members in the cabinet. Hamas agreed to support the government without direct participation in it. The United States and most of its allies cautiously backed the new setup, but Israel denounced the government because of its ties to Hamas, which it continues to view as a terrorist group. Prior to the beginning of the latest Hamas-Israeli clash in July 2014, the leaders of Hamas and Fatah had agreed in principle to hold elections for all Palestinians, including those in Gaza and the West Bank, at the end of 2014. However, the renewed fighting involving Hamas greatly complicated those plans. Another Hamas-Fatah unity agreement, brokered by Egypt in October 2017, has similarly run into major obstacles, and the two factions remained far apart as of August 2018. Indeed, the "unity" government announced in 2014 has been unified in name only. Efforts to achieve a unity government continue, with the Israeli government claiming that it will not negotiate with a Palestinian unity government if it includes Hamas.

In August 2015, Mahmoud Abbas resigned as chairman of the PLO's Executive Committee. This prompted calls for a convention of the Palestinian National Council (PNC), which was to take up the resignation of Abbas and several other individuals. Amid popular protests, however, the convention was postponed indefinitely, leaving Abbas and his supporters in limbo. Abbas's resignation was seen as an attempt to force new elections for the PLO's Executive Committee, which appeared deadlocked because of the continued rift between Hamas and Fatah.

Despite serious setbacks for the PLO, it is today recognized by the UN and more than 100 countries as the "sole legitimate representative of the Palestinian people."

Amy Hackney Blackwell, Paul G. Pierpaoli Jr., Spencer C. Tucker, and Sherifa Zuhur

### See also
Abbas, Mahmoud; Arafat, Yasser; Begin, Menachem; Camp David Accords; Fatah, al-; Gaza Strip Disengagement; Hamas; Intifada, First; Intifada, Second; Israel; Lebanon; Lebanon Civil War; Lebanon-Israeli War; Madrid Conference; Netanyahu, Benjamin; Oslo Accords; Palestinian National Authority; Popular Front for the Liberation of Palestine; Popular Front for the Liberation of Palestine–General Command; Sabra and Shatila Massacre; Sharon, Ariel; Terrorism; West Bank

### References
Abbas, Mahmud. *Through Secret Channels: The Road to Oslo: Senior PLO Leader Abu Mazen's Revealing Story of the Negotiations with Israel.* Reading, UK: Garnet, 1997.

Aburish, Said K. *Arafat: From Defender to Dictator.* New York: Bloomsbury, 1998.

Cobban, Helena. *The Palestinian Liberation Organization.* Cambridge: Cambridge University Press, 1984.

Gabriel, Richard. *Operation Peace for Galilee: The Israeli-PLO War in Lebanon.* New York: Farrar, Straus and Giroux, 1985.

Hart, Alan. *Arafat: A Political Biography.* Rev. ed. London: Sidgwick and Jackson, 1994.

Kushner, Arlene. *Disclosed: Inside the Palestinian Authority and the PLO.* Philadelphia: Pavilion, 2004.

Livingstone, Neil C., and David Haley. *Inside the PLO.* New York: William Morrow, 1990.

Rubin, Barry. *Revolution until Victory? The Politics and History of the PLO.* Cambridge, MA: Harvard University Press, 2003.

## Palestinian Islamic Jihad

Militant nationalist Palestinian group. Harakat al-Jihad al-Islami fi Filastin, known as the Palestinian Islamic Jihad (PIJ), was established by Fathi Shiqaqi, Sheikh Abd al-Aziz al-Awda, and others in the Gaza Strip during the 1970s. Several different factions identified with the name Islamic Jihad, including the Usrat al-Jihad, founded in 1948; the Detachment of Islamic Jihad, identified with the Abu Jihad contingent of Fatah; the Islamic Jihad Organization al-Aqsa Battalions, founded by Sheikh Asad Bayyud al-Tamimi in Jordan in 1982; Tanzim al-Jihad al-Islami, led by Ahmad Muhanna; and several non-Palestinian groups. This has caused much confusion over the years. Also, the PIJ movement portrayed itself as being a part of a jihadi continuum rather than a distinct entity.

While in Egypt in the 1970s, Shiqaqi, al-Awda, and the future director-general of the PIJ, Ramadan Abdullah Shallah, embraced an Islamist vision similar to the Egyptian Muslim Brotherhood. But they rejected the moderation forced on that organization by the Egyptian government's aim of political participation in tandem with *dawa* (proselytizing and education). The Palestinian group distinguished itself from secular nationalists and antinationalist Islamists in calling for grassroots organization and armed struggle to liberate Palestine as part of the Islamic solution.

Shiqaqi returned to Palestinian territory, and the PIJ began to express its intent to wage jihad (holy war) against

Israel. Israeli sources claim that the PIJ developed the military apparatus known as the Jerusalem Brigades (Saraya al-Quds) by 1985, and this organization carried out attacks against the Israeli military, including an attack known as Operation GATE OF MOORS at an induction ceremony in 1986. The PIJ also claimed responsibility for the suicide bombing in Beit Led, near Netanya, Israel, on January 22, 1994. In the attack, 19 Israelis were killed and another 60 were injured.

Shiqaqi spent a year in jail in the early 1980s and then in 1986 was jailed for two more years. He was deported to Lebanon along with al-Awda in April 1988. The PIJ established an office in Damascus, Syria, and began support and services in Palestinian refugee camps in Lebanon.

Shallah had meanwhile completed a doctorate at the University of Durham, served as the editor of a journal of the World and Islam Studies Enterprise, and taught briefly at the University of South Florida. When Shiqaqi was assassinated by unidentified agents (allegedly members of the Israeli Mossad) in Malta in 1995, Shallah returned to lead the PIJ. His Florida associations led to the trials of Dr. Sami al-Arian and Imam Fawaz Damra and others who allegedly supported the PIJ in the United States.

The PIJ emerged prior to Hamas. The two organizations were rivals despite the commonality of their nationalist perspectives, but Hamas gained a much larger popular following than the PIJ, whose estimated support is only 4–5 percent of the Palestinian population in the territories. The PIJ developed a following among university students at the Islamic University in Gaza and other colleges and became very active in the Al-Aqsa (Second) Intifada, which began in September 2000.

In Lebanon, the organization competes with Fatah, the primary and largest political faction in the Palestine Liberation Organization (PLO). Like Hamas and secular nationalist groups known as the Palestinian National Alliance, the PIJ rejected the 1993 Oslo Accords and demanded a full Israeli withdrawal from Palestinian lands. The group has a following among Palestinian refugees and at Ain Hilweh but also suffers from the political fragmentation of Palestinian and Islamist organizations there.

The Palestinian Authority (PA) closed down a publication sympathetic to the PIJ but eventually allowed it to reopen. In June 2003 under significant international pressure, Syria closed PIJ and Hamas offices in Damascus, and Shallah left for Lebanon. Khalid Mishaal went to Qatar, but both later returned to Syria.

In the Palestinian territories, the PIJ continues to differ with Hamas. Hamas successfully captured a majority in the Palestinian elections of January 2006. Hamas moderates are also considering the recognition of Israel and a two-state solution. The PIJ, in contrast, had called for Palestinians to boycott the 2006 elections and refused any accommodation with Israel. It continued to sponsor suicide attacks after 2004 in retaliation for Israel's military offensives and targeted killings of PIJ leaders, including Louay Saadi in October 2005. The PIJ claimed responsibility for two suicide attacks in that year.

Israeli authorities continue to highlight Iranian-PIJ links. They cite Shiqaqi's early publication of a pamphlet that praised Ayatollah Ruhollah Khomeini for the 1979 Islamic revolution based on sharia (Islamic law) and for recognizing the Palestinian cause. Iran is a major financial supporter of the PIJ. Following the combined Israeli and Egyptian blockade of Gaza and the corresponding squeeze on Hamas that began in early 2014, the PIJ has seen its power steadily increase, thanks in part to strong Iranian financial support. Syria also provided financial assistance, as did Hezbollah in Lebanon.

SHERIFA ZUHUR

**See also**
Fatah, al-; Hamas; Hezbollah; Intifada, Second; Jihad; Muslim Brotherhood; Oslo Accords; Palestine Liberation Organization

**References**
Abu-Amr, Ziad. *Islamic Fundamentalisms in the West Bank and Gaza: Muslim Brotherhood and Islamic Jihad.* Bloomington: Indiana University Press, 1994.
Journal of Palestine Studies. "The Movement of Islamic Jihad and the Oslo Process: An Interview with Ramadan Abdullah Shallah." *Journal of Palestine Studies* 28 (1999): 61–73.
Knudsen, Are. "Islamism in the Diaspora: Palestinian Refugees in Lebanon." *Journal of Refugee Studies* 18(2) (2005): 216–234.

## Palestinian National Authority

The Palestinian [National] Authority (PA or PNA) is an interim self-governing entity authorized by the 1993 Oslo Accords and established in 1994 to govern what would be the Palestinian autonomous regions of the West Bank and the Gaza Strip and what Palestinians specified as a future autonomous state. The Oslo Accords were finalized during a series of secret meetings between Israel and the Palestine Liberation Organization (PLO). The accords scheduled incremental Israeli withdrawals from the designated territories as refined in ensuing agreements. Israel, as scheduled, withdrew from Jericho on May 13, 1994; the Gaza Strip on May 18, 1994; Janin on November 13, 1995; Tulkarem and Nablus on December 11, 1995; Qalqiliyya on December 16, 1995;

Bethlehem on December 21, 1995; Ramallah on December 27, 1995; and 80 percent of Hebron on January 17, 1997.

The autonomous areas were initially chosen so that the PA would govern 91 percent of the Palestinian populace. The PA was given control over 85 percent of the Gaza Strip. (The Jewish settlements comprised the other 15 percent.) Prime Minister Ariel Sharon imposed an Israeli withdrawal from these settlements in August 2005 despite some Israeli governmental and popular opposition and in the absence of any agreement with the Palestinians. The PA was also initially given control over 39.7 percent of the West Bank.

The Oslo Accords specified that the PA would have control over all civilian- and security-related issues in most of the urban areas of the autonomous regions, termed Area A, but would have control over only civilian affairs in certain rural areas, termed Area B. By 1997 the urban areas under the control of the PA included most of the major Arab population centers in the West Bank except East Jerusalem. Israel retained control over all travel, civilian affairs, and security in Area C; all of the remaining disputed territories; all Israeli settlements and military installations and access to them in all of the autonomous regions; the Jordan Valley; connecting roads between Palestinian communities; and any common borders.

The PA's elected presidency is its highest-ranking political office. The Palestinian Legislative Council (PLC), representing the Gaza Strip and the West Bank, was originally composed of 88 elected members but now has 132 from 16 electoral districts in the West Bank and the Gaza Strip. The PLC elects a member from its ranks for the president to declare as prime minister, an office it first created in March 2003. The prime minister ostensibly reports to the president. Even though the president and prime minister share power, in theory at least the preponderance of power rests with the prime minister. The prime minister, with the approval of the PLC, chooses a cabinet to run the PA's government agencies. As chief of the national security services, the prime minister also directs the PA's security forces. As head of state, the president represents the PA in negotiations with governmental entities apart from the PA.

The PA is headquartered in Ramallah. Since the death of President Yasser Arafat in November 2004, the ability of the PA to govern has been challenged by various Palestinian subgroups. The PA is also constrained by the Israeli government and military. This was made clear following the January 2006 PLC elections, when militantly Islamist Hamas won a majority of seats. A Hamas prime minister, Ismail Haniyeh, was then chosen to govern with previously elected Fatah PA president Mahmoud Abbas.

The PA regulates businesses within its borders and levies taxes and duties that are collected by Israel to be distributed back to the PA. The PA is responsible for social services, education, and health care within the regions it governs and represents the Palestinians in all negotiations with Israel. The PA is also responsible for publicly denouncing and preventing any Palestinian terrorism against Israel. Attempts to carry this out have placed the PA at odds with groups within its own ranks, however.

Funding for the PA comes from duties and taxes as well as aid from Western nations, Russia, and some Arab states. Most Western aid was cut off, however, after the 2006 election of the Hamas-oriented PLC. This meant that the PA was unable to provide many of the educational, health care, and other social services of its mandate. PA employees, especially its police and security agencies, also went unpaid for months. The lack of sufficient indigenous sources of income coupled with a history of corruption and patronage, along with the freezing of donor funds, left the PA largely unable to meet its basic responsibilities.

The Oslo Accords limit the PA to an official uniformed security force (police force) totaling 30,000 personnel. Although the PA officially claims less than this figure, external sources estimate the true size at 40,000–80,000 men. The force is restricted to armored cars and a limited number of automatic weapons, but external estimates judge its capabilities to be greater.

The unemployment rate and the number of people living below the regional poverty level were substantial before the creation of the PA. However, continued violence and curfews, the Israeli Security Fence, and strict Israeli border control have cost jobs and prevented Palestinians from entering Israel, where they were historically employed as guest workers.

The Oslo Accords envisioned the withdrawal of Israel from the proposed autonomous regions and the transfer of administrative responsibilities to the PA during a five-year period to be followed by a second phase beginning in 1999 that would develop a permanent solution. However, despite repeated final status agreements signed at the 2000 Camp David Summit, the 2001 Taba Summit, and the 2003 Geneva Draft Permanent Status Agreement, an official peace agreement between Israel and the PA remains elusive.

The elusive issues are the same ones that existed before establishment of the PA, including the status of Jerusalem, the Palestinian right of return, recognition of the right of Israel to exist, security issues, economic concerns, and borders. The PA remains committed to the creation of a

Palestinian state with its capital in Jerusalem. The sporadic violence followed by suicide bombings from 1996 troubled many, but the spirit of Oslo did not truly break down until the Second (al-Aqsa) Intifada.

Following the signing of the Oslo Accords, Arafat immediately returned to the region from his exile in Tunisia and in 1994 appointed a 19-member interim PA. Planned elections were delayed for 18 months beyond the intended date. The Israelis blamed the delay on Arafat's determination that he be able to control the election result, while the interim PA asserted that the delay was prompted by the need to create an administrative system from scratch, the logistics of setting up an election, and Israeli intransigence in dealing with Arafat.

The first elections for the presidency and the 88-member PLC occurred on January 20, 1996. Arafat was elected president, and his Fatah party held 55 of the 88 PLC members in March 1996.

Additional areas of the West Bank were placed under PA control in 1997, but Israel halted additional withdrawals called for under the October 23, 1998, Wye River Agreement owing to the continued failure of the PA to enforce the agreed-upon security provisions of the agreement. The agreement also allowed the PA to open the Gaza International Airport in Rafah, although Israel maintained control over its security so that the facility could not be used to launch terrorist attacks or import weapons. The airport opened in November 1998 but was closed and then completely razed by Israel in December 2001 following the outbreak of the Second Intifada.

The signing of the Oslo Accords and the creation of the PA effectively ended the violence of the First Intifada (1987–1993). The Second Intifada began in September 2000 after Israeli politician Sharon brought troops onto the Haram al-Sharif (Temple Mount). The Second Intifada ended most discussions concerning the implementation of the Oslo Accords, for as the violence increased and suicide bombings became more prevalent, Israel responded by attacking PA infrastructure and facilities and reoccupying territory previously ceded to the PA. Israel also added to the tension by doubling the number of Jewish settlements in the West Bank between 1991 and 2001.

In March 2003 the PLC created the position of prime minister and named Abbas to the position, which he held from March to October 2003. Although considered a moderate, he was a longtime PLO associate of Arafat. Arafat saw the addition of a PA prime minister as weakening his position as PA president, leading to escalating tension between the two. Israel and the United States had both cut off all contact with Arafat and dealt only with Abbas, further isolating the PA president. A short lull in the cycle of Palestinian violence and Israeli reprisals soon ended, and Abbas resigned. His successor, Ahmad Quray (Qurei), also struggled with Arafat regarding administration of the PA and control of its security forces, but Arafat retained firm control of both the PLO and the PA.

Although never formally assuming the title, Rawhi Fattuh, then PLC Speaker of the house, became interim PA president following Arafat's death on November 11, 2004. Fattuh held this post until Abbas, elected PLO chairman after Arafat's death, was elected president of the PA on January 9, 2005.

Although Abbas's attempts to reengage the U.S. Road Map to Peace proposal were challenged by most militant Palestinian groups, he and Israeli prime minister Sharon agreed in an early 2005 summit to suspend hostilities. This agreement effectively ended the Second Intifada and led to the March 2005 reestablishment of PA control of Jericho and a few northern West Bank towns over which Israel had taken control early during the conflict.

While continuing to encourage new Jewish settlements in the West Bank against the extremely vocal opposition of the Israeli settlers, Sharon commenced a unilateral withdrawal of all Israeli military and civilians from the Gaza Strip in August 2005. The withdrawal and razing of the settlements, completed on September 12, ceded control of all of Gaza to the PA. While the PA benefited from the appearance of having successfully negotiated a withdrawal on quite favorable terms to itself, the jobs lost when Israeli farms and industries no longer provided employment drove more than 75 percent of the population of the Gaza Strip below the poverty line.

A pledge of $50 million and continued support of a free Palestinian state from the United States in May 2005 coupled with the Israeli withdrawal from Gaza led Abbas to set PLC elections for January 25, 2006. However, when Hamas did well in local elections (December 15, 2005), Abbas unsuccessfully sought to postpone the PLC election.

Violence continued within Gaza and against Israel after the Israeli withdrawal. Abbas's power dissipated rapidly when Sharon experienced a debilitating stroke on January 4, 2006, that ultimately ended his premiership. The elections that Abbas had called but could not now cancel led to a Hamas majority in the expanded 132-seat PLC. Although Abbas remained as PA president, his party's hold on the PA was severely weakened. Hamas selected Ismail Haniyeh as the new PA prime minister, and he formed a new PA government. Israel's opposition to Hamas, owing to the latter's previously stated refusal to recognize the right of Israel to exist, caused the European Union (EU) and the United States to withhold financial support that together totaled approximately $1 billion in 2005 alone. Some other nations also terminated aid, while other nations froze it.

This loss of aid and worsening unemployment situation exacerbated the PA's economic crisis and stoked tensions between Fatah and Hamas. In June 2006, Hamas operatives dug a tunnel from inside Gaza to an IDF border outpost inside Israeli territory and captured an Israeli soldier in June 2006, taking him back into Gaza. Israel responded by invading Gaza and arresting PA leaders in the West Bank, primarily members of Hamas.

The situation worsened as political friction between Fatah and Hamas grew and the potential for civil war increased. Abbas called for early parliamentary elections, which many Palestinians rejected as a gambit to undo the previous Hamas victory. Instead, a truce was negotiated between Fatah and Hamas representatives meeting in Mecca in February 2007.

On March 17, 2007, Abbas managed to assemble a Palestinian unity government that included both Hamas and Fatah and with Hamas leader Ismail Haniyeh as prime minister. Despite the agreement, in May violence between Hamas and Fatah escalated. Then on June 14 in an unexpected move, Hamas fighters seized control of Gaza. In retaliation, Abbas dissolved the Hamas-led unity government and declared a state of emergency. On June 18 having been assured of EU support, Abbas dissolved the National Security Council and swore in an emergency Palestinian government. Concurrently, the United States ended its 15-month embargo on the PA and resumed aid to it in an effort to strengthen Abbas's government, now limited to the West Bank. On June 19 Abbas cut off all ties and dialogue with Hamas, pending the return of Gaza. In a further move to strengthen the perceived moderate Abbas, on July 1 Israel restored financial ties to the PA. The situation remained stalemated, with Gaza under increasing economic and diplomatic isolation.

Despite attempts to reconcile Hamas and Fatah, the political stalemate continued; meanwhile, Palestinians in the Gaza Strip suffered considerable deprivation because of Israel's blockade of Gaza and the dearth of foreign aid. Increasing rocket and mortar fire from Gaza into Israel brought the December 2008–January 2009 Gaza War between the Israel Defense Force (IDF) and Hamas. This was replicated in the Gaza War of November 2012. That November also the United Nations (UN) voted to recognize Palestine as a nonmember UN observer state.

The Hamas-Fatah rift was seemingly healed in the spring of 2014, when both sides agreed to a power-sharing arrangement. Abbas formed a new unity government in early June; although Hamas pledged to support the new setup, none of its members actively participated in the government. Abbas now seemed to exert at least some control over Gaza, but his position was quickly undermined by renewed fighting between the IDF and Hamas in the Gaza War of July–August 2014. This fighting undermined the unity government, with Hamas and Fatah remaining estranged.

Talks were held in Qatar in February 2016 in an attempt to heal the rift between Fatah and Hamas but without success. Hamas charged that Israel and the United States were conspiring to prevent the implementation of a lasting unity government. Fatah meanwhile held firm in its assertion that Hamas had reneged on significant portions of the 2014 power-sharing plan. No parliamentary elections have been held since 2006, and a presidential election has not taken place since 2005. The PA remains effectively split between the administrations of Abbas and Hamas in the Gaza Strip. In early July 2016, Abbas announced that the PA would discontinue its cooperation with the 2002 Quartet on the Middle East, alleging that the group was siding with Israel to the detriment of the Palestinians.

On October 12, 2017, in Cairo, representatives of the PA and Hamas met to sign a unity agreement that would end their decade-long feud. No doubt influenced by the dire conditions facing the 2 million residents of Gaza, Hamas agreed to hand over government of Gaza to the PA. Difficulties lay ahead, however, as the PA was refusing to give up control of its rockets and mortars aimed at Israeli, which was one of the key PA conditions. The Israeli government also voiced objection to any agreement not recognizing Israel and disarming Hamas. The 2017 unity deal has yet to take effect, with Hamas and the PA remaining apart on key issues. At the same time, Egypt's government has been engaged in talks with Hamas to help broker a compromise to the impasse.

The PA also had to wrestle with U.S. president Donald Trump's decision, announced in December 2017, reversing decades of U.S. policy by recognizing Jerusalem as the capital of Israel. In May 2018, the U.S. embassy was officially moved to the city. On this news, protests and rioting broke out in the Palestinian areas, and Abbas announced that the PA no longer regarded the United States as a neutral broker in the peace process.

RICHARD M. EDWARDS, PAUL G. PIERPAOLI JR.,
AND SPENCER C. TUCKER

**See also**

Abbas, Mahmoud; Arafat, Yasser; Cairo Accord; Fatah, al-; Gaza War of 2006; Gaza War of 2008–2009; Geneva Accord; Hamas; Intifada, First; Intifada, Second; Israeli Security Fence; Oslo Accords; Palestine Liberation Organization; Right of Return, Palestinian; Settlements, Israeli; Sharon, Ariel; Wye River Agreement

**References**

Abbas, Mahmoud. *Through Secret Channels: The Road to Oslo; Senior PLO Leader Abu Mazen's Revealing Story of the Negotiations with Israel.* Reading, UK: Garnet, 1997.

Gelvin, James L. *The Israel-Palestine Conflict: One Hundred Years of War.* New York: Cambridge University Press, 2005.

Hall, John G. *Palestinian Authority: Creation of the Modern Middle East.* Langhorne, PA: Chelsea House, 2002.

Makovsky, David. *Making Peace with the PLO: The Rabin Government's Road to the Oslo Accord.* Boulder, CO: Westview, 1996.

Pappe, Ilan. *A History of Modern Palestine: One Land, Two Peoples.* Cambridge: Cambridge University Press, 2003.

Parsons, Nigel Craig. *The Politics of the Palestinian Authority: From Oslo to Al-Aqsa.* London: Routledge, 2003.

# Palestinian Right of Return

*See* Right of Return, Palestinian

# Palmach

Jewish fighting force numbering at its height a few thousand soldiers. It was created jointly by the British and the Jewish Haganah on May 15, 1941. Haganah (Hebrew for "defense"), the Jewish underground self-defense and military organization formed in 1920, was the precursor of the Israel Defense Force (IDF). Haganah leadership realized the need for a permanently mobilized military organization to defend Jewish settlements that from time to time came under harassment from Arab bands. More important to the British was that if Axis forces were ever to enter the British Mandate for Palestine, Palmach (Palmakh) would fight them as well.

The new elite Palmach, which is the Hebrew abbreviation of *plugot mahats* (strike force), was originally commanded by Yitzhak Sadeh. Composed of 9 assault teams, it was trained and equipped by the British and dispersed throughout Palestine, including 1 team in Jerusalem. A third of its members were young women. Palmach eventually grew to 12 assault teams that initiated scouting and sabotage missions as well as preemptive strikes into Syria and Lebanon. Yigal Allon, Moshe Dayan, Yitzhak Rabin, Chaim Bar-Lev, Uzi Narkiss, and Ezer Weizman were some of its more notable members.

Palmach was officially disbanded when the British defeated the German forces at El Alamein in the summer of 1942 and the threat to the British position from Syria and Lebanon had abated after the Allied invasion of Syria. Haganah converted Palmach after its supposed dissolution into an underground commando force and initially assigned it to the protection of the Yishuv (Jewish settlements) in Palestine in August 1942. Yitzhak Tabenkin, head of the kibbutzim union, conceived of a plan that assigned Palmach platoons to various kibbutzim. These would provide the Palmachniks (Palmach members) with food, shelter, and other needs as they arose. In return, Palmach protected the kibbutz to which they were assigned, worked in the agricultural enterprises of the kibbutz, and participated in Zionist education. This combination of training, protection, education, and work was called Akhshara Meguyeset, or Drafted/Recruited Training. Each Palmachnik was to train 8 days a month, stand guard 14 days a month, and rest 7 days a month. However, Palmachniks were always on call in case of an attack.

The role of Palmach was not limited to the protection of the Yishuv. By 1943 Palmach had organized itself into six regular companies and a like number of special units. The Ha-Makhlaka Ha-Germanit, or German Department, operated against the Nazi infrastructure in the Middle East and the Balkans. The Ha-Makhlaka Ha-Aravit, or Arab Department (known also as the Arab Platoon because members often dressed in Arabic attire), operated against Arab militias. After the formation of Israel, they formed the basis of the border police and IDF infiltration units. The Palyam was the sea force of Palmach and focused on facilitating the illegal entry of Jewish refugees from Europe in violation of the British white paper of 1939 that limited Jewish immigration to Palestine. Palmach's Sabotage Units eventually formed the nucleus of the IDF Engineering Corps. The Palmach Air Force consisted of British-trained Jewish pilots who, however, had no aircraft until 1948, when they commenced observation and scouting operations. Additionally, Zionist youth movement participants aged 18–20 were formed into Nahal (Hebrew acronym for *noar halutzi lohem,* meaning "fighting pioneer youth") or nucleus groups. They were trained by Palmachniks and eventually formed the basis of the Nahal settlements, created as strategic strongholds in case of war.

Palmachniks received basic training in physical fitness, small arms, topography, squad operations, and Krav Maga (Hebrew for "contact combat"), a martial art developed in Czechoslovakia in the 1930s. Most Palmachniks also received additional training in one or more of the following combat specialties: sabotage and explosives, reconnaissance, sniping, light and medium machine gunnery, and mortars. Group and platoon training also included live-fire drills using artillery, machine guns, and mortars. Palmach officer training emphasized the development of independent and innovative field commanders who took initiative and led by example.

When it was clear that the British were unwilling to create a Jewish state or allow the immigration of large numbers of Jewish refugees into Palestine, Palmach attacked British infrastructure such as bridges, railways, radar stations, and police stations during 1945 and 1946. These attacks stopped when the British arrested en masse many of the Palmach and Haganah leadership on June 29, 1946, a date known in Israeli history as the Black Sabbath.

Palmach units assumed responsibility for protecting the Jewish settlements from Arab militias when the Israeli War of Independence (1948–1949) erupted following the partition of Palestine and the formation of the State of Israel. These Palmach units persevered until Haganah relieved them. Palmach was then formed into two units of the newly created IDF, the Negev Brigade and Yiftah Brigade. These units stopped the Egyptian Army in the Negev and then seized the Gaza Strip and Sharm El Sheikh.

Many Palmachniks entered Israeli politics, including Rabin, Dayan, Bar-Lev, Mordechai Gur, Mati Peled, Yair Tsaban, Shulamit Aloni, Rehavam Zeevi, and Rafael Eitan. Indeed, Palmachniks dominated the IDF command structure for many years and helped shape its distinctive ethos.

RICHARD M. EDWARDS

### See also
Dayan, Moshe; Eitan, Rafael; Haganah; Rabin, Yitzhak

### References
Bar-On, Mordechai, ed. *A Never-ending Conflict: A Guide to Israeli Military History*. Westport, CT: Praeger, 2004.
Goldstein, Yaacov N., and Dan Shomron. *From Fighters to Soldiers: How the Israeli Defense Forces Began*. Brighton, UK: Sussex Academic, 1998.
Van Creveld, Martin. *The Sword and the Olive: A Critical History of the Israeli Defense Force*. New York: PublicAffairs, 2002.

## Palmyra

Palmyra is the Greek name for the city of Tadmor, located in an oasis in central Syria. Palmyra was a major hub for trade with the East. Occupied since 2000 BCE, Palmyra was settled by people from many civilizations: Assyrian, Semitic, Arab, Greek (from the Hellenistic age), and Persian. These cultures are all evident in the site's art, architecture, and archaeology. The dominant language of the Palmyrenes was Aramaic; their cultural identification was probably Semitic.

Mark Antony attempted without success to conquer Palmyra, but the early Roman emperors accepted Palmyra's de facto independence due to the popularity in Rome of luxury goods from India and China (especially spices and silk textiles). Palmyra remained a free city until Septimius Severus incorporated it into the adjacent Roman province. However, the Roman Army recruited units of Palmyrene auxiliaries, especially archers and cavalry.

In the mid-third century as the Roman Empire threatened to fragment under the stress of barbarian invasions and civil war, Palmyra became an independent realm, the "Palmyrene Empire," ruled by Septimius Odenathus and then by his widow Zenobia. Odenathus seems to have been confirmed as "Ruler of Tadmor" (attested in Palmyrene inscriptions) by Emperor Philip as a bulwark against Persia. Emperor Gallienus (r. 260–268) granted Odenathus the title *corrector totius Orientis* (emperor's deputy in the East), permitted to command Roman troops. Odenathus succeeded in reconquering part of Mesopotamia from the Persians and took the native title "king of kings." Around 267 he was acclaimed imperator by his troops. Gallienus, faced with many other rivals for the purple, tolerated this state of affairs. Odenathus died mysteriously, perhaps assassinated, circa 268 and succeeded by his widow Queen Zenobia.

Zenobia governed Palmyra as regent for her son Septimius Vaballathus but aggressively sought to expand the Palmyrene empire. She appointed Septimius Zabdas as her general. Palmyra pushed forward into Roman Arabia (where the culture was similar). Zabdas defeated the *dux* (commander) of Roman Arabia, sacked the garrison city of Bostra, and proceeded to capture Judaea and invade Egypt. Zabdas and Zenobia captured Alexandria despite the resistance of the Roman prefect of Egypt, whom the Palmyrenes defeated. Zenobia then sought to consolidate Palmyrene control of Syria. Coins show that Zenobia and Vaballathus increasingly took Roman imperial titles, Zenobia being *sebaste* (augusta) and Vaballathus *sebastos* (augustus), then the formal Latin titles augusta and augustus on coins minted at Alexandria and Antioch.

Emperor Aurelian could no longer tolerate this rivalry and reconquered Palmyra for the Roman Empire. His legion first captured Tyana, a city in Cappadocia at the edge of Palmyrene influence. He then defeated Palmyrene forces in the Battle of Immae in Syria and forced Zenobia to flee from Emesa in Syria to Palmyra. Aurelian then besieged Palmyra; attempting to flee to the Persians, Zenobia was captured by the Romans. Aurelian court-martialed Zenobia and her generals and advisers, putting the latter to death but sparing Zenobia. Diocletian (284–305) built walls and an army camp in Palmyra as a frontier outpost.

The extensive ancient archaeological remains of the city of Palmyra were a major tourist destination before the onset of the Syrian Civil War (2011–). The extremist Islamic State of Iraq and Syria (ISIS) seized control of the city in 2015. ISIS demolished many of the city's ancient treasures, including the 1,800-year-old Arch of Triumph and the nearly 2,000-year-old Temple of Baalshamin, as well as the Temple of Bel. The group also beheaded the antiquities expert who oversaw the ruins. The Syrian Army retook Palmyra on March 27, 2016. ISIS made a major effort to regain control of Palmyra on December 10, but some 64 Russian air strikes in support of the Syrian Army drove the rebels out. The Russians claimed that they had killed 300 of the militants and destroyed a dozen tanks and armored vehicles.

SARA E. PHANG AND SPENCER C. TUCKER

**See also**
Aurelian, Emperor; Islamic State of Iraq and Syria; Odenathus; Zenobia

**References**
Southern, Pat. *Empress Zenobia: Palmyra's Rebel Queen.* London: Continuum, 2008.
Watson, Alaric. *Aurelian and the Third Century.* London: Routledge, 1999.

# Pan-Arab Congress (September 8, 1937)

Conference of some 400 Arab leaders that convened on September 8, 1937, in Bludan, Syria. The Pan-Arab Congress took place in the middle of the Great Palestinian Rebellion in Palestine (1936–1939), sometimes called the Arab Revolt. More specifically, the congress met during the second major phase of the rebellion (July 1937–October 1938). The rebellion, which was aimed primarily at British interests in Palestine, also saw widespread violence against Jews, whose numbers in Palestine had been steadily increasing. By 1936, Palestinian Arabs had grown weary and annoyed with British policies that had allowed more and more Jewish immigrants into Palestine. Many Arabs had also grown fearful that Jewish purchases of Arab land were relegating the Palestinian Arabs to a decidedly second-rate status and threatening their economic well-being.

The Arab Revolt was led by two primary groups. The first was the politically conscious Arab elite, dominated by the two rival clans of the Husseini family (led by the mufti of Jerusalem, Haj Amin al-Husseini) and the Nashashibi family (represented by Fakhri al-Nashashibi). The second (and true center of the leadership) resided among local committees that had emerged in Jerusalem, Nablus, Jaffa, Tulkarm, and elsewhere.

The primary triggering mechanism of the hastily convened Pan-Arab Congress, however, was the 1937 Peel Commission, sponsored by the British government. As a response to the violence of the uprising, the British government had charged the Peel Commission with making recommendations that would ease Arab-Jewish tensions and bring an end to the rebellion.

Issued in July 1937, the Peel Commission Report concluded that the Arab Revolt was the result of the Palestinians' drive for independence and their enmity toward the concept of a Jewish state in Palestine. To bring an end to the violence, the Peel Commission recommended the partitioning of Palestine into Jewish and Palestinian states (the latter to be part of Transjordan) and common areas controlled by the mandate (e.g., Jerusalem).

The Palestinian Arabs—and most other Arabs—were incensed with the Peel Commission's conclusion that partition was necessary. Instead of mitigating Palestinian anger, the report served only to fan the flames of resentment. Violence reached new heights in the late summer and early autumn of 1937, and by September as many as 10,000 well-armed Palestinian guerrillas were prowling the countryside. They were joined by at least several hundred Arab fighters, sponsored by the Arab Higher Commission, from other states.

It was amid this incredibly tense political and military atmosphere that the Pan-Arab Congress convened. The meeting resulted in unanimous support for the Palestinians' right to a homeland and took considerable pains to condemn the Peel Commission and the suggestion of a bifurcated Palestine. The conferees also called for scrapping the 1917 Balfour Declaration, immediately suspending all Jewish immigration to Palestine, ending the British Mandate, and creating with all due haste a Palestinian state. For Jews already living in Palestine, the Pan-Arab Congress agreed to give them guaranteed minority status. In addition, the congress agreed to create a permanent executive committee to help Palestinians economically and to engage in public relations activities. Finally, delegates voted to expand the Arab economic boycott to include British as well as Jewish goods.

The 1937 Pan-Arab Congress not only gave voice to Palestinian grievances but also unified the effort to help them attain a homeland. Also, Syria quickly emerged as the linchpin of the rebellion in Palestine. Syria hosted key leaders of the insurgency and funneled money to the Palestinian cause. The Arab Revolt continued for almost two additional years, with many more deaths and casualties.

PAUL G. PIERPAOLI JR.

**See also**
Arab Revolt in Palestine; Balfour Declaration; Husseini, Haj Amin al-; Palestine, British Mandate for; Peel Commission; Syria

**References**
Gelvin, James L. *The Israel-Palestine Conflict: One Hundred Years of War.* New York: Cambridge University Press, 2005.
Morris, Benny. *Righteous Victims: A History of the Zionist-Arab Conflict, 1881–2001.* New York: Vintage Books, 2001.
Porath, Yehoshua. *The Palestinian National Movement, 1929–1939: From Riot to Rebellion.* London: Cass, 1974.
Swedenburg, Ted. *Memories of Revolt: The 1936–1939 Rebellion and the Palestinian National Past* Minneapolis: University of Minnesota Press, 1995.

## Pan-Arabism and Pan-Arabist Thought

Philosophical and political movements based on the need to reinvest pride in Arab identity after centuries of dominance by the Ottoman Empire. Beyond this basic Arabism were versions of Arab nationalism that called for the solidarity of Arab peoples and movements for Arab unity, implying a political union of Arab governments. Pan-Turkism had arisen at the end of the 19th century and the early 20th century, and the revival of Arab identity came in response to it. Other responses to Western encroachments were Pan-Islamist in orientation. Arab nationalism, sometimes with a Pan-Arab program, contrasted with such movements in calling for the appropriate response of Arab nations against increased Western imperial expansion. Pan-Arabism ultimately developed into such political doctrines in the region as Baathism, Nasserism, and, more generally, Arab nationalism. The application of these doctrines was to have far-reaching consequences for power relations in the Middle East and beyond.

In the second half of the 19th century, a variety of Middle Eastern intellectuals began to theorize about the future of the Islamic world in relation to the increasingly powerful imperial nations of Europe. One influential movement was that of Pan-Islamism. Led by Jamal ad-Din al-Afghani, early Pan-Islamists were fiercely anti-imperialist and framed their desires for parity with the West along religious lines. Afghani did not believe that the West was superior to the Muslim East. Rather, he believed that over time Middle Eastern governments and religion had become corrupt and lost touch with the true message of Islam.

For Afghani, there were two major Islamic tenets that needed to be revised in order for the Muslim world to become as powerful as the West: unity and action. Unity of the Muslim world was crucial in the eyes of Afghani. He looked back to the early Muslim kingdoms and the success of early Islam as something that could be achieved anew in the Middle East. Muslims need only unify behind a progressive Islam, which would encourage its followers throughout the world to forget their ethnic and national differences and see themselves as part of one supernation of believers. In doing so, Muslims would actively unite against European expansionism and economic exploitation.

One of Afghani's most influential students was Muhammad Abduh, a well-respected theologian who ultimately became the mufti of Egypt in 1899. Abduh formulated one of the most influential modern interpretations of Islam in a book titled *Risalah al-Tawhid* (A Treatise on the Oneness of God), published in 1897. It asserted not only that Islam and modernity were compatible but also that modernity complemented Islam rather than restricted it. Abduh founded the Salafiyya movement, which called for the reintroduction into Sunni Islam of a legal principle of Islamic law allowing for more reinterpretation (*ijtihad*). As Pan-Islamists, both Afghani (who was not an Arab) and Abduh were concerned about Islamic affairs more than Arab affairs; however, Abduh was also involved in an Egyptian uprising against the British. Punished for his views, he took up the reform of al-Azhar University, which has also fostered Pan-Islamism.

Abd al-Rahman al-Kawakibi (1849–1903), a journalist from Aleppo, was of Kurdish descent. He spent the last three years of his life in Cairo and published two key books in which he voices disgust toward the corruption of the Ottoman Empire, which ruled large segments of the Arab world. He blamed the decline of Muslim rule on the fact that non-Arabs had taken control of the Middle East. He looked at Islam as the greatest achievement of the Arabs, and because God had chosen to reveal Islamic teachings to an Arab prophet in Arabic, the Arabs were an ideal people for leadership. He wanted to see the restoration of an Arab caliphate, which, he believed, would hasten a revival in the region as well as in the religion. Kawakibi's ideology gave some Arabs a framework for opposing the Ottomans, which eventually took on nationalist tones.

Arab nationalism also evolved from Syrian nationalism and a movement of revival for the Arabic language called the *nahda,* or renaissance. Many of these Arab nationalists were Christians, including Jurji Zaydan, who wrote histories and novels; Ibrahim al-Yaziji, who established a secret society in 1875 that focused on Arab pride and rejected the Ottoman claim to the caliphate; and Najib Azury, who founded the Ligue de la Patrie Arabe (League of the Arab Fatherland) in 1903 in Cairo and wrote *The Awakening of the Arab Nation* in 1905. By 1913 other secret nationalist societies had formed and survived rounds of suppression from the Ottoman government.

As the Ottoman Empire collapsed at the end of World War I and Britain and France secured control over much of the Middle East, other Arab intellectuals challenged European expansionism. It is in the ideas of these thinkers that the foundations of Pan-Arabism were laid.

One of the most noted individuals who focused his efforts on Arab nationalism was a Syrian Arab named Sati al-Husri, who had become known during the Ottoman era as a bureaucrat committed to educational reform. After the collapse of Ottoman rule in 1918, Husri introduced Arabist or Arab nationalist values into the Iraqi educational curriculum in the interwar years, when he headed the Ministry of Education in King Faisal I's Iraqi government. In the 1920s and 1930s, Husri wrote a series of pamphlets—*Arabism First, On Arab Nationalism* and *What Is Nationalism?*—in which he called for the creation of a single, united, and independent Arab state. He believed that the Arab people constituted one nation and that the Arabic language was the primary marker of that fact, as all who spoke Arabic shared other cultural attributes. Because the Arabic speakers existed before Islam, both Muslim and Christian Arabs should be united under this nation. Husri hoped that the common language, shared culture, and shared history would inspire Arabs to found a modern nation-state and successfully combat the external Western forces then dominating the region.

Another pair of influential thinkers who helped to establish the Baath Party along with Zaki al-Arsuzi and others were the Syrian intellectuals Michel Aflaq and Salah al-Din al-Bitar. Both had studied at the Sorbonne in Paris in the 1930s. Like many of their era, they were attracted to socialist ideology, particularly its anti-imperialism and messages of social justice. They called their new movement the Baath (Arabic for "resurrection"). Its principles were socialism, unity, and freedom. They expressed an Arab nationalist agenda in the context of social restructuring to build a powerful and independent Arab society. In part, their movement was a reaction to the pro-French attitudes of other elites and the identification with a past Phoenician identity by some Lebanese at the time. Members of the Baath movement believed that the Arabs could regain their confidence only with unity. That unity would hearken back to Arab greatness under the conquering caliphs of early Islam and would put the Arab world on par with the West. In that way, Aflaq and Bitar were influenced by Kawakibi. Indeed, the Baath movement, although a secular philosophy inclusive of Muslims and Christians, idealized Islam as a cultural system and a symbol of what the Arab world was capable of producing. Baathism's inclusive rhetoric also appealed to non-Muslim Arabs who wished to see their nation resurrected as well. The ideology of the Baath movement was coupled with two other powerful political developments in the Arab world: the dispossession of the Palestinians from their homeland and the emergence of Nasserism in Egypt during the rule of President Gamal Abdel Nasser.

Many Pan-Arab thinkers called on Egypt to take the lead in promoting the Arabist cause, and such ideas took hold during the 1930s and 1940s. In 1945 the Arab League was formed in Cairo in the hopes of forging greater cooperation between Arab nations in the postwar period. The league was a coalition of Egypt, Syria, Lebanon, Iraq, and Transjordan (later Jordan). The leaders of these states pledged to support one another in building economic, political, and cultural strength and cooperation.

In May 1948 during the Israeli War of Independence, the member nations of the Arab League invaded Palestine to halt the formation of the State of Israel, but they were defeated by the Israelis in December. The defeat of Arab armies was a turning point for the Arab nationalist movement. The loss of Palestine to the Israelis was made more bitter by the humiliating crisis of the Palestinian refugees, who had fled and for several years lived only on Palestinian and Arab aid until the refugee camps were organized. For Arabs throughout the world, the shared rhetoric and considerable efforts taken to restore the Palestinians to their homeland and defeat the Israeli state became a powerful tool of political unification.

Nasser ultimately became the most well-known spokesperson for Arab nationalism. During his period in power (1952–1970), he promoted Arab unity and pride in the Arab nation to rally Egyptian resistance to the Western powers and Israel in the 1956 Suez War and to oppose what he regarded as British and U.S. plans to divide the region. He convinced Jordan and Syria not to join the British-sponsored Baghdad Pact of 1954, and in 1956 he successfully faced off against the

The return of British-held Shalufa military base to Egyptian control. Egyptian prime minister Gamal Abdel Nasser hands the flag to the new Egyptian army base commander, March 22, 1955. (ullstein bild via Getty Images)

Western powers and nationalized the Suez Canal. Nasser, a brilliant orator, proclaimed the Arab nation to be one nation and stated that "the Arab people are one people" in a speech following the failure of the British, French, and Israelis in the Suez Crisis to force a popular coup against his government. Later, he defined Egypt's embrace of Arabism to be a progressive and populist cause, in contrast to the Arabism espoused by traditional monarchies, such as Saudi Arabia.

As the propaganda war grew between Egypt and Saudi Arabia because of their conflict in Yemen and efforts to be the dominant influence in the region, Nasser utilized the Voice of Cairo, a powerful radio network broadcast throughout the Arab world and beyond, to spread the doctrines of Arab unity and Arab socialism.

In late 1957 Syrian politicians turned to Nasser and asked him to join a union of the two countries, since they were at that time under threat by a rival faction. In February 1958 the United Arab Republic (UAR), the political unification of Syria and Egypt, was founded. Baath leaders believed that the union would ensure their control over Syria, while the Egyptians saw the move as the first of several possible unions. Millions of Arabs saw the unification of Syria and Egypt as a dream combination; they ardently hoped that the UAR was the beginning of a new Arab superstate that could challenge Western hegemony.

It was not to be. It soon became clear that resentment existed among the Syrian bourgeoisie, who could justifiably claim that the administrative arrangements based on Egypt's demographic preponderance did not grant Syria an equal voice. Some of the Egyptian bureaucrats and officials who went to Syria were highly unpopular there. The unification also demonstrated that stated resistance to the programs of land reform and industrialization in Syria were politically destabilizing. The UAR was not a well thought-out formation but rather a hasty attempt by the Syrian opposition to capitalize on Nasser's power in a way that he could not refuse. In September 1961 Syrian military units staged an insurrection against the Egyptian commanders, and the UAR came to an end. Nasser accepted this defeat, but his subsequent statements were bitter and dwelt on the issues of class struggle that led to the union's failure, thus contributing to the discourse on Arab socialism at that time.

The failure of the UAR was followed by a lengthy Egyptian military involvement in Yemen and then in 1967 by the humiliating defeat of Egypt, Syria, and Jordan by the Israelis in the Six-Day War. The war brought great territorial losses for the Arab side and dramatic increases in the number of Palestinian refugees. For the Arab world, it appeared that Arab unity was now more necessary than ever. Yet the governments of the Arab nations were further divided by the 1967 defeat. Moreover, with the 1967 defeat it was clear to Palestinians that their cause could not be left in the hands of the Arab states. Although the Palestinian cause remained a symbol for Arab unity, real action for change was moved away from the Arab League and concentrated in the Palestine Liberation Organization (PLO) and other Palestinian movements.

In the 1970s and 1980s, Arab leaders employed the rhetoric of Arab nationalism, or Baathism, to rally their populations behind a number of issues, particularly the struggle against Israel. Saddam Hussein of Iraq in particular used the Arab cause as a rationale for his policies. But in 1990 an event occurred that spelled increasing factionalism in the Arab world. When Iraq invaded Kuwait in August 1990, the Western powers, led by the United States working through the United Nations, convinced a number of other Arab nations to join their alliance against Iraq. Egypt and Syria committed troops to the Persian Gulf War in exchange for debt cancellation and other economic rewards, while

Saudi Arabia agreed to host coalition forces. The punishing defeat of Iraq in February 1991 dimmed hopes for a unified approach by Arab nations.

Today, a significant number of people, parties, and governments still employ Arab nationalism and Arab unity as the framework for their policies, even though a larger segment of the population is searching for other alternatives to political, social, and economic problems. Many have turned instead to the numerous Islamist or Muslim fundamentalist/extremist movements, with the two best known being Al Qaeda and the Islamic State of Iraq and Syria (ISIS).

Nancy L. Stockdale and Sherifa Zuhur

**See also**
Al Qaeda; Arab League; Egypt; Hussein, Saddam; Iraq; Islamic State of Iraq and Syria; Nasser, Gamal Abdel; Palestine Liberation Organization; Persian Gulf War, Overview; Syria; United Arab Republic

**References**
Hourani, Albert. *Arabic Thought in the Liberal Age, 1798–1939*. New York: Cambridge University Press, 1983.
Khalidi, Rashid, et al., eds. *The Origins of Arab Nationalism*. New York: Columbia University Press, 1993.
Tibi, Bassam. *Arab Nationalism: Between Islam and the Nation-State*. New York: St. Martin's, 1997.

# Paraetacene, Battle of (317 BCE)

Important battle of the Second War of the Diadochi (Greek for "successors") of 319–315 BCE. These wars followed the death of Alexander III the Great in 323 and were fought by his generals over control of the territory he had conquered. Antigonus I Monophthalmus ("the One-eyed," so called because of the loss of one of his eyes in battle) and Eumenes of Cardia were two of the most effective of the Diadochi generals. The battles of Paraetacene in 317 BCE and Gabiene in 316 were the last of the engagements of the war in Asia Minor. Both should be noted as the first pitched battles in the Hellenistic world involving a large number of war elephants on both sides.

Eumenes commanded around 35,000 infantry, 6,000 cavalry, and 120 elephants. He positioned light cavalry fronted by elephants and light infantry on his left flank. The veteran *sarissa* phalanx fronted by elephants was in the center, while heavy cavalry occupied the right. There were also both advance and rear guards of slaves or pages. Antigonus's deployment was identical but with his 30 best elephants in echelon on his left. He had a similar number of infantry, 10,600 cavalry, and 65 elephants.

Antigonus's left-wing commander insubordinately attacked first, charging Eumenes's right wing. They were winning the battle until Eumenes counterattacked with light cavalry and infantry. Eumenes's veterans then defeated the enemy phalanx in the center. Antigonus personally led a heavy cavalry charge between Eumenes's phalanx and left wing, bypassing the elephant screen, and easily routed the surprised cavalry to salvage a draw by winning on the left, with Eumenes victorious everywhere else.

Eumenes's veterans in the phalanx refused to leave their baggage undefended and so abandoned the battlefield. Antigonus forced his men to encamp on the field and thus claimed a victory. Antigonus may have lost up to 8,000 men and Eumenes up to 5,000.

The inconclusive Battle of Paraetacene was followed by the decisive clash between the two armies at Gabiene in 316.

Graham Wrightson and Spencer C. Tucker

**See also**
Antigonus I Monophthalmus; Diadochi, Wars of the; Gabiene, Battle of

**References**
Devine, Albert M. "Diodorus' Account of the Battle of Paraitacene (317 B.C.)." *Ancient World* 12 (1985): 75–86.
Hackett, John. *Warfare in the Classical World*. London: Sidgwick & Jackson, 1989.
Pietrykowski, Joseph. *Great Battles of the Hellenistic World*. Barnsley, UK: Pen and Sword, 2009.

# Parthian Empire (247 BCE–224 CE)

Ancient power in present-day Iran and Iraq. The Arsacid Persians—or Parnis—entered history as one of three nomadic tribes making up the Dahae, a Scythian confederacy that lived east of the Caspian Sea. After abandoning the Dahae region (ca. 250 BCE), the Parnis settled in the Seleucid province of Parthava, which later became "Parthia." Under their semimythical leader, Arsaces I, they soon won independence from the Seleucids, prompting Arsaces to found the Arsacid dynasty.

During the course of the next two centuries, the Arsacids slowly dismantled the Seleucid Empire. They first absorbed smaller neighboring territories such as Hyrcania, Bactria, and Media. But after several victories against the Seleucids, the Arsacids set their sights on the more profitable regions of Mesopotamia. Babylonia in particular, with its numerous large cities, eventually became the hub of the Arsacids' new empire, which stretched from the Euphrates River in the West to the Indus River in the East.

The collapse of the Seleucids might have taken the Arsacids all the way to the Mediterranean. But by the mid-first-century BCE, Rome was already asserting its authority in eastern Asia Minor and Syria. The Roman triumvir Crassus's unprovoked attack on Persia in 53 BCE permanently marred any chance of lasting peace between Rome and Persia. During the next 300 years, the two empires engaged each other in a vicious cycle of invasions and counterattacks that, in the end, did little to alter the overall political makeup of the Near East.

While neither Arsacid Persia nor Rome ever permanently overcame the other, their long conflict did diminish the Arsacids' prestige at home. The Roman emperor Trajan's invasion of Persia (114–117 CE) was the first to sack the Arsacids' main capital at Ctesiphon. But several of Trajan's successors (Lucius Verus in 165, Septimius Severus in 197, and possibly Caracalla in 215) temporarily seized the capital as well. Although the Romans never held Ctesiphon for long, the city's repeated capture made later Arsacid kings seem weak in the eyes of Persia's nobility.

Civil war, which was a constant bane for the Arsacids, also intensified as royal family members vied with each other for power. By the third century, the nobility's waning confidence in the royal line finally led it to look elsewhere. In 224 CE, an internal revolt of Persian vassals deposed the last Arsacid ruler, Artabanus V. The revolt's leader, Ardashir, the son of Sasan, then established a new dynasty, the Sassanid, which proved to be a much more difficult foe for Rome in the ensuing decades.

The Arsacid Persians' political system has been described as feudal. The king, who was required to be an Arsacid, wielded absolute power at the top of the social structure. The only check on his authority was a dual council of nobles and Magi, a special tribe of Zoroastrian priests, that elected each new Arsacid ruler. Below the king, court officials and local administrators, chosen from the Arsacid family or from Persia's seven noble clans, ran the empire's minor kingdoms and larger cities. Although the Arsacids constructed Ctesiphon early on as their main capital, their court remained itinerant for much of its history. Frequent travel allowed kings to supervise administrators in the provinces more closely. But to prevent corruption or rebellion in far-flung regions, Persian monarchs also employed spies, who were often referred to as the king's "eyes" and "ears."

Other than personal troops and retainers, Arsacid kings had no standing army. When war occurred, the kings called on their vassals to supply local contingents of soldiers. Because the rulers relied on their subordinates for troops, gathering a large army could be time-consuming and unreliable. Disgruntled vassals might rally when summoned, but they could just as easily refuse. Worse still, they could—and frequently did—join rebellions against the king. On the other hand, if an Arsacid monarch was popular and had his vassals' support, he could amass a considerable fighting force.

Cavalry units made up the bulk of the Persian Army. Of these, there were two principal types. Cataphracts were the Persians' heavy cavalry. They fought by charging with a lance and were nicknamed *clibanarii* (iron pot-men) because both horse and rider wore armor covering them from head to foot. Persian horse archers, by contrast, were much more famous and feared. They used a powerful composite bow and inspired dread because of a tactic called the Parthian shot. In battle, horsemen would feign a retreat, lure their enemies into a pursuit, and then turn and fire backwards in their saddles to devastating effect.

Like most Mesopotamian cultures, Arsacid Persia's primary economic activity was agriculture. But Persia's strategic position along the famed Silk Road also made the Persians wealthy as traders. They operated as middlemen, facilitating the exchange of slaves, textiles, and spices from the Far East for raw materials, precious metals, and manufactured goods from the Roman Empire. Persian merchants grew rich marking up trade goods flowing in both directions, but the Persian king and aristocracy also profited by levying hefty tolls and taxes.

Nor were the Persians shy about flaunting their wealth. At court, the Persian king sat on a throne made of pure gold. Nobles wore copious amounts of jewelry, and both men and women used cosmetics to improve their appearance. Persian men were typically bearded and styled their hair in elaborate curls. They wore loose-fitting robes, similar to the Asian caftan, but trousers for riding. The aristocracy's favorite pastimes were banqueting and hunting, which the Persians may have done on specially constructed animal preserves.

Arsacid religion was probably some blend of Zoroastrianism and the nomadic (perhaps animistic) rituals. Arsacid kings were, for example, keepers of the eternal flame, and we know that fire worship was the cornerstone of many Zoroastrian rituals. Yet we also know that the Arsacids' successors, the Sassanids, often accused the Arsacids of being heretics to Zoroastrianism. There may be some truth to this, because Arsacid kings were buried first at Nisa and then at Arbela; strict Zoroastrians, in contrast, preferred exposing their dead. However, one should also remember that the Arsacids ruled over a vast multiethnic empire—one that included not just Zoroastrian and nomadic beliefs but also Semitic, Greek, Jewish, and Christian religions. Aspects of these other religions could have easily influenced Arsacid religious practices.

JOHN POIROT

**See also**
Ardashir I; Carrhae, Battle of; Crassus, Marcus Licinius; Roman-Parthian Wars; Roman-Sassanid Wars; Trajan

**References**
Campbell, Brian. "War and Diplomacy: Rome and Parthia, 31 BC-AD 235." In *War and Society in the Roman World*, ed. John Rich and Graham Shipley, 213–240. London: Routledge, 1993.
Colledge, M. A. R. *The Parthians*. New York: Frederick A. Praeger, 1967.
Debevoise, N.C. *A Political History of Parthia*. Chicago: University of Chicago Press, 1938.
Yarshater, E., ed. *The Cambridge History of Iran*, Vol. 3. Cambridge: Cambridge University Press, 1983.

## Passarowitz, Treaty of (July 21, 1718)

The Treaty of Passarowitz, also known as the Treaty of Požarevac, signed between the Ottoman Empire and Habsburg Austria and the Republic of Venice at Požarevac in Ottoman territory (now Serbia) on July 21, 1718, ended the Ottoman-Habsburg War of 1716–1718 and the Ottoman-Venetian wars of 1716–1718.

The Ottoman-Habsburg War of 1716–1718 saw the Ottomans win important victories over the Venetians but suffer defeats at the hands of the Habsburgs, led by Prince Eugene of Savoy. Under the treaty's terms, the Porte agreed to relinquish to the Habsburgs the Banat of Temeswar, most of Serbia, and parts of northern Bosnia and Lesser Walachia (Oltenia). Venice lost its possessions on the Peloponnesus peninsula and on Crete but retained the Ionian Islands and Dalmatia.

ALEXANDER MIKABERIDZE

**See also**
Ottoman-Habsburg Wars; Venetian-Ottoman Wars

**References**
Fleet, Kate, Suraiya Faroqhi, and Reşat Kasaba, eds. *The Cambridge History of Turkey*. 3 vols. Cambridge: Cambridge University Press, 2006–2008.
Hochendlinger, Michael. *Austria's Wars of Emergence: War, State and Society in the Habsburg Monarchy, 1683–1797*. London: Longman, 2003.

## *Patria*, Destruction of (November 25, 1940)

French ship blown up at Haifa, Palestine, on November 25, 1940. Early in November 1940, three ships carrying Jewish immigrants sailed for Palestine from the Romanian port of Tulcea. In effect, the German government saw an opportunity to create difficulties for the British and abetted the departure of the refugees and the ships. On November 1, the *Pacific* arrived at Haifa with some 1,100 illegal Jewish immigrants from Germany and Austria. A few days later, the *Milos* arrived with another 700 immigrants from Czechoslovakia.

The year 1940 was a difficult one for the British, with a number of setbacks in World War II. Germany had defeated France, and Britain was the only major military opponent remaining against the Germans and Italians. There were fears in London that the Axis powers would soon conquer Egypt and take the Suez Canal. In these circumstances and despite the documented persecution of Jews by Germany, London was anxious to placate the Arabs regarding Jewish immigration into Palestine. The German government saw in these circumstances an opportunity to embarrass the British.

Warned in advance of the arrival of the ships, British authorities secured the aging *Patria*, a 12,000-ton French transport. They then transferred the immigrants to it, supposedly for reasons of quarantine. The British then announced that the immigrants would not be admitted to Palestine and would instead be shipped on to Mauritius in the Indian Ocean for the duration of the war, after which a decision would be rendered as to where the immigrants would be sent.

On November 24, 1940, the *Atlantic*, the third ship carrying illegal immigrants, arrived at Haifa. The British then prepared to transfer its passengers to the *Patria* as well, refusing all appeals to the contrary from Jewish representatives. The Zionists in Palestine did all they could to persuade the British to change their minds. A general strike had no impact.

Finally, on November 21 a mine was smuggled aboard the ship by members of the Jewish self-defense organization, Haganah. The plan was to blow a small hole in the ship's hull, forcing the British to disembark the passengers. Unfortunately, when the mine went off at 9:00 a.m. on November 25 as passengers from the *Atlantic* were being transferred to it, the *Patria* sank almost immediately. Some 267 people died, including 50 crew members and British soldiers and policeman. Later the members of Haganah claimed that the *Patria* was in such poor condition at the time that it would have sunk at sea anyway, with far greater loss of life.

Following this incident and ensuing widespread outrage, British authorities decided to make an exception and allow the 1,560 survivors of the *Patria* to enter Palestine, although the number of refugees was to be deducted from subsequent Jewish immigration quotas. Immigrants not yet transferred from the *Atlantic* were not included in the special consideration and were indeed deported to Mauritius on December 9, 1940. After the war they were given the option to return to Palestine, and more than 80 percent chose to do so.

SPENCER C. TUCKER

**See also**
Holocaust; Palestine, British Mandate for

**References**
Chazan, Meir. "The *Patria* Affair: Moderates vs. Activists in Mapai in the 1940s." *Journal of Israeli History* 22, no. 2 (2003): 61–95.
Israeli, R., and M. N. Penkower. *Decision on Palestine Deferred: America, Britain and Wartime Diplomacy, 1939–1945.* New York: Routledge, 2002.
Ofer, S. "The Rescue of European Jewry and Illegal Immigration to Palestine in 1940: Prospects and Reality; Berthold Storfer and the Mossad le'Aliyah Bet." *Modern Judaism* 4, no. 2 (1984): 159–181.
Shepherd, Naomi. *Ploughing Sand: British Rule in Palestine, 1917–1948.* New Brunswick, NJ: Rutgers University Press, 1999.

# Patrona Halil Revolt (September 28, 1730)

An armed uprising in Istanbul (Constantinople) that ended the reign of Sultan Ahmed III (r. 1703–1730). The revolt marked a realignment of forces within the Ottoman government and was the only Ottoman uprising of the 18th century not instigated by the army.

Though support for the centralized government of the Ottoman sultan had traditionally come from the military elite and the ulema (learned Muslim leaders), the reforms that Ahmed had tried to introduce had a French-influenced secular trend that was disturbing to these two groups. The reforms did not succeed in improving the economy, and inflation, taxation, and banditry made life difficult for common people. When the Ottoman military was defeated by the forces of Nadir Shah on Persia in 1729, these strands of discontent all came together in opposition to Ahmed III.

On September 28, 1730, an Albanian sailor (some sources say shopkeeper) named Patrona Halil (also spelled Khalil) led a mob uprising in Istanbul, buoyed by popular anger over the sultan's opulent lifestyle and new taxes imposed as a consequence of the defeat by Persia. The rebels, who included janissaries, lynched the grand vizier and his son-in-law, the commander in chief of the Ottoman Navy. The ulema provided the movement with legitimacy by defining a religious basis for it. The opposition to him was such that Ahmed was forced to abdicate on October 1, succeeded by his nephew Mahmud I. Ahmed died in captivity in 1736.

Mahmud I (r. 1730–1754) was forced to spend the first months of his rule trying to suppress the rebellion and an uprising among the Janissaries that followed in 1731. On November 25, 1730, meanwhile, Halil was lured to Topkapi Palace on the pretext of receiving an imperial honorific and there seized by the sultan's guards and promptly executed.

The Patrona Halil Revolt marked the beginning of an anti-Western, religiously oriented current of opinion in the Ottoman Empire that existed throughout the 18th and 19th centuries alongside the desire for reform based on Western models.

KAREN MEAD AND SPENCER C. TUCKER

**See also**
Nadir Shah; Ottoman-Safavid Wars

**References**
Aksan, Virginia. *Ottoman Wars 1700–1870: An Empire Besieged.* Harlow, UK: Longman, 2007.
Shaw, Stanford J. *History of the Ottoman Empire and Modern Turkey.* 2 vols. New York: Cambridge University Press, 1977.

# PEACE FOR GALILEE, Operation
*See* Lebanon-Israeli War

# Peel Commission (August 1936– July 7, 1937)

Commission to study the British-held mandate in Palestine. In August 1936 the British government appointed a Royal Commission of Inquiry headed by Lord Robert Peel to examine the effectiveness of the mandate system and to make proposals concerning future British policy in Palestine. Peel was the former secretary of state for British-held India. Members of the Royal Commission arrived in Jerusalem on November 11, 1936. While all of the committee's members were experienced in foreign affairs, none had any particular connection to either the Arab cause or the Jewish cause.

The Peel Commission, as it came to be called, was established at a time of increasing violence in Palestine. Indeed, serious clashes between Arabs and Jews broke out in 1936 and were to last three years. The commission was charged with determining the cause of the unrest and judging the merit of grievances on both sides. Chaim Weizmann gave a memorable speech on behalf of the Zionist cause. However, the mufti of Jerusalem, Haj Amin al-Husseini, refused to testify in front of the commission. Instead, he demanded full cessation of Jewish immigration into Palestine. Although the Arabs continued to boycott the commission officially, there was a sense of urgency to respond to Weizmann's speech. The former mayor of Jerusalem, Raghib Bey al-Nashashibi, was thus sent to explain the Arab perspective through unofficial channels.

The commission returned to Britain on January 18, 1937, and published its report on July 7, 1937. The Peel Commission attributed the underlying cause of the Arab Revolt of 1936–1939 to the Arabs' desire for independence and their hatred and fear of the establishment of a Jewish homeland in Palestine. Therefore, the commission recommended freezing Jewish immigration to Palestine at 12,000 people per year for five years. It also urged that a plan be developed for formal partition of the territory.

With regard to partition, the commission recommended that the mandate be eventually abolished except for a corridor surrounding Jerusalem and stretching to the Mediterranean coast just south of Jaffa and that the land under its authority be apportioned between an Arab and an Israeli state. The Jewish side was to receive a territorially smaller portion in the midwest and the north, from Mount Carmel to south of Be'er Tuvia as well as the Jezreel Valley and the Galilee, while the Arab state was to receive territory in the south and mideast, which included Judaea, Samaria, and the Negev Desert.

The Peel Commission recommended that until the establishment of the two states, Jews should be prohibited from purchasing land in the area allocated to the Arab state. To overcome demarcation problems, the commissioners proposed that land exchanges be carried out concurrently with the transfer of population from one area to the other. Demarcation of the precise borders of the two states would be entrusted to a specialized partition committee.

These recommendations marked the beginning of the end of British rule in Palestine. The British government accepted the recommendations of the Peel Commission regarding the partition of Palestine, and Parliament announced its endorsement of the commission's findings. Among Jews, bitter disagreements erupted between supporters and opponents of the partition proposal, while the Arabs rejected it outright. Ultimately, the plan was shelved. A new commission, the Woodhead Commission, was subsequently established to determine borders for the proposed states.

MOSHE TERDIMAN

**See also**

Arab Nationalism; Balfour Declaration; Husseini, Haj Amin al-; Palestine, British Mandate for; Zionism

**References**

Ayaad, Abdelaziz A. *Arab Nationalism and the Palestinians, 1850–1939.* Jerusalem: Passia, 1999.

Cohen, Aharon. *Israel and the Arab World.* New York: Funk and Wagnalls, 1970.

*Palestine Royal Commission Report Presented by the Secretary of State for the Colonies to Parliament by Command of His Majesty, July 1937.* London: HMSO, 1937.

Swedenburg, Ted. *Memories of Revolt: The 1936–1939 Rebellion and the Palestinian National Past.* Minneapolis: University of Minnesota Press, 1995.

## Pelagius of Albano (ca. 1165–1230)

Cardinal and papal legate during the Fifth Crusade (1217–1221). Pelagius was born Pelagio Galvani around 1165 at Gusendos, León. He was a cardinal and canon lawyer in the Catholic Church and later a leader of the Fifth Crusade. Little is known of his earlier life, although he claimed to have been a Benedictine monk. Pope Innocent III created him cardinal-deacon of St. Lucia in Septasolio (1206/1207–1211), cardinal-priest of St. Cecilia (1211–1213), and cardinal-bishop of Albano (1213–1230). By 1213, Pelagius's skill as a papal auditor earned him the unenviable task of reforming Latin and native ecclesiastics in the recently established Latin Empire of Constantinople while facilitating the union of the Roman and Greek Orthodox Churches. Although nominated to the Latin patriarchate of Antioch, Pelagius returned to Italy by 1215 and was appointed legate for Pope Innocent III's long-planned crusade to the Holy Land. As legate, Pelagius was to combine the reform of the church in Outremer with serving as peacekeeper and disciplinarian for the crusading army. Delayed by affairs in Cyprus, he joined the crusading army then besieging the port of Damietta in Egypt in 1218.

As head of the papally subsidized Roman fleet and dispenser of the crusading funds forwarded from Europe, Pelagius was initially only one of many spiritual and military leaders in the army, but he soon assumed a decisive leadership role during ensuing crises. With the support of other clergymen, he promulgated laws governing the army and wielded his legatine powers of excommunication and ability to grant indulgences to hold the army together in anticipation of the advent of the crusade's presumed leader, Holy Roman emperor and king of Sicily Frederick II. Because they expected reinforcements, Pelagius and other parties rejected the truces offered by Ayyubid sultan of Egypt al-Kamil both before and after the capture of Damietta.

In 1221 after the departure of John of Brienne, king of Jerusalem, and the arrival of Frederick II's representative, Duke Ludwig I of Bavaria, Pelagius urged the army to advance. He supported his arguments partly with prophecies circulating in the crusader camp that a Christian King David and a Western emperor (glossed as Frederick II) would take Cairo in the near future. Although some contemporary chroniclers and poets blamed the army's subsequent defeat and surrender to al-Kamil following Pelagius's inept strategy, the army's variable supply of funding and men and Frederick II's delayed participation sealed the crusade's disastrous denouement.

Immediately after his release by al-Kamil, Pelagius attempted to resolve the contested succession to the principality of Antioch, which threatened to further weaken the Frankish states in Outremer. He also strove to redress conflicts between the Latin and Greek clergy in Cyprus, which were similar to those he had previously encountered in the empire of Constantinople. He later became involved in the planning of Frederick II's crusade at the councils of Ferentino (1223) and San Germano (1225). After Pope Gregory IX excommunicated Frederick for failing to depart on the crusade in 1227, the pope took advantage of the emperor's absence to dispatch Pelagius and the legate Pandulf to Sicily with a papal army in support of John of Brienne's claim to the western emperorship, which John abandoned after his election as Latin emperor of Constantinople. After Frederick II's victorious return to Europe, Pelagius participated in negotiations between the emperor and Gregory IX before his death at Monte Cassino on January 30, 1230.

JESSALYNN BIRD

**See also**
Crusades in the Holy Land, Christian; Frederick II, Holy Roman Emperor; Outremer

**References**
Donovan, Joseph P. *Pelagius and the Fifth Crusade.* Philadelphia: University of Pennsylvania Press, 1950.
Maleczek, Werner. *Papst und Kardinalskolleg von 1191 bis 1216: Die Kardinäle unter Coelestin III. und Innocenz III.* Vienna: Verlag der Österreichischen Akademie der Wissenschaften, 1984.
Powell, James M. *Anatomy of a Crusade, 1213–1221.* Philadelphia: University of Pennsylvania Press, 1986.

# Pelekanon, Battle of (June 10–11, 1329)

Battle fought near Nicomedia, Bithynia (modern-day Maltepe, Turkey), in northeastern Anatolia during June 10–11, 1329, between forces of the Byzantine Empire led by Emperor Andronicus II and John Cantacuzene and an Ottoman Beylik army led by Bey Orhan I. The battle was the first between a Byzantine emperor and an Ottoman bey.

When Andronicus II ascended the Byzantine throne in 1328, the once mighty Byzantine Empire had shrunk to only a small portion of its greatest extent. Most of Anatolia had already been lost to the Ottomans, who were then laying siege to the important Byzantine cities of Nicomedia and Nicaea, both in northwestern Asia Minor. Andronicus assembled an expeditionary force of some 4,000 men with the goal of raising the sieges of these two cities and restoring the southern Byzantine border. Informed of the Byzantine movements, Orhan I set up camp with an army of some 8,000 men in the hills at Pelekanon on the road to Nicomedia in order to block Andronicus's approach to that besieged city.

On June 10, Orland I dispatched a small force of some 10,000 cavalry against the Byzantines in an effort to lure them forward against his prepared positions. The Byzantines refused to take the bait, however. They drove off the Ottoman cavalry but then halted. Additional indecisive combat occurred later that day, with the Byzantines preparing to withdraw. Aggressive Turkish action led to a pitched battle, however. Both Andronicus and Cantacuzene sustained slight wounds in the fighting, but a false report that the emperor had been slain created panic in the Byzantine forces, and the ensuing retreat became a rout. The Byzantines suffered heavy casualties before the survivors were able to escape to Constantinople by water.

Andronicus made no further effort to relieve the two besieged cities, which then fell to the Ottomans, Nicaea in 1331 and Nicomedia in 1337. The psychological implications of the Byzantine defeat in the Battle of Pelekanon were immense, and never again did the Byzantines attempt to restore their control over territory in Asia.

SPENCER C. TUCKER

**See also**
Byzantine Empire; Byzantine Empire Civil War; Ottoman Empire

**References**
Bartusis, Mark C. *The Late Byzantine Army: Arms and Society, 1204–1453.* Philadelphia: University of Pennsylvania Press, 1997.
Mango, Cyril, ed. *The Oxford History of Byzantium.* New York: Oxford University Press, 2002.

Nicol, Donald M. *The Last Centuries of Byzantium, 1261–1453.* 2nd ed. New York: Cambridge University Press, 1993.
Norwich, John Julius. *Byzantium: The Decline and Fall,* Vol. 3. New York: Knopf, 1996.

## Pelusium, Battle of (525 BCE)

The first major battle fought between the ancient Egyptians and the Achaemenid Empire (First Persian Empire). Fought in 525 BCE at Pelusium, an important city on the eastern stretches of the Nile Delta, the battle was one of the most decisive on Egyptian soil, as it gave Persian king Cambyses II control of Egypt.

The generally accepted source for the battle is the Greek historian Herodotus. He states that the conflict was sparked by deteriorating relations between Persian king Cambyses II (r. 529–522) and Egyptian pharaoh Amasis II (r. 570–526). Herodotus reports that Cambyses requested of Amasis an Egyptian physician, probably an ophthalmologist, and that Amasis agreed. The person selected, however, resented this imposition and out of spite persuaded Cambyses to ask the pharaoh for his daughter in marriage in the full knowledge that this would probably not be acceptable to Amasis. Amasis was indeed unwilling to see his daughter marry the king of Persia but also did not want to spark a war, so he sent Nitetis, daughter of Apries, the previous pharaoh, whom Amasis had defeated and killed. Cambyses discovered the ruse and, infuriated, vowed to avenge the insult. Cambyses was apparently abetted and assisted in the Persian king's plan to invade Egypt by one Phanes of Halicarnassus, who had been a close adviser to Amasis but had broken with the pharaoh and managed to escape to Persia, where he then became a close adviser to Cambyses and helped convince him to embark on the conquest of Egypt. Herodotus relates that Psamtik was so enraged by the defection of Phanes of Halicarnassus that he ordered his sons seized and cut them one by one and drained their blood, mixing it with wine, which he himself drank and ordered his advisers to do the same.

Although he already controlled the Neo-Babylonian Empire and northern Arabia, Cambyses was able to secure a pledge of safe passage for his army from the local ruler for the shorter march route along the road from Gaza across the Sinai to Pelusium. Gaza, however, resisted the Persian invasion but was taken following a lengthy siege.

Amasis had died in 526, six months before Cambyses reached Egypt, and his son Psamtik III (Psammenitus) became pharaoh. He assembled the Egyptian forces and placed his army along the fork of the Red Sea and the river Nile. Meanwhile, Egyptian hopes of an alliance with the Greeks against the Persians evaporated, with the tyrant Polycrates of Samos, who possessed a large fleet, siding with the Persians and supplying them with 40 triremes. Cyprus, a traditional Egyptian ally, also refused support. Psamtik, who had scant military experience, was thus entirely dependent on his own resources.

The decisive battle occurred at Pelusium near present-day Port Said. We know nothing of the battle. Apparently it was over quickly, ending in an Egyptian rout. One source gives the Egyptian losses as 50,000 killed, with the Persians losing only 7,000. Psamtik and his men then fled to the port city of Memphis.

Polyaenus, a retired Macedonian general turned historian, relates the oft-repeated story that Cambyses captured Pelusium by a ruse. Knowing that the Egyptians held cats sacred and would not injure them on any account, Cambyses had his men paint cats on their shields and drive cats and other animals sacred to the Egyptians in front of them during the attack, and the Egyptians did not dare to shoot their arrows for fear of wounding the animals. After the battle, Cambyses then had his men hurl the cats at the departing Egyptians.

Herodotus relates that Cambyses sent a ship with a herald to Memphis in an effort to convince the Egyptians to surrender, but the Egyptians attacked it and killed all those aboard. Cambyses then laid siege to Memphis and took its surrender at a cost of only some 200 Persian dead for 2,000 Egyptians. Psamtik was captured after the fall of Memphis and allowed to live under Persian control but was subsequently executed after attempting a revolt against the Persians. Meanwhile, Egypt passed under Persian control with Cambyses as its pharaoh, beginning the Twenty-Seventh Dynasty. Egypt remained a Persian possession for nearly two centuries until the arrival of Alexander III of Macedon (the Great) in 332 BCE.

Spencer C. Tucker

**See also**
Achaemenid Empire; Cambyses II; Egypt, Ancient

**References**
Herodotus. *The Histories.* Suffolk, UK: Penguin Books, 1975.
Ruzicka, Stephen. *Trouble in the West: Egypt and the Persian Empire, 525–332 BC.* New York: Oxford University Press, 2012.

## Perdiccas (365–321 BCE)

Macedonian general who fought with Alexander III the Great during the latter's invasion of Persia and then was one of the Diadochi (successors) who fought to control Alexander's empire after his death in 323. Born in 365 in the Macedonian province of Orestis and possibly of royal descent, Perdiccas occupied a prominent position in Alexander the Great's court, including serving as a bodyguard. Perdiccas was a member of the Royal Hypaspists at the time of Macedonian king Philip II's assassination in 336 and was among those who pursued and killed his murderer. In many sources Perdiccas is often linked to events that highlight the lack of discipline of his soldiers, but much of this negativity likely stemmed from Ptolemy I Soter's history, for he and Perdiccas became serious rivals after Alexander's death.

Following the death of Hephaestion in 324, Perdiccas effectively became Alexander's second-in-command. Perdiccas was one of the most influential marshals when Alexander died and was said to have been given the king's signet ring just before his death. Perdiccas supported the right of Alexander's unborn child for the kingship and was poised to seize sole regency before Philip III Arrhidaeus was put forward as another candidate.

A compromise followed that limited Perdiccas's power, although he remained *chiliarch*. Perdiccas then set about eliminating rivals almost immediately, executing another general, Meleager, and having 300 of his supporters crushed to death by elephants. Perdiccas also had Alexander's wife Stateira and her sister murdered (so they could not be used as political pawns), and he annulled Alexander's last plans: to cancel Craterus's instructions to assume the regency of Macedonia.

Seeking a strong alliance, Perdiccas married Antipater's daughter Nicaea but soon aimed higher and secretly courted Alexander's sister Cleopatra as well. Perdiccas was successful in campaigns to conquer Cappadocia with Eumenes of Cardia, which made the army well disposed toward Perdiccas for a time.

In 321 Perdiccas faced a confrontation with Antipater, Craterus, and Antigonus I Monophthalmus, who feared his growing power, but Perdiccas turned his attentions instead to Egypt. He had arranged for Alexander's body to be transported to Macedonia in a magnificent funeral procession, through which Perdiccas hoped to be seen as Alexander's legitimate heir. Ptolemy intervened, however, and had the funeral procession and body stolen and brought to Egypt. This prompted Perdiccas to attempt to eliminate Ptolemy once and for all; however, the campaign was a disaster. In attempting to reach an island opposite Memphis, Perdiccas lost at least 2,000 men to the Nile (and to the crocodiles). Unwilling to suffer any longer under Perdiccas's leadership,

his prominent generals, including Seleucus I Nicator and Peithon, stole into his tent and murdered him in the night.

CHARLOTTE M. R. DUNN

**See also**

Alexander III the Great; Antigonus I Monophthalmus; Diadochi, Wars of the; Eumenes of Cardia; Ptolemy I Soter; Seleucus I Nicator

**References**

Austin, Michel. *The Hellenistic World from Alexander to the Roman Conquest.* 2nd ed. Cambridge: Cambridge University Press, 2006.

Heckel, Waldemar. *The Marshals of Alexander's Empire.* New York: Routledge, 1992.

Waterfield, Robin. *Dividing the Spoils: The War for Alexander the Great's Empire.* New York: Oxford University Press. 2011.

## Pergamum

Name of a city and kingdom situated in western Asia Minor. The city of Pergamum (modern-day Bergama in Izmir Province, Turkey) was situated on a towering hill on the north side of the broad Caicus Valley in Mysia in western Anatolia. It is first mentioned in historical sources by the Greek general and historian Xenophon, who says that the town surrendered voluntarily to Thibron the Spartan in 399, but the city only rose to prominence in the Hellenistic period, when it became the capital of the Attalid kingdom of Pergamum. After the death of Attalus III of Pergamum in 133, the city and kingdom of Pergamum briefly became the capital of the Roman province of Asia.

The Macedonian general and Diadochi (meaning "successors," those generals of Alexander the Great who fought after his death to control the vast empire he had conquered) Lysimachus chose Pergamum as a secure treasury and appointed Philetaerus as the garrison commander. However, Philetaerus switched his allegiance to another Diadochi, Seleucus I Nicator, in 282, just before the downfall of his former master.

At first Pergamum was nominally under Seleucid rule, but following his victories over the Galatians in the 230s, Attalus I of Pergamum declared himself king, thereafter pursuing a vigorous policy of resistance to Seleucid rule in Asia Minor. Pergamum was to become the heart of the Attalid kingdom that came to control much of Asia Minor. Attalus I of Pergamum allied himself with Rome against Philip V of Macedon during both the First and Second Macedonian Wars.

In 201 Philip V of Macedon besieged Pergamum and, perhaps out of frustration at his inability to take such a

## Asia Minor in 189 BCE

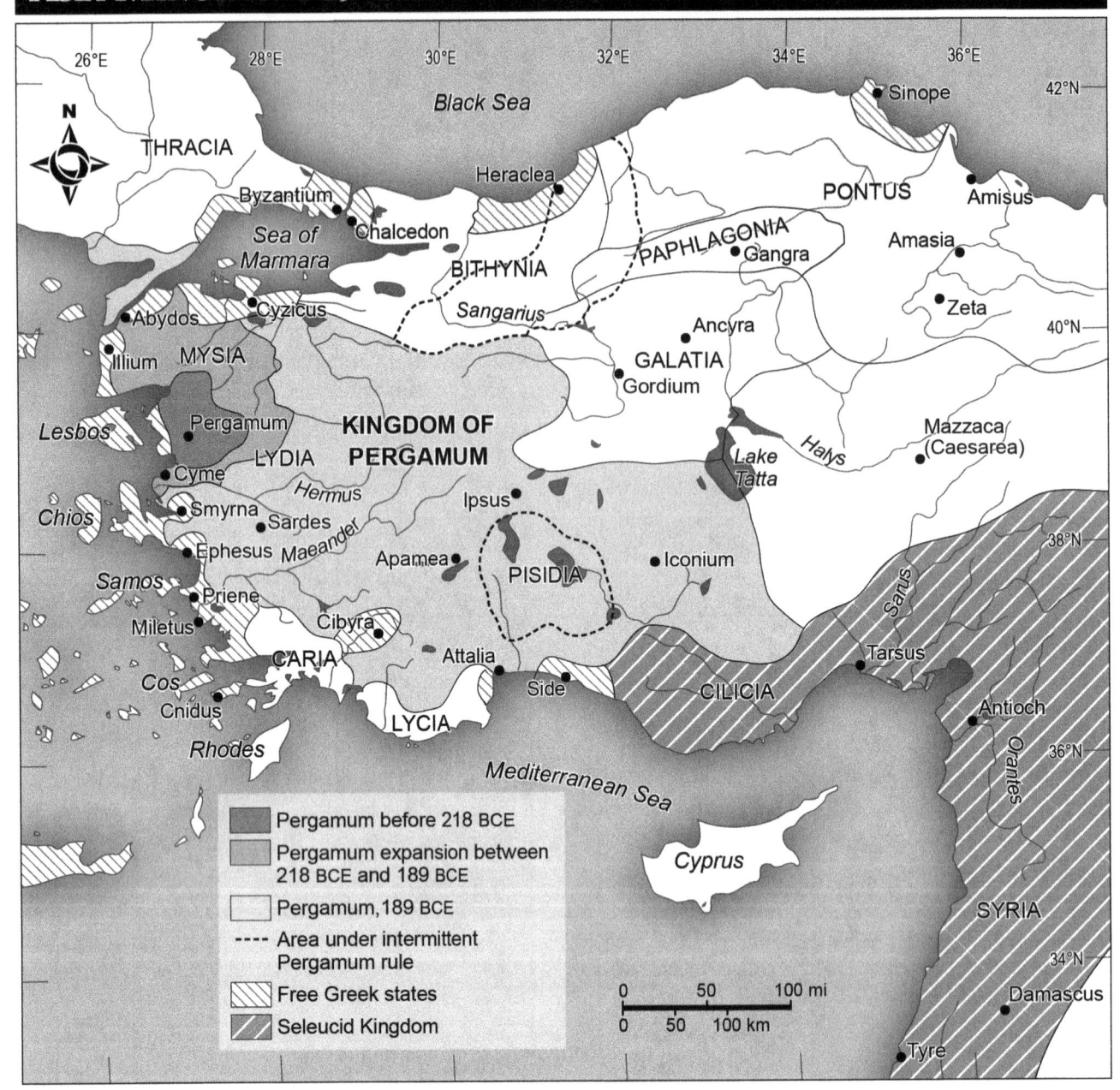

well-fortified and well-defended city, resorted to impiously laying waste to the religious sanctuaries of the lower city. Pergamum was again besieged unsuccessfully in 192–191 by Seleucus, the son of Antiochus III the Great. Under Eumenes II of Pergamum, the city and kingdom of Pergamum once again allied to Rome against Perseus during the Third Macedonian War. Between 156 and 154 Prusias II of Bithynia invaded Pergamene territory and, like Philip V of Macedon before him, resorted to despoiling the sacred places, including the Nicephorium, without making any real attempt to take the city itself.

Pergamum was an excellent example of well thought-out town planning, evolving and expanding over time. The palace and citadel occupied the top of the hill, while other buildings were built in terraces on the slopes of the hill including a large and splendid theater. The citadel at Pergamum contained arsenals and barracks; the city also boasted a magnificent library, regarded as being second only to the Great Library of Alexandria, and a museum. The city housed the Great Altar of Zeus and the temple to Athena Nicephorus and was also famous for its Sanctuary of Asclepius. At the height of its power, Pergamum was one of the most beautiful, important, wealthy, and powerful of the cities of the Hellenistic World.

DAVID HARTHEN

**See also**
Antiochus Hierax; Diadochi, Wars of the; Eumenes I of Pergamum; Eumenes II of Pergamum; Lysimachus; Seleucus I Nicator; Xenophon

**References**
Evans, Richard. *A History of Pergamum: Beyond Hellenistic Kingship.* London: Bloomsbury Publishing, 2012.
Hansen, Esther V. *The Attalids of Pergamon.* Ithaca, NY: Cornell University Press, 1971.

# Persia, Arab Conquest of (642–671)

The Arab conquest of Persia began a few years after the Arab Muslim victory at Qadisiyya (636) and the subjugation of Iraq. In fact, Caliph Umar (Omar) had forbidden his commanders to cross the Zagros Mountains to attack the Persians after defeating them at Jalula. He intended that these mountains would be the natural boundary between the Persian and Arab domains. However, this was not a compromise that Sassanid shah Yazdagird III (r. 632–651) was ready to make, and he issued a call to arms and gathered his forces at Nihawand with the intention of reconquering Iraq.

Umar dispatched an army under Numan ibn Amr ibn Muqarrin to face the Sassanids and ordered the governors of Basra and Kufa to send troops to support him. The Muslim army of some 30,000 men found a numerically superior Persian force in a strong defensive position at Nihawand in 642. The Sassanid soldiers were protected by trenches and spiked obstacles that were meant to arrest any advance by the Arab cavalry.

Despite his forces being better equipped and more organized and experienced than those Arabs who fought at Qadisiyya a few years earlier, Numan was unable to break through the Persian defenses. After two days of futile attacks, the Arabs feigned a retreat to lure the Persians into the open. The ruse was successful. Sensing victory, the Persians abandoned their strong defenses to pursue the Arabs, who then wheeled about and faced the Persians on open ground. The Arabs inflicted a major defeat on Yazdagird III's army despite its numerical superiority but themselves suffered heavy losses, including Numan. The Battle of Nihavand is known to the Arabs as "the victory of victories," for although Shah Yazdagird III escaped, the Sassanids were never able to field an army against the Arabs again.

Following Nihawand, the Arabs set out to conquer Persia. However, unlike the conquest of Syria, Egypt, and Iraq, this endeavor was a long and slow process, extending over three decades. Sassanian Persia was rather decentralized, and its different regions were ruled by local princes and dynasties that put up stiff resistance to the Arab advance.

The Arab armies conquered Persia region by region, sometimes allying with one Iranian prince against another. Nihawand, Rayy, Qum, Ardabil, Hamadan, Istakhr, Merv, and other major centers all fell to the advancing Arabs as they systematically conquered all of Persia. Khurasan was the last province to fall and was fully pacified in 671. However, despite the Arab military successes, rebellions against caliphal rule flared up frequently even as late as the middle Abbasid period.

ADAM ALI

**See also**
Iran; Qadisiyya, Battle of; Sassanid Empire; Umayyad Caliphate

**References**
Frye, Richard N. *The Golden Age of Persia: The Arabs in the East.* London: Weidenfeld and Nicolson, 1975.
Jandora, John W. *The March from Medina: A Revisionist Study of the Arab Conquests.* Clifton, NJ: Kingston, 1990.
Zarinkub, Abd al-Husain. "The Arab Conquest of Iran and Its Aftermath." In *The Cambridge History of Iran,* Vol. 4, ed. R. N. Frye. Cambridge: Cambridge University Press, 1975.

# Persia, 18th-Century Wars of Succession

A series of power struggles shook Persia between 1725 and 1796. The first began in the wake of the 1722 invasion of the Afghan tribes that resulted in the collapse of the Safavid dynasty; Shah Sultan Husain abdicated that same year and died in 1726. This marked the twilight of the Safavid power but also served as a launching pad for Afshar Turkmen commander Nadir Khan.

In the ensuing political chaos Nadir chose to side with Tahmasp Mirza, the surviving heir to the Safavid throne. Tahmasp chose him as his principal military commander and gave him the title Tahmasp Quli Khan (Servant of Tahmasp). Throughout the 1720s Nadir gained a series of major victories, first in 1725–1726 crushing Malek Mahmud Sistani, who claimed the crown, and then defeating the Abdali Afghans near Herat in May 1729 and the Gilzi (Ghilzais) Afghans at Mihmandust and Murchakhur in the fall of 1729. Nadir expelled the Afghans from the former Safavid capital of Isfahan, where Tahmasp was installed as a shah but with actual authority in the hands of Nadir. In 1730 Nadir announced the Safavid restoration to the Ottomans, but just two years later he deposed Tahmasp in favor of an infant son, who himself was deposed in 1736 when Nadir Khan became Nadir Shah.

During the next decade Nadir Shah conducted numerous campaigns that revived the Persian Empire, which stretched from India to Caucasus. Despite his military successes, Nadir came to be regarded as a cruel and capricious tyrant and faced a number of internal revolts in 1746. A group of Afshar and Qajar officers organized a conspiracy against Nadir and assassinated him in June 1747.

Nair's death plunged Iran into another civil war. The empire that Nadir had forged with his sword disintegrated as soon he breathed his last, for his military commanders immediately scrambled for power. One of them, Karim Khan of the Zand tribe who exerted influence in southern Iran, entered into an alliance with Ali Mardan Khan, leader of the Bakhtiari tribe, who controlled central Iran. The two men seized Isfahan in 1757 and restored Shah Ismail III, the grandson of the last Safavid shah, to the throne, although they retained real power in their own hands. After Ali Mardan broke the alliance, Karim Khan had him killed and took control of southern and central Persia. He gradually came to control western Iran, defeating the rival Azad Khan near Qazvin and extending his authority to Azerbaijan. In early 1750s, Karim Khan defeated the rival Qajar tribesmen and limited their authority to Mazanderan.

By the early 1770s, Karim Khan controlled all of Persia (except for Khurasan, where he tolerated the rule of the blind Shah Rukh, Nadir Shah's grandson). Karim Khan never claimed the title of shah, instead maintaining the powerless Shah Ismail III, grandson of the last Safavid shah, on the throne and himself ruling as *vakil* (deputy, regent). His pragmatic and commonsense policies restored peace in his realm, reorganized the fiscal system, promoted agriculture and commerce, and presided over a building boom, particularly in his capital of Shiraz.

Karim Khan's death in 1779 brought another period of anarchy for Persia as a power struggle ensued among his successors until 1789, when Lutf Ali became the dominant political figure. Yet, Lutf Ali was not secure in his authority and faced a challenge from rival Qajar tribesmen whom Karim Khan had managed to control. The Qajars were led by Agha Muhammad Khan, who besides his political ambitions had a personal score to settle with the Zand. In 1759 Agha Muhammad's father had lost control of western Iran to Karim Khan Zand, and Agha Muhammad was captured, castrated, and kept at the Zand court in Shiraz for 16 years. Although well treated, he was nonetheless a prisoner.

In 1779 upon Karim Khan's death, Agha Muhammad escaped and gradually succeeded in establishing his authority in Iran's northern provinces. In 1782–1784 he conducted a successful campaign against Ali-Morad Khan Zand, one of the claimants of the Zand throne, becoming undisputed master of the northern half of Persia. He moved his capital to Tehran, where he was enthroned (but not crowned) by 1789, laying the foundation for the Qajar dynasty.

During 1790–1794, Agha Muhammad continued his struggle against other pretenders. Although his forces suffered repeated defeats at the hand of Lotf Ali Khan, Agha Muhammad eventually triumphed over the Zands, sacking their last refuge in Kerman. There all males were either killed or blinded, and as many as 20,000 women and children were enslaved.

Agha Muhammad now controlled most of Persia and sought to reclaim the former Safavid territories as well. He first turned to the Caucasus, where the Georgian kingdom of Kartli-Kakheti, once a Safavid tributary, established an alliance with Russia against Persia and the Ottoman Empire. Agha Muhammad demanded Georgian recognition of his sovereignty and upon being rejected invaded southern Caucasia in 1796. The Georgian Army, heavily outnumbered, was defeated at Krtsanisi in September 1795, and the Georgian capital city of Tiflis (Tbilisi) was razed.

After capturing Erivan, Agha Muhammad crowned himself as the shah of Iran in March 1796, girding himself with a sword that had belonged to Safavid Shah Ismail.

Alexander Mikaberidze

### See also
Agha Muhammad Khan Qajar; Gulnabad, Battle of; Isfahan, Siege of; Karim Khan Zand, Muhammad; Nadir Shah

### References
Axworthy, Michael. *A History of Iran: Empire of the Mind*. New York: Basic Books, 2008.
Axworthy, Michael. *Nader Shah: From Tribal Warrior to Conquering Tyrant*. New York: I. B. Tauris, 2006.
Farmanfarmaian, Roxane. *War and Peace in Qajar Persia: Implications Past and Present*. New York: Routledge, 2008.
Perry, John R. *Karim Khan Zand*. Oxford, UK: Oneworld, 2006.

# Persian (Achaemenid) Empire
*See* Achaemenid Empire

## Persian Cossack Brigade

A unit in the late 19th-century Perisan Army that can best be explained as a result of the confluence of the "Great Game" with the moribund Qajar dynasty. The Berigad-e qazzaq, or Cossack Brigade, was operational between 1879 and 1921. It contained Persian troopers and, until 1920, Russian officers. Along with two other foreign-led units, the South Persia Rifles and Gendarmerie, it was one of the most effective units in the Qajar military.

Naser al-Din Shah (1848–1896), attempting to modernize his army, hired French, Austrian, Italian, and Russian advisory teams. Russia, long in competition with Great Britain for domination of Central Asia, saw such an effort as beneficial for promoting its influence in Persia. During the 30 years of the brigade, upwards of 120 Russian officers and noncommissioned officers served in it as leaders and technical advisers. Up to the last year of its existence, the Cossack Brigade always served two masters: the shah and the tsar, with the tsar having the final word.

By 1900, the brigade numbered 2,000 men; two years later it was 8,000 men. Involved in minor military expeditions until the Constitutional Revolution (1906–1911), it then joined reactionary forces to bombard the Majles (parliament) building in Tehran on June 23, 1908. This action killed hundreds of people and permanently blackened the unit's image with Persian liberals.

The brigade survived, however, and even expanded to division size during World War I. Although the 1917 revolutions in Russia brought an end to tsarist domination in Persia, Russia continued to direct the Cossack Brigade until 1920. Completely Persianized that year, the brigade fell under the influence of Allied forces then in Persia.

On January 14, 1921, British general Edmund Ironside, then commanding the Allied force in Persia, chose Reza Khan, commander of the Tabriz Battalion, to lead the 3,000–4,000-man Cossack Brigade as a brigadier general and the first Persian so selected. The next month, supported by the British, he marched with the brigade on Tehran, and on February 21 he seized control of the government in a largely bloodless coup d'état. The Persian Brigade subsequently furnished a number of leaders for the future Reza Shah's military.

JOHN P. DUNN AND SPENCER C. TUCKER

### See also
Iran; Reza Shah Pahlavi

### References
Cronin, Stephanie. *The Army and the Creation of the Pahlavi State in Iran, 1910–1926.* London: Tauris Academic Studies, 1997.

Farmanfarmaian, Roxane, ed. *War and Peace in Qajar Persia: Implications Past and Present.* London: Routledge, 2008.

Kazemzadeh, F. "The Origin and Early Development of the Persian Cossack Brigade." *American Slavic and East European Review* 15 (1956): 351–363.

Rabi, Uzi, and Ter-Oganov, Nugzar. "The Russian Military Mission and the Birth of the Persian Cossack Brigade: 1879–1894." *Iranian Studies* 42, no. 3 (2009): 445–463.

## Persian Front, World War I

A secondary fighting front during World War I, Persia was nonetheless of great strategic importance. A vast empire bordering most of the focal points of Great Power rivalry in Central and South Asia yet stricken with an utterly weak central government and persistent feudal and tribal structures, Persia (present-day Iran) represented a power vacuum that almost by default became a battleground for the Great Powers in the war. Persia was extremely important to both sides because of its strategic location and because of recently developed British-controlled oil fields. Vulnerable to foreign intervention, it was ruled by the weak and vacillating 17-year-old Ahmad Shah. His minuscule military consisted largely of the 8,000-man Cossack Brigade commanded by Russian officers and a Swedish gendarmerie of 7,000 men led by Swedish officers who favored the German side.

Supposedly, foreign troops entered Persia during the war to uphold the shah's authority. In reality, British troops entered southern Persia to protect the Anglo-Persian oil installations around Abadan and keep open the sea route through the Persian Gulf. Western Persia became a convenient extension of the Anglo-Ottoman front in Mesopotamia and the Russo-Ottoman front in the Caucasus. In central Persia, British, Russian, Ottoman, and German forces and missions battled for dominance over what little central power the monarchy possessed; in eastern Persia, Britain tried to shield its Indian empire from German and later Russian interference. In 1918 northern Persia became the springboard for British intervention in the Russian Civil War (1918–1922).

The Ottoman Empire was not the only power that hoped to take Persian territory. Minister of War Enver Pasha was pursuing his fantastic Pan-Turkic schemes when he ordered the Van Jandarma (paramilitary police) Division into Persia in December 1914, simultaneously with the Caucasian offensive of the Third Army. In spite of some success in bringing local tribes on their side, the Ottoman invaders were unable to secure a permanent foothold in Persia. In the spring of 1915, Russian forces drove them back. Late in 1915 Russia reinforced its forces, commanded by General Nikolai N. Baratoff.

That December the Russians advanced on Hamadan, Tehran, and Qum, driving the Ottomans back farther and bringing most of northwestern Persia under Russian control. Seesaw action continued through the winter of 1915–1916, with inconclusive engagements between Turkish, Russian, and Persian tribal forces in which little ground actually changed hands. On February 25, 1916, Baratoff took Kermanshah.

In the spring of 1916 in order to support the Russian defense in the Caucasus, Baratoff received orders to move on Khaniqin. His advance, however, collided with a renewed Ottoman effort in Persia. Ali Insan Pasha's Ottoman XIII Corps of three crack infantry divisions totaling 25,000 men hit the scattered Russians and drove them back. On June 26 the Ottomans were in Karind, and on July 2 they reached Kermanshah.

Operating at the extreme end of a fragile supply line through hostile country, Baratoff had no real hope of stopping the Ottoman thrust. The Allies considered a diversionary attack on the Ottoman flank by the British Expeditionary Force in Iraq, but this did not materialize. On August 9, Ali Insan took Hamadan. Realizing that he had little chance of permanently holding vast stretches of territory deep in Persia with his small force, he advanced no farther. The Russians remained firmly entrenched on the mountain passes just beyond Hamadan.

A lull occurred in Persia during the winter of 1916–1917. In the spring the Ottoman XIII Corps was withdrawn from Persia to help fend off the British advance in Mesopotamia. Baratoff followed, and on March 31, 1917, he retook Qasr-i-Shirin. The Ottoman invasion of Persia was over.

In central and southern Persia, the first two years of the war saw German influence increasing. German diplomatic personnel succeeded in winning over local tribes to oppose the British and Russians, and the Germans even managed to incite revolts in southern Persia. The Germans also sent a military mission to Tehran to train Persian troops under German leadership, and German expeditions traversed the country toward Afghanistan, hoping to win Emir Habib Allah of Afghanistan to their side and thus exert pressure on British India. If the British overstated the case in their claim that Persia was virtually a German colony in 1915–1916, it was nevertheless obvious that upholding British influence there would require additional resources.

The British response was multifaceted. Britain asked its Russian allies to bring pressure to bear on the central government by advancing on Tehran. The British also reinforced with units of the Indian Army their position in the Persian Gulf and in southern Persia, and in Fars and Kerman the British raised an indigenous force under their control. Known as the South Persian Rifles, the force later expanded to two brigades of more than 6,000 men. Finally, in the vast expanses of eastern Persia, the British established a military cordon to prevent German incursions into Afghanistan.

In southeastern Persia, the British maintained throughout the war the so-called Seistan Force, later styled the East Persian Cordon Field Force. It consisted of several Indian squadrons and companies and some 100 indigenous troops. British forces in southern and eastern Persia spent the rest of the war upholding British influence and quelling tribal unrest in continuous small wars.

In northeastern Persia the Russians controlled vast expanses bordering their Central Asian provinces. In 1916 after the Russian advance in northwestern Persia, the Germans found themselves cut off from their lines of communications.

The Russian Revolutions of March and November 1917 dramatically changed the military situation in Persia. Internal unrest sapped Baratoff's force and loosened the Russian hold on northwestern Persia. Simultaneously, the Ottomans again pushed into the Caucasus region with the aim of finally securing a Pan-Turkic empire. Meanwhile, German progress in southern Russia posed a threat not only to the British position in Persia but also to its influence in Afghanistan.

To remedy this situation, the British dispatched to northern Persia forces under Major General L. C. Dunsterville. A confusing strategic situation developed when the Ottoman Ninth Army advanced southeast into Persia and took Tabriz while Dunsterville moved his troops, known as Dunsterforce, north to secure a road to the vital oil-producing region around Baku. The British forces were finally drawn into the Russian Civil War, at times fighting alongside the counterrevolutionary White forces against the Bolsheviks in northern Persia, Caucasia, and Turkistan.

The Ottomans meanwhile tried to hold on to Azerbaijan even after the Armistice of Mudros (October 30, 1918). Only on November 7, 1918, did British forces finally enter Baku. The British intervention in Transcaspia (Turkistan) continued into March 1919, when Russian White forces took over from them.

DIERK WALTER

**See also**
Caucasus Front, World War I; Enver Pasha; Iran; Mesopotamian Theater, World War I; Ottoman Empire

**References**

Allen, W. E. D., and Paul Muratoff. *Caucasian Battlefields: A History of the Wars on the Turco-Caucasian Border, 1828–1921.* Cambridge: Cambridge University Press, 1953.

Butler, Daniel Allen. *Shadow of the Sultan's Realm: The Destruction of the Ottoman Empire and the Creation of the Modern Middle East.* Dulles, VA: Potomac Books, 2011.

Ellis, C. H. *The Transcaspian Episode, 1918–1919.* London: Hutchinson, 1963.

Erickson, Edward J. *Ordered to Die: A History of the Ottoman Army in the First World War.* Westport, CT: Greenwood, 2000.

Majd, Mohammad Gholi. *Persia in World War I and Its Conquest by Great Britain.* Lanham, MD: University Press of America, 2003.

Moberly, Frederick James. *Operations in Persia, 1914–1919.* London: HMSO, 1929.

# Persian Gulf

Inland sea located in the Middle East, considered by most geographers to be a part of the Indian Ocean. The Persian Gulf, also referred to as the Arabian Gulf by Arab countries, encompasses an area of some 96,525 square miles and connects to the Gulf of Oman and the Arabian Sea via the Straits of Hormuz to the east. To the west, the Persian Gulf is fed by the confluence of the Tigris and Euphrates Rivers via the Shatt al-Arab waterway.

Nations bordering the Persian Gulf include Iran, Oman, the United Arab Emirates, Saudi Arabia, Qatar, Bahrain, Kuwait, and Iraq in the far northwest. Iraq's only access to the gulf is through the Shatt al-Arab waterway, wide in some areas but in others a marshy delta that can be easily blocked in time of war. The eastern portion of the Shatt al-Arab is controlled by Iran, a bitter and longtime rival of Iraq.

The Persian Gulf also contains a number of small islands, mostly all considered offshore or barrier islands. The gulf is quite shallow, with an average depth of just 160 feet. Its deepest portion is approximately 300 feet deep. Because of the climate of the region, which is hot and very dry, high evaporation rates render the Persian Gulf quite salty; parts of the gulf contain up to 40 percent salt. The southern coastline is rather flat, while the Iranian coastline is mountainous. Over the past 6,000 years the size of the Persian Gulf has steadily decreased, and silt and sediment draining from the Shatt al-Arab continue slowly to reduce the amount of water area.

The Persian Gulf is strategically significant not only because of its location and connection to the Arabian Sea but also because of its rich petroleum and natural gas resources. There are many oil fields and wells located in the gulf, including Al-Safaniya, the world's largest producing oil field. Also, the gulf is used to transport oil via large oceangoing tankers, and nations such as Kuwait, Bahrain, Qatar, and others operate major oil port facilities and refineries on or near the coast. In addition to petrochemical resources, the Persian Gulf has historically been quite rich in wildlife, including fish and major coral reefs. For many years Persian Gulf pearl-producing oysters were highly prized, but their numbers have been drastically reduced in the last 75 years or so.

The Persian Gulf's natural resources have come under enormous pressure since the discovery of oil in the region in the 1920s and 1930s and with the rapid industrialization of the region. Pollution, overharvesting of fish and other wildlife, and a lack of concern—until fairly recently—about what gets put into the gulf have all imperiled its delicate ecosystem. The gulf has been the scene of numerous large oil spills, including one in 1983, several large spills during the 1980–1988 Iran-Iraq War, and again in 1991, when the Iraqis dumped as many as 6 million barrels of oil into the water during the Persian Gulf War, precipitating an ecological catastrophe. The results of that conflict are still impacting gulf waters and beaches.

In the late 1980s, the Persian Gulf was also the scene of a series of tanker wars precipitated by Iraq and Iran during their eight-year-long war. The conflict led the United States to implement Operation EARNEST WILL during 1987–1988 in order to protect Kuwaiti and other neutral oil tankers plying the gulf from attack. It was the largest naval convoy program since World War II.

PAUL G. PIERPAOLI JR.

**See also**

EARNEST WILL, Operation; Iran-Iraq War; Shatt al-Arab Waterway

**References**

Palmer, Michael A. *Guardians of the Gulf: A History of America's Expanding Role in the Persian Gulf, 1833–1992.* New York: Free Press, 1992.

Waterlow, Julia. *The Red Sea and the Arabian Gulf.* Orlando, FL: Steck-Vaughan, 1997.

# Persian Gulf War, Air Campaign (January 17–February 28, 1991)

Called by British Air Vice Marshal R. A. "Tony" Mason the "apotheosis of 20th-century airpower," the stunningly successful coalition air campaign prompted many to claim that Operation DESERT STORM may well be the first time in history in which a war was won from the air. As brilliant as subsequent land operations proved to be, the powerful Iraqi forces had already sustained devastating blows delivered by combined air operations of the coalition forces before the ground campaign commenced. This success resulted from both effective planning and skillful execution.

The precise execution of some of the air strikes during the campaign, presented so effectively on television, made it look too easy, almost facile. The public failed to grasp that such expertise was the result of long years of careful effort, superb training, and a brilliant procurement effort that had been under siege for many years.

Following the Iraqi occupation of Kuwait on August 2, 1990, Iraqi president Saddam Hussein rejected demands from the world community that he withdraw his troops. Acting under the authority of United Nations (UN) resolutions, U.S. president George H. W. Bush then put together a grand coalition, including Arab states, to oust the Iraqi Army from Kuwait by force.

The buildup of U.S. forces there, first to protect Saudi Arabia and then to allow offensive operations against Iraq, known as Operation DESERT SHIELD, began on August 7, 1990. The most visible and immediate measure of support came in the form of airpower when the U.S. Air Force dispatched 48 McDonnell F-15C/D Eagles from Langley Air Force Base, Virginia, to Dhahran, Saudi Arabia. The longest operational fighter deployment in history, this nonstop flight required about 17 hours and seven en route in-flight refuelings. It proved to be the first step in the largest buildup of airpower in the history of the Middle East. By September 2 more than 600 aircraft were in place, buttressed by U.S. Navy and U.S. Marine Corps forces and by the deployed ground forces of Great Britain, France, and the Arab coalition nations. Iraq was effectively ringed by airpower, with two carrier battle groups operating in the Red Sea and four others in the Persian Gulf.

Despite this show of force, coalition forces did not arrive in the Persian Gulf with an air war plan in hand. The creation of the plan is still a matter of debate. Briefly, maverick Colonel John Warden III, author of *The Air Campaign: Planning for Combat* (1988), was called upon to furnish an air war plan to Lieutenant General Charles A. Horner, commander of both U.S. Central Command (CENTCOM) air forces and the Joint Force Air Component.

Warden and 20 colleagues in the Pentagon put forward what they called INSTANT THUNDER (so named to signal its difference from the attenuated and ineffective Operation ROLLING THUNDER of the Vietnam War). Horner believed that INSTANT THUNDER was insufficiently detailed. Warden was then sent home, and Brigadier General Buster C. Glosson was ordered to transform the plan into a usable document. Ironically, as developed, the plan followed the broad brush strokes of Warden's ideas.

From Glosson's efforts, aided by Warden's Pentagon group, a new plan emerged from which the daily Air Tasking Order could be created. Targets were selected and apportioned to the constituent air elements of the coalition forces, along with recommendations for aircraft types, numbers, and weapons to be used.

Ultimately the air plan called for securing and maintaining air superiority; attacking Iraqi political and military leadership by destroying the command and control networks; severing Iraqi supply lines; destroying all Iraqi chemical, biological, and nuclear capabilities; and destroying the elite Republican Guard units. In essence, the plan required history's most intensive air battlefield preparation prior to a land offensive.

Iraq appeared to be a formidable opponent, with the typical effective Soviet-style integrated air defense system. This latter included perhaps 1,012 aircraft, many of them flown by pilots with combat experience gained in the war with Iran; 7,000 antiaircraft guns; 16,000 surface-to-air missiles (SAMs); and a surprisingly modern command, control, and communications system.

The United States and its coalition allies possessed a powerful strike force of 2,614 aircraft. The countries represented in the air war and the number of aircraft they supplied were as follows: United States, 1,990; Saudi Arabia, 339; Great Britain, 73; France, 66; Kuwait, 43; Canada, 28; Bahrain; 24; Qatar, 20; United Arab Emirates, 20; Italy, 8; and New Zealand, 3. Of the total, 1,838 were fighters, bombers, or attack aircraft, and 312 were tankers.

Some crucial elements of the strike force were as yet unproven, particularly one of the key aircraft in the developed air plan, the Lockheed F-117A Nighthawk stealth fighter. It had been employed in Operation JUST CAUSE, the U.S. intervention in Panama, without notable success. Furthermore, there was no way of knowing whether or not the Iraqis and their military suppliers had crafted a defense against such aircraft.

On the expiration of the UN Security Council ultimatum, coalition military operations against Iraq, known as Operation DESERT STORM, commenced on January 17, 1991. To achieve maximum surprise, air operations actually began on the morning of January 16, when seven B-52G Stratofortresses departed Barksdale Air Force Base, Louisiana, carrying AGM-86Cs, nonnuclear cruise missiles. These were reinforced by some 100 Tomahawk land-attack missiles launched by ships stationed in the Red Sea and the Persian Gulf. The missile combination coincided with a stealthy but piloted attack force. The latter consisted first of 10 F-117As, which took off from Khamis Mushayt in southern Saudi Arabia at 12:22 a.m. on January 17. Also in action were the sophisticated U.S. Air Force MH-53J Pave Low and U.S. Army AH-64 Apache helicopters, the latter using their withering firepower in a direct attack on Iraqi early-warning radar systems. The stealth bombers dropped laser-guided bombs to cripple Iraq's air defense system, their success verified by the sudden end of Iraqi television transmissions. A lethal array of bombers, fighters, tankers, electronic warfare aircraft, and Wild Weasels (suppression of enemy air defense aircraft) were soon airborne.

This was the beginning of a savage campaign that devastated Iraqi air defenses and decisively defeated the Iraqi Air Force. The value of the F-117As had been firmly established; these aircraft had not been detected by the Iraqi radar, nor had any succumbed, as statistically they might have, to any one of many antiaircraft shells illuminating the night sky over Baghdad.

The air campaign proceeded flawlessly. Every one of coalition commander General H. Norman Schwarzkopf's requirements and every feature of General Glosson's plan was met. Coalition forces scored 41 air-to-air victories during the war and 2 more in the following month. The United States suffered 35 losses in combat, while coalition forces lost eight aircraft, six of the latter being Royal Air Force Tornados lost in low-level attacks on heavily defended airfields. Twenty-two U.S. aircraft were also lost in noncombat accidents.

Sandstorms proved to be a significant deterrent to air operations, but the single most important factor that distracted planners from executing the air war plan as originally conceived was the emphasis given to the elimination of the Iraqi Scud threat. The Scud was a Soviet-developed tactical ballistic missile widely sold abroad. Iraq possessed some 600 Scuds, and these posed a strategic rather than a tactical threat. The Scud was not accurate but had the great advantage of being easily dispersed, and many were on mobile missile launchers. The principal coalition worry was the certainty of an Iraqi Scud attack on Israel and military response by the Jewish state that would unhinge the coalition. Iraq had carefully surveyed Israel for such an attack for that exact reason.

The United States applied great pressure on Israel not to intervene in the war, but if Scuds caused significant damage to the Jewish state, it would be difficult for the Israeli government to resist public pressure for retaliation. Iraq fired its first two Scuds against Israel on January 17, followed by 7 more the next day. In all 42 were fired at the Jewish state. In return for Israeli restraint, the United States supplied U.S. Army Patriot PAC-2 missiles and prepared an intensive Scud hunt that consumed an immense amount of time and resources. Iraq also fired Scuds against Saudi Arabia. Ultimately, the coalition flew some 2,500 sorties against the Scuds and their missile launchers, detracting from the other aerial effort but diminishing the Scud threat so that firings dropped to 1 or less per day.

The coalition air campaign gutted the fighting strength of the Iraqi forces. In the 43-day war, the coalition flew some 110,000 sorties (a sortie being 1 flight by an individual aircraft). This effort placed an immense demand on aerial refueling capacity, with U.S. Air Force tankers refueling just under 46,000 aircraft (including U.S. Air Force, U.S. Navy, U.S. Marine Corps, and coalition units) and off-loading an incredible 110 million gallons of aviation fuel.

The coalition flew more than 44,000 combat sorties and dropped more than 84,000 tons of bombs. Of this amount, some 7,400 tons changed the shape of warfare, for they were precision-guided munitions (PGMs) with a much greater capability than those that had debuted in the Vietnam War. U.S. Air Force F-117s dropped more than 6,600 tons of PGMs, with U.S. Navy and U.S. Marine Corps aircraft contributing the remainder. Although fewer than 10 percent of the total tonnage expended, PGMs accounted for more than 75 percent of the damage inflicted on key Iraqi targets. The inventory of PGMs included Paveway bombs and Maverick, Hellfire, Tomahawk, and AGM-86C missiles as well as high-speed antiradiation missiles and a few other missile types.

Interestingly, the very success of the PGM may have sown the seeds of future difficulties in the Persian Gulf. The incredible accuracy of the PGM permitted F-117As to completely dislocate Iraqi command and control capability while inflicting only minor damage on the Iraqi capital. This led to a general perception that the value of the PGM lay not only in its lethality but also in its ability to avoid collateral damage. The PGM made warfare much more refined and much easier on the civilian populace. In the subsequent 2003 Iraq War, the even more extensive use of PGMs inflicted decisive damage on Iraq's military capability, but this did not convince the populace that it was—or indeed could be—defeated. This situation was unique in modern warfare. Thus, as successful as the 1991 air campaign was in destroying the Iraqi electrical grid, fuel economy, and transport system and the Iraqi Air Force, it did not make a lasting impression on Saddam Hussein or the Iraqi people.

Nevertheless, the air campaign had a catastrophic effect on the Iraqi military's ability to resist. Schwarzkopf had stipulated the requirements for the degradation of Iraqi effectiveness that would be necessary before an attack was begun. He reported that this had been achieved, for when he made his land attack, intelligence estimates claimed that one-third of the Iraqi divisions were at 50 percent or lower strength, one-third at 50–75 percent, and one-third at full strength.

The considerable Iraqi armored force was decimated by tank plinking by A-10 Thunderbolt IIs (Warthogs) and helicopters. The Warthog's outstanding performance rescued it from retirement and launched an entirely new career in U.S. Air Force service.

On February 24, 1991, the ground campaign began, its key being a massive armor attack on the western flank of the Iraqi Army, with the goal of cutting off and destroying Iraqi Republican Guard divisions in Kuwait. The ground forces were able to accomplish this assembly and execution in complete security, for the Iraqi forces were bereft of airpower, had no insight into coalition movements, and were for the most part immobile. Coalition forces were thus able to achieve a ground victory with only the most minor losses. The decimated Iraqi forces crumbled before the coalition ground offensive, and a cease-fire was granted after only 100 hours of ground warfare.

The great coalition victory was thus accomplished largely as a consequence of airpower's pummeling of the Iraqi Army in the weeks before the ground war began. The U.S. Air Force and U.S. Navy had put together a force of aircraft varying in age from more than 40 years (the B-52) to just a few years (the F-117A). The U.S. Air Force had labored under funding shortages and procurement limits for decades, yet it managed to field an intricate system of satellites, airborne command and control, stealth fighters, air superiority fighters, tankers (also 40 years old), and airlift so as to create a force that was unbeatable. Much was owed to the crews who operated the weapons. Satellites were tweaked to provide an optimum result for the combat theater. Ancient aircraft reached new reliability standards. Obsolete aircraft such as the A-10, B-52, and F-4G Wild Weasels suddenly assumed new stature. Both stealth munitions and PGMs proved themselves. All of this effort and its resultant validation prepared the U.S. Air Force for the coming years of almost continuous combat but completely failed to convince the U.S. Congress and the public of the requirement to update aging systems.

WALTER J. BOYNE

**See also**
Persian Gulf War, Overview; Schwarzkopf, H. Norman, Jr.

**References**
Hallion, Richard P. *Storm over Iraq: Air Power and the Gulf War.* Washington, DC: Smithsonian Institution Press, 1997.
McFarland, Stephen L. *A Concise History of the United States Air Force.* Washington, DC: Air Force History and Museum Program, 1997.
Warden, John A., III. *The Air Campaign: Planning for Combat.* Washington, DC: National Defense University Press, 1988.

## Persian Gulf War, Cease-Fire Agreement (April 6, 1991)

Agreement of April 6, 1991, under which Iraq formally accepted the United Nations (UN) terms for a cease-fire following the Persian Gulf War. The ground assault phase of the war commenced on February 24, 1991, and quickly routed the Iraqi military from Kuwait. Three days later, Iraqi foreign minister Tariq Aziz notified the UN that his country would comply with 3 of the 12 UN resolutions concerning a cessation of hostilities if the Security Council brokered a cease-fire. The council rejected the proposal that same day and asserted that Iraq must unconditionally agree to all 12 resolutions.

Meanwhile, chairman of the U.S. Joint Chiefs of Staff General Colin L. Powell briefed President George H. W. Bush that coalition forces had liberated Kuwait and eliminated Iraq's ability to threaten its neighbors. This assessment, combined with the desire to avoid the impression that the United States was employing excessive force, prompted Bush to unilaterally announce that military operations would be suspended at 8:00 a.m. the following day, February 28, 100 hours after the ground campaign had begun. Bush stressed that the suspension of hostilities would be temporary unless Iraq met certain conditions, including the release of prisoners of war, the revelation of the location of mines, and compliance with all UN Security Council resolutions.

Isolated fighting occurred during the next two days, but on March 3, 1991, Iraqi president Saddam Hussein dispatched deputy chief of staff of the ministry of defense Sultan Hashim Ahmad al-Jabburi al-Tai, assisted by Lieutenant General Salah Abud Mahmoud, to meet at Sawan Airfield in southern Iraq with coalition commander General H. Norman Schwarzkopf and Saudi prince Khalid bin Sultan to sign a cease-fire agreement. Shwarzkopf addressed such issues as a prohibition on Iraq's use of fixed-wing aircraft, the return of captured Iraqi territory, and prisoners of war.

Unfortunately, the decision not to include helicopters in the no-fly prohibition allowed Iraq to employ them against the Shia uprising in southern Iraq.

UN Security Council Resolution 686, passed on March 2, created the framework for the subsequent formal cease-fire. Among other provisions, it required Iraq to renounce its claims on Kuwait, return all seized Kuwaiti property, return all prisoners of war, and pay war damages. On April 3, the Security Council passed the most complete list of 34 mandates in Resolution 687. It reiterated earlier provisions and added additional measures, such as requirements that Iraq abandon weapons of mass destruction programs, faithfully pay its international debts, affirm that it would not aid international terrorists, and recognize Kuwaiti sovereignty. Iraq formally accepted these terms on April 6.

Iraqi acceptance of the UN terms did not end conflict between Iraq and the international community. In subsequent years, the Hussein regime employed helicopters to punish ethnic groups inside its borders in violation of UN mandates and threatened air patrols over northern and southern Iraq in the no-fly zones. Iraq's eventual refusal to cooperate with weapons inspectors from the UN Special Commission on Iraq (UNSCOM) largely contributed to the American-Anglo decision to invade the country and topple Hussein in March 2003.

MATTHEW J. KROGMAN

**See also**
Hussein, Saddam; Persian Gulf War, Overview; Schwarzkopf, H. Norman, Jr.

**References**
Bacevich, Andrew J., and Efraim Inbar, eds. *The Gulf War of 1991 Reconsidered*. Portland, OR: Frank Cass, 2003.
Gow, James, ed. *Iraq, The Gulf Conflict and the World Community*. London: Brassey's, 1993.
Yetiv, Steve A. *Explaining Foreign Policy: U.S. Decision-Making and the Persian Gulf War*. Baltimore: Johns Hopkins University Press, 2004.

# Persian Gulf War, Ground Campaign (February 24–28, 1991)

On paper, Iraq appeared formidable. Its army numbered close to 1 million men, and it possessed some 4,200 main battle tanks (MBTs)—of which 1,000 were modern T-72s—along with 2,800 armored personnel carriers (APCs) and about 3,100 artillery pieces. Iraqi president Saddam Hussein ultimately deployed 42–43 divisions to Kuwait, with most positioned along the border with Saudi Arabia. At the time their strength was believed to be about 540,000 men, but the best postwar analysis places it at no more than 336,000. The Iraqi Navy was negligible, but the Iraqi Air Force counted more than 1,000 aircraft of all types.

Coalition assets in the Persian Gulf region assembled in Operation DESERT SHIELD, which was designed to protect Saudi Arabia and prepare for the liberation of Kuwait. The United States put together an impressive coalition of 34 nations that included Saudi Arabia, Egypt, and Syria as well as Britain, France, and many other states. Coalition ground forces numbered some 540,000 men from 31 countries, with 3,318 tanks and 3,850 artillery pieces plus some 1,800 combat aircraft from 12 nations and a large naval force in the Persian Gulf and Red Sea.

Hussein remained intransigent but also quiescent, allowing the buildup of coalition forces in Saudi Arabia to proceed unimpeded. When the deadline for Iraq to withdraw from Kuwait passed on January 15, 1991, coalition commander U.S. Army general H. Norman Schwarzkopf unleashed Operation DESERT STORM. It began with a massive air offensive, striking targets in Kuwait and throughout Iraq, including Baghdad. In only a few days the coalition had established absolute air supremacy over the battlefield. The air campaign destroyed important Iraqi targets along the Saudi border. Night after night Boeing B-52 Stratofortresses dropped massive bomb loads in classic attrition warfare; many Iraqi defenders were simply buried alive.

At the same time, Schwarzkopf mounted an elaborate deception to convince the Iraqis that the coalition was planning a marine amphibious assault against Kuwait. This feint pinned down a number of Iraqi divisions. In reality, Schwarzkopf had planned a return to large-scale maneuver warfare, which tested the U.S. Army's new AirLand Battle concept.

Schwarzkopf's campaign involved three thrusts. On the far left 200 miles from the coast, the XVIII Airborne Corps of the 82nd Airborne Division and the 101st Airborne Division (Air Assault), supplemented by the French 6th Light Armored Division and the U.S. 24th Infantry Division (Mechanized) and 3rd Armored Cavalry Regiment, were to swing wide and cut off the Iraqis on the Euphrates River, preventing resupply or retreat. The center assault, the mailed fist of the VII Corps, was to be mounted some 100 miles inland from the coast. It consisted of the following heavily armored coalition divisions: the U.S. 1st and 3rd Armored Divisions, the 1st Cavalry Division, the 1st Infantry (Mechanized) Division, and the British 1st Armored Division. The VII Corps's mission was to thrust deep, engage, and then destroy the elite Iraqi Republican Guard divisions. The third

M-60A1 main battle tanks of the 1st Tank Battalion, U.S. 1st Marine Division, advance toward Kuwait City during the third day of the ground offensive phase of Operation DESERT STORM, February 26, 1991. (U.S. Department of Defense)

and final thrust was to occur on the coast. It consisted of the U.S. I Marine Expeditionary Force of two divisions, a brigade from the U.S. Army 2nd Armored Division, and allied Arab units and was charged with driving on Kuwait City. Schwarzkopf saw this as chiefly a holding action, believing that it would be several days before the forces here would be able to break through the heavily defended Iraqi Saddam Line. By that time the other two thrusts would have cut off the Iraqi forces, trapping them in Kuwait.

On February 24 coalition forces executed simultaneous drives along the coast, while the 101st Airborne Division established a position 50 miles behind the border. As it turned out, the marines were able to break through the Iraqi defenses in a matter of hours. As the marines moved up the coast toward Kuwait City, they were hit in the flank by Iraqi armor. In the largest tank battle in the history of the U.S. Marine Corps, the marines, supported by coalition airpower, easily defeated the Iraqis. The battle was fought in a surrealist day-into-night atmosphere caused by the smoke of oil wells set afire by the retreating Iraqis.

As the marines, preceded by a light Arab force, prepared to enter Kuwait City, Iraqi forces fled north toward Iraq with whatever they could steal. Thousands of vehicles and personnel were caught in the open on Highway 80 from Kuwait City at Mutla Ridge and there pummeled by air and artillery along what became known as the "Highway of Death." Although media images of the destruction were dramatic and caused concerns in Washington over their effect on public opinion, coalition troops found only about 200 Iraqi corpses amid the vehicle wreckage but did round up several thousand Iraqi prisoners hiding nearby in the desert.

The coalition now came up against an Iraqi rear guard of 300 tanks covering the withdrawal north toward Basra of four Republican Guard divisions. In perhaps the most lopsided tank battle in history, the Iraqi force was defeated at a cost of only one American fatality.

Lieutenant General Frederick Franks Jr., commander of the VII Corps to the west, angered Schwarzkopf by insisting on halting on the night of February 24 and concentrating his forces rather than risking an advance through a battlefield littered with debris and unexploded ordnance and the possibility of casualties from friendly fire. When the VII Corps resumed the advance early on February 25, its problem was not the Iraqis but rather the supply of fuel; because of the speed of the advance, the M1 Abrams tanks needed to be refueled every eight to nine hours.

The afternoon of February 27 saw the VII Corps engaged in some of its most intense combat. Hoping to delay the coalition, an armored brigade of the Medina Republican Guard Division established a six-mile-long skirmish line on the reverse slope of a low hill, digging in their T-55 and T-72 tanks. The advancing 2nd Brigade of the 1st Armored Division came over a ridge, spotted the Iraqis, and took them under fire from 2,500 yards. The American tankers used sabot rounds to blow the turrets off the dug-in Iraqi tanks. The battle was the single-largest armor engagement of the war. In only 45 minutes, U.S. tanks and aircraft destroyed 60 T-72 and 9 T-55 tanks as well as 38 Iraqi armored personnel carriers.

Coalition tanks, especially the M1A1 Abrams and the British Challenger, proved their great superiority over their Soviet counterparts, especially in night fighting. Of 600 M1A1 Abrams that saw combat, none were penetrated by an enemy round. Conversely, the M1A1's 120mm gun proved lethal to Iraqi MBTs. It could engage the Iraqi armor at 3,000 meters (1.86 miles), twice the Iraqis' effective range, and its superior fire-control system could deliver a first-round hit while on the move. Overall, the coalition maneuver strategy bound up in AirLand Battle worked to perfection. As the VII Corps closed to the sea, the XVIII Corps to its left, with a much larger distance to travel, raced to reach the fleeing Republican Guard divisions before they could escape to Baghdad.

In only 100 hours of ground combat, coalition forces had liberated Kuwait, but President Bush now stopped the war. He feared the cost of an assault on Baghdad and also the possibility that Iraq might then break up into a Kurdish north, a Sunni Muslim center, and a Shiite Muslim south. A fragmented Iraq would be very much to the advantage of the radical Islamist regime in Iran.

The Persian Gulf War was among the most lopsided in history. Iraq lost a majority of its tanks, other armored vehicles, and artillery. In contrast, the coalition lost 4 tanks, 9 other combat vehicles, and 1 artillery piece. In human terms, the coalition sustained 500 casualties (150 dead), many of these from accidents and friendly fire. Iraqi casualties have been estimated at between 25,000 and 100,000 dead, but the true figure is unknown. The coalition also took 80,000 Iraqis prisoner. Perhaps an equal number simply deserted.

SPENCER C. TUCKER

**See also**
Hussein, Saddam; Kuwait, Liberation of; Persian Gulf War, Overview; Schwarzkopf, H. Norman, Jr.

**References**
Dunnigan, James F., and Austin Bay. *From Shield to Storm: High-Tech Weapons, Military Strategy, and Coalition Warfare in the Persian Gulf.* New York: William Morrow, 1992.
Romjue, John L. *American Army Doctrine for the Post–Cold War.* Washington, DC: Military History Office and U.S. Army Training and Doctrine Command, 1997.
Scales, Robert H. *Certain Victory: The U.S. Army in the Gulf War.* Washington, DC: Brassey's, 1994.
Schubert, Frank N., and Theresa L. Kraus, eds. *The Whirlwind War: The United States Army in Operations Desert Shield and Desert Storm.* Washington, DC: U.S. Government Printing Office, 1995.
Schwarzkopf, H. Norman, with Peter Petre. *It Doesn't Take a Hero: General H. Norman Schwarzkopf, the Autobiography.* New York: Bantam Books, 1993.

# Persian Gulf War, Naval Operations (January 17–February 28, 1991)

Iraq has less than 50 miles of coastline on the Persian Gulf. Indeed, Iraqi president Saddam Hussein's determination to increase Iraqi access to the gulf was a key factor not only in the war with Iran (1980–1988) but also in prompting the invasion and occupation of Kuwait in August 1990. Access to Umm Qasr, the principal Iraqi naval base, had been a matter of contention between the two states.

Given the limited Iraqi access to the sea, its navy was quite small and consisted of several dozen vessels centered on missile boats but also some amphibious ships, a few minesweepers, and other vessels. Because of this, most coalition naval action during the Persian Gulf War was centered on support of coalition ground operations, minesweeping, and a deception to convince Hussein to retain sizable forces along the coastal stretches of Iraq and Kuwait to prevent a coalition amphibious assault.

The coalition naval effort was a vast one. Operations DESERT SHIELD and DESERT STORM included naval units in the Persian Gulf, the Gulf of Oman, the Gulf of Aden, the Red Sea, and the eastern Mediterranean. Although U.S. Navy ships comprised the bulk of the force, 23 nations contributed naval assets. The U.S. Navy provided a total of 189 ships and some 450 aircraft; Great Britain provided the next largest number of ships, at 33, while France furnished 21. Altogether, coalition nations other than the United States committed 144 ships. Vice Admiral Henry H. Mauz Jr., commander of the U.S. Seventh Fleet, headed the Naval Component Central Command and coordinated the naval effort from August 1990 to December 1, 1990, when he was succeeded by U.S. Navy vice admiral Stanley Arthur.

By the time the war began on January 17, 1991, the U.S. and coalition navies had already registered a major contribution to the subsequent coalition success. With the passage of United Nations Security Council Resolution 665 on August 25, 1990, coalition naval forces choked off Iraqi seaborne commerce. Although some goods came into Iraq by land through Jordan and by air, the seven-month-long Maritime Interception Operations not only largely denied Iraq access to weapons, spare parts, and other military supplies but also reduced Iraqi oil exports to a mere trickle, starving the Iraqi government of its major source of revenue.

With the beginning of the war, most coalition naval forces continued their work of maritime interdiction and minesweeping, while naval units of the Gulf Cooperation Council (GCC) states patrolled the areas near to and within their territorial waters. Only the U.S. and British navies actively participated in Operation DESERT STORM. Coalition naval goals in the war were fourfold: to destroy Iraqi naval units, to deny Iraq the use of oil platforms for military purposes, to drive back Iraqi surface forces in the Persian Gulf from south to north; and to protect against any Iraqi threat to coalition forces and countries in the Gulf region.

The Persian Gulf War saw the first major employment of land-attack cruise missiles. Indeed, during the conflict the U.S. Navy launched 282 Tomahawk land-attack missiles (TLAMs) against key Iraqi air defense posts, radar systems, and communications facilities. The majority of the Tomahawks were expended in the first two days of the war. Altogether, 16 U.S. Navy ships, including the battleship *Wisconsin*, and 2 submarines launched TLAMs. The submarine *Louisville* (SSN-724) launched eight of these while submerged in the Red Sea, and the *Pittsburgh* (SSN-720) launched four others while submerged in the Mediterranean Sea.

On January 24, 1991, U.S. Navy SEALs recaptured the first Kuwaiti territory in an assault on Qaruh Island, taking 67 Iraqis prisoner. On January 29, marines landed on Umm Al-Maradim. Although that island had been abandoned by the Iraqis, the marines discovered maps indicating the location of Iraqi mines in the northern Persian Gulf, and they destroyed abandoned Iraqi equipment.

The major naval action of the war occurred on January 29–30 in the Battle of Bubiyan (also known as the Bubiyan Turkey Shoot). Bubiyan is an island off the northern coast of Kuwait, close to the Iraqi border. The battle occurred when Iraqi Navy units were detected believed to be attempting to flee to Iran. It involved U.S. Navy and Canadian Air Force airplanes and Royal Navy and resulted in the destruction of some two dozen Iraqi naval vessels of all types, in effect eliminating the Iraqi Navy as an offensive threat.

At the same time, Hussein mounted a ground assault on Khafji, on the Saudi-Kuwaiti border. Naval gunfire provided important support to the defenders in this battle of January 29–February 1, and the Iraqis were driven off. U.S. and British ships also destroyed concurrent Iraqi coastal commando raids. By early February also, coalition naval forces had established control of the northern Persian Gulf.

Indeed, the chief threat to the coalition naval forces came in the form of mines. Both the U.S. Navy cruiser *Princeton* (CG-59) and the amphibious assault ship *Tripoli* (LPH-10) were seriously damaged by Iraqi mines off Kuwait, and 12 sailors were wounded, 6 of them seriously. The *Tripoli* was able to continue operations for several days before it had to retire to Bahrain for repairs, while the *Princeton* had to be placed under tow and was hors de combat for the remainder of the war.

The final action of the Iraqi Navy occurred on February 25, when the Iraqis launched two Silkworm antiship missiles from land in the direction of the U.S. battleship *Missouri* (BB-63). The missiles were detected, and the *Missouri* fired its SRBOC chaff. The U.S. guided missile frigate *Jarrett* (FFG-33) was then some three miles distant. Its Phalanx system, operating in the automatic target-acquisition mode, fixed upon the *Missouri*'s chaff, and four Phalanx rounds hit the *Missouri*, but there were no injuries. One Silkworm was intercepted in midflight by a British Sea Dart missile from the destroyer HMS *Gloucester* (D96), in the first validated engagement of a missile by a missile during combat at sea. The second Silkworm fell harmlessly into the sea.

During February 20–22 helicopters attacked Faylakah Island, and on February 23, the evening before the ground offensive began, a 14-man SEAL team simulated an assault at Mina Saud, Kuwait. Employing high-speed boats, they detonated explosives and opened up on the beach with heavy machine guns and grenade launchers. These assaults were part of a successful coalition effort to convince the Iraqis that a large-scale assault there was imminent. Indeed, this deception carried out by the U.S. Navy was an important part of the coalition war plan. It had commenced with amphibious training exercises along the Saudi coast during Operation DESERT SHIELD and included public allusions to statements by coalition commander U.S. Army general H. Norman Schwarzkopf that an amphibious attack would be mounted against Kuwait. The deception tied down a number of Iraqi divisions in eastern Kuwait that might otherwise have been employed in the defense of southern Kuwait against the coalition ground offensive launched from Saudi Arabia.

U.S. and British naval units provided important support to coalition forces during the ground phase of the war in shore bombardment but also primarily in air support. In naval gunfire support, the battleships *Missouri* and *Wisconsin* together fired 1,083 shells from their highly accurate 16-inch guns against ground targets, while U.S. Navy and Marine Corps aircraft flew some 24,000 sorties during the war.

SPENCER C. TUCKER

**See also**
Bubiyan Island, Battle of; Hussein, Saddam; Iran-Iraq War; Schwarzkopf, H. Norman, Jr.

**References**
Marolda, Edward, and Robert Schneller. *Shield and Sword: The United States Navy and the Persian Gulf War.* Annapolis, MD: U.S. Naval Institute Press, 2001.
Pokrant, Marvin. *Desert Storm at Sea: What the Navy Really Did.* Westport, CT: Greenwood, 1999.

# Persian Gulf War, Overview (January 17–February 28, 1991)

On July 17, 1990, Iraqi president Saddam Hussein threatened military action against Kuwait for its overproduction of oil quotas that had helped drive down the world price of oil. Iraq was heavily in debt as a consequence of the Iran-Iraq War (1980–1988) and wanted the price of oil to be as high as possible. Hussein also sought concessions on the vast sums that Iraq owed to Kuwait for loans during the war. He wanted control of Bubiyan and Warbah islands to improve Iraqi access to the Persian Gulf and an end to what he claimed was Kuwaiti slant drilling into the major Iraqi Rumaila oil field. Undergirding all this was Iraq's long-standing claim that Kuwait was an Iraqi province.

In mid-July 1990, American spy satellites detected Iraqi forces massing along the Kuwaiti border. U.S. analysts assumed that it was most likely a show of force by the Iraqis to extract concessions from Kuwait. U.S. policy was in any case unclear, and Washington had tacitly supported Iraq in its war with Iran. However, for some time Washington had been concerned over Iraq's expanding nuclear industry and its development of chemical and biological weapons, which had been employed in the war against Iran as well as against Kurds within Iraq itself.

On July 25 new U.S. ambassador to Iraq April Glaspie met with Hussein on behalf of the George H. W. Bush administration. The Iraqis would later claim that her remarks allowed Hussein operational freedom in the Persian Gulf. Hussein probably believed that any move against Kuwait would not be challenged by the United States, certainly not by war. For its part, the U.S. State Department did not believe that Hussein would actually mount a full-scale invasion of Kuwait. Washington expected at most only a limited incursion to force the Kuwaitis to accede to Iraq's demands regarding the price of oil. Certainly all of Washington underestimated Hussein's ambition.

With Iraqi Army divisions now on the Kuwaiti border, on July 31 Iraqi and Kuwaiti officials met in Jeddah. There Iraq presented Kuwait with a list of demands, including the writing off of some $12–14 billion in loans extended to Iraq during the Iran-Iraq War, giving up control of some territory along their common border, and a lease on Bubiyan and Warba islands in order to facilitate the shipment of Iraqi oil.

With Kuwait rejecting the Iraqi demands, on August 2, 1990, four elite Iraqi Republican Guard divisions invaded Kuwait and seized key military installations, including air bases and airports. Another division of commandos and special forces employed small craft and helicopters to assault Kuwait City. The Kuwaitis were caught by surprise, with their far smaller forces not on alert. Within two days the Iraqis had seized full control, and on August 8 Iraq formally announced the annexation of Kuwait as its 19th province.

On news of the Iraqi invasion, President Bush had immediately convened the National Security Council, the Central Intelligence Agency (CIA), and the military leadership headed by chairman of the Joint Chiefs of Staff General Colin Powell. U.S. Central Command (CENTCOM) commander General H. Norman Schwarzkopf was also present. Washington was concerned about Kuwait but also about the stranglehold that Iraq might now have over Kuwait's neighbor, Saudi Arabia, which had the world's largest oil reserves. Bush and others of his generation saw Hussein's aggression as a challenge akin to that of Adolf Hitler and made much of the supposed contrast between dictatorship (Iraq) and democracy (Kuwait). Powell and other officers who had fought in Vietnam, however, resisted waging another unpopular war in a faraway country. Most certainly, the Pentagon overestimated Iraq's military prowess.

On August 2, the United Nations (UN) Security Council passed Resolution 660 condemning the Iraqi invasion, and UN Resolution 661 of August 6 called for sanctions against Iraq. On August 8, President Bush ordered the deployment of forward forces to Saudi Arabia in Operation DESERT SHIELD. The air, ground, and naval units were sent to bolster the Saudis and to demonstrate U.S. resolve in support of diplomacy.

The buildup of forces by CENTCOM was massive. The U.S. Army provided the bulk of the forces, including armor, infantry, and airborne units from the United States and Europe. The marines also contributed two divisions, while offshore there were two carrier battle groups with full complements of aircraft and a U.S. Marine Corps fleet force. The U.S. Air Force deployed several wings of combat aircraft as well as transports and support units.

President Bush deserves considerable credit for forging an impressive international coalition and then holding it together. Allied support arrived in the form of an armored division and two armored brigades from Britain and a light armored division from France. Saudi Arabia, Syria, and Egypt also provided forces. Other nations furnishing military assistance were Argentina, Australia, Bahrain, Belgium, Canada, Czechoslovakia, Denmark, Germany, Greece, Italy, Kuwait, the Netherlands, Norway, Oman, Poland, Portugal, Qatar, Spain, and the United Arab Emirates. Other nations including Japan furnished financial, medical, and logistical support. Altogether, the force in theater numbered some 665,000 troops. Opposing them, Hussein in January 1991 deployed some 546,700 men, 4,280 tanks, 2,880 armored personnel carriers, and 3,100 artillery pieces. General Schwarzkopf commanded the combined coalition forces.

When Hussein refused to yield, an air campaign dubbed INSTANT THUNDER began early on January 17. A massive air offensive, it commenced with stealth bombers and fighters and cruise missiles destroying the Iraqi air defense network. Large numbers of Iraqi aircraft were destroyed on the ground, and Hussein ordered those remaining flown to Iran.

In retaliation, Hussein launched Scud missiles against targets in Saudi Arabia and Israel in an attempt to draw Israel into the war and split the coalition of Arab states against him. Washington responded by dispatching Patriot antiaircraft missile batteries to Israel.

A major objective of the air campaign was to eliminate Iraq's highly mobile Scud force, but this was not achieved. At the same time, airpower inflicted tremendous casualties on the dug-in Iraqis, and the capital of Baghdad came under heavy attack. The A-10 "Warthog" ground-attack aircraft proved highly effective against Iraqi armor, destroying several hundred tanks during the course of the war.

With his forces now being seriously degraded by coalition airpower and determined to begin what he threatened would be "the mother of all battles," Hussein ordered his commanders to attack across the Saudi border. Only at Khafji during January 29–31 did such a battle occur, but it was beaten back by Saudi and Qatari forces and U.S. marines supported by artillery and airpower.

In only a few days the coalition had established absolute air supremacy over the battlefield. Iraq possessed nearly 800 combat aircraft and an integrated air defense system controlling 3,000 antiaircraft missiles, but it was unable to win a single air-to-air engagement. Air superiority ensured success on the ground. The air campaign also destroyed important Iraqi targets along the Saudi border. Night after night B-52s dropped massive bomb loads in classic attrition warfare, and many Iraqi defenders were simply buried alive.

Operation DESERT STORM, the ground war, began at 4:00 a.m. on February 24, Iraqi time. Schwarzkopf succeeded in convincing the Iraqis that the coalition planned an amphibious assault against Kuwait, and this tied down a number of Iraqi divisions that otherwise could have been committed against the real coalition land operations.

Schwarzkopf's offensive plan involved three major thrusts. The far left flank, some 200 miles from the coast, consisting of U.S. and French forces, had the greatest distance to cover. It was to swing wide and deep in order to cut off the Iraqi forces in Kuwait at the Euphrates River. The powerful center assault of heavily armored U.S. and British divisions had the mission of engaging and destroying the elite Iraqi Republican Guard divisions. The third and final thrust on the right flank along the coast consisted of U.S. Marine Corps, U.S. Army, and allied Arab units. They were charged with the liberation of Kuwait City.

On February 24 coalition forces began simultaneous drives along the coast while the 101st Airborne Division established a position 50 miles behind the border. Marine forces advancing on Kuwait City were hit in the flank by Iraqi armor, and in the largest battle in U.S. Marine Corps history, the marines and supporting aircraft turned back the Iraqis. Day had turned to night as the Iraqis set fire to Kuwaiti oil wells.

In many Iraqi units discipline completely collapsed, and individuals desperately fled northward, hoping to regain Iraq in whatever conveyance they could secure, including a great many civilian vehicles loaded with loot from Kuwait City. Thousands of these vehicles and the people in them were caught in the open on the highway running north and there destroyed by coalition aircraft and artillery fire. U.S. forces then encountered and destroyed some 300 Iraqi tanks seeking to cover the withdrawal northward of four Republican Guard divisions.

Meanwhile, the advance of the VII Corps was slowed, forced to halt on the night of February 24. Its major problem turned out to be not the Iraqis but fuel. The afternoon of February 27, however, saw the VII Corps engaged in intense combat with an armored brigade of the Medina Republican Guard Division seeking to delay its advance. The Iraqis had established a six-mile-long skirmish line on the reverse slope of a low hill, digging in their T-55 and T-72 tanks there. The advancing 2nd Brigade of the 1st Armored Division came over a ridge, spotted the Iraqis, and took them under fire from 2,500 yards. The American tankers used sabot rounds to blow the turrets off the dug-in Iraqi tanks. The battle was the largest armor engagement of the war. In only 45 minutes, U.S. tanks and aircraft destroyed 60 T-72 tanks, 9 T-55 tanks, and 38 Iraqi armored personnel carriers. As the VII Corps closed to the sea, the XVIII Corps to its left, with a much larger distance to travel, raced to cut off the Republican Guard divisions fleeing northward before they could escape the coalition trap.

In only 100 hours of ground combat, coalition forces had liberated Kuwait. On February 28, however, President Bush stopped the war. Images on American television of the destruction of the so-called Highway of Death leading from Kuwait City suggested a completely beaten foe. This was not the case, but Bush had to weigh the cost of an assault on Baghdad and that an invasion of Iraq could well break up the coalition, with the defection of some of its Arab members. The administration also feared that with the collapse of Saddam Hussein's regime, long-standing grievances would come to the fore, and Iraq might then break up into a Kurdish north, a Sunni Muslim center, and a Shiite Muslim south. The Bush administration wanted to keep Iraq intact to counter a resurgent Iran.

The war was declared at an end at 8:01 a.m. on February 28 local time. With its air portion, the war had lasted just 43 days. In the 100-hour ground war, coalition forces liberated Kuwait, but the war was halted earlier than many thought should have been the case. Iraq thus escaped with its best Republican Guard troops largely intact. A cease-fire agreement was concluded on March 3.

The war was among the most lopsided conflicts in history. Iraq lost 3,700 tanks, more than 1,000 other armored vehicles, and 3,000 artillery pieces. The victors lost 4 tanks, 9 other combat vehicles, and 1 artillery piece. The coalition sustained 500 casualties (150 dead), many of these from accidents and friendly fire, while Iraqi casualties totaled between 25,000 and 100,000 dead, with the best estimates being around 60,000. Eighty thousand Iraqis were taken prisoner. Perhaps an equal number simply deserted.

The war ended probable Iraqi pressure on oil prices through the threat of military intervention in Saudi Arabia. Kuwait, the object of the war, had been restored to independence, although a massive and costly cleanup effort would be required to deal with the environmental disaster caused by the deliberate release of oil into the Persian Gulf and the torching of Kuwaiti oil fields by withdrawing Iraq troops. Much damage would have to be repaired in Kuwait itself, all to be funded by Iraqi reparations. Kuwait was little changed politically. This was hardly a war for democracy against dictatorship as Bush had trumpeted, and Kuwait remained securely under the control of the affluent.

The employment of Western military forces in the Middle East, even if they were allied with those from Arab states, fueled Muslim extremism and brought the birth of the Al Qaeda terrorist organization. Its founder, the wealthy Saudi Osama bin Laden, had been outraged at the Saudi Arabian government's decision to allow American armed forces into the desert kingdom. Al Qaeda was to play a major role in bringing about the Iraq War of 2003.

Saddam Hussein, hardly humbled by the outcome of the conflict, remained firmly in power, his intransigence intact. He constantly stymied the work of the UN Special Commission observers sent to Iraq to ensure compliance with the UN resolutions outlined in the cease-fire agreement and in Security Council Resolution 687. To many foreign observers, Hussein appeared to be bent on efforts to revive his weapons of mass destruction (WMD) programs, making UN searches of possible facilities for these as difficult as possible.

Hussein was not long in wreaking vengeance on those who had risen against him, especially the Kurds in northern Iraq and the majority Shiites in the south of the country. These populations, who had risen up in support of coalition forces, now found themselves at Hussein's mercy. The United States, Britain, and France were forced to maintain air assets in the region and use these to enforce no-fly zones in the north and south and from time to time carry out air strikes or fire cruise missiles from ships.

The war did not translate, as many had hoped and President Bush had claimed, into a new era in the Middle East. The Israeli-Palestinian issue remained unresolved. Indeed, the Bush administration seems to have had no broad plan for Iraq or the region apart from evicting Iraq from Kuwait. By weakening Iraq, the United States had strengthened Iran, its chief rival for regional dominance and the major state sponsor of terrorism in the region. (Iran also benefited directly militarily, as it now had the bulk of the Iraqi Air Force.)

Disillusionment in the region with the United States found expression a decade later in 2003, when President George W. Bush took the United States into war with Iraq for a second time. This time there was no broad Arab support. While the new war removed a cruel dictator from power, Iraq descended into sectarian violence, and the problems of the Middle East appeared as intractable as ever.

SPENCER C. TUCKER

### See also

Iran-Iraq War; Iraq; Hussein, Saddam; Kuwait, Iraqi Invasion of; Kuwait, Iraqi Occupation of; Kuwait, Liberation of; Persian Gulf War, Air Campaign; Persian Gulf War, Cease-Fire Agreement; Persian Gulf War, Ground Campaign; Persian Gulf War, Naval Operations; Schwarzkopf, H. Norman, Jr.

### References

Atkinson, Rick. *Crusade: The Untold Story of the Persian Gulf War.* Boston: Houghton Mifflin, 1993.

Freedman, Lawrence, and Efraim Karsh. *The Gulf Conflict, 1990–1991: Diplomacy and War in the New World Order.* Princeton, NJ: Princeton University Press, 1993.

Hilsman, Roger. *George Bush vs. Saddam Hussein: Military Success! Political Failure?* Novato, CA: Lyford Books, 1992.

Marolda, Edward J., and Robert J. Schneller Jr. *Shield and Sword: The U.S. Navy and the Persian Gulf War.* Washington, DC: Naval Historical Center, 1998.

Scales, Robert H. *Certain Victory.* Washington, DC: Office of the Chief of Staff, United States Army, 1993.

Schwarzkopf, H. Norman. *It Doesn't Take a Hero.* New York: Bantam Books, 1992.

## Peshmerga

Armed Kurdish insurgents operating chiefly in Kurdistan (southeastern Turkey, northern Iraq, northwestern Iran, and northern Syria). Peshmerga (meaning those facing death) are Kurdish irregular fighters whose origins predate the 20th century. Although primarily Kurdish men, they has come to include women and non-Kurds. The fighters' chains of command were the successive leaders of the Kurdistan Democratic Party (KDP), namely Mullah Mustafa Barzani and, following his death, his successor and son Masoud Barzani, currently the president of the Kurdistan Regional Government (KRG), as well as the Patriotic Union of Kurdistan (PUK) led by Jalal Talabani. The Peshmerga in Turkey fall under the auspices of the Kurdistan Workers' Party (PKK).

In Iraq, the KDP and PUK comprise the current government of the KRG, by which the Peshmerga are largely governed. Historically, they have played a pivotal role in shaping Kurdish nationalist aspirations for independence since the early 1920s, particularly as a result of the dissolution of the Ottoman Empire after World War I and the quest for a Kurdish homeland.

The historical development of the Peshmerga was concurrent with the rise and fall of various Kurdish rebellions following the collapse of the Ottoman Empire. Failed promises by the Allied Powers after World War I to grant Kurds local autonomy and possible independence as suggested in the Treaty of Sèvres (1920) helped solidify the Kurds' quest for independence thereafter. The 1920s witnessed various Kurdish uprisings led by Sheikh Mahmud Barzinji of Sulamaniyah, all of which were promptly quashed by the Iraqi government and the British Royal Air Force. In 1931, Sheikh Barzinji died in one such uprising. This critical juncture witnessed the rise of Mullah Mustafa Barzani as the leader of the Kurdish movement in Iraq and the first solidification of the Peshmerga as a united force.

Throughout the 1930s and 1940s the Kurdish nationalist movement remained largely dormant, as Barzani was forced into exile first in the Soviet Union, then Iran, and finally Western Europe. However, the ouster of Reza Shah's dictatorship in Iran enabled Kurdish intellectuals along with various Barzani followers to declare an independent Kurdistan in the Mahabad region, in northwestern Iran. This saw the swift dissolution of the Imperial Iranian Army there, which was replaced by the National Army composed of Peshmerga. However, Mahabad, or the Republic of Kurdistan, succumbed to an Iranian invasion in 1946 during which both external influences and internal divisions, primarily between Iranian and Iraqi Kurds, shifted the power of the Peshmerga. In exile, Mustafa Barzani, greatly influenced by Marxist-Leninist ideals, solidified the Kurdish movement by the creation of the KDP, the political arm of which provided for the support of the Peshmerga. Instability in Iraq fueled by the decline of the Hashemite monarchy throughout the 1940s and 1950s created an opportunity for the KDP and the Peshmerga to affirm their position as a force to be reckoned with during the 1958 revolution in Iraq.

The 1958 coup witnessed the overthrow of the Iraqi monarchy by General Abd al-Karim Qasim. At the onset, Qasim favored the integration of Barzani and the KDP into the Iraqi political fabric; Qasim also legalized the KDP and the Peshmerga as political entities while recognizing Kurds as distinct but integral people of Iraq under Article 23 of the newly drafted constitution. This ephemeral success was short-lived, however, as Qasim's Pan-Arabist ideology blunted any demands for Kurdish autonomy within Iraq.

Kurdish Peshmerga, the soldiers of Iraqi Kurdistan, prepare to conduct a combined arms live-fire exercise near Erbil, Iraq, on October 11, 2016, during Combined Joint Task Force Operation INHERENT RESOLVE. (U.S. Army)

Under the leadership of Barzani, the Peshmerga occupied the northern region of Zakho stretching to the Iranian border as a result of the Kurdish revolt of 1962. The revolt had brought an unrelenting bombardment of Kurdish villages and towns across the northeastern frontier. Soon thereafter, Qasim's regime was quickly overthrown by the Baathist rise to power in 1963. The Baathists would prove steadfastly intolerant of Kurdish demands and would quickly increase their military campaign against the Peshmerga and the KDP. The Peshmerga launched counterattacks, which sustained their position and demands for autonomy by controlling much of the northern frontier by 1968.

The growing strength of the KDP and the Peshmerga led to the 1970 Manifesto on Kurdish Autonomy, a proposal drafted by the Baath Party to dilute the rise of Kurdish power, particularly in the north. The ultimate futility of the manifesto led to the 1974 uprising headed by Barzani along with an estimated 50,000 trained Peshmerga. Geopolitical events forced Barzani to abandon the struggle and seek refuge in Iran along with thousands of trained fighters and civilians.

The 1988 Iraqi offensive against Kurds in northern Iraq saw the destruction of hundreds of Kurdish and non-Kurdish villages perceived as being in support of Peshmerga. Labeling the Peshmerga as traitors, the Saddam Hussein regime engineered the 1988 chemical weapons offensive against the town of Halabja, a PUK and Peshmerga stronghold. Kurdish leaders along with thousands of Peshmerga and civilians sought refuge in nearby countries. Estimates place the total number of militant and civilian deaths at some 100,000.

After the 1991 Persian Gulf War, the Peshmerga became an even more vital military force. The creation of the northern no-fly zone by the United Nations (UN) in 1991 provided an opportunity for Kurdish parties to regroup and form the National Front of Kurdistan, which unified the Peshmerga as a force. In doing so, the Peshmerga, aided by Western powers, were able to secure key Iraqi government strongholds, namely Kirkuk, Arbil, and Sula-maniyah, during 1991–1992. Although friction between Kurds and the Iraqi Army continued, the creation of the no-fly zone enabled leaders of the KPD and the PUK to establish the Kurdish

National Assembly, which sought to unite the two major factions of the Peshmerga.

Currently, the Peshmerga are part of the official military force of the KRG, established in 2006. Its mandate seeks the implementation of law and order in the KRG and throughout Iraq and has been instrumental in sustaining security both inside and outside Kurdish-controlled territories in coordination with the Iraqi, U.S., and coalition militaries. Since 2003 the two parties comprising the KRG have signed the Kurdistan Regional Government Unification Agreement, which oversees the administration of various governmental departments, most specifically the Department of Peshmerga Affairs, all in an effort to bolster Kurdish self-rule. Because of Kurdish unity and the presence of the Peshmerga, northern Iraq has been relatively free of the fighting that has plagued the rest of Iraq since 2004 with the exception of the campaigns against Ansar al-Islam and the Turcomen and Arab conflicts with the Kurds. It should be noted, however, that in the past the Peshmerga have battled each other in tribal and intra-Kurdish conflicts. The classification of the Peshmerga as an irregular force is rather disingenuous, given its current position within the Iraqi Army.

In 2012 the Kurdish leadership began a program of unifying the Kurdish forces of the PUK and the KDP, both of which had operated as separate entities. Completed in 2014, it provided a force of 19 brigades. The Peshmerga has also organized its own Special Operations Forces. The Peshmerga has had funding problems and suffered from a lack of ammunition as well as heavy weapons. The former problem has been resolved, with the Iraqi government and other countries, including the United States, supplying ammunition to assist the Peshmerga in fighting the Islamic State of Iraq and Syria (ISIS or ISIL). Despite calls for this, however, the U.S. government has been reluctant to supply heavy weaponry to the Peshmerga, given the Iraqi government's strong opposition.

Although ISIS captured the city of Mosul, Peshmerga fighters, assisted by U.S. air strikes, were able to retake strategic Mosul Dam and played a key role in the ISIS siege of the Kurdish city of Kobanî in Syria, on the frontier with Turkey. They also played an important role in the retaking of Mosul by Iraqi government forces in July 2017. By the summer of 2018, the future of the Peshmerga appeared somewhat more uncertain. Turkey's campaign to neutralize Kurdish fighters in northern Iraq had placed limitations on the Peshmerga's freedom of action, as had the late 2017 declarations by both the Syrian and Iraqi governments that ISIS had been defeated. With the need to defeat ISIS gone, the Peshmerga's role has become increasingly unclear. Certainly, with the Iraqi-Kurdish independence declaration in September 2017, which was strongly opposed by Iraq's government and many other players in the region, nations such as the United States have been somewhat more reluctant to further empower the Peshmerga. Nevertheless, in the summer of 2018 Peshmerga leaders vowed that their forces would reenter Kirkuk. The Peshmerga had largely evacuated the city in the aftermath of the September 2017 Kurdish independence referendum.

Peshmerga forces are armed with a wide variety of weapons from many nations. Reportedly they have some 2,000 armored vehicles (perhaps 100 of these PT-76 tanks along with a smaller number of T-55 main battle tanks) as well as Soviet artillery and some helicopters.

In addition to northern Iraq, the Peshmerga is an influential force in Turkey, Iran, and Syria.

Shamiran Mako

**See also**
Hussein, Saddam; Iraq; Islamic State of Iraq and Syria; Kobanî, Siege of; Kurds; Qasim, Abdul Karim

**References**
Barkey, J. Henri, and Ellen Laipson. "Iraqi Kurds and Iraq's Future." *Middle East Policy* 12(4) (Winter 2005): 66–76.
Chaliand, Gerard, ed. *People without a Country.* London: Zed, 1980.
Chapman, Dennis P. *Security Forces of the Kurdistan Regional Government.* Costa Mesa, CA: Mazda, 2011.
Gunter, M. Michael. *The Kurds of Iraq.* New York: St. Martin's, 1992.
Lawrence, Quil. *Invisible Nation: How the Kurds' Quest for Statehood Is Shaping Iraq and the Middle East.* New York: Walker, 2008.
McDowall, David. *A Modern History of the Kurds.* New York: I. B. Tauris, 2000.
O'Balance, Edgar. *The Kurdish Struggle, 1920–94.* London: Macmillan, 1996.
O'Leary, Brendan, John McGarry, and Khaled Salih, eds. *The Future of Kurdistan in Iraq.* Philadelphia: University of Pennsylvania Press, 2005.
Yildiz, Kerim, and Tom Blass. *The Kurds in Iraq: The Past, Present and Future.* London: Pluto, 2004.

# Peter the Hermit (1050?–1115)

Preacher, charismatic figure, and leader of one of the so-called people's expeditions during the First Christian Crusade in the Holy Land (1096–1099). Peter was also known as Peter of Amiens, having been born in or near that city in northern France around 1050.

Peter the Hermit is one of the most problematic individuals associated with the entire crusade movement. Supposedly, while undertaking a pilgrimage to Jerusalem (there is some question as to whether this actually occurred), Peter had experienced a vision of Christ asking him to preach in favor of an expedition to rescue the Christians in the East and to liberate the Church of the Holy Sepulchre. Peter is said to have received a letter from the patriarch of Jerusalem confirming this calling and, upon his return, to have informed Pope Urban II of his divinely ordained mission before going to preach the crusade.

In the spring of 1096 Peter set out from Cologne, reportedly with some 40,000 men, women, and children. Their numbers probably included some soldiers. As they made their way south from the Rhineland, Peter had difficulty controlling his followers, and a number of Jews were slain. At the end of July, perhaps 30,000 members of this so-called People's Crusade arrived at Constantinople (modern-day Istanbul), where they camped outside the city walls. His undisciplined followers carried out acts of violence, and Byzantine emperor Alexius I Komnenus had them ferried across the Bosporus to Asia Minor, instructing them to await his orders and not to proceed into Ottoman territory. There they allegedly continued their wrongdoings and, under the inadequate command of Peter, who lacked authority, strayed too far into Ottoman territory and were slaughtered at Kibotos (October 22, 1096). The emperor, not sorry to be rid of them, rescued the survivors, including Peter, and had them disarmed.

Despite his demonstrated incompetence and, according to at least one source, a possible attempt to desert from the army in January 1098, Peter became the ambassador of the entire crusader armies to treat with Ottoman leader Karbugha, who had laid siege to Antioch (modern-day Antakya, Turkey) in June 1098. The crusaders there were starving and had lost most of their horses. Peter's diplomatic effort came to naught, but the crusaders at Antioch sortied from the city and were victorious on June 28, 1098, miraculously assisted, it was claimed, by celestial warriors.

Following the crusader capture of Jerusalem (July 15, 1099), Peter organized the processions and prayers that the crusaders hoped would bring them victory against a Muslim relieving army but ended in a crusader defeat at Ascalon (modern-day Tel Ashqelon, Israel) on August 12, 1099.

A few much-debated documents claim that on his return to Europe, Peter founded a church at the monastery of Neufmoutier, Huy, in modern-day Belgium. This was supposedly where he died (perhaps on July 15, 1115) and was buried.

JEAN FLORI AND SPENCER C. TUCKER

**See also**
Antioch, Sieges of; Ascalon, Battle of; Crusades in the Holy Land, Christian; Jerusalem, Crusader Siege of

**References**
Blake, Ernest O., and Colin Morris. "A Hermit Goes to War: Peter the Hermit and the Origins of the First Crusade." *Studies in Church History* 22 (1985): 79–107.
Coupe, Malcolm D. "Peter the Hermit, a Reassessment." *Nottingham Medieval Studies* 31 (1987): 37–45.
Flori, Jean. "Faut-il réhabiliter Pierre l'Ermite?" *Cahiers de Civilisation Médiévale* 38 (1995): 35–54.
Morris, Colin. "Peter the Hermit and the Chroniclers." In *The First Crusade: Origins and Impact,* ed. Jonathan P. Phillips, 21–34. Manchester, UK: Manchester University Press, 1997.

## Petraeus, David Howell (1952–)

U.S. Army officer, commander of the Multi-National Force–Iraq (2007–2008), commander of the U.S. Central Command (CENTCOM) (2008–2010), commander of the International Security Assistance Force in Afghanistan (2010–2011), and director of the U.S. Central Intelligence Agency (CIA, 2011–2012). Born on November 7, 1952, in Cornwall, New York, David Howell Petraeus graduated 10th in his class from the United States Military Academy, West Point, in 1974. Commissioned a second lieutenant of infantry, he graduated from Ranger School and then held a variety of command and staff positions, with alternating assignments for professional military and civilian academic education. He graduated from the Army Command and General Staff College in 1983, then earned a master's degree (1985) in public administration and a doctorate in international affairs (1987), both from Princeton University. His doctoral dissertation dealt with the U.S. Army in Vietnam and the lessons learned there.

Petraeus returned to West Point as an assistant professor of international relations and then was a military fellow at Georgetown University's School of Foreign Service. In 1995 he was assigned to the United Nations (UN) mission during Operation UPHOLD DEMOCRACY in Haiti. Petraeus commanded a battalion in the 101st Airborne Division (1991–1993) and a brigade in the 82nd Airborne Division, (1995–1997). He was promoted to brigadier general in 1999.

As a major general, Petraeus commanded the 101st Airborne Division (Air Assault) in the invasion of Iraq in March 2003. The division engaged in the Battles of Karbala and Najaf as well as the feint at Hilla. Petraeus later oversaw the administration and rebuilding of Mosul and Niveveh Provinces. Subsequently, he commanded the Multinational Security

Transition Command–Iraq and the North Atlantic Treaty Organization (NATO) Training Mission–Iraq between June 2004 and September 2005. Petraeus's next assignment was as commanding general of Fort Leavenworth, Kansas, and the U.S. Army Combined Arms Center, where he had responsibility for the doctrinal changes to prepare the army for its continued efforts in Afghanistan and Iraq. He also coauthored *Counterinsurgency (Field Manual 3–24)*.

On January 5, 2007, Petraeus, now a lieutenant general, was selected by President George W. Bush and later unanimously confirmed by the U.S. Senate to command the Multi-National Force–Iraq. Petraeus took formal command on February 10, 2007, replacing Lieutenant General George Casey. The Petraeus appointment was the keystone in Bush's troop surge strategy in Iraq designed to bring an end to the insurgency and sectarian violence there.

In April 2007 Petraeus reported to the U.S. Congress regarding the progress of the Bush administration's surge strategy, begun that January. Meeting considerable skepticism, Petraeus stated confidently that the strategy, given time, would show positive results. At the same time, he firmly argued against setting a timetable for the withdrawal of ground troops from Iraq. Petraeus was promoted to four-star rank in December 2007.

By the spring of 2008, Petraeus could point to a significant reduction in sectarian and insurgency-based violence in Iraq. In addition, the Iraqis themselves seemed increasingly willing and able to take over security and policing tasks. As a result, U.S. and coalition troop withdrawals accelerated throughout 2008, and violence in Iraq hit four-year lows. Petraeus received considerable credit in the United States for this accomplishment. On October 1, 2008, he took command of CENTCOM.

During congressional hearings, Petraeus was careful to point out that talk of victory in Iraq was still premature. As the head of CENTCOM, he was responsible for U.S. military operations in 20 nations, from Egypt to Pakistan, as well as the ongoing conflicts in Afghanistan and Iraq.

On June 24, 2010, the same day that he removed General Stanley A. McChrystal as commander of U.S. and NATO forces in Afghanistan, U.S. president Barack Obama tapped Petraeus as McChrystal's successor, thereby sending a signal that there was no change in U.S. Afghanistan policy. Then on April 28, 2011, Obama nominated Petraeus to become the new director of the CIA. Confirmed by the Senate on June 20 in a vote of 94 to 0, Petraeus was sworn in on September 6.

On November 8, 2012, however, Petraeus, who had been married for 37 years, submitted his letter of resignation with the admission that he had engaged in an extramarital affair. Since his resignation, Petraeus has held teaching positions at the City University of New York (CUNY) and the University of Southern California. He also serves on several corporate and organization boards in addition to engaging in occasional consulting work. In 2013, he was named a nonresident senior fellow at Harvard University's John F. Kennedy School of Government. In 2014 he was named a visiting professor at the University of Exeter in England, and in 2016 the Belfer Center for Science and International Affairs at Harvard University announced a new project involving Petraeus in order to explore the link between policy and operations at the theater level of military command. That same year, Petraeus and retired astronaut Mark Kelly announced formation of the gun control group Veterans Coalition for Common Sense. In late 2016, Petraeus was on President-elect Donald Trump's short list of potential secretaries of state. That position went to Rex Tillerson, however.

Marcel A. Derosier

**See also**
Iraq Insurgency; Iraq War; Multi-National Force–Iraq; Troop Surge, U.S., Iraq War

**References**
Atkinson, Rick. *In the Company of Soldiers: A Chronicle of Combat*. New York: Henry Holt, 2005.
Day, Thomas L. *Along the Tigris: The 101st Airborne Division in Operation Iraqi Freedom: February 2003–March 2004*. Atglen, PA: Schiffer, 2007.
Fontenot, Gregory, et al. *On Point: The United States Army in Iraqi Freedom*. Annapolis, MD: Naval Institute Press, 2005.

## PHANTOM STRIKE, Operation (August 15, 2007–January 2008)

An Iraq War (2003–2011) Multi-National Force–Iraqi Army offensive launched on August 15, 2007. The attackers numbered some 28,000 troops, many of whom were present as a result of the George W. Bush administration's troop surge, which had begun earlier in the year. Following on the heels of recent coalition offensive operations, which began in June 2007, including FARDH AL-GANOON (the Baghdad Security Plan) and PHANTOM THUNDER (a nationwide counteroffensive), Operation PHANTOM STRIKE was designed to root out remaining Al Qaeda in Iraq terrorists and Iranian-backed extremist elements (including the Mahdi Army) and to reduce sectarian violence, with the goal of restoring law and order for the Iraqi people.

PHANTOM STRIKE was led by U.S. Army lieutenant general Ray Odierno, then commander of the Multi-National Corps–Iraq. It was a joint mission conducted with the Iraqi Security Force. Opposing them were Abu Omar al-Baghdadi and Abu Ayyub al-Masri, leaders of Al Qaeda in Iraq. PHANTOM STRIKE was begun one month before General David Petraeus, commander of all coalition forces in Iraq, was to report to the U.S. Congress on progress in Iraq.

During the operation, coalition and Iraqi security forces went into previously unsecured regions and attempted to eliminate terrorist groups from safe havens in the capital city of Baghdad and the provinces of northern Babil, eastern Anbar, Salahuddin, and Diyala. Considerable emphasis was placed on destroying the terror cells in Baghdad, Diyala, and central and northern Iraq. Largely an intelligence-driven operation, PHANTOM STRIKE had coalition forces move into previous no-go zones and establish local security forces and intelligence networks designed to pinpoint the exact makeup and location of Sunni and Shia extremist groups while also rooting out Al Qaeda operatives. The experiences of the Baghdad Security Plan and PHANTOM THUNDER shaped PHANTOM STRIKE.

In the operation, coalition and Iraqi security forces launched dozens of raids in and around Baghdad. These included units of varying sizes and composition. Among those American and Iraqi units participating in the total operation were troops of the 3rd Stryker Brigade Combat Team, the 2nd Infantry Division, the 3rd Brigade Combat Team, the 1st Cavalry Division, the 25th Combat Aviation Brigade, and the 1st and 4th Iraqi Army Divisions.

Strike forces went into action by land and air. In some of the attacks, it was a matter of getting in and out quickly. In others, the forces remained for an extended period in order to keep the insurgents on the defensive and thus turn former safe insurgent areas into places too risky for them to return. Commanders of the surge forces were told only to take territory they could hold. As part of General Petraeus's new counterinsurgency strategy, PHANTOM STRIKE saw coalition forces moving out of their bases and into neighborhoods across Baghdad and other major urban centers in the country in order to establish a security area based on the doctrine of clear, control, and retain (CCR).

PHANTOM STRIKE marked the last military offensive of Operation PHANTOM THUNDER and lasted until January 2008. From June 16 to August 19, 2007, alone, some 1,196 insurgents were killed and another 6,702 were captured. The precise number of killed or captured during the entire effort is uncertain. Eleven U.S. military personnel died during the operation; the number of Iraqi government casualties is unknown. The operation was termed a success in that insurgent groups were ejected from their strongholds in northern Babil, eastern Anbar, and Diyala Provinces and the southern outskirts of Baghdad. Furthermore, the raids conducted during PHANTOM STRIKE gathered valuable information on Al Qaeda and Iranian-backed terror cells countrywide. PHANTOM STRIKE was followed by Operation PHANTOM PHOENIX (January 8–July 28, 2008).

CHARLES FRANCIS HOWLETT

**See also**
Al Qaeda; Iraq Insurgency; Iraq War; Petraeus, David Howell

**References**
Filkins, Dexter. *The Forever War.* New York: Knopf, 2008.
Roggio, Bill. "Coalition, Iraqi Forces Launch Operation Phantom Strike." *Long War Journal,* August 13, 2007, http://longwarjournal.org/archives.
West, Bing. *The Strongest Tribe: War, Politics, and the Endgame in Iraq.* New York: Random House, 2008.

## PHANTOM THUNDER, Operation (June 16–August 14, 2007)

Corps-size operation during the Iraq War (2003–2011). Operation PHANTOM THUNDER was carried out by coalition forces in Iraq (American and Iraq security forces) and commenced on June 16, 2007, under the command of General David Petraeus (Multi-National Force–Iraq, overall headquarters) and Lieutenant General Raymond Odierno (Multi-National Corps–Iraq, major troop force). The operation was part of the U.S. troop surge strategy implemented in January 2007 and was designed to root out extremist groups, including Al Qaeda. PHANTOM THUNDER comprised several subordinate operations, including ARROWHEAD RIPPER in Diyala Province, MARNE TORCH and COMMANDO EAGLE in Babil Province, FARDH AL-QANOON in Baghdad, ALLJAH in Anbar Province, and special forces attacks against the Mahdi Army in southern Iraq. In preparation for this campaign against the so-called Baghdad Belt, an additional five American brigades were deployed to Iraq between January and June 2007.

As the buildup commenced, Operation LAW AND ORDER began on February 14, 2007, in an effort to resecure Baghdad, where estimates ran as high as almost 70 percent of the city under insurgent control. The operation became part of PHANTOM THUNDER when American and Iraqi forces moved to clear Sunni insurgents, Al Qaeda fighters, and Shiite militiamen from the north and south of the city. The United States wanted to take quick advantage of the arrival of 30,000 additional troops, so the offensive was begun as soon as possible. During LAW AND ORDER, 311 insurgents were killed.

Operation MARNE TORCH began on June 16 in Arab Jabour and Salman Pak, major transit points for insurgent forces in and out of Baghdad. By August 14, some 2,500 allied troops had killed 88 insurgents, captured more than 60 suspected terrorists, destroyed 51 boats, and destroyed 51 weapons caches.

On June 18, Operation ARROWHEAD RIPPER commenced when multinational troops assaulted Al Qaeda forces in the city of Baquba in Diyala Province with nighttime air strikes. As the ground forces moved in, intense street fighting engulfed the center of the city near the main market. By August 19, U.S. and Iraqi forces had killed 227 insurgents.

Multinational forces began Operation COMMANDO EAGLE on June 21 in the Mahmudiyyah region southwest of Baghdad. The area was known as the "Triangle of Death" because 3 U.S. soldiers had been kidnapped and killed there in mid-May 2007. Employing Humvee-based attacks supported by helicopter gunships, the operation resulted in roughly 100 insurgents killed and more than 50 captured.

Operations FARDH AL-QUANOON and ALLJAH were also conducted by multinational forces, this time west of Baghdad. The primary targets were Fallujah (Alljah), Karma, and Thar Thar. Allied planners developed a concept of attack similar to the one that had secured Ramadi in 2003. On June 17 a raid near Karma killed a known Libyan Al Qaeda fighter and six of his aides. Four days later, six Al Qaeda leaders were killed and five were captured near Karma. By the end of July, ground commanders reported that Karma and Thar Thar had been secured.

Throughout the summer, U.S. air strikes also proved effective against insurgents in Fallujah. However, on June 22 insurgents retaliated with two suicide bombing attacks on off-duty police officers that left four dead. On June 29 U.S. forces killed Abu Abd al-Rahman al-Masri, a senior Egyptian Al Qaeda leader, east of Fallujah. They also captured and killed many others in the ensuing weeks. Fallujah proved hard to secure, and while officials declared it secure in late August, periodic incidents continued to occur well into 2008.

The final part of PHANTOM THUNDER was the action against the Mahdi Army. In June, Iraqi Special Forces, the core of the joint Iraqi-American operation, killed and captured dozens of Mahdi Army troops.

Several lesser operations were also conducted against retreating insurgent forces in which an additional 234 were killed by August 14, when the operation officially ended and Operation PHANTOM STRIKE began. Operation ARROWHEAD RIPPER continued for another five days until street fighting in Baquba ended. This action then blended into Operation PHANTOM STRIKE.

Official reports of the action stated that coalition and Iraqi security forces had pushed into areas previously not under their control and had killed or expelled insurgent forces from northern Babil, eastern Anbar, and Diyala Provinces as well as from the southern outskirts of Baghdad. During the operation, Iraqi and coalition forces conducted intelligence raids against Al Qaeda in Iraq and the Iranian-backed cells nationwide.

Iraqi and coalition forces conducted 142 battalion-level joint operations, detaining 6,702 insurgents, killing 1,196, and wounding 419. Of this number, 382 were high-value targets. They captured 1,113 weapons caches and neutralized more than 2,000 improvised explosive devices (IEDs) and vehicle-borne IEDs. Of the approximately 28,000 U.S. and Iraqi military personnel who took part in PHANTOM THUNDER, 140 American soldiers died; the number of wounded has not been determined. Of the Iraqi security forces who fought with the Americans, 220 died; the number of wounded is not known. An additional 20 Iraqis died fighting in U.S.-allied militia units.

WILLIAM P. HEAD

**See also**
Al Qaeda in Iraq; ARROWHEAD RIPPER, Operation; Iraq Insurgency; Iraq War; PHANTOM STRIKE, Operation; Troop Surge, U.S., Iraq War

**References**
Institute for the Study of War Military Analysis and Education for Civilian Leaders. "Operation Phantom Thunder," http://www.understandingwar.org/operation/operation-phantom-thunder.
Roggio, Bill. "Operation Phantom Thunder: The Battle of Iraq." *Long War Journal*, June 21, 2007, http://www.longwarjournal.org/archives/2007/06/operation_phantom_fu.php.

# Pharnabazus (?–ca. 370 BCE)

Pharnabazus was a Persian noble who governed the satrapy of Dascylium (Phrygia) circa 413–370 BCE. This period coincided with the latter stages of the Second Peloponnesian War (431–404), Sparta's postwar operations in Asia Minor, and the Corinthian War (395–388/387). Pharnabazus therefore had considerable contact with the Greeks both as an ally and an opponent.

Pharnabazus adopted a pro-Spartan line in the course of the Greek operations in his region during the Peloponnesian War, presumably because he saw the Athenians as a greater threat. He provided financial and other support to the Peloponnesian fleet and directly fought against Athens at Abydus, Cyzicus, and Chalcedon. However, he later encouraged the Athenians to negotiate support from Persian king Darius II, probably to ensure that the Peloponnesians did not become too powerful.

Pharnabazus had an interesting relationship with his fellow satrap Tissaphernes. Ironically, although the Peloponnesians regarded Pharnabazus as the more honest of the two to deal with during their war with Athens, his territory was later the main target of Spartan operations, largely because of Tissaphernes's intrigues.

Although hampered by the superior quality of the opposing Greek hoplites and navy, Pharnabazus seems to have been a solid military commander. His use of cavalry against foragers from the Ten Thousand during 401–400 and against Agesilaus II (395) was highly effective. For a Persian aristocrat he showed an unusual interest in naval operations, including commanding the fleet at Cnidus (394) with Conon.

Pharnabazus was also apparently an effective administrator and politician. Not only did he serve as satrap for some 40 years, but he was also given the Great King's daughter as a wife and was entrusted with two (albeit unsuccessful) commands to recover Egypt (in 385 and 374 BCE).

IAIN SPENCE

**See also**
Achaemenid Empire; Hellespont Campaign; Ten Thousand, March of the

**References**
Briant, Pierre. *From Cyrus to Alexander: A History of the Persian Empire.* Winona Lake, IN: Eisenbraun, 2002.
Waters, Matt. *Ancient Persia: A Concise History of the Achaemenid Empire.* Cambridge: Cambridge University Press, 2014.

# Phase Line Bullet, Battle of (February 26, 1991)

Battle during the 1991 Persian Gulf War that led to the destruction of the 9th Mechanized Brigade of the Iraqi Republican Guard Tawakalna Division. The battle occurred on February 26, 1991, in southern Iraq and involved units of Major General Paul E. Funk's 3rd Armored Division and the 9th Armored Brigade of the Iraqi Tawakalna Republican Guard Division commanded by General Ayad Futayh al-Rawi. It was one of the few battles during the war in which entrenched and prepared Iraqi infantry were able to repulse American armor. It was also notable for the adverse weather conditions in which it was fought and for the American friendly fire casualties.

The Tawakalna Division (also known as the 3rd Mechanized Division) had distinguished itself during the war with Iran (1980–1988) and was regarded as one of the best Iraqi units. It had led the invasion of Kuwait in August 1990 and then assumed a defensive position near the western Kuwaiti border. The division included two mechanized brigades and one armored brigade. At the beginning of the war the division was near full strength, with 220 T-72 tanks and 278 infantry fighting vehicles. Because it had taken up its position before the air campaign began, the division was largely intact by the commencement of the ground campaign on February 24.

The coalition strategic plan included a turning movement by forces in western Saudi Arabia. The American XVIII Corps on the far left flank would move north and east through largely unprotected deserts in southern Iraq to cut off escape routes to Baghdad. The American VII Corps to its right under Lieutenant General Frederick Franks Jr. would also drive north and then wheel east in a more shallow movement to roll up the Iraqi forces in southern Iraq and Kuwait and destroy them before they could withdraw. Funk's 3rd Armored Division was part of the VII Corps.

By February 26 the coalition plan was unfolding as expected, although the VII Corps was somewhat behind schedule. Thousands of Iraqi soldiers had surrendered, most without a fight, and many coalition soldiers believed that the rest of the campaign would see little action. That morning as the VII Corps moved east, it encountered and defeated Iraqi units, with the 2nd Armored Cavalry Regiment destroying two Iraqi armored brigades. The 3rd Armored Division headed for Phase Line Bullet, one of the lines drawn to mark the allied advance. Weather conditions now deteriorated, with a sandstorm reducing visibility. The smoke from hundreds of oil well fires set by the Iraqis also helped to bring visibility near zero, forcing the advancing U.S. units to employ thermal lights.

Around 3:00 p.m. an advance unit of the 3rd Armored Division encountered heavy Iraqi resistance near Phase Line Bullet, about 80 miles from Kuwait City. This unit was Alpha Troop, 4th Squadron, 7th Cavalry Regiment, commanded by Captain Gerald Davie. It consisted of 14 M3 Bradley armored fighting vehicles. Iraqi surprise was nearly complete because the unit had just received word from division headquarters that no Iraqi units remained between it and the Kuwaiti border to the east. The first indication that something was amiss was when the Americans saw a line of Iraqi armored personnel carriers only some 325 yards ahead. As Davie later admitted, this was about one-tenth the preferred range. Iraqi small-arms and heavy machine-gun fire, along with rocket-propelled grenades (RPGs) and Sagger antitank missiles, raked the American formation. Fortunately, Sagger accuracy was adversely affected by the weather conditions.

Alpha Troop responded with 25mm fire from the Bradley turret guns, machine-gun fire, and TOW antitank missiles. The U.S. fire had little effect, however, as many of the Iraqi vehicles were in dug-in fighting positions. They were also supported by a dozen field artillery batteries to the rear along with mortars near the line.

The ensuing engagement lasted about two hours. Realizing that his unit was also receiving main gun tank rounds and running out of ammunition, Davie ordered a withdrawal. Before they were able to withdraw, however, a majority of the Bradleys had received varying damage. U.S. M-1 Abrams tanks positioned to the rear fired in support of A Troop and destroyed at least one Iraqi T-72 tank and several armored personnel carriers (APCs), but at least one Abrams mistook the Bradleys for Iraqi vehicles and fired on them. Two Bradleys were hit by Abrams tank fire, with two American soldiers killed.

General Funk recognized that a hasty assault on the entrenched Iraqi position could be costly and ordered his screening forces to probe the position, identify weak points, and then push through if possible. The 1st Brigade, on the right, sent a company from the 3rd Battalion, 5th Cavalry, forward. They were joined by two other companies in Bradleys. Because of the poor visibility, the battalion was much closer to the Iraqis than normal, and thermal sights used in poor visibility were not working as well as expected because of the weather and the oil smoke. Even so, the battalion was able to call in artillery support as it identified Iraqi tanks and other vehicles. Iraqi field artillery was quickly silenced, but the American forces here were unable to advance. On the left, scouts from the 4th Battalion, 32nd Armor, identified Iraqi T-72 tanks advancing. They managed to destroy the leading tank but were unable to move any farther.

The action was confused, and the Americans were unable to break through until early on the morning of February 27. The Battle of Phase Line Bullet was an unexpected setback for the Americans. Four Bradleys had been destroyed, and 10 others were damaged. Two Americans had been killed by friendly fire, and another 12 were wounded by both Iraqi and American fire. The 3rd Armored Division's advance was held up by at least 12 hours. When the American forces moved forward after the battle, they found 6 Iraqi T-72 tanks either destroyed or disabled by their crews. Eighteen Iraqi APCs were also destroyed or abandoned, along with some field artillery and other weapons. Iraqi casualties are unknown.

The Battle of Phase Line Bullet did not change the course of the war. It did, however, demonstrate that the Iraqis were capable of putting up a good fight when their troops had the best equipment and proper training and when weather and terrain forced the Americans to fight in close proximity, thereby negating the overwhelming U.S. advantage in stand-off firepower.

TIM J. WATTS

**See also**
Persian Gulf War, Ground Campaign; Republican Guard, Iraq

**References**
Atkinson, Rick. *Crusade: The Untold Story of the Persian Gulf War.* New York: Mariner Books, 1994.
Bin, Alberto, Richard Hill, and Archer Jones. *Desert Storm: A Forgotten War.* Westport, CT: Praeger, 1998.

## Philippe II, King (1165–1223)

King of France. Born in Gonesse in the Val-d'Oise on August 21, 1165, Philippe of the House of Capet was the son of French king Louis VII and his third wife Adèle of Champagne. In declining health, Louis had his son crowned king at Rheims on November 1, 1179, before dying on September 18, 1180. As king, Philippe's goals were first to protect his royal domains and then to expand them. Not known as a warrior, Philippe for the most part accomplished his aims by governmental reforms, adroit diplomacy, and manipulation of the feudal system. An example of this was his marriage in 1180 to Isabella, daughter of Count Baldwin V of Hainaut. She gave him a son, the future Louis VIII.

Philippe remarried following the death of Isabella in 1190. This second marriage, in 1193, was to the beautiful and pious Ingeborg, sister of the king of Denmark. But for reasons unclear, Philippe disliked her almost immediately after their marriage and had her consigned to a monastery. His subsequent efforts to secure a divorce were refused by Popes Celestine III and Innocent III. Not until 1196 was Philippe finally able to marry his mistress, Agnes of Meran, whose children by him were legitimized.

Philippe defeated a major revolt against him in Champagne and Flanders (1181–1185) and then, as with his father, supported several rebellions by the sons of Henry Plantagenet: Henry "the Young King" (d. 1183), Geoffroy (d. 1186), and finally Richard, who came to be known as Richard the Lionheart. Eventually defeated at Le Mans, the elder Henry sought refuge in Chinon, where he died in 1189. However, his successor Richard would prove to be an even more dangerous rival for Philippe.

In response to the capture of Jerusalem by Saladin in 1187, both Richard and Philippe took the cross at Gisors on January 21, 1188. Their departures on the Third Crusade (1189–1192) were delayed by the deaths of Henry II and of Isabella, however. Richard and Philippe departed Vézelay on July 4, 1190, with the intention of meeting in Sicily, where the animosity between them grew. Richard indeed outshone Philippe in his splendor and also rejected his long-standing fiancée, Philippe's half sister Alice, whom he claimed had been the concubine of Henry II. Philippe released Richard from his engagement for the payment of 10,000 marks. Richard then married Berengaria of Navarre in Cyprus, which he seized before landing in triumph at Acre (modern-day Akko, Israel). Philippe was already there, having been involved in the siege of Acre, held by Saladin's troops, since April 20, 1191. The crusader assaults on the city often took place without the two kings, both of whom were suffering from an illness that caused fever as well as loss of hair and nails. Philippe in particular was severely ill. Acre finally capitulated on July 12, 1191. The town was to be surrendered, the Muslims were to free 1,200 Christian captives and pay a ransom of 200,000 bezants, and Saladin was to return the relic of the True Cross, which he had captured at the Battle of Hattin in 1187.

Although Jerusalem had still not been recovered, Philippe II soon decided to return to France. His own illness and the illness of his only son (then four years old) as well as rumors of attempts to poison him were all put forward by Philippe and his court, but his motivations were probably political: the count of Flanders, Philippe of Alsace, had died at Acre on June 1, and Philippe II wanted to assert his right of succession over Artois and thus extend his domains toward the north.

As soon as he returned to France, Philippe took advantage of Richard's absence from his domains by supporting the rebellion of his brother John, lord of Ireland. When Richard was captured by Duke Leopold V of Austria and handed over to Emperor Henry VI, Philippe and John offered 100,000 marks to have him kept a prisoner. Richard's mother Eleanor, however, succeeded in obtaining his freedom, and Richard returned to England in March 1194. He immediately attacked Philippe, defeating him at Fréteval on July 4. Though he managed to evade capture, Philippe lost his treasury and numerous chancery documents. Hostilities continued, with Richard having the upper hand, until the king of England died at Châlus (April 6, 1199).

A protracted war with Richard I along the Epie River (1192–1199) ended poorly for Philippe, who suffered defeats at Fréteval (July 1194) and Courcelles (September 1198). When Richard was killed in 1199, Philippe was able to take advantage of the succession of John I to expand his realm, confirmed in the Treaty of Le Goulet in May 1200. Philippe then fought John in a protracted campaign (1202–1206), ravaging Angevin holdings in France and capturing the important fortress of Château Gaillard (March 6, 1204) as well as taking Normandy, Maine, Touraine, Anjou, and most of Poitou.

John then allied with Holy Roman emperor Otto IV to attack Philippe. John invaded southern France but was beaten there by a French army under Philippe's son Louis at La Roche-aux-Moines (July 2, 1214). Meanwhile, Philippe personally led French forces against an allied force under Otto IV that had invaded from the north. In one of the most decisive battles of the medieval period, Philippe defeated the combined English, German, and Flemish army in the great Battle of Bouvines (July 27, 1214). During the fighting Philippe was at one point pulled to the ground from his horse by enemy soldiers but was rescued by his bodyguards. Among the French prisoners were Count Ferrand of Flanders and the earl of Salisbury. Otto IV barely escaped but soon lost his throne.

Philippe spent most of the remainder of his reign at peace, strengthening his territory through administrative reforms. He greatly improved the city of Paris and extended a charter to the University of Paris in 1200. Philippe II, known as Philippe Auguste (Philip Augustus), died at Nantes, France, on July 14, 1223.

A ruler of great ability, Philippe II achieved remarkable success in the expansion of his realm, doubling its size and making France the mot powerful country in Europe.

JEAN FLORI AND SPENCER C. TUCKER

**See also**
Crusades in the Holy Land, Christian; Hattin, Battle of; Richard I, King; Saladin

### References

Bradbury, Jim. *Philip Augustus: King of France, 1180–1223*. London: Longman, 1996.
Duby, Georges. *The Legend of Bouvines: War, Religion, and Culture in the Middle Ages*. Berkeley: University of California Press, 1990.
Flori, Jean. *Philippe Auguste, roi de France*. Paris: Tallandier, 2002.
Hallam, Elizabeth M. *Capetian France: 987–1328*. London: Longman, 1980.

## Philomelion, Battle of (1116)

Major battle that occurred in the autumn of 1116 at Philomelion (Latinized as Philomelium and today's Aksehir, Turkey) in central Anatolia. Fought during the Byzantine-Seljuk Wars, the Battle of Philomelion pitted a Byzantine army under Emperor Alexios I Komnenos against forces of the Sultanate of Rum led by Sultan Malik Shah I (not to be confused with Malik Shah I of the Great Seljuk Empire [r. 1072–1092]).

The Byzantines profited from the success of the First Christian Crusade in the Holy Land (1096–1099). They were able to retake the Aegean coasts and much of the interior of western Anatolia. However, with the failure of the Crusade of 1101, the Seljuk and Danishmendid Turks resumed offensive military operations against the Byzantines, and Malik Shah recovered central Anatolia.

The Byzantines were unable to prevent Turkish raids into the areas of Anatolia they had so recently retaken but were able to turn back a Turkish effort to take Nicaea in 1113. In 1116 Byzantine emperor Alexios I Komnenos, old and suffering from a terminal illness, personally took the field with his army campaigning in northwestern Anatolia and was able to defeat the Turks in a minor battle at Poemanenon. Upon receiving reinforcements, he decided to mount a major raid into Turkish-controlled territory.

The Seljuk capital of Iconium was probably Alexios I's initial objective, but apparently he abandoned this in favor of a show of force and the evacuation of Christians in Turkish-controlled areas. As he proceeded, Alexios employed a new battle formation of his own making. Known as the parataxis, it was essentially a defensive formation in the form of a hollow square of infantry with the army's baggage in the center and cavalry within the square but able to mount attacks in any direction. This proved to be a highly efficient means of dealing with the Turkish tactic of essentially massed attacks by horse archers. During the Third Crusade (1189–1192) English king Richard I would employ a similar formation in the Battle of Arsuf (September 7, 1191).

The Byzantines moved through Santabaris and then took the city of Philomelion by assault. Alexios then sent out small detachments to round up the Christian populations in the area for removal. Informed of the approach of a large Seljuk force, Alexios ordered his army to withdraw back to Byzantine territory. The arm took assumed the parataxis formation, with the evacuated Christians joining the baggage train in the center of the formation.

The initial Seljuk force, commanded by an officer known as Manalugh, was confused by the Byzantine formation and did not press the attack. The next day, however, the rest of the Seljuk force came up under Sultan Malik Shah and attacked simultaneously the van and rear of the Byzantine formation. The Byzantine cavalry mounted two counterattacks, the first apparently unsuccessful, with Alexios I's son Andronikos among those killed. The second Byzantine counterattack, led by Nikephoros Bryennios the Younger, Alexios's son-in-law, was successful, putting to flight that part of the Seljuk force led in person by Malik Shah, who barely escaped. A subsequent night attack by the Seljuks was rebuffed.

The next day Malik Shah again attacked, his troops completely surrounding the Byzantine formation. Again the Seljuk attacks met rebuff, and the day following Malik Shah sent an emissary to Alexios with a peace proposal. The two rulers then met in person and reached agreement, with Malik Shah apparently agreeing to cease his raids into Byzantine territory and perhaps even recognizing Byzantine control over eastern Anatolia.

The Byzantine campaign was remarkable for the high level of discipline shown by the Byzantine army, Alexios having shown that he could move with impunity through Turkish-dominated territory. His own reverse at Philomelion probably contributed to Malik Shah's demise, for that same year he was deposed, blinded, and then murdered by his brother Mas'ud. Alexios meanwhile died in 1118, leaving the task of reconquering all of Asia Minor to his eldest son and successor, John II Komnenos.

Spencer C. Tucker

### See also

Alexios I Komnenos; Arsuf, Battle of; Byzantine Empire; Byzantine-Seljuk Wars; Crusades in the Holy Land, Christian; Danishmendid Dynasty; Rum, Sultanate of

### References

Birkenmeier, John W. *The Development of the Komnenian Army: 1081–1180*. Leiden: Brill, 2002.

France, J. *Victory in the East: A Military History of the First Crusade.* Cambridge: Cambridge University Press, 1994.

Haldon, John. *Byzantium at War, AD 600–1453.* Oxford, UK: Osprey, 2002.

Mango, Cyril. *The Oxford History of Byzantium.* New York: Oxford University Press, 2002.

Norwich, John Julius. *A Short History of Byzantium.* New York: Vintage Books, 1997.

Runciman, Stephen. *A History of the Crusades.* Harmondsworth, UK: Pelican Books, 1971.

## Phoenicia

Phoenicia, like ancient Greece, was not a nation but rather a group of city-states linked by a common language, culture, ethnic origin, and religious practices. In the Bible the Phoenicians are referred to as the Canaanites, a West Semitic people. But the more common name used to describe them—Phoinikes, meaning "red men"—appears to have come from the Greek. Scholars have debated the etymology, but it is generally agreed that it is derived from the reddish-purple dye they produced from sea snails and traded abroad. The Phoenicians identified themselves as natives of their particular city (Sidonians, Tyrians, and so on).

It is ironic that the people who with the Phoenician script gave us the basis of the modern Western alphabet left behind very little written material. It is in the writings of other peoples and the archaeological record that we learn most about them. The Phoenicians first really appear in the historical record in the mid-14th-century Armana correspondence, letters exchanged between the Phoenicians and Egyptians. These letters show how they had established themselves in well-defended walled cities of the Levant. Their main centers were Tyre, Sidon, Byblos, Berytus (modern-day Beirut), Sarepta, and Arwad, but they also established colonies westward across the Mediterranean, the most famous being the great city of Carthage.

Phoenician cities are recorded as fielding light infantry units supplemented by chariots and archers, but it was their navies that provided their most powerful defensive force. The Phoenicians built and operated the greatest navies of the Mediterranean throughout most of the classical and Hellenistic periods. Greek historian Herodotus claims that Phoenician sailors circumnavigated Africa around 600, and it is generally believed that their ships traded as far west as Cornwall for tin. Their merchant fleets certainly regularly serviced cities as far away as Spain, Africa, Sicily and Cyprus.

In the Levant, the Phoenicians had access to extensive cedar forests and other timber, useful for shipbuilding as well as to trade with their dominant neighbors: Egypt and later the Assyrians and Babylonians. From the 530s Phoenicia came under Persian control but generally was able to enjoy a level of autonomy.

The Greeks believed that Cadmus, the legendary founder of the Greek city-state of Thebes, was Phoenician, but the relationship with the Greeks was often more hostile, given overlapping colonial and maritime interests. To some extent Greek colonizers were more interested in agricultural land than the trade-oriented Phoenicians, but there was significant scope for conflict in areas such as Sicily.

Persia relied heavily on Phoenician fleets in its wars with the Greeks and Egypt. Phoenician service to Persia earned the Phoenicians a degree of independence and important mercantile privileges. Herodotus tells us that the fleet from Tyre was pivotal in Cambyses's successful Egyptian campaign of 525 BCE. Herodotus also describes the Phoenicians as the "most committed" of Persia's allies in the Battle of Lade in 494. The Athenian Cimon was unsuccessful in ending Phoenician control of Cyprus in 450, and the resulting Peace of Callias (449) saw the Athenian fleets barred from Cyprus. Consequently, the Phoenician Cypriot city of Citium flourished.

Persian rule of Phoenicia ended with the conquests of Alexander the Great, who captured Tyre after a protracted siege in 332. After changing hands several times in the decades following Alexander's death in 323, for most of the third century Phoenicia was controlled from Egypt by the Ptolemies. But the Seleucids regularly contested Ptolemaic control and themselves ruled Phoenicia for the greater part of the second century. After a period of Armenian rule, Phoenicia became part of the Roman Empire in 65.

JAMES MCDONALD

**See also**

Cambyses II; Cyprus; Greco-Persian Wars; Syrian-Egyptian Wars; Tyre and Gaza, Sieges of

**References**

Knapp, A. Bernard. *The History and Culture of Ancient Western Asia and Egypt.* Chicago: Dorsey, 1988.

Markoe, Glenn E. *The Phoenicians.* London: British Museum Press, 2000.

## PILLAR OF DEFENSE, Operation

*See* Gaza War of 2012

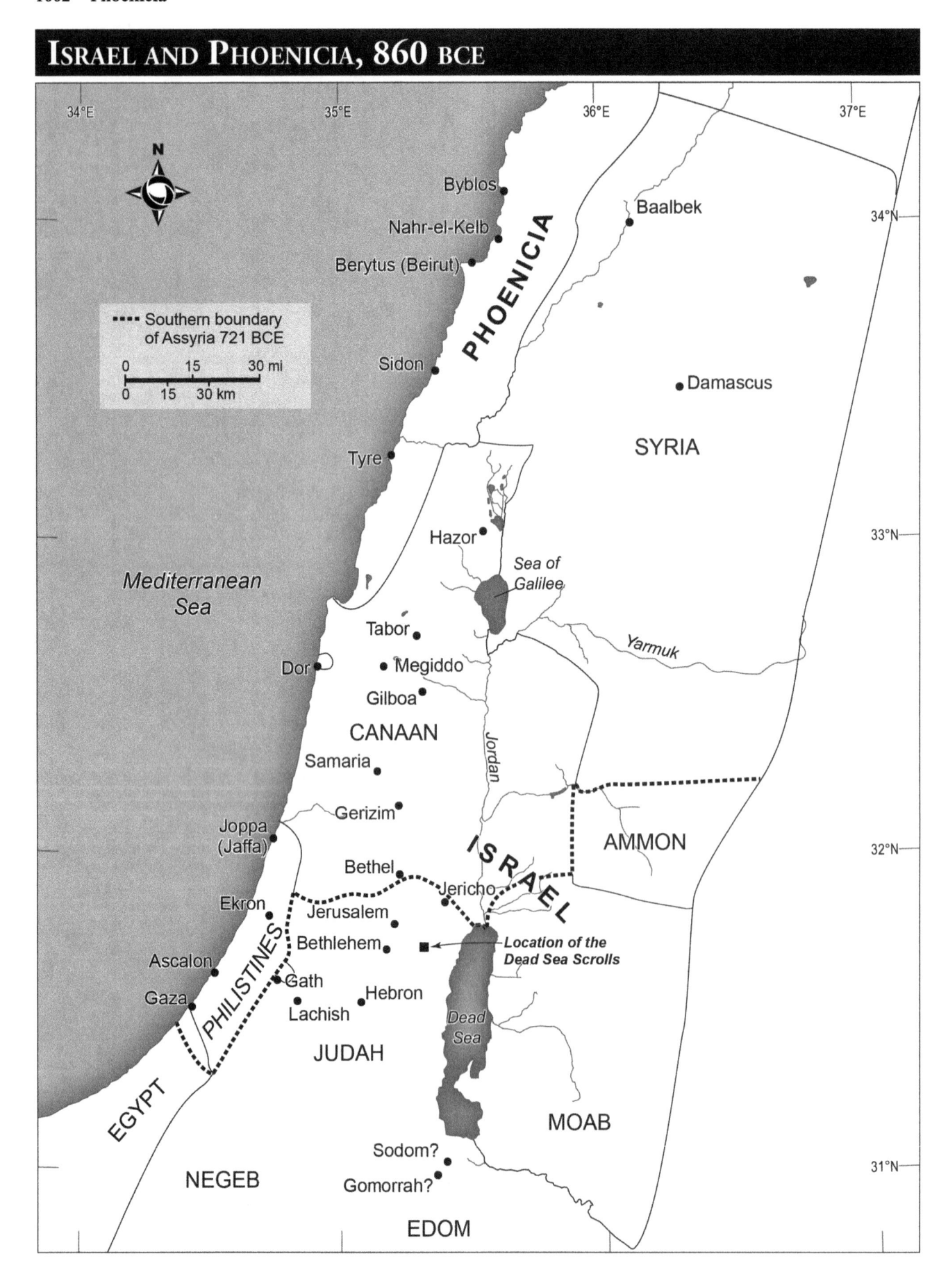

# Phoenicia

## Israel and Phoenicia, 860 BCE

# Pompeius Magnus, Gnaeus (106–48 BCE)

Roman general and political leader. Born on September 29, 106 BCE, in Picenum, Italy, Gnaeus Pompeius (Pompey) fought under his father in the Social War (91–88). During the civil war of 88–82 between Gaius Marius and Lucius Sulla, Pompey switched sides early to Sulla, raising three legions to support the latter's march on Rome in 83. Pompey married Sulla's daughter Amelia and then secured Sicily and North Africa for Sulla. Returning to Rome, while still in his 20s Pompey celebrated a triumph and was accorded the title "magnus" (great) in March 79.

Following Sulla's death, Pompey received from the Senate a commission to suppress a rebellion led by M. Aemilius Lepidus during 78–77 BCE. Successful at this, Pompey then received from the Senate authority to campaign in Spain, where he defeated forces under Quintus Sertonius (77–72). Returning to Italy in 71, Pompey took part in putting down the great slave revolt led by Spartacus (the Third Servile War) in 73–71 and was elected consul in 70.

In 67 Pompey received from the Senate a grant of extraordinary powers for a three-year period to end piracy in the Mediterranean. Accomplishing this feat in only six months and with a large fleet at his disposal, Pompey secured command against King Mithridates VI of Pontus, who had invaded Asia Minor in 66. Pompey defeated Mithridates, forcing him to commit suicide in 63. Pompey then went on to subdue Asia Minor and annex Syria and Judaea to the Roman Empire during 66–62.

Returning to Rome in 61 BCE, Pompey celebrated yet another triumph and requested land for his soldiers. When the Senate resisted this, he joined the First Triumvirate with Julius Caesar and Marcus Licinius Crassus in 60, securing land for his soldiers. At first Pompey was the most powerful figure in the combination, but with the death of Crassus in Syria following the Battle of Carrhae in 53, Caesar became the more powerful. Jealous of his rival, Pompey, who had received command in Spain, governed it through legates and remained in Rome during 61–50, and following the death of his fourth wife, Caesar's daughter Julia, in 54, Pompey became more inclined to side with the Senate aristocrats against Caesar, securing his own illegal election as sole consul in 52.

Caesar refused to obey senatorial decrees and invaded Italy in 49. Defeated in Italy, Pompey relocated to Illyria, while Caesar campaigned in Spain during 49–48. Caesar then took up the pursuit of his opponent and, evading Pompey's command of the sea, landed forces in Illyria. Pompey and his allied Senate forces outmaneuvered Caesar's smaller army near Dyrrhacium but failed to capitalize on it in the spring of 48. Finally, the two sides met in the decisive encounter near Pharsalus where, against his better judgment, Pompey allowed himself to be talked into utilizing his larger army to fight there, and Caesar was victorious in the Battle of Pharsalus (August 3, 48). Pompey then fled to Egypt, only to be murdered on his arrival by one of his lieutenants on September 28, 48 BCE.

A superb commander and trainer of legionnaires, Pompey in his early years was a brilliant general and secured the eastern Mediterranean for Rome. In his later years a defender of the status quo, he proved to be an ineffective campaigner and no match for Julius Caesar as general or strategist.

Spencer C. Tucker

## See also
Caesar, Gaius Julius; Carrhae, Battle of; Crassus, Marcus Licinius; Mithridates VI Eupator Dionysius; Roman-Parthian Wars

## References
Greenlaugh, Peter L. *Pompey, the Republican Prince*. Ithaca, NY: Cornell University Press, 1986.

Leach, John. *Pompey the Great*. Totowa, NJ: Book Club Associates, 1978.

Seager, Robin. *Pompey the Great*. Berkeley: University of California Press, 1979.

# Pontus (281 BCE–62 CE)

An ancient kingdom in Anatolia. Pontus was located in northern Anatolia and extended from the coast of the Black Sea south to Cappadocia and Armenia and from the Halys River to Colchis. It was a fertile region, with good deposits of iron, copper, and silver. Pontus had a largely tribal nature, with a powerful nobility and priestly caste. The Greek colonies along its coast seem to have been originally founded for trade (especially in local metals).

The kingdom of Pontus was founded under Mithridates I Ctistes (r. 302–266 BCE). His successors developed significant alliances with the Seleucid Empire, increased the power of the monarchy, and reduced the power of the nobility and priests. Mithridates V Euergetes (r. 151–120) in particular extended Pontic territory, changed the character of his court to make it more Greek, and developed strong ties with Rome. He supported Rome in the Third Punic War (149–146) and during the slave revolt in Pergamum (133–129).

Pontus reached its greatest extent and power under Mithridates VI Eupator, who reigned in his own right during

113–163 CE. However, his attempts to annex Cappadocia led to three wars against Rome, each of which Mithridates lost, culminating in the dissolution of Pontus as an independent entity in the year 62.

IAIN SPENCE

**See also**
Diadochi, Wars of the; Mithridates VI Eupator Dionysius; Seleucid Empire

**References**
Green, Peter. *Alexander to Actium: The Historical Evolution of the Hellenistic Age.* Berkeley: University of California Press, 1990.
Pastor, Luis B. "Nullis umquam nisi domesticis regibus. Cappadocia, Pontus and the resistance to the Diadochi in Asia Minor." In *After Alexander: The Time of the Diadochi (323–281 BC),* ed. Víctor A. Troncoso and Edward M. Anson, 183–198. Oxford, UK: Oxbow Books, 2013.

# Popular Front for the Liberation of Palestine

Marxist-Leninist organization founded in 1967 that seeks to create a socialist state for Palestinians. The Popular Front for the Liberation of Palestine (PFLP) has always been opposed to the existence of Israel and has committed numerous terrorist attacks since 1968, focusing on Israeli and moderate Arab targets. Founded by George Habash on December 11, 1967, just after the Six-Day War, the PFLP arose from the merger of the Arab Nationalist Movement, which Habash had founded in 1953, with the Palestine Liberation Front and Youth for Revenge. Habash created the PFLP to represent the Palestinian working class and stated that its goal was the creation of a democratic socialist Palestinian state and the elimination of Israel. Habash saw the elimination of Israel as a necessary step in purging the Middle East from Western capitalist influences. He also claimed after the 1967 Arab defeat that it would be necessary to combat the Arab regimes before that could be accomplished. Although Habash was himself a Palestinian Christian, he wanted the PFLP to be an entirely secular organization based on Marxist principles and socialism and positioned on the vanguard of a world socialist revolution.

The PFLP quickly spread into other Arab countries and acquired financial backing from Syria and Jordan. The group joined the Palestine Liberation Organization (PLO) in 1968 and immediately generated two splinter factions, the terrorist organization Popular Front for the Liberation of Palestine–General Command (PFLP-GC) and the orthodox Marxist Democratic Front for the Liberation of Palestine.

Most members of the PFLP were trained as guerrillas. The group soon became known for its terrorist activities, especially its airliner hijackings, many of which targeted the Israeli airline El Al. Most of the early attacks were coordinated by Wadi Haddad, known as "The Master." On July 23, 1968, the PFLP commandeered an Israeli El Al airplane on its way from Rome to Tel Aviv and landed it in Algeria, mistakenly believing that Major General Ariel Sharon, later to become an Israeli prime minister, was on board. The group held the passengers and crew captive until August 31.

Other hijackings and attacks followed. On December 26, 1968, PFLP guerrillas shot at an El Al jet about to leave Athens for Paris, killing 1 passenger. On February 18, 1969, its members attacked another El Al jet in Zurich, killing the copilot. Two days later they bombed a supermarket in Jerusalem. That August, the PFLP hijacked a TWA flight flying from Rome to Tel Aviv and forced it to land in Damascus. One of the leaders of this attack was Leila Khaled, who had joined the Arab Nationalist Movement in 1958 at the age of 14. She was arrested in Damascus but was quickly released. On September 9, 1969, 6 Palestinians threw grenades at Iraqi embassies in Bonn and The Hague and at the El Al office in Brussels. The PFLP also attacked a bus at the Munich airport on February 10, 1970. On February 21, 1970, the group detonated a barometric pressure device on Swissair Flight 330, flying from Zurich to Tel Aviv. The bomb damaged the plane sufficiently that the crew was unable to return to the Zurich airport. The jet crashed and killed all on board, including 38 passengers and 9 crew members.

On September 6, 1970, the PFLP launched its most ambitious hijacking scheme yet. Group members simultaneously hijacked jets in Brussels, Frankfurt, and Zurich and forced them to fly to Cairo or Zarqa, Jordan. The group hijacked a fourth plane three days later. They blew up the three aircraft in Zarqa on September 12. The PFLP announced that the hijackings were intended to teach the Americans a lesson and to punish them for supporting Israel. On September 16, 1970, King Hussein of Jordan formed a military government and began attacking Palestinian guerrillas in Jordan. He ultimately expelled the PLO from the country. This crisis, which became known as Black September, reinforced Habash's claim that Arab regimes were inhibiting the Palestinian guerrilla movement.

Khaled, who had undergone six months of cosmetic surgery to disguise her appearance, and her colleague Patrick Arguello attempted to hijack a fourth aircraft departing from Amsterdam on September 6. They failed in this task. Arguello was shot, and Khaled was overpowered and then

Members of the Popular Front for the Liberation of Palestine wave Soviet- and Egyptian-supplied weapons. The photo was published in 1969. (Library of Congress)

imprisoned in London. This arrest provoked the PLFP to seize five more civilian airplanes in an effort to persuade British authorities to release Khaled. She was released after 28 days in exchange for 56 Western hostages.

In 1973 Habash agreed that the PFLP would cease terrorist activities abroad, on the advice of the Palestinian National Council. Thereafter he restricted his terrorist activity to Israel, Jordan, and Lebanon. On May 30, 1972, the PFLP attacked Lod Airport in Israel, killing 24 people. Two months later on July 9, 1972, Israelis killed PFLP member and creative writer Ghassan Kanafani. Throughout the 1970s the group attacked numerous Israeli targets. The PFLP withdrew from the PLO in 1974, complaining that the PLO was no longer interested in destroying Israel completely and seemed instead to be willing to compromise.

When the First Intifada began on December 8, 1987, elements of the PFLP organized terrorist attacks in the Gaza Strip and the West Bank. In 1990 the Jordanian branch of the PFLP was converted into an actual political party, the Jordanian Popular Democratic Party. Habash stepped down as leader on April 27, 2000, and was replaced by Abu Ali Mustafa. He was killed on August 27, 2001, when an Israeli helicopter fired rockets at his office in the West Bank town of Ramallah. The PFLP retaliated on October 17, 2001, by killing Rehavam Zeevi, the Israeli minister of tourism. Ahmed Sadat became secretary-general of the organization on October 3, 2001. The armed militia of this group continued its terrorist activity in the early 2000s, using car bombs and other small-scale bombing techniques and sometimes simply shooting targets. Sadat was subsequently arrested by the Palestinian Authority (PA) and held in Jericho.

The PFLP opposed the 1993 Oslo Accords, partially because of its resentment of Fatah control over the PLO and subsequently the PA. The group has maintained its Marxist-Leninist beliefs, and this has always contributed to its smaller size and led to its decline as Islamism became much more influential.

After the Oslo Accords the PFLP had difficulty establishing itself in the West Bank and the Gaza Strip. At that time, Hamas enjoyed rapidly rising popularity in the wake of its successful strategy of suicide bombings devised by Yahya Ayyash, known as "the Engineer." The collapse of the Soviet

Union coupled with the rise of radical Islam and particularly the popularity of Islamist groups Hamas and Palestinian Islamic Jihad served to greatly diminish the role of the PFLP in Palestinian politics and armed resistance. Despite this, the organization retains considerable influence within the PLO, since no new elections have been held for the Palestine National Council (PNC).

The PLO's agreement with Israel in September 1993 and ensuing negotiations led the PFLP to establish contacts with Islamic fundamentalist groups linked to Iran, including Palestinian Hamas and Hezbollah in Lebanon.

The PFLP is politically important in the Ramallah area, the eastern districts and suburbs of Jerusalem, and Bethlehem as well as the primarily Christian Refidyeh district of Nablus, but it has little strength in the rest of the West Bank and is of threat politically to Hamas in Gaza. In the 2006 Palestinian legislative elections, the PFLP won 4.2 percent of the popular vote and 3 of the 132 seats in the Palestinian Legislative Council.

When it was formed in the late 1960s, the PFLP supported the established line of most Palestinian guerrilla fronts and ruled out any negotiated settlement with Israel that would result in a two-state solution. Habash and other leaders advocated one state with an Arab identity in which Jews were entitled to live with the same rights as any minority. The PFLP declared that its goal was to create "a people's democratic Palestine, where Arabs and Jews would live without discrimination, a state without classes and national oppression, a state which allows Arabs and Jews to develop their national culture."

The PFLP platform called for revolution in conservative or monarchist Arab states such as Morocco and Jordan and the right of return of all Palestinian refugees to their homes in pre-1948 Palestine. As of 2018, the PFLP continued to insist that Hamas is a vital part of the Palestinian national movement and thus should be included in any future peace deals.

AMY HACKNEY BLACKWELL AND SPENCER C. TUCKER

**See also**
Intifada, First; Oslo Accords; Palestine Liberation Organization; Popular Front for the Liberation of Palestine–General Command; Terrorism

**References**
Hourani, Albert. *A History of the Arab Peoples.* Cambridge, MA: Harvard University Press, 1991.
Popular Front for the Liberation of Palestine. *A Radical Voice from Palestine: Recent Documents from the Popular Front for the Liberation of Palestine.* Oakland, CA: Abraham Guillen, 2002.

Smith, Charles D. *Palestine and the Arab-Israeli Conflict: A History with Documents.* 6th ed. New York: Bedford/St. Martin's, 2006.

# Popular Front for the Liberation of Palestine–General Command

Militant Palestinian organization that carried out military-style operations and terrorist attacks against Israeli targets and Arab political opponents. Founded in October 1968 as a splinter group of the Popular Front for the Liberation of Palestine (PFLP) and the Arab Nationalist Movement, the Popular Front for the Liberation of Palestine–General Command (PFLP-GC), led by Ahmad Jibril, a former Palestinian officer in the Syrian Army, dedicated itself to conducting armed revolutionary action. It did so as a result of ideological debates about political strategies and directions among the more militant groups of that period. Based in Syria and Lebanon, the PFLP-GC is an organization of negligible size (a few hundred fighters) and limited influence within the Palestinian nationalist movement.

The roots of the organization can be traced to the experiences of dispossession shared by many Palestinians. The group's founder, Ahmad Jibril, was born in Jaffa in present-day Israel in 1928. Although his family relocated to Syria in late 1947, he yearned for a return to Palestine. Together with like-minded Palestinians serving in the Syrian Army during the 1950s and early 1960s, he conducted covert cross-border raids into Israel. In 1965 he and other army veterans formed the Palestine Liberation Front (PLF).

Jibril's militancy grew out of the Arab defeat in the 1967 Six-Day War. Following this, in October 1967 the PLF joined the Palestinian wing of the Arab Nationalist Movement to found the PFLP led by George Habash. However, within a year Jibril withdrew from the collaboration, reportedly over disputes involving control and command. He then formed the PFLP-GC.

The new organization quickly established itself as one committed to mounting spectacular operations with skill and tenacity. In February 1970 the group killed 47 people in its first major terrorist attack, bringing down a Swissair passenger plane bound for Israel. Just four years later, a team of 3 PFLP-GC fighters killed another 18 people in a raid to seize hostages in the northern Israeli town of Qiryat Shmona. Major attacks also targeted the Palestine Liberation Organization (PLO) as the myriad Palestinian groups became embroiled in the Lebanese Civil War and feuded over leadership of the nationalist movement. And even as the PFLP-GC was increasingly marginalized by its affiliation with both Syrian and Libyan interests, the group's actions still served to inspire and support the popular Palestinian drive to end the Israeli occupation.

In late November 1987 only days before the outbreak of the First Intifada (1987–1993), an innovative operation saw the PFLP-GC employ hang gliders to ferry guerrillas into northern Israel and attack army positions, underscoring the group's desire to defy the political realities on the ground.

With ongoing backing from Syria and bases in Lebanon, the PFLP-GC continued to have a role in the Palestinian nationalist movement. However, its future has been tenuous since the death of Jibril's son, Muhammad Jihad, whose assassination in Beirut on May 20, 2002, robbed the group of its commander of armed operations and the heir apparent to overall leadership.

With the beginning of the Syrian Civil War in March 2011 and despite some opposition from within the PFLP-GC leadership, the organization allied itself with the Syrian government under President Bashar al-Assad. The PFLP-GC was based in Yarmouk Camp, a nearly one-square-mile district of Damascus. Originally outside the city and an unofficial refugee camp, Yarmouk was home to the largest number of Palestinian refugees in Syria (112,550 registered residents in 2004 but down to only some 20,000 in 2014). During the ensuing fighting, the PFLP-GC assisted the Syrian Army in fighting Syrian rebels in and around Yarmouk.

Opposition from a number of Palestinian refugees to the alliance with the Assad government led to the shooting deaths of a number of Yarmouk residents on June 5, 2011, however. Then on August 3, 2012, 21 civilians were killed when Syrian Army forces shelled Yarmouk. Palestinian president Mahmoud Abbas sharply criticized the Syrian Army for this and also criticized the PFLP-GC for bringing Palestinians into the civil war. On December 5, 2012, there was fighting in Yarmouk between Syrian rebel forces, including the Free Syrian Army, and a number of Palestinians formed into the Liwa al-Asifa, or Storm Brigade. By December 17 the rebels had won control of Yarmouk. Thereafter an agreement was reached between the Syrian government and the rebels to establish Yarmouk as a neutral zone, with all armed groups withdrawing. The agreement also called for the PFLP-GC to be dismantled and its weapons surrendered.

Intermittent government shelling of Yarmouk and armed clashes rendered the agreement problematic at best. Reportedly many PFLP-GC fighters defected to the rebels, and Jibril fled Damascus for the Mediterranean port city of Tartus. That December the Palestinian National Council denounced Jibril and expelled him for his role in the Syrian Civil War.

JONAS KAUFFELDT AND SPENCER C. TUCKER

### See also
Abbas, Mahmoud; Assad, Bashar al-; Intifada, First; Israel; Lebanon; Palestine Liberation Organization; Popular Front for the Liberation of Palestine; Syria; Syrian Civil War; Terrorism

### References
Katz, Samuel M. *Israel versus Jibril: The Thirty-Year War against a Master Terrorist.* New York: Paragon House, 1993.

O'Neill, Bard E. *Armed Struggle in Palestine: A Political-Military Analysis.* Boulder, CO: Westview, 1978.

Sayigh, Yezid. *Armed Struggle and the Search for State: The Palestine National Movement, 1949–1993.* New York: Oxford University Press, 2000.

Shemesh, Moshe. *The Palestinian Entity, 1959–1974: Arab Politics and the PLO.* 2nd ed. London: Frank Cass, 1996.

## Popular Front for the Liberation of the Occupied Arabian Gulf

Insurgent group in Oman that opposed the rule of reactionary Said bin Taimur, sultan of Oman from 1932 to 1970. Initially known as the Dhofar Liberation Front (DLF) and led by Mussalim bin Nufl, the group enjoyed the support of Ghalib bin Ali, the exiled imam (religious leader) of Oman, who claimed power himself. British forces assisting the sultan had put down the imam's revolt in Jebel Akhdar in 1955, but Saudi Arabia, which had its own claims on part of Oman, supported him, as did Egyptian leader Gamal Abdel Nasser, who regarded British interference in the region as a threat to Arab nationalism.

Thus, in June 1957 the exiled Ghalib bin Ali led a new revolt against the sultan. After major fighting near Nizwa on July 15, 1957, Said requested British military assistance. This aid, mostly in the form of air support, enabled him to crush the revolt by mid-August. An effort by Arab states in the United Nations to censure the British for their intervention failed to win approval. In 1958 Said sold the port city and district of Gwadar on the Arabian Sea in coastal Balochistan to Pakistan.

In 1962 the DLF began a sabotage campaign and then in June 1965 led a revolt in the Omani province of Dhofar. Britain's decision to withdraw from Aden in 1967 led to the creation of the Marxist People's Republic of South Yemen (PRSY), which was quick to support the revolt in Dhofar. At a DLF congress in August 1968, however, the nationalist leadership led by Mussalim was ousted by hard-line

Marxists, and the DLF became the Popular Front for the Liberation of the Occupied Arabian Gulf (PFLOAG), which in 1971 became the Popular Front for the Liberation of Oman and the Arabian Gulf.

The PFLOAG secured arms from China and the Soviet Union, and some of its members received military training in the Democratic People's Republic of Korea (DPRK, North Korea). The PFLOAG made steady gains in western Dhofar, but on July 23, 1970, Sultan Said bin Taimur was overthrown by his progressive-minded son, Qaboos bin Said. Qaboos pledged to apply his country's considerable oil wealth for the benefit of his people and called on the British for support. They responded with the Special Air Service. The resultant comprehensive counterinsurgency program included a "hearts and minds" component and amnesty for the rebels. At the same time, government forces and the British worked to cut rebel resupply. Aircraft proved to be a major asset, as did aid from Iran.

From a peak of some 2,000 active fighters and 3,000 militia in 1968, PFLOAG declined to about 800 activists and 1,000 militia by 1974. In August 1974 PFLOAG divided into the Popular Front for the Liberation of Oman and the Popular Front for the Liberation of Bahrain. Omani government forces made steady gains, and the insurgency was declared at an end in January 1976, although isolated incidents continued into 1983.

Spencer C. Tucker

### See also
Dhofar Rebellion; Oman

### References
Beckett, Ian F. W. *Encyclopedia of Guerrilla Warfare.* Santa Barbara, CA: ABC-CLIO, 1999.

Halliday, Fred. *Revolution and Foreign Policy: The Case of South Yemen, 1967–1987.* Cambridge: Cambridge University Press, 1990.

## Portuguese Colonial Wars in Arabia (1507–1650)

Moorish control over Portugal from the eight century and the reconquest fostered a strong anti-Islamic and anti-Arabic element to Portuguese nationalism. As Portuguese exploration and trade increased, entrepôts on the Arabian Peninsula grew in importance as midway points between Africa and the Indies and because Arab traders controlled much of the trade in East Africa and engaged in trade with the Indies, as did the Persians.

The Portuguese crown charged Afonso de Albuquerque with an attack on Aden, but given limited resources he instead engaged in raids against the Arabian Peninsula and then an attack on the Persian sultanate of Hormuz in 1507. He took that and made it a tributary state, garrisoned by the construction of a fort, but the following year the sultanate rose in revolt and regained its independence.

After 1510 as governor of the Estado da Índia, Albuquerque attempted to control key geographic points to secure shipping routes and the spice and gold trades. In 1513 Albuquerque assaulted Aden as a step to control the Red Sea and to strike against Egypt, which competed with the Portuguese as middleman in the spice trade between the Indies and Europe. The fortress proved too difficult to take, however.

Albuquerque returned in 1515, however, and retook Hormuz. Though located on the Persian side of the Persian Gulf, Hormuz controlled key ports on the Arabic side. Thus, when Hormuz became a tributary of the Portuguese crown, those ports went over to the Portuguese as well. Hormuz became a captaincy with a captain appointed for three years who headed a local garrison to provide military protection and ensure local control. In 1521 Hormuz revolted, but in 1523 the Portuguese restored order and replaced the shah with a new ruler. Subsequent rebellions against Portuguese authority occurred in Hormuz and cities on the Arabian side of the gulf throughout the 16th century, but they were put down. From Hormuz, the Portuguese engaged in raids in the Red Sea and Arabia.

Ottoman Empire forces seized Egypt in 1517, expanded into the Arabian Peninsula, and took control of trade in the Red Sea. In 1551 the Portuguese captured Al Qatif in Arabia from the Ottomans. The Ottomans in turn attacked Muscat as well as Bahrain, which they failed to take. By 1554 the Portuguese eliminated Ottoman sea power in the Persian Gulf and fortified Muscat as well as Bahrain, ensuring Portuguese control of trade in the area.

In 1581 the Ottomans destroyed Muscat, and in 1602 Shah Abbas drove the Portuguese from Bahrain. More troubling than the Ottoman threat, however, was increased competition from the British and Dutch in Africa, the Indies, and Arabia. The British East India Company allied with Persians to seize Hormuz; the British provided naval support to blockade the port while the Persians besieged the city, resulting in Hormuz's fall in 1622. Even so, a series of fortresses in the Persian Gulf and on the Arabian Peninsula provided Portugal with influence in the region, although Portugal no longer held a monopoly on trade in the gulf.

As in India, North European powers played on indigenous people's animus against Portuguese abuses and trading practices. Aided by the Dutch and British, Oman developed as a sea power and seized the main Portuguese stronghold on the Arabian Peninsula of Muscat in 1650. Oman then challenged Portuguese trade in Africa and also attacked Portuguese commerce in the Indian Ocean.

MICHAEL K. BEAUCHAMP

**See also**
Abbas I the Great; Mamluk-Ottoman Wars

**References**
Newitt, Malyn. *A History of Portuguese Overseas Expansion, 1400–1668.* New York: Routledge, 2005.
Subrahmanyam, Sanjay. *The Portuguese Empire in Asia, 1500–1700: A Political and Economic History.* London: Longman, 1993.

## PRAYING MANTIS, Operation (April 18, 1988)

Retaliatory strike against Iranian targets carried out by the U.S. Navy that resulted in a major naval action. On April 14, 1988, the U.S. Navy guided missile frigate *Samuel B. Roberts* struck a mine in the central Persian Gulf. The warship was involved in Operation EARNEST WILL, the 1987–1988 operation in which U.S. Navy warships provided escorts to tankers in the Persian Gulf during the 1980–1988 Iran-Iraq War. The *Samuel B. Roberts* was badly damaged in the blast, which blew a 15-foot hole in the ship's hull. Although no crewmen were killed, 10 were badly wounded and had to be medevacuated. After a five-hour struggle, the crew of the *Samuel B. Roberts* managed to save its ship.

U.S. Navy divers subsequently recovered other mines in the area. These were identified as having the same identification numbers as Iranian mines seized the previous September from the Iranian Navy minelayer *Iran Ajr*. With the United States having previously warned Iran not to lay mines in the Gulf, four days later the navy responded with Operation PRAYING MANTIS.

In the operation the U.S. Navy committed the aircraft carrier *Enterprise,* one amphibious transport dock ship, one guided missile cruiser, four destroyers, and three frigates. The punitive operation was directed at the Sassan and Sirri inoperable oil platforms in the Gulf, which the Iranians had armed. Iranian personnel on the Sassan platform were given the chance to abandon it for a tugboat there, but they chose instead to open fire on the American ships. The U.S. Navy destroyer *Merrill* immediately used its own 5-inch gun to neutralize the Iranian fire. U.S. marines then went aboard the platform, collected intelligence data, and left explosive charges that damaged it. The American ships then attacked the Sirri platform.

In response, the Iranians sent half a dozen Boghammar speedboats to attack various targets in the Gulf, including an American supply ship and a Panamanian ship. Two U.S. Navy A-6E Intruder aircraft from the *Enterprise* were then directed to the speedboats and brought them under attack. Employing cluster munitions, the aircraft sank one of the speedboats and damaged several others. The surviving speedboats then fled to Iranian-controlled Abu Musa Island. The *Joshan,* an Iranian Combattante II Kasman-class fast-attack gunboat, then moved against the U.S. Navy guided missile cruiser *Wainwright* and its accompanying frigates *Simpson* and *Bagley,* firing a Harpoon missile at them. The American warships returned fire with Standard and Harpoon missiles, which destroyed the Iranian ship's superstructure but did not sink it; this was subsequently accomplished by naval gunfire. Although two Iranian U.S.-built McDonnell Douglas F-4 Phantom aircraft approached the *Wainwright,* they were driven off.

The Iranian frigate *Sahand* then departed Bundar Abbas in another effort to attack the American ships. It soon came under attack from two A-6Es on combat air patrol that used missiles and laser-guided bombs to set the ship afire. The fire reached the ship's magazines, and the resulting explosions sent it to the bottom. A sister ship to the *Sahand,* the *Sabaland,* also sortied. An A-6E dropped a laser-guided bomb on it, severely damaging the frigate and leaving it dead in the water. An Iranian tug appeared and took the frigate in tow. Pursuant to orders, the A-6Es did not continue the attack.

The daylong battle was the U.S. Navy's largest engagement involving surface warships since World War II and also saw the first surface-to-surface missile engagement in the navy's history. The battle was entirely one-sided. In it, the U.S. forces had damaged the two Iranian offshore oil platforms, sank one of the Iranian frigates and the gunboat, damaged the other frigate, and sank as many as three of the speedboats. U.S. losses were one helicopter to an accident and its two marine crewmen killed. Iranian personnel losses are unknown.

Shortly after PRAYING MANTIS, the United States extended its naval protection to all non-Iranian shipping in the Persian Gulf. The engagement probably helped push Iran into agreeing to a cease-fire with Iraq to end its eight-year-long war, convincing the Iranian leadership that the United States was now firmly on the side of Iraq in the conflict.

SPENCER C. TUCKER

**See also**
EARNEST WILL, Operation; Iran-Iraq War; Persian Gulf

**References**
Palmer, Michael A. *Guardians of the Gulf: A History of America's Expanding Role in the Persian Gulf, 1833–1992.* New York: Free Press, 1992.
Peniston, Bradley. *No Higher Honor: Saving the USS Samuel B. Roberts in the Persian Gulf.* Annapolis: Naval Institute Press, 2006.
Wise, Harold L. *Inside the Danger Zone: The U.S. Military in the Persian Gulf 1987–1988.* Annapolis, MD: Naval Institute Press, 2007.

## PRIME CHANCE, Operation (1987–1989)

An American special forces operation in the Persian Gulf that occurred between August 1987 and June 1989. Operation PRIME CHANCE was intended to prevent Iranian Revolutionary Guards from mining the shipping lanes used by international oil tankers. PRIME CHANCE coincided with Operation EARNEST WILL, an effort by the U.S. Navy to escort unarmed tankers through the Persian Gulf. PRIME CHANCE was the first operation in which helicopter pilots used night-vision goggles and forward-looking infrared vision devices in combat. It was also significant for the high degree of interoperability displayed by the special forces from different services.

Between 1980 and 1988, Iran and Iraq waged a brutal war of attrition. Unable to force a decision on land, the Iranian Revolutionary Guards began to attack international oil tankers carrying oil from Iraq and countries friendly to Iraq (including Kuwait) as they traversed the Persian Gulf. In December 1986, Kuwait requested that 11 of its tankers be reflagged as American ships so they would receive protection from the U.S. Navy. After U.S. president Ronald Reagan approved the request on March 10, 1987, the navy began preparing for Operation EARNEST WILL. After the tanker *Bridgeton* hit a mine laid by Iranians on July 24, 1987, during the first convoy, a secret operation was put in place to bring a halt to the Iranian mining.

Code-named PRIME CHANCE, the operation included helicopters and pilots from the U.S. Army's 160th Special Operations Aviation Regiment (Airborne) (SOAR[A]). SOAR pilots were trained to fly and fight at night, when the Iranians minelayers were most active. The operation's forces also included navy SEALS and Mark III patrol boats. U.S. marines guarded PRIME CHANCE's floating bases, and air force flight controllers monitored airborne operations.

The first PRIME CHANCE components arrived in the Persian Gulf on August 5, 1987. Two detachments of helicopters were formed, each with an MD Helicopters MH-6 Little Bird light transport helicopter and two AH-6 Little Bird attack helicopters, along with crew and support personnel. The first operations were flown from the decks of navy frigates and the command ship *La Salle*. On August 8, 1987, the detachments flew their first missions escorting convoys and guarding minesweeping detachments. Soon afterward, operations were transferred to two large oil-servicing barges, the *Hercules* and *Wimbrown VII*, that were converted into floating mobile sea bases.

The barges allowed PRIME CHANCE to be independent of land bases and released navy ships for other operations. Each barge was converted by erecting hangars for the three helicopters of each detachment, 10 small boats, ammunition and fuel, workshops, and accommodations for more than 150 men. The mobile sea bases became operational in October 1987.

Typically, missions took place after sunset. The helicopters usually flew only 30 feet above the water, with the pilots relying on night-vision goggles. The MH-6s were used to spot Iranian boats and ships in the shipping lanes. Once they located Iranian targets, the MH-6 crews would call in the AH-6 gunships, which would attack the Iranians. When operating with conventional naval forces, the AH-6s would rely on information from the warships' radar and that of their SH-60 Seahawk helicopters. The patrol boats began operating on September 9, 1987, and were in close contact with the helicopters as well.

On September 21, the special forces enjoyed their first success. One helicopter detachment from the frigate *Jairett* soon spotted the Iranian ship *Iran Ajr*. As the Americans watched, the ship extinguished its lights and began laying mines in the shipping lanes used by tankers. After receiving permission, the helicopters attacked the *Iran Ajr* with miniguns and high-explosive and flechette antipersonnel rockets. The attack continued until the ship stopped and the crew abandoned it. The next morning, a SEAL team boarded the *Iran Ajr* while two patrol boats stood by. The SEALs found nine mines on board along with documents showing where the Iranians had dropped other mines and papers implicating Iran in mining international waters. Twenty-three Iranians were rescued and taken prisoner. The *Iran Ajr* was scuttled by American forces on September 26.

The American forces quickly realized that the Iranians spent their daylight hours near the oil and gas separation platforms in Iranian waters, then moved into international waters after dark. The Iranians usually used the Middle Shoals Buoy, a navigation aid used by tankers, as their assembly point before laying mines. On October 8, PRIME CHANCE participants laid an ambush for the Iranians. The attack helicopters found three Iranian boats at the buoy and exchanged fire with them until all three were sunk. Patrol boats picked up five survivors.

Forces from PRIME CHANCE also took part in Operations NIMBLE ARCHER (October 1987) and PRAYING MANTIS (April 1988). In both operations, conventional forces destroyed Iranian oil platforms in response to attacks on American ships. After PRAYING MANTIS, Iranian interference with neutral shipping dropped dramatically. PRIME CHANCE patrols continued after the Iranian-Iraqi cease-fire of July 1988, with the last forces returned to the United States in June 1989. Between June 1987 and June 1989, 259 ships were escorted in 127 convoys.

TIM J. WATTS

**See also**
EARNEST WILL, Operation; Iran-Iraq War; PRAYING MANTIS, Operation

**References**
Partin, John W. *Special Operations Forces in Operation Earnest Will/Prime Chance I.* MacDill AFB, FL: U.S. Special Operations Command, History and Research Office, 1998.
Stubblefield, Gary. *Inside the Navy Seals.* Osceola, WI: Motorbooks International, 1995.
Wise, Harold Lee. *Inside the Danger Zone: The U.S. Military in the Persian Gulf, 1987–88.* Annapolis, MD: Naval Institute Press, 2007.

## PROTECTIVE EDGE, Operation
*See* Gaza War of 2014

## PROVIDE COMFORT, Operation (1991)

A 1991 humanitarian relief mission carried out in northern Iraq by the United States and several of its military allies. Following the coalition victory over Iraq in the Persian Gulf War, in March 1991 Kurds living in northern Iraq revolted against the rule of Iraqi president Saddam Hussein. The Kurds composed about one-fifth of Iraq's population and had long claimed northern Iraq (Kurdistan) as their ancestral home.

Initially the rebellion went well, and demoralized Iraqi soldiers fled from the Kurdish Peshmerga (meaning "those who face death") fighters. However, after dealing with a similar Shiite revolt in southern Iraq, Hussein sent his reconstructed military north to fight the Peshmerga. The lightly armed Kurdish fighters could not contend with Iraqi tanks, artillery, and helicopter gunships. The Iraqis also employed chemical weapons against the Kurds. The Iraqis recaptured Kurdish cities one by one until only the city of Zakho, near the Turkish border, remained. On March 31, 1991, an Iraqi offensive against Zakho began. Fearing another chemical attack, most of the city's Kurds fled into the nearby mountains, where they joined a growing stream of Kurdish refugees.

Because of Turkish government concerns regarding absorbing thousands of stateless Kurds, its armed forces prevented the refugees from entering Turkey. Consequently, Kurdish refugees were caught in a vice between the Iraqi military and the Turkish border. Here the Kurds lived without shelter on cold mountain slopes, suffering from hunger, exposure, and disease. The international aid group Doctors Without Borders reported no health care while diseases such as measles, cholera, typhus, and dysentery raged through refugee camps. A humanitarian disaster loomed, with an estimated 750,000 people in danger of imminent death. Aid workers reported that about 1,500 Kurds were dying each day.

President George H. W. Bush did not want American forces to become involved in what he viewed as an Iraqi civil war, so he resisted calls for American intervention. However, on April 5, 1991, the United Nations Security Council passed Resolution 688 condemning the repression of Iraqi Kurds. Resolution 688 provided the legal basis for responding to the crisis.

President Bush then bowed to public pressure as well as requests from the United Kingdom and France and committed American resources to a relief effort. This decision marked the beginning of what became Operation PROVIDE COMFORT. On April 5, 1991, U.S. Air Force major general James L. Jamerson assumed command of a joint task force, the goal of which was to assist dislocated civilians living in northern Iraq. Jamerson's first task was to organize and manage the delivery of emergency relief. The second objective was to create a sustained relief effort.

Operation PROVIDE COMFORT was a particular challenge for Turkey. That country has had a long and uneasy history with the Kurds, most of whom live in southern Turkey near the border with Iraq. Kurdish guerrillas used bases inside Iraq to launch raids against Turkey. Inside Turkey itself, a sizable and restive Kurdish minority presented a challenge to the

A British soldier with an L85A1 assault rifle protecting Kurdish children in Zakhu, northern Iraq in 1991. The soldier was part of Operation PROVIDE COMFORT, a multinational effort to protect Kurds in northern Iraq in the aftermath of the 1991 Persian Gulf War and deliver humanitarian aid to them. The operation occurred from March 1991 through June 7, 2001. (U.S. Department of Defense)

central government. Moreover, by mid-April 1991, fleeing refugees who had managed to make it across the border had overwhelmed Turkey's capacity to provide assistance. Turkish president Turgut Özal accepted a United Nations plan to move refugees back into northern Iraq. Thereafter, Turkey offered vital logistical support to the mission.

On April 6, 1991, Joint Task Force Provide Comfort deployed to Incirlik Air Base at Adna, Turkey. American fighter aircraft provided aerial security. Two days later, six C-130 Hercules cargo aircraft delivered 27 tons of supplies, including dehydrated combat rations, blankets, and water. The next day, a growing international force that included units from Denmark, Spain, Japan, New Zealand, and Australia joined the effort. From start to finish four countries—the United States, the United Kingdom, France, and Turkey—were the major contributors to the mission.

On April 16, 1991, Bush expanded PROVIDE COMFORT to include multinational forces with the additional mission of establishing temporary refuge camps in northern Iraq. This was first labeled "Express Care." On April 17 when it had become apparent that a ground presence in northern Iraq was also necessary, Lieutenant General John M. D. Shalikashvili (who later became chairman of the Joint Chiefs of Staff) replaced Jamerson as commander. Jamerson served as his deputy commander, and U.S. Marine Corps brigadier general Anthony Zinni became chief of staff. Two subordinate joint task forces (JTFs)—designated Alpha and Bravo—were also established.

JTF Alpha entered the mountains of southeast Turkey with the goal of alleviating the dying and suffering while stabilizing the situation. Commanded by U.S. Army brigadier general Richard Potter, JTF Alpha was composed primarily of the 10th Special Forces Group (10th SF). A special subunit began organizing to provide the first phase of emergency relief, called Express Care. Some 200 U.S. Army Special Forces personnel provided the ground component of Express Care. On April 13, only six days after the decision to commit American resources, the first special forces teams entered the refugee camps inside northern Iraq. Their mission was to help organize the camps while receiving and distributing supplies. Planners initially thought that this first phase would last 10 days.

It soon became clear that relief efforts were inadequate to meet the crisis. Participants in the relief effort found 12 major refugee camps along the Iraqi border. Each camp had an estimated 40,000 refugees, all of whom lacked food, clean water, and medical care. The initial phase of emergency aid expanded to first 30 days and then 90 days.

The second component, JTF Bravo, centered on the 24th Marine Expeditionary Unit under Major General Jay Garner. Its mission was to prepare the town of Zakho in northern Iraq as a transit point for the Kurdish refugees and to facilitate their eventual return home. An important part of this mission was to transfer responsibility over to nongovernment organizations. Task Force Encourage Hope (later renamed Joint Task Force Bravo) was also formed to construct a series of resettlement camps where dislocated civilians could find food, shelter, and security.

The formal decision to expand PROVIDE COMFORT's mission from emergency relief to comprehensive sustainment required organizational changes. More than just U.S. Army and Marine Corps forces were involved, and 12 countries sent military forces. Thirty-six sent financial assistance or supplies. Thirty-nine civilian relief agencies cooperated in PROVIDE COMFORT. Accordingly, in recognition of the international character of the operation, on April 9, 1991, Joint Task Force Provide Comfort became Combined Task Force Provide Comfort.

The emergency phase of Operation PROVIDE COMFORT stabilized the situation. Attention then turned to building temporary camps in the lowlands so refugees could move to a more accessible location. Coalition forces established a demilitarized zone inside northern Iraq to protect the Kurds. Air units operating from Incirlik enforced a no-fly zone above the 36th parallel to prevent Iraqi interference. Within this zone, JTF Bravo established transit camps where refugees could live in safety until they returned home. The refugees enjoyed better sanitation facilities at these lowland camps. Here Kurdish officials could also assume administrative tasks. This was in keeping with the operational plan to transition rapidly from military to civilian control.

The city of Dohuk proved to be a major obstacle to the successful return of Kurdish refugees. Located near the Turkish border, this former Kurdish stronghold was a powerful symbol to thousands of refugees, but they refused to leave their camps until coalition forces had secured Dohuk. The Iraqis, in turn, refused to depart from Dohuk. Several armed encounters took place between Iraqi and coalition forces. Exasperated by Iraqi harassment, General Shalikashvili ordered an American military response. Before this took place, however, the situation changed dramatically.

After meeting with Saddam Hussein, on May 18, 1991, the leader of the Kurdish Democratic Party, Masoud Barzani, announced a tentative agreement concerning Kurdish autonomy. It established a Kurdish Autonomous Zone in northern Iraq. The next day, Shalikashvili met with an Iraqi general to forge an agreement regarding the city of Dohuk. It was designated an "open" city where the Iraqis would allow limited humanitarian and related groups to operate. Turkey agreed to allow a multinational force to remain on Turkish soil along the Turkish border with Kurdistan. These events eased tensions and encouraged hundreds of thousands of refugees to leave the mountains and return home. The last refugee camp closed on June 7, 1991.

By mid-July, military forces assigned to Operation PROVIDE COMFORT had pulled out of Iraq; a residual force in southeastern Turkey was left to keep the Iraqis in check. A military coordination center remained in Iraq to link the armed forces and civilian relief workers, and the United Nations assumed responsibility for the refugee camps.

Operation PROVIDE COMFORT was the first post–Cold War humanitarian intervention conducted principally by the United States. During the operation, from April to July 12,316 American and 10,926 coalition military personnel served. It was fundamentally a military operation, implemented and managed by military officers. In conjunction with civilian relief agencies, they met the operational objectives of stopping the suffering and resettling the refugees, first in transit camps and them back in their homes.

In late July 1991 after coalition military forces departed northern Iraq, Operation PROVIDE COMFORT II began. It was essentially a show of force designed to deter Hussein from launching further attacks against the Kurds and had a limited humanitarian component. PROVIDE COMFORT II ended on December 31, 1996.

JAMES ARNOLD

See also
Hussein, Saddam; Iraq No-Fly Zones; Kurds; Kurds, Massacres of; Peshmerga

References
Brown, Ronald J. *Humanitarian Operations in Northern Iraq, 1991 with Marines in Operation Provide Comfort.* Washington, DC: History and Museums Division Headquarters, U.S. Marine Corps, 1995.

Cuny, Frederick C. *Northern Iraq: One Year Later.* Washington, DC: Carnegie Endowment for International Peace, 1992.

Rudd, Gordon W. *Humanitarian Intervention: Assisting the Iraqi Kurds in Operation Provide Comfort, 1991.* Washington, DC: Department of the Army, 2004.

Seiple, Chris. *The U. S. Military/NGO Relationship in Humanitarian Intervention.* Carlisle Barracks, PA: Peacekeeping Institute, Center for Strategic Leadership, U.S. Army War College, 1996.

## Pruth, Treaty of (July 23, 1711)

Peace accord signed between Russia and the Ottoman Empire to end the Russo-Ottoman War of 1710–1711. The treaty was signed on July 23, 1711, near the Pruth River, where Tsar Peter I of Russia had conducted an unsuccessful campaign against the Ottomans. The Russian ruler was compelled to restore to the Ottomans the fortress of Azov, which he captured in 1697, and to destroy the fortresses of Taganrog, Bogoroditsk, and Kamennyizaton. The Ottomans pledged to expel Swedish king Charles XII (who had fled to the Porte after being defeated by Peter's army in the Battle of Poltava in 1709) and agreed to maintain peaceful relations with Poland and the Cossacks. The treaty was an important political victory for the Ottoman Empire in its struggle against the rising Russian state.

ALEXANDER MIKABERIDZE

**See also**
Russo-Ottoman Wars

**References**
Massie, Robert K. *Peter the Great: His Life and World.* London: Gollancz, 1981.
Phillips, Edward J. *The Founding of Russia's Navy: Peter the Great and the Azov Fleet, 1688–1714.* Westport, CT: Greenwood, 1995.

## Ptolemaic Kingdom (305–30 BCE)

The Ptolemies ruled an empire centered on Egypt for most of the Hellenistic period. The dynasty was named after its founder, Ptolemy I Soter, who ruled Egypt as king from 305 to 283/282 BCE. Ptolemy I had been a general under King Alexander III the Great of Macedon. All of Ptolemy I's successors were also called Ptolemy. A feature of the dynasty was corule: fathers frequently associated a son with them as king, and it was not unknown for siblings to rule together. It was also not uncommon for brothers and sisters to marry. As a foreign (Macedonian) dynasty ruling over a largely Egyptian population, this was one method of ensuring dynastic purity. In addition to internal security issues arising because the dynasty was non-Egyptian, much of the history of Ptolemaic Egypt onward revolved around conflict with the Seleucid Empire based in Syria.

The Ptolemies preserved their rule by maintaining firm control of the military and adapting Egyptian culture and practices. Nevertheless, there were occasional revolts, and the Ptolemies (as in many successor kingdoms) tended to maintain the core of the army as Macedonian or Greek. The training of Egyptians as Macedonian-style phalangites prior to the Battle of Raphia in 217 was an exception to this.

Ptolemy I Soter substantially expanded Egyptian territory to include Palestine, Phoenicia, and parts of Asia Minor. Ptolemaic naval power was demonstrated with his acquisition of Cyprus and the Aegean islands. Ptolemy I also came to control most of Syria south of Lebanon and Damascus as well as other places in Asia Minor and the Aegean islands. Much of this was achieved at the expense of the Antigonids; however, the region of Coele-Syria (essentially the coast and inland of Lebanon) became a particularly contested region between the Seleucids and Ptolemies.

The Ptolemies experienced mixed success against the Seleucids. They achieved their greatest power under Ptolemy III Euergetes in the Third Syrian-Egyptian War (246–241), but defeat in the Fifth Syrian-Egyptian War (202–195) eliminated Ptolemaic power in Asia Minor and Coele-Syria. Only Roman intervention saved Egypt from conquest in the Sixth Syrian-Egyptian War (170–168). Clever diplomacy ensured Ptolemaic independence until the last Ptolemaic ruler, Cleopatra VII, committed suicide in 30 BCE after the defeat at Actium, ending the dynasty. Egypt then became a Roman province.

IAIN SPENCE

**See also**
Antigonus I Monophthalmus; Antiochus III Megas; Caesar, Gaius Julius; Cleopatra VII; Demetrius I Poliorcetes; Diadochi, Wars of the; Egypt; Ptolemy I Soter; Ptolemy II Philadelphus; Ptolemy IV Philopator; Ptolemy V Epiphanes; Ptolemy VI Philometor; Syria; Syrian-Egyptian Wars

**References**
Fischer-Bovet, Christelle. *Army and Society in Ptolemaic Egypt: Armies of the Ancient World.* Cambridge: Cambridge University Press, 2014.
Green, Peter. *Alexander to Actium: The Historical Evolution of the Hellenistic Age.* Berkeley: University of California Press, 1990.
Manning, Joseph G. *The Last Pharaohs: Egypt under the Ptolemies, 305–30 BC.* Princeton, NJ: Princeton University Press, 2010.

## Ptolemy Ceraunus (ca. 320–279 BCE)

Ptolemy, named Ceraunus (Keraunus) for "Thunderbolt," was born around 210 BCE, the eldest son of King Ptolemy I of Egypt by his first wife, Eurydice, daughter of Antipater. When he was pushed aside from the succession to make way for Ptolemy II Philadelphus, Ptolemy Ceraunus sought to secure reinstatement by allying first with Lysimachus and then with Seleucus I. Ptolemy Ceraunus was with Seleucus when he defeated Lysimachus in the Battle of Corupedium in 281 but personally assassinated him just after he had landed in Thracian Chersonese.

Ceraunus placed himself at the head of Seleucus's army and took over Lysimachus's kingdom. Ceraunus also obtained the Macedonian throne by making an agreement with Pyrrhus, ruler of Epirus, then preoccupied with his Italian expedition, and defeating Macadonian king Antigonus II Gonatas in a sea battle. After only one year of Ptolemy Ceraunus's rule, in 279 the Celts mounted their first invasion of Macedonia. His hastily levied army was badly defeated, and he was captured and beheaded. Ptolemy Ceraunus had a high sense of entitlement owing to his birth but was ruthless and incapable.

Douglas Kelly

### See also
Corupedium, Battle of; Lysimachus; Ptolemy I Soter; Ptolemy II Philadelphus; Seleucus I Nicator

### Reference
Grainger, John D. 1990. *Seleukos Nikator: Constructing a Hellenistic Kingdom.* New York: Routledge, 1990.

---

## Ptolemy I Soter (367–282 BCE)

Ptolemy I Soter was a general and biographer of Alexander III (the Great) of Macedon. After Alexander's death, Ptolemy became ruler of Egypt (304–282 BCE) and founder of the Ptolemaic dynasty. Born in 367 to the Macedonian nobleman Lagus and Arsinoe (although ancient authors mention rumors that he was an illegitimate son of Philip II), Ptolemy was one of Alexander's closest childhood friends and participated in the latter's invasion of the Persian Empire from the beginning. Ptolemy took part in the Battle of Issus (333) and accompanied Alexander to the oracle of Ammon at Siwah in the Libyan desert in 331. In December 330 Ptolemy was appointed *somatophylax,* one of Alexander's seven bodyguards and trusted deputies. Ptolemy's first independent command was against Bessus, the last Achaemenid king, whom he captured and handed over to Alexander for execution. During the campaign in the Indian subcontinent, Ptolemy was in command of the advance guard at the siege of Aornus and fought at the Battle of the Hydaspes in 326.

After Alexander's death in 323, the principal officers of the Macedonian Army gathered for a meeting to discuss the future of his empire. It was Ptolemy's arguments that convinced the other generals that they should divide the conquered territories among themselves, and Ptolemy was given the satrapy of Egypt. In order to strengthen his position over the imperial regent Perdiccas, Ptolemy managed to bring Alexander's body for burial in Egypt. In 322 Ptolemy allied himself with Antipater against Perdiccas, while in 316 he joined forces with Cassander, Seleucus I Nicator, and Lysimachus to resist Antigonus's ambition to reconstitute the whole of the Macedonian Empire under his rule.

At the same time, Ptolemy tried to turn his capital city, Alexandria, into the most important city in the eastern Mediterranean. He founded the museum and the library and initiated the construction of the Pharos, the lighthouse that would come to be considered one of the seven wonders of the ancient world. Ptolemy was a very effective administrator and managed to win the support of the local Egyptian population by marrying an Egyptian woman, restoring ancient Egyptian temples and offering sacrifices to Egyptian gods, and establishing the cult of Serapis, which fused Egyptian and Greek religious elements.

As with all of the Diadochi (successors of Alexander), Ptolemy assumed the title of king (and in his case also pharaoh). His success in defending Rhodes against an assault by Demetrius I Poliorcetes's in 304 earned him the title "Soter" (Savior). Ptolemy's memoirs offer a detailed description of Alexander's campaigns and was the main source of the account written by the later historian Arrian. Ptolemy I died in 282 and was succeeded by his second son, Ptolemy II Philadelphus, who was already coregent since 285. The dynasty of the Ptolemies lasted for some 300 years.

Ioannis Georganas

### See also
Alexander III the Great; Alexander III's Invasion of the Persian Empire; Antigonus I Monophthalmus; Demetrius I Poliorcetes; Diadochi, Wars of the; Egypt; Lysimachus; Perdiccas; Ptolemaic Kingdom; Ptolemy II Philadelphus; Seleucid Empire; Seleucus I Nicator

### References
Bevan, Edwyn. *The House of Ptolemy: Egypt under the Ptolemaic Dynasty.* Chicago: Ares Publishing, 1985.
Ellis, Walter. 2010. *Ptolemy of Egypt.* New York: Routledge, 2010.

## Ptolemy II Philadelphus (308–246 BCE)

Son of Ptolemy I Soter, king of Egypt and joint ruler with his father from 285. Born in 308 BCE, Ptolemy Philadelphus (Sister-loving) married his sister Arsinoe who displaced his existing wife (also an Arsinoe.) She reputedly exercised considerable influence over him until her death in 270. In 279 Magas, Ptolemy's half brother, the governor of Cyrenaica, rebelled. In 274 Magas and his father-in-law, Antiochus II, launched a coordinated attack on Ptolemy. This First Syrian-Egyptian War (274–271) ended in stalemate. The Second Syrian-Egyptian War (260–253) was sparked by Ptolemy. This war also ended with no appreciable gains for either side, although it caused Ptolemy considerable financial difficulties and temporarily damaged Ptolemaic naval power in the Aegean. Ptolemy II Phiadelphus died in 246 BCE.

IAIN SPENCE

**See also**

Egypt; Ptolemaic Kingdom; Seleucid Empire; Syria; Syrian-Egyptian Wars

**References**

Manning, Joseph G. *The Last Pharaohs: Egypt under the Ptolemies, 305–30 BC.* Princeton, NJ: Princeton University Press, 2010.

McKechnie, Paul, and Philippe Guillaume, eds. *Ptolemy Philadelphus and His World.* Leiden: Brill, 2008.

## Ptolemy III Euergetes (r. 246–221 BCE)

King of Egypt. Ptolemy III's birth date is unknown; indeed, virtually nothing is known of him until his marriage in 245 BCE to Berenice II, daughter of Magas, king of Cyrene, which reunited Egypt and Cyrenaica, divided since 258. The son of King Ptolemy II Philadelphus, Ptolemy Euergetes (meaning "benefactor") came to the throne in 246 shortly after the death of Antiochus II of Syria. Antiochus's death sparked a succession dispute pitting his first wife (Laodice) and her son Seleucus II Callinicus against Ptolemy's sister, Berenice (Antiochus's second wife) and her son. Ptolemy began the Third Syrian-Egyptian War (246–241) by marching north to support his sister and continued it after his sister and nephew were murdered. Despite some reverses, the war ended with Ptolemaic territory at its greatest ever extent. Although many of the gains seem either ephemeral or perhaps exaggerated, Ptolemy did secure the valuable prize of Seleucia-in-Pieria (Antioch's port).

Ptolemy III poured considerable money into Greece to counter Macedonian power, initially supporting Aratus of Sicyon but then Sparta and the Aetolian League. Despite this, Ptolemy lost naval control in the Aegean to Antigonus II Gonatas. Ptolemy did, however, retain sufficient sea power in the east to allow him to operate with relative impunity against the Seleucid Navy. Ptolemy also enjoyed a reputation for good government and sound financial management. He died in 221 BCE and was succeeded by Ptolemy IV Philopator.

IAIN SPENCE

**See also**

Egypt; Ptolemaic Kingdom; Seleucid Empire; Syria; Syrian-Egyptian Wars

**Reference**

Manning, Joseph G. *The Last Pharaohs: Egypt under the Ptolemies, 305–30 BC.* Princeton, NJ: Princeton University Press, 2010.

## Ptolemy IV Philopator (ca. 244–205 BCE)

King of Egypt. Son of Ptolemy III Euergetes, Ptolemy IV Philopator (father-loving) became king on his father's death in 221 BCE and ruled until his own death in 205. Ptolemy had a troubled reign, although after a run of defeats and territorial losses Egypt unexpectedly secured victory in the Fourth Syrian-Egyptian War (219–217). However, the resistance seems to have been directed by Sosibius, Ptolemy's minister, who took the unusual step of training Egyptians in the Macedonian phalanx. This was critical in the Egyptian victory in the Battle of Raphia (217) but may to have led to postwar internal issues.

During Ptolemy IV's reign the Egyptian priests seem to have taken a more independent line, and the Thebaid revolted around 205 and could not be recovered for some time. The same year Ptolemy was assassinated by two of his ministers, Sosibius and Agathocles.

IAIN SPENCE

**See also**

Egypt; Ptolemaic Kingdom; Raphia, Battle of; Seleucid Empire; Syria; Syrian-Egyptian Wars

**Reference**

Manning, Joseph G. *The Last Pharaohs: Egypt under the Ptolemies, 305–30 BC.* Princeton, NJ: Princeton University Press, 2010.

## Ptolemy V Epiphanes (ca. 210–180)

King of Egypt. Born around 210 BCE, Ptolemy V Epiphanes (Made Manifest) was the son of Ptolemy IV Philopator. Under the rule of Ptolemy V, Syria and most of Egypt's other foreign possessions were lost. Sosibius and Agathocles, two of Ptolemy IV's ministers, murdered Ptolemy V's father and mother, and Ptolemy V, age five, was officially installed as king. Sosibius became his guardian and banished a number of capable figures so that he and his clique could control the boy king and with him Egyptian affairs. Seleucid king Antiochus III the Great and Philip V of Macedon were well aware of Egyptian weakness and took advantage of the situation to seize Egypt's Asia Minor and Aegean possessions.

When Sosibius retired about 202, Agathocles then became Ptolemy's guardian. Soon, however, Agathocles provoked Tlepolemus, the governor of Pelusium (Egypt's eastern frontier city), who rebelled and marched on Alexandria, where a mob demanded the death of those who had killed Ptolemy IV. The mob soon killed Agathocles and his family. Tlepolemus, however, proved incompetent and did not retain power for long.

Meanwhile, Antiochus III invaded Coele Syria, beginning the Fifth Syrian-Egyptian War (202–195). Ptolemy's forces mounted a counteroffensive and captured Jerusalem, but in 201 Antiochus returned and defeated the Egyptians, securing Egyptian holdings in Asia Minor. Roman pressure prevented Antiochus from invading Egypt proper and finally halted the war. As part of the ensuing peace treaty, Cleopatra I, a daughter of Antiochus, was married to Ptolemy.

The situation within Egypt remained chaotic, however, with widespread internal revolts. In 197 Ptolemy V campaigned against rebels in the Nile Valley and demonstrated great cruelty toward the surrendering rebel leadership. Troubles in Upper Egypt continued until around 186, when Ptolemy extended the authority of the governor of Thebes to include all of Upper Egypt. This decree is inscribed on the Rosetta Stone; discovered at the Rosetta mouth of the Nile in 1799, it provided the key to understanding the hieroglyphics, or pictographic writing, of ancient Egypt and thereby unlocked much of the secrets of ancient Egyptian civilization. In 187–186 Ptolemy V succeeded in regaining the Thebaid.

Ptolemy retained the existing Egyptian alliances in Greece. Late in his reign an able eunuch was sent to recruit Greek mercenaries, but Ptolemy V's plans for them are unknown. He died suddenly, in 180, leaving two sons and a daughter, with the queen as their regent.

IAIN SPENCE AND SPENCER C. TUCKER

### See also
Antiochus III Megas; Ptolemaic Kingdom; Syria; Syrian-Egyptian Wars

### Reference
Manning, Joseph G. *The Last Pharaohs: Egypt under the Ptolemies, 305–30 BC*. Princeton, NJ: Princeton University Press, 2010.

## Ptolemy VI Philometor (ca. 186–145 BCE)

Egyptian king. Born around 186 BCE, Ptolemy VI was the son of Ptolemy V Epiphanes. Ptolemy VI Philometor (Mother-loving) ruled jointly with his mother, Cleopatra I, during 180–176. He ruled alone from 176–170 and again from 163–145, but from 169 to 164 he ruled jointly with his brother Ptolemy VIII (Euergetes II) and with his sister/wife Cleopatra II. Ptolemy VI's reign was marked by internal dissension, and he was he was exiled in 164–163.

During Ptolemy VI's reign, Egypt lost the Sixth Syrian-Egyptian War (170–168) to Antiochus IV Epiphanes, only retaining Egypt because of Roman intervention. Ptolemy VI Philometor died in 145 of wounds incurred fighting Alexander I Balas, ruler of the Seleucid kingdom during 150–146.

IAIN SPENCE

### See also
Alexander I Balas; Antiochus IV Epiphanes; Egypt; Ptolemaic Kingdom; Seleucid Empire; Syria; Syrian-Egyptian Wars

### Reference
Manning, Joseph G. 2010. *The Last Pharaohs: Egypt under the Ptolemies, 305–30 BC*. Princeton, NJ: Princeton University Press, 2010.

## Pyramids, Battle of the (July 21, 1798)

On July 1, 1798, French General Napoleon Bonaparte's expeditionary force, dubbed the Army of Egypt, landed at Alexandria, Egypt. Informed that a British squadron under Rear Admiral Horatio Nelson had already arrived at that port and was looking for the French, Bonaparte ordered his men to disembark. The French quickly took Alexander, although the soldiers, many of whom were beguiled by tales of fabulous Egyptian wealth, were soon discouraged by the great poverty of that place and in the towns they subsequently encountered.

Leaving some of his force to garrison Alexandria and Rosetta, Bonaparte set off with the bulk of his men for Cairo. The march was difficult, made so by extreme heat and the lack of water caused by the Egyptians filling cisterns on the French march route across the desert. After more than a week, the French last reached the Nile at al-Rahmaniya. On July 13 near Shubra Khit an Egyptian force of some 14,000 men (4,000 cavalry and 10,000 infantry) commanded by Murad Bey attacked the French. Informed that the French had virtually no cavalry, Murad Bey reportedly said that he would slice through the French as if they were watermelons. The result was quite different. The Egyptian force was soundly defeated, although the bulk of the attackers and their leaders escaped.

Bonaparte and the army then resumed the march on Cairo. On July 21, close to that city and perhaps 10 miles from the famous Pyramids of Giza the French force of perhaps 20,000 men (3,000 cavalry and 17,000 infantry) again came under attack by Murad Bey, this time with a force variously estimated at between 21,000 and 40,000 men (but exaggerated by Bonaparte as 78,000). Bonaparte had 25,000. Bonaparte's divisions advanced en echelon and on being attacked formed into hollow squares, with baggage, noncombatants and cavalry in the centers and artillery on the corners. Bonaparte reportedly famously addressed the men with "Forty centuries of history look down on you."

In what Bonaparte chose to call the Battle of the Pyramids (also known as the Battle of Embabeh), the Mamluks engaged in a series of wild charges extending over some two hours that only served to demonstrate the superiority of massed musket fire over the archaic tactic of the charge with drawn saber. Some 7,000–8,000 Egyptians died in the fighting, and perhaps 1,000 others drowned in an effort to escape by swimming across the Nile. French losses were given as 29 dead and 260 wounded.

Word of the Battle of the Pyramids added immensely to Bonaparte's military reputation in Europe and gave Bonaparte Cairo, which the French troops entered on July 24. A week later on August 1, however, Nelson returned to Aboukir Bay and, in what the British (who also knew how to identify a battle for maximum propaganda value) referred to as the Battle of the Nile, immediately attacked and largely destroyed the French warships riding at anchor there, effectively cutting Bonaparte's army off in Egypt.

Spencer C. Tucker

**See also**
Aboukir Bay, Battle of; Bonaparte, Napoleon; Egypt, French Invasion and Occupation of; Nelson, Horatio

**References**
Chandler, David G. *The Campaigns of Napoleon.* New York: Macmillan, 1966.
Herold, J. Christopher. *Bonaparte in Egypt.* New York: Harper & Row, 1962.
Markham, J. David. *Napoleon's Road to Glory: Triumphs, Defeats & Immortality.* London: Brassey's, 2003.
Schur, Nathan. *Napoleon in the Holy Land.* London: Greenhill, 1999.
Strathern, Paul. *Napoleon in Egypt.* New York: Bantam, 2007.

# Q

## Qaboos bin Said al-Said (1940–)

Sultan of Oman since 1970. Qaboos bin Said al-Said was born the son of Sultan Said ibn Tamir on November 18, 1940, in Salalah, Dhofar Provincee. Qaboos spent seven years in Britain during his youth and attended the Royal Military Academy at Sandhurst. He returned to Oman in 1965, much influenced by Western ideas; as a result, his very conservative father placed him under virtual house arrest.

On July 23, 1970, during the Dhofar Rebellion (1962–1976), Qaboos, aided by loyal military forces, staged a coup d'état and deposed his father, who then went into exile in Great Britain. Sultan Qaboos then set about trying to modernize his country and bring it into the international political mainstream. As such, he oversaw the construction of new roads and the extension of educational opportunities and greatly improved medical care for his people. With assistance from Britain, he also defeated the insurgency of the Dhofar Rebellion in 1976.

Sultan Qaboos maintained strong ties with the United States, sometimes alienating other Arab countries. Indeed, he was one of only two Arab leaders to support the 1978 Camp David Accords signed by Israel and Egypt and brokered by the United States. In 1985, Qaboos began to cultivate relations with the Soviet Union. He also attempted to assume a stronger stance in regional politics. In 1981, he brought Oman into the Gulf Cooperation Council. He also worked hard to stabilize the region in the wake of the 1991 Persian Gulf War, which he strongly supported and to which he dispatched troops.

In 1996, the sultan issued a decree promulgating a new basic law that clarified royal succession, provided for a legislative council and a prime minister, and guaranteed basic civil liberties for Omani citizens. Qaboos, who still rules with an iron hand, holds the positions of prime minister and minister of foreign affairs, defense, and finance. His rule has been fairly progressive, however, especially vis-à-vis Persian Gulf standards, and since 1994 he has appointed numerous women to government posts.

In October 2004 as a result of many of the sultan's reforms, which included the institution of universal suffrage in 2003, Oman held its first free elections for the economic advisory council, known as the Shura Majlis Council. Still, Sultan Qaboos continues to exercise absolute power, and government institutions operate in a merely advisory capacity. During the so-called Arab Spring when protests erupted across the Arab world with demands for democratic change, the Omani government arrested a number of protest leaders who, however, were later released. There has also been concern over the succession, as there was no heir apparent.

Qaboos has been a cooperative partner in the U.S.-led war on terrorism since September 2001, allowing coalition forces overflight and basing rights. He was less supportive of the Iraq War of 2003. Under Qaboos, Oman, unlike most of the Arab states of the Persian Gulf, has maintained normal relations with Iran. As a result, Oman has often been an intermediary between the United States and Iran.

PAUL G. PIERPAOLI JR.

**See also**
Arab Spring; Camp David Accords; Dhofar Rebellion; Gulf Cooperation Council; Iraq War; Oman; Persian Gulf War, Overview

**References**
Kechichian, Joseph A. *Oman and the World: The Emergence of an Independent Foreign Policy.* Santa Monica, CA: Rand Corporation, 1995.
Owtram, Francis. *A Modern History of Oman: Formation of the State since 1920.* London: I. B. Tauris, 2004.

## Qadisiyya, Battle of (November 16–19, 636)

Decisive battle between an Arab Muslim army commanded by Saad ibn Abi Waqqas and a Sassanid Persian army commanded by Rustem. The battle occurred at that location in Iraq during November 16–19, 636, and is also known as the Battle of al-Qādisiyyah, Qadisiyyah, Kadisiya, and Ghadesiyeh. The two sides had met in several engagements prior to the Battle of Qadisiyya, with the Muslims winning most of them except the Battle of the Bridge in November 634. Qadisiyya was the final decisive clash between the two sides that decided the fate of Iraq. Saad's army is said to have numbered between 9,000 and 12,000 men, in addition to reinforcements arriving from the Syrian front during the course of the battle that numbered between 1,500 and 6,000 troops. The Sassanids greatly outnumbered the Arabs, with Rustem probably commanding between 30,000 and 80,000 men supported by a small number of elephants.

The Arabs took up a defensive position with a canal in front of them and marshes guarding their flanks. Initially the Sassanids had the upper hand in the fighting owing to their numbers and armament; however, the Arabs succeeded in neutralizing the elephants by blinding them, which caused a stampede that disrupted the Sassanid lines. Furthermore, the Arabs were heartened by the arrival of the Syrian reinforcements. After three days of heavy fighting the Sassanids grew disheartened and finally dispersed when the Muslims broke through their center in a night attack on the last day of the battle, in which Rustem died.

The remnants of the Sassanid army were besieged in Ctesiphon. It surrendered in November 637. The Battle of Qadisiyya led to the Islamic conquest of Persia and was key to the conquest of Iraq.

ADAM ALI

**See also**
Persia, Arab Conquest of

**References**
Glubb, John Baggot. *The Great Arab Conquests.* London: Hodder and Stoughton, 1963.
Jandora, John W. *The March from Medina: A Revisionist Study of the Arab Conquests.* Clifton, NJ: Kingston, 1990.
Zarinkub, Abd al-Husain. "The Arab Conquest of Iran and Its Aftermath." In *The Cambridge History of Iran,* Vol. 4, ed. R. N. Frye. Cambridge: Cambridge University Press, 1975.

## Qalawun (ca. 1222–1290)

Mamluk sultan of Egypt (r. 1279–1290) and founder of a dynasty that lasted 100 years. Qalawun was born around 1222, a Kipchak Turk by origin. He became a mamluk (slave-soldier) in the 1240s after being sold to a member of Sultan al-Kamil's household. Qalawun was known as al-Alfi (the Thousander) because he was purchased for 1,000 gold dinars. Later he served al-ali Ayyub as a member of the Bariyya corps of soldiers. Qalawun became an emir under Sultan Baybars I (r. 1260–1277).

After Baybars's death, Qalawun succeeded to the throne following a brief power struggle. He then set about consolidating his position. This involved setting aside the mamluks of Baybars in favor of his own as well as installing those loyal to him in important positions. He also put down a revolt in Syria by Sunqur al-Ashqar with the support of the Bedouin leader Isa ibn Muhanna.

In 1281 Qalawun faced a long-expected invasion of Syria by the Ilkhan Abaka, who had sought to break Mamluk power in the region. Qalawun's victory in the Second Battle of Homs (October 29) followed by Abaka's death shortly thereafter left him free to continue the Mamluk military campaign against the Frankish states of Outremer, which were politically weak and divided. The sultanate had previously concluded a number of truces with individual Frankish powers; now, Qalawun found pretexts for declaring them void and defeating his enemies piecemeal.

In 1285 the sultan accused the Hospitallers of Margat of attacking Muslims, and after a brief campaign he took the stronghold in late May. He then moved against the castle of Maraclea, which Prince Bohemund VII of Tripoli ordered to be surrendered so as to preserve his own truce with the

Mamluks. In 1287 after an earthquake destroyed some of the fortifications at Laodikeia in Syria, Qalawun took the city, claiming that it was not covered by his truce with Bohemund, as the city lay outside the boundaries of the county of Tripoli. In 1289 Qalawun attacked Tripoli (modern-day Trâblous, Lebanon), eventually storming the town and massacring much of the population. He then razed the city and ordered it rebuilt on a new site.

In an attempt to save Acre (modern-day Akko, Israeli), the last Christian possession in the area, Pope Nicholas IV called a crusade in February 1290, though many Western monarchs simply used the crisis to strengthen their economic interests in Egypt. During the preparations for his campaign against Acre, however, Qalawun died in Cairo on November 10, 1290. Qalawun's son and successor Khalil ended the Frankish occupation of the Near East.

BRIAN ULRICH

### See also
Baybars I; Bohemund VII of Antioch-Tripoli; Crusades in the Holy Land, Christian; Homs, Second Battle of

### References
Amitai-Preiss, Reuven. *Mongols and Mamluks: The Mamluk-Ilkhanid War, 1260–1281.* Cambridge: Cambridge University Press, 1995.
Holt, Peter M. *The Age of the Crusades: The Near East from the Eleventh Century to 1517.* London: Longman, 1986.
Irwin, Robert. *The Middle East in the Middle Ages: The Early Mamluk Sultanate, 1250–1382.* London: Croom Helm, 1986.
Northrup, Linda S. *From Slave to Sultan: The Career of al-Mansur Qalawun and the Consolidation of Mamluk Rule in Egypt and Syria (678–689 A.H./1279–1290 A.D.).* Stuttgart: Steiner, 1998.

# Qarmatians

A dissident faction of the early Ismailis and named after Hamdan Qarmat, the first chief missionary (*da'i*) of the Ismailis in Iraq. The early Ismaili movement appeared in Iraq and many other regions of the Islamic world from around 870 CE. As Shiite Muslims, the Ismailis aimed to replace the Sunni-Abbasid established order with a new Shiite caliphate ruled by the Ismaili imam.

The majority of the early Ismailis recognized a line of seven such imams, starting with Prophet Muhammad's cousin and son-in-law Ali (d. 661) and ending with Muhammad ibn Ismail, a grandson of Imam Ja'far al-Sadiq (d. 765), who was also acknowledged as the Mahdi, or the restorer of true Islam, and justice in the world. Meanwhile, Muhammad ibn Ismail remained in hiding, and the Ismailis awaited his reappearance. The central leaders of the early Ismaili movement, who traced their ancestry to Ali, did not initially claim the imamate openly. Instead, they acted as the *hujjas* (full representatives) of the hidden seventh imam/Mahdi, Muhammad ibn Ismail.

In 899 soon after his own accession to the central leadership of the Ismaili movement, Abd Allah al-Mahdi, future founder of the Fatimid caliphate, claimed the imamate for himself and his successors. The doctrinal reform of Abd Allah split the Ismaili movement into two rival factions. On one side, there were those loyal Ismailis who accepted Abd Allah's reform and maintained continuity in the Ismaili imamate; they also recognized Abd Allah's successors to the Fatimid caliphate as their imams. By contrast, a dissident Ismaili faction, initially led by Hamdan Qarmat and his chief assistant Abdan, retained its original doctrine and continued to expect the return of Muhammad ibn Ismail as the Mahdi and final imam. Henceforth, the term "Qarmatian" was more specifically applied to those dissident Ismailis who did not acknowledge Abd Allah al-Mahdi (d. 934) and the later Fatimid caliphs as their imams.

Qarmatian communities existed in different parts of Arabia, Yemen, Iraq, Iran and Central Asia. But the Qarmatians found their main stronghold in eastern Arabia, then known as Bahrayn. There, in 899 Abu Sa'id al-Jannabi (d. 913) founded the Qarmatian state. He was succeeded by several of his sons, including Abu Tahir al-Jannabi (d. 944). The Qarmatians of Bahrayn indulged in continuous pillaging raids into surrounding regions, remaining hostile to both the Sunni Abbasids and the Ismaili Shiite Fatimids. Several Qarmatian missionaries, including especially Abu Hatim al-Razi (d. 934) and Muhammad al-Nasafi (d. 943), attained prominence in Iran and Central Asia, where they converted a Samanid emir and other rulers.

By the time the Qarmatian state of Bahrayn was finally uprooted by local tribesmen in 1077, the Qarmatian groups of other regions, who had continued to await the return of their hidden Mahdi, had either disintegrated or joined the loyal Ismaili camp led by the Fatimids. The Qarmatians were generally condemned and refuted by the Muslim majority as heretics, while the Qarmatians of Bahrayn also received occasional praise for the communal and egalitarian principles that informed the sociopolitical organization of their state.

FARHAD DAFTARY

See also

Kharijites; Shia Islam

**References**

Daftary, Farhad. "Carmatians." In *Encyclopaedia Iranica,* Vol. 4, 823–832. New York: Bibliotheca Persica, 2000.

Daftary, Farhad. *The Isma'ilis: Their History and Doctrines.* 2nd ed. Cambridge: Cambridge University Press, 2007.

Halm, Heinz. *The Empire of the Mahdi: The Rise of the Fatimids.* Translated by M. Bonner. Leiden: E. J. Brill, 1996.

Madelung, Wilferd. "The Fatimids and the Qarmatis of Bahrayn." In *Mediaeval Isma'ili History and Thought,* ed. F. Daftary, 21–73. Cambridge: Cambridge University Press, 1996.

## Qasim, Abdul Karim (1914–1963)

Iraqi general and leader of a 1958 coup that overthrew the British-imposed monarch King Faisal II, sweeping away the last vestiges of colonial rule in Iraq. Abdul Karim Qasim (Kassem), son of a Sunni Arab and a Shia Kurdish mother, was born in a poor section of Baghdad on November 21, 1914. His father raised corn along the Tigris River. The poverty he experienced as a young boy influenced Qasim's later efforts at social reform. He attended school in Baghdad, and at age 17, following a brief period teaching elementary school (1931–1932), he enrolled in the Iraqi Military College. Two years later in 1934 he graduated as a second lieutenant. In 1935 he took part in suppressing unrest in the middle Euphrates region of Iraq.

In 1941 Qasim graduated with honors from the al-Arkan (General Staff) College and became a staff officer. In 1942 while stationed in Basra near the Persian Gulf, he struck up a friendship with Abd al-Salam Arif. The two men shared a desire to overthrow the Iraqi monarchy. In 1945 Qasim commanded a battalion against rebellious Kurdish tribesmen in northern Iraq, a campaign that earned him the highest Iraqi military decoration.

In 1948 during the Israeli War of Independence (1948–1949), Qasim commanded a battalion of the Iraqi 1st Brigade in Palestine. Following the Arab defeat, he attended a senior officers' school in Britain. Upon his return to Iraq, he was promoted to colonel and a year later attained the rank of brigadier general. During the Suez Crisis of 1956, he commanded Iraqi troops in Jordan, where his schooling and his combat experience earned him respect and prominence.

In 1956 Qasim helped organize and then headed the central organization of the Free Officers, a clandestine association working to overthrow the Iraqi monarchy. He worked closely with Arif waiting for the right moment to mount a

Iraqi general Abdul Karim Qasim, leader of the 1958 coup that overthrew the government and King Faisal II. The coup ended the last vestiges of colonial control of Iraq. (Central Press/Hulton Archive/Getty Images)

coup. That time came in 1958 when a revolt broke out in Jordan followed by a crisis in Lebanon, and the Iraqi monarchy ordered troops into Jordan.

Arif's battalion entered Baghdad on July 13 en route to Jordan, but the next day his troops occupied the central radio studio and proclaimed the overthrow of the king. The following day King Faisal II, the crown prince, some other members of the royal family, and Prime Minister Nuri al-Said Pasha were all assassinated. Qasim arrived in Baghdad with his troops after the assassinations. Some historians attribute the apparent delay in his arrival to a calculated decision to allow Arif to take the initial risk. Regardless, Qasim became prime minister and minister of defense, with Arif as deputy prime minister and interior minister.

Disputes soon arose between Qasim and Arif over the direction of the revolutionary government. Arif was more popular with the crowds than Qasim, and this also led to tension. Arif favored the unionist wing of the Baathists who first argued for unity with Egypt and later Syria, while Qasim was attempting to balance the Baath Party with its several factions against the Arab nationalists and the communists. These tensions eventually resulted in a showdown with Arif and his imprisonment on charges of conspiracy.

Qasim allowed the Communist Party to operate, and he embarked on serious land reform to address rural poverty. The new government launched a series of attacks on opponents that prompted a public outcry. Two incidents in particular inspired revulsion. The first occurred in March 1959 when Qasim's communist allies, after crushing a revolt by army units in Mosul, went on a rampage, killing anticommunist supporters of the rebellion. The second incident occurred later that summer when Kurdish communists were involved in massacres, particularly of Turcomen in Kirkuk.

Meanwhile, Qasim launched several important domestic and foreign policy reforms. First, he addressed the maldistribution of land by limiting the size of holdings. Second, he expanded women's rights in the areas of marriage, divorce, and inheritance. Third, in a highly successful move, he reduced the influence of oil companies by confiscating large amounts of land held by the foreign-owned Iraq Petroleum Company. This step prepared the way for full nationalization in 1973.

In foreign affairs Qasim followed a policy of nonalignment, but his actions, including substantial arms purchases from communist bloc nations, tilted Iraq toward the Soviet Union. Relations with Egypt deteriorated, encouraging unionists to contemplate Qasim's overthrow. In October 1959 the Iraqi branch of the Arab Baath Socialist Party concluded that Qasim's policies, particularly his antagonism toward Egypt and alliance with the communists, necessitated his removal. The Baathists plotted to kill Qasim in the streets of Baghdad. Their attempt on October 7 only wounded him. Several of the conspirators fled Iraq, including the young Saddam Hussein.

Following this attempt on his life, Qasim permitted the free organization of political parties but only if they did not threaten national unity. In practice, this meant that no independent party could exist, a fact confirmed in late 1960 when Qasim suppressed all parties. His increasingly narrow support became restricted to segments of the military, and he lived an increasingly isolated existence, barricaded in the office of the Ministry of Defense.

Qasim's growing unpopularity was exacerbated by two military failures. One was the inability to quell a Kurdish rebellion in northern Iraq. The second was his bungled attempt to absorb Kuwait in 1961, when he announced that the small Persian Gulf nation was in reality a renegade Iraqi province. When British and later Arab League troops moved to protect Kuwait, Qasim was forced to back down. Another blow came in the form of an Iraqi economic slump. All these factors led to growing disaffection in the army, Qasim's last bastion of support. On February 8, 1963, a military coup led by Arif Baathists toppled Qasim. Following a bloody street battle, he was captured and executed.

Qasim achieved much in societal reform, health, education, housing for the poor, and agriculture, but perhaps his greatest accomplishment was the establishment of a truly independent Iraq.

NEIL HAMILTON AND SPENCER C. TUCKER

### See also
Baath Party; Faisal II, King of Iraq; Iraq; Israeli War of Independence; Nasser, Gamal Abdel; Suez Crisis; United Arab Republic

### References
Batatu, Hanna. *The Old Social Classes and the Revolutionary Movements of Iraq: A Study of Iraq's Old Landed and Commercial Classes and of Its Communists, Ba'thists and Free Officers.* Princeton, NJ: Princeton University Press, 1978.

Dann, Uriel. *Iraq under Qassem: A Political History, 1958–1963.* New York: Praeger, 1969.

Khadduri, Majid. *Republican Iraq: A Study in Iraqi Politics during the Revolution of 1958.* Oxford: Oxford University Press, 1969.

Makiya, Kanaan [Khalil, Samir al-]. *Republic of Fear: The Politics of Modern Iraq.* Berkeley: University of California Press, 1998.

Marr, Phebe. *The Modern History of Iraq.* 2nd ed. Boulder, CO: Westview, 2003.

## Qassam, Izz ad-Din al- (1882–1935)

Arab nationalist and militant credited with helping to instigate the Great Palestinian Rebellion (or Arab Revolt) of 1936–1939. Born in Jaballah, Syria, in 1882, Izz ad-Din al-Qassam was sent at age 14 to Cairo to study at al-Azhar University. He returned to Syria in 1903, then went back to Alexandria, Egypt, to try to create an armed force to fight the Italians in Libya. He also studied sharia (Islamic law).

In 1922 al-Qassam moved to Haifa in the British Mandate for Palestine. He led a masjid and taught militant and charismatic religious leaders who believed in the necessity of armed struggle, and he was also a representative of the Naqshabandi Sufi order and was elected the head of the Young Men's Muslim Association in 1928. He was then made a registrar for the Islamic court in the Haifa area. Al-Qassam attracted many followers, particularly from among the lower classes, and believed in both Arab and Muslim solidarity.

Al-Qassam argued for the immediate departure from Palestine of both the British and the Jews. When Mufti Haj Amin al-Husseini rejected al-Qassam's plan to transfer funds dedicated to mosque repairs in order to purchase weapons, al-Qassam proceeded to organize a military effort on his own in response to the British firing on a crowd of Palestinian demonstrators. He was killed on November 20, 1935, while leading a group against the British at Ya'bud outside the town of Jenin.

Al-Qassam is regarded by Palestinian militants as a hero and martyr. His followers, the Qassamiyun, or Izz ad-Din al-Qassam Brigades, fought in the 1936–1939 Arab Revolt. The Hamas military divisions and the Qassam rocket, which is employed by both Hamas and Hezbollah, are named for him.

SPENCER C. TUCKER

**See also**
Arab Revolt in Palestine; Hamas; Hezbollah; Husseini, Haj Amin al-

**References**
Nafi, Basheer M. "Shaykh 'Izz Al-Din Al-Qassam: A Reformist and a Rebel Leader." *Journal of Islamic Studies* 8, no. 2 (1997): 185–215.
Schleifer, Abdullah. "Izz al-Din al-Qassam: Preacher and Mujahid." In *Struggle and Survival in the Modern Middle East*, ed. Edmund Burke III, 164–178. Berkeley: University of California Press, 1993.
Sherman, A. J. *Mandate Days: British Lives in Palestine, 1918–1948.* Baltimore: Johns Hopkins University Press, 2001.
Wasserstein, Bernard. *The British in Palestine: The Mandatory Government and Arab-Jewish Conflict.* London: Blackwell, 1991.

# Qatar

Qatar, officially the State of Qatar, is located in Southwest Asia and comprises the Qatar Peninsula on the northeastern coast of the Arabian Peninsula and, at 4,416 square miles, is a bit smaller than the U.S. state of Connecticut. Qatar's sole land border is to the south with Saudi Arabia. The remainder of Qatar is surrounded by the Persian Gulf. A strait separates Qatar from the nearby island of Bahrain, and Qatar also shares sea borders with the United Arab Emirates and Iran.

Qatar's population in 2018 was some 2.45 million. About 80 percent of the people live in the capital city of Doha and its suburbs. Qatar is a hereditary constitutional monarchy, headed by an emir. Some 67.7 percent of Qataris are Muslim, and Islam is the state religion, with the vast majority of Muslims belonging to the Salafi sect of Sunni Islam. Another 13.8 percent are Christians (almost all of these foreigners), while 13.8 percent are Hindu and 3.1 percent are Buddhist. Other religions and religiously unaffiliated people make up the remaining 1.6 percent. Qatar is regarded as the most conservative of the states, after Saudi Arabia, of Gulf Cooperation Council members.

Qatar enjoys considerable per capita wealth and a modern infrastructure. Indeed, Qatar has the world's highest per capita income as a result of possessing the world's third-largest natural gas and oil reserves. It has used this wealth to become a major power in the Arab world. It also enjoys great influence beyond the region through its highly regarded Al Jazeera Media Network.

Qatar has been inhabited for some 50,000 years. In 224 CE it became part of the Sassanian Empire. Islam was introduced in 621. Qatar was known for its trade in pearls and for a purple dye and as a horse and camel breeding center. Ruled by Bahrain during 1783–1868, in 1871 it became part of the Ottoman Empire. Qatar shook off Ottoman rule in the Arab Revolt in 1916 during World War I (1914–1918). Qatar became a British protectorate on November 3, 1916, when Sheikh Abdullah bin Jassim Al Thani signed a treaty in which he pledged not to enter into relations with any other power without the prior consent of the British government. The British pledged in return to protect Qatar from seaborne attack. Another treaty between Qatar and Britain on May 5, 1935, provided Qatar further protection against internal and external threats.

Although Qatar's vast oil holdings were discovered in 1939, exploitation was delayed by World War II. Following the independence of India and Pakistan in 1947, British interest in the Persian Gulf region declined considerably. At the same time, the considerable wealth from oil production led the people of Qatar to support independence. On January 24, 1968, British prime minister Harold Wilson announced his government's decision to let the treaties with the emirates lapse in three years. This was reaffirmed in March 1971 by Prime Minister Edward Heath. Qatar then joined other states of the eastern Persian Gulf in a federation. Regional disputes, however, led Qatar to resign and declare its independence from this coalition of small states that would become the United Arab Emirates (UAE), and on September 3, 1971, Qatar became an independent sovereign state. On February 22, 1972, Sheikh Khalifa bin Hamad Al Thani deposed his cousin Sheikh Ahmed bin Ali Al Thani as ruler of Qatar.

# Qatar

On January 26, 1982, Qatar joined with Saudi Arabia, Bahrain, Kuwait, Oman, and the UAE in establishing a joint military command structure and integrated air defense system. This move was prompted by the perceived threats posed by the Islamic Republic of Iran, the ongoing Iran-Iraq War (1980–1988), and the Soviet-Afghan War (1979–1989).

The United States established diplomatic relations with Qatar in March 1973. Since then, relations between the two governments have been mainly cordial. Qatar has only a small military establishment numbering only some 11,000 troops, 34 tanks, and about a dozen aircraft. Its most extensive role in combat operations came during January 29–31, 1991, in the first battle of the 1991 Persian Gulf War when a Qatari tank battalion and Saudi troops, backed by American artillery and air support, repulsed an Iraqi cross-border assault on the Saudi city of Khafji. During that war U.S., French, and Canadian aircraft staged from Qatar. The era since the end of the Persian Gulf War has been marked by greater political, economic, and military cooperation with the West and the United States in particular, as the 1990 Iraqi invasion of Kuwait and the resulting threat to other small Persian Gulf states forced Qatar to significantly alter its defense and foreign policy priorities.

On June 27, 1995, Crown Prince Hamad bin Khalifa Al Thani carried out a bloodless coup, overthrowing the repressive regime of his father, Emir Sheikh Khalifa bin Hamad Al Thani. The crown prince vowed to liberalize Qatar, and during the next several years he allowed women far more freedom, including the right to vote in municipal elections; ended censorship; introduced Qatar's first constitution; and established Al Jazeera. He also permitted the construction of U.S. military facilities.

Strains with Saudi Arabia and Bahrain and aspirations for a more assertive and influential position in foreign affairs explain Qatar's recent foreign policy, which has become more Western oriented. On June 23, 1992, Qatar and the United States signed a bilateral defense cooperation agreement that provided the United States access to Qatari bases, the prepositioning of U.S. military equipment in the nation, and future joint military exercises. Qatar also allowed construction of an extensive American military air base—Al Udeid—in the country, which served as the command center for the Anglo-American invasion of Iraq in March 2003. Presumably for this reason, Iraq launched Scud missiles at Qatar upon the commencement of the conflict. Al Udeid boasts the longest runway (15,000 feet) in the Persian Gulf region and currently houses some 5,000 U.S. troops. It is equipped to accommodate as many as 10,000 troops and 40 aircraft in a 76,000-square-foot hangar. Qatar also allowed the construction of the As-Sayliyah Army Base, the largest prepositioning facility for U.S. equipment in the world.

Shortly after the terror attacks against the United States on September 11, 2001, Qatar granted the Americans permission to deploy warplanes to Al Udeid, and these flew missions in Afghanistan during the U.S.-led invasion of Afghanistan (Operation ENDURING FREEDOM) in the fall of 2001 to overthrow the Taliban government, which had given sanctuary to Osama bin Laden and his Al Qaeda terrorist organization.

In the months leading up to the U.S. and British-led invasion of Iraq (Operation IRAQI FREEDOM, the Iraq War) in 2003, the United States moved significant troops, weapons, and equipment, along with its Air Operations Command Center, from Prince Sultan Air Base in Saudi Arabia to Qatar, the consequence of Saudi Arabia's opposition to the invasion. Indeed, during the Iraq War, Saudi Arabia forbade the U.S. from using its territory to launch attacks against Iraq.

In March 2005, a suicide bombing carried out by an Egyptian with suspected ties to Al Qaeda in the Arabian Peninsula killed a British teacher, shocking the country, which had not previously experienced such acts of terrorism. Qatar firmly aligned itself with the United States and NATO in the latter's intervention in the 2011 Libyan Civil War. It has also been, along with the United States, the chief supplier of arms and financial support for the rebels battling the regime of Syrian president Bashar al-Assad in the ongoing Syrian Civil War (2011–) and has hosted several meetings of representatives of states supporting the rebels. On September 23, 2014, Qatar Air Force planes took part in a U.S. and Arab coalition attack on Islamic State of Iraq and Syria (ISIS) rebels in Syria. Qatar has also served as a base for U.S. aircraft taking part in the fight against ISIS. These included the B-1 and B-52 strategic bombers, the latter from April 2016. Qatar has also been active in trying to broker a peace agreement with the Taliban in Afghanistan.

On June 25, 2013, Sheikh Tamim bin Hamad Al Thani became the emir of Qatar upon his father ceding power. Sheikh Tamim stated his intention to improve the welfare of Qatari citizens by improving both advanced health care and education. He has also supported major improvements in the country's infrastructure in preparation for the hosting of the 2022 World Cup, the first Arab country to do so.

During 2013–2014 Qatar earned the enmity of some of its Persian Gulf neighbors, especially Saudi Arabia, Bahrain, and the United Arab Emirates, because of its support of the Muslim Brotherhood, a group that is both feared and despised in those nations. On March 26, 2015, Qatar sent aircraft to participate in the Saudi Arabian–led military intervention in Yemen against Iranian-backed Houthi rebels. Qatar's relations with the West seemed solid.

On June 5, however, in a surprise announcement, Saudi Arabia, Egypt, the United Arab Emirates, and Bahrain severed ties with Qatar, opening up the worst rift in years among some of the most powerful states in the Arab world. This move dramatically escalated the sharp disagreement over Qatar's support of the Muslim Brotherhood. At the same time, however, the other four Arab states accused Doha of supporting regional archrival Iran by broadcasting radical Islamic propaganda over the Qatari state-run satellite television network Al Jazeera and encouraging Iranian-backed militants in Saudi Arabia's restive and largely Shiite Muslim-populated eastern region of Qatif and in Bahrain. The four states also cut off all transport ties with Qatar and gave its citizens within their countries two weeks to leave. Qatar was also expelled from the Saudi-led coalition fighting in Yemen.

It seemed clear to many analysts that the Saudis and Emiratis felt emboldened by the results of the first foreign visit undertaken by U.S. president Donald Trump, when he visited Saudi Arabia, expressed strong backing for that nation, and encouraged an Arab alignment against Iran and Islamic extremism. Oil prices rose on the news, with Qatar being the largest supplier of liquefied natural gas (LNG) and a major seller of condensate, a low-density liquid fuel and refining product derived from natural gas.

Then on June 23, 2017, Saudi Arabia, the United Arab Emirates, Bahrain, and Egypt sent Qatar a list of demands with a 10-day time frame to comply, which sharply escalated what was already the worst crisis among the Persian Gulf states in years. It includes a demand that Qatar shut down the Al Jazeera news network and its affiliates, halt development of a Turkish military base in the country, reduce its diplomatic ties with Iran, cut all ties to extremist organizations, cease interfering in the four countries' affairs, and end the practice of extending Qatari nationality to citizens of the four countries.

Qatar rejected the demands. Shuttle diplomacy by U.S. secretary of state Rex Tillerson (all the countries involved are allies of the United States) to try to relieve the impasse failed, but in mid-July the countries that had cut ties eased their stance somewhat, stating that they were no longer insisting on these precise 13 conditions or had set a time limit for compliance. No direct talks had been scheduled, however. As of early 2019, the diplomatic impasse involving Qatar and its neighbors had yet to be resolved. That same month, press reports emerged claiming that Tillerson, who was forced from his post in March 2018, had stopped Saudi Arabia and the United Arab Emirates from attacking Qatar in the summer of 2017.

STEFAN BROOKS AND SPENCER C. TUCKER

**See also**
Saudi Arabia; Yemen Civil War

**References**
Blanchard, Christopher. *Qatar: Background and U.S. Relations.* Washington, DC: Congressional Research Service, Library of Congress, 2005.
Cleveland, William F. *A History of the Modern Middle East.* Boulder, CO: Westview, 2004.
Fromherz, Allen J. *Qatar: A Modern History.* Washington, DC: Georgetown University Press, 2012.
Kamrava, Mehran. *Qatar: Small State, Big Politics.* Cornell, NY: Cornell University Press, 2015.
Roberts, David. *Qatar: Securing the Global Ambitions of a City-State.* London: Hurst, 2016.
Ulrichsen, Kristian Coates. *Qatar and the Arab Spring.* Oxford: Oxford University Press, 2014.

# Qawuqji, Fawzi al- (1890–1976)

Arab nationalist and military commander. Born in Tripoli in present-day Libya in 1890, Fawzi al-Qawuqji (Kaukji) pursued a military career and served as a junior officer in the Ottoman Army during World War I. In the wake of the defeat, he joined the struggle to assert Arab interests in the face of European occupation and Zionist inroads in Palestine.

Al-Qawuqji greatly resented the British and French occupation of Arab lands after World War I and became a regional leader of the Great Syrian Revolt (1925–1927), which sought unsuccessfully to end French rule there. After the resistance faded, he fled via Iraq to the Hejaz in western Arabia with the other fighters and Sultan al-Atrash.

Defeat and exile did not deter al-Qawuqji, who emerged as a key figure in the Arab drive for self-determination. For a time he served as a military adviser to Ibn Saud, future king of Saudi Arabia. In 1932 al-Qawuqji made his way to Iraq, where he joined the Iraqi Army and became an instructor at the military college in Baghdad. Over the next few years, his image as a fervent Arab nationalist and a legendary military figure seemingly made him the ideal man to lead the next regional uprising. In 1936 he was encouraged to take command of contingents of armed volunteers in the struggle against British rule in Palestine and the stream of Jewish immigrants into the mandate.

Despite numbering only in the hundreds of men, al-Qawuqji's forces quickly elevated the quality of Arab resistance, as they included both veteran fighters and professional soldiers. However, facing thousands of British troops and an Arab decision to suspend the fighting, his men eventually had to retreat back across the Jordan River in October 1936.

During al-Qawuqji's brief stay in Palestine, he also embroiled himself in local politics and generated a mutual enmity for Haj Amin al-Husseini, the mufti of Jerusalem. The bitter rivalry between the two men, in a sense symbolic of Arab divisions over the fate of Palestine, would intensify during the decade following the 1939 defeat of the Arab Revolt in the mandate. As fellow nationalists, al-Qawuqji and al-Husseini reluctantly collaborated, first during the failed Iraqi uprising against the British in 1941 and later as joint exiles in Nazi Germany, but throughout those years the friction between them grew.

Tensions hardly lessened with al-Qawuqji's appointment in 1947 to be field commander of the Arab Liberation Army (ALA), a motley fighting force sponsored by the Arab League and intended for deployment to Palestine. Organized and trained in southern Syria, the ALA gradually slipped into the mandate during the early months of 1948, and by April shortly after al-Qawuqji arrived to assume direct command, the ALA of some 7,500 men was poised to begin major operations.

The ALA, heavily influenced by Syrian interests (Syrians made up about a third of the force), was as much sent to block the ambitions of Jordan and those of al-Husseini as to fight Jewish military forces. During the weeks before the neighboring Arab states directly joined the conflict, al-Qawuqji failed to achieve any significant successes on the field of battle, and it is even asserted that he intentionally withheld men and supplies from assisting the Palestinian forces loyal to al-Husseini. The ALA commander later rejected such criticisms. He instead blamed the Arab League for poor logistical support and attributed the overall defeat of Arab forces to the lack of a unified command.

Al-Qawuqji's participation in the Israeli War of Independence ended by November 1948. His remaining ALA forces, unable to further resist a superior enemy, retreated permanently from Palestine. The defeat disillusioned al-Qawuqji greatly, as he soon retired from military service and withdrew entirely from public life. He published his memoirs in 1975 and died in Beirut, Lebanon, in December 1976.

JONAS KAUFFELDT

### See also
Arab League; Arab Liberation Army; Husseini, Haj Amin al-; Israeli War of Independence; Zionism

### References
Morris, Benny. *Righteous Victims: A History of the Zionist-Arab Conflict, 1881–2001.* New York: Vintage Books, 2001.

Pollack, Kenneth M. *Arabs at War: Military Effectiveness, 1948–1991.* Lincoln: University of Nebraska Press, 2002.

Porath, Yehoshua. *The Palestinian Arab National Movement: From Riots to Rebellion.* London: Frank Cass, 1977.

Provence, Michael. *The Great Syrian Revolt.* Austin: University of Texas Press, 2005.

Rogan, Eugene L., and Avi Shlaim, eds. *The War for Palestine: Rewriting the History of 1948.* Cambridge: Cambridge University Press, 2001.

## Qibya Massacre (October 14, 1953)

Israeli assault on the West Bank village of Qibya on October 14, 1953, that resulted in the deaths of some 60 Palestinians and the nearly wholesale destruction of the town. At the time, the West Bank was under Jordanian administration. Code-named Operation SHOSHANA by the Israel Defense Force (IDF), the Qibya attack was launched soon after nightfall and carried out by a unit of Israeli paratroopers, a specialized force of counterinsurgency troops known as Unit 101 that was commanded by Major Ariel Sharon, who would much later become Israeli prime minister.

The Israeli government asserted that the Qibya raid was in retaliation for a steady stream of Palestinian attacks and incursions via Jordan and the West Bank that had killed scores of Israeli citizens since late 1949. In 1953 the pace and severity of the Palestinian raids had increased dramatically, so much so that 32 Israelis had died from January to September alone. The immediate triggering event was the October 12, 1953, murders of a Jewish woman and her two young children in the village of Yehud, Israel. Determined to exact revenge on the Palestinians, Israeli defense minister Pinhas Lavon, in consultation with Prime Minister David Ben-Gurion, made plans for a quick and heavy retaliation. Qibya was chosen because of its close proximity to the Israeli border and the fact that several Palestinian attacks had seemed to come from there.

The assault on Qibya commenced with an Israeli artillery strike as IDF ground forces moved into position. Roads leading to and from the village were mined to prevent the Jordanians from sending in reinforcements and to cause maximum damage to fighters trying to flee the town. IDF forces maintain that they conducted a house-to-house search to warn civilians to leave the area. Palestinians dispute that this occurred. After the village had been secured militarily, IDF troops blew up a number of homes that had not already been leveled by the artillery barrage. Many Palestinians thus died because they either never received the warnings from the IDF or could not leave their homes as they were being fired on. At dusk the following morning, 60 Palestinians lay dead and an undetermined number were injured. The dead included a high percentage of women and children. Forty-five houses, the village mosque, the school, and water facilities lay in ruins. The Israelis then withdrew across the border in the early hours of the morning.

A high degree of uncertainty and conflicting stories exist as to what precisely happened in Qibya that night. The IDF claimed that it had given fair warning to the villagers before the fight began, but it is also likely that the initial artillery strike killed several villagers, who at that point would have had no warning at all. Sharon said he believed that all the homes demolished by explosives had been empty, but other reports claim that those who died in their homes had been forced at gunpoint to remain in them and had not been given the chance to escape before they were blown up.

Initially, the Israeli government sought to downplay the raid. Indeed, when news of the raid first came to light, Ben-Gurion's government denied having had anything to do with it. Ben-Gurion claimed that it had been carried out by civilians. This denial did not wash, however, and as word of the massacre circulated, the Israeli government came under harsh criticism from many Israelis. On the international front, the Qibya Massacre was a public relations catastrophe for the Israelis. Virtually every Western nation including the United States denounced the attack, and the United Nations (UN) Security Council passed a resolution that November condemning the raid. Clearly, the Qibya Massacre only served to enrage Palestinian guerrillas all the more.

PAUL G. PIERPAOLI JR.

**See also**
Ben-Gurion, David; Israel; Sharon, Ariel; West Bank

**References**
Laqueur, Walter, and Barry Rubin, eds. *The Israel-Arab Reader: A Documentary History of the Middle East Conflict.* London: Penguin, 2001.
Morris, Benny. *Israel's Border Wars, 1949–1956: Arab Infiltration, Israeli Retaliation, and the Countdown to the Suez War.* Oxford, UK: Clarendon, 1993.
Pappe, Ilan. *The Making of the Arab-Israeli Conflict, 1949–1951.* London: Tauris, 1994.

## Qilij Arslan I of Rum (1079–1107)

Izz al-Din Qilij Arslan I was the third sultan (r. 1092–1107) of the Seljuk Sultanate of Rum in western Anatolia. He reigned during 1092–1107 and thus faced the First Christian Crusade in the Holy Land (1096–1099).

Born in 1079, Qilij Arslan I (Sword Lion) was the son of Sulaymān I Ibn Qutlumush, the founder of the Rum Sultanate. When Sulaymān died in combat at Shaizar in Syria (ca. 1086) fighting against the Great Seljuk sultan Malik Shah I and his brother Tutush I, ruler of Syria, the young Qilij Arslan was among those taken hostage and spent some years in captivity in Baghdad, during which time his sultanate was ruled by his uncle Abu'l Qasim (1086–1092). Qilij Arslan's liberation following Malik Shah's violent death (1092) coincided with Abu'l Qasim's death in Nicaea at the hands of Malik Shah's agents, so Qilij Arslan managed to ascend his throne. From the outset of his reign he established contacts with Chaka, the ambitious emir of Smyrna (modern-day İzmir, Turkey), whose son-in-law he became, while his belligerent activities were directed against the Danishmendids in eastern Anatolia.

In August 1096 Qilij Arslan's troops decimated the rabble led by Peter the Hermit and constituting one of the so-called people's expeditions of the First Crusade who were the first crusaders to cross into Asia Minor. The following year while he was engaged besieging Danishmendid Melitene, Qilij Arslan's capital of Nicaea (modern-day Iznik, Turkey) was besieged by the combined armies of the First Crusade and the Byzantines. The Byzantines became masters of the city and of the sultan's wife and family, despite Qilij Arslan's attempt to relieve the city (May–June 1097). However, Byzantine emperor Alexios I Komnenos soon returned the captives to the sultan, who, now in coalition with the Danishmendids, confronted the crusaders at Dorylaion on July 17, 1097, and suffered a grave defeat at their hands.

Having lost his capital, Qilij Arslan selected Ikonion (modern-day Konya, Turkey), which was to become his new headquarters early in the 12th century, though it seems that the actual transferral of the new Rum Seljuk capital was associated with his successors Malik Shah II (1107–1116) or Mas'ud I (1116–1155). Qilij Arslan allied with the Danishmendids in two victorious battles against crusaders in 1101 at Mersivan and Herakleia (modern-day Ereğli, Turkey); Bohemund I of Antioch was captured in these engagements but released by the Danishmendids in 1104.

In the last eventful period of his reign, in 1104 Qilij Arslan took advantage of the death of Danishmendid emir Malik Ghazi to resume war with the Danishmendids, demanding half the ransom gained for Bohemund. As a result, Bohemund allied with the Danishmendids against Rum and the Byzantines. In 1106 Qilij Arslan captured Melitene (modern-day Malatya, Turkey) and Martyropolis (modern-day Silvan, Turkey), and in 1107 he seized Mosul. However, when he attempted an invasion of Mesopotamia, he faced a massive coalition under great Seljuk sultan Mehmed I (r. 1105–1118) and was killed in a hotly contested battle at the Khabur River on July 3, 1107, which was to assume legendary proportions in early Turkish epics.

ALEXIOS G. C. SAVVIDES

**See also**
Alexios I Komnenos; Bohemund I of Antioch; Crusades in the Holy Land, Christian; Danishmendid Dynasty; Dorylaion, Battle of; Malik Shah I; Rum, Sultanate of; Tutush I

**References**
Cahen, Claude. *Pre-Ottoman Turkey, c. 1071–1330.* London: Sidgwick & Jackson, 1968.
Talbot-Rice, Tamara. *The Seljuks in Asia Minor.* London: Thames & Hudson, 1961.
Wittek, Paul. *The Rise of the Ottoman Empire.* London: Royal Asiatic Monographs, 1938.

## Qilij Arslan II of Rum (ca. 1115–1192)

Sixth Seljuk sultan of Rum (r. 1156–1192) in whose reign the sultanate, centered on Ikonion (modern-day Konya, Turkey), assumed a leading role in Anatolian affairs by defeating the Byzantines, annexing the two Danishmendid emirates, and contracting an alliance with the Holy Roman emperor and crusading leader Frederick I Barbarossa (r. 1155–1190).

Izz ad-Din Qilij Arslan II (Sword Lion) was born around 1115, the son of Sultan Mas'ud I (d. 1156). Although his brother's claim to the succession was supported by Nur al-Din, the ruler of Muslim Syria, Qilij Arslan II finally prevailed. Among his first tasks was to thwart a possible alliance between Nur al-Din and Byzantine emperor Manuel I Komnenos, with whom Qilij Arslan had signed an ineffectual treaty in 1158. It was to prevent such an alliance that he visited Constantinople in 1161–1162, where he was magnificently received for three months by Manuel and a new treaty was signed. However, this treaty was not observed, since in 1173/1174 the sultan signed another treaty with Byzantium's bitter Western enemy, Frederick I Barbarossa.

Manuel I then decided to invade Anatolia, where he strengthened the fortresses of Dorylaion and Choma-Soublaion (1175/1176). Rejecting Qilij Arslan II's peace offer, he was eventually badly defeated in September 1176 at Myriokephalon, in west-central Anatolia. This victory enabled the sultan to expand his conquests at the expense of Byzantium until the mid-1180s.

Meanwhile, between 1174 and 1177/1178 Qilij Arslan II succeeded in annexing the strongholds of the two Danishmendid dynasties of Sebasteia (modern-day Sivas, Turkey) and Melitene (modern-day Malatya, Turkey). In the last years of his reign when the Byzantines contracted alliances with Saladin (1184–1185 and 1189–1192) and the Rupenids of Cilicia solidified their grip on the Taurus-Antitaurus area, Qilij Arslan II faced difficulties with his nine ambitious sons, each of whom ruled an important Anatolian city as emir but aspired to the throne. During 1189/1190 the eldest son, Qub al-Din, defeated his old and sick father at Ikonion.

Despite an alliance with Saladin, Qilij Arslan II was unable to stop the German forces of Frederick I in Anatolia in 1190 during the Third Crusade. The Seljuk capital was taken, but following the death of his eldest son Qub al-Din in 1191, it was restored to Qilij Arslan, who lived there until his death in August 1192 under the protection of his youngest and favorite son, Kay-Khusraw I, who succeeded him. The other sons continued to fight over territory in Anatolia.

ALEXIOS G. C. SAVVIDES

**See also**
Crusades in the Holy Land, Christian; Frederick I or Frederick Barbarossa; Manuel I Komnenos, Emperor; Myriokephalon, Battle of; Nur al-Din; Saladin

**References**
Cahen, Claude. *Pre-Ottoman Turkey, c. 1071–1330*. London: Sidgwick & Jackson, 1968.
Rice, Tamara Talbot. *The Seljuks in Asia Minor*. London: Thames & Hudson, 1961.
Savvides, Alexios G. C. *Byzantium in the Near East: Its Relations with the Seljuk Sultanate of Rūm in Asia Minor, the Armenians of Cicilia, and the Mongols, A.D. c. 1192–1237*. Thessaloniki: Byzantine Research Centre, 1981.
Vryonis, Speros, Jr. *The Decline of Medieval Hellenism in Asia Minor and the Process of Islamization from the 11th through the 15th Century*. Berkeley: University of California Press, 1971.

# Quran

The principal religious and sacred text of Islam. The Quran (Koran, al-Karim, or Noble Quran) of the Muslim faith derives from the Arabic verb meaning to declaim or recite. This text is so named because the Quran is composed of divine revelations dictated to Prophet Muhammad by the angel Gabriel from about 610 CE until Muhammad's death in 632. Muslims hold that the Quran in the holy original Arabic is the literal word of Allah transmitted to Prophet Muhammad (the Messenger) for humanity. Reading of the Quran is a duty for every Muslim. Specially trained reciters or readers (*qari*' or *muqri*') present the Quran in a format called *tajwid*, a chanting in the musical modal system (*maqamat*) set to the natural rhythm of the Arabic words, with their longer or shorter syllables. The *tajwid*, which today may be enjoyed in audio recordings or over the radio, allows the listener to hear the voice of the text.

Epic poetry and other forms of oral literature were especially prized in pre-Islamic Arabian society. Hence, Quranic recitation provided Muslims a literary as well as a religious experience and an opportunity to reflect on the meaning of the text as well.

According to tradition, Prophet Muhammad was illiterate, but like the other men of Mecca, he used to retreat to the hills beyond the city to spend time reflecting or meditating. At his retreat in a cave on Mount Hira, when he heard a voice commanding him to "read," Muhammad protested that he did not know how or what to read. The mysterious voice was that of the archangel Gabriel, and his words were the first of the Quran:

> Read [Iqra']: In the name of thy Lord who created,
> Created a man from Alaq [a "clinging" clot, or small amount of fetal material].
> Read: And thy Lord is the Most Generous,
> Who taught [the use of] the pen,
> Taught man that which he knew not.

This verse has been interpreted to mean that the omnipotent Allah (God) had the ability to bring and teach his Message even to an illiterate man. This passage, from the sura al-Alaq (96:1–5), was revealed to Muhammad in Mecca and is the first of thousands to be given to the prophet over the next 23 years, signaling the beginning of the divine revelation that was the Quran and the message of Islam.

The Quran is not a story of the prophet's life, but some understanding of his experience is helpful to the outsider seeking to comprehend the text. After 13 years, the ruling elite in Mecca, who were threatened by the growing crowds of followers and the messages of monotheism and strict moral codes that Muhammad was spreading, put pressure on the 53-year-old prophet to leave. In 622 after the pressures were multiplied by the deaths of his wife, Khadija, and his uncle, Abi Talib, Muhammad fled with his followers to the town of Yathrib, later renamed Madinat al-Nabi (City of the Prophet) on a journey now known as the Hijra. While the Muslims were living in Medina, the early and basic concepts and practices of the faith were defined, although some changed after Mecca was reconquered. Also, the Kaaba, or holy site where the Black Rock is located, was cleansed of its idols.

Early on, some of the prophet's companions and his wives had partial collections of the Quran, and other collections were written down. These were different in the ordering of the suras and the number of verses they contained. Many Quran reciters worked from memory and not written texts. There were different versions, including variant spellings and even more important differences. After a major battle when many Quranic reciters were killed, Omar asked the caliph Abu Bakr to assemble one written version of the Quran, which he then did. The caliph Uthman revised the Quran, creating a committee that met and approved one version based on their understanding of the text and the Qurayshi dialect. Uthman burned all the other versions of the Quran he could find and distributed this official version 23 years after the prophet's death. The recension was controversial to different parties, especially the Shia Muslims. By the ninth century Uthman's form, or codex, was vocalized, meaning that the normally unwritten Arabic vowels were included to stabilize its meaning. Some suggest that because of an inability to destroy all variant versions, a tradition states that Prophet Muhammad had approved seven valid readings of this text. More than seven exist, however.

The Quran is organized into the basic divisions of *ayat,* or verses; sura, chapters with titles that concern particular themes; and *juz,* which is simply a section that is a 30th of the entire Quran. Muslims use this division to read the Quran over a one-month period, or they might divide it into 7 sections. There are 114 suras in the Quran, each of a different length, from just 3 to 286 verses, or *ayat.* Many of the shorter, more dramatic suras were revealed at Mecca, while the longer, more legalistic suras were revealed at Medina. The Quran is arranged so that the longest suras are at the beginning of the text.

Exegesis, or explanations of the Quran, are called *tafsir,* and these are a very important part of religious studies as well as a basis for Islamic law, or sharia. The Quran is most important as the ultimate authority in sharia. The Quran is used as liturgy—that is, in prayer—and devout Muslims recite a portion each night (or more often).

The Quran has also served as a basis for education. The goal of learning to read in Arabic is the completion of a Quran reading, often at a young age. The *kuttab,* or Quranic school, was found throughout the Muslim world. The Quran also serves various social purposes. It is read in funeral sittings and recited at public events or conferences. Contests in Quran reading are held. Calligraphy is based on the Quran.

The most basic aspect of the Quran is that it is proof of Allah's existence and gives information about his nature, which is at once powerful, tender, and mystical: "He is the First and the Last, the Outward and the Inward; and He is the Knower of every thing" (37:3). This is based on the notion of *tawhid,* or unicity or monotheism, that is demonstrated in a multiplicity of ways.

Theology as expressed in the Quran begins with monotheism. The unity of Allah, his attributes, and the descriptions of Heaven, Hell, and the angels are all supported by the Quran. Another basic message in the Quran concerns the nature of humankind, who have been warned through the revelations to follow the Straight Path, or divine law, and must also overcome their tendencies toward insecurity, haste, and panic. If humans honor their pact with Allah, maintaining their trust in him and living according to his rules, they will be rewarded. If not, they will be grievously punished.

During the seventh century, the Arabs at Mecca were polytheistic. Moreover, their society benefited the wealthy and the powerful. According to the Quran, however, the disenfranchised, orphans, and the poor are the responsibility of the Muslim community, for wealth comes from Allah and must be used for the good of his community. Another important message of the Quran has to do with living in accordance with Allah's will and avoiding sin, for the Day of Judgment and the Resurrection will come when all shall be reckoned with.

The term "Islam" means "submission" or "surrender to Allah," while the term "Muslim" means "one who submits." This does not, as in English, have any tinge of self-abasement.

Rather, it implies one who trusts completely in God and thus in his revelation, the Quran. The Quran describes the Muslim community, or *ummah,* in its covenant with Allah, as a "community in a state of surrender" (*ummah muslimah*) in which Muslims are accountable and responsible for their actions. The opposite of Islam is *kufr,* which means that one covers up, obscures, or denies Islam and all of its requirements.

The Quran is seen as the final in a series of revelations that began with the book of Genesis and the story of Adam and Eve as revealed to Moses and through the gospels of Christ to the revelations given to Muhammad. The Quran continues to build its credibility by drawing a holy line of succession from Abraham to Muhammad (and thus all of Islam) as prophesied in Genesis 21:12. The Quran makes various references to prophets within and excluded from the Bible. The Quran refers to Jews and Christians (as well as Zoroastrians) as "Peoples of the Book," meaning that they and their scripture are to be respected and that they are not infidels or polytheists. However, in places the Quran also criticizes Christians and Jews for failing to follow the dictates of their own holy scriptures and not heeding the teachings of their prophets. The Quran also commands its followers to "struggle in the way of Allah," meaning to engage in jihad. This is interpreted to mean an armed struggle in battle as well the struggle to fulfill all the elements of faith (*iman*) in Islam.

Muslims recite and learn the Quran in Arabic, as it is in that form that it is considered to be the literal word of Allah. Muslim clerics maintain that any translation of the words of the Quran is not divine speech. As the majority of Muslims are non-Arabic speakers, the requirement to learn and study the Quran in Arabic meant study of the Arabic language—even more so for scholars of the Quran—since many historic texts and commentaries that pertain to the Quran are also in Arabic. The book itself is treated with reverence. Translations typically were described as works of commentary, and there was resistance to the early 20th-century suggestion that Turkish be a language of worship. However, some popular translations, such as that by Abdullah Yusuf Ali in English, are very close to the original text, and these have helped to create and sustain Muslim scholarship and discussion about the Quran in other languages. Meanwhile, works of commentary on the Quran have led to discussions that are relevant to the political and social challenges facing Muslims today.

B. Keith Murphy and Sherifa Zuhur

**See also**
Bible; Shia Islam; Sunni Islam

**References**
'Ali, Abdullah Yusuf. *The Meaning of the Holy Qur'an.* Beltsville, MD: Amana, 2001.
Ayoub, Mahmoud. *The Qur'an and Its Interpreters.* 2 vols. Albany, NY: SUNY Press, 1984, 1992.
Nelson, Kristina. *The Art of Reciting the Quran.* Austin: University of Texas Press, 1985.
Rahman, Fazlur. *Major Themes of the Qur'an.* Minneapolis: Biblioteca Islamica, 1980.

## Qurna, Battle of (December 4–9, 1915)

British amphibious operation against Ottoman forces in Mesopotamia. Qurna is located at the junction of the "Old" Euphrates River with the Tigris River, 40 miles north of Basra (modern-day Iraq). For half of the year, the Euphrates flooded its shallow bed, turning the surrounding desert into an immense lake.

Following their defeat at Basra in November 1914, Ottoman Army colonel Subhi Bey's forces fell back on Qurna to resupply and reinforce. British area commander Lieutenant General Sir Arthur Barrett's orders called for him to secure Basra but also allowed him to move up the river as far as he believed necessary to protect that port.

On December 3 Barrett dispatched upriver in steamers a combined force of two Indian battalions and a double company from the Royal Norfolk Regiment, along with some sappers and several field guns. The next morning the assault force went ashore, covered by naval gunfire from accompanying British gunboats.

Concealed Ottoman artillery in Muzereh Village opened heavy fire on the British vessels. The guns were difficult to locate from the river, and the ships took a number of hits. Hit at the waterline, the *Miner* was forced to withdraw. Despite taking damage, the British ships lent effective gunnery support to the troops ashore. Shells from the *Espiègle* set Muzereh on fire and drove the Ottoman troops from their concealed positions in date palm groves.

Because the Ottoman defensive positions had been only partially completed, British and Indian Army land forces were able to control the riverbank opposite Qurna. Heavy Ottoman gunfire, however, forced the British to retire for the night and await reinforcements.

At dawn on December 6, Major General C. I. Fry arrived with the remaining Norfolks, two additional Indian Army battalions, and a mountain battery. Altogether, the British committed some 2,100 men to the fight. Subhi Bey's troops meanwhile had reoccupied their old positions, and both sides were forced to reengage once again along the same lines. British land forces made steady progress, and the Ottomans were eventually forced to retreat again across the Tigris to Qurna.

On the morning of December 8, the British warships moved past the river junction, enabling them to fire into the town. Meanwhile, two Indian battalions and some sappers, supported by mountain guns, marched up the left bank well away from the river, then turned toward it. Soon the British were ferrying troops a mile and a half north of Qurna. Ottoman communications were now cut, and the escape route was closed.

British vessels continued shelling Qurna until the next day, December 9, when Fry demanded and received Subhi Bey's unconditional surrender. During the battle the British land force sustained 27 dead and 292 wounded; 2 sailors were also killed, and 2 others were wounded. Some 1,000 Ottoman soldiers (including 42 officers) surrendered. The capture of Qurna solidified the British hold on Basra.

CHRISTOPHER J. RICHMAN

### See also
Mesopotamian Theater, World War I

### References
Barker, A. J. *The Bastard War: The Mesopotamian Campaign of 1914–1918.* New York: Dial, 1967.
McEntee, Girard Lindsley. *Military History of the World War.* New York: Scribner, 1943.
Moberly, F. J. *The Campaign in Mesopotamia, 1914–1918.* 3 vols. Nashville: Battery Press, 1997–1998.
Townshend, Charles. *Desert Hell: The British Invasion of Mesopotamia.* Cambridge, MA: Belknap Press of Harvard University Press, 2011.

## Qutb, Sayyid Ibrahim Husayn Shadhili (1906–1966)

Egyptian Islamist theorist, educator, and leader of the Muslim Brotherhood incarcerated and executed by the Egyptian government. Sayyid Qutb received considerable attention when, in the wake of the September 11, 2001, Al Qaeda terrorist attacks on the United States, Westerners researched the older literature on Islamic revivalism and extremism in an effort to understand the roots of Al Qaeda. Sayyid Qutb was born on October 9, 1906, and raised in the village of Musha in Asyut Province of Upper Egypt. His father came from a family of landowners and was politically active, while his mother was deeply religious.

Qutb had a traditional Islamic education alongside a modern education in the Egyptian national education system. Around 1921, Qutb left Musha and moved to Cairo, where he trained to become a teacher of Arabic language and literature. At this time the Wafd Party and other groups were promoting Egyptian nationalism and ever since the revolution of 1919 had demanded the expulsion of Britain from the country. In 1922 the British government finally granted Egypt nominal independence and a degree of self-government.

Qutb was influenced by key members of the Wafd Party, and during this period in his life he worked for the Egyptian Ministry of Education, taught, published poetry, and wrote works of literary criticism. In 1945 he was appointed director general of culture. As part of his work and also to remove him from the limelight because of controversial statements he made opposing the government, Qutb was sent to the United States from 1948 to 1950 to study and report on its educational system. He was briefly in Washington, D.C., and also studied for several months at Colorado State in Greeley, Colorado.

While he was in the United States, in 1949 Qutb published one of his most important books, *al-Adala al-ijtima'iyya fi-l-Islam* (*Social Justice in Islam*). This book thoughtfully analyses the failure of Muslim-led governments to uphold the need for social justice and recommends a major shift in order to secure an Islamic system that would bring about this condition. The Muslim Brotherhood of Egypt's commitment to social justice is one of its continuous planks. In recent accounts of Qutb's life, it is claimed that he became anti-Western as a result of allegedly morally licentious behavior he observed. It is true that Qutb did not like the aura of certain mixed sex events he saw, but his more significant criticisms of American life centered on the lack of true spirituality and the racism he observed in this period prior to the civil rights movement.

Qutb was already familiar with the Muslim Brotherhood movement in Egypt. In the late 1940s the secret militant wing of the organization battled with the Egyptian government, and Egyptian government agents assassinated the leader of the Muslim Brotherhood, Hassan al-Banna, in 1949.

On his return to Egypt, Qutb resigned his government position and joined the Muslim Brotherhood in 1951, declaring that he was "born" in that year. He became the editor in chief of *al-Ikhwan al-Muslimin,* the organization's weekly publication, and then the head of its Propaganda Department and a member of the Working Committee. In

1952 Qutb published his monumental work on the Quran, *Fi Dhilal al-Quran,* which is simultaneously exegesis (a *tafsir,* or interpretation) and a work on the aesthetics of the Quran.

When the Egyptian Revolution of 1952 occurred, members of the Muslim Brotherhood had hopes that they would be able to operate legally. Some of the members of the Free Officers Movement that had overthrown the previous regime were allied with the Muslim Brotherhood. However, the organization had clashed with the leader of the Muslim Brotherhood in 1949, and Qutb aligned himself with it. Many members of the Muslim Brotherhood were jailed in 1951 when the movement was banned in Egypt, and Qutb himself was arrested in 1954. He was held in prison until 1964 on charges of promoting antigovernment activities, and copies of his books were ordered destroyed. Indeed, much of the recent characterization of him as a mastermind of radicalism springs from his struggle with the regime of Egyptian strongman Gamal Abdel Nasser.

In Qutb's book *Ma'alim fi Tariq (Milestones on the Road)* of 1964, he outlines the inevitability of conflict between an oppressive state that does not operate under Islamic principles and oppresses those supporting an Islamic society, equating it to the suppression of early Muslims. Qutb charged that the oppressors were in essence no longer Muslims, as they embraced the world of *jahiliyyah* (the term for the pre-Islamic environment), or barbarism. He instructs those struggling for Islam that they must embrace martyrdom, not by choice but because it is a matter of conflict between the forces that support Islam and those that oppose it. While this argument did not explicitly identify the rulers as nonbelievers as later radicals did in the 1970s, it paved the way for that interpretation. Death by martyrdom or in revolutionary jihad is the fate of those locked in the struggle.

The book was banned, and in 1965 Egyptian authorities rearrested Qutb, along with other leaders of the Muslim Brotherhood. Qutb was brought to trial, found guilty, and executed by hanging in Cairo on August 29, 1966.

Some of the many Islamists jailed in the 1960s became more radical, but when most were released in 1971 by the Egyptian government of Anwar Sadat, they forswore violence and agreed to operate as a movement and were not a legalized political party. However, other more radical groups began to organize. Qutb's ideas are similar to some of those espoused by the radical Takfir wa-l Higrah and the Gama'at Islamiyya, which arose in the 1970s. More recently, those dedicated to jihad in contemporary extremist organizations such as Al Qaeda make use of the same ideological constructs of jihad, which are part of Islamic history. What radicalizes them and causes them to pursue radical means is identical to that which confronted Qutb—a state power intent on their eradication

RUSSELL G. RODGERS AND SHERIFA ZUHUR

**See also**
Al Qaeda; Islamic Radicalism in the 20th and 21st Centuries; Muslim Brotherhood; Nasser, Gamal Abdel; Sadat, Anwar

**References**
al-Qaradawi, Yusuf. *The Eye of the Beholder: The Muslim Brotherhood over the Past 70 Years.* Cairo, Egypt: Al-Falah Foundation, 2003.
Binder, Leonard. *Islamic Liberalism: A Critique of Development Ideologies.* Chicago: University of Chicago Press, 1988.
Moussalli, Ahmad. *Moderate and Radical Islamic Fundamentalism: The Quest for Modernity, Legitimacy and the Islamic State.* Gainesville: University of Florida Press, 1999.

## Quwatli, Shukri al- (1891–1967)

Syrian political leader and president of Syria (1943–1949 and 1953–1958). Shukri al-Quwatli was born in 1891 in Damascus, Syria, which was then part of the Ottoman Empire. His family owned land and engaged in trade. Al-Quwatli attended secondary school in Damascus and college in Istanbul, where he earned a degree in political science and associated with Arab nationalists. Returning to Syria, he joined Fatah, a secret Syrian nationalist organization opposing Ottoman rule.

In 1916 Ottoman authorities arrested al-Quwatli for his association with Fatah. Fearful that under torture he would reveal information about comrades in Fatah, he attempted suicide by slashing his wrists but was saved from death at the last minute by colleague and friend Dr. Ahmad Qadri. This event made al-Quwatli a nationalist hero in Syria.

Following the end of World War I and the collapse of the Ottoman Empire, al-Quwatli became a civil servant and helped to organize the Arab Independence Party, a radical group seeking Syrian nationhood. In 1920, however, Syria passed under French control as a League of Nations mandate. When the Syrians resisted this arrangement, French troops expelled the Syrian monarch, King Faisal I.

Forced into exile himself, al-Quwatli lived for a time in Egypt and then in Geneva. In exile, he worked with Syrian, Lebanese, and Palestinian nationalists to establish the Syrian-Palestinian Congress. In 1922 France separated Lebanon from Syria and centralized its control. The French also built roads and schools, established the University of

Damascus, and reformed agriculture. Yet their high-handed policies angered the nationalists and produced the Great Syrian Revolt of 1925–1927. Having returned to Syria in 1924, al-Quwatli participated in these events.

Exiled again in 1927, al-Quwatli raised money for the Arab nationalist movement. He returned to Syria under an amnesty in 1932 and developed his landholdings into the Syrian Conserves Company, which produced fruit and vegetables for export. At the same time, he continued to raise money for the nationalist cause. Al-Quwatli joined the National Bloc, which rejected armed conflict in favor of popular protests and negotiated concessions to secure greater Syrian autonomy. He was uncomfortable with this moderate approach but used his influence to ensure that the National Bloc did not agree to unfavorable terms.

When the French resisted meaningful concessions, in 1936 al-Quwatli helped organize a 50-day general strike. This led to negotiations and a French agreement to allow Syrian independence. In elections to establish a transitional government, al-Quwaitli was returned to the legislature and served as minister of defense and finance. In 1938, however, he resigned to protest the Syrian government's acquiescence to changes in the independence treaty that were more favorable to France. As it turned out, the French government did not ratify the treaty.

During World War II on March 20, 1941, al-Quwatli demanded Syria's immediate independence. Food shortages and unemployment plagued Syria, and nationalist riots had become widespread. On September 27, 1941, France formally recognized Syrian independence. However, French troops remained, and elections were delayed. Finally, in August 1943 al-Quwatli was chosen president by Syria's new legislature, and following further riots in 1945 and al-Quwatli's insistence that French troops remain in their barracks, France withdrew them in April 1946, commencing Syria's complete independence.

As leader of Syria, al-Quwatli embraced Pan-Arabism and led Syria into the League of Arab States in 1945. He also attempted agricultural reforms, but his administration suffered from continued economic difficulties brought by the devaluation of the French franc, by misspending, and in 1948 by Israel's defeat of the Syrian forces during the Israeli War of Independence (1948–1949).

On March 30, 1949, although al-Quwatli had in 1948 secured reelection, he was ousted in a bloodless coup and charged with corruption. Held in a hospital for a month, he was then released to go into exile, first in Switzerland and later in Egypt. This coup began a series of similar upheavals. Two additional coups occurred in 1949, and a new constitution was adopted in 1950. The following year, the Nationalist Party (successor to the National Bloc), which was dominated by the business leaders in Damascus, sought al-Quwatli's return, but another coup led to a military dictatorship, and he did not return to Syria until 1954.

Al-Quwatli regained the presidency in 1955, but in the power shift to the military the position of president had been greatly weakened. He supported Egypt in the Suez Crisis of 1956. He also supported the merger of Egypt and Syria into the United Arab Republic (UAR), resigning the Syrian presidency in 1958 so that Egyptian leader Gamal Abdel Nasser could serve as president of the UAR. Al-Quwatli quarreled with Nasser in 1959, however, and was again forced into exile, ending his political career. Al-Quwatli died in Beirut, Lebanon, on June 30, 1967, but was subsequently given a state funeral in Damascus by the successor Baath Party leadership.

Neil Hamilton and Spencer C. Tucker

### See also
Franco-Syrian Treaty; Israeli War of Independence; Mandates, League of Nations; Nasser, Gamal Abdel; Suez Crisis; Syria; United Arab Republic

### References
Devlin, John F. *Syria: Modern State in an Ancient Land.* Boulder, CO: Westview, 1983.

Hitti, Philip Kuri. *History of Syria, including Lebanon and Palestine.* 2 vols. Piscataway, NJ: Gorgias, 2002.

Khoury, Philip. *Syria and the French Mandate: The Politics of Arab Nationalism, 1920–1945.* Princeton, NJ: Princeton University Press, 1987.

Seale, Patrick. *The Struggle for Syria: A Study of Post-War Arab Politics, 1945–1958.* New Haven, CT: Yale University Press, 1987.

Tibawi, Abdul L. *A Modern History of Syria including Lebanon and Palestine.* London: Macmillan, 1969.

# R

## Rabat Summit (October 26–29, 1974)

A meeting of 20 Arab heads of state as well as leaders of the Palestine Liberation Organization (PLO) in Rabat, Morocco, in October 1974. Convened as the seventh summit of the Arab League, the conference produced a series of resolutions on October 28 and 29, the most notable of which conferred upon the PLO de facto Arab recognition as the sole and legitimate representative of the Palestinian people. The same meeting also welcomed Somalia to the Arab League. The summit met exactly one year after the 1973 Yom Kippur War and was an attempt to solidify the Arab position vis-à-vis Israel and the West as well as an effort to deal with the Palestinian question in a coherent and uniform fashion. It was in this period that the idea of a Palestinian state in the West Bank and the Gaza Strip began to take shape, although neither the Arab states nor the Palestinians were in full agreement at this time. The summit also dealt with a variety of other issues, including the Palestinian situation in the wake of the 1973 Yom Kippur War. Some conference participants were concerned that areas such as the West Bank might be returned to Jordanian control. In fact, Palestinians in the West Bank had taken part in a series of demonstrations, strikes, and sit-ins that rejected both Israeli occupation and any restoration of Jordanian rule. Prior to the conference, PLO officials had met clandestinely with officials from President Richard M. Nixon's administration in hopes of securing U.S. recognition of the PLO. Such recognition was not forthcoming.

Arafat believed that it was important for the PLO to push for formal recognition from as many Arab countries as possible. Thus, as plans for the Rabat Summit progressed, Palestinian leaders made their case clearly: they would walk out of the meeting if the Arab League refused to grant the PLO formal recognition as the solitary representative of the Palestinian people. Once the meeting began, Arafat demanded that any land earmarked for Palestinian settlement (such as the West Bank) be turned over to the PLO. This included land won in war or sacrificed for peace. The Jordanians balked at this because Jordan was home to such a large number of Palestinians whose interests could lie either with Jordan, where they had the right to citizenship, or with the West Bank.

After some hard-fought wrangling, the conferees hammered out a compromise. It stated that the Palestinians had a right to their own homeland but that its territory was not to be limited to the West Bank exclusively. Even more important for the short term, the summit issued a resolution, which passed unanimously, acknowledging the PLO as the sole legitimate Palestinian representative body. Arafat had won his point. Finally, the summit resolutions promised cooperation between the PLO and Arab nations but warned against meddling in the PLO's internal affairs, just as the Arab League advised against member interference in all of its member states.

The Rabat Summit formalized the PLO's legitimacy in the Arab world and also codified Arab acceptance of the PLO's claims to the West Bank. Not surprisingly, King Hussein of Jordan, having experienced such tensions with the PLO leadership, recoiled at the summit's conclusions and at first refused to endorse the resolutions. Indeed, some sources allege that he signed on to them only after he had been promised some $300 million per year in subsidies from Persian Gulf and other oil-producing Arab states. Other sources emphasize Hussein's desire to implement fully the summit's intentions. In terms of the Arab-Israeli conflict, the Rabat Summit sent an unambiguous signal to Israel that the Arab world was united in its advocacy of a Palestinian state. In succeeding years Hussein gave the more than 900,000 Palestinians in the West bank the opportunity to choose either a Jordanian or Palestinian identity. The Rabat resolutions also meant that Jordan's House of Representatives, at that point made up only of West Bank politicians, would have to be reorganized. Jordan continued its responsibilities in the West Bank, however, including paying the salaries of civil servants and teachers there.

PAUL G. PIERPAOLI JR.

**See also**
Arab League; Arafat, Yasser; Hussein ibn Talal, King of Jordan; Jordan; Palestine Liberation Organization; West Bank; Yom Kippur War

**References**
Al-Shuaibi, Issa. "The Development of Palestinian Entity-Consciousness." *Journal of Palestinian Studies* 9(3) (1979): 50–70.
Nassar, Jamal R. *The Palestine Liberation Organization: From Armed Struggle to the Declaration of Independence.* New York: Praeger, 1991.
Norton, Augustus Richard, and Martin Harry Greenberg, eds. *The International Relations of the Palestine Liberation Organization.* Carbondale: Southern Illinois University Press, 1989.
Rabinovich, Abraham. *The Yom Kippur War: The Epic Encounter That Transformed the Middle East.* New York: Schocken, 2005.

## Rabin, Yitzhak (1922–1995)

Israeli army general, diplomat, leader of the Labor Party, and prime minister of Israel (1974–1977 and 1992–1995). Born in Jerusalem on March 1, 1922, Yitzhak Rabin moved with his family to Tel Aviv the following year. He graduated from the Kadoori Agricultural High School in 1940 and then went to work at the Kibbutz Ramat Yochanan, where he joined Palmach, an elite fighting unit of Haganah, the Jewish self-defense organization that ultimately became the Israel Defense Force (IDF).

In 1944 Rabin was second-in-command of a Palmach battalion and fought against the British mandate authorities. He was arrested by the British in June 1946 and spent six months in prison. He became chief operations officer of Palmach in 1947.

Rabin spent the next 20 years fighting for Israel as a member of the IDF. During the 1948–1949 Israeli War of Independence he commanded the Harel Brigade and fought for Jerusalem. He participated in the armistice talks and served as a deputy to Yigal Allon. During 1956–1959 Rabin headed the Northern Command. During 1959–1961 he was chief of operations, and during 1961–1964 he was deputy chief of staff of the IDF. On January 1, 1964, he became IDF chief of staff and held this position during the Six-Day War in 1967. Following the Israeli capture of the Old City of Jerusalem in the war, he was one of the first to visit the city, delivering what became a famous speech on the top of Mount Scopus at the Hebrew University.

On January 1, 1968, Rabin retired from the army and shortly thereafter was named Israeli ambassador to the

Yitzhak Rabin, Israeli army general, diplomat, leader of the Labor Party, and prime minister of Israel (1974–1977 and 1992–1995). Rabin's assassination on November 4, 1995, by a Jewish right-wing extremist fanatic dealt a perhaps fatal blow to the peace process. (Israeli Government Press Office)

United States. He held this position until the spring of 1973, when he returned to Israel and joined the Labor Party. He was elected to the Knesset (Israeli parliament) in December 1973. Prime Minister Golda Meir appointed Rabin to her cabinet as minister of labor in April 1974. Meir retired as prime minister in May 1974, and Rabin took her place on June 2.

As prime minister, Rabin concentrated on improving the economy, solving social problems, and strengthening the IDF. He also sought to improve relations with the United States, which played a key role in mediating disengagement agreements with Israel, Egypt, and Syria in 1974. Egypt and Israel signed an interim agreement in 1975. That same year Israel and the United States signed their first memorandum of understanding. The best-known event of Rabin's first term as prime minister was the July 3–4, 1976, rescue of hostages of Air France Flight 139 held at Entebbe, Uganda.

In March 1977 Rabin was forced to resign as prime minister following the revelation that his wife Leah held bank accounts in the United States, which was at that time against Israeli law. Menachem Begin replaced him, and Rabin was praised for his integrity and honesty in resigning.

Between 1977 and 1984 Rabin served in the Knesset as a member of the Labor Party and sat on the Foreign Affairs and Defense Committee. He published his memoirs, *Service Notebook*, in 1979. He served as minister of defense in the national unity governments between 1984 and 1990. In 1985 he proposed that IDF forces withdraw from Lebanon and establish a security zone to protect the settlements along the northern border of Israel.

In February 1992 Rabin was elected chairman of the Labor Party in its first nationwide primary. He led the party to victory in the June elections. He became prime minister for the second time that July. In an effort to achieve peace in the Middle East, he signed the joint Declaration of Principles with Palestine Liberation Organization (PLO) chairman Yasser Arafat, shaking hands with him on September 13, 1993, during the Oslo Peace Accords. This agreement created the Palestinian Authority (PA) and gave it some control over the West Bank and the Gaza Strip. Rabin, Arafat, and Shimon Peres shared the 1994 Nobel Peace Prize for their efforts to achieve peace. In 1995 Rabin continued his negotiations, signing an agreement with Arafat expanding Palestinian autonomy in the West Bank.

A number of ultraconservative Israelis believed that Rabin had betrayed the nation by negotiating with the Palestinians and giving away land they considered rightfully theirs. On November 4, 1995, right-wing extremist Yigal Amir shot Rabin after a peace rally in Kings of Israel Square, afterward renamed Yitzhak Rabin Square. Rabin died of his wounds soon afterward in Ichilov Hospital in Tel Aviv. November 4 has since become a national memorial day for Israelis. Numerous squares, streets, and public foundations have been named for Rabin, who is revered by many for his efforts on behalf of peace.

AMY HACKNEY BLACKWELL

**See also**
Allon, Yigal; Arafat, Yasser; Begin, Menachem; Haganah; Meir, Golda Mabovitch; Oslo Accords; Palestinian National Authority; Palmach; Zionism

**References**
Freedman, Robert Owen, ed. *Israel under Rabin*. Boulder, CO: Westview, 1995.
Kurzman, Dan. *Soldier of Peace: The Life of Yitzhak Rabin, 1922–1995*. New York: HarperCollins, 1998.
Makovsky, David. *Making Peace with the PLO: The Rabin Government's Road to the Oslo Accord*. Boulder, CO: Westview, 1996.
Rabin, Yitzhak. *The Rabin Memoirs*. 1st English-language ed. Boston: Little, Brown, 1979.
Slater, Robert. *Rabin of Israel*. Rev. ed. New York: St. Martin's, 1993.
Tessler, Mark. *A History of the Israeli-Palestinian Conflict*. Bloomington: Indiana University Press, 1994.

## Rafah Tunnels

Rafah, a city of some 150,000 people, lies at the far southern end of the Gaza Strip, adjacent to the Egyptian border and only about three miles from what was once the Gaza International Airport. Rafah saw fighting in both the 1956 Sinai Campaign and the 1967 Six-Day War. Under the terms of the 1993 Oslo Accords, Israel controlled a narrow strip of land between the Gaza and Egyptian borders, running in an almost straight line from the southernmost corner of the strip near the town of Kerem Shalom in Israel north-northwest to the Mediterranean coast. The road running along this narrow buffer zone is called the Philadelphi Road.

Following the Israel-Egypt Peace Treaty in 1979, Rafah became a key center for smuggling between Egypt and Palestinian-held territory. Tunnels dug from Rafah under the Philadelphi Road and to the Egyptian side served as a major conduit for contraband cigarettes, pirated cassette tapes and videos, and drugs. With the start of the Second (al-Aqsa) Intifada in September 2000, the Rafah Tunnels became the major entry point for weapons, ammunition, and explosives into Gaza, all in violation of the Oslo Accords. The tunnels were also used to exfiltrate terrorists and suicide bombers to attack Israel within its borders. Emerging on the Egyptian side, the terrorists would proceed southward into the Sinai and then cut back to the east, entering Israel through the porous border between the Sinai and the trackless southern Negev Desert.

During the passage of time, the Rafah Tunnels became complex and sophisticated. To camouflage the entrances in Rafah, almost all are built on private property or within homes. In some cases the homes belong to the tunnel's owners, members of the various militant groups or criminal gangs. In other cases, private citizens with no other connections to the tunnel operations are paid quite well for the use of their property. Both the criminal and militant groups use small children to move material back and forth through the tunnels.

The packed clay subsoil in the area is relatively easy to dig yet firm enough to support tunnels. The tunnel builders could dig down 90 feet and more before starting the horizontal section, which can run anywhere between 500 and 2,000 feet. The construction of a single tunnel could take more than three months. The tunnels were reinforced with wooden supports, and most had some sort of ventilation system. Some were outfitted with lighting and phone lines, and some even had trolleys running their horizontal lengths.

For security purposes, tunnel construction work was carried out in hours of darkness. Dirt and sand were removed from the excavation sites in flour sacks and dispersed in remote locations. Once the tunnel was operational, its entrance in a private home was concealed under furniture, under showers or bathtubs, or behind specially constructed double walls.

To counter the smuggling operations through the tunnels, the Israel Defense Force (IDF) constructed a 12-feet-deep underground barrier along the Philadelphi Road. This only forced the tunnelers to go deeper, which also made their operations more difficult for the Israelis to detect with listening devices. The IDF also built an aboveground wall along the road to shield its soldiers from snipers in Gaza while conducting operations against the tunnels.

The Egyptian government has operated against the tunnels on their side of the border, but the Israelis complained that the Egyptians were not sufficiently aggressive or effective. Nonetheless, in 2002 and 2003 the Egyptians intercepted more than two tons of explosives headed into Gaza. Prodded by the U.S. Coordinating and Monitoring Mission (USCMM), the Palestinian Preventive Security Organization (PSO) in Gaza headed by Muhammad Dahlan conducted raids in Rafah during August 23–24, 2003, that seized five tunnels. Israeli intelligence, however, dismissed the action as a show raid, claiming that all of those tunnels were old and inactive. Israeli intelligence also told USCMM officials that at least two of the tunnels were owned by officers in other Palestinian security organizations who had been forewarned about the PSO raid.

As a result, the Israeli government has on occasion sent IDF forces into Rafah itself to find the tunnel entrances and then physically destroy the tunnels. Most all such incursions have met with stiff opposition and usually result in casualties on both sides. Experience has shown that once a tunnel is found, filling in its entrance with dirt or even cement will rarely keep it closed for very long. Most tunnels have multiple openings. The only way to neutralize the tunnel completely is with large explosive charges, which almost always results in the complete destruction of the private home where the tunnel originates. The incursions and the destruction of private homes in Rafah create even more resentment among the Palestinians as well as far wider public relations problems for the Israelis.

During Operation PILLAR OF DEFENSE (November 14–21, 2012), Israeli air strikes rendered more than 100 tunnels inoperative, but many of them were repaired and back in operation within a span of several weeks. During the 2014 Gaza War, IDF land forces invaded Gaza, with the primary objective being destruction of the cross-border; the Israelis claimed 31 tunnels destroyed. In August 2014, the IDF announced that it had successfully tested a system employing sensors and special transmitters to locate the tunnels.

Egyptian government policy toward the Rafah Tunnels has varied. In 2009, Egypt began the construction of an underground barrier to block existing tunnels and make new ones harder to dig. In 2011, however, Egypt relaxed restrictions at its border with the Gaza Strip, allowing Palestinians to cross freely. Later that same year, however, Egyptian forces began sealing a series of tunnels between its territory and the Gaza Strip. This intensified when on August 5, 2012, radical Islamists killed 16 Egyptian border police in a terror attack. Egyptian action against the tunnels intensified after 2013 and the coup d'état that toppled the pro-Hamas Egyptian government. Among effective Egyptian measures against the tunnels has been pumping saltwater into them and filling them with sewage.

DAVID T. ZABECKI AND SPENCER C. TUCKER

See also
Egypt; Gaza Strip; Gaza War of 2014; Hamas; Intifada, Second; Oslo Accords

**References**

Guyatt, Nicholas. *Absence of Peace: Understanding the Israeli-Palestinian Conflict.* New York: St. Martin's, 1998.

Tessler, Mark. *A History of the Israeli-Palestinian Conflict.* Bloomington: Indiana University Press, 1994.

# Ramadan War

*See* Yom Kippur War

# Ramadi, Fall of (November 21, 2014–May 17, 2015)

The 2014–2015 Battle of Ramadi, also known as the Fall of Ramadi and the Battle of Abu Muhannad Al Sweidawi, was part of an Islamic State of Iraq and Syria (ISIS) offensive to take control of all of Anbar Province in Iraq. Located only 68 miles west of the Iraqi capital of Baghdad, Ramadi was the capital of Anbar and one of the Iraqi government's last strongholds in that vast province. ISIS already controlled most of Anbar Province, and taking Ramadi would give it control of a large swath of territory from the western outskirts of Baghdad north through Syria and to the Turkish border.

ISIS first established a presence in the city in October 2014, but the real battle for control of the city dates from November 21, 2014, to May 17, 2015. Fighting at Ramadi effectively ended on May 14, 2015, when ISIS insurgents seized hold of government buildings, but the last Iraqi Army and special forces troops did not flee the city until May 17.

On November 21, 2014, ISIS fighters launched a coordinated assault from the east and west against the city. ISIS was able to take advantage of a sandstorm that prevented U.S. aircraft from attacking their columns. The heaviest fighting in the battle for the city occurred at the government complex in the center of the city. In the fighting ISIS employed both mortars and car bombs.

In April 2015, ISIS renewed its offensive in Ramadi. With ISIS having the upper hand, some 100,000 people fled the city amid warnings that it was about to fall. On May 14, 2015, ISIS fighters raised their flag over the local government headquarters in Ramadi and employed mosque loudspeakers to proclaim victory. Anbar governor Sohaib al-Rawi characterized the situation as "dire." On May 17, government forces and officials still in the city withdrew entirely, escorted by tanks.

Ramadi was the first major city taken by insurgents since the Iraqi security forces and militias had undertaken an offensive against them late in 2014. Iraqi Army troops and militia forces in the battle were estimated to number some 6,000, while ISIS had only some 600 fighters. Casualty figures remain in dispute. Casualties on the government side are said to have been some 200 killed or missing, while ISIS lost more than 68 killed. Prior to May 14, the Iraqi government claimed that ISIS had executed 658 civilians in and around the city, and during May 14–17 it executed another 500 civilians and captured Iraqi military personnel.

Considerable recrimination occurred following the government defeat. U.S. secretary of defense Ashton Carter criticized the performance of the Iraqi forces. Noting their great numerical advantage in the battle, he blamed the defeat on their lack of will to fight, while many in the Iraqi government blamed the defeat on insufficient U.S. air support. In any case, the U.S. Defense Department sought to play down the ISIS success and stated that the militants are on the defensive in Iraq, with the government retaining control of key facilities, infrastructure, and lines of communication in the Ramadi area. While the fighting was raging in Ramadi and the government was losing control in Anbar Province, Iraqi forces did register some progress in Diyala Province. Assisted by coalition air strikes, Kurdish Peshmerga forces, Iraqi military and police, and Shiite militias retook the strategic towns of Jalawla and Saadiya. And in October 2015, the government forces retook Baiji refinery, the country's largest, which had been lost to ISIS in June 2014, although it would be years before the badly damaged refinery could be put back in full operation.

Spencer C. Tucker

**See also**

Inherent Resolve, Operation; Iraq; Islamic State of Iraq and Syria

**References**

Arango, Tim. "Key Iraqi City Falls to ISIS as Last of Security Forces Flee." *New York Times,* May 17, 2015.

Schmitt, Eric, and Helene Cooper. "ISIS Fighters Seized Advantage in Iraq Attack by Striking during Sandstorm." *New York Times,* May 18, 2015.

"US: Iraqi Forces Lack Will to Fight ISIL: Pentagon Chief Says Iraqi Forces Show No Will to Fight ISIL, while Senior Iraqi MP Says the US Has Failed to Help." *Al Jazeera,* May 25, 2015.

# Ramadi, First Battle of (April 6–10, 2004)

Military engagement during the Iraq War (2003–2011) between U.S. forces and Iraqi insurgents (mainly Sunnis) on April 6–10, 2004, in Ramadi in central Iraq. Ramadi is the capital of Anbar Province, with a 2004 population of some 450,000. The city lies along the Euphrates River 70 miles west of Baghdad on the main highway that continues eastward to the Iraqi capital and to the west across the Syrian desert to Jordan. Most of the city's inhabitants are Sunni Muslims. The battle was precipitated when Sunni forces in Ramadi arose in rebellion against U.S. forces garrisoned there.

Situated in the western part of the so-called Sunni Triangle, Ramadi's population had long been a center of support for the government of deposed Iraqi dictator Saddam Hussein and as such became a focal point for anticoalition forces following the March 2003 invasion of Iraq. In the days immediately after the fall of Baghdad in April 2003, the *muqawama* (resistance), including those who supported the former regime as well as Sunni Iraqis opposed to the invasion and Iraqi and foreign jihadists, began to fight coalition forces. The insurgents routinely ambushed lightly armored coalition vehicles and attacked convoys with small arms and rockets, set off bombs in public places and near police stations, and planted improvised explosive devices (IEDs), which they detonated by remote control to destroy or disable coalition vehicles. While U.S. forces sought to maintain a low-profile presence in the city and engaged in efforts to win the support of the city's population through constructive projects, they found that many of the Sunnis held them in contempt.

U.S. troops were blamed when a bomb-making group accidentally set off a charge in a local mosque and when another device exploded in the city's marketplace. By September 2003, the U.S. camp at Ramadi was coming under nightly mortar and artillery fire, with 19 soldiers having been killed and more than 100 wounded. The Americans sought to turn the city over to Iraqi officials, but insurgents also targeted these alleged collaborators. The resistance also became increasingly brazen, and there were large, noisy pro-Hussein public demonstrations in the city's streets.

Thus, 13 months after the coalition invasion, Ramadi had become one of the most perilous places in all of Iraq. When members of the Iraqi Governing Council agreed on a new constitution in March 2004 and drafted plans for elections the following January, an upsurge in violence occurred in Anbar Province. The most dramatic incident in this escalation occurred in Fallujah, another epicenter of the insurgency located just 30 miles east of Ramadi. There a mob lynched four American civilian contractors who had been dragged from an ambushed convoy, desecrated their burned bodies, and hanged the corpses on a bridge over the Euphrates on March 31, 2004. As coalition forces moved to pacify Fallujah, insurgents in Ramadi confronted U.S. marines there at a level of intensity not seen since the early days of the war.

The worst of the Battle of Ramadi from the American perspective occurred on April 6, the first day of pitched battle. The 2nd Battalion, 4th Marine Regiment, 1st Marine Division, which was charged with maintaining order in the city, received intelligence that insurgents intended to seize a government building. Marine patrols entered the city to carry out a sweep in support of loyalist Iraqis to prevent the takeover and to disperse antigovernment elements. On their way, they fell into well-laid ambushes set up by scores of fighters who were thought to be former members of the Special Republican Guards. Thus, the marines of Golf Company, who were carrying out the foot patrols, came under sniper fire, ran into insurgent ambushes, and spent much of the day pinned down and taking casualties. As other units moved to relieve the beleaguered marines, they too were ambushed. Several platoons engaged in firefights before they could extricate themselves with the help of other marines as well as members of the U.S. Army's 1st Brigade, 1st Infantry Division, which committed M1 Abrams tanks and Bradley Fighting Vehicles to the fight.

The deadliest of the attacks that day took place in the city's marketplace, where a group of perhaps 50 anticoalition fighters set up a .50-caliber machine gun on a rooftop and took positions atop other buildings or in nearby shops and behind trees with AK-47 assault rifles, rocket-propelled grenade launchers, and other small arms. There they waylaid a group of some 20 marines from Echo Company who had entered the marketplace in three Humvees followed by two trucks. The hard-pressed marines were unable to call in helicopter support, which was then committed elsewhere, and the heavy machine-gun fire ripped apart the lead vehicle with all but one of its occupants trapped inside. With the arrival of reinforcements and the marines able to move forward again, they found that many of their Iraqi opponents had fled. Ten marines were killed and many others were wounded in this action.

Heavy fighting occurred in Ramadi during the next few days. On April 7, the marines returned in force to complete their original mission. They came under similar ambushes and sustained additional casualties but no combat deaths in a series of firefights that occurred throughout the day. The marines also inflicted heavy losses on the insurgents. Ultimately, the marines conducted street-by-street and house-by-house raids that led to the capture of dozens of suspects and the seizure of arms caches. Altogether before the battle ended on April 10, the marines suffered 16 killed in action and 25 wounded. Insurgent losses remain unclear, as many of those killed or wounded were removed before U.S. forces regained the upper hand; however, most estimates put insurgent casualties at around 250 killed and hundreds more wounded.

The insurgency greatly increased in intensity with the fighting in March and April 2004. Heretofore, coalition leaders had continued to hope that they would win the battle for the hearts and minds of Iraqi civilians. Now, many wondered whether this was possible. Others questioned whether there were sufficient numbers of boots on the ground to quell a growing resistance that was developing new and more lethal tactics. Rather than the desultory hit-and-run efforts mounted by the insurgents in the past, the marines at Ramadi encountered well-coordinated attacks, with their opponents proving themselves adept at ambushes, laying down suppression fire, and making effective use of cover and concealment. Although the marines had won this battle, they and other forces in Iraq still faced a stiff resistance in many other towns and districts of Iraq that would not easily be extinguished.

GEORGE L. SIMPSON JR.

### See also
Fallujah, First Battle of; Iraq War; Sunni Triangle

### References
Fitzgerald, Paula M. "Marines Recall Ar Ramadi Battle." *Marine Corps News*, April 19, 2004.

Negus, Steve. "The Insurgency Intensifies." *Middle East Report* (Fall 2004): 22–27.

Swanson, David, with Joseph L. Galloway. "Battle at Ramadi." *Philadelphia Inquirer*, August 15, 2004, A-4.

## Ramadi, Recapture of (November 25, 2015–February 9, 2016)

Battle fought during November 25, 2015–February 9, 2016, by the Iraqi Army and associated militia forces to retake the city of Ramadi from the Islamic State of Iraq and Syria (ISIS). Although greatly outnumbered by the Iraqi government defenders, ISIS had captured the city at scant cost to themselves in May 2015. Airpower was a major factor in the outcome of this new battle; between July 2015 and late February 2016, the United States, Britain, and other nations carried out more than 850 air strikes in the Ramadi area.

On July 13, 2015, Iraqi forces supported by Shiite and Sunni progovernment militias began a major offensive to recapture the bulk of Anbar Province from ISIS. Ramadi is the capital of Anbar and is located only some 68 miles west of Baghdad. Driving on the city from the west and south, on July 13 Iraqi forces captured the Ramadi Olympic stadium in western Ramadi and reached the eastern part of the city. By August 11, Iraqi forces appeared poised for a final drive. Yet operations then stalled.

In early October, Iraqi forces resumed the offensive, securing several areas north and west of the city, and by midmonth the Iraqi troops had encircled the city. This accomplished, on November 25, 2015, they began the battle to take the city. Supported by coalition air strikes, Iraqi forces secured the Palestine Bridge over the Euphrates River and cut ISIS's supply line into the city. Air-dropped leaflets on November 29 warned of an imminent government attack and urged civilians in the city to leave. Few were able to do so, however; ISIS having warned that anyone attempting to escape would be killed.

Major Iraqi ground operations commenced on December 4, with the army entering the city proper for the first time on December 8 and securing the key district of Tamim in southwestern Ramadi, separated from the rest of the city by the Euphrates tributary of the al-Waar River. Iraqi forces also recaptured the Anbar Operation Control Center near the Palestine Bridge. Still, most of the city remained under ISIS control. On December 10, ISIS forces blew up the Warrar Dam, leaving the Qassim Bridge as the last working bridge in Ramadi.

On December 22, using a temporary bridge over the al-Warrar River, Iraqi forces drove in a three-pronged attack into the city center and toward the main government complex. Royal Air Force aircraft provided excellent close air support. By December 25, Iraqi government and militia forces had entered the al-Haouz district, perhaps 500 yards from the main government complex, which fell two days later. This enabled Baghdad to declare that it had full control of the city. On December 30, 2015, Iraqi prime minister Haider al-Abadi visited Ramadi and raised the Iraqi flag at the government complex before being forced to leave by ISIS mortar fire.

Nonetheless, ISIS still controlled some 30 percent of Ramadi, and the pockets of resistance had to be rooted out one by one. On January 3, 2016, the Iraqi government declared that it had retaken 80 percent of the city. Two days later the Iraqi Army captured the Bruwana district in western Ramadi. Iraqi military operations then slowed in an effort to limit civilian casualties. ISIS continued a strong presence in eastern Ramadi. On January 8, the Iraqi Army recaptured al-Malab district in southeastern Ramadi, and the next day it took the Andalus district, the Ramadi Great Mosque, and

Maaref University, all in eastern Ramadi. ISIS control was now largely limited to districts in the eastern city outskirts. Fighting continued, with Ramadi finally declared secured on February 9.

Iraq had committed to the battle some 10,000 men of its army, 3,000 Shiite militiamen, and 250 tribal fighters against an estimated 1,100 to 2,000 ISIS fighters. Iraqi losses were on the order of 300 killed and 1,000 wounded. Half a million civilians had been displaced and some 150 killed, although the latter figure seems low. ISIS losses have been estimated at between 1,000 and 2,000 killed. Perhaps 80 percent of Ramadi had been destroyed in the fighting and would have to be rebuilt. Owing to the success of the combination of ground encirclement and close air support, these were employed in the retaking of Fallujah, which had been captured by ISIS in January 2014 and was retaken by the government during May 23–June 28, 2016.

SPENCER C. TUCKER

**See also**
Abadi, Haider al-; Iraq; Islamic State of Iraq and Syria; Ramadi, Fall of

**References**
Al-Jawoshy, Omar, Sewell Chan, and Kareem Fahimdec. "Iraqi Forces Fighting ISIS for Ramadi Push toward City Center." *New York Times*, December 22, 2015.

Al Jazeera Staff. "Iraq Army Enters Last ISIL Stronghold in Ramadi." Al Jazeera, February 9, 2016.

"Reclaiming the Ruins from Islamic State: By Retaking Ramadi, Iraq's Security Forces Have Won a Morale-Boosting Victory." *The Economist*, January 2, 2016.

Tilghmanm, Andrew. "No End in Sight for Iraq Fight against ISIS in Ramadi." *Military Times*, September 15, 2015.

# Ramadi, Second Battle of (June 17– November 15, 2006)

Battle during the Iraq War (2003–2011) in which U.S. Army and Marine Corps forces, along with elements of the Iraqi Army, fought for control of Ramadi, the capital of Anbar Province in western Iraq. After U.S.-led forces took Fallujah for the first time during November–December 2004, Ramadi became the center of the growing insurgency in Iraq. In this city of some 400,000 people, about 80 miles west of Baghdad, insurgent leaders created the Islamic State of Iraq, a coalition of Islamist fighting groups that included Al Qaeda in the Land of the Two Rivers, meaning Iraq. At the time, marine leaders believed that if Ramadi remained in insurgent hands, all of Anbar Province would be insecure.

In June 2006 with the situation worsening, the U.S. command dispatched the 1st Brigade Combat Team of the 1st U.S. Armored Division to the Ramadi area preparatory to attacking the insurgents. There were fears that another full-scale Fallujah-style assault might kill or injure many noncombatants and do great damage to the city. However, U.S. commanders were determined to proceed with caution, and they carefully planned their operation, which involved some 5,500 U.S. soldiers and marines and 2,000 Iraqi Army troops.

By June 10, the U.S. and Iraqi troops had cordoned off Ramadi, and a growing number of air strikes were mounted on specific targets. U.S. forces, using loudspeakers, warned residents to evacuate before the impending attack. The main goal of the operation was to sever insurgent supply and reinforcement lines into Ramadi. The Americans also planned to set up locations outside Ramadi where noninsurgent Iraqis from the city could find safe haven.

Operations began in earnest on June 18 when two U.S. mechanized columns and an Iraqi Army unit of some 2,000 men entered Radami's suburbs from the south and cut off two access routes into the city. Concurrently, marine units captured and held the western portion of the city center, controlling the river and its two main bridges. While armored forces sealed off the city's eastern exits, marine units established outposts east of Ramadi along the main road between Baghdad and Syria.

With these key points secured, several hundred coalition forces, supported by AC-130 gunships, moved into eastern Ramadi. The gunships killed several insurgents as coalition troops established an outpost in Ramadi's Mulab neighborhood to allow U.S. and Iraqi troops to better patrol this problem area. There they discovered numerous weapons caches and improvised explosive device (IED) components in many homes.

While this part of the operation met with some success, the Americans soon found themselves in intense street fighting throughout the city. Insurgents would mount widely scattered attacks simultaneously and then disappear. On July 24, the jihadist forces launched a major attack, and while they suffered heavy casualties, they continued to press toward their main objective, the Ramadi Government Center in which dozens of marines were barricaded.

To meet the threat, U.S. troops demolished several smaller surrounding structures, with the plan to turn the area into a park later. Still, all the coalition troops who ventured into the city faced IEDs, suicide attacks, and patrol ambushes. Sniper fire was nearly constant.

U.S. Army soldiers patrolling the streets of Ramadi, Iraq, on August 16, 2006, during the Second Battle of Ramadi (June 17–November 15, 2006). (U.S. Army)

In early July, U.S. troops captured the Ramadi General Hospital, which had been used as an insurgent barracks. Coalition wounded who had been taken to the hospital were found beheaded, and nearly every room on every floor of the seven-story building was rigged with explosive devices.

On August 21, the insurgents killed and defiled the body of Sunni sheikh Abu Ali Jassim, who had encouraged many of his tribesmen to join the Iraqi police in their efforts to root out the insurgents. In response, with funding and organizational efforts coming from the coalition, on September 9, 2006, 50 sheikhs from 20 tribes from across Anbar Province formally organized an anti-insurgent council, named Anbar Awakening. Some of its members had been fighters with Al Qaeda in Iraq. However, as the council gained strength, its tribal members began attacking Al Qaeda fighters in the suburbs of Ramadi. By October, representatives from many tribes in northern and western Ramadi had joined the Anbar Awakening.

In mid-September 2006, new marine units relieved those holding western Ramadi. Throughout the next three months, truck bombs as well as suicide and sniper attacks continued. U.S. Navy SEAL Michael A. Monsoor was posthumously awarded the Medal of Honor for having thrown himself on a grenade that threatened the lives of the other members of his team on September 29, 2006.

One of the more tragic events in the battle occurred in mid-November when, during a firefight, an air attack in central Ramadi inadvertently killed more than 30 civilians, many of them women and children. The Battle of Ramadi also marked the first time insurgents employed chlorine bombs. On October 21, 2006, they detonated a car bomb of two 100-pound chlorine tanks, injuring three Iraqi policemen and a civilian.

The battle formally ended on November 15. It had claimed the lives of 75 American soldiers and marines, and more than 200 were wounded. U.S. officials estimated insurgent dead at 750. The number of Iraqi Army deaths are not known. Coalition forces claimed to have secured 70 percent of the city by the end of November.

On December 1, 2006, with insurgents still entrenched in parts of Ramadi, the United States launched Operation

SQUEEZE PLAY. Supported by Anbar Awakening tribal fighters, by January 14, 2007, coalition forces had secured a much larger portion of the city and killed or captured roughly 200 additional insurgents.

By the spring of 2007, U.S. officials believed that they had finally gained control over all of Ramadi. On June 30, 2007, a group of 64 insurgents attempted to infiltrate the city but were wiped out by U.S. marines, who had been alerted to the threat by Iraqi police.

WILLIAM P. HEAD

**See also**
Al Qaeda in Iraq; Anbar Awakening Movement; Fallujah, Second Battle of; Iraq War; Ramadi, First Battle of

**References**
Barnes, Julian E. "In Ramadi, the Battle Is Ever Changing." *Los Angeles Times*, August 6, 2006, A5.
Campbell, Donovan. *Joker One: A Marine Platoon's; Story of Courage, Sacrifice, and Brotherhood.* New York: Random House, 2008.

# Ramesses II the Great (ca. 1303–1213 BCE)

Regarded by many scholars as Egypt's greatest pharaoh, Ramesses II, known as Ramesses the Great (Ramesses is also rendered as Rameses or Ramses), was born around 1303 BCE, the son of Pharaoh Seti I (r. 1290–1279) and Queen Tuya. In his early teens Ramesses accompanied his father on military campaigns in Libya and Palestine. At age 14, Ramesses was appointed prince regent by his father and became pharaoh in 1279 on Seti's death. The third pharaoh of the Nineteenth Dynasty, Ramesses ruled until his death in 1213. Reportedly he had more than 200 wives and concubines, 96 sons, and 60 daughters, most of whom predeceased him.

Ramesses proved to be an able military leader who built the Egyptian Army into a formidable force totaling as many as 100,000 men. He employed this army to secure Egyptian trade, take back land in Asia Minor that had been lost earlier to the Hittites, and secure Egypt's borders.

Ramesses was tested early as pharaoh, for the Sherden pirates, a formidable group of the so-called Sea People probably operating from the coasts of Ionia, western Anatolia, or Sardinia had been preying on trading vessels in the eastern Mediterranean, disrupting Egyptian trade. In the second year of his reign Ramesses laid a trap for the pirates. Placing a small number of decoy ships off the Nile Delta, he secreted large naval forces nearby. The sea pirates took the bait and were soon surrounded by Egyptian naval forces issuing from both sides. The Egyptians captured or sank virtually all the pirate ships. The captured crews were pressed into Egyptian military service; later some formed an elite bodyguard for the pharaoh.

Ramesses then embarked on a land campaign in Canaan against a Hittite vassal state. The Egyptians had long had an uneasy relationship with the Hittites, who controlled much of Asia Minor. Hittite king Suppiluliuma I (r. 1344–1322) had taken a number of important Egyptian trading centers in Canaan and Syria. Although Seti I had recaptured the important center of Kadesh in Syria, Hittite king Muwatalli II (r. 1295–1272) had then taken it back.

The campaign in Canaan was successful, with the king of the vassal state mortally wounded in battle. Ramesses reportedly made a number of royals prisoner (probably Hittite as well as Canaan), taking them back with him to Egypt afer plundering their territories and exacting tribute.

Ramesses was determined to control Kadesh in Syria. In 1274 he led some 20,000 men in four divisions into Syria. After a long march, his forces arrived at their goal. Two Hittite spies were captured, and once tortured, they revealed the location of the Hittite army, which they said was nowhere near. Reassured, Ramesses made camp to await the arrival of all of his forces. The spies, however, had been deliberately sent to reveal false information. The main Hittite army now fell on that part of the Egyptian army then with Ramesses, completely overrunning one division, which was entirely unprepared for battle. Ramesses refused to panic and gave orders for the other two divisions to come up, while he himself demonstrated great personal bravery and rallied his remaining men. When reinforced, he attacked.

The battle ended in a draw, and Ramesses then withdrew his forces back to Egypt. He trumpeted a great victory, although the Battle of Kadesh had nearly ended in his defeat and death. The Hittites, however, remained under pressure from both the Egyptians and the Assyrians.

Ramesses was also a great builder. During his long reign he ordered the construction of temples, monuments, and cities throughout his realm. These include the vast tomb complex known as the Ramesseum at Thebes, the temples at Abu Simbel, the great hall at Karnak, the complex at Abydos, and hundreds of other buildings, monuments, and temples. Many consider his reign the height of Egyptian art and culture, demonstrated by the famous tomb of his first wife and favorite, Queen Nefertari.

Ramesses also ordered construction of a new city, Pi-Ramesses in the Nile Delta, to serve as his new capital and

A 19th-century illustration of Ramesses II in his chariot during the Battle of Kadesh, in 1274 BCE. (New York Public Library)

advance base for operations to the east. A sizable arms industry was soon established there, with Egyptian workers fashioning large quantities of weapons and chariots for the army.

These preparations complete, Ramesses again moved into Syria in a third campaign there in the seventh year of his reign. He divided his army into two forces, one led by himself and the other by his son Amun-her-khepeshef. His son's army drove the warriors of the Shasu tribes across the Negev Desert as far as the Dead Sea, capturing Edom-Seir and securing Moab. Meanwhile, Ramesses attacked Jerusalem and Jericho before rejoining his son's army at Moab. Together they moved on Hesbon, Damascus, and to Kumidi, gaining control of Upi, the land around Damascus.

During the next two years, Ramesses continued his Syrian campaigning. Crossing the Dog River (Nahr al-Kalb), his men moved north into Amurru, reaching as far north as Dapur, territory that had last been under Egyptian control under Thutmose III more than a century earlier. Having reestablished Egyptian control of Canaan, Ramesses led his army northward to near present-day Beirut.

Much of this was for naught, however, for within a year the Hittites had regained control of the territory between Amurru and Kadesh so that the next year Ramesses again marched against Dapur, taking a number of towns. With neither the Egyptians nor Hittites able to inflict a decisive defeat on the other and with the Hittites also under pressure from the Assyrians, in 1258 Ramesses concluded a treaty with new Hittite king Hattusili III at Kadesh to end the conflict. This treaty, the terms of which are preserved in inscriptions, is said to be the earliest known peace treaty in world history.

Ramesses also campaigned south of the first cataract of the Nile into Nubia, and apparently Egyptians forces also ventured some 200 miles into coastal Libya, at least as far as Zawiyet Umm el-Rakham.

Ramesses died at age 90 in July or August 1213 BCE. He had built extensively throughout Egypt and Nubia, and his cartouches are prominently displayed even in buildings that he did not construct. Colossal statues of him are also found all over Egypt. Buried in a tomb in the Valley of the Kings, his mummified remains were later moved but discovered in 1881. They are now on display in the Cairo Museum. Although other Egyptian rulers, notably Ramesses III (r. 1186–1155), may be said to have been more effective rulers or military leaders, Ramesses the Great accomplished much in his long reign, and nine other pharaohs took the name of Ramesses in his honor.

SPENCER C. TUCKER

**See also**
Egypt, Ancient; Kadesh, Battle of; Thutmose III, Pharaoh

**References**
Dodson, Aidan, and Dyan Hilton. *The Complete Royal Families of Ancient Egypt*. London: Thames & Hudson, 2004.
Grimal, Nicolas. *A History of Ancient Egypt*. Oxford, UK: Blackwell, 1992.
Kitchen, Kenneth. *Pharaoh Triumphant: The Life and Times of Ramesses II, King of Egypt*. London: Aris & Phillips, 1983.
Kuhrt, Amelie. *The Ancient Near East c. 3000–330 BC*, Vol. 1. London: Routledge, 1995.
Tyldesley, Joyce. *Ramesses: Egypt's Greatest Pharaoh*. London: Viking/Penguin Books, 2000.

## Ramla, First Battle of (September 7, 1101)

Battle fought on September 7, 1101, between crusader forces under King Baldwin I of Jerusalem and a Fatimid army commanded by Sa'ad al-Dawla al-Qawa-misi. The battle occurred at the town of Ramla (Rameleh) on the road from Jerusalem to Ascalon (modern-day Tel Ashqelon, Israel), the latter being the largest Fatimid fortress in Palestine. From Ascalon Egyptian vizier al-Afdal Shahanshah mounted a series of attacks into the newly founded crusader kingdom during 1099 to 1107 in an effort to regain the Fatimid possessions in Palestine lost to the Christian crusaders in 1099 during the First Crusade (1096–1099).

The Egyptian invasion force, estimated as high as 10,000 men, reached Ascalon in mid-May 1101 and advanced on Ramla but withdrew back to Ascalon when Baldwin arrived with relieving forces. From May to August, there was a stalemate while the Egyptian army awaited reinforcements, and Baldwin was content to wait on developments. On September 4, the Egyptians again advanced on Ramla.

Baldwin then had only 260 cavalry and 900 infantry at his disposal. He divided this force into five divisions and then attacked. The battle occurred on September 7, and the fighting was fierce. The first two Frankish divisions were completely destroyed, and the third, suffering heavy losses, broke and fled back to Jaffa (modern-day Tel Aviv–Yafo, Israel), pursued by the Egyptian left wing. Baldwin, commanding the reserve division, attacked and broke the Egyptian center, and the entire Egyptian army then fled back to Ascalon, pursued so closely by the Frankish army that most of the Egyptian force was destroyed.

ALEC MULINDER AND SPENCER C. TUCKER

**See also**
Baldwin I of Jerusalem; Crusades in the Holy Land, Christian; Ramla, Second Battle of; Ramla, Third Battle of

**References**
Brett, Michael. "The Battles of Ramla (1099–1105)." In *Egypt and Syria in the Fatimid, Ayyubid and Mamluk Eras*, ed. Urbain Vermeulen and Daniel De Smet, 17–39. Leuven, Belgium: Peeters, 1995.
Röhricht, Reinhold. *Geschichte des Königreichs Jerusalem (1100–1291)*. Innsbruck: Wagner, 1898.
Runciman, Steven. *History of the Crusades*. 3 vols. Cambridge: Cambridge University Press, 1954.

## Ramla, Second Battle of (May 17, 1102)

Battle between a Christian force of crusaders and Franks of Outremer under King Baldwin I of Jerusalem and an Egyptian army commanded by Sharaf al-Ma'ali Samā' al-Mulk, a son of Fatimid vizier al-Afdal Shahanshah. The battle occurred on May 17, 1102, and is known for the town of Ramla (Rameleh) in southwestern Palestine on the road from Jerusalem to Ascalon (modern-day Tel Ashqelon, Israel), the latter being the largest Fatimid fortress in Palestine. From Ascalon, Fatimid vizier al-Afdal mounted a series of attacks into the newly founded crusader kingdom during 1099 to 1107 in an effort to regain the Egyptian territory in Palestine lost to the Christian crusaders in 1099 during the First Crusade (1096–1099). In September 1101, Baldwin had defeated a large Egyptian invasion force here.

In May 1102 the Egyptians began a siege of Ramla, plundering the surrounding lands. Spurred into a precipitate show of force, Baldwin gathered 700 cavalry, many of them recently arrived members of the crusading expeditions of 1101–1102, and advanced toward Ramla. The battle took place at Yazur, some 10 miles from Jaffa (modern-day Tel Aviv–Yafo, Israel) on May 17. The Egyptians surprised Baldwin, who took a hasty decision to attack rather than retreat. The Christian force was surrounded and massacred. A few knights cut their way through the encircling Egyptians and managed to reach Jaffa, but most of the survivors were forced to take refuge in Ramla. Baldwin and a few companions escaped that night, and the following morning the Egyptians stormed Ramla. The surviving knights defended a tower, but all were quickly captured or killed. Christian casualties included Stephen, count of Blois, and Stephen, count of Burgundy.

The Christian defeat in this battle placed the Kingdom of Jerusalem in great peril, but it was saved from collapse by Baldwin's ensuing decisive victory in the Battle of Jaffa on July 4, 1102.

ALEC MULINDER AND SPENCER C. TUCKER

**See also**
Baldwin I of Jerusalem; Crusades in the Holy Land, Christian; Jaffa, Battle of; Ramla, First Battle of; Ramla, Third Battle of

**References**
Brett, Michael. "The Battles of Ramla (1099–1105)." In *Egypt and Syria in the Fatimid, Ayyubid and Mamluk Eras,* ed. Urbain Vermeulen and Daniel De Smet, 17–39. Leuven, Belgium: Peeters, 1995.
Mulinder, Alec. "The Crusade of 1101–1102." Unpublished PhD dissertation, University of Wales at Swansea, 1996.

# Ramla, Third Battle of (August 27, 1105)

Third battle fought at Ramla (Ramleh) in southwestern Palestine between the Christian force of crusaders and Franks of Outremer under King Baldwin I of Jerusalem and an Egyptian army commanded by Sharaf al-Ma'ali Sama' al-Mulk, a son of Fatimid vizier al-Afdal Shahanshah. The battle occurred on May 17, 1102, and is known for the town of Ramla on the road from Jerusalem to Ascalon (modern-day Tel Ashqelon, Israel), the latter being the largest Fatimid fortress in Palestine. From Ascalon, Fatimid vizier al-Afdal mounted a series of attacks into the newly founded crusader kingdom during 1099–1107 in an effort to regain the Egyptian territory in Palestine lost to the Christian crusaders in 1099 during the First Crusade (1096–1099). Although victorious in the First Battle of Ramla on September 7, 1101, on May 16, 1102, Baldwin and the crusaders had suffered a major defeat here.

At the beginning of August 1105 an Egyptian force of perhaps 5,000 men, composed primarily of Arab cavalry, Sudanese infantry, and mounted Turkish bowmen together with allies from Damascus, gathered at Ascalon. Informed of events, King Baldwin I gathered a force of 500 horsemen and 2,000 infantry at Jaffa (modern-day Tel Aviv–Yafo, Israel), then advanced and met the allied Egyptian and Damascene army at Ramla on August 27. The battle was hotly contested, with the Egyptian infantry repelling repeated attacks by the Frankish cavalry. At one point a counterattack by the Damascene mounted archers caused great havoc in the Frankish ranks and nearly carried the day, but Baldwin attacked with his own division and routed the attackers. Many of the Egyptian cavalry on the Muslim left flank departed the battle to try to plunder Haifa (modern-day Hefa, Israel), without success, while the remainder of the cavalry was forced to retreat; despite these setbacks, the Egyptian infantry was able to withstand numerous mounted assaults and was only overcome following the collapse of the infantry's Damascene allies.

The Muslim force retreated to Ascalon. Having suffered many casualties, the Franks were unable to pursue the enemy and were content to plunder their camp. The Third Battle of Ramla marked the last large-scale Fatimid attempt to reconquer Palestine from the Franks.

ALEC MULINDER AND SPENCER C. TUCKER

**See also**
Baldwin I of Jerusalem; Crusades in the Holy Land, Christian; Ramla, First Battle of; Ramla, Second Battle of

**References**
Brett, Michael. "The Battles of Ramla (1099–1105)." In *Egypt and Syria in the Fatimid, Ayyubid and Mamluk Eras,* ed. Urbain Vermeulen and Daniel De Smet, 17–38. Leuven, Belgium: Peeters, 1995.
Runciman, Steven. *History of the Crusades.* 3 vols. Cambridge: Cambridge University Press, 1954.

# Raphia, Battle of (June 22, 217 BCE)

Battle fought on June 22, 217 BCE, between the armies of Seleucid king Antiochus III the Great and King Ptolemy IV Philopator of Egypt during the Fourth Syrian-Egyptian War. The battle occurred at Raphia (present-day Rafah in the Gaza Strip).

Antiochus commanded a force of some 62,000 infantry, 6,000 cavalry, and 102 Indian elephants. Ptolemy's forces numbered 70,000 infantry, 5,000 cavalry, and 73 African elephants. Nearly half of Ptolemy's phalanx at Raphia was composed of Egyptians armed and trained to fight as a Macedonian phalanx. This reliance by Ptolemy on Egyptian (rather than Greek and Macedonian) troops led to increased Egyptian influence within the Ptolemaic administration.

Antiochus opened the battle with an elephant attack against the elephants on Ptolemy's left wing. Ptolemy's outnumbered elephants fled, causing havoc among the Ptolemaic Agema (Royal Guard) and cavalry who were stationed on the same wing. Antiochus followed up his success by launching the remainder of his troops on his right wing against Ptolemy's shaken left wing, driving them back. But at this crucial moment Antiochus left the battlefield in pursuit of Ptolemy's defeated left wing. Ptolemy's cavalry on his right wing then outflanked Antiochus's left wing and with the support of elephants, Greek mercenaries, Gauls, and Thracians drove off Antiochus's left wing. Finally, Ptolemy's phalanx, consisting of some 25,000 Macedonians and 20,000 Egyptians, secured the victory in the center.

Ptolemy did not aggressively follow up this victory. However, Antiochus's losses and the risk of Ptolemy advancing into Syria proper caused Antiochus to withdraw from Coele-Syria and conclude peace, which lasted until 202.

DAVID HARTHEN

**See also**
Antiochus III Megas; Egypt; Ptolemaic Kingdom; Ptolemy IV Philopator; Seleucid Empire; Syria; Syrian-Egyptian Wars

**Reference**
Grainger, John D. *The Syrian Wars.* Leiden: Brill, 2010.

# Reagan Plan (September 1, 1982)

Middle Eastern peace initiative put forth by U.S. president Ronald W. Reagan on September 1, 1982. The so-called Reagan Plan (or Reagan Peace Plan) came on the immediate heels of the August 12, 1982, cease-fire agreement between the Palestine Liberation Organization (PLO) and Israel, both of which had been heavily involved in the Lebanese Civil War (1975–1990). One of the terms of this agreement was that the PLO would abandon its operational base in Lebanon, resulting in the exodus of some 15,000 Palestinian fighters by September 1, 1982. PLO chairman Yasser Arafat relocated the PLO's headquarters to Tunisia shortly thereafter. The war in Lebanon had been a protracted and tragic affair for all involved and had left the country a virtual wasteland. Thus, in order to breathe new life into the moribund Middle East peace process and to begin the process of rebuilding in the region, the Reagan administration unveiled its plan to coincide with the September 1 deadline.

The Reagan Plan had six primary points. First, the Palestinians would achieve autonomy in the Gaza Strip and the West Bank after elections that would constitute a Palestinian governing entity. Full autonomy would be achieved after a five-year transitional period. Second, Israel would bar the construction of any more settlements in disputed or occupied territories. Third, the United States would not support a fully independent Palestinian state in the West Bank or the Gaza Strip. The United States would also not tolerate Israeli control over these areas. Fourth, the United States supported a negotiated settlement over the disputed areas and believed that an autonomous Palestinian entity under Jordanian jurisdiction offered the best potential for an enduring peace. Fifth, Israel would withdraw from Gaza and the West Bank entirely in exchange for peace. Sixth, Jerusalem would remain intact and not be divided, subject to future negotiations.

The Reagan Plan had been drawn up in great secrecy and was not divulged to either the Israelis or Arab nations until its formal announcement on September 1. Implicit in the announcement was the fact that the United States would continue to refuse any contacts with the PLO until it officially recognized Israel and accepted United Nations (UN) Resolutions 242 and 338. Another condition not initially made public was that the United States would not press for the dismantlement of any Israeli settlements until after the five-year transitional period had ended.

Israel's Likud government, led by Menachem Begin, flatly rejected the plan. Indeed, Begin allegedly said that reading the plan was the "saddest day" of his life. The Labor Party, however, believed that the Reagan Plan might provide a solid base from which negotiations would follow. In several aspects, the plan echoed the party's own approach to peace. The PLO rejected the plan, albeit for different reasons. Arafat's biggest problem with the plan was that it provided no mechanism for full Palestinian sovereignty and self-determination. The PLO also refused to accept the plan because it had not been previously consulted, and the Americans refused to meet with its leadership. On the other hand, the PLO had to have been heartened somewhat by the Americans' call for a freeze on new Israeli settlements and their opposition to Israeli claims of sovereignty over the West Bank and the Gaza Strip.

Jordan also rejected the Reagan Plan and by so doing essentially rendered the entire initiative moot because it depended on Jordanian control over an autonomous Palestinian Authority (PA). Some have argued that the plan was destined to fail because it addressed only part of the larger Palestinian problem. Indeed, it did not mention the plight and status of as many as 2.5 million Palestinian refugees, did not earmark any additional land to the Palestinians besides Gaza and the West Bank, and did not speak to UN-mandated specifications for restitution to those Palestinians who lost their property since 1948.

PAUL G. PIERPAOLI JR.

**See also**
Arafat, Yasser; Begin, Menachem; Gaza Strip; Hussein ibn Talal, King of Jordan; Lebanon Civil War; Palestine Liberation Organization; West Bank

### References

Gabriel, Richard. *Operation Peace for Galilee: The Israeli-PLO War in Lebanon.* New York: Farrar, Straus and Giroux, 1985.

Hart, Alan. *Arafat: A Political Biography.* Rev. ed. London: Sidgwick and Jackson, 1994.

Laham, Nicholas. *Crossing the Rubicon: Ronald Reagan and U.S. Policy in the Middle East.* Aldershot, Hampshire, UK: Ashgate, 2004.

Rubin, Barry. *Revolution until Victory? The Politics and History of the PLO.* Reprint ed. Cambridge, MA: Harvard University Press, 2003.

# Red Sea

The large body of water separating the continents of Africa and Asia. The most northern of all tropical seas, the Red Sea dominates the physical and geopolitical landscape of the Middle East. Egypt, Sudan, Eritrea, and Ethiopia lie on its western borders; Saudi Arabia and Yemen are on its eastern borders; and Egypt, Israel, and Jordan are at its northern apex.

In the north the Red Sea is separated by the Sinai Peninsula into two channels. The first is the Gulf of Suez. Lying to the west, it is about 180 miles long and some 20 miles wide on average. To the east is the Gulf of Aqaba. It is roughly 100 miles in length with an average width of about 15 miles.

The Red Sea is some 1,450 miles in length from its northern edge, where the city of Suez is located, to its southern boundary at the Straits of Bab al-Mandab, where it connects via the Gulf of Aden to the Indian Ocean. The Red Sea is never more than 200 miles in width. Why the Red Sea was so named remains obscure. It may be from a misinterpretation of the Hebrew word for "Reed Sea" or from the occasional abundance of blooms of red algae that cause so-called red tides.

The Red Sea is connected to the Mediterranean Sea to the north via the Suez Canal, which opened to ship traffic in 1869. The Red Sea varies in depth from more than 8,000 feet in the central trench, where there are numerous metal-rich deposits, to less than 2,000 feet. There are extensive shallow-water shelves around its periphery that are well developed in the Gulf of Suez. The tidal flow ranges from about 2 feet close to the mouth of the Gulf of Suez to some 3 feet near the Gulf of Aden. The central region is virtually tideless. The predominance of an arid climate and torridly hot temperatures in the region means that evaporation is high, resulting in the highest salinity concentrations of all the nonlandlocked seas.

Among important cities along the Red Sea's coastal plain are Jiddah in Saudi Arabia and Port Sudan in Sudan. Along the Sinai coast lie the cities of Eilat, Israel; Aqaba, Jordan; and Sharm El Sheikh, Egypt. All have capitalized on the rich geological and ecological resources of the region to develop economically important tourism industries. Much of this is based on the abundance of near-coastal coral reefs in shallow waters, which provide many opportunities for ecotourism and other marine activities.

The Red Sea is not merely a key geographic feature and important economic resource. It is also a significant piece of the geopolitical equation in the Middle East. Indeed, the Suez Canal is critical to the regional power balance, as was shown in the 1956 Suez Crisis. The closing off of the Gulf of Aqaba and the Strait of Tiran to Israeli shipping from 1949 to 1956 represented a significant hardship for the Israelis. The strait was again briefly closed in 1967 prior to the Six-Day War. While the area was blockaded, Israeli ships bound for the East had to circumnavigate the African continent, adding many days and considerable expense to such voyages. During the Iran-Iraq War (1980–1988), the Gulf of Aqaba was crucial to the Iraqis as a resupply route via Jordan.

ANTOINETTE MANNION

**See also**

Aqaba, Gulf of; Sharm El Sheikh; Strait of Tiran Crisis; Suez Canal; Suez Crisis

**References**

Ghisotti, Andrea. *The Red Sea.* Florence, Italy: Casa Editrice Bonechi, 1995.

Mallory, Kenneth. *The Red Sea.* New York: Franklin Watts, 1991.

# Reform Judaism and Zionism

A branch of Judaism that originated in Germany in the early 1800s and is now the dominant movement in North American Judaism. Although its doctrines have changed over time, Reform Judaism has a history of liberalism and progressivism. Reform Judaism's emphasis on Judaism as a religion rather than a nationality initially put it at odds with Zionism and the creation of a Jewish homeland, but changing world events have done much to reconcile these two ideological strains of Judaism.

Reform Judaism has its roots in the Jewish Enlightenment (Haskalah) of the late 18th and early 19th centuries. During this period, German Jewish intellectuals used the expanded rights and freedoms granted to Jews during the 18th-century European Enlightenment as a basis for a new form of Judaism. Reform Jews argued that Judaism was a religion, not a nationality. This meant that Jews should work to integrate themselves into the larger civic structure of the nation. To this end, certain aspects of Jewish religious observation were changed to streamline them with non-Jewish practices. For instance, previously banned musical accompaniment was incorporated into religious observations, and services were conducted in German rather than Hebrew. Other practices that set Jews apart from their non-Jewish neighbors, such as circumcision and the following of dietary restrictions, were also abolished. In addition to their ideological basis, these changes had a practical purpose. They helped stem the flow of conversions to Christianity by Jews who found their religion overly rigid, difficult to understand, and a source of alienation.

Reform Judaism spread to other European states, including Britain, the Netherlands, Denmark, Hungary, and Austria. It was brought to the United States by a wave of almost 150,000 Jewish immigrants from German-speaking countries between 1840 and 1870. Although the American Reform movement had many important intellectual and religious leaders, the most important was undoubtedly Isaac Mayer Wise. A Bohemian rabbi who immigrated to the United States in 1846, Wise wrote the first prayer book edited for American Jews in 1857. He also established many important institutions in American Reform Judaism, including the Union of American Hebrew Congregations in 1873, the Hebrew Union College in 1875, and the Central Conference of American Rabbis (CCAR) in 1889. Although Reform Judaism met with opposition from the Orthodox Jewish community as it had in Europe, it quickly became the dominant form of Judaism in the United States. The 1885 Declaration of Principles (also known as the Pittsburgh Platform) was the first official statement made by American Reform rabbis.

By the 1930s, however, Reform Judaism had begun to reincorporate elements of traditional Jewish observation that it had previously eschewed. The changing landscape of Reform Judaism was addressed in a series of platform statements issued by the CCAR in 1937, 1976, 1997, and 1999. Reform Judaism remains more liberal than Orthodox Judaism. For instance, Reform Judaism welcomes gay and lesbian Jews and allows members to trace their Jewish lineage through either the mother or the father rather than just the mother.

This gradual evolution of doctrine in Reform Judaism can be best exemplified by the movement's attitude toward Zionism and Israel. Many of the first leaders of the Reform movement believed that pushing for the creation of a Jewish homeland in Israel undermined the concept of Judaism as a religious rather than national identity. They maintained that Jews should not think of themselves as exiled from Israel but instead should embrace the place of their birth as their homeland. It was feared that working for the creation of a Jewish state would only further alienate the Jewish population. A desire to create a Jewish homeland would promote dual loyalties and might even be seen by non-Jewish authorities as treasonous. However, after the 1917 Balfour Declaration, which pledged Britain's support for the creation of a Jewish homeland in the Middle East, Reform Judaism began to warm to the Zionist cause.

The 1948 creation of the State of Israel significantly helped to infuse Zionism into the Reform movement. In 1997 in accordance with the centennial of the World Zionist Organization (WZO), the CCAR issued "Reform Judaism and Zionism: A Centenary Platform" (also known as the Miami Platform) in which it formally declared its support of Israel and Zionism. Today, a small number of Reform Jews maintain anti-Zionist positions.

PAUL G. PIERPAOLI JR.

### See also
Ashkenazic Judaism; Zionism

### References
Greenstein, Howard R. *Turning Point: Zionism and Reform Judaism.* Otterup, Denmark: Scholars Press, 1981.
Kaplan, Dana Evan. *American Reform Judaism: An Introduction.* Piscataway, NJ: Rutgers University Press, 2003.
Meyer, Michael A. *Response to Modernity: A History of the Reform Movement in Judaism.* Detroit: Wayne State University Press, 1995.

## Regime Change, Iraq War

"Regime change" is a phrase that first appeared in the American vocabulary in the early 2000s. Generally, the term refers to action taken by external actors to replace another state's government. In its contemporary American usage, "regime change" refers to President George W. Bush's policy goal of removing Iraqi president Saddam Hussein from power. The stated belief that Iraq had weapons of mass destruction (WMD) and possible links with Al Qaeda were the chief reasons advanced by the Bush administration for the U.S.-led invasion of Iraq in March 2003 (Operation IRAQI FREEDOM). Regime change was mentioned with the suggestion that a democratic Iraq would transform the Middle East. When no WMD were found and no link with Al Qaeda was proven, regime change became the Bush administration's chief justification for the war, this despite the fact that when candidate Bush was first running for president in 2000, he had attacked the Democrats for foreign interventions and "nation building."

Although the descriptor "regime change" is relatively new, the ideas behind it are not. Indeed, the United States has been involved in a number of military and diplomatic conflicts with similar goals. The invasion of Iraq was the first action in which the goal of regime change was explicitly named but was not the first operation that the United States has undertaken to that end.

The origins of the U.S. aspiration for Iraqi regime change lie in the Persian Gulf War of 1991, in which the United States, under the urging of President George H. W. Bush, went to war with Saddam Hussein's Iraq in order to expel the Iraqis from Kuwait, which they had invaded and occupied. In November 1998, President Bill Clinton signed the Iraq Liberation Act, which referred specifically to the "regime" of Saddam Hussein and the importance of ousting it. In George W. Bush's estimation, the goal of regime change, along with the presumed threat of WMD and the assumption that Hussein had ties to terrorist networks, necessitated military action. In his now famous State of the Union address on January 29, 2002, President Bush identified Iraq as part of a global "Axis of Evil," which also included Iran and North Korea. This speech presaged his new foreign policy strategy of preemption and was a break with past policy toward Iraq that had emphasized sanctions and localized bombing operations. General Colin Powell, then secretary of state, made the case for an invasion of Iraq before the United Nations Security Council in February 2003; Powell later apologized for the faulty intelligence upon which he had relied.

Hussein was captured on December 13, 2004, with the promise that he would be tried before an Iraqi court. He was tried, found guilty, and executed in December 2006. In the meantime, the Iraqi government and military were restructured, and democratic elections were held in January 2005. U.S. and coalition troops spent years training and equipping Iraqi soldiers and police.

The Iraq War had varied outcomes. No WMD were discovered, and the Central Intelligence Agency (CIA) established that there were no clear links between the Hussein government and the Al Qaeda terrorist organization that had carried out the September 11, 2001, attacks on the United States. The goal of regime change was realized, although the Iraqi government remains unstable, and insurgent activity against the Shiite-dominated government and terrorist bombings continues as Iraq struggles to secure control of territory lost to the Islamic State of Iraq and Syria (ISIS).

Although most recognized that Hussein was a despotic and violent ruler, significant portions of the international community remained unconvinced that regime change in Iraq was a goal worth pursuing, especially given skepticism over WMD or ties with Al Qaeda, as evidenced by the reluctance of the United Nations Security Council to support military action against Iraq. Regime change is generally not recognized as adequate cause for invading a sovereign nation, especially given the lack of any evidence indicating that Saddam Hussein posed an immediate threat. Furthermore, many scholars, activists, and world leaders expressed concern that regime change was simply American imperialism by another name.

REBECCA ADELMAN

See also
Bush Doctrine; Chemical Weapons and Warfare; Hussein, Saddam; Iraq War

References
Bolton, M. Kent. *U.S. Foreign Policy and International Politics: George W. Bush, 9/11, and the Global Terrorist Hydra.* Upper Saddle River, NJ: Pearson/Prentice Hall, 2005.
Everest, Larry. *Oil, Power, and Empire: Iraq and the U.S. Global Agenda.* Monroe, ME: Common Courage, 2004.

## Religious Sites in the Middle East, Christian

Jerusalem, the principal holy city for Christianity, contains the traditional tomb of Jesus and the route Jesus traveled to his crucifixion after his condemnation by the Roman procurator Pontius Pilate. The city is also the place of Jesus's crucifixion (Golgotha). The Church of the Holy Sepulchre, in the northwest quarter of the Old City of Jerusalem, sits atop what most of Christendom believes to be the site of both Jesus's tomb and his crucifixion. The original church was built by Constantine the Great, the first Roman emperor (CE 306–337) to profess his Christianity. It was destroyed, however, in 1009. A new structure went up in the mid-12th century that underwent major renovations during the 19th century and major restorations in the mid-20th century.

The Via Dolorosa (Street of Sorrows) is a street in the Old City of Jerusalem that is the supposed path trod by Jesus to Golgotha. It is divided by the Roman Catholic Church into the 14 Stations of the Cross, which pilgrims follow to remember Jesus's steps to his death. The final 5 stations, the last being the laying of Jesus's body in the tomb, are within the walls of the Church of the Holy Sepulchre.

There remains a dispute over the correct site of both Jesus's crucifixion and his burial. Some Protestants, most notably British general Charles George Gordon in the late

19th century, asserted that both the tomb (the Garden Tomb) and Calvary (Golgotha, the place of the Skull) are in East Jerusalem, just north of the walls of the Old City. The uncertainty arises because the inhabitants of Jerusalem fled to Pella in 66 CE during the Jewish uprising and subsequent destruction of the Second Temple by the Roman general Titus in 70. There was no tradition of the correct location until Constantine ordered its determination in 325, which was carried out at best subjectively.

Other significant Christian sites in Jerusalem include the Garden of Gethsemane (near the base of the Mount of Olives) where Jesus was betrayed and the Tomb of the Virgin Mary close by. Farther up on the Mount of Olives is the traditional place where Christians believe Christ made his final ascent to Heaven. A mosque currently sits on the site, which is venerated by Muslims.

The Church of the Nativity in Bethlehem (the House of Bread) is the second major holy site for Christendom in the Middle East. It was built by Saint Helena (248–328), the mother of Constantine the Great, on the site identified by Saint Justin the Martyr who lived in the second century. The Church of the Nativity is administered by the Greek, Roman, and Armenian churches.

Bethlehem, Jesus's traditional birthplace, has been under control of the Palestinian Authority (PA) since 1995. Palestinian militants fleeing the Israel Defense Force' (IDF) Operation DEFENSIVE SHIELD seized the church on April 2, 2002, and set fire to a portion of the building. They were deported to Cyprus and European Union countries following a negotiated settlement 38 days later.

Nazareth, the town where Jesus grew up, is located some 15 miles west of the southern end of the Sea of Galilee. The shore of the Sea of Galilee itself is the site of much of Christ's early ministry, especially Capernaum, the original home of Simon Bar Jonah (later known as Saint Peter), and the Mount of Beatitudes near Tabgha, the traditional site of the Sermon on the Mount.

A less accepted and less venerated Christian holy site is what is believed to be the Church of John the Baptist. It was erected by Byzantine emperor Anastasius (r. 491–518) to mark the spot on the bank of the Jordan River where Jesus is thought to have left his outer garments before being baptized by John the Baptist. There are, however, several places along the Jordan that claim to be the site of the baptism.

Israel allows unrestricted access to all religious shrines and holy sites. Nevertheless, entry checkpoints into Israel from the West Bank and Gaza limit access to the religious sites in Israel and Jerusalem in particular. The Israeli Security Fence, however, does restrict access to and from Bethlehem, Hebron, and the Jordan River. Israel does allow the appropriate religious authorities to administer their respective holy places. In Jerusalem, for example, the Church of the Holy Sepulchre is administered by the Greek Orthodox, Roman Catholic, Armenian Orthodox, and Coptic Churches. Each controls a separate section of the church.

RICHARD M. EDWARDS AND DAVID T. ZABECKI

**See also**
Religious Sites in the Middle East, Jewish; Religious Sites in the Middle East, Muslim

**References**
Bahat, Dan. *The Illustrated Atlas of Jerusalem.* New York: Simon and Schuster, 1990.
Crown-Tamir, Hela. *How to Walk in the Footsteps of Jesus and the Prophets: A Scripture Reference Guide for Biblical Sites in Israel and Jordan.* Jerusalem: Gefen, 2000.
Mansour, Atallah. *Narrow Gate Churches: The Christian Presence in the Holy Land under Muslim and Jewish Rule.* Carol Stream, IL: Hope Publishing House, 2004.
Poole, Karen, ed. *Jerusalem & the Holy Land.* New York: Dorling Kindersley, 2007.

## Religious Sites in the Middle East, Jewish

Jerusalem is the principal holy city for Judaism and was made the ancient capital of the United Kingdom of Israel by King David in the 10th century BCE. It remained the capital of the Southern Kingdom of Judah in the Divided Kingdom. Jerusalem is the current capital of the State of Israel, although it is unrecognized as such by the majority of the world community. With the exception of the Israel Defense Force (IDF), it is the location of the primary offices of all the branches of the Israeli government and the Israeli parliament (Knesset).

Jerusalem is the site of King Solomon's Temple (the First Temple) and the Second Temple erected during the rule of the Persian Darius (522–486 BCE). The Second Temple was completely rebuilt starting around 19 BCE under the reign of Herod the Great. The temple was destroyed by the Roman general Titus in the Jewish revolt that ended at Masada in 70 CE. The only surviving remnant of the Second Temple is the Western Wall, which was actually a retailing wall at the base of the Temple Mount erected during Herod's reconstruction.

The Western Wall is also known as the Wailing Wall, so called by Europeans who saw pious Jews bemoaning the destruction of the Temple and praying for its restoration, and is a place of Jewish prayer and pilgrimage. The wall is central to the plans for a new temple by such groups as the Temple Mount Faithful Movement. Even though the cornerstone for this new temple was laid in July 2001, the building of a Third Temple on the site of the first two is highly problematic.

Currently, the Temple Mount is occupied by the al-Aqsa Mosque, Islam's third-holiest site. Both access to the Noble Sanctuary and the potential encroachment on the precinct by the proposed new temple have led to many clashes between Jews and Muslims since the Israelis captured the Old City of Jerusalem in the 1967 Six-Day War. The latest such disturbance began with a visit by Prime Minister Ariel Sharon on September 28, 2000, to the al-Aqsa precinct. This event triggered the Second (al-Aqsa) Intifada.

The Tomb of David, located on Mount Zion just outside the walls of the Old City, is the traditional burial place of ancient Israel's greatest king. Until the Israeli capture of the Old City in 1967, the Tomb of David was the major site for Jewish prayers because Jews were not allowed access to the Western Wall. Also outside the current-day walls of the Old City and just to the south of the Temple Mount lie the excavated ruins of the City of David, the original city of Jerusalem conquered by King David about 1004 BCE.

The Kidron Valley also lies outside the current-day Old City walls in East Jerusalem, between the Mount of Olives to the east and the high ground of the Temple Mount and Mount Zion to the west. The Kidron is known in the Bible as the Valley of Jehoshaphat, meaning "the valley where God will judge." It is the site of many significant Jewish tombs, including the Tomb of Bene Hezir, the Tomb of Zechariah, and the Pillar of Absalom.

The Tomb (Cave) of the Patriarchs and Matriarchs in Hebron (ancient Judaea and now the southern part of the West Bank) is the second-holiest site in Judaism. It is the purported burial place of the great patriarchs and matriarchs buried as couples—Abraham and Sarah, Isaac and Rebecca, Jacob and Leah, and Adam and Eve—and is sacred to Muslims as well. Hebron was the capital of Judah, the Southern Kingdom, and the first capital of the United Kingdom before Jerusalem. Hebron came under Israeli control in the Six-Day War. The Jewish settlements built in Hebron since then remain a flashpoint in Israeli-Palestinian relations, despite the 1997 Hebron Protocol. Both a mosque (Sanctuary of Abraham) and a synagogue are built on top of the tomb. Jacob's second wife is buried in the Tomb of Rachel on the Jerusalem-Hebron Road near the Iron Gate of Israel's security fence at Bethlehem's northern entrance. Both tombs are holy to Jews and Muslims, who claim a common ancestry through Abraham.

Tzfat, or Safed, is sacred to Jews as the site of the writing of much of the Jerusalem (Palestinian) Talmud (400–550 CE) and for the development of Jewish kabbalistic mysticism (15th and 16th centuries). Tiberias is considered sacred as the last meeting place of the Sanhedrin (426 CE), as an ancient center of Jewish learning, and for the tombs of the ancient Jewish scholars.

RICHARD M. EDWARDS AND DAVID T. ZABECKI

**See also**
Intifada, Second; Religious Sites in the Middle East, Christian; Religious Sites in the Middle East, Muslim; Sharon, Ariel; Six-Day War

**References**
Bahat, Dan. *The Illustrated Atlas of Jerusalem.* New York: Simon and Schuster, 1990.
Crown-Tamir, Hela. *How to Walk in the Footsteps of Jesus and the Prophets: A Scripture Reference Guide for Biblical Sites in Israel and Jordan.* Jerusalem: Gefen, 2000.
Hoffman, Lawrence A. *Israel: A Spiritual Travel Guide; A Companion for the Modern Jewish Pilgrim.* 2nd ed. Woodstock, VT: Jewish Lights, 2005.
Mansour, Atallah. *Narrow Gate Churches: The Christian Presence in the Holy Land under Muslim and Jewish Rule.* Carol Stream, IL: Hope Publishing House, 2004.
Poole, Karen, ed. *Jerusalem & the Holy Land.* New York: Dorling Kindersley, 2007.

## Religious Sites in the Middle East, Muslim

The Middle East is home to all of the holiest shrines of Islam. The three holiest Islamic sites are Mecca, Medina, and the al-Aqsa Mosque in Jerusalem. Other venerated sites are located in Damascus, Cairo, Najaf, Karbala, Qum, Mashhad, and Fez, to mention only a few. Also important in Palestine are Khalil (Hebron), Jericho, and numerous other mosques and tombs of holy persons.

The holy sites in Israel and Palestine remain a focal point of the Palestinian-Israeli conflict because there is no freedom of worship for Muslims at these religious sites and also because of certain groups that propose to destroy them in order to rebuild the Temple. Israel restricts access to all religious sites for Palestinians, allowing entry only to those who are permitted to reside or travel in that specific area. Thus, Muslims who wish to visit the al-Aqsa Mosque must first obtain permission to visit Israel, which is restricted by many Muslim nations, and they will then most likely be

The al-Aqsa Mosque, among the holiest of Muslim sites, situated in the Old City of Jerusalem. (Dmitry Bomshtein/iStockphoto.com)

denied entry to the country by Israel. Even Muslims from European nations and Turkey who can obtain entry must then satisfy soldiers at entry checkpoints. More recently, Israel's security fence restricted access to and from the West Bank and Gaza.

An Islamic waqf, a trust or endowment that is required to be administered by Muslims, has been instead controlled by Israel. The endowment is delegated to representatives approved by Israel, and since Oslo there has been an agreement that Palestinian security personnel will guard entry to the al-Aqsa complex in East Jerusalem. This is a site holy to both Islam and Judaism and has been a source of conflict since long before Israel gained control of it after the 1967 Six-Day War. The principal reason that Israeli prime minister Ehud Barak and Palestine Liberation Organization (PLO) chairman Yasser Arafat were unable to reach an agreement at the Camp David talks in July 2000 was the failure to reconcile Jewish and Muslim claims to the Bayt Maqdis, or al-Aqsa complex, known to Israelis as the Temple Mount.

Mecca, in Saudi Arabia, was the birthplace of Prophet Muhammad and is Islam's holiest site. Muslim religious obligations include the pilgrimage (hajj) to Mecca, held annually during the Dhul-Hijjah (month of hajj), the last month of the Islamic calendar. Devout Muslims are expected to make at least one hajj if they can afford to do so.

Mecca's Great Mosque (Masjid al-Haram) is constructed around the Kaaba (meaning "cube"), the holiest place in Islam. Muslims believe that the Kaaba, a windowless granite and masonry cube covered with a black silk cloth, was built by Adam and then rebuilt by Ibrahim (Abraham). According to Islamic tradition, Muhammad in 605 CE placed in its southeastern corner a gift, known as the Black Stone, from the angel Gabriel. The Zamzam, a dome-covered sacred well created by Allah, is located 115 feet from the Kaaba and provides water for the pilgrims.

Muhammad was welcomed in Medina after finding few adherents in Mecca. Medina was the nucleus of the new Muslim community until the rise of the Umayyad caliphs, when the capital was moved to Damascus in 661. It is home to the Mosque of the Prophet. This mosque contains the tombs of Muhammad and his daughter Fatima. It also houses the tomb of Omar, the second caliph. The caliphs were the political successors to Muhammad. However, prayer was conducted in the direction of Jerusalem for many years, and this only later was changed to Mecca after the reconquest of that city.

The third-holiest Islamic site is the Bayt al-Maqdis, later known as the Haram al-Sharif (Noble Sanctuary) at the end of the Old City of Jerusalem (al-Quds). The al-Aqsa Mosque (Masjid al-Aqsa, meaning the "farthest mosque") is both a building and a complex of buildings. The site is dominated and bounded by two major structures, the al-Aqsa Mosque building on the east and the Dome of the Rock on the west.

The Dome of the Rock, or the Mosque of Omar, is a *mashhad* (shrine) for pilgrims. It is not a mosque used for public worship. The Dome of the Rock surrounds and covers a large rock (the Noble Rock). From this rock, Islamic tradition believes that Muhammad, at the end of his Night Journey from Mecca to Jerusalem in 621 CE, ascended in the company of Gabriel through the heavens to Allah. Before returning to Earth Muhammad met at the rock with the prophets, including Moses, and negotiated the number of the obligatory Islamic prayers. According to a prophetic tradition (*hadith*), the site is so sacred that Muslims believe that a single prayer there is equivalent to 500 normal prayers. Some Jewish traditions assert that the rock was the platform upon which Abraham intended to fulfill God's divine command to sacrifice Isaac.

The Tomb (Cave) of the Patriarchs and Matriarchs in Hebron (ancient Judaea and now the West Bank) is the burial place of Ibrahim and his family. He was the father of Ishmael, the ancestor from whom all Arab peoples believe they descended. The Orthodox Jewish settlements in Hebron that went up after the 1967 Six-Day War remain a flashpoint in the Palestinian-Israeli conflict despite the 1997 Hebron Protocol. The Sanctuary of Ibrahim, a mosque, and a synagogue are built atop the tomb. Muslims consider the cave too sacred to enter. The Oak of Ibrahim (Oak of Mamre), sitting just over a mile west of Hebron, is believed to be the place where three angels told Ibrahim that his wife Sarah would bear his son Isaac. Also at Hebron is the tomb of Fatima, the daughter of Imam Husayn.

Although the prophet Moses died on Mount Nebo in present-day Jordan, his tomb, Maqam al-Nabi Musa near Jericho, is also venerated in Islam.

Throughout Israel and especially in the Negev, there are the tombs of Muslim saints. Those in the Negev are venerated by the Bedouins, who also believe that they may be cured by visiting these tombs. Oil or fabric scraps may be left to acquire the charismatic blessing of the saint. Just outside the city of Herzliya is the tomb of Alin ibn Alim, known as the Mashhad Sayyidna Ali.

There are also sites holy to the Druzes such as the grave of the prophet Jethro at Nabi Shu'ayb. Rather than a gravestone, a huge Christ's Thorn jujube tree was the focus and prayer site for pilgrims and is called the Sidrat Nabi Shu'ayb. There are numerous Islamic sites, historic mosques, and centers of Islamic scholarship outside of Palestine, but this does not detract from its importance. Religiously, Muslims consider all of Palestine a *waqf*.

For the Shia Muslims, the four most important sites are the holy cities of Najaf and Karbala in present-day Iraq and also two places in the cities of Mashhad and Qum in Iran. Mashhad is the burial place and shrine of Imam Reza (766–818), the eighth Shia imam to follow Prophet Muhammad. For the Twelver Shia Muslims this imam was one of the infallible successors to Muhammad, descended through his son-in-law Ali. Qum, also in Iran, is a center for Shia Islamic studies and is a counterpart to the city of Najaf, known as Najaf the Noble, to Muslims in Iraq. Ayatollah Ruhollah Khomeini taught in both cities. Qum is also home to the gold-plated dome shrine to Fatima the Pure, the sister of Imam Reza. Karbala is a city important to Shiites because Imam Husayn and his forces were murdered here, and these deaths are honored annually in the mournful holiday of Ashura.

RICHARD M. EDWARDS AND SHERIFA ZUHUR

### See also
Arafat, Yasser; Barak, Ehud; Camp David Accords; Israeli Security Fence; Khomeini, Ruhollah; Palestinian National Authority; Religious Sites in the Middle East, Christian; Religious Sites in the Middle East, Jewish; Six-Day War

### References
Bahat, Dan. *The Illustrated Atlas of Jerusalem.* New York: Simon and Schuster, 1990.

Canaan, Taufik. *Mohammedan Saints and Sanctuaries in Palestine.* London: Luzac, 1927.

Crown-Tamir, Hela. *How to Walk in the Footsteps of Jesus and the Prophets: A Scripture Reference Guide for Biblical Sites in Israel and Jordan.* Jerusalem: Gefen, 2000.

Mansour, Atallah. *Narrow Gate Churches: The Christian Presence in the Holy Land under Muslim and Jewish Rule.* Carol Stream, IL: Hope Publishing House, 2004.

Nasr, Seyyed Hossein, and Ali Kazuyoshi Nomachi. *Mecca the Blessed, Medina the Radiant: The Holiest Cities of Islam.* New York: Aperture, 1997.

Poole, Karen, ed. *Jerusalem & the Holy Land.* New York: Dorling Kindersley, 2007.

Taragan, Hana. "The Tomb of Sayyidna 'Ali in Ar[sdotu]uf: The Story of a Holy Place." *Journal of the Royal Asiatic Society* 14 (2004): 83–102.

# Republican Guard, Iraq

Iraqi military formation created in 1978 that served as the elite force of Iraqi president Saddam Hussein's army. The Republican Guard was permanently disbanded after the Iraq War (Operation IRAQI FREEDOM) that began in 2003. Throughout its existence, the Republican Guard was one of the mainstays of Hussein's regime and received the best equipment, training, and personnel. When first constituted, the Republican Guard was a palace guard of one brigade. At the outbreak of the Iran-Iraq War in 1980, the Republican Guard was expanded to take on the role of an elite offensive force, and by 1988 it numbered seven divisions and had been redesignated as the Republican Guard Forces Command (RGFC). The total strength of this force was estimated at 50,000 men and 400 tanks in seven divisions. There were an additional 10,000 troops in the Special Republican Guard, which was composed of the most loyal troops, usually stationed close to Baghdad.

The names of the seven divisions reflected either past military victories or past monarchs, such as the 6th Nebuchadnezzar Division named after the sixth-century BCE king of Babylon. Republican Guard divisions were organized similarly to those of the regular army, apart from the fact that the tank battalions had more tanks. However, soldiers in the Republican Guard were volunteers rather than conscripts and received subsidized housing and new cars as incentives. These incentives were to help ensure the loyalty of the Republican Guard to Hussein and his regime. Many members of the Republican Guard were either from the Tikrit area or from other bases of support for the regime. In terms of equipment, much of the armored forces of the Republican Guard were equipped with Soviet-produced T-72 tanks, and training in their use was more thorough than in the regular army.

The Republican Guard was not under the control of the defense ministry but instead served as Iraq's special security apparatus. By 1990 the RGFC was officially under the command of Saddam Hussein's son Qusay, although it is possible that he directed only the Special Republican Guard, which guarded the palaces and important headquarters of the regime.

The Republican Guard was the main strike force in the Iraqi invasion of Kuwait in August 1990, and its destruction was a high priority for the coalition forces that drove Iraqi forces from Kuwait in the Persian Gulf War of 1991. Following the war Hussein rebuilt the Republican Guard, although, as with the rest of the Iraqi Army, it was not to pre-1990 standards.

In 1995 an attempted military coup against Hussein led a battalion of the Republican Guard from the al-Dulaymi tribe to rebel as well. The battalion was subsequently defeated by two loyal brigades, and the clans of the al-Dulaymi tribe were severely punished. In July 1995 the Republican Guard was purged of all officers whom Hussein suspected of disloyalty. In 2002 there were reports that the Republican Guard was being trained in urban warfare and guerrilla tactics. The U.S. military claimed that former guardsmen constituted many of the insurgent forces in Iraq that fought the coalition and new Iraqi government after 2003.

Before the March 2003 Anglo-American invasion of Iraq (Operation IRAQI FREEDOM), the Republican Guard was dug in along the Tigris River close to Baghdad. It was then thought to number between 55,000 and 60,000 troops; some estimates placed the number as high as 75,000–80,000 (including some 7,000–12,000 Special Republican Guards). The force had at its disposal between 350 and 450 Soviet-made T-62 and T-72 tanks and various other armored and unarmored mechanized vehicles. When some of these units advanced to meet the U.S. drive on the capital, they were largely destroyed by U.S. air strikes. Those that escaped the aerial bombardment were annihilated during the Battle for Baghdad during April 3–12, 2003; particularly hard hit during that engagement was the Special Republican Guard. Following the end of official hostilities in May 2003, coalition forces broke up any remaining Republican Guard formations. Some of its personnel, however, were subsequently recruited into internal security formations because of their comparatively high level of training.

RALPH MARTIN BAKER

### See also
Baghdad, 2003 Battle of; Hussein, Saddam; Iraq War

### References
Carhart, Tom. *Iron Soldiers: How America's 1st Armored Division Crushed Iraq's Elite Republican Guard.* New York: Pocket Books, 1994.

Ripley, Tom. *Desert Storm Land Power: The Coalition and Iraqi Armies.* London: Osprey, 1991.

Xenos, Nicolas. *Republican Guard: Leo Strauss, Foreign Policy, and the American Regime.* Oxford, UK: Routledge, 2006.

# Resht, Treaty of (February 1, 1732)

Treaty between Persia and Russia signed on February 1, 1732, at Resht (Rasht) in Gilan Province, Persia. In the 1720s, the two powers were involved in a brief war that left parts of Persia under Russian control. The Russian involvement in Persian affairs, however, withered away following Russian tsar Peter I's death in 1725. At the same time, Persia's domestic situation improved following the rise of the maverick Nadir Khan, who consolidated power and sought to recover Persian territorial losses of the earlier years. Thus, he negotiated the Treaty of Resht that restored Astrabad, Mazandaran, and Gilan to Iran, while the territory north of the Kura River remained temporarily under Russian control. Three years later, Russia accepted the Treaty of Ganja by which it gave up all of its previous Persian conquests, including Baku, Derbent, and Tarqu.

ALEXANDER MIKABERIDZE

**See also**
Nadir Shah; Russo-Persian Wars

**References**
Avery, Peter, et al., eds. *The Cambridge History of Iran: From Nadir Shah to the Islamic Republic*, Vol. 7. Cambridge: Cambridge University Press, 1991.

Ward, Steven. *Immortal: A Military History of Iran and Its Armed Forces*. Washington, DC: Georgetown University Press, 2009.

## Revisionist Zionism

A form of Zionism that gained hold after 1925. Revisionist Zionism argued that the British Mandate for Palestine should be revised to create a sovereign Jewish state encompassing both sides of the Jordan River. Revisionist Zionists also held that Zionism should shift its emphasis from social and economic development in Palestine to the immediate creation of a Jewish state aligned with the United Kingdom.

Vladimir Jabotinsky founded Revisionist Zionism in 1925 as a variant of Theodor Herzl's Political Zionism. Jabotinsky was the Russian-born Jewish Zionist who helped found the Jewish Legion that fought for the British in World War I. Israel's present-day Likud and Kadima Parties and many prominent Israeli politicians are inheritors of the Revisionist legacy.

Revisionist Zionism is part of the pantheon of Zionist movements that developed at the end of the 19th century in response to increased Jewish persecution in Europe. Zionism sought to resolve this growing problem by seeking to create a legal (guaranteed) Jewish homeland in Palestine. These Zionist movements spanned the spectrum from the purely secular to the purely religious.

Revisionist Zionism was one of the major influences in Jewish Palestine following World War I. Jabotinsky's experience in World War I led him to believe that swift and strong retaliatory action could forestall Arab attacks on the Yishuv (Jewish community in Palestine). Jabotinsky was one of the founders of the United Jewish Appeal (Keren Hayesod), the main Zionist fund-raising organization, and in 1921 he was elected to the Executive Council of the World Zionist Organization (WZO) that was chaired by Chaim Weizmann. Jabotinsky disagreed with the measured goals advocated by Weizmann. Thus, in 1923 Jabotinsky resigned and then in 1925 formed the Revisionist Zionist Alliance, also known as the Alliance of Revisionists-Zionists. Jabotinsky's Revisionist Zionism sought to change the WZO's moderate plan and the timetable of the other Zionist movements to a more aggressive plan with speedier implementation. Revisionism advocated shifting the emphasis of Zionism away from social and economic development in Palestine to the immediate creation of a Jewish state in Palestine. Jabotinsky advocated massive European immigration into Palestine, rapidly producing a Jewish voting and fighting majority; the immediate creation of a Jewish state in Palestine; and the creation of a Jewish self-defense organization.

The Revisionists advocated two additional revisions. Jabotinsky rejected what he perceived to be the fanciful hope of David Ben-Gurion's Labor Zionism that a Jewish state would eventually arise from an established Jewish working and middle class flourishing in Palestine and asserted that more direct and immediate action was needed. Revisionism also sought to revise, reexamine, or realign the relationship of Zionism to the British mandatory government in Palestine and to the United Kingdom itself. Weizmann and Ben-Gurion emphasized and promoted the independent settlement of Palestine with the approval of the dominant world communities. Revisionism originally advocated a more direct alliance with the British.

Revisionists under Jabotinsky's leadership sought to develop a symbiotic relationship with the United Kingdom and through that relationship alter the British Mandate for Palestine to be more favorable to Zionism. Jabotinsky tried to bring this change about through worldwide and internal social and political pressure on the British government by using petitions, demonstrations, and other forms of public appeal and protest. He also sought to reason with the British, arguing that it was in the United Kingdom's best interest to have a loyal friend in the region, something the British had learned in World War I. Jabotinsky also argued that British aid and cooperation would be reciprocated by a strong Zionist state with European, particularly British, roots. He even asserted that such a Zionist state would be a loyal autonomous extension of the United Kingdom, allowing it to project power into the region with minimal military commitment.

Jabotinsky used the latter reasoning to argue for the revision of the 1922 decision by the League of Nations to divide the mandate into two geographical units, one east of the Jordan River and one west of the Jordan River that remained under the direct administration of the British. The Emirate of Transjordan had been created as a semiautonomous political division of the British Mandate for Palestine east of the Jordan River, encompassing an area roughly equivalent to the 1942–1965 Kingdom of Jordan. The creation of Transjordan was an attempt to appease the Arab nations in light of the 1917 Balfour Declaration that expressed official British support for a Jewish homeland in Palestine. Jabotinsky argued that this appeasement would create neither a loyal nor a strong British advocate and partner in the region and that he and other Zionists had demonstrated their loyalty to the United Kingdom when they had fought with the British in World War I. Jabotinsky pressed the British to convert all of the mandate east and west of the Jordan River into a dependable sovereign Jewish state with a proven pro-British propensity. Such a friend would be achieved in part by a British-sponsored, -promoted, and -funded mass Jewish immigration from Europe into the mandate, and this would make European Jewry the majority in Palestine. Jabotinsky also advocated the formation and sponsorship of two Jewish Legion groups to be stationed in Palestine and military training of Jewish youths for self-defense and potential mobilization if needed.

The British rejected Jabotinsky's ideas and even barred his return to Palestine following the Sixteenth World Zionist Congress in 1929, but these ideas were implemented in the Yishuv. Revisionist settlers brought their Betar youth movement into the Yishuv and created their own self-defense force, the Irgun Tsvai Leumi (National Military Organization), based on theories of Middle East warfare advocated by Jabotinsky.

Irgun was a right-wing paramilitary Zionist underground movement in Palestine during 1931–1948 known for immediate and harsh retaliation for attacks on the Jewish community in Palestine and its advocacy of military action against the British. The Irgun movement itself was classified by the British as a terrorist organization, and many of its operations were declared terrorist by the Jewish Agency for Palestine, Haganah, and the Histadrut (Israeli trade union). Haganah, organized after the Arab riots of 1920–1921, was the main Jewish self-defense and military organization during 1920–1948 in Palestine. Jabotinsky, one of the founders of Haganah, led the organization against Arab riots in Jerusalem during Passover in 1920. His swift response was deemed criminal by the British mandatory government, and he was sentenced to 15 years' hard labor but was soon granted amnesty and released. Irgun was created in 1931 as an alternative to what the Revisionists perceived was Haganah's overly restrained responses to Arab attacks on the Yishuv. The Revisionists sought in similar fashion to confront and at times counter with force what they perceived as the British mandatory government's pro-Arab bias.

Jabotinsky founded the Betar youth movement, also known as Beitar, in Riga, Latvia, in 1923. He asserted five major goals for Betar: teach Jewish youths to defend themselves, prepare the youths of the Yishuv to protect their homes against Arab attacks, prepare the youths of the Yishuv to fight for a Jewish state in Palestine, prepare the youths of the Yishuv to lead the Jewish state in Palestine, and encourage Jewish youths from outside Palestine to immigrate to Palestine.

Menachem Begin exemplified the ideals of Jabotinsky and Betar. Begin joined Betar when he was 16 years old and in 1932 led the Organization Department of Betar Poland before graduating from the University of Warsaw in 1935. He assumed the leadership of Betar Czechoslovakia in 1936, and in 1938 Betar Poland's 100,000 members engaged in self-defense, weapons, agricultural, and communications training, and transported immigrants to Palestine whom the British deemed illegal. Begin advocated the establishment of a Jewish national homeland in Palestine by conquest and pushed Betar and Jabotinsky to adopt this position at the 1938 Betar convention. Begin openly criticized the Jewish Agency for Palestine and worldwide Zionism as being too timid in their approach to a Jewish state and forcefully advocated the Revisionist Zionists' belief that a Jewish homeland must be created in Palestine and if need be by military action. Begin joined Irgun in 1942 and commanded the organization from 1943 to 1948. Irgun stopped its attacks on the British during 1941–1943 as World War II worsened and supported the Allies against Germany and Germany's Arab allies in the Middle East. It was under Begin's leadership that Irgun declared war on the British in February 1944 and resumed attacks on Arab villages and British interests. Some Betar graduates also joined the more radical Stern Gang, also known as Lehi (Jewish Freedom Fighters).

Ever the Anglophile, Jabotinsky disagreed with the attacks on the British and asserted that the real enemy was the Arabs and that the British could still be enticed to side with the Yishuv. Irgun and Lehi, on the other hand, felt it necessary to war against both the British and the Arabs. Jabotinsky and the Irgun-Lehi branch of Revisionist Zionism also disagreed on the status of the Arabs in Palestine and their status in the future Jewish state. An essential element of almost all of the

Zionist strategies was the creation of a Jewish majority that would vote for a Jewish state. Almost all Zionists sought to produce this Jewish majority through *aliya* (mass immigration). Many argued, however, that aliya should be augmented by a correlative strategy, the outmigration of the Arab population. Most Zionists argued for a voluntary transfer encouraged through economic incentives and sanctions. Still others advocated involuntary transfer (i.e., expulsion). It was this latter technique that was used during 1948–1949 to reduce the Palestinian Christian population in West Jerusalem by 50 percent following the Israeli War of Independence (1948–1949).

The argument for transfer was simply that reductions in the Arab population hastened the creation of the Jewish majority and created a more stable and secure state by decreasing the danger of having pockets of Arabs living within the Jewish state. The Revisionists generally supported involuntary transfer. The Irgun-Lehi branch of Revisionism adamantly opposed any power sharing with Arabs in Palestine and advocated their involuntary expulsion. Jabotinsky never made a clear statement concerning transfer.

Although Revisionism advocated shifting the emphasis of Zionism away from social and economic development in Palestine, it did not ignore those needs. Revisionism created a labor union, the National Labor Federation, and health services to compete with the community services offered by Labor Zionism's Histadrut (General Federation of Laborers in the Land of Israel).

Labor Zionism was strongest in the rural Jewish communities of Palestine, in the kibbutzim and moshavim, and with the working class. Revisionism had few followers in the areas dominated by Labor Zionism. General Zionism dominated the Yishuv middle class. Revision was strongest in Poland and Eastern Europe. This strength was primarily due to the pervasiveness of Betar in the Jewish communities there that were formed from the remnants of World War II Holocaust survivors.

As the 1920s and 1930s passed with what the Revisionists saw as little progress toward the creation of a Jewish state and as attacks on the Yishuv grew in the face of what some Revisionists asserted was a profound British pro-Arabism, the Revisionists became more strident in their demands for action. The Revisionists' more aggressive approach was rejected by the WZO in 1935, and the Revisionists resigned from the WZO. The Revisionists returned to the WZO in 1946 and asserted that the position of the WZO had come into line with Revisionism with the 1942 Biltmore Program's rejection of the binational solution to Palestine in favor of the immediate creation of a Jewish state in Palestine.

Revisionist Zionism diverged into three distinct branches at the end of the 1930s: the centrists, Irgun and Lehi, and the national messianists. All three branches advocated the creation of a Jewish state spanning the Jordan River with boundaries similar to those of Israel after the conquest of the land of Canaan under Joshua. The centrists favored the voluntary transfer of the Arab population, a British parliamentary form of government, and a more cooperative approach seeking the long hoped for alliance with the United Kingdom. Irgun and Lehi opposed any power sharing, favored Arab expulsion, and saw the British as being as much the enemy as the Arabs. Irgun and Lehi did favor a parliamentary form of government such as that in the United Kingdom. The national messianists opposed any power sharing, favored Arab expulsion, and opposed any agreements or alliances with any foreign powers. The national messianists leaned more toward an authoritarian, theocratic (divinely directed) regime, choosing the leader as God had chosen David and Saul.

Betar members and former members played important roles in the fight against the British during the time of the mandate and in the creation of Israel and in all branches of the Israeli military. Betar and Revisionist Zionism also produced two more Israeli prime ministers besides Begin—Yitzhak Shamir and Ehud Olmert—as well as Israel's former defense minister Moshe Arens. Betar remains active in support of worldwide Jewry and continues to encourage *aliya* to Israel through its young adult and university campus programs in North America.

RICHARD M. EDWARDS

**See also**
Balfour Declaration; Begin, Menachem; Ben-Gurion, David; Haganah; Herzl, Theodor; Irgun Tsvai Leumi; Jabotinsky, Vladimir Yevgenyevich; Lohamei Herut Israel; Palestine, British Mandate for; Reform Judaism and Zionism; Zionism

**References**
Baume, Judith Taylor. *The "Bergson Boys" and the Origins of Contemporary Zionist Militancy.* Translated by Dena Ordan. Syracuse, NY: Syracuse University Press, 2005.
Brenner, Lenni. *The Iron Wall: Zionist Revisionism from Jabotinsky to Shamir.* London: Zed, 1984.
Brenner, Michael. *Zionism: A Brief History.* Translated by Shelley Frisch. Princeton, NJ: Markus Wiener, 2003.
Kaplan, Eran. *The Jewish Radical Right: Revisionist Zionism and Its Ideological Legacy.* Madison: University of Wisconsin Press, 2005.
Morris, Benny. *Righteous Victims: A History of the Zionist-Arab Conflict, 1881–2001.* New York: Vintage, 2001.
Sachar, Howard M. *A History of Israel: From the Rise of Zionism to Our Time.* 3rd ed. New York: Knopf, 2007.

## Reza Shah Pahlavi (1878–1944)

Shah of Iran. Reza Pahlavi, who ruled Iran as Reza Shah Pahlavi, was born on March 16, 1878, in Alasht, a town in Mazanderan Province. When he was less than a year old his father, Abbas Ali Khan, a major in the Persian Army, died. Reza's mother moved with him to Tehran, where she remarried and sent her son to live with an uncle. At age 16 Reza joined the military in the Persian Cossack Brigade. Although he did not secure formal schooling, he proved himself intelligent and talented, and he advanced through the military ranks, being promoted to gunnery sergeant and then commissioned a lieutenant. By 1912 he was a captain, and in 1915 he was promoted to colonel.

During World War I both Russia and Great Britain expanded their influence in Persia. By the end of the conflict, thanks to the chaos of the Bolshevik Revolution in Russia, the British had secured a virtual protectorate over Persia. Russian Bolsheviks were active in the country, however.

On January 14, 1921, British general Edmund Ironside, then commanding the Allied force in Persia, chose Reza Khan, commander of the Tabriz Battalion, to lead the major Persian military formation, the 3,000–4,000-man Cossack Brigade, as a brigadier general and the first Persian so selected. The next month, supported by the British, he marched with the brigade on Tehran, and on February 21 he seized control of the government in a largely bloodless coup d'état.

Although military actions extended well into 1922, Reza Khan was able to pacify the entire country. At first minister of war and commander of the army, on October 28, 1923, he became prime minister of Persia, serving in that capacity until November 1, 1925, when the Majles (parliament) officially deposed the weak Ahmad Shah Qajar, the last shah of

Reza Shah Pahlavi, ruler of Iran from 1941 until the monarchy was overthrown in 1979, at his desk in Tehran, November 1960. (Bettmann/Getty Images)

the Qajar dynasty, and on December 12 selected Reza Khan as shah. Three days later he established the Pahlavi dynasty with himself as Reza Shah Pahlavi I.

Reza Shah laid the foundations of the modern Iranian state. Looking to Western nations as his model, he instituted agricultural reforms, introduced Western economic practices, promoted secular education, and began modernization of the country's transportation system. Reza Shah also built up the country's military establishment. These and other reforms threatened the status of the Shia Muslim clerics in Iran, who began to oppose the shah and policies that were seen as impinging on their authority. Desiring to stress the country's pre-Islamic traditions and to include Iranians who were not from Fars (the central province), Reza Shah in 1935 changed the country's name from Persia to Iran.

Germany had a significant economic influence and presence in Iran prior to the outbreak of World War II, for in the 1930s Reza Shah had turned to it for economic assistance. His admiration of Germany, which had no tradition of imperial intervention in Iran or in the Middle East, was well known, as was his distrust of Britain and the Soviet Union.

Reza Shah declared Iran neutral in the war. After the Germans attacked the Soviet Union in June 1941, however, Iranian involvement became inevitable. The Soviet Union was now allied with Britain, and as German forces drove farther eastward and threatened the Caucasus, the strategic significance of Iran grew. The Allies were determined to protect the British-controlled oil fields in Khuzestan and to use Iran and, in particular, its newly built Trans-Iranian railroad to transport military supplies to the Soviet Union. The British and Soviet representatives in Iran demanded that the government expel German nationals and allow the Allies to utilize the railroad to transport war materials. When Reza Shah refused on the grounds of Iranian neutrality, the Allies invaded and occupied the country.

On August 25, 1941, Soviet forces entered Iran from the northwest, while the British entered from Iraq. The Allied forces suppressed Iranian military and naval resistance in just three days. Reza Shah was forced to abdicate on September 16, 1941. Sent into exile, he died in Johannesburg, South Africa, on July 25, 1944. He was succeeded as shah by his 22-year-old son, Mohammad Reza Pahlavi.

SPENCER C. TUCKER

**See also**
Iran; Reza Shah Pahlavi

**References**
Abrahamian, Ervand. *A History of Modern Iran.* Cambridge: Cambridge University Press, 2008.
Ansari, Ali. *A History of Modern Iran since 1921: The Pahlavis and After.* Boston: Longman Publishing, 2003.
Katouzian, Homa. *The Persians: Ancient, Medieval, and Modern Iran.* New Haven, CT: Yale University Press, 2010.
Majd, Mohammad Gholi. *Persia in World War I and Its Conquest by Great Britain.* Lanham, MD: University Press of America, 2003.
Wilber, Donald N. *Iran: Past and Present.* Princeton, NJ: Princeton University Press, 1955.

# Rhodes, Demetrius's Siege of (305–304 BCE)

Siege of the island of Rhodes by forces under Demetrius I Poliorcetes during 305–304 BCE. The son of Antigonus I Monophthalmus, Demetrius besieged Rhodes at his father's instruction. The island controlled access to the Aegean Sea, and its capture was necessary if Antigonus, one of the Diadochi (successors of Alexander III of Macedon, Alexander the Great), who ruled over much of Asia Minor and northern Syria were to proceed with his goals of liberating Greece and conquering Macedonia.

Rhodes enjoyed friendly relations with King Ptolemy I of Egypt, and Demetrius was concerned that the islanders might supply him with ships in fighting Egypt. Indeed, the Rhodians had refused a summons to fight against Egypt. Demetrius arrived at Rhodes with some 200 warships and 150 auxiliary vessels. A large number of private vessels also accompanied the invaders, their owners intent on plunder. Rhodes would have surrendered had Demetrius not demanded entry into the city with his fleet. The Rhodians sent away all those unwilling or unable to fight, leaving some 7,000 men as well as freeing those slaves who opted to stay. Demetrius led a large army and fleet with experienced engineers and a siege train. He also used his own vessels and enlisted the privately owned ships to blockade Rhodes's harbors. The city and main harbor, however, were strongly fortified.

Demetrius attacked the main harbor and the city walls. A large floating boom proved unsuccessful, and he was unable to prevent reinforcements of supplies and troops from entering the city. After weeks of fighting Demetrius gained a foothold, but a storm forced him off, destroying many of his ships and his siege towers and allowing the Rhodians to regain the harbor. Demetrius delayed for a few days rebuilding his towers, then abandoned the harbors and attempted land assaults. Demetrius failed to prevent Rhodian ships sallying out and capturing valuable supplies. Demetrius attacked repeatedly with the famed siege engine, the Heliopolis (about 135 by 65 feet and mounted on eight wheels 15 feet in height), but was repulsed. He launched a night attack through a breach in the walls, but 1,500 mercenary reinforcements dispatched by Ptolemy were instrumental in defeating this only foray by the attackers into the city itself.

After a year of failure at Rhodes, Antigonus ordered Demetrius to make peace. Deemtrius concluded a treaty with Rhodes that he trumpeted as a success, for Rhodes agreed not to join Egypt in Antigonus's war against Ptolemy. The Heliopolis was abandoned. Several years later its metal plating was melted down by the Rhodians and used to create the Colossus of Rhodes in celebration of their victory. A statue of Helios, the Greek god of the sun, it stood some 108 feet high (about the same height as the U.S. Statue of Liberty) and was the largest statue of the ancient world. Touted as one of the Seven Wonders of the Ancient World, the statue was destroyed in the earthquake of 226 BCE and never rebuilt.

GRAHAM WRIGHTSON AND SPENCER C. TUCKER

**See also**
Antigonus I Monophthalmus; Demetrius I Poliorcetes; Diadochi, Wars of the; Ptolemy I Soter

**References**
Billows, Richard A. *Antigonus the One-Eyed*. Berkeley: University of California Press, 1990.
Bosworth, A. Brian. *The Legacy of Alexander: Politics, Warfare and Propaganda under the Successors*. Oxford: Oxford University Press, 2002.

# Rhodes, Suleiman's Siege of (July 28–December 21, 1522)

Rhodes is the largest of the Dodecanese Islands in the eastern Mediterranean and lies only about 10 miles from Anatolia. The Knights of St. John (Hospitallers) controlled Rhodes in the 16th century in what was the last Christian holding in the eastern Mediterranean. The Knights of St. John had been in possession of Rhodes since 1310 and over the years had extensively fortified both its harbor and its high ground. The knights used the island, astride major Ottoman shipping lanes, to raid Muslim shipping throughout the eastern Mediterranean. This had led Sultan Mehmed II (the Conqueror) to mount an unsuccessful three-month siege of the island in 1480.

Continued raiding from Rhodes induced Ottoman sultan Suleiman (Süleyman) I to plan a major effort against the island. In 1522 Suleiman assembled some 400 ships, 100,000 men, and heavy siege artillery. On Rhodes the grand master of the Knights of St. John, Auguste de Villiers de L'Isle-Adam, commanded only about 5,700 men: 700 knights drawn from all over Christendom, 500 mercenaries from Crete, 500 Genoese, 50 Venetians, and 4,000 men-at-arms from other places.

The knights did what they could to prepare for the attack. They closed off the entrance to the port with great chains, laid in supplies, and even demolished some buildings to create better fields of fire. Each of the principal defensive positions on the island was held by a particular language grouping.

The Ottoman fleet arrived off Rhodes on June 26. It sailed north and anchored off Parambolino in the north, where the Ottoman troops came ashore uncontested. Among the artillery brought ashore were 40 bombards and 12 large basilisks. The Ottoman engineers took about a month to position their ordnance, opening fire on July 28 with explosive shell in what is believed to have been its first recorded use in battle in history.

When this shelling failed to have the desired effect, at the end of August the Ottomans commenced mining operations. The defenders were well aware of this and dug countermines, setting off explosions against the Ottoman tunnels and venting them to disperse the blasts.

Attempts in early September to take the principal Christian stronghold, commanded by the grand master in person, were unsuccessful. The knights also launched a number of effective counterattacks. Had the Christian powers provided assistance, the Ottomans might have been forced to lift the siege, but the two principal Christian rulers, Holy Roman emperor Charles V and French king François I, were then at war with one another.

Suleiman's forces had suffered heavily in the fighting, and morale among them was low; Suleiman is said to have lost upwards of half his force. In recognition of both the tremendous costs of the siege and the heroic Christian defense, on December 10 he offered to discuss a Christian surrender on honorable terms. The onset of winter, their own precarious position, dwindling numbers and supplies, and unrest among the civilian population all prompted the knights to negotiate. On December 21 an agreement was reached. Suleiman allowed the knights to depart the island with the full honors of war, their arms, their religious relics, and the treasury of the order. Such civilians as wished to leave could also depart and take with them portable possessions.

The knights departed Rhodes on January 1, 1523. The siege had lasted 145 days. Suleiman, at least temporarily, had removed the last serious threat to Ottoman naval power in the eastern Mediterranean and Aegean. For five years the knights were homeless, but they eventually took up residence in Malta, from which they continued to harry Ottoman shipping, inducing Suleiman in 1565 to order military operations against that island, but these were unsuccessful.

SPENCER C. TUCKER

**See also**
Suleiman I

**References**
Brockman, Eric. *The Two Sieges of Rhodes: The Knights of St. John at War, 1480–1522.* New York: Barnes & Noble, 1995.
Kinross, Lord (John Patrick). *The Ottoman Centuries: The Rise and Fall of the Turkish Empire.* New York: William Morrow, 1977.
Prata, Nicholas C. *Angels in Iron.* Huntingdon Valley, PA: Arx Publishing, 1997.

# Richard I, King (1157–1199)

King of England. Richard, the third child of King Henry II of England and Eleanor of Aquitaine, was born at Oxford, England, on September 8, 1157. He received the duchy of Aquitaine in 1168 and Poitiers in 1172 but joined his brothers Henry and John in rebellion against their father during 1173–1174. Richard soon acquired the reputation of a formidable military commander during fighting in France. On the sudden death of his older brother Henry in 1183, Richard became heir to the throne and, on the death of Henry II in 1189, became king of England as Richard I and also inherited his father's lands in France.

Almost immediately on ascending the throne, Richard left to campaign in the Holy Land on the Third Crusade (1189–1192), there to join French king Philippe II Auguste. Betrothed to Philippe's sister and wishing to marry another, Richard secured release from the engagement by a large cash payment and transfer of lands in France.

On his way to the Holy Land, Richard seized Cyprus from the Byzantine Empire. He arrived in Palestine in June 1191, where his goal was to recapture Jerusalem, held by the brilliant Muslim leader Saladin. Richard first besieged and then captured Acre (July 12, 1191), sharing the honor with Philippe II. When Philippe returned to France shortly thereafter, Richard was sole commander of the Christian forces in the Holy Land. After rebuilding Acre, Richard launched a carefully planned movement down the coast against Jaffa (modern-day Tel Aviv, Israel). Ships with provisions accompanied the army along the shore. Saladin sought to attack Richard's 8,500-man army en route but in the Battle of Arsuf (September 7, 1191) was driven off at a cost of 700 crusader casualties against 7,000 Muslims. Arriving at Jaffa a few days later, the crusaders restored the city's defenses, which Saladin had earlier destroyed.

Richard then sought to negotiate a truce with Saladin that would secure joint control of the Holy Land. In the meantime, he strengthened the cities that would protect his supply lines in a possible campaign against Jerusalem. Saladin, however, mounted numerous smaller attacks along Richard's supply lines to wear down Richard's forces. With dissension mounting among his subordinate commanders, Richard also faced treason against him in England on the part of his young brother John in league with Philippe II. Finally, Richard and Saladin reached agreement that would allow Muslims and Christians free access throughout the Holy Land and permit continued Christian control of the coastal strongholds.

On October 9, 1192, Richard departed the Holy Land to return to England. His ship was wrecked in the Adriatic and driven ashore near Venice. Traveling in disguise, Richard was recognized and taken prisoner in Vienna in December by Duke Leopold of Austria, who was allied to Philippe II. Richard was held captive and then turned over to Holy Roman emperor Henry VI until the payment of a large ransom in February 1194. Returning to England, Richard reclaimed his throne and was there crowned a second time on April 7. Almost immediately he again departed in May 1194 for France, where he waged an intermittent campaign against Philippe II. During the next five years, Richard regained all the fortresses and lands taken by the French king earlier. Richard also ordered the strengthening of many castles and the building of others. He was struck in the shoulder by an arrow in the Siege of Châlus in the Limousin. The wound became infected, and he died there on April 6, 1199.

Known as "Richard Coeur de Lion" (Richard the Lionheart), King Richard was a brave and skillful commander of undoubted ability. A careful planner, he well understood the importance of logistics. As king, Richard was, however, largely indifferent to the situation of his people, and he had little impact on English history.

SPENCER C. TUCKER

**See also**
Arsuf, Battle of; Crusades in the Holy Land, Christian; Saladin

**References**
Brundage, James A. *Richard Lion Heart: A Biography.* New York: Scribner, 1974.
Riley-Smith, Jonathan, ed. *The Oxford History of the Crusades, 1189–1311.* New York: Oxford University Press, 1997.

## Richard of Cornwall (1209–1272)

Leader of an English expedition to the Holy Land during 1240–1241 in the wake of that of Thibaud IV of Champagne and later titular king of the Romans (1257–1272). Born on January 5, 1209, at Winchester Castle, Hampshire, England, Richard was the second son of King John of England and was named after his illustrious crusading uncle, King Richard I the Lionheart. The younger Richard was created earl of Cornwall by his older brother, King Henry III, in 1227.

Richard's crusade took place in the context of the political situation in England, which had been disturbed by the revolt of Richard Marshal in 1233. Richard took the cross in 1236 alongside Gilbert Marshal in order to seal a reconciliatory alliance with the Marshal family, also marrying Gilbert's sister Eleanor. The crusade aimed to coincide with the end in 1239 of a 10-year truce with Egypt. Pope Gregory IX granted Richard the use of money raised from vows that had been redeemed by cash payments and from legacies intended for the aid of the Holy Land. This grant was unprecedented, a significant moment in the evolution of crusade finances, as redemptions had previously been granted to individual crusaders, not to a commander.

The proposed English crusade was nearly blown off course by papal politics, in particular the conflict between Richard's brother-in-law, Emperor Frederick II, and Pope Gregory IX. Fearing that Richard's presence in Outremer would further the ambitions of Frederick II (whose son Conrad IV was titular king of Jerusalem) in the East, Gregory attempted to block Richard's departure, or at least to direct his crusade to the defense of the Latin states in Greece or of papal interests in Italy. However, in an oath taken at Northampton in November 1239, the English barons swore not to be turned aside from Outremer. Ironically, Frederick was scarcely more enthusiastic to see English or French armies intervening in "his" Kingdom of Jerusalem, but Richard and the emperor grew closer diplomatically after the former's departure, and Richard seems to have been granted a measure of authority to act in Frederick's name in the East.

Richard's presence in the East was characterized by diplomacy and construction rather than battle. The defeat of Thibaud IV of Champagne by the Egyptian Ayyubids at Gaza (November 13, 1239) and internal dissension within the Kingdom of Jerusalem made any offensive by the crusaders impossible. Richard contented himself with assisting in the reconstruction of the fortifications at Ascalon (modern-day Tel Ashqelon, Israel) and concluding a treaty with the sultan of Egypt confirming the Christian possession of Jerusalem. The impression of Richard's diplomatic achievements was exaggerated by his own skillful propaganda as well as by his achievement in securing the release of French prisoners taken at Gaza. In reality, his efforts could be seen as undermining those of Thibaud before him, who had sensibly negotiated with the Ayyubid sultan of Damascus. Although junior to the sultan of Egypt, only the Damascene sultan was realistically able to dispose of territory in Palestine.

Richard never returned to the East, but his involvement in crusading and his relations with Frederick II may explain his later involvement in affairs overseas. Richard repeatedly turned down papal offers of the crown of Sicily between 1247 and 1254 but assumed the title of king of the Romans in 1257 in an ambitious attempt to make himself Holy Roman emperor. He met Pope Innocent III at Lyons in 1250 as part of negotiations concerning Henry III's proposed crusade, which was later subsumed in papal plans for Henry to intervene in Sicily. Richard later played an important role as adviser to his nephew Edward (the future King Edward I) in the latter's crusade of 1271–1272.

Richard assisted Henry against Simon de Montfort's rebels in the Second Barons' War (1264–1267). In December 1271, Richard suffered a stroke that paralyzed his right side and robbed him of speech. He died on April 2, 1272, at Berkhamsted Castle in Hertfordshire, England.

MICHAEL R. EVANS

#### See also
Crusades in the Holy Land, Christian; Frederick II, Holy Roman Emperor; Gaza, Battle of

#### References
Denholm-Young, Noel. *Richard of Cornwall*. Oxford, UK: Blackwell, 1947.

Lloyd, Simon. *English Society and the Crusades*. Oxford: Oxford University Press, 1988.

Tyerman, Christopher. *England and the Crusades*. Chicago: University of Chicago Press, 1988.

## Ridda Wars (632–633)

Prophet Muhammad died unexpectedly at Medina on June 8, 632. His death sparked a power struggle that developed into what became known as the Ridda Wars or Wars of Apostasy (*ridda*) that lasted until June 633. The success of the Quarish leadership at Medina led by Abu Bakr set the stage for the vast Islamic conquests that followed.

The struggle involved taxes and power. Shortly after Muhammad's death, his follower Omar (Umar) ibn al-Khattab announced the news. Immediately the men of

Medina, who had invited Muhammad and his followers (*muhajirun*) into their city of Medina, began to discuss who should be chosen from among themselves as leader. Before they could take action, however, Umar hailed Abu Bakr, the father of Muhammad's wife Aisha, as the new caliph (Khalifat Allah, meaning "lieutenant of God").

With political power consolidated at Medina, Abu Bakr directed a series of campaigns that forced the rebellious Arab tribes to submission. Most of these had joined Muhammad to share in the booty from conquest. For some, it was a matter of ending the Muslim taxes or of independence. Others, such as the Banu Hanifa of Yamama in eastern Arabia, asserted the claim of their own prophet, a man named Musaylimah.

In August 632, the Bedouin tribes at Dhu al-Qasa some 30 miles east of Medina moved against that city. Abu Bakr after a night march led his forces in a dawn attack that drove the Dhu al-Qassa Bedouins into the desert. In September Abu Bakr put Khalid ibn al-Waleed, an experienced warrior, in charge of the Muslim army. In October he defeated the Dhu al-Qassa Bedouins and their allies the Banu Asad, led by their prophet Talaith at the Battle of Buzaka 60 miles east of Medina.

The Battle of Yamama (the Garden of Death) was fought in December 632 on the sandy plain of Aqaraba in southeastern Nejed. It ended in defeat for Musaylimah and the Banu Hanifa but with significant Muslim losses, many of whom had been companions of Muhammad. In November, Muslim forces led by Hudaifa bin Mihsan defeated the Omani chief Dhul Taj at the Battle of Daba. By February 633 Oman was subdued following the death of Dhul Taj in the Battle of Dibba Al-Baya. By the spring of 633 Yemen was in Muslim control.

The Ridda Wars gave Abu Bakr control of the Arabian Peninsula and its warring tribes.

Andrew J. Waskey

### See also
Bakr, Ahmad Hassan al-

### References
Donner, Fred M., trans. *The History of al-Tabari: The Conquest of Arabia,* Vol. 10. Albany, NY: State University of New York Press, 1993.

Glubb, John Bagot. *The Great Arab Conquests.* New York: Barnes & Noble Books, 1963.

Kennedy, Hugh. *The Great Arab Conquests: How the Spread of Islam Changed the World We Live In.* Philadelphia: Da Capo, 2007.

Shufani, Ilyas. *Al-Riddah and the Muslim Conquest of Arabia.* Toronto: University of Toronto Press, 1973.

## Right of Return, Palestinian

An internationally recognized principle that holds that an ethnic, religious, or national group has the right to settle in—or become a citizen of—the country that it considers to be its homeland, regardless of national changes that may have occurred in that state. Usually, the right of return involves ethnically dispersed or displaced peoples. In the Middle East, it applies to Palestinians who were driven from their homes and homeland during the various Arab-Israeli wars since 1948. The Palestinians' right of return to lands now controlled by Israel has been a perennial sticking point in Arab-Israeli relations and continues to present a major impediment to a lasting peace in the region.

At present there are an estimated 7.2 million Palestinian refugees worldwide, with 4.3 million residing in refugee settlements throughout the Middle East. Most refugees live in the Gaza Strip, the West Bank, Lebanon, Syria, Egypt, Iraq, and Jordan. The vast majority of these refugees were displaced from their ancestral homeland (lands now controlled by Israel) during the 1948–1949 Israeli War of Independence and the 1967 Six-Day War. This number also includes the children and even grandchildren of those first displaced in 1948 and 1967. Palestinians believe that these refugees and their offspring have an unalienable right to return to their homes. In fact, many of them retain legal documents, deeds, and even keys to homes and businesses that they owned prior to the diaspora.

Indeed, the Palestinians' belief that they have an absolute right to return to areas now controlled by Israel is far from unfounded. United Nations (UN) Resolution 194 (specifically Article 11), passed by the General Assembly on December 11, 1948, calls for the return of all refugees from the conflict "at the earliest practicable date." The UN made no distinction between Israeli and Palestinian refugees. Quite naturally, the Palestinians have used this resolution as the linchpin of their right of return. Over the years, the UN has also specified that the right of return applies to both Palestinians and their direct descendants. This stands in contrast to its normal policies regarding refugees, which usually hold that only those actually displaced have a right of return and that the right does not extend to descendants. To bolster their claims further, Palestinians also point to the UN's Universal Declaration of Human Rights, which was adopted on December 10, 1948, just one day prior to UN Resolution 194. That document holds that an individual has the right to "leave any country, including his own, and to return to his country."

But while the Palestinian right of return seems justified based on the various UN dictates, the issue is far more complicated to put into practice, especially after so many years have passed since the Palestinian diaspora. From the Israeli perspective, the issue raises several critical concerns. First, Israel maintains that as a sovereign nation, it must be the sole arbiter of Israeli immigration policy. Arguing that every nation has the right to set its own policies in this regard, the Israelis insist that to surrender to the right of return would involve surrendering a piece of their sovereignty. Second and perhaps more important, the Israeli government claims that allowing 4 million Palestinians to return to Israel would threaten the very survival of the nation and seriously alter the ethnic and national identity of the state. It has repeatedly been argued that relatively few of the 4 million would want to return. However, Israel refused to discuss this issue even with its inclusion in the Oslo Accords, and otherwise liberal negotiators argued that it was Palestinians who were unreasonable in advancing such a position. Many of the property rights that predate the founding of Israel have actually been argued in court and settled in favor of Palestinians, but the government has refused to honor these rulings.

Besides Israeli concerns, there are other potential roadblocks in the right of return. One is certainly determining the Palestinians who became refugees in 1948 and 1967. Another is determining the exact circumstances of their departure. Be that as it may, there are fairly accurate figures for Palestinian refugees that have been kept by the UN over the years. In 1951, for example, the UN determined that there were approximately 860,000 Palestinians who lost their homes, livelihoods, or both as a result of the Arab-Israeli conflict that began in 1948. After Israel annexed the West Bank and the Gaza Strip in 1967, there were an additional 300,000 Palestinians who left their homeland. Most went to neighboring Jordan.

Most Israelis see the right of return as a fundamental issue that is not to be implemented, for to agree to do so would be a tacit admission that their very existence as a people and a nation might be at risk. Indeed, they equate the concept with Israel's destruction. But the likelihood that anywhere near 4 million Palestinians would stream into Israel if the right of return is granted is highly unlikely. A recent survey of Palestinians living in Jordan, Lebanon, the Gaza Strip, and the West Bank indicated that only about 10 percent would actually attempt to return to their homes if allowed. The vast majority preferred to stay where they were or wait for the creation of a bona fide Palestinian nation. Thus, the number of likely Palestinian refugees returning to Israel would be far less than 4 million, perhaps only 1 million to 1.5 million or even fewer. This blunts Israeli assertions that the right of return would drastically alter or destroy their nation. Still, even with this knowledge, many Israelis (even some of whom support a limited right of return) argue that an influx of even several hundred thousand Palestinians would be enormously expensive and would create major challenges in terms of infrastructure, housing, education, health care, etc.

In the final analysis, the right of return continues to stand as a contentious and outstanding issue that would benefit from serious efforts at negotiation. Most Arabs assert that no peace can be brokered without allowing Palestinians the right of return. The 1993 Oslo Accords were negotiated chiefly because both sides consented to take up the issue in future talks. And the 2000 Camp David discussions between Palestine Liberation Organization (PLO) chairman Yasser Arafat and Israeli prime minister Ehud Barak in part broke down because Barak would not consent to a right of return.

PAUL G. PIERPAOLI JR.

**See also**

Arafat, Yasser; Barak, Ehud; Gaza Strip; Israel; Israeli War of Independence; Oslo Accords; Palestine Liberation Organization; Six-Day War; West Bank

**References**

Aruri, Naseer Hasan, ed. *Palestinian Refugees: The Right of Return.* London: Pluto, 2001.

Bowker, Robert. *Palestinian Refugees: Mythology, Identity, and the Search for Peace.* Boulder, CO: Lynne Rienner, 2003.

Ginat, Joseph, Edward J. Perkins, and Hassan bin Talal, eds. *Palestinian Refugees: Traditional Positions and New Solutions.* Norman: University of Oklahoma Press, 2002.

United Nations. *The Right of Return of the Palestinian People.* New York: United Nations, 1979.

# Rogers Plan (December 9, 1969)

Comprehensive peace initiative for the Middle East put forward by U.S. secretary of state William P. Rogers in 1969 in the aftermath of the 1967 Six-Day War. The Rogers Plan was unveiled on December 9, 1969.

Peace efforts in the ongoing Arab-Israeli conflict had been under way since the end of the Six-Day War. On November 22, 1967, some five months after the cessation of hostilities, the United Nations (UN) Security Council passed Resolution 242 calling for the withdrawal of Israeli troops from occupied territories. The following day the Security Council appointed Swedish diplomat Gunnar Jarring as special envoy to the Middle East, with the task of negotiating with all parties concerned in the Middle East dispute. Over the next 18 months, Jarring was unsuccessful in his attempts to hammer out a lasting peace arrangement. In the meantime, the War of Attrition continued to threaten the region with another full-scale war.

With the advent of the Richard Nixon administration in January 1969, the United States began pushing hard for an end to the War of Attrition and, more importantly, a comprehensive peace settlement between Israel and its Arab neighbors. Indeed, Nixon's focus on détente with the Soviet Union played a sizable role in this renewed American commitment to Middle East peace. Because the Soviet Union did not have diplomatic relations with Israel at the time, U.S. policy makers sought to take a tougher line against the Israelis in an effort to curry favor with the Kremlin.

By 1969, the Soviets had presented their own peace plan calling for a bilateral arrangement between Egypt and Israel. In March, Rogers met with Israeli ambassador to the United States Yitzhak Rabin and called for an Israeli withdrawal from occupied territories gained in the Six-Day War. Tel Aviv rejected the request, claiming that such a move offered no guarantee of security from future Arab attacks. Rogers then presented the proposal to the Soviets and Arabs, who refused to deal bilaterally with the Israelis and asked instead for a UN-sponsored proposal.

Hostilities meanwhile continued, with sporadic fighting occurring between Israeli and Egyptian forces. In September 1969, Israeli prime minister Golda Meir visited Washington and consulted personally with Nixon and Rogers. Rabin was also a party to most of the discussions, in which the Israelis informed the Americans that peace proposals without security arrangements were not acceptable. Throughout the fall, Nixon had continued to confer with both Meir and Rabin.

At the same time, the U.S. Department of State was readying a comprehensive peace proposal to be presented to all sides. On December 9, 1969, Rogers took the initiative and unveiled the so-called Rogers Plan in the course of a prescheduled speech. The proposal called for cooperation among the United States, the Soviet Union, the United Kingdom, and France in helping the Jarring Mission arrive at an agreement acceptable to all parties. The plan also envisaged a central role for the UN as per the spirit of Resolution 242. For the first time in U.S.-Israeli relations, such a proposal had not been revealed to the Israelis beforehand. Indeed, both Meir and Rabin were caught off guard by the announcement.

More specifically, the Rogers Plan requested the withdrawal of Israeli forces from Egyptian territory to the heretofore internationally recognized border. Egypt, for its part, would have to commit specifically to a binding peace settlement. The status of Jerusalem would be determined in accordance with consultations among Israel, Jordan, and the international community. The plan also addressed the issue of Palestinian refugees rendered homeless by the 1948 and 1967 wars. Finally, the Rogers Plan reiterated the U.S. commitment to peace and cooperation with all parties concerned in the region.

Immediately after the Rogers speech, Rabin was called home for consultations. On December 22, 1969, Israel formally rejected the Rogers Plan following a contentious cabinet debate. The Israelis refused to consider a proposal that did not address the question of its long-term security. In 1970, 70 U.S. senators and 280 U.S. congressional representatives also rejected the Rogers Plan on the grounds that it ran counter to the interests of Israel. For his part, Egyptian president Gamal Abdel Nasser had also rejected the proposal.

The War of Attrition continued until full-scale war again erupted in the October 1973 Yom Kippur War. In the interim, the failure of both the Jarring Mission and the Rogers Plan strained U.S.-Israeli relations considerably. It was not only the content of the plan that had angered the Israelis. They were also resentful that Rogers had announced it without prior consultation with Tel Aviv.

PATIT MISHRA AND PAUL G. PIERPAOLI JR.

**See also**
Expellees and Refugees, Palestinian; Jarring Mission; Meir, Golda Mabovitch; Nasser, Gamal Abdel; Rabin, Yitzhak; Six-Day War; War of Attrition; Yom Kippur War

**References**
Bailey, Sydney D. *Four Arab-Israeli Wars and the Peace Process.* New York: St. Martin's, 1982.
Dupuy, Trevor N. *Elusive Victory: The Arab-Israeli Wars, 1947–1974.* Garden City, NY: Military Book Club, 2002.
Herzog, Chaim. *The Arab Israeli Wars: War and Peace in the Middle East from the War of Independence to Lebanon.* Westminster, MD: Random House, 1984.

## Rognvald Kali Kolsson (ca. 1099–1158)

Earl of Orkney (1136–1158) and leader of a crusade to the Holy Land in 1151–1153. Born around 1099, Kali Kolsson, as he was originally known, belonged to a family that had ruled Orkney as a semi-independent earldom under the Norwegian Crown since the 10th century. Although he was born in and grew up in Norway, Kali had a claim to the earldom of Orkney through his mother Gunnhild, sister of the martyred earl St. Magnus I Erlendsson (d. 1115).

In 1129 Kali's title to half of Orkney was recognized by Sigurd, king of Norway, and at this time he adopted the name Rognvald after an 11th-century earl. Rognvald contracted an alliance with William the Old, bishop of Orkney, and Maddad, earl of Atholl, who was married to Margaret, sister of the ruling earl, Paul II Hakonsson (1123–1136). This alliance enabled Rognvald to mount a successful invasion of Orkney in 1135, capturing and disposing of Earl Paul. Rognvald's rule as earl was marked by his promotion of the cult of St. Magnus, notably in the construction of a new cathedral dedicated to him at Kirkwall.

In 1150 Rognvald decided to embark on an expedition to the Holy Land. He left Orkney in the charge of Maddad's son Harald, whom he had accepted as joint earl in 1138. Rognvald's decision was influenced by one Eindredi Ungi, a Norwegian with extensive experience in the East who evidently hoped to recruit Norsemen for service in the Varangian units of the Byzantine emperor. The timing of the expedition suggests that it may also have been connected with wider (but ultimately fruitless) efforts in 1150 to launch a new crusade in response to the advances of Nur al-Din in northern Syria.

Rognvald's crusade is described somewhat confusedly in the *Orkneyinga Saga*, but its itinerary can be reconstructed with reasonable certainty. Crusaders from Orkney and Norway, including Bishop William and Eindredi, sailed from Orkney with 15 ships in the summer of 1151 and, after a short stay in Galicia, on to southern France. They wintered in Narbonne, giving military assistance to Aimery, count of Narbonne, against his enemies. Eindredi went on to Constantinople (modern-day Istanbul, Turkey), but Rognvald and the others sailed for the Holy Land in early 1152, capturing en route a Muslim ship. These proved to be the only warlike activities of the Orkney crusaders. In August 1152 they visited Jerusalem and the Jordan River, then returned home via Constantinople, Italy, Denmark, and Norway.

Rognvald arrived in Orkney by Christmas 1153 to find the earldom being disputed between Harald Maddadsson and Paul II's nephew, Erlend III Haraldsson (1151–1154). A period of civil war between the three earls ended in 1154 when Rognvald and Harald joined forces and captured and killed Erlend. Four years later Rognvald was killed, the result of a feud while hunting in Caithness.

ALAN V. MURRAY

**See also**
Crusades in the Holy Land, Christian; Nur al-Din

**References**
Macquarrie, Alan. *Scotland and the Crusades, 1095–1560*. Edinburgh, UK: Donald, 1997.
*The Orkneyinga Saga*. Edited and translated by Alexander B. Taylor. Edinburgh, UK: Oliver and Boyd, 1938.
Taylor, Alexander B. "Studies in the Orkneyinga Saga." *Proceedings of the Orkney Antiquarian Society* 11 (1933): 45–49.
Thomson, William P. L. *History of Orkney*. Edinburgh, UK: Mercat, 1987.

## Romani, Battle of (August 4–5, 1916)

Battle during the 1916 Sinai Campaign. The battle occurred near the town of Romani, 23 miles east of the Suez Canal and 3 miles south of the Mediterranean coast. By late May 1916, the British had established a railhead at Romani as the first step in their planned advance across the Sinai Peninsula. Local Ottoman forces, reinforced with troops fresh from the Ottoman victory on the Gallipoli Peninsula, were determined to disrupt these plans and launch another attack against the Suez Canal.

To this end, an 18,000-strong Ottoman expeditionary force centered on the veteran 3rd Infantry Division set out for Romani in late July under the command of German lieutenant colonel Friedrich Kress von Kressenstein. Progress was slow because of the presence of two Austro-Hungarian heavy artillery batteries and the difficulties of transporting them in sandy terrain. Kressenstein hoped to outflank and then trap and destroy the British garrison at Romani. The heavy guns and a single infantry regiment were to pin down the British defenders while the bulk of his force attempted to attack the British right flank.

British commander Lieutenant General Sir Archibald Murray anticipated Kressenstein's line of attack and had deployed his forces accordingly. An infantry force of 11,000 men centered on the 52nd (Lowland) Division manned the Romani defenses, while about 3,000 men of Major General Henry "Harry" Chauvel's Australian and New Zealand Mounted Division screened the desert expanses to the south of the railhead.

With his mounted troops in the path of the main Ottoman attack, Murray intended to use two brigades to fight a delaying action until it was clear that the Ottoman force was fully committed. Then the remaining two brigades of the Australian and New Zealand Mounted Division were to counterattack and take the Ottomans in the flank. As the Ottoman expedition approached the outskirts of Romani,

Murray reinforced the position and added the British 5th Mounted Brigade to his mounted force.

At 2:00 a.m. on August 4, Kress von Kressenstein launched his main assault. Ottoman infantry and Australian light horsemen shot and bayoneted one another in the darkness as the Ottomans strove to break through to the rear of Romani. The Ottoman attack was pressed home with fierce determination and drove the Australians back farther than Murray had planned. Nonetheless, by midmorning the Australian line was still holding, and the momentum of the Ottoman advance had been halted. At that point, Chauvel ordered the rest of his division and the 5th Mounted Brigade to attack the now-exposed Ottoman left flank. Fighting continued throughout the day, but by nightfall the Ottoman troops were forced to withdraw. Meanwhile, at Romani itself the garrison had come under sustained bombardment, though the Ottoman diversionary attack had been easily contained.

The following day, August 5, the British began their pursuit of the retreating Ottoman troops. To Murray's disappointment, this was not as effective as hoped. The British infantry were unable to meet the required pace under the harsh Egyptian sun, and the task was left to the five mounted brigades, which had already borne the brunt of the battle. For the next five days under increasingly unfavorable and trying conditions, the Australian, New Zealand, and British horsemen harried the Ottoman force as it fell back to prepared positions at Bir el Abd, but they could not destroy it.

Despite this, Romani was still a significant British victory, and the Ottoman Army would never again threaten the Suez Canal. Ottoman casualties numbered some 9,200, of which more than 4,000 were taken prisoner. British casualties totaled 1,130, the bulk of which were Australians.

DAMIEN FENTON

**See also**
Kress von Kressenstein, Friedrich Sigismund Georg; Murray, Sir Archibald James; Sinai Campaign of 1916–1917

**References**
Erickson, Edward J. *Ordered to Die. A History of the Ottoman Army in the First World War.* Westport, CT: Greenwood, 2000.
Gullet, Henry S. *Official History of Australia in the War of 1914–18,* Vol. 7, *The Australian Imperial Force in Sinai and Palestine.* Melbourne, Australia: Government Printer, 1923.
MacMunn, George, and Cyril Falls. *Official History of the Great War: Military Operations, Egypt and Palestine, from the Outbreak of the War with Germany to June 1917.* London: HMSO, 1928.
Powles, Charles G. *Official History of New Zealand's Effort in the Great War,* Vol. 3, *The New Zealanders in Sinai and Palestine.* Wellington, New Zealand: Whitcombe and Tombs, 1922.

# Roman-Parthian Wars (53 BCE–215 CE)

Rome's wars with the Parthian Empire (Arsacid Persia) spanned almost three centuries. Finding a single cause is difficult. Part of the answer lies in the expansionist nature of ancient empires. During the first two centuries BCE, Rome and Persia experienced rapid growth. Therefore, in some sense, they were destined to collide.

But in many early encounters, Rome also took a high-handed approach to diplomacy. Thus, when Persian king Mithridates II dispatched an ambassador to Roman dictator Lucius Cornelius Sulla to open formal relations, Sulla rather infamously treated the envoy as a social inferior, seating him across from one of Rome's minor client-kings. Roman general Lucius Licinius Lucullus used threats and intimidation tactics to ensure Persian neutrality while conducting military operations in Armenia in 69 BCE, and he may even have planted spies in the Persian king's entourage. Finally, in 66 Gnaeus Pompeius Magnus (Pompey the Great) promised the Upper Mesopotamian province of Gordyene to the Armenians, conveniently ignoring the fact that he had already guaranteed the same territory to Persia. When the Persians protested, Pompey ordered forces into Gordyene to clear out Persian settlers by force.

Rome's condescension toward Persia was rooted in beliefs about Roman racial superiority. Most Romans considered Easterners culturally and genetically inferior—even subhuman. The Romans inherited many of these prejudices from the Greeks, who, ever since the Greek Persian Wars, had regarded non-Greeks as barbarians. In the Greco-Roman mind-set, barbarians were thought to be effeminate, decadent, and servile. They were certainly not considered adept warriors or worthy military adversaries. And this, more than any other reason, may be why Sulla, Lucullus, and Pompey initially treated the Persians with such disdain. These same stereotypes also helped motivate Crassus's and Mark Antony's early attempts to conquer Persia (53 and 36 BCE). Both generals believed that the Persians would be easy prey.

The Roman-Parthian Wars began when Roman governor of Syria Marcus Licinius Crassus invaded Persia in 53 BCE. Persia was embroiled in civil war, and one of the parties had asked Rome to intervene. Crassus set out from Antioch with seven legions. However, local guides led the Romans deep into Upper Mesopotamia. Unaccustomed to desert warfare, the Romans stumbled into a Persian ambush near Carrhae. The Persians pressed their advantage with barrages of arrows and heavily armored cavalry shock troops. Most of Crassus's soldiers were casualties; Crassus himself was slain while trying to negotiate his army's surrender. The Battle of Carrhae ranks as one of the most disastrous Roman defeats.

In 37 BCE Phraates IV acceded to the Persian throne. He then secured his position by murdering all 30 of his brothers. He also persecuted the Persian nobility, who again turned to the Romans for relief. Mark Antony, whose purview at the time included the eastern Roman Empire, believed that a Persian victory would help him in his propaganda war against Octavian. But on campaign Antony became preoccupied besieging Praaspa, a stronghold in Media Atropatene. Poor logistical planning and allied desertions allowed Phraates to capture the Roman baggage train. Inadequately provisioned, Antony was forced to call off the siege. On the long march home, harried by the Persians and plagued by disease and shortage of water, the Romans lost almost 25,000 soldiers.

Now emperor, Octavian Augustus could not afford another eastern war; Rome's civil wars had sapped the empire's manpower. He also wished to avoid the mistakes of both Crassus and Antony. Octavian therefore negotiated with Persia and in 20 BCE gave assurances that Rome would respect the Euphrates boundary and not attempt another invasion. In exchange, the Persians returned Crassus's military standards and accepted Roman hegemony over Armenia, which served as a buffer zone between the empires. Although Octavian had earned no military victory, the return of the standards inspired jubilation in Rome. Octavian even celebrated a triumph and housed the recovered standards in the temple of Mars the Avenger.

The disasters at Carrhae and Praaspa changed Roman perceptions about Persia. This new view, combined with losses that Rome sustained during its civil wars, persuaded Octavian that conquering Persia outright was no longer a feasible option. He therefore turned to diplomacy. But while the return of the Roman standards bought a century of peace, it came with a cost. Although the Armenian buffer zone helped end the cycle of invasions and retaliatory raids so characteristic of the Late Republic, it was only a temporary fix. And when conflict resumed at the end of the first century, Rome's stake in Armenia actually exacerbated affairs in the East by giving the two superpowers another point of contention.

The return of the Roman standards also gave Rome a military advantage vis-à-vis Persia. This was partly the result of Persia's almost incessant state of civil war. Without the threat of Roman invasion, Persia's royal family, the Arsacids, occupied much of their free time feuding with each other. Constant civil unrest alienated Persia's nobility, who in turn incited their own rebellions. By the time of Trajan's invasion in 114, the Persian state was in such disarray that it was only able to offer nominal resistance.

Moreover, the peace under Octavian's rule also gave Rome time to learn from its Late Republican errors. By the second century, Roman commanders no longer underestimated Persia's cavalry capabilities or Mesopotamia's environment. Trajan and his later imitators employed larger cavalry contingents to negate the Persians' mobility advantage. The Romans began to develop heavily armored cavalry in imitation of the Persians. Many of Trajan's successors also followed his well planned invasion route down the Euphrates to ensure that their armies had a constant water supply.

Rome's friendly relations with Persia, begun by Octavian, continued for half a century. But when Nero became emperor in 54 CE, the Persian king Vologaeses I decided to test the young ruler's resolve. Violating the treaty, Vologaeses installed his brother, Tiridates, on the Armenian throne. In response, Nero dispatched Gnaeus Domitius Corbulo to the East. Although Corbulo drove the Persians out of Armenia twice, the surrender of Corbulo's cocommander, Caesennius Paetus, in 62 forced Nero to compromise. Nero agreed to recognize Tiridates as Armenia's king and even held an elaborate investiture ceremony in Rome.

By the second century, fear of slacking legionary discipline and desire for personal aggrandizement led emperors to revive Rome's earlier more belligerent attitude toward the East. Starting with Trajan, emperors began rushing to war for even insignificant diplomatic slights. Trajan's war (114–117), for instance, began as a relatively minor quarrel over Armenian succession when Persian king Osroes deposed Armenia's ruler without first consulting Rome. Osroes soon regretted his decision, however, when it became clear that Rome was mobilizing for a full-scale invasion. Osroes tried to backpedal, offering Trajan a different pro-Roman candidate. However, the emperor ignored the offer and invaded Persia anyway. Thus, scholars believe that Trajan used the Armenian crisis as a pretext and that his real motive was personal glory.

Trajan's eastern campaign of 114–117 ushered in a new phase in Romano-Persian relations. Trajan shunned the Julio-Claudians' diplomatic compromises, preferring instead to conquer Persia outright. He invaded Armenia in 114, deposed its pro-Persian monarch, and organized the kingdom into a Roman province. He then did the same to Upper Mesopotamia. For these victories, the Senate awarded Trajan the title "Optimus Princeps" (Best Citizen).

Having met little resistance, Trajan decided to attack Ctesiphon. In 116 his army marched south along the Euphrates accompanied by a Roman supply fleet in the river. North of the capital, Trajan transferred his flotilla overland to the Tigris. The size of the Roman army unnerved the Persian king, who fled, abandoning his family and golden throne to Trajan.

Trajan, however, had difficulty consolidating his new provinces. Soon after Ctesiphon's fall, anti-Roman revolts broke out in Mesopotamia, Armenia, and Judaea. When Trajan died on his way home in 117 CE, his successor, Hadrian, relinquished Rome's claims beyond the Euphrates.

A half century later another dispute over Armenia sparked a new war during 163–165, under the coemperors Marcus Aurelius and Lucius Verus. Verus's commanders, Statius Priscus and Avidius Cassius, relied heavily on Trajan's strategy. Priscus occupied Armenia first, and then Cassius followed Trajan's route down the Euphrates. After sacking Seleucia, Cassius stormed Ctesiphon and burned the Persian king's palace. A sudden outbreak of plague, however, forced the Romans to withdraw.

Septimius Severus fought two campaigns in Mesopotamia. The first, in 195, was a punitive expedition against local rulers who had supported Severus's political rival, Pescennius Niger. The next year while Severus was in Gaul, the Persian king reclaimed his lost territory and raided Syria. Severus's second Mesopotamian expedition in 197, which also followed Trajan's course, was therefore aimed at Persia's heart. After minimal resistance, Severus again captured Ctesiphon.

Severus's son Caracalla, who styled himself as a new Alexander the Great, also attacked Persia during 215–216 and may have taken Persia's capital after luring King Artabanus V into a trap. However, Caracalla's own guards assassinated him soon afterward. The emperor's sudden death spurred Artabanus to counterattack. After a heated three-day battle near Nisibis, the new Roman emperor, Macrinus, retreated ignominiously. Artabanus forced Macrinus to pay 200 million sesterces to secure the Romans' safe withdrawal.

The Persian king's good fortune did not last long. A revolt led by the "Neo-Persian" Ardashir ended in the ouster in 224 of Artabanus V, the last Arsacid ruler of Persia. Henceforth, Rome's contests in the East were not with the Arsacids but instead with Ardashir's successors, the Sassanid dynasty. The Romans were not responsible for ending the Arsacid dynasty—the internal revolt had accomplished this—but Rome's numerous second-century invasions and repeated sacking of Ctesiphon directly contributed to the Arsacids' downward spiral and eventual collapse.

JOHN POIROT

**See also**
Caesar, Gaius Julius; Carrhae, Battle of; Crassus, Marcus Licinius; Parthian Empire; Septimius Severus, Emperor; Trajan

**References**
Bennett, Julian. *Trajan: Optimus Princeps.* Rev. ed. Bloomington: Indiana University Press, 2001.
Campbell, Brian. "War and Diplomacy: Rome and Parthia, 31 BC–AD 235." In *War and Society in the Roman World,* ed. John Rich and Graham Shipley, 213–240. London: Routledge, 1993.
Isaac, Benjamin. *The Limits of Empire: The Roman Army in the East.* Rev. ed. Oxford, UK: Clarendon, 1992.
Mattern, Susan P. *Rome and the Enemy: Imperial Strategy in the Principate.* Berkeley: University of California Press, 1999.

## Roman-Sassanid Wars (232–440)

In 224 CE the Persian Empire's Arsacid dynasty was supplanted by the Sassanids, a dynasty from Fars or Pars (Greek Persis). The Sassanids proved much more aggressive toward Rome. This came at a particularly bad time for the Roman Empire, which was then being torn by civil war and facing Germanic invasions. The first Sassanid king, Ardashir I (r. 224–242), raided both Mesopotamia and Syria in 230. He also demanded the cession of all former territories wrested from Persia by Rome.

Rome rejected the Persian demands, and in 232 Emperor Alexander Severus took the field. Proceeding from Antioch, he marched against the Sassanid capital of Ctesiphon, south of modern-day Baghdad, but the Persians defeated another Roman army, and the Romans sustained additional losses during a retreat in Armenia. There was also a mutiny in the Roman legion in Syria with an attempt to place another ruler on the throne, but Alexander Severus put it down and went on to celebrate a triumph in Rome in 233.

There was only a brief respite, for Ardashir resumed his attacks during 238–240. The Sassanids took several cities in Syria and Mesopotamia. Among these were Carrhae and Nisibis, taken by Ardashir's son, Shapur.

Ardashir died in 242, but the fighting continued under his son, Shapur I, who reigned from 242 to 270, although some sources have him as a coregent from 240. In 242 young

Roman emperor Gordian III set out against the Sassanians with a large force. The Romans passed the winter in Antioch while Shapur was busy putting down unrest in Khwarezm and Gilan. Under Gordian, the Romans won a number of battles and recaptured Carrhae and Nisibis before defeating a Sassanian army at Resaena. Gordian subsequently invaded eastern Mesopotamia with the intention of taking Ctesiphon. The Romans proceeded down the Euphrates but were blocked by the Sassanids short of their goal in the Battle of Misiche in early 244 and defeated. Gordian was killed in battle, although it is not clear that it was here. His successor, Philip (r. 244–249), was well aware of the need to proceed to Rome to secure his accession and hastily concluded peace with the Sassanids. This included recognition of Armenia as being within the Persian sphere of influence and payment of a considerable indemnity in gold to the Persians. His power secure, Philip subsequently violated the treaty and seized lost territory.

Shapur I invaded Mesopotamia in 250, but trouble arose in Khorasan, and Shapur I had to shift there before resuming his invasion of the eastern Roman territories. In 253 he defeated a Roman army said to number some 60,000 men in the Battle of Barbalissos. Shapur then laid waste to the Roman province of Syria, capturing Antioch among other Syrian cities.

Shapur I then reconquered Armenia and incited Anak the Parthian to murder king of Armenia Khosrov II in 252. Anak was, however, soon murdered by Armenian nobles. Shapur then made his son Hormizd I king of Armenia. With Armenia now part of the Sassanian Empire, Georgia soon followed suit.

Emperor Valerian (r. 253–260) marched against Shapur. In 257 he recovered Antioch and again secured Roman control of Syria, only to be badly defeated and taken prisoner by Shapur in the Battle of Edessa in 260. A commemorative Persian relief and inscription (the *Res Gestae Divi Saporis*) at Naqsh-e-Rostam boasts of Shapur I's humbling the "caesars" Gordian III, Philip, and Valerian. Shapur then advanced into Asia Minor. He captured Caesarea in modern Israel, then deported its citizens to the southern Sassanian provinces.

Shapur then invaded Anatolia but was there defeated by Septimius Udaynath (Latinized as Odenathus), who had been granted Roman citizenship and was ruling Palmyra. Shapur then plundered eastern Syria. Odaenathus stayed on the side of Rome; assuming the title of king, he led the Palmyrene Army and attacked and defeated the Persians before they could cross the Euphrates to the eastern bank.

Odenathus then sided with Emperor Gallienus, son of Valerian, who ruled with his father from 253 and alone from 260 to 268. Gallienus's succession was contested by Fulvius Macrianus. Odenathus crushed the rebellion, whereupon Gallienus had little choice but to confirm Odenathus as ruler in the east.

In 262, Odenathus crossed the Euphrates and recovered Carrhae and Nisibis. He then drove on Ctesiphon, laying siege to the Persian capital in 264. The city withstood the siege, and Odenathus was obliged to withdraw. Nonetheless, he had retaken all the Roman territory in the east occupied by the Persians since 252.

Odenathus died in 268, and his widow, Queen Zenobia, ruling for her young son Vaballathus, developed imperial ambitions and invaded Roman Syria and Egypt. Emperor Aurelian (r. 270–275) defeated Zenobia and returned the "Palmyrene Empire" to the Roman Near East.

The Sassanids suffered from their own dynastic strife in the 270s–280s, preventing the Persian Empire from further aggression. Roman emperor Carus (r. 282–283) mounted an expedition against Persia but died and was succeeded by his son Numerian (r. 283–284), who was forced to retreat. Numerian's successor Diocletian (r. 284–305) and his caesar Galerius (293–305, then augustus during 305–311) renewed the Roman war against the Persian Empire around 296. The winner of a dynastic conflict in the Sassanid Empire, Narses (r. 293–302), proved to be an aggressive ruler. Galerius's initial expedition suffered a defeat somewhere between Callinicum and Carrhae. In 297, however, Garlerius successfully swept through Armenia, defeating Narses's forces. In 298 Galerius campaigned through Mesopotamia, capturing Ctesiphon and the Sassanid king's family. Narses was forced to sue for peace, agreeing to the Peace of Nisibis in 299 in which he conceded to the Romans all territory up to the Tigris, which became the boundary of the Roman and Persian Empires. With this victory and settlement, Galerius had avenged the defeat and capture of Valerian in 260 and restored Roman prestige. The Arch of Galerius at Thessalonica boasts of Galerius's conquest of Mesopotamia.

During the Tetrarchic civil warfare of 306–313 and most of the reign of Constantine I (r. 306–337), the Sassanid Persians were not a threat. Sassanid king Hormizd II (r. 303–309), the son of Narses, was succeeded by Shapur II (Shapur the Great, r. 309–379), who ascended the throne as an infant. Reaching adulthood, Shapur II developed more aggressive intentions toward Rome, allegedly breaking the Treaty of Nisibis in 337. In his last years Constantine seems to have planned a war against Persia, perhaps motivated by religion, hoping to avenge Sassanid persecution of Christians within the Persian Empire. Constantine died from natural causes as he was setting out for this expedition, so little is known about his exact plans.

What is certain is that Constantine's son, Constantius II (r. 337–361), inherited this conflict and waged war off and on with the Persian Empire during 337–350 and 358–361, mainly in the form of siege warfare. Notable engagements were the Battle of Singara and the Siege of Amida in 359. Constantius elevated his cousins Gallus and then Julian to the rank of caesar to take command while he fought Magnentius and then the Persians. Gallus fell to an alleged conspiracy, but Julian's military success in Gaul resulted in his being acclaimed augustus by his troops. The Roman Empire was on the brink of civil war when Constantius died from an illness in 361.

Julian (r. 361–363) succumbed to the ambition of his predecessors Crassus, Mark Antony, Trajan, Septimius Severus, Caracalla, Valerian, and Galerius in hoping to conquer the Persian Empire in imitation of Alexander the Great's achievement. Though Julian defeated the Persians at Ctesiphon, overall his expedition in 363 was pyrrhic, being costly for the Roman Army and fatal for Julian. Burning his fleet and leading his army farther into Sassanid territory, Julian died from a wound received in battle. He had no heir, and the army elevated Jovian (r. 363–364), a guards officer distinguished mainly for his great stature. To extricate the Roman Army from Julian's fiasco, Jovian made a humiliating peace with the Persians, ceding back to them the Roman territories won by Galerius. Jovian died soon after in 364, suffocated by fumes from a charcoal brazier in his bedroom.

The reigns of Valentinian (r. 364–375) and Valens (r. 364–378) were marked by a return to status quo conflict and negotiation with Persia, principally over Armenia, long a buffer client state of either empire. During the conflicts of the fifth-century Roman Empire Sassanid Persia was not an active threat, waging only two short conflicts with Rome in 421–422 and 440.

Conflict with Persia would resume in the sixth century, particularly in the reign of Byzantine emperor Justinian (r. 527–565). Emperor Heraclius (r. 610–641) inflicted the most extensive Byzantine conquests in Sassanid territory that were then lost to the Arab conquest in the 630s and 640s.

Rome and Persia influenced each other during the third century CE and later, seen in both empires' adoption of heavily armored cavalry (*cataphractarii*) and in general the Roman Empire's increasing reliance on cavalry. Whether features of Later Roman imperial ceremonial, such as prostration (adoration of the purple), was derived from Persian influence or from Hellenistic practices is uncertain.

SARA E. PHANG AND SPENCER C. TUCKER

### See also
Alexander Severus, Roman Emperor; Ardashir I; Constantine I; Galerius, Roman Emperor; Gordian III, Emperor; Jovian; Julian, Emperor; Odenathus; Palmyra; Valens, Emperor; Valerian, Emperor; Zenobia

### References
Dodgeon, M. H., and S. N. C. Lieu. *The Roman Eastern Frontier and the Persian Wars (AD 226–363): A Documentary History.* London: Routledge, 1991.

Frye, Richard N. "The Sassanians." In *Cambridge Ancient History,* Vol. 9, *The Crisis of Empire, A.D. 193–337,* 461–480. Cambridge: Cambridge University Press, 2005.

Lendon, J. E. *Soldiers and Ghosts: A History of Battle in Classical Antiquity.* New Haven, CT: Yale University Press, 2005.

Lenski, Noel. *Failure of Empire: Valens and the Roman State in the Fourth Century AD.* Berkeley: University of California Press, 2002.

Potter, David S. *The Roman Empire at Bay: AD 180–395.* London: Routledge, 2004.

## Roman-Seleucid War
*See* Syrian-Roman War

## Rommel, Erwin Johannes Eugen (1891–1944)

German Army general who played a prominent role in the World War II North Africa Campaign but was defeated in Egypt. Born in Heidenheim, Württemberg, on November 15, 1891, Erwin Johannes Eugen Rommel joined the German Army as an officer cadet in 1910. Graduating from officers training school at Danzig (present-day Gdansk, Poland), he was commissioned in January 1912.

Rommel was wounded in September 1914 during the World War I German invasion of France. On his recovery he fought with distinction on the Romanian and Italian fronts. In the Battle of Caporetto (October 24–November 12, 1917) his men took 9,000 Italian troops prisoner and captured 81 guns. Promoted to captain, he was also awarded the Pour le Mérite.

Rommel remained in the Reichswehr after the war. He commanded an infantry regiment, then was an instructor in the Infantry School during 1929–1933. There he wrote

*Infantry Attacks,* a textbook on infantry tactics based on his World War I experiences. After commanding an infantry battalion, he taught briefly at the War Academy in 1938 and then had charge of Chancellor Adolf Hitler's army security detachment.

Rommel used his access to Hitler to secure command of the 7th Panzer Division in 1940, leading it in spectacular fashion in the invasion of France (May 10–July 11). Promoted to Generalleutnant in February 1941, Rommel received command of the Afrika Korps (German forces sent in Libya). An aggressive, bold commander, he employed his German and Italian forces in daring attacks and was tenacious in battle. Rommel's skill as a field commander earned him the sobriquet "Desert Fox." Promoted to General der Panzertruppen in July 1941 and Generaloberst in January 1942, Rommel was elevated to Generalfeldmarschall (field marshal) in June 1942.

Rommel's drive into Egypt was halted by British Empire forces under General Claude Auchinleck in the First Battle of El Alamein (July 1–27, 1942), some 66 miles west of Alexandria. Rommel's forces were then defeated by British forces under General Bernard Montgomery's Eighth Army in the Second Battle of El Alamein (October 23–November 11, 1942). Driven westward, Rommel conducted a skillful withdrawal west across Lybia and into Tunisia. Returning to Germany for reasons of health, he was assigned on his recuperation as commander of Army Group B with responsibility for northern Italy. He then had charge of the German coastal defenses, where he worked to strengthen the so-called Atlantic Wall.

Appointed commander of Army Group B in France in January 1944, Rommel believed, based on his experiences in France, that if an Allied invasion was to be stopped it would have to be at the beach, but his superior, German commander in chief, West, Generalfeldmarschall Karl Rudolf Gerd von Rundstedt and Hitler disagreed, planning to draw the Allies inland and destroy them in maneuver warfare.

When the invasion occurred (June 6, 1944), Rommel was in Germany. He was badly wounded on July 17, 1944, in an air attack that caught his staff car on the road. Not a fanatic Nazi, Rommel grew despondent over Hitler's estrangement from reality but failed in his efforts to convince Hitler that the war was lost. Approached about joining in a plot to overthrow Hitler, Rommel refused to participate but also failed to inform the authorities. In the aftermath of the unsuccessful attempt on Hitler's life, Rommel was given the choice of a trial for treason or suicide. He chose the latter, dying of poison near Ulm on October 14, 1944, and was accorded a full military funeral, the German government claiming that he had died of battle wounds.

Annette Richardson

**See also**
El Alamein, First Battle of; El Alamein, Second Battle of

**References**
Douglas-Home, Charles. *Rommel.* New York: Saturday Review Press, 1973.
Fraser, David. *Knight's Cross: A Life of Field Marshal Erwin Rommel.* New York: HarperCollins, 1994.
Heckmann, Wolf. *Rommel's War in Africa.* Translated by Stephen Seago. Garden City, NY: Doubleday, 1981.
Lewin, Ronald. *Rommel as Military Commander.* London: Batsford, 1968.
Rutherford, Ward. *The Biography of Field Marshal Erwin Rommel.* London: Hamlyn, 1981.
Young, Desmond. *Rommel.* London: Collins, 1967.

## Rum, Sultanate of (1080–1307)

Islamic sultanate in Anatolia (Asia Minor), with its capital first at Nicaea (modern-day Iznik, Turkey) and then at Ikonion (modern-day Konya), ruled by a branch of the Seljuk family from 1080/1081 to 1307/1308. The name Rum, deriving from the Bilad al-Rum of Muslim authors, relates to the formerly Rhomaic (i.e., Byzantine) territories of Anatolia. Indeed, the Sultanate of Rum occupied central and eastern Anatolia.

The sultanate's foundation and consolidation period is intertwined with the careers of the able Sulayman I ibn Qutlumush, who perished fighting against a large Great Seljuk coalition in 1085 or 1086, and with Qilij Arslan I, who lost his capital of Nicaea to the Byzantines in 1097 during the First Crusade (1096–1099). The latter faced the crusade of 1101 in coalition with the Danishmendids, winning two important victories at Mersivan and Herakleia, but then met his death in Syria against Seljek ruler Riwan of Aleppo in 1107. By the early 12th century, the Seljuks of Rum had moved their capital to the Cappadocian town of Ikonion, from which comes the alternative appellation of their state as Sultanate of Konya.

For most of the 12th century the sultans of Rum had to wage wars against their Anatolian rivals, the Turkophone Danishmendids of Caesarea in Cappadocia (modern-day Kayseri) and Sebasteia (modern-day Sivas) as well as against the Byzantine Empire. The sultans also faced attacks by the Christian armies of the Second Crusade (1147–1149) and the Third Crusade (1189–1192). Under the Komnenian emperors Alexios I and John II (ca. 1112–1140), the Byzantines succeeded in wresting from the Seljuks a significant section of their former western and northwestern Anatolian possessions. However, Seljuk-Byzantine relations then went through fluctuating phases, especially in the reigns of Qilij Arslan II of Rum and Manuel I Komnenos of Byzantium. In 1161–1162 the sultan was magnificently received in Constantinople, but the treaty concluded was soon proven a dead letter, for in 1173–1174 Qilij Arslan II made a pact with bitter Byzantine enemy Holy Roman emperor Frederick I Barbarossa. Shortly afterward the sultan thwarted Manuel I's invasion of Rum (1174–1175) by defeating him at the Battle of Myriokephalon in September 1176.

Qilij Arslan II crowned his successes by annexing the two Danishmendid emirates in 1174–1178, though his final years were spent in agonizing strife, as his sons bickered over the succession. In the course of the Third Crusade (1189–1192), Qilij Arslan II lost his capital to the armies of Frederick I and soon afterward died a broken man, naming as his successor one of his younger sons, Kay-Khusraw I. It was during this period that the Byzantine Empire failed to exploit its contacts with the Zangids; a firm alliance with Nur al-Din (d. 1174) might have prevented its defeat at Myriokephalon, while a more effective collaboration with Saladin (with whom the last Komnenos, Andronikos I, and the first Angelos, Isaac II, signed treaties between 1184/1185 and 1192) might have led to a gradual reconquest of Asia Minor, most of which had been lost to the Rum Seljuks by the late 12th century.

From the late 12th to the late 13 centuries there was considerable social, institutional, cultural, and artistic contact and interplay between Rum Seljuks and Anatolian Christians, mostly evidenced by the phenomenon of mixed marriages that prove both were not only opponents in battlefields but also shared a common cultural heritage.

In his first reign Kay-Khusraw I attempted to expand his territories at the expense of the Byzantine Empire, but he was temporarily toppled by his brother Rukn al-Din Sulayman Shah II, who continued his brother's policy and also attacked Cilician Armenia and Georgia but died suddenly while preparing a major expedition in the Caucasus. Meanwhile the exiled Kay-Khusraw I, who had found refuge in Constantinople in 1197–1203/1204, was reinstated at Ikonion. Since his Byzantine benefactors, the Angeloi, had been toppled in 1204, he became hostile toward their successors at Nicaea, the Laskarids, as well as to the latter's allies, the Cilician Armenians. He succeeded in capturing the important southern Anatolian port of Attaleia (modern-day Antalya) in 1207, but in 1211 the Seljuks were defeated at Antioch on the Maeander by the Laskarids and their Italian mercenaries, and Kay-Khusraw I was killed.

The operations of Kay-Khusraw's successors were directed mainly against the Grand Komnenoi of the empire of Trebizond, from whom Kay-Kawus I (r. 1211–1220) took Sinope in 1214, but the Seljuk army of Kay-Qubadh I (r. 1220–1237) failed to capture Trebizond in 1222–1223 (a previous unsuccessful attempt having taken place in 1205–1206). Kay-Qubadh also faced attacks from John III Doukas Vatatzes of Nicaea between 1222–1225 and 1231, and he also led an expedition against Crimea (1227–1228) and participated in an eastern alliance that defeated the Khwarazm Shah Jalal ad-Din Mangubirtī in 1231.

The brunt of the imminent Mongol invasion of Anatolia, however, was reserved for Kay-Qubadh's successor, Kay-Khusraw II, shortly after an internal religious insurrection led by Baba Isaq (1240/1241) had threatened the Rum throne. On June 26, 1243, the Mongol Ilkhans under Baidju crushed the forces of the Rum Seljuks and their Latin and Trapezuntine allies at Satala (modern-day Köse Dağ). It was now too late for the Nicaean-Seljuk alliance of August 1243 to be effective, and from then onward the Rum Sultanate declined to the status of a protectorate of the Mongol Ilkhanid empire, in which most of the sultans were mere puppets in the hands of Ilkhanid governors.

The period from the mid-13th century, with a long list of ineffectual Seljuk nominal sultans, witnessed a gradual spread of Turkoman emirates (beyliks) in Anatolia. The most powerful of these developed into the Ottoman Empire.

ALEXIOS G. C. SAVVIDES

**See also**
Basian, Battle of; Crusades in the Holy Land, Christian; Frederick I or Frederick Barbarossa; Myriokephalon, Battle of; Nur al-Din; Saladin; Seljuk Dynasty

**References**
Cahen, Claude. *Pre-Ottoman Turkey, c. 1071–1330.* London: Sidgwick & Jackson, 1968.
Kafesoğlu, İbrahim. *History of the Seljuks.* Ed. Gary Leiser. Carbondale: Southern Illinois University Press, 1988.
Köprülü, Mehmed Fuad. *The Seljuks of Anatolia: Their History and Culture according to Local Muslim Sources.* Salt Lake City: University of Utah Press, 1992.
Langdon, J. *Byzantium's Last Imperial Offensive in Asia Minor, 1222 or 1225 to 1231.* New Rochelle, NY: Caratzas, 1992.
Rice, Tamara Talbot. *The Seljuks in Asia Minor.* London: Thames & Hudson, 1961.
Savvides, Alexios G. C. *Byzantium in the Near East: Its Relations with the Seljuk Sultanate of Rum in Asia Minor, the Armenians of Cilicia and the Mongols, A.D. c. 1192–1237.* Thessaloniki: Byzantine Research Centre, 1981.

Savvides, Alexios G. C. "Kilij Arslan I of Rum, Byzantines, Crusaders and Danishmendids." *Byzantiaka* 21 (2000): 365–377.

Savvides, Alexios G. C. "Suleyman Shah of Rum, Byzantium, Cilician Armenia and Georgia, A.D. 1197–1204." *Byzantion* 73 (2003): 96–111.

# Russo-Ottoman Wars (1676–1911)

The Russian Empire and the Ottoman Empire shared a long border and were rivals for centuries. They competed for territory and influence in the Balkans, the Crimea, the Caucasus, and Central Asia. Although the two empires were often in conflict with each other because of their alliances with other Great Powers in Europe, the early Russo-Ottoman Wars were caused mainly by Russia's desire to establish a warm-water port on the Black Sea, which lay under Ottoman control.

### Early History

The first formal diplomatic contact between the Ottomans and what was then the principality around Moscow known as Moscovy occurred in 1492 when the Muscovite embassy arrived at Istanbul (Constantinople) to discuss trade. Early Russo-Ottoman relations were marked by clear distinction in status between the powerful Ottoman state and the rising Russian principality. The sultans refused Russian offers of alliance and oftentimes relegated Russian affairs to their vassal khans of the Crimea, who conducted periodic raiding expeditions in the southern provinces of Muscovy. By the mid-16th century, however, Muscovite Rus became strong enough to resist the Crimean Khanate, and Tsar Ivan IV (r. 1533–1584) destroyed the Kazan and Astrakhan Khanates, important allies of the Crimean Tatars, in 1552–1556.

Since the Black Sea was bordered by the Ukraine to the north, Ukraine was an area of constant struggle between Russia, Poland, the Ottoman Empire, and the Don Cossacks for most of the 17th century. In 1637–1642 the Don Cossacks captured Azov, an important Ottoman fortress, which they offered to Tsar Mikhail of Russia; the first Romanov ruler declined it, however, to avoid a direct conflict with the Porte.

### The Russo-Ottoman War of 1676–1681

In 1654 following a powerful Cossack uprising against Poland, Russia signed the Treaty of Pereyaslav with the Cossacks. This granted Russia control over parts of eastern Ukraine. The Russian expansion, however, provoked a war with Poland and the Crimean Khanate, supported by the Ottoman Empire. In 1672 the Ottoman Army occupied parts of southern Ukraine, and a preliminary contest between Russia and the Ottoman Turks began in 1676 after the Cossacks, under Ivan Samoilovich, hetman of the Left-Bank Ukraine, asked for Russian assistance against the Ottomans, who supported his rival Hetman Petro Doroshenko. The Russian army, supported by Ukranian allies, captured the Cossack capital of Chyhyryn in 1676. The following year Ibrahim Pasha led a large Ottoman army in an invasion of Ukraine. It besieged Chyhyryn, although Russian attack soon forced it to retreat. In 1678 the Ottomans again besieged Chyhyryn, capturing it in August. During the next two years, the two sides limited their actions to raids and border attacks before the Treaty of Bakhchisarai, signed in 1681, established a buffer zone between the Ottoman and Russian-controlled regions of Ukraine.

### Russo-Ottoman War of 1686–1700

In 1686 in the wake of the Ottoman defeats against the Holy League (the Habsburgs, Venice, Poland and the Papacy), Russia, under regent Sofia Alekseyevna, joined the war and organized two invasions led by Prince Vasily Golitsyn, of the Crimean Khanate, in 1687 and 1689. Both ended disastrously for Russian arms, contributing to a discontent that resulted in the ouster of Sofia by her brother Peter. In 1695, Peter I (the Great) took personal command of a force that sought to capture the Ottoman fortress of Azov on the northern shore of the Sea of Azov, an inlet of the Black Sea.

Most of the Russian troops approached the area by traveling down the Don and Volga Rivers. Because the Russians had no navy, however, they were unable to cut off Ottoman access by water to Azov, and the Ottoman defenders turned back the Russians with heavy losses. Peter then took a year to build a navy at the Don River city of Voronezh.

In the spring of 1696, the Russians again approached Azov with some 75,000 men. This time, half the force traveled in the new warships down the river, and half proceeded overland. As the land force engaged the fortress's defenders, the naval force was able to defeat the Ottoman warships and blockade the fortress from the sea. The Russians captured the city on July 28, 1696. The Treaty of Constantinople of 1700 compelled the Porte to acknowledge Russian control of the fortresses of Azov, Taganrog, Pavlovsk, and Mius.

### Russo-Ottoman War of 1711 (the Pruth Campaign)

Encouraged by his military success against the Swedes, whom he crushed in the Battle of Poltava in 1709, Peter decided to force the Ottomans to open Constantinople and the straits to Russian commerce and gain free passage to the Mediterranean Sea. Hoping to incite an anti-Ottoman rebellion among the Orthodox Christian population of the Danubian Principalities (Walacia, Moldavia, and Bessarabia), Peter launched an ill-prepared campaign in the basin of the Pruth River, where he was defeated at Stanileshti (July 1711) and was surrounded by Ottoman (and Crimean) forces under Grand Vizier Baltaci Mehmet Pasha. On July 21, 1711, Peter accepted the Treaty of Pruth. It required him only to restore Azov and its surrounding territory back to the Ottomans. Considering Peter's desperate situation, the Ottomans certainly missed an opportunity for greater concessions.

**Russo-Ottoman War of 1735–1739**
In 1735 after a long period of occupation with European rather than Ottoman affairs, Russia, in league with the Habsburgs and Persia, declared a new war on the Ottomans. It came in the wake of the War of the Polish Succession (1733–1738), which had seen raids by the Crimean Tatars. Russian troops under Field Marshal Burkhard Christoph von Munnich and General Peter Lacy twice invaded the Crimea. They captured Perekop, Azov, and Ochakov but were later forced to retreat owing to logistical difficulties and an epidemic of the plague. In 1739 the Russians advanced into southern Ukraine, defeating the Ottomans at Stavuchany and capturing Khotin and Yassy. Meanwhile, the Hasburgs, whose troops had been less successful than those of Russia, were forced to agree to the Treaty of Belgrade in 1739. With its ally gone and war with Sweden looming, Russia chose to sign the Treaty of Nissa in October 1739. In it Russia restored to the Porte portions of Moldavia and Bessarabia, including the city of Khotin, and promised to dismantle the fortifications at Azov, which it retained as a port. The Ottomans, however, opened the Black Sea to Russian commercial activity.

**Russo-Ottoman War of 1768–1774**
Under Russian empress Tsarina Catherine II (the Great, r. 1762–1796) the Russo-Ottoman conflict entered a new stage determined by Russia's role in the partitions of Poland. In 1768 with Russian forces having invaded Poland and having pledged six years earlier to aid Poland in such circumstances, Sultan Mustafa III declared war on Russia in late 1768. This time, Catherine made sure Russia was well prepared for war. Russian troops led by Field Marshal P. A. Rumyantsev advanced into Moldavia and in 1770 defeated the Ottomans under Kaplan Girey and Ivazzade Halil Pasha at Larga and Kagul; the defeat at Kagul, one of the worst in Ottoman history, was so decisive that it spurred the Ottomans into introducing Western-influenced reforms into their army.

By the summer of 1770, Moldavia was occupied by the Russians. Meanwhile, the Russian fleet, under the command of Count Alexis Orlov, reached the coast of Greece, where it won the naval Battle of Chios on July 5, 1770. Two days later, Orlov's ships completely destroyed the Ottoman fleet at Chesma Bay. In 1772, the Russian fleet bombarded Beirut to assist local rebels against the Porte and conducted diplomatic negotiations with the mamluk leader Ali Bey of Egypt. A Russian expeditionary force was also sent to eastern Georgia, where King Erekle II scored a major victory over the Ottomans at Aspindza in 1770.

After a failed attempt at negotiations in 1772, hostilities resumed in earnest. Russian forces under General Alexander Suvorov advanced to the Danubian Principalities. Crossing the Danube in 1773 and 1774, they scored a decisive victory at Kozluca (now Suvorovo) in 1774, which forced Ottoman commander Muhsinzade Mehmed Pasha to sue for peace.

The Treaty of Kuchuk-Kainardji of July 1774 granted Russia additional territory on the shores of the Black Sea along with the right of navigation on the sea and free passage for Russian merchant ships through the straits. The Crimean Khanate gained independence from the Porte. Encouraged by such success, Empress Catherine invaded and annexed the Crimean Khanate in 1783 and ended Ukrainian autonomy in 1786. At the same time, Russia extended its authority to southern Caucasia, where it established a protectorate over the eastern Georgian kingdom.

**Russo-Ottoman Wars of 1787–1791**
The Ottomans spent the next decade reorganizing their army and fleet. Both sides complained of infringements of the Treaty of Kuchuk-Kainardji, while in 1786 Empress Catherine II's triumphal procession through the annexed Crimea only further infuriated the Porte. On August 19, 1787, Sultan Abdul Hamid I, influenced by the vociferous prowar ulema, refugee Crimean Tatar nobles, and Grand Vizier Hoca Yusuf Pasha, declared war on Russia. Russian leaders welcomed the war, as it provided an opportunity to expand their influence in the Black Sea littoral and to realize Empress Catherine II's long-standing Greek Project, the reestablishment of a Byzantine state on Ottoman territory with Constantinople as its capital. Once the war began, the Habsburgs joined in on the side of Russia.

The Ottomans were caught ill-prepared for the war and failed in their attempt to prevent further Russian expansion, let alone recover territories lost earlier. Although they successfully dealt with the Habsburgs in the Banat (parts of present-day Romania, Serbia and Hungary), the Ottomans could not arrest the Russian advance. The Russian Black Sea fleet was victorious at Kinburn (1787) and Fidonisi (1788), Field Marshal Pyotr Rumyantsev captured Yassy and Khotin (1788), and Prince Gregory Potemkin seized Ochakov (1788) in the Crimea. In 1789, Russian forces under Potemkin, Suvorov, and Rumyantsev invaded the Danubian Principalities and defeated Hasan Pasha's army at Focşani (July) and at Rymnik (September). Following these two defeats the Ottoman army withdrew in complete confusion, abandoning Bessarabia and Walacia to the Russians.

In 1790, Gazi Hasan Pasha replaced Hasan Pasha as commander of the Ottoman forces in the Balkans. But with his army in disarray and lacking supplies and quality recruits, the new commander could not rectify the situation. In December 1790 in one of the bloodiest battles of the 18th century, Suvorov's forces stormed the powerful Ismail fortress on the Danube and secured control of the lower Dniester and Danube Rivers. Continued Russian successes in the Caucasus and on the Black Sea compelled the Ottomans to sign the Treaty of Jassy on January 9, 1792, whereby they ceded the entire western Ukrainian Black Sea coast to Russia.

**Russo-Ottoman War of 1806–1812**
This new Russo-Ottoman conflict must be understood within the context of the Napoleonic Wars in Europe. As French emperor Napoleon I scored decisive victories over the Russo-Austrian coalition in 1805, Sultan Selim III adopted pro-French policies, which alarmed Russia. The immediate cause for hostilities was the sultan's dismissal of two pro-Russian rulers of the Danubian principalities, which violated the provisions of earlier agreements. In late 1806, two Russian armies crossed the Dniester River and occupied the Danubian Principalities. The Porte declared war on Russia but could not dislodge the Russian force. During the next three years Russian armies gradually expanded their theater of operations, reaching the Danube River in 1809 and defeating the Ottomans at Frasin, Rassevat, and Tataritsa. In 1810 the Russians crossed the Danube, capturing Hirsovo, Razgrad, Silistra, Ruse, and Shumla and advancing into Bulgaria. At the same time, Russia provided considerable support to the Serbs in the First Serbian Uprising (1804–1813) and conducted successful operations in western Georgia and eastern Anatolia, where an Ottoman army under Yusuf Ziya Pasha was routed at Arpa Su (1808). The Russian Navy defeated the Ottomans in the Aegean Sea in 1807 and blockaded the Dardanelles Straits.

Ottoman military efforts were greatly constrained by domestic difficulties as a series of internal political crises shook Istanbul in 1807–1808. Sultan Selim III's effort to modernize the army provoked a violent response from the ulema and the Janissaries who overthrew the sultan in the spring of 1807. New sultan Mustafa IV's reign proved to be brief, as he was overthrown in 1808. These power struggles occupied the attention of the Ottoman high command and provincial notables, forcing them to adopt a defensive posture against the Russians. In 1811 Sultan Mahmud launched a counteroffensive led by Ahmet Pasha, but the Russians, under Mikhail Kutuzov, surrounded and starved that force into submission at Ruse in November 1811. Nevertheless, as the chances of a full-scale Franco-Russian war increased, Russia sought a quick end to the struggle with the Ottomans. In May 1812 Russia agreed to the rather disadvantageous Treaty of Bucharest, which restored all of the Danubian Principalities, except Bessarabia, to the Ottoman Empire.

**Russo-Ottoman War of 1828–1829**
Under Tsar Nicholas I (r. 1894–1917), the question of the independence of Greece became central to Russo-Ottoman relations. In 1827 Russia, France, and the United Kingdom took joint action against the Porte, and their combined fleets destroyed the Egyptian fleet in the decisive Battle of Navarino Bay on October 20. Later after Russo-British cooperation had come to an end, Russia continued to support the Greeks and declared war on the Ottoman Empire on April 26, 1828, seeking to engage the Ottoman Army before extensive military reforms launched by Sultan Mahmud II could take effect. A Russian army quickly advanced into the Danubian Principalities, reaching the Danube River.

Once again the Ottoman military was ill-prepared, with the Janissaries having been destroyed by Mahmud in 1826 and the Ottoman fleet shattered at Navarino Bay a year later. Russia exploited its naval supremacy to establish reliable supply lines to support its land forces. Crossing the Danube, the Russian army captured Silistra and Vidin as the Ottomans under Husrev Pasha fell back to the defensive line in the Balkan mountains. In 1829 Russia opened a second front in the war in southern Caucasia, where Russian troops captured Poti, Ardahan, Kars, and Erzurum and besieged Trabzon. The Russian advance into the Balkan Mountains resulted in a decisive victory at Adrianople (Edirne), which opened a route to Istanbul. To prevent catastrophe, the Ottomans agreed to the Treaty of Adrianople (Edirne), the terms of which were highly favorable to Russia.

**Russo-Ottoman War (Crimean War) (1853–1856)**

The cause of the war lay in a dispute between France and Russia over control of religious sites in the Holy Land. When the Ottoman government allowed Roman Catholics equal rights with Greek Orthodox Christians in 1852, Russia (the self-appointed protector of the Orthodox Church) began to exert strong military and political pressure on the Porte. After the Ottomans allowed an Anglo-French squadron to sail through the Dardanelles, Russia deployed troops to the borders of Moldavia and Walachia, both of which were under Ottoman rule; sent a commission to Istanbul (Constantinople) to seek Russian rights to protect Orthodox Christians; and suggested to the British ambassador a plan to partition the Ottoman territories.

When the commission failed to resolve matters, Russia occupied Moldavia and Walachia over the protests of France and Britain. The Ottoman government declared war on Russia on October 16, 1853. Government officials in France and Britain who wanted to maintain the balance of power in Europe and keep the Russians out of the Mediterranean decided to support the Ottomans and declared war on Russia in March 1854.

The Crimean War was fought on three main fronts. On the Danubian front, some 82,000 Russian troops under General M. Gorchakov faced Omer Pasha's army of some 150,000 men, while General V. Bebutov's corps of 30,000 men was charged with countering Abdi Pasha's army of up to 100,000 men on the Caucasian front.

In the Caucasus, the war began in November 1853 with the Ottoman offensive toward Aleksandronopol and Tiflis. The Russian forces successfully repelled this attack, scoring major victories at Akhaltsikhe (November 26) and Bashgedikler (December 1). The cold winter weather caused a lull in operations in the Caucasus until the spring of 1854. Meanwhile, the Russians launched an offensive on the Danubian Front but failed in early November to break through the Ottoman positions at Oltenitsa. The Ottoman counterattacks were repelled at Cetati, Giurgiu, and Keleres between January and March 1854. On November 30, 1853, the Russian Navy secured supremacy in the Black Sea with its decisive victory at Sinope, which exposed the Ottoman capital to direct Russian attack.

Alarmed by the Russian success, Britain and France sent fleets to protect the Ottoman coastline of the Black Sea in January 1854, prompting Russia to declare war against them on February 21. In March 1854 the Russians launched a major offensive in the Danubian Theater, crossing the Danube at Braila, Talata, and Izmail and occupying Isaccea, Tulcea, and Macin. In May the strategic fortress of Silistra was besieged, and anti-Ottoman uprisings were incited in Bulgaria. However, following Austrian threats, Russia was forced to abandon its newly acquired territory, move its army across the Danube, and allow Austria to occupy Moldavia and Walachia. In the Caucasus, Mustafa Sarif Pasha regrouped the Ottoman forces, incited north Caucasian mountaineers to attack Russian forces in eastern Georgia, and launched offensives toward Alexandropol and Kutaisi. The Ottoman attacks, however, failed in all directions. During the summer of 1854, Russian routed the Ottomans on the Chorokh River (June 16) and at the Chingil Pass (July 29), captured the fortress of Bayazid (July 31), and won a major battle over the main Ottoman army at Kürük-Dar (August 5).

These Russian victories, however, were negated by the Anglo-French-Sardinian invasion of the Crimea, where the tide of war turned against Russia as it suffered defeat at Inkerman, Alma, Chernaya, Malakov, and Sevastopol. Russian troops were more successful in the Caucasus. The Ottoman attack in Abkhazia was repelled by General I. Bagration-Mukhranskii on the Inguri and Tskhenistskali Rivers in early November, while General Nikolai Muravyev launched an offensive toward Erzurum and captured the strategic fortress of Kars on November 28. Nonetheless, Russian defeats in the Crimea, especially the great siege of Sevastopol (October 17, 1854–September 9, 1855), decided the outcome of war and forced Emperor Alexander II to sue for peace.

The Treaty of Paris (March 30, 1856) reduced the prestige and territories of Russia and maintained the Ottoman Empire without strengthening it. Moldavia and Walachia (which would unite as Romania in 1858) became self-governing territories under the guardianship of European powers. The treaty also demanded that Russia remove its warships on the Black Sea and that the Danube River remain open as an international commercial river.

**Russo-Ottoman War of 1877–1878**

Although Ottoman power continued to decline, the empire still controlled most of the Balkan Peninsula. While Greece was independent, Romania, Serbia, and Montenegro were autonomous principalities. In 1875 and 1876 uprisings occurred in Herzegovina, Bosnia, and Macedonia. Then in mid-1876 the Bulgarians also rose, only to be slaughtered by the Ottomans. Serbia and Montenegro then declared war on the Ottoman Empire. Russia saw an opportunity to recoup its prestige lost in the Crimean War and secure a warm-water port on the Mediterranean.

While the major European powers discussed intervention, the Ottomans, led by Osman Nuri Pasha, were winning the war. With it clear by the autumn of 1876 that they would soon capture Belgrade, Russia demanded an armistice, which the Ottomans accepted. A conference at Constantinople in December failed, and in March 1877 Serbia made peace with the Porte. Sentiment in Russia was then so strong for intervention that despite warnings of bankruptcy, Tsar Alexander II declared war in April 1877.

As the Ottomans controlled the Black Sea with ironclad warships, a Russian land invasion proved necessary. In late April 1877 two Russian armies invaded: one in Caucasia, advancing on Kars, Ardahan, and Erzurum, and the other in the Balkans. Romania was essential to a Russian drive down the eastern part of the Balkan Peninsula, and following agreement of Romanian cooperation, Russian troops crossed the Prut (Pruth) River into Moldavia. The Ottomans responded by shelling the Romanian forts at the mouth of the Danube, whereupon on May 21 Romania declared both war on the Ottoman Empire and its independence. Serbia reentered the war in December. Bulgarian irregular forces fought with Russia, and Montenegro remained at war as it had been since June 1876.

Russian forces under nominal command of Grand Duke Nicholas, brother of the tsar, crossed the Danube on June 26 and took Svishtov (Sistova) and Nikopol (Nicopolis) before advancing to Pleven (Plevna, Plevne), some 25 miles south of Nikopol. The Bulgarians acclaimed the Russians as liberators. Russian general Nikolai P. de Krüdener, who had actual command, sent forces across the Balkan Mountains into Thrace, then back toward Shipka Pass through the mountains to defeat the Ottomans. Russian troops, assisted by Bulgarian partisans, also raided in the Maritza Valley, seemingly threatening Adrianople.

Ottoman general Mehmed Ali defeated the Russians in the south, driving them back to the Balkan Mountains with heavy losses. To the north the main Russian armies

Depiction of Russian forces attacking the Ottoman entrenchments during the great Siege of Pleven in present-day Bulgaria during July 19–December 10, 1877. The illustration is from the magazine *The Graphic*, August 25, 1877. (De Agostini/Getty Images)

encountered a formidable obstacle in Ottoman forces sent to the Danube under capable general Osman Nuri Pasha, who soon had entrenched his men at Pleven. Ottoman engineers created in the rocky valley there a formidable fortress of earthworks with redoubts, trenches, and gun emplacements.

The ensuing Siege of Pleven (July 19–December 10, 1877) saw the Russians commit 120,000 men and 5,000 guns. Other Russian forces under General Ossip Gourko ravaged the countryside, preventing Ottoman supply columns from reaching Pleven from the south. The Russians also easily defeated and turned back the poorly trained Ottoman relief force. On December 10, his men short of ammunition and reduced to starvation, Osman Nuri Pasha surrendered. The battle cost the Russians 40,000 dead or wounded. The Ottomans lost 25,000 dead or wounded and 43,340 prisoners.

Russia imposed harsh terms in the Treaty of San Stefano on March 3, 1878, leaving the Ottoman Empire only a small strip of territory on the European side of the Straits. Romania, Serbia, and Montenegro were enlarged, but the major territorial change was the creation of a new large autonomous Bulgaria, including most of Macedonia from the Aegean Sea to Albania. This would make Bulgaria the largest of the Balkan states, though the assumption was that it would be dominated by Russia. The treaty did not last, however. Britain and Austria-Hungary threatened war if it was not revised, and Russia agreed to an international conference that met in Berlin in June and July 1878.

Under the terms of the Treaty of Berlin, Bulgaria was divided into three parts: Bulgaria proper (the northern section) became an autonomous principality subject to tribute to the sultan. Eastern Rumelia, the southeastern part, received a measure of autonomy, and the rest of Bulgaria was restored to the sultan. Romania, Serbia, and Montenegro all became independent, and Greece received Thessaly. Russia received from Romania the small strip of Bessarabia lost in the Crimean War in 1856 and territory around Batum, Ardahan, and Kars that it had conquered in the Caucasus, while Romania had to be content with part of the Dobrudja. Austria-Hungary secured the right to occupy and administer, though not annex, Bosnia and Herzegovina.

The region continued to smolder, however. During 1912–1913 there were two Balkan wars, both of which threatened to become wider conflicts. Then in June 1914 the assassination of Austrian archduke Franz Ferdinand led to a third Balkan war that this time became World War I.

ALEXANDER MIKABERIDZE AND SPENCER C. TUCKER

**See also**
Adrianople, 1713 Treaty of; Bakhchisarai, Treaty of; Constantinople, 1700 Treaty of; Kuchuk Kainardji, Treaty of; Pruth, Treaty of

**References**
Aksan, Virginia. *Ottoman Wars 1700–1870: An Empire Besieged.* New York: Longman, 2007.
Badem, Candan. *The Ottoman Crimean War (1853–1856).* Leiden: Brill, 2012.
Barker, A. J. *The War against Russia.* New York: Holt, Rinehart, and Winston, 1971.
Baumgart, Winfried. *The Crimean War: 1853–1856.* New York: Oxford University Press, 1999.
Herbert, Frederick William von. *The Defense of Plevna, 1877.* Ankara, Turkey: Ministry of Culture, 1990.
Jelavich, Barbara. *History of the Balkans: Eighteenth and Nineteenth Centuries.* Cambridge: Cambridge University Press, 1983.
Jelavich, Charles, and Barbara Jelavich. *The Establishment of the Balkan Nation States, 1804–1920.* Seattle: University of Washington Press, 1986.
Kinross, Lord (John Patrick). *The Ottoman Centuries: The Rise and Fall of the Turkish Empire.* New York: William Morrow, 1977.
Mikhailovsky-Danilevsky, Alexander. *Russo-Turkish War of 1806–1812.* Translated and edited by Alexander Mikaberidze. 2 vols. West Chester, OH: Nafziger Colletion, 2002.
Shaw, Stanford J. *History of the Ottoman Empire and Modern Turkey.* 2 vols. New York: Cambridge University Press, 1976–1977.

# Russo-Persian Wars (1722–1911)

A series of conflicts between the Russian Empire and Persia in the 18th through 20th centuries. Prior to the 18th century the two powers had sporadic contacts, although commercial activity between Persia and Muscovite Russia increased following Tsar Ivan IV's conquest of Kazan and Astrakhan in the late 16th century and the Russian expansion into the northern Caucasus in the 17th century. The reign of the Russian tsar Peter I the Great (r. 1682–1725) saw a major transformation in the nature of Russo-Persian relations. Despite Russia's exhaustion after the Great Northern War (1700–1721), Peter turned his attention to the Caspian Sea region, but he lacked a legitimate excuse to declare war on Persia.

Peter did not have long to wait. In August 1721, Shah Sultan Hussein freed Daud Khan of Dagestan with a hope that he would support the shah against the Afghans who had rebelled in 1709. However, Daud Khan instead attacked and sacked Shemaka, an important Persian trade center in eastern Caucasia. The attack claimed the lives of several thousand residents, including a few Russian merchants. Daud Khan then appealed to the Ottoman Empire for protection. Upon receiving this news, Tsar Peter seized it as a casus belli by claiming he was reclaiming Persian land against a common enemy; if Persia protested, Russia could then demand an indemnity. At the same time, King Vakhtang VI of Kartli (eastern Georgia), who had been long mistreated by the Persians, appealed to Russia for help and offered to join a campaign against Persia.

**Russo-Persian War of 1722–1723**

As Afghan tribesmen attacked Persia from the east, Russian troops advanced to Astrakhan where Tsar Peter arrived on June 29, 1722. The Russian ruler dispatched an envoy to the shah offering help in defeating the Afghans in exchange for certain provinces along the Caspian Sea. If Persia refused, Peter still planned to occupy the Caspian provinces to prevent an Ottoman presence there. While the Russian envoy was delivering Peter's message, Russian forces seized the Persian cities of Derbent (Darband), but their progress then stalled owing to the loss of a large number of ships in a storm at sea and an epidemic that killed most of the horses in the Russian cavalry. Compelled to retreat to Astrakhan, Peter left garrisons at Tarqu, Derbent, and Baku. The Georgian-Armenian army, which gathered under the leadership of Vakhtang VI at Ganja, was abandoned to face Persian retribution.

Although Tsar Peter soon lost interest in the Caspian region, his forces continued the campaign and captured Rasht (Resht) in late 1722. When the local Persian governor demanded the Russians withdraw, a minor battle took place between Russian and Persian forces near Resht (March 28, 1723), which ended with a Russian victory and the loss of perhaps 1,000 Persian lives. At the same time, the Ottomans, threatened by Russian penetration into the Caspian region, responded by launching an invasion of eastern Georgia and seizing Tiflis (Tbilisi).

Alarmed by the Ottoman attack, Shah Tahmasp, who had replaced Sultan Hussein in 1722, agreed to negotiate with the Russians. By the Treaty of St. Petersburg, signed on September 23, 1723, Russia gained control of Derbent, Baku, and the coastal areas in between as well as the provinces of Gilan, Mazandaran, and Astrabad. The shah also received Russian troops for domestic peacekeeping.

When the treaty reached Isfahan in April 1724, Shah Tahmasp refused to ratify it; by then it was clear that the Russian forces in the region were too small to pose a major threat to Persia. Still, the news of a Russo-Persian accord precipitated a crisis between Russia and the Ottoman Empire, which openly declared that it would not permit any other power to establish itself on the Caspian Sea. War was avoided through French mediation that resulted in the Treaty of Constantinople (June 24, 1724), by which the Ottomans received Azerbaijan and most of southern Caucasia (Georgia and Armenia), while the Russians retained the three Caspian provinces of Persia and captured territories. The treaty specified that if Persia refused to accept the treaty, both Russia and the Porte would make common cause against Iran to enforce the treaty and install a puppet ruler.

The Russian involvement in Persian affairs, however, withered away following Tsar Peter's death in 1725. In February 1732, Nadir Khan negotiated the Treaty of Rasht that restored Astrabad, Mazandaran, and Gilan to Persia, while the territory north of the Kura River remained temporarily under Russian control. Three years later, Russia accepted the Treaty of Ganja by which it gave up all of its previous conquests, including Baku, Derbent, and Tarqu.

**Russo-Persian War of 1796**

Following the death of Nadir Shah in 1747, Iran descended into political chaos, while Russia remained preoccupied with the Ottoman Empire. Yet, by the 1780s Russia showed growing interest in Georgia, where King Erekle of Kartli-Kakheti (eastern Georgia) appealed for Russian help against the Ottomans and the Persians. Anarchy in Persia created favorable conditions for Russian penetration into the Caucasus and the Caspian region. In 1781 a Russian expedition, led by Count Voinovich, landed near Astrabad with a goal of establishing a fortified base to facilitate subsequent conquest of the northern Persian provinces. However, Agha Muhammad Khan, the new leading contender in Iran's power struggle, quickly realized the threat and had the members of the expeditions arrested and deported. Although Agha Muhammad Khan tried to smooth over relations with Russia, Empress Catherine II felt slighted by the incident and refused to accept the envoy. The relations between the two powers gradually deteriorated, with the Russians supporting Agha Muhammad Khan's opponents, while Agha Muhammad imposed tariffs on Russian products.

In 1783, eastern Georgia and Russia signed the Treaty of Georgievsk that which placed Georgia under Russian protection. The arrival of Russian troops in Georgia greatly alarmed the Persians, who still considered Georgia a Persian vassal state. In 1784, Russia became embroiled in another conflict with the Ottomans and recalled its troops from Georgia.

For the next 10 years Empress Catherine's attention was centered on European affairs, away from the Caucasus.

This allowed Agha Muhammad to attempt restoring Persian authority in defiant Georgia. In 1795, he led a major invasion of Georgia, unleashing the full force of his wrath on its capital of Tbilisi, where thousands of residents were massacred and some 15,000 others were taken into captivity.

Russia provided no military help to stop the Persian invasion, but after Agha Muhammad left Georgia, the Russian authorities proposed a plan for an invasion of Persia. Led by Count Valerian Zubov, the Russian expedition aimed at overthrowing Agha Muhammad and replacing him with a more pro-Russian candidate. The Russian troops set out from Kizlyar in April 1796 and captured Derbent on May 10. By mid-June, they were in control of most of Azerbaijan, including Baku, Shemakha, and Ganja, and by early November, Zubov was poised to invade Persia. The death of Empress Catherine put an end to this prospect, however. Her successor Paul had other plans and ordered the troops back to Russia.

**Russo-Persian War of 1804–1813**
Eight years passed before a new conflict erupted between Russia and Persia. Agha Muhammad's successor, Fath Ali Shah Qajar, sought to consolidate his authority by securing land near the Caspian Sea's southwestern coast and in southern Caucasus. At the same time, new Russian emperor Alexander I was also determined to extend Russian sovereignty over the disputed territories across the Caucasus mountain range. In 1801, Russia annexed the Georgian kingdom of Kartli-Kakheti while the appointment of Prince Paul Tsitsianov (Tsitsishvili) as Russian commander in chief in the Caucasus greatly accelerated Russian expansion in the region. Despite his Georgian origins, Tsitsianov was a die-hard Russian imperialist who believed in Russia's mission civilisatrice in Asia.

Between 1802 and 1804, Tsitsianov proceeded to impose Russian rule on the western Georgian kingdom of Imereti and the principalities of Mingrelia and Guria as well as the khanates located around Georgia. Some submitted without a fight, but Ganja resisted, prompting a Russian attack. Ganja was ruthlessly sacked, with some 3,000 people killed and thousands more expelled to Persia. Russian attacks on the khanates, which Persia considered its vassal territories, served as a casus belli for Fath Ali Khan. On May 23 Persia demanded a Russian withdrawal from southern Caucasia and, following Russian rejection of this, declared war on Russia. In the spring of 1804, Tsitsianov's army of 3,000 troops marched to the Erivan Khanate after its ruler Muhammad Khan refused to accept Russian sovereignty. In June, the Russians besieged Erivan and engaged Persian forces in the region. On June 22, the Russians defeated Persian detachments at Gumry (Leninakan) while Tsitsianov himself scored a victory over Persian crown prince Abbas Mirza not far from the Echmiadzin Monastery (near Erivan) on July 2–3. Following these defeats, the Persian forces withdrew to regroup while Tsitsianov continued to exert pressure on local khanates.

In 1805 Karabagh, Shakki, and Shirvan recognized Russian authority, while the Russians conducted raids against Baku and Resht. Although Tsitsianov was assassinated near Baku in February 1806, the Russians repelled a Persian attack in Karabagh in the summer of 1806 and occupied Derbent and Baku. Inconclusive warfare persisted until 1812, as Russia, preoccupied with events in Europe, was unable to devote considerable resources to the Caucasian theater, while Persia was unable to deal with the Russian threat. Persian forces suffered defeats on the Aras (Araxes) and Zagam Rivers in 1805 as well as at Karakapet in 1806, Karababa in 1808, Ganja in 1809, and Meghri, the Aras River, and Akhalkalaki in 1810.

In 1812, as French emperor Napoleon I launched his invasion of Russia, Abbas Mirza led some 20,000 men into the khanate of Talysh (southern Azerbaijan) and captured the fortress of Lenkoran on August 21. By October, the Persians reached the Aras River and attacked a small Russian detachment of some 2,000 men under the charismatic General Petr Kotlyarovskii but suffered an unexpected defeat on October 31. On January 13, 1813, the Russians stormed Lenkoran, forcing Persia to sue for peace.

Negotiated with British mediation and signed at the village of Gulistan on October 14, 1813, the peace treaty confirmed the Russian victory in the war and forced Fath Ali Shah to relinquish claims to southern Caucasia. Persia lost all its territories north of the Aras River, which included Dagestan, all of Georgia, and parts of Armenia and Azerbaijan (Karabagh, Ganja, Shirvan, Baku, etc.). The shah also surrendered Persian navigation rights on the Caspian Sea and granted Russia exclusive rights to maintain warships in the Caspian Sea as well as capitulatory rights to trade within Persia. Russia in return promised to support Crown Prince Abbas Mirza as heir to the Iranian throne after the death of Fath Ali Shah.

**Russo-Persian War of 1825–1828**
The leaders of Persia did not regard the Treaty of Gulistan as definitive and considered it more as a truce that allowed

Persia time to regroup. The Caucasus was, however, peaceful for 13 years as Fath Ali Shah sought to secure foreign support and modernize his forces. Abbas Mirza played an important role in Persian military reforms, believing that the introduction of European-style regiments would enable Persia to defeat Russia and regain the territory lost earlier. He sent Persian students to Europe to learn Western tactics and employed British and French officers (as well as a few renegade Russian officers) to train and drill the Persian forces. He also tried to introduce a new recruitment system to create a more predictable supply of manpower and to make himself independent of the local elites. Abbas Mirza had to overcome public resistance to reforms as the population and ulema disliked changes, the European appearance of new regiments, and the presence of "infidel" instructors. Although Persia received British subsidies to defray the cost of military reforms, training and equipping new regiments proved very expensive, adversely affecting the Qajar finances. The reformed army had some success in campaigns against the Ottomans in 1821–1823, but it proved to be ill-prepared for the second Russo-Persian war that broke out in 1826.

The continued Russian encroachment into the southern Caucasian territories as well as mistreatment of Muslim population seriously strained Russo-Persian relations. General Alexei Yermolov, the new Russian commander in the Caucasus, shared his predecessor Tsitsianov's worldview toward "Asiatics" and was firmly committed to war as a means of achieving Russia's political goals. In May 1826, Russian forces occupied Mirak in Erivan khanate in violation of the Treaty of Gulistan. In response, Iranian forces invaded the Karabagh and Talysh khanates, where local elites switched sides and surrendered to the Persians the major cities of Lenkoran, Kuba, and Baku. Although Abbas Mirza was able to seize the initiative and regain considerable territory in the first months of the war, the Persian offensive soon stalled.

The Russian garrison at Shusha heroically defended the fortress for 48 days, which allowed Yermolov to rush reinforcements to the theater of war. The Russian counterattack soon shattered the Persian forces, first crushing Muhammad Mirza (future Muhammad Shah of Iran) on the banks of the Shamkhor River (September 15) and then defeating Persian forces under Abbas Mirza himself at Ganja (September 26).

In October, Russian troops under General I. Paskevizh stormed Erivan. In 1827, the Russians drove Abbas Mirza back into Persia, taking Nakhichevan, Abbasabad, Meren, Urmiya, Ardabil, and Tabriz. By 1828, Persia had lost all of its southeast Caucasian territories and was forced to sue for peace.

Signed at Turkmanchai on February 22, 1828, the treaty was the definitive acknowledgment of the Persian loss of the Caucasus region to Russia and of the permanent division of Azerbaijan. The treaty required Iran to cede sovereignty over the khanates of Yerevan, Nakhichevan, Talysh, Ordubad, and Mughan in addition to regions that Russia had annexed under the Treaty of Gulistan. The Aras River was declared the new border between Persia and Russia. Persia also had to agree to pay vast reparations of 20 million rubles in silver and also transferred to Russia the exclusive right to maintain a Caspian Sea fleet. In addition, capitulatory rights guaranteed Russia preferential treatment for its exports, which generally were not competitive in European markets, and exempted Russian subjects from Iranian Persian jurisdiction.

### Russo-Persian Conflict of 1911

The Persian Revolution of 1906–1909 forced Muzaffar al-Din Shah to accept a constitution (January 7, 1907), but he died just a week later. His successor, Muhammad Ali Shah, came to power and stayed there, with the assistance of the Russian-controlled Cossack Brigade. The first National Consultative Assembly (the Majles), which opened in October 1907, was suppressed in 1908 by the officers of the Persian Cossack Brigade. However, the following year the second Majles forced Muhammad Ali to flee to Russia and installed the young Ahmad Shah (r. 1909–1925). In 1911, the Majles hired American financial adviser William Morgan Shuster to modernize the Persian economy, but his moves to collect revenue throughout the country soon angered both Russia and Britain, which had divided Persia into spheres of influence since 1907.

Russia issued an ultimatum demanding Shuster's dismissal, and when the Majles refused, the Russian army seized Tabriz and advanced to Tehran. The shah's regents hastily dismissed Shuster and dissolved the Majles in December 1911. For the next three years Russia effectively ruled Peria, but with the beginning of World War I in 1914, the Russian troops were withdrawn from the north of the country.

ALEXANDER MIKABERIDZE

### See also
Abbas Mirza; Agha Muhammad Khan Qajar; Gulistan, Treaty of; Nadir Shah; Resht, Treaty of

**References**

Avery, Peter, et al., eds. *The Cambridge History of Iran: From Nadir Shah to the Islamic Republic,* Vol. 7. Cambridge: Cambridge University Press, 1991.

Baddeley, John Frederick. *The Russian Conquest of the Caucasus.* London: Longmans, Green, 1908.

Dubrovin, Nikolai. *Istoriia voiny i vladychestva russkikh na Kavkaze.* 6 vols. St. Petersburg: Tipografiya Departamenta udelov, 1871–1888.

Farmanfarmaian, Roxane. *War and Peace in Qajar Persia: Implications Past and Present.* New York: Routledge, 2008.

Fasai, Hasan ibn Hasan, and Heribert Busse. *History of Persia under Qajar Rule.* New York, Columbia University Press, 1972.

Kazemzadeh, F. *Russia and Britain in Persia, 1864–1914: A Study in Imperialism.* New Haven, CT: Yale University Press, 1967.

Lang, David M. *The Last Years of the Georgian Monarchy, 1658–1832.* New York: Columbia University Press, 1957.

Ward, Steven. *Immortal: A Military History of Iran and Its Armed Forces.* Washington, DC: Georgetown University Press, 2009.

# S

## Saadabad Pact (July 8, 1937)

Treaty of nonaggression signed by Afghanistan, Iraq, Iran, and Turkey on July 8, 1937, at the Saadabad Palace in Tehran. Italy's invasion of Ethiopia and the increasing threat posed by Italy in the Near East exacerbated the security concerns of the regional countries. Under these circumstances, on October 2, 1935, Turkey, Iran, and Iraq reached an agreement in Geneva on consultation and nonaggression. Afghanistan readily declared its intention to join. Yet the conclusion of the treaty was delayed until 1937, when Iran's outstanding border disputes with Afghanistan and Iraq were finally resolved.

Having reiterated their commitment to the General Treaty for Renunciation of War of 1928 (the Kellogg-Briand Pact), the parties pledged not to engage in acts of aggression against each other, ranging from declaration of war to assisting an aggressor; to consult in case an international dispute arises that might have an impact on parties' interests; to respect the inviolability of common borders; to prevent establishment of organizations on their own territory that aimed to threaten security of other parties; and not to intervene in others' domestic affairs. Despite the fact that no party has officially denounced the Saadabad Pact, it became obsolete after World War II.

Tuba Ünlü Bilgiç

**See also**
Baghdad Pact

**References**

Gönlübol, Mehmet, et al. *Olaylarla Türk Dış Politikası Cilt I (1919–1973)*. Ankara: Ankara Üniversitesi Siyasal Bilgiler Fakültesi Yayınları, 1987.

"No. 4402 Treaty of Non-Aggression between the Kingdom of Afghanistan, the Kingdom of Iraq, the Empire of Iran and the Republic of Turkey, Signed at Teheran, July 8th, 1937." *League of Nations Treaty Series* 190 (1938): 21–28.

## Sabra and Shatila Massacre (September 16–18, 1982)

Mass Phalangist killing of inhabitants of the Sabra and Shatila refugee camps in Beirut, Lebanon, during September 16–18, 1982. The incident occurred as part of the Lebanese Civil War (1975–1990) and following the Israeli invasion of Lebanon in 1982. Estimates of the number of individuals killed ranged from 700–1,800 to more than 3,500. Included among the dead were many women, children, and elderly, some of whom were raped or castrated and killed in the most brutal ways possible. In addition, bulldozers were used to destroy dwelling places in the camps, and a number of camp residents were hauled off in trucks, never to be seen again. Hospitals in each camp were attacked, and in one case a crowd of 500 persons escaped from the hospital but was driven back into the camp by Israelis.

The massacre created a firestorm of international outrage and resulted in significant political and military repercussions in Israel. At the time, Israel Defense Force (IDF) occupied the area that included Sabra and Shatila. The IDF was in direct contact with the militia that committed the massacre, surrounded the camps, and gave the Phalangist forces access into the camps. The IDF subsequently prevented civilians and residents from exiting the camps and escaping what went on there. The IDF was thus responsible, along with the Phalangist forces, for actions that took place in the camps. Most IDF personnel would later claim that they were not aware of the actions within the camps because they were patrolling the perimeter areas only. Worse still, it was later confirmed that the Lebanese Christian Phalangist militia had been invited to Sabra and Shatila by top-level Israeli military officials to flush out Palestine Liberation Organization (PLO) fighters who were supposedly using the refugee camps as safe havens. Israeli journalists and others later presented evidence revealing that this plan was concocted not to flush out fighters but instead to kill camp residents, destroy the buildings there, and terrorize Palestinians who remained in Beirut into leaving. Israeli defense minister Ariel Sharon claimed that there were as many as 2,000 fighters in the camps who had not been part of the September 1 evacuation from Beirut.

The mission involving the Phalangists had been approved by Sharon and was carried out by IDF chief of staff General Rafael Eitan. Those who believe that the operation was planned in advance argue that the Phalangists deliberately waited until after the September 1 evacuation of the Palestinians and then used the assassination of Lebanon's Maronite Christian president Bashir Jumayyil (Gemayel) as the pretext for their actions. The Israeli forces later argued that the Phalangists seemed determined to exact revenge for the assassination on the Palestinians—any Palestinians. The deliberate methods used, including carving the sign of the cross on victims, dismemberment, rape, torture, the killing of children, and the destruction of buildings, point instead to much more than the actual claim made at the time: pursuit of what Israelis called terrorists, PLO fighters who were in fact not in evidence. The idea that this was a revenge spree for the death of Jumayyil was also problematic, as it was quickly known that the Syrians and not the PLO were behind his murder because of his alliance with Israel. Furthermore, the Phalangists were accompanied by southern Lebanese under Saad Haddad's command, pointing additionally to Israeli foreknowledge or coordination.

Israeli soldiers, who had already sealed off the Sabra and Shatila camps, admitted the Phalangists and Haddad's fighters into them on September 16, 1982. The Phalangist and South Lebanon Army (SLA) personnel then began an indiscriminate 62-hour killing spree that involved the murder of many innocent Palestinians. All the while, IDF forces were providing illumination flares for nighttime operations and were observed monitoring activities from rooftop observation posts. Some Phalangists would later claim that they had made specific reports to Israelis about the killings, including those of civilians. The bloodletting continued unabated, as IDF troops barred exits from the camps. It is hard to believed that Israeli commanders were not aware of the activities inside Sabra and Shatila. Additional Phalangist and SLA troops came into the camps. The medical staff, mostly Europeans, were forced out of the Gaza Hospital at Sabra after the Palestinians and a Syrian medic were killed. Israelis took custody of the Europeans and later released them. Not until the morning of September 18 did the militia units leave the camps.

A little more than an hour after the Phalangists left the refugee camps, foreign journalists caught their first glimpses of the carnage. What they saw was deeply disturbing. Inside the camps were many hundreds of dead bodies, some of which had been mutilated. Included among the dead were women, children, and the elderly. Journalists saw evidence of the discarded Israeli illumination flares as well. By noon local time on September 18, the first reports of the massacre had hit the news wires. At least a quarter of the victims were Lebanese, and the remainder were Palestinian. The Red Cross tallied 350 dead, the Israelis claimed 700–800 dead, several foreign journalists claimed 2,000 dead, and an Israeli journalist claimed 3,000–3,500 dead, a figure that most Palestinians cite as fact. Whatever the number, the Sabra and Shatila Massacre was horrific, and the event elicited sharp international condemnations and strong reactions in Israel. In December 1982 the United Nations (UN) General Assembly denounced the killings, calling them an act of genocide.

Amid street protests condemning the killings and genuine outrage in Israel, the Israeli government established a commission of inquiry to investigate the incident on September 28, 1982. Israeli Supreme Court justice Yitzhak Kahan headed the inquiry. On February 8, 1983, after a detailed investigation, the Kahan Commission issued its report on the massacre at Sabra and Shatila. The report concluded that while the Phalangists themselves were directly accountable for the killings, Israeli forces were indirectly responsible. Defense Minister Sharon was deemed personally responsible for the incident because of his complacency and his failure to anticipate the obvious: that the Phalangists were driven by revenge and therefore should not have been allowed into the camps. The report recommended that Sharon be removed as minister of defense, and he resigned shortly thereafter. Chief of Staff Eitan was also held partially accountable, and he too was forced to resign his post. In addition, the director of Israeli military intelligence, Yehoshua Saguy, was required to resign.

The Kahan Commission was and remains a controversial inquiry. Many people, both inside Israel and beyond, claim that it was motivated mainly by political expediency. Some hold that it was an outright distortion of the true facts and dimensions of the massacre. Indeed, Noam Chomsky termed the Kahan Commission a "shameful whitewash," while Israeli journalist Shimon Lehrer claims that its conclusions were "untenable." The Israeli writer Benny Morris alleges that the IDF provided bulldozers to bury as many dead as possible so as to lessen the grim impact of the event. Elie Hubayka (Hobeika), the Phalangist commander whom most consider responsible, was killed in a bomb blast in 2002, allegedly to prevent his testimony to the International Court in The Hague, where Palestinians had hoped to charge Sharon. The probable reason that no charges were made against the Lebanese perpetrators (with the exception of those in the SLA) is that the Taif Agreement was forged on the understanding that war crimes, massacres, kidnappings, and assassinations as well as battle casualties could not be prosecuted, as that would render the cessation of violence impossible.

PAUL G. PIERPAOLI JR. AND SHERIFA ZUHUR

**See also**
Eitan, Rafael; Lebanon; Lebanon Civil War; Lebanon-Israeli War; Palestine Liberation Organization; Sharon, Ariel

**References**
Al-Hout, Bayan Nuwayhed. *Sabra and Shatila: September 1982.* London: Pluto, 2004.
Black, Ian, and Benny Morris. *Israel's Secret Wars: A History of Israel's Intelligence Services.* New York: Grove, 1994.
Brynen, Rex. *Sanctuary and Survival: The PLO in Lebanon.* Boulder, CO: Westview, 1990.
Chomsky, Noam. *Fateful Triangle: The United States, Israel, and the Palestinians.* Cambridge, MA: South End Press, 2002.
Kapeliouk, Amnon. *Sabra et Chatila: Enquête sur un massacre.* Paris: Seuil, 1982.

Morris, Claud. *Eyewitness Lebanon: Eyewitness Evidence of 91 International Correspondents.* London: Morris International, 1983.

## Sadat, Anwar (1918–1981)

Egyptian nationalist leader, vice president (1966–1970), and president (1970–1981) of Egypt. Born on December 25, 1918, in Mit Abu al-Kum, Egypt, in a family of 13 children, Anwar Sadat attended the Royal Egyptian Military Academy, from which he graduated in 1938 as a second lieutenant. His first posting was in the Sudan, where he met Gamal Abdel Nasser, fellow nationalist and future Egyptian president. Stemming from their mutual disdain of British colonial rule, Sadat and Nasser helped form the secret organization that would eventually be called the Free Officers Group, composed of young Egyptian military officers dedicated to ending British rule and ousting King Farouk I. During World War II, Sadat was jailed for conspiring with the Axis powers to expel British forces from Egypt.

Sadat was an active participant in the July 23, 1952, coup against King Farouk engineered by the Free Officers Group. Farouk abdicated and left Egypt on July 26. When Egypt was declared a republic in June 1953, Major General Mohammad Naguib became its president, and Nasser became vice president. In October 1954 after an attempt on Nasser's life, Naguib was removed from office, while Nasser consolidated his power. In February 1955 Nasser became prime minister and seven months later became president. Sadat meanwhile served loyally under Nasser, acting as his chief spokesman and one of his closest personal confidants and advisers.

In 1964 Sadat became vice president of Egypt. He became president upon Nasser's death in September 1970. Egypt's relationship with the Soviet Union, once robust, was now showing signs of serious strain. At the time of his death, in fact, Nasser had been moving away from the Soviet Union. Part of the reason for this had been the reduction in equipment that the Soviets were willing to sell to Egypt. On July 18, 1972, Sadat ordered all Soviet advisers to leave the country, to be followed by pilots and other army technicians.

Despairing of the failure of negotiations to achieve the return of the Sinai Peninsula, lost to Israel as a consequence of the 1967 Arab-Israeli War, on October 6, 1973, Sadat led Egypt, along with Syria, into a war with Israel. Although Egyptian and Syrian forces were ultimately defeated in the war, initial military successes that saw Egyptian forces cross the Suez Canal and inflict heavy losses on the Israelis and Sadat's determination earned him great respect from the Egyptian people and lifted the morale of the nation, which had been badly shaken by Nasser's heavy-handed rule and economic difficulties. At war's end, the United States and the Soviet Union both were concerned about the balance of power in the Middle East and thus negotiated a cease-fire agreement that was generally favorable to Egypt, allowing Sadat to claim a victory of sorts.

Realizing that only the United States could elicit any substantive concessions from Israel, Sadat completely severed relations with the Soviet Union in March 1976 and began working with the Americans toward a peace settlement with the Israelis. In a courageous move in November 1977, Sadat became the first Arab leader to officially visit Israel, there meeting with Prime Minister Menachem Begin and even addressing the Israeli Knesset. In September 1978 Sadat signed the Camp David Accords, ushering in a comprehensive peace agreement with Israel. The accords were highly unpopular in the Arab world, however, especially among fundamentalist Muslims, and led to Egypt's expulsion from the Arab League.

Although the Camp David Accords were in the long run beneficial for Egypt, many in the Arab world saw them as a great betrayal and viewed Sadat as a traitor. In September 1981, Sadat's government cracked down on extremist Muslim organizations and radical student groups, in the process arresting more than 1,600 people. Sadat's strong-arm tactics angered many in the Arab community and only exacerbated his problems, which included economic stagnation and charges that he had forcibly quashed dissent.

On October 6, 1981, Sadat was assassinated in Cairo while reviewing a military parade commemorating the Yom Kippur War. His assassins were radical fundamentalist army officers who belonged to the Islamic Jihad organization that had bitterly denounced Sadat's peace overtures with Israel and his suppression of dissidents the month before. Sadat was succeeded in office by Hosni Mubarak.

DALLACE W. UNGER JR.

**See also**
Begin, Menachem; Camp David Accords; Nasser, Gamal Abdel; Yom Kippur War

**References**
Beattie, Kirk J. *Egypt during the Sadat Years*. New York: Palgrave, 2000.
Finklestone, Joseph. *Anwar Sadat: Visionary Who Dared*. Portland, OR: Frank Cass, 1996.
Hirst, David, and Irene Beeson. *Sadat*. London: Faber and Faber, 1981.
Sadat, Anwar. *In Search of Identity: An Autobiography*. New York: Harper and Row, 1978.

# Saddam Line, Persian Gulf War

Following the Iraqi invasion and occupation of Kuwait on August 2, 1990, Iraqi Army engineers constructed a network of fortifications along Kuwait's southern border with Saudi Arabia. Known as the Saddam Line, these fortifications were designed to inflict casualties and slow any invasion. The overall Iraqi defensive plan was quite straightforward. Behind the Saddam Line, the Iraqis positioned mechanized and infantry divisions in a second line designed to contain and counterattack any breech of the first line. Finally, the Iraqis held elite Republican Guard divisions in reserve for a strategic counteroffensive. The Iraqi intention was to contain any coalition advance, inflict heavy casualties, and force the enemy to the negotiating table.

The Saddam Line itself consisted of two belts of mines, sand berms, and concrete bunkers. The Iraqis also constructed a network of ditches that could be flooded with oil from Kuwaiti wells, then set afire to turn the battlefield into a smoky inferno. Farther north, the Iraqis had sited some 800 South African–manufactured 155mm long-range artillery pieces. The Iraqi artillery was preregistered to concentrate fire on likely invasion routes from Saudi Arabia.

Breaking the Saddam Line posed challenges for coalition military planners. However, the coalition's relentless six-week aerial bombing campaign significantly reduced the combat capability of Iraqi troops manning the Saddam Line, many of whom were Shiite conscripts who had little enthusiasm for the war. Indeed, a number of them had deserted or surrendered even before the coalition ground offensive began on February 24, 1991.

Coalition forces attacking into southern Kuwait, primarily the U.S. 1st and 2nd Marine Divisions, used line charges fired from armored personnel carriers to blast a narrow path through the Saddam Line's minefields. The line charges, propelled by rockets, consisted of heavy cords with attached explosives that detonated when the rope had fallen to the ground. M60 Patton and M1 Abrams tanks equipped with steel plows then widened the pathway. Coalition forces also employed conventional mine-detecting equipment.

Clearing and widening the minefields proved to be a laborious task, especially because the Iraqis had used British-manufactured L-9 Bar mines captured from Kuwaiti stockpiles. Made of plastic, the Bar mines could not be located by the American mine detectors, which were effective only against metal mines. Some of the line charges also failed to detonate properly. The mine-clearing process took so long that some marine tanks ran out of gas and had to be refueled between the first and second Iraqi lines, a highly dangerous procedure. Several marine tanks and vehicles were disabled or destroyed by Iraqi mines. Had Iraqi artillery not suffered such serious losses from the air campaign, the marines might well have taken heavy casualties. Regardless, the marines were able to force a number of passages through the Saddam Line on February 24. Surviving Iraqi defenders in the Saddam Line were not inclined to put up significant resistance, and the way into Kuwait was soon open.

PAUL WILLIAM DOERR

**See also**
Persian Gulf War, Overview

**References**
Gordon, Michael R., and General Bernard E. Trainor. *The Generals' War: The Inside Story of the Conflict in the Gulf.* New York: Little, Brown, 1995.
Pollack, Kenneth M. *Arabs at War: Military Effectiveness, 1948–1991.* Lincoln: University of Nebraska Press, 2002.

# Sadeh, Yitzhak (1890–1952)

Israeli soldier and founder of the Palmach. Yitzhak Sadeh was born in Lublin, Poland, on August 10, 1890. Having completed his basic education, he joined the Imperial Russian Army. Sadeh saw considerable action in World War I and was one of the first officers to be commissioned in the Red Army following the November 1917 Bolshevik seizure of power. In 1918 he was a major in command of a battalion. During the ensuing civil war he developed his skills in mobile warfare and small unit tactics.

In 1920 Sadeh immigrated to Palestine and joined Haganah, the Jewish underground self-defense organization. In 1929 he took part in the defense of Haifa. In 1936 as a response to Arab threats, he formed the Nodedet (Patrol). By 1937, this force had become known as the Fosh and operated as a mobile force to protect Jewish settlements throughout Palestine.

In 1938 Sadeh worked closely with British Army captain and militant Zionist Orde Wingate to set up the Special Night Squads, which consisted of both British and Jewish troops. In 1941 Haganah leadership ordered Sadeh to form the Palmach (Phugot Machaz, or Strike Companies), a permanently mobilized Jewish military force. The Palmach was essentially an armed youth movement, but Sadeh quickly trained its recruits into a highly effective military force. He also aided in bringing numbers of illegal Jewish immigrants into Israel.

At the start of the 1948–1949 Israeli War of Independence, Sadeh helped defend territory under attack by the Syrians. The Palmach was absorbed into the newly established Israel Defense Forces (IDF). Later in 1948, he took command of the 8th Brigade in the IDF. The 8th Brigade was, on paper at least, an armored brigade and included the battalion of jeep commandos raised by Major Moshe Dayan. These forces captured the Lod Airport and took part in operation KHOREV, reaching El Arish in the Sinai.

Following the end of the war, Sadeh left the military as a major general and pursued a literary career under the pen name of Y. Noded. While in the Palmach, he had been given the nickname "The Old Man" because so many of the recruits were only in their teens. Nevertheless, his charisma and outgoing personality made him a vital figure in establishing the ethos of the Israeli military. Sadeh died in Tel Aviv on August 21, 1952.

RALPH MARTIN BAKER

**See also**
Dayan, Moshe; Haganah; Israeli War of Independence; Palmach; Wingate, Orde Charles

**References**
Goldstein, Yaacov N., and Dan Shomron. *From Fighters to Soldiers: How the Israeli Defense Forces Began.* Brighton, UK: Sussex Academic, 1998.
Kurzman, Dan. *Genesis 1948: The First Arab-Israeli War.* New York: Da Capo, 1992.

# Sadr, Muqtada al- (1973–)

Influential religious figure in the Iraqi Shia community, leader of the Sadriyun that included the Mahdi Army militias, and considered by many to be the most populist of Iraqi Shiite leaders. The fourth son of the famous Iraqi cleric Muhammad Sadiq al-Sadr, Muqtada al-Sadr was born in Baghdad on August 12, 1973. Sadr became a political leader with an enhanced following as a consequence of

Iraqi Shiite cleric Muqtada al-Sadr photographed following a meeting with Iraqi parliament speaker Salim al-Jabouri on April 5, 2015, in the holy city of Najaf. (Haidar Hamdani/AFP/Getty Images)

his nationalist stance against the coalition presence in Iraq, beginning in 2003.

Sadr acquired a loyal following of his own and, during a period of political truce with the Iraqi government, sought to enhance his standing by continuing his own religious training. Like his father and Iraq's highest Shiite religious authority, Grand Ayatollah Sayyid Ali Husayn al-Sistani, Sadr drew support from a network of mosques but also from extensive charitable and social services provided to impoverished Shia communities in various areas of Baghdad. He also has followers in many other cities and areas of southern and central Iraq. Sadr became especially popular in the large slum areas in Baghdad, including the Thawra area, which became known as Sadr City due to the strength of his followers there.

The elder Sadr, a revered member of the Iraqi Shiite clergy, was assassinated, along with his two elder sons, in 1999. It is widely believed that the assassination was ordered by Iraqi leader Saddam Hussein.

Despite his opposition and that of his followers to Hussein's dictatorial government, Muqtada al-Sadr spoke out fiercely against the U.S.-led coalition following its invasion of Iraq in 2003. Sadr's opposition was based on both political and religious considerations. After the U.S. Coalition Provisional Authority (CPA) closed Sadr's newspaper *al-Hawza* on March 28, 2004, and numerous attacks against him in the American-funded Iraqi press, Sadr mobilized his militia, known as the Mahdi Army. This was to protest what he perceived as the CPA's attempt to eliminate his organization prior to the transfer of authority to Iraqi officials, scheduled for June 30, 2004. The subsequent protests turned violent when a key Sadr aide was arrested on April 3, 2004. The situation was further inflamed two days later when CPA administrator L. Paul Bremer issued a warrant for Sadr's arrest and essentially declared him an outlaw. Sadr's Mahdi Army subsequently seized control of several cities in southern Iraq, provoking the worst crisis for the U.S.-led occupation since the spring of 2003, especially as the Mahdi Army held the loyalty of the most fiercely anti-Baathist groups in the country.

During the ensuing week of violence Sadr sought refuge in the Imam Ali Mosque in Najaf, the holiest shrine in Shia Islam. Sadr's popularity soared during this period because he appeared to be the only Iraqi leader willing to actively resist the occupation. All others, even Ayatollah Sistani, appeared to be passively silent or even acquiescent to the Western authorities. Sadr declared a cease-fire on April 10, 2004, ostensibly to observe a three-day religious holiday, but momentum had also shifted as the CPA retook certain key bases in southern cities. In subsequent negotiations, the CPA called for Sadr to surrender but refrained from overt attempts to arrest him.

In late August 2004 following more than three weeks of renewed fighting between Mahdi Army fighters and U.S. forces, Sadr's forces withdrew from the Imam Ali Mosque. Sadr issued a statement urging his fighters to lay down their arms in line with an agreement he had reached with Ayatollah Sistani. On August 27, 2004, members of the Mahdi Army began surrendering their arms to Iraqi police. But Iraqi prime minister Iyad Allawi renewed the violence when he refused to honor the tenuous truce; fighting ensued, especially in Sadr City. Sadr, in an attempt to distance himself from the acrimony, was thereafter careful not to involve himself directly in Iraqi politics.

In October 2006 the Mahdi Army seized control of Amarah in southern Iraq. A pitched battle ensued between Iraqi security forces and the militiamen. Sadr implored the Mahdi soldiers to lay down their arms, and some have speculated that he had not authorized the Amarah offensive and had lost control of Mahdi Army groups in that area. Sadr's plea was largely ignored. In February 2007 the U.S. media reported that Sadr had fled to Iran in anticipation of the security crackdown attendant with the U.S. troop-surge strategy. Sadr, however, had merely gone into seclusion in Iraq, and during his two-month hiatus he sharply condemned the U.S.-led occupation and called for Iraqi security forces not to cooperate with occupation forces. In 2008 in response to myriad negotiations with Iranian and Iraqi leaders following several months of brutal fighting between the Mahdi Army and Iraqi government forces, Sadr called for a truce and implored the Mahdi Army to lay down its arms.

Sadr continued to condemn the U.S. government and coalition forces' occupation in Iraq, as that was the primary concern of his followers. In late 2008 he called for attacks against U.S. troops in Iraq in retaliation for the Israeli incursion into the Gaza Strip seeking to defeat the radical Palestinian group Hamas. However, this was largely a rhetorical gesture, as his followers continued to observe the truce in place.

In 2010, Sadr urged all Iraqis to participate in that year's national elections. He also continued to call for the withdrawal of all foreign forces from Iraq. The next year, Sadr reached an uneasy agreement with Prime Minister Nuri al-Maliki; meanwhile, Sadr's followers controlled a sizable bloc in Iraq's parliament. After the withdrawal of U.S. troops from Iraq in December 2011, Sadr took a more moderate stance, eschewing violence and urging peace in an increasingly unstable Iraq. In February 2014, he stunned many by officially withdrawing from Iraqi politics and disbanding his party's structure. This move was seen as a boost to al-Maliki's reelection bid in the April 2014 elections.

Sadr was behind a demonstration said to number 1 million people on February 26, 2016, in Tahrir Square, Baghdad, to protest corruption and the Iraqi government's failure to deliver on promised reforms. Then on March 18 Sadr's followers staged a sit-in outside the Green Zone, the heavily fortified Baghdad district with government offices and foreign embassies. Sadr called the Green Zone "a bastion of support for corruption." On March 27, he himself entered the Green Zone while urging followers to remain outside and peaceful. Sadr remains one of the most influential figures in Iraq, despite not holding any official title in the Iraqi government.

Following a Syrian government chemical attack against its own people in April 2017, Sadr called for Syrian president Bashar al-Assad to step down. In April 2018 Sadr offered to act as an intermediary between Saudi Arabia and Iran, which by then were at loggerheads over a variety of weighty issues. In the May 2018 Iraqi parliamentary elections Sadr's Saairun electoral coalition captured 54 seats, which was a major victory for Sadr and gave him increased clout in Iraqi politics. After the elections he denounced any U.S. involvement in the formation of a new Iraqi government, claiming that the United States was an "invader country" and thus had no right to interfere in Iraqi politics. Although U.S. policy makers were not entirely happy with the outcome of the elections, many tacitly agreed that Sadr's strong showing was still preferable to Iran gaining more political ground in Iraq.

PAUL G. PIERPAOLI JR.

**See also**
Allawi, Ayad; Bremer, Lewis Paul, III; Hussein, Saddam; Sistani, Sayyid Ali Hisayn al-

**References**
Cockburn, Patrick. *Muqtada: Muqtada al-Sadr, the Shia Revival, and the Struggle for Iraq.* New York: Scribner, 2008.
Iraq-Business News. "The New Maqtada al-Sadr Seeks Moderate Image." March 13, 2013, http://www.iraq-businessnews.com/2013/03/13/the-new-muqtada-al-sadr-seeks-moderate-image/.
Nasr, Vali. *The Shia Revival: How Conflicts within Islam Will Shape the Future.* New York: Norton, 2006.

## Sadr City, Battle of (March 26–May 11, 2008)

Iraq War battle during March 26–May 11, 2008. In the Battle of Sadr City, coalition forces principally fought elements of the Mahdi Army. Sadr City is one of nine administrative districts of Baghdad and home to more than 1 million Shia Muslims, many of them poor. Part of the district had been known as Thawra and was termed Saddam City by the Americans in 2003. American forces in the coalition then began to call the area "Sadr City" from the strength there of Muqtada al-Sadr's followers, known as the Sadriyun.

Coalition forces in Iraq had long sought permission from Iraqi prime minister Nuri al-Maliki to subdue the Jaysh al-Mahdi (JAM) militias, which they called the Mahdi Army. The Sadriyun, or Sadrists, possessed militias just as did the Dawa Party and the Supreme Council of the Islamic Revolution in Iran (SCIRI). However, these militias also clashed with them, and therefore the coalition had to some degree been influenced by the competition of the various Shia political forces. The Americans claimed that certain elements from the Jaysh al-Mahdi were obtaining arms from Iran, although their competitors, such as the Badr Brigades, were more clearly linked with Iranian support, or at least had been in the past. Maliki was reluctant to approve coalition operations against fellow Shiites, particularly as he might not have been elected had it not been for his good relations with Muqtada al-Sadr and his followers. Also, the largest Shia party in the country had been even closer to Iran than the Sadriyun, who were seen as an Iraqi-based party. Another concern was the vulnerability of the poor civilian population of Sadr City. However, under pressure from Washington, when 12 rockets were launched from the Sadr City area into the Green Zone on March 25, 2008, Maliki approved a joint Iraqi-American response.

Forces of the Iraqi Army 11th Division entered Sadr City on March 26, supported by the U.S. Army 3rd Brigade Combat Team of the 4th Infantry Division, commanded by Colonel John Hort. As the Iraqis moved in, American combat engineers began construction of a concrete barrier across the southern one-third of Sadr City in order to push insurgent forces back beyond rocket range of the coalition-controlled Green Zone. An American Stryker brigade and other supporting coalition units, including troops from the 2nd Stryker Cavalry Regiment, succeeded over the course of a month in building a three-mile-long wall across the southern third of the neighborhood. The concrete "Gold Wall" was constructed from sections 12 feet high by 5 feet wide, placed individually by crane. The Gold Wall and the construction of barriers has been highly criticized by Iraqis and others who believe that defense of perimeters or erection of "sanitized zones" is untenable in the long run.

The fighting in Sadr City was some of the heaviest in the Iraq War. Significantly, for the first time an unmanned aerial vehicle (UAV), or drone, was placed under the direct control of a battlefield commander. Utilizing helicopters and armed and unarmed UAVs and leveraging the persistent surveillance ability of the surveillance drones, which could follow a target on the ground for hours, American forces were able to strike insurgent targets deep within Sadr City. Precision attacks directed or conducted by UAVs killed numerous insurgent mortar and rocket teams.

The heaviest fighting took place on April 28 as militia forces, emboldened by the lack of American air support during a heavy sandstorm, attacked along the heavily contested area of al-Quds Street, known to allied forces as Route Gold. Dozens of militia fighters were killed in ensuing firefights. Mahdi Army forces marshaled heavy firepower to oppose the construction of the concrete wall. Although they employed .50-caliber sniper rifles and RPG-29 rockets and detonated more than 120 Iranian-made mines with explosively forged projectiles against coalition forces, the militias failed to prevent construction of the wall.

Of the some 2,000 American troops in the battle, 6 were killed. Some 5,000 men of the Iraqi Army took part in the battle; their casualty figures were not reported. The Mahdi militia numbered perhaps between 2,000 and 4,000 members; they are believed to have sustained some 700–1,000 casualties.

The forces of the Supreme Islamic Iraqi Council (Majlis al-A'la al-Islami al-'Iraqu, or SIIC), formerly known as the SCIRI, are heavily represented in the new Iraqi Army; consequently, the action was understood as one of intrasectarian and political warfare. Muqtada al-Sadr went into seclusion but called for his fighters to adhere to a truce; otherwise, this campaign could have led to a much wider popular rebellion against the new Iraqi government. Unfortunately, violence continued in Baghdad, with numerous large-scale suicide bombings there and in other cities in the spring of 2009. These, however, were primarily Sunni attacks on Shia or Iraqi and coalition forces or against the Awakening Shaykhs.

The Battle of Sadr City was seen as a significant victory for coalition forces; however, it came at the expense of Prime Minister Maliki's impartiality and credibility to some degree, making him appear to be a creature of the coalition. Sadrist forces and Maliki reached a cease-fire agreement on May 11, 2008, bringing an end to the major fighting in Sadr City.

SHAWN FISHER AND SHERIFA ZUHUR

**See also**
Iraq Insurgency; Maliki, Nuri Muhammed Kamil al-; Sadr, Muqtada al-

**References**
Gordon, Michael R., and Stephen Farrell. "Iraqi Troops Take Charge of Sadr City in Swift Push." *New York Times,* May 21, 2008.
Gordon, Michael R., and Alissa J. Rubin. "Operation in Sadr City Is an Iraqi Success, So Far." *New York Times,* May 22, 2008.
Gordon, Michael R., and Bernard E. Trainor. *The Endgame: The Inside Story of the Struggle for Iraq, from George W. Bush to Barack Obama.* New York: Vintage, 2013.

# Safavid Dynasty (1501–1722 and 1729–1736)

The Safavids came to the throne of Iran (then known in the West as Persia) in 1501 and ruled until 1722 and then again from 1729 to 1736. The Safavid dynasty was certainly one of the most important dynasties in Iranian/Persian history, and many scholars believe that it marks the beginning of modern Iran. One of the largest dynasties of the Persian Empire territorially following the seventh-century Muslim conquest, at its height the Safavids ruled all of present-day Iran, Azerbaijan, and Armenia as well as most of Georgia, the northern Caucasus, Iraq, Kuwait, Afghanistan, and parts of Turkey, Syria, Pakistan, Turkmenistan, and Uzbekistan. The Safavids also established the Twelver school of Shia Islam as the official religion of the empire. This greatly aided the establishment of a national consciousness among the many different ethnic and religious communities constituting the empire.

The Safavids were of largely Kurdish and Azerbaijani descent from the city of Ardabil in Azerbaijan, and about 1399 they switched from Sunni to Shiite Islam. From Ardabil they would establish their control over much of Greater Iran as the first native dynasty since the Sassanians in 224–651 to rule over a unified Iranian state.

The Safavid dynasty was founded by Ismail, who ruled as Shah (king) Ismail I during 1501–1524. Ismail invaded Shirvan to avenge his father, who had been killed during a siege of Derbent in Dagestan. Ismail then embarked on a campaign of conquest. Securing sufficient Turkmen support, in July 1501 he captured Tabriz from the Ak Koyunlu, or White Sheep Uzbek Confederation, whereupon he proclaimed himself shah of Azerbaijan with Shia Islam as the state's official religion.

Although at first they ruled only Azerbaijan and southern Dagestan, the Safavids were in fact well placed to rule all of Persia, which was then wracked by dynastic conflict and fragmentation with accompanying religious diversity. A year after taking Tabriz, Ismail laid claim to most of Persia and in the next decade conquered what remained, bringing all of Iran under his rule. Ismail also conquered the Iraqi provinces of Baghdad and Mosul and, despite the fact that they were predominantly Sunni Muslim, imposed Shia Islam on them.

On August 23, 1514, however, Ismail suffered a major military reverse in the Battle of Chaldiran at the hands of Sunni rival Ottoman sultan Selim I. This Ottoman victory gave the Ottomans control of eastern Anatolia. Ismail I died in 1524 and was succeeded by his son Tahmasp I, age 10. Another influential shah, he ruled until 1576 in the longest reign of any Safavid ruler. Tahmasp mounted multiple invasions in the Caucasus. He also began the practice of population relocation of the border peoples, forcing hundreds of thousands of Circassians, Georgians, and Armenians to relocate to the Iranian heartland. Iran came under Turkmen forays under Tahmasp's incompetent successors Ismail II (r. 1576–1577) and Mohammad I (r. 1577–1587), however.

A coup d'état against the inept Mohammad I brought to power in 1587 his son, Shah Abbas I, known as Abbas the Great (r. 1587–1629), at age 16. Abbas turned out to be the greatest of the Safavid monarchs. Realizing the inadequacy of his own military, he made peace with the Ottomans on unfavorable terms in 1590 and directed his military efforts against the Uzbeks instead. In 1598 he recaptured Herat and Mashhad, both of which had been lost by his father earlier in the Ottoman-Safavid War (1578–1590). Ongoing pressure from the Ottomans and the Usbeks, however, led Abbas to relocate the Safavid capital to Isfahan in 1598.

In 1599 Abbas hired the English artillerist Sir Robert Sherley to carry out major reforms in his army. The new military force thus created was trained and armed along regular European lines and paid from the royal treasury. Abbas also greatly centralized the administrative system of his country.

In 1602, taking advantage of internal problems in the Ottoman Empire and its involvement in Europe, Abbas invaded the eastern Ottoman Empire. In 1603 he captured Tabriz, and in 1604 he secured Yerevan (Erevan, Erivan). Shirvan and Kars also fell. Abbas thus regained the territory lost to the Ottomans the decade before. In 1603 also he expelled the Portuguese traders from Bahrain.

Determined to reverse this situation, Ottoman sultan Ahmed moved against Abbas with some 100,000 men and joined battle with Abbas and his army of some 62,000 men at Sis in present-day Azerbaijan on September 9, 1606. Abbas won a crushing victory that resulted in his securing Azerbaijan, Kurdistan, Baghdad, Mosul, and Diarbekh.

In 1613 Abbas sent an army into Georgia to force it to acknowledge his suzerainty. In a punitive campaign, he devastated Kakheti and Tbilisi and deported as many as 200,000 Georgians into the Iranian heartland. During his reign he would also remove to the Iranian interior some 300,000 Armenians and 100,000–150,000 Circassians.

Because the Ottomans considered Georgia to be within their sphere of influence, this brought renewed war between the two empires in 1616. The Ottomans invaded Armenia and laid siege to its largest city, Yerevan (Erevan), but were forced to raise the siege in the winter of 1616–1617. A year later the Ottomans again invaded and moved against Tabriz, but lack of success here led to peace talks and Ottoman recognition of Iranian control of both Azerbaijan and Georgia.

In 1622 Abbas led a Safavid army into present-day Afghanistan, capturing Kandahar. That same year, assisted by English ships, Abbas captured Hormuz, retaking it from the Portuguese.

In 1623 the Ottomans again went to war against the Safavids in an effort to recapture the territory lost in the two earlier wars. This time the Ottomans focused on Baghdad. Their effort there during 1625–1626 was unsuccessful, although some border warfare between the two empires continued thereafter.

Abbas expanded commercial links with the Dutch East India Company and established firm diplomatic ties with the major European governments, which had been initiated by Ismail I. During Abbas I's reign Isfahan became one of the world's largest and most beautiful cities, with the construction of many new mosques and other structures.

Abbas I's last years were troubled. Three of his sons survived into adulthood. Believing that they were plotting against him, Abbas had them either killed or blinded. Abbas died in 1629, succeeded by his grandson, Shah Safi (r. 1629–1642). Safi proved ineffectual. His son Abbas II (r. 1642–1666) was another strong ruler, but those shahs who followed presided over the deterioration of the dynasty, seemingly more interested in a lavish lifestyle, strong drink, and the royal harem than the act of ruling. Shahs Suleiman I (r. 1666–1694) and Husayn (r. 1694–1722) were both weak rulers.

Increasingly, the Iranian frontiers were under attack. In 1709 Afghan Ghilzai Pashtun chieftain Mir Wais Khan commenced a rebellion in Kandahar and defeated a Safavid army. In 1722, Russian tsar Peter I the Great began the Russo-Persian War (1722–1723), capturing many of Iran's Caucasian territories. Also in 1722 Isfahan fell to an Afghan army led by Mahmud Hotak, who proclaimed himself shah and ruled until 1725, when he was succeeded by his cousin Ashraf Hotak. In 1729 the son of Sultan Husayn recovered Isfahan and ascended the throne as Shah Tahmasp II, but he was the last of the Safavids. In 1732 he was deposed by his Afsharid lieutenant Nadr Qoli Beg, the future Nadir Shah.

Despite their demise in 1736, the Safavids left behind a unitary and strong state, noted for its commercial wealth, its achievements in the arts, and the spread of Shia Islam.

SPENCER C. TUCKER

### See also
Abbas I the Great; Constantinople, 1590 Treaty of; Ismail I, Shah; Nadir Shah; Nasuh Pasha, Treaty of; Ottoman-Safavid Wars; Russo-Persian Wars; Selim I, Sultan; Shia Islam

### References
Blow, David. *Shah Abbas: The Ruthless King Who Became an Iranian Legend.* New York: I. B. Tauris, 2009.

Jackson, Peter, and Laurence Lockhart, eds. *The Cambridge History of Iran,* Vol. 6, *The Timurid and Safavid Periods.* Cambridge: Cambridge University Press, 1986.

Newman, Andrew J. *Safavid Iran: Rebirth of a Persian Empire.* London: I. B. Tauris, 2006.

Savory, Roger. *Iran under the Safavids.* Cambridge: Cambridge University Press, 2007.

Sicker, Martin. *The Islamic World in Decline: From the Treaty of Karlowitz to the Disintegration of the Ottoman Empire.* Westport, CT: Praeger, 2001.

## Saif al-Dawla (926–967)

Founder of the Hamadanid dynasty in Syria famous for his prolonged struggle against the Byzantine Empire. Saif (Sayf) al-Dawla was born Abu al-Hasan Ali Ibn Hamdan on June 22, 916, into a prominent family. His grandfather Ibn Hamdan, the lord of Mardin, rebelled against the Abbasid caliph during 894–895, while his father Abu al-Haija perished in the power struggle in Baghdad in the early 930s. The young Abu al-Hasan initially ruled at Wasit in modern-day Iraq and, with his brother Nasir al-Dawla, actively participated in the political struggles in Baghdad. Saif al-Dawla helped Caliph al-Muttaki consolidate his authority in the 940s, for which the caliph granted him the surname Saif al-Dawla (sword of the state).

Saif al-Dawla also exploited the weakness of the Abbasid caliphate to expand his own realm. In 944 with the support of the local Banu Kilab tribe, he invaded Syria and that October captured Aleppo from the Ikhshidid dynasty of Egypt. In 945, he besieged Damascus but failed to capture it. Muhammad ibn Tughj al-Ikhshid then took the field against Saif and, victorious at Qinnasrin, compelled the Hamdanid prince to sign a peace treaty. The accord established a mutually recognized frontier in Syria, with Saif gaining Qinnasrin and Aleppo while the rest of Syria, including Damascus, stayed under the Ikhshidid control. To keep Saif at bay, al-Ikhshid pledged to send annual gifts in compensation for Saif's abandoning his claims to Damascus.

In July 946 al-Ikhshid died in Damascus, and Saif al-Dawla broke the treaty and marched upon the city, which he captured. He then advanced into Palestine, hoping to exploit the moment to extend his authority. However, he was defeated by the Ikhshidid army, led by the black eunuch Abu'l-Misk Kafur, near Nasira in December 946 and forced to withdraw into northern Syria, while Kafur reoccupied Damascus.

After regrouping, Saif returned to Damascus in the spring of 947 but again suffered defeat at Marj Rahit. Following these reverses, Saif agreed to accept a new peace treaty with the Ikhshidids, who allowed him to retain north Syria in order to create a buffer from the Byzantines, but no longer paid the Hamdanids tribute. The newly established frontiers in Syria, with the Hamdanid-controlled north and the Egyptian-ruled south, remained intact until the rise of the Egyptian mamluks in the mid-13th century.

Unable to defeat the Ikhshidids, Saif turned his attention to the Byzantine Empire. He had targeted the Byzantine realm as early as 936–938, with his early raids into Byzantine territory producing enormous booty. In December 944 Saif scored a decisive victory over the Byzantine army, led by a certain Pantherios, near Aleppo. Beginning in 949, Saif embarked on a series of raids (*razzias*) that turned him into a leader of the holy war (jihad) against the Byzantines during the next 20 years. In 949, he raided the Byzantine province of Lycandus, but the Byzantines drove him out and sacked the border towns of Germanicea and Theodosiopolis.

In 950, encouraged by Byzantine defeats in Crete, Saif set out on an ambitious raid deep into Byzantine territory, plundering Lycandus and Charsianum. He defeated Domestic of the Schools (commander in chief) Bardas Phokas in the valley of Lycus and then turned for home with vast booty. But Byzantine forces under Leo Phokas ambushed Saif in a mountain pass between Lycandus and Germanikeia, inflicting heavy losses.

Spurning a Byzantine offer of peace, Saif raided the regions of Melitene and Lycandus in 951 and 952. A year later he won a great victory near Germanikeia, killing the *patrikios* Leo Maleinos, severely wounding Bardas Phokas, and capturing his son Constantine. This was followed by more victories in the course of the next three years during which Saif rebuilt the ruined border fortresses of Germanikeia, Adata, and Samosata. In 953–954 he laid waste to the Melitene region, and two years later he invaded the Byzantine Empire as far inland as Harsan in Armenia, capturing several fortress and devastating the entire region.

Saif's military successes prompted the Byzantines to focus their efforts against him. Emperor Constantine VII made treaties with neighboring rulers and sought military aid from them against Saif. Constantine then launched a series of expeditions to break Saif's power. In 956, brilliant young Byzantine commander John Tzimiskes raided Hamdanid territory. A year later, the domestic Nikephorus Phokas destroyed Saif's major fortress of Adata, while in 958 Tzimiskes sacked Dara and Samosata on the Euphrates and defeated Saif near Aleppo, taking thousands of captives back to Constantinople.

In the spring of 959 the Byzantines raided Qurus, just 40 miles from Aleppo. Three years later, Nikephoros Phokas led an even greater invasion of Cilicia and Syria, defeating Saif near Aleppo and capturing that place on December 23, 962. As Phokas continued his campaign, the Byzantines plundered much of northern Syria, including Saif's palace, which they destroyed.

By then Saif suffered from a serious illness that left him partially paralyzed. Nevertheless, he continued his struggle against the Byzantines, scoring an important victory near Aleppo during a new Byzantine invasion in 964. But in 965–966 Nikephorus Phokas reduced the numerous Muslim fortresses beyond the Taurus range, Cilicia, and northern Syria. Broken in body but not spirit, Saif died at Aleppo on February 9, 967. Although his struggle against the Byzantines ultimately proved unsuccessful, he brilliantly interpreted the role of *ghazi* leader, engaging the best Arabic poets of the time to sing praises to his rule.

ALEXANDER MIKABERIDZE

**See also**
Byzantine-Muslim Wars; Kafur, Abu al-Misk

**References**
Canard, Marius. *Saif al-Dawla: Quelques receuil de texts relatives à l'émir Saif al-Dawla*. Algiers: n.p., 1934.
Shepard, Jonathan, ed. *The Cambridge History of the Byzantine Empire*. Cambridge: Cambridge University Press, 2008.
Treadgold, Warren. *A History of the Byzantine State and Society*. Palo Alto, CA: Stanford University Press, 1997.

## Sakarya, Battle of the (August 23–September 13, 1921)

Important battle of the Greco-Turkish War (1919–1922). Following the Greek defeat in the Second Battle of İnönü (March 26–31, 1921), Greek king Constantine assumed personal command in the field. With his army reinforced, in mid-July he launched an offensive with the goal of taking Ankara. Constantine was optimistic, believing that the Turkish Nationalist forces would be forced to stand and fight to defend their capital and could therefore be decisively defeated. Despite assistance from Bolshevik Russia, the Turks were chronically short of both equipment and supplies.

Constantine's feint toward the Turkish right flank at Eskişehir distracted Ismet İnönü Pasha, while the major Greek effort fell on the Turkish left at Kara Hisar. The Greeks then wheeled to the north and swept toward Eskişehir, defeating the Turks in a series of frontal assaults and flanking movements. Despite a fierce Turkish counterattack, Constantine's forces defeated Ismet in the Battle of Kutahya-Eskişehir on July 17 and again advanced to the Sakarya River, some 50 miles west of Ankara. Ismet Pasha was determined to fight to the end, but Mustafa Kemal prevailed on him, and

Ismet then disengaged and withdrew to the Sakarya River, some 30 miles to the north and only 50 miles from Ankara.

Mustafa Kemal now assumed personal command of the Turkish forces. The resulting long and sanguinary Battle of the Sakarya (Sakkaria) River, during August 23–September 13, 1921, centered on a series of hilltop positions held by the Turks and repeated efforts by the Greeks to dislodge them. Both sides employed artillery, while the Greeks had 18 aircraft and the Turks 2. The battle pitted as many as 120,000 Greeks against some 96,000 Turks. Although their positions changed hands a number of times, the Turks managed to hold. The battle claimed about 23,000 Greek casualties, while the Turks lost as many as 38,000 killed, wounded, captured, or deserted.

With the onset of winter, his forces short of ammunition, and his 350-mile supply line westward threatened, Constantine decided to withdraw. Although Turkish casualties were considerably higher, the battle was tactically inconclusive. However, the Turks had halted the Greek advance, and so it must be counted as a strategic Turkish victory. The war then entered a period of stalemate. Kemal used this time to build up his military strength and solidify his support within the Ottoman Empire.

Spencer C. Tucker

**See also**
Ataturk, Mustafa Kemal; Greco-Turkish War

**References**
Mango, Andrew. *Atatürk: The Biography of the Founder of Modern Turkey.* Woodstock, NY: Overlook, 2000.
Pope, Nicole, and Hugh Pope. *Turkey Unveiled: Ataturk and After.* London: John Murray, 1997.

# Saladin (1138–1193)

Egyptian vizier (1169–1171) and sultan (1174–1193) and the principal opponent of the Frankish kingdoms of Outremer in the second half of 12th century. Born in Takrit in upper Mesopotamia (present day Iraq) in the Abbasid Caliphate in 1138, Salah-al din Yusuf ibn Ayyub (the honorific Saladin is a European corruption of his honorific Arabic title *Sala al-Din,* meaning "righteousness of the faith"). He was a Kurd and the son of Najm ad-Din Ayyub, governor of Damascus. Saladin received a traditional Sunni religious education. Saladin's uncle, Shirkuh, was a key assistant to Syrian ruler Nur al-Din. Saladin joined the military as a teenager and campaigned with Nur al-Din.

In 1164 Nur al-Din dispatched troops under Shirkuh and Saladin to Egypt to help the Fatimid dynasty defeat Christian crusaders under King Amalric I of Jerusalem. Saladin distinguished himself fighting against Amalric I in the Battle of Cairo (April 11, 1167). He then helped Shirkuh drive the crusaders from Egypt (January 1169). Shirkuh then became virtual ruler of Egypt as vizier (prime minister) under the Fatimids.

On Shirkuh's death in 1169, Saladin succeeded him as vizier with the full support of Nur al-Din. He then consolidated his power and in 1171 terminated the Fatimid dynasty altogether, beginning the Surni Ayyubid dynasty. Saladin moved the capital to Cairo and worked to strengthen Egypt both militarily and economically. He carried out raids against the crusaders, ordered the successful invasion and conquest of Yemen, and crushed pro-Fatamid rebellions in Upper Egypt.

On the death of Nur al-Din in 1174, Saladin marched on Damascus, which he secured without fighting on invitation of its governor. In 1175 Saladin conquered both Hama and Homs, inviting the animosity of his former Zengid lords, who had been rulers of Syria. He defeated the Zengid army in the April 13, 1175, Battle of the Horns of Hama and as a consequence was proclaimed by Abbasid caliph al-Mustadi as sultan of Egypt and Syria. On November 25, 1177, Saladin suffered a major defeat at the hands of the Franks in the Battle of Mont Giscard in southern Palestine. However, he recovered from this setback, and in the Battle of Marj Ayyun (Marj Ayyoun) on June 10, 1179, he defeated a crusader army led by King Baldwin IV of Jerusalem.

After additional conquests in northern Syria and Jazira and escaping two attempts on his life by the Assassins, Saladin returned to Egypt. By 1182, he had taken Aleppo and completed the conquest of Muslim Syria. Although his efforts to secure the Zengid stronghold of Mosul were unsuccessful, its leaders did agree to recognize Saladin's sovereignty and contribute forces to his campaigns. Other victories by Saladin included conquest of the Artuqid towns of Mayyafariqin and Mardin and the fortress of Amida (modern-day Diyarbakir, Turkey) in 1183.

Having secured control of most of today's Syria and Iraq, in 1187 Saladin proclaimed jihad (holy war) against the crusader states in an effort to drive the Christians from Outremer. In the Battle of Cresson (May 1, 1187), Saladin defeated a small crusader force, causing the crusaders to assemble a large force against him at Acre.

Saladin laid siege to Tiberius in June to draw the crusaders there from Acre, which occurred. When the crusaders arrived at Tiberius, they assumed that they would find water for their horses at the Lake of Tiberius (Sea of Galilee), but

Saladin had assembled a large force to block their access to the lake. He then attacked and utterly defeated the crusaders in the Battle of Hattin (July 4, 1187). During the next several months, Saladin captured most of the Christian cities of Palestine, including Jerusalem, which fell following a two-week siege (September 20–October 2).

As a consequence of Saladin's military successes, the Christian states of Europe mounted the Third Crusade (1189–1192), of which the preeminent figure was King Richard I of England (Richard the Lionheart). The crusaders laid siege to Acre and took it (July 12, 1191). After having strengthened Acre, including rebuilding its walls, Richard I led a large crusader force down the coast to Jaffa (today Tel Aviv, Israel). En route near Arsuf, Saladin attacked Richard (September 7, 1191) but was defeated at a cost of some 7,000 Muslims slain for only 700 crusaders. Despite this, Saladin continued to hold Jerusalem. Finally, Richard and Saladin negotiated a truce on September 2, 1192, in which Muslims and Christians were granted free access in Palestine, allowing Christian pilgrims to visit Jerusalem, but the crusaders were left holding coastal cities and Saladin in control of the interior of Palestine. Returning to Damascus, Saladin fell ill there and died on March 4, 1193.

A highly effective general and strategist, Saladin was also an excellent administrator and organizer. A sincere Muslim, he nonetheless never allowed religion to influence his policies.

Spencer C. Tucker

**See also**
Acre, 1189 Siege of; Al-Adil; Arsuf, Battle of; Assassins; Ayyubid Dynasty; Cresson, Battle of; Crusades in the Holy Land, Christian; Hattin, Battle of; Jaffa, Battle of; Mont Giscard, Battle of; Nur al-Din; Richard I, King; Zangi, Imad ad-Din

**References**
Ehrenkreutz, Andrew S. *Saladin.* Albany: State University of New York Press, 1972
Gibb, Hamilton, A. R. *The Life of Saladin.* Oxford, UK: Clarendon, 1973.
Humphreys, R. Stephen. *From Saladin to the Mongols: The Ayyubids of Damascus, 1193–1260.* Albany: State University of New York Press, 1977.
Lev, Yaacov. *Saladin in Egypt.* Leiden, Netherlands: Brill, 1999.
Lyons, Malcom Cameron, and D. E. P. Jackson. *Saladin: The Politics of the Holy War.* Cambridge: Cambridge University Press, 1982.
Newby, P. H. *Saladin in His Time.* New York: Dorset, 1992.
Regan, Geoffrey. *Lionhearts: Saladin, Richard I, and the Era of the Third Crusade.* New York: Walker, 1999.
Sivan, Emanuel. *L'Islam et la croisade.* Paris: Librairie d'Amérique et d'Orient, 1967.

# Salafism

Islamic fundamentalist school of thought. The term "Salafism" is derived from the Arabic *salaf* in reference to the early generations of Muslims, especially those close to Prophet Muhammad. It is often connected to the *sahabah,* or those who saw and spoke to the prophet at least once in their lifetime. A key concept behind Salafism is that those closest to the prophet would best know his mind and actions and would thus provide the clearest examples of how one was to live life as a devout Muslim. Within Islam there is no clear core of fundamental law, and as a result it is important for a Muslim to connect with those principles laid out by Prophet Muhammad in order to be able to do the right things to gain *jannah,* or paradise. Salafism, which has informed the worldview of organizations such as the Muslim Brotherhood and Al Qaeda, is often equated in the West with radicalism, violence, and terrorism, but most Muslims who abide by the precepts of Salafism are neither violent nor radical.

The term "Salafism" is fairly new, although the use of the root word appears in a number of early *hadith,* or sayings of the prophet and his companions, as well as other writings such as the *tafsir* (exegesis) of al-Tabari and Ibn Kathir. The modern term was popularized in the late 1800s by several Muslim thinkers, including Jamal ad-Din al-Afghani and his disciple Muhammad Abduh, mainly in response to British colonialism in the Middle East, Afghanistan, and India. In essence, it was a revival movement of early or, as some would claim, authentic Islam after hundreds of years of domination by Christian Europe.

Jamal ad-Din al-Afghani (1838–1897) was born and raised in eastern Iran and was probably Shiite by doctrinal association. Nevertheless, in his effort to see the revival of Islam as a counter to British colonial policy, he strove to hide his doctrinal sympathies, focusing instead on building a philosophical opposition movement to oppose British occupation of Muslim lands. He traveled extensively and typically portrayed himself in ways that were not consistent with his background and training. In each instance when his benefactors, whether in Great Britain, Egypt, or Istanbul, became suspicious of him and his motives, al-Afghani would depart to another area of the world to continue his self-appointed mission to throw off the British yoke. Wherever he went he continued to preach the revival of the Islamic community, or *ummah,* as based on the lives of the prophet and his early companions.

In his desire to defeat British colonialism, al-Afghani was willing to engage in a wide range of political and insurgency-type activities, ranging from simple fund-raising to endorsing assassination attempts against those Middle Eastern rulers he considered to be British puppets. He spoke openly of killing the leader of Persia, Nasir ad-Din Shah, and one of his disciples eventually carried out the deed in 1896. Although supportive of the Ottoman Empire as the current seat of the Islamic Khalifate, al-Afghani spent his last years in Istanbul virtually as a political prisoner of the empire's sultan and died of cancer in 1897.

Al-Afghani's influence almost vanished after his death, but later his name would be resurrected as a folk hero to the revived Islamic movement in the Middle East. The principles of Salafism would be pushed eloquently by one of his main disciples, Muhammad Abduh (1849–1905). Abduh collaborated with al-Afghani on a number of publishing projects and helped to popularize Salafist ideas through what became known as the Islamic League. He was savvy politically and was able to secure the position as grand mufti of Egypt in 1899, a post he held until his death.

In some ways Abduh's influence was greater than al-Afghani's because he was seen by many as more moderate and mainstream, even though his ideas were essentially no different than his mentor's. Abduh's writings were more readily accepted and included a *tafsir* of the Quran along with other works defending the unity of Allah from Christian influences stemming from British colonial policy.

Abduh's ideas would have a tremendous impact on the thinking of Hassan al-Banna (1906–1949) and the founding of the Muslim Brotherhood in Egypt in 1928. The focus of the brotherhood as well as other revivalist Muslim societies was initially based on personal piety and raising money through the imposition of *zakat*, or the charitable tax. Soon these activities turned to political activism, and the brotherhood surged to the forefront of political thought in the struggle against British colonial occupation of the country. Al-Banna was assassinated in 1949, and the ideas of the brotherhood spread throughout the Middle East and into the rest of the Islamic world, especially through such apologists as Sayyid Qutb (1906–1966) and Yusuf al-Qaradawi (1926–), and has in large measure become the foundation of the Islamic revival movement.

The principles of Salafism revolve around several key issues that involve the literal interpretation of the Quran and adopting certain aspects of the lifestyle of the prophet and his companions. Shunning Western dress and grooming became important outward displays of this movement, although this was not always consistently done for political reasons. Coupled with this was a revival of interest in the writings of the Hanbalite jurist Ibn Taymiyyah (1263–1328), who discussed the conflict inherent between the *salaf* (predecessors) and the *khalaf*, or the authentic believers of the prophet with those who are merely substitutes of the real thing.

This led to sporadic conflict in the Muslim world between the members of the Salafist movement and the governments of the region. Efforts by Arabic governments to suppress Salafism culminated in the judicial execution of Sayyid Qutb by the Egyptian government of Gamal Abdel Nasser in 1966 and the destruction of the town of Hama, which had become the base of the movement in Syria, by the government of Hafez al-Assad in 1982 in which close to 30,000 people died. However, these attempts to destroy the movement were only temporary. Rebounding from these setbacks, the Muslim Brotherhood continued its political activities throughout the Islamic world, spreading even into Europe and the United States.

Another important aspect of the Salafist movement is the rejection in general of the concept of *taqlid* and the call to revive *ijtihad*. *Taqlid*, often incorrectly translated as "blind following," stresses the need for Muslims to simply follow the rulings of a particular *madhhab*, or school of law, without doing the necessary research themselves. This is a convenient approach, for it does not require an inordinate amount of time and energy to be expended on learning the fundamentals of Islam, particularly those considered well established a few hundred years after the death of Prophet Muhammad. Taking a ruling on faith, Muslims can practice their religion on the basis of these early rulings by those much more learned.

The weakness of *taqlid*, however, is obvious, as for Muslims to be truly devoted followers it is best to learn the foundational material themselves. This requires long hours of study and sometimes even formal training to become well versed in the early writings of Islam. This approach reopened the door to *ijtihad*, being the revival of personal interpretation of Quranic texts as well as other early writings. For many centuries, the learned within Islam had considered *ijtihad* closed because of the solidification and codification of Islamic practice through the *maddhabs* (school of thought). Salafism called for the return of *ijtihad* to allow typical believers to make up their minds for themselves, and this led to a massive revival in interest in the classical and medieval works of Islam. Translations of the hadith and sunna writings flourished, and the works of medieval scholars such as Qadi Iyad (544–1149), Ibn Taymiyyah, and Ibn Qayyim (1292–1350) were resurrected. Even the writings of some early Sufi scholars such as Imam Ghazzali became popular, although the Salafist movement by and large considers Sufism a heretical interpretation of Islam.

The return of *ijtihad* meant that many devout Muslims began to question some aspects of the juristic rulings from later scholars of the *maddhabs* while still retaining interest in the rulings of the founders of those schools. This revival of personal interpretation had significant influence on bringing back the earliest teachings regarding *zakat* (alms giving), the proper forms of prayer, and the need to engage in jihad. *Zakat* became the means for the Salafists to influence local politics through provision of welfare and family support, while jihad became more than an inward struggle, returning to the prophet's own conception that jihad was a form of warfare to make Islam supreme. This revival not only spawned such groups as the Muslim Brotherhood but also led to a whole series of other lesser groups generally striving for the same goals, being the imposition of Islamic sharia in the Muslim world and a return to evangelistic operations to spread Islam throughout the non-Muslim world. The Salafist movement's teachings can be found in virtually every Islamic revival today, largely because those teachings were built on the earliest ideas and writings of the prophet and his companions.

RUSSELL G. RODGERS

### See also
Al Qaeda; Islamic Radicalism in the 20th and 21st Centuries; Muhammad, Prophet of Islam; Muslim Brotherhood; Quran; Sharia; Shia Islam; Sunni Islam

### References
'Abduh, Muhammad. *Risalat al-Tauhid* [The Theology of Unit]. Translated by Ishaq Musa'ad and Kenneth Craig. Kuala Lumpur, Malaysia: Islamic Book Trust, 2004.

Al-Hashimi, Muhammad Ali. *The Ideal Muslim Society: As Defined in the Qur'an and Sunnah*. Riyadh, Saudi Arabia: International Islamic Publishing House, 2007.

Al-Qaradawi, Yusuf. *The Eye of the Beholder: The Muslim Brotherhood over the Past 70 Years*. Cairo: Al-Falah Foundation, 2003.

Keddie, Nikki. *An Islamic Response to Imperialism: Political and Religious Writings of Sayyid Jamal ad-Din "al-Afghani."* Translated by Nikki Keddie and Hamid Algar. Berkeley: University of California Press, 1968.

Philips, Abu Ameenah Bilal. *The Evolution of Fiqh: Islamic Law & the Madh-habs*. Kuala Lumpur, Malaysia: A. S. Noordeen, 2005.

## Saleh, Ali Abdullah (1942–2017)

President of the Republic of Yemen (1990–2012) and, prior to that, president of the Yemen Arab Republic (North Yemen) during 1978–1990. Ali Abdullah Saleh al-Sanhani al-Humairi was born on March 21, 1942, into the Sanhan tribe at Bait el-Ahmar village, some 12 miles southeast of Sana'a. In 1968 Saleh joined the Kingdom of Yemen's military, serving in the infantry. After attending the kingdom's Military Academy during 1960–1963, he was commissioned a second lieutenant in the Tank Corps.

Saleh took part in the army coup of 1962, which brought the removal of King Muhammad al-Badr and establishment of the Yemen Arab Republic. During the North Yemen Civil War of 1962–1970 Saleh served in the Tank Corps. Promoted to major in 1969, he received additional military education in the Higher Command and Staff Course in Iraq during 1970–1971 and was promoted to lieutenant colonel. He became a full colonel in 1976 and assumed command of a mechanized brigade. In 1977 his mentor, president of North Yemen Ahmed bin Hussein al-Ghashmi, appointed Saleh military governor of Ta'izz.

Following the assassination of al-Ghashmi on June 24, 1978, Saleh became one of the four members of a provisional presidency council ruling the country. On July 17, Saleh was elected by the parliament as president of the Yemen Arab Republic and commander of its armed forces.

As president, Saleh relied heavily on family members, especially his seven brothers, who received key positions. Beneath these were Sanhan tribal members and members of al-Ghasnmi's Hamdan Sana'a tribe. Saleh's regime was characterized by rampant corruption, as he greatly enriched himself and his family at the expense of the people of what is one of the world's poorest nations. In August 1978, Saleh ordered the execution of 30 officers charged with conspiring to overthrow his government. Promoted to major general in 1980, Saleh was elected secretary-general of the General People's Congress party in August 1982, and reelected president of the Yemen Arab Republic in 1983.

In 1990 following prolonged negotiations, the two Yemens, North and South, agreed to unify. Saleh became president of the unified country, while Ali Salim al-Beidh, secretary-general of the Yemeni Socialist Party in South Yemen, became vice president. A staunch ally of Iraqi president Saddam Hussein, Saleh supported the Iraqi invasion of Kuwait in August 1990. When Yemen, then a member of the UN Security Council, abstained from a number of votes condemning Iraq and voted against the resolution authorizing the use of force, the Saudi Arabian government expelled some 800,000 Yemenis, creating staggering unemployment and an economic crisis in Yemen.

Following food riots in major towns in 1992, a new coalition government was formed. In 1993, complaints by southerners that the northerners were completely dominating Yemeni affairs led to a brief civil war during May–June 1994,

Ali Abdullah Saleh, photographed on May 21, 2008. Saleh was president of the Republic of Yemen (1990–2012) and, before that, president of the Yemen Arab Republic (North Yemen) during 1978–1990. (Khaled Fazaa/AFP/Getty Images)

with the northern part of the Yemeni army victorious over the secessionists.

In December 1997, the parliament approved Saleh's promotion to field marshal. Two years later, he became Yemen's first directly elected president, winning an announced 96.2 percent of the vote. Following that election, the members of parliament agreed to extend the presidential term from five to seven years, extended its own terms from four to six years, and created a 111-member presidentially appointed council of advisers with legislative authority.

Although Saleh had announced in July 2005 that he would not seek another presidential term, he changed his mind in June 2006, saying he was bowing to "popular pressure and appeals of the Yemeni people." Saleh won the September 2006 election with an announced 77.2 percent of the vote.

In early 2011 as part of the demand for democratic changes that swept much of the Arab world and was known as the Arab Spring, protests began in Yemen demanding an end to Saleh's three-decades-long heavy-handed, autocratic, and corrupt rule. Confronted with these, on February 2, 2011, Saleh announced that he would not seek reelection in 2013 but would serve out the remainder of his term. On March 10, 2011, Saleh announced that there would be a referendum on a new, more liberal constitution. On March 18, however, at least 52 people were killed and more than 200 injured when security forces fired on unarmed demonstrators in Sana'a. Saleh denied that the security forces were even present.

With protests mounting and civil war looming, on April 23 Saleh agreed to step down under a plan whereby he would receive immunity from criminal prosecution and yield power to Vice President Abd Rabbuh Mansur Hadi. Although he had earlier pledged to resign within a month, on May 23 Saleh refused to sign the agreement, leading to renewed protests and the withdrawal of the Gulf Cooperation Council (GCC) from mediation efforts.

On June 3, 2011, a bomb in the presidential compound badly injured Saleh and killed four of his bodyguards. The prime minister, deputy prime ministers, and many other prominent officials were also injured. Although government spokesmen tried to downplay the attack by saying that Saleh was only lightly wounded, the next day he was flown to Saudi Arabia for treatment. On June 4, Vice President Hadi became acting president in Saleh's absence. On September 23, Saleh returned to a Yemen increasingly in turmoil with gun battles in the streets of Sana'a and more than 100 people killed.

Although Saleh dithered, on November 23 he flew to Riyadh under a government transition plan hammered out by the GCC by which he ceded all presidential powers to Vice President Hadi. In late January 2012 Saleh arrived in the United States for further medical treatment, returning to Sana'a on February 25 only hours before Hadi was to take the oath of office. With widespread protests occurring, on February 27 Saleh formally ceded power.

Saleh, who had described governing Yemen as "dancing on the head of snakes," continued active involvement in Yemeni politics. Operating behind the scenes, he abetted the Houthi insurgency that led to the Houthi capture of Sana's and the flight of President Hadi's government. On July 28, 2016, Saleh and the Houthi rebels announced a formal alliance to fight the Saudi-led military coalition battling the Houthis, now supported by Iran. The new governing body had 10 members: 5 from Saleh's General People's Congress and 5 from the Houthis.

On December 2, 2017, Saleh shattered the alliance between his own followers and the Houthis. In a televised statement he denounced the latter as a "coup militia" and called on his followers to take back territory held by the Houthis. On December 4, 2017, Saleh was killed in Sana'a, reportedly as he was attempting to flee to Saudi-held territory. All of this only complicated the possibility of securing a deal that would end the fighting in Yemen that had devastated the country and had placed some 7 million people at risk of death from starvation.

SPENCER C. TUCKER

**See also**
Gulf Cooperation Council; Yemen; Yemen Civil War

**References**
Clark, Victoria. *Yemen: Dancing on the Heads of Snakes.* New Haven, CT: Yale University Press, 2010.
Day, Stephen W. *Regionalism and Rebellion in Yemen.* Cambridge: Cambridge University Press, 2012.
Dresch, Paul. *A History of Modern Yemen.* New York: Cambridge University Press, 2001.
Mackintosh-Smith, Tim. *Yemen: The Unknown Arabia.* New York: Overlook, 2014.
Rabi, Uzi. *Yemen: Revolution, Civil War and Unification.* London: I. B. Tauris, 2014.

# Samawah, Battle of (March 30–April 4, 2003)

Early Iraq War battle involving U.S. and Iraqi troops. The fighting occurred in Samawah, about 170 miles to the southeast of Baghdad. Beginning in late March, the U.S. Army's 2nd Brigade, 82nd Airborne Division, swept through Samawah to rid it of Iraqi resistance. From March 22 to 25 on its way to Baghdad, the U.S. 3rd Infantry Division encountered hostile fire from Iraqi troops in Samawah. Although U.S. artillery and air strikes hammered Iraqi positions within the city, the decision was then made to skirt the city so that the 3rd Infantry Division could move directly to Baghdad. At the same time, on March 25 the 2nd Brigade, 82nd Airborne Division, received orders to assault Samawah and clear it of hostile forces.

On March 30 at approximately 3:00 a.m. the 2nd Brigade reached the outskirts of Samawah. Inside the city were elements of the Iraqi Republican Guard, Fedayeen Saddam, and the regular Iraqi Army. Toward daybreak U.S. forces began to advance into the city, expecting to meet stiff resistance on its perimeter; they encountered no such resistance and no organized defenses there. However, U.S. troops began to encounter heavy Iraqi small-arms fire and assaults by rocket-propelled grenades (RPGs) as they neared a concrete factory just inside the perimeter. At about 3:00 p.m. that same day, U.S. commanders called in air strikes, conducted by U.S. Navy F-18 Hornets, that leveled a warehouse next to the plant, temporarily neutralizing resistance there.

That evening the 2nd Battalion, 325th Infantry Regiment, began a feint against the bridges spanning the Euphrates River. The hope was to draw in Iraqi Republican Guard units so they would be distracted and thus unable to conduct a rearguard action against American forces. At the same time, U.S. air strikes occurred against the north bank of the river, allowing the 2nd Brigade to capture the bridges, cross them, and dig in north of the river. At around dawn the next day American troops pulled back, having accomplished their objective. The remainder of that day, fighting was light and sporadic.

Iraqi resistance inside Samawah was concentrated in and near the concrete factory. On April 2, U.S. forces (mainly from the 1st Battalion, 325th Infantry Regiment) finally took the entire concrete factory complex, assisted by AC-130 Spectre gunships. This action permitted other forces to move into the city and take control. The operation culminated in an attack on the headquarters of an Iraqi paramilitary group on April 4.

U.S. tactics were designed to demoralize the enemy while keeping American casualties to a minimum; much of the fighting involved concentrated short attacks into the city followed by carefully staged withdrawals. Meanwhile, U.S. air strikes were called in against entrenched Iraqi positions, such as the local Baath Party headquarters, a school building being used as a shelter, and even a soccer field. By nightfall on April 4 Samawah had been secured, with just 1 U.S. combat death and 6 wounded. The Iraqi side suffered at least 50 dead and 23 taken prisoner.

PAUL G. PIERPAOLI JR.

**See also**
Iraq War

**References**
Gordon, Michael R., and Bernard E. Trainor. *The Endgame: The Inside Story of the Struggle for Iraq, from George W. Bush to Barack Obama.* New York: Vintage, 2013.
Keegan, John. *The Iraq War: The Military Offensive, from Victory in 21 Days to the Insurgent Aftermath.* New York: Vintage, 2005.
Murray, Williamson, and Robert H. Scales Jr. *The Iraq War: A Military History.* Cambridge, MA: Belknap, 2005.

# Samita Incident (December 1972–April 1973)

Incident in which the Iraqi government sought to annex Samita, several miles south of Umm Qasr. It was only one of a series of incidents in which Iraq sought to take territory from Kuwait.

After Iraq became independent from the Ottoman Empire, a major goal of Iraqi leaders was the acquisition of the emirate of Kuwait. Even before oil was discovered in Kuwait in 1937, King Ghazi of Iraq made public statements about annexing Kuwait and encouraged the Kuwaiti people to overthrow al-Sabah family rule. The strong British presence in both countries limited the amount of direct pressure the Iraqis could put on the Kuwaitis, however. The situation changed after World War II. In 1958, the Iraqi monarchy strongly encouraged Kuwait to join a union of Jordan and Iraq to form a single state. The concept of Arab unity was very strong at the time, and Egypt and Syria had just formed the United Arab Republic.

The 1958 revolution that overthrew the Iraqi monarchy put an end to the movement to unify Jordan, Iraq, and Kuwait, but it did not end Iraqi interest in Kuwaiti territory. In June 1961, a treaty between Great Britain and Kuwait that gave Britain control over the emirate was replaced by a treaty of friendship acknowledging Kuwaiti independence. Iraqi prime minister Abd al-Karim Qasim condemned the new treaty as illegal because Iraq held that the original treaty that had ended Kuwait's association with the Ottoman Empire was also illegal. His threats regarding Kuwaiti independence prompted the emirate to request assistance from Great Britain, which responded by stationing some 8,000 troops, along with supporting air units, in or near Kuwait. This British assistance was sufficient force to deter Iraqi leaders, who also faced a rebellion by Kurds in northern Iraq at the time.

Kuwaiti leaders were uncomfortable with having to rely on British armed forces, however, because this appeared to impinge on their independence and keep them in colonial status, and they thus turned to the Arab League for assistance. Thanks to an Iraqi boycott, Kuwait was accepted for membership in the league on July 20, 1961. Kuwait then requested Arab forces to protect it from Iraq, and the Arab League members eventually dispatched 3,300 troops. Although these did not actually replace British troops already in place, the Arab forces were politically more acceptable.

Qasim was overthrown in February 1963, and an Iraqi government apparently friendly to Kuwait replaced him. Arab forces were then gradually withdrawn from Kuwait. The Kuwaiti government sought to establish friendly relations with Iraq by making a number of long-term financial loans to that nation, and on October 4, 1963, an agreement was signed between the two countries that appeared to guarantee Kuwaiti independence. Kuwaiti leaders were sufficiently encouraged by developments that they terminated the treaty with Great Britain guaranteeing military assistance.

The Iraqi government, however, continued to try to impinge on Kuwait's sovereignty. At different times, it demanded ownership or occupation of Bubiyan and Warba Islands off the narrow tip of Iraq that borders the Persian Gulf. Kuwaiti financial aid kept the Iraqis from pressing the issue too hard, however.

In April 1969, the Iraqi government tried another tack. It requested permission to station troops on Kuwaiti soil to protect the newly built port of Umm Qasr from Iranian attack. Following considerable pressure, Kuwaiti defense minister Shaikh Sa'd al-Sabah gave his verbal consent. Iraqi troops were to be allowed to occupy two square kilometers of land on the Kuwaiti side of the border, just south of Umm Qasr near al-Samita, better known just as Samita. In fact, Iraqi troops had already begun crossing the border before Sheikh Sa'd had given his assent to what became the "unwritten agreement."

Even after relations between Iraq and Iran had cooled, Iraqi troops remained in Kuwait near Umm Qasr. In December 1972, protected by their troops, the Iraqis commenced construction of a paved road to Samita. When Kuwait protested, in March 1973 the Iraqi government presented a draft treaty that would give Iraq virtual sovereignty over the area, including oil drilling and exporting rights. The Kuwaiti government rejected the treaty out of hand. Iraq responded by reinforcing its border garrison in Kuwait and by establishing a new post at Samita. The Kuwaitis already had an outpost in Samita, however, and tensions immediately rose.

On March 20, 1973, Kuwaiti soldiers approached the Iraqi troops and road construction crew under orders to eject them from Kuwaiti territory. The Iraqi commander warned the Kuwaitis to withdraw, and when they refused, Iraqi troops opened fire. In the ensuing brief firefight, two Kuwaitis and one Iraqi were killed.

Two days later, the Kuwait government lodged a formal protest with the Iraqis. Arab League secretary-general Mahmoud Riad and Syrian foreign minister Abdel Halim Khaddam visited both capitals in an effort to mediate the situation, and on April 5 Iraq withdrew its troops to the old border, but the Iraqi government continued to claim parts of Kuwait, including Bubiyan and Warba islands.

The Samita Incident attracted little attention in the West because it was quickly resolved, but it had long-term significance. The first Kuwaiti action to protect its territory without British protection, it nonetheless revealed that Kuwaiti leaders had allowed Iraqi troops to occupy part of the emirate's territory for years, undercutting Kuwait's claims for its existing borders. Because the crisis was brokered by the Arab League, it may have encouraged Iraqi leader Saddam Hussein 17 years later to believe that a move against Kuwait would have only limited international impact.

TIM J. WATTS

**See also**
Iraq; Kuwait; Qasim, Abdul Karim; Umm Qasr, Battle of

**References**
Finnie, David H. *Shifting Lines in the Sand: Kuwait's Elusive Frontier with Iraq.* Cambridge, MA: Harvard University Press, 1992.
"Iraq and Kuwait Clash at Border." *New York Times,* March 21, 1973.

## Samu Raid, West Bank (November 13, 1966)

Retaliatory military raid by Israel Defense Force (IDF) on the Palestinian village of Samu (Samoa, Samoa) in the West Bank, not far from the city of Hebron, on November 13, 1966. At the time, the West Bank was under Jordanian control. In the months leading up to the Samu Raid, Israel had come under attack by a number of Palestinian guerrillas who had been staging increasingly destructive assaults, many of which had involved civilians. However, the majority of these attacks had been emanating from neighboring Syria. Those responsible for them were members of Fatah, the military faction of the Palestine Liberation Organization (PLO). Nevertheless, when a mine exploded near the Israeli-Jordanian border, resulting in the deaths of three Israeli policemen (a fourth police officer was seriously injured), the Israeli government decided to respond with a major incursion and assault into the West Bank.

The IDF assembled a large strike force of about 400 men reinforced by 10 tanks and 40 trucks for transport. Aircraft of the Israeli Air Force provided cover for the ground operation. Dubbed Operation SHREDDER, the raid began in the early hours of November 13, 1966. As the force crossed into the Jordanian-held West Bank, it initially encountered little resistance. Moving toward the settlement of Rujm al-Madfa, IDF forces leveled the police station there. Still encountering light resistance, the assault force continued toward Samu, the next major village. Here the town's inhabitants fled in panic as the IDF soldiers targeted homes, blowing them up or bulldozing them with their tanks.

By now, the Jordanians had managed to mobilize a small counterforce. An armored column, smaller in number than the Israelis, it began advancing toward Samu. As the Jordanians approached, the Israelis partly surrounded them in a near-perfect ambush. The ensuing short battle resulted in the deaths of 15 Jordanian soldiers and the wounding of 54 others. The Israelis suffered 1 dead and 10 wounded. Meanwhile, Jordanian fighters were scrambled to provide air cover but arrived too late. In a momentary dogfight, the Israelis shot down a Jordanian fighter before the Jordanian planes withdrew. Casualties went beyond military personnel, however, and when the raid and brief battle had ended, 3 Arab civilians were among the dead, and an additional 96 civilians were wounded.

The Samu Raid did not go well from the Israeli perspective. The Israelis suffered casualties, lost equipment, and engendered the wrath of the international community. In the Middle East, the operation fanned the flames of Arab resentment against Israel during a time in which Arab-Israeli tensions were already running high. Indeed, just six months after the Samu Raid, the June 1967 Six-Day War broke out. And more than one Arab government would name the raid as a contributing factor to the conflict. In the United States, President Lyndon B. Johnson's administration was far from pleased with the Israeli action, arguing that it was too large, was not commensurate with the provocation, and ignored the fact that Syria had been supporting the lion's share of attacks against Israel. U.S. policy makers were also in a quandary, because Jordan was one of the few Arab nations in the Middle East that had continued to remain a fairly reliable friend and ally of the United States.

The United Nations (UN) Security Council, in Resolution 228, formally censured Israel for its attack on the West Bank. In Jordan, the attacks brought widespread unrest and riots in Jordan's cities. A number of Jordanians were outraged by the government's seeming ineffectiveness in preventing or blunting the attack, and still others were incensed that nothing had been done to safeguard Palestinian civilians residing in the West Bank.

PAUL G. PIERPAOLI JR.

**See also**
Israel; Jordan; Six-Day War; West Bank

**References**
Broyles, Matthew. *The Six-Day War.* New York: Rosen, 2004.
James, R. S., and Rebecca Stettof. *The West Bank and Gaza Strip.* New York: Chelsea House, 1988.
Parker, Richard B., ed. *The Six-Day War: A Retrospective.* Gainesville: University Press of Florida, 1996.

# Sanchez, Ricardo S. (1951–)

U.S. Army general who commanded coalition forces in Iraq from June 2003 to June 2004. Born on May 17, 1951, in Rio Grande City, Texas, Ricardo S. Sanchez began his military career in the Reserve Officers' Training Corps program at the University of Texas at Austin and Texas A&I University (now Texas A&M–Kingsville). A 1973 graduate of the latter institution, Sanchez was commissioned in the U.S. Army as a second lieutenant that same year. He served in both infantry and armor units early in his career. His military education included both the Command and General Staff College and the U.S. Army War College. He also earned a master's degree in operations research and systems analysis engineering from the Naval Postgraduate School.

As a lieutenant colonel, Sanchez served in the Persian Gulf War in command of the 2nd Battalion, 69th Armor, 197th Infantry Brigade. His outstanding performance contributed to his early promotion to colonel in September 1994. During 1994–1996 he commanded a brigade of the 1st Infantry Division (Mechanized) at Fort Riley, Kansas.

Sanchez was then an investigator in the Office of the U.S. Army Inspector General Agency and served in various roles at U.S. Southern Command. After promotion to brigadier general in November 1998, Sanchez was assistant division commander (support) of the 1st Infantry Division during 1999–2000. During 2000–2001 he was deputy chief of staff for operations, U.S. Army Europe and Seventh Army, Germany. During 2001–2003 he commanded the 1st Armored Division, being promoted to major general in July 2002. Promoted to lieutenant general in August 2003, from July 2003 to June 2004 Sanchez was commanding general of the V Corps, U.S. Army Europe and Seventh Army, Germany, to include duty as commanding general, Combined Joint Task Force 7, in the Iraq War.

With the rapid withdrawal of U.S. Central Command (CENTCOM) and its Combined Forces Land Component Command (CFLCC), Sanchez by default became the commander of coalition ground forces in Iraq, the top military position in Iraq. This critical period after the end of major hostilities saw the emergence of the Iraqi insurgency, the deaths of Uday and Qusay Hussein, and the capture of deposed Iraqi president Saddam Hussein. The major challenges facing Sanchez were the reestablishment of essential services and basic security and ending the counterinsurgency. According to multiple sources, communications between Sanchez and L. Paul Bremer, head of the Coalition Provisional Authority, were strained and often nonexistent. This poor communication and lack of unified leadership is

U.S. Army lieutenant general Ricardo S. Sanchez commanded coalition ground forces in Iraq, the top military position there, from June 2003 to June 2004. This critical period after the end of major hostilities saw the emergence of the Iraqi insurgency. His tenure was marked by the controversy involving prisoner abuse at U.S.-run Abu Ghraib Prison. (Charles Ommanney/Getty Images)

often cited as one of the contributors to the turmoil that followed the end of major conflict in Iraq. Compounding Sanchez's problems during this period was the fact that he was essentially a corps commander with little more than a corps staff yet was responsible for commanding an entire theater. With the vacuum created by the rapid withdrawal of the CFLCC, Sanchez was left with a staff that was nowhere near large enough for his responsible span of control or trained and experienced at the higher level of theater operations.

Despite progress in certain areas, this period of the Iraq War was marked by a burgeoning insurgency, widespread lawlessness, and the challenge of detaining thousands of prisoners. The most glaring controversy during Sanchez's tenure was the prisoner abuse at Abu Ghraib Prison. In September 2003 Sanchez approved in writing 29 interrogation methods authorized for use with Iraqi detainees. At the direction of CENTCOM, 10 of those methods were later repealed after having been deemed unacceptably aggressive. However, the actual methods employed at Abu Ghraib went beyond even what Sanchez had authorized, as evidenced by the graphic photographs that were ultimately seen on worldwide media. On January 16, 2004, Sanchez issued a press release announcing the investigation of "detainee abuse at a Coalition Forces detention facility."

Sanchez left his post in June 2004. Ultimately several low-ranking military members were court-martialed over the abuse scandal. Sanchez believed that he was denied his fourth star and was forced into retirement on November 1, 2006, because of it.

In 2008 Sanchez published his autobiography, *Wiser in Battle: A Soldier's Story,* a sweeping indictment of the handling of the Iraq War by Defense Secretary Donald Rumsfeld and the George W. Bush administration. Sanchez now lives in Texas. In 2012 he intended to run as a Democrat for an open U.S. Senate seat representing Texas, but he ultimately withdrew from the race for personal reasons.

BENJAMIN D. FOREST

### See also
Abu Ghraib; Bremer, Lewis Paul, III; Iraq; Iraq Insurgency; Iraq War

### References
Gordon, Michael R., and General Bernard E. Trainor. *Cobra II: The Inside Story of the Invasion and Occupation of Iraq.* New York: Pantheon Books, 2006.

Ricks, Thomas E. *Fiasco: The American Military Adventure in Iraq.* New York: Penguin, 2006.

Sanchez, Ricardo S., and Donald T. Phillips. *Wiser in Battle: A Soldier's Story.* New York: Harper, 2008.

## San Remo Conference (April 19–26, 1920)

International summit held in San Remo, Italy, during April 19–26, 1920, to discuss unresolved issues arising from World War I (1914–1918) and the Paris Peace Conference of 1919. The most pressing issue at San Remo was the official disposition of Middle Eastern territories formerly belonging to the Ottoman Empire, which had dissolved as a result of the war. In attendance at the San Remo Conference were the prime ministers of France, Great Britain, and Italy and top-level representatives from Greece, Belgium, and Japan.

In regard to the disposition of lands in the Middle East, the San Remo Conference simply codified and elaborated upon the secret Sykes-Picot Agreement of 1916 in which the French and British agreed to create spheres of control in the Middle East. Although other issues were discussed at the meeting including the particulars of the 1919 Treaty of Versailles and the creation of a peace treaty with the Turks, the main item on the agenda was the establishment of mandates. In this case, mandates would be administered via the League of Nations, although the mandate powers (France and Great Britain) would administer their mandate governments with almost complete autonomy.

The mandates were organized into three categories depending on the location and sociopolitical development of the nations involved. The mandates in the first category included Iraq and Palestine, to be administered by the British, and Syria and Lebanon, which fell under French aegis. Unlike the other mandates in this category, the people of Palestine would not be treated as citizens of a nation-state because of the varied ethnic and religion makeup of the region.

Not surprisingly, many Arabs viewed the British Mandate for Palestine with considerable trepidation particularly given the 1917 Balfour Declaration, which seemed to suggest that the British favored the creation of a Jewish homeland in Palestine. Furthermore, many Arabs believed that Arabs living in Palestine had been singled out by denying them political autonomy. Indeed, as early as December 1920, Arab leaders were already planning for the formation of an autonomous Palestinian state within the borders of the British mandate.

PAUL G. PIERPAOLI JR.

### See also
Balfour Declaration; Mandates, League of Nations; Palestine, British Mandate for; Sykes-Picot Agreement; World War I, Impact on the Middle East

### References
Méoouchy, Nadine, and Peter Sluglett, eds. *The British and French Mandates in Comparative Perspective,* Vol. 93. Leiden: Brill Academic, 2004.

Sherman, A. J. *Mandate Days: British Lives in Palestine, 1918–1948.* Baltimore: Johns Hopkins University Press, 2001.

## San Stefano, Treaty of (March 3, 1878)

Important treaty regarding the Ottoman Empire. Signed on March 3, 1878, the Treaty of San Stefano ended the Russo-Ottoman War of 1877–1878. Highly favorable to Russia, it called for the creation of the autonomous principality of Bulgaria, whose territory would extend from the Danube River to the Aegean Sea. Under Article 7, a prince elected by the people but approved by the sultan would rule over Bulgaria, while Article 8 called for the Ottoman evacuation of Bulgaria and deployment there of Russian forces for two years. Russia also compelled the Ottomans to cede territory to Montenegro and recognize its independence. Serbia was granted independence and received the cities of Nis and Leskovac. The Porte was forced to grant autonomy to Bosnia-Herzegovina under Austrian and Russian supervision and to recognize the independence of Romania. In the Caucasus, the Ottoman Empire lost Ardahan, Artvin, Batum, Kars, Olti, and Beyazit to Russia. Under Article 24, the straits of the Bosporus and the Dardanelles were declared open to all neutral ships in peacetime and in war, assuring Russia of naval access to the Mediterranean.

The treaty, so advantageous to Russia, was rejected by the Great Powers, notably Austria and Britain, which were concerned about the spread of Russian authority into the Balkan Peninsula. As tensions between the Great Powers escalated, German chancellor Otto von Bismarck negotiated a new agreement at the Congress of Berlin in June 1878 that was far less generous to the Russians.

ALEXANDER MIKABERIDZE

### See also
Russo-Ottoman Wars

### Reference
Macfie, A. L. *The Eastern Question, 1774–1923*. London: Longman, 1989.

## Saracen

The term "Saracen" (Latin, Sarracen; French, Sarrasin) was widely used in the period of the Middle Ages in Europe as an indiscriminate term for "Muslim." Originally designating one ethnic group in the Arabian Peninsula, by late antiquity it had become a synonym for Arabs and was employed by Latin chroniclers of the 8th and 9th centuries to describe the Muslim Arab invaders in the Mediterranean region. In the 12th century, chroniclers of the First Crusade (1096–1099) and poets of the chansons de geste (Old French epic poems) applied the term to Turks, Arabs, and other Muslims, creating a colorful and wildly inaccurate portrait of Saracens who worshipped pantheon idols, chief among them Mahomet. At the same time, theologians offered polemical refutations of the Lex Sarracenorum (Law of the Saracens), as they generally called Islam. The travel narratives and romances of the later Middle Ages often blend literary topoi of pagan Saracens with more realistic depictions of Islam. The term "Saracen" gradually fell into disuse by the 17th century, to be replaced by "Turk," "Mohammedan," and "Moslem."

JOHN TOLAN

### See also
Crusades in the Holy Land, Christian

### References
Camille, Michael. *The Gothic Idol: Ideology and Image-Making in Medieval Art*. Cambridge: Cambridge Press, 1989.
Ramey, Lynn. *Christian, Saracen and Genre in Medieval French Literature: Imagination and Cultural Interaction in the French Middle Ages*. New York: Garland, 2001.
Tolan, John. *Saracens: Islam in the Medieval European Imagination*. New York: Columbia University Press, 2002.
Tolan, John, ed. *Medieval Christian Perceptions of Islam: A Collection of Essays*. New York: Garland, 1996.

## Sargon of Akkad (ca. 2350–2279 BCE)

Sargon of Akkad, also known as Sargon the Great, was the founder of a Sumero-Akkadian dynasty in southern Mesopotamia and the creator of the first empire in recorded human history. He was the ruler of Akkad, a city near Babylon, and claimed to have conquered powerful Syrian states, including Mari and Ebla. His conquests may have reached as far as the Mediterranean Sea.

As is the case with many ancient figures, Sargon's early years are somewhat of a mystery. He was probably born around 2350 BCE. His parentage is undetermined. Some historians theorize that he had pastoral upbringing or that he was the child of a priestess. According to legend, the young Sargon began life as Moses did—cast adrift on a river (in this case the Euphrates River) by his mother. He was rescued and raised by others, in this case a farm family, not a royal one. However, he managed to become cupbearer to Ur-Zababa, the king of Kish. Sargon later succeeded Ur-Zababa and made war against Sumer.

Sargon, whose reign is typically said to have begun circa 2334 BCE, united his Semitic people. He took control of cities up the Euphrates River and conquered Sumer. He also marched on Mesopotamia and possibly as far as present-day Syria and Lebanon, with rumors of conquests in lands as far-flung as Egypt, Asia Minor, and India.

At some point during his reign, Sargon advanced toward the Sumerian cities in the south, conquered Ur, and defeated Lugalzagesi of Uruk, who had claimed to be the leader of the Sumerian cities. After the conquest of the south of Mesopotamia, Sargon proceeded to establish Akkadian as the language of bureaucracy, creating a Sumero-Akkadian synthesis of cultures. To ensure legitimacy in that area, he made his daughter, Enheduanna, the high priestess of Ur, one of the more important cities.

Sargon claimed to have controlled territory from Persia to Asia Minor and the Mediterranean Sea (possibly including Cyprus). By placing so much land under one ruler, previously uncooperative peoples became more open to relations with neighboring tribes, and a freer exchange of goods and ideas resulted. In addition, new gods and religions were frequently adopted from conquered peoples.

According to a Sumerian list of kings, Sargon ruled for 56 years, but his reign ended with parts of the empire in revolt. Following his death circa 2279 BCE, Sargon became the subject of historical narratives for nearly the next two millennia that described his rise to power and his military campaigns. The Akkadian Empire lasted some 200 years.

MARK W. CHAVALAS

### See also
Akkad; Mesopotamia; Sumer

### References
Kramer, S. N. *History Begins at Sumer.* New York: Doubleday, 1959.

Liverani, Mario, ed. *Akkad: The First World Empire.* Padua, Italy: Sargon, 1993.

## Sarikamish, Battle of (December 22, 1914–January 17, 1915)

The first major battle of World War I on the Caucasian front. Ottoman minister of war Enver Pasha sought to take advantage of Russian preoccupation with Germany and Austria-Hungary to launch an offensive through Armenia to recover territory in Caucasia lost to the Russians in the Russo-Ottoman War of 1877–1878. For Ottoman leaders the oil fields of Baku were the ultimate prize, but Enver had even more ambitious plans. While both sides faced daunting logistical problems in this first Ottoman strategic initiative of the war, Ottoman leaders needed to come to grips with the fact that Caucasia was 500 miles from the nearest Ottoman railhead at Konia.

Following the declaration of war, Enver took personal command of the Turkish Eastern Army, consisting of the Third and Second Armies. He hoped to surprise the Russians, but his offensive was slow to develop because of both logistical problems and harassment by Armenian and Kurdish tribesmen. It also occurred in the dead of winter in the worst possible weather conditions. Kars guarded the route from the Ottoman advanced base of Erzurum to the middle of Caucasia. A railroad led from the Black Sea to the Caspian Sea with branch lines on both sides. One of these ran through Kars to Sarikamish (Sarıkamış). Enver hoped to capitalize on his superior numbers of 150,000 men against some 100,000 Russians under General Viktor Myshlaevsky. Russian forces were also split between their headquarters at Tbilisi and the frontier bases of Kars and Ardahan.

Enver divided his forces to move against the two Russian frontier bases, hoping to entrap his enemy. The Ottoman offensive from Erzurum began on November 18, but both axes of the advance made only slow progress, in part because of deteriorating weather conditions. The Russians soon halted the smaller Ottoman Second Army's drive on Ardahan, allowing Myshlaevsky time to concentrate 60,000 men under his chief of staff, Major General Nikolay Yudenich, at Kars. Although ordered to retreat, Yudenich instead advanced to meet the Turkish Third Army east of the town of Sarikamish, located 30 miles inside Russian territory between Kars and Erzurum.

The Battle at Sarikamish opened on December 26 and lasted until January 4. Both sides had only a few artillery pieces. On December 27, the Russian repulsed the Ottomans from Sarikamish. The Ottoman 28th Division reached the Kars Road but was driven back from it. However, the Ottoman 30th Division then took Alisofu south of the road and railway line, isolating the Russians.

The decisive day of the battle was December 29, when some 18,000 Ottomans supported by about 20 guns faced 14,000 Russians with 34 guns. The Russians managed to repulse the Ottoman 30th and 31st Divisions, and the Ottomans were also forced to withdraw from Alisofu. Although the Ottoman 17th Division managed to penetrate Sarikamish proper, it was annihilated there, with about 800 men taken prisoner. Reinforced on December 31 from Kars, Yudenich saw a chance to surround the Ottomans.

On January 1 Enver ordered a retreat, evading pursuit by January 4. The Battle of Sarikamish had effectively destroyed the Turkish IX Corps. Exact casualty figures for both sides are unknown. The Ottoman attack on Ardahan was also beaten back on January 4, and two weeks later what remained of both Ottoman armies were back in their base of Erzurum, their strength reduced to only some 18,000 men. Perhaps 30,000 may have died of the bitter cold weather. Unfortunately for the Russians, their winter victory over the Ottomans was not decisive. Although Yudenich was promoted to lieutenant general and received command of the Russian Caucasus Army, he was seriously short of supplies and equipment and was unable to capitalize on the situation beyond mounting a number of probing attacks. Enver meanwhile was forced to shelve plans for a new spring offensive following the Allied naval assault on the Dardanelles and the resulting Gallipoli campaign.

Spencer C. Tucker

**See also**
Caucasus Front, World War I

**References**
Erickson, Edward J. *Ordered to Die: A History of the Ottoman Army in the First World War.* Westport, CT: Greenwood, 2000.
Stone, Norman. *The Eastern Front, 1914–1917.* New York: Scribner, 1975.

# Sassanid Empire (224–651)

The Sassanid (Sasanid, Sassanian, Neo-Persian) Empire (224–651) was founded by Ardashir, governor of Istakhr, a district in the province of Fars in southern Persia (modern-day Iran). Ardashir, who was a vassal of the Arsacid Empire (Parthian Empire), rose against ruling Arsacid king Artabanus IV and killed him on the battlefield. The death of Artabanus IV signaled the end of the Arsacid dynasty.

After overthrowing the Parthian state, Ardashir imposed his authority over the countries and provinces ruled by the Arsacids. In 225 he forced into submission the Kushans, who ruled the territories comprising modern Pakistan, Afghanistan, and vast regions in southern Central Asia. Ardashir then marched against Roman-held Mesopotamia, attacking Nisibis in present-day southeastern Turkey on the Syrian border. Ardashir's son, Shapur I, fought and/or negotiated with three Roman emperors: Gordian III, Philip the Arab, and Valerian. These campaigns culminated in the capture of Roman emperor Valerian by the Persians in 260. Thus, the early Sassanian rulers laid the foundation for a powerful empire, which at its zenith ruled a vast territory extending from Central Asia to Syria.

The Sassanid rulers were known as *shahanshah* (king of kings). Ardashir I abolished the decentralized structure he had inherited from the Arsacids and, in distinct contrast, established an absolutist monarchy and a highly centralized state. Additionally, Ardashir's successors reversed the tolerant attitude of the Arsacids toward the different religious communities of the empire and introduced Zoroastrianism as the state religion.

Local kings who refused to obey the authority of the Sassanian king of kings were replaced by members of the Sassanian royal family, usually the sons of the ruling monarch. This does not mean, however, that the Sassanians destroyed the powerful landowning families, such as the Suren and Karen families. Closely allied with the Arsacid ruling family, they retained their vast landholdings and the special privileges they had enjoyed during the Parthian period. Indeed, in the second half of the fifth century CE as the Sassanian state declined, the landed nobility resurfaced, and the very families that had played an important role during the Arsacid era began to play a central role in the political life of the Sassanian Empire.

Although the Roman Empire remained the principal adversary of the Sassanian state, starting in the fifth century a new threat emerged from Central Asia. The nomadic Kidarites and Hephthalites invaded the eastern provinces of the Sassanian state and forced the Sassanian monarchs Bahram V (r. 421–439), Yazdegerd II (r. 439–457), and Peroz I (r. 459–484) to spend much of their reigns on countering the Hephthalite threat. In 484 the Hephthalites defeated and killed Sassanian monarch Peroz on the battlefield. The victory over the Sassanian army and the death of the Persian king allowed the Hephthalites to invade eastern Iran, forcing the Sassanians to sue for peace and pay an annual tribute.

The humiliating defeats at the hands of the Hephthalites undermined the power and legitimacy of the Sassanian state. Sassanian monarch Kavad I saw the need for social and economic reforms, including curtailing the power of the empire's ruling classes, namely the Persian nobility and the Zoroastrian priesthood. Not surprisingly, Kavad was thus attracted to the teachings of Mazdak, a member of the Zoroastrian religious hierarchy who preached against the greed, arrogance, and unchecked power exhibited by the country's ruling classes. According to Mazdak, the source of evil and suffering in the world was the human fixation with satisfying self-centered desires without any regard for the hardships and needs of fellow human beings. To liberate the human soul from the forces of evil and to create a just and peaceful society free of competition and violence, human beings had to abandon greed and selfishness and share the existing resources of their society, including private property and women.

Mazdak's ideas and Kavad's support for them posed a direct threat to the established privileges of the ruling classes, particularly the Persian nobility and the Zoroastrian religious hierarchy. This formidable coalition was sufficiently powerful to depose Kavad I in 496 and force him to seek refuge with the Hephthalites, among whom he had lived as a hostage after his father's defeat. In 499, Kavad managed to convince the Hephthalites to assist him in raising an army and regaining his throne. The deposed king marched against his opponents and defeated them. Kavad ascended the Sassanian throne for a second time, but he realized that his authority would not be fully secure unless he appeased the anti-Mazdak nobility and priests.

The ruling dynasty was itself divided from within among the pro-Mazdak and anti-Mazdak factions. Among the contenders to the throne, Mazdak and his followers favored the older son of Kavad, Kavus, who sympathized with the ideas and objectives of their movement. The younger son, Khosrow, a fervent opponent of Mazdak, was the preferred candidate of the anti-Mazdak nobility and the Zoroastrian priesthood. After the death of Kavad in 531, Khosrow seized the throne and suppressed the Mazdakite movement by executing Mazdak and many of his followers.

During the reign of Khosrow I Anushiravan (r. 531–579), the Sassanian state introduced a series of important reforms that aimed at curtailing the power of the Persian nobility and the Zoroastrian religious establishment and increasing the power of the central government by expanding the size of the Sassanian central government and strengthening the position of the Sassanian king of kings vis-à-vis the provincial power centers. The first and perhaps most important of these reforms was restructuring the archaic tax system of the empire. In the traditional system, taxes were levied on the yield of land. Therefore, from year to year the amount of the tax varied. Khosrow abolished the system based on yearly variation and replaced it with a fixed sum. The Sassanian king also reorganized the administrative structure of his empire. He established a governmental system based on a council of ministers or a divan headed by a prime minister. Khosrow also reduced the power of the great feudal families who enjoyed enormous influence in the royal court. This did not mean, however, that he attacked the privileges of the dominant economic classes by destroying the prevailing class structure. In fact, Khosrow defended the traditional division of the Iranian society into priests, warriors, government officials, and the members of the third estate, which incorporated peasants, artisans, and merchants.

Khosrow also reorganized the Sassanian Army. To centralize the decision-making process under his direct control, the post of the supreme commander in chief was abolished in favor of four commanders responsible for the security of the eastern, western, northern, and southern regions of the empire. Each commander reported directly to the Sassanian king. The king also appointed margraves (commanders) of the frontiers, who also received their orders directly from the Sassanian monarch.

The Sassanian Empire reached its greatest extent during the reign of Khosrow's grandson, Khosrow II Parvez (r. 590–628). In 603 Persian armies invaded Mesopotamia and Asia Minor. The Sassanian forces quickly marched to upper Mesopotamia and laid siege to the well-fortified Roman fortress of Dara, which was captured in 604. Another Sassanian army attacked Roman forces in Armenia. In 607 the Persian armies struck again, this time seizing Theodosiopolis in northern Syria in 608 and the important city of Edessa in present-day southern Turkey in 609. In 611, Khosrow II captured Caesarea in the central Anatolian region of Cappadocia. In the same year new Byzantine emperor, Heraclius (r. 610–641), sent a delegation to the Sassanian court, but Khosrow refused to recognize Heraclius as the legitimate ruler and ordered the execution of his ambassadors. Meanwhile, the Persians continued their military advance westward. They seized Antioch once again and reached the Mediterranean coast in 612. In 613 Persian forces defeated a Roman army led by Heraclius and occupied Syria and Palestine, including the city of Jerusalem. There they seized the True Cross of Christian tradition and transported it back to the Sassanian capital of Ctesiphon in 614. To the north, the Persians moved from Cappadocia and quickly reached the Asian shores of the Bosporus in 614. The capital of the Eastern Roman Empire now seemed within their grasp. Since the time of the Persian Achaemenid Empire, no Persian ruler had amassed as much territory. At this point, a second Byzantine embassy arrived at the Persian court and pleaded for peace. Emperor Heraclius likewise arrived in the Persian camp with a plea for negotiations. Khosrow, however, rejected a peace settlement.

The Persian armies resumed their offensive in Asia Minor in 617. In 618 Khosrow deployed his forces in Palestine with the goal of attacking Egypt. His invasion of Egypt succeeded, and the port city of Alexandria was secured in 619. Only a year later, the Persian conquest of Egypt was complete. The fall of Egypt allowed Khosrow to concentrate his main forces in Asia Minor and attack the heartland of the Byzantine state and eventually its capital of Constantinople. In 622 the Persian forces attacked Asia Minor and advanced rapidly. By 623 they had reached Ancyra (modern-day Ankara), while their naval forces seized the island of Rhodes and several other islands in the eastern Aegean.

At this historic juncture, Heraclius mounted a counterattack and surprised the Persians with a swift and determined march against eastern Asia Minor and western Iran. As Khosrow's army disintegrated and the Persian king fled, Heraclius entered Azerbaijan and then reached the important Zoroastrian temple at Shiz, which contained the sacred fire of Adur Gushnasp (Azar Goshnasp), and destroyed it. Though defeated, the Persian commanders fought back and forced

Heraclius and his army to evacuate Azerbaijan. Under relentless attack from Persian forces, Heraclius retreated to eastern Asia Minor. Determined to drive the Byzantine forces from eastern Asia Minor, Persian forces under General Shahrbaraz attacked the Byzantine forces in southeastern Anatolia and northern Syria, forcing them to retreat. Shahrbaraz then continued his westward march, targeting Constantinople, which he reached in the summer of 626.

Battles fought in the summer of 626 would prove devastating for the Sassanians and seal the fate of Khosrow and his armies. As the Persian armies suffered significant losses, an army of Turks allied with the Byzantine emperor invaded, devastating urban and rural communities in the Caucasus and Azerbaijan. Although the Sassanian forces already suffered significant losses in 626, the next year proved even more disastrous. A massive Turkish invasion from the north devastated the Caucasus region. The strategic town of Darband as well as the town of Partaw, the capital of Albania (Iranian Eran), were overrun. A Byzantine army also pushed south toward Azerbaijan and northern Iraq where, at the Battle of Nineveh, it defeated the Sassanian forces, which had been sent to block Heraclius's advance against the Persian capital of Ctesiphon in southern Iraq.

Twenty-four years of incessant warfare had exhausted the Sassanian state. Outraged by Khosrow's setbacks, obstinacy, and intransigence, a group of army officers joined by sons of several prominent families organized a plot to overthrow him and replace him with his son Kavad Shiruya (Shiroy). On the evening of February 23, 628, the plotters staged their coup. Shiruya was released from detention, and a herald proclaimed him the king of kings. The gates of the jails were also opened, and all prisoners, including Byzantines, were allowed to escape. Khosrow fled the palace but was later captured. Two days later, his son Shiruya ascended the throne as Kavad II.

The new monarch, who had initially promised to restore peace and reverse the harsh policies of his father, initiated a bloodbath by killing all of his brothers. He then ordered the execution of his father. The Sassanian Empire never recovered from this bloodbath. Shiruya died a few months after he had seized the throne. The Persian state began to disintegrate thereafter.

As army commanders, courtiers, and powerful members of the Persian nobility battled among themselves and eliminated one another, Sassanian territory was invaded on all sides by powerful neighbors. Turks breached the eastern borders of the empire, while the Khazars invaded its northern provinces by using the Caucasus region to raid Armenia, Azerbaijan, and Asia Minor. In the end, however, it was a powerful force from the Arabian Peninsula that brought the collapse of the Sassanian state. The Sassanian Empire came to an end when Arab Muslims defeated the Persian armies at Qadisiyyah in 636 CE and again at Nahavand in western Iran in 642. The last Sassanian king of kings, Yazdegerd III, was killed in 651 near Marv in Central Asia.

Mehrdad Kia

**See also**
Ardashir I; Khosrow I Anushiravan; Parthian Empire; Shapur I the Great; Shapur II the Great; Zoroastrianism

**References**
Daryaee, Touraj. *Sasanian Persia: The Rise and Fall of an Empire.* London: I. B. Tauris, 2013.
Frye, R. N. "The Political History of Iran under the Sasanians." In *The Cambridge History of Iran,* Vol. 3 (I), *The Seleucid, Parthian and Sasanid Periods.* Cambridge: Cambridge University Press, 1983.
Pourshariati, Parvaneh. *Decline and Fall of the Sasanian Empire: The Sasanian-Parthian Confederacy and the Arab Conquest of Iran.* London: I. B. Tauris, 2008.
Rawlinson, George. *The Sixth Great Oriental Monarchy.* Tehran: Imperial Organization for Social Services, 1976.

## Saudi Arabia

The Kingdom of Saudi Arabia is located in Western Asia. Constituting nearly the entire Arabian Peninsula, Saudi Arabia occupies some 830,000 square miles and is thus nearly three times the area of the U.S. state of Texas. Saudi Arabia, second in size in the Arab world only to Algeria, borders on Jordan, Iraq, and Kuwait to the north; the Persian Gulf, Qatar, and the United Arab Emirates to the east; Oman and Yemen to the south; and the Red Sea to the west. Saudi Arabia's capital is Riyadh, which is also its largest city, with a population of some 6 million.

Arabs predominate in the kingdom, and Saudi Arabia is an absolute monarchy. The ruling House of Saud has historical ties to the Wahhabi sect of Islam, which is a branch of Sunni Islam and the official state religion. Adherents prefer the term "Salafism" rather than "Wahhabism," but what is described as the true faith by adherents is seen by many in the West as intolerant or at best ultraconservative. Regardless, Saudi Arabian law and society are based on a strict interpretation of Islamic law. Virtually all Saudi citizens are Muslims, and the vast majority (75–90 percent) are Sunni Muslims, with the remainder being Shiites. Saudi Arabia is home to the two holiest places in the Muslim

# Saudi Arabia

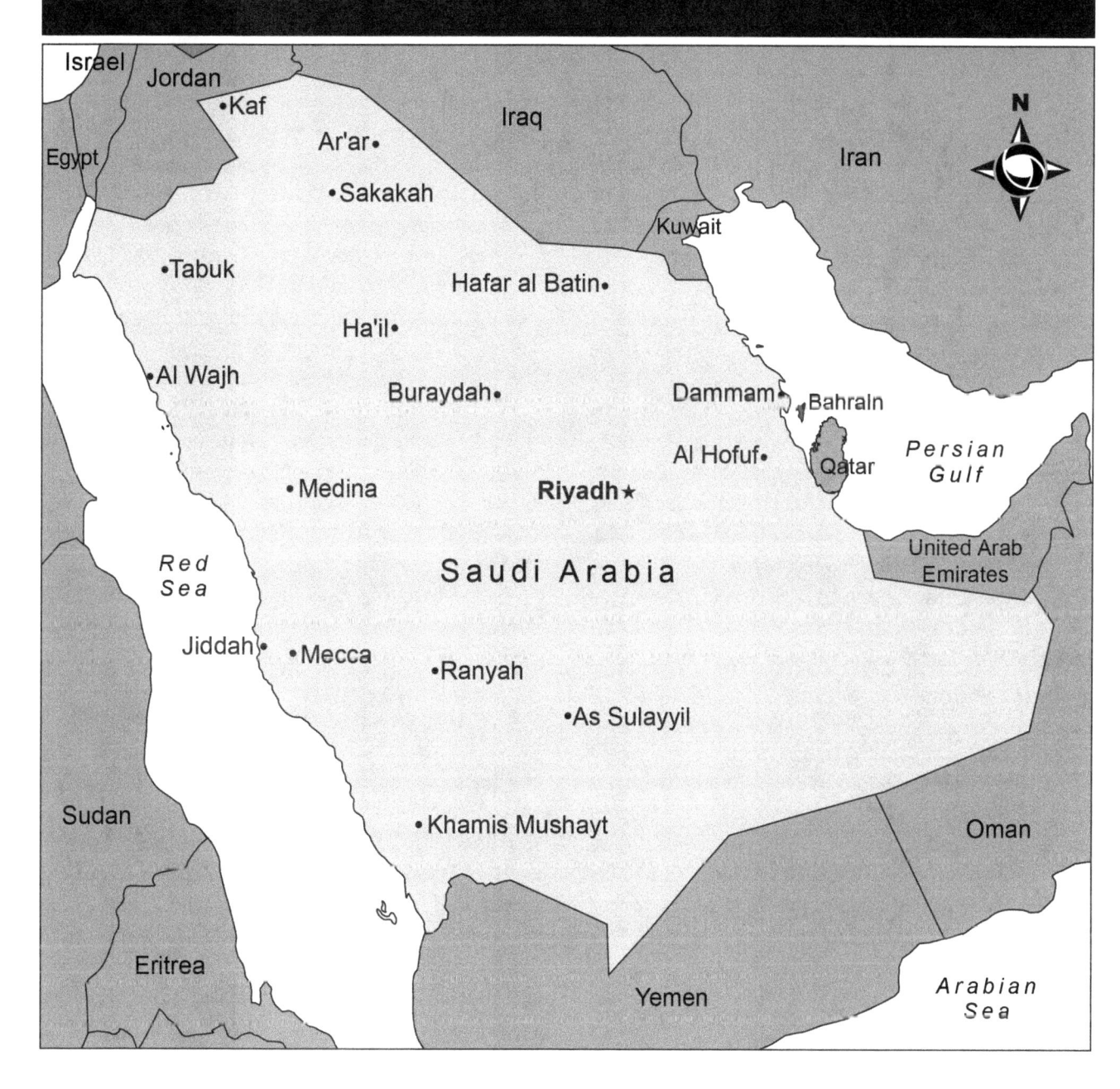

world, Al-Masjid al-Haram in Mecca and Al-Masjid an-Nabawi in Medina.

Some 1.5 million Christians live in Saudi Arabia. Almost all of them are foreign workers, but they are not permitted to practice their faith openly. Saudi Arabia also forbids religious conversion from Islam and punishes it by death. There are perhaps 390,000 Hindus, again foreign workers, in the kingdom.

Saudi Arabia had a total population in 2016 of some 32.158 million. A high percentage of these are foreign workers. The figure varies widely according to source, with the Saudi Arabian government putting it at about one-third of the total. One source estimates the leading foreign populations and country of origin as follows: Pakistan, 1.5 million; India, 1.3 million; Egypt, 900,000; Yemen, 800,000; Bangladesh, 500,000; the Philippines, 500,000; Jordanians and Palestinians, 260,000; Indonesia, 250,000; Sri Lanka, 350,000; Sudan, 250,000, Syria, 100,000; and Turkey, 100,000. Perhaps 100,000 Westerners also reside in Saudi Arabia, most of them in compounds or gated communities.

Saudi Arabia possesses the world's largest oil reserves, something that was to give it immense influence in the region and in the world as a whole. This seemingly endless supply of oil led to the creation of a quasi-socialist state in which an astonishing 90 percent of Saudis worked for the government and enjoyed subsidies for water, electricity, and gas. Health care and education are also free.

What would become the Kingdom of Saudi Arabia was early peopled by nomadic tribes surviving in a hostile desert environment. Two population centers developed in Mecca and Medina. The Islamic prophet Muhammad (ca. 571–632) was born in Mecca, and in the early 600s he led a military effort that ended with his securing control of both Mecca and Medina and uniting the tribes into a single Islamic religious state.

Muhammad's followers aggressively expanded the territory under Islamic control until it reached as far west as the Iberian Peninsula and as far east as present-day Pakistan. With other areas far richer in terms of resources and wealth, Arabia was soon eclipsed as the center of Islamic power. From the 10th century the sharif of Mecca, who ruled the Hejaz, was the leading figure, but most of the territory that would become modern Saudi Arabia remained under tribal rule. The sharif was hardly independent, as most of the time he owed allegiance to one of the Islamic empires in Baghdad or Cairo and then in Istanbul. In the 16th century the Ottoman Empire came to control the coastal areas on the Red Sea and the Persian Gulf (the Hejaz, Asir, and Al-Ahsa) and claimed suzerainty over the Arabian interior. Actual Ottoman control varied during the course of the next four centuries, however.

In 1744 in central Arabia, Muhammad bin Saud, founder of the dynasty that continues to rule Saudi Arabia, formed an alliance with Muhammad ibn Abd al-Wahhab, who founded the Wahhabi movement (Wahhabism), a strict puritanical form of Sunni Islam. The alliance was formalized in the marriage of Muhammad ibn Abd al-Wahhab's daughter to Abdul Aziz bin Muhammad bin Saud (son and successor of Muhammad ibn Saud), who ruled from 1765 to 1803. The descendants of these two families have remained closely linked ever since.

This alliance gave Saud control of the area around Riyadh. He then rapidly expanded his control until he ruled most of what today constitutes Saudi Arabia. Ottoman viceroy of Egypt Muhammad Ali Pasha invaded and destroyed this "state" in 1818. By 1824, however, Saud had established a new state in Nejd. For the remainder of the 19th century the Al Saud family dueled with another ruling family, the Al Rashid, to see which would control the Arabian interior. By 1891 the Al Rashid family won out, and the Al Sauds were forced into exile in Kuwait.

In 1902, Abdulaziz ibn Abdul Rahman ibn Faisal ibn Turki ibn Abdullah ibn Muhammad al-Saud (known in the Arab world as Abdulaziz and in the West as Ibn Saud), then age 27, recaptured control of Riyadh. The role played by Ibn Saud in the history of Saudi Arabia cannot be overstated. Securing the assistance of the Ikhwan, a tribal army inspired by Wahhabism, by 1913 Ibn Saud had conquered Arabia's easternmost province of Al-Ahsa from the Ottomans.

The British were eager to protect their imperial lifeline to India, and during World War I (1914–1918) when the Ottoman Empire was fighting against them on the side of the Central Powers, on December 26, 1915, the British signed the Treaty of Darin with Ibn Saud, securing the latter's benevolent neutrality. With Ibn Saud holding aloof from direct involvement in the war, British authorities in Cairo that same year had entered into negotiations with Hussein bin Ali, sharif of Mecca and a rival of Ibn Saud, to lead a Pan-Arab revolt against the Ottoman Empire with the pledge of the creation of a united Arab state at the end of the conflict.

Although the Arab Revolt of 1916–1918 greatly aided the British forces in their defeat of the Ottoman forces in the Middle East and helped bring finis to the Ottoman Empire, it did not lead to the creation of a single independent Arab state. Indeed, the British and French had secretly agreed to divide control of the region among themselves. The result was the creation of new states as League of Nations mandates, formed from territory of the former Ottoman Empire. The British had de facto control of Palestine, Transjordan, and Iraq, while the French controlled Syria and Lebanon.

Ibn Saud had avoided involvement in the Arab Revolt, choosing instead to continue his struggle with the Al Rashids. After World War I, he received support for that effort from the British, including munitions. He launched his campaign in 1920, leading to their defeat by 1922. On November 3, 1921, Ibn Saud had taken the title "Sultan of Nejd." His victory doubled the size of Saudi territory.

Assisted by the Ikhwans, on August 24, 1924, Ibn Saud invaded the Hejaz and drove on Mecca. Sharif Hussein abdicated on October 3, succeeded by his son Ali. Mecca surrendered to Ibn Saud on October 14. On December 8, 1925, Ali, who had withdrawn to Jidda, also abdicated, and Ibn Saud's forces took Jidda on December 23. Now in effective control of the entire area, on January 8, 1926, Ibn Saud declared himself king of the Hejaz. A year later he added the title "King of Nejd," although both kingdoms were administered separately.

Following the conquest of the Hejaz, the Ikhwan leadership wanted to expand Wahhabism northward, and they began raids into the British protectorates of Transjordan, Iraq, and Kuwait. This greatly concerned Ibn Saud, who was anxious not to antagonize the British. Another point of contention between him and the Ikhwans was Ibn Saud's domestic program, which the Ikhwans said smacked of modernism. They also objected to an influx of non-Muslims into the kingdom. Fighting began in 1927 between the Ikhwans and forces loyal to Ibn Saud, and a two-year civil war ensued. The decisive engagement in the so-called Ikhwan Revolt was the Battle of Sabilla (March 29–31, 1929). Ibn Saud's forces were victorious, and the Ikhwan leaders were massacred. On September 23, 1932, Ibn Saud merged his two kingdoms of the Hejaz and Nejd to form the Kingdom of Saudi Arabia.

The ruling House of Saud has dominated Saudi Arabia for its entire modern history. Ibn Saud ruled the kingdom until his death on November 9, 1953, and all succeeding kings have been his sons, of which he had more than 50. The present ruler, Salman, is said to be Ibn Saud's 25th son.

Despite its vast size, however, Saudi Arabia was one of the world's poorest countries, apparently bereft of natural resources and dependent economically to a considerable extent on religious pilgrimages to its holy sites. That changed in 1938 with the discovery of significant oil deposits by the American-owned California-Arabian Standard Oil Co., which paid royalties for the right to extract and ship Saudi oil. The importance of oil during World War II enhanced the U.S.-Saudi relationship, and in 1944 the Arab-American Oil Corporation (ARAMCO) was formed.

President Franklin Roosevelt helped cement the growing relationship between the United States and Saudi Arabia when he met with Ibn Saud aboard the U.S. Navy cruiser *Quincy* in Egypt's Great Bitter Lake on February 14, 1945, the first time that the Saudi king had left his country. The Saudi monarchy has maintained close economic and strategic ties to the United States ever since, although that relationship has not always been a smooth one.

Because of the growing strategic importance of the Middle East and its oil reserves to geopolitics, during the Cold War (1945–1991) both the United States and the Soviet Union sought increased influence in the region. The Soviets endorsed the rise of secular, socialist Arab nationalist regimes in Egypt, Iraq, and Syria, and Soviet military assistance was crucial to these nations in their ongoing struggle with the State of Israel after its establishment in 1948. The United States tightened its ties to the royal regimes in Iran and Saudi Arabia.

In September 1962 civil war broke out in the Kingdom of Yemen (North Yemen) and came to involve Saudi Arabia. On the death of Imam Ahmed on September 19, Crown Prince Seif al-Islam Mohammed al-Badr assumed the throne of the Kingdom of Yemen. However, a republican revolt began on September 27 in the capital city of Sana'a (Sanaa, Sana) when rebels headed by Colonel Abdullah al-Sallal proclaimed the establishment of the "Free Yemen Republic" and easily seized key locations in Sana'a and moved against Al-Bashaer Palace, capturing it the next day. Meanwhile, an insurgency was ongoing in South Yemen, which remained under British rule until 1967.

Al-Badr escaped into far northern Yemen, where he received the support of royalist tribes and also the Saudi monarchy. President Gamal Abdel Nasser of Egypt meanwhile decided to back al-Sallal, even sending Egyptian forces. Indeed, by late 1965 there were some 55,000 Egyptian troops in North Yemen. Saudi Arabian leaders were greatly angered by Nasser's move, seeing this as a direct challenge to their influence. By the mid-1960s, the royalists also secured the help of Iraq, Jordan, Pakistan, Iran, and Britain as well as covert assistance from Israel, while the Soviet Union and several other communist bloc nations supported the republican side. The conflict thus became politicized along Cold War lines, with the United States, the United Kingdom, and other Western powers siding with the royalists. Attempts by the United Nations (UN) to bring about an end to the fighting were unsuccessful.

The Egyptian forces initially performed poorly, and in January 1964 the royalists laid siege to Sana'a. When the Egyptians staged air strikes on Najran and Jizan, staging areas within Saudi Arabia for the royalist forces, this almost led to war between the two countries. U.S. president John F. Kennedy supplied air defense systems to Saudi Arabia and also dispatched U.S. aircraft to Dhahran Airbase, demonstrating the American commitment to defend Saudi Arabia.

The war becomes a stalemated guerrilla conflict and a huge drain on the Egyptian treasury and military. Indeed, the presence in Yemen of so many trained troops and so much equipment certainly impacted the June 1967 Six Day War. Egypt's ignominious defeat in that conflict forced Nasser to begin withdrawing his troops from Yemen. That same year the British withdrew from South Yemen. By 1969, both sides in the struggle agreed that the first step to ending the war was the withdrawal of all foreign troops from Yemeni territory. On April 14, 1970, Saudi Arabia recognized the republican government of Yemen in return for the inclusion of royalists in several key government posts.

The Israeli issue greatly complicated U.S.-Saudi relations. The Saudis strongly objected to the 1948 formation of Israel and opposed the displacement of Palestinian Arabs. Although the Saudis played only a minor military role in the Israeli War of Independence (1948–1949), they contributed significant funds to Palestinian causes. Indeed, Saudi Arabia became a primary source of economic aid for the Palestine Liberation Organization (PLO). While PLO support for Iraqi president Saddam Hussein during the Persian Gulf War of 1991 effectively curtailed Saudi financial support, the Saudis continued to insist on a comprehensive peace settlement that would include the right of return for Palestinian refugees.

Despite its opposition to Israel, the Saudi government maintained only perfunctory relations with Arab nationalist regimes in Syria, Egypt, Iraq, and Jordan, Israel's principal enemies. Thus, Saudi Arabia did not participate in the Arab-Israeli wars of 1956, 1967, and 1973. As American support for Israel increased after the 1967 war, however, the Saudis sought to influence American policy, and the Arab-Israeli confrontation laid the foundation for the 1973 oil embargo.

Saudi oil was largely controlled by American oil companies until the early 1970s, when the House of Saud negotiated the gradual takeover of ARAMCO by Saudi interests. This transfer of control had begun by 1973. When Egypt and Syria attacked Israel in October 1973, prompting the Yom Kippur War, Saudi Arabia's King Faisal obtained U.S. president Richard Nixon's assurances of American nonintervention. The Israelis suffered severe reversals in the opening stages of the conflict, however, prompting Nixon to send U.S. military assistance to Israel beginning on October 19. The next day, working through the Organization of Petroleum Exporting Countries (OPEC), the Saudi government implemented an oil embargo directed at the United States. This severely impacted the U.S. economy, with prices at the pump rising 40 percent during the five months of the crisis. Even after the embargo ended, oil prices remained high for the rest of the decade.

Saudi Arabia emerged from the crisis as the clear leader of OPEC and with renewed respect in the Arab world. Massive increases in oil revenues (from $5 billion in 1972 to $119 billion in 1981) helped transform Saudi Arabia into an affluent, urbanized society with generous government subsidies and programs for its citizens and no taxation. The U.S.-Saudi relationship eventually recovered and remained close; indeed, Saudi Arabia often used its influence in OPEC to keep oil prices artificially low from the mid-1980s to late 1990s.

Such policies, however, had a downside. When oil prices dipped dramatically during 1981–1985, the Saudi economy plunged into recession, presenting the government with significant domestic unrest. A similar scenario was played out in the late 1990s. This time the Saudis acted aggressively, hiking oil prices in 2000 and 2001 to right their foundering economy. An effort begun by the Saudis in November 2014 to keep production high and thereby sharply lower prices, with one aim being to drive the U.S. oil companies into bankruptcy, was not successful.

Despite the considerable power the Saudis wielded in international relations beginning in the 1970s and the tremendous increase in wealth as a result of oil revenues, the House of Saud maintained strict control over Saudi society, culture, and law. Opposition emerged to King Faisal, however, particularly from conservatives. On March 25, 1975, Faisal was assassinated by his nephew, the stated reason being revenge for the death of his brother who had been killed by Saudi Defense Force members during a demonstration in 1965. Faisal was succeeded by his half brother, Khalid bin Abdulaziz al-Saud.

On November 20, 1979, Juhayman al-Otaybi, a member of an influential Nejd family, led hundreds of followers, many of them theology students at the Islamic University in Medina, to seize control of the Grand Mosque in Mecca. Al-Otaybi declared his brother-in-law Mohammed Abdullah al-Qahtani to be the Mahdi, or redeemer, whom Muslims believe will arrive on Earth several years before Judgment Day. This event triggered a full-scale political crisis. Fighting lasted until December 4, when the mosque was finally secured. The military suffered 127 dead and 451 injured, while the insurgents lost 117 killed and suffered an unknown number of wounded. On January 9, 1980, 63 of the rebels were publicly beheaded in the squares of eight different Saudi cities.

The Saudis continued to oppose Israel's treatment of the Palestinians and its continued presence in the occupied territories. Saudi relations with Egypt also declined precipitously after the 1978 signing of the Camp David Accords between Israel and Egypt. The Saudis objected to any individual peace deals with Israel that did not settle the entire Arab-Israeli conflict and address the plight of the Palestinian Arabs and the refugees of the 1948–1949 war.

On August 7, 1981, Crown Prince Fahd presented an eight-point proposal to resolve the Arab-Israeli conflict and give the Palestinians an independent state. Loosely based on UN Resolutions 242 and 338, the plan called for recognition of Israel but with Israel to withdraw from territories captured in 1967, including East Jerusalem (but not the whole city). Israel was also to dismantle its settlements, recognize the PLO as the representative of the Palestinian people, and agree to the establishment of an independent Palestinian state with Jerusalem as its capital. There were also to be secure guarantees of peace. Fahd's plan was not popular at home with the Saudi intelligentsia, middle class, and clergy, who were strongly critical of any proposal that recognized Israel. At the Twelfth Arab Summit Conference, held in Fez, Morocco, on September 9, 1982, however, the Arab League adopted a version of the Fahd plan, which became known as the Fez Initiative. It received a mixed reception in the Arab capital because it implicitly recognized Israel but found support among European countries, anxious to secure their oil supplies. At the time the United States was more interested in what became known as the Reagan Plan that kept Jordan in place as the sovereign in the West Bank. On April 26, 2002, during a trip to the United States, Saudi crown prince Abdullah presented an eight-point Mideast peace proposal to U.S. president George W. Bush. Similar to Fahd's 1981 plan, it was rejected by the Israeli government.

Saudi Arabia strongly backed Iraq during the Iran-Iraq War (1980–1988), providing some $20 billion to help fund the Iraqi war effort. Thus, the Saudis were greatly angered when Iraqi president Saddam Hussein decided to invade and annex Kuwait beginning on August 2, 1990, especially as the Saudis had been trying to broker a deal between the two states. U.S. president George H. W. Bush immediately rushed forces to Saudi Arabia (Operation DESERT SHIELD) and took the lead in the formation of an international coalition to force Iraq to withdraw.

The Saudis took the highly unusual step of allowing foreign troops into their territory, from which the coalition invasion of Kuwait would be mounted. This decision, which led to the presence in the kingdom of some half million foreign troops, most of them Americans, was billed as a protective measure to keep Iraq from continuing its offensive into Saudi Arabia itself. It did, however, cause a negative reaction among influential ultraconservatives in Saudi Arabia, who claimed that the foreigners were defiling Islamic traditions and law and that this was thus a motivation behind the formation of the Al Qaeda Islamic terrorist organization, headed by Saudi citizen Osama bin Laden.

Saudi Arabia was confirmed as a significant regional military force during the ensuing 1991 Persian Gulf War. Two Arab task forces were organized under the command of Saudi prince Khalid ibn Sultan al-Saud, with the Saudi ground commitment totaling nearly 50,000 men. The Saudis deployed some 270 tanks and 930 other armored fighting vehicles as well as artillery and more than 250 aircraft that flew 6,852 sorties. Saudi forces took part in the Battle of Khafji (January 29–February 1, 1991) and in the four-day ground war that began on February 24, and they helped drive the Iraqis from Kuwait.

U.S.-Saudi relations suffered following the September 11, 2001, terrorist attacks on the United States, which involved 15 Saudi Arabian nationals or citizen. The Saudis, however, strongly disapproved of the U.S.- and British-led invasion of Iraq (Operation IRAQI FREEDOM) that began in March 2003, and they refused to allow use of their territory as a base of operations for the invasion. The Saudis disapproved because of the likelihood of Iraqi fratricide following regime change and the advantage that a destabilized Iraq would create for Iran. However, many Saudis were also concerned that if the coalition forces pulled out too soon, Iraq would degenerate into full-scale civil war.

The U.S. engagement in Iraq also provided a rationale for Saudis who opposed their government's alliance with America. Indeed, some joined the insurgents in Iraq. At the same time, an effort to close down U.S. military operations in the kingdom had been in progress for some time, and by August 2003 all remaining U.S. troops had been withdrawn.

During 2003–2005 a series of attacks by a hitherto unknown group calling itself Al Qaeda fi Jazirat al-Arabiyya (Al Qaeda in the Arabian Peninsula, AQAP) attacked and killed a number of Westerners. These included the bombing in May and November 2003 of housing compounds for foreign workers and an attack on the American consulate in Jeddah. Attacks and attempted sabotage by this group continued despite numerous arrests and the deaths of most of the AQAP leadership, a strong counterterrorism effort carried out by Saudi authorities, and a thorough reeducation program designed by the Saudi Ministry of the Interior. The Saudis also cooperated with numerous American requirements such as exerting control over Islamic charitable groups, addressing extremism in parts of the Islamic educational system, cutting off funding to the *mutawa'in* (morals police), and providing information to the international counterintelligence effort.

In January 2011 as revolution swept Egypt and sparked what became known as the Arab Spring, protests occurred in Jeddah. The demonstrations were quickly crushed, and a number of people were arrested. The following month, however, the Saudi government announced a major multibillion-dollar initiative designed to ameliorate living conditions for its poorer citizens. In March, the government rolled out a plan that would provide some 500,000 new housing units and create at least 60,000 new jobs. The plan was estimated to cost $93 billion. In a bid to further mollify Saudis, King

Abdullah declared that women would be able to vote beginning in 2015 and would be eligible for positions on the Shura Council. This was seen as a major political reform measure in a profoundly conservative nation that had all but excluded women from public life.

On March 14, 2011, following massive prodemocracy demonstrations in neighboring Bahrain, Saudi Arabia acted on a request from that government and sent some 150 vehicles and 1,000 troops eastward into Bahrain via the long 12-mile causeway that connects the two states. The stated goal here was to protect Bahrain's government offices and end the demonstrations. While expressing concern, the U.S. government refused to condemn the Saudi move, which was regarded as a signal by Saudi leaders that concessions by the Bahrainian monarchy could empower Saudi Arabia's own Shia minority and benefit Iran.

The Sunni-Shia religious confrontation has come to impact much of Saudi foreign policy. Saudi Arabia has assumed the former Iraqi role of opposing the spread of Iranian influence in Lebanon, Syria, and Yemen. Thus, the Saudis have strongly supported opposition forces battling the Iranian-backed Syrian government of President Bashar al-Assad in the Syrian Civil War (2011–present), first with funds and then by early 2013 with small arms shipped through Jordan. Saudi demands that Assad resign brought the severing of diplomatic ties between the two states.

The Saudis have also viewed the rise of the Islamic State of Iraq and Syria (ISIS) with great concern. On September 23, 2014, Saudi aircraft joined those of the United States and some other Arab states in striking ISIS targets in Syria. In September 2014, Saudi Arabia reportedly encouraged air attacks against radical Islamists in Libya carried out by the United Arab Emirates, Qatar, and Egypt. Then in December 2015, the Saudi government announced the formation of a coalition of 34 predominantly Muslim nations to fight terrorism, specifically referencing such activity in Syria, Iraq, the Sinai, Yemen, Libya, Mali, Nigeria, Pakistan, and Afghanistan. The new coalition's joint operations center is based in Riyadh.

Saudi Arabia also intervened more forcefully in the Yemen Civil War that had begun on March 19, 2015. With clear evidence that Iran had been arming the Shiite Muslims there, on March 26 Saudi Arabia and its Persian Gulf region allies launched air strikes in an effort to counter the Iran-allied Houthi rebel forces besieging the southern city of Aden. The Saudi military intervention in Yemen, primarily through airpower with attendant civilian casualties, continues.

On January 4, 2016, after rioters stormed the Saudi embassy in Tehran amid a row over the Saudi execution of prominent Shia Muslim cleric Sheikh Nimr al-Nimr and 46 others condemned for alleged terrorist activities, Saudi Arabia terminated diplomatic relations with Iran.

King Abdullah bin Abdulaziz al-Saud died at age 90 on January 22, 2015. He was succeeded by his 79-year-old brother, Salman bin Abdulaziz, whose brother Prince Muqrin, a decade younger, became the new crown prince. Salman has been both defense minister and deputy prime minister.

Saudi Arabia's crackdown on dissent and history of human rights abuses remained the subject of harsh criticism from Western nongovernmental organizations such as Amnesty International and Human Rights Watch. In April 2016, however, in a significant step Saudi Arabia stripped its religious forces of their powers to arrest, urging them to act "kindly and gently" in enforcing Islamic rules. Then in May, King Salman reshuffled the government and replaced a number of key cabinet ministers. With the price of oil at low levels and unlikely to rise any time soon, the regional order that Saudi Arabia had long supported apparently in tatters, civil war raging in Syria and Yemen, and an intensified challenge from regional rival Iran, Salman sought to reduce the kingdom's dependence on oil as a source of revenue while also improving the quality of life for the kingdom's citizens. Cabinet changes included the reshuffling of the duties of the oil ministry and the replacement of its long-standing minister, Ali al-Naimi.

At the same time, normally close relations with the United States had deteriorated. The Saudis were upset regarding the lack of U.S. support for embattled Egyptian president Hosni Mubarak, and Saudi leaders also wanted a robust U.S. effort to topple Syrian president Bashar al-Assad, whose regime was closely aligned with Iran. Saudi Arabia was also upset not to be included in the initial negotiations between the United States and Iran regarding the latter's nuclear program, which were conducted in secret in Oman in 2013.

There was also the Saudi military intervention in the Yemeni Civil War beginning in 2015. The Obama administration supplied the Saudis with arms (indeed, Saudi Arabia is the major foreign purchaser of U.S. military hardware, accounting for nearly 10 percent of U.S. arms sales abroad between 2010 and 2015). The administration also provided intelligence and aerial refueling to allow the Saudis to prosecute the war. Yet there were sharp disagreements, for Washington called for restraint, especially on targeting areas with high civilian populations. Mounting civilian casualties and the destruction of hospitals, schools, and infrastructure needed to transport food created a humanitarian crisis, with much of the population on the verge of famine. In its last few months in office, the Obama administration suspended the sale of precision-guided missiles to Saudi Arabia. The new Donald Trump administration moved to reverse this, and secretary of defense Jim Mattis visited Saudi Arabia in April 2017 and offered U.S. support for the Saudi war effort in Yemen as a way of getting at Iran.

Then in May, Trump made Saudi Arabia his first foreign destination as president. In Riyadh the president signed a new arms deal with the desert kingdom amounting to nearly $110 billion, this in addition to $55 billion in deals with U.S. companies also announced during Trump's visit. This was about more than enhancing Saudi Arabia militarily, however. King Salman understood that his kingdom could no longer rely simply on oil revenues alone. These deals were designed in large part to jump-start the Saudi economy and diversify it, creating new private-sector jobs and allowing the kingdom to cut back on government employment and subsidies. This plan, known as Vision 2030, is designed to privatize the education, health care, agriculture, mining, and defense sectors and to sell off Saudi ARAMCO, perhaps the wealthiest company in the world with an estimated worth of some $1 trillion. King Salman also empowered his 31-year-old son, Deputy Crown Prince Mohammed bin Salman, to slowly modernize Saudi society while quickly diversifying the economy.

On June 5 in a surprise announcement, Saudi Arabia, Egypt, the United Arab Emirates, and Bahrain severed ties with Qatar, opening up the worst rift in years among some of the most powerful states in the Arab world. This move dramatically escalated the sharp disagreement over Qatar's support of the Muslim Brotherhood. At the same time, however, the other four Arab states accused Doha of supporting regional archrival Iran by broadcasting radical Islamic propaganda over the Qatari state-run satellite television network Al Jazeera and encouraging Iranian-backed militants in Saudi Arabia's restive and largely Shiite Muslim-populated eastern region of Qatif and in Bahrain. The four states also cut off all transport ties with Qatar and gave its citizens within their countries two weeks to leave. Qatar was also expelled from the Saudi-led coalition fighting in Yemen.

It seemed clear to many analysts that the Saudis and Emiratis felt emboldened by the alignment of their regional interests toward Iran and Islamic extremism with those of the Trump administration. Oil prices rose on the news, with Qatar being the largest supplier of liquefied natural gas (LNG) and a major seller of condensate, a low-density liquid fuel and refining product derived from natural gas.

In June 2017 King Salman shook up the Saudi political scene when he named his 31-year-old son Mohammed bin Salman in place of the king's nephew, Mohammed bin Nayef (age 57), as the new crown prince and hence next ruler of Saudi Arabia. Mohammed was then defense minister. This move appeared to be an affirmation that the Saudis remain committed to an aggressive approach to the Middle East, prompting fears of a greater escalation with Saudi rival Iran and challenges to traditional U.S. policies in the region. The new crown prince has been deeply involved in three controversial Saudi foreign policy moves: the brutal campaign against Iran-backed militants in the civil war in Yemen, the recent push against U.S. partner nation Qatar, and efforts since 2016 to slash even limited engagement with Iran, all of which have been largely ineffective.

At the same time, the Saudi government has attempted to institute limited—though significant—social reform, including a 2017 decree that permitted Saudi women to drive automobiles, an activity that had previously been forbidden. King Salman has also attempted to reform Saudi governing institutions and rejuvenate the country's economy.

In November 2017 Salman's government ordered the arrest of at least 10 members of the royal family, including 4 cabinet ministers as well as a number of former ministers. Among the detained princes was Al-Waleed bin Talal, one of the world's richest men. The most important cabinet change was the removal of Prince Miteb bin Abdullah as minister of the National Guard. Prince Miteb, the favorite son of the late king Abdullah, had been considered the most likely to one day replace King Salman before the rise of Prince Mohammed in 2015. The move consolidated Miteb's control of the security apparatus of the desert kingdom, which had previously been divided among a number of princes. The stated purpose of this extraordinary action was to curb corruption in the kingdom. Mohammed pledged to end corruption at the highest levels and will head a new anticorruption body, but the changes were seen primarily as yet another move to strengthen Mohammed's hand.

At the same time, the Saudi government increased its campaign against the growing influence in the region of its archrival Iran by securing on November 19, 2017, the support of most of the 22 members of the Arab League in condemning the actions of Iran's ally Hezbollah in Lebanon, branding it a "terrorist organization."

During the summer of 2018, Saudi Arabia began ramping up its oil output in an attempt to stabilize and reduce oil prices, which had peaked at more than $70 per barrel. The Saudis had come under increased pressure by the Trump administration, which insisted that oil prices were too high and threatened the global economy. In August 2018, various press reports indicated that Saudi Arabia and the United Arab Emirates had planned to attack Qatar during the summer of 2017 in a bid to force that country to conform to its demands. According to those same reports, U.S. secretary of state Rex Tillerson, who resigned in March 2018, convinced both nations not to attack Qatar. As of early 2019, the Saudis' impasse with Qatar had still not been resolved. That same month, Saudi Arabia became embroiled in a major diplomatic contretemps with Canada, going so far as to expel that country's ambassador and withdrawing Saudi students from Canadian universities. The row began after Raif Badawi, a Saudi citizen who had publicly rebuked Saudi officials and religious leaders, was arrested and jailed in Saudi Arabia for his derogatory blogs. Canada had previously granted asylum and citizenship to Badawi's family. When Badawi was arrested, Canada protested, and the spat took on a life of its own.

Meanwhile, Saudi crown prince Mohammad bin Salman moved with a heavy hand, holding members of the royal family hostage until they agreed to turn over substantial funds, refusing to end Saudi Arabia's participation in the civil war in Yemen, and ordering the murder of Saudi dissident and *Washington Post* correspondent Jamal Khashoggi, who was a U.S. resident. This brought considerable international condemnation but Saudi government denials of the crown prince's culpability. Despite overwhelming evidence to the contrary, the Trump administration refused to recognize the crown prince's role in the murder and indeed stressed the importance of U.S.-Saudi ties.

ROBERT S. KIELY, SPENCER C. TUCKER, AND SHERIFA ZUHUR

### See also
Al Qaeda; Al Qaeda in the Arabian Peninsula; Arab League; Arab Oil Embargo; Arab Revolt in Palestine; Arab Spring; Assad, Bashar al-; Bahrain; Bin Laden, Osama; Fahd, ibn Abd al-Aziz al-Saud; Hezbollah; Hussein, Saddam; Hussein ibn Ali ibn Mohammed; Ibn Saud, King; Iran-Iraq War; Islamic State of Iraq and Syria; Khalid bin Sultan, Prince; Kuwait; Lebanon; Muhammad, Prophet of Islam; Nasser, Gamal Abdel; Organization of Petroleum Exporting Countries; Ottoman Empire; Persian Gulf War, Overview; Qatar; Religious Sites in the Middle East, Muslim; Saudi-Hashemite War; Saudi-Kuwaiti War; Saudi-Ottoman War; Saudi-Rashidi Wars; Saudi-Yemeni War; Syrian Civil War; Wahhabism; Yemen; Yemen, Civil War in the North; Yemen, Civil War in the South; Yemen Civil War; Yom Kippur War

### References
Aarts, Paul, and Carolien Roelants. *Saudi Arabia: A Kingdom in Peril*. New York: Hurst, 2015.

Cooper, Andrew Scott. *The Oil Kings: How the U.S., Iran, and Saudi Arabia Changed the Balance of Power in the Middle East*. New York: Simon and Schuster, 2011.

Darlow, Michael, and Barbara Bray. *Ibn Saud: The Desert Warrior Who Created the Kingdom of Saudi Arabia*. New York: Skyhorse Publishing, 2009.

Hourani, Albert. *A History of the Arab Peoples*. Cambridge, MA: Harvard University Press, 1991.

House, Karen Elliott. *On Saudi Arabia: Its People, Past, Religion, Fault Lines and Future*. New York: Vintage, 2012.

Lacey, Robert. *Inside the Kingdom: Kings, Clerics, Modernists, Terrorists, and the Struggle for Saudi Arabia*. New York: Penguin, 2009.

Lacey, Robert. *The Kingdom*. New York: Harcourt Brace Jovanovich, 1982.

Lewis, Bernard. *The Middle East*. New York: Scribner, 1997.

Wynbrandt, James. *A Brief History of Saudi Arabia*. New York: Checkmark, 2004.

Zuhur, Sherifa. *Saudi Arabia: Islamic Threat, Political Reform and the Global War on Terror*. Carlisle Barracks, PA: Strategic Studies, 2005.

## Saudi-Hashemite War (1919–1925)

A conflict fought between the Hashemite dynasty of Hejaz and Ibn Saud of the Nejd over supremacy in Arabia. As descendants of Prophet Muhammad, the Hashemites (taking their dynastic name from the great-grandfather of Muhammad, Hashim ibn Abd al-Manaf), were entitled to use the title of sharif. For centuries they ruled Mecca but were subordinate to Great Powers, be it the Mamluks of Egypt or the Ottoman Empire. When World War I began in 1914, Ibn Saud, the powerful emir of the Nejd, offered Sharif Hussein bin Ali of Mecca and the rulers of Hail and Kuwait to adopt a neutral stance, avoid involvement in European hostilities, and seek self-determination for the Arab peoples. But Arab rulers' interests did not coincide, and no agreement was reached. For the next two years Ibn Saud refrained from providing any real support to any side, bidding his time to see which way the wind would blow.

Meanwhile, in 1916 Sharif Hussein, with British encouragement, declared the Arab Revolt against the Ottomans and proclaimed himself "King of the Arabs" even though he lacked the forces necessary to exert his authority beyond the Hejaz. Ibn Saud was infuriated by Hussein's claim of power over all of Arabia and demanded negotiations concerning the Nejd-Hejaz border and the extent of suzerainty over frontier tribes. Hussein rejected Ibn Saud's demands and insulted him in his response, calling him "either mad or drunk" for making such claims.

In response Ibn Saud became involved in a political crisis that was unfolding in the Hashemite states between

King Hussein and Khalid ibn Mansur ibn Luwai, emir of the al-Khurma oasis. Khurma, the crucial strategic gateway between Hejaz and Nejd, was under Hashemite control, but insulted by the king, its emir Khalid defected to Ibn Saud's side. When in July 1918 Hussein dispatched a detachment to seize al-Khurma, Ibn Saud clandestinely sent his Ikhwan troops to protect Khalid, who defeated the Meccan force.

Britain could not ignore Ibn Saud, the strongest of the Arab leaders, and gave him generous financial subsidies in the hope of inciting him to attack pro-Ottoman polities in Arabia. In December 1917 a British deputation, led by Lieutenant Colonel Robert Edward Hamilton, sought to spur Ibn Saud to action against Jabal Shammar. The Saudi leader promised energetic action if given modern arms.

In early 1918, however, British forces achieved a breakthrough in Palestine and occupied Jerusalem, making Ibn Saud's support irrelevant. Furthermore, Hussein concluded a peace treaty with Jabal Shammar, while the British became concerned that Ibn Saud's campaign might be detrimental to their chief ally, Sharif Hussein. Thus, in the fall of 1918 as Ibn Saud gathered some 5,000 men against Shammar, the British ordered him to end the campaign. The Saudi leader was furious at this duplicity and concluded that Britain was not interested in his success.

With Ottoman forces defeated and his army free after capturing Medina, Hussein thought the time ripe to deal with Ibn Saud and began reviving the issue of al-Khurma. The conflict soon transcended political dimensions and gained religious overtones as a struggle between the Wahhabis of the Nejd against the Orthodox Sunni Hashemites. Ibn Saud's official passivity regarding the al-Khurma dispute placed Hussein in an awkward position, since the king's claim of Ibn Saud's challenge to his sovereignty appeared to many as unreasonable and overly aggressive. Yet, Hussein was in a difficult position. Abstention from military action would make him appear weak and allow the spread of Wahhabi ideas. But if he was aggressive he would undermine his religious legitimacy in the eyes of the many, since he would be fighting against the Islamic revival movement. Hussein finally decided to organize a new expedition against al-Khurma.

The British understood that the new campaign would provoke a direct clash between the rulers of Hejaz and Nejd, but largely ignorant of the strength of Ibn Saud, they believed that his forces would be quickly routed. In May 1919, Hussein's son Abdallah led the Hashemite Army to Turaba, an oasis some 80 miles from al-Khurma, which he seized and plundered on May 21. Ibn Saud warned Abdallah that continued Hashemite presence at Turaba or advance on al-Khurma would provoke a war, but neither side was willing to compromise. The Ikhwan force under Sultan ibn Bijad, Hamud ibn Umar, and Khalid advanced stealthily to Turaba and surprised the slumbering enemy in their camp on May 25–26. In just a few hours the entire Hashemite Army was annihilated, with some hundreds killed and thousands fleeing; Abdallah himself barely escaped with his life.

The Battle of Turaba proved to be the turning point in the Saudi-Hashemite conflict. The loss of the army, the sole independent means of defending his sovereignty, placed Hussein in a very weak position vis-à-vis Ibn Saud. In early July 1919 Ibn Saud arrived in Turaba with about 10,000 men, ready to invade Hejaz. But on July 4 he received a British ultimatum to stop his campaign and return to Nejd or face a war. Unwilling to fight Britain, Ibn Saud submitted to the British demands. His first, rather easy, victory over the Hashemites had convinced him, however, that he would ultimately triumph over Hejaz. He ordered his troops to evacuate the region but also called upon local tribesmen to join his struggle, and many of them responded positively.

During the next four years Ibn Saud was preoccupied with consolidating his authority and expanding into new regions of Arabia. He annexed Jabal Shammar in 1920–1921, defeated Kuwait and defined the border with Iraq and Transjordan in 1922, and simultaneously conquered the Asir emirate in southern Arabia. King Hussein, understanding that a military conflict with Ibn Saud was inevitable, tried to prepare for it by increasing taxes to strengthen the army. Yet government corruption and increased taxes caused resentment among many tribesmen, who fled to Ibn Saud's court. By early 1923, Ibn Saud decided to conquer Hejaz but was unsure about Britain's position. He welcomed the worsening of relations between London and King Hussein, who refused to ratify the Treaty of Versailles in protest of the Anglo-French partition of Ottoman Empire territory.

In March 1924 Hussein proclaimed himself a caliph, hoping to consolidate his authority among the Arabs. Yet, this decision proved to be highly unpopular and turned many Arabs from him. In July 1924 Hussein recognized the Soviet Union, causing alarm among the British, who were worried that they might lose control over Hejaz.

At the same time, Ibn Saud decided to begin the conquest of the Hejaz. This decision was enthusiastically supported by the Ikhwans, who hoped to "purify" the holy sites of Islam. To test Britain's position, Ibn Saud launched a preliminary attack on al-Taif in early September 1924; the city was captured and viciously sacked by the Ikhwans for three days, prompting the Saudi leader to issue a strict order against any such atrocities. With no British response forthcoming, Ibn Saud advanced his forces toward Mecca. King Hussein's son Ali tried to stop the Ikhwans at al-Hada but was routed in late September. The nobility of Mecca and Jidda, who believed that the main reason for war was a quarrel between Ibn Saud and Hussein, pressured the king to abdicate, which he did in favor of his son Ali on October 6, 1924.

Hussein's abdication did not placate Ibn Saud, whose troops entered Mecca without a fight in mid-October 1924. With Britain's tacit blessing, Ibn Saud himself arrived in Mecca on December 5 and demanded that King Ali abdicate and leave the Hejaz at once. Upon Ali's refusal Ibn Saud advanced against the Hashemite king, besieging Jidda (where Ali was in residence) on January 4, 1925, and against Medina in early February.

As the yearlong siege of Jidda unfolded, Ibn Saud busied himself with diplomacy to consolidate his conquests. Neither King Abdallah of Transjordan nor Faisal of Iraq were willing to jeopardize their authority to assist their brother Ali in his struggle against the Saudi ruler. Demonstrating his political acumen, Ibn Saud agreed to concede some land in northern Arabia in exchange for Britain's recognition of his annexation of Hejaz, which was formalized in the al-Hada agreement of November 2, 1925.

Learning about the al-Hada agreement and the surrender of Medina on December 6, King Ali realized that he was abandoned and capitulated in Jidda on December 22, 1925. The nobility and ulema of Mecca and Jidda swore allegiance to Ibn Saud as "the King of Hejaz and the Sultan of Nejd and her dependencies." The first state to recognize Ibn Saud's authority was the Soviet Union, on February 16, 1926.

ALEXANDER MIKABERIDZE

### See also
Hussein ibn Ali ibn Mohammed; Ibn Saud, King; Saudi-Kuwaiti War; Saudi-Ottoman War; Saudi-Rashidi Wars

### References
Al-Enazy, Askar. *The Creation of Saudi Arabia: Ibn Saud and British Imperial policy, 1914–1927.* New York: Routledge, 2010.

Bowen, Wayne. *The History of Saudi Arabia.* Westport, CT: Greenwood, 2008.

Kostiner, Joseph. *The Making of Saudi Arabia, 1916–1936: From Chieftancy to Monarchical State.* Oxford: Oxford University Press, 1993.

McLoughlin, Leslie J. *Ibn Saud: Founder of a Kingdom.* New York: St. Martin's, 1993.

Troeller, Gary. *The Birth of Saudi Arabia: Britain and the Rise of the House of Sa'ud.* London: F. Cass, 1976.

Vassiliev, Alexei. *The History of Saudi Arabia.* London: Saqi Books, 1998.

## Saudi King as Custodian of the Two Holy Mosques

The title taken by the king of Saudi Arabia as the temporal protector of al-Masjid al-Haram (the Sacred Mosque) in Mecca and the Masjid al-Nabawi (the Prophet's Mosque) in Medina, both of which are located in Saudi Arabia. These two mosques are, respectively, the first and second most holy places in all of Islam. Mecca and the Sacred Mosque are so central to Islam that Muslims who are able to do so are required to make at least one pilgrimage there in their lifetime (known as *hajj*). They are also obliged to pray five times per day facing in the direction of Mecca (*qiblah*). Because Medina is not far from Mecca, many Muslims also extend their pilgrimage to include a visit to the Prophet's Mosque.

The title "custodian of the two holy mosques" goes back centuries, but it was originally reserved for the chief caliph who oversaw Mecca and Medina. However, when the caliphate in the Arabian peninsula lost temporal authority in the region, the grand sharif of Mecca took up the mantle of custodian of the two holy mosques. This lasted until the early 20th century. As the House of Saud began to gain more control over the Arabian Peninsula, it began to assert its control over Mecca and Medina. In 1925, King Abd al-Aziz al-Saud (Ibn Saud) decisively defeated Hashemite sharif Hussein ibn Ali and took control of Mecca and the Sacred Mosque. This ended nearly 700 years of Hashemite control of Mecca. The following year Ibn Saud was crowned king of the Hejaz (modern-day western Saudi Arabia), which included both Mecca and Medina.

From that time forward, the royal House of Saud has exercised temporal control over these holy sites. As the Saudis consolidated their control on the Arabian Peninsula, they moved to solidify their control over Mecca and Medina. Not until 1982 did Saudi king Fahd bin Abdul Aziz (King Fahd) formally adopt the honorific title "custodian of the two holy mosques," though this was a mere formality because the House of Saud had been exercising de facto control for decades.

Many Muslims and other Arab nations take a dim view of Saudi control of Mecca and Medina. Many Muslims are suspicious of the Saudi royal family, partly because they are Wahhabi but also because they see them as attempting to fulfill the role of caliph, which many would consider anathema, if not blasphemous. Also, their immense wealth (mainly from oil revenues) and closeness with the West have led many Arabs to question Saudi motives and loyalties. On the positive side, the late King Fahd spent hundreds of millions of dollars expanding and improving the holy sites in Mecca and Medina, including the installation of air-conditioning in the Sacred Mosque and its environs.

PAUL G. PIERPAOLI JR.

**See also**
Fahd, ibn Abd al-Aziz al-Saud; Ibn Saud, King; Medina, Siege of; Saudi Arabia; Wahhabism

**References**
Al-Rasheed, Madawi. *A History of Saudi Arabia*. Cambridge: Cambridge University Press, 2002.
Peters, F. E. *Mecca: A Literary History of the Muslim Holy Land*. Princeton, NJ: Princeton University Press, 1994.
Waines, David. *An Introduction to Islam*. Cambridge: Cambridge University Press, 1995.
Wintle, Justin. *The Timeline of Islam*. New York: Barnes & Noble, 2004.

## Saudi-Kuwaiti War (1921–1922)

In the late 19th century, the small sheikhdom of Kuwait found itself in the center of a power struggle between Britain, Persia, and the Ottoman Empire. Although nominally under Ottoman authority, Kuwait cut its ties with the empire in 1896 and sought support from Britain. In 1899, Kuwait and Britain signed a treaty of cooperation that guaranteed Kuwait's integrity and domestic self-rule but granted Britain control over its foreign policy. Following World War I, during which Britain incited an Arab rebellion against the Ottomans, Kuwait faced a serious threat from the rising power of Ibn Saud, who sought to unite Arabia under his control. Kuwait's southern and western borders were undefined, and this served as a cause of friction between the two states.

In 1920, a dispute over a small border oasis led to the start of hostilities. Faisal al-Duwaish, leader of the Saudi Mutair Ikhwan warriors, defeated the Kuwaiti army led by Sheikh Du'aij al-Sabah. Kuwaiti ruler Sheikh Salim al-Mubarak al-Sabah (r. 1917–1921) ordered a defensive wall built around Kuwait, which was completed in two months. Facing continued Saudi attacks, Kuwait invoked the 1899 agreement with Britain and requested British intervention.

In late 1920, Ibn Saud resumed hostilities and with his commander Faisal al-Duwaish attacked the Kuwaiti village of Al-Jahra on October 10. Saudi troops captured the village but failed to dislodge Kuwaiti troops from a small fort. The arrival of Kuwaiti reinforcements drove the Saudis out into the desert, where they came under attack from British aircraft. Although a Kuwaiti victory, the Battle of Al-Jahra led to a Saudi blockade of Kuwait that lasted for several years. The death of Sheikh Salim in 1921 and the accession of new sheikh Ahmad al-Jaber al-Sabah (r. 1921–1950) played an important role, since the new Kuwaiti ruler established friendly relations with Ibn Saud.

The British intervention eventually led to a conference at Uqayr in eastern Arabia where negotiations produced the Protocol of Uqayr (December 2, 1922). Ibn Saud preferred a "tribal frontier," that is, a nondemarcated flexible border allowing the sphere of influence of the state to be determined by the movements and grazing of its tribes. But the British delegation insisted on the Western concept of territorial demarcation, and the final agreement specified the territory belonging to each side and created the Saudi-Kuwaiti neutral zone, where both sides held equal rights. The zone survived until the 1960s when, following the discovery of oil, the two states agreed to divide the territory.

ALEXANDER MIKABERIDZE

**See also**
Ibn Saud, King; Saudi-Hashemite War; Saudi-Ottoman War; Saudi-Rashidi Wars

**References**
Casey, Michael S. *The History of Kuwait*. Westport, CT: Greenwood, 2007.
Kostiner, Joseph. *The Making of Saudi Arabia, 1916–1936: From Chieftancy to Monarchical State*. Oxford: Oxford University Press, 1993.

## Saudi-Ottoman War (1911–1913)

The Ottoman Empire's military resources were stretched to the breaking point in the decade before World War I. Soldiers not only defended the empire from external threats posed by Russia and Italy but were also widely employed as a gendarmerie in far-off Arabia. This dual role created headaches for military planners, and as the Balkans were so much closer to Istanbul, the empire's widely dispersed military assets facilitated internal unrest.

Nowhere was this more obvious than in the Arabian Peninsula. Although not yet counted as being valuable for its natural resources, Arabia contained the Holy Cities of Mecca and Medina. As the caliph of Sunni Islam, the Ottoman sultan secured prestige and political authority in helping pilgrims visit these cities. Sultan Abdulhamid II (r. 1876–1909) argued that the survival of the empire rested on four points: supporting Islam, maintaining the dynasty, keeping the Holy Cities under Ottoman control, and holding Istanbul.

Keeping the Holy Cities under Ottoman control became a challenge during 1911–1913, when the empire faced three simultaneous threats in the Balkans, Africa, and Arabia. In the latter region, religious leaders such as Imams Muhammad of Yemen and Muhammad ibn Ali al-Idrisī of Asīr led major uprisings against Ottoman rule. These conflicts were dangerously close to the Holy Cities and required considerable Ottoman resources.

Nor was Yemen the Ottoman Empire's only problem in Arabia. On the other coast, after three decades of relative peace, Ottoman client tribes faced a powerful enemy in the House of Saud. Forces under Ibn Saud recaptured Riyadh in 1902. Two years later, Ibn Saud secured Unaizah. Despite the support of eight Ottoman battalions, the sultan's client tribes went down to defeat, with Ibn Saud's forces conquering most of al-Hasa by 1913. When his forces took Hufuf on May 4, it was with the full knowledge that Ottoman military disasters in Thrace in the First Balkan War were pulling potential reinforcements away from Arabia. Ottoman military reverses in the Balkans in fact led to a drawing off of Ottoman troops from Iraq and prevented any Ottoman counteroffensive in Arabia

As a consequence of the Saudi-Ottoman War, Ibn Saud was able to establish the Saudi Arabian state.

JOHN P. DUNN

**See also**

Ibn Saud, King; Saudi-Hashemite War; Saudi-Kuwaiti War; Saudi-Rashidi Wars

**References**

Anscombe, Frederick. *The Ottoman Gulf: The Creation of Kuwait, Saudi Arabia and Qatar*. New York: Columbia University Press, 1997.

Habib, John. *Ibn Sa'ud's Warriors of Islam: The Ikhwan of Nejd and Their Role in the Creation of the Saudi Kingdom, 1910–1930*. Leiden: Brill, 1978.

# Saudi-Rashidi Wars (1887–1921)

A prolonged conflict between the houses of Saud and Rashid (Rasheed) over control of the Arabian Peninsula. The House of Saud first came to prominence in the 18th century when Muhammad ibn Saud (1710–1765), with the help of religious cleric Muhammad ibn Abd al-Wahhab, managed to establish the first Saudi state in Nejd (central Arabia) in 1744. By the mid-19th century, the Saudi state had been through many ups and downs, including an Egyptian military occupation until 1840.

Following the Egyptian withdrawal, Nejd descended into internecine warfare among the tribes. In early 1843, Saudi leader Faisal bin Turki bin Abdullah Al Saud (1785–1865), who was captured by the Egyptians in 1838, returned to Nejd and reclaimed authority with the help of his old friend Abdallah Al Rashid, ruler of Jabal Shammar (in north Arabia), who provided the Saudi leader with troops and money. The relationship between Faisal and Abdallah remained amicable throughout their lives, and this continued following the accession of Talal ibn Abdallah in 1847. Faisal died in December 1865 and was succeeded by Abdul Rahman bin Faisal (1845–1928), who faced a prolonged power struggle against his own brother Saud bin Faisal, who seized Riyadh in 1871. However, Saud's authority was weak, and many tribes refused to obey him, chief among these the al-Radhids of Jabal Shammar.

Like the Saudis, the house of al-Rashid experienced violent succession crises between 1868 and 1872. In March 1868 Talal al-Rashidi committed suicide. His brother and successor Mitab was killed just 10 months later by his nephew Bandar ibn Talal, who in turn was assassinated by his uncle Muhammad ibn Abdallah Al Rashid in 1872. During the reign of Muhammad Al Rashid (r. 1872–1897), the Jabal Shammar reached the height of its power, made possible by the continued Saudi strife.

Between April 1871 and December 1876, Riyadh saw seven changes of power as the Saudi princes fought for authority and in the process lost much of it. By the mid-1880s Saudi authority was largely limited to the town of Riyadh, as numerous tribes and oases broke away from them and surrendered (voluntarily or forcibly) to the Rashidis, whose prestige and power continued to rise. In 1887 Abdallah ibn Faisal, one of the Saudi pretenders who briefly held authority in Riyadh, was ousted from the Saudi capital by his nephews.

Abdullah appealed for help to Muhammad al-Rashid, who eagerly seized this opportunity to interfere in Saudi affairs on the pretext of "saving" the legitimate ruler. Leading a strong military force, he recaptured Riyadh and appointed his loyal commander Salim Al Subhan as its emir, while Abdallah ibn Faisal was kept in virtual captivity in Hail. Salim Al Subhan quickly moved against the remaining Saudi claimants, whom he routed in August 1888. The following year, the once proud Saudi emir Abdallah died as an Al Rashidi vassal, with his former kingdom largely gone. Although he was succeeded by Abdul Rahman bin Faisal, real authority in Riyadh was in the hands of Salim Al Subhan. In 1890, Abdul Rahman bin Faisal organized a revolt against the al-Rashidis and repelled their subsequent attack on Riyadh. By the end of the year, he organized a broad coalition of anti-Rashidi tribes and attacked Muhammad al-Rashid's forces. What ensued was probably one of the largest campaigns fought in Arabia in the 19th century, with several thousand men on each side. The two armies fought a series of battles near Mulaida in the Qasim region throughout December 1890 before Muhammad al-Rashid routed his opponents in January 1891; Abdul Rahman bin Faisal then fled to Kuwait for safety.

Muhammad al-Rashid was now the undisputed ruler of central Arabia. His supremacy lasted for six years as he tried to revive the exhausted and devastated country. His death in 1897 marked the start of a new wave of tribal conflict. The new al-Rashidi emir, Abd al-Aziz, faced a series of uprisings, and his callous repression only stoked continued resistance among the tribes. Within a decade he had squandered most of the inheritance bestowed to him by Muhammad al-Rashid. Relying increasingly on Ottoman support, Abd al-Aziz was perceived by many Arabs as an instrument of Ottoman oppression, and the House of Saud naturally attracted these discontent tribesmen.

In 1900, the fugitive Saudi emir Abdul Rahman bin Faisal began preparations to reclaim his authority. The British government supported him, as it was interested in weakening the al-Rashids, who were firmly pro-Ottoman. In January 1901 a Saudi-Kuwaiti force invaded Nejd, hoping to capture Riyadh, but was routed by Abd al-Aziz near al-Sarif Oasis in March. At the same time, one detachment of the Kuwaiti-Saudi force, commanded by young Abd al-Aziz Al Saud, who became known to Europeans under his kin name Ibn Saud, managed to capture Riyadh but was forced to abandon it after learning about the defeat of the main force.

Al-Rashidi forces, supported by the Ottomans, then invaded Kuwait but were unable to captured an important fort at al-Jahra, while the British sent a warship to help the Kuwaitis exert pressure on the Ottomans. Abd al-Aziz al-Rashid's withdrawal allowed the Saudis to regroup, and this time Ibn Saud convinced his father to entrust military command to him. During November–December 1901 accompanied by only 40 men, Ibn Saud moved into eastern Arabia and recruited tribesmen hostile to the al-Rashidis. During January 12–15, 1902, this small group of men infiltrated Riyadh, where they assassinated the al-Rashidi governor and massacred the entire garrison, losing only two men killed and three wounded. This daring attack captured the imagination of many tribesmen and greatly enhanced the young Saudi's reputation. In May 1902 with his father declining the honor, the ulema and notables of Riyadh declared Ibn Saud emir.

While Abd al-Aziz was mobilizing his forces to recapture Riyadh, Ibn Saud mounted attacks throughout Nejd, seeking to rally tribesmen dissatisfied with al-Rashidi rule. The Saudi-Rashidi rivalry meanwhile attracted attention from the Great Powers as well. Germany and the Ottoman Empire threw their support behind the al-Rashidis, while Britain supported the Saudis.

In 1902 Abd al-Aziz set out with his army for Riyadh but was unable to capture it, as it was heavily fortified. Ibn Saud turned to hit-and-run tactics against his stronger opponent, and skirmishes continued from September to November, when an epidemic forced Abd al-Aziz to withdraw. Regrouping, the Rashidi leader launched an attack on Kuwait, Ibn Saud's principal ally, in January 1903 but was repelled by joint Saudi-Kuwaiti forces a month later. Abd al-Aziz's renewed attack on Riyadh failed in the spring of 1903 as well, and this allowed Ibn Saud to create a nucleus of the emirate of Riyadh that his ancestors once ruled.

In the summer of 1903, the Saudis prevailed in the struggle over Sudair Province, then defeated the al-Rashidi force near Anaiza in March 1904 and captured Buraida in Qasim Province in June. These successes, however, alarmed the Porte, which sent 2,000 men and six artillery pieces to reinforce Abd al-Aziz. Despite his enemy's superior strength, Ibn Saud engaged the Ottoman al-Rashidi forces at al-Bukairiya in mid-July 1904 and defeated them. His men inflicted heavy losses on the Ottoman al-Rashidi force, capturing all its cannon and killing the Ottoman commander. Abd al-Aziz fled to Shunana, hoping to secure additional Ottoman assistance, but was attacked and routed by Ibn Saud in late September.

Infuriated by such defeats, Ottoman authorities in Istanbul sent 3,000 more troops to Nejd. Ibn Saud refrained from hostilities against the Ottomans but targeted the Rashidis, whom he defeated again in Qasim on April 13, 1906. Abd al-Aziz died in the fighting. His head was briefly put on display before being thrown to the dogs.

In the summer of 1906, Ibn Saud reached the Rashidi capital of Hail. Although unsuccessful in efforts to capture it, he defeated the new Rashidi emir Mitab ibn Abd al-Aziz. These successes empowered the Saudi leader, who successfully pressured the Ottomans, whose numbers had declined from some 4,500 to fewer than 1,000, the result of desertions, disease, and skirmishes, to abandon Arabia in October–November 1806.

Rashidi emir Mitab was assassinated by his own nephews in late December 1906, and the new Rashidi leadership proved to be unpopular and incompetent. The Rashidi emirate steadily declined between 1907 and 1910 and was unable to take advantage of the Saudi preoccupation with rebellious tribes. In late 1907, Ibn Saud routed a joint force of the

Rashidis and other tribes near Tarafiya and reasserted his authority in the Qasim region.

By then the rising Saudi emirate prompted concerns among various Arab leaders including the sheikh of Kuwait, who had long supported Ibn Saud, and Sharif Husain of Mecca, who was alarmed by the rise of a new emirate on his eastern borders. Thus, between 1907 and 1915 Ibn Saud was preoccupied with local revolts and campaigns to various regions, which prevented him from fully concentrating on the Rashidis. During World War I the British insisted that Ibn Saud neutralize the Rashidis, the pro-Ottomans in Arabia. In early 1915, Ibn Saud led some 3,000 men toward Hail but encountered the Rashidi forces near the Jarrab well (north of al-Zilfi), where an inconclusive battle was fought in late January.

Unable to confront the Saudis alone, the Rashidis sought alliance with other groups, including the Kuwaitis, but also suffered from internal divisions. In March 1920 Emir Saud was assassinated by his cousin Abdallah ibn Talal, who was in turn shot dead the same year, relinquishing the title to Abdallah ibn Mitab. A low-intensity conflict between the Rashidis and Saudis continued until late 1920, when a joint Rashidi-Kuwaiti force attempted to invade Saudi territory but was routed near al-Jahra in October 1920. In 1921, Ibn Saud concluded a peace treaty with Kuwait and then turned to deal with the isolated Rashidis.

In April–May, Ibn Saud defeated the Rashidi forces and besieged Hail, which surrendered in August following a two-month siege. Abdallah ibn Mitab was taken as a prisoner to Riyadh, where he died in 1952. On November 1, 1921, the Rashidi emirate of Jabal Shammar was incorporated into the nascent Saudi state, which controlled the whole of central Arabia.

ALEXANDER MIKABERIDZE

**See also**
Ibn Saud, King; Saudi-Hashemite War; Saudi-Kuwaiti War; Saudi-Ottoman War

**References**
Al-Enazy, Askar. *The Creation of Saudi Arabia: Ibn Saud and British Imperial Policy, 1914–1927*. New York: Routledge, 2010.
Armstrong, H. C. *Lord of Arabia*. London: Arthur Barker, 1934.
Bowen, Wayne. *The History of Saudi Arabia*. Westport, CT: Greenwood, 2008.
McLoughlin, Leslie J. *Ibn Saud: Founder of a Kingdom*. New York: St. Martin's, 1993.
Troeller, Gary. *The Birth of Saudi Arabia: Britain and the Rise of the House of Sa'ud*. London: F. Cass, 1976.
Vassiliev, Alexei. *The History of Saudi Arabia*. London: Saqi Books, 1998.

# Saudi-Yemeni War (1934)

A brief conflict between Saudi Arabia and Yemen caused by disputed boundaries. In 1918 following their defeat in World War I, Ottoman forces were withdrawn from the southern regions of Arabia where the Mutawakkilite Kingdom of Yemen had emerged. Fourteen years later, Ibn Saud proclaimed the merger of the Nejd and Hejaz kingdoms into the Kingdom of Saudi Arabia, but its southern borders with Yemen remained undemarcated and disputed.

Yemeni king Yahya Muhammad Hamid ed-Din actively interfered in Saudi affairs and supported opponents of Ibn Saud. In February 1934 Saudi-Yemeni negotiations took place in Abna but failed to resolve differences. Ibn Saud demanded recognition of the Saudi rights in Najran, Yemeni evacuation of the border area mountains, and the expulsion of his opponents sheltered in Yemen. The Yemeni delegation rejected these demands.

Ibn Saud waited for the end of the pilgrimage before issuing an order on March 20 for his forces to attack Yemen. The war proved to be short but sharp. One Saudi army, under Crown Prince Saud, stalled against the Yemeni forces of Crown Prince Ahmad in the highlands. However, Saudi prince Faisal, leading well-trained Saudi troops equipped with modern British weaponry, including tanks, routed the Yemeni forces in the lowlands, driving them out of Najran, penetrating far down Yemen's Red Sea coast, and capturing the major port town of Hodeida.

Such successes, however, aroused concerns among the European powers and threatened to undermine the regional balance of power. The leaders of Britain, Italy, and France, concerned over their colonial possessions in Africa, sent warships to Hodeida. On May 12 following just seven weeks of fighting, Ibn Saud announced a cease-fire and willingness to negotiate.

The war officially came to an end on May 20, 1934, with the signing of the Treaty of Taif between Ibn Saud and Yemeni king Yahya. The treaty defined the Yemeni-Saudi border from the Red Sea to a southern tip of Najran, provided for an indemnity of 100,000 pounds in gold to be paid to Saudi Arabia, and asserted Saudi sovereignty over the provinces of Asir and Najran. Initially the provinces were placed under temporary Saudi rule, but in 1994 Saudi Arabia claimed permanent ownership of the territories. After a round of border clashes the two states agreed to demarcate the border, but as of 2016 this had not been accomplished.

ALEXANDER MIKABERIDZE

**See also**
Ibn Saud, King; Saudi-Hashemite War; Saudi-Kuwaiti War; Saudi-Ottoman War; Saudi-Rashidi Wars

**References**
Gause, Gregory F. *Saudi-Yemeni Relations: Domestic Structures and Foreign Influence.* New York: Columbia University Press, 1990.
Leatherdale, Clive. *Britain and Saudi Arabia, 1925–1939: The Imperial Oasis.* New York: Routledge, 1983.

## SCATHE MEAN, Operation (January 17, 1991)

Part of air operations at the beginning of Operation DESERT STORM in 1991 intended to force the Iraqis to turn on their radars and track large numbers of decoys that would confuse and overwhelm their tracking systems. Operation SCATHE MEAN was to follow initial air strikes by conventionally armed cruise missiles and Lockheed F-117 stealth fighters targeting the major Iraqi air defense control centers. Coalition planners hoped that the Iraqis would also fire some of their surface-to-air (SAM) missiles at the decoys. In any event, coalition aircraft armed with high-speed antiradiation missiles (HARM) would attack the radars, helping to blind Iraqi air defenses. The operation was a great success, leaving the Iraqis unable to seriously challenge coalition strike aircraft.

In 1981, Israel had launched a surprise attack on Iraq's Osiraq nuclear reactor. The raid was a complete success and prompted Iraqi president Saddam Hussein to order the construction of a new air defense system. Companies from several countries provided parts for the new system. French engineers working on the system dubbed it "Kari" ("Iraq" in French spelled backwards). Although Kari employed radars from different countries, including China and Italy, its heart was a centralized command structure of mainframe computers collecting data from different sources in order to provide a clear picture of the situation to controllers in Baghdad. The central authorities could then decide how best to deal with an incoming threat.

Kari was based on the Soviet Union's air defense system. By integrating radars, surface-to-air missiles (SAMs), and antiaircraft artillery, Kari was expected to make air strikes by coalition aircraft very costly. The weakness turned out to be its highly centralized control. Under Kari, intercept operations centers fed information to sector operations centers, which in turn sent information to Air Defense Headquarters in Baghdad. The coalition air plan concentrated the first strikes against the command facilities in Baghdad, including the communications and power nodes. Essentially, the plan was to break the Iraqi air defense system into component parts and then destroy each. Because Baghdad was so heavily defended, stealth fighters and cruise missiles were assigned to the initial attacks.

Although U.S. war planners believed that they could disable the Iraqi central command structure, they recognized that the Iraqi air defenses remained dangerous. The navy's Strike Projection Evaluation and Anti-Air Research (SPEAR) study group had been studying how to overcome antiaircraft defenses since 1983, when the navy lost two aircraft against relatively weak Syrian air defenses. SPEAR shared its knowledge of Iraqi air defenses with the group in Saudi Arabia preparing the air campaign. The air force had a similar study group known as Checkmate. One of the plans to come out of Checkmate was to use decoys to fool the Iraqi defenses. The idea was based on the success enjoyed by the Israelis against Syrian air defenses in 1982.

One of the problems that planners faced was obtaining a sufficient number of decoys to fool the Iraqi defenses. The U.S. Navy had purchased more than 1,000 Tactical Air Launched Decoys (TALDs) that were based on decoys used by the Israelis in 1982. They weighed between 400 and 450 pounds each, and up to six could be carried on a single wing pylon of a naval aircraft. The TALDs were unpowered gliders, but they had a glide ratio of 10 to 1, so they could fly more than 60 miles upon being released. With an ability to reach speeds up to 460 miles per hour and the capability to return radar signatures similar to any military aircraft, the TALDs would fool the Iraqis into thinking a major air attack was under way.

The U.S. Air Force role in Operation SCATHE MEAN was somewhat different because it had no decoys or drones suitable for the operation. Instead, it secured 44 BQM-74 Chukar drones from the navy. The navy typically used the Chukars as targets. They were powered by a turbojet engine that gave the drone a top speed of nearly 600 miles per hour. The gyroscopes used to control the Chukars' flight path were not as accurate as hoped, but the planners believed they would work. Brigadier General Larry Henry, known as "Poobah," headed the air force operation, which became known as "Poobah's Party."

To launch the Chukars, the air force had to assemble the equipment and a team. Because the drones were not standard air force equipment, expertise regarding them was in short supply. Ordinarily, the Chukars would be launched from a Lockheed DC-130 Hercules director aircraft, but none was available for duty in the Persian Gulf. Instead, Henry made the decision to use ground launchers. A dozen launchers were found in the navy's stockpiles and made available. Rocket-assisted takeoff packs were found in Belgium and flown to Saudi Arabia. Trucks were purchased from a California commercial trucking firm, and tool kits were bought at Sears. Field gear for the personnel was purchased at military surplus stores.

The only air force personnel with experience in ground-launched missiles were those who had been trained to launch nuclear-tipped cruise missiles. Those weapons had been eliminated in the 1987 Intermediate-Range Nuclear Forces Treaty, but a training unit was still operational in Arizona. Personnel from the unit were then formed into the 4468th Tactical Reconnaissance Group and sent to Saudi Arabia. They arrived in two six-launcher teams near the Iraqi border on October 15, 1990. One team was based near King Khalid Military City near Kuwait, while the other was near Ar'ar, a town in western Saudi Arabia that was a base for U.S. special forces.

On January 17, 1991, the air campaign began. After F-117s and cruise missiles had hit targets in and around Baghdad, Operation SCATHE MEAN began. Twenty-five TLADs were launched by Navy Grumman A-6 Intruders, apparently heading toward Iraqi targets. At 3:48 a.m. (local time), the Chukars were launched from Saudi Arabia. Although 38 decoys were supposed to be launched in groups of 3, only 37 were actually sent on their way. The Iraqi defenders, deprived of central control and determined to prevent more strikes on the capital, lit up their radars and began tracking the decoys. As they identified targets, they began launching their Soviet-made SAMs. To the Iraqis, they seemed to be scoring many successes. As the TLADs reached the end of their range, they descended off the radar scopes, like so many aircraft being shot down. As the Chukars approached from Saudi Arabia, the Iraqis launched interceptor aircraft. One group of three was intercepted, while the others made it to their targets in and around Baghdad.

As the Iraqis turned on radars to track the decoys, U.S. Marine Corps and U.S. Navy McDonnell Douglas F/A-18 Hornets and U.S. Air Force McDonnell Douglas F-4G Phantom II/Weasel aircraft launched more than 200 HARM missiles. Many Iraqi radars were destroyed, creating huge holes in their defenses for later air strikes. The loss of radars and the wasting of many SAMs on decoys were severe blows from which the Iraqi air defenses never recovered. Although coalition aircraft continued to be lost until the end of the war, the numbers were quite low. Indeed, most fell to unguided antiaircraft artillery or individually launched missiles.

The 4468th Group was disbanded after the war, and a single BQM-74C was donated to the U.S. Air Force Museum at Wright-Patterson Air Force Base (Ohio) to commemorate the success of Operation SCATHE MEAN.

TIM J. WATTS

**See also**
Persian Gulf War, Air Campaign; Persian Gulf War, Overview

**References**
Gordon, Michael R., and General Bernard E. Trainor. *The Generals' War: The Inside Story of the Conflict in the Gulf.* New York: Little, Brown, 1995.
Murray, Williamson. *Air War in the Persian Gulf.* Baltimore: Nautical & Aviation Publishing, 1995.
Olsen, John Andreas. *Strategic Air Power in Desert Storm.* Portland, OR: Frank Cass, 2003.

# Schwarzkopf, H. Norman, Jr. (1934–2012)

U.S. Army officer and commander of coalition forces during Operations DESERT SHIELD and DESERT STORM (the Persian Gulf War). H. Norman Schwarzkopf Jr. (Known as "Stormin' Norman") was born on August 22, 1934, in Trenton, New Jersey. His father, Herbert Norman Schwarzkopf, disliked his own first name and gave his son only its first letter. The elder Schwarzkopf had graduated from the U.S. Military Academy, West Point, and, following his military career, headed the New Jersey State Police. In the late 1940s Schwarzkopf Jr. accompanied his father to Iran, where the elder Schwarzkopf helped establish and train that country's national police. This experience gave the young Schwarzkopf a lasting interest in Islamic culture and history.

Schwarzkopf followed his father in attending West Point, graduating in 1956. He received advanced infantry and airborne training at Fort Benning, Georgia, and later served with the 101st Airborne Division in Kentucky and the 6th Infantry Division in Germany. He was in Berlin during the crises there in 1960 and 1961. In 1964, Schwarzkopf earned a master's degree in mechanical engineering from the University of Southern California, specializing in the development of precision-guided missiles, and in 1965 he began a three-year teaching assignment at West Point.

The war in Vietnam cut short his teaching. Captain Schwarzkopf served a tour as an adviser to the Republic

As commander of the U.S. Central Command during 1988–1991, Army general H. Norman Schwarzkopf directed the highly successful international military coalition that drove Iraqi forces from Kuwait in the Persian Gulf War in 1991. (U.S. Department of Defense)

of Vietnam Airborne Division before returning to the academy. Promoted to lieutenant colonel in 1968, Schwarzkopf attended the U.S. Army Command and General Staff College, and in 1969 he returned to Vietnam as a battalion commander, where he earned a Silver Star and was twice wounded. There he also acquired his reputation as a tough, no-nonsense commander willing to risk his own life for his men. In 1970, now a colonel, Schwarzkopf returned to the United States in a body cast. On his recovery, he studied at the Army War College. He then served in Alaska, Washington state, Hawaii, Germany, and Washington, D.C.

Schwarzkopf was promoted to brigadier general in 1978 and assigned as assistant division commander of the 8th Infantry Division (Mechanized) in the Federal Republic of Germany. Promoted to major general in 1982, Schwarzkopf assumed command of the 24th Infantry Division (Mechanized) at Fort Stewart, Georgia. A year later, he was an adviser to the navy in Operation URGENT FURY, the U.S. invasion of Grenada. Earning the confidence of the naval commanders, he was appointed deputy commander of the joint task force. He learned valuable lessons from the experience, especially the need for more effective coordination and control in joint operations.

In 1984, Schwarzkopf returned to the Pentagon in the Office of Deputy Chief of Staff for Operations. In 1986, he was promoted to lieutenant general and took command of the I Corps at Ft. Lewis, Washington. After only one year in that assignment, he returned to the Pentagon as the army's deputy chief of staff for operations.

Promoted to full general in 1988, Schwarzkopf was assigned as commander of the U.S. Central Command (CENTCOM), headquartered at Tampa, Florida. CENTCOM was tasked primarily with potential U.S. operations in the Middle East and Southwest Asia. Although at the time Schwarzkopf assumed CENTCOM command the possibility of U.S. military action in those regions seemed remote to American military planners, this situation changed dramatically in August 1990.

Following the Iraqi invasion of Kuwait on August 2, 1990, Schwarzkopf established a forward headquarters in Riyadh, Saudi Arabia, and played a key role in building the international coalition that carried out the United Nations mandate to restore the independence of Kuwait. Schwarzkopf doubted the ability of airpower alone to cause Iraqi leader Saddam Hussein to withdraw his forces from Kuwait and insisted on a large buildup of ground forces to do the job. Operations DESERT SHIELD and DESERT STORM proved highly successful, with coalition forces winning the ground war within only 100 hours in February 1991. Despite the overwhelming success of DESERT STORM, during the war Schwarzkopf's relations with his subordinates and his superiors in Washington, D.C., were often rocky. Many subordinates resented his bullying, confrontational manner of command, and his interaction with the Joint Staff and the army staff was often difficult. Although he was immensely popular with the American public, those who worked with him did not share this perception.

Reportedly, Schwarzkopf opposed the George H. W. Bush administration's decision to end the war without the destruction of the Iraqi Republican Guard. Yet Schwarzkopf himself made the decision in the cease-fire agreement that allowed the Iraqis to continue to fly helicopters, which very much surprised the Iraqi delegates. This decision greatly aided the Iraqi government in crushing insurrections against the Hussein regime.

Schwarzkopf returned to the United States a national hero, aided considerably by his ability to deal quite effectively with the press. He retired from the army in August 1991 and published his best-selling memoir, *It Doesn't Take a Hero*, in 1992. He then was a member of several corporate boards. Schwarzkopf was sharply critical of Secretary of Defense Donald Rumsfeld's management of the Iraq War but supported President George W. Bush's reelection bid in 2004 and Republican senator John McCain's presidential bid in 2008. Following a long illness, Schwarzkopf died at his home in Tampa, Florida, on December 27, 2012.

DEBORAH KIDWELL, PAUL G. PIERPAOLI JR.,
AND SPENCER C. TUCKER

**See also**
Persian Gulf War, Overview

**References**
Cohen, Roger, and Claudio Gatti. *In the Eye of the Storm: The Life of General H. Norman Schwarzkopf.* New York: Farrar Straus and Giroux, 1992.
Morris, M. E. *H. Norman Schwarzkopf: Road to Triumph.* New York: St. Martin's, 1993.
Schubert, Frank N., and Theresa L. Kraus, eds. *The Whirlwind War: The United States Army in Operations Desert Shield and Desert Storm.* Washington, DC: United States Army Center of Military History, 1995.

Schwarzkopf, H. Norman. *It Doesn't Take a Hero: The Autobiography: H. Norman Schwarzkopf.* New York: Diane Publishing, 1992.
Woodward, Bob. *The Commanders.* New York: Simon and Schuster, 1991.

## SCORPION, Operation

A plan for ground operations during the 1991 Persian Gulf War to occupy western Iraq. Operation SCORPION was never implemented, but its supporters believed that the operation, also known as the Western Excursion, would prevent Iraqi Scud missiles from being fired at Israel, which would have threatened a breakup of the military coalition against Iraq. They also believed that the operation offered an opportunity to destabilize the regime of President Saddam Hussein and force a change in the Iraqi government. The cost to American personnel would be minimal, it was hoped, while Iraqi ground forces that moved to oust the Americans could be arrested by American airpower. U.S. Secretary of Defense Richard (Dick) Cheney was the plan's chief supporter.

When Saddam ordered his forces to occupy Kuwait in August 1990, the first American objective was to prevent the Iraqis from moving on and occupying the Saudi Arabian oil fields. When sufficient forces had been assembled to prevent this, under the code name DESERT SHIELD, planners then began to address how to force the Iraqis from Kuwait. The United Nations had authorized tough economic sanctions against Iraq, and many members of the George H. W. Bush administration hoped that these would force Hussein to withdraw. Even so, military commanders began to plan how to use force if necessary to accomplish American goals.

By October 1990, the U.S. Army's XVIII Airborne Corps was fully in place in Saudi Arabia. Even with supporting units, including marines on amphibious assault ships in the Persian Gulf, this force was outnumbered by Iraqi forces defending Kuwait. Coalition theater commander U.S. Army general H. Norman Schwarzkopf had organized a planning group to develop options to drive the Iraqis out of Kuwait with the forces at hand. All plans proceeded from the assumption that the coalition organized to liberate Kuwait could rapidly secure air supremacy.

On October 10 and 11, military planners from Schwarzkopf's command presented their preliminary plans to President Bush and his national security team. The original plan consisted mainly of a direct attack on Iraqi defenses in Kuwait. Planners estimated that American forces could suffer up to 10,000 casualties, with 1,500 killed in action. Because one important domestic political consideration was to limit American casualties, the plan was deemed unacceptable. One concrete result of the October conferences was to confirm that Bush expected that a military solution would be required. He then approved the transfer of additional forces to Saudi Arabia. American ground, naval, and air forces in the theater would double by the beginning of 1991.

Rejection of the original military plan led chairman of the Joint Chiefs of Staff General Colin L. Powell to organize a planning staff at the Pentagon to develop alternatives. Because a direct attack into Kuwait had been implicitly rejected, the planners looked to a left-hook scenario that would have coalition forces move farther west to envelop the Iraqis in Kuwait.

By the late fall of 1990, a certain amount of friction had developed between Powell and Cheney. Cheney favored a more immediate military solution than Powell. Cheney had his own staff develop a plan to force the Iraqis from Kuwait as well as to meet other political objectives. The genesis of what became Operation SCORPION came from former Stanford University professor Henry Rowen, who was assistant defense secretary for international security affairs, responsible for Southwest Asia and the Middle East. Rowen was looking forward to returning to Stanford, and even after the invasion of Kuwait, he found time to take a vacation to France in September. While there, he read *The History of the Arab Peoples* by Sir John Bagot Glubb, who had commanded the British Arab Legion during the 1930s and 1940s. Glubb recorded how he had led the legion from Transjordan across western Iraq in 1941, when Iraq revolted against British control. Rowen realized that Arab armies had maneuvered across the desert for centuries. Surely the U.S. Army, with its far greater logistic capabilities, could do the same. Rowen found that a two-lane asphalt highway, known as the Tapline Road, ran from western Iraq into Saudi Arabia and paralleled the border with Iraq. He believed that it could be utilized for supply purposes.

When Rowen returned to the United States, he shared his idea with Paul Wolfowitz, a key Cheney aide. Wolfowitz saw potential in the plan and took it to Cheney. Cheney had Wolfowitz set up a secret planning team in the Pentagon to flesh out the possibilities. Wolfowitz picked retired U.S. Army lieutenant general Dale Vesser, who had been planning officer for the Joint Chiefs of Staff, to head the team. Cheney recognized that a plan developed by a retired general officer was more likely to be accepted by military commanders than one seen as coming strictly from civilians. Vesser and his team were instructed not to discuss their work with anyone else, including Powell.

Vesser was initially skeptical but came to embrace the plan. Basically, it called for American airborne forces, including the 82nd and 101st Airborne Divisions, to be moved by air into western Iraq. Presumably they would be able to occupy most of the region with little difficulty because only one low-grade Iraqi division was based there. The region was also sparsely populated, which would lower civilian casualties. The airborne units were to be supported by mechanized forces that would move up the Tapline Road with supplies and armor support.

Cheney and his team saw this plan as making the best use of American advantages in airpower and mobility. They expected that the first result would be the destruction or capture of the Iraqi Scud missiles located in western Iraq. Air force planners believed that coalition aircraft could knock out the Scuds before they could be launched.

Another benefit from Operation SCORPION was that it would sever road communications between Baghdad and Jordan, cutting supplies flowing to Iraq through Jordan, a significant hole in the blockade authorized by United Nations sanctions.

Cheney also expected that Iraqi Republican Guards, the most effective Iraqi troops, would be called upon to drive the Americans out of western Iraq. As they moved along the roads, coalition aircraft would be able to attack and significantly degrade them. The weakened divisions could then be defeated by American ground forces with fewer American casualties.

Finally, some planners believed that having U.S. forces within 60 miles of Baghdad would bring the overthrow of Hussein. Baghdad itself could be cut off from outside aid, and dissidents would be encouraged to rise up and revolt. While Cheney discounted this possibility, it remained attractive to some planners.

Cheney then had Powell and the Joint Chiefs of Staff briefed on Operation SCORPION. The joint chiefs quickly dismissed it as failing to meet American objectives and for logistical shortcomings. Nonetheless, when Powell was in Saudi Arabia in late October, Cheney took the plan to President Bush and briefed him on it. It was unprecedented for the civilian secretary of defense to go around his military commanders to present a plan directly to the president. Powell was furious, as were most other military leaders. They viewed it as a signal that Cheney had lost faith in their abilities. It also highlighted the tension that often exists between civilian and military leaders in wartime.

Although Operation SCORPION was not accepted, it did help convince Pentagon planners to move the main ground effort farther west. The final plan for DESERT STORM had the main U.S. effort west of the Wadi al-Batin, much farther west than had been originally planned.

TIM J. WATTS

**See also**
Schwarzkopf, H. Norman, Jr.

**References**
Gordon, Michael R., and General Bernard E. Trainor. *The Generals' War: The Inside Story of the Conflict in the Gulf.* New York: Little, Brown, 1995.
Rowen, Henry S. "Inchon in the Desert: My Rejected Plan." *National Interest* 40 (Summer 1995): 34–39.

## Seleucid Empire (312–63 BCE)

The Seleucid Empire was ruled by the dynasty of the same name and centered on Syria during 312–63 BCE. The empire was named after its founder, Seleucus I Nicator (r. 312–281), a general under Alexander III the Great. From their base in Syria, the Seleucids ruled an empire consisting of the eastern and largest part of Alexander's conquests. At its largest extent, the Seleucid Empire stretched from the northern Levant and parts of Asia Minor in the West to the Indus River Valley in the East.

In the settlement following Alexander's death, Seleucus was made commander of the Companion cavalry under the regent Perdiccas. After the death of Perdiccas, Seleucus was given charge of the satrapy of Babylon, but he was soon driven out by Antigonus. Seleucus sought refuge at the court of King Ptolemy I Sotar in Egypt and in 312 was restored by Ptolemy to his satrapy. Thereafter, Seleucus expanded his kingdom to include nearly all of the former eastern empire of Alexander.

Seleucus was succeeded by his half-Bactrian son Antiochus I Soter (r. 281–261 but coregent from 292). Antiochus defeated an invasion of Celts into Anatolia in 275. He also fought in the First Syrian-Egyptian War against the Ptolemies over Coele-Syria. Seleucus's son Antiochus II Theos (r. 261–246) succeeded his father. During his reign, the Parthian and Bactrian satrapies broke away from Seleucid control. The Second Syrian-Egyptian War was fought to a stalemate. Peace was made in 253, and Antiochus married Ptolemy II's daughter Berenice, divorcing his first wife Laodice I. But in 246, the king left Berenice and reunited with Laodice, who then allegedly poisoned him.

Laodice then had Berenice and her infant son Antiochus killed and proclaimed her son Seleucus II Callinicus king. To avenge the murder of his sister and nephew, Ptolemy III launched the Third Syrian-Egyptian War, attacking the coast of Asia Minor and marching deep into the Seleucid realm, perhaps as far as Babylon. Civil war (the so-called War of the Brothers) then occurred between Seleucus II and his brother Antiochus Hierax. It was waged intermittently during the next 20 years. During it, Seleucus II partially recovered his eastern empire but lost Asia Minor to Hierax and then to Attalus I, king of the breakaway kingdom of Pergamum.

Seleucus's son Seleucus III Ceraunus succeeded to the throne in 225 but was assassinated in 223, allowing his brother, Antiochus III the Great (r. 223–187), to take the throne. After reconquering his eastern empire and Asia Minor but losing the Fourth and Fifth Syrian Wars to Ptolemy IV and Ptolemy V, Seleucus III lost the Syrian-Roman War, and the Romans forced him to withdraw from Asia Minor beyond the Taurus Mountains and the Halys River.

Antiochus III was succeeded by his son Seleucus IV Philopator (r. 187–175), who plundered the Temple in Jerusalem and was later assassinated by his minister Heliodorus. Seleucus's younger brother Antiochus ejected Heliodorus and became king. He ruled as Antiochus IV Epiphanes during 175–164 and defeated Ptolemy VI and the Egyptians in the Sixth Syrian War. Antiochus IV was on the verge of taking Egypt when the Romans ordered him to stand down in 168. He also sacked Jerusalem and persecuted the Jews, sparking the revolt of the Maccabees in 167.

Epiphanes's son Antiochus V Eupator (r. 163–161) succeeded to the throne at age 9 even though his cousin, 22-year-old Demetrius I Soter, son of Seleucus IV, was capable of ruling. But Demetrius was in detention in Rome, where he had been living as a hostage since his father's reign. The Romans, being informed that Eupator was in breach of the Seleucid treaty with Rome, sent envoys to Syria to oversee the hamstringing of the king's elephants and the destruction of his ships.

Demetrius escaped from Rome in 162. Returning to Syria, he deposed his cousin. Demetrius recovered Babylonia and Cappadocia and continued to persecute the Jews. He was deposed by a pretender, Alexander Balas, in 150. Balas (r. 150–145) was in turn deposed by Demetrius's son Demetrius II Nicator.

The later Seleucid monarchs exhausted themselves in dynastic quarrels and lost their grip on all but the Syrian heartland of their empire. Tigranes II the Great of Armenia took over the Seleucid Empire in 83 but was forced to surrender to the Roman general Gnaeus Pompeius Magnus, Pompey the Great, in 66. Tigranes's Seleucid holdings were annexed into the new Roman province of Syria in 64–63 BCE.

PAUL J. BURTON

**See also**

Alexander III the Great; Antiochus I Soter; Antiochus III Megas; Antiochus IV Epiphanes; Antiochus VII Sidetes; Antiochus Hierax; Demetrius II Nicator; Diadochi, Wars of the; Pompeius Magnus, Gnaeus; Ptolemy I Soter; Ptolemy II Philadelphus; Ptolemy III Euergetes; Ptolemy IV Philopator; Ptolemy V Epiphanes; Ptolemy VI Philometor; Seleucus I Nicator; Syria; Syrian-Egyptian Wars; Syrian-Roman War

**References**

Bevan, Edwyn R. *The House of Seleucus.* 2 vols. London: Edward Arnold, 1902.

Grainger, John D. *Seleukos Nikator: Constructing a Hellenistic Kingdom.* New York: Routledge, 1990.

Musti, Domenico. 1984. "Syria and the East." In *The Cambridge Ancient History,* Vol. 7, Part I, *The Hellenistic World,* 2nd ed., ed. Frank W. Walbank, Alan E. Astin, Martin W. Frederiksen, and Robert M. Ogilvie, 175–220. Cambridge: Cambridge University Press, 1984.

## Seleucus I Nicator (ca. 358–281 BCE)

Macedonian officer of Alexander I the Great and one of the Successors (Diadochi). Born in Macedon around 358, Seleucus rose to prominence as an infantry general in the wars of Alexander III the Great. After the death of Alexander, Seleucus was appointed by Perdiccas as commander of the Companion Cavalry. In the wars of the Diadochi that followed Alexander's death, Seleucus at first centered his power on Babylon, from where he would establish the Seleucid Empire and the Seleucid dynasty.

Seleucus accompanied Perdiccas in his bid to oust Ptolemy from Egypt but appears to have turned on Perdiccas and might even have been one of Perdiccas's murderers. At the Triparadisus Conference circa 321–320, Seleucus was given the satrapy of Babylonia. However, in 320 he was driven from Babylon by Antigonus I Monophthalmus. Seleucus then sought sanctuary with Ptolemy and served under him as a naval commander.

Following the Battle of Gaza in 312, which saw Ptolemy and Seleucus defeat Demetrius I Poliorcetes, Seleucus regained Babylon with Ptolemy's support. Seleucus went on to conquer Media and Persia and extended his conquests toward India. In 305 following the example of the other Diadochi, he assumed the title of king and as a result of a settlement with the Mauryan king Chandragupta (Sandrokottos or Androcottus in Greek and Latin texts), Seleucus received 500 war elephants in exchange for ceding provinces in the east. This large force of elephants would prove decisive when Seleucus and his allies Cassander and Lysimachus defeated Antigonus I and Demetrius I at the Battle of Ipsus in 301. Antigonus was killed, and Demetrius, isolated from his father's main force, was forced to flee.

Following the Battle of Ipsus, the victors divided up the Antigonid territorial possessions between them, with Seleucus receiving Syria. However, Ptolemy I Soter, who had taken no part in the war against Antigonus, had occupied the southern part of Syria, Coele Syria. Seleucus, who had been aided by Ptolemy in the past, took no military action against him but moved his capital from Seleucia on the Tigris and established his new capital at the recently founded city of Antioch on the Orontes. At the same time Seleucus founded three other cities in northwestern Syria: Seleucia in Pieria, Apamea, and Laodicea. This strategic move served to halt any further northern expansion by Ptolemy, and these four cities were to be the core of the future Seleucid Empire.

In 292, Seleucus made his son Antiochus satrap of Bactria and his coregent. In 285 Seleucus took Demetrius I Poliorcetes prisoner and imprisoned him in Apamea. In 281 Seleucus intervened in Lysimachus's affairs, the latter having had his son assassinated, and at the Battle of Corupedium Seleucus was victorious, and Lysimachus fell in the fighting. Lysimachus's territory now fell into Seleucus's possession, but Seleucus was murdered by Ptolemy Ceraunus, son of Ptolemy I and a fugitive at Seleucus's court, also in 281. Seleucus was succeeded by his son Antiochus I.

DAVID HARTHEN

**See also**

Alexander III the Great; Antigonus I Monophthalmus; Antiochus I Soter; Corupedium, Battle of; Diadochi, Wars of the; Ipsus, Battle of; Lysimachus; Perdiccas; Ptolemy Ceraunus; Ptolemy I Soter; Syria

**References**

Grainger, John D. 1990. *Seleukos Nikator: Constructing a Hellenistic Kingdom.* New York: Routledge, 1990.

Waterfield, Robin. 2011. *Dividing the Spoils: The War for Alexander the Great's Empire.* New York: Oxford University Press.

## Selim I, Sultan (1470–1520)

Ottoman sultan who during his brief eight-year reign greatly expanded the empire to include the entire Mamluk Sultanate of Egypt. Selim I was also known as Yavuz, meaning "The Stern" or "The Steadfast" but often rendered in English as "The Grim." Selim was born in 1470 in Amasya, in today's north-central Turkey, one of five sons of Sultan Bayezid II (r. 1481–1512). By 1512 two of the five had died, leaving Selim, Ahmed, and Korkut as contenders to succeed their father.

The Ottoman Empire had come under pressure from Ismail of Persia, founder of the Safavid dynasty, who in 1502 had proclaimed himself shah. Ismail rejuvenated Persia, but he also switched the state religion from Sunni to Shia Islam. By 1510 Ismail had established his firm control over all of Persia and was threatening the neighboring Sunni states to the west in an effort to spread Shia Islam. Soon there were armed clashes along the Ottoman border. Bayezid's failure to deal effectively with this threat proved to be his downfall.

Taking advantage of widespread discontent over Batezid's inactivity regarding Persia, Selim promoted a coup by the Janissaries (April 25, 1512) that forced Bayezid to abdicate in favor of him. Selim then caused his brothers Ahmed and Korkut and his nephews to be put to death, while Bayezid died in mysterious circumstances en route to his birthplace. His position at home now secure, Selim renewed treaties with Venice and Hungary that allowed both states trade concessions within the Ottoman Empire, and he also concluded a formal alliance with the Mamluks of Egypt, who were also concerned about Persian expansion.

Having secured his flanks, in 1514 Selim assembled a large army and moved east through Anatolia, slaughtering all those who had converted to Shiite Islam and invading Persia. Ismail withdrew before the Ottoman advance, hoping to lure the Ottomans into the mountains of northern Persia, and practiced a scorched-earth policy that created supply problems for the Ottomans. Selim engaged and defeated the Persians at Chaldiran, near the Persian capital of Tabriz (August 23, 1514), in a battle decided largely by Ottoman gunpowder artillery and small arms. Selim then took Tabriz (September 5) and sacked it. Concerned about the onset of winter, Selim then withdrew. In 1515 Selim reorganized eastern Anatolia, then was victorious in Cilicia in southeastern Anatolia, incorporating it into the Ottoman Empire.

In 1516 as Selim was preparing to again invade Persia, Mamluk sultan al-Gawri, fearful of Selim's intentions, moved his army north into Syria. Selim used this Mamluk threat as s an excuse to attack. He won an overwhelming victory in the Battle of Marj Dabiq (August 24, 1516). Sultan al-Gawri was killed, and his army was destroyed. Selim quickly occupied Syria, then offered terms to new Mamluk sultan Tuman Bey, who rejected them.

Selim's army crossed the Sinai Desert in January 1517 and destroyed a second Mamluk army in a single battle, at Ridaniya (January 24). Tuman Bey escaped but was captured and executed in April. His death brought an end to the Mamluk dynasty and marked the beginning of Egypt's incorporation into the Ottoman Empire. While in Cairo, Selim received the sharif of Mecca, who surrendered Islam's holy cities of Mecca and Medina. Bedouin tribes from Arabia also pledged their allegiance.

Following his conquest of the Mamluk Empire, Selim returned to Istanbul and reorganized the army and administration of the empire. He extended the *devshirme* system of bringing into the army Christian boys, thereby enlarging the Janissary Corps that was the backbone of the Ottoman Army. He also completed the move of the Ottoman government from Edirne (Adrianople) to Istanbul. Selim ordered construction of a new palace and ordered construction of a new shipyard to enable enlargement of the Ottoman Navy. At the same time, he expanded existing shipyards and brought to Istanbul the leader of the Mamluk Red Sea fleet, along with his commanders and artisans. By the end of his reign, the Ottoman Navy was acknowledged as the most powerful in the Mediterranean.

In 1519 Shiite Muslims in Anatolia revolted, led by Celal, who claimed that he was the Mahdi (Islamic messiah). Selim completely destroyed the rebels. In July 1520 Selim departed Istanbul for Edirne, probably to plan a campaign against Hungary, but died at Çorlu on September 22, 1520, possibly of anthrax.

An exceptionally able military commander who greatly enlarged the territory of the Ottoman Empire, making it the dominant power of the Islamic world, Selim paved the way for his son and successor, Suleiman I the Magnificent.

RICHARD SAUERS AND SPENCER C. TUCKER

See also

Bayezid II; Chaldiran, Battle of; *Devshirme* System; Ismail I, Shah; Janissaries; Marj Dabiq, Battle of; Ottoman Empire; Ottoman-Safavid Wars; Suleiman I

References

Barber, Noel. *The Sultans.* New York: Simon and Schuster, 1973.
Kinross, Patrick Balfour. *The Ottoman Centuries: The Rise and Fall of the Turkish Empire.* New York: Morrow, 1977.
Shaw, Stanford J. *History of the Ottoman Empire and Modern Turkey.* 2 vols. New York: Cambridge University Press, 1976.

## Selim III, Sultan (1761–1808)

Ottoman sultan. The first son of Sultan Mustafa III (r. 1757–1774), Selim was born in Istanbul on December 14, 1761. Thanks to the liberal and companionate approaches of his father and his uncle, Sultan Abdulhamid I (r. 1774–1789), Selim enjoyed unusual freedom and an excellent education. An accomplished composer of classical Ottoman music, he was also a talented poet. In addition, he showed great interest in European military reforms.

Selim III ascended the throne during the Ottoman-Habsburg-Russian War of 1787–1791. He was unable to change the course of the war, but he used its disastrous outcome for the Ottoman Empire to convince many traditional and conservative Ottoman officials of the necessity for reform.

Selim officially began his military reforms with the publication in 1792 of new regulations for the Kapikulu Corps (imperial regular army) and Timarli Sipahi (provincial cavalry corps). This effort largely ended in failure. But the radical part of his reforms were launched secretly and involved creation of a modern European-style infantry corps as the core of a totally modern military establishment. The new infantry corps was known as the Nizam-i Cedid (literally new regiment or order). This became the name of Selim's entire reform package and era.

The first regiment was established at Levend in 1795 and the second at Üsküdar in 1799. Selim also ordered the establishment of additional units, albeit under the control of the *ayans* (provincial magnates). At least nine provinces in Anatolia carried this out, and for the first time recruitment of villagers began. The size of the corps rose from 9,300 in 1801 to 24,000 in 1806. In 1795, the Mühendishane-i Berri Hümayun (the Imperial Military Engineering School) was established. It was not only the first modern Ottoman military school but also the first modern high school in the empire.

Unfortunately, while this process of modernization was still under way, a new war began. In 1798, French forces under General Napoleon Bonaparte invaded Egypt with the goal of threatening British India. Despite French victories on land, the British Royal Navy destroyed the French fleet in the Battle of the Nile (Aboukir Bay), cutting the French off in Egypt. Napoleon's subsequent invasion eastward was stymied thanks to his unsuccessful siege of Acre in 1799.

The foreign problems confronting the empire did not end with peace with France in 1802. In 1806 Russian forces invaded the principalities of Moldavia and Walacia, beginning a war with the Ottomans that would last until 1812. Once again the Ottoman military performed poorly and in spite of numerical superiority lost most of the pitched battles and only displayed limited and ineffective resistance in the defense of fortresses. A series of rebellions further destabilized the empire. Selim was also handicapped by being unable to unite the different reformist groups.

On May 25, 1807, opposition to his reforms became unrest and then outright revolt, in the Kabakchi Mustafa Rebellion, named for its leader. The rebels soon took control of Istanbul. With the bulk of the Ottoman Army off fighting the Russians, Selim tried to appease the rebels by accepting their initial demands, including the execution of some of his reformist officials and close associates. This only encouraged those who opposed the sultan and his reforms, and on May 29 Selim was forced to abdicate in favor of Mustafa IV.

Fourteen months of near chaos ensued until Alemdar Mustafa Pasha, an Ottoman official in present-day Bulgaria and supporter of Selim, led a march on Istanbul. Selim III was killed on July 28, 1808, during Mustafa's effort to rescue him. Mustafa then crushed the rebels, removed Mustafa IV, and gave the throne to the sole survivor of the House of Osman, young prince Mahmud, who became sultan as Mahmud II (r. 1808–1839).

MESUT UYAR

**See also**
Aboukir Bay, Battle of; Acre, 1799 Siege of; Bonaparte, Napoleon; Ottoman Empire; Russo-Ottoman Wars

**References**
Shaw, Stanford J. *Between Old and New: The Ottoman Empire under Sultan Selim III 1789–1807.* Cambridge, MA: Harvard University Press, 1971.
Zorlu, Tuncay. *Innovation and Empire in Turkey: Sultan Selim III and the Modernization of the Ottoman Navy.* New York: I. B. Tauris, 2008.

## Seljuk Dynasty (1016–1153)

Turkic dynasty of Central Asiatic origin that conquered and came to rule Persia, Iraq, and much of the Near East from the early 11th century through mid-12th century.

By the middle of the 10th century, the Muslim world consisted of a patchwork of peoples and states in the lands of the former Arab Empire, united and divided by the religion of Islam. That world had been founded by the Arab conquests four centuries earlier, when the last of the barbarians to assault the Roman Empire and the last of the heretics to challenge its faith, had invaded and unified a Near and Middle East previously partitioned between the empires of Rome and Persia. In the middle of the 10th century, this world was in turn invaded by fresh barbarians: Berbers from the Sahara and Turkomans from Central Asia. Even more than the Arabs, these barbarians were nomads of the arid zone from the Atlantic to Mongolia. And as in the case of the Arabs, their invasions were testimony to the attraction of the civilized world for the peoples on its periphery, who were drawn into its affairs by its wealth on the one hand and by its religion and its politics on the other.

At the end of the 10th century the emirate of the Samanid dynasty in Central Asia, an offshoot of the Abbasid Empire, collapsed. Its territories were divided between the Turkoman Qarakhanids in Transoxania and the Ghaznawids in Khurasan and Afghanistan. Unlike the immigrant Qarakhanids, the Turkoman Oghuz (also known as Ghuzz), who occupied the steppes beyond the Aral Sea, remained largely pagan. In the first half of the 11th century, however, a Muslim faction of the Oghuz, nomadic warriors in search of pasture and military service, moved south into Qarakhanid and then Ghaznawid territory. These were the Seljuk (Selçük) clan, named after their ancestor, and they came into conflict with both the Qarakhanids and the Ghaznawids, a dynasty founded by a Turkish *ghulam* (slave-soldier, pl. *ghilman*) in the service of the Samanids. The Seljuks established a large empire in Central Asia, with its capital at Ghazni (modern-day South Kabul).

Mahmud of Ghazni (r. 998–1030) came to the throne at age 27 and was the first ruler to be proclaimed sultan, meaning "authority." To justify his rule, Mahmud of Ghazni turned to war against the internal and external enemies of Islam, that is, the Shiites in Iraq and Persia and Hindus of the Indian subcontinent. The Shiite Buyid dynasty in western Persia held power over the Sunni Abbasid caliphate at Baghdad; the Shiiite Fatimids in Egypt claimed the caliphate for themselves. As recognized champions of the Abbasids, Mamud and his son Mas'ud not only persecuted the Ismailis, the followers of the Fatimids within their dominions, but also set out to overthrow the Buyids and ultimately the Fatimids. But their ambitions were cut short at the Battle of Dandanqan in 1040, when Mas'ud's ponderous army was routed by the Seljuks, who had overrun the province of Khurasan. From the battlefield, the Seljuk leader Tughril Beg (r. 1016–1063) sent the news of his victory to Baghdad, thereby taking upon himself the championship of the Abbasid caliphate and Sunni Islam.

With the Ghaznawids confined to Afghanistan and northwestern India, their dominions in northeastern Persia were divided between Tughril and his brothers Chagri and Musa Yabghu in a family dominion like that of the Qarakhanids in Transoxania. What might in consequence have remained yet another regional power, without pretensions or prospects, was transformed into a great new empire by this active championship.

Leaving Chagri to establish a local dynasty in Kirman in southeastern Persia, Tughril resumed the drive of the Ghaznawids to the west. Between 1040 and 1055 he took over the Buyid dominions in western Persia and Iraq, and between 1055 and 1060 he secured Baghdad against the attempt of the Fatimids to win it for themselves. By the time of his death in 1063, he had married the daughter of the Abbasid caliph and received from him a plethora of titles: king of the East and the West, pillar of the faith, and so on. These confirmed him as the sultan, the hereditary ruler of the world on behalf of the caliph.

Tughril's nephew Alp Arslan (d. 1073) and Alp Arslan's son Malik Shah I (d. 1092) ensured that this role did not die with him and was justified by further conquest. In 1071 Alp Arslan routed the Byzantines at the Battle of Manzikert in Armenia, adding Anatolia not only to the Seljuk realm but also to the Islamic world. Between 1078 and 1086 Malik Shah I and his brother Tutush I took the bulk of Syria, while in the northeast the Qarakhanids of Transoxania were forced into submission. The ambition to conquer Egypt was never pursued, but at the death of Malik Shah I, Islam in Asia was predominantly under Seljuk rule.

The Seljuk Empire was a family affair, divided among brothers and their sons in accordance with Turkoman custom and exposed to their rivalry. But at the same time, it was not a Turkoman empire in the sense of nomadic tribesmen ruling over settled populations. The princes were khans, or chieftains, to the nomads who followed them, but as heirs to the Ghaznawids and the Buyids, they were rulers who relied less on the folk than the household for their forces, and from the outset they depended on the secretarial class of the Muslim world for their administration.

The Turkoman tribesmen who accompanied the Seljuks into the Muslim world and migrated in search of pasture for their sheep through the highlands of Persia into Anatolia largely escaped, and indeed resisted, their control. The twin threats of devolution and dissidence were only overcome with the creation of a centralized regime by two great viziers (*wazirs*) brought up in the service of the Ghaznawids, al-Kunduri and Niam al-Mulk. They did so as politicians as well as administrators, whose powers of appointment and patronage created networks of clients around their own extensive households and enabled them to command obedience from the Seljuks themselves, from their colleagues, and from their subordinates. As politicians they lived dangerously between the confidence of the sultan and the royal ladies on the one hand and the intrigues of their rivals on the other: Niam al-Mulk had al-Kunduri put to death and before his own murder in 1092 was protesting his loyalty against the calumnies of his enemies. But for more than 30 years they reined back the centrifugal forces underlying the supremacy of the king of the East and the West.

The Siyasat-nama (Book of Government) by Niam al-Mulk is a prescription for government that relies heavily on Ghaznawid practice and example, not least for the acculturation of the Turks, who were to be trained up as *ghilman,* loyal and disciplined warriors in the household of the prince. What has been called the despotic and monolithic Ghaznawid state could not be re-created; the household of the sultan was only the greatest of many such retinues, which gave each prince a greater or lesser degree of independence. Devolution was nevertheless kept in check by the size of his household, coupled with that of Niam al-Mulk himself, and by the appointment of its members as provincial governors and *atabegs* (father dukes), senior commanders who acted as tutors of junior princes, whose mothers they often married. It was more formally controlled by the use of *iqa',* a grant of revenue in payment for military service that under the Seljuks became a grant of local or provincial government.

At the same time Niam al-Mulk set out to ground the pretensions of the sultan to the role of defender of the faith in more than titles and occasional warfare. In the name of Sunni Islam he founded the Niamiyya at Baghdad, the most famous of a series of colleges of religious education designed to inculcate the true faith as well as to bring it under the patronage and control of the state. The foundation of such a madrassa (religious college) became a hallmark of the pious prince, concerned with his image in the public eye.

On their entry into the Islamic world, the Seljuks were Turkoman nomads, fighting on horseback with composite bows and curved swords but without armor, opposing their mobility to the more static formations of the armies they encountered. During the next 100 years of warfare, the Turkomans acquired helmets and a certain amount of body armor, while the Seljuks themselves adopted the style of the *ghulam,* the so-called slave-soldier, recruited as boys from the Turkish populations of Central Asia and trained up to be fully armored cavalrymen in the armies of the Islamic world from the ninth century onward. Their principal innovation was to provide the Turkoman bow in addition to sword and spear. Seljuk armies thus came to consist of squadrons of heavy household cavalry supported by Turkoman and other ethnic auxiliaries, with all the advantages of armor, archery, and mobility. Such squadrons under their individual commanders were nevertheless limited in size, and large armies were the exception. By the end of the Seljuk period, the term *ghulam* had been generally replaced by *mamlūk* (pl. *mamalik*), most obviously in Egypt, where the Seljuk warrior was introduced by Saladin.

The image of piety supplemented that of defender of the faith, employed by Tughril to create his empire and to justify the power of a rank outsider over the Islamic world. That justification, however, at the expense of Shiite Islam, provoked a radical new challenge and a radical new threat. The Siyasat-nama barely mentions the Fatimids, nominal enemies who had evidently ceased to serve the Seljuk purpose of empire building. But it vehemently attacks the Ismailis, followers of the Fatimids under their leader Hasan-i Sabbah, who in 1090 seized the castle of Alamut in northwestern Persia as a base for revolution.

Directed against the Seljuks as the champions of Sunni Islam, the threat of insurrection not only forced the regime to go to war in the mountains, but also in 1092 Hasan's alarming campaign of assassination may have claimed the life of Niam al-Mulk. Whoever arranged it, the murder of the great vizier was the beginning of the end for the empire he had striven to consolidate. The death of Malik Shah I a few weeks later curtailed the sultan's plan to depose the reigning caliph and thus bring the Abbasid caliphate completely under his control. Instead, it opened the way to a struggle for the succession from which the empire never fully recovered.

Malik Shah I's sons Mamud and Barkiyaruq were minors, fought over by the factions at court and challenged by their uncle Tutush I in Syria. Barkiyaruq succeeded to the throne in 1094. Tutush was killed in 1095, but from 1097 to his death in 1105, the new sultan was challenged by his half brothers Muhammad Tapar (d. 1118) and Sanjar (d. 1157). The ensuing warfare divided the empire between Barkiyaruq in Iraq and western Persia and his rivals in the northeast and placed the contestants in the hands of the military.

As the shifting loyalties of the *atabegs* came to dominate the conflict, Syria was abandoned to the sons of Tutush at Damascus and Aleppo, while the Seljuks of Rum (Anatolia) were left to fight off the Byzantines and crusaders at Ikonion (modern-day Konya, Turkey). The unsuccessful attempt of the *atabeg* of Mosul, Karbugha, to relieve Antioch (modern-day Antakya, Turkey) in 1098 was the most that was done to halt the progress of the First Christian Crusade in the Holy Land (1096–1099). In Persia itself, Hassan-i Sabbah extended his mountain kingdom, while his assassins claimed their victims, and Shahdiz outside Isfahan fell into Ismaili hands.

The conflict ended with the death of Barkiyaruq in 1105 and the accession of Muhammad Tapar (r. 1105–1118), under whom the unity of the empire was restored. Shahdiz was recovered in 1110, and the expansion of Alamut halted. Between 1110 and 1115 two attempts were made by the *atabegs* of Mosul on behalf of the sultan to organize a joint campaign in Syria against the Frankish states of Outremer. Both, however, failed in the face of Syrian hostility to any attempt to recover the country for the empire. Mosul itself, under successive *atabegs*, was semi-independent, while Diyar Bakr and Mayyafariqin on the upper Euphrates were taken over by the Turkoman Artuqid dynasty.

### Great Seljuk Sultans

| | |
|---|---|
| Tughril Beg | 1055–1063 |
| Alp Arslan | 1063–1072 |
| Malik Shah I | 1072–1092 |
| Mamud I | 1092–1094 |
| Barkiyaruq | 1094–1105 |
| Malik Shah II | 1105 |
| Muhammad Tapar | 1105–1118 |
| Sanjar | 1118–1157 |

This shrinkage of the empire back toward the east was confirmed by the death of Muhammad Tapar in 1118. The sultanate then passed to Ahmad Sanjar, the fourth son of Malik Shah I, who had governed Khurasan since 1097 and remained identified with this first conquest of the dynasty. Sanjur ruled from 1118 to 1157. Left to rule over western Persia and Iraq, the sons and grandsons of Muhammad steadily lost control of their territory to their *atabegs*, whose principalities came to stretch from the Caspian Sea and the Caucasus through Mosul in northern Iraq to Luristan and Fars in western and southern Persia. By 1152 they had even lost Baghdad to the Abbasids, who had taken advantage of Seljuk weakness to create their own state. In Khurasan itself, Sanjar's position was seriously weakened by defeat at the hands of the Qara Khitay in Transoxania in 1141 and collapsed in 1157, when he was defeated by Oghuz Turkish tribesmen and died.

Like the Ghaznawids before them, the Great Seljuks thus met their fate in the same region and at the hands of the same people whom they had led to the original victory at Dandanqan. Just as in 1040, their dominions in eastern Persia, including Kirman under the descendants of Tughril's brother Chagri, were overrun by the victors, while an empty title passed to the line of Muhammad in what was left of their empire in the west. From 1161 to 1191 their sultanate was under the control of the *atabeg* Eldigüz and his successors, whose power extended from Azerbaijan as far as Isfahan. It ended in heroic suicide when Tughril III ousted the Eldiguzids, only to go to war with the formidable Khwarazm Shah and die in battle in 1194.

The great difference between the victory of the Oghuz in 1157 and the victory of the Seljuks in 1040 was the absence of either a great religious or a great political cause. After the death of Sanjar, the Turks behaved as the Seljuks might have done without the championship of the caliphate and Islam and remained as a horde in eastern Persia; there was no mantle for their leader Malik Dinar to inherit. This failure on the part of the Great Seljuks to maintain the ideal as well as the reality of universal empire is symptomatic of the growing conviction that might is right—in other words, the ruler who had the power to govern had the authority to do so—and anticipated the coming of the pagan Mongols and their ready acceptance by the counterparts of Niam al-Mulk in the 13th century. It was left to the Zangids, the dynasty of the Seljuk *atabeg* at Mosul, to gradually rediscover the principle of religion for empire and to have their henchman Saladin to put it once again into practice.

Michael Brett

**See also**

Alp Arslan; Barkiyaruq; Byzantine-Seljuk Wars; Georgian-Seljuk Wars; Ismailis; Malik Shah I; Seljuk War of Succession

**References**

Ayalon, David. *The Mamluk Military Society.* London: Variorum, 1979.

Bosworth, Clifford Edmund. *The New Islamic Dynasties.* Edinburgh, UK: Edinburgh University Press, 1996.

Bosworth, Clifford Edmund. "The Political and Dynastic History of the Iranian World (A.D. 1000–1217)." In *The Cambridge History of Iran,* Vol. 5, *The Saljuk and Mongol Periods,* ed. J. A. Boyle, 1–202. Cambridge: Cambridge University Press, 1968.

Cahen, Claude. "The Turkish Invasion: The Selchükids." In *A History of the Crusades,* Vol. 1, ed. Kenneth M. Setton et al., 135–176. 2nd ed. Madison: University of Wisconsin Press, 1969.

Humphreys, R. Stephen. *Islamic History: A Framework for Inquiry.* 2nd ed. London: Tauris, 1991.

Klausner, Carla L. *The Saljuk Vezirate: A Study of Civil Administration, 1055–1194.* Cambridge, MA: Harvard University Press, 1973.

Lambton, Anne K. S. "The Internal Structure of the Saljuk Empire." In *The Cambridge History of Iran,* Vol. 5, *The Saljuk and Mongol Periods,* ed. J. A. Boyle, 203–283. Cambridge: Cambridge University Press, 1968.

Morgan, David O. *Medieval Persia, 1040–1797.* London: Longman, 1988.

Niam al-Mulk. *The Book of Government or Rules for Kings.* Translated by Hubert Darke. London: Routledge and Kegan Paul, 1960.

Nicolle, David. *The Armies of Islam, 7th–11th Centuries.* London: Osprey, 1982.

Tahir al-Din Nishapuri. *The History of the Seljuq Turks.* Translated by K. A. Luther, ed. C. E. Bosworth. Richmond, UK: Curzon, 2001.

## Seljuk War of Succession (1092–1105)

The Great Seljuk Empire came to its height under Sultan Malik Shah (r. 1073–1092). His death in 1092 launched a struggle for the succession from which the empire never fully recovered. The first signs of weakness in the Seljuk Empire came in the wake of the assassination of Seljuk vizier Nizam al-Mulk in October 1092. A month later, Malik Shah himself died while hunting in circumstances that are still disputed by historians. The deaths of two most powerful men in the empire plunged it into disarray.

Malik Shah's eldest son Barkiyaruq was still a youth at the time of his father's death and faced a prolonged power struggle involving his uncles and half brothers. He first had to deal with Terken Khatun, Malik Shah's ambitious wife, who suppressed the news of Malik Shah's death and had her son Mahmud recognized as the sultan's successor. Once the demise of the sultan became known, Barkiyaruq rallied his supporters and advanced against Mahmud, who was in Isfahan. Barkiyaruq was victorious in fighting at Burudjird in January 1093 and then laid siege to Isfahan, which finally surrendered. Barkiyaruq let Mahmud retain Isfahan and Fars but claimed the rest of the Seljuk Empire for himself.

Hardly had Barkiyaruq crushed this threat than he faced new challenges. In 1093 Barkiyaruq defeated his maternal uncle, who led a rebellion in Azerbaijan. Later the same year, Barkiyaruq's paternal uncle Tutush disputed Barkiyaruq's claim to the sultanate, secured the support of all the Turkic leaders of Syria, and invaded Iraq, capturing Mosul. In the summer of 1093, Tutush confronted his nephew in battle at al-Rayy. There some of Tutush's allies switched sides and joined Barkiyaruq, forcing Tutush to retire to Damascus. Barkiyaruq consolidated his authority in Iraq (his name was mentioned in the mosque prayers in February 1094), but his uncle still remained a potent threat.

Tutush soon collected a new army and occupied Anatolia, Iraq, and much of western Iran, winning recognition as sultan from the Abbasid caliph in Baghdad. However, on February 26, 1095, Barkiyaruq defeated his forces in a battle at the village of Dashlu, south of the Caspian Sea, where Tutush was killed. Barkiyaruq's victory had devastating consequences for Seljuk unity in Syria. Tutush left five sons who became embroiled in a power struggle and fought a bitter civil war in Syria.

Barkiyaruq meanwhile was preoccupied with the threat posed by his other uncle, Arslan Arghun, who launched a rebellion in Khurasan in 1096–1097. After the revolt was crushed, Barkiyaruq faced another challenge from his younger brother Muhammad Tapar, who rebelled in Azerbaijan in 1098. Barkiyaruq advanced against him, but many of his troops went over to the other side, forcing him to take flight to Persia. He returned with a new army in 1100 and reclaimed part of Iraq before suffering a major defeat at the hands of Muhammad at Hamadhan in April 1101. Barkiyaruq and Muhammad negotiated a peace in 1101 that recognized the former as the sultan and granted the former domains in Iraq and Azerbaijan. But the truce was quickly broken, and the fighting resumed with changing success throughout the next three years, exhausting Seljuk military power and crippling the economy of the empire. By early 1105 on Barkiyaruq's death, Muhammad controlled most of Anatolia, Iraq, and much of Persia and thus had restored the unity of the Seljuk Empire. Still, the prolonged civil war greatly limited the ability of the Great Seljuks to respond effectively to the threat posed by the First Christian Crusade in the Holy Land that reached Syria and Palestine in 1096–1099.

ALEXANDER MIKABERIDZE

**See also**
Malik Shah I; Seljuk Dynasty

**References**
Boyle, J. ed. *The Cambridge History of Iran,* Vol. 5, *The Saljuk and Mongol Periods.* Cambridge: Cambridge University Press, 1968.

Lambton, A. K. S. *Continuity and Change in Medieval Persia.* London, Tauris, 1988.

Zahir al-Din Nishapuri. *The History of the Seljuq Turks.* Trans. K. A. Luther, ed. C. E. Bosworth. Richmond, UK: Curzon, 2001.

## Sennacherib (?–681 BCE)

King of Assyria from 705 BCE to 681 BCE and king of Babylon from 704 to 703 BCE and 688 to 681 BCE. Sennacherib was known for his building program in Assyria and military campaigns against various Southwest Asian states, including Judah, Palestine, and Babylon. Although his date of birth is unknown, Sennacherib was a younger son of Assyrian king Sargon II, who reigned between 722 and 705 BCE. Sennacherib, whose name means "Sin (Assyrian moon god) has replaced his brothers," is sometimes referred to as Sennecherib or Sin-ahhe-eriba. Sennacherib had several wives, the most significant being Naqui-Zakutu, and at least four sons: Ashur-nadin-shum, whom Sennacherib placed on the throne of Babylonia between 699 and 694 BCE; Adrammelech; Sharezer; and Esarhaddon.

Sennacherib became king on Ab (July–August 20, 705 BCE), when his father was killed while on campaign against the Cimmerian tribesmen in the Taurus Mountain region of modern-day Turkey. Sennacherib initially ruled from Ashur rather than his father's capital in Dar-Sharrukin, but in 701 BCE he moved his capital to Nineveh, which underwent significant changes during his reign. In addition to upgrading his palace there and restoring older palaces and temples, he also built new ones. Other improvements in Nineveh included widening or constructing new roads, constructing canals and aqueducts, and increasing the availability of water for the city's inhabitants. Other Assyrian cities and regions also benefited from public buildings, temples, and water projects constructed during his rule.

Although one of the most well-known primary sources of information about his rule is King Sennacherib's Prism, a six-side clay prism with writing on the sides that discusses his restoration of Nineveh and his palace there, the prism focuses primarily on his military campaigns. Additional source material on his campaign against Judah is also found in parts of the Old Testament books II Kings and Isaiah. Although most scholars believe that Sennacherib waged eight major military campaigns during his tenure, a few scholars argue that he waged a second campaign against Judah (in essence a ninth), which is not listed on the prism.

Although the campaign against King Hezekiah and Judah is well known, the majority of Sennacherib's military operations were directed against Babylonia. Between 703 and 689 BCE, Sennacherib engaged in four campaigns there. Babylonia's former king, Merodach-Baladan, a member of the Chaldean tribe of Bît Yakin who had lost the throne to Sargon II, regained control over Babylonia with the assistance of Elamites and Aramaeans, proclaiming himself king.

Sennacherib launched his first campaign in 703 BCE and successfully defeated the Babylonians and their allies but failed to capture Merodach-Baladan, who escaped into the swamps in southern Mesopotamia. In 700 BCE, Sennacherib fought and defeated Merodach-Baladan and his armies in a second campaign. In 694 BCE, Sennacherib waged a successful third campaign against the Bît Yakin, Babylon, and Elam, which included a combined naval and ground operation. In his final campaign circa 691–689 BCE against Elam, Babylonia, and their allies, he fought a major battle at Hallulê around 691 BCE. Both Sennacherib and his opponents claimed victory; however, Sennacherib besieged and destroyed the city of Babylon in 689 BCE.

In 701 BCE, Sennacherib launched a major campaign against lands along the Mediterranean coast and Palestine. Although he successfully defeated or forced the surrender of Sidon, Ashkelon, and other states in the region, he enjoyed only partial success against the Kingdom of Judah. Despite conquering at least 43 cities in Judah, his siege of its capital of Jerusalem failed. However, Hezekiah was forced to pay tribute to Sennacherib. Sennacherib's other three campaigns, which were successful, were against the Kassites, other rebelling tributary states, and other tribes in northern Iran.

Sennacherib ruled the empire until he was murdered on Tebet (December–January) 20, 681 BCE. Although some sources claim that only one of Sennacherib's sons murdered him, Hebrew sources and at least one Assyrian source state or imply that at least two of his sons were involved in the plot. Hebrew texts claim that Adrammelech and Sharezer killed their father while he was worshipping in a temple in Nineveh, attempting to prevent their favored younger brother Esarhaddon from succeeding to the throne. This did not prevent Esarhaddon from becoming king of Assyria that same year, however.

Iraqi president Saddam Hussein, who liked comparing himself to great leaders of the past and in particular Nebuchadnezzar and Saladin, also sometimes invoked Sennacherib. In fact, Hussein reportedly compared his invasion and defeat of Kuwait in August 1991 to Sennacherib's sack of Babylon. In 1985 Hussein began rebuilding on the site of ancient Babylon, a project never brought to fruition, however.

Wyndham E. Whynot

**See also**
Assyrian Empire; Hussein, Saddam; Mesopotamia

**References**
DeCamp, L. Sprague. *The Ancient Engineers*. New York: Barnes & Noble Books, 1993.
Gallagher, William. *Sennacherib's Campaign to Judah: New Studies*, Vol. 18, ed. B. Halpern and M. H. E. Weippert. Boston: Brill, 1999.
Healy, Mark. *The Ancient Assyrians*. London: Osprey, 2003.

# Sephardic Judaism

One of the two principal branches of Judaism whose origins can be traced to the Iberian Peninsula, North Africa, and the eastern Mediterranean. During the Middle Ages, Judaism diverged into two cultures that differed in laws, customs, liturgy, and language. While Ashkenazic Judaism evolved and flourished in Central and Eastern Europe, the environs of the Holy Roman Empire, Sephardic Judaism evolved and flourished in the Moorish Iberian Peninsula, primarily Spain and North Africa.

Sephardic customs and halakic (Jewish law) rulings are based on the Palestinian Talmud and ritual traditions. Ashkenazic customs and halakic rulings meanwhile are based on the Babylonian Talmudic and ritual traditions. This division of Sephardic and Ashkenazic Judaism can be seen in the structure of the chief rabbinate of Israel that represents all of Judaism in Israel and is the final arbiter of halakic and kashruth (Jewish food laws). The chief rabbinate has two chief rabbis, one Sephardic and one Ashkenazic. The Jewish community in Rome predated the destruction of the Solomonic Temple and the diaspora and along with Yemenite, Ethiopian, and Oriental Jewry is neither Sephardic nor Ashkenazic.

Sephardic Judaism derives its name from the Hebrew term "Sefarad" (Spain). Rulers Ferdinand and Isabella expelled the Jews from Spain in 1492 along with the last of the Moors. These Sephardim were dispersed throughout the Mediterranean region and the Ottoman Empire. A number also settled in Southwest Asia, France, Italy, the Spanish Americas (present-day U.S. Southwest, Mexico, Central America, and South America), Brazil, the Netherlands (including the former Dutch possessions of Aruba, Suriname, and Curacao), Hungary, Denmark, Germany, Austria, and England. Benjamin Disraeli, a Sephardic Jew who converted to Anglicanism, served two terms as the British prime minister in the late 19th century. The majority of the Jews of this Sephardic diaspora settled in Morocco and North Africa, however.

The first Jewish congregation in North America, Shearith Israel (New York, 1684), was founded by Sephardim. But by 1751 Ashkenazim dominated the American Jewish community. Sephardic Jews, who represented 97 percent of world Jewry in the 11th century, comprised only 8 percent in 1931 before the decimation of Ashkenazic Jews in the Nazi Holocaust. The Sephardim now comprise approximately 15 percent of world Jewry.

In addition to their differences in Talmudic traditions, Sephardic and Ashkenazic Jews differ in their indigenous languages and in some legal and ritual practices. Ladino, a hybrid of Judeo/Hebrew-Castilian/Spanish, is the traditional vernacular of Sephardic Jewry. Yiddish (Judeo/Hebrew-German) is the traditional vernacular language of Ashkenazic Jews. Just as the Gileadites and the Ephramites of biblical times varied in their pronunciation of "Shibboleth," Sephardim and Ashkenazim vary in their pronunciation of one Hebrew consonant and some vowels.

Sephardim and Ashkenazim also vary in some halakic and kashruth (kosher) practices. Sephardim eat rice, corn, peanuts, legumes, peanuts, and millet during the observance of Passover (Pesach). Ashkenazim abstain from these foods. Sephardim and Ashkenazim also vary in some other halakic and kashruth practices. Sephardim are generally stricter than Ashkenazim in their understanding of which meats are kosher. There are also differences in the permissibility of specific slaughter practices.

Although they have much in common, Sephardic and Ashkenazic Torah and worship practices also differ. The terms "Sephardic" and "Ashkenazic" are often used to refer to liturgical traditions (*nusackh*). Those traditions vary in the content of the prayers, the order of the prayers, their text and the melodies, and the prayer book (*Siddur*). Sephardic brides and grooms do not refrain from meeting for one week prior to their wedding, while Ashkenazic brides and grooms do. Sephardic Torahs stand during a Torah service, and Ashkenazic Torahs lie flat. The Sephardic understanding of Jewish law is based on the writings of Rabbi Joseph Caro, and the Ashkenazic understanding of Jewish law is based on the writings of Rabbi Moses Isserles.

Sephardim and Ashkenazim have generally lived together peacefully where both have settled, with the possible exception of the Sephardic migration to France following the French withdrawal from Morocco in 1956 and Algeria in 1962. Sephardim and Ashkenazim rarely intermarry. Sephardim have maintained their religious and variant ethnic heritages by settling or grouping themselves according to their countries or culture of origin. Thus, among the myriad of cultures from which and into which the Sephardim have settled, they have formed Castilian, Aragonian, Catalonian, Portuguese, Cordovan, Romaniotes, Mallorcan, Sicilian, Sevillian, Moroccan, Algerian, and numerous other culturally and geographically rooted congregations.

Even though the Ashkenazim, Sephardim, and Mizrahi Jews have lived peacefully with one another and fought together to preserve the State of Israel since 1948, present-day Israel continues to be dominated by Ashkenazic Jews of European descent. This peaceful and fruitful coalition is endangered by a rising Mizrahi post-Zionist backlash that asserts that Mizrahi, or Arab Jews, are discriminated against by Israel's Ashkenazic Jewish political establishment. These Mizrahim contend that the Zionist immigration policies that promoted Ashkenazic Jewish immigration from the late 19th through the 20th centuries reduced Mizrahi Jews to second-class citizenship. This, they argue, has created social, political, and economic discrimination that separates Sephardic and Mizrahi Israelis from Ashkenazic Israelis.

RICHARD M. EDWARDS

**See also**
Ashkenazic Judaism

**References**
Assis, Yom Tov. *The Jews of Spain: From Settlement to Expulsion.* Jerusalem: Hebrew University of Jerusalem, 1988.
Bartlett, John R. *Jews in the Hellenistic World: Josephus, Aristeas, the Sibylline Oracles, Eupolemus.* Cambridge: Cambridge University Press, 1985.

## September 11, 2001, Attacks on the United States

On September 11, 2001, the United States suffered a series of coordinated suicide attacks perpetrated by members of the Islamic terrorist group Al Qaeda, which was then based in Afghanistan and led by Osama bin Laden. On that day, 19 Al Qaeda terrorists hijacked four commercial American jetliners and crashed them into prearranged targets. Two of the airplanes crashed into the Twin Towers of the World Trade Center in New York City. Another plane crashed into the Pentagon, the headquarters of the Department of Defense, in northern Virginia. A fourth plane crashed into a field near Shanksville in rural Somerset County, Pennsylvania, after some passengers, having been informed of the other suicide airplane attacks from cellular phone communications with family members, attempted to storm the cockpit and regain control of the plane from the hijackers. The White House or the Capitol were the most likely suspected targets of this plane. Excluding the hijackers, a total of 2,974 people died in the attacks, including 246 from all four planes in which there were no survivors.

The attacks crippled not only New York City and its economy but also sectors of the U.S. economy. Particularly hard hit were the airline and insurance industries, which suffered billions of dollars of losses. The September 11 attacks were the worst terrorist attacks ever committed against the United States, and the resulting death toll surpassed that of the December 7, 1941, Japanese attack on Pearl Harbor.

The George W. Bush administration responded to the attacks by declaring a global war on terror; the next month the United States invaded Afghanistan, toppling the Taliban government that had given sanctuary and support to bin Laden and Al Qaeda. The U.S. government also enacted the Patriot Act in October 2001, a sweeping law designed to protect the country against terrorism by enhancing the power of the federal government to conduct criminal and intelligence investigations, engage in espionage, and conduct searches for communications records.

The four airliners hijacked—American Airlines Flights 11 (Boston to Los Angeles) and 77 (Dulles, Virginia, to Los Angeles) and United Airlines Flights 175 (Boston to Los Angeles) and 93 (Newark to San Francisco) were all bound for the West Coast from the East Coast. Al Qaeda deliberately chose the flights because of their long distance, which meant that the large airplanes (Boeing 757s and 767s) would be carrying considerable amounts of jet fuel, thereby intensifying the destruction and explosions once the planes crashed. It is suspected that at least some of the hijackers had previously flown on some of the same flights from the East Coast in preparation for their suicide operations.

It is not entirely clear how exactly the hijackers gained control of the cockpits of each of the four planes, as federal aviation rules mandated that cockpit doors remain closed and locked during flight. The hijackers were armed with box cutters, however, and also mace or pepper spray. According to some passengers on some of the planes, the terrorists claimed to have bombs as well, although this was probably a ruse to control the passengers. According to the September 11 Commission Report, the hijackers probably gained access to the then-unreinforced cockpit doors by forcing a flight attendant to open them. Other theories hold that they may have stabbed the flight attendants to obtain a cockpit door key or somehow lured the captain or first officer out of the cockpit. During cell phone conversations as the drama unfolded, some passengers on American Airlines Flight 11 reported that two flight attendants had been stabbed; passengers on United Airlines Flight 175 revealed that both pilots had been killed and a flight attendant stabbed. However, passengers on American Airlines Flight 77 and United Airlines Flight 93 reported no in-air injuries or deaths, but the cockpit voice recorder of United 93 indicated that a woman, most likely a flight attendant, was being held in the cockpit and struggled with one of the hijackers who either killed or otherwise silenced her.

None of the airport security checkpoint supervisors recalled the 19 hijackers or reported anything suspicious regarding their screening; they were apparently allowed to clear security unimpeded. The September 11 Commission, which investigated the events, concluded that the quality

Fires still burn amid the rubble and debris of the World Trade Center in New York City in the area known as Ground Zero two days after the September 11, 2001, terrorist attacks. (U.S. Department of Defense)

of the screening was "marginal at best," particularly given the fact that 2 of the hijackers had set off metal detectors and were then hand-wanded and allowed to proceed. The security screeners never resolved what had set off the metal detector in the first place, and airport video footage showed that one of the hijackers was carrying an unidentified item clipped to his back pocket that escaped any scrutiny. In addition, although some of the hijackers were selected by a computerized prescreening program known as Computer Assisted Prescreening Passenger System (CAPPS) to identify passengers who should be subjected to special security measures, this only meant that the hijackers' checked bags were held off the plane until it was confirmed that they were aboard the aircraft. CAPPS did not trigger any further scrutiny of what they carried on the planes with them.

American Airlines Flight 11 and United Airlines Flight 175 crashed into the North and South Towers of the 110-story World Trade Center at 8:48 a.m. and 9:30 a.m local time, respectively. At 9:59 a.m. and 10:26 a.m. the South and North Towers, respectively, collapsed due to massive structural failure, killing a total of 2,603 in both buildings (including 341 New York firefighters and 2 paramedics, 23 New York City police officers, and 37 Port Authority police officers); another 24 people remain listed as missing. The collapse of the two huge buildings also brought down neighboring office towers and badly damaged others, all of which occurred in a densely populated part of the city.

According to a 2005 report by the National Institute of Standards and Technology of the U.S. Department of Commerce titled "Final Report on the Collapse of the World Trade Center Towers," the impact of both planes as they crashed ignited thousands of gallons of jet fuel, which melted the thermal insulation, or fireproofing, on the interior core steel-support columns of the World Trade Center. This caused the floors to sag and then collapse. In so doing, they pulled and collapsed the exterior, or perimeter, columns of the buildings, reducing their ability to support the floors above. This explains why neither tower collapsed immediately upon impact with the aircraft. The aircraft impacts did not cause the towers to collapse; instead, it was the ensuing fires from the exploding jet fuel that ultimately brought the buildings down. The South Tower collapsed more quickly than the North Tower because there was more aircraft damage to the central core of the building, which then collapsed the exterior or perimeter support structure of that building. The report also found no evidence to substantiate some of the principal conspiracy theories alleging that the World Trade Center was destroyed by some elements of the U.S. government by means of a controlled implosion using explosives.

Meanwhile, American Airlines Flight 77 crashed at 9:37 a.m. local time into the Pentagon, killing 125 people, while United Airlines Flight 93 plowed into a field in Shanksville, Pennsylvania, at 10:03, killing all 40 passengers and crew aboard. It is clear from the cockpit voice recorder that the hijackers, who had gained access to the plane's controls, were aware of the passengers' assault against the cockpit and pitched the plane so that it crashed into an empty field.

The motives for the attacks of September 11, 2001, date from Al Qaeda's declaration of jihad, or holy war, against the United States in February 1998. Bin Laden decried American foreign policy in the Middle East, including America's military presence in Saudi Arabia—the site of Islam's two holiest shrines. According to bin Laden, American support for Israel and dictatorial Arab states such as Egypt and Saudi Arabia allegedly constituted proof of Americans' anti-Islamic policies. Sadly, the attacks of September 11, 2001, were but a tragic and devastating culmination of escalating attacks by Al Qaeda against U.S. targets around the world, including the August 1998 U.S. embassy bombings in Kenya and Tanzania and the October 2000 attack on USS *Cole* at Aden.

The fallout from the attacks was both long-lasting and far-reaching. No commercial air traffic was allowed for several days after the attacks, the stock market was closed for nearly a week, and the U.S. economy tilted toward recession as consumer spending plummeted in the weeks and months after the disaster. The attacks helped shape the Bush Doctrine, which would seek to prevent further attacks by launching preemptory strikes against nations or regimes likely to launch terrorist assaults on the United States. The 2003 invasion of Iraq was a case in point. That conflict and the Afghanistan War have both dragged on, seemingly without resolution. Although the Iraq War was officially declared at an end in December 2011, sectarian violence continues there, as does the challenge of terrorism, principally in the form of the Islamic State of Iraq and Syria (ISIS). Finally, the September 11 attacks shattered Americans' sense of invulnerability, which has helped the federal government erect a pervasive and powerful internal security state to complement the broader national security state.

STEFAN BROOKS

**See also**

Al Qaeda; Bin Laden, Osama; Bush Doctrine; *Cole,* USS, Attack on; Terrorism

**References**

Bernstein, Richard. *Out of the Blue.* New York: Times Books, 2002.

New York Magazine Editors. *September 11, 2001: A Record of Tragedy, Heroism and Hope.* New York: Harry N. Abrams, 2001.

*The 9/11 Commission Report: The Final Report of the National Commission on Terrorist Attacks upon the United States.* New York: Norton, 2004.

Talbot, Strobe, and Nayan Chanda, eds. *The Age of Terror: America and the World after September 11.* New York: Basic Books, 2002.

## Septimius Severus, Emperor (ca. 145–211)

Roman emperor (r. 191–211). Lucius Septimius Severus, founder of the Severan dynasty, was born circa 145 in Leptis Magna, a city in Roman North Africa. His father entered the senatorial order, and Severus was thus of senatorial rank and prior to 193 followed a regular senatorial career, holding the consulship in 190. Severus was governor of Upper Pannonia when Emperor Commodus (r. 181–192) was assassinated and Pertinax became emperor. The Praetorians assassinated Pertinax after only three months, on March 28, 203. Twelve days later, Severus was acclaimed emperor by his troops at Carnuntum. He then marched on Rome, claiming to avenge Pertinax.

At Rome Didius Julianus, who became another short-lived emperor, was assassinated on Severus's approach, and Severus entered Rome to unanimous support on June 19, 193. He punished the disloyalty of the Praetorians (and their impiety for murdering emperors) by disbanding the Guard and discharging its members en masse without benefits. He recruited a new Guard not from Italy, as hitherto had been the case, but instead from the Danubian legions. He also enlisted three new legions, raised military pay, and granted serving soldiers the right to marry.

Pescennius Niger revolted and was proclaimed emperor in Syria in April 193. After consolidating his position at Rome, Severus marched his army east and defeated Niger at Cyzicus and Nicaea by the winter of 193. Niger died in the spring of 194. Severus punished Syria by dividing it into two smaller provinces. He then campaigned aggressively against the Persians, perhaps to punish them for supporting Niger, but victory against Persia was also a traditional Roman goal.

His campaign was successful, with both Mesopotamia and Osrhoene added to the Roman Empire.

Clodius Albinus, Roman ruler in Britain and Severus's erstwhile ally, revolted and invaded Gaul. Severus declared war on Albinus, invaded Gaul, and defeated Albinus at Lyons in February 197. Severus then took reprisals against the supporters of Albinus, putting to death 29 senators.

Severus left Rome for another Persian campaign in 198, capturing Ctesiphon. He then organized Mesopotamia as a Roman province. He also visited Egypt and reorganized its administration.

Severus promoted his two sons as intended heirs, renaming his son Bassianus as Marcus Aurelius Antoninus (invoking the memory of the admirable Marcus Aurelius) and raising him to the rank of caesar and then, after the capture of Ctesiphon, coaugustus. Imperial edicts from 198 to 211 have Severus and Antoninus (Caracalla) as coemperors. Severus's second son, Geta, was only elevated to the rank of caesar. Severus stayed in Italy during 203–208, then traveled to Britain with his sons and campaigned in Scotland. He elevated Geta to the rank of Augustus in 210. Septimius Severus died from natural causes at York in north Britain in 211, succeeded by his sons Caracalla and Geta, though Geta would rule only briefly, being assassinated by Caracalla, who ruled from 211 to 217.

Severus has been termed a "military monarch" by modern scholars for his emphasis on military power. He proved to be a ruthless and aggressive military leader, and on his deathbed he allegedly told his sons, "Be harmonious, enrich the soldiers and despise everyone else."

SARA E. PHANG

### See also
Alexander Severus, Roman Emperor; Roman-Parthian Wars

### References
Birley, Anthony R. *Septimius Severus: The African Emperor*. Rev. ed. New Haven, CT: Yale University Press, 1988.
Campbell, J. B. 1984. *The Emperor and the Roman Army, 31 BC–AD 235*. Oxford, UK: Clarendon.
Potter, David S. 2004. *The Roman Empire at Bay: AD 180–395*. London: Routledge.
Smith, R. E. 1972. "The Army Reforms of Septimius Severus." *Historia* 21: 481–500.

# Serbian-Ottoman War (1876)

War in which Serbia and Montenegro fought the Ottoman Turks in support of an uprising in Bosnia and Herzegovina. The conflict intensified the crisis in the Balkans that culminated in the Russo-Ottoman War of 1877–1878.

In the second half of the 19th century, most of the Balkan states lived under strict Ottoman rule. In 1875 the Ottoman Empire passed a law effecting a rigid collection of taxes in Bosnia, despite a bad agricultural year in 1874. Coupled with that economic burden was a proposed Ottoman constitution intended to appease the Balkan states. The main feature of that constitution was an assembly that would represent all the peoples of the Ottoman Empire.

Despite that offer, Serbians in Herzegovina and other Balkan areas rebelled with limited but notable success, and ethnic nationalism among the Balkan states began to grow. The combination of Orthodox Christian beliefs and a Slavic cultural identity produced the idea that a federation of Serbs, Croatians, Slovenes, and Bulgarians was not only preferable to Ottoman rule but was also the Balkan states' right as an ethnic group. Rebellion raged in Bosnia in 1875 and spread to Bulgaria and other regions the following year.

Ottoman officials were especially harsh in repressing the Bulgarian revolt. For Russia, a major supporter of the Pan-Slavism movement, what became known as the Bulgarian Horrors was the last straw. After Serbia declared war on the Ottoman Empire on June 30, 1876, the Ottomans defeated a united Serbian front, but Russia then presented to the Ottoman sultan an ultimatum for peace. In addition to Russia's involvement, Great Britain was threatening to fight the Ottomans in protection of Balkan Christians, though it simultaneously stated its intention to honor earlier alliances with the Ottomans against the Russians.

These conflicts necessitated a conference, and the Great Powers met in Istanbul to discuss peace between Serbia and the Ottomans. The sultan would not agree to Russian terms, however, and the conference fell apart. The Serbians then signed an independent peace with the Ottoman Empire that preserved the status quo.

Following the peace in late 1876, Russia declared war against the Turks in 1877. The Ottomans, although weakened by their suppression of the recent revolts, put up a strong fight but eventually succumbed. That war culminated in the Congress of Berlin in 1878. Through that settlement, the European powers recognized Serbia, Montenegro, Romania, and part of Bulgaria as independent states. The settlement also gave other areas of the Ottoman Empire to various countries for control and administration. The Ottoman Empire was not dismantled, yet its significant territorial losses left it a shadow of its former self.

STACY KOWTKO

### See also
Montenegrin-Ottoman Wars; Russo-Ottoman Wars

**References**

Cox, John K. *The History of Serbia*. Westport, CT: Greenwood, 2002.

Jelavich, Barbara. *History of the Balkans: Eighteenth and Nineteenth Centuries*. New York: Cambridge University Press, 1983.

# Settlements, Israeli

Four issues dominate the Israeli-Palestinian conflict as the most difficult to resolve if a peace settlement is to be achieved. These are the status of Jerusalem, Palestinian refugees (and their right of return), borders, and settlements. Although the term "settlement" is used broadly within Israel to describe residential communities and neighborhoods settled by Jewish pioneers, the term is more specifically used to describe residential communities built in the areas occupied by Israel after the June 1967 Six-Day War.

Jewish settlements are located in the West Bank and the Golan Heights, areas that are widely considered by the international community and the United Nations as territory belonging to a future Palestinian state. East Jerusalem is a separate issue, because unlike the other two areas it was annexed by Israel following the 1967 war, thereby bringing the entire city under Israeli control. Israel has not, however, annexed the West Bank, part of which remains under military law and controlled by the Israeli military.

In September 2016 there were 126 Israeli settlements in the West Bank (excluding East Jerusalem) with a population of some 420,000 settlers. Territorially, they are spread across the West Bank. The 1993 Oslo Accords divided the West Bank into three areas: A, B, and C. Most of the settlements are in Area C, which constitutes some 60 percent of the area of the West Bank and is entirely under Israeli control. Area B, with some 20 percent of the West Bank area, is under the joint control of Israel and the Palestinian Authority. Area A, also with about 20 percent, is under the full control of the Palestinian Authority.

Most settlers live in settlement blocs, those areas with a high number of Jewish settlements. The three main blocs are Ariel in the north, Ma'ale Adumim near Jerusalem, and Gush Etzion in the southern West Bank. Other settlements lie apart from these blocs. The settlers are motivated for a wide range of reasons. Religious and nationalist Jews (and many evangelical Christians in the United States) believe that the West Bank is part of historic Israel, territory promised the Jews in the Old Testament and containing a number of sites holy to them. Many other Jews are attracted to the settlements for financial reasons, as the settlements are subsidized by the government. Quality of life and ease of access to work are motivations for many others.

Outposts differ from settlements and are illegally built settlements, many of which have been ordered razed by the Israeli courts. Peace Now, a left-wing organization that tracks settlement growth, lists 97 Israeli outposts in the West Bank.

The settlements are controversial because although a number might end up as part of Israel in a two-state solution, a great many others would be in territory belonging to a Palestinian state. As settlement construction expands, it renders a two-state solution increasingly difficult and indeed at some point impossible. Thus, a string of east-west Jewish settlements in the northern West Bank threatens to separate the West Bank into northern and southern segments. This in itself might end the possibility of a two-state solution. Palestinians have long claimed, with considerable justification, that the growth of settlement construction is a way for Israel to seize control of the land in a way that would be almost impossible to undo. For this reason, Palestinians have demanded a freeze in settlement construction before negotiations can resume. Right-wing prime minister Benjamin Netanyahu, who said publicly that he opposes a two-state solution but then reversed this, claims that settlement expansion is a function of natural growth within existing settlements and that the refusal of the Palestinians to accept Israel as a Jewish state within any borders is the chief obstacle to peace.

The settlements are in fact illegal under international law. The Fourth Geneva Convention, which concerns civilian populations during a time of war, states in Article 49 that "The Occupying Power shall not deport or transfer parts of its own civilian population into the territory it occupies." In 2012, Netanyahu's government published the Levy Commission Report rejecting the applicability of the Fourth Geneva Convention to the West Bank. The report held that the West Bank was never a legitimate part of any Arab state. Regardless, United Nations Security Council resolution 2334 of December 2016, which the United States did not veto, reaffirms the Fourth Geneva Convention position. The resolution states that settlements have "no legal validity" and indeed are "a flagrant violation under international law."

East Jerusalem is a special problem, as both Israel and the Palestinians claim the city as the capital of their state. From 1948 to 1967 Jerusalem was divided by the Green Line, the cease-fire line of 1948 between Israel and Jordan. Although the city is now under Israeli governance, the distinction remains. Under international law, settlements in East Jerusalem are no different than settlements in the West Bank. In late June 1967, Israel expanded the boundaries of West Jerusalem to include East Jerusalem, applying Israeli law to the entire city and declaring a unified Jerusalem as the capital of Israel. No other country recognizes this annexation, but there are 200,000 Jews along with 300,000 Palestinians living in East Jerusalem.

The Golan Heights is also considered occupied territory. It was taken by Israel from Syria in the Six-Day War of 1967. Unlike the West Bank, Israel has applied Israeli law to the Golan, effectively annexing it, an action not recognized by the international community.

Israel has, however, withdrawn some settlements in the past. During 1982–1989 it withdrew settlements in the Sinai as part of the 1979 peace deal with Egypt and in 2005 did the same in the Gaza Strip and in some areas of the northern West Bank.

In April 2017 after new U.S. president Donald Trump took office, Netanyahu's government announced a sharp increase in planned settlement construction with plans to build 25,000 new housing units, 15,000 of which would be in East Jerusalem. Under previous U.S. administrations, the State Department routinely and strongly criticized such plans. Indeed, Israeli-U.S. relations under Trump's predecessor, President Barack Obama, sharply deteriorated to an all-time low largely on the settlements issue. Initially the Trump administration was mostly silent on the issue, but Trump eventually claimed that continued Israeli settlement construction was "unhelpful," indicating that his administration would neither strongly oppose nor encourage such activity. However, in the spring and summer of 2018, Washington declined to specifically condemn Israel's announcement that it would be building more than 2,000 new settler homes in the West Bank.

Spencer C. Tucker

**See also**
Gaza Strip; Golan Heights; Israeli Security Fence; Netanyahu, Benjamin; Oslo Accords; Palestine Liberation Organization; Six-Day War; West Bank

**References**
Efrat, Elisha. *The West Bank and Gaza Strip: A Geography of Occupation and Disengagement.* New York: Routledge, 2006.
Gorenberg, Gershom. *The Accidental Empire: Israel and the Birth of the Settlements, 1967–1977.* New York: Times Books, 2006.
Lein, Yehezkel. *Land Grab: Israel's Settlement Policy in the West Bank.* Jerusalem: B'Tselem, 2002.

# 73 Easting, Battle of (February 26, 1991)

During Operation desert storm, the ground portion of the Persian Gulf War, the U.S. VII and VIII Corps undertook a left hook into the western Iraqi desert in which they skirted the western limit of Iraqi frontier defenses, the so-called Saddam Line. Both corps then made a great right turn with the intention of cutting off Iraqi forces remaining in Kuwait. On February 26 Lieutenant General Frederick M. Franks Jr.'s VII Corps came into contact with Iraqi major general Salah Aboud Mahmoud's Republican Guard Tawakalnah Division.

The Iraqis had been hastily redeployed to take up improvised defensive positions along the western side of the Wadi al-Batin that marked the Kuwaiti-Iraqi border. They hoped to delay the VII Corps long enough to allow their forces in Kuwait to escape. The Battle of Wadi al-Batin refers to the VII Corps' attack on the Tawakalnah Division, while the Battle of 73 Easting was a part of the larger overall Battle of Wadi al-Batin. "73 Easting" is simply a Global Positioning System (GPS) coordinate. The battle is notable as one of the few engagements during the war in which an outnumbered American force faced a larger Iraqi force in a stationary defensive position.

The main American force involved in the battle was the 2nd Armored Cavalry Regiment (2nd ACR), commanded by Colonel Don Holder. It consisted of eight troops, each of about 120 soldiers in 20–30 armored vehicles. Three troops of the 2nd ACR were most involved in the 73 Easting actions. Eagle Troop, commanded by Captain Herbert R. McMaster, took the lead and did most of the fighting, followed by Ghost Troop and Iron Troop.

Eagle Troop was acting as a reconnaissance unit for the VII Corps when it encountered the 18th Brigade of the Tawakalnah Division late in the afternoon of February 26. The Iraqis had deployed T-72M1 tanks supported by BMP infantry fighting vehicles, while the Americans had M1A1 Abrams tanks and M4 Bradley armored fighting vehicles. Weather conditions at the time were poor, with a heavy storm limiting visibility and preventing the Americans from calling in air strikes. However, the Abrams tanks and Bradleys had the advantage of thermal sights, and the Abrams' main gun far outranged that of the T-72. American tanks could also fire on the move, and the Iraqis could not.

Eagle Troop found itself in a seam between the Iraqi 18th Brigade and the adjacent Iraqi 12th Armored Division. Surprised, the Iraqis quickly opened fire. U.S. Army normal procedure called for the reconnaissance units to wait for heavier supporting units to catch up, but Iraqi fire was so intense that McMaster had no choice but to engage. At the start of the fighting, Eagle Troop numbered only 9 Abrams tanks and 12 Bradleys.

The tank-on-tank battle was over quickly, with 37 T-72s and 32 other vehicles destroyed in just 40 minutes. Ghost and Iron Troops moved up to join in the battle. However, Iraqi resistance at 73 Easting proved to be unexpectedly determined, as they maneuvered their tanks in an attempt to outflank the American tanks rather than remaining in stationary defensive positions as was their normal operating procedure.

Iraqi troops typically surrendered or broke and fled when their tanks were knocked out, but the infantry of the Tawakalnah Division continued to resist, employing rocket-propelled grenades. Ghost Troop was heavily counterattacked after nightfall and had to call in an artillery bombardment that included 2,000 howitzer rounds and 12 rockets. Iraqi opposition finally ended some six hours after the battle first began.

The U.S. 1st Infantry Division arrived later that night to pass through the battle scene and continue the U.S. advance. American losses in the battle were minimal, with the Iraqis destroying only one Bradley. A second Bradley was hit by friendly fire. Despite the ferocity of their resistance, the Iraqis proved ultimately ineffective in countering the American advance. Altogether, the Iraqis lost 113 armored vehicles and suffered some 600 casualties.

The first defeat for the Iraqi Republican Guard in the war, the Battle of 73 Easting allowed the 1st Infantry Division to move into the heart of the Iraqi defenses and then on into Kuwait. In seeking to explain how three troops of an armored cavalry regiment could destroy an entire Iraqi brigade, commentators have stressed superior U.S. equipment and training.

Paul William Doerr

**See also**
Persian Gulf War, Overview; Republican Guard, Iraq; Wadi al-Batin, Battle of

**References**
Gordon, Michael R., and Bernard E. Trainor. *The General's War: The Inside Story of the Conflict in the Gulf.* New York: Little, Brown, 1995.
Macgregor, Douglas. *Warrior's Rage: The Great Tank Battle of 73 Easting.* Annapolis, MD: Naval Institute Press, 2012.
Pollack, Kenneth M. *Arabs at War: Military Effectiveness, 1948–1991.* Lincoln: University of Nebraska Press, 2002.
Scales, Robert. *Certain Victory: The U.S. Army in the Gulf War.* Washington, DC: Brassey's, 1994.

## Severus Alexander
*See* Alexander Severus, Roman Emperor

## Sèvres, Treaty of (August 10, 1920)

Peace treaty between 13 Allied Powers (most notably France, Great Britain, and Italy) and the Ottoman Empire signed on August 10 1920, in an exhibition room at the Manufacture nationale de Sèvres porcelain factory in Sèvres, France. The treaty marked the beginning of the dissolution of the Ottoman Empire.

Although the Armistice of Mudros had ended World War I hostilities with the Ottoman Empire in October 1918, the Treaty of Sèvres took another 20 months to conclude. As with many other treaties that ended the war, its terms were presented by the winners to the losers without negotiation. Unlike many other treaties, few of its terms were ever implemented. In 1923 the Treaty of Lausanne superseded most of the terms of the Treaty of Sèvres. It was thus the shortest lived of the treaties ending World War I.

Although the Allies (specifically France and Great Britain) did not envision the destruction of the Ottoman Empire in 1914, the Treaty of Sèvres confirmed what had become an established fact. Sultan Mehmed VI remained in power, but the treaty provisions made him a virtual prisoner to the interests of the victorious nations. Consistent with realities on the ground, Sèvres removed all predominantly Arabic-speaking regions from Turkish control. The region of the Hejaz (in what is now Saudi Arabia) became an independent kingdom and was named a signatory to the treaty.

The creation of an Arabian state notwithstanding, the treaty denied independence to much of the Middle East, which passed under French and British control as mandates under the aegis of the League of Nations. While nominally free of foreign rule, Arabia was in reality under British suzerainty. Palestine and Mesopotamia were to be British mandates, while Syria and Lebanon became French mandates. The mandates were supposed to lead to eventual independence under the supervision of the League of Nations. The United States, displeased at what it saw as the furtherance of European imperialism in the region and never itself at war with the Ottoman Empire, declined to participate in the treaty negotiations. Nevertheless, U.S. president Woodrow Wilson secured the right to determine the borders of the new state of Armenia.

The treaty was an immediate disappointment to Arab leaders. The British had made grandiose promises of independence during the war to Arab leaders such as Sharif Hussein of the Hejaz. In return for staging rebellions in the Arab parts of the Ottoman Empire, the British had pledged to Hussein and other Arab leaders that they would support the creation of independent Arab states.

The Treaty of Sèvres fell far short of those guarantees. Instead, it upheld the secret Sykes-Picot Agreement of 1916 wherein Britain and France agreed to divide former Ottoman territories among themselves, although the treaty added the cloak of the mandate system. The treaty also reaffirmed the Balfour Declaration of 1917 in which Great Britain stated that it viewed with favor the creation of a Jewish homeland in Palestine. Nevertheless, the Great Powers took no definitive steps in that direction.

The treaty did not deal with the humiliations of the Capitulations, which granted special rights and had been solidified between the states of Western Europe and the Ottoman Empire since the 16th century. These involved unequal trade terms between the Great Powers and the Ottoman Empire and granted the right of extraterritoriality to foreign nationals. Under the terms of the Treaty of Sèvres, the Capitulations were effectively continued.

In addition, the treaty made the Bosporus and the Dardanelles an international waterway. This provision was mostly intended to prevent the Russian Bolshevik regime from claiming ownership of the straits. Armenia, the scene of an appalling genocide during the war, was made independent, and Kurdistan received significant autonomy. Great Britain landed a force under General George Milne to guarantee the neutrality of the straits and ensure control of Constantinople.

The real humiliation for the Ottomans lay in the settlement of the Ottoman European and Anatolian boundaries. Greece acquired all of European Ottoman territory except for the immediate area around Istanbul (Constantinople), which now came under international control. The Greeks were also awarded the city of Smyrna (Izmir), several Aegean islands, and large parts of western Anatolia. These areas were to remain under Greek control for five years, after which the Greeks were to conduct a plebiscite. Britain and France presumed that this vote would result in the annexation of these areas to the Kingdom of Greece. Finally, Ottoman finances were placed not in its hands of but rather under the supervision of British, French, and Italian financiers.

The principal architect of the treaty, British prime minister David Lloyd George, regarded it as the triumph of Romantic Hellenism and Christendom. He seems to have immediately recognized, however, that Great Britain could not enforce these terms. The Greeks were already showing an appetite for more of Anatolia than the treaty permitted, and Britain was facing intense domestic pressures to demobilize.

Most importantly, Turkish nationalists were showing determination to resist many of the terms laid out in the treaty. Brilliantly led by Mustafa Kemal (Ataturk), hero of the Gallipoli Campaign, the nationalists planned to overturn Sèvres. Most nationalists understood that reviving the Ottoman Empire and recapturing the lost Arab lands could not and should not be accomplished. They bristled, however, at any ethnically Turkic lands falling under foreign control. Kemal set out to regain all Anatolian and Armenian lands for Turkey.

Only Greece decided to meet Kemal with military force. The Greeks had 150,000 troops in Turkey, and Greek premier Eleuthérios Venizélos was determined to use them to crush Kemal's nationalists. Kemal, however, carried out a brilliant military campaign in the Greco-Turkish War of 1920–1922. His forces recaptured Smyrna and its hinterland, then turned north to move on Istanbul (Constantinople). The Italians, who had come to view Greece as a more immediate rival than Turkey, agreed to withdraw their occupation troops after a defeat at Kemal's hands in central Anatolia. The Italian decision led the British and French also to quit Turkey. Within only two years the Treaty of Sèvres had been superseded by the Second Treaty of Lausanne, signed on July 24, 1923.

MICHAEL S. NEIBERG

**See also**
Arab Revolt in Palestine; Armenians and the Armenian Genocide; Ataturk, Mustafa Kemal; Balfour Declaration; Gallipoli Campaign; Hussein ibn Ali ibn Mohammed; Lausanne, Second Treaty of; Mandates, League of Nations; Ottoman Empire; Ottoman Empire, Post–World War I Revolution in; Sykes-Picot Agreement

**References**
Fromkin, David. *A Peace to End All Peace: The Fall of the Ottoman Empire and the Creation of the Modern Middle East.* New York: Holt, 1989.
Helmreich, Paul. *From Paris to Sèvres: The Partition of the Ottoman Empire at the Peace Conference of 1919–1920.* Columbus: Ohio State University Press, 1974.
Macfie, A. L. *The End of the Ottoman Empire, 1918–1923.* London: Longman, 1998.
MacMillan, Margaret. *Paris, 1919: Six Months That Changed the World.* New York: Random House, 2002.
McCarthy, Justin. *The Ottoman Peoples and the End of Empire.* London: Hodde Arnold, 2001.

## Shakur, Yusuf bin Raghib (1928–)

Syrian general and commander of Syrian armed forces against Israel in the Yom Kippur War of October 1973. Yusuf bin Raghib Shakur was born in 1928 near Homs, Syria. Upon graduation from secondary school he attended the Military Academy in Homs. He then took an advanced course in artillery at Châlons-sur-Marne, France, in 1949 and also pursued higher military studies in the Soviet Union.

A gifted linguist, Shakur is fluent in Arabic, French, English, Spanish, Russian, and Armenian. These language skills brought him diplomatic assignments, and he served as Syrian consul general to Venezuela and Brazil during 1961–1964.

Following his return to Syria, Shakur became the director of security forces. He was promoted to colonel and then to brigadier general before the Six-Day War with Israel in 1967, in which he saw action. He was promoted to major general in 1970 not only for his military accomplishments but also for his loyalty to Hafez al-Assad, who assumed power in Syria that year. In April 1972 following the appointment of Mustafa Tlas as minister of defense, Shakur was moved into his former post as chief of staff of the Syrian armed forces.

In his new position Shakur was closely involved in planning for war with Israel in 1973. The idea for a joint Egyptian-Syrian invasion of Israel originated with Egyptian president Anwar Sadat, and Shakur participated in a final review of the plans with his Egyptian counterparts in Alexandria in the summer of 1973. Among the chief concerns were how to deceive the United States and Israel into believing that the massing of Syrian forces along Israel's northern and southern borders was simply in connection with routine autumn maneuvers.

The beginning of the Yom Kippur War on October 6, 1967, caught Israel completely off guard. Shakur committed substantial resources to exploit the initial Syrian success achieved in the Golan Heights, the primary territory that Syria hoped to recover from Israel in the war. Although Syrian forces fought hard and well, Shakur's commanders often failed to exercise initiative in what was a developing situation. Hoping for a knock-out punch, Shakur committed too much of his available armor too soon in unfavorable territory and thus lacked the resources to meet the inevitable Israeli counterattack.

Shakur and the remainder of the Syrian high command were also not aware that their Egyptian allies had different goals for the war. The strategy of a simultaneous invasion from north and south had been designed to split the Israel Defense Force (IDF), but Egypt had limited goals. Sadat merely hoped to provoke new peace negotiations. Syria, however, sought an all-out military victory. This divergence in strategies enabled the Israelis to concentrate their attention on the Syrian forces in the Golan Heights and prevent a Syrian breakthrough there.

On October 8 the Israelis halted the Syrian drive in the Golan Heights and began counterattacking. Under this Israeli pressure Shakur authorized a Syrian withdrawal, which was initially accomplished in good order. A subsequent all-out Israeli push, however, reached almost to Damascus and was halted only by the injection of Iraqi and Jordanian armor units and the cease-fire accepted by Syria on October 22.

Assad made Shakur one of the scapegoats for the Syrian military failure in the war. In the reshuffling that followed the conflict, Shakur was forced into retirement in August 1974.

Spencer C. Tucker

### See also
Assad, Hafez al-; Sadat, Anwar; Syria; Yom Kippur War

### References
Herzog, Chaim. *The War of Atonement: October, 1973*. Boston: Little, Brown, 1975.
Pollack, Kenneth M. *Arabs at War: Military Effectiveness, 1948–1991*. Lincoln: University of Nebraska Press, 2002.
Rubin, Barry, and Thomas A. Keaney, eds. *Armed Forces in the Middle East: Politics and Strategy*. Portland, OR: Frank Cass, 2002.
Seale, Patrick. *Assad of Syria: The Struggle for the Middle East*. Berkeley: University of California Press, 1988.

## Shallah, Ramadan Abdullah Mohammad (1958–)

Leader of the Palestinian Islamic Jihad (PIJ). Born in Sajaya in the Gaza Strip on January 1, 1958, Ramadan Abdullah Mohammad Shallah studied at Zagaziq University in Egypt, where he became friends with Fathi Shiqaqi, the founder of Islamic Jihad of Palestine. Returning to Gaza, Shallah worked for a time at Al-Azhar University. He established Islamic Jihad in the West Bank.

Shallah returned to Egypt in 1984 and then went on to the United States, where he studied political science and economics. He then settled in Britain, where he earned a doctorate in banking and economics from the University of Durham. He also helped coordinate activities of Islamic Jihad in Europe. In 1991 he moved to the United States, becoming director of the World and Islam Studies

Enterprise in Tampa, Florida; publishing a journal, *Qira'at Siyasiya* (Political Readings); and teaching as an adjunct professor at the University of Florida. Following the assassination of Shiqaqi by Mossad, the Israeli intelligence service, Shallah was selected in October 1995 to succeed him as head of Islamic Jihad.

On November 27, 1995, the U.S. government listed Shallad as a "Specially Designated Terrorist." A federal district court in Florida indicted both Shallah and fellow PIJ member Abd Al Aziz Awda on Racketeer Influenced and Corrupt Organizations Act charges of alleged involvement in racketeering activities to include bombings, murders, extortion, and money laundering to support PIJ activities. This caused both men to be added to the U.S. Federal Bureau of Investigation Most Wanted Terrorists list in February 2006.

In March 2014 Shallah, who resides in Damascus, Syria, claimed that the PIJ and Hamas were responsible for launching more than 100 rockets into southern Israel.

SPENCER C. TUCKER

**See also**
Fatah, al-; Palestinian Islamic Jihad; Shiqaqi, Fathi

**References**
Abu-Amr, Ziad. *Islamic Fundamentalism in the West Bank and Gaza: Muslim Brotherhood and Islamic Jihad.* Bloomington: Indiana University Press, 1994.

Hatina, Meir. *Islam and Salvation in Palestine: The Islamic Jihad Movement.* Syracuse, NY: Syracuse University Press, 2001.

# Shamir, Yitzhak (1915–2012)

Israeli politician and prime minister (1983–1984, 1986–1992). Yitzhak Shamir was born Yitzhak Jaziernicki on October 15, 1915, in Ruzinoy, Poland (now in Belarus). While a young man, he joined the Polish Betar Zionist youth movement. He studied law in Warsaw but then left Poland for the British Mandate for Palestine in 1935, where he ultimately enrolled in Jerusalem's Hebrew University.

That same year, 1935, Jaziernicki formally changed his name to Shamir. He then joined the Irgun Tsvai Leumi (National Military Organization), a right-wing paramilitary Zionist underground movement. Irgun was known for its immediate and harsh retaliation for Arab attacks on the Jewish community in Palestine and its advocacy of military action against the British mandatory government.

When Irgun split into right-wing and left-wing factions in 1940, Shamir affiliated himself with the more militant Lohamei Herut Israel (Israel Freedom Fighters), classified by the British as a terrorist organization and later known as the Stern Gang (after its founder, Avraham Stern). Shamir was arrested by the British in 1941 and escaped from their custody in 1943 following the death of Stern in 1942. Shamir became one of the organization's leaders who reformed it and renamed it Lehi. It was under Shamir's leadership that in 1944 Lehi assassinated Walter Edward Guinness, Lord Moyne, heir to the Guinness fortune and British minister resident in the Middle East.

Shamir served as Lehi's principal director of operations until he again was arrested by the British in 1946 and exiled to a prison camp in Eritrea. Shamir escaped in 1947 to the neighboring French colony of Djibouti and, although granted political asylum by France, returned to Israel in 1948 to command Lehi until it was disbanded in 1949. Shamir directed the 1948 assassination of Count Folke Bernadotte, the United Nations (UN) representative in the Middle East, whom Shamir and his collaborators saw as anti-Zionist and in league with the British.

Shamir served as a Mossad (Israeli intelligence service) operative from 1955 to 1965 and then engaged in business until he joined Menachem Begin's Herut movement (which became the Likud Party) in 1973. Shamir was elected to the Knesset (Israeli parliament) that same year and in 1975 became Herut's chairman. Likud's victory in the national elections in May 1977 saw Begin become Israel's first non-Labor prime minister and Shamir become Speaker of the Knesset. Begin immediately challenged King Hussein of Jordan, President Hafez al-Assad of Syria, and President Anwar Sadat of Egypt to meet to negotiate a peace treaty. Sadat subsequently agreed to the Camp David Accords and the Israel-Egypt Peace Treaty that extended full Egyptian diplomatic recognition to Israel in exchange for the return of the Sinai Peninsula, which Israel had seized in the Six Day War in 1967. Shamir presided over the ratification of the treaty in the Knesset.

Following the resignation of Moshe Dayan, Shamir served as Israel's foreign minister during 1980–1983. In that capacity he oversaw the posttreaty normalization process with Egypt, reestablished diplomatic contacts with African countries severed during the Yom Kippur War in 1973, and negotiated a peace agreement for Galilee with Lebanon. This latter was later revoked by the Lebanese under Syrian pressure soon after Begin's resignation as prime minister in October 1983.

Shamir succeeded Begin as both the leader of Likud and prime minister. Shamir's inability to decrease the inflation racking Israel's economy led to an indecisive national election in July 1984 and the formation of a government of national unity that allied Likud with the Labor Party headed by Shimon Peres. Peres served as prime minister with Shamir as vice premier until October 1986, when the two rotated positions and Shamir again became prime minister. While serving in these capacities, Shamir and Defense Minister Moshe Arens collaborated with U.S. president Ronald Reagan and Defense Secretary Caspar Weinberger to advance U.S.-Israeli strategic cooperation and free trade.

Following another indecisive election in 1988, Likud and Labor formed a new coalition government that retained Shamir as prime minister but did not have the rotation arrangement of its predecessor agreement. When this coalition government failed in 1990, Shamir formed a new government that included members of some ultraconservative parties and excluded Labor.

In 1991 Shamir's government ordered the rescue of thousands of Ethiopian Jews in Operation SOLOMON. At Washington's urging, Shamir did not retaliate in 1991 for unprovoked Iraqi Scud missile attacks during the Persian Gulf War that were designed to bring Israel into the conflict and break up the allied coalition. In September 1991 Shamir's government participated in the Madrid Peace Conference, which led to the 1993 peace accords between Israel and the Palestine Liberation Organization that began Israel's withdrawal from the West Bank and the Gaza Strip.

Shamir's premiership ended in 1992 with the defeat of Likud in general elections. He resigned from the leadership of Likud in March 1993, although he retained his seat in the Knesset until 1996. Shamir died in Tel Aviv on June 30, 2012.

RICHARD M. EDWARDS

### See also
Begin, Menachem; Camp David Accords; Irgun Tsvai Leumi; Israel-Egypt Peace Treaty; Lohamei Herut Israel; Madrid Conference; Persian Gulf War, Overview

### References
Brinkley, Joel. *The Stubborn Strength of Yitzhak Shamir*. New York: New York Times, 1988.
Enderlin, Charles. *Shamir*. Paris: O. Orban, 1991.
Shamir, Yitzhak. *Summing Up: An Autobiography*. London: Orion, 1994.

## Shapur I the Great (ca. 215–270)

The second monarch of the Persian Sassanian dynasty (224–651) who ruled from 240 to 270. Born around 215, possibly in Gor, Shapur was the son of Ardashir I (r. 224–240), the founder of the Sassanian state. Ardashir had defeated and killed Artabanus IV, the last king of the Parthian Arsacid dynasty, on the battlefield in 224.

Shapur was chosen by his father as coruler in either 239 or 240, and after Ardashir I died, Shapur assumed sole rule of the vast Sassanian Empire, which by then stretched from Central Asia to Syria. The first years of Shapur's reign were spent on consolidating his rule and suppressing internal rebellions against the Sassanian central government. Once he had completed these, Shapur shifted his focus to the west and the threat posed by the Roman Empire.

Ardashir I had already adopted an offensive posture toward the Romans by invading and occupying several key urban centers in Mesopotamia. Before Ardashir's death, Emperor Gordian III (r. 238–244) organized a large army to retake the territory lost in Mesopotamia. In 243, Gordian succeeded in reestablishing Roman rule over Antioch, Nisibis (modern-day Nusaybin), and Carrhae (modern-day Harran), both in present-day southeastern Turkey. He then moved south toward Ctesiphon, the Sassanian capital located in modern-day southern Iraq.

Battle was joined between the two sides at Misiche or Massice in Mesopotamia in 244, and the Sassanians emerged victorious. The Romans were forced to withdraw, and Emperor Gordian was either killed on the battlefield or murdered by his own officers shortly after the battle. Gordian was succeeded by Marcus Julius Philippus (commonly known by his sobriquet of Philip the Arab), who ruled during 244–249. Philip the Arab concluded a peace treaty with Shapur I whereby Philip ceded Armenia and Mesopotamia. He also agreed to pay a large indemnity of 500,000 gold dinarii to the Persian king. After this victory, Misiche was renamed Peroz Shapur (Shapur Victorious).

Hostilities between the two empires resumed, however, when the Romans reneged on the peace treaty and intervened in Armenia. In 256, the Sassanians defeated a 60,000-man Roman army at Barbalissos in northern Syria. This opened the eastern portion of the Roman Empire to attack and led to the Sassanian capture of Antioch, followed by Dura Europos on the right bank of the Euphrates River in eastern Syria. Shapur I ravaged Syria before returning home.

Humiliated by the defeats they had suffered at the hands of Shapur and determined to recapture the territory they had lost, the Romans attacked again during the reign of Roman emperor Valerian (r. 253–260) with a force of 70,000 men. After seizing Edessa (modern-day Sanliurfa in southeastern Turkey), Shapur led the Sassanian army against the Romans. Many of the Roman soldiers died of the plague, and

Relief depicting Shapur I, Persian ruler during 240–270. He defeated Roman forces under the emperors Gordian III and Valerian, taking the latter prisoner, and was recognized as Shapur the Great. (Steve Estvanik/Dreamstime.com)

in 260 Valerian became the first Roman emperor to become the prisoner of a foreign power when he was taken prisoner, along with a number of Roman commanders, senators, and engineers, during negotiations with Shapur. The disintegration of the Roman army allowed Shapur to attack and devastate Syria, northern Mesopotamia, and Asia Minor. The Sassanians raided and plundered the major urban centers of the region, including Antioch, Edessa, Konya, and Caesarea. The Sassanians were, however, surprised when the ruler of the important commercial city of Palmyra, who had remained loyal to the Romans, attacked the Persian forces and captured Nisibis.

It is generally believed that many Romans captured by Shapur were sent to Fars in southern Iran, where they were employed in the construction of the city of Bishapur. Valerian never saw Rome again and died in captivity. Three rock reliefs at Bishapur celebrate Shapur's victories over the Romans.

During Shapur's reign, around 242 CE the Iranian prophet Mani visited the Sassanian court. Mani dedicated one of his books, *Shapurakan* (*The Book of Shapur*), to the Persian monarch. Shapur I granted Mani the right to preach his religion in the provinces of the Sassanian Empire. Some have suggested that Mani tried to convert Shapur to his religion but failed, although Manichaean sources claimed that the Iranian prophet did convert Mihrshah, a brother of Shapur, to the new religion. Shapur's decision to allow Mani to preach his religion without fear of persecution may indicate that the Zoroastrian priesthood did not enjoy sufficient power over the Sassanian dynasty to prevent competing religious doctrines and movements from carrying out their missionary activities within the empire.

Shapur I, recognized as Shapur the Great, died most probably in 270 and was succeeded by his son Hormozd Ardashir, who ascended the Sassanian throne as Hormozd I. Hormozd was not the oldest son of Shapur and had previously served as king of Armenia.

MEHRDAD KIA

### See also
Ardashir I; Gordian III, Emperor; Sassanid Empire; Valerian, Emperor

### References
Curtis, John. *Mesopotamia and Iran in the Parthian and Sasanian Periods.* London: British Museum Press, 2000.

Daryaee, Touraj. *Sasanian Iran (224–651 CE): Portrait of a Late Antique Empire*. Costa Mesa, CA: Mazda Publishers, 2008.
Frye, Richard Nelson. *The Heritage of Persia*. Cleveland, OH: World Publishing Company, 1963.
Frye, Richard Nelson. "The Political History of Iran under the Sasanians." In *The Cambridge History of Iran*, 3:116–180. Cambridge: Cambridge University Press, 1983.
Rawlinson, George. *The Seventh Great Oriental Monarchy or the Geography, History, and Antiquities of the Sassanians or New Persian Empire*. New York: Dodd, Mead, 1882.
Tabari. *The History of al-Tabarī*, Vol. 5, *The Sāsānids, the Byzantines, the Lakhmids, and Yemen*. Translated by C. E. Bosworth. Albany: State University of New York Press, 1999.
Tabari. *Tarikh-e Tabari*. Translated from Arabic into Persian by Abol Qassem Payandeh. Tehran: Asatir Pulications, 1984.

# Shapur II the Great (309–379)

Shapur II, also called Shapur the Great, was a ruler of the Persian Sassanid Empire. Born in 309, possibly in Firuzabad, Shapur was crowned king prior to his actual birth. Following the death of Shapur's father, Hormizd II, Persian nobles had killed his eldest son, blinded the second, and imprisoned the third, thereby reserving the throne for the unborn child of one of Hormizd's wives. The crown was placed on her belly, and Shapur was therefore born king. Little is known of Shapur's childhood or early adulthood, although his mother and magnates ran the government until his independent rule at age 16.

Following a raid by Arabs across the Persian Gulf from Bahrain that penetrated into the Persian interior, Shapur retaliated by conquering Bahrain and advancing into the Nejd, the central region of the Arabian Peninsula. Angered by the decision of Emperor Constantine I (r. 324–337) to make Christianity the state religion of Rome, Shapur made Zoroastrianism the state religion of Persia and began the persecution of Christians. Although Persia and Rome had been at peace for 40 years, Shapur attacked Rome's eastern territories in 337, commencing two prolonged wars (337–350 and 358–367). Shapur won most of the engagements in the field, including that of Singara (Sinjar, Iraq) against Emperor Constantius II (r. 337–361) in 344, but he was unable to take the fortified Roman cities, especially strategically important Nisibis in Mesopotamia, which under Roman general Lucilianus withstood sieges in 337, 344, and 349.

A series of destructive raids by the Scythians beginning in 349, most notably those led by Grumbates in the eastern part of Shapur's empire, forced Shapur to conclude a hasty truce with the Romans in 350 so he could deal with this new threat. Finally defeating Grumbates in Khorasan in 358, Shapur enlisted Grumbates and incorporated his highly effective Scythian light cavalry in his own army.

Shapur then returned to his campaign against the Romans. In 359 he besieged the important frontier city of Amida (modern-day Diyarbakir in southeastern Turkey). Although Shapur took Amida following a 73-day siege, it was at such great cost that he had to suspend operations until the next spring.

Shapur renewed operations in 360, taking other Roman fortified cities but bringing a Roman invasion by a large and well-equipped army under new emperor Julian (Julian the Apostate, r. 361–363) in 363. Accompanying Julian was the Persian prince Hormozd, whom the Romans expected to place on the throne after their anticipated victory over Shapur II. Julian split his forces in two. The main Roman army moved into southern Mesopotamia and attacked the Persian capital, Ctesiphon, near modern Baghdad in present-day Iraq. Another Roman army moved directly east to join forces with the Armenian king who was allied with the Romans. Though he defeated a small Persian force outside Ctesiphon on May 29, 363, Julian was unable to penetrate the strong Sassanian defenses of the capital city. As Shapur and the Persian army approached Ctesiphon, Julian and his officers burned the boats that had transported them to southern Mesopotamia and marched eastward to confront the Sassanian king in battle. Shapur avoided a set-piece battle and instead in the Battle of Samara mounted a surprise cavalry attack. In the ensuing fighting Julian received a mortal wound, dying three days later. He was succeeded by one of his generals, the inept Jovian (r. 363–364), who was forced to cede to Shapur Roman Mesopotamia, including the cities of Nisibis (modern-day Nusaybin, Turkey) and Singara in northern Iraq; give him a free hand in Armenia; and pay an enormous tribute.

Shapur then invaded Armenia, capturing by treachery its king, Arshak II, the ally of Rome. Shapur's efforts to force the conversion of the Christianized Armenians to Zoroastrianism brought fierce resistance, secretly supported by Rome. Learning of this, Shapur again declared war on Rome (373), but although he gradually gained a military advantage, he also realized that conquering all of Armenia was beyond his present means, and he concluded peace in 377. By the time of his death at Bishapur in 379, however, Shapur had secured not only Roman Macedonia but also the territory of present-day Afghanistan and Pakistan to the east. He removed the captured peoples from cities he had conquered, resettling them elsewhere in the Persian Empire.

This brought an infusion of Hellenic culture into the Sassanid Empire.

A strong and effective ruler and a capable general, Shapur II greatly expanded the territorial extent of the Persian Empire. He also brought his realm back into conflict with Rome, a step that would fatally weaken both empires.

SPENCER C. TUCKER

**See also**

Constantine I; Constantius II, Emperor; Julian, Emperor; Roman-Sassanid Wars; Sassanid Empire; Zoroastrianism

**References**

Daryaee, Touraj. *Sasanian Iran (224–651 BCE): Portrait of a Late Antique Empire.* Costa Mesa, CA: Mazda Publishers, 2008.

Fisher, William Bayne, et. al. *The Cambridge History of Iran.* Cambridge: Cambridge University Press, 1968.

Frye, Richard Nelson. *The Heritage of Persia.* Cleveland: World Publishing, 1963.

Frye, Richard N. *The History of Ancient Iran.* München, Germany: C. H. Beck, 1984.

Gagé, Jean. *La montée des Sassanides et l'heure de Palmyre.* Paris: A. Michel, 1964.

Huart, Clément. *Ancient Persia and Iranian Civilization.* New York: Barnes & Noble, 1972.

Rawlinson, George. *The Seventh Great Oriental Monarchy or the Geography, History, and Antiquities of the Sassanians or New Persian Empire.* New York: Dodd, Mead, 1882.

Sykes, Sir Percy. *A History of Persia.* 3rd ed. London: Macmillan, 1930.

# Sharia

Sharia, literally "the path leading to the watering place," is Islamic law as ordained by Allah. Systematized during the eighth and ninth centuries, sharia represents the legal and social modality of a people based on the revelation of Prophet Muhammad. Unlike canon law, sharia not only represents religious law but also covers a wide range of secular laws and ordinances, including military law. Sharia, however, was (and still is) subject to various interpretations, and during the course of the centuries four major schools—Maliki, Shafi'i, Hanbali, and Hanafi—have emerged within Sunni Islam, while Shia jurisprudence developed its own peculiar variations; this entry will deal with the sharia of Sunni Islam.

Under sharia, an Islamic state's principal goals were to carry out God's law and seek to establish Islam as the dominant world ideology. To achieve these goals, Muhammad's successors were willing to embark on prolonged conquests in the name of Islam, justifying such actions with the concept of *jihad*. Yet as the Muslim expansion grinded to a halt, the Muslim authorities had to adjust to the reality of Muslim and non-Muslim realms. As a result, the world was divided into two spheres: the dar al-Islam (abode of Islam), the area under Muslim rule and subject to Islamic law where Muslims enjoyed full rights of citizenship while non-Muslims were tolerated but granted only partial rights and subject to special rules, and the Dar al-Harb (abode of war), territory outside the world of Islam whose inhabitants were denoted as unbelievers. Since sharia called for Islam's worldwide dominion, the two abodes were in theory constantly at war with each other. Some Muslim jurists also made subdivisions within this division, adding dar al-Muwadaah or dar al-Sulh (abodes of truce) where the non-Muslim rulers have reached a truce with the Muslims, generally in return for the payment of tribute.

An Islamic state was under obligation to enforce sharia, recognize no authority but its own, and spread Islam. If non-Muslims refused to accept Islam or pay the *jizya* (poll tax), they would be subject to *jihad* (commonly described as holy war), which sought to transform the Dar al-Harb into the Dar al-islam. This legal responsibility to wage war was a product of the early Arab society and state that came about as a result of rapid expansion. Sharia condemned the pre-Islamic Arab practices (e.g., intertribal raids, vendettas, etc.) and prohibited all types of violence (whether directed against Muslims or non-Muslims), leaving jihad as the sole legal violence that, however, had to be directed against non-Muslims. Yet, jihad was not the only legal means of interacting with non-Muslims, and sharia recognized negotiation, arbitration, and treaty making as legitimate alternatives.

Although sharia prohibited all forms of violence and declared jihad as the sole legal war, Islamic history is full of conflicts between Muslim rulers or factions who, in theory, violated the doctrine. Muslim jurists often considered these conflicts as *harb* (secular) wars that were caused by man's sins, recklessness, and pride. The Quran specifies that "If two parties among the Believers fall into a quarrel, make ye peace between them: but if one of them transgresses beyond bounds against the other, then fight ye (all) against the one that transgresses until it complies with the command of Allah; but if it complies, then make peace between them with justice, and be fair: for Allah loves those who are fair (and just)" (49:9).

Muslim jurists have distinguished four different ways in which a believer can stay true to Allah: by his heart, his tongue, his hands, and the sword. The first type refers to the internal struggles that all people experience to remain true to the laws of God, and Prophet Muhammad himself considered it the most important type of jihad, often called greater jihad. The second and third types refer to a person's daily struggles to be good and honest, support the right, and battle the wrong. However, the fourth type, oftentimes called lesser jihad, implies the outer and often violent struggle in defense of the true religion of Islam.

Sharia declares that Islam cannot tolerate *shirk* (associating other gods with Allah) and mandates that all Muslim religious leaders ensure that no unbeliever denies Allah and his favors (*niam*). This concept was initially developed in an effort to combat polytheism and allowed exception for the *dhimmis* (e.g., Christians, Jews) who agreed to pay the poll tax. Although in theory jihad implied a state of permanent war between dar al-Islam and dar al-Harb, in reality Islamic states often made peace with non-Muslims, and Muslim jurists had to produce new interpretations of sharia to justify such suspensions of jihad. They thus agreed that when the Islamic state entered a period of decline, jihad had to be interrupted by a peace in which the jihad duty assumed a dormant status.

In its basic form, lesser jihad can be directed against non-Muslims or against Muslims who have reneged from Islam, espoused dissenting views, or threatened public order. The great Muslim jurist al-Mawardi, known as Alboacen in the West, distinguished between the "wars against polytheists and apostates" and "wars of public interest." In the first group, the most violent form of jihad is reserved for those who refuse to acknowledge Allah. They are denounced as pagans or idolaters and are subject to death. "Fight and slay the Pagans wherever ye find them, and seize them, beleaguer them, and lie in wait for them in every stratagem (of war)." (Quran, 9:5) "So when you meet in battle those who disbelieve, then smite the necks until you have overcome them" (Quran, 47:4). Muslim jurists argued that the *dhimmis* (often called the people of the book or scriptuaries), who believe in Allah but have distorted their scriptures, are subject to jihad but are only partially liable to punishment.

Thus, unlike "pagans," who have a choice of Islam or war, the dhimmis can also choose to pay a poll tax. Among other types of jihad, the *al-ridda*, or apostasy jihad, is directed against those Muslims who have reneged from Islam. Muslim jurists suggested first starting mediation to convince such apostates to return to Islam and, if they refused, to declare jihad that would be subject to the same rules as the war against dar al-harb. The same principles applied to *al-baghi*, the type of jihad directed against those Muslims who embrace unorthodox forms of Islam.

"Wars of public interest" included fighting belligerents, highway robbers, and deserters who harassed peaceful populations. "The punishment of those who wage war against Allah and His Messenger, and strive with might and main for mischief through the land is: execution, or crucifixion, or the cutting off of hands and feet from opposite sides, or exile from the land: that is their disgrace in this world, and a heavy punishment is theirs in the Hereafter" (Quran 5:33). Another type of war, the *ribat*, is based on the Quranic instruction to protect the frontiers of dar al-Islam and refers to military outposts set up along the frontiers of the Islamic realm. "Make ready your strength to the utmost of your power, including steeds of war, to strike terror into (the hearts of) the enemies, of Allah and your enemies, and others besides, whom ye may not know, but whom Allah doth know" (Quran 8:60).

Muslim jurists disagree whether this directive has a defensive character or not, with some *hadith* (prophetic tradition) specifying that jihad is offensive in character, since its goal is to combat the unbelievers, while the *ribat* is defensive, aiming at protecting the believers. The *ribat* was particularly significant in Spain, where the Muslims endured the centuries-long Reconquista conducted by the Christians; thus, medieval Muslim scholars, such as Ibn Hudhayl, argued that the *ribat* in Spain was the most indispensable duty of the believers.

Sharia recognizes jihad as a collective responsibility of the Muslim community, not an individual duty (*fard 'ayn*) such as the Five Pillars of Islam. As such, jihad is considered a state instrument and must be declared and conducted under specific rules outlined by sharia. Jihad cannot be launched by an individual—although if the dar al-Islam is attacked, jihad becomes the duty of every believer—and only an *imam* (ruler, head of state) had the responsibility of declaring it. Such a call could be made in a public speech, in a prayer, or in special communications that were issued in the name of the *amir al-muminin* (commander of the faithful). Yet jihad does not imply an immediate start of hostilities, since the Quran (17:16) requires a request to be made to the adversary to embrace Islam or pay the poll tax. Refusal to accept either offer would then provoke the fighting, although some Muslim jurists argued in favor of renewing an invitation before attacking. Once the invitation was issued, a Muslim leader could wait for a response for several days (usually three) during which he was allowed to negotiate with the enemy. During early Muslim conquests, this grace period oftentimes led to surrender and peaceful settlement in Iraq, Syria, and Egypt. This practice was also quite prevalent during the Christian crusades in the Holy Land.

Once an invitation to embrace Islam was rejected, however, sharia allowed the start of actual war, which, however, had to be conducted for the glory of Islam and not material aggrandizement or personal glory. Muslim jurists agreed that unnecessary destruction and excessive killing were prohibited but, as expected, disagreed on details. The jihadists in theory had the right to kill any *harbi* (resident of dar al-harb) who refused to accept Islam, provided the *harbi* was not killed perfidiously or with unnecessary cruelty. But the jurists agreed that noncombatants (women, children, monks, the elderly, and those who were physically or mentally disabled) could not be maltreated unless they directly participated in violence either by action or advice. The killing of craftsmen, wage earners, and farmers who did not do battle and those (e.g., merchants) who followed an army but did not participate in battle was prohibited as well. Jurist Malik ibn Anas prohibited the destruction of the flock and beehives, Muhammad ibn Idris ash-Shafii believed that all inanimate objects (including plants) had to be destroyed, and Abu Hanifa an-Numan argued that everything that the jihadist could not take had to be destroyed, thus authorizing the wholesale destruction of settlements.

Muslim armies were not allowed to start a war during the sacred months (*al-ashur al-haram*), although Quranic dictates conflicted in this respect. "They ask thee concerning fighting in the Prohibited Month. Say: 'Fighting therein is a grave (offence); but graver it is in the sight of Allah to prevent access to the path of Allah, to deny Him, to prevent access to the Sacred Mosque, and drive out its members'" (Quran 2:217). Some jurists prohibited Muslims from using some weapons, for example, poisoned arrows, although permitting poison or other materials to despoil enemy water supplies. If the defenders of the besieged city took Muslims captive, the Muslim army was advised to use limited means of violence, with some jurists even calling for complete cessation of assault. Abu Hanifa argued that Muslims could use siege machines and arrows against a besieged location even if they kill Muslims held captive there so long as their intention was to kill the *harbis*. Shafii, however, stated that catapults could be used against military installations but not toward inhabited houses. At the same time, Abu Hamid al-Ghazali believed that the killing of captive Muslims during a siege was justified on the basis of public interest (*istislah*).

During battle, sharia denied the Muslim combatant the right to kill his foe if the latter withdrew and ceased to fight. "If they withdraw from you but fight you not, and (instead) send you (guarantees of) peace, then Allah Hath opened no way for you (to war against them)" (Quran 4:90). However, an enemy can be killed in surprise through the use of agents, the spread of rumors to undermine morale, or ruses and stratagems.

Upon a Muslim victory, the Quran prohibited collective punishment of the defeated, proclaiming "that no bearer of burdens can bear the burden of another" (53:38). Nevertheless, the holy book also tolerates acts of vengeance and reciprocation of punishment: "as for those who have piled up evil deeds, the recompense of an evil deed is its like" (40:40) and "the recompense of any evil deed is an evil like it" (53:31). Once a siege or battle was finished, sharia prohibited mutilation of the bodies of dead *harbis* and called for their burial.

War traditionally produced plenty of spoils, and sharia regulated the process of acquiring, dividing, and maintaining them. Sharia distinguished between *ghanima* (property), *asra* (prisoners of war), and *sabi* (women and children) spoils that Muslims could obtain during war. Sharia made a distinction between property acquired by Muslims by force and property acquired by chance or occupied as a result of a peace settlement.

While Islam recognized the right of non-Muslims to ownership, taking property as spoils during war was considered just punishment because of the refusal of the defeated to embrace Islam. Nevertheless, the taking of property required an imam's permission, since it would otherwise be considered objectionable (*makruh*) and potentially theft. Muslim jurists agreed that only those who participated in battle could claim spoils, but some recommended that reinforcements, which were on the way to the battle or were prevented from participating by some extraordinary event, should also receive a share.

If a Muslim perished in battle, his share had to be given to his offspring. The division of spoils had to take place after the Muslim victory was complete and could be done on the battlefield or back at home, leaving the final decision in the hands of imams. Hanafi jurists, however, prohibited sharing spoils outside the dar al-Islam.

The Quran (8:41) specifies that "out of all the booty that ye may acquire [in war], a fifth share is assigned to Allah, and to the Messenger, and to near relatives, orphans, the needy, and the wayfarer." Thus, one-fifth of the spoils had to be given to the state, yet Islamic law schools were divided regarding how this share should be managed. Maliki jurists thought that the share should distributed evenly among the members of the Muslim community. Hanafi scholars argued that it should be divided into three parts for Prophet Muhammad and the caliph as his successor, the prophet's relatives, and the poor, orphans and wayfarers. The Hanbali school recommended dividing it into six parts for every group mentioned in the Quranic *ayat*. The remaining four-fifths of the booty was divided among the male participants of the battle, while any women and children present received either no share or smaller shares. Maliki, Shafi'i, and Hanbali jurists agreed that a cavalryman should receive three parts (two for the horse and one for the rider) and infantryman only one part. Exercising the power of *tanfil* (supererogation), an imam could grant additional shares (*nafal*) to certain participants, but the jurists disagreed on the amount that could be dispersed in such fashion. Prisoners of war (*asra*) oftentimes constituted a large proportion of the spoils and could be released on ransom payment (*fida*), exchanged for Muslim captives, made slaves, or executed. Sharia prohibited killing the *sabi* (women and children) but permitted their enslavement.

ALEXANDER MIKABERIDZE

**See also**
Dar al-Islam and Dar al-Harb; Quran; Sunni Islam

**References**
Firestone, Reuvan. *Jihād: The Origin of Holy War in Islam.* Oxford: Oxford University Press, 1999.
Haleem, Harfiyah Abdel. *The Crescent and the Cross: Muslim and Christian Approaches to War and Peace.* New York: Palgrave Macmillan, 1998.
Johnson, James Turner. *The Holy War Idea in Western and Islamic Traditions.* University Park: Penn State University Press, 1997.
Khadduri, Majid. *War and Peace in the Law of Islam.* Baltimore: Johns Hopkins University Press, 1955.

## Sharm El Sheikh

Egyptian coastal city on the Red Sea, now a major resort and tourist destination, located on the southern tip of the Sinai Peninsula. After the Israeli War of Independence (1948–1949) ended, the Egyptian government closed the Strait of Tiran to Israeli shipping. Because of the negative impact that the closure caused to the Israeli economy, the Israel Defense Force (IDF) had long planned for a military operation that would seize Sharm El Sheikh and reopen the straits. When the 1956 Suez Crisis began, the IDF's plan to cross the Sinai included an assault against the city. As the main attack smashed toward the Suez Canal in October 1956, the IDF's 9th Infantry Brigade attacked southward from Eilat toward Sharm El Sheikh, beginning on October 29.

Traversing difficult terrain and overcoming stiff Egyptian resistance along the west coast of the Gulf of Aqaba, the 9th Brigade reached the outskirts of the city on November 4. Meanwhile, the 202nd Parachute Brigade had been dropped on al-Tur, 40 miles west of Sharm El Sheikh, in support. The combined Israeli force began its attack on November 4. After the Egyptians repulsed a night attack, the Israelis broke through early on the morning of November 5. By 9:00 a.m. Sharm El Sheikh was in IDF hands, and an internationally negotiated truce began the next day.

Sharm El Sheikh remained under Israeli control until March 11, 1957, when the Israelis were promised that the straits would remain open under international law to all shipping. In order to monitor the Strait of Tiran, United Nations Emergency Forces (UNEF) were then stationed in Sharm El Sheikh.

Sharm El Sheikh remained under United Nations supervision until May 1967, when Egyptian president Gamal Abdel Nasser ordered all UNEF forces out of the Sinai, to include Sharm El Sheikh. When the Six-Day War began in June 1967, the IDF had planned for a combined naval-airborne attack to seize the city once more. With the stunning success of the overall Israeli war plan, IDF chief of staff Yitzhak Rabin moved up the attack against Sharm El Sheikh, afraid that an early cease-fire might prevent the IDF from taking that city. Meanwhile, the Egyptian garrison there had been ordered to retreat without a fight.

The Israelis cancelled a planned paratroop assault against al-Tur and dropped their airborne troops directly into Sharm El Sheik on June 7, 1967. With support from naval forces, the IDF took the city virtually without a fight, as most of the defenders had already been withdrawn. Israel immediately declared the Strait of Tiran open to international shipping.

During the 15 years of Israeli occupation of the Sinai Peninsula, the city was renamed Mifratz Shlomo. In 1982, three years after the initial Israel-Egypt Peace Treaty was signed, Israel returned Sharm El Sheikh to the Egyptians.

Known today for its vibrant tourism, upscale hotels and resorts, fishing, and deep-sea diving, Sharm El Sheikh has been the site of several diplomatic conferences. On September 4, 1999, the city hosted a joint peace conference that produced the Sharm El Sheikh Memorandum, which implemented parts of the interim agreements reached via the Oslo II agreement of September 1995 to include the Israeli transfer of portions of the West Bank to the Palestinian Authority (PA). Another summit held at Sharm El Sheikh on October 17, 2000, failed to stem the violence of the Second (al-Aqsa) Intifada. New terrorist cells have threatened Sinai tourism beginning with a series of bombings during 2004–2006, the first of which targeted Israeli tourists at Taba. Since around the summer of 2015, air flights to Sharm El Sheikh have been severely disrupted owing to the rise of the Islamist militant group ISIS (the Islamic State of Iraq and Syria).

THOMAS D. VEVE

**See also**
Geography of the Middle East; Islamic State of Iraq and Syria; Israel-Egypt Peace Treaty; Nasser, Gamal Abdel; Red Sea; Sinai Campaign of 1956; Six-Day War; Strait of Tiran Crisis; Suez Crisis

**References**
Herzog, Chaim. *The Arab-Israeli Wars: War and Peace in the Middle East from the War of Independence to Lebanon.* Westminster, MD: Random House, 1984.
Oren, Michael B. *Six Days of War: June 1967 and the Making of the Modern Middle East.* Novato, CA: Presidio, 2003.

## Sharon, Ariel (1928–2014)

Israeli Army general, politician, and prime minister (2001–2006). Ariel Sharon was born Ariel Scheinermann (also known by the diminutive Arik) on February 27, 1928, in Kfar Malal, Palestine, to Russian immigrants. In 1942 at age 14 he joined the Gadna, the paramilitary youth organization of Haganah, the Jewish defense force that protected kibbutzim (collective-farming settlements) from Arab attacks.

Sharon commanded an infantry company in the Alexandroni Brigade during the Israeli War of Independence (1948–1949) and was severely wounded by Jordanian forces in an effort to relieve the besieged Jewish population of Jerusalem during the Second Battle of Latrun. Following the war he founded and commanded a special commando unit (Unit 101) that specialized in reconnaissance, intelligence gathering, and retaliatory raids designed to punish and deter Palestinian and Arab protagonists while enhancing Israeli morale.

Sharon was criticized for targeting both Arab soldiers and noncombatants and was condemned for the killing of 69 civilians, half of whom were women and children, during a raid on the West Bank village of Qibya in the fall of 1953. In an effort to end the criticism, in 1954 Unit 101 was folded into the 202nd Paratrooper Brigade. However, it continued to attack military and civilian targets, including a raid on the Kalkiliya police station in October 1956.

During the 1956 Suez Crisis, Sharon commanded the 202nd Brigade in the Israeli invasion of the Sinai Peninsula, capturing the strategically important Mitla Pass at the onset. Later he received heavy criticism for taking the pass rather than merely holding the ground east of it, which claimed 38 Israeli dead and hindered Sharon's military advancement during the next several years.

Ariel Sharon (1928–2014), Israeli army general, politician, and prime minister (2001–2006). Sharon was one of the founders of the right-wing Likud Party in 1973 and as defense minister under Prime Minister Menachem Begin, he designed and executed Israel's 1982 invasion of Lebanon. As prime minister, he withdrew Israeli forces from the Gaza Strip during 2004–2005. (Israeli Government Press Office)

After studying at the British Staff College in Camberley, England, in 1957, Sharon commanded an infantry brigade and then the Israeli Army Infantry School. In 1962 he earned his bachelor of law degree from the Hebrew University of Jerusalem. He was appointed chief of staff of the Northern Command in 1964 and then in 1966 headed the Israel Defense Force (IDF) Training Department.

Sharon was promoted to major general just before the 1967 Six-Day War, when forces under his command again took Mitla Pass. He assumed leadership of the Southern Command in 1969. Sharon retired from the IDF in June 1972, only to be recalled to command the armored division that crossed the Suez Canal into Egypt at the end of the 1973 Yom Kippur War. His direction of that crossing and the subsequent encirclement of Egyptian forces is widely considered one of the masterpieces of tactical command in modern mobile warfare.

Sharon helped found the Likud Party in September 1973 and was elected to the Knesset in December 1973. He resigned in 1975 to serve as security adviser to Prime Minister Yitzhak Rabin until 1977 and then became minister of agriculture in Prime Minster Menachem Begin's first government (1977–1981). In this position Sharon actively promoted the construction of Jewish settlements in the occupied Arab territories. In June 1981 he became Begin's minister of defense, and in this position he designed and prosecuted Israel's 1982 invasion of Lebanon, known as Operation PEACE FOR GALILEE for the ostensible intent to force the Palestine Liberation Organization (PLO) Katyusha rockets out of the range of Israel's northern border and to destroy the terrorist infrastructure there. Sharon and Begin, however, deliberately expanded the invasion to include a drive against Beirut. Although the PLO was driven from Lebanon, the invasion intensified the Lebanese Civil War, allowing Syria to become entrenched in the politics of that country.

The Israeli presence in force lasted three years (a limited Israeli force remained until 2000) and resulted in such a high number of Palestinian civilian deaths that worldwide public opinion turned against Israel. Following the September 1982 massacre of Palestinians at the Sabra and Shatila refugee camps by Israel's Lebanese Christian Phalangist allies, Sharon was found to be indirectly responsible for failing to provide adequate protection for the refugees and thus resigned as Begin's minister of defense. This event overshadowed Sharon's diplomatic rapprochement with a number of African nations and his role in developing the first strategic cooperation agreement with the United States (1981), Operation MOSES (1984), and a free trade agreement with the United States (1985).

Sharon served in various Israeli governments as a minister without portfolio (1983–1984), minister of industry and trade (1984–1990), and minister of construction and housing and chairman of the ministerial committee on immigration and absorption (1990–1992). The latter post allowed him to double the number of Jewish settlements throughout the West Bank and the Gaza Strip during his tenure in office. He hoped that these would not only provide a strategic buffer for Israel proper but would also reduce the possibility of the return of these territories (Judaea and Samaria) to Palestinian Arabs.

Sharon then served on the Knesset's Foreign Affairs and Defense Committee (1992–1996) and as minister of national infrastructure (1996–1998) under Prime Minister Benjamin Netanyahu. As foreign minister (1998–1999), Sharon led Israel's permanent status negotiations with the Palestinian Authority and sought to promote long-term solutions to the region's water disputes and inadequacies.

Sharon assumed the leadership of the Likud Party after Ehud Barak's victory in the general elections of May 1999 led to the resignation of Netanyahu. The failure of Barak's land for peace initiative at the Camp David Summit in 2000 coupled with the collapse of his governing coalition and the eruption of Palestinian violence led to Barak's defeat by Sharon in the general election of February 2001, even though much of the civil violence was precipitated by Sharon's visit to the Temple Mount on September 28, 2000. The ensuing violence was known as the Second (al-Aqsa) Intifada (2000–2004).

Palestinians charged that Prime Minister Sharon pursued a policy of confrontation and nonnegotiation. On July 2004, he also angered the French government when he called for French Jews to emigrate to Israel following an upswing in anti-Semitic incidents in France. With 600,000 Jews, France had the largest Jewish population after the United States and Israel.

In 2004 Sharon began a bold policy of disengagement, or unilateral withdrawal, from the Gaza Strip, a policy opposed by his own Likud Party but supported by the Labor Party, the U.S. government, and many European nations. Sharon completed the withdrawal from Gaza of all Israeli settlers on August 30, 2005, and the destruction of all Israeli settlements and the complete withdrawal of the Israeli military on September 11, 2005.

Sharon narrowly defeated a challenge to his leadership of Likud by Netanyahu on September 27, 2005, and then on November 21, 2005, resigned his Likud position, dissolved parliament, formed a new center-right party known as Kadima (Forward), and set new elections for March 2006. Perhaps the most controversial of Sharon's projects as prime minister was a security wall designed to separate and secure Israel proper from territory to be ceded to the Palestinians.

On December 18, 2005, Sharon was hospitalized for what was thought to be a minor ischemic stroke. He suffered a massive cerebral hemorrhage on January 4, 2006, before planned surgery could be accomplished. He underwent several brain surgeries but remained in a persistent vegetative state. On April 11, 2006, the Israeli cabinet declared Sharon incapacitated and ended his prime ministership three days later, naming Ehud Olmert as interim prime minister. Sharon died in Ramat Gan, Israel, on January 11, 2014.

RICHARD M. EDWARDS

**See also**

Arafat, Yasser; Barak, Ehud; Begin, Menachem; Gaza Strip; Intifada, Second; Israeli Security Fence; Lebanon-Israeli War; Mitla Pass; Netanyahu, Benjamin; Palestine Liberation Organization; Palestinian National Authority; Rabin, Yitzhak; Suez Crisis; Yom Kippur War

**References**

Finkelstein, Norman H. *Ariel Sharon*. Minneapolis: First Avenue Editions, 2005.

Gelvin, James L. *The Israel-Palestine Conflict: One Hundred Years of War*. New York: Cambridge University Press, 2005.

Kimmerling, Baruch. *Politicide: Ariel Sharon's War against the Palestinians*. London: Verso, 2003.

Miller, Anita, Jordan Miller, and Sigalit Zetouni. *Sharon: Israel's Warrior-Politician*. Chicago: Academy Chicago Publishers, 2002.

Sharon, Ariel, and David Chanoff. *Warrior: An Autobiography*. 2nd ed. New York: Simon and Schuster, 2001.

# Shatt al-Arab Waterway

A 120-mile waterway formed by the confluence of the Tigris and Euphrates Rivers at al-Qurnah in the Basra Governorate in southern Iraq and fed by a number of Iranian tributaries, of which the Karun River is the largest. The waterway traverses the eastern edge of the Fao (al-Faw) Peninsula and empties into the Persian Gulf near Kuwait. The waterway's southern half delineates the border between Iraq and Iran. Shatt al-Arab is Arabic for the "Stream, River, or Coast of the Arabs." The Shatt al-Arab is Iraq's only access to the sea and is thus essential to the exportation of Iraqi oil and the importation of goods and commodities. Iran uses the waterway for the same purposes.

Alluvial deposits from the waterway's feeder rivers have created an expansive marsh that remains the home of the 5,000-year-old Marsh Arab culture and people. These deposits continue to expand the delta at the mouth of the waterway on the Persian Gulf. The Shatt al-Arab shrinks from a width of half a mile at its mouth to 120 feet at the Iraqi port city of Basra. Constant dredging is necessary to keep the waterway open to Basra and the Iranian port cities of Abadan and Khorramshahr. The legal course of the waterway is disputed between Iraq and Iran, because in the distant past the Tigris and Euphrates Rivers flowed into the Persian Gulf more to the west than they do today and because the shifting delta now separates Abadan from the gulf by some 30 miles. About 1,000 years ago, the city was situated at the head of the Gulf.

The earliest known dispute over the waterway was resolved by the 1639 CE Treaty of Zuhab between Safavid Persia and the Ottoman Empire, the territory of which included current-day Iraq, and Persia, renamed Iran in 1935. A later dispute was resolved by the 1847 Second Treaty of Erzurum, with the British supporting the Ottoman claim to both banks of the waterway and the Russians supporting the Persian claim to the eastern bank, which granted Persia rights of navigation on the waterway. The dispute continued, and a 1913 protocol signed in Constantinople gave Persia control of the eastern bank with expanded control to the middle of the waterway at Abadan and Khorramshahr, allowing easier navigation into and out of Iranian ports. World War I, however, halted implementation of this protocol. A 1935 British-led international commission gave Iran control of the approaches to Abadan and Khorramshahr while granting the new state of Iraq complete control of the rest of the Shatt al-Arab and its delta.

As the economic importance of oil exportation to Iraq and Iran increased in the 1960s and 1970s, so did tensions and disputes over the Shatt al-Arab. The 1975 Iran-Iraq Algiers Accord divided sovereignty using straight lines connecting at the waterway's deepest points (the *thalweg* principle), with Iraq controlling the waterway westward of the line and Iran to eastward.

Believing that Iraq's greatest weakness was the Shatt al-Arab, the artery through which Iraq's oil passed, Iraqi president Saddam Hussein in 1980 verbally abrogated the 1975 accord, claimed sovereignty over both banks, and invaded Iran, sparking the Iran-Iraq War (1980–1988). Iraq initially took control of the waterway during the war. Iraqi fears about the waterway were realized when in 1987 Iran captured Iraq's al-Faw Peninsula, blocking most of Iraq's export-import activities. The original pre-1980 accord boundaries were restored when the war ended in 1988. Hussein renounced his stated abrogation of the Algiers Accord in 1990, mollifying Iran prior to Iraq's 1990 invasion and occupation of Kuwait.

Although the 1991 Persian Gulf War removed Hussein's forces from Kuwait, the cessation of the war before Hussein was ousted led President George H. W. Bush to urge an internal revolt against Hussein. Responding to this call, the Marsh Arabs joined a short-lived (March 1991) Shiite uprising in southern Iraq. Hussein brutally crushed the rebellion and began draining the marshes by channeling the Tigris and Euphrates Rivers directly into the Shatt al-Arab, essentially converting the wetlands into a desert. This decimated and dispersed the Marsh Arab population.

The waterway was an initial target in the Anglo-American–led 2003 Iraq invasion that ousted Hussein and overthrew Iraq's Sunni-led Baathist government. British

Royal Marines employed the 1987 Iranian tactic and captured the al-Faw Peninsula, severing Iraq's main economic artery. Restoration of the marshlands began in 2003 following the end of organized Iraqi military resistance, and by 2007 the marsh had been restored to approximately 50 percent of the area it comprised prior to the Iraq-Iran War.

In June 2004 the Iranians seized British marines patrolling the waterway, releasing them a few days later. United Nations Security Council Resolution 1723, passed in 2006, mandated that the British patrol, interdict contraband on, and keep the waterway open from Basra to the Persian Gulf. On May 23, 2007, the Iranians seized 15 Royal Navy personnel patrolling the waterway but released them 13 days later. The incident increased the already strained relations between Iran and the West.

RICHARD M. EDWARDS

**See also**
Erzurum, Second Treaty of; Fao Peninsula; Hussein, Saddam; Iran; Iran-Iraq War; Iraq; Iraq War; Marsh Arabs; Persian Gulf War, Cease-Fire Agreement; Persian Gulf War, Overview

**References**
Brown, Sarah Graham. *Sanctioning Saddam: The Politics of Intervention in Iraq.* London: I. B. Tauris, 1999.
Coughlin, Con. *Saddam: His Rise and Fall.* New York: Harper Perennial, 2005.
Karsh, Efraim. *The Iran-Iraq War 1980–1988.* Oxford, UK: Osprey, 2002.
Keegan, John. *The Iraq War.* New York: Knopf, 2004.
Ochsenschlager, Edward L. *Iraq's Marsh Arabs in the Garden of Eden.* Philadelphia: University of Pennsylvania Museum Publication, 2004.
Schofield, R. N. *Evolution of the Shatt al Arab Boundary Dispute.* Middlesex, UK: Kingston Press, 1986.
Tripp, Charles. *A History of Iraq.* New York: Cambridge University Press, 2000.

# Shaw Commission (August 1929– March 31, 1930)

Commission dispatched by the British government to Palestine to investigate Arab violence against Jews that occurred there in August 1929. The riots had resulted following a confrontation in Jerusalem at the location of the Western (Wailing) Wall, the most sacred of Jewish sites, and the al-Aqsa Mosque precinct, Islam's third-holiest site. The proximity of these two sacred religious sites provided a volatile setting. The Western Wall had been the scene of confrontation between Jews and Arabs on every Jewish holy day when Jews sought to go there to pray.

On August 16, 1929, a right-wing Jewish youth group secured permission from the British authorities for a march to the Western Wall to commemorate the fast of the Ninth of Ab. Learning of this, the Muslim leadership in Jerusalem hastily organized a counterdemonstration near the wall, replete with inflammatory speeches. Some minor clashes then occurred between the two groups. During the next week, Muslim agitators traveled throughout Palestine and urged Arab peasants to come to Jerusalem in order to protect the al-Aqsa Mosque against Jewish attacks.

During the night of August 23 and the next day, crowds of Arabs moved into Jerusalem near the al-Aqsa Mosque and at noon on August 24 attacked the orthodox Jewish quarter. Jews also came under Arab attack elsewhere in Palestine, such as Hebron and Safed. British authorities were obliged to call in additional troops from Egypt, and it was not until August 28 that order was restored. By that date, 133 Jews had been killed and 399 others wounded. The Arab side lost 87 killed and 91 wounded. The riots proved to be a turning point in the history of the mandate, for hopes that both Arab and Jew might live together in the same state now dimmed considerably.

The Colonial Office in Prime Minister Ramsay MacDonald's Labour government then dispatched a commission headed by Sir Walter Shaw to report back on the causes of the riots and to make recommendations to prevent a reoccurrence. Shaw was a retired chief justice of the Turkish Straits Settlements. The commission, which conducted formal hearings in Palestine during a five-week period, issued its report on March 31, 1930.

The Shaw Commission's report blamed the Arabs for the rioting but also found fault with the British authorities and police for failing to provide adequate security. The report concluded that widespread Arab dissatisfaction over the intentions of Jews in Palestine, including Arab concern for their economic future, was the chief factor behind the rioting. The report noted that the British government had promised to provide but had never issued a statement that spelled out its obligations to the non-Jewish population of Palestine. Pending that, the commission urged that the British government tighten Jewish immigration into Palestine and restrict Jewish land purchases so that Jews could not evict Arab tenants. London should also ensure that the Jewish Agency be made to understand that it had no role in the government of Palestine.

Zionists received the Shaw Commission's report with shock and anger. Worse was to come. In May, the British government sent Sir John Hope Simpson, a retired Indian civil servant and authority on agricultural economies, to

Palestine. He spent three months there and on October 20, 1930, issued a massive report that held that the land available to Arabs was less than had been thought previously and that Arabs were being driven off the land by Jewish land purchases. He blamed Arab poverty on Jewish land purchases and concluded that steps should be immediately taken to restrict Jewish immigration into Palestine. The report's conclusions were embodied in a white paper issued by the British government the same day that called for restrictions on Jewish purchases of land and suspending Jewish immigration into Palestine as long as there was extensive poverty in Palestine. The white paper also called on Zionist leaders to rethink their national home policy. Greeted by a storm of protest, the white paper was quickly withdrawn.

SPENCER C. TUCKER

### See also
Palestine, British Mandate for; Religious Sites in the Middle East, Jewish; Religious Sites in the Middle East, Muslim; Zionism

### References
Sachar, Howard M. *A History of Israel: From the Rise of Zionism to Our Time.* 3rd ed. New York: Knopf, 2007.

Sanders, Ronald. *The High Walls of Jerusalem: A History of the Balfour Declaration and the Birth of the British Mandate for Palestine.* New York: Holt, Rinehart and Winston, 1983.

# Shazly, Saad el- (1922–2011)

Egyptian military officer and diplomat largely responsible for the planning and successful execution of the Egyptian Suez Canal offensive in the Yom Kippur War (Ramadan War) of 1973. Born in Basyoun, Gharbiya, Egypt, on April 1, 1922, Saad el-Shazly began his military career by attending the Egyptian Military Academy during 1939–1943. His first combat assignment was as a platoon leader in the Egyptian Army in the Israeli War of Independence (1948–1949). His performance in combat earned him a nomination to the Junior Officer's Command Course and Military Staff College, from which he graduated in 1952 with a master's degree in military science. A year later Shazly was selected to attend the U.S. Army Infantry School at Fort Benning, Georgia. Upon his return to Egypt he was assigned to Egypt's Parachute School, which he commanded from 1954 to 1956.

Shazly faced combat for the second time as a paratroop company commander in the 1956 Sinai Campaign. In 1958 he attended the Command Leadership Course in the Soviet Union and was later appointed chief of staff of a paratroop brigade. Between 1960 and 1961 he commanded the Egyptian United Nations (UN) contingent in the Congo. During the next two years he was the Egyptian military attaché to the United Kingdom. In 1965 he went to Yemen as part of the Egyptian forces intervening in the Yemeni Civil War.

By 1967 Shazly had been promoted to the rank of major general. As a special task force commander in the June 1967 Six-Day War, he was tasked with cutting off the Israeli city of Eilat in an attempt to deny Israeli forces access to the Gulf of Aqaba. The Israelis preempted this move, however, effectively cutting off his force. Shazly successfully avoided decisive engagements and eventually led his troops out of Israeli encirclement to safety.

After the end of the Six-Day War, Shazly was seen as the most qualified Egyptian officer to lead and train the Egyptian Special Forces. His two-year tenure brought significant improvements to their training program, including the establishment of al-Saiqa (commandos) and the Mizidat (paratroops).

In September 1970 Anwar Sadat assumed the Egyptian presidency and immediately initiated a political and military restructuring. As a result, Shazly, now a lieutenant general, became chief of the General Staff of the Egyptian armed forces on May 16, 1971. Later that year he was named assistant secretary-general for military affairs for the Arab League.

After the losses in the Six-Day War, Sadat sought to strike back at Israel and recapture at least a portion of the Sinai Peninsula in an attempt to force the Israelis to negotiate. As such, Shazly and his staff developed an attack plan that focused on crossing the Suez Canal and establishing strong defensive positions that would lure the Israel Defense Force (IDF) into a killing zone. Unlike his predecessors, Shazly managed to synchronize air, ground, and naval forces. The plan worked, and the Egyptians were able to cross the canal. They then used their Soviet-supplied defensive firepower, in the form of antiaircraft missiles, to drive off Israeli aircraft and also used antitank missiles to destroy counterattacking Israeli armor.

With this success, Sadat then sought to expand the offensive in an attempt to regain the whole of the Sinai. Shazly strongly opposed any additional advances beyond the coverage of the Egyptian surface-to-air missile (SAM) batteries. Sadat disregarded his advice. Upon the successful Israeli counteroffensive, Shazly pleaded with Sadat to withdraw Egyptian troops that were in danger of encirclement. Shazly later orchestrated an ineffective counterattack. On October 20, 1973, after continued pleas and requests to shift troops to address possible encirclement, Sadat removed Shazly from his post in the field. Shazly was officially fired in December 1973.

As a result of his open protests, Shazly was sent abroad as Egypt's ambassador to the United Kingdom in 1974. A year later, he was appointed Egypt's ambassador to Portugal. Shazly openly criticized the Arab-Israeli peace process and predicted failure for the 1978 Camp David Summit. He argued that the only solution to the Arab-Israeli conflict was a military one and criticized Sadat for being weak, even calling for the Egyptian leader's overthrow.

Forced into permanent exile in Libya, Szhazly eventually settled in Algeria, where he founded the Egyptian National Front opposition party in March 1980. While in exile he was tried in absentia and court-martialed for allegedly disclosing classified information in his memoirs, which were published in 1976. Found guilty, he was sentenced in absentia to three years in prison.

After 14 years of exile Shazly returned to Egypt in 1992 and was immediately imprisoned. Although Egypt's High Court reversed the earlier sentencing, Shazly ended up serving out his full sentence. Shazly died in Cairo on February 10, 2011.

VADIM KONSTANTINE SIMAKHOV

### See also
Egypt; Sadat, Anwar; Sinai Campaign of 1956; Six-Day War; Suez Crisis; Yom Kippur War

### References
Aboul-Enein, Youssef. "Egyptian General Saad-Eddine El-Shazly: Controversial Operational Thinker and Architect of the 1973 Yom-Kippur War." *Infantry* (January–February 2005): 20–24.

An-Nahar Arab Report Research Staff. "General Saaduddin Shazli." In *The October War: Documents, Personalities, Analyses and Maps,* ed. Riad N. el-Rayyes and Dunia Nahas, 176–178. Beirut, Lebanon: An-Nahar Press Services S.A.R.L., 1973.

El Shazly, Saad. *The Arab Military Option.* San Francisco: American Mideast Research, 1986.

El Shazly, Saad. *The Crossing of the Suez.* San Francisco: American Mideast Research, 1980.

## Shia Islam

The smaller of the two predominant branches of Islam. Adherents to Shia Islam account for 12–15 percent of all Muslims worldwide. The Sunni sects or schools of Islam account for 67 percent. Shiism is divided into several major subgroups: the Ithna Ashariyya, called Twelvers by Westerners and Jafariyya by adherents, for their school of Islamic law; the Ismailiyya (Seveners); and the Zaydiyya (Fivers), named according to the prominent figures in the chain of religious leaders (imams) that each recognizes as constituting the proper line of leadership succession from Prophet Muhammad. Shiism is the dominant branch of Islam in Iran (90 percent of the population), Iraq, Lebanon, Bahrain, Azerbaijan, and Yemen. Shiism also has adherents in Syria, East Africa, India, Pakistan, Afghanistan, Turkey, Qatar, Kuwait, the United Arab Emirates, and the Eastern Province of Saudi Arabia. Shiism accounts for a small percentage of the Islamic population in South Asia and Europe, although Shiism's presence in the latter, particularly Great Britain, is increasing.

The Shiites were originally referred to as the Shiat Ali (Party of Ali). Upon the prophet's death, they preferred the succession of Ali ibn Abi Talib, the son-in-law of Muhammad by marriage to Muhammad's only surviving daughter Fatima. Some suggest that in the mixture of southern and northern Arab Muslim tribes, it was the southerners, Aws and Khazraj of Medina, who most strongly supported hereditary rights in leadership. Ali accepted Abu Bakr as caliph (*khalifa*), or political leader of the Muslims, but his supporters agitated again when Uthman became the third caliph. Uthman was so disliked for nepotism and the enrichment of his Umayyad relatives that a revolt occurred in which he was killed. Ali's followers recognized him as the fourth caliph in 656 CE. However, the Umayyads claimed the caliphate for Muawiya, and this led to two civil wars in Islam and Ali's assassination in 661. Following Ali's death, his son Hasan was forced to abdicate, and his other son Husayn fought the Umayyads and was killed at Karbala. With the accession of the Umayyads, its preachers regularly cursed Ali in their Friday sermons.

While all Muslims revere Prophet Muhammad and his family, Sunni Muslims also recognize the prophet's early companions at Medina for their political role and strength as transmitters of *hadith*, the short texts relating Muhammad's words, actions, or preferences. In contrast, the Shiites extend the notion of the prophet's family, the Ahl al-Bayt (People of the House), from the prophet, his daughter Fatima, and Ali on to Ali's sons Hasan and Husayn and the succession of imams who followed them.

Shiites believe that Ali was the first imam. The imam is the sole legitimate successor of the prophet. Each imam designates his own successor. In Shia Islam, each imam is held to have special knowledge of the truth of the Quran, Muhammad's *sunna* (traditions or practices), and Islam. The *aimah,* or chain of imams, is believed to be infallible, sinless, and personally guided by Allah (God) and is also believed to possess the divine authority over Islam and humanity granted to Ali by Muhammad.

Shiites and Sunnis hold to the same views of Allah, who has omnipotence over all beings, and yet Allah is also believed to be, as expressed in his other names, Merciful and Beneficent, closer to man than his own jugular vein and one who cares deeply about his creation. In both, there is also a dynamic between faith and the acceptance of divine will with the responsibility of the human believer. Indeed, apart from the differences in the Shia view of leadership, the two sects are very similar in many aspects. They diverge, however, in their legal systems.

The Shiites recognize all the same religious duties as the Sunnis, which are described in the study of Islam in the West as the five pillars with two additional duties. However, the Ismailiyya sect and its subsects also stress the inner truths, or esoteric knowledge of Islamic principles. The Shiites stress the unicity or oneness (*tawhid*) of Allah, a strict monotheism, and the avoidance of any trace of polytheism. They support social justice (*adalah*), which means equity within society, and aid to the oppressed and the needy. As with Sunni Muslims, the Shiites adhere to the principle of the *hisba,* or commanding the good and forbidding the reprehensible. This refers to all that is licit or recommended in Islamic law as opposed to sins that are forbidden. Entrance into Paradise is based on doing more good than evil or on martyrdom. All Muslims, Shia as well as Sunni, respect the prophets, including Abraham, Moses, Jesus, and Muhammad, whom they believe revealed to humans the true religion of Allah.

The concept of the *aimah* (imamate)—that specific leaders are appointed by Allah and then by other imams (*nass*, or "designation")—grew in strength thanks to the sixth imam, Jafar al-Sadiq (d. 765). His followers developed the Twelver legal and theological tradition. The last of these 12 imams, Muhammad al-Mahdi, did not make himself known at the death of the 11th imam, al-Hasan al-Askari. Al-Mahdi is believed to be hiding on Earth, neither alive nor dead but in a state of occultation, and will return at the Day of Judgment and the Resurrection (Qiyamah), when Allah will decide the fate of all humanity, Muslim and non-Muslim alike.

The Twelvers believe that al-Mahdi was the son of al-Hasan, born in 869. The Shiites believe that al-Mahdi was in hiding from the caliph and that between the years 874 and 941 he communicated by letters with his people. During this period, called the Lesser Occultation, the community recognized four regents for Muhammad al-Mahdi. In his last letter, he wrote that he would no longer communicate with humanity. Thus, the period from 941 to the present is known as the Greater Occultation.

In Islam, every human is held accountable for his or her deeds. The deeds of each individual are judged by Allah and weighed on a scale. If the good outweighs the evil, then the individual gains entrance into Paradise. If the evil outweighs the good, the individual spends eternity in Hell. The Shiites further believe that the prophets, imams, and martyrs can intercede with Allah for a soul on the Day of Judgment and may seek this intercession (*shafaa*), if possible, through prayer, religious rituals, or appeals to the Fourteen Infallibles: Prophet Muhammad, his daughter Fatima, and the 12 imams. They also seek redemption through the ritual of repentance performed on the Day of Ashura, the commemoration of Imam Husayn's death.

Shiism's Twelvers, the largest Shia group, proclaim the necessity of obligatory religious duties or acts of outward worship. The first is the *shahada,* or testimony that there is no God but God and that Muhammad is his prophet and Ali his imam. The next is prayer (*salat*), recited five or more times a day. The third is fasting (*sawm*) during the daylight hours for all of the month of Ramadan, the ninth month of the Islamic calendar. The fourth religious practice is the pilgrimage (*hajj*), a journey to the holy city of Mecca that should be made at least once during a person's life if he or she is physically and financially able to undertake it. The fifth religious practice is the paying of *zakat,* a voluntary tax that is used to support the poor, spread Islam, or sometimes other purposes such as aid to travelers and the funding of jihad. The assessment of *zakat* should be 2.5 percent of one's income and assets in any given year. (All Muslims also give gifts of money during and at the end of Ramadan and the Id al-Adha, but these are not technically *zakat.*) Another form of tithing, the *khums* is a 20 percent tax on all annual profits from any source levied on all adult males and is used to support the mosque and the clerics. Jihad is also a commanded duty in Shiism and refers to the struggle of the faithful to please Allah as well as to defend Islam by waging war. The idea of the *walaya* is important in Shiism (but also in Sufi Islam), as is the *tabarra*. These mean a special reverence for all members, past and descended, of the household of Prophet Muhammad, the Ahl al-Bayt, and the guardianship of the imamate and the disassociation from all enemies of the Ahl al-Bayt.

In addition to the Shia groups mentioned above, there are others. The Druzes are an offshoot of the Ismailiyya sect, and the Alawites found in Syria and Turkey are a distinct sect. The Shaykhiyya of Basra and Bahrain are a subsect of the Ithna-Ashariyya, or Twelver Shia, influenced by Akhabari thought. Sunni Muslims and some Shiites, however, consider the Alawi sect deviant because of some of its syncretic practices. Nonetheless, it was declared a licit school of Islam in a fatwa issued by Imam Musa al-Sadr in order to legitimate the rule of President Hafez al-Assad, an Alawi, in Syria. Although all branches of Islam believe in a divine savior, Mahdi, who will come at the Day of Judgment, the Twelver branch of Shiism holds that the 12th imam, or Hidden Imam since he is in occultation, is the Mahdi and call him Imam Mahdi.

In Iran, many believe that Imam Mahdi will reappear from a well at the mosque in Jamkaran just outside of the holy city of Qum, Iran. The site is frequently visited by Shiite pilgrims who drop messages into the well hoping that the Hidden Imam will hear them and grant their requests. Along with Imam Mahdi's return at the Day of Judgment, there are various beliefs about other millenarian events and wars that will occur before this period.

Since the disappearance of the 12th imam, the Shia *ulema* (clerics) have served as his deputies, interpreting the law and leading the Shiite faithful under the authority of the Hidden Imam. In Twelver Shiism it is believed that four persons acted as the deputies or special vice-regents (*wakala al-khassa*) of the Hidden Imam during the Lesser Occultation. These persons were called the *bab* (gate) or *naib* (deputy) for the imam. From 941 there have been no overt claims of a *bab* except for Sayyid Ali Muhammad, known as The Bab, who established Babism in the 19th century, and the Shaykhi Shia, who put forth the idea of the perfect Shia who lives in each age. Generally in this period, the idea is that there is a *wakala al-amma*, or a general idea of vice-regency delegated to the Shia clerics. When Ayatollah Ruhollah Khomeini and his government established the system of rule of the cleric (*vilayat-e faqih*) in Iran, he was referred to as the *naib al-Imam*, or deputy of the Hidden Imam. The idea of rule of the cleric, developed from the increasingly activist opinions of one branch of Shiism—the *usulis* (*usuliyya*)—who opposed the *akhbaris*, a different intellectual tradition. Khomeini's official title became "Supreme Faqih" (Jurist), and he served with the Council of Guardians as its supreme religio-political authority. However, his successor, Ali Husayni Khamenei, was not the most senior of the possible clerics to follow Khomeini and was granted the title of ayatollah more as a political appointment.

Ismaili Shiites, also known as Ismailiyya, or the Seveners, are followers of the living Aga Khan and constitute the second-largest branch of Shia Islam. Ismailis believe that the imamate is a position that continues unbroken since the caliphate of Ali, although the living imams since the 7th imam serve as regents awaiting the return of the Hidden Imam. Ismailis acknowledge only six of the 12 imams and assert that the real 7th Imam was Ismail Ibn Jafar. Other Muslims assert that Ismail's son Muhammad was the 7th imam and that he is presently occulted awaiting the end of time to reveal himself as the last imam. The Ismaili movement spread through missionary activity as a secret organization beginning in the later ninth century. It split in a factional dispute about leadership in 899. Ismaili Shiites are found primarily in South Asia, Syria, Saudi Arabia, Yemen, China, Tajikistan, Afghanistan, and East Africa but have in recent years immigrated to Europe and North America.

Ismailis mandate the same religious practices as the Twelvers, but their emphasis is on an inner or deeper interpretation of each that can make them distinct. As with the Twelvers, the Ismailis evince love and devotion (*walaya*) for Allah, the prophets, the Ahl al-Bayt, the imam, and the Ismaili *dai* (preacher) and also believe in personal purity and cleanliness (*taharah*). The third pillar is prayer, and the fourth is almsgiving, or purifying religious dues. The fifth is the fast, and the sixth is the pilgrimage. The seventh pillar is jihad.

Zaydis, also known as Zaydiyya or the Fivers, are in theology and the view of the law closer to a Sunni school of the law. Zaydism is strongest in India, Pakistan, and Yemen. Zaydis derive their name from Zayd ibn Ali ibn Abi Talib, the son of Husayn ibn Ali ibn Abi Talib (626–ca. 680), the grandson of Prophet Muhammad. Most Zaydis regard Husayn as the third rightful imam. After Ali, Hasan, and Husayn, the Zaydis assert that the succession of the imamate was determined by engaging in armed rebellion against evil caliphs. Although Zayd's rebellion against the corrupt Umayyad caliph Hisham ibn Abd al-Malik (691–743) in 740 was unsuccessful, the attempt was sufficient to make Zayd the fourth Zaydi imam.

Zaydism does not support the infallibility of the imams and asserts that no imam after Husayn receives any divine guidance. Zaydis reject the Hidden Imam and the idea that the imamate must be passed from father to son, although they do believe that the living imam must be a descendant of Ali. Zaydi Islamic law (*fiqh*) is most like the Sunni Hanafi school.

While there was never a concept of Sunni Islam as a sect, the non-Alid Muslims accepted the institution of the caliphate even though the caliph was not a spiritual descendant of the prophet. Still, the caliph received an oath of allegiance from his people and had to be pious and promote and protect Islam. Alids (supporters of Ali), later the Shiites, accepted their temporal rulers but did not regard them as being spiritually legitimate in the manner of the imams. For purposes of survival, they could deny their Shia beliefs if need be in the practice known as *taqqiya* (dissimulation). Non-Shia Muslims accepted the authority of the first three caliphs—Abu Bakr, Umar, and Uthman—and often cited hadith that are traced to the companions (*sahaba*) of the prophet as well as Prophet Muhammad himself. The *hadith* explain the practice or beliefs of the prophet and constitute his way, or sunna. Shia Muslims often cite hadith as having passed through the Ahl al-Bayt or relating back to the imams. Minor differences pertain to the times for prayer and the commencement of holidays.

Shia Islamic education is centered in Najaf and Karbala in Iraq and in Qum and Mashhad in Iran, with additional centers of learning elsewhere. Shia clerics from Lebanon typically studied in Iraq or in Iran. The most prominent Shia theorist in Iran following the Islamic Revolution was probably Abd al-Karim Sorush, who is famous for his idea of the expansion and contraction of Islamic law (*qabz va hast-e shariat*). The most senior cleric in Iraq today is the Shia Grand Ayatollah al-Sayyid Ali al-Husseini al-Sistani. The clerical establishment in Iraq is referred to as the *hawza*, and its duty is to train the future clerics of Shiism.

Alongside the hadith traceable to Prophet Muhammad, Sunni Islam most highly regards the testimony of the companions as it passed through the ages, while Shia Islam also highly regards the teachings of the 12 imams and their representatives. The testimony of the companions is sometimes at variance with Shia traditions in interpretations (*tafsir*) of the Quran, Islamic history, and the practices (*sunna*) of Muhammad.

Sunnis and Shiites have different approaches to jurisprudence, or the making of Islamic law, and therefore also in the issuance of *fatwas* to broader religious questions of Muslims. The different Sunni schools of law use as sources (*usul al-fiqh*) the Quran, the hadith, analogy (*qiyas*), and *ijma*, or the consensus of the community at Medina or of the jurists. In earlier periods, these legal schools also used *ray* (opinion of the jurist) or *ijtihad*, a particular technique of intellectual problem solving. In the 10th century, the Sunni jurists decided to stop using *ijtihad* so as to avoid the introduction of too many innovations into sharia. However, the Shia legal school of the Twelvers retained this principle. Consequently, Shia cleric-jurists who train in this technique and qualify receive the title *mujtahid*, or one who can enact *ijtihad*.

There are various ranks of clerics in Shia Islam in addition to the *mujtahid*, such as the elevated designations of ayatollah and grand ayatollah that other clerics should agree on. In addition, the Shiite may follow his or her own preferred *marja* (source). Above all of these clerics, there may be one agreed-upon *marja-e taqlid* (source of emulation of the age).

These are not the only differences between Sunni and Shia Islam. Other legal and sociocultural or even economic differences exist in such countries as Lebanon and Saudi Arabia, where the Shiites have been an underclass. Both Sunni and Shia Islam have produced Sufi movements or brotherhoods. Both have also produced militant versions of Islamism, including parties that aim at Islamic governance. There has been some effort to recognize Shiism in Sunni Islam. Indeed, al-Azhar University did so and teaches Shiism as a *madhhab*, or legal school of Islam, in spite of the fact that the government of Egypt outlawed Shiism. It should also be noted that Shia and Sunni Muslims had coexisted peacefully and frequently intermarried in Iraq. Shia Muslims were often members of the Communist Party or the Baath Party, and the clerics began an Islamic movement in Iraq in part to dissuade youths from joining the secular parties. This resulted in Iraqi president Saddam Hussein's suppression of the Shia Islamist movement. Sadly, the end of Hussein's rule brought Shia-Sunni sectarian conflict to Iraq, fueled in part by Sunni Islamists and nationalists who viewed the new Shia-dominated majority as conspirators with the Americans and who called the Shia apostates or renegades.

RICHARD M. EDWARDS AND SHERIFA ZUHUR

### See also
Iran; Iraq; Jihad; Khomeini, Ruhollah; Quran; Saudi Arabia; Sistani, Sayyid Ali Hisayn al-; Sunni Islam; Syria

### References
Ajami, Fouad. *The Vanished Imam: Musa al-Sadr and the Shia of Lebanon*. Ithaca, NY: Cornell University Press, 1986.

Daftari, Farhad. *The Isma'ilis: Their History and Doctrines*. Cambridge: Cambridge University Press, 1990.

Fuller, Graham E., and Rend Rahim Francke. *The Arab Shi'a: The Forgotten Muslims*. Hampshire, UK: Palgrave Macmillan, 2001.

Gregorian, Vartan. *Islam: A Mosaic, Not a Monolith*. Baltimore: Brookings Institute Press, 2004.

Halm, Heinz. *Shi'a Islam: From Religion to Revolution*. Princeton, NJ: Markus Wiener, 1997.

Momen, Moojan. *An Introduction to Shi'i Islam: The History and Doctrines of Twelver Shi'ism*. New Haven, CT: Yale University Press, 1987.

Nasr, Seyyed Hossein. *Islam: Religion, History, and Civilization*. New York: HarperCollins, 2003.

Sachedina, A. A. *Islamic Messianism: The Idea of the Mahdi in Twelver Shi'ism*. Albany, NY: SUNY Press, 1981.

Sobhani, Ayatollah Jafar, and Reza Shah Kazemi. *Doctrines of Shi'i Islam: A Compendium of Imami Beliefs and Practices.* London: Tauris, 2001.

## Shiqaqi, Fathi (1951–1995)

Cofounder of the Islamic Jihad of Palestine organization. Born in the Gaza Strip in 1951 to a Palestinian family that had fled Jaffa during the Israeli War of Independence (1948–1949), Fathi Shiqaqi studied mathematics in Beirut and then medicine at the Zagazig University in Egypt during the 1970s. Graduating with a degree in medicine, he worked as a doctor in Egypt, where he joined the Muslim Brotherhood. He practiced medicine for a time in Jerusalem, then returned to Gaza in 1981.

In Gaza in the early 1980s, Shiqaqi and Sheikh Abd al-Aziz Awda founded Islamic Jihad of Palestine, which carried out suicide bombings inside Israel. The U.S. government subsequently designated Islamic Jihad as an international terrorist organization. Reportedly, Shiqaqi was the first to publish a booklet that legitimized suicide martyrdom attacks, which he called sacrifices, as justifiable in *jihad* (holy war).

Arrested by the Israelis in 1983, Shiqaqi was imprisoned for a year. Again arrested in 1986, he was again imprisoned and then was deported in 1988. He settled in the Palestinian refugee camp at Yarmuk in Damascus, Syria. There in January 1994 he played a leading role in creating the National Alliance, a coalition of eight Palestine Liberation Organization (PLO) groups, Islamic Jihad, and Hamas. Early the next year, he sharply disagreed with Sheikh Awda over both the funding and organization of Islamic Jihad.

Shiqaqi rejected the 1993 Oslo Peace Accords and was said to have been behind a number of suicide bombings in Israel in 1995. He was shot to death, allegedly by several agents of Mossad, the Israeli intelligence service, in front of the Diplomat Hotel in Sleima, Malta, on October 26, 1995. Reportedly, he was on his way to Libya to meet with its strongman, Muammar Gaddafi, to secure funding for Islamic Jihad terrorist activities. Shiqaqi's funeral, held in Damascus on November 1, was attended by some 40,000 people. Ramadan Abdullah Shallah succeeded Shiqaqi as head of Islamic Jihad.

Spencer C. Tucker

### See also
Jihad; Palestinian Islamic Jihad; Shallah, Ramadan Abdullah Mohammad

### References
Abu-Amr, Ziad. *Islamic Fundamentalism in the West Bank and Gaza: Muslim Brotherhood and Islamic Jihad.* Bloomington: Indiana University Press, 1994.

Hatina, Meir. *Islam and Salvation in Palestine: The Islamic Jihad Movement.* Syracuse, NY: Syracuse University Press, 2001.

## Shishakli, Adib al- (1909–1964)

Syrian Army general and strongman of Syria (1949–1954). Adib al-Shishakli was born in 1909 in Hamah, Syria, then part of the Ottoman Empire. By the time he joined the military, France ruled Syria under a League of Nations mandate. Shishakli studied at the Syrian military academy in Damascus and was commissioned in the Special Troops organized by France. Early on he joined the Syrian Social Nationalist Party, which was headed by Antun Saada and advocated a Greater Syria.

Syria achieved independence as a consequence of World War II, and in 1948 during the Israeli War of Independence (1948–1949) Shishakli served as a deputy commander of the Arab Liberation Army (ALA) sponsored by the Arab League against the Jewish forces. The ALA had a poor combat record in the war, and this was one factor in a coup in March 1949 in which Shishakli played a role and that brought Husni al-Zaim to power in Syria.

Zaim distrusted Shishakli and soon dismissed him. In August 1949, however, Shishakli participated in a coup that toppled Zaim and brought Sami al-Hinnawi to power. Hinnawi became chief of staff of the army, and longtime Syrian nationalist Hashim al-Atasi became prime minister. When Atasi sought to secure a union with Hashemite Iraq, Shishakli strongly objected and in December 1949 was the prime mover behind yet another coup that toppled Hinnawi. Shishakli now took power himself.

At first, Shishakli was content running things behind the scenes and allowed the Syrian parliament to continue to function. By 1951, however, his opposition to the pro-Iraqi bent of the People's Party led him to organize another coup in November 1951, during which he assumed complete power and ordered the arrest of the prime minister, his cabinet, and a number of other key leaders. Shishakli suppressed most Syrian political parties and appointed his associate, Colonel Fawzi Salu (later promoted to general), as chief of state, premier, and minister of defense. Nonetheless, it was Shishakli who now openly controlled affairs.

Throughout those early years of his rule, Shishakli pursued several goals. His experience in the fighting with Israel made him acutely aware of the failings of the Syrian military, and he worked hard to build up and improve the armed forces. He sometimes spoke of his wish to transform Syria into the "Prussia of the Arab states." A strong Syrian nationalist, he made the Druze minority a particular target of his campaign against so-called centrifugal tendencies, even shelling their strongholds.

In foreign affairs, Shishakli sought improved relations with the West, but he continued an uncompromising stance toward Israel. He also very much feared the expansion of Egyptian president Gamal Abdel Nasser's Pan-Arabism. Shishakli nonetheless refused to join the Middle East defense organization, sponsored by the United States (although it was not a member), that became the 1955 Baghdad Pact. Although tempted, he also rejected a U.S. offer of financial assistance in return for Syrian acceptance of Palestinian refugees and an effort to turn them into Syrian citizens.

In August 1952 Shishakli banned all political organizations and created a one-party state based on his own Arab Liberation Movement. In June 1953 he assumed more of the trappings of power by becoming premier and then securing the presidency of Syria by means of a popular referendum. This same referendum also provided approval for a new constitution that increased the presidential powers.

In January 1954, resistance to Shishakli's government became more open. Prominent Syrian political leaders had refused to support his Arab Liberation Movement, the Druze community engaged in violent demonstrations, and others followed suit. By February, elements within the army had determined that Shishakli had to go. The coup on February 25, 1954, in which the Baath Party also played an important role began in the mutiny of troops in Aleppo and rapidly spread. Forced to resign, Shishakli sought exile first in Lebanon, then in Saudi Arabia, and subsequently in France.

Although reportedly Shishakli subsequently negotiated with foreign agents concerning a possible coup attempt to topple the more pro-Soviet Syrian government and replace it with one headed by himself, nothing came of these efforts. In 1957, moreover, the Syrian government tried Shishakli in absentia on charges of conspiracy to overthrow the government. In 1960 Shishakli thought it prudent to move to a more distant location, and he settled in Brazil. There on September 27, 1964, he was assassinated by a Druze militant for his attacks on the Druze minority of Syria during his presidency.

SPENCER C. TUCKER

### See also
Baghdad Pact; Druzes; Nasser, Gamal Abdel; Pan-Arabism and Pan-Arabist Thought; Syria

### References
Lenczowski, George. *The Middle East in World Affairs.* 4th ed. Ithaca, NY: Cornell University Press, 1980.

Pipes, Daniel. *Greater Syria: The History of an Ambition.* New York: Oxford University Press, 1990.

Roberts, David. *The Ba'th and the Creation of Modern Syria.* New York: St. Martin's, 1987.

## Shomron, Dan (1937–2008)

Dan Shamron was an Israeli Army officer and chief of staff of the Israel Defense Forces (IDF) during 1987–1991. Shomron was born on August 5, 1937, at Ashdot Yaacov in the British Mandate for Palestine. He graduated with a BA in geography from Tel Aviv University. Drafted into the IDF in 1956, he continued in its service.

Although as a junior officer he was trained in armored warfare, Colonel Shomron commanded a paratroop unit at the Suez Canal during the Six-Day War (1967) and later as a brigadier general commanded the 401st Armored Brigade defending the Suez Canal at the beginning of the Yom Kippur War (1973). Rallying from the initial Egyptian attacks, Shomron and his unit then crossed the Suez under the command of Major General Ariel Sharon on October 14, 1973.

In 1974 Shomron commanded the IDF's Infantry and Paratroopers Branch and in this capacity had overall operational command of Operation THUNDERBOLT in July 1976. This operation successfully liberated the Israeli passengers and crew of Air France Flight 139 held hostage at the Entebbe Airport in Uganda.

As head of the IDF's Southern Command (1978), Shomron directed the dismantling of Israeli settlements and military bases in the Sinai Peninsula mandated by the 1978 Camp David Accords. He was on study leave in the United States when Israel invaded Lebanon in September 1982. In 1983 Major General Shomron was directed to integrate all of the IDF infantry, armor, artillery, and engineer corps into a single field command. He then assumed command of this new organization with the title of chief of the Ground Forces Command, reporting directly to the IDF chief of staff. Promoted to lieutenant general, Shomron succeeded Moshe Levi as the IDF chief of staff on April 19, 1987, and held that position until April 1, 1991.

During the Persian Gulf War (1990–1991) when Iraq launched Scud missiles against Israel in an effort to draw it into the fighting and unhinge the coalition against Iraq, Shomron authorized the deployment of American Patriot missiles and cautioned Israel's Prime Minister Yitzhak Shamir against retaliation against Iraq. As IDF chief of staff, Shomron also began the process of converting the IDF into a smaller and smarter army, reduced the number of its special operations, hinted publicly at an Israeli nuclear capability, and oversaw the Israeli initial response to the First Intifada (1987–1993). Later, he asserted that there was no military solution to the intifada.

Although Shomron had no formal higher education or experience in business, following his retirement as chief of staff in 1991 he became chairman of the Israel Military Industries (later Ta'as Israel Industries). He remained in that position until 1995, when Ta'as was unable to provide the Labor government of Israel with accurate financial records. Shomron remained active in business and in 2004 signed a cooperative agreement with the Israeli defense contractor Bynet Systems for an artificial intelligence video motion detector–based system for securing installations and settlements.

In 1995 Shomron helped found the Third Way political party that later joined Likud. He served as Likud prime minister Benjamin Netanyahu's chief negotiator in finalizing the 1997 Hebron Protocol with the Palestine Liberation Organization (PLO). Shomron criticized any loosening of Israeli gun control laws that would make private firearms more readily available and increase the already high Israeli violent crime rate. He advocated trading territory for peace and asserted that there could be no peace unless Hamas was challenged and a strong Palestinian leadership that was willing to negotiate emerged. He also served on the Committee for the Prevention of Destruction of Antiquities on the Temple Mount; the International Advisory Board of the Begin-Sadat Center for Strategic Studies at Bar-Ilan University; and the presidium of the Israeli Media Watch that monitors, reports, and responds to political and cultural media bias against Israel.

Shomron died on February 26, 2008, in Herzliya, Israel.

RICHARD EDWARDS

**See also**
Camp David Accords; Entebbe Hostage Rescue; Hamas; Intifada, First; Netanyahu, Benjamin; Persian Gulf War; Shamir, Yitzhak; Six-Day War

**References**
Goldstein, Yaacov N., and Dan Shomron. *From Fighters to Soldiers: How the Israeli Defense Forces Began.* Brighton, UK: Sussex Academic, 1998.

Porat, Yesha Yahu Ben. *Entebbe Rescue.* New York: Delacorte, 1977.
Van Creveld, Martin. *The Sword and the Olive: A Critical History of the Israeli Defense Force.* New York: PublicAffairs, 2002.

## Shultz Plan (March 4, 1988)

Middle East peace proposal formally enunciated by U.S. secretary of state George P. Shultz on March 4, 1988. The Shultz Plan was part of President Ronald Reagan's response to the First Intifada, which had broken out in the occupied territories the preceding year. Dozens of people had already been killed during the uprising since it first began in December 1987. The plan was also part of an American attempt to become more actively engaged in the ongoing Arab-Israeli peace process. Since 1983, U.S. policy makers had shied away from active engagement in the Middle East. The reasons for this are multifaceted. The abortive U.S. involvement in the Lebanese Civil War, the failure of the 1982 Reagan Plan, and the October 1983 destruction of the U.S. Marine Corps barracks in Beirut in which 241 Americans died all had forced Reagan to reverse course and pull American troops out of the region. These negative experiences had convinced the Americans that peace in the Middle East was a chimera. Also, the renewed Cold War with the Soviets and then negotiations with the Soviets beginning in late 1985 had diverted the Reagan administration's attention from the problems in the Middle East.

By the late 1980s, however, the Reagan administration realized that the United States could no longer stay out of the Middle East. Yet the Palestinians would not make the Americans' jobs any easier. The U.S. State Department had tried on more than one occasion to engage the Palestine Liberation Organization (PLO), but the organization refused to alter its goal of destroying Israel. And as long as this persisted, the United States refused to enter into negotiations with the PLO. In October 1987 just weeks before the First Intifada began, Shultz asserted in a speech—which was clearly a precursor to the Shultz Plan—that the Palestinians had to be involved in the peace process. Yet he also said that "there isn't a role in the peace process for people whose tactics are violent." Shultz seemed to be holding out a vision of direct U.S.-PLO talks in return for that group's denunciation of violence.

The Shultz Plan had three primary parts. First, immediate negotiations involving all pertinent parties that accepted United Nations (UN) Resolutions 242 and 338 and denounced violence. The talks would be sponsored by the five permanent members of the UN Security Council.

Second, the Palestinians would be part of the Jordanian delegation that would negotiate for all the Palestinians a three-year period of transitional self-government in the occupied territories (Gaza and the West Bank). Third, the initial multination conferences would be spun off into binational negotiations in which the details of the larger negotiations would be hammered out. The secretary of state's plan was predicated in part on the 1978 Camp David Accords, the 1982 Reagan Plan, and peace ideas prescribed by Israeli foreign minister Shimon Peres and King Hussein of Jordan.

The Shultz Plan initially caused quite a stir. And to make headway in getting it accepted, Shultz embarked on a flurry of shuttle diplomacy in and around the Middle East that lasted from March to June 1988. While the plan was generally accepted by Peres, Israeli prime minister Yitzhak Shamir had grave reservations and was especially suspect of the land for peace formula, which would have given the Palestinians control over land currently occupied by Israel. He also disagreed with the three-year transitional period that Shultz had proposed, believing that it should be considerably longer. Thus, there was a split within Israel over the plan and an overt rift between the foreign minister and the prime minister.

The Egyptians and Jordanians ultimately gave the Shultz Plan a lukewarm endorsement but with few large reservations. Syria expressed serious concerns with the plan, as did the PLO, which had not yet denounced violence against Israel. When Shultz traveled to the West Bank and Gaza to talk with key Palestinian leaders, none would meet with him, apparently on orders of the PLO.

As the summer of 1988 approached, Shultz had made little headway in getting the key players in the region to sign on to the plan. Israel was proving intransigent, as were the Palestinians. As with the Reagan Plan that preceded it, the Shultz Plan fell short on specifics. It did not offer any breakthroughs on Palestinian self-determination and did not specifically include the PLO. Without the PLO's participation, no peace settlement could be brokered. After June, Shultz continued to press his case for the plan, but the little momentum he had gained initially was gone. While he could say that no party had rejected the plan outright, neither was it met with much zeal.

The Shultz Plan became a dead letter after the November 1988 elections ushered Reagan's vice president, George H. W. Bush, into the Oval Office. Yet Shultz's laudable effort set the stage for important developments in the Middle Eastern peace process. By laying out the exact conditions under which the United States would engage with the PLO, the Shultz Plan forced a lively internal debate among PLO factions and their leaders. The plan, in fact, had given PLO chairman Yasser Arafat the opportunity to seize the initiative and overcome hard-line resistance within the organization. In so doing, he outflanked them by announcing, with much fanfare, the November 15, 1988, Algiers Declaration. This statement implied PLO acknowledgment of Israel and a vow to cease and desist from engaging in or promoting terrorism. Although it was not enough to satisfy Washington, it was nevertheless a historic step toward a direct U.S.-PLO dialogue. The Shultz Plan also laid the groundwork for the Oslo Accords of 1993.

PAUL G. PIERPAOLI JR.

**See also**
Algiers Declaration; Arafat, Yasser; Intifada, First; Lebanon Civil War; Oslo Accords; Palestine Liberation Organization; Reagan Plan; Shamir, Yitzhak

**References**
Laham, Nicholas. *Crossing the Rubicon: Ronald Reagan and U.S. Policy in the Middle East.* Aldershot, Hampshire, UK: Ashgate, 2004.
Quandt, William B. *The Peace Process: American Diplomacy and the Arab-Israeli Conflict since 1967.* Washington, DC: Brookings Institution, 1993.
Rubin, Barry. *Revolution until Victory? The Politics and History of the PLO.* Reprint ed. Cambridge, MA: Harvard University Press, 2003.
Shultz, George P. *Turmoil and Triumph: My Years as Secretary of State.* New York: Scribner, 1993.

## Siffin, Battle of (July 26–28, 657)

Decisive military event in the first Muslim civil war (First Fitna) of 656–661. The battle took place during July 26–28, 657, on the plains of Siffin in what is now now al-Raqqah (ar-Raqqah, Rakka, and Raqqa), Syria, and was between the forces of the fourth caliph, Ali ibn Abi Talib, and those led by Syrian governor Muawiyah.

The conflict between Ali and Muawiyah began with the assassination of Uthman ibn Affan, the third caliph of Islam. Ali, a kinsman of Prophet Muhammad, was selected to succeed Uthman. Muawiyah, who was related to Uthman, refused to recognize Ali as caliph because he blamed Ali for failing to prevent Uthman's murder and then not taking action against those responsible. Muawiyah gathered an army of those opposed to Ali at his capital of Damascus.

Ali led an army of possibly 90,000 troops into Syria to put down the rebellion. Muawiyah's forces, estimated to be

120,000 but possibly fewer, marched out to meet them on the plains of Siffin. The two sides came together in May 657 near the Euphrates River. There they remained for some 100 days. Most of the time was spent in negotiations, with the principal fighting occurring during July 26–28. Led by General Malik al-Ashtar, Ali's forces gained an advantage over Muawiyah's troops early on. Muawiyah, however, instructed his soldiers to fix on their spears copies of the Quran and to shout its proclamation that Muslims should not shed other Muslims' blood. A substantial part of Ali's army refused to fight at this point, and Ali agreed to put their dispute up for arbitration.

In the ensuing negotiations, Muawiyah's delegate Amr ibn al-As outmaneuvered Ali's representative, Abu Musa, and Ali's authority as caliph was called into question. Although weakened by this, Ali remained as caliph of the fractured Islamic world until his assassination in 661 by a member of the Kharijite sect, which held that Ali had betrayed Islam at Siffin when he put the issue of the succession up for human— as opposed to divine—arbitration. With Ali out of the way, Muawiyah became caliph. He was founder of the powerful Umayyad dynasty of caliphs.

The Battle of Siffin increased the division between the groups that would eventually split into the Sunni and Shia branches of Islam. The Sunnis, as represented by Muawiyah, believed that the line of caliphs passed through the descendants of Muhammad's wife Aisha. The Shiites, however, believed that Muhammad had instead proclaimed Ali as his successor. The followers of Shia Islam venerate Ali as second only to Muhammad in holiness.

RYAN HACKNEY

**See also**
Ali ibn Abi Talib; Islamic Civil War, First; Muawiyah I

**References**
Esposito, John. *The Oxford History of Islam.* New York: Oxford University Press, 2000.
Hourani, Albert. *A History of the Arab Peoples.* Cambridge, MA: Belknap Press, 1991.
Robinson, Francis, ed. *Cambridge Illustrated History of the Islamic World.* New York: Cambridge University Press, 1996.

# Sinai Campaign of 1916–1917 (March 1916–January 1917)

The World War I Sinai campaign grew out of British attempts to improve and rationalize their defense of the Suez Canal. In response to criticism of the initial British policy of merely defending the west bank of the canal, construction of three defensive lines extending some 11,000 yards beyond the east bank had been authorized in late 1915. However, these developments only exacerbated the need to maintain a sizable garrison in Egypt, as the new defenses required an estimated six infantry divisions and five mounted brigades to adequately man them.

While British forces in Egypt had at times exceeded this number, the large force maintained there was a reflection of Egypt's strategic role as the main staging point for British operations from Mesopotamia to Salonika. Even the evacuation of the Gallipoli Peninsula in January 1916 provided only a temporary influx of units, as most were sent to France as soon as they had been rebuilt. Given the incessant demands of other fronts, the British Imperial General Staff balked at the idea of having such a large force tied down on static defensive duties in Egypt. This was the problem confronting newly appointed commander of the Egyptian Expeditionary Force Lieutenant General Sir Archibald Murray in early 1916. His response was progressively to abandon the canal defenses in favor of adopting a strategy of active defense.

There were three invasion routes across the Sinai available to Ottoman forces: the coastal route from El Arish to Qantara, a central route from El Kossaima to Ismailia, and a southern route from El Kossaima to Nekhl and thence to Suez. Murray argued that the most effective way to defend the canal was to advance across the coastal route and capture El Arish. From there the British could threaten the flank of any Ottoman force trying to pass through El Kossaima and thus neutralize the other two routes. With El Arish under his control, Murray estimated that he would only need five divisions and four mounted brigades to defend all of Egypt. Furthermore, these troops could be used to threaten southern Palestine and tie down a disproportionate number of Ottoman troops instead of the other way around.

Initially the Imperial General Staff was reluctant to back Murray's proposal in full but gave him permission to advance as far as Katia Oasis, about 25 miles east of the canal. Projecting a large British force across the Sinai, even by the coastal route, was no easy task. Local oases could not support a force of any significant strength, and Murray had to build a railway and water pipeline to accompany his advance.

Work began in early March 1916 and was carried out by the locally recruited Egyptian Labour Force under the direction of British engineers. The rate of construction essentially determined the pace of the British advance. By the middle of May the railhead had reached the oasis of Romani, but thereafter progress slowed as the British engineers confronted the treacherous sand dunes of the Sinai Desert. Furthermore, while the extension of the more intricate water pipeline always lagged behind that of the railway, this became particularly critical in the desert zone, where oases were few and far between.

Opposing Murray was the Ottoman VIII Corps, effectively commanded by its German chief of staff Lieutenant Colonel Friedrich Kress von Kressenstein. The flurry of British activity was quickly brought to his attention. Recognizing the seriousness of the threat, Kress did his best to disrupt Murray's plans. On April 23 he launched a raid against British outposts around Katia and destroyed the better part of a regiment of British cavalry. Kress followed this by assembling a force of 18,000 men to attack the British railhead at Romani. This led to the only set-piece battle of the Sinai campaign, a decisive defeat for the Ottoman force during August 4–9. Thereafter Ottoman efforts were restricted to small-scale raids and actions. Kress was unable to offer more vigorous resistance during the rest of 1916 because of a lack of manpower. His pleas for reinforcements were largely ignored by the leadership in Istanbul (Constantinople) for whom the focus that year was on offensive operations against the Russians in the Caucasus.

Encouraged by his victory at Romani and the Arab Revolt, the British General Staff finally granted Murray permission to carry out his original plan. As engineers and laborers toiled away, they were guarded by Murray's infantry divisions, while his mounted troops ranged as far forward as possible, driving Ottoman forces before them. By December 1, 1916, the British railhead had reached Bir el Mazaar, and Murray was poised to attack the Ottoman garrison at El Arish. However, it was withdrawn before Murray launched his assault. British forces entered El Arish unopposed on December 22, 1916. The loss of the entire Ottoman garrison at nearby Magdhaba on December 23 saw Kress order the withdrawal of all remaining Ottoman outposts in the Sinai Peninsula except, for political reasons, the village of Rafa on the Sinai Palestine border. This pointless gesture resulted in the capture of Rafa and the destruction of its garrison by Murray's horsemen on January 9, 1917. With that action, the Sinai campaign effectively came to a close.

Murray had achieved everything he originally set out to do. The British now dominated the entire Sinai Peninsula, and the Suez Canal would never again be threatened by Ottoman forces. However, this success, coupled with the failure of Allied offensives on every other front in 1916, led to pressure from London for Murray to expand upon his original plan to threaten southern Palestine. The objective of the Egyptian Expeditionary Force was now no longer the protection of the Suez Canal but rather the capture of Jerusalem.

DAMIEN FENTON

**See also**
Gallipoli Campaign; Kress von Kressenstein, Friedrich Sigismund Georg; Murray, Sir Archibald James; Palestine and Syria Campaign, World War I; Romani, Battle of; Suez Canal

**References**
Erickson, Edward J. *Ordered to Die: A History of the Ottoman Army in the First World War.* Westport, CT: Greenwood, 2000.
Gullet, Henry S. *Official History of Australia in the War of 1914–18,* Vol. 7, *The Australian Imperial Force in Sinai and Palestine.* Melbourne, Australia: Government Printer, 1923.
Keogh, Eustace G. *Suez to Aleppo.* Melbourne, Australia: Wilke, 1954.
MacMunn, George, and Cyril Falls. *Official History of the Great War: Military Operations, Egypt and Palestine, from the Outbreak of the War with Germany to June 1917.* London: HMSO, 1928.
Powles, Charles G. *Official History of New Zealand's Effort in the Great War,* Vol. 3, *The New Zealanders in Sinai and Palestine.* Wellington, New Zealand: Whitcombe and Tombs, 1922.
Wavell, Colonel A. P. *The Palestine Campaigns.* London: Constable, 1928.
Woodward, David R. *Hell in the Holy Land: World War I in the Middle East.* Lexington: University Press of Kentucky, 2006.

# Sinai Campaign of 1956 (October 29–November 6, 1956)

On October 29, 1956, Israeli forces invaded the Egyptian Sinai Peninsula, opening what became known as the Sinai Campaign. The Israeli attack had been prearranged with the governments of Britain and France, which would then intervene militarily, claiming they were protecting the Suez Canal from fighting between Egypt and Israel but in reality to secure the Suez Canal.

On July 26, 1956, Egyptian president Gamal Abdel Nasser nationalized the Suez Canal, heretofore owned and operated by a company controlled largely by the British. This action and Nasser's support for Algerian rebels fighting France as well as his support for raids against Israel led to the opening of secret talks among the French, Israeli, and British governments regarding common action designed to topple Nasser from power and remove any military threat by Egypt to Israel. The Israelis were especially anxious to end the blockade imposed by Egypt on the Strait of Tiran at the southern tip of the Sinai Peninsula. The blockade cut off the Israeli port of Eilat at the head of the Gulf of Aqaba, halting Israeli shipping from that port with East Africa and Asia. The Israelis also wanted to wipe out Palestinian fedayeen guerrillas located on Egyptian territory, especially in the Gaza Strip. Fedayeen attacks on Israel had been a major problem for Israel.

Israeli leaders were anxious that the attack be carried out soon. A year earlier on October 27, 1955, Egypt had arranged for the purchase of a large quantity of Soviet military equipment from Czechoslovakia. This included some 230 tanks and 200 modern jet aircraft, including 120 MiG-15 and MiG-17 fighters and 50 Ilyushin IL-28 bombers. Much of this equipment was superior to anything in the Israeli arsenal. In June 1956, however, the Egyptians had not fully integrated the new weapons into their military establishment. Thus, only about 30 pilots had been fully trained to fly the MiG-15, and only 10 bomber crews were trained in the IL-28. In all, in October 1956 the Egyptian Air Force numbered about 254 aircraft, including 84 British Gloster Meteor and de Havilland Vampire fighters.

Intelligence deception aided the Israelis in gaining surprise at the start of the war. The Egyptians believed that the bulk of Israeli forces were in place facing Jordan and that no major attack on Egypt was imminent. With the nationalization of the canal, the Egyptians had positioned a large part of their military assets in the Nile Delta area to defend against a possible British and French attack there. As a result, Egyptian defenses in the Sinai were undermanned. The Egyptian defensive plan for the Sinai had called for a force of four infantry divisions, one armored division, and several independent infantry battalions, all to be deployed in a defense in-depth. The armored division was to act as a mobile reserve. However, in October 1956 only one-third of the Egyptian Army, about 30,000 men, was stationed in the Sinai, a far smaller force than was required. Egyptian troops there were organized into two divisions and a number of scattered smaller independent units. Nonetheless, two infantry divisions and the sole armored division were positioned in the Ismailia area just across the canal and could presumably easily move into the Sinai if necessary. On the upside, the Egyptians had constructed extensive field fortifications around the Sinai towns of Rafah and Abu Ageila. Former German Army officer Wilhelm Frambecher had overseen their construction and had also drawn up the Egyptian defense plan for the Sinai.

Egyptian minister of defense and commander in chief General Abdel Hakim Amer was supremely confident of victory should any armed clash occur. He had announced on September 3 that the Egyptian Army was "prepared to the smallest detail." Indeed, just a few days before the start of the Israeli invasion, Amer traveled to Jordan and then on to Syria to sign the new tripartite Arab pact. He was in Syria when the fighting began. Israeli intelligence discovered the return route of his aircraft, and an Israeli jet shot it down. Amer was not aboard, having decided to remain in Syria an additional day, but 18 senior officers died in the crash, which was a serious blow to Egyptian military operations.

When fighting began on the afternoon of October 29, 1956, Israel had concentrated 45,000 men in 10 brigades, including 1 armored and 3 mechanized brigades with some 200–250 tanks. Israel also had 136 aircraft, 54 of them jet fighters: 16 Dassault Mystre IVAs, 22 Dassault Ouragans, and 16 Gloster Meteors. There were also 42 propeller aircraft—29 P-51D Mustangs and 13 de Havilland Mosquitos—for ground-attack missions. Although the Israeli Air Force was at great disadvantage in terms of number of aircraft as well as their technical quality, these disadvantages were more than offset by far superior pilot training and expertise.

Israel Defense Force (IDF) chief of staff Lieutenant General Moshe Dayan developed the Israeli strategic plan. It called for the chief initial Israeli attacks to come in the central Sinai against the Abu Ageila complex and Mitla Pass. Four of the Israeli brigades were committed to the central Sinai effort. Three other Israeli brigades would then attack Rafah and the Gaza Strip before turning west and heading toward the canal. Two brigades would be held in reserve, while another would strike south toward Sharm El Sheikh.

The Sinai offensive began with an Israeli parachute battalion of the 202nd Brigade dropped on the eastern side of Mitla Pass on the afternoon of October 29. This key terrain feature guarded the approach to the Suez Canal, 30 miles west. The pass was of major strategic importance and was heavily defended by the Egyptians. The paratroopers established a defensive perimeter and then settled in for the night, while the remainder of the brigade, under command of Major Ariel Sharon, raced for Mitla Pass to link up with the paratroopers. Sharon's unit easily brushed aside scant Egyptian resistance and linked up with the airborne unit the next morning. Over the next several days, heavy fighting occurred at the pass as Sharon violated orders by attempting to take the pass rather than merely holding the ground east of it. The fighting there claimed 38 Israeli dead, and Sharon subsequently came in for heavy criticism.

It took perhaps a dozen hours for the Egyptians to figure out Israeli intentions. Nasser and key military leaders all assumed that the thrust against Mitla Pass was the main attack, and they committed major resources, including the

Israeli tanks in the Sinai Desert during the 1956 Sinai Campaign. (Israeli Government Press Office)

4th Armored Division, against it. Other Israeli forces meanwhile easily broke through Egyptian border defenses in the central and southern Sinai. South of Abu Ageila, the Israeli 4th Infantry Brigade easily overran Egyptian defenses at Qusaymah. The Egyptians there simply broke and ran. Part of the 4th Brigade then continued into the central Sinai, screening Sharon's more southerly advance. The Israelis then moved against Abu Ageila itself and adjacent Umm Qatif. There the Egyptians beat back a number of Israeli attacks between October 29 and November 1. Despite losing Abu Ageila, the Egyptian garrison at Umm Qatif fought on stubbornly. The Israelis did not take it until Nasser ordered a general retreat from the Sinai. However, Egyptian counterattacks farther north were completely unsuccessful.

Additional Israeli units bypassed Egyptian strongpoints and poured into the Sinai. The 4th Armored Division had already crossed the Suez Canal and moved into the Sinai to block the Israeli advance. However, the Egyptians had difficulty piecing together what was happening in the Sinai because of their poor communications.

On October 30, meanwhile, the British and French governments issued an ultimatum, nominally to both the Egyptian and Israeli governments but in reality only to Egypt, expressing the need to "separate the combatants" and to protect the security of the Suez Canal. The ultimatum demanded that both sides withdraw their forces 10 miles from the canal. The Egyptian and Israeli governments were given 12 hours to reply. The Israelis immediately accepted the ultimatum, while the Egyptians promptly rejected it. On the evening of October 31, therefore, the British and French began air strikes against the Egyptians.

Nasser concluded that the British and French threat was the more serious. Therefore, the 4th Armored Division, which had been advancing slowly into the Sinai, was ordered to turn around and head back to the canal. The Israelis thus were able to occupy the central Sinai with minimal opposition. At the same time, on November 1 Nasser ordered all Egyptian Army units in the Sinai to begin a withdrawal toward the canal. Egyptian forces thus finally abandoned Umm Qatif and began pulling out of their defenses in the Gaza Strip and Rafah. This Egyptian retreat soon turned into a catastrophic rout as the withdrawing Egyptian columns came under heavy attack from Israeli Air Force aircraft.

In sharp contrast to the superb support rendered to its ground units by the Israeli Air Force, the Egyptian Air Force played virtually no role in the fighting. It mounted several strikes against the Israelis at Mitla Pass, but the lack of trained pilots as well as poor maintenance meant that most Egyptian jets remained on the ground for much of the war. Indeed, many Egyptian aircraft were moved to southern Egypt simply to avoid their destruction. The Egyptians carried out exactly one bombing raid on Israeli territory, sending six bombers to attack an Israeli air base near Jerusalem. However, five of the Egyptian bombers failed to find Israel and had to return to base. The sixth bomber located Jerusalem but dropped its bomb load in an open field. The raid was a testimony to the abysmal state of Egyptian training.

Besides suffering Israeli air attacks, the retreating Egyptian columns simply moved too slowly to escape the much more mobile Israeli forces. Some Egyptian Army units could fight well from static defenses, as they did at Umm Qatif and Mitla Pass, although other formations broke and ran at the first sign of an Israeli attack. In mobile warfare, the Egyptians were completely outclassed by the Israelis. Egyptian weaknesses in this became abundantly clear during the retreat to the Suez Canal after November 1. The marksmanship of Egyptian tank crews was especially poor, even though they operated superior tanks. Possibly half of Egypt's new Soviet-built tanks remained immobilized during the war because of maintenance problems in the harsh desert environment. Egyptian advances and counterattacks also moved far too slowly. Had the Egyptian 4th Armored Division moved quickly into the Sinai, the entire Israeli plan of attack might have come undone. Its snail's pace advance contrasted sharply with the rapid attacks of the Israelis. Egyptian counterattacks seemed completely disorganized, and they were unable to operate around the vulnerable flanks of Israeli units.

The Israeli conquest of the Sinai proceeded rapidly after November 1. The Israelis broke into Egyptian defenses at Rafah, meeting sporadic resistance. Gaza was quickly overrun as additional Israeli columns stormed along the north shore of the Sinai toward the canal. Finally, in the south the Israelis captured Sharm El Sheikh at the very tip of the Sinai Peninsula, ending the Egyptian blockade of the Strait of Tiran. By November 3, major combat operations in the Sinai were virtually at an end, with only mopping up remaining.

Meanwhile, British and French airborne assaults began on November 5. The British captured Port Said, while the French took Port Fuad. Egyptian defenses crumbled quickly under the British and French air and commando attacks. Once again Egyptian counterattacks failed, despite the bravery of many Egyptian soldiers. The British and French both prepared to move south and seize the rest of the Canal Zone, but international pressure, chiefly from the United States, forced a cease-fire at midnight on November 6.

Estimates vary, but in the brief conflict the Egyptians suffered about 1,000 troops killed in action, 4,000 wounded, and just under 6,000 taken prisoner. The Egyptians also lost at least 215 aircraft and 100 tanks. The usual tally given for Israeli casualties is 189 dead and some 900 wounded. The Israelis lost only 15 aircraft. The British and French counted 26 dead and 129 wounded.

In December 1956 the British and French withdrew their forces from Port Said and Port Fuad, while the Israelis withdrew from the Sinai in March 1957. A specially created United Nations (UN) Emergency Force then took up station in Sharm El Sheikh and in the Gaza Strip.

The Israelis, at least, had achieved their objectives. They defeated the Egyptian Army, lifted the blockade of the Strait of Tiran, and smashed Palestinian fedayeen operations in Gaza. The British and French failed to accomplish their goals. Curiously, Nasser emerged from the war with his reputation enhanced in the Arab world, even though the Egyptians had fared badly in the actual fighting. Many Arabs saw Nasser as a hero for having stood up to the old colonial powers and to Israel. Egypt's military losses could be excused on the grounds that the British and French had intervened and that Egypt could not have been expected to defeat these forces. Egyptian Army leaders also concluded that it had nothing to learn from the Sinai Campaign, again because they had supposedly lost to the British and the French. The British and French intervention allegedly meant that the Egyptian defenses in the Sinai were not fully manned and that their best units could not engage the Israelis. Although partially true, this line of reasoning ignored serious Egyptian Army shortcomings in tactics, training, leadership, communication, and control revealed during the fighting.

The Egyptians paid a heavy price for ignoring the lessons of 1956 when they next fought Israel in 1967. The Israelis, by contrast, learned a great deal from the war and made major efforts to improve their armed forces. Indeed, the Israelis made mobility, maneuver, and air supremacy the keystones of their armed forces doctrine.

PAUL WILLIAM DOERR

**See also**
Amer, Abdel Hakim; Aqaba, Gulf of; Dayan, Moshe; Egypt; Gaza Strip; Israel; Nasser, Gamal Abdel; Sharon, Ariel; Strait of Tiran Crisis; Suez Canal; Suez Crisis

### References

Bregman, Ahron. *Israel's Wars, 1947–93*. London: Routledge, 2000.

Dayan, Moshe. *Diary of the Sinai Campaign*. Cambridge, MA: Da Capo, 1991.

Dupuy, Trevor N. *Elusive Victory: The Arab-Israeli Wars, 1947–1974*. Garden City, NY: Military Book Club, 2002.

Pollack, Kenneth M. *Arabs at War: Military Effectiveness, 1948–1991*. Lincoln: University of Nebraska Press, 2002.

Sheffy, Yigal. "Unconcern at Dawn, Surprise at Sunset: Egyptian Intelligence Appreciation before the Sinai Campaign, 1956." *Intelligence and National Security* 5, no. 3 (1990): 7–56.

Troen, Selwyn. *The Suez-Sinai Crisis, 1956: Retrospective and Reappraisal*. Ed. Moshe Shemesh. New York: Columbia University Press, 1990.

## Sinai I and Sinai II Agreements (January 19 and September 4, 1974)

Comprehensive cease-fire agreements between Israel and Egypt. Sinai I was signed on January 19, 1974, while Sinai II was signed on September 4, 1974. The United States played a critical role in both agreements. After the Yom Kippur War of October 1973, Israel and Egypt began a process of negotiations that would lead to the Israeli withdrawal from most of the territory it had captured from Egypt, not just in 1973 but also in the Six-Day War of June 1967. This was a significant departure from what had happened following previous conflicts. In 1956 the United States pressured Israel as well as Britain and France to give up all territories seized from Egypt in October during the Suez Crisis and the Sinai Campaign. In 1967 Israel kept all territories gained. Thus, the Sinai I and Sinai II agreements ushered in a new era in Israeli-Egyptian relations that would ultimately lead to formal diplomatic relations by 1978.

The Sinai agreements followed the October 6 surprise attack by Egyptian forces on the Bar-Lev Line defending the Suez Canal line in Sinai and the Syrian assault on Israeli positions on the Golan Heights. Although the Egyptians and Syrians secured early successes, the Israelis rallied, and by the time the United Nations (UN) had brokered a cease-fire on October 24, Israel was within artillery range of Damascus and had crossed the canal and was in position to threaten Cairo. Serious talks now began, this time with significant results in the Sinai.

U.S. secretary of state Henry Kissinger played a key role in structuring the Sinai agreements. He hoped to prevent the Middle Eastern conflict from escalating into a wider war or conflict with the Soviets, and he also wanted to enhance the position of the United States in the Middle East. Keeping these strategic goals in mind, he understood that achieving a durable agreement would require a step-by-step approach, breaking each issue into discrete parts for resolution. He was also willing to be an active participant in the negotiations, focusing on specific tactical goals for each step of the way. This involved frequent trips to the Middle East, soon dubbed shuttle diplomacy, as he sometimes functioned as the conduit for proposals and counterproposals between Israel and Egypt.

The Sinai I process began even before the UN cease-fire. Kissinger's first goal was Soviet agreement to a cease-fire. Kissinger met with Soviet premier Leonid Brezhnev in Moscow on October 21, 1973. Brezhnev agreed to a cease-fire. Kissinger's task was then to attain Israeli agreement. Israel reacted positively but wanted continued U.S. arms shipments and a face-to-face meeting between Kissinger and Israeli prime minister Golda Meir.

The preliminary Israeli agreement led to UN Resolution 338, ordering a cease-fire within 12 hours. This allowed sufficient time for Kissinger to fly to Tel Aviv, where he obtained Meir's commitment. The guns fell silent about 7:00 p.m. on October 22, an hour after Kissinger flew back to Washington.

The lull in the fighting did not last, however. Because the Israeli military had cut off the Egyptian Third Army east of the Suez Canal, the Egyptians tried to escape. That gave Israel the chance to open fire and further denigrate Egyptian forces. UN Resolution 339, passed on October 23, reaffirmed Resolution 338 and called for a return to the lines of the previous day. The fighting ended on October 24. Intense negotiations continued in Washington and New York, leading to UN Resolution 340 on October 25, again reaffirming Resolution 338 and authorizing a UN buffer force in the Sinai. Both sides then agreed to it. Kissinger's step by step process had thus far worked to prevent expansion of the conflict and broker a cease-fire.

Maintaining the cease-fire required more work, and Kissinger led the effort. The first discussions in Washington resulted in the Israeli agreement to allow nonmilitary supplies to reach the Third Egyptian Army in exchange for return of Israeli prisoners held by Egypt. On November 5, 1973, Kissinger set off for the Middle East for several weeks of negotiations. He concentrated on talks with Arab leaders in Morocco, Egypt, Saudi Arabia, and Jordan and dispatched others to treat with Tel Aviv. Another trip in December included meetings between Meir and Kissinger as well as meetings in Cairo, Riyadh, and Damascus in preparation for a general conference on Middle East problems in Geneva on December 21.

Kissinger could not obtain Syrian agreement to participate in the Geneva talks, but his approach did lead to a settlement between Israel and Egypt in the Sinai after Geneva and another set of shuttle diplomacy in January 1974. On January 18, 1974, both the Egyptian and Israeli sides agreed to extend the cease-fire indefinitely. Egypt accepted a UN observer force, reduced its demands to maintain armored forces in the Sinai, and agreed to allow Israeli shipping through the Suez Canal and out of the Gulf of Aqaba. Israel received assurances of major U.S. military aid, while Egypt received a promise from the Americans to work toward implementation of UN Resolution 242, passed in November 1967. Hostilities between Israel and Egypt would not resume, and the United States had now become the dominant superpower in the Middle East.

The question now was how much more could be accomplished in Israeli-Egyptian relations. The negotiations that led to Sinai II would answer this decisively. The cast of players in the negotiations changed, as President Gerald Ford replaced Richard Nixon and Yitzhak Rabin replaced Meir. But Anwar Sadat remained in control of Egypt, and Kissinger remained as secretary of state. As with Nixon, Ford gave Kissinger a great deal of leeway in negotiations. Kissinger continued his course of step-by-step diplomacy with personal involvement in almost all of the negotiations. The Egyptians' goal was for Israel to concede to more concessions. These included withdrawal from the key passes in the Sinai, limiting Israel's intelligence gathering abilities, and the return of oil-producing regions to Egypt. Israel, in turn, demanded a path to ultimate peace with its Arab neighbors, especially Egypt, in return for concessions. Kissinger wanted the United States to remain the major superpower in the Middle East with influence on both sides of the conflict.

Following preliminary posturing, diplomacy resumed with meetings among Ford and both Sadat and Rabin in June 1975. Kissinger carefully managed shuttle diplomacy that involved the U.S. ambassador to Egypt traveling back and forth between Cairo and Washington, while Kissinger concentrated his efforts with a visit to Tel Aviv in August 1974. By August 31, he had persuaded both sides to agree to what would become the Sinai II Agreement.

Sinai II was formally signed in Geneva on September 4, 1974. Israel agreed to a return of the oil fields and withdrawal from key Sinai passes. The United States committed itself to continue arms supplies and economic aid to Israel, along with support for a UN presence in the Sinai and support for oil supplies to replace those from the Sinai. Egypt agreed to concessions on Israeli trade through the Suez Canal and the Gulf of Aqaba and to limitations on the size of forces kept in the Sinai. Although Israel was not completely satisfied with the wording of Sinai II regarding U.S. guarantees in case of Soviet intervention in the Middle East, Kissinger had essentially ended any effective Soviet role in the region.

Following direct talks between Sadat and Israeli prime minister Menachem Begin at Camp David in 1978, Egypt and Israel finally made peace with each other on September 17, 1978. That peace has been sustained. In the final analysis, it was Sinai I and Sinai II that paved the way.

Daniel E. Spector

**See also**
Begin, Menachem; Camp David Accords; Meir, Golda Mabovitch; Rabin, Yitzhak; Sadat, Anwar; Sinai Campaign of 1956; Six-Day War; Suez Crisis; Yom Kippur War

**References**
Herzog, Chaim. *The War of Atonement: October, 1973*. Boston: Little, Brown, 1975.
Quandt, William B. *The Peace Process: American Diplomacy and the Arab-Israeli Conflict since 1967*. Washington, DC: Brookings Institution, 1993.

## Sinai Peninsula

The Sinai Peninsula is the triangle-shaped peninsula belonging to Egypt that links Africa and Asia. The peninsula is part of West Asia, while the remainder of Egypt is part of North Africa. The Sinai is bordered by the Gulf of Suez and the Suez Canal on the west and the Gulf of Aqaba and the Negev Desert on the east. The Mediterranean Sea is to the north, and the Red Sea is to the south. The Sinai constitutes an area of some 23,166 square miles and is almost entirely desert and high mountains.

During ancient Egyptian times the Sinai was inhabited by the Monitu people, who called it the Country of Turquoise, and both turquoise and copper were mined in the region. Arab tribes have resided there since before Islam. From 1260 the peninsula was controlled by the Egyptian Mamluks. In 1518 the Ottoman Turks defeated the Mamluks and took control of the Sinai and the rest of Egyptian territory. In 1882 the British took control of Egypt, and in 1906 the Porte agreed, under British pressure, to hand over control of the Sinai to Egypt. British authorities then set the border of the Sinai, which is now the border between Egypt and Israel. The Ottomans reoccupied the Sinai during World War I, but it was returned to Egyptian control thereafter. The British maintained a governor in the Sinai until 1936, when they withdrew from all areas except for the Suez Canal region.

In response to the 1948 creation of the State of Israel, a huge number of Bedouins in the Sinai were expelled, and others were prevented from reentering. During the Israeli War of Independence (1948–1949) Egyptian troops traversed the Sinai Peninsula, where they were met and halted by Israeli forces. Israeli forces occupied much of the northeastern corner of the Sinai during the war, but British and American pressure forced them to withdraw.

In 1956 Egyptian president Gamal Abdel Nasser instituted a blockade of the Israeli port of Eilat. During the ensuing Suez Crisis the Israeli, British, and French governments worked out a secret plan whereby Israel would invade the Sinai followed by French and British moves to reestablish control of the canal. Israeli forces drove deep into the Sinai toward the canal, prompting the excuse of British and French military intervention to allegedly protect the canal. The United States forced all three countries to withdraw from Egyptian territory. Subsequently, a United Nations Emergency Force (UNEF) took up position along the Egyptian-Israeli border.

In the spring of 1967 Nasser reinforced Egyptian troops in the Sinai, ordered the UNEF observers to depart, and reimposed a blockade of Eilat. Israel's response was the preemptive air strike of June 5, 1967, that wiped out the Egyptian Air Force and opened what became known as the Six-Day War. This time Israel occupied the entire Sinai.

In the 1973 Yom Kippur War Egyptian forces crossed the Suez Canal, penetrating the Israeli Bar-Lev Line, and proceeded a short distance into the Sinai. Although the Egyptians were at first successful, the Israelis soon gained the upper hand. They crossed over the canal and isolated an Egyptian army on the east bank when a cease-fire was declared. Under the subsequent Sinai Disengagement Agreements, Israel agreed to withdraw its forces west of the canal and from an additional strip of the western Sinai, allowing the Suez Canal to be reopened under Egyptian control.

In 1979 Israel and Egypt signed a peace agreement in accordance with the Camp David Accords of a year earlier. The peace treaty stipulated that the entire Sinai was to be returned to Egyptian control. Israel completed its withdrawal from the peninsula in 1982. The Israeli pullout required that several Jewish settlements be destroyed.

According to biblical tradition, Jabal Musa (Mount Sinai) is where Moses received the Ten Commandments from God. The monastery of Saint Catherine at the foot of the mountain is said to be the world's oldest Greek Orthodox monastery and is a major tourist attraction. There has been little development in the Sinai except for tourism. Economic conditions have been quite difficult for the Bedouins, particularly in the north, and Palestinians. Several Sinai coastal cities that are popular tourist destinations for Egyptians as well as Israelis and other nationals have seen terrorist attacks, most of them against tourists as in October 2004 when explosions in Taba killed more than 30 people, a number of them Israelis. Attacking the tourist industry is seen as a means to force the government to pay attention to the difficult economic conditions for many there. These attacks became more frequent after the 2011 Egyptian Revolution, including an Egyptian-Israeli border attack in 2012 that killed 16 Egyptian soldiers. Also on the rise are kidnappings of refugees by Bedouins, who then hold their captives for ransom. Egyptian president Abdel Fattah el-Sisi has mounted a strong effort against the militants in the Sinai and securing the border area with the Gaza Strip. The latter effort has included the dismantling of tunnels into Gaza.

On October 31, 2015, the Sinai witnessed the crash of Metrojet Flight 9268, a Russian-registered chartered jetliner. All 224 passengers and crew on board were killed. The aircraft was blown out of the sky by a bomb shortly after taking off from Sharm El Sheikh's airport. It was the deadliest air crash in Russian history and the deadliest to occur on Egyptian soil. The Islamic State of Iraq and Syria's (ISIS) Sinai Branch claimed responsibility for the bombing. The disaster compelled President El-Sisi to step up efforts to rid the Sinai of ISIS and other extremist groups. On November 24, 2017, terrorists in the Sinai struck again. Some 40 gunmen attacked a mosque in the northern Sinai and killed 331 people. Another 122 were injured. It was the deadliest terror attack in Egyptian history. In February 2018, Egyptian air and ground assets struck back at terrorist targets all across the Sinai in a major retaliatory operation.

Spencer C. Tucker

### See also
Aqaba, Gulf of; Bar-Lev Line; Camp David Accords; Egypt; Israeli Air Strikes Beginning the Six-Day War; Nasser, Gamal Abdel; Sinai Campaign of 1956; Six-Day War; Suez Canal; Suez Crisis

### References
Beck, John A. *The Land of Milk and Honey: An Introduction to the Geography of Israel.* St. Louis: Concordia, 2006.
Henriques, Robert D. Q. *A Hundred Hours to Suez: An Account of Israel's Campaign in the Sinai Peninsula.* New York: Viking, 1957.
Orni, Ephraim. *Geography of Israel.* Philadelphia: Jewish Publication Society of America, 1977.
Quandt, William B. *Camp David: Peacemaking and Politics.* Washington, DC: Brookings Institution Press, 1986.

## Siniura, Fuad (1943–)

Lebanese businessman and politician, prime minister (July 18, 2005–November 9, 2009), and acting president (November 23, 2007–May 25, 2008). Fuad Siniura (Siniora) was born in the coastal city of Sidon, Lebanon, on November 22, 1943, and is a Sunni Muslim. A fluent English speaker, he received a master's degree in business administration from the American University of Beirut, where he was a lecturer during the 1970s. His career background is in banking and finance. Siniura held an important post within the Central Bank of Lebanon from 1977 to 1982. He became a financial adviser and subsequently a close political ally to Rafik Hariri, Lebanon's two-time prime minister who was assassinated in 2005.

Siniura served in both of Hariri's cabinets, as minister of state during 1992–1998 and as finance minister during 2002–2004. While he was at the Finance Ministry, critics complained about his handling of the state budget and ballooning national debt. Highlights of Siniura's tenure in the Hariri administration included his efforts to secure international economic assistance for Lebanon in 2002 to combat debt caused by the country's 15-year civil war and enormous reconstruction costs. Siniura is probusiness and a proponent of free trade.

With the elections in May and June 2005, an alliance led by Saad Hariri, the son of Rafik Hariri, won control of Lebanon's National Assembly. On June 30, 2005, Lebanese president Émile Lahoud appointed Siniura prime minister to succeed Najib Mikati. A member of Hariri's Future Movement political party, Siniura formed his cabinet on July 19, 2005.

Siniura's cabinet was the first in more than a decade to have a majority of members who opposed Syrian influence in Lebanon. Syria, which had a military presence in the country for 29 years, withdrew its forces from Lebanon in April 2005. The withdrawal left Lebanon free from foreign occupation by the forces of Israel and Syria (along with Palestinian groups) for the first time in 35 years. The cabinet was also the first to include a minister from Hezbollah.

Upon taking office, Siniura promised to implement a reform program begun by Hariri. In April 2006 Siniura visited Washington, D.C., and met with President George W. Bush and members of his administration.

In response to the devastating conflict between Hezbollah fighters in Lebanon and Israel that began on July 12, 2006, Siniura presented a seven-point plan in Rome on July 27, 2006. It called for an immediate and comprehensive cease-fire and the release of Lebanese and Israeli prisoners and detainees (through the International Committee of the Red Cross), the withdrawal of Israel's army from Lebanon, the deployment of a United Nations international force in southern Lebanon to conduct humanitarian and relief work and ensure the stability of the region, the extension of Lebanese armed forces throughout its territory, the enforcement of the armistice agreement signed by Lebanon and Israel in 1949, and the international community's commitment to assist Lebanon with relief, reconstruction, and the rebuilding of its national economy.

Siniura's government lost support during the crisis because of the devastation wrought by the Israeli attacks on the country. Many Lebanese criticized Siniura's tearful addresses to the nation, since it was Hezbollah and not the government that had responded with assistance and because it was understood that some coordination had occurred between the government and the Israelis. Also, Siniura's government was powerless to prevent Lebanese pro-Syrian elements from acting. On November 21, 2006, assassins shot to death Minister of Industry Pierre Gemayel, the fourth high-level outspoken Lebanese critic of Syria to be assassinated since the murder of Hariri. After repeated calls for changes in the government and the cabinet, six ministers resigned from it in November, bringing about a constitutional and governmental crisis. This was followed, beginning on December 1, 2006, by huge public demonstrations and picketing against Siniura. These were sponsored by the pro-Syrian parties of Amal, Hezbollah, and the Free Patriotic Movement of Michel Aoun that launched a campaign of street demonstrations with the goal of securing a veto power in the government.

Lebanese affairs were further paralyzed by the opposition's refusal to attend the parliament and vote for a new president, on the expiration of Lahoud's term of office. Siniora was thus acting president until the new president could be voted into office. This state of affairs and the demonstrations continued for 17 months until May 7, 2008, when Hezbollah, Amal, the Syrian Social Nationalist Party, and other groups mounted an effort to take power in Beirut. The Rafik Hariri International Airport and a number of other locations came under siege. Some 200 people were killed in the few days of fighting.

The siege in Beirut came to an end after Lebanese leaders met in Doha in Qatar and in the Doha Agreement of May 21, 2008, promised the Lebanese political minority veto power. The agreement also led to the election as president of Michel Suleiman and a pledge by the various factions that armed force would not be employed to secure political gain.

Siniora left the premiership on November 9, 2009. He is currently a member of parliament and heads the Future Movement.

Spencer C. Tucker

**See also**

Doha Agreement; Hezbollah; Lebanon; Lebanon, Israeli Operations against; Lebanon Civil War

**References**

Harris, William. *Lebanon: A History, 600–2011.* New York: Oxford University Press, 2014.

Levitt, Matthew. *Hezbollah.* Washington, DC: Georgetown University Press, 2016.

Traboulsi, Fawwaz. *A History of Modern Lebanon.* 2nd ed. London: Pluto, 2012.

## Sinope, Battle of (November 30, 1853)

Decisive Russian naval victory over the Ottoman Empire early in the Crimean War (1853–1856). In late November 1853, Ottoman vice admiral Osman Pasha was proceeding north along the western Black Sea coast with a force of seven sailing frigates, two corvettes, and several transports to resupply Ottoman land forces. Osman flew his flag on the 60-gun frigate *Avni Illah.* Caught by a storm in the Black Sea, he took his ships into the Ottoman port of Sinope (Sinop). Although Osman's largest guns were only 24-pounders, the anchorage was protected by 84 guns, some of them possibly landed from the ships.

Russian admiral Paul S. Nakhimov soon arrived at Sinope with three ships of the line of 84 guns each: the *Imperatritsa Maria* (flagship), *Chesma,* and *Rostislav.* He also had two frigates. He secured from Sebastopol three additional ships of the line: the 120-gun *Veliky Knyaz Konstantin, Tri Sviatitelia,* and *Parizh.* Their main armament comprised new 68-pounder shell guns.

A thick mist on the morning of November 30 masked the approach of the Russian ships into the harbor. The Ottomans barely had time to clear for action before battle was joined at 10:00 a.m. Within half an hour, the *Veliky Knyaz Konstantin* had sunk an Ottoman frigate and silenced the Ottoman shore batteries. The battle nevertheless raged until 4:00 p.m. Only one Ottoman vessel, the paddle steamer *Taif* of 12 guns, managed to escape; the remaining ships were all sunk. The Russians admitted to 37 dead, while Ottoman losses were upwards of 3,000 men.

Although the Ottomans were badly outgunned at Sinope, the inequity of the losses conclusively demonstrated the superiority of shell over shot against wooden ships. The Russian *Imperatritsa Maria* had been struck by 84 cannon balls without sustaining major damage, for example, while the Ottoman fleet had been destroyed. The battle heightened world interest in the construction of ironclad warships for protection against shell.

The battle also produced a wellspring of support in Britain and France for the Ottoman Empire. The British press labeled this legitimate act of war "a foul outrage" and a "massacre."

Spencer C. Tucker

**See also**

Russo-Ottoman Wars

**References**

Barker, A. J. *The War against Russia, 1854–1856.* New York: Holt, Rinehart and Winston, 1970.

Lambert, Andrew, ed. *Steam, Steel and Shellfire: The Steam Warship, 1815–1905.* London: Conway Maritime; Annapolis, MD: Naval Institute Press, 1993.

## Sisi, Abdel Fattah el- (1954–)

President of Egypt since 2014. Abd el-Fattah Saeed Hussein Khalil el-Sisi was born on November 19, 1954, in Zagazig in Old Cairo. He graduated from the Egyptian Military Academy, but his military education also included the Egyptian Command and Staff College, the Joint Services Command and Staff College in the United Kingdom, and the Army War College in the United States. Most of his military service was in mechanized infantry units, but he was also military attaché in Saudi Arabia. As director of military intelligence, Sisi was the youngest member of the Supreme Council of the Armed Forces during the Egyptian revolution of 2011 that ousted Hosni Mubarak.

In August 2012, new Egyptian president Mohamed Morsi appointed Sisi minister of defense and then commander of the Egyptian armed forces. Following the mass protests against what many Egyptians perceived to be the increasing influence of the Muslim Brotherhood in the Morsi government, the military presented an ultimatum to the president. On Morsi's rejection of this, the military seized power on July 3, 2013. Sisi was the key player in this coup that removed Morsi from office.

The new Egyptian leaders promptly abrogated the recently approved Egyptian Constitution of 2012 and pledged a new constitution and fresh elections. Although the Egyptian military now controlled the national affairs, Adly Mansour was interim president. The government banned the Muslim Brotherhood and also moved against some liberals who opposed the new regime. On August 14, 2013, Egyptian security forces carried out what became known as the Rabaa massacre against opposition demonstrations in that place, in which 638 people died (595 of them civilians and 43 police officers), with at least 3,994 people injured. This action by

Egyptian president Abdel Fattah el-Sisi speaks during a meeting with Russian president Vladimir Putin on December 11, 2017, in Cairo. As Egyptian minister of defense, Sisi was the key figure in the July 3, 2013, coup that ousted President Mohamed Morsi. Sisi subsequently resigned from the military and was himself elected Egyptian president, taking office on June 8, 2014. (Mikhail Svetlov/Getty Images)

the Egyptian security forces resulted in considerable international criticism and led U.S. president Barack Obama to halt weapons transfers from the United States to Egypt.

On January 27, 2014, Sisi was promoted to field marshal, and on March 26, 2014, he formally retired from the military and announced that he was running for president in the new election for Egypt's leader. Held in May, it saw only two candidates: Sisi and Hamdeen Sabahi. With only 47 percent of eligible Egyptian voters participating, Sisi was declared the winner with 97 percent of the vote. He took up office on June 8, 2014.

As president, Sisi has projected a hands-on, hardworking, commonsense approach to governing and has called on his ministers to do the same. Much of his energy has been focused on righting the troubled Egyptian economy, stagnant for nearly a decade. He told Egyptians that they would have to sacrifice in the short term and sought to set the example by donating half his salary and half his personal assets to the treasury and encouraging prominent Egyptians to do the same. He also ordered that maximum wage caps be enforced.

With almost 90 percent of the Egyptian population living in poverty, Egyptian governments had regularly kept fuel and food prices low to avoid widespread unrest, such as had occurred in the 1977 Bread Riots. Sisi, however, sharply raised fuel prices as part of an effort to cut government subsidies constituting nearly a quarter of the state budget. Taxes were raised on a number of items.

Energy is a particularly vexing problem, with Egypt importing most all its needs in that area. Indeed, the energy crisis helped bring down former president Morsi. Early on in the Sisi presidency, problems in that sector grew worse for a variety of reasons, with blackouts throughout Egypt. Much has been achieved in that area since then, however.

To raise needed revenue, Sisi invested in Suez Canal construction, completed in August 2015, with financing from Egyptian sources only. It doubled capacity from 49 to 97 ships a day and more than doubled revenue. New economic development projects have also been undertaken, a major effort is under way to build a modern road network, and Sisi has announced plans to build a new capital city near Cairo. He has also undertaken the elimination of unsafe city slums with construction of new housing units for the poor.

From a religious family, Sisi has nonetheless called for the reform and modernization of Islam. He had endeavored to regulate mosque sermons and remove content from school textbooks that might glorify violence and incite hatred of non-Muslims. To show support for the large Coptic Christian population in Egypt, he became the first Egyptian president to attend a Christmas service.

In foreign affairs, Sisi mended relations with Israel that had suffered under his predecessor. Sisi supports the two-state solution that would establish a Palestinian state on lands occupied by Israel in 1967 with East Jerusalem as its capital. Although he was critical of Israeli military action in the 2014 Israel Gaza conflict, Egypt brokered the ceasefire. Egypt then hosted an international donor conference seeking to raise $4 billion to reconstruct the Gaza Strip. The Sisi administration has cooperated with Israel against Hamas, which it blames for the killing of 16 Egyptian soldiers in 2012.

Egyptian relations with Turkey deteriorated following Morsi's ouster, as then prime minister and now president of Turkey Recep Erdoğan characterized Morsi's ouster as a coup and called Sisi an illegitimate president. Erdoğan's demands for the reinstatement of Morsi led to the ouster of Turkey's ambassador to Egypt.

At the same time, Egypt's relations with Saudi Arabia, Kuwait, and the United Arab Emirates have remained close. Together, they have given more than $20 billion to assist Egypt since Morsi's overthrow. In return, Egypt has participated in the Saudi Arabian–led military intervention in Yemen, and the Sisi administration agreed to return to Saudi Arabia Tiran and Sanafir, two Egyptian-administered islands in the Gulf of Aqaba. However, Sisi has said that he supports the presidency of Bashar al-Assad in Syria, if only for the sake of regional stability.

Egyptian relations with Russia significantly improved under Sisi. This coincided with the sharp deterioration in relations with the United States, once considered Egypt's most important supporter. Unlike Washington, Moscow supported Sisi from the start, and Russian president Vladimir Putin was the first to congratulate Sisi on his inauguration as president. Sisi subsequently visited Moscow to meet with the Russian leader. In 2014 Egypt concluded a multibillion-dollar arms deal with Russia following U.S. president Barack Obama's freezing of arms transfers from the United States to Egypt.

Tensions with the United States arose after Morsi's overthrow and the Rabaa Massacre. Sisi was also bitter over Washington's earlier lack of support for Mubarak. Washington not only held up the transfer of arms to Egypt but also cancelled the Bright Star joint military exercise with the Egyptian Armed Forces. Although the arms transfer was subsequently largely lifted, the election of Donald J. Trump as U.S. president in November 2016 and his apparent lack of concern for human rights abuses in other countries was expected to significantly improve relations between the two countries. Thus, Egypt was not included among the countries in Trump's travel ban against a number of Arab states. Sisi received a warm welcome when he met with Trump in Washington in April 2017, and Trump praised his governing prowess.

By 2018 many problems remained, however, including terrorist attacks in the Sinai carried out by Islamist extremists against Copts but also Sufi Muslims, especially a 2017 attack on a Sufi mosque in the Sinai that killed 311 worshippers and wounded many others. These called into question Sisi's clampdown on political freedoms as justified in combating Islamic extremism. And Sisi continued to be accused of authoritarian rule. Indeed, many of his detractors say that his regime is democratic in name only and that he has encouraged a cult of personality.

Sisi handily won the March 2018 presidential election, although he faced only token opposition. His victory permitted him at least another four years in office. That same spring Sisi vowed to strengthen his country's ties to Washington, and in June 2018 he approved a parliamentary measure that would make it easier for U.S. aid to flow into Egypt.

One measure of shifting influence in the Middle East came in the form of Sisi's decision on December 1, 2017, to allow Russian access to Egyptian air space and bases. This marked the greatest Russian penetration of Egypt since President Anwar Sadat expelled Soviet advisers in 1973. Since then, Egyptian-Russian ties have continued to grow.

SPENCER C. TUCKER

**See also**
Egypt; Erdoğan, Recep Tayyip; Gaza War of 2014; Hamas; Morsi, Mohamed; Mubarak, Hosni; Muslim Brotherhood

**References**
Kingsley, Patrick. "Abdel Fatah al-Sisi: Behind the Public Face of Egypt's Soon-to-Be President." *The Guardian,* May 22, 2014.
Kirkpatrick, David D. "Islamists Debate Their Next Move in Tense Cairo." *New York Times,* August 15, 2013.
Springborg, Robert. "Sisi's Islamist Agenda for Egypt." *Foreign Affairs* 90, no. 3 (July 2013): 26–32.
Weymouth, Lally. "Rare Interview with Egyptian Gen. Abdel Fatah al-Sissi [sic]." *Washington Post,* August 3, 2013.

## Sistani, Sayyid Ali Hisayn al- (1930–)

Islamic cleric and the most imposing traditional religious authority in Iraq, author of some 38 books, and a key presence in post-2003 Iraq, where he is regarded as the spiritual leader of Iraqi Shia Muslims. Grand Ayatollah Sayyid Ali Husayn al-Sistani was born in Mashhad, Iran, on August 4, 1930, into a sayyid family that traced its lineage to Prophet Muhammad. Sistani began his religious training in Mashhad and then moved to Qum, Iran, to study Islamic jurisprudence and theory when the supreme and only *marja'-e mutlaq* (source of emulation) of his time, Muhammad Husayn Burujerdi, taught there.

Sistani moved to Najaf, Iraq, in 1951. There he attended lectures by Grand Ayatollahs Abu al-Qassim Khoi and Sheikh Hussayn Hilli. Upon his return to Mashhad, Sistani received the certificate of *ijtihad* by both Khoi and Hilli. *Ijtihad* is a source of law in Jafari jurisprudence involving independent deductive and creative reasoning attainable only after sufficient study and with acknowledgment by certain clerics.

Sistani later returned to Najaf to teach, remaining a quietist during the Islamic revival and rise of activist parties, such as the Islamic Dawa Party, and surviving when other Shiite clerics were persecuted by the Baathist government. Sistani served as the prayer imam in Khoi's own mosque from 1987 to 1993 and announced his status as a *marja' al-taqlid* (religious source of emulation) after Khoi's death. This led to challenges to his authority by clerics in Qum, but Sistani shrugged them off thanks largely to responses of his *wakil* (agent) and son-in-law Javad Shahrastani.

Sistani's mosque was closed in 1994, and he was placed under house arrest. Sistani rarely traveled except for pilgrimages, but he went to London in 2004 to be treated for a heart condition.

Grand Ayatollah Sistani and his *wakils*, including Shahrastani, built and continue to maintain a vast network of adherents and centers of learning and charity. This includes a main office in Qum, which manages his mosques, scholarly libraries, charities, schools, hospitals, seminaries, the publishing of Islamic legal codes, and the distribution of preachers' and students' salaries. The main office also manages the transfers to other agents of his international network, which consists of mosques, charitable organizations, Internet sites, and seminaries, all of which operate on a multimillion-dollar budget. Sistani's activities in Najaf further the *hawzah* (scholarly establishment) there, shaping the future role of clerics, supporting pilgrims and other religious traffic to Iraq's holy cities, and managing educational, Internet, and publishing outlets.

Beyond his religious reach, since 2003 Sistani has significantly impacted the political life of Iraqis, facilitating the integration of clerical influence in the country with government agencies, for the dominant political parties are Islamist and have been extremely powerful within the various ministries. Indeed, he helped move the Iraqi polity more toward an Islamic democratic system than the secular, liberal democracy envisioned by American administrators during 2003–2011.

From the beginning of the Iraqi occupation, the Americans realized that Sistani was an important contact point for them, but they did not fully understand his beliefs or stances vis-à-vis Islamic life and government, Iraqi sovereignty, Iran's role in the country, or Shiism. He refused to meet with them, as he did not support a lengthy military occupation of Iraq and did not wish to be compromised. Communications were thus carried on through intermediaries.

With his thick Iranian accent and his image as a cleric steeped in the Iranian tradition, Sistani has garnered ire from those who oppose Islamic clerics, the Shiites, and Iran in general. He could have initially more forcefully opposed the American occupation, but he instead urged Iraqi cooperation to build stability and independence. However, on June 26, 2003, Sistani's office called for an immediate general election instead of the formation by the Coalition Provisional Authority (CPA) of a transitional government. He then opposed the CPA-supported plan for caucuses that would precede an election. His followers staged protests throughout Iraq and ultimately defeated the plan. Sistani, however, was sustaining his legacy as a quietist scholar who had to preserve clerical independence from politicians and the media. At the same time, he had to oppose undue Western interference in Iraqi affairs.

Sistani nevertheless encouraged all Iraqis to participate in the 2005 elections as their Islamic duty. The result was the emergence of a democratically elected coalition of Shiite parties with an Islamist agenda. One may conclude that Sistani's interpretation of the role of the cleric (*ulema*) differs from that of the late Ayatollah Ruhollah Khomeini's in that Sistani does not argue for *vilayat al-faqih* (rule of the cleric) and opposes authoritarianism. Instead, he holds that the cleric's role in Muslim society is a holistic defense of Islam.

Sistani has decried the civil and sectarian violence that has convulsed Iraq since 2005, calling for restraint in revenge attacks against Sunni Iraqis, although his ability to moderate these conflicts, or inter-Shiite conflict, in central and southern Iraq is limited. He opposed the Iraqi government's 2008 attacks on the Mahdi Army, the militia controlled by cleric

Muqtada al-Sadr, because of the need for Iraqi unity. Sistani did not favor the proposed mutual security agreement between Iraq and the United States, which became operational after the United Nations (UN) Security Council's authorization of U.S. troop presence in Iraq ended in December 2008.

In more recent years, Sistani has urged Iraqis to unify in the face of threats from militant Islamists, most notably appealing directly to Iraqis to fight the Islamic State of Iraq and Syria (ISIS) in June 2014. He has also decried violence against Iraqi Christians. In the spring of 2014, Sistani was mentioned as a possible recipient of the Nobel Peace Prize.

Sherifa Zuhur

**See also**
Iraq; Islamic State of Iraq and Syria; Sadr, Muqtada al-; Shia Islam

**References**
Friedman, Thomas L. "A Nobel for Sistani." *New York Times*, March 20, 2005.
Khalaji, Mehdi. *The Last Marja: Sistani and the End of Traditional Religious Authority in Shiism.* Policy Focus #59. Washington, DC: Washington Institute for Middle Eastern Affairs, September 2006.
Rahimi, Babak. *Ayatollah Sistani and the Democratization of Post-Ba'thist Iraq.* Special Report No. 187. Washington, DC: U.S. Institute of Peace, June 2007.

## Six-Day War (June 5–10, 1967)

In the spring of 1967 the Middle East was poised on the brink of a new war. Israel's neighbors still refused to recognize Israel as an independent state, but their military defeats in the Israeli War of Independence of 1948–1949 and the 1956 War sparked by the Suez Crisis had made even the most belligerent Arab leaders reluctant to embark on a new conflict. Indeed, the fighting after 1956 had shifted to a low-intensity struggle marked by Palestinian raids against the Jewish state from Israeli neighbors Syria and Jordan. Yasser Arafat's al-Fatah movement was a leader in this effort.

Israel met this undeclared war on its territory by retaliatory strikes against guerrilla camps and villages in the Golan Heights of Syria and in Jordan. The year 1965 saw an Arab attempt to divert the flow of the Jordan River, and this brought a series of Israel Defense Force (IDF) attacks against the diversion sites in Syria. This in turn led to a mutual defense pact between Egypt and Syria against Israel, signed on November 4, 1966.

On November 13, 1966, the IDF mounted a large-scale attack on Es Samu in Jordan, a Palestinian refugee camp held by the Israelis to be a base for Syrian terrorists. Then on April 7, 1967, two decades of sporadic raids across the Israel-Syria border exploded into an aerial battle over the Golan Heights, with IDF aircraft downing six Syrian Mikoyan-Gurevich MiG-21 jet aircraft, after which IDF warplanes flew over Damascus in a show of force.

With Israeli's chief supporter of the United States heavily engaged in Vietnam, the leaders of the Soviet Union saw an opportunity to alter the balance of power in the Middle East that would favor their client states of Egypt and Syria. On May 13, the Soviets provided the Egyptian government with false information that Israel was mobilizing troops along the Syrian border. As a consequence, on May 16 Egyptian president Gamal Abdel Nasser declared a state of emergency (Israel's subsequent protestations that the Soviet report was untrue were ignored) and the next day the Egyptian and Syrian governments proclaimed a state of "combat readiness." Jordan also mobilized.

As a consequence of this belligerency, Nasser's popularity soared in the Arab world, and this emboldened him. On May 16 also, Nasser requested that with Egyptian forces massing in the Sinai and the possibility of an Israeli attack on Egypt, the United Nations Emergency Force (UNEF), stationed in the Sinai, should depart immediately. Since the 1956 War UNEF had served as a buffer between Egyptian and Israeli forces. UNEF complied on May 19. The day before, Syria and Egypt placed their armed forces on maximum alert, while the Iraqi and Kuwaiti government announced their forces were also mobilizing.

In a meeting with the Arab press, Nasser also announced Egypt's intention to close the Strait of Tiran to Israeli shipping. The straits were the principal avenue for Israeli trade with Asia and the transit point for 90 percent of its oil imports. Closing the straits to Israel would severely disrupt the Israeli economy. Indeed, Israel had already let it be known that it would consider such a step to be justification for war. Nasser knew that Israel would probably react militarily, but he assumed that the United States would not support the anticipated Israeli military response, while Egypt and its allies would have the support of the Soviet Union. The Kremlin, however, reacted negatively to Nasser's announcement. Having stirred the pot, it now urged restraint. Responding to a hot-line message to Soviet leaders from U.S. president Lyndon Johnson, the Soviets on May 27 insisted that the Egyptians not strike first.

Nasser's proposal regarding the Strait of Tiran was apparently in part bluff. He assumed that the threat of closing the straits would at least force Israel to withdraw its supposed

1188 Six-Day War

# BALANCE OF FORCES, MAY 14–24, 1967

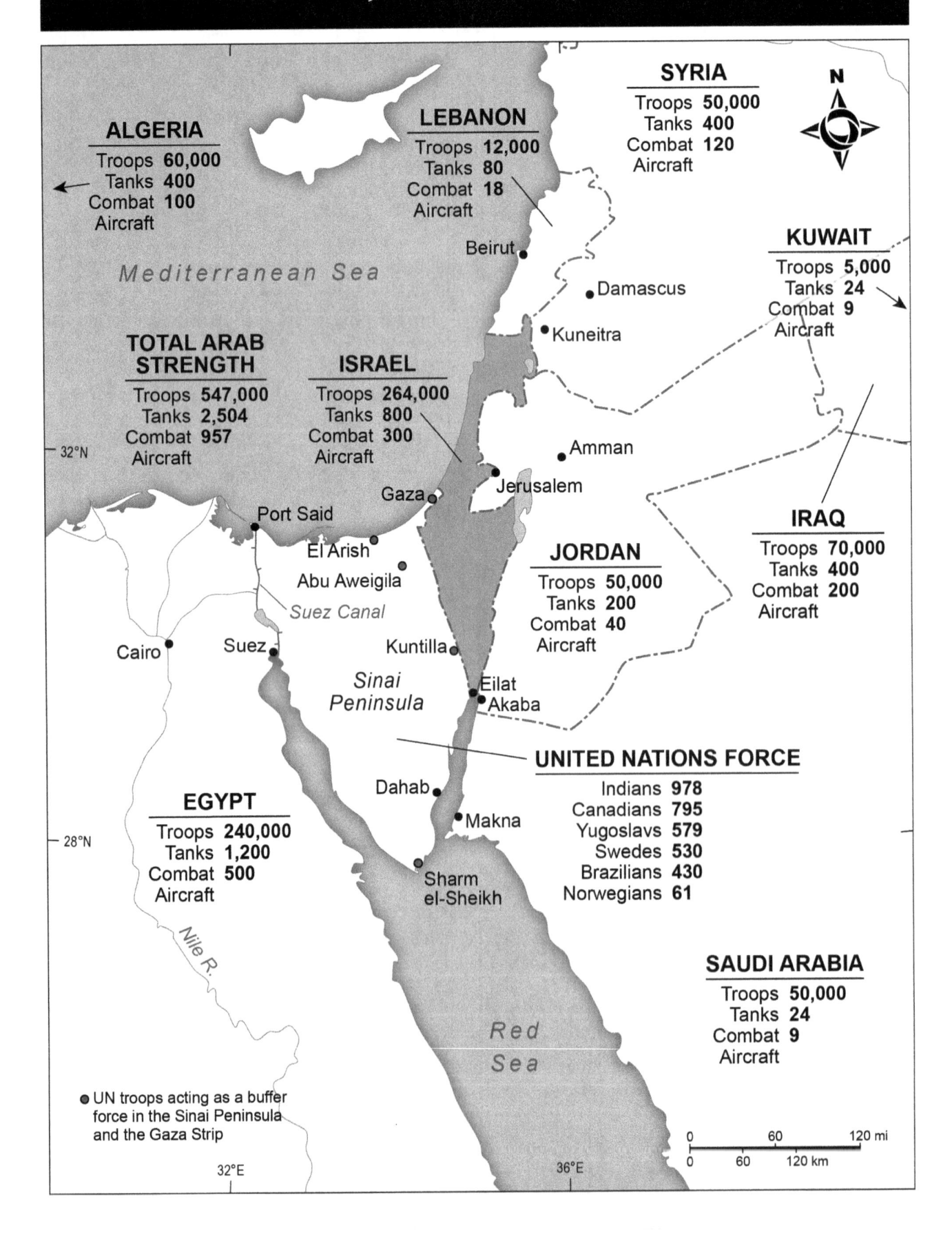

**ALGERIA**
Troops 60,000
Tanks 400
Combat Aircraft 100

**LEBANON**
Troops 12,000
Tanks 80
Combat Aircraft 18

**SYRIA**
Troops 50,000
Tanks 400
Combat Aircraft 120

**KUWAIT**
Troops 5,000
Tanks 24
Combat Aircraft 9

**TOTAL ARAB STRENGTH**
Troops 547,000
Tanks 2,504
Combat Aircraft 957

**ISRAEL**
Troops 264,000
Tanks 800
Combat Aircraft 300

**JORDAN**
Troops 50,000
Tanks 200
Combat Aircraft 40

**IRAQ**
Troops 70,000
Tanks 400
Combat Aircraft 200

**EGYPT**
Troops 240,000
Tanks 1,200
Combat Aircraft 500

**UNITED NATIONS FORCE**
Indians 978
Canadians 795
Yugoslavs 579
Swedes 530
Brazilians 430
Norwegians 61

**SAUDI ARABIA**
Troops 50,000
Tanks 24
Combat Aircraft 9

● UN troops acting as a buffer force in the Sinai Peninsula and the Gaza Strip increased forces along the Syrian border, greatly enhancing his own standing in the Arab world. On May 22, however, Egyptian minister of defense Field Marshal Abdel Hakim Amer ordered Egyptian forces to close the Strait of Tiran the next day. A countermanding order from Nasser would have signaled weakness on his part, and the Egyptian leader issued orders to the Egyptian military to prepare for war.

On May 20, meanwhile, Israel completed a partial mobilization. The Arab states were also mobilizing, and Iraqi and Algerian forces began moving to Syria and Egypt. On May 26, Nasser announced that if Israel were to strike either Egypt or Syria, it would result in a general war, with the Arab goal "the destruction of Israel." On May 30, Jordanian king Hussein arrived in Cairo, and Egypt and Jordan concluded a mutual security pact.

On paper, the balance of forces heavily favored the Arab states. At the beginning of June 1967, Israel had mobilized 230,000 men, 1,100 tanks, 200 artillery pieces, 260 combat aircraft, and 22 naval vessels. Egypt and Syria together had 263,000 men, 1,950 tanks, 915 artillery pieces, 521 combat aircraft, and 75 naval vessels. Counting Iraqi and Jordanian forces, the Arab advantage swelled to 409,000 men, 2,437 tanks, 1,487 artillery pieces, 649 combat aircraft, 90 naval vessels.

Now certain that there would be war and unwilling to allow the Arab forces time to fully mobilize their larger resources, on June 4, despite strong U.S. opposition, Israeli prime minister Levi Eshkol authorized a preemptive strike against Israel's strongest enemy, Egypt. Minister of Defense General Moshe Dayan passed the word to Lieutenant General Yitzhak Rabin and the Israeli General Staff.

The Arab-Israeli War of 1967, known to history as the Six-Day War, commenced on the morning of June 5. For all practical purposes, the war was over by noon. The Israeli Air Force offensive of that day remains one of the most stunning successes in modern warfare.

Destruction of the Egyptian Air Force was essential if the Israeli Army was to enjoy success on the ground, yet Israel was outnumbered by Egypt and Syria two to one in combat aircraft. Also, it would be difficult for Israel to defend against Egyptian and Syrian air attacks because the attackers would come from two different directions and also because Israel was too small in area for early warning systems to provide sufficient time for Israeli fighters to scramble. The Israeli capital of Tel Aviv was 25 minutes' flying time from Cairo but only 4.5 minutes from the nearest Egyptian air base at El Arish.

The initial Israeli air attack plan relied on accurate, timely, and precise intelligence information. It called for a first-strike against Egypt, the most formidable of Israel's opponents. Israeli aircraft were to take off from airfields all around Israel and fly west, under radio silence and at low altitude to avoid radar, out over the Mediterranean, then turn south to strike Egyptian airfields as simultaneously as possible. Rather than attacking at dawn, the strikes were timed to coincide with the return of Egyptian aircraft to base from morning patrols, when most Egyptian pilots would be having breakfast.

The Israeli Air Force (IAF) was certainly one of the best-trained air forces in the world and was well prepared for its mission. The air crews had been thoroughly briefed as to objectives and procedures. IAF ground crews were also highly trained and able to reduce turnaround time between missions to a minimum. Thus, Israeli aircraft could fly up to four sorties a day versus only half that number for their opponents. The operation was, however, extremely risky in that it employed almost all Israeli bomber and fighter aircraft, leaving only a dozen fighters behind to fly combat air patrol in defense of Israel itself.

The IAF achieved complete tactical surprise, going into action at 7:45 a.m. (8:45 a.m. Cairo time). One unexpected development was that Egyptian field marshal Abdel Hakim Amer and his deputy, General Mamoud Sidky, were in the air, flying from Cairo to inspect units in the Sinai, when the attacks commenced. Unable to land in the Sinai, they returned to Cairo, so during 90 minutes two key Egyptian commanders were out of touch with their units and unable to give orders.

The first IAF attack wave struck 10 Egyptian airfields, hitting all of them within 15 minutes of the scheduled time. On their final approach to their targets, the Israeli pilots climbed to make their aircraft suddenly visible on radar in order to induce Egyptian pilots to attempt to scramble in hopes of catching them in their aircraft on the ground. Only four Egyptian aircraft, all trainers, were in the air at the time of the first strikes, and all were shot down. Subsequent waves of Israeli attacking aircraft, about 40 per flight, arrived at 10-minute intervals. These met increased Egyptian opposition, mostly in the form of antiaircraft fire. Only eight Egyptian MiGs managed to take off during the strikes and all were shot down.

In all, the IAF attacked 17 major Egyptian airfields with some 500 sorties (a sortie being one mission by one individual aircraft) in just under three hours, wiping out half of Egyptian Air Force strength of 431 combat aircraft. Most of the Egyptian aircraft were destroyed by accurate Israeli cannon fire, but the Israelis also dropped 250-, 500-, and

1,000-pound bombs. Special bombs with 365-pound warheads, developed to crack the hard-surface concrete runways, were dropped on Egyptian airfields west of the Suez Canal, but none of these were employed against the Sinai airfields, which the Israelis planned for subsequent use by their own aircraft.

Later that same day, June 5, Israeli aircraft struck Syria and Jordan. Following an Iraqi air strike on Israel, IAF aircraft also attacked Iraqi air units based in the Mosul area. With its opposing air forces largely neutralized, the IAF could then turn to close air support and other missions in support of Israeli mechanized ground forces, which had begun operations in the Sinai simultaneously with the initial air attacks. In all, during the war, the Arab side would lose 390 aircraft of their prewar strength of 969 aircraft of all types (Egypt, 286 of 580; Jordan, 28 of 56; Syria, 54 of 172; Iraq, 21 of 149; and Lebanon, 1 of 12). Total IAF losses were 32 aircraft shot down of 354 of all types at the beginning of the war, only 2 to aerial combat.

Israeli ground forces were also on the move against Egypt. The Egyptians, it should be noted, were handicapped by the fact that 50,000 of their best troops were tied down in the ongoing civil war in Yemen. Israeli ground forces sent against Egypt consisted of a mechanized brigade under Colonel Yehuda Resheff, a mechanized division commanded by Major General Israel Tal, an armored division under Major General Avraham Yoffe, and a mechanized division under Major General Ariel Sharon. Tal's division drove into the Rafah–Al Arish area, Resheff advanced into the Gaza Strip, and Sharon moved toward fortifications in the area of Abu Ageila and Kusseima. Yoffe headed southward toward the central Sinai to cut off an Egyptian retreat.

On June 6 Egyptian troops in Gaza surrendered to Resheff's forces. Meanwhile, Tal's mechanized division and Yoffe's armored division linked up. Sharon sent part of his mechanized division to Rafah and Al Arish and the remainder toward Nakhl and Mitla Pass, while Yoffe attacked the main Egyptian force at Jabal Libni in central Sinai. Egyptian Army commander Field Marshal Amer ordered all Egyptian units in the Sinai to withdraw.

On June 7, the major elements of Tal's mechanized division arrived at Bir Gifgafa, while his northern task force passed Romani. The leading brigade of Yoffe's armored division arrived at the eastern end of Mitla Pass out of fuel and short of ammunition. Egyptian forces quickly surrounded it, but shortly thereafter Yoffe's other brigade arrived and relieved the first. Sharon's mechanized division advanced closer to Nakhl, while other units captured northeastern Sinai, and Israeli air and amphibious forces secured Sharm El Sheikh.

On June 8 Egyptian armored units attempted to provide cover for other forces withdrawing from the Sinai. Tal's mechanized division drove them back, however, advancing toward the Suez Canal between Qantara and Ismailiyya. Meanwhile, Yoffe's armored division transited Mitla Pass and reached the canal opposite Port Suez, while Sharon's mechanized division captured Nakhl and moved through Mitla Pass. By the end of the day, the Sinai was firmly under Israeli Army control. Egypt had lost 80 percent of its military equipment and had some 11,500 troops killed, 20,000 wounded, and 5,500 taken prisoner. IDF losses were 338 killed.

On June 9 the United Nations Security Council called for a cease-fire. This left Israel in control of the Sinai east of the Suez Canal. While Israel accepted it immediately, Egypt did not agree to the cease-fire until the next day, June 10. On June 9, meanwhile, Nasser had offered his resignation as president, but it was rejected, the consequence of large Egyptian public demonstrations.

Israeli leaders had urged King Hussein of Jordan to stay out of the war, informing him at the onset of fighting that the dispute was with Egypt. Hussein wanted to avoid participation but came under heavy pressure to act. He was also deceived by early broadcasts from Cairo claiming major Egyptian military successes. Hussein hoped to satisfy his allies with minimum military action short of all-out war. Jordanian 155mm "Long Tom" guns went into action against Tel Aviv, and Jordanian aircraft attempted to strafe a small airfield near Kfar Sirkin. These steps, however, led the Israeli government to declare war on Jordan.

The Jordanians commenced firing on Israeli territory from their part of Jerusalem. Israeli brigadier general Uzi Narkiss then commenced an offensive against Jerusalem with three brigades under Colonel Mordechai Gur. The Israelis surrounded the Old City, defended by Jordanian forces under Brigadier General Ata Ali. That same day in the Battle of Jenin-Nablus, Major General David Elazar, who headed the Israeli Northern Command, received orders to seize Jenin and Nablus and advance to the Jordan River. Elazar dispatched one division and an armored brigade toward Jenin.

On June 6 the Israelis continued their attacks on the Old City but encountered fierce Jordanian opposition. They were able, however, to prevent Jordanian efforts to relieve the Old City. An Israeli tank brigade seized Ramallah, and another captured Latrun. The road between Tel Aviv and Jerusalem was open to Jewish traffic for the first time since 1947. To the north, Jenin fell after midnight to the Israelis after fierce combat.

On June 7 Gur's forces stormed the Old City, forcing the Jordanians to withdraw. That same day, the Israelis captured Bethlehem, Hebron, and Etzion. At the same time, despite Jordanian counterattacks, the Israelis advanced on and seized Nablus. Jordanian forces then withdrew across the Jordan River, and both Israel and Jordan agreed to a cease-fire to take effect at 8:00 p.m.

To the north, at the onset of fighting Syria had positioned on the Golan Heights six brigades on line, with six others in reserve east of Quneitra (Kuneitra). For four days Israeli commander of the Northern Front Major General David Elazar engaged in artillery duels against the Syrians, who showed no signs of wishing to initiate offensive action. On June 8, however, a United Nations–brokered cease-fire collapsed, the consequence of artillery fire from both sides.

On June 9, with resources released from other fronts, Elazar initiated major offensive action in an advance toward the Dan-Banyas area along the foothills of Mount Hermon. The Israelis broke through the first line of Syrian defenses in the northern Golan, with three brigades poised to follow. Other units forced their way north of the Sea of Galilee, while Elazar ordered units recently engaged in the Jenin-Nablus area to attack the Golan south of the Sea of Galilee.

Syrian defenses rapidly deteriorated on June 10 as Israeli forces drove into the northern Golan. The Israelis resisted calls from the United States not to occupy the Golan Heights or to agree to a cease-fire and advanced on Quneitra from the north, west, and southwest. Troops from the Jordanian front pushed northeastward toward the Yarmouk (Yarmuk) Valley and occupied the southern Golan. The Israelis then surrounded Quneitra and captured it. Only when the Golan Heights were firmly in their hands did the Israelis agree to a cease-fire. It went into effect on the Syrian front at 6:30 p.m. on June 10.

Fighting also occurred at sea. In the last few days just before the beginning of the war, during June 3–4 the Israelis trucked landing craft by day from the Mediterranean to Eilat, then returned them at night. This deception led the Egyptians to believe that the Israelis were massing resources at Eilat for operations in the Gulf of Aqaba and caused the Egyptians to shift naval assets into the Red Sea, redressing the imbalance of naval forces in the Mediterranean.

With the start of the war on June 5, Israeli and Egyptian naval units clashed off Port Said. An Israeli destroyer and several motor torpedo boats reached Port Said and were there met by two Egyptian Osa-class missile boats. After an inconclusive battle, the Egyptian missile boats withdrew into the harbor. Israeli frogmen entered the harbors of both Port Said and Alexandria and inflicted some damage on Egyptian ships at Alexandria before they were taken prisoner. On June 6 as a consequence of the Israeli air attacks and the advance on land, Egyptian naval units withdrew from Port Said to Alexandria.

On the night of June 6–7, three Egyptian submarines shelled the Israeli coast near Ashdod and north and south of Haifa, but Israeli air and naval forces returned fire and drove them off. On June 7, with the Israeli capture of Sharm El Sheikh, Israeli warships were able to transit the Strait of Tiran to the Red Sea unobstructed.

On June 8 the *Liberty*, a U.S. electronic intelligence-gathering ship, was steaming in international waters some 13 miles off El Arish on the Sinai Peninsula when it came under attack by Israeli air force and naval units. Thirty-four American personnel died in the attack; another 172 were wounded, many seriously. Although their ship was badly damaged, the *Liberty*'s crewmen managed to keep it afloat, and it was able to make Malta under its own power, escorted by ships of the U.S. Sixth Fleet. The Israeli government later apologized for the attack and paid nearly $13 million in compensation. The reasons for the attack and charges of a cover-up have been the topics of conspiracy theories, but inquiries in both the United States and Israel have concluded that it was a matter of mistaken identity.

In June 2017 on the 50th anniversary of the start of the war, what has been characterized as the war's "last secret" was revealed: during the conflict Israeli scientists raced during the war to assemble a nuclear device to be used in case of an impending Israeli defeat. The secret contingency plan was revealed by retired IDF brigadier general Itzhak Yaakov, who headed IDF weapons development, to historian Avner Cohen in interviews in 1999 and 2000 well before Yaakov's death in 2013. It would have involved the detonation of a nuclear devise atop a mountain in the Sinai in order to intimidate Israel's enemies into withdrawing.

In all, the Six-Day War claimed on the Israeli side some 800 dead, 2,440 wounded, and 16 missing or prisoners. Arab losses, chiefly Egyptian, were estimated at 14,300 dead, 23,800 wounded, and 10,500 missing or prisoners. Israel lost 100 tanks and 40 aircraft, while the Arab side lost 950 tanks and 368 aircraft.

The war vastly increased the amount of territory controlled by Israel. From Egypt, Israel gained all of the Sinai east of the Suez Canal, including the Gaza Strip; from Jordan, it secured the entire east bank of the Jordan River and the Old City of Jerusalem; and from Syria, it added the Golan Heights. Despite calls by the United Nations and the passage

Gunfire and rocket damage to the U.S. Navy intelligence-gathering ship *Liberty*, inflicted when it came under attack by Israeli forces off the Sinai Peninsula on June 8, 1967. (U.S. Navy)

of Security Council Resolution 242 of November 17, 1967, which called for the Israelis to return the captured territories and the Arab states to negotiate peace treaties with Israel, it would be 12 long years and more fighting before the first formal peace treaty between Israel and an Arab nation, Egypt, with the return of the Sinai.

Indeed, warfare between the two sides simply entered a new stage in what would become known as the War of Attrition, with Egypt and Syria supporting enhanced terrorist attacks against Israel. By 1969, Arafat's al-Fatah had gained complete control of the Palestine Liberation Organization (PLO), which supported terrorist activities against Israeli citizens around the world.

The territorial acquisitions by Israel as a consequence of the war made securing a Middle East peace settlement much more difficult. Although Israel returned the Sinai to Egypt in 1978 and withdrew from the Gaza Strip in 2005, it has showed a marked reluctance to yield up the Golan Heights, the West Bank, and Old Jerusalem. Politically conservative Israelis and Ultra-Orthodox Jews consider the West Bank part of the ancient Jewish state, not to be given up on any basis. Yet, some 1.7 million Arabs constitute 21 percent of the Israeli population, raising issues of Israel's survival both as a Jewish state and a democracy. Increasing construction of Jewish settlements and Israel's determination to retain significant parts of the West Bank and all of Jerusalem certainly constitute major barriers to a comprehensive peace settlement. All of these may be traced to the 1967 Six-Day War.

Spencer C. Tucker

**See also**

Amer, Abdel Hakim; Arafat, Yasser; Dayan, Moshe; Egypt; Elazar, David; Eshkol, Israel; Levi; *Liberty* Incident; Nasser, Gamal Abdel; Rabin, Yitzhak; Sharon, Ariel; Syria

**References**

Bowen, Jeremy. *Six Days: How the 1967 War Shaped the Middle East*. London: Simon and Schuster, 2003.

Bregman, Ahron. *Israel's Wars: A History since 1947*. London: Routledge, 2002.

Broa, William J., and David E. Sanger. "Israeli's 1967 Doomsday Plan: A Nuclear Display." *New York Times*, June 4, 2017.

Finkelstein, Norman G. *The Rise and Fall of Palestine: A Personal Account of the Intifada Years*. Minneapolis: University of Minnesota Press, 1996.

Friedman, Thomas L. *From Beirut to Jerusalem*. New York: Anchor, 1990.

Gawrych, George W. *The Albatross of Decisive Victory: War and Policy between Egypt and Israel in the 1967 and 1973 Arab-Israeli Wars*. Westport, CT: Greenwood, 2000.

Goldschmidt, Arthur. *Modern Egypt: The Formation of a Nation State*. Boulder, Co: Westview, 2004.

Hammel, Eric. *Six Days in June: How Israel Won the 1967 Arab-Israeli War*. New York: Simon & Schuster, 1992.

Herzog, Chaim. *The Arab Israeli Wars*. New York: Random House, 1982.

Morris, Benny. *Righteous Victims: A History of the Zionist-Arab Conflict, 1881–2001*. New York: Vintage, 2001.

Mutawi, Samir A. *Jordan in the 1967 War*. Cambridge: Cambridge University Press, 2002.

Ochsenwald, William, and Sydney Nettleson Fisher. *The Middle East: A History*. Boston: McGraw-Hill, 2004.

Oren, Michael B. *Six Days of War: June 1967 and the Making of the Modern Middle East*. New York: Presidio, 2003.

Parker, Richard B. *The Six-Day War: A Retrospective*. Gainesville: University Press of Florida, 1996.

Pollack, Kenneth. "Air Power in the Six-Day War." *Journal of Strategic Studies* 28, no. 3 (2005): 471–503.

Pollack, Kenneth. *Arabs at War: Military Effectiveness, 1948–1991*. Lincoln: University of Nebraska Press, 2002.

Sachar, Howard M. *A History of Israel from the Rise of Zionism to Our Time*. New York: Knopf, 1967.

## Smyrna Crusade (1344–1348)

A joint Christian crusade carried out by the so-called Holy League (Sancta Unio) against the powerful Turkoman ruler of the Aydin emirate, Umur Begh or Umur Pasha (r. 1334–1348), who had his capital at Smyrna (modern-day İzmir, Turkey), a stronghold on the western Anatolian coast.

The crusade was preached during August–September 1343 by Pope Clement VI and undertaken by a united western fleet carrying forces of the papacy, the Venetians, the Knights Hospitallers, the Lusignan kingdom of Cyprus, and some other minor Latin rulers of the Aegean region. The operation's main target was Smyrna itself, held since 1317 by the Aydin Turkomans and used since 1326–1329 as their base for piratical operations in the southeastern Mediterranean. The crusade operations of 1343–1344 came as a sequel to an earlier abortive attempt by the Holy League to seize the port during the autumn and winter of 1334. Its failure left Umur Begh's position strengthened until the early 1340s.

The Holy League Crusade met with success on October 28, 1344, when a surprise Christian attack led by titular Latin patriarch of Constantinople Henri of Asti occupied the port and the lower citadel of the town. Umur Begh's prestige thus received a severe blow, and he was then forced to mount land attacks aimed at recapturing the harbor of Smyrna and dislodging the crusaders from the lower town. During the period of the emir's counterattacks, the Christians received assistance from a new crusading fleet headed by Humbert II, dauphin of Viennois, who was officially appointed leader of the crusade by Clement VI.

In an attempt to neutralize Umur Begh's efforts to retake Smyrna, Humbert led repeated unsuccessful operations in the Aegean between early 1345 and late 1346, using as his base from mid-1346 the island of Chios, recently captured by the Genoese. It was only in late April–early May 1347 that his forces (chiefly the Hospitallers) scored a victory over a united Turkoman fleet from the emirates of Aydin and Sarukhan near the island of Imbros.

Umur Begh was killed in battle during April–May 1348 (according to the dating of the contemporary Byzantine historian Nikephoros Gregoras) during one of his raids against lower Smyrna. Umur's demise occurred just as his former ally, the Byzantine usurper-emperor John VII Kantakouzenos (1347–1354), was on the verge of joining the Holy League, while Clement VI had since 1347 been contemplating a peace treaty with Aydin, having, however, rejected it in February 1348.

Umur's brother and successor, Hizir (Hidir Begh), eventually signed a treaty with the Latins on August 18, 1348. Smyrna remained in Latin hands until its seizure by Timur Lenk (Tamerlane) in the autumn of 1402, following the latter's victory over the Ottomans at the Battle of Ankara (July 20, 1402).

Alexios G. C. Savvides

**See also**
Nikopolis, Crusade in; Tamerlane

**References**
Ahrweiler, Hélène. "L' histoire et la géographie de la region de Smyrne entre les deux occupations turques, 1081–1317." *Travaux et mémoires* 1 (1965): 1–204.
Inalcık, Halil. "The Rise of the Turcoman Principalities in Anatolia, Byzantium and Crusades." *Byzantinische Forschungen* 9 (1985): 179–217.
Lemerle, Paul. *L' Emirat d'Aydin, Byzance et l' Occident: Recherches sur "La Geste d'Umur Pacha."* Paris: Bibliothèque Byzantine, 1957.
Setton, Kenneth. *The Papacy and the Levant, 1204–1571,* Vol. 1. Philadelphia: American Philosophical Society, 1976.
Zachariadou, Elizabeth. *Trade and Crusade: Venetian Crete and the Emirates of Menteshe and Aydin, 1300–1415.* Venice: Institute for Byzantine and Post-Byzantine Studies, 1983.

## SOUTHERN WATCH, Operation (1992–2003)

Coalition surveillance and air policing operation of southern Iraq from August 26, 1992, to March 19, 2003. Operation SOUTHERN WATCH was to prevent Iraqi fixed- and rotary-wing military aircraft from flying in Iraqi airspace south of the 32nd parallel (33rd parallel after 1996). The operation effectively established a southern no-fly zone to enforce United Nations (UN) Security Council Resolution 688, passed on April 5, 1991.

Following the end of the Persian Gulf War in February 1991, Iraqi leader Saddam Hussein ordered his military forces to repress Shiite Muslims in southern Iraq who had revolted against his rule. In April UN Security Council Resolution 688 demanded that Hussein end the attacks, but the Iraqi dictator refused.

On August 26, 1992, U.S. president George H. W. Bush announced that a coalition of UN-member military forces would begin air policing operations of Iraq below the 32nd parallel to ensure Iraq's compliance with Resolution 688. The coalition barred all Iraqi fixed- and rotary-wing aircraft from flying in the designated area. The U.S. Central

Command (CENTCOM) activated Joint Task Force Southwest Asia (JTF-SWA) as the command and control organization for coalition forces monitoring the southern no-fly zone, and the mission was dubbed Operation SOUTHERN WATCH. Lieutenant General Michael A. Nelson, then commander of CENTCOM Air Forces, became the first commander of JTF-SWA, headquartered in Riyadh, Saudi Arabia. Besides the United States, the other coalition partners were Great Britain, France, Russia, and Saudi Arabia.

Coalition air forces flew the first SOUTHERN WATCH sortie on August 27, 1992. At first Iraq complied with the no-fly restrictions, but Hussein soon began challenging SOUTHERN WATCH operations after the UN decision of November 24, 1992, to retain sanctions against Iraq. On December 27, 1992, a U.S. Air Force F-16 Fighting Falcon, patrolling the no-fly zone, encountered an Iraqi MiG-25 Foxbat. After the Iraqi pilot locked his air-to-air radar onto the F-16, the American pilot destroyed the Foxbat with an air-to-air missile. Shortly afterward, Hussein moved surface-to-air missiles (SAMs) into southern Iraq below the 32nd parallel. Because of the threat this posed to coalition pilots flying SOUTHERN WATCH missions, the coalition ordered Hussein to remove them. He ignored the demand.

On January 6, 1993, the United States, Russia, France, and the United Kingdom agreed to work together to enforce Resolution 688. A week later, coalition aircraft destroyed Iraqi SAM sites and their command and control units in southern Iraq, and on January 17, 1994, coalition naval forces disabled an Iraqi nuclear facility with Tomahawk cruise missiles to emphasize the need for Iraq to comply with UN Security Council Resolution 687, which had demanded the destruction of all Iraqi weapons of mass destruction (WMD).

On April 18, 1993, an F-4G Phantom II fired a missile into an Iraqi antiaircraft position after its radar had illuminated the aircraft. On June 26, 1993, the United States launched Tomahawk missiles against targets in Iraq in retaliation for an April 1992 Iraqi government plan to assassinate former president George H. W. Bush during a visit to Kuwait.

Because the first nine months of 1994 passed without any Iraqi challenges in the SOUTHERN WATCH area, JTF-SWA began to withdraw forces in February 1994. By late spring almost 20 aircraft, about 300 personnel, and almost 1,000 tons of equipment had redeployed to their home stations in the United States. However, in October 1994 Iraq began to move troops toward Kuwait after the coalition refused to set a date to end sanctions against Iraq.

Coalition forces then deployed additional forces into the theater in Operation VIGILANT WARRIOR. In response, the UN Security Council passed Resolution 949, which prohibited Iraq from using its forces to threaten neighboring countries or UN operations in Iraq, from deploying units south of the 32nd parallel and from enhancing its military capabilities in southern Iraq.

After another Iraqi confrontation in September 1996, JTF-SWA continued to monitor the airspace south of the 32nd parallel in southern Iraq with aircraft from the American, British, French, and Saudi Arabian air forces from land bases in the region and from U.S. Navy carrier groups in the Arabian Gulf and the Red Sea. Coalition naval forces also provided maritime intercept operations in the northern Red Sea and the Arabian Gulf in support of UN sanctions against Iraq. By this time, the U.S. Air Force had deployed over 6,000 personnel to support Operation SOUTHERN WATCH air operations over southern Iraq. Aircraft included the F-4 Phantom II, F-15 Eagle, and F-16 Fighting Falcon and the KC-135R Stratotanker for refueling coalition strike aircraft. Between August 1992, when SOUTHERN WATCH began, and the end of January 1997, U.S. Air Force aircraft and crews had flown more than 28,800 sorties (68 percent of the total sorties) in support of the coalition operation.

After the June 1996 bombing of the Khobar Towers in Saudi Arabia, the U.S. Air Force relocated the majority of its SOUTHERN WATCH forces at Prince Sultan Air Base to Al Kharj, Saudi Arabia, located to the southeast of Riyadh, and instituted additional force protection measures throughout the U.S. Central Command's area of responsibility.

In November 1998, U.S. president William J. Clinton warned Saddam Hussein that the coalition would use force if he continued to hamper UN weapons inspectors looking for Iraqi weapons of mass destruction. When Hussein continued to do so, the coalition conducted Operation DESERT FOX during December 16–19 to show its resolve in supporting the UN's weapons inspections. Coalition air forces attacked installations associated with Iraq's development of weapons of mass destruction, national command and control systems, air defense facilities, Republican Guard facilities, airfields, and the Basra oil refinery, which was involved in the illegal production of petroleum products for export.

After DESERT FOX began, France ended its participation in SOUTHERN WATCH air operations on December 16, 1998, contending that the American and British air forces had conducted attacks against Iraqi targets for more than a year, contributing to the continuing tensions. France, however, still retained men and equipment in the region.

By early 2001, coalition pilots had entered the southern no-fly zone 153,000 times since the start of SOUTHERN

WATCH without losing any pilots. Since December 1998, the Iraqis had illuminated coalition aircraft with their radar or attacked them with antiaircraft weapons on 500 occasions. In the same period, CENTCOM reported that Iraqi aircraft violated the southern no-fly zone more than 150 times, often trying to lure coalition aircraft north of the 33rd parallel into so-called SAM-bushes. Although some published reports indicated that coalition air operations had caused the deaths of 175 civilians and wounded nearly 500 others between January 1999 and April 2000, coalition aircraft did not target civilian populations or infrastructure and sought to avoid injury to civilians and damage to civilian facilities.

During 2001 and into 2002, U.S. and British aircraft launched sporadic attacks against Iraqi command centers, radars, and communications centers in southern Iraq. Coalition aircraft hit only about 40 percent of the targets, but these attacks sparked adverse opinion in the foreign press, reflecting growing world skepticism about U.S.-British policy toward Iraq. Then, attacks by Iraqi antiaircraft defenses on coalition aircraft, followed by retaliatory air strikes, began to occur almost weekly.

In June 2002, American and British forces stepped up their attacks to degrade Iraqi air defense and communication targets all over southern Iraq to soften them up in preparation for a future invasion of Iraq. Lieutenant General Michael Mosley revealed the existence of this operation, called SOUTHERN FOCUS, in mid-2003. Later revelations discovered that these attacks were part of a preplanned operation to degrade the Iraqi air-defense system in preparation for the planned invasion of Iraq. This operation continued until the beginning of the invasion of Iraq (Operation IRAQI FREEDOM) in March 2003. By that time, coalition air forces had flown nearly 300,000 sorties in support of Operation SOUTHERN WATCH and related operations.

In December 2002, the U.S. Air Force sent an RQ-1 Predator unmanned reconnaissance aircraft, armed with infrared AIM-92 Stinger air-to-air missiles, to patrol the no-fly zone in an attempt to bait Iraqi fighters into a fight. An Iraqi MiG-25 spotted the unmanned aerial vehicle and attacked. Both aircraft fired missiles at each other, but the Iraqi aircraft was outside the range of the Stinger. While the U.S. missile fell short, the Iraqi missile hit the Predator, destroying it. This mission was the first time an unmanned aircraft had been used in air-to-air combat.

During the decade of its duration, Operation SOUTHERN WATCH sparked a number of both good and bad results. First, it provided a major impetus for the U.S. Air Force to reorganize itself into 10 Aerospace Expeditionary Forces (AEFs) that could handle regular, extended, or temporary deployments. Additionally, the need for combat-ready forces produced equipment upgrades and modernization for Air National Guard and Air Force Reserve units, which provided 10 percent of the U.S. Air Force's deployed aerospace expeditionary forces. On the down side, the operation contributed significantly to fast-paced operations that caused major readiness problems throughout the air force. In May 2000, for example, one-third of U.S. Air Force combat units were not fully ready for war, largely because manning and spare parts shortages had reduced its readiness to the lowest level in 15 years. Many believed that the long-term sustained air operations of SOUTHERN WATCH contributed significantly to this problem.

ROBERT B. KANE

**See also**
DESERT FOX, Operation; Hussein, Saddam; Iraq No-Fly Zones; VIGILANT WARRIOR, Operation

**References**
Boyne, Walter J. *Beyond the Wild Blue: A History of the U.S. Air Force, 1947–2007.* 2nd ed. New York: Macmillan, 2007.
Byman, Daniel L., and Matthew C. Waxman. *Confronting Iraq: U.S. Policy and the Use of Force since the Gulf War.* Santa Monica, CA: Rand Corporation, 2000.
Hines, Jay E. "From Desert One to Southern Watch: The Evolution of the U.S. Central Command." *Joint Forces Quarterly* (Spring 2000): 42–48.
Kitfield, James. "The Long Deployment." *Air Force Magazine* 83 (July 2000): 31–36.
Knights, Michael Andrew. *Cradle of Conflict: Iraq and the Birth of Modern U.S. Military Power.* Annapolis, MD: Naval Institute Press, 2005.

## South Lebanon Army

Israeli-trained and -funded Lebanese Christian militia that grew out of the Lebanese Civil War (1975–1990) and helped control and administer the Israeli security zone in southern Lebanon from 1982 to 2000. The South Lebanon Army (SLA), also known as the Free Lebanon Army, numbered 5,000–10,000 fighters at its peak strength in the early 1980s.

Conflict between the Palestine Liberation Organization (PLO) and the broader Palestinian Resistance Movement and some elements in Lebanon began to grow as the Palestinian resistance increased attacks on northern Israel. The Lebanese Civil War began on April 13, 1975, when Phalangist (Christian militia) forces ambushed a bus carrying Palestinians back from a political rally. Syria entered the war in May 1976 on the side of the Lebanese National Movement, an alliance of Druzes, Muslims, and some Christians, after the Lebanese Army began to disintegrate in March 1976. Lebanese Army major Saad Haddad, whose battalion had been allowed to withdraw after being besieged by the PLO in southern Lebanon, joined 400 Christian soldiers who occupied the southern Lebanon border town of Qlaya since leaving the Lebanese Army in 1968 in response to the growing power of the PLO. This new group became known as the Free Lebanon Army (FLA), and its members were still drawing Lebanese government salaries until 1979.

Although a cease-fire in November 1976 brought some calm to Lebanon, the many internal Lebanese issues that had actually sparked the civil war remained unsolved. Israel increased its support of the FLA, while the Palestinians continued their incursions into northern Israel. Israel responded to these attacks by invading southern Lebanon in March 1978 and creating a security zone defended by Israeli forces as well as the approximately 2,000-member SLA. This invasion resulted in a huge loss of life on the Lebanese side, turning many in the area more firmly against Israel and the SLA. The Israel Defense Force (IDF) withdrew in June 1978. On April 18, 1979, Haddad declared the security zone, roughly 62 miles long and 6–12 miles wide with a population of 100,000 people (60 percent Shiite Muslim and 35 percent Christian), to be Independent Free Lebanon, also known as the Government of Free Lebanon. The government of Lebanon did not recognize his claim. The FLA was renamed the South Lebanon Army in May 1980.

During 1980–1982 the ferocious and complex civil war in which Christians fought Christians and Muslims fought Muslims as well as each other continued. Seeing the chaos and weakness of the Lebanese government, Israeli leaders claimed that they feared the growing influence and power of Syria and the PLO in Lebanon. Following PLO attacks on Israeli diplomats in London and Paris, Israeli forces invaded Lebanon on June 6, 1982. The Israeli invasion, known as Operation PEACE FOR GALILEE, sought to secure an area that would push the PLO's Katyusha rockets beyond the range of Israel's northern border. The Israelis also hoped to destroy the terrorist infrastructure that had developed in Lebanon.

After effecting the ouster of the PLO, the IDF hoped to push all remaining Palestinian civilians out of Beirut if possible. The IDF surrounded Beirut and then moved into West Beirut following the assassination of Lebanon's president-elect Bashir Gemayel on September 14, 1982. On September 17, 700–3,500 Palestinian civilians, including women and children, were massacred in the Sabra and Shatila refugee camps by Lebanese Christian Phalangists who were authorized to enter the camps and were monitored there by the IDF. The Phalangist force responsible for the massacre included 150 SLA fighters. While the latter denied their participation in the attacks, survivor testimony noted their southern accents and uniforms.

From 1982 to 2000 the SLA was supplied and supported by Israel, while the SLA administered the security zone and fought the Islamic Resistance movement composed mostly of Lebanese Shiites, Hezbollah, Amal, Islamic Amal, and some Palestinians. Although the PLO was effectively driven from Lebanon by Operation PEACE FOR GALILEE, the Israeli presence in force lasted until 2000 and resulted in such a high number of Palestinian civilian deaths that worldwide public opinion turned against Israel. A treaty ending the engagement was signed on May 17, 1983, only to be revoked by the Lebanese under Syrian pressure soon after Menachem Begin resigned as prime minister of Israel.

SLA head Haddad died of cancer in January 1984 and was replaced by Antoine Lahad. Israel partially withdrew from Lebanon in 1985 but continued to operate in the security zone and supply and support the SLA. In 1985 the SLA occupied Jezzin and its environs, 12 miles north of the security zone, and also opened a detention center in al-Khiam. Amnesty International later accused the SLA of using the al-Khiam facility for torture. Israel contended that al-Khiam was exclusively controlled by the SLA. However, many Lebanese who survived their stay in Israeli-run prison camps from 1982 or who were kidnapped into detention without charges attested to the same types of torture.

Israel redeployed infantry and armor into the security zone in May 1991 in support of its 1,000 soldiers garrisoned there and the approximately 2,500-member SLA. The IDF also deployed soldiers to Jezzin in July 1991. The 1991 SLA-IDF positions remained the status quo until 1999. Ehud Barak was elected prime minister of Israel in May 1999, and in June 1999 he initiated the withdrawal of the IDF and the SLA from the Jezzin area. Hezbollah reentered Jezzin in June 1999. Israel announced its complete withdrawal from southern Lebanon in April 2000 and completed that withdrawal on May 24, 2000. The SLA was too small to hold the security zone against the much larger Hezbollah force without the direct support of Israeli armor and infantry. Barak's rapid withdrawal was blamed in part for the collapse of the SLA.

Once the Israeli withdrawal had been completed, the Lebanese government began hunting down SLA members so they could be brought to trial for various war crimes. Lahad petitioned the Lebanese government for mercy, but the petition was denied. Approximately 4,000 SLA fighters and their families sought refuge in Israel. Some SLA members sought asylum in Europe, with Germany accepting the largest number. More than 3,000 former SLA members were in the custody of the Lebanese government by June 2000, and 2,700 of those were tried by military courts before the year ended. Approximately one-third of those tried were sentenced to less than a month of imprisonment, and one-third were sentenced to one year of imprisonment. The 21 SLA members sentenced to death eventually had their sentences reduced, and 2 SLA members convicted of torture at al-Khiam continue to serve life sentences.

Even though some of the SLA members who fled to Europe and Israel were allowed to return, others were barred from reentry for various spans of time. Those who stayed in Israel were given full citizenship and financial packages equivalent to those given to new immigrants to Israel. The Israeli Knesset Finance Committee agreed on April 6, 2006, to pay the families of each SLA veteran 40,000 Israeli shekels in seven annual installments.

RICHARD M. EDWARDS

### See also
Barak, Ehud; Begin, Menachem; Hezbollah; Lebanon; Lebanon Civil War; Lebanon-Israeli War; Palestine Liberation Organization; Sabra and Shatila Massacre; Syria

### References
Bechara, Souha. *Resistance: My Life for Lebanon.* Translated by Gabe Levine. Brooklyn, NY: Soft Skull, 2003.
Bregman, Ahron. *Israel's Wars: A History since 1947.* 2nd ed. New York: Routledge, 2002.
Fisk, Robert. *Pity the Nation: The Abduction of Lebanon.* 4th ed. New York: Nation Books, 2002.
Schiff, Ze'ev, and Ehud Ya'ari. *Israel's Lebanon War.* Translated by Ina Friedman. New York: Touchstone, 2002.

## South Yemen Civil War (January 13–24, 1986)

Fighting in South Yemen (the People's Democratic Republic of Yemen), known as the South Yemen Civil War, the Events of '86, or simply The Events. With the end of the Aden Emergency (1963–1967), the leftist National Liberation Front (NLF) assumed power in what became the People's Republic of South Yemen. In 1978 the NLF changed its name to the Yemeni Socialist Party (YSP). It became the only legal political party in South Yemen. The YSP, however, was a broad coalition of leftist groups, and there was considerable infighting among them. The civil war of January 1986 resulted from the rivalry that developed between the two leading YSP factions: that led by Abdul Fattah Ismail, the principal Marxist proponent, and the other by South Yemen president Ali Nasir Muhammad. Abdul Fattah Ismail had been de facto president of South Yemen during 1969–1980 before Ali Nasser returned from exile.

On January 13, 1986, in Aden, Ali Nasir's bodyguards opened fire on members of the YSP Politburo as it was about to meet. Ali Nasir's supporters were not in the room when this occurred, and the assassins killed Vice President Ali Ahmads Nair Antar, Defense Minister Saleh Muslik Qassem, and YSP disciplinary head Ali Shayi Hadi. Although Abdul Fattah Ismail survived the attack, he died later that day, apparently from naval gunfire on the city from forces loyal to Ali Nasir.

Fighting immediately spread through Aden between the supporters of the two factions and continued for 12 days, with anywhere from 4,000 to 10,000 people killed. Ali Nasser was ousted on January 25. Some 60,000 people, including Ali Nasser and his supporters, fled South Yemen into North Yemen, and much of the city of Aden was in ruins.

Former Politburo member Ali Salem al-Beidh was the new secretary-general of the YSP. He became vice president of Yemen following its unification in 1990.

SPENCER C. TUCKER

### See also
Aden Emergency; Yemen

### References
Day, Stephen W. *Regionalism and Rebellion in Yemen.* Cambridge: Cambridge University Press, 2012.
Dresch, Paul. *A History of Modern Yemen.* New York: Cambridge University Press, 2001.
Fraihat, Ibrahim. *Unfinished Revolutions: Yemen, Libya, and Tunisia after the Arab Spring* New Haven, CT: Yale University Press, 2016.

## Special Night Squads

Military formations in the British Mandate for Palestine consisting of both British soldiers and members of Haganah, the secret Jewish self-defense organization. The Special Night Squads were organized as a consequence of the Arab Revolt (1936–1939), when Arab militants and terrorists attacked Jews and their property in Palestine. The Special Night Squads were established in 1938 by British captain Orde Charles Wingate, who was attached to British military intelligence in Galilee. Despite his Arabist training and the pro-Arab sentiment of the British administration in Palestine, Wingate learned Hebrew and became a fanatical Zionist.

Wingate secured official permission to organize the Special Night Squads, which were designed to protect Jewish settlements against Arab attack. Active in Lower Galilee and in the Jezreel Valley, the squads operated at night and set ambushes for Arab raiders conducting attacks on the Jewish settlements. The Special Night Squads also attacked known Arab terrorist bases and helped protect the Iraq-Haifa oil pipeline. A special squad also patrolled the Palestine Electric Corporation high-voltage cable located in the Sharon Plain. Although the squads were highly successful in both offensive and defensive operations, they were also much criticized for their ruthless, brutal methods, including the torture of prisoners.

Wingate both commanded the squads and participated in a number of their raids until his politically inspired transfer from Palestine at the end of 1938. His passport was stamped with the words that he was not to be allowed to reenter Palestine. The British administration then greatly limited the effectiveness of the squads, and they were completely disbanded in late 1939. Among the members of the Special Night Squads were future Israeli leaders Moshe Dayan and Yigal Allon. Many regard the Special Night Squads as Britain's first special forces, the predecessor of the Special Air Service formed in October 1941.

Spencer C. Tucker

**See also**
Allon, Yigal; Arab Revolt in Palestine; Dayan, Moshe; Haganah; Palestine, British Mandate for; Wingate, Orde Charles

**References**
Kaniuk, Yoram. *Commander of the Exodus.* New York: Grove, 2001.
Katz, Sam. *Israeli Units since 1948.* London: Osprey, 1988.

## Special Republican Guards

Elite military unit created in 1992 by Iraqi president Saddam Hussein to protect his regime and himself from revolt or assassination by other Iraqi military units. The Special Republican Guards (SRG) was composed of men from clans and towns (such as Tikrit) that were particularly loyal to Hussein. They were better paid and received more benefits than members of the regular army or the Republican Guards and had the best military equipment at their disposal. After the fall of Hussein's government in April 2003, the SRG was believed to have been responsible for much of the violence of the Iraqi insurgency that followed.

During the 1991 Persian Gulf War, most of Hussein's elite Republican Guard units suffered heavy casualties. Although those who survived remained loyal to Hussein and helped maintain him in power, he apparently feared that some might turn on him. For that reason, in 1992 (some sources say 1995) Hussein created the SRG. From the very beginning, the SRG was intended to protect the regime from internal foes more than from external threat. To ensure loyalty, SRG members were recruited from Hussein's clan and those closely allied to it. The members were also required to be from Tikrit, Bayji, Sharqat, or other smaller towns in the region in which Hussein was born. Recruits were almost always Sunni Muslims rather than Kurds or Shiites. By insisting on these membership criteria, Hussein was able to better ensure that the SRG would be loyal to him and his family through ties of family, regional origin, and shared religion. In addition to better pay than their military compatriots, members of the SRG received enlistment bonuses and subsidized housing, which were not offered to other units.

The SRG was the only armed force allowed to garrison Baghdad. Regular army troops were never stationed in the city, and Republican Guard divisions were stationed in the city's outer defenses. The SRG was under the authority not of the Defense Ministry but rather of the State Special Security Apparatus, which was tightly controlled by Hussein himself. Indeed, the commander of the SRG was Qusay Hussein, the dictator's son.

The SRG was originally composed of one brigade but later was expanded to five brigades with a total of 14 battalions of 1,300 to 1,500 men each. Four of the brigades were mechanized infantry, equipped with the best weapons available in Iraq. A fifth brigade was armored, equipped with T-72 main battle tanks. Antiaircraft weapons were also available, including handheld weapons and antiaircraft artillery. Because the SRG's purpose was to protect the regime, it had to be able to resist assaults by regular military units. At its peak, the SRG numbered about 26,000 men. By March 2003, however, its strength had declined to some 12,000 troops.

The SRG's duties included protecting Hussein's various presidential palaces and residences along with his farms and other real estate holdings. The SRG also guarded key installations in Baghdad. The 1st Brigade in particular was charged with presidential security. Various units drove and maintained the limousines used by Hussein and provided security for motorcades and members of the government and their families. One gruesome task assigned to the 1st Brigade was the apprehension and execution of military officers and government leaders accused of disloyalty to the regime. Other units are believed to have been charged with guarding sites that might have contained weapons of mass destruction (WMD).

In 1998 a dispute between the Iraqi government and the United Nations (UN) arose when weapons inspectors wanted to examine SRG facilities believed to contain WMD. Although the situation was resolved without violence, the episode convinced some intelligence experts that Hussein continued to work on forbidden weapons and used his most loyal units to keep prying eyes away.

During the March 2003 Anglo-American–led invasion of Iraq, many American military leaders believed that the SRG would be their most dangerous opponent. While the Republican Guard was largely destroyed outside of Baghdad, the SRG was first encountered in the fighting for Baghdad International Airport on April 4. In a three-hour engagement with troops of the U.S. 3rd Infantry Division, the SRG was soundly defeated. Three tanks were destroyed, and an estimated 250 SRG members were killed; American losses were 1 dead and 8 wounded. Following this battle, the SRG largely melted into the population. Fears that SRG members might fight house to house for Baghdad proved unfounded. On May 23, 2003, the provisional Iraqi government ordered the SRG dissolved.

Former SRG members are believed to have launched the insurgency against coalition forces in the Sunni triangle around Tikrit during the summer of 2003. Ironically, the Sons of Iraq and Anbar Awakening home guard militias were funded, trained, and equipped by the Americans beginning in 2007; they contained cadres composed of former SRG members.

TIM J. WATTS

### See also
Anbar Awakening Movement; Baghdad, 2003 Battle of; Hussein, Saddam; Iraq; Iraq Insurgency; Republican Guard, Iraq

### References
Carlisle, Rodney P. *Iraq War*. New York: Facts on File, 2005.
Keegan, John. *The Iraq War: The Military Offensive, from Victory in 21 Days to the Insurgent Aftermath*. New York: Vintage, 2005.
Woods, Kevin M., and Michael R. Pease. *The Iraqi Perspectives Report: Saddam's Senior Leadership on Operation Iraqi Freedom; From the Official U.S. Joint Forces Command Report*. Annapolis, MD: Naval Institute Press, 2006.

## Speicher Massacre
*See* Camp Speicher Massacre

## *Stark* Incident (May 17, 1987)

Iraqi cruise-missile attack on the U.S. Navy Perry-class frigate *Stark* (FFG-31) in the Persian Gulf on May 17, 1987. The attack occurred during the Iran-Iraq War (1980–1988), which saw both sides routinely firing on cargo and tanker vessels in the Persian Gulf. Fearing that such activity would disrupt oil supplies to the West, the Ronald Reagan administration dispatched U.S. Navy warships to escort tankers in the Persian Gulf.

At 8:00 p.m. on May 17, 1987, an Iraqi Mirage F-1 Falcon fighter aircraft departed Iraq's Shaibah Air Base on a routine antishipping patrol. The crew of a U.S. Airborne Warning and Control System (AWACS) aircraft detected the Mirage as it broke over the Persian Gulf 10 minutes later. The *Stark* was informed and itself detected the Mirage at 9:40 p.m. when it was 200 nautical miles distant. With there being no indication of anything other than a routine patrol, the crew of the *Stark* was unprepared. Captain Glenn Brindel of the *Stark* ordered two messages sent, identifying his vessel as a U.S. Navy warship and calling on the pilot to identify himself. There was no response.

At 22 miles distant from the *Stark*, the Mirage pilot launched an AM-39 Exocet antiship cruise missile; at 15 miles he launched a second missile, then veered off. The messages to the Iraqi aircraft actually occurred after the missile launches. At approximately 10:10 p.m., one of the ship's lookouts detected an incoming missile and notified the ship's Combat Information Center (CIC). By then, it was too late for the crew to take action.

Both of the radar-guided missiles, traveling at Mach 0.8, slammed into the ship's port side. One hit beneath the bridge, and the other hit just aft of the first missile, almost in the superstructure's center. The first missile did not detonate, but its fuel ignited and caused a large damaging fire. The single warhead detonation all but destroyed the ship's CIC, eliminating most of its combat systems, electronics, and a third of its firefighting equipment. The crew fought fires throughout the night and ultimately saved the ship. They then took it to Bahrain under its own power. The frigate lost 37 crewmen killed; 8 others died of their wounds, while 21 other injured men survived.

The subsequent U.S. Navy investigation found several problems with the ship's design and shortcomings in the *Stark*'s watch standing and training procedures. The ship's electronic countermeasures system had a blind zone off the bow and had been facing the Iraqi fighter at the time of the Exocet launches. However, the failure to detect the incoming missiles was as much due to complacency as systems shortcomings. Two critical weapons stations were not manned during the incident, one of them because the assigned watch stander had departed his station to run personal errands. Brindel had not been called to the CIC, nor was he kept constantly informed of the situation until the final moments before the missile struck. More importantly, the ship's executive officer was present in the ship's CIC, and neither noticed the empty weapons control stations or took any action to increase the ship's combat readiness until the incoming missile had been detected when it was too late.

The *Stark* incident illustrated the deadliness of antiship cruise missiles and proved the "win big or die" nature of modern sea combat. It also triggered political debate in Washington about the wisdom of operating U.S. warships in the Persian Gulf when Europe and Asia received a far greater proportion of their oil from that region than did the United States. However, the Reagan administration perceived that U.S. credibility was at stake and continued the naval patrols and tanker escorts in the Persian Gulf, soon to be dubbed Operation EARNEST WILL, which would endure until December 1989.

The poststrike investigations forced Brindell's retirement and resulted in letters of reprimand for the executive officer and the tactical action officer on watch that evening as well as disciplinary proceedings against the individual who had departed his assigned watch station. U.S. Navy warships intensified their quick-reaction drills and other combat readiness training for ships destined for Persian Gulf duty. Also, the Perry-class frigates received upgrades to their electronic warning and countermeasures systems to eliminate blind zones. The *Stark* was taken back to the United States on a special heavy-lift ship. The extensive repairs required led to the *Stark* being out of service for more than 18 months.

CARL OTIS SCHUSTER

**See also**
EARNEST WILL, Operation; Iran-Iraq War; Persian Gulf

**References**
Cooper, Tom, and Farzaad Bishop. *The Iran-Iraq War in the Air, 1980–1988*. Atglen, PA: Schiffer Publishing, 1991.
Karsh, Efraim. *The Iran-Iraq War, 1980–1988*. Oxford, UK: Osprey, 2001.
Levenson, Jeffrey L., and Randy L. Edwards. *Missile Inbound: The Attack on the Stark in the Persian Gulf*. Annapolis, MD: Naval Institute Press, 1997.
Wise, Harold L. *Inside the Danger Zone: The U.S. Military in the Persian Gulf, 1987–1988*. Annapolis, MD: Naval Institute Press, 2007.

## STEEL CURTAIN, Operation (November 5–22, 2005)

A major anti-insurgent operation during the Iraq War (2003–2011) mounted by U.S. marines and Iraqi forces during November 5–22, 2005, as part of the broader al-Sayyad operation that aimed to control the resistance in the Euphrates River Valley, deal with Anbar Province, and also establish control by the Iraqi Army in the Al Qaim region. Operation STEEL CURTAIN (also known as AL-HAJIP ELFULATHI) was important in that it was the first military operation of the war to include significant numbers of Iraqi Army personnel recruited and trained by the coalition government for Iraq. Thus, for the first time Iraqi soldiers took the lead in some of the house-to-house searches and extensively patrolled in insurgent areas. The U.S. command considered the operation to be a success, although it was costly in terms of civilian casualties and the creation of strong tensions.

After the fall of President Saddam Hussein's regime in April 2003, many U.S. leaders considered the war in Iraq to be effectively at an end. This proved not to be the case when a major insurgency broke out that summer and intensified over the succeeding months. Some of the resistance came from Islamist groups, but all wanted American troops out of Iraq. The resistance activity was particularly intense in Anbar Province, in western Iraq adjoining the Syrian border, but was not restricted to this area. The Anbar region is dominated by Sunni tribes, and they expected nothing but violence and a diminution of their role in Iraq under a government dominated by Shiites.

This region had long been used by smugglers. Consisting mostly of rough desert terrain, the province held many routes for men, arms, and supplies to flow from Syria to desert camps and urban locations inside Iraq. Major urban centers included Husaybah, Karabilah, and Ubaydi. Ubaydi in particular was considered a key location for insurgents and was heavily fortified. Indeed, the earlier Operation MATADOR in May 2005 had been an attempt to secure Ubaydi. Although coalition forces took the city, they failed to garrison it, and insurgents quickly resumed control over the city.

Most observers believed that coalition success in Iraq would depend on whether or not a viable Iraqi military could be established. When Hussein was forced from power, the United States took what many now consider to be the unwise course of completely disbanding the Iraqi military as part of the attempt to rid the country of Baathist influences. This decision left a power vacuum that coalition forces could not fill and forced the building of a new Iraqi Army from scratch. The process was slow and difficult, but Operation STEEL CURTAIN appeared to be an opportunity to speed along the process.

In June 2005 U.S. forces launched Operation SPEAR, an effort to oust insurgents from Anbar Province. Only some 100 Iraqi soldiers participated. By November 2005, however, the number of Iraqi soldiers nationwide had increased dramatically. Special efforts had also been made to recruit and station new units in and around Anbar. Two Iraqi division headquarters were formed, along with four brigade headquarters. Ten infantry battalions were recruited and deployed to Anbar. A total of 15,000 Iraqi soldiers were stationed in the province by November 2005, with 1,000 deployed to help the American troops in STEEL CURTAIN.

The most hopeful sign for the coalition was that some of the new troops were locally recruited. A number were assigned to specially trained Scout Platoons, also known as Desert Protectors. Comparisons were made between the Scout Platoons and Native Americans recruited by the U.S. cavalry during the 19th-century Native American wars in the American West. As with the Native American units, the Scout Platoons were familiar with the territory in which STEEL CURTAIN took place. They served as a liaison between American units and local tribal leaders, and the scouts also provided information about which individuals belonged in the area and which individuals might be foreign fighters. American military leaders also viewed the increased number of recruits as a sign that the local population was increasingly unhappy with the foreign fighters, especially members of Al Qaeda.

In July 2005 coalition forces launched Operation HUNTER, an effort to clear the Euphrates River Valley. Coalition planners recognized that in the western provinces most of the insurgents in 2005 were Al Qaeda operatives. The goal of Operation HUNTER was to force the insurgents from the region and cut off the supply lines that funneled fresh resources and men into Iraq and permitted operatives to escape to camps in Syria and beyond. Unlike earlier anti-insurgent campaigns, Operation HUNTER was also expected to establish a permanent Iraqi Army presence in the area.

American operational forces for STEEL CURTAIN included marines of the 3rd Battalion, 6th Marine Regiment, and the 2nd Battalion, 1st Marine Regiment. Both were part of the 2nd Marine Division. The marines were reinforced with supporting units and specialists, including forward air controllers, to total approximately 2,500 troops.

STEEL CURTAIN began on November 5 with an assault on Husaybah. It took coalition forces four days to clear the city. Many of the insurgents forced from Husaybah fled to Karabilah. Another four days were needed to secure Karabilah. The final phase of the operation was to secure Ubaydi. Fighting in this center of Al Qaeda operations was difficult and more protracted, involving house-to-house combat. After seven days, coalition commanders declared the city secure.

Operation STEEL CURTAIN officially ended on November 22. Iraqi soldiers were praised for their participation in the operation, especially their work inside the cities. Unlike earlier operations, the coalition forces established forward operating bases in the region as they cleared out the Al Qaeda insurgents. The goal was to establish an ongoing presence that would prevent the return of Al Qaeda.

Coalition losses in STEEL CURTAIN were relatively light. Ten marines were killed and 30 others were wounded. Losses among the Iraqi troops are unknown. Coalition spokesmen claimed that 139 insurgents were killed and another 256 captured. The operation also resulted in hundreds of civilian casualties and the destruction of much of Husaybah, including government buildings, schools, and two mosques. Iraqi citizens were also very angry and upset because they were not allowed to reclaim their dead.

Five Al Qaeda terrorist organization leaders were killed in the air strikes on Husaybah. Although planners had hoped to capture or kill Jordanian-born Al Qaeda associate Abu Musab al-Zarqawi, he was not among them but was killed in an American air strike in June 2006.

Coalition leaders considered the operation a success and held that the new Iraqi Army could now aid in operations against insurgents. Only three weeks after the conclusion of STEEL CURTAIN on December 15, the Iraqi provisional government held the first democratic election in years. A permanent legislative body was elected. Although many in the Al Qaim and Anbar regions refused to take part, the reduction in the harassment and intimidation of voters was considered an important goal of STEEL CURTAIN and similar coalition military operations.

TIM J. WATTS

### See also
Al Qaeda in Iraq; Iraq Insurgency; Iraq War

### References
Benhoff, David A., and Anthony C. Zinni. *Among the People: U.S. Marines in Iraq.* Quantico, VA: Marine Corps University, 2008.

Navarro, Eric. *God Willing: My Wild Ride with the New Iraqi Army.* Washington, DC: Potomac Books, 2008.

West, Bing. *The Strongest Tribe: War, Politics, and the Endgame in Iraq.* New York: Random House, 2008.

## Stern, Avraham (1907–1942)

Fervent Zionist and founder and leader of the Lehi (Lohamei Herut Israel) terrorist group, also known as the Stern Gang. Avraham Stern was born in Suwałki, Poland, on December 23, 1907. He studied at the Hebrew High School there but immigrated to Palestine in 1925 before graduating and continued his high school studies in Jerusalem. He then studied philosophy and classical languages at Jerusalem's Hebrew University. Fluent in Latin and Greek, Stern won a scholarship to study in Florence, Italy. There he was impressed by dictator Benito Mussolini as well as Italian fascism.

A natty dresser and a womanizer, Stern on his return to Palestine sought a calling to which he could dedicate his talents, as academic work no longer held his attention. Considered a gifted albeit eccentric poet, he failed in his attempts to make a living from writing. Instead, he turned to politics.

By the late 1920s Stern embraced Revisionist Zionism, a movement founded by Vladimir Jabotinsky. Revisionist Zionists agreed with mainline Zionists on the goal of establishing a Jewish state in Palestine, but its approach was more militant and envisioned an armed struggle to achieve the end. Palestine was then ruled by Britain under a League of Nations mandate, and tensions between Jews and Arabs owing to increased Jewish migration into Palestine and Jewish land purchases there spilled over into violence. Stern became an active member of Haganah, the Jewish self-defense organization that helped to protect Jews against Arab attack. Stern participated in the defense of Jewish homes and shops in Jerusalem during the Arab Riots of 1929 in which some 133 Jews were killed and 400 injured in Jerusalem, Hebron, and Safed.

Although the British finally quelled the riots, sporadic violence continued throughout the next decade. Indeed, the official response from the British government seemed to favor the Arabs in that London sought means to curb Jewish immigration and land purchases in Palestine. Stern was convinced of the need to organize a more active defense of Jewish interests. In 1931 he helped found the radical group known as the Irgun Tsvai (Zvai) Leumi (National Military Organization [IZL], commonly referred to as Irgun). It advocated counterterrorist tactics against the Arabs and the military liberation of Palestine. Subsequently, Stern directed a training program that emphasized the use of small arms and explosives. He quickly rose through the ranks and became Irgun's top field commander.

Despite Stern's success, in 1937 he formed a splinter group of Irgun commonly referred to as the IZL. By that time, he was drifting away from Jabotinsky and turned to Abba Achimeir, whose Brith Habiryonim faction was even more radical than the Revisionists. Achimeir and Stern agreed to take a more aggressive approach regarding their enemies. Designed with such tactics in mind, the IZL prepared for a campaign of terror. Stern's watchwords were "study, train, and think," but his emphasis was on the use of force.

Formation of the IZL coincided with another Arab uprising known as the Arab Revolt, which began in 1936, as Haj Amin al-Husseini, grand mufti of Jerusalem, led a successful general strike. For the next three years, unrest was commonplace throughout the country. British authorities seemed unable or unwilling to end the violence and continued to offer peace plans and then retract them. Stern organized a bombing campaign and instructed his IZL squads to "kill, be killed, but do not surrender."

*Staunch Zionist Avraham Stern was the leader of the Lehi underground Jewish terrorist organization that became known as the "Stern Gang." Stern was tracked down and killed by British authorities in Palestine on February 12, 1942. (Israeli Government Press Office)*

By 1938, civil government had largely broken down in Palestine. Martial law brought a semblance of peace, but new British policies helped push Stern into a different strategy. Recognizing the strong possibility of a world war, London opted to protect Britain's significant Middle Eastern holdings by placating Arab opinion. On May 17, 1939, an official British white paper declared that only 75,000 more Jews would enter Palestine. After that, local Arabs would decide immigration policy. To Zionists in Palestine, the white paper was a dangerous blow against their future. Furthermore, few Western countries were willing to accept Jewish refugees.

Stern saw Britain's decision as a declaration of war. He called for action but was overruled by Jabotinsky. To avoid controversy, Stern returned to Poland. There, he hoped to expand IZL operations and recruit fighters. Although he established a daily newspaper, *Die Tat* (Action), the German invasion of September 1, 1939, interrupted Stern's mission. Escaping back to Palestine, Stern made a complete break with Jabotinsky and the IZL, which argued the need for cooperation with the British, who had gone to war against Germany on September 3. Stern, asserting that World War II was a conflict "between Gog and Magog," called instead for a campaign against Great Britain. A year later, Stern formed his last underground unit, Lohamei Herut Israel (Fighters for Israel's Freedom, also known as Lehi for its Hebrew acronym). Recruited chiefly from the IZL, Lehi numbered about 200 men and women. Although Lehi was small in size, its members were dedicated and extremely dangerous. Lehi lived up to Stern's dark poetry, for assassination, bombing, and robbery were all Lehi tactics.

British authorities labeled Lehi the Stern Gang, and during 1940–1941 Stern led a clandestine existence that required numerous safe houses, codes, and a quick wit. His alias, Yair, was picked to honor Eliezar ben Yair, the Zealot leader who had defied the Roman armies from the fortress of Masada centuries before. In a controversial action, Stern sent agents to contact Nazi Germany. Arguing that "the enemy of my enemy is my friend," he attempted to forge an alliance between Lehi and the Abwehr, Germany's military intelligence service. Although nothing came of that tentative outreach, word of Stern's activities caused most Jews to sever all ties with Lehi.

In January 1942 following a bomb explosion in Tel Aviv that killed three policeman, British authorities offered a reward of £1,000 for Stern's arrest. Cut off from support and now hunted, he went into hiding. He escaped several dragnets but was finally discovered in Tel Aviv. On February 12, 1942, six British policemen broke into his safe house and shot him on the spot. In 1978 an Israeli postage stamp was issued in Stern's honor, and he is also memorialized in the town of Kochav Yair (Yair's Star), after his nickname.

SPENCER C. TUCKER

**See also**

Arab Revolt in Palestine; Gog and Magog; Haganah; Husseini, Haj Amin al-; Irgun Tsvai Leumi; Jabotinsky, Vladimir Yevgenyevich; Palestine, British Mandate for; White Paper of 1939; Zionism

**References**

Bell, J. Bowyer. *Terror Out of Zion: Irgun Zvai Leumi, Lehi and the Palestine Underground, 1929–1949*. New York: St. Martin's, 1979.

Bethell, Nicholas. *The Palestine Triangle: The Struggle for the Holy Land, 1935–48*. New York: Putnam, 1979.

Brenner, Lenni. *The Iron Wall: Zionist Revisionism from Jabotinsky to Shamir*. London: Zed, 1984.

## Stern Gang

*See* Lohamei Herut Israel

## St. Petersburg, Treaty of (September 12, 1723)

Peace treaty signed in the wake of the Persian campaign of Emperor Peter I of Russia. In 1722 in an attempt to expand Russian influence to the Caspian Sea, Peter I secured an alliance with eastern Georgia and launched a successful campaign against the Persians along the western shores of the Caspian Sea. By late August he captured Derbent (southern Dagestan) but was then forced by stormy weather to return back to Russia. A Russian flotilla, however, conducted successful raids and occupied Resht (December 1722) and Baku (July 1723). These successes compelled Persia, which had just suffered a devastating Afghan invasion, to sue for peace.

Russia and Iran signed the peace treaty in St. Petersburg on September 12, 1723. The agreement forced Persia to cede all lands on the western and southern coast, including Derbent, Baku, Shirvan, Gilan, Mazandaran, and Astrabad. In return, Russia pledged to provide military support to Persia against the Ottoman Empire.

The Persian government initially refused to ratify the treaty, but the Russian threat of further military action forced it to consent to the cession of these provinces. In 1732, Russia agreed in the Treaty of Resht to return the above-mentioned territories to Persia in exchange for Persian assistance against the Ottoman Empire.

ALEXANDER MIKABERIDZE

**See also**
Russo-Ottoman Wars

**Reference**
Kazemzadeh, F. "Iranian Relations with Russia and the Soviet Union to 1921." In *The Cambridge History of Iran*, ed, W. B. Fisher et al., 314–350. Cambridge: Cambridge University Press, 1991.

# Strait of Tiran Crisis (1956–1967)

The Strait of Tiran, a strategically important three-mile-long narrow body of water between the Sinai Peninsula and the island of Tiran that connects the Red Sea to the Gulf of Aqaba, is the westernmost passage of the Strait of Tiran. Egyptian closure of the waterway helped precipitate the opening of hostilities during both the 1956 Suez Crisis and the 1967 Six-Day War. The eastern shore of the Strait of Tiran is part of Saudi Arabia, while the western shore is at the southern tip of the Sinai Peninsula, overlooked by the Egyptian city of Sharm El Sheikh. All shipping to and from the Israeli port of Eilat and the Jordanian port of Aqaba must pass through these narrow straits.

In the aftermath of the Israeli War of Independence (1948–1949), Egypt closed the Strait of Tiran from 1949 to 1956. This action was in violation of both the 1949 armistice agreement and international law. As such, the Israel Defense Force (IDF) General Staff planned for a preemptive war that would begin with an attack to reopen the strait.

The Israelis found common cause with the British and French when Egyptian president Gamal Abdel Nasser nationalized the Suez Canal on July 26, 1956. The Israeli government secretly conspired with the British and French governments whereby the IDF would attack across the Sinai, providing the British and French an excuse to intervene with their forces allegedly to protect the canal. Cooperating with its allies, the IDF hoped to be able to reopen the Strait of Tiran to Israeli shipping but also to destroy Egyptian military forces in the Sinai and halt fedayeen terrorist attacks originating from the Gaza Strip.

The IDF's Sinai Campaign, launched on October 29, 1956, proved to be a huge success. During the final phase of the campaign, the IDF's 9th Infantry Brigade captured Sharm El Sheikh and reopened the Strait of Tiran on the night of November 2–3.

Now in complete control of the Sinai, the Israelis were not content with a mere armistice. They refused to evacuate the Sinai until they secured international promises that would guarantee unfettered Israeli access to the Strait of Tiran. After 17 nations had agreed that Israel was entitled to the right of passage through the waterway, on March 1, 1957, Israel began to withdraw its forces. All IDF personnel had departed the Sinai by March 11.

Recognizing Egypt's blockade of the strait as a violation of international passage, United Nations (UN) Resolution II of February 2, 1957, called for a UN Emergency Force (UNEF) to be placed in the Sinai upon Israel's withdrawal. An element of the UNEF was garrisoned at Sharm El Sheikh to ensure that the waterway remained open to all international shipping. The United States further pledged to the Israelis that it would consider any blockade of the Strait of Tiran to be an act of war against Israel and thus subject to an Israeli military response. Further protections were afforded Israel in April 1958 when the UN Conference on the Law of the Sea adopted the Convention on the Territorial Sea and Contiguous Zone, which forbade any future blockade of the strait.

As Israeli-Egyptian tensions heated up again in 1967, President Nasser demanded that the UNEF be withdrawn from the Sinai. In a mistaken decision, UN secretary-general U Thant complied with the request without seeking the counsel of the General Assembly. On May 23, 1967, Nasser announced that Egypt had again closed the Strait of Tiran to Israeli shipping. The following day, he announced that the waterway had been mined. Both moves were in blatant violation of international law.

The Israeli government first sought a diplomatic solution to the crisis by asking both the United States and the UN to secure reopening the Strait of Tiran, as had been promised in 1957. With no sign of international action against Egypt, however, Israel launched the Six-Day War on June 5, 1967. The IDF General Staff planned Operation LIGHTS to seize Sharm El Sheikh and open the waterway. Although originally planned as a night offensive, with paratroops landing at A-Tur to support a naval assault, the IDF conducted a morning attack on June 7, when it was determined that most of the Egyptian forces had already withdrawn. After a brief fight, the Israelis declared the strait reopened. The Israelis remained in control of the Strait of Tiran until 1982, when they evacuated Sharm El Sheikh under the provisions of the 1978 Camp David Accords and the 1979 Israel-Egypt Peace Treaty. The eastern part of the Sinai, including the strait, is currently demilitarized and remains under the supervision of the Multinational Force and Observers.

Thomas D. Veve

**See also**
Aqaba, Gulf of; Camp David Accords; Eilat, Israel; Geography of the Middle East; Israel-Egypt Peace Treaty; Nasser, Gamal Abdel; Red Sea; Sharm El Sheikh; Sinai Campaign of 1956; Six-Day War; Suez Canal; Suez Crisis

**References**
Halderman, John W., ed. *The Middle East Crisis: Test of International Law.* Dobbs Ferry, NY: Oceana, 1969.
Herzog, Chaim. *The Arab-Israeli Wars: War and Peace in the Middle East from the War of Independence to Lebanon.* Westminster, MD: Random House, 1984.
Oren, Michael B. *Six Days of War: June 1967 and the Making of the Modern Middle East.* Novato, CA: Presidio, 2003.
Smith, Charles D. *Palestine and the Arab-Israeli Conflict: A History with Documents.* 6th ed. New York: Bedford/St. Martin's, 2006.

# St. Sabas, War of (1256–1270)

A conflict between the Genoese and the Venetian merchant communes in Acre (modern-day Akko, Israel) in the Latin Kingdom of Jerusalem. Fought during 1256–1270, it escalated into a civil war that embraced the whole of the Kingdom of Jerusalem. The conflict developed out of rival claims by the Genoese and the Venetians to the monastery of St. Sabas, which lay on the boundary between their respective quarters in Acre, and was fueled by their competition for the maritime trade of the Mediterranean. The Genoese had the upper hand early in the war, but this situation was reversed when Venice and Pisa signed a 10-year military alliance.

Early in 1256 the Genoese seized the monastery and attacked the Venetian quarter with the support of the Pisans. They were repulsed, but both sides proceeded to set up siege engines and use these to bombard each other.

The Kingdom of Jerusalem was divided by the conflict. John of Arsuf initially backed the Genoese, while some barons, led by John of Jaffa, favored the Venetians. Philip of Montfort, lord of Tyre and Toron, used the opportunity to expel the Venetians from Tyre (modern-day Soûr, Lebanon) and allied himself with the Genoese. In July 1257 the Pisans changed sides to join Venice. The fraternities in Acre sided with the Venetians, as did the Templars and the Teutonic Knights, while the Hospitallers supported the Genoese. The communes from southern France opposed the Genoese, and consequently the Catalan communes backed them.

The Venetians gained ground when John of Jaffa successfully manipulated the regency laws to bring Plaisance of Antioch to power in the Kingdom of Jerusalem. As *bailli* (regent), she ordered the crown vassals to support Venice. Both sides were reinforced by new arrivals from Europe, and the struggle continued both on land and at sea.

In 1257, a Venetian fleet commanded by Lorenzo Tiepolo broke through the harbor chain at Acre, destroyed several Genoese ships, and then landed men to restore control of the Venetian quarter, seize the disputed property, and destroy the fortifications at St. Sabas. Tiepolo's men were unable to take control of the Genoese portion of the city, however, which was defended by some 800 men and some 50–60 siege engines.

In June 1258 Philip of Montfort, with the support of the Hospitallers, led an army south to attack Acre while the Genoese launched an assault from the sea. The Venetian and Genoese fleets clashed and the latter were defeated, losing many men and a number of galleys. Philip and the Hospitallers were forced to withdraw.

The position of the Genoese in Acre become untenable, and they abandoned the city in favor of Tyre. Intermittent fighting continued in the 1260s, with both sides employing Muslim mercenaries. In 1266 the Genoese concluded an alliance with Egyptian sultan Baybars (Baibars) I, who was to provide some soldiers for an attack on Acre, but the promised Genoese fleet that was to support the operation never arrived. The next year, however, the Genoese managed to capture the Tower of Flies in the city and blockade the city for 12 days until a Venetian flotilla forced them to withdraw. The conflict was finally resolved in the signing of a pact between the Venetians and Genoese in 1270. In 1282, the Genoese finally received control of their portion of the city.

Much of Acre had been destroyed in the fighting, which also damaged its trade and exacerbated the factional divisions within Outremer, weakening its ability to withstand external threats. According to one Christian chronicler, the war resulted in the deaths of some 20,000 people, a major loss considering the relatively small population of Outremer at the time.

Linda Goldsmith and Spencer C. Tucker

**See also**
Baybars I; Crusades in the Holy Land, Christian; Jerusalem, Latin Kingdom of; Outremer

**References**
Boucheron, Patrick. *Les Villes d'Italie: Vers 1150–vers 1340.* Paris: Belin, 2004.

Racine, Pierre. *Les villes d'Italie: Du milieu du XIIe siècle au milieu du XIVe siècle.* Paris: CNED, 2004.

Renouard, Yves. *Les villes d'Italie de la fin du Xe siècle au début du XIVe siècle.* Paris, Centre de Documentation Universitaire, 1963.

Richard, Jean. *The Crusades: c. 1071–c. 1291.* Cambridge: Cambridge University Press, 1999.

## Suez Canal

Canal linking the Mediterranean Sea and the Red Sea and one of the world's most important shipping lanes. Just more than 100 miles in length, the Suez Canal, which opened in 1869, has been a source of great controversy since its construction in the mid-19th century. Although the canal had been built by Egyptian labor, control of the canal and its revenues remained in French and British hands until 1956, when it was nationalized by Egyptian president Gamal Abdel Nasser.

From its inception, the Suez Canal has been the source of diplomatic struggles. Although a canal had cut through the Sinai Peninsula in ancient times, it was filled in during the Abbasid era in the 8th century. However, as the centuries passed, engineers and local rulers speculated about the possibility of creating a new canal that would connect the Red Sea and the Mediterranean Sea. In the 18th century, European trade in India led to an increased desire to find a faster route between the subcontinent and Europe. A canal through the Sinai Peninsula would serve to eliminate the long journey to India around Africa's Cape of Good Hope.

However, despite years of speculation, it was not until 1854 that the modern Suez Canal project began, the brainchild of French entrepreneur Ferdinand de Lesseps. Planning commenced when the khedive (viceroy) of Egypt, Said Pasha, granted de Lesseps a concession for the canal's construction. During the next several years, de Lesseps and his Compagnie Universelle du Canal Maritime de Suez (Universal Maritime Company of the Suez) sold shares to numerous European investors in an effort to raise the funds necessary to build the canal.

In 1856 Said Pasha granted the French company the right to operate the canal for 99 years. This concession became a source of immense consternation among Egyptians, and anger was further inflamed by de Lesseps's shady business practices. When he was unable to sell all of the necessary shares to European investors, de Lesseps announced that Said Pasha had purchased those remaining. In reality, the Egyptian leader had not done so and did not have the money to do so. To protect his honor and that of his country, Said Pasha borrowed vast amounts of money from European banks to acquire the shares, using Egypt's cotton crops and other natural resources as collateral. This was the beginning of a long legacy of debt that would cripple the Egyptian economy. Meanwhile, profits to European financiers soared.

Construction on the canal began in 1859 and took a decade to complete. In the first years of building, Egyptian corvée (indentured) labor was used to dig the canal by hand at great expense to the life and liberty of the Egyptian population. The corvée practice was perceived as a further insult among the Egyptians. In the final years of construction, dredging machines and other mechanized equipment from Europe were employed, and in November 1869 to great fanfare the canal finally opened. In consequence, ships could now pass between the Mediterranean Sea and the Red Sea, greatly cutting the time and expense of a journey between Europe and Asia.

In 1875 Ismail Pasha, now khedive of Egypt, offered for sale his nation's shares in the canal to pay back loans made to Egypt by European lenders. By now two-thirds of the tonnage transiting the canal was British, and the British government could not be indifferent to its control. Thus, British prime minister Benjamin Disraeli, without waiting for parliamentary consent, boldly and quickly purchased the shares for Great Britain (176,602 of the total of 400,000 shares) at a cost of £4 million. The British government was now the largest shareholder in the company. Egypt was also completely cut out of the canal's profits, a condition that would last until 1949 when the Suez Canal Company granted Egypt 7 percent of the canal's profits.

For nearly a century, Egyptians watched helplessly as foreign governments and investors made huge profits from the canal built on their soil and with their labor. Meanwhile, Britain occupied Egypt in 1881 ostensibly to restore order following antiforeign riots there and in so doing reduced the sovereignty of the Egyptian monarchy to puppet status. The Egyptian population and politicians harbored great resentment, and this resentment eventually found a voice in the policies of Egyptian nationalist leader Nasser.

A leader of the 1952 Free Officer Coup against King Farouk I, Nasser became the undisputed leader of Egypt by 1954 and was elected president (as the only candidate) in 1956. A man of modest background who spoke of social justice, Nasser was a leading light in the international Non-Aligned Movement and a founder of modern Arab nationalism.

In 1955 Nasser had announced plans to build a new high dam at Aswan and had secured funding from the World

Bank, with the United States and Great Britain as the primary lenders. However, when Egypt purchased weapons from Soviet-allied Czechoslovakia and recognized the People's Republic of China, the United States, followed by Britain, pulled out of the loan program. In response, Nasser determined that the only way his country could raise the money necessary for the dam's completion was by seizing control of the Suez Canal. Thus, on July 26, 1956, Nasser's troops took control of the Suez Canal Zone.

Britain and France, the two primary shareholders in the Suez Canal Company, not only feared the loss of their profits but also worried that the Egyptians would restrict their supplies of oil. At the same time, Israel was in crisis because Nasser had coupled the Suez seizure with a blockade of Israeli shipping through the Strait of Tiran. These three nations clandestinely plotted to band together, depose Nasser, and reassert control over the canal.

The event known as the Suez Crisis began on October 29, 1956, when Israel sent forces into Egypt's Sinai Peninsula. Meanwhile, as per the secret plan they had hatched with the Israelis, the British and French sent both Egypt and Israel an ultimatum regarding the canal. When Egypt rejected their demands, prepositioned British and French forces attacked Egypt, even landing troops.

Angered at having been caught by surprise by the British and French action, U.S. president Dwight Eisenhower brought heavy diplomatic and financial pressure on Britain to withdraw. When the British announced that they would do so, France and Israel were forced to follow suit. The Soviet Union also applied pressure, but it was the U.S. move that was decisive. Nasser found himself an instant hero not only in Egypt and the larger Arab world but also in countries fighting against imperial oppression.

From 1956 until 1975 the Suez Canal was closed to Israeli shipping while Israel and Egypt continued to skirmish across their border. In 1967 the canal closed during the June Six-Day War, with ships scuttled in the waterway and with Israel's occupation of the Sinai. The canal remained closed to all traffic until June 1975. During this long period, the Suez Canal Zone was the site of many engagements between Egypt and Israel. However, the Suez Canal reopened to ships in 1975. When peace was achieved between Egypt and Israel in 1979, Israeli troops withdrew from the Sinai, and Egypt once again took full control of the waterway. Today all ships are able to pass through the Suez Canal, one of the most important shipping lanes of the world.

Nancy L. Stockdale

### See also
Egypt; Nasser, Gamal Abdel; Sinai Campaign of 1956; Six-Day War; Suez Crisis

### References
Gorst, Anthony, and Lewis Johnman. *The Suez Crisis*. London: Routledge, 1997.
Karabell, Zachary. *Parting the Desert: The Creation of the Suez Canal*. New York: Knopf, 2003.
Schonfield, Hugh Joseph. *The Suez Canal in Peace and War, 1869–1969*. Coral Gables, FL: University of Miami Press, 1969.

## Suez Canal, World War I Ottoman Operations against

Key Allied line of communication and transportation. The Suez Canal is a strategic man-made channel connecting the Mediterranean Sea and the Red Sea through the Isthmus of Suez. In World War I, India, Australia, and New Zealand added nearly 3 million men to the manpower of the British Isles, and the Suez Canal was a key transportation link for these troops and supplies moving in support of Allied operations in the Middle East and in Europe. German kaiser Wilhelm II saw the canal as key to the English position in the Middle East, and he reportedly stated at the start of the war that he looked forward to "cutting England's jugular vein."

When the Ottoman Empire officially joined the Central Powers on October 31, 1914, the most immediate threat to Britain's canal zone defenses came from Ottoman land forces in the Sinai Desert and Palestine. The British General Staff had begun formulating defense plans for the canal as early as 1888, and by 1914 there were four railway tracks on both sides of the canal and ample rolling stock permitting swift and rapid concentration of troops and equipment at threatened points. Moreover, the Suez Canal Zone was fortified with long-range guns along canal banks operating in tandem with large-caliber artillery on warships, all capable of firing ordnance a significant distance into the relatively flat desert to the east.

The Ottoman high command ordered Djemal Pasha and his Second Army to take the canal. Djemal's force numbered some 30,000 men and 5,000 camels to carry water for a desert transit. His plan envisaged a surprise attack coupled with an uprising by the Egyptian people in a jihad (holy war).

The Ottoman surprise element vanished, however, when aerial reconnaissance from French seaplanes spotted the advancing Ottoman troops. Additional warships were moved into the canal, and British troops dug in on the west side of the waterway, as commanders planned on using the canal itself as the first line of defense. On visiting the canal before assuming his duties as minister of war, Field Marshal Lord Kitchener had remarked, "Gentlemen, are you defending the canal, or is the canal defending you?"

The Ottomans and their accompanying German advisers launched their attack on February 3, 1915, with the main body of 20,000 troops assaulting the central canal sector between Toussoum and Serapeum. A second element struck Kantara, about 30 miles north of the main thrust. A third detachment moved against Canal Defense Forces 5 miles south of Little Bitter Lake, about 40 miles south of the main body. Intense fighting ensued amid a raging sandstorm. The expected uprising among the Egyptians failed to materialize, however, and the Ottoman attacks were repulsed.

Kitchener believed that the true defense of the Suez Canal, and of Egypt, was on the Palestine border. By January 1916 three army corps of British imperial troops were quartered along the canal, and preparations were under way for the creation and deployment of the Egyptian Expeditionary Force (EEF) to commence offensive operations to clear the Sinai and Gaza and take Palestine. Simultaneously, however, the Ottoman Fourth Army and elements of the Eighth Army were engaged in training new troops and preparing for a second offensive against the canal.

In the summer of 1916, German lieutenant colonel Friedrich Kress von Kressenstein was preparing to lead another attack on the canal. For the first two years of the war, Kressenstein, with the help of Bedouin tribesmen in Sinai, kept substantial British forces tied down in the Suez Canal Zone. In June and July 1916, Kressenstein received Ottoman reinforcements. A squadron of German aircraft also arrived and carried out raids on Port Said. One German plane even managed a flight to Cairo, where it dropped a few bombs. In July 1916, Kressenstein advanced from Al Arish with 20,000 men and attacked British positions between Romani and Kantara.

British forces here, commanded by General Sir Archibald J. Murray, had been preparing for offensive action themselves, and they inflicted heavy losses on the attackers and took more than 4,000 prisoners. British forces then went on the offensive, clearing the Sinai Desert, securing Gaza, and taking Palestine and Jerusalem in December 1917.

JAMES B. MCNABB

### See also
Djemal Pasha, Ahmed; Egypt; Kress von Kressenstein, Friedrich Sigismund Georg; Murray, Sir Archibald James

### References
Farnie, D. A. *East and West of the Suez Canal: The Suez Canal in History, 1854–1956.* Oxford, UK: Clarendon, 1969.

Ford, Roger. *Eden to Armageddon: World War I in the Middle East.* Cambridge, UK: Pegasus, 2010.
Longwood, William F. *Suez Story: Key to the Middle East.* New York: Greenberg, 1957.
Mansfield, Peter. *The British in Egypt.* New York: Holt, Rinehart and Winston, 1972.
Monroe, Elizabeth. *Britain's Moment in the Middle East, 1914–1956.* Baltimore: Johns Hopkins University Press, 1963.

## Suez Canal and Egypt, World War II Campaigns for Control of (1940–1942)

Eastern North Africa was a major combat theater in World War II. The stakes here were high, with the fighting largely over control of Egypt and the Suez Canal. Great Britain depended on the canal for access to Middle Eastern oil and raw materials from Asia. The canal and the Mediterranean Sea were the primary lifeline to Britain's overseas dominions.

Fighting in North Africa had begun in the late summer of 1940 when Italian dictator Benito Mussolini sought to take advantage of the defeat of France and the weakness of Britain. On August 6 Italian forces invaded British Somaliland from Italian East Africa; it fell to the Italians in two weeks. Then on September 13, 1940, Field Marshal Rudolfo Graziani invaded Egypt from Tripoli. Graziani had at his disposal some 250,000 troops in Libya; British commander in chief of the Middle East General Sir Archibald Wavell had only 100,000 soldiers to defend Egypt, Sudan, and Palestine. The British army, however, was far better organized, trained, equipped, and led. This began a critical campaign over control of the Suez Canal. It was so important for the British that at the height of the Battle of Britain, British prime minister Winston Churchill had to divert vitally needed military resources to the Near East.

Fortunately for the British, Graziani moved at a snail's pace on a narrow front along the coast. This allowed British outpost forces to fall back and Wavell to reinforce. Within three days, however, Graziani's men had reached Sidi Barrani, Egypt, where they established a number of fortified camps. Meanwhile, Wavell gathered two divisions at Mersa Matruh, while General Sir Henry M. Wilson, commander of British forces in Egypt, prepared for a counterattack.

Wavell's North African offensive, delayed by the need to dispatch forces to Greece, finally began on December 9, 1940, when Major General Richard N. O'Connor hurled his Western Desert Force against the Italians. Largely drawn from the Indian Army, the Western Desert Force was only a quarter of the Italian strength in numbers. Despite this, the Western Desert Force was able to roll up the Italian strongpoints.

Within a week the British had not only ejected the Italians entirely from Egypt but had also secured 38,000 prisoners and great quantities of war matériel. After a two-week pause to resupply, on January 1 O'Connor's men assaulted the remnants of Graziani's force at Bardia. On January 5 supported by naval bombardment, they took the Italian positions. Tobruk on the coast fell on January 22, 1941. Then on February 5 at Beda Fomm on the Gulf of Sirte, the remaining Italian forces surrendered. In this brilliant campaign of just two months' duration, the Western Desert Force had advanced 500 miles, destroyed 9 Italian divisions, and taken more that 130,000 Italian and Libyan prisoners, 380 tanks, and 845 guns. British losses were 500 killed, 1,373 wounded, and 55 missing.

In January 1941 Wavell sent some 70,000 men against 110,000 Italian troops in East Africa. Addis Ababa fell on April 5, and a month later Emperor Haile Selassie returned to power, although the last Italian troops in East Africa did not surrender until November 27.

The Western Desert Force could have driven on to Tripoli and cleared the Axis out of Africa completely, but as previously noted, Wavell was forced to halt O'Connor's offensive in order to shift assets to Greece. In January 1941 the first German reinforcements had arrived in North Africa in the form of 500 aircraft of the X Air Corps. German bombers soon neutralized Benghazi as a base for the Western Desert Force.

In February 1941 Lieutenant General Erwin Rommel arrived in Tripoli and assumed command of the newly created Afrika Korps. Rommel, a charismatic commander who led from the front, began an offensive against O'Connor's weakened force. Striking with the 21st Panzer Division and two Italian divisions (one armored and one motorized), he drove back the British at El Aghella on March 24, 1941. He then sent the Afrika Korps in a reprise of O'Connor's advance in reverse. The Italian forces followed the coastal road to Derna, while the 21st Panzer Division sliced across the desert of Cyenaica for the port of Tobruk. O'Connor's 2nd Armored Division, endeavoring to delay the Axis drive, was split. One brigade, short of fuel, was cut off at Derna and forced to surrender on April 6. The remainder of the division was captured the next day. The 9th Australian Division reached Tobruk. Unfortunately for the Allied cause, on April 17 O'Connor was captured by a German patrol while on reconnaissance.

Wavell was determined to hold Tobruk in order to deny it to the Axis as a supply port but also to provide a threat to Rommel and the Afrika Korps from the flank. Wavell reinforced Tobruk by sea, inserting the 7th Australian Division along with some tanks. On April 10 Rommel launched a determined attack on the port but was thrown back after three days of savage fighting. He then encircled Tobruk from the land and besieged it. Rommel's supply situation was by now difficult, especially given the fact that the Allies, thanks to Ultra radio intercepts and their possession of Malta, were extracting a steady toll of Italian shipping across the Mediterranean.

Under pressure from Churchill, on June 15 Wavell prematurely launched Operation BATTLEAXE, a two-division effort (one armored and one infantry) in an effort to relieve Tobruk. The battle played out over three days, but the attackers, split into six small semi-independent task forces and committed piecemeal, failed in their effort. On July 1 Churchill replaced Wavell with General Sir Claude Auchinleck. In effect, Wavell became the scapegoat for Churchill's own decision to expand the already stretched-thin theater to include Greece and Crete.

During July–October both sides built up their strength to renew the offensive. The Western Desert Force, now renamed the Eighth Army and with General Alan Cunningham in command, was built up to 7 divisions and 700 tanks supported by 1,000 aircraft. Rommel also reorganized the Italian-German Panzerarmee Afrika of 10 divisions (4 German and 6 Italian), along with 260 German and 154 Italian tanks supported by 120 German and 200 Italian aircraft.

Auchinleck attacked first, on November 18. Cunningham's Eighth Army, utilizing new U.S. Stuart light tanks, struck west from its base at Mersa Matruh. Rommel checked the British thrust in a series of uncoordinated battles around Sidi-Rezegh, and Axis forces also halted a sortie from Tobruk. Rommel then took the offensive, slashing into the British rear areas. Cunningham considered withdrawal, but Auchinleck insisted on a stand, and Rommel was halted. The Axis forces then withdrew to the west and south of Tobruk. Auchinleck, displeased with Cunningham's performance, replaced him with Major General Neil M. Ritchie.

At the end of December under British pressure, Rommel withdrew to his original position at El Agheila in Cyrenaica, 459 miles from the main Axis base of Tripoli. Axis personnel losses were 8,900 killed or wounded and 28,500 missing or taken prisoner; Commonwealth casualties totaled 17,700.

Undaunted, in January 1942 Rommel launched a second offensive. Striking on a narrow front, he drove the widely dispersed British forces back beyond Benghazi, where Auchinleck dug in. Having outrun their supply lines, Axis forces halted. During the course of the next four months, both sides rested and resupplied. The Eighth Army, reinforced to 125,000 men with 740 tanks and 700 aircraft, confronted an Axis force of 113,000 men, with 570 tanks and 500 aircraft. The Eighth Army established a heavily mined and fortified line extending from Gazala on the coast 40 miles south to Bir Hacheim, held by Major General Marie Pierre Koenig's Free French Brigade Group. Auchinleck concentrated his armor behind the French to protect the Eighth Army's open left flank.

Rommel struck on May 28, concentrating his resources to the south. Although the Italian forces failed to take Bir Hacheim, Rommel's panzers swept south of the British, then turned north inside their line. But the British held, and Rommel's tanks were running out of fuel. On May 31, however, Italian infantry managed to penetrate the British minefield belt between Bir Hacheim and Gazala and open a supply route to Rommel. This forced the French to evacuate Bir Hacheim, and on June 13 Ritchie ordered a general retirement.

During the next two weeks the British withdrew in disorder back into Egypt. Tobruk fell on June 21 to a well-planned air and ground attack, the Germans taking 33,000 prisoners. Along with the vital port, the Axis forces captured 2,000 tons of much-needed fuel and 2,000 wheeled vehicles.

The British fell back to Mersa Matruh, about 100 miles inside Egypt. Rommel, promoted to field marshal for his victory at Gazala, pursued. Auchinleck relieved Ritchie and personally assumed command of the Eighth Army. Rommel had only 60 operational tanks, but he still attacked at Mersa Matruh on June 26 and routed four British divisions in three days of fighting. The British then fell back again another 120 miles to the east to Alam el Halfa ridge between El Alamein on the Mediterranean and the Qattara Depression 40 miles south. This was less than 100 miles from Alexandria.

Auchinleck was determined to hold near El Alamein. Although under constant pressure from Rommel's forces, Auchinleck improvised a fluid defensive line anchored on Ruweisat Ridge a few miles south of the El Alamein perimeter. The First Battle of El Alamein (July 1–27, 1942) began on July 1 with Rommel attacking, intending to sweep around El Alamein, but Auchinleck skillfully battled Rommel to a standstill over the course of three weeks of fighting. Auchinleck then launched a major counterattack on July 21–22 but made no progress. Exhausted, both sides paused to regroup, and the fighting front stabilized only 70 miles from Alexandria. Rommel's offensive had cost the British 75,000 casualties and the Axis only 40,000, but his forces were now stretched thin, and his logistical situation had worsened, thanks to a British naval and air buildup in the theater.

The Allies had superior equipment and numbers. Their basic problem was that they did not understand the employment of combined arms: tanks, antitank guns, and infantry all working in concert. It was only through bitter experience that the British learned how to conduct mobile warfare effectively. The Americans would have to learn the same lesson in 1943.

Despite the fact the British had finally halted Rommel's advance, Churchill relieved Auchinleck in early August and replaced him with General Sir Harold Alexander as commander in chief of the Middle East. Sir William Gott was promoted to general and placed in command of the Eighth Army. On August 7 while flying to Cairo to take up his appointment, Gott was killed when a German fighter attacked his airplane. Churchill then selected Lieutenant General Bernard L. Montgomery to succeeded Gott in command of the Eighth Army.

On August 31, 1942, Rommel launched what he believed would be the final attack to carry the Axis forces to the Nile. Montgomery, however, had made extensive preparations around El Alamein based on a plan developed by Auchinleck. Montgomery also had the advantage of knowing Rommel's plan through Ultra intercepts. Rommel intended to sweep around to the south of Ruweisat Ridge and cut off El Alamein from the rear. However, the British had laid extensive minefields and had heavily fortified Alam el Halfa Ridge behind and southeast of El Alamein. Rommel's attack ran short of fuel and stalled by September 3. Montgomery counterattacked immediately but halted as soon as the Axis forces were pushed back to their starting positions. Taken together, the Battles of Ruweisat Ridge and Alam el Halfa marked the real operational turning point of the war in North Africa.

Montgomery used the time after the Battle of Alam el Halfa to carefully plan a set-piece counterattack from El Alamein. Rommel meanwhile returned to Germany on sick leave. When Montgomery finally launched the attack, the British had an overall force superiority ratio of three to one. Rommel immediately returned from Germany when the Battle of El Alamein started on October 23, 1942. The Allies tried for five days to break through the Axis positions and sustained 10,000 casualties in the process. On October 31, Montgomery renewed the attack with strong support from the Royal Air Force. Critically short of fuel and ammunition, Rommel was forced to disengage on November 3. The following day, the 1,400-mile Axis withdrawal to Tunisia began.

For the next three months, Montgomery followed rather than aggressively pursued Rommel and the Axis forces across the northern coast of Africa. Rommel reached the Tunisian border at the end of January 1943. By the time he got there, however, another Allied force was waiting for him.

On November 8, 1942, four days after Rommel began his long withdrawal, the British and Americans initiated Operation TORCH, the invasion of Northwest Africa, with U.S. lieutenant general Dwight D. Eisenhower in overall command. The ultimate objectives were the Tunisian city of Tunis and the port and airfield complex at Bizerte.

The Germans reacted by sending troops from Sicily to Tunisia on November 9. For the Germans, control of the Tunis complex was critical to prevent Rommel from being trapped between Montgomery in the east and the newly formed British First Army in the west. On November 28 the Allies reached Tebourba, only 12 miles from Tunis, but an Axis counterattack drove them back 20 miles in seven days. In January 1943, the winter rains and resulting mud brought mechanized operations to a halt in northern Tunisia. The Axis side had temporarily won the race.

Waiting for better weather in the spring, the Allies continued to build up their forces. Bizerte and Tunis both fell on May 7. The last Axis forces surrendered on May 13. Axis losses in Tunisia alone totaled 40,000 dead or wounded, 240,000 prisoners, 250 tanks, 2,330 aircraft, and 232 vessels. British and American casualties were 33,000 and 18,558, respectively. For the entire North African Campaign, the British suffered 220,000 casualties. Total Axis losses came to 620,000, which included the loss of three field armies. The losses were large for what amounted to a secondary theater for both sides.

SPENCER C. TUCKER AND DAVID T. ZABECKI

**See also**
Alam el Halfa, Battle of; Auchinleck, Sir Claude John Eyre; Cunningham, Sir Alan Gordon; El Alamein, First Battle of; El Alamein, Second Battle of; Mersa Matruh, First Battle of; Mersa Matruh, Second Battle of; Montgomery, Bernard Law; O'Connor, Richard Nugent; Rommel, Erwin Johannes Eugen

**References**
Atkinson, Rick. *An Army at Dawn: The War in North Africa, 1942–1943*. New York: Henry Holt, 2002.
Barnett, Correlli. *The Desert Generals*. New York: Viking, 1961.
Greene, Jack, and Alessandro Massignani. *Rommel's North African Campaign*. Conshocken, PA: Combined Publishing, 1999.
Pitt, Barrie. *The Year of Alamein, 1942*. New York: Paragon House, 1990.

# Suez Crisis (July 26, 1956– March 6, 1957)

The Suez Crisis was one of the major events of both the Cold War and the Arab-Israeli wars. The crisis ended Britain's pretensions to be a world superpower and fatally weakened Britain's hold on what remained of its empire. The Suez Crisis also placed a dangerous strain on U.S.-Soviet relations, strengthened the position of Egyptian leader Gamal Abdel Nasser throughout the Middle East, and distracted world attention from the concurrent Soviet military intervention in the Hungarian Revolution.

The crisis had its origins in the development plans of Nasser, who had come to power in Egypt following a 1952 military coup. As strongman and ultimately president of Egypt, Nasser hoped to enhance his prestige and improve the quality of life for his nation's burgeoning population by carrying out long-discussed plans for construction of a high dam on the upper Nile River south of Aswan to provide electric power. To finance the project, Nasser sought assistance from the Western powers. But at the same time, he had been endeavoring to build up and modernize the Egyptian military. Toward that end he had sought to acquire modern weapons from the United States and other Western nations. When the U.S. government refused to supply the advanced arms, which it believed might be used against Israel, in 1955 Nasser turned to the communist bloc. That September with Soviet encouragement, he reached a barter arrangement with Czechoslovakia for substantial quantities of weapons, including jet aircraft and tanks, in return for Egyptian cotton.

This arms deal impacted on the Aswan High Dam construction project for which Nasser had sought Western financing. In December 1955 Washington declared its willingness to lend $56 million for financing the dam, while Britain pledged $14 million and the World Bank $200 million. The condition to the aid was that Egypt provide matching funds and that it not accept Soviet assistance.

Nasser was unhappy with the Western conditions. With expectations of a Soviet counteroffer, the controlled Egyptian press launched an all-out propaganda offensive against the West, especially the United States. But when no Soviet offer was forthcoming, Nasser finally accepted the Western aid package on July 17, 1956. Much to his chagrin, two days later U.S. secretary of state John Foster Dulles announced that it had been withdrawn. Britain immediately followed suit. The official U.S. reasons were that Egypt had failed to reach agreement with Sudan over the dam (most of the vast lake created by the dam would be in Sudanese territory), and the Egyptian part of the financing for the project had become uncertain. The real reasons were objections from some U.S. congressmen, especially southerners fearful of competition from Egyptian cotton and Dulles's determination to teach Nasser and other neutralists a lesson. Dulles was angry over Nasser's flirtation with the communist bloc to include the arms purchases and was especially upset over Egypt's recent recognition of the People's Republic of China.

Nasser's response to this humiliating rebuff came a week later on July 26 when he nationalized the Suez Canal. He had contemplated such a move for some time, but the U.S. decision prompted its timing. In 1955 the canal produced net revenues of nearly $100 million, of which Egypt received only $2 million. Seizure of the canal would not only provide additional funding for the Aswan High Dam but would also greatly enhance Nasser's prestige in the Arab world.

The British government regarded the sea-level Suez Canal, which connected the eastern Mediterranean with the Red Sea across Egyptian territory, as its lifeline to Middle Eastern oil and the Far East. Indeed, fully 60 percent of all oil consumed in Western Europe passed through the canal. The canal, which had opened in 1869, had quickly altered the world's trade routes, and two-thirds of the tonnage passing through the canal was British. In 1875 the British had purchased the 44 percent of canal shares owned by Egyptian khedive Ismail Pasha, and in 1878 Britain acquired Cyprus from the Ottoman Empire, further strengthening its position in the eastern Mediterranean. The British also increased their role in Egyptian financial affairs, and in 1882 they intervened militarily in Egypt. Britain in effect controlled Egyptian affairs through World War II.

In 1954 Nasser succeeded in renegotiating the 1936 treaty with the British to force the withdrawal of British troops from the Suez Canal Zone. The last British forces departed on June 13, only six weeks before Nasser nationalized the canal.

The British government took the lead in opposing Nasser. London believed that Nasser's growing popularity in the Arab world was encouraging Arab nationalism and threatening to undermine British influence throughout the Middle East. British prime minister Anthony Eden developed a deep and abiding hatred of Nasser. For Eden, ousting Nasser from power became nothing short of an obsession. In the immediate aftermath of Nasser's nationalization of the canal, the British government called up 200,000 military reservists and dispatched military resources to the eastern Mediterranean.

The French government also had good reason to seek Nasser's removal. It sought to protect France's own long-standing interests in the Middle East, but more to the point, the French were now engaged in fighting the National Liberation Front (NLF) in Algeria. The Algerian War, which began in November 1954, had greatly expanded, and Nasser was a strong and vocal supporter of the NLF. There were many in the French government, now led by socialist premier Guy Mollet, and the military who believed that overthrowing Nasser would greatly enhance French chances of winning the Algerian War. This position found considerable support when on October 18, 1956, the French intercepted the Egyptian ship *Athos* and found it loaded with arms and documents proving Egyptian support for the NLF.

Israel was the third leg in the triad of powers arrayed against Nasser. Egypt had instituted a blockade of Israeli ships at the Gulf of Aqaba, Israel's outlet to the Indian Ocean. Also, Egypt had never recognized the Jewish state and indeed remained at war with it following the Israeli War of Independence (1948–1949). In 1955 Israel mounted half a dozen cross-border raids, while Egypt carried out its own raids into Israeli territory by fedayeen (guerrilla fighters).

During the months that followed Egyptian nationalization of the Suez Canal, the community of interest among British, French, and Israeli leaders developed into secret planning for a joint military operation to topple Nasser. The U.S. government was not consulted and indeed opposed the use of force. The British and French governments either did not understand the American attitude or, if they did, believed that Washington would give approval after the fact to policies undertaken by its major allies, which the latter believed to be absolutely necessary.

The British government first tried diplomacy. Two conferences in London attended by the representatives of 24 nations using the canal failed to produce agreement on a course of action, and Egypt refused to participate. A proposal by Secretary of State Dulles for a canal users' club of nations also failed, as did an appeal to the United Nations (UN) Security Council. On October 1 Dulles announced that the United States was disassociating itself from British and French actions in the Middle East and asserted that the United States intended to play a more independent role.

Meanwhile, secret talks were going forward, first between the British and French for joint military action against Egypt. Military representatives of the two governments met in London on August 10 and hammered out the details of a joint military plan known as MUSKETEER that would involve occupation of both Alexandria and Port Said. The French then brought the Israeli government in on the plan, and General Maurice Challe, deputy chief of staff of the French

Egyptian Army soldiers taken prisoner by British and French forces following their invasion of Egypt during the Suez Crisis. The photograph was taken on November 3, 1956. The soldiers' steel helmets are in the foreground. (Israeli Government Press Office)

Air Force, undertook a secret trip to the Middle East to meet with Israeli government and military leaders.

The Israelis were at first skeptical about British and French support. They also had no intention of moving as far as the canal itself. The Israelis stated that their plan was merely to send light detachments to link up with British and French forces. They also insisted that British and French military intervention occur simultaneously with their own attack.

General André Beaufre, the designated French military commander for the operation, then came up with a new plan. Under it, the Israelis would initiate hostilities against Egypt in order to provide the pretext for military intervention by French and British forces to protect the canal. This action would technically be in accord with the terms of the 1954 treaty between Egypt and Britain that had given Britain the right to send forces to occupy the Suez Canal Zone in the event of an attack against Egypt by a third power.

On October 23 Mollet and French foreign minister Christian Pineau met in the Paris suburbs at Sèvres with Israeli prime minister David Ben-Gurion, Defense Minister Shimon Peres, and chief of the Israeli General Staff Lieutenant General Moshe Dayan. The French agreed to provide additional air cover for Israel. French ships supposedly searching for Egyptian arms shipments to the Algerian rebels would move to the Israeli coast immediately, and French aircraft flown by French pilots would be repositioned in Israel. That afternoon British foreign secretary Selwyn Lloyd and Foreign Office undersecretary of state Patrick Dean joined the discussions. The British, while staunchly prointervention, were deeply concerned about their position in the Arab world and were not anxious to be seen in collusion with the Israelis. Thus, an Israeli strike toward the canal through the Sinai would enable the British to have it both ways: they could join the French in demanding of Nasser the right to protect the canal. When he refused, as he certainly would, they could join the French in destroying the Egyptian Air Force, eliminating the one possible threat to Israeli success on the ground. All parties agreed to this new plan, dubbed the "Treaty of Sèvres" and signed by Dean, Pineau, and Ben-Gurion.

On October 23, meanwhile, unrest began in Hungary. The next day Soviet tanks entered Budapest to put down what had become the Hungarian Revolution. French and British planners saw this major crisis event as providing them a degree of freedom of action.

On the afternoon of October 29 Israeli forces began Operation KADESH, the invasion of the Sinai Peninsula. Sixteen C-47 transports took off from Israeli fields, each with a paratroop platoon. The objective of the 395-man paratroop battalion was the key Mitla Pass, 156 miles from the Israeli border and only 45 miles from the canal. Meanwhile, the remainder of Colonel Ariel Sharon's 202nd Parachute Brigade would race for the pass in French-provided trucks, linking up with the paratroopers within 36 hours. This operation was designed to trigger a major Egyptian response and threaten the canal in order to justify the planned British-French response.

The announced objective of KADESH was the eradication of the fedayeen bases, but it was begun so as to appear to the Egyptians as if it was the beginning of an all-out war. Dayan's detailed plan called for nothing less than a weeklong lightning advance that would end with Israeli forces securing the entire Sinai and a total victory over Egypt. The destruction of Nasser's prestige in the Arab world and final Egyptian recognition of the impossibility of an Arab military victory over Israel were the goals rather than destruction of the Egyptian Army or acquisition of its new Soviet equipment.

A day later, October 30, the British and French governments issued an ultimatum, nominally to both the Egyptian and Israeli governments but in reality only to Egypt, expressing the need to separate the combatants and demanding the right to provide for the security of the Suez Canal. The ultimatum called on both sides to withdraw their forces 10 miles from the canal and gave them 12 hours to reply. The Israelis, of course, immediately accepted the ultimatum, while the Egyptians just as promptly rejected it.

At dusk on October 31, British and French aircraft struck Egyptian airfields and military installations from bases on Cyprus and Malta and from aircraft carriers. The aircraft attacked four Egyptian bases that day and nine the next. On November 1, meanwhile, a British and French naval task force sailed from Malta to join with other ships at Cyprus. In all, the landing force numbered some 80,000 men: 50,000 British and 30,000 French. There were 100 British and 30 French warships, including 7 aircraft carriers (5 British) and the French battleship *Jean Bart,* hundreds of landing craft, and some 80 merchant ships carrying 20,000 vehicles and stores. Yet when Eden reported to the House of Commons on events, he encountered a surprisingly strong negative reaction from the opposition Labour Party.

Also, following the initial British and French military action, the Egyptians immediately sank a number of ships in the canal to make it unusable. The Israelis meanwhile swept across the Sinai in only four days against ineffective Egyptian forces. Finally, on November 5 British and French paratroopers carried out a vertical envelopment of Port Said at the Mediterranean terminus of the canal, while at the same time French and British destroyers carried out a shore bombardment against those targets likely to impede a landing. Early on November 6, British troops began coming ashore at Port Said and the French at Port Fuad. A single day of fighting saw the ports in allied hands. French and British forces then began a virtually unopposed advance southward along the canal.

U.S. president Dwight D. Eisenhower had already entered the picture. On October 31 he described the British attack as "taken in error." He was personally furious at Eden over events and is supposed to have asked when he first telephoned the British leader, "Anthony, have you gone out of your mind?" The United States applied immediate and heavy financial threats, both on a bilateral basis and through the International Monetary Fund, to bring the British government to heel. Eisenhower also refused any further dealings with Eden personally.

The Soviets, preoccupied by Hungary, took some five days to come to the conclusion that the United States was actually opposing the British and French action. On November 5, Moscow threatened to send "volunteers" to Egypt. This proved to be a further embarrassment for the British government, but it was U.S. pressure that was decisive. Nonetheless, the world beheld the strange spectacle of the United States cooperating with the Soviet Union to condemn Britain and France in the UN Security Council and call for an end to the use of force. Although Britain and France vetoed the Security Council resolution, the matter was referred to the General Assembly, which demanded a cease-fire and withdrawal.

Israel and Egypt agreed to a cease-fire on November 4. At midnight on November 6, the day of the U.S. presidential election, the British and French governments also accepted a cease-fire, the French only with the greatest reluctance. By the time the cease-fire went into effect, the French and British controlled about half of the canal's length. French and British losses in the operation were 33 dead and 129 wounded. Egyptian losses are unknown.

A 4,000-man UN Emergency Force (UNEF) authorized on November 4 and made up of contingents from the Scandinavian countries, Brazil, Colombia, India, and Indonesia then arrived in Egypt to take up positions to keep Israeli and Egyptian forces separated. At the end of November the British and French governments both agreed to withdraw their forces from Egypt by December 22, and on December 1 Eisenhower announced that he had instructed U.S. oil companies to resume shipping supplies to both Britain and France. Under pressure from both the United States and the UN, Israel withdrew its forces from the Sinai, to include the Gaza Strip, during February 5–March 6, 1957. A UN observer force of 3,500 men then took up station in Gaza, at Sharm El Sheikh, and along the Sinai border. Although Israel had been assured that Egyptian forces would not return to Gaza, they were there within 48 hours of the Israeli withdrawal.

Nasser and Arab self-confidence were the chief beneficiaries of the crisis. The abysmal performance of Egyptian military forces in the crisis was forgotten in Nasser's ultimate triumph. Nasser found his prestige dramatically increased throughout the Arab world. Israel also benefited. The presence of the UN force guaranteed an end to the fedayeen raids, and Israel had also broken the Egyptian blockade of the Gulf of Aqaba, although its ships could still not transit the Suez Canal. The crisis also enhanced Soviet prestige in the Middle East, and the UN emerged with enhanced prestige, helping to boost world confidence in that organization.

The Suez Crisis ended Eden's political career. Ill and under tremendous criticism in Parliament from the Labour Party, he resigned from office in January 1957. Events also placed a serious, albeit temporary, strain on U.S.-British relations. More importantly, they revealed the serious limitations in British military strength. Indeed, observers are unanimous in declaring 1956 a seminal date in British imperial history that marked the effective end of Britain's tenure as a Great Power. The events had less impact in France. Mollet left office in May 1957 but not as a result of the Suez intervention. The crisis was also costly to both Britain and France in economic terms, for Saudi Arabia had halted oil shipments to both countries.

Finally, the Suez Crisis could not have come at a worse time for the West, because the event diverted world attention from the concurrent brutal Soviet military intervention in Hungary. Eisenhower believed, rightly or wrongly, that without the Suez diversion there would have been far stronger Western reaction to the Soviet invasion of its satellite.

Spencer C. Tucker

### See also
Aqaba, Gulf of; Baghdad Pact; Ben-Gurion, David; Egypt; Gaza Strip; Hussein ibn Talal, King of Jordan; Israel; Nasser, Gamal Abdel; Sharon, Ariel; Sinai Campaign of 1956; Strait of Tiran Crisis; Suez Canal

### References
Beaufre, André. *The Suez Expedition, 1956*. Translated by Richard Barry. New York: Praeger, 1969.
Cooper, Chester L. *The Lion's Last Roar: Suez, 1956*. New York: Harper and Row, 1978.
Eden, Anthony. *The Suez Crisis of 1956*. Boston: Beacon, 1968.
Freiberger, Steven Z. *Dawn over Suez: The Rise of American Power in the Middle East, 1953–1957*. Chicago: Ivan R. Dee, 1992.
Gorst, Anthony, and Lewis Johnman. *The Suez Crisis*. London: Routledge, 1997.
Hahn, Peter. *The United States, Great Britain, and Egypt, 1945–1956: Strategy and Diplomacy in the Early Cold War*. Chapel Hill: University of North Carolina Press, 1991.
Kelly, Saul, and Anthony Gorst, eds. *Whitehall and the Suez Crisis*. London: Routledge, 2000.
Kingseed, Cole C. *Eisenhower and the Suez Crisis of 1956*. Baton Rouge: Louisiana State University Press, 1995.
Kyle, Keith. *Suez: Britain's End of Empire in the Middle East*. London: Weidenfeld and Nicolson, 1991.
Louis, William R., and Roger Owen, eds. *Suez, 1956: The Crisis and Its Consequences*. New York: Oxford University Press, 1989.
Varble, Derek. *The Suez Crisis, 1956*. London: Osprey, 2003.

## Suicide Bombings

Suicide bombings are when an explosive is delivered and detonated by a person or persons who expect to die in the explosion along with the intended target or targets. In recent years the number of suicide bombings or attacks has risen exponentially, not just in the Middle East. Certainly, the September 11, 2001, terror attacks against the United States represented the worst—and most dramatic—example of a suicide operation. Other shocking attacks have taken place in Bali, Jakarta, Madrid, London, Paris, and Brussels, in addition to those in Iraq, Afghanistan, Pakistan, Syria, and Lebanon.

Suicide bombers employ several different techniques. Japanese (kamikaze) pilots in World War II were known for crashing their airplanes straight into targets. Kamikazes exacted a heavy toll on Allied warships at the end of World War II. The Tamil Tigers of Sri Lanka utilized suicide bombings during their long struggle against the central government in 1983–2009. Other attackers have employed bombs secured in cars or trucks.

Individual suicide bombers often strap explosives and shrapnel to their bodies or wear vests or belts specially designed for the purpose. They then drive or walk to their targets. Typical targets include crowded shopping areas, restaurants, and buses. Suicide bombers may also approach softer targets directly linked to the military or police, such as a line of recruits in the street during the Iraq War. Detonating the explosives kills and injures people in the vicinity and can also destroy property. One technique is to send two or more suicide bombers against a single target; after the first blast, the second bomber works his way into the crowd of responders and then detonates his explosives.

An explosion in an enclosed area is more destructive than one in the open, and suicide bombers pick their targets accordingly. Forensic investigators at the site of a suicide bombing can usually identify the bomber and the general type of device he or she used. A suicide vest decapitates the bomber; a belt cuts the bomber in two.

The explosive devices themselves are easily constructed. They might include an explosive charge, a battery, a cable, a light switch detonator, and a custom-made belt or vest to hold the explosives. Scrap metal might be employed to act as shrapnel, which in the blast would kill or maim those nearby. Explosives may also be carried in a briefcase or other bag. The bomber sets off the explosives by flipping a switch, using a cell phone, or pressing a button, sometimes remotely.

Muslim extremists in the latest wave of violence might leave a written note or a video, which is partially a statement of their intent and partially a will and settlement of any debts. Suicide bombings have been employed in the Middle East since the late 1970s. The Islamic resistance employed them in Syria against the Baathist government. During the Lebanese civil war, car bombings evolved in some cases into suicide attacks.

In response to the Israeli invasion of Lebanon in 1982, the Islamic Resistance planned bombing attacks. In November 1982 an Islamic Resistance suicide bomber destroyed a building in Tyre, Lebanon, killing 76 Israelis. The Organization of Islamic Jihad and other militant Islamist groups including Hezbollah as well as numerous Christians carried out another 50 suicide attacks between 1982 and 1999. A massive suicide truck bombing of their barracks at the Beirut Airport in October 1983 killed 305 people and caused American and French peacekeeping forces to quit Lebanon.

The belief held by many that such attacks bring martyrdom has encouraged suicide bombings in countries all over the world. In 1995 a suicide bomber dressed as a priest attempted to assassinate Pope John Paul II in Manila.

Suicide attacks by Palestinians began after the First Intifada but were not regular events; however, many more took place during the Second (al-Aqsa) Intifada. The first Palestinian suicide bombing occurred in April 1994 in the West Bank. Hamas explained that its basic policy was only to attack Israeli soldiers, but if Palestinian civilians were slaughtered in deliberate attacks, then it would break that policy. There were 198 known suicide-bombing attacks in Israel and Palestine between 1994 and July 2002, which killed 120 people. Because many of the bombers were intercepted and/or the attacks otherwise failed, the numbers of casualties were far lower than in the numerous suicide attacks carried out in Iraq after 2003.

Attacks increased after the beginning of the Second Intifada in September 2000. Although suicide bombings comprised only a small percentage of actual attacks launched by Palestinians against Israelis, they accounted for perhaps half the Israelis killed between 2000 and 2002. In 2005 Hamas ordered a cease-fire that, however, was not binding on the other groups that had engaged in attacks: the Abu Ali Mustafa Brigades of the Popular Front for the Liberation of Palestine, Islamic Jihad, and the al-Aqsa Martyrs Brigades. During 2005 there were seven attacks killing 23, and then in 2006 only two attacks.

Many of the suicide attackers in Lebanon in the 1980s were Christians; Palestinian suicide bombers have been presumed to be Muslims, although there are many Christians in the Palestinian national movement. It is obvious from the Tamil, Japanese, and anarchist violence that the motivation is primarily nationalist, and in fact Islam strictly forbids suicide and engaging recklessly in jihad so as to obtain martyrdom. According to classical doctrine, there are set rules regarding who may participate in jihad, and these exclude children, those with dependants, and also, traditionally, women. The main religious justification is that under circumstances of military occupation, jihad is required of Muslims. Among convocations of clerics who have met on this issue, most acknowledge that jihad is licit for Palestinians and in other occupied countries, although many object to suicide attacks.

For most Muslims, suicide is anathema. Many would-be suicide bombers are motivated by the desire to combat social injustice; others find irresistible the temptation of martyrdom with its promise of rewards in paradise. Martyrdom has its own history in early Islam, and it is believed that martyrs are cleansed of their sins and will have special power to intercede on behalf of their relatives and close friends on the Day of Judgment. The families of suicide bombers are often extremely proud of their loved ones and praise them publicly as heroes. Suicide bombers also believe that they will be remembered as popular heroes. Would-be Palestinian suicide bombers have often used the argument that all Israelis serve in the military, at least as reserves, and therefore are combatants and not really civilians.

In Iraq, the suicide attacks after the coalition invasion of March 2003 were initially directed against coalition forces but then turned to Iraqi government officials, police, military personnel, and civilians. These attacks spiked in 2005 before falling markedly beginning in 2007. In 2003 there were 25 suicide bombings; in 2005, there were 478. Suicide attacks continued to decline in Iraq for several more years but spiked again after the departure of U.S. and coalition troops in late 2011 and during the rise of the Islamic State of Iraq and Syria (ISIS) in 2014–2015. Indeed, as ISIS and allied extremist insurgents gained ground in Iraq after 2011, the number of suicide attacks skyrocketed and were occurring throughout the country.

In August 2015, a suicide bombing perpetrated by ISIS killed 76 civilians and injured 200 more at a Baghdad market. In July 2016, a massive suicide bomb killed 215 people in Baghdad and wounded 175 others; it was the worst bombing in that city since the Iraq War era. During 2015–2016 as Iraqi and coalition forces steadily eroded ISIS's influence in Iraq and Syria, ISIS operatives increasingly turned to suicide bombings as a means of employing asymmetrical warfare.

There are differing attitudes in the various states where suicide attacks have occurred. While most all people fear such attacks, many citizens support the notion of armed resistance. Since Al Qaeda and groups similar to it have been active, counterterrorist agencies, police, and gendarmeries around the world have been focusing on ways to prevent suicide bombings. Suicide bombings are part of asymmetric warfare. Advantages for any group employing this tactic are that bombers require no escape and are not expected to live to reveal information. Also, the materials for the explosive devices are inexpensive.

Al Qaedist tactics have created new rules of jihad, which are somewhat different from the past. For example, in a collective jihad, women, children, and parents of dependant children, or the children of the elderly, were not to volunteer for jihad, but in the five-year period when such attacks were most prevalent in Israel and in more recent times in Iraq, bombers have come from both genders, although most were men. It is a common assumption that suicide bombers are drawn from the poor and desperate, but most suicide bombings show this to be untrue; the bombers were rather the ideologically committed of different backgrounds. Sometimes those who were recruited to such actions were chosen for their psychological predispositions not to suicide but rather to suggestibility and were prevented, if possible, from contacting their families once their mission was set.

In recent years suicide bombings have occurred with increasing frequency in many nations, including Pakistan, Yemen, Turkey, Nigeria, Bangladesh, Belgium, and France. Many of the perpetrators have been self-avowed jihadist extremists or operatives carrying out missions on behalf of groups such as Al Qaeda, ISIS, Boko Haram, and al-Shabaab.

Understandably, suicide bombings are enormously unsettling. Suicide bombers turn up when they are least expected as their victims go about their daily business, and victims and bystanders are taken completely by surprise. The victims are often civilians, and children make up a sizable percentage of those killed. Because the bomber has no concern for his or her own life, it is difficult to prevent such attacks. In some countries, individuals and businesses have hired security guards who are specially trained to spot potential bombers. Airport and general transport security has now been increased worldwide.

AMY HACKNEY BLACKWELL AND SHERIFA ZUHUR

**See also**
Al Qaeda; Hamas; Hezbollah; Intifada, First, Intifada, Second; Iraq; Iraq War; Islamic Radicalism in the 20th and 21st Centuries; Islamic State of Iraq and Syria; Jihad; Lebanon; Palestinian Islamic Jihad

**References**
Friedman, Lauri S. *What Motivates Suicide Bombers?* Farmington Hills, MI: Greenhaven, 2004.
Khosrokhavar, Farhad. *Suicide Bombers: Allah's New Martyrs.* Translated by David Macey. London: Pluto, 2005.
Rosenthal, Franz. "On Suicide in Islam." *Journal of the American Oriental Society* 66 (1946): 239–259.

# Suleiman I (1494–1566)

Ottoman sultan. Born on November 8, 1494, at Trabzon on the east coast of the Black Sea, Suleiman (Süleyman I, Süleiman the Lawgiver, Süleiman the Magnificent) was the son of Sultan Selim I. Suleiman was educated in the Topkapi Palace schools in Istanbul (Constantinople). At age 17 in order that he secure administrative experience, Suleiman was appointed governor of first Kaffa (Theodosia) and then of Manisa, with a brief period at Edirne.

Suleiman succeeded his father on the latter's death and ascended the throne as the 10th Ottoman sultan on September 30, 1520. In May 1521 he led Ottoman forces in an invasion of South-Central Europe and captured Beograd (modern-day Belgrade) on August 29, which he made his principal base for further operations into Central Europe against both Hungary and Habsburg Austria. Suleiman then turned his attention to the eastern Mediterranean, laying siege to and taking the island of Rhodes off the eastern coast of Anatolia, which was held by the Knights of St. John (July 28–December 21, 1522).

After suppressing a mutiny among the Janissaries in Istanbul (January 1525), Suleiman invaded Hungary, defeating the Hungarians in the important Battle of Mohács (August 29, 1526) and occupying the city of Buda (September 10). He then established his control over most of Hungary. Suleiman returned to Istanbul but resumed the campaign three years later, this time against Austria. Suleiman's forces reached Vienna (September 23, 1529), but unusually heavy rains precluded him from bringing up the heavy siege engines required to take the city, and with the onset of winter he abandoned the effort after only three weeks on October 15.

Suleiman formed an alliance with French king François I against Holy Roman emperor Charles V. Thereafter Suleiman regularly campaigned against Charles but occasionally was distracted by war against the Persians. Campaigning in Mesopotamia, Suleiman captured Baghdad (December 1534). In additional campaigning against Persia, he took and destroyed the city of Tabriz (August 1535).

Following the Habsburg invasion of Hungary in 1542, Suleiman undertook another campaign against that country in 1543, moving up the Danube and capturing Gran (Esztergom) in August and Stuhlweissenburg (Szekesfehérvár) in September. He then concluded peace with Emperor Charles V in 1544. Suleiman campaigned in Armenia (1545–1549), taking Van and Tabriz (1548). In his final effort against Persia, he invaded and ravaged much of Georgia and western Persia (1552–1555). Under the terms of peace concluded with Persia in 1555, Suleiman added territory to his empire as far east as the Caspian Sea.

At the same time, thanks in large part to his capable naval commander, Khair ed-Din Barbarossa, Suleiman established Ottoman dominance over the western Mediterranean, including the Aegean Islands. An Ottoman fleet also secured much of the eastern Mediterranean (1552–1555), and most of North Africa accepted Ottoman suzerainty. Ottoman fleets also raided Sicily and Minorca during 1558–1561.

Domestically, Suleiman accomplished a great deal. He reformed the Ottoman administrative structure, improved education, codified and simplified the laws (leading to the appellation of *kanuni*, or lawgiver), and carried out a major building program in Istanbul. In defiance of custom, he married the favorite in his harem, Roxanna, a former captive from Galicia. She managed to discredit his first son, later executed on Suleiman's orders.

Suleiman resumed warfare against the Habsburgs in 1566, planning to besiege Vienna. He most usually accompanied his armies in the field, and he died in the course of this campaign on September 5, 1566, near Saigetvár, Hungary.

Probably the greatest of Ottoman rulers and at war almost constantly throughout his nearly 46-year reign (the longest of any Ottoman sultan), Suleiman greatly expanded Ottoman power, reigning over a population of some 20 million to 30 million. His rule saw the height of Ottoman influence, but decline set in soon thereafter.

SPENCER C. TUCKER

**See also**
Hayreddin Barbarossa; Janissaries; Ottoman Empire; Ottoman-Habsburg Wars; Ottoman-Hungarian Wars; Ottoman-Safavid Wars; Rhodes, Suleiman's Siege of; Tahmasp I, Shah

**References**
Bridge, Anthony. *Suleiman the Magnificent: Scourge of Heaven*. New York: F. Watts, 1983.
Clot, Andre. *Suleiman the Magnificent*. Trans. Matthew J. Reisz. London: Saqi Books, 1992.
Kunt, Metin, and Christine Woodhead. *Suleyman the Magnificent and His Age: The Ottoman Empire in the Early Modern World*. New York: Longman, 1995.

## Sumer

Located in the Tigris-Euphrates River Valley, Sumer was the first in a long line of Mesopotamian cultures to dominate the Near East in the ancient world. The cradle of one of the most ancient civilizations, Sumer was the birthplace of written language and the notion of city. Sumer was located in modern-day southern and central Iraq, a region that in ancient times was dense with marshlands. Although non-Semitic peoples drained many of the marshes before the establishment of Sumerian culture, it was the Sumerians who brought immense prosperity to the region.

Scholars believe that the Sumerians migrated to Mesopotamia from Asia Minor circa 3300 BCE. Within 300 years, they established all of the tools for building the first major collection of cities tied together by a single culture and economy: surplus agriculture, extensive trade in manufactured goods, and a consolidated religious system based on animist beliefs. Between 3000 and 1900 BCE, the Sumerian city-states struggled for political power among themselves. Such cities as Kish, Ur, Erech, Lagash, and Larsa dominated the region for several centuries, combining military power with economic dominance.

Trade was an important vehicle for Sumerian success. Goods such as leathers, metal wares, and pottery were traded extensively. Construction was also an important activity. Annual floods and regular seismic activity made sturdy construction important, and masons were valued for their fine work.

The Sumerians used their written language, expressed in cuneiform, to establish bureaucracies previously unknown in scale. Indeed, cuneiform, the oldest-known written language in human history, rose in prominence with the fortunes of Sumer. The wedge-shaped symbols of cuneiform allowed for abstract expression previously unknown, making it possible for the Sumerians to record everything from tax records to literary works. Because of its value to government and religion, the Sumerians' language spread relatively widely and was eventually adopted as the script of many other Mesopotamian cultures.

Fighting between various Sumerian city-states in the period after 2500 BCE eventually weakened unity among the Sumerians and the Sumerian economy. A series of invasions also hobbled Sumer. Elamites and Akkadians both took control of Sumer during the subsequent centuries. The conquerors adopted many aspects of Sumerian society, including cuneiform and the building of ziggurat complexes.

The almost constant warfare among the Sumerian city-states for 2,000 years spurred the continuous development of military technology and technique far beyond any similar developments found elsewhere in the Near East. The first Sumerian war for which there is detailed evidence occurred between the states of Lagash and Umma in 2525 BCE. The importance of that war lies in a commemorative stele that Eannatum of Lagash erected to celebrate his victory. The stele is called the Stele of Vultures for its portrayal of birds of prey and lions tearing at the flesh of the corpses of the dead as they lay on the desert plain. This is the first important pictorial portrayal of war during the Sumerian period. The stele indicates that Sumerian troops fought in a phalanx formation organized six files deep with an eight-man front, a formation somewhat similar to that used in archaic Greece. Fighting in phalanx requires discipline and training, hence the soldiers portrayed on the stele were probably professionals. Another indication of their professionalism is the presence of titles associated with military command. The Stele of Vultures, then, seems to provide evidence of the world's first standing professional army.

The stele also provides the first historical evidence of soldiers wearing helmets. The appearance of the helmet marks the first defensive response to the killing power of an important offensive weapon: the mace. In Sumer, the presence of a well-crafted helmet indicates a major development in military technology that was so effective that it drove the mace from the battlefield.

The first representation of the military application of the wheel is also depicted on the stele, which shows Eannatum riding in a chariot. Certainly, the Sumerian invention of the chariot has to be ranked among the major military innovations in history. The Sumerians are also credited with the invention of the wheeled cart, which became the standard vehicle for logistical transport in the Near East until the time of Alexander the Great.

By 1900 BCE, the Sumerians no longer considered themselves unique; rather, they had been subsumed into the cultures of their conquerors. However, their reign over the Tigris-Euphrates River Valley, which lasted more than 1,000 years, laid the foundation for many civilizations to come.

Nancy L. Stockdale and Richard A. Gabriel

**See also**
Akkad; Mesopotamia

**References**
Charvat, Peter. *Mesopotamia before History*. London: Routledge, 2002.
Kramer, S. N. *History Begins at Sumer*. New York: Doubleday, 1959.

## SUMMER RAINS, Operation
*See* Gaza War of 2006

## Sunni Islam

The largest of the two predominant branches of Islam. Approximately 67 percent of Muslims worldwide are adherents of Sunni Islam. The word "Sunni" is rarely used by Muslims themselves. It derives from a medieval phrase, *Ahl al-Sunna wa al-Jama'a*, meaning those who live according to Prophet Muhammad's model and who congregate. In the early period, this term did not refer to all Muslims but rather to those who were engaged in Islamic scholarship and learning. The *sunna*, or way of Prophet Muhammad, refers to his practice of Islam during his 23 years of life following the initial revelation of Allah's words to him. It is mostly in the West that Muslims are differentiated as Sunni or Shia. If asked, a Muslim may instead identify oneself by a school of Islamic law or jurisprudence, such as the Hanafi school, which was the official legal doctrine of the Ottoman Empire. If a contemporary Muslim is identified as a Sunni, in some countries this indicates the person's stronger religiosity or that he or she is an Islamist (frequently called a fundamentalist in the West).

In contrast with the more institutionalized clerics, courts, and systems of Sunni Muslim learning, Sufi Islam is a mystical movement within Islam that recognizes personal guides (*shaykh* or *pir*) and is organized into brotherhoods (*tariqat*). There are Shia as well as Sunni Sufi orders.

Sunni Muslims do not adhere to the doctrine of the *a'imah,* or imams, as do several sects of Shia Muslims. In the past, Sunnis generally judged the validity of the caliph (the temporal political and military leader) or the caliphate (Islamic government) itself by his or its adherence to the faith and the order and harmony that he or it maintained. In contrast with the Shias, Sunni Muslims believe that Abu Bakr, Omar, and Uthman—the first three Rashidun caliphs following Muhammad—were legitimate successors of Muhammad and that they are of equal standing with the fourth caliph, Ali, Muhammad's son-in-law. Ali became the fourth caliph in 656 CE after the murder of Caliph Uthman and was himself assassinated in 661.

It was not a requirement that the political and religious leadership in Sunni Islam trace its lineage through Ali, although the requirements of a caliph as defined by the scholar Abu al-Hasan Ali Ibn Muhammad Ibn Habib al-Mawardi (972–1058) indicated that he must be of Prophet Muhammad's Quraysh tribe. Any link to the Ahl al-Bayt, the immediate family members of the prophet, was highly regarded. Sunnis ascribe no particular religious importance to the position of imam and emphasize the historic role of the caliphate in governing Islam. For example, according to most Sunni schools of law, an offensive (and collective) jihad can only be declared by the caliph, the successor to Prophet Muhammad and the lawful temporal and spiritual authority for the entire Islamic community. This was highly problematic, as the caliphs lost their real authority in 1055, regaining it only partially until the Mongol sack of Baghdad in 1258. When the Ottoman sultans later declared themselves to be caliphs in order to wage jihad, their religious claim was questioned by other Muslims. By this period, Muslims understood the caliphate as an ideal structure but one that could be replaced by other forms of authority.

In the absence of the caliphate, Muslim politics had continued under the precept that other rulers, sultans, or emirs would rule to the best of their ability in accordance with sharia, or Islamic law, and "order the good and forbid the evil," a key principle in Islam. Clerics (*ulema*), those who possess *ilm* (religious knowledge), were to be consulted by the ruler, issue *fatawa,* and help to guide the believers.

Disputes have occurred over the duly Islamic nature of rulers or their governance and have given rise to purist, separatist, or millenarian movements. For example, an early Muslim group, the Khwaraij (Kharijites), called for a return to the piety of the prophet and refused to acknowledge certain caliphs. A Kharijite actually killed Ali ibn Abi Talib. However, among the capital sins in Islam are sedition and regicide. In the late 19th century, the Mahdist movement in the Sudan fought against the British in the belief that their leader was the Mahdi and that his appearance heralded the Day of Judgment.

To justify Islamic rule the Ottomans, who were Sunni Muslims, later governed under a particular theory called the circle of equity in which mutual responsibilities were to provide equity and justice. In the 20th century both Sunni- and Shia-politicized Islamic movements have argued for a more intensely Islamic government. The Muslim Brotherhood, Hamas, Hezbollah, Gamaat Islamiya, and Al Qaeda have all taken this position. These groups draw on very important arguments about governance and the state that have developed in Islamic history. The Muslim Brotherhood rejected jihad as armed struggle and seeks to change society through education. Hezbollah and Hamas argue for both armed struggle and education. Gamaat Islamiya and Al Qaeda focused on armed struggle until the truce between Gamaat Islamiya and the Egyptian government in 1999.

In general, Sunnis believe that the individual interpretation of Islamic law by scholars may vary. Their legal schools employ a principle of lawmaking known as *ijma,* or consensus, that is not employed by the Shia legal schools. However, there are differences in where legal scholars locate that consensus. There is no central authority in Sunni Islam, so Muslims may seek advice from various clerics or authorities, and advice columns in newspapers and on the Internet all provide differing opinions to them.

Muslims believe that the Quran is the literal word of God pronounced in Arabic by the angel Gabriel to Muhammad over a period of 23 years. Any desecration of the Quran is therefore a desecration of the very words of Allah. Although the Quran is the final statement of Allah to humanity, where it does not offer explicit advice on a matter a Muslim may appeal to a jurist to look to the prophet's sunna as recorded in the hadith, or collected materials concerning the tradition, behavior, practices, and sayings of the prophet. They may also use *qiyas,* or types of analogy, in determining the licitness of any action, or behavior, or the principle of *ijima,* a kind of consensus.

The hadith are sometimes related by the companions (*sahabh*) of Muhammad or by his wives. An important companion was Abu Bakr, also known as "The Most Truthful" (*al-Siddiq*), the first caliph. The next companions in level of importance are the next two caliphs, Omar and Uthman. Shiites reject the top ranking of the testimony of these companions, asserting the primacy of Ali. Although these three are important companions, Sunnis consider anyone who knew or even saw Muhammad, accepted his teachings, and died as a Muslim to be a companion. Early Sunni scholars identified these companions and listed them in various reference texts. This identification was essential because their testimonies and their reputation for veracity affirm and determine the content of the hadith and therefore the sunna.

There are many collections of these original oral traditions, but they are graded according to their soundness with six respected collections, two of which—that of Muslim and al-Bukhari—are considered most reliable. However, many Muslims repeat and believe in hadith that are not necessarily the most sound, and since the reform movement of the 19th century, some Muslims believe that the hadith brought many unwanted innovations or, conversely, too much imitation of tradition (*taqlid*) into Islam. Shia Islamic law generally uses hadith that pertain to Muhammad as told to members of Ali's family. These variations lead to some differences in Sunni Islamic law and Shia Islamic law.

Muslims must practice their faith through demonstrated religious rituals and obligations. Many sources speak of five religious practices or duties, often referred to as the Five Pillars. The first pillar is called bearing witness (*shahadah*) and is the recitation of the creed or confession of faith, called the Testimony of Faith: "There is no God, but Allah; and Muhammad is His prophet." Shiites generally add "and Ali ibn Abi Talib is the friend of God" to the *shahadah.* The *shahadah* is also uttered as part of the Muslim call (*adhan*) to prayer and is part of the Tashahud segment of the prayers recited at least five times daily. The second pillar is prayer (*salat*), performed at least five times a day (dawn, noon, midafternoon, sunset, and evening). Muslims purify themselves before prayer by washing their hands, face, mouth, nose, ears, and feet. During prayer, all Muslims face Mecca. The third pillar is fasting (*sawm*) during the daylight hours for all of the month of Ramadan, the ninth month of the Islamic lunar calendar. This fasting means that no food or beverages are consumed and that there is no smoking or sexual intercourse. Those who are sick are excused from fasting.

The fourth pillar is almsgiving, effectively a tax (*zakat*) levied on one's assets at the end of the year. It is used for the community's poor, the promotion of Islam, and the maintenance of the mosque and other religious institutions. The fifth pillar is the required pilgrimage (*hajj*) once in a lifetime to the holy city of Mecca re-creating Muhammad's pilgrimage there in 632.

The responsibility for performing these duties falls on the individual, but stricter Muslims hold that it is the duty of the state to command the good and enforce their performance. There are other strictures. For example, Muslims must not drink alcohol, not simply as a forbidden substance but because it clouds alertness and judgment and makes it impossible to pray. Pork is forbidden, as are games of chance. Many Muslim women believe that covering their heads is a required individual duty, but others do not. Modest behavior is, however, required of both men and women.

Many Westerners know little about Muslims with the exception of the Five Pillars. Yet ethical behavior is very important to Islamic belief, including the protection of the weak and aid to the poor and socially disadvantaged. Islam seeks to promote an ethical life lived within a community. It is more difficult in many ways to be a good Muslim while fulfilling one's obligations to family and community than to live as a hermit, and Prophet Muhammad is said to have promoted marriage and discouraged celibacy or an extreme ascetic lifestyle. Many of the rules regarding relations between men and women, which non-Muslims find very strict and hard to understand, are indeed intended to provide a moral and ethical grounding for the community.

Muslims are concerned with *iman,* or faith, and many religio-philosophical principles guide them. The most basic aspect of Islam is belief in Allah and the oneness (*tawhid*) of Allah. This monotheism is expressed in many ways. Muslims believe in the prophets and believe that they brought important messages to mankind, but Muhammad is considered the Seal of Prophecy, or the last prophet. Nonetheless, Jesus, Moses, Abraham, and others are revered. However, Muslims believe that the Jews did not heed the word of God and that the Jews changed the revelation of Moses to support their assertion that they, and not the descendants of Ishmael, are the chosen people of Allah. The Christians, Sunnis argue, distorted the revelation of Jesus because the doctrine of the Trinity violates the idea of the oneness of Allah.

Muslims recognize the scriptures as revelations of Allah. Allah was the creator, but he did not simply create the world and humankind and leave humans to fend for themselves. Rather, Allah provided revelations for the guidance of men. The Quran is the transcending revelation of Allah that cannot be contradicted by any other revelations of Allah. Still, Muslims recognize other revelations, which include the Jewish and Christian holy scriptures as well as the Zoroastrian texts.

Muslims believe in the angels (*malaika*) who are the servants of Allah. Angels were not given the free will that Allah granted to humans. Their duties include recording all human deeds, ensouling the fetus at 120 days of gestation (although some Islamic scholars believe ensoulment occurs on the 40th day), watching over and caring for creation, gathering souls at death, and much more.

All Muslims also believe in the Day of Judgment and in the Resurrection (*qiyama*), when Allah will return to judge all of humanity, Muslim and non-Muslim, including the dead. After the Resurrection, every human is held accountable for his or her deeds. The deeds of each individual are judged by Allah and weighed on a scale. If the good outweighs the evil, then the individual gains entrance into Paradise. If the evil outweighs the good, the individual spends eternity in Hell.

In the pre-Islamic era, referred to as the *jahilliya*, or time of barbarity, people believed entirely in preordination. Islam rejects this passivity because people possess free will and can thus choose to do good or evil and are held accountable for their decisions. At the same time, it is difficult to retain faith in the face of tragedy, poverty, or disaster. The Muslim belief in the omnipotence of God, his transcendence and simultaneous immanence, is meant to solace the believer.

The application of reason, in the form of Hellenic philosophical arguments to law and theology in order to derive the correct rules and meaning of the Quran and the sunna, gave rise to multiple Sunni traditions, or schools of law and theology. These schools share the basic theology described above and assert the primacy of the Quranic revelation, but there are notable differences.

Sunni Islamic law (sharia) is based on the Quran and the sunna as nuanced by the particular hadith collection accepted. Different scholars using different assumptions, reasoning, hermeneutics (guiding interpretive principles), and source materials arrived at different applications of Islamic law organized into schools known as *madhahib*. Muslims assert that sharia never changes but that the understanding and application (*fiqh*) do. For example, the Quran and derived sharia never envisioned the use of the telegraph. Thus, the application of the sharia to the use of the telegraph was a matter of interpretation. In addition to the usual sources of law, jurists took into account *maslaha*, public benefit or the common good, in considering new technology.

There are four major schools of law in Sunni Islam, yet there have been other schools that have died out and smaller schools that continue to exist. The various schools predominate in different regions. These dominant Sunni schools of law are Hanbali, Hanafi, Maliki, and Shafi'i, and all use the Quran as their primary source.

Hanbali is the strictest tradition and has fewer than 10 percent of Sunnis as adherents. It was founded by Ahmad ibn-Hanbal and is the dominant tradition on the Arabian Peninsula, although it has adherents in Iraq and Syria as well. The clear statements of the Quran and the sunna as transmitted through its accepted hadith override any opinion from any source.

Hanafi is the largest school. It was founded by Abu Hanifa and encompasses 30 percent of Sunnis. Its adherents are mainly in Turkey, Central Asia, the Balkans, Iraq, Afghanistan, Pakistan, India, Bangladesh, lower Egypt, Russia, and parts of China. Both the Mongol Empire and the Ottoman Empire promoted the Hanafi tradition. When Ottoman sultan Selim the Grim (1512–1520) captured Palestine, he imposed Hanafi law on the region. The official judicial traditions and systems in contemporary Syria, Jordan, and Palestine are derived from the Hanafi tradition.

Maliki has approximately 15 percent of Sunnis as adherents. It was founded by Malik ibn Anas and has adherents in North Africa and West Africa, particularly upper Egypt, Algeria, Tunisia, Morocco, Mauritania, and Libya as well as the Sudan, Kuwait, Dubai, and Abu Dhabi. The Maliki school derives its *fiqh* through consensus more than any of the other traditions. The Malikite system of lawmaking is built on the Quran and the hadith, supplemented by the consensus of the people (*ijma*), analogy (*qiyas*), and the agreed practice of the people of Medina. In addition, Malik considered the statements of the prophet's companions, the public good (*masalih mursala*), customary law (*urf*), common practice (*adat*), and several other legal principles.

Shafi'i was founded by Muhammad ibn Idris al-Shafi and has adherents in the southern Arabian Peninsula, Syria, Indonesia, Malaysia, the Philippines, Sudan, Ethiopia, Somali, North Yemen, and lower Egypt. The Shafi'i school utilizes the *usul al-fiqh* (roots of lawmaking) in a way that places *ijma* ahead of analogy, the Quran, the sunna of the prophet, and consensus.

Historically, there were many Sunni schools and trends in theology. Among the important or well-known trends were the Mutazilah, whose doctrine was abandoned, and the Ashariyya, Maturidiyyah, and Salafism (which has at least two versions).

The Mutazilah school was established in Iraq by Wasil bin Ata (699–749). Abbasid caliph al-Mamun (813–827) made Mutazila theology the state religion and persecuted all dissenters. At the time, Muslims had debated the uncreatedness versus the created (man-made) nature of the Quran. Mutazilites did not accept the doctrine of the uncreated Quran, but with their downfall Muslims accepted precisely that doctrine. They took an intermediate position on the question of sin, asserting that Muslims who commit grave sins and die without repentance are neither believers nor nonbelievers. The Mutazilites rejected anthropomorphic interpretations of God. For instance, the phrase "hand of God" might refer symbolically to God's power.

The Ashariyya school was founded by Abu al-Hasan al-Ashari (873–935) and became the dominant Sunni theology in that era. It emphasizes divine revelation and stresses the understanding of that revelation through the application of human reasoning.

The Maturidiyyah was founded by Abu Mansur al-Maturidi (d. 944). Maturidis believe that the existence of Allah as understood in Islam can be derived through reason alone and that such is true of major concepts of good and evil, legal and illegal. Salafism, a reform movement in Islam, actually developed in two different contexts in 18th-century Arabia and in 19th-century Egypt and the Ottoman Empire. The 19th-century to early 20th-century reformers Jamal al-Din al-Afghani, Muhammad Abduh, Qasim Amin, and Rashid Rida initiated a discussion about the decline of the Muslim world and the reforms it should carry out to overcome the negative influence of Western colonialism and imperialism. While al-Afghani looked for an Islamic ruler who would stand up to the West and believed that Pan-Islam could solve the problem, Muhammad Abduh, an Egyptian jurist, recommended reform of Islamic education and methodology in which blind imitation of the past would cease. He thought that Sunni Muslims should consider a return to *ijtihad* (a Shia methodology of lawmaking) to meet contemporary requirements, and he wanted Western sciences introduced into the educational curriculum. Qasim Amin argued for an end to enforced marriages, female seclusion, and lack of education, while Rashid Rida pursued a somewhat stricter idea of a cleansed Islamic way of life.

Earlier, a strictly monotheistic sect of Islam was developed under Muhammad abd al-Wahhab in Arabia and referred to as Wahhabism by that leader's enemies. Its adherents were known both as Ikhwans (Brethren) and Salafis because they wanted to cleanse Islamic practice and society of its un-Islamic accretions and innovations (*bid'a*) that had arisen through cultural synthesis. The Wahhabis adhered to the Hanbali school of law, although some Salafis speak of rejecting all legal tradition and utilizing only the Quran and the sunna. The Salafis were anti-Ottoman, anti-Shia, and anti-Sufi and opposed such practices as Sufi ceremonies and visiting tombs. These Salafis called for jihad in its active form with which they, in alliance with the Saud family, drove out first the Ottomans and then in a later historical period the al-Rashids and the Hashemites.

Osama bin Laden was a neo-Salafi. He believed that the Saudi Arabian royal family does not strictly uphold Wahhabi or Salafi values and should be militantly opposed for its alliance with the West. Other Salafis have been part of the resistance in post-2003 Iraq to U.S. occupation and the new Iraqi government.

Some Salafis consider the Shias to be renegades or apostates, apostasy being a capital crime in Islam. Shiites feared and hated the Wahhabis because of their raids on their areas, but this is not true of all Sunnis and Shia who, in general, lived peacefully alongside each other in prewar Iraq. Some charge that the United States and Israel as well as certain Arab countries are heightening fears in the region of a Shia crescent of influence running from Iran to the Shias of Iraq and the Persian Gulf states and then to the Shias of Lebanon. Such discourse could create more problems between Muslims in the region. Therefore, clerics in Saudi Arabia, Egypt, and elsewhere are trying to quiet sectarian discord or at least represent Shia as a legitimate *madhhab*, or legal school of Islam.

RICHARD M. EDWARDS AND SHERIFA ZUHUR

**See also**
Al Qaeda; Hezbollah; Jihad; Medina, Siege of; Quran; Shia Islam; Wahhabism

**References**
Ahmed, Akbar S. *Islam Today: A Short Introduction to the Muslim World.* Rev. ed. London: Tauris, 1999.
Armstrong, Karen. *Islam: A Short History.* New York: Modern Library, 2002.
Esposito, John L. *The Oxford History of Islam.* New York: Oxford University Press, 2000.
Esposito, John L. *What Everyone Needs to Know about Islam.* New York: Oxford University Press, 2002.
Fuller, Graham E., and Rend Rahim Francke. *The Arab Shi'a: The Forgotten Muslims.* Hampshire, UK: Palgrave Macmillan, 2001.
Gregorian, Vartan. *Islam: A Mosaic, Not a Monolith.* Baltimore: Brookings Institute Press, 2004.

Sachiko, Muratam, and William C. Chittick. *The Vision of Islam.* New York: Paragon House, 1994.

Salamah, Ahmad Abdullah. *Shia & Sunni Perspective on Islam: An Objective Comparison of the Shia and Sunni Doctrines Based on the Holy Quran and Hadith.* Jedda, Saudi Arabia: Abul-Qasim Publication House, 1991.

## Sunni Triangle

The region of Iraq that is populated largely by Sunni Muslims and was at the epicenter of the Iraqi insurgency during the Iraq War (2003–2011). Beginning in 2013, a large portion of the area was taken over by the Islamic State of Iraq and Syria (ISIS), which is a Sunni extremist group that is rabidly anti-Shia.

The Sunni Triangle begins near Baghdad, then extends west to Ramadi and north to Tikrit. Each side of the triangle is roughly 125 miles long. This region, which lies generally northwest of the capital city of Baghdad, is densely populated. Tikrit, the birthplace of former Iraqi president Saddam Hussein, was one of the epicenters of the insurgency after 2003. Also lying within the triangle are the cities of Mosul, Fallujah, Samarra, and Baqubah, all of which were heavily involved in the insurgency. Hussein's strong tribal and familial connections to the area traditionally made it the strongest base of support for his regime, and many of his advisers, confidantes, and military commanders hailed from the area.

The term "Sunni Triangle" did not enter the popular lexicon until 2003 after a *New York Times* story that ran on June 10 used it to describe the area in which the growing insurgency was based. The Sunni Triangle witnessed several major offensives conducted by coalition forces designed to flush out and neutralize Iraqi insurgents. The first was Operation RED DAWN, launched in December 2003. Its goal was the capture of the deposed Hussein. On December 13, 2003, Hussein was found alive and captured in ad-Dawr, a small village not far from his hometown of Tikrit. His apprehension was a significant public relations and morale boost for coalition forces occupying Iraq.

On April 4, 2004, coalition forces implemented Operation VIGILANT RESOLVE, an attempt to capture control of Fallujah from insurgent forces. The operation precipitated the First Battle of Fallujah, which lasted until May 1, 2004. U.S. forces were unsuccessful in their endeavor, and they sustained 27 killed in the fighting. The prematurely terminated operation proved to be a public relations nightmare for the United States, as it drove home the notion that its forces were now waging a dangerous and increasingly ineffective counterinsurgency.

During the Second Battle of Fallujah (November 7–December 23, 2004), U.S. forces, working in concert with Iraqi forces, were successful in wresting control of the city from the insurgents. At the time, the Pentagon termed the vicious combat at Fallujah as the worst urban fighting in which American forces had been involved since the January–March 1968 Battle of Hue during the Tet Offensive of the Vietnam War. The victory at Fallujah was costly, however. U.S. forces suffered 95 killed; Iraqi forces reported 11 killed. At least 1,350 insurgents died in the fighting, while another 1,500 were taken captive.

During November 8–16, 2004, American and allied Iraqi Security Forces fought Iraqi insurgents in the Battle of Mosul. It was designed to coincide with the Second Battle of Fallujah. U.S.-led forces were only partly successful in seizing control of Mosul, as a number of insurgents remained in the western third of the city from which they engaged in hit-and-run tactics. Despite the capture of Fallujah and other counterinsurgency operations, the Sunni Triangle remains among the most dangerous regions of Iraq for U.S. and allied forces.

In early 2013 ISIS began seizing large swaths of the Sunni Triangle and by early 2014 had seized Fallujah, Ramadi, and virtually all of Anbar Province. The Iraqi government under Nuri al-Maliki proved incapable or unwilling to stop the militants, and by late 2014 ISIS forces were within 60 miles of Baghdad. This serious turn of events necessitated the redeployment of some 3,000 U.S. military "advisers" to Iraq in the late summer of 2014, at which time the United States also began an aerial bombardment campaign against ISIS targets in western and northern Iraq; in the fall, the campaign was extended to include air strikes against ISIS targets in Syria. At the same time, the Barack Obama administration assembled a broad international military coalition, including a number of Arab nations, to defeat ISIS. After more than three years of heavy fighting, in December 2017 the Iraqi government declared victory over ISIS, with virtually all of the Sunni Triangle back under Iraqi control.

PAUL G. PIERPAOLI JR.

**See also**

Fallujah, First Battle of; Fallujah, Second Battle of; Hussein, Saddam; Maliki, Nuri Muhammed Kamil al-; Iraq Insurgency; Islamic State of Iraq and Syria

**References**

Buzzell, Colby. *My War: Killing Time in Iraq.* New York: Putnam, 2005.

Hashim, Ahmed. *Insurgency and Counter-insurgency in Iraq.* Ithaca, NY: Cornell University Press, 2005.
Keegan, John. *The Iraq War: The Military Offensive, from Victory in 21 Days to the Insurgent Aftermath.* New York: Vintage, 2005.
Ricks, Thomas E. *Fiasco: The American Military Adventure in Iraq.* New York: Penguin, 2006.

## Sykes-Picot Agreement (May 16, 1916)

Agreement reached between the British, French, and Russian governments regarding claims of territory belonging to the Ottoman Empire. In the spring of 1915 British high commissioner in Egypt Sir Henry McMahon promised Sharif Hussein ibn Ali of Mecca British support for an Arab state under Hussein in return for Arab military support against the Ottoman Empire. Confident of British support, in June 1916 two of Hussein's sons proclaimed the Arab Revolt. The French government was alarmed over this, and on October 24 McMahon informed Hussein of limitations on a postwar Arab state. Britain was to have direct control of the Baghdad-Basra region so that the area west of Hama, Homa, Aleppo, and Damascus could not be under Arab control. Any Arab state east of the Hama-Damascus area would have to seek British advice. McMahon also warned Hussein that Britain could make no promises that would injure French interests.

Aware of the British agreement with Hussein, Paris pressed London for recognition of its own claims in the Ottoman Empire. Englishman Sir Mark Sykes and Frenchman François Georges Picot were appointed by their respective governments to conduct the negotiations, and because discussions of the future of Asiatic Turkey necessarily affected the Russians, the two proceeded to Petrograd in the early spring of 1916 and there presented their draft agreement. They secured Russian support in the formal Sazonov-Paléologue Agreement of April 26, 1916, named for Russian foreign minister Sergei D. Sazonov and French ambassador to Russia Georges Maurice Paléologue. It is most often known as the Sykes-Picot Agreement, however. The agreement was officially concluded on May 16, 1916.

The Sykes-Picot Agreement provided extensive territorial concessions to all three powers at the expense of the Ottoman Empire. Russia was to receive the provinces of Erzerum, Trebizond, Van, and Bitlis (known as Turkish Armenia) as well as northern Kurdistan from Mush, Sairt, Ibn Omar, and Amadiya to the border with Persia (Iran). France would secure the coastal strip of Syria, the vilayet of Adana, and territory extending in the south from Ayntab and Mardin to the future Russian border to a northern line drawn from Ala Dagh through Kaysariya Ak-Dagh, Jidiz-Dagh, and Zara to Egin-Kharput (the area known as Cilicia). Britain would secure southern Mesopotamia with Baghdad as well as the ports of Haifa and Acre in Palestine. The zone between the British and French territories would be formed into one or more Arab states, but this was to be divided into British and French spheres of influence. The French sphere would include the Syrian hinterland and the Mosul province of Mesopotamia, while the British would have influence over the territory from Palestine to the Persian border. The agreement also provided that Alexandretta would become a free port, while Palestine would be internationalized.

The parties involved agreed to maintain strict secrecy regarding the plan. Despite this, the Italian government learned of its existence by early 1917 and forced the French and British governments to agree in the St. Jean de Maurienne Agreement of April 17, 1917, that Italy would receive a large tract of purely Turkish land in southern Anatolia and a sphere of influence north of Smyrna. This was the final agreement among the Allies regarding the future partition of the Ottoman Empire. It was contingent on the approval of the Russian government, which was not forthcoming because of revolutionary upheaval there. Hussein did not learn of the Sykes-Picot Agreement until December 1917 when the information was published by the Bolshevik government of Russia and relayed to Hussein by the Turks, who vainly hoped thereby to reverse his pro-British stance.

The Sykes-Picot Agreement proved a source of bitter conflict between France and England at the 1919 Paris Peace Conference. French premier Georges Clemenceau expected to receive British support for French claims to Lebanon, Cilicia, and Syria. He based this belief on a December 2, 1918, meeting in London with British prime minister David Lloyd George where, in a verbal understanding without witnesses, Clemenceau agreed to modify the Sykes-Picot Agreement. Recognizing the British role in victory in the Middle East, Clemenceau agreed that the oil-producing area of Mosul, assigned to France in the Sykes-Picot Agreement, would be transferred to the British sphere. Palestine, which had been slated for some form of international status, would also be assigned to the British. In return, Clemenceau believed that Lloyd George had promised British support for French claims to Syria and Cilicia.

At the Paris Peace Conference, however, Lloyd George jettisoned the Sykes-Picot Agreement. Appealing to U.S. president Woodrow Wilson's principles of national self-determination, Lloyd George argued that the Arab Revolt entitled the peoples of Lebanon and Syria to self-rule. Lloyd George wanted Hussein's son Emir Faisal, who was under British influence, to rule Lebanon and Syria. But Lloyd George also insisted that Britain retain control of Iraq and Palestine. Clemenceau protested. The standoff was resolved on April 24, 1920, at the San Remo Conference, whereby the British and French governments reached agreement on mandates in the Middle East. Britain would receive Palestine and Iraq, while France secured Lebanon and Syria. Self-determination was thus rejected.

Spencer C. Tucker

**See also**
Faisal I, King of Iraq; Hussein ibn Ali ibn Mohammed

**References**
Andrew, Christopher, and A. F. Kanya-Forstner. *The Climax of French Imperial Expansion, 1914–1924*. Stanford, CA: Stanford University Press, 1981.
Kent, Marian, ed. *The Great Powers and the End of the Ottoman Empire*. London: Routledge, 1996.
Lenczowski, George. *The Middle East in World Affairs*. 4th ed. Ithaca, NY: Cornell University Press, 1980.
Nevakivi, Jukka. *Britain, France and the Arab Middle East, 1914–1920*. London: Athlone, 1969.
Tanenbaum, Jan Karl. *France and the Arab Middle East, 1914–1920*. Philadelphia: American Philosophical Society, 1978.
Tauber, Eliezer. *The Arab Movements in World War I*. London: Frank Cass, 1993.

# Syria

The Syrian Arab Republic borders on Jordan and Israel to the south, Lebanon and the Mediterranean Sea to the west, Turkey to the north, and Iraq to the east. Occupying 71,479 square miles, Syria is thus slightly larger than the U.S. state of North Dakota. Syria's 2018 population was some 18.285 million. Its capital of Damascus is one of the world's oldest cities. Syrian Arabs and some 600,000 Palestinian Arabs constitute some 74 percent of the population. Kurds, most of whom live in northeastern Syria, are about 10 percent of the population, or some 1.6 million people. Smaller Syrian ethnic groups include Turkmen, Circassians, Greeks, and Armenians (most of whom arrived there during World War I). Syria was once home to a large number of Jews, but most immigrated either to Europe or Latin America and then to the new State of Israel. Today only a few Jews remain. Sunni Muslims number about 74 percent of the population, while some 13 percent are Shias (Alawites, Twelvers, and Ismailis). Christians make up 10 percent, with the majority being orthodox. Some 3 percent are Druzes. Despite their minority status, Alawites dominate the Syrian power structure. President Bashar al-Assad is an Alawite, as are other leading figures in the government and military.

Syria is home to one of the world's oldest civilizations, preceded perhaps only by those of Mesopotamia. The Kingdom of Ebla was founded in northern Syria around 3500 BCE. A succession of empires and kingdoms followed: Akkadian, Old Babylonian, Old Assyrian, Yamhad, Hittite, and Egyptian. From the 12th century BCE, Canaanites known as Phoenicians dominated the eastern Mediterranean coast. They established colonies through the Mediterranean, including Carthage. Syria was then part of the Neo-Assyrian Empire, followed by the Neo-Babylonian Empire. The Achaemenid Persian Empire held sway until conquered by King Alexander III (the Great) of Macedon. After his death, it became part of the Seleucid Empire. The Greeks introduced the name "Syria" for the region, basing it on "Assyria."

Syria briefly came under Armenian control but was conquered by the Roman Empire in 64 BCE. The division of the Roman Empire in 295 CE saw Syria become part of the Eastern Roman (Byzantine) Empire. The Arabs conquered Syria by 640, and the Umayyad dynasty made Damascus its capital (the Abbasid dynasty moved the capital to Baghdad in 750). Arabic became the dominant language.

Syria passed under Muslim Egyptian control in 887. During the crusades of 1096–1291 a number of Christian city-states were established on the eastern Mediterranean, the most important of these being Antioch. After rule by the Seljuk Turks, Syria was conquered in the late 12th century by the Kurdish warlord Saladin, founder of the Ayyubid dynasty in Egypt. The Mongols invaded in 1260 but were defeated by Mamluks from Egypt. In 1400 Muslim conqueror Timur (Tamerlane) invaded, sacked Aleppo, and took Damascus.

In 1516 Ottoman Empire forces invaded the Mamluk Sultanate of Egypt, conquered Syria, and incorporated it into their empire. Ottoman rule lasted until the end of World War I. The Ottoman leaders had chosen to join the war on the side of the Central Powers, and defeat brought an end to the empire, which shrank to Anatolia and a small bit of Europe. During the war the Armenians had rebelled, seeking independence. This forced the Ottoman government to divert troops there from major campaigns elsewhere, and in an effort to stabilize the situation, the government forcibly relocated the Armenians to Deir ex-Zor in the Syrian Desert. Inadequate water, food, clothing, and medical supplies brought the deaths of as many as 1.2 million Armenians in

# SYRIA

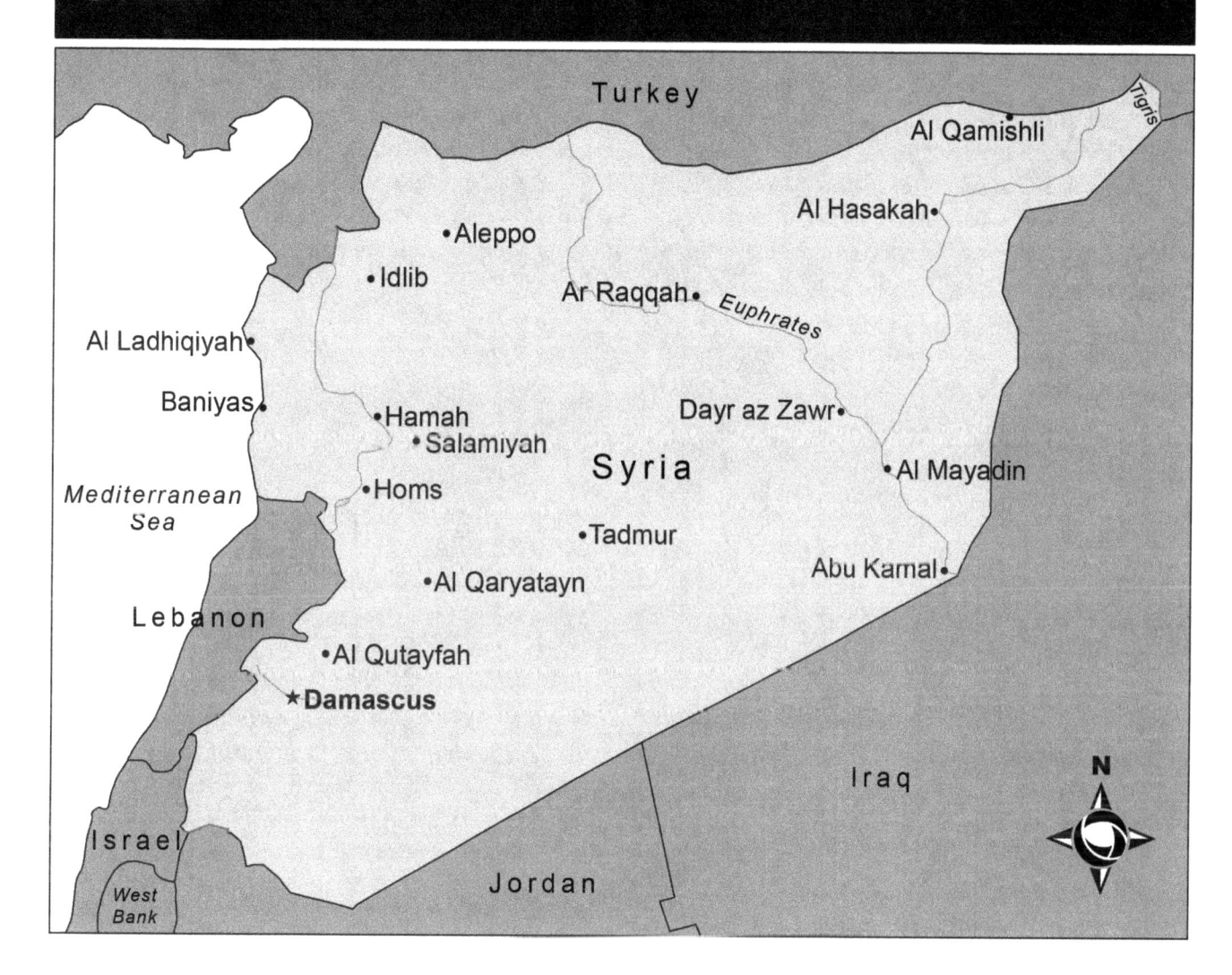

the forced march, which has been called the Armenian Massacre and, controversially, the Armenian Genocide.

During the war, in 1916 French diplomat François Georges-Picot and Briton Mark Sykes reached a secret agreement on behalf of their governments to divide much of the Ottoman Empire into spheres of influence. With their borders arbitrarily drawn by Britain and France, four new states were created in Syria and Lebanon (to be controlled by the French) and Iraq and Palestine (to pass under British control).

On March 8, 1920, Faisal bin Hussein of the Hashemites established a short-lived independent Kingdom of Syria as Faisal I. He had led the Arab Revolt against the Ottomans during World War I and been promised establishment of an Arab kingdom by the British. His reign lasted only until July 24, when the French Army of the Levant defeated his forces in the Battle of Maysalun. French troops then occupied Syria. Syria and Lebanon were officially recognized as French mandates by the League of Nations in 1923.

In 1925 a prominent Arab Druze, Sultan al-Atrash, led a revolt that spread to include all of Syria and parts of Lebanon. Al-Atrash's forces won several battles against the French, with the most notable being al-Kafr (July 21, 1925) and al-Mazraa (August 2–3, 1925). Although France dispatched troops from Morocco and Senegal, the revolt simmered on until the spring of 1927. Although captured and sentenced to death, al-Atrash escaped to Transjordan and was eventually pardoned. He returned to Syria in 1937.

In 1934 the French government proposed independence for Syria under an arrangement beneficial to France. Strong opposition to this was organized in Syria by nationalist leader Hashim al-Atassi. In September 1936 in Paris, Syria and France negotiated a new treaty that called for immediate recognition of Syrian independence as a sovereign republic but with full emancipation to occur during a 25-year period. The previously autonomous Druze and Alawite regions were to be incorporated into Syria, but not so with Lebanon, with which the French signed a similar treaty in November. The treaty with Syria pledged curtailment of French intervention in Syrian domestic affairs as well as a reduction in the number of French troops and military bases. For its part, Syria pledged to support France in times of war, including the use of its airspace, and allowed France to retain two military bases. There were also political, economic, and cultural provisions. Atassi was elected president of Syria in November.

The treaty was stillborn, because faced with the threat to French security posed by Germany under Adolf Hitler, the French legislature refused to ratify it. In 1940 during World War II Germany defeated France, and Syria passed under the control of the Vichy French government.

A pro-Axis coup against the British in Iraq in April 1941 led to fighting between British forces and the Iraqi military and caused Berlin to demand from the Vichy government the right to ship arms and supplies through Damascus to Iraq. The Vichy government acquiesced, and French high commissioner to Syria Henri Dentz granted German and Italian aircraft landing rights in Syria for Axis aircraft on their way to Iraq.

The British government responded with an invasion of Syria and Lebanon in June 1941 by British, Australian, and Free French forces as well as the Transjordan Arab Legion. By mid-July the Allies fully controlled both Syria and Lebanon. Syria was then turned over to the Free French authorities. Although they recognized Syrian independence, the French continued to occupy the country and declared martial law, imposed strict press censorship, and arrested political subversives.

In July 1943 under pressure from its allies, the Free French government-in-exile announced new Syrian elections. A nationalist government came to power that August, electing Syrian nationalist Shukri al-Quwatli as president. France granted Syria independence on January 1, 1944, but the country remained under Allied occupation for the rest of the war. On February 26, 1945, Syria declared war on the Axis powers and became a member of the United Nations (UN) the next month.

In early May 1945 anti-French demonstrations erupted throughout Syria, whereupon French forces bombarded Damascus, killing some 400 people before the British intervened. A UN resolution in February 1946 called on France to evacuate the country, and by mid-April all French and British forces had departed Syrian soil. Evacuation Day, April 17, is celebrated as a Syrian national holiday.

Syria was a cofounder of the Arab League on March 22, 1945. The league advocated Pan-Arab nationalism but without the consolidation of states and the resultant problems that would have ensued. The Arab League was also aimed at blocking the creation of a Jewish state in Palestine, which the Syrian government strongly opposed.

Syria played a relatively small role in the failed Israeli War of Independence (1948–1949) that arose from the creation of the State of Israel in May 1948. At the beginning of the fighting Syria had only some 4,500 troops to commit, almost all of whom were dispatched to the Syrian-Palestinian border. These were repelled with heavy casualties early in the fighting. Quwatli was widely blamed for the setback and reacted by firing his defense minister and chief of staff. As time progressed, Syrian troops enjoyed some modest success but then remained rather quiescent for the rest of the war.

The Israeli victory and disagreements regarding a possible Syrian union with Iraq torpedoed Quwatli's government. He was overthrown in a bloodless military coup on March 29, 1949, by former chief of staff Husni al-Za'im. After a brief imprisonment, Quwatli was allowed to go into exile in Egypt. This first Syrian military coup shattered that country's democratic rule and set off military revolts. Two more coups quickly followed.

On August 14, 1949, Za'im was himself overthrown in a coup headed by Colonel Sami al-Hinnawi that included Lieutenant Colonel Adib al-Shishakli. After the coup, Hinnawi ordered Za'im and Prime Minister Muhsin al-Barazi executed. Hinnawi was the titular head of the military junta ruling Syria, but Shishakli was its strongman and on December 19, 1949, mounted the third coup of that year. Shishakli governed with a heavy hand until 1954.

Growing discontent eventually led to another coup on February 24, 1954, in which Shishakli was overthrown. The plotters included members of the Syrian Communist Party, Druze officers, and members of the Baath Party. Shishakli resigned rather than risk civil war and then fled abroad.

The period 1954–1958 in Syria was marked by party politics and weak national governments. Late in 1954 elections were held to install a civilian government. In the end, a coalition of the People's Party, the National Party, and the Baath Party emerged, with National Party chief Sabri al-Asali as its head. The coalition was a shaky one. In succeeding years the Baathists, who combined Arab nationalism with socialist economic policies, became the most powerful political force in Syria.

In October 1955 Syria signed a defense pact with Gamal Abdel Nasser's Egypt, and Syria followed Egypt's lead in cultivating relations with the Soviet bloc, including arms purchases. On February 1, 1958, Syria and Egypt joined to form the United Arab Republic (UAR) as a step toward realizing Nasser's dream of one large Pan-Arab state. Many Syrians had assumed that this would be a federation of equals, but Egypt completely dominated, imposing Nasser's centralized socialistic political and economical system on a weaker Syria. A strong backlash from Syrian business interests and the military resulted in yet another coup on September 28, 1961, and the end of the UAR.

The new coup saw the establishment of the Syrian Arab Republic. Elections on December 1, 1961, for a new National Assembly resulted in the selection of Nazzim al-Qudsi as president. Another army coup occurred on March 28, 1962; although Qudsi was retained as president, there were other personnel changes. On September 13, 1962, Khalid al-Azm became prime minister. He quickly dissolved the parliament and announced that he would govern by decree until new elections in one year.

Yet another military coup on March 8, 1963, brought a new government, largely controlled by the Baath Party. The government nationalized most industrial and large commercial concerns and engaged in land reforms, redistributing land to the peasants. One significant development was the decline in political influence of the Syrian Sunni Muslim majority and dominance of the Alawite minority.

A schism in the Baath Party resulted in more instability, and on February 26, 1966, the radical wing of the party staged yet another coup and removed the military government of Salah al-Din al-Bitar. There was some fighting, and the coup claimed perhaps 400 lives. The victorious faction was principally Alawite Muslim. The two key figures in the coup were Salah Jadid and Hafez al-Assad. The new regime tightened Syria's ties with both the Soviets and Egyptians.

Syria fought Israel again in the June 1967 Six-Day War, with disastrous consequences. This time, Syria's defeat included the loss of the Golan Heights to the Israelis. The outcome of the war eviscerated the ruling government, and when Syrian forces had to pull back after attempting to aid the Palestinians in Jordan during Black September (1970), the scene was set for yet another change of government. On November 13, 1970, General Assad, now Syrian minister of defense, seized power in a bloodless coup. Assad referred to this as the "Corrective Resolution," which essentially ousted from power civilian Baathists in favor of the military Baathists. An ardent Baath nationalist himself, Assad sought to strengthen ties to other Arab states, de-emphasize Syrian reliance on the Soviet Union, and defeat Israel.

In early 1971 Assad was elected president and immediately began to consolidate his power. He would rule the country until his death in 2000. He modernized and greatly enlarged the Syrian Army (it went from about 50,000 men in 1968 to 500,000 men in 1986). To fortify his own power, he saw to it to that only trusted figures were in command positions, and he also greatly increased the security apparatus, composed primarily of Alawites. He engaged in modest economic reforms, with the state playing a central role in economic planning and implementation. Assad's tactics could be brutal, and there was little room for dissent or democracy.

Syria joined with Egypt in the 1973 October Yom Kippur (Ramadan) War with Israel. At the beginning of the fighting, Syria launched a massive ground attack that included 1,500 tanks (900 in the initial attack and 600 in reserve) and 144 batteries of artillery in an attempt to retake the Golan Heights. After some initial success and although Syrian forces this time fought quite well, the Israelis rallied and drove the attackers back beyond their original positions. Syria did regain control over a small portion of the Golan Heights as a result of negotiations after the war.

In the late 1970s and 1980s, Sunni Muslim fundamentalists began challenging the Baath Party's secular outlook. From 1976 to 1982, urban areas all across Syria became hotbeds of political unrest. Assad brutally crushed a February 1982 uprising by the Muslim Brotherhood in Hama. Large parts of the old city were destroyed. Estimates of the dead, including 1,000 soldiers, range from 10,000 to 40,000, with 20,000 being a likely figure.

Assad also sent his army into Lebanon in June 1976, ostensibly as a peacekeeping force during the civil war there that had broken out the year before. The troops stayed on, however, with Assad siding with the Muslims who were fighting Christian militias. By the mid-1980s, Syrian forces had become the preponderant political and military force in Lebanon. Although the Lebanese Civil War was declared to have ended in 1990, Syrian troops were not withdrawn from Lebanon until April 2005. As a result of the long Syrian presence in Lebanon, nearly 1 million Syrians moved into Lebanon to seek work. In 1994 the Lebanese government granted citizenship to 250,000 Syrians, a move that for obvious reasons was controversial among the Lebanese people.

On June 6, 1982, substantial Israeli forces began an invasion of southern Lebanon to attack Palestine Liberation Organization (PLO) forces that had been striking northern Israeli from Lebanon. There was also heavy fighting between the Israelis and Syrian forces in and over the Bekaa Valley in which Israel downed a substantial number of Syrian aircraft before a cease-fire took hold between Israel and Syria on June 11.

At the same time, the 1980s saw the Assad regime taking harder-line Arab positions and moving closer to the Soviets, accompanied by massive arms purchases. Assad's get-tough approach in regional politics included the funding and encouragement of terrorism both in the Middle East and internationally. He openly supported the radical Kurdish Workers' Party in its insurgency against the Turkish government. When some 10,000 Turkish troops massed on the Syrian border, however, on October 21, 1998, Assad agreed to halt all Syrian aid to the rebels.

Assad, always a pragmatist, sought to ameliorate relations with the West as the Soviet Union imploded in 1990. When Iraq invaded Kuwait in August 1990, Assad was the first Arab leader to denounce the attack. Syria provided 20,000 troops to the international coalition that defeated Iraqi forces in the 1991 Persian Gulf War. Assad's frontline position in the war reflected both his desire to strengthen relations with the West and his strong dislike of Iraqi dictator Saddam Hussein. Although Hussein was a Baathist at least in name, Assad saw himself as the predominant leader in the region.

In 1991 Assad's government entered into peace negotiations with Israel in an effort to regain the Golan Heights, although the process broke down with no firm agreement in January 2000. After 30 years in power, Assad died unexpectedly on June 10, 2000. His oldest son, Basil al-Assad, was the presumed heir apparent but had died in an automobile accident in 1994, and the mantle passed to his younger brother, Bashar al-Assad, who had studied medicine and then trained in ophthalmology, including at the Western Eye Hospital in London. After his brother's death, Bashar al-Assad enrolled in the military academy at Homs and became a colonel in the Syrian Army in 1999.

In 2000, Assad was elected secretary-general of the Baath Party and stood as a presidential candidate. The People's Assembly amended the Syrian Constitution to lower the minimum presidential age to 35, and Assad was elected president for a 7-year term. A general referendum soon ratified the decision.

A reform movement emerged during the first year of Assad's rule, dubbed the Damascus Spring. Some Syrians hoped that their young president—who had announced governmental reforms, an end to corruption, and economic liberalization—would open Syria to a greater degree. Indeed, reformers hoped to end the State of Emergency Law, which allowed for the abuse of legal and human rights. Assad released some political prisoners from the notorious Mezze Prison, and certain intellectual forums were permitted. However, by mid-2001 Assad reined in the reformists, some of whom were imprisoned and accused of being Western agents.

Under Assad, Syria opened somewhat in terms of allowing more media coverage, although censorship remained a contentious issue. Cellular phones became prevalent, and Syria finally allowed access to the Internet, whereas under Hafez al-Assad even facsimile machines were prohibited. Economic reform and modernization received top priority. Job creation, the lessening of Syria's dependence on oil revenue, the encouragement of private capital investments, and the mitigation of poverty were goals in the economic sphere. The government created foreign investment zones, and private universities were legally permitted, along with private banks. Employment centers were established after 2000, and Bashar al-Assad announced his support for an association with the European Union. However, these changes were too few and too gradual to instill much confidence in Syrian modernization. Assad's pledges of democratic reform failed to materialize.

After the September 11, 2001, terrorist attacks against the United States, Syria pledged its cooperation in the so-called war on terror. But with the beginning of the U.S.-led Iraq War in 2003, which Assad refused to support, U.S.-Syrian relations sharply deteriorated. Syria's continued support of militant Palestinian groups and terrorist organizations such as Hezbollah in Lebanon seriously strained relations with the United States and much of the West. To make matters worse, Syria's long and porous border with Iraq to the east served as a conduit for Syrian weaponry and terrorist fighters involved in the ensuing insurgency in Iraq. U.S. president George W. Bush's administration repeatedly warned Damascus not to aid the Iraqi insurgents, but the warnings were little heeded.

Although Syrian troops were finally out of Lebanon by 2005, evidence suggests that the Syrians continued to involve themselves in the internal politics of that nation. Indeed, most observers agree that Syrian operatives were responsible for the assassination of former Lebanese prime minister Rafik Hariri in February 2005. By late 2006 there were fears that Syria, working in tandem with Iran, was attempting to undermine the shaky government in Lebanon in a bid to exert de facto control over that country.

The Arab Spring, a reform movement that began with a revolution in Tunisia in December 2010 and impacted much of the Arab world, brought on the Syrian Civil War. On March 15, 2011, as in other Arab countries, demonstrators took to the streets in Damascus to demand democratic reforms, action against widespread corruption, and the release of political prisoners. Syrian security forces opened fire on the demonstrators, but the protests quickly spread. Daraa became a major opposition center, and Assad unleashed his military there. In the two weeks it took the government forces to secure the city, some 244 civilians died, along with 81 soldiers. Another 1,000 people were arrested. Despite this brutal show of force, demonstrations against the government spread and became full-scale civil war. By the end of 2012, the fighting had claimed an estimated 60,000 lives and showed no sign of abating.

In these circumstances Assad announced a series of modest reform measures, such as formally ending the five decades of emergency law in Syria and dissolving the security courts that had angered locals with unfair and corrupt adjudication. He also issued a decree legalizing political parties and indicated that he was even open to changing the constitution. However, such reforms were rendered hollow by the harsh reality of the actions of the government security forces.

The revolt was fueled by the long-standing resentments felt by the majority Sunnis as well as by minority Christians, Druzes, and others against rule by the minority Alawites. Much of the fighting was along sectarian lines, with the Sunni areas experiencing the brunt of the government attacks. Thus, the Syrian people were not only fighting for fundamental governmental reform but were also revisiting historic rivalries.

Establishing a united political and military front against the Assad regime proved immensely difficult. The UN, the Arab League, and the international community held that intervening in the conflict without an established opposition political and military leadership in place would bring failure. By August 2011 the Free Syrian Army had been established. A conglomeration of the country's opposition forces, it included defected members of Assad's military. The next month, the Syrian National Council and National Coordinating bodies were set up in Turkey. Despite these bodies, opposition unity remained tenuous at best.

The Assad regime had an overwhelming advantage in heavy weaponry in the form of aircraft, tanks, and artillery and enjoyed strong support and outright military assistance from Shiite Iran and from Russia, which had long had close ties with Syria and was determined to maintain its naval base in the Syrian city of Tartus on the Mediterranean. The Syrian government also had active support from Hezbollah in Lebanon.

The Syrian opposition looked to neighboring countries for assistance. Some Salafists and other jihadists joined the insurgency. A number of fighters who had fought the Americans and security forces in Iraq relocated to Syria and pushed an Islamist agenda. The most notorious of these organizations was the Islamic State of Iraq and Syria (ISIS), which soon held brutal sway over a substantial portion of central Syria and northern Iraq. The presence of ISIS and other Islamic extremist groups made putting together a broad-based coalition extremely difficult. The U.S. government was especially loath to become involved and provided only limited small arms and trainers. Jordan, Saudi Arabia, and some other countries also provided aid. Finally, in September 2014 in Operation INHERENT RESOLVE, coalition forces began operations in Syria against ISIS although not the Assad regime itself. Since then the U.S. government has deployed small contingents of ground troops to Syria, and other coalition partners have sent their own small troop deployments. INHERENT RESOLVE, however, has consisted chiefly of air support for anti-ISIS and some antigovernment rebels. In September 2015 Russia intervened in the war, ostensibly to defeat ISIS, although its unspoken primary goal was to shore up Assad's regime. As of 2019 Russian involvement in Syria continued, as did Operation INHERENT RESOLVE.

Fighting seesawed back and forth in the Syrian Civil War (March 25, 2011–). It was difficult to determine with any accuracy the casualty total from the war because Assad would not permit access to the international media, but it certainly was horrendous. Estimates of the number of dead through the early months of 2019 run as high as 560,000, with as many as 2 million more wounded. In addition, as many as 11 million Syrians, or almost half of the country's prewar population, had been internally displaced, while another 5.1 million people were refugees in other nations. Multinational human rights organizations have also accused the Syrian government of massive human rights violations, including torture, the direct targeting of civilians and hospitals (with such indiscriminate antipersonnel weapons as barrel bombs), and the use of chemical weapons. The civil war has also led to a major resettlement crisis in Europe.

In 2019, the civil war continued with no immediate end in sight. Nevertheless, in November 2017 Assad declared victory over ISIS in Syria, and by August 2018 he had significantly strengthened his position over antigovernment insurgents. Indeed, by then it had become increasingly likely that he would remain in power for some time to come, probably with continued Russian support. Assad has vowed that he will retake "every inch" of Syria from those he refers to as "terrorists."

Larissa Mihalisko, Paul G. Pierpaoli Jr.,<br>and Spencer C. Tucker

**See also**

Achaemenid Empire; al-Atrash, Sultan; Alawites; Alexander III the Great; Armenians and the Armenian Genocide; Assad, Bashar al-; Assad, Hafez al-; Arab Spring; Ayyubid Dynasty; Baath Party; Babylonian Empire, Neo-; Black September; Byzantine Empire; Crusades in the Holy Land, Christian; Druzes; Faisal I, King of Iraq; Golan Heights; Hezbollah; Inherent Resolve, Operation; Israeli War of Independence; Kurds; Lebanon; Lebanon Civil War; Lebanon-Israeli War; Mandates, League of Nations; Maysalun, Battle of; Nasser, Gamal Abdel; Palestine Liberation Organization; Persian Gulf War, Overview; Quwatli, Shukri al-; Saladin; Seleucid Empire; Shia Islam; Shishakli, Adib al-; Six-Day War; Sunni Islam; Sykes-Picot Agreement; Syria and Lebanon Campaign; Syrian Civil War; Syrian-Egyptian Wars; Syrian-Roman War; Tamerlane; Umayyad Caliphate; United Arab Republic; Yom Kippur War

**References**

Ajami, Fouad. *The Syrian Rebellion*. Stanford, CA: Hoover Institution, Stanford University, 2012.

Darraj, Susan Muaddi. *Bashar al-Assad*. New York: Chelsea House, 2005.

George, Alan. *Syria: Neither Bread nor Freedom*. London: Zed Books, 2003.

Glass, Charles. *Syria Burning: A Short History of a Catastrophe*. New York: Verso, 2016.

Herzog, Chaim. *The Arab-Israeli Wars: War and Peace in the Middle East from the War of Independence to Lebanon*. Westminster, MD: Random House, 1984.

Lesch, David W. *The New Lion of Damascus: Bashar Al-Assad and Modern Syria*. New Haven, CT: Yale University Press, 2005.

Lesch, David W. *Syria: The Fall of the House of Assad*. New Haven, CT: Yale University Press, 2012.

Leverett, Flynt. *Inheriting Syria: Bashar's Trial by Fire*. Washington, DC: Brookings Institution Press, 2005.

Lustick, Ian. *From War to War: Israel vs. the Arabs, 1948–1967*. New York: Garland, 1994.

Maoz, Moshe, and Avner Yaniv, eds. *Syria under Assad: Domestic Constraints and Regional Risks*. London: Croom Helm, 1987.

McHugo, John. *Syria: A Recent History*. London: Saqi, 2015.

Pipes, Daniel. *Greater Syria: The History of an Ambition*. New York: Oxford University Press, 1990.

Pollack, Kenneth M. *Arabs at War: Military Effectiveness, 1948–1991*. Lincoln: University of Nebraska Press, 2002.

Rabil, Robert G. *Embattled Neighbors: Syria, Israel, and Lebanon*. Boulder, CO: Lynne Rienner, 2003.

Roberts, David. *The Ba'th and the Creation of Modern Syria*. New York: St. Martin's, 1987.

Rubin, Barry, and Thomas A. Keaney, eds. *Armed Forces in the Middle East: Politics and Strategy*. Portland, OR: Frank Cass, 2002.

Seale, Patrick. *Assad of Syria: The Struggle for the Middle East*. Berkeley: University of California Press, 1988.

Solomon, Brian. *Chemical and Biological Warfare*. New York: H. W. Wilson, 1999.

Starr, Stephen. *Revolt in Syria: Eye-witness to the Uprising*. New York: Columbia University Press, 2012.

Torr, James D. *Weapons of Mass Destruction: Opposing Viewpoints*. San Diego: Greenhaven, 2005.

## Syria and Lebanon Campaign (June 8–July 14, 1941)

Middle Eastern campaign during World War II. The growing German commitment in the Balkans and the Mediterranean encouraged those in Iraq who favored the Axis side to stage a coup on April 2, 1941. The coup brought to power Rashid Ali al-Gaylani, who was closely linked with the violently anti-British mufti of Jerusalem, Haj Amin al-Husseini. The Arab nationalists hoped that a German victory would end British control of Iraq. Encouraged by the Germans, who promised air support and promised to persuade the Vichy French in Syria to provide material assistance, Rashid Ali refused the British the right to transit troops through Iraq and ordered Iraqi government forces to surround the British air base at Habbaniya, 25 miles west of Baghdad. With the British fully committed in the Western Desert, Greece, and East Africa, it seemed an opportune time for the Iraqi nationalists to move.

British commander in the Middle East General Sir Archibald Wavell, rightly apprehensive about losing British communications with India and the supplies of Iraqi oil, ordered a minor offensive. The besieged garrison at Habbaniya attacked on May 2. A 5,800-member-strong column, Habforce, was hastily organized from the 1st Cavalry Division in Palestine. Habforce made a 500-mile transdesert dash to reach Habbaniya on May 19, by which time the 10th Indian Division had landed in Basra.

Although Axis planes flew to Syria in support and were involved in the fighting, the Iraqis moved a month too early, before the Germans were able to offer effective assistance. The Germans were themselves too slow in reacting, and the British captured Baghdad on May 31.

Alarmed by evidence provided by code breaking that Vichy high commissioner in Syria General Henri Ferdnand Dentz, who buttressed his pro-Vichy patriotism with a strong personal Anglophobia, had supplied weapons to the Iraqis and freely cooperated with the Germans, the British worried that Germany—supported by vehemently anti-British French admiral Jean Darlan, who now exerted considerable influence in Vichy France—would extend its victories beyond Crete and through Syria into the Middle East.

This fear combined with the threat posed to the British base in Egypt by the French Army of the Levant, a force of 45,000 hard-core professional soldiers that included four battalions of Foreign Legionnaires, convinced the British to launch Operation EXPORTER, the invasion of Syria and Lebanon. On June 8, a hastily concocted force consisting of the 21st and 25th Australian Brigades, the 5th Indian Brigade, and the weak 1st and 2nd Free French Brigades, all commanded by General Maitland "Jumbo" Wilson, invaded in three drives—through Daraa to Damascus, through Merjayun to Rayak, and along the coast from Haifa to Beirut.

The British had hoped for a peaceful occupation by guaranteeing the independence of Syria and Lebanon, but Dentz was aware of negotiations between Vichy France and Germany that would culminate in the Paris Protocols and was determined to demonstrate solidarity with Germany. By the end of the first phase of the Allied invasion on June 13, it was evident that the Vichy French showed no sympathy with Free French ambitions, and all advances were stalled by fierce fighting at Kissoué, Mezze, the Litani River, and especially Merjayun.

Damascus finally fell on July 22, and with the conclusion of Operation BATTLEAXE in the Western Desert, the British were able to bring up two fighter and three bomber squadrons. Meanwhile, Habforce and Major General William Slim's 10th Indian Division invaded Syria from Iraq against Palmyra and Aleppo on June 21 to isolate Dentz's force.

The campaign for Syria and Lebanon also involved naval operations. Vice Admiral E. L. S. King commanded a British force of three cruisers, eight destroyers, and a landing ship with a small commando unit. Opposing them was a Vichy French force of two large destroyers, a sloop, and three submarines. The naval portion of the campaign consisted of small skirmishes as the British carried out both coastal landings and shore bombardments. Vichy French forces damaged several of the British warships through both air and naval attack, necessitating the dispatch of other ships. The French lost to air attack on June 21 just 50 miles from Syria one of two large destroyers dispatched from Toulon. The other French destroyer made it safely to Beirut on June 21 but was damaged there in bombing the next day. The Vichy French government considered dispatching the battle cruiser *Strasbourg* from Toulon but, with the campaign too far gone, decided against it.

After five weeks of bitter fighting, Dentz capitulated on July 11, and an armistice known as the Acre Convention was signed on July 14. Although its terms were generous, the immediate results of the armistice did little to encourage belief in any French desire to see the defeat of Nazi Germany. Only 5,668 troops, 1,006 of whom were native Frenchmen, opted to join Free French Forces rather than be repatriated to France.

This tragic, regrettable episode, which cost the lives of 3,500 men, was a short but sour campaign imbued with resentment, particularly between the Vichy and Free French Forces who wreaked sacrilegious vengeance on each other. For the British, however, the campaign consolidated their flank and guarded against any German attack through Turkey.

A few weeks later Britain, in unison with the Soviet Union, occupied Iran to guarantee the transfer of Lend-Lease supplies through Iran to Russia. In the process, Britain secured its position in the Middle East. Thus, in the midsummer of 1941 Germany consolidated its position in the Balkans, while Britain dominated the entire Middle East. The British commander was liberated from all other preoccupations but that of defeating Axis forces in Libya, and for the first time he could concentrate all his force on a single task.

PAUL H. COLLIER

**See also**
Husseini, Haj Amin al-; Iran; Iraq; Lebanon; Syria

**References**
Mockler, Anthony. *Our Enemies the French*. London: Cooper, 1976.
Pitt, Barrie. *The Crucible of War*, Vol. 1, *Wavell's Command*. London: Cassell, 2001.
Warner, Geoffrey. *Iraq and Syria, 1941*. London: Davis-Poynter, 1974.
Zweig, Ronald W. *Britain and Palestine during the Second World War*. Suffolk, UK: Boydell, 1986.

# Syrian Civil War (March 25, 2011–)

The Syrian Civil War (also known as the Syrian Insurgency and the Syrian Uprising) began on March 15, 2011, and is ongoing. Prompted by the Arab Spring protest movement throughout the Middle East and North Africa, it has grown into a prolonged and costly conflict, the deadliest of the 20th century. The war has devastated large sections of the country, displaced much of the population, and produced a humanitarian crisis with an attendant refugee crisis that has threatened to overwhelm social services in Southern Europe and impacted politics in much of the West.

The conflict in Syria began as a protest movement demanding democratic reforms and action against corruption and escalated into an attempt to overthrow the dictatorial regime of the Assad family. President Hafez al-Assad ruled the country with an iron fist from 1970 to 2000. His son and successor, Bashar al-Assad, has held the presidency ever since. Bashar al-Assad regarded the protests as a major threat to his regime, and his reaction was to clamp down hard.

On March 18, the Syrian Army was called in to suppress the protesters for fear that they might get out of hand and bring down the regime, as had occurred with President Hosni Mubarak in Egypt. The Syrian military employed harsh tactics. In the ensuing Siege of a protest center of Daraa (April 25–May 5, 2011), some 6,000 army troops supported by tanks and helicopters moved against the city. By the time it had been secured, as many as 244 civilians had been killed along with 81 soldiers. Some 1,000 people were arrested. Nonetheless, the demonstrations increased, becoming full-scale civil war.

The military response in cities such as Daraa and Deir al-Zor, far from cowing the demonstrators, brought larger protests from civilians and also from some defected members of the Syrian military, prompting even harsher attacks by the Assad regime. In July 2012, fighting began in Syria's largest city of Aleppo, with a population of 2.5 million. By the end of 2012, the widespread civil strife in Syria had already claimed an estimated 60,000 lives and showed no signs of abating.

In the wake of the uprisings, Assad attempted to address some concerns raised by protesters, such as formally ending five decades of emergency law in the country and dissolving the security courts that had angered locals with unfair and corrupt adjudications. He also issued a decree legalizing political parties and indicated that he was even open to changing the constitution. However, such measures were offset by the concurrent actions of the government security forces against the protesters, especially in Daraa and in Damascus, where in one day 100 people were killed, a 13-year old boy was tortured and killed, and 15 young students were arrested for writing antigovernment slogans on a wall. By late June, many Syrian cities witnessed massive antiregime demonstrations, which then encountered Assad's security forces.

Sunni Muslims constitute some 74 percent of the population of Syria, but the country had been ruled for half a century by the Alawite (Shia) sect, which numbers only about 13 percent and to which the Assad family belongs. The demonstrations brought to the fore long-standing resentments regarding this held by the Sunnis as well as by minority Christians, Druzes, and others. Much of the fighting was along sectarian lines, with the Sunni areas experiencing the brunt of the government attacks. Thus, the Syrian people were not only fighting for fundamental governmental reform but were also revisiting historic rivalries. It was no surprise that cities such as Hama, Daraa, and Deir al-Zor, where there had been past sectarian violence, should see heavy fighting.

Establishing a united political and military front against Assad's forces proved challenging for the opposition and remains so. The United Nations, the Arab League, and the international community long argued that intervening in the conflict without an established political and military opposition leadership in place would be a disaster. The Free Syrian Army (FSA), a conglomeration of the country's opposition forces and made up of defected members of Assad's military, had been formed by August 2011. The next month, the Syrian National Council and National Coordinating bodies were established in Turkey. Despite these, opposition unity remained tenuous at best.

The Assad regime enjoyed the support of Iran. Shiite Iran, already locked in an intense rivalry with Sunni Saudi Arabia, sought to bolster its coreligionist Alawites against the Syrian Sunni majority, with Iranian weaponry finding its way to Syria through Iraqi air space. The regime also received diplomatic support and some arms from the Russian Federation, a major trading partner that maintains an important naval base in the Syrian city of Tartus on the Mediterranean. Then, in September 2015 when it appeared that the Assad regime might be losing the civil war, the Russians sent units of their own air force into action. This direct Russian military intervention was probably the key factor in tipping the balance in Assad's favor and certainly impacted the protracted Battle of Aleppo, which Assad's forces won in December 2016. Islamist Shiite Hezbollah militias from Lebanon also provided important assistance to the government side.

The Syrian opposition looked primarily to neighboring Sunni countries for assistance. Some Salafists and other jihadists joined the uprising, although fighting on their own. A number of individuals who had fought the Americans and security forces in Iraq transitioned to Syria to pursue an Islamist agenda. Concerns abounded that the uprising in Syria would disrupt the delicate Sunni-Shia balance in neighboring countries. Lebanon was particularly vulnerable, and fighting triggered by the Syrian crisis occurred

Members of the Free Syrian Army fire into the air in celebration of their return to Qusayr after an attack on Syrian regime forces in the village of Nizareer, near the Lebanese border in Homs province, May 12, 2012. (AFP/Getty Images)

along sectarian lines in Tripoli and other cities. There was also some violence in Israel, Iraq, Turkey, and Jordan. Also, the Syrian Kurds sought to form their own polity, while Syrian Christians, fearing repression under a new Syrian regime, sought support from their coreligionists in Lebanon and Iraq. Turkey has played a critical role in the conflict by providing sanctuary to tens of thousands of Syrian refugees and also hosted the opposition leadership until September 2012, when the latter moved back into Syria. Turkish president Recep Tayyip Erdoğan became an outspoken opponent of Assad and urged, without success, the imposition of a no-fly zone over part of Syria.

Attempts by the United Nations, the Arab League, and the Gulf Cooperation Council to bring an end to the violence proved futile. So too was Assad's prompting of parliamentary elections on May 7, 2012, which saw opposition forces reject the elections altogether.

Assad's forces routinely shelled civilian neighborhoods and cities and increasingly relied on artillery and airpower in an effort to defeat the opposition forces (which Assad referred to as terrorists). The cities of Homs and Bab Amr each endured more than a month of shelling, driving civilians out of the cities and forcing a temporary rebel withdrawal in March 2012. Opposition forces, albeit somewhat disorganized, mounted regular attacks against government targets such as the Damascus intelligence headquarters and military buildings. Suicide attacks increased during 2012, as did the use of roadside bombs.

During 2012, attacks by security forces against civilians and opposition forces increased dramatically. In the town of Daraya, an August battle between rebels and security forces brought the massacre of more than 300 people. Increasing government firepower against the Syrian civilian population led to major defections, including in July 2012 Brigadier General Manaf Tlas, a longtime close friend of Assad, as well as several Syrian ambassadors and legislators.

In July 2012, Syrian rebels began to retake some of the towns they had been driven from earlier, capturing a military base near Aleppo. Their downing of military aircraft indicated improved weaponry and tactics. By November 2012, the military balance appeared to be tipping toward the opposition as its fighters edged closer to Assad's stronghold of Damascus. Concerns in December 2012 that Assad would employ chemical weapons in a last-ditch effort against the opposition brought warnings by the United States and West European governments that such a step would have serious consequences. In midmonth Syria for the first time employed Scud missiles against rebel concentrations, while the United States dispatched to Turkey Patriot missile batteries and 400 troops to man them in a largely symbolic gesture designed to help protect the long Turkish border with Syria against possible Syrian missile or aircraft attack.

In July 2013 the war, which had seemed to be going in favor of the rebels, again turned toward the government side when on June 5 Assad's forces captured the key city of Qusair near the Lebanese border. The battle for Qusair saw Hezbollah militia units from Lebanon fighting on the Syrian government side. With Hezbollah strongly supported by Iran, this action angered many Sunni Muslims and raised the prospect of a widened Middle Eastern War along sectarian lines that would spread to at least Lebanon. On June 15, 2013, the Egyptian government broke diplomatic ties with Syria and called for the overthrow of Assad.

Also on June 15, the American government, following similar announcements by France and Britain, concluded that the Syrian government had indeed employed chemical weapons against its own people. This finding led the Barack Obama administration, while backing off its threat of air strikes, to declare that it would provide military support to the Syrian rebels. On June 22, representatives of 11 states, including the United States, met in Doha, Qatar, and pledged increased aid to the rebels. It was not clear what form this aid would take, but clearly the rebels, badly divided among themselves and armed basically with small arms, were outgunned by Syrian government forces, with tanks, artillery, and aircraft. Under the threat of direct Western military action, Syria did agree to give up its chemical weapons stockpile, reportedly one of the world's largest, and reportedly the last of these were shipped out of the country in June 2014 for destruction.

By the summer of 2014 fighters of the self-proclaimed extremist Islamic State of Iraq and Syria (ISIS) had come to control considerable territory in northern Syria and in Iraq, indeed threatening Baghdad. ISIS had also committed widespread atrocities against non-Muslims and executed U.S. and British hostages. On September 15 an international conference took place in Paris to deal with the threat posed by ISIS, with the Obama administration taking the lead in forging an international coalition, known as Operation INHERENT RESOLVE and numbering nearly 40 nations to assist in the fight against ISIS. The irony here is that the coalition was in effect strengthening Assad's hand in the Syrian Civil War.

Meanwhile, in late September 2014, ISIS launched a major offensive with the goal of securing the predominantly Kurdish Syrian city of Kobanî on the Turkish border, in the process displacing a reported 200,000 Kurds. On September 23, the United States launched cruise missiles. Its aircraft and those of allied Arab nations also attacked ISIS targets in Syria. This was the first U.S. military offensive in the war-torn country but was limited to ISIS targets. The air strikes were centered on the city of Raqqa, the declared capital of ISIS's self-proclaimed Islamic State, but some 20 targets were struck, including ISIS command and control and training facilities. Bahrain, Saudi Arabia, the United Arab Emirates, Jordan, and Qatar all assisted in the operation.

Among the targets in the air strikes was the presumed headquarters of the Khorasan group, an affiliate of the Al Qaeda umbrella terrorist organization and now working in league with Al Qaeda's Syrian affiliate, the al-Nusra Front. Coalition aircraft then dropped supplies and commenced bombing operations to assist Kobanî's defenders. Turkish president Erdoğan sent tanks and troops to the border, but he refused to allow Turkish troops to intervene. He did, however, ultimately permit aid and certain Kurdish fighters to cross from Turkey into Syria in defense of the city.

Israel has also been involved to the fighting in Syria to a limited extent. It has responded with artillery fire to cross-border fighting, shot down Syrian aircraft, and conducted several bombing raids in Syria, even close to Damascus, reportedly to prevent sophisticated weaponry supplied by Iran from transiting Syria to Hezbollah in Lebanon.

The civil war created a refugee crisis of immense proportion, with millions of people displaced both inside Syria and abroad. The greatest burden has been borne by the neighboring states of Turkey, Lebanon, Jordan, Iraq, and Egypt, which together had absorbed by December 2014 some 3.8 million refugees. This crisis continued to worsen with no end to the war in sight. The United States was the largest donor of humanitarian aid to alleviate the crisis, at $3 billion. Other wealthy nations such as the People's Republic of China and the Persian Gulf states contributed little.

With the ongoing fighting, the death toll continued to climb. In August 2014 the United Nations set the toll from three years of fighting from March 2013 to April 2014 at more than 191,000 people, while in January 2015 the Syrian Observatory of Human Rights claimed that 76,000 people died in the war in 2014 alone, including more than 3,500 children, with the total for the war at 206,000. This was nearly double the estimated number of deaths for 2013.

The Syrian Kurds used the war to establish a political entity of their own. The largest ethnic group in the world without their own state, Kurds constitute significant minorities in Turkey, Syria, Iraq, and Iran and have long sought an independent nation. The Syrian Kurds sought to emulate the Iraqi Kurds who had taken advantage of the situation on the ground to establish their own autonomous region. In Syria this was known as Rojava. In 2015, the People's Protection Units joined forces with Arab, Assyrian, Armenian, and some Turkmen groups to form the Syrian Democratic Forces (SDF), while most Turkmen groups remained with the FSA.

The de facto autonomous Kurdish region in Syria consists of three cantons (Afrin, Jazira, and Kobani) in northern Syria as well as adjacent areas such as the Shahba region. This largely Kurdish region, known as Syrian Kurdistan or Western Kurdistan, is regarded by Kurdish nationalists as one of the four parts of Greater Kurdistan to include parts of southeastern Turkey (Northern Kurdistan), northern Iraq (Southern Kurdistan), and northwestern Iran (Eastern Kurdistan). Since December 2016 and adoption of a constitutional document, the polity governing Rojava has been known as the Democratic Federation of Northern Syria. Neither the Syrian government nor any international state or organization recognize this as an autonomous area, however. Supporters consider this a model for a federalized Syria as a whole. It appeared extremely doubtful that the Syrian government would permit this should it win the civil war.

In September 2015, Russia directly intervened in the war when its aircraft joined those of the Syrian Air Force in indiscriminate attacks on rebel civilian centers. This included the bombing of clearly marked hospitals and schools. Syrian aircraft also employed so-called barrel bombs and cluster munitions. Certainly the injection of Soviet aircraft into the war was a major factor in the Syrian government victory in the Battle for Aleppo. The biggest victory for Assad in the war to date, that battle lasting four and a half years ended in a government victory in December 2016.

With the Western powers unable to agree on a unified forceful response in Syria, with the opposition sharply divided among secular fighters and Islamists, and with Iran and Russia firmly supporting Assad (indeed, in a warning to the West, Russian president Vladimir Putin announced that Russia would proceed with the sale to the Syrian government of advanced antiaircraft missiles), peace in Syria remained as elusive as ever.

On April 6, 2017, in the first U.S. direct military action against the Syrian government, new U.S. president Donald Trump ordered a missile strike against the Shayrat Airfield from which Syrian aircraft had taken off two days earlier and dropped chlorine gas cylinders on a rebel-held town in Idlit Province. The air strike killed some 70 people, including at least 10 children, and wounded many more. Publication of the graphic images of the results of the Syrian attack led Trump to order the retaliatory strike, saying that the United States would not permit the use of chemical weapons. A total of 59 Tomahawk missiles were fired at the airfield from U.S. warships in the Mediterranean. These were directed against aircraft, hardened aircraft shelters, and support facilities. Reportedly 9 Syrian military personnel were killed and 9–20 aircraft were destroyed.

In another escalation of the conflict, following a dramatic June 7 attack by ISIS terrorists in Tehran that killed 12 people and wounded 46 (6 attackers also were killed), Iran struck back on June 18. In the first time it had employed missiles against another country in three decades, the Islamic Revolutionary Guard Corps announced the launching of several ground-to-ground midrange missiles from bases in Kermanshah Province in western Iran against ISIS forces in the Deir Ezzor region in eastern Syria.

In yet another escalation of the conflict, on June 18, 2017, two U.S. Navy aircraft shot down a Syrian fighter after it had attacked SDF positions in the town of Ja'Din just south of Tabqah in Syria. It was the first U.S. shootdown of a Syrian piloted aircraft since the United States commenced air operations in Syria. The incident occurred after a threatened attack by pro-Syrian regime troops and the U.S.-backed anti-ISIS group of the SDF. Regime tanks, artillery, and technical vehicles were advancing on the SDF position, forcing the coalition to use the de conflict ion hotline established with the Russians in an attempt to turn the regime troops back. When this proved unsuccessful, coalition aircraft performed strafing runs near the regime positions, halting their advance. Following this, however, the Syrian jet again flew over the SDF positions and, despite warnings, dropped bombs, whereupon it was shot down by the U.S. aircraft.

Moscow responded to the shootdown several days later by threatening to target as hostile all aircraft flown by the United States and its allies in the anti-ISIS coalition. The Russians also said that they had suspended use of the hotline with the United States created in 2015 to prevent collisions of their aircraft in Syrian airspace. In late July 2017 after having met several times with Russian president Putin at the G-20 Meeting in Hamburg, U.S. president Trump in a highly controversial move ordered the U.S. Central Intelligence Agency (CIA) to discontinue a program of arming and training anti-Assad rebels in Syria, no doubt part of Trump's much-touted pro-Russia policy. Critics of the decision pointed out that it removed a pressure point on Assad, on the Iranians, and on the Russians.

On October 4, Syrian government forces, supported by intense Russian air strikes and Iranian-backed militia on the ground, took control of the remainder of the Syrian provincial capital city of Deir al-Zour. Meanwhile, the ISIS stronghold of Raqqa had come under siege by INHERENT RESOLVE coalition forces. This capital city of the self-proclaimed ISIS caliphate fell to largely Kurdish U.S.-supported forces on October 17. On November 9, 2017, Assad's government declared victory over ISIS in Syria. By then Assad's position had been significantly strengthened, as he vowed to take back every inch of territory still held by what he termed "terrorists."

With no end of the war in sight, its human cost has continued to grow. Syria's prewar population was some 23 million. By the late summer of 2018, estimates of the number of dead from the war ranged from 350,000 to 500,000, with as many as 2 million wounded. In addition, as many as 11 million Syrians, or almost half of the country's population, had been internally displaced, and 5.1 million were refugees abroad, a large number of these in Jordan and Lebanon as well as in Western and Central Europe.

A number of peace initiatives, including the March 2017 Geneva peace talks on Syria led by the United Nations, failed to produce agreement. Throughout much of 2018, peace negotiations were taking place in Sochi, Russia, chiefly among warring Syrian parties, while peace talks in Astana, Kazakhstan, also continued into the summer of 2018. The latter involved Turkey, Russia, and Iran. None of these more recent efforts, however, seemed poised to yield any breakthrough in the peace process.

By early 2018, events seemed to be going very much in Assad's favor, however. By then, the Syrian government was estimated to hold 55.7 percent of Syrian territory with the majority of the country's population. The SDF controlled 27.4 percent, various other rebel groups held 15.6 percent, and ISIS held only 2 percent. The area of Syrian government control was chiefly in the south and west of the country. Kurdish control was in the north and south of the country.

Assad's forces continued to make headway against antigovernment forces as 2018 progressed. During January–February, government forces continued to hammer away at rebel positions in the Hama Governate and Ghouta, situated east of Damascus. During these operations, Syrian government forces shot down an Israeli warplane in response to an Israeli cross-border raid. On April 7, 2018, a Syrian government chemical attack, which killed 70 Syrian civilians, was reported in Douma. A week later, U.S., French, and British air assets struck Syrian government targets in retaliation. Nevertheless, Assad's forces soon entered Douma, which helped end the long siege of eastern Ghouta. On May 1, the United States announced that its coalition forces were engaged in a final sweep of areas where small pockets of ISIS fighters remained in a bid to clear all ISIS elements from Syria by the fall of 2018. In June, Syrian government forces and its allies commenced the Southern Syrian Offensive, which ended on July 31. By then, Assad's forces had retaken control of Daraa and Quneitra Provinces.

Meanwhile, on July 16, 2018, Trump and Putin met in Finland, where the subject of Syria became a major topic of discussion. While they both agreed that a quick resolution to the Syrian Civil War was needed, there was little firm agreement over how that should be accomplished. Trump wanted Iranian troops withdrawn from Syria, while Putin demurred on that point. Both leaders did, however, agree that Iranian troops should be kept away from the Israeli-Syrian border to protect Tel Aviv's interests. Trump pledged U.S. humanitarian aid to Syria, even without a peace settlement, although that seemed to contradict long-term U.S. policy that had held back such aid so long as Assad remained in power. Finally, both men agreed that current peace talks should continue, with Russia maintaining a primary role in them.

Observers, however, pointed out that Russia faces an almost impossible task, given the deeply conflicting interests of the United States, Israel, Iran, Syria, and Turkey in the civil war. It seemed increasingly clear as the late summer of 2018 set in that Assad would remain in power for the foreseeable future and that the United States and other Western governments had begun to tacitly accept this as a foregone conclusion. On August 2, Israel declared the Syrian Civil War essentially over. In the meantime, growing tensions between Washington and Tehran in July and August 2018 were further complicating efforts to rein in Iranian activities in Syria.

Multinational human rights organizations have charged the Syrian government with being guilty of massive human rights violations, including torture, the direct targeting of civilians and hospitals with antipersonnel weapons, and the use of poison gas. The civil war also created a major crisis resettlement crisis in Europe with direct impact on the political situation in those countries involved.

SPENCER C. TUCKER

### See also
Aleppo, Battle for; Al Qaeda; Assad, Bashar al-; Erdoğan, Recep Tayyip; INHERENT RESOLVE, Operation; Iraq; Islamic State of Iraq and Syria; Kobanî, Siege of; Kurds; Lebanon

### References
Ajami, Fouad. *The Syrian Rebellion*. Stanford, CA: Hoover Institution, Stanford University, 2012.
Glass, Charles. *Syria Burning: A Short History of a Catastrophe*. New York: Verso, 2016.
Lesch, David W. *Syria: The Fall of the House of Assad*. New Haven, CT: Yale University Press, 2012.
McHugo, John. *Syria: A Recent History*. London: Saqi, 2015.
Sorenson, David S. *Syria in Ruins: The Dynamics of the Syrian Civil War*. Santa Barbara, CA: Praeger Security International, 2016.
Starr, Stephen. *Revolt in Syria: Eye-witness to the Uprising*. New York: Columbia University Press, 2012.

## Syrian-Egyptian Wars (274–168 BCE)

### First Syrian-Egyptian War (274–271 BCE)
The First Syrian-Egyptian War was fought between King Antiochus I Soter of Syria and Ptolemy II Philadelphus of Egypt. The root cause of the series of six Syrian-Egyptian Wars was the competing Seleucid and Ptolemaic claims to the lands of Coele-Syria (roughly the area of modern-day Lebanon, Israel, and Palestine). The Seleucid claim was based on the fact that Syria was granted to Seleucus I Nicator in the settlement following the defeat of Antigonus Monophthalmus after the Battle of Ipsus in 301. The Ptolemaic claim was based on the conquests of Ptolemy I Soter in the region in 302–301 BCE. Initially in 301, in recognition of his friendship with Ptolemy, Seleucus ceded his claim to Coele-Syria south of the Eleutherus River (the modern-day Nahr al-Kabir, on the northern border of Lebanon) but later asserted his rights to the land and declared that Ptolemy had wrongly taken it from him, thus setting the stage for the Syrian-Egyptian Wars.

The immediate cause of the First Syrian-Egyptian War was the coordinated attack on Ptolemaic possessions by Antiochus II and his son-in-law Magas, who had been ruling Ptolemaic Cyrenaica since 301 but then rebelled against Ptolemy II in 279.

Magas was forced to call off his invasion of Egypt (most likely in 275) even before Antiochus could begin his attack on Coele-Syria. Egyptian forces invaded Syria in 274, perhaps by sea. These were apparently driven out by Seleucid troops, who then moved well south of the Eleutherus River line, perhaps to the borders of Egypt itself, since an inscription locates Ptolemy and his sister-wife Arsinoe at the eastern edge of the Nile Delta supervising the construction of defensive works. Ptolemy eventually recovered his position in Coele-Syria, and peace was made on the basis of the status quo before the war in 271.

The war ended in stalemate, with Antiochus preoccupied with Galatian attacks in Asia Minor. Magas remained in possession of Cyrenaica.

### Second Syrian-Egyptian War (260/259–ca. 253 BCE)
The Second Syrian-Egyptian War was fought between Antiochus II of Syria and Ptolemy II Philadelphus of Egypt. Around 262 or 261 BCE, Ptolemy installed his eldest son, Ptolemy Epigonus, as ruler of Ephesus, thus directly challenging Seleucid control of Asia Minor. Epigonus rebelled against his father in 260 or 259 while his friend Timarchus, ruler of Miletus on behalf of the Ptolemies, set himself up as tyrant of that city. After Epigonus was killed by his soldiers, Ptolemy took direct control of Ephesus. Meanwhile, Antiochus II attacked Timarchus in Miletus, which Ptolemy chose to regard as an infringement on his sphere, thus sparking the Second Syrian-Egyptian War.

Ptolemy successfully invaded Syria and Cilicia but was quickly driven out in unknown circumstances. Meanwhile, Antiochus secured an alliance with Rhodes and wrested Ephesus from Ptolemy's control. Peace was made around 253 and sealed with a marriage alliance: Antiochus married Ptolemy's daughter Berenice.

The Ptolemies temporarily lost their possessions in Asia Minor and influence in the Aegean. The costs of the war compelled Ptolemy to intensify his taxation regime in Egypt. While Antiochus was preoccupied with the war, Parthia seceded from the Seleucid Empire. Antiochus also had to acquiesce to the permanent settlement of the Galatians in Asia Minor and the formation of a separate kingdom of Cappadocia there.

### Third Syrian-Egyptian War (246–241 BCE)
The Third Syrian-Egyptian War was fought between Seleucus II Callinicus of Syria and Ptolemy III Euergetes of Egypt. When Antiochus II died, allegedly by poisoning at the hands of his divorced wife Laodice, a successionist dispute broke out between Laodice, who claimed the throne for her son, Seleucus II, and Berenice, daughter of Ptolemy II Philadelphus, who supported her son Antiochus's claim to the throne. Berenice called upon her brother Ptolemy III to support Antiochus's claim. Meanwhile, Laodice and Seleucus secured the murder of Berenice and her son.

In 246 BCE Ptolemy marched north and was welcomed at Seleucia-by-Pieria and then at Antioch, where he discovered that his sister and nephew had been killed. Ptolemy then occupied Cilicia and Syria and marched perhaps as far east as the Euphrates and Babylon (reports that he reached Bactria are probably exaggerated). Ptolemy regained Ephesus as well. Seleucus mustered a fleet against Ptolemy, but it was destroyed in storms. Ptolemy was nonetheless recalled to Egypt by an outbreak of unrest there.

The course of the war after this is unclear. Aradus in Coele-Syria fell under Ptolemy's control for a few years but reverted to near independence in the Seleucid sphere soon afterward. Ephesus, Miletus, Samos, and parts of Hellespontine Thrace, including Aenus and Maronea, all became Ptolemaic possessions before the war was over. Seleucus retook Damascus before peace was concluded in 241.

Under the terns of the peace, the Ptolemaic empire reached its greatest extent at Seleucid expense. Ptolemaic control over Seleucia-by-Pieria was a particularly important prize, though its possession by Egypt virtually guaranteed further conflict between the two kingdoms.

## Fourth Syrian-Egyptian War (221–217 BCE)

The Fourth Syrian-Egyptian War was fought between Antiochus III the Great of Syria and Ptolemy IV Philopator of Egypt. Antiochus was a young man of enormous ambition and energy when he came to the Seleucid throne in 223 BCE. He immediately set about trying to restore his empire to its greatest extent. A succession crisis in Egypt offered the opportunity. Ptolemy IV succeeded his father Ptolemy III amid civil disturbances and court intrigue, including the murder of Philopator's mother Berenice II and his brother Magas. In these circumstances, Antiochus began planning the conquest of Coele-Syria. Antiochus's opportunism may have been compounded by his desire for revenge against the Ptolemaic regime for the assistance it provided Attalus I of Pergamum against Seleucid interests in Asia Minor.

Antiochus marched into Coele-Syria in 221 with the aim of retaking Seleucia-by-Pieria, a Ptolemaic possession since the Third Syrian-Egyptian War. Antiochus was forced to call off the invasion, however, after Molon, his renegade commander of the Upper Satrapies, defeated the king's generals sent against him. After defeating Molon, Antiochus resumed the war against Ptolemy, ignoring the incipient rebellion of his commander in Asia Minor, Achaeus, whose revolt may have been instigated by Ptolemy.

Upon his return to Coele-Syria in 219, Antiochus took Seleucia-by-Pieria. Then Theodotus, Ptolemy's commander in the region, defected to Antiochus, turning over to him Ptolemais and Tyre. Antiochus began advancing southward, laying siege to Ptolemy's cities, while Ptolemy's ministers, Sosibius and Agathocles, managed to secure a four-month truce with the Seleucid king during the winter of 219–218. This gave Ptolemy the time he needed to assemble and train a massive land army, numbering some 20,000 men.

In the spring of 218 Antiochus resumed operations, taking Ptolemaic cities by surprise and by siege and also overwhelming Ptolemy's generals in battles on land and sea. In the summer of 217, the Seleucid and Ptolemaic armies clashed in the Battle of Raphia in southern Palestine. Antiochus was defeated and sued for peace.

Antiochus was forced to withdraw from Coele-Syria entirely, while Ptolemy failed to follow up his victory by attacking Seleucid territory, choosing instead to return to Egypt.

## Fifth Syrian-Egyptian War (202–195 BCE)

The Fifth Syrian-Egyptian War was fought between Antiochus III the Great of Syria and Ptolemy V Epiphanes of Egypt. Like the Fourth Syrian-Egyptian War, this war originated from Antiochus being able to take advantage of a succession crisis in Egypt to attack Coele-Syria. Shortly after the accession of the five-year-old Ptolemy V to the Egyptian throne in 204 BCE, Antiochus struck a secret pact with Philip V of Macedon to attack Ptolemaic lands and divide the kingdom between themselves.

Antiochus attacked Coele-Syria in the spring of 202 and seized Damascus. He then began a long siege of Gaza, which fell at the end of the summer of 201. Ptolemy's governor in the region, Ptolemaeus, son of Thrasea, defected to Antiochus in late 202 or 201. Ptolemy's ministers then charged Scopas the Aetolian with the defense of Coele-Syria. He began his invasion in a surprise winter campaign (201–200) and retook Palestine. In the latter half of 200, Scopas's forces clashed with Antiochus's at the Battle of Panium. Antiochus was victorious, and he began reestablishing Seleucid authority in Palestine. He then turned to the Phoenician coastal cities and blockaded Scopas in Sidon until the summer of 199, when the city surrendered. Antiochucs also captured Berytus and Byblos and successfully besieged Ptolemais, Tyre, and perhaps Joppa. By early 198, Coele-Syria was under Seleucid control.

In 197, Antiochus attacked Ptolemaic possessions in Asia Minor. His fleet took all the Ptolemaic ports on the south and Aegean coasts, and his land army removed all remaining Ptolemaic forces from inland Cilicia and Lycia.

Peace was made by 195, and Antiochus's daughter Cleopatra was betrothed to Ptolemy. They were married in the winter of 194–193.

The Fifth Syrian-Egyptian War undid the results of the third and fourth wars, eliminating all outposts of Ptolemaic power from Asia Minor and Coele-Syria for good. The Seleucid dream of reestablishing its ancestral claims to Coele-Syria had finally been achieved.

### Sixth Syrian-Egyptian War (170–168 BCE)

The Sixth Syrian-Egyptian War was fought between Antiochus IV Epiphanes of Syria and Ptolemy VI Philometor of Egypt. Antiochus III's daughter Cleopatra, wife of Ptolemy V and mother of Ptolemy VI Philometor, died in 176 BCE after ruling jointly with her young son since the death of her husband in 180. An anti-Seleucid backlash in Egypt followed, and in 170 Philometor's regents Eulaeus and Lenaeus declared war on Antiochus IV.

By 169, Antiochus defeated an Egyptian army at Pelusium on the eastern edge of the Nile Delta. Eulaeus and Lenaeus were overthrown by an anxious Egyptian populace and replaced with Comanus and Cineas, who negotiated with Antiochus. Antiochus took his nephew Ptolemy VI under his guardianship, making him effectively the ruler of Egypt. Unhappy with this, the Alexandrians appointed Philometor's younger brother, Ptolemy VIII Physcon, king. Antiochus laid siege to Alexandria in 169 but failed to take it and withdrew.

During the course of the winter, Philometor and Physcon were reconciled, provoking Antiochus into attacking Egypt again. The Ptolemies requested protection from Rome, but the latter was too preoccupied with the Third Macedonian War against Perseus to offer any help. Antiochus took Memphis and Cyprus and marched on Alexandria. However, at Eleusis, on the city's outskirts, he was met by a Roman delegation led by a former consul, C. Popilius Laenas, the Romans having just defeated Perseus at the Battle of Pydna. Antiochus held out his hand to Laenas, but the latter refused to shake it, instead handing him a copy of the senatorial decree ordering him to stand down. Antiochus said that he would have to consult his advisers before giving his response, but Laenas drew a circle around the king in the sand with a stick, ordering him to respond before he stepped out of the circle. Antiochus acquiesced, and Laenas took his hand and greeted him as a friend and ally of Rome.

The Seleucids then withdrew from Egypt and never attacked it again. More significant, however, is the fact that all states in the Hellenistic East had to be mindful of and answer to the power of Rome.

PAUL J. BURTON

**See also**
Antiochus I Soter; Antiochus III Megas; Antiochus IV Epiphanes; Diadochi, Wars of the; Egypt; Ptolemy I Soter; Ptolemy II Philadelphus; Ptolemy III Euergetes; Ptolemy IV Philopator; Ptolemy V Epiphanes; Ptolemy VI Philometor; Raphia, Battle of; Seleucid Empire; Seleucus I Nicator; Syria

**References**
Grainger, John D. *The Syrian Wars.* Leiden: Brill, 2010.
Gruen, Erich S. *The Hellenistic World and the Coming of Rome.* Berkeley: University of California Press, 1984.

## Syrian-Roman War (192–188 BCE)

The Syrian-Roman War pitted Seleucid king Antiochus III the Great and the Aetolian League against Rome. The war was caused by mutual mistrust, Roman fear of Antiochus's power and ambitions, and, according to Roman historian Polybius, the anger of the Aetolians, who invited the king to liberate Greece, that is, to replace Rome as the arbiter of Greek freedom. Aetolian anger stemmed from perceived slights against the league by the Romans, especially Rome's failure to reward the Aetolians sufficiently for their loyalty and service to Rome during the Second Macedonian War.

Lengthy diplomatic preliminaries, stretching across almost five years, preceded the actual outbreak of war. In 196 BCE T. Quinctius Flamininus, the Roman liberator of Greece, warned Antiochus not to infringe upon the autonomy of the Greek states of Asia Minor and to relinquish control of the former possessions of Philip and Ptolemy in Asia Minor. At the conference at Lysimacheia in September 196, the Roman commissioners in charge of the settlement of the Second Macedonian War demanded that Antiochus leave the Greek cities of Asia alone, evacuate Thrace, and reconcile with Ptolemy. Antiochus defended his activities in Thrace and Asia Minor as a reassertion of traditional Seleucid prerogatives, questioned Rome's right to interfere in his sovereign affairs, and announced a marriage alliance with Ptolemy.

In late 194, Antiochus sent envoys to Rome to request a formal treaty of alliance to clarify his status, power, and sphere of interest vis-à-vis that of Rome. This the Romans refused, demanding that Antiochus withdraw from Thrace (while conceding, if he complied, that the king could do as he wished with the Greek states of Asia Minor). The next year during a conference that was interrupted by the death of Antiochus's son Antiochus, the Romans reiterated their demands concerning Thrace and the Greek cities, while the king's minister Minnio, speaking on the absent king's behalf, reasserted Seleucid ancestral rights. Talks broke down when it was clear that neither side was prepared to budge.

In 192, the Aetolian League made Antiochus its *strategos* (general) for 192–191 and invited the king to cross the Aegean to Greece. Antiochus embarked with 10,000 men—too few to anticipate a war with Rome, which, even at this late date, was by no means a foregone conclusion. War only became inevitable when Antiochus's men attacked a detachment of Roman troops at Delium. The Roman consul M. Acilius Glabrio crossed to Greece in 191 with a substantial force. Antiochus took his relatively small army to Thermopylae to make his stand against the Romans, as much for strategic reasons (small numbers would be most effective in the narrow space) as for the historical symbolism of the place: like the Spartans in 480, the king could pose as the champion of Greek freedom against the barbarian aggressors, the Romans, who would be cast in the role of the invading Persians. The Romans, however, used the same path around the pass by which the Spartans had been betrayed in 480 and easily defeated the Seleucid forces. Antiochus fled back to Asia.

Roman forces commanded by Consul L. Cornelius Scipio launched an amphibious campaign in Asia Minor in 190. The combined Roman-Rhodian fleet defeated the Seleucid Navy (a portion of which was under the command of Hannibal, now exiled from Carthage) in two battles at Eurymedon and Myonessus. The consul Scipio (alongside his brother and adviser P. Cornelius Scipio Africanus, Hannibal's conqueror in the Second Punic War), having been escorted to the Hellespont through Macedon and Thrace by Philip V, launched a land invasion of Asia Minor. Antiochus's attempts to negotiate a solution failed when Scipio demanded that he evacuate Asia west of the Taurus and pay all war-related expenses. The Romans and a coalition of their allies, including Eumenes II of Pergamum, defeated the forces of Antiochus at Magnesia-by-Sipylum (Magnesia ad Sipylum) in Lydia in 189.

Antiochus sued for peace, which was granted in the Peace of Apamea (formalized in 188). The king was forced to withdraw from all lands west of the Taurus Mountains and the Halys River; pay 15,000 talents, 500 immediately, 2,500 upon ratification of the peace, and 1,000 each year over 12 years; hand over Hannibal and other advisers as well as 20 hostages; and give up all war elephants and retain no more than 12 warships. Antiochus's territory in Asia Minor was partitioned between Pergamum and Rhodes.

Meanwhile in Greece, the Romans and Philip V of Macedon fought Antiochus's allies, the Aetolians. After the Battle of Thermopylae, the Romans laid siege to the Aetolians at Heraclea while Philip besieged Lamia. Macedonian forces also took control of Athamania, an Aetolian League ally. Heraclea soon fell, and Glabrio ordered Philip to call off the siege of Lamia. In the summer of 191, the Aetolians sought a truce and talks with the Romans, but negotiations failed when a dispute arose over the nature and terms of surrender. After the truce expired, the war began again.

As the war with Antiochus and Roman attention shifted eastward, the Aetolians and their allies the Athamanians recovered most of their losses from Philip. After the Battle of Magnesia, however, the Romans returned to Greece. The Aetolians, lacking all hope of carrying the war on without Antiochus, sued for peace, which was granted in 189 on condition that they pay a 500-talent indemnity, give up any gains from the recent war, and not expand the league in future. They also signed a treaty of alliance promising to "respect the majesty of the Roman people" in the future.

PAUL J. BURTON

**See also**

Antiochus III Megas; Eumenes II of Pergamum; Magnesia, Battle of

**References**

Burton, Paul J. *Friendship and Empire: Roman Diplomacy and Imperialism in the Middle Republic (353–146 B.C.)*. Cambridge: Cambridge University Press, 2011.

Eckstein, Arthur M. *Rome Enters the Greek East: From Anarchy to Hierarchy in the Hellenistic Mediterranean, 230–170 B.C.* Malden, MA: Blackwell, 2008.

Grainger, John D. *The Roman War of Antiochus the Great*. Leiden: Brill, 2002.

# T

## Taalat Pasha, Mehmed (1874–1921)

Ottoman politician, one of the triumvirate of leaders controlling Ottoman affairs just before and during World War I. Born in 1874 at Edirne in Thrace, near Adrianople, in the Ottoman Empire (but today in Bulgaria), Mehmed Taalat Pasha began his career as a postman and telegraph operator before becoming involved in political activities of the reformist Committee of Union and Progress (CUP), for which he was jailed during 1893–1895. After his release he became chief secretary of posts and telegraphs for the Salonika district and began a rapid rise in the CUP's ranks, finally becoming one of the leading Young Turks of the 1908 revolution.

Shortly after the CUP ousted the liberal Ottoman government in 1913, Taalat Pasha was appointed the empire's secretary of the interior. In that role, he joined Enver Pasha and Djemal Pasha in the triumvirate that effectively controlled Ottoman policy until 1918. Taalat Pasha was physically attractive, humorous, and approachable and was considered the most able of the three, acquiring a reputation as the "Danton" of the revolution, despite his concerted efforts to force the Turkish language and culture onto the empire's Albanians, Arabs, and other minorities.

In 1914 Taalat Pasha favored an Ottoman alliance with Russia, but he was unable to negotiate an acceptable arrangement and was ultimately overruled by Enver Pasha, who preferred aligning with the Central Powers. After allying with Germany, the three Young Turks covertly sanctioned German vice admiral Wilhelm Souchon's bombardment of Odessa, Sevastopol, and Novorossiysk, an act of aggression that precipitated a declaration of war by Russia, France, and Great Britain and for which the Young Turks only retroactively sought support of the rest of the CUP.

Taalat Pasha was named grand vizier of the Ottoman Empire in February 1917, a post he was forced to resign from after Bulgaria dropped out of the war in October 1918. Taalat Pasha fled to Germany, where he remained in retirement until March 15, 1921, when he was assassinated in Berlin by an Armenian revolutionary.

Jack E. McCallum

### See also
Djemal Pasha, Ahmed; Enver Pasha; Ottoman Empire; Ottoman Empire, Entry into World War I

### References
Aksakal, Mustafa. *The Ottoman Road to War in 1914: The Ottoman Empire and the First World War.* Cambridge: Cambridge University Press, 2010.

Butler, Daniel Allen. *Shadow of the Sultan's Realm: The Destruction of the Ottoman Empire and the Creation of the Modern Middle East.* Dulles, VA: Potomac Books, 2011.

Kinross, Lord John Patrick Balfour. *The Ottoman Centuries: The Rise and Fall of the Turkish Empire.* New York: Morrow Quill Paperbacks, 1977.

Lewis, Bernard. *The Emergence of Modern Turkey.* 3rd ed. New York: Oxford University Press, 2002.

Turfan, M. Naim. *The Rise of the Young Turks: Politics, the Military and Ottoman Collapse.* New York: I. B. Tauris, 2000.

## Tahmasp I, Shah (1514–1576)

Influential Safavid ruler of Persia whose reign saw a continued conflict with the Ottoman Empire. Born at Isfahan on February 22, 1514, Tahmasp was the eldest son of Shah Ismail, the founder of the Safavid dynasty, and came to power at the tender age of 10 in 1524. Unable to rule, Ismail was controlled by Qizilbash tribal leaders, whose rivalries eventually led to civil strife in 1526. Seeking to exploit Persia's internal weakness, the Uzbeks invaded its northeastern province of Khurasan but were defeated in battle at Jam in 1528.

By 1533 Tahmasp, now 19, asserted royal authority and began to rule in his own right. Exploiting Ottoman preoccupation in Europe, where Suleiman I the Magnificent conducted major campaigns in Serbia and Hungary, Tahmasp sought to stir up rebellion in the eastern provinces of the Ottoman Empire and opened diplomatic negotiations with the Habsburgs on the creation of a Habsburg-Safavid alliance against the Ottomans. In response, the Ottomans, led by Grand Vizier Ibrahim Pasha, who was later joined by Suleiman himself, invaded Iraq. During the course of the next eight years, the Ottomans captured Baghdad, Bitlis, and Tabriz. Tahmasp avoided pitched battles and waged a scorched-earth strategy. Tabriz, recaptured by Tahmasp in early 1535, was sacked later that year by Suleiman. Although major military operations ended, minor skirmishes and border fighting persisted for almost a decade.

Between 1540 and 1553, Tahmasp also conducted military campaigns in the southern Caucasus, primarily targeting the eastern Georgian kingdoms of Kartli and Kakheti, where he captured and resettled thousands of Georgians who soon become an important new element in Persian society. In 1544, Tahmasp also became involved in Indian political affairs after he sheltered the Mughal emperor Humayn, who had been overthrown and forced to flee from India. With Tahmasp's help, Humayn was able to reestablish his rule in 1555.

In 1548, Tahmasp's conquests of Tabriz and Van provoked a second campaign by Suleiman. Yet again, the shah adopted a scorched-earth policy, laying waste to the Armenian highlands. The Ottomans, however, reclaimed Tabriz and Van as well as additional fortresses in Armenia and Georgia.

Following a three-year hiatus, the war resumed in earnest. Tahmasp's attack on Erzurum in 1552 led to a counterattack by Suleiman, who reclaimed Erzurum and invaded western Persia in 1553–1554. Unable to defeat the Ottomans, Tahmasp chose to negotiate, signing the Treaty of Amasya in 1555. Under its terms, the two powers settled their spheres of influence, with Persia receiving Azerbaijan, eastern Armenia, eastern Kurdistan, and the eastern Georgian kingdoms, while the Ottomans secured all of western Georgia, Arabia, Iraq, and western Armenia and Kurdistan. Kars was declared neutral, and its fortress was destroyed.

Tahmasp spent the last years of his life in seclusion, particularly after becoming ill in the mid-1570s. A generous patron of the arts, he commissioned various artistic works, including the famous *Shahnama-yi Shah Tahmaspi* with dozens of exquisite miniature paintings. Even before his death at Qazvin on May 14, 1576, his sons from Georgian, Circassian, and Turkoman wives quarreled over the succession, which turned into an open conflict upon his passing.

ALEXANDER MIKABERIDZE

**See also**
Jam, Battle of; Ottoman-Safavid Wars; Suleiman I

**References**
Newman, Andrew J. *Safavid Iran: Rebirth of a Persian Empire*. London: I. B. Tauris, 2009.
Savory, Roger M. *Iran under the Safavids*. Cambridge: Cambridge University Press, 1980.

## Taif Accords (October 22, 1989)

Agreement made among Lebanese leaders at Taif, Saudi Arabia, that was to bring an end to the 25-year-long Lebanese Civil War, stabilize the Lebanese political scene, and force Israeli troops out of southern Lebanon. The Taif Accords (also known as the Taif Agreements, the National Reconciliation Accord, and the Document of National Accord) were signed on October 22, 1989, at Taif and ratified on November 4, 1989. The agreement was based in part on the 1985 Damascus Agreement, which was never implemented.

The Taif Accords were designed to decrease *ta'ifiyya* (sectarianism). The accords set forth the basis of the country itself and the role and duties of key officials. The document defines itself as a "coexistence charter." Section A defines Lebanese identity as belonging to all and opposes identification on any other basis. Sectarianism is addressed in Section G, which calls for the abolition of the practice of hiring and appointing individuals according to their religion and for an end to mention of their sect on the national identity card. The accords spell out the duties of the president, the prime minister, the Chamber of Deputies (the legislature), the ministers, the cabinet, and the courts. The agreement also decentralized the country administratively.

The Taif Accords could not be implemented right away, as fighting in Lebanon continued. The accords were also considered controversial due to the circumstances at the time they were formulated, when Lebanon was divided between two presidents, one defying Syrian influence and the other being the ally of the Syrians. Critics also claimed that the accords essentially legitimized the presence of Syrian troops in Lebanon (they would not be withdrawn until 2005) and thereby gave Damascus a considerable say in Lebanese affairs.

Not all Lebanese leaders accepted the Taif Accords, and President Michel Aoun, a Maronite Christian, rejected the agreement out of hand. He in fact called for the dissolution of the Chamber of Deputies when the agreement was being negotiated, which detractors of the accords say made it an illegal document. While Syria understandably supported the agreement, Druze leaders criticized it, declaring it too generous to Sunni Muslims in Lebanon. In the long run the accords were never entirely implemented, and the forced withdrawal of Syrian troops in 2005 rendered the accords partly moot.

In the political realm, the accords addressed the imbalance of representation in the Lebanese parliament by granting equal representation (50/50) to both Christians and Muslims. This overrode the old formula, which had given Christians a much larger representative proportion than their numbers should have yielded, by a 6 to 5 ratio. In this it reflected the new demographic realities of the country. The legislature was expanded from 108 to 128 seats, and the exact proportion of representatives was specified. The cabinet was similarly divided equally between Muslims and Christians. The agreement also required the president (who must be a Christian) to designate the prime minister in consultation with the Chamber of Deputies.

To ensure that the civil war would be brought to a close, the accords called for the disbanding of all national and nonnational militias and the return of Lebanese evacuees to their point of origin. Most militias were indeed disarmed, although Hezbollah continued to operate within Lebanon, legally from a Lebanese perspective because of the continued occupation of southern Lebanon by Israel and its proxy Lebanese force. Finally, the agreement required a two-thirds vote among the Council of Ministers to alter the new governmental setup and provide for the protection of minority rights within Lebanon.

The Taif Accords also called for a redeployment of Syrian troops within Lebanon upon consultation with the Beirut government, although the Syrians effectively dictated such policies until they were finally forced out in 2005. Between 1990 and 2005 Damascus had an advisory role or even the last word in certain disputes with the Lebanese government and forced upon it a number of disadvantageous agreements. Implicit in the accords was the expectation that Syrian troops would gradually be withdrawn from Lebanon. The United States was a key player in a campaign to pressure the Syrians to withdraw from Lebanon. When this failed to occur within a reasonable time period, the international community condemned the continuing Syrian occupation. In May 2004 the George W. Bush administration invoked sanctions against Syria, in part because its policies were not in keeping with the spirit of the Taif Accords. Syrian troops finally departed in April 2005 after the assassination of former Lebanese prime minister Rafik al-Hariri provoked mass demonstrations in Lebanon. Many Lebanese linked Hariri's murder to a conspiracy either launched by the Syrian government or at least carried out with its knowledge, although Damascus continues to claim that it had no connection to the murder.

PAUL G. PIERPAOLI JR. AND SHERIFA ZUHUR

**See also**
Fatah, al-; Hezbollah; Lebanon; Lebanon Civil War; Syria

**References**
Deeb, Marius. *Syria's Terrorist War on Lebanon and the Peace Process.* New York: Palgrave Macmillan, 2003.
Long, David E., and Bernard Reich. *The Government and the Politics of the Middle East and North Africa.* Boulder, CO: Westview, 2002.
Picard, Elizabeth. *Lebanon, a Shattered Country: Myths and Realities of the Wars in Lebanon.* New York: Holmes and Meier, 2002.

# Taji Bunkers, Attacks on (January 17– February 27, 1991)

Coalition air assault during the Persian Gulf War on Iraq's Taji bunkers between January 17 and February 27, 1991. The Taji bunkers were two specially fortified installations at Taji Airfield, some 20 miles northwest of Baghdad, that contained Iraqi government communication and control facilities. Coalition air attacks utilizing conventional bunker-busting bombs failed to inflict significant damage on the bunkers early in the war, leading the U.S. Air Force to employ a new bomb developed after the start of the buildup of forces in Saudi Arabia preceding the war in what was one of the most rapidly developed weapons in military history.

Before the Persian Gulf War, Iraq had begun to fortify sensitive facilities throughout the country. These were protected by steel-reinforced concrete and/or were dug deep into the earth. Special bunkers were prepared underground for

Iraqi leader Saddam Hussein and his chief subordinates to allow them to direct operations in safety in the event of war.

Taji One and Taji Two at Taji Airfield were two of the most heavily fortified bunkers. Located 30 to 50 feet underground, they were protected by a 2-foot-thick slab of reinforced concrete. The bunkers covered approximately the same area as a U.S. football field and featured a series of hardened concrete cylindrical corridors 8 feet in diameter. A central corridor tube connected to other areas, including living quarters, communications facilities, and armories. Reports indicated that the bunkers could house 1,200 Republican Guards for up to a month. The bunker complex was also said to be one of three utilized by Iraqi leader Saddam Hussein.

On the first night of the war, January 17, 1991, F-117 Nighthawk stealth aircraft attacked the bunkers with standard bunker-busting bombs. These were 2,000-pound GBU-27 precision laser-guided bombs with a BLU-109 hardened steel warhead to break through earth and reinforced concrete. Although direct hits were registered, the bombs were unable to penetrate the bunkers. Air force planners had anticipated this development, and already at the end of October 1990 Lieutenant General Thomas Ferguson, commander of the Systems Command Aeronautical Systems Division, directed his team to develop alternatives able to destroy reinforced bunkers deep underground. Eleven were put forward, including the use of an unmanned Boeing 727 or 737 flying bomb. None were available before the air campaign began, however.

As the air campaign progressed, engineers at the Air Force Development Test Center offered another alternative. They suggested a heavy bomb dropped from a B-52 Stratofortress from a high altitude, which would have sufficient kinetic energy to penetrate Iraqi defenses. To develop the weapon quickly, engineers would have to utilize components already available. The idea was approved on February 1, 1991.

The first problem was finding a tube for the bomb canister that would be able to withstand the enormous forces of impact. A Lockheed engineer remembered that the U.S. Army had stored a number of 8-inch howitzer gun barrels. Several were available at the Watervliet, New York, arsenal. Workers there immediately began to modify the barrels into bomb canisters. Engineers decided that the proposed original 6,500-pound bomb should be reduced to about 5,000 pounds so it could be carried by F-111 Aardvark bombers or F-15 Eagle fighters.

Work had begun by February 11. The barrels were cut down, the chrome liners were removed, and machinists bored out the interior to a 10-inch diameter. One end of the tube was modified to allow the insertion of a BLU-109 warhead. On February 16 the first two modified barrels were delivered to Eglin Air Force Base in Florida to be converted into bombs and tested.

Wind-tunnel testing on scale models had already indicated the bombs' aerodynamic characteristics, and tests that would have taken two years were either completed in a week or simply not done. The modified barrels were then fitted with laser-guidance packages at Eglin. One bomb was filled with concrete, while the other was filled with 630 pounds of molten Tritonal explosive. The completed bombs weighed 4,700 pounds and were 13 feet long with 2.25-inch-thick walls. After being carried on an F-111E to test how the bomb would handle in the air, both test bombs were flown to Tonopah Test Range in Nevada.

On February 24, the first day of the ground war, the first bomb, loaded with concrete, was dropped to test the guidance system. It penetrated more than 100 feet into the ground. On February 26 the second bomb was tested on a rocket sled to try its penetrating power. It penetrated 22 feet of steel-reinforced concrete and then traveled half a mile beyond.

Two other bomb casings were delivered to Eglin on February 23. Engineers immediately loaded them with Tritonal and placed them in a C-141 Starlifter for delivery on February 27. Within five hours of landing, two F-111s at Taif Air Base in Saudi Arabia had been armed with the bombs. Because a cease-fire was imminent, Washington had ordered that no bombing occur after 5:00 a.m. local time, but the air force was determined to test the GBU-28 in combat.

The plan had called for four F-111s to deliver the two bombs, but this was reduced to two by February 27. The two Aardvarks departed Taif in predawn darkness and headed north. They were refueled by a tanker aircraft south of the Iraqi border. The F-111s were accompanied by F-15C fighter escorts and F-4G Phantom II Weasels, which took out an Iraqi antiaircraft site en route.

On approaching their target, the two F-11ls turned on their afterburners in order to effect a steep climb to be able to develop sufficient kinetic energy for the GBU-28 to penetrate the bunkers. This caused some pilot nervousness, as the afterburner plumes were visible to area Iraqi air defenses.

Both aircraft were to run over the target, with the first F-111 to guide the GBU-28 to its target by laser. If the first aircraft could not get a good fix, then the second would use its laser to guide the bomb home. After the first bomb was dropped, the two aircraft would circle about and repeat the process, with the second aircraft leading.

The lead pilot called out a good fix and guided the first bomb home solo, but he then called on the second pilot to switch from the planned secondary target to the primary, with no reason given. The second F-111 failed to secure the target on its first and second passes but found it on the third run. The targeted bunker was painted with the Pave Tack laser for 60 seconds before the drop and throughout the bomb's flight. The F-111s then returned to base, refueling en route.

Video of the attack indeed indicated that the first aircraft had missed the intended target, but the second bomb scored a direct hit, as indicated by smoke pouring from the bunker vents seven seconds after impact. Casualties in the attack are unknown, but some hold that the hasty Iraqi cease-fire on the following day may have had something to do with the fact that the last Iraqi command bunkers were no longer safe.

The process of bringing the GBU-28 from planning stage to delivery in less than six weeks was unprecedented. The U.S. Air Force continued work in other penetration weapons, especially thermobaric bombs.

TIM J. WATTS

**See also**
Persian Gulf War, Overview

**References**
Gordon, Michael R., and General Bernard E. Trainor. *The Generals' War: The Inside Story of the Conflict in the Gulf.* New York: Little, Brown, 1995.

Murray, Williamson. *Air War in the Persian Gulf.* Baltimore: Nautical and Aviation Publishing Company of America, 1995.

# Talmud

An extensive set of interpretations of the writings (or scriptures) of the Torah dealing with the law, customs, ethics, and history of the Jewish people. The Torah is the first of three parts of the written Hebrew Bible. The Torah is also essentially the same as the first five books of the Christian Old Testament—Genesis, Exodus, Leviticus, Numbers, and Deuteronomy—often referred to as the Five Books of Moses and the Pentateuch. The Talmud began as an oral commentary on the Torah and was designed to offer insights into the writings of the Torah as well as how to interpret and apply the laws mandated in the Torah. The Talmud also treats issues relating to Jewish history, ethics, and traditions.

Jews of the orthodox tradition believe that God handed down the Oral Torah directly to Moses, who then taught it to others. In this fashion, it was handed down from generation to generation. However, the oral teaching of the Talmud lasted only until the second century CE. At that time, much of it was written down in the form of the Mishna (repetition), which is a compilation of all the laws contained in the Torah.

In the succeeding few centuries, more commentaries were written by rabbis and Jewish scholars both in Babylon and Jerusalem. These newer writings came to be known as the Gemara (Completion), a set of commentaries on the various teachings of the Mishna. Taken together, the Mishna and Gemara make up the Talmud. By the fifth century, most of the writings had been completed.

There are two different Talmuds. The so-called Jerusalem Talmud consists of the Gemara writings and interpretations compiled by scholars, mostly in the Galilee town of Safed. The Babylonian Talmud was compiled by rabbis and scholars in Babylonia. The latter Talmud is the most expansive, and it is the one that many Jews mean when they reference the Talmud.

The Talmud has not remained a static set of writings or interpretations, however. Over the centuries, rabbis and scholars added to it and provided new interpretations of the old laws and scriptures. Currently, a new commentary is being prepared for the Mishna, Gemara, and older commentaries.

Reading the Talmud and comprehending its meaning is not always an easy task. Thus, it is no surprise that reading and interpreting it have often been left to rabbinic scholars and rabbis, although many observant Jews make a habit of reading a little bit of the Talmud daily. The writing is often not linear and can have large gaps in reasoning as well as interpretation. References to passages in the Torah are sometimes little more than a few words, making familiarity with the Torah essential for full comprehension. The writings also may provide more than one interpretation of a law or custom without explicitly stating which interpretation is the preferred one. It takes a well-trained eye and a learned scholar to navigate around such complexities.

The Mishna is organized into six *sedarim* (orders), and each order has one or more sections known as *masekhtot* (tractates). The first seder is called *Zera'im* (Seeds) and contains 11 tractates. Zera'im covers agricultural laws, tithing, blessings, and prayers. The second seder is *Mo'ed* (Festival), containing 12 tractates. This section deals primarily with laws relating to the Sabbath and the observance of festivals and holidays. The third seder is *Nashim* (Women), with 7 tractates, and covers subjects relating to marriage, divorce, and certain oaths. The fourth seder is *Nezikin* (Damages) and includes 10 tractates. Nezikin covers criminal and civil laws and the functions of courts. The fifth seder, comprising 11 tractates, is *Kodashim* (Things Holy) and speaks to dietary laws, sacrificial ceremonies, and the laws guiding the temple. *Toharot* (Purity), the sixth seder with 12 tractates, interprets things that are both pure and impure. Taken as a corpus of writings, the Mishna covers religious, social, and judicial laws and interpretations that are meant to guide observant Jews' lives on a daily basis, the oral law as handed down to Moses.

In the 300 years or so after the Mishna had been written down, rabbinic scholars in both Babylonia and Safed began debating and discussing the Mishna. Many of the Gemara writings are in the form of legal syntheses based on the Mishna or Torah and appear in the form of a Socratic, or dialectical, exchange between fictional or anonymous characters. One voice asks the question (*makshan*), and another voice replies (*tartzan*).

Because the work proceeded independently in Palestine and Babylon, the Gemara is divided in like fashion. The first is called the Palestinian Talmud (ca. fourth century CE), while the second is known as the Babylonian Talmud (ca. fifth century CE). The Babylonian Talmud is usually the one referred to when the general term "Talmud" is invoked and includes the Mishna as the entire body of work. During the course of the centuries, rabbinic scholars have placed considerably greater emphasis on the Babylonian Talmud. Part of this preference may stem from the fact that the Babylonian Talmud is far easier to read and interpret than the Palestinian version. The Babylonian Talmud, however, is more than four times the size of the Palestinian Talmud.

The first complete edition of the Babylonian Talmud was printed in the mid-16th century in Italy. In modern times, Orthodox Jews eschew any attempt to apply historical syntheses or interpretations to the Talmud and do not attempt to second-guess the writers and interpreters of the Talmud. Some modern scholars claim that because it is not possible to cobble together all of the various versions and interpretations of the Talmud, it is unwise to try to reinterpret the law. Others claim that it is indeed possible to reconstruct the corpus of writings and apply historical segmentation to them.

Not all Jews embrace the Talmud as an absolute and authoritative text. Reform Judaism tends to view the Talmud as a guide to moral conduct and inspiration but does not ascribe to it the sacrosanct nature that Orthodox Jews lend to it. Jews of the Conservative tradition have made the Talmud a central part of their system of belief but tend to see it more as a historical guide rather than an inviolable set of laws.

Paul G. Pierpaoli Jr.

**See also**
Ashkenazic Judaism; Hasidic Judaism; Mizrahi Judaism; Sephardic Judaism

**References**
Biale, David. *Cultures of the Jews: A New History.* New York: Schocken, 2002.

Dimont, Max. *Jews, God and History.* New York: Simon and Schuster, 1962.

Robinson, George. *Essential Judaism: A Complete Guide to Beliefs, Customs, and Rituals.* New York: Pocket Books/Simon and Schuster, 2001.

Seltzer, Robert. *Jewish People, Jewish Thought.* New York: Macmillan, 1980.

# Tamerlane (1336–1405)

Mongol ruler. Born near Kesh south of Samarkand in Transoxania (now Uzbekistan) on April 6, 1336, Timur (Tamerlane, Timur-e-leuk, Timur the Lame, Tamburlane) was of Turco/Mongol descent and the son of a Central Asian lord. He became known as Timur the Lame, Tamerlane, for a leg injury suffered as a youth. Tamerlane belonged to a Mongol clan that had adopted Islam as its religion and Turkish as its language. He claimed his legitimacy to rule as a relative of Genghis Khan, which is probably untrue.

Tamerlane soon became involved in the struggle that occurred in the breakup of the Mongol Empire established by Genghis Khan. Establishing his military reputation by 1360, Tamerlane joined with his brother-in-law, Amir Husayn, to secure all Transoxania (1364–1370). With the assassination of Husayn in 1369, Tamerlane assumed sole rule.

Tamerlane next campaigned against and defeated the rulers of Khwarizm and Jatah (today Tajikistan) during 1370–1380. He then invaded and conquered all of eastern Persia, including Khorasan, during 1383–1385. Tamerlane then returned to defeat an invasion from Russia (1385–1386) led by his former lieutenant Toktamish, whom he had helped become ruler of the Blue Horde and then the Golden Horde of most of the Russian principalities. Tamarlane took the remainder of Persia, including the territory of present-day Armenia, Azerbaijan, and Mesopotamia, during 1386–1387. Toktamish invaded again and was again defeated (1388 and 1389), on the last occasion in the Battle of Syr Dar'ya (November or December 1389).

Tamerlane invaded Russia in 1390 and crushed Toktamish in the Battle of the Kondurcha River (June 18, 1391) but was forced to return to Persia to put down a revolt there (1392). Tamerlane then reconquered Armenia, Azerbaijan, Fars, and Iraq. He took Mesopotamia and Georgia in 1395. He then defeated yet another invasion by Toktamish (1395), winning the Battle of Terek (April 15). In retaliation, Tamerlane invaded and ravaged most of southern Russia and Ukraine, reaching to Moscow (1396).

Tamerlane returned to Persia to crush revolts (1396–1397), then went on to invade India and defeat Mahmud Tughluk's army at Panipat (December 17, 1398). Taking Delhi, his men killed tens of thousands of people and virtually destroyed the city. He then captured Meerut and withdrew back to the Punjab (March 1399).

Tamerlane next invaded Syria, defeating the Mamluk army in the Battle of Aleppo (October 30, 1400). He then sacked both Aleppo and Damascus. Laying siege to Baghdad in 1401, he captured the city and massacred its population for rebelling against him. Invading Anatolia, he defeated the Ottoman Turk army of Sultan Bayezid I before Ankara (July 20, 1402), then captured Smyrna (Izmir) and received tribute from the sultan of Egypt and Byzantine emperor John I. Tamerlane returned to Samarkand in 1404.

Tamerlane was preparing an invasion of China (which had driven out the Mongols in 1389) when he fell ill and died at Otrar, near Chimkent (now Shymkent, Kazakstan), on January 19, 1405.

A brilliant tactician and master of highly mobile warfare, Tamerlane created a vast empire that encompassed much of Western and Central Asia. The empire was held together chiefly by fear, however, for Tamerlane lacked any sense of what constituted effective rule. He knew only reprisal to include the destruction of cities and the slaughter of rebellious inhabitants. Ironically, Tamerlane was also known as a patron of the arts, especially architecture. After his death, his empire was divided among his sons and grandsons.

SPENCER C. TUCKER

### See also
Ankara, Battle of; Baghdad, 1401 Siege of; Bayezid I; Mamluk Sultanate

### References
Manz, Beatrice Forbes. *The Rise and Fall of Tamerlane.* Cambridge: Cambridge University Press, 1989.
Marozzi, Justin. *Tamerlane: Sword of Islam, Conqueror of the World.* New York: Da Capo, 2006.
Nicolle, David. *The Mongol Warlords: Genghis Khan, Kublai Khan, Hulegu, Tamerlane.* London: Brookhampton, 1998.
Sokol, Edward D. *Tamerlane.* Lawrence, KS: Coronado, 1977.

## Tammuz I Reactor

Iraqi nuclear reactor destroyed by Israeli aircraft in 1981 while in the final stages of construction. The Tammuz I reactor was also known as the Osiraq reactor. Beginning in the late 1950s, the Iraqi government headed by Saddam Hussein had sought to acquire nuclear technology. Iraq claimed that this effort was for peaceful purposes, but many governments, most notably Israel, surmised that the ultimate Iraqi goal was the production of nuclear weapons. Iraq's first foray into the nuclear field came in 1959 when it entered into an agreement with the Soviet Union to build a small five-megawatt research reactor near Baghdad. The project was completed in 1968, but its small size and close supervision by Soviet technicians frustrated Iraq's goal of acquiring a facility capable of producing weapons-grade plutonium by-products.

In light of this Iraq began to look to other sources, notably France and Italy, for more sophisticated nuclear technology. After the 1973–1974 Organization of Petroleum Exporting Countries (OPEC) oil embargo, Iraq's huge energy reserves gave it a powerful bargaining chip as it negotiated an agreement with France for nuclear technology. In 1978 a French-led consortium signed a formal agreement to construct a nuclear plant with the Iraqi government. The terms of the agreement stipulated that Iraq would provide France with oil at discounted prices and agree to large purchases of French military hardware in exchange for construction of a nuclear complex centered on a 70-megawatt nuclear reactor.

Fuel for the proposed reactor was to be 93 percent enriched (weapons-grade) uranium. The project was originally named Osiraq, an Iraqi derivation of the name of a similar reactor in France. However, the name was soon changed to Tammuz to commemorate the time of the year in which the ruling Iraqi Baath Party came to power.

Italian firms would provide expertise in the extraction of weapons-grade plutonium from the reactor's spent fuel. As the reactor complex neared completion in 1980, the Israeli government embarked on a public information campaign designed to alert the world to the dangers of allowing Iraq to acquire nuclear technology. There were also indications by then that Israel had conducted several covert intelligence and sabotage missions against scientists and equipment associated with the program.

In September 1980 Iraq invaded neighboring Iran, triggering the eight-year-long Iran-Iraq War. One of the first Iranian Air Force targets was the Tammuz I reactor. In September 30, 1980, a raid by Iranian bombers failed to inflict serious damage on the facility but did precipitate an evacuation of several hundred French and Italian workers and brought construction on the site to a standstill. By the spring of 1981, however, many of the technicians had returned, and work was proceeding, with a target date for completion of the complex later that year.

Israeli aircraft struck the Tammuz I reactor site on June 7, 1981. The mission, more than a year in planning and rehearsals, involved eight F-15 Eagle fighter-bombers with six F-15 Fighting Falcon fighters flying cover. The strike package flew the 700-mile approach at low altitudes. Battle damage assessment indicated that the reactor building was struck and completely destroyed by 14 bombs.

Iraqi attempts to rebuild Tammuz I in the 1980s were slowed by a diversion of resources to the war with Iran and a breakdown in negotiations with France for the reconstruction of the reactor. The Tammuz site was again heavily bombed by coalition aircraft in 1991 during the Persian Gulf War, after which there were no significant efforts to rebuild.

ROBERT M. BROWN

**See also**
Iran-Iraq War; Iraq; Osiraq Raid; Persian Gulf War, Overview

**References**
Claire, Rodger W. *Raid on the Sun: Inside Israel's Secret Campaign That Denied Saddam the Bomb*. New York: Broadway, 2004.
Nakdimon, Shelomoh. *First Strike: The Exclusive Story of How Israel Foiled Iraq's Attempt to Get the Bomb*. New York: Summit Books, 1987.
Perlmutter, Amos, Michael Handel, and Uri Bar-Joseph. *Two Minutes over Baghdad*. 2nd ed. London: Frank Cass, 2003.

# Tancred (ca. 1076–1112)

Prince of Galilee (1099–1101) and regent of the principality of Antioch (1101–1103 and 1104–1112). Born around 1076, Tancred was a scion of the Norman dynasty of Hauteville in southern Italy. His father was Odo "the Good Marquis," and his mother was Emma, a daughter of Robert Guiscard, duke of Apulia and Calabria.

In 1096 Tancred joined his maternal uncle, Bohemund of Taranto, in the First Crusade (1096–1099) and early on distinguished himself as one of its leaders, especially in the fighting at Nicaea (modern-day Iznik, Turkey) and Dorylaion (near modern-day Eskişehir, Turkey). Indeed, Tancred's uncle gave him command of a company of knights. Tancred then moved into Cilicia, where he clashed with Baldwin of Boulogne, brother of Godfrey of Bouillon, regarding possession of Tarsos (modern-day Tarsus, Turkey). Tancred rejoined the main crusader forces at Antioch (modern-day Antakya, Turkey), where he played a significant role in the siege and conquest of the city.

After the establishment of Bohemund's principality at Antioch in 1098, Tancred continued toward Jerusalem, joining first Raymond of Saint-Gilles and then Godfrey of Bouillon. Tancred became one of the most important commanders in Godfrey's army. In June 1099 Tancred conquered Bethlehem on Godfrey's behalf and, having joined him at the siege of Jerusalem, commanded raids to obtain materials for building siege machines and ladders. During the conquest of the Holy City (July 15, 1099), Tancred seized the mosques of the Temple Mount and claimed lordship of the area.

Following establishment of Frankish rule in Jerusalem, Tancred proceeded northward and conquered Tiberias (modern-day Teverya, Israel), Nazareth (modern-day Nazerat, Israel), Mount Tabor, and other places in Galilee. Godfrey of Bouillon then gave him these territories as fiefs. Tancred took the title of prince of Galilee, and by campaigning in the areas of the Golan and the Terre de Suète, he enlarged his principality into the northern Transjordan.

In 1100 Tancred commanded the land forces at the siege of Haifa (modern-day Hefa, Israel), hoping thereby to secure an outlet for his principality on the Mediterranean. Supported by Daibert of Pisa, the new patriarch of Jerusalem, Tancred took advantage of Godfrey's death on July 18, 1100, to establish his men in Haifa castle. However, his ambitions in this regard were checked by Baldwin of Boulogne, Godfrey's brother, who came from Edessa to become the first Latin king of Jerusalem and appointed Tancred's rival Geldemar Carpinel as lord of Haifa.

The clash between Tancred and King Baldwin I, who had been rivals since the march through Cilicia, was cut short as a result of the capture of Bohemund by the Danishmendid Turks in 1101. Tancred was appointed regent in Antioch and relinquished his Galilean principality to the king. As regent of Antioch, Tancred distinguished himself militarily, fighting against the Armenians of Cilicia and the Byzantines, who were based in the port of Laodikeia (modern-day Al-Lādhiqīyah, Syria), and against the Turkish lords of Aleppo and elsewhere in northern Syria.

After Bohemund's release in 1103, Tancred became regent of Edessa during the captivity of Count Baldwin II (of Bourcq). Called to Antioch upon Bohemund's departure to return to Europe in 1104, he became its effective ruler until his death. According to his uncle's wish, in 1107 Tancred married Cecilia, who was the daughter of King Philip I of France and Bertrada of Montfort and was then in her childhood.

During the next few years Tancred's rule in Antioch was uncontested. His combined military and diplomatic talents enabled him to enlarge the principality to the south by annexing Laodikeia, Jabala, and Margat, connecting the principality with the county of Tripoli, and establishing a protectorate over Muslim Aleppo. In the dispute regarding the succession to the county of Tripoli, he supported William-Jordan, cousin of Raymond of Saint-Gilles, in his claims against Bertrand, who was backed by King Baldwin I. In 1108 Baldwin restored Tancred's title of prince of Galilee and returned to him the ownership of the Temple area of Jerusalem, though the foundation of the abbey of the Temple of the Lord prevented Tancred from exercising any effective authority there.

Tancred's main activity was concentrated in northern Syria, where the rising power of Mawdud, emir of Mosul, threatened both Antioch and Edessa. Tancred's power reached its peak with the failure of Mawdud's attack against the Frankish states in 1111. Tancred died in the fall of 1112.

A young adventurer belonging to a cadet branch of his family, Tancred demonstrated great military ability and diplomatic skills. These were, however, counterbalanced by his hard, self-seeking, faithless, and unscrupulous character; he was unpopular even among his own men. Yet his achievements and prestige became the basis for the growth of his romantic image to the point that he became a popular hero, particularly among the romanticists of the 19th century.

ARYEH GRABOIS

See also
Antioch, Principality of; Baldwin I of Jerusalem; Crusades in the Holy Land, Christian; Edessa, County of; Godfrey of Bouillon; Jerusalem, Crusader Siege of; Jerusalem, Latin Kingdom of; Mawdud

References
Murray, Alan V. *The Crusader Kingdom of Jerusalem: A Dynastic History, 1099–1125*. Oxford, UK: Prosopographica & Genealogica, 2000.
Nicholson, Robert L. *Tancred: A Study of His Career and Work in Their Relation to the First Crusade and the Establishment of the Latin States in Syria and Palestine*. Chicago: University of Chicago Press, 1940.
Rheinheimer, Martin. *Das Kreuzfahrerfürstentum Galiläa*. Frankfurt am Main: Lang, 1990.
Runciman, Steven. *A History of the Crusades*, Vols. 1–2. Cambridge: Cambridge University Press, 1953.

# Tanzimat

Turkish for "reorganization." Tanzimat was the period of Ottoman reforms from 1839 to 1876 during which Ottoman sultans and government reformers tried to modernize the Ottoman Empire, secure its territorial integrity against growing nationalism and aggressive European powers, encourage the development of Ottomanism, and more thoroughly integrate non-Muslims and non-Turks into Ottoman society by enhancing their civil liberties and granting them equality.

Sultans Mahmud II (r. 1808–1839) and Abdul Mecid I (1839–1861) and European-educated bureaucrats, such as Ali Pasha, Fuad Pasha, Ahmed Cevdet Pasha, and Midhat Pasha, provided the initial impetus for the Tanzimat reforms. They realized that since the late 1600s the Ottoman Empire had declined politically, militarily, and geographically as the European powers increased their military power. The reformers recognized that the old religious and military institutions no longer met the needs of the empire in the modern world and sought to adopt successful European practices.

Mahmud II provided the initial impetus for the reforms, but his successor Abdul Mecid I took the first official step by proclaiming the Imperial Rescript of the Rose Chamber on November 3, 1839. The most significant provision of the rescript was the elimination of the millet system by which each religious group had its own autonomous religious community and the declaration of legal equality for both Muslim and non-Muslims in the empire. In 1856, the Ottoman government proclaimed full legal equality to all Ottoman subjects, regardless of religion. The Nationality Law of 1869 made all inhabitants of the empire Ottoman citizens, regardless of religion or ethnic nationality.

The rescript abolished the so-called head tax on non-Muslims and tax farming. The government created a regular method of establishing and collecting taxes by salaried tax collectors. The government also allowed the recruitment of non-Muslims for the Ottoman Army, reorganized the army, established a regular recruitment method, and fixed the length of military service.

The rescript also promised a number of administrative reforms. These included guarantees of security for the lives, honor, and property of all Ottoman subjects; the introduction of the first Ottoman paper banknotes (1840); a modern financial system with a central bank, treasury bonds, and a decimal currency; the reorganization of the civil and criminal codes; the establishment of the first modern universities and academies (1848); and the establishment of a prototype parliament (1876). The reforms also created a system of state schools to educate prospective government officials. The government created defined administrative districts with a governor with specified duties and an advisory council to better serve that territory.

The rescript also called for the expansion of roads, canals, and railroads to provide better communication and transportation within the empire. To further modernize the economy, the government replaced guilds with factories and established in Istanbul the first Ottoman stock exchange in 1866.

The rescript was a clear move toward Westernization. The sultan hoped that by adopting Western standards, he could sufficiently appease European governments so they would not interfere in Ottoman internal affairs and also prevent the empire from falling under European control.

The Tanzimat reforms had mixed results. Many of those educated in the schools established during the Tanzimat period became progressive leaders and thinkers of the Turkish Republic, including such individuals as Mustafa Kemal Ataturk. Many Christians in the Balkans rejected the reforms, however, as these eliminated the autonomy and special privileges enjoyed under the millet system. In fact, the reforms spurred some provinces to rebel. Groups such as the Muslim Brotherhood opposed the loss of cultural traditions and the position of religion in Ottoman society.

The Great Powers themselves contributed to the internal opposition to the reforms. After the Crimean War (1853–1856), the European powers demanded increased sovereignty for the ethnic communities within the empire, undermining the Ottoman government's attempt to provide legal equality for all citizens and promote Ottomanism, a feeling of belonging to a cosmopolitan Ottoman nationality. The Christian middle class increased its economic and political power, while the Muslims received none of these benefits and were ultimately left worse off by the reforms. As a result, the Ottoman Empire saw the radicalization of a portion of the Muslim population with anti-Western sentiment and the rise of nationalist groups, such as the Young Ottomans.

The reforms peaked in 1876 with the implementation of a constitution that provided some limits on the sultan's autocratic powers. Unfortunately, the Ottoman ministers had deposed Abdul Aziz on May 30, 1876, and his nephew Murad succeeded him. Murad in turn was deposed, and Abdulhamid II became sultan on August 31, 1876. Although Abdulhamid signed the empire's first written constitution, he quickly turned against it, and the Tanzimat period came to an end.

Robert B. Kane

**See also**
Abdulhamid II; Mahmud II, Sultan; Ottoman Empire

**References**
Howard, Douglas A. *The History of Turkey*. Westport, CT: Greenwood, 2001.
Lewis, Bernard. *The Emergence of Modern Turkey*. London: Oxford University Press, 1961.
Shaw, Stanford J., and Ezul Kural Shaw. *History of the Ottoman Empire and Modern Turkey*, Vol. 2, *Reform, Reaction and Republic: The Rise of Modern Turkey, 1808–1975*. Cambridge: Cambridge University Press, 1977.

# Task Force Normandy (January 17, 1991)

A joint military force collectively named Task Force Normandy and consisting of U.S. Army and U.S. Air Force helicopters that paved the way for the opening of the air campaign for Operation DESERT STORM, which marked the beginning of the military campaign to expel Iraqi forces from Kuwait. Task Force Normandy involved elements of the U.S. Army's 1st Battalion, 101st Aviation Regiment, 101st Airborne Division, commanded by Lieutenant Colonel Richard "Dick" Cody, and the U.S. Air Force's 20th Special Operations Squadron (SOS) of the 1st Special Operations Wing, commanded by Lieutenant Colonel Richard L. Comer. Their mission was to destroy two Iraqi air defense radar sites some 25 miles inside Iraq. It was imperative that this be carried out simultaneously so as not to alert Baghdad that hostilities had begun.

The first of six rehearsals for the mission occurred on October 10, 1990, and the last occurred on January 10, 1991, one week prior to the actual combat mission. The rehearsals focused on flying without communication, blackout, visual signals, drop-offs, and formations. The 101st employed nine uniquely configured AH-64 Apache helicopters for the conduct of the mission. The U.S. Air Force's 20th SOS deployed four MH-53J Pave Low III helicopters to accompany the AH-64s. The MH-53J was selected not only for its unique combat search and rescue (CSAR) capabilities but also for its advanced terrain-following and terrain-avoidance radar system, making it the ideal platform for such an operation.

The Pave Lows were to escort the Apaches into Iraq, allowing the latter to destroy the radar sites with their Hellfire missiles. Armed with a 20-pound high-explosive antitank (HEAT) warhead, each missile required no further guidance after launch and could hit its target without the launcher being in line of site of the target.

Because the Apaches were not as technologically advanced as the Pave Lows, the crews came up with a creative way for the army helicopters to update their navigational systems. The air force crews strung together chemical lights and dropped them out of the back of their aircraft at certain points. When the army helicopters flew over the lights, they then updated their own navigational systems. On the day of the actual attack, the MH-53Js used their Global Positioning System (GPS) receivers and terrain-following radars to move the attack force to within nine miles of the target, undetected and with pinpoint accuracy.

Each AH-64 was armed with 8 Hellfire missiles as well as 19 2.75-inch rockets and 7 flechette rockets. Each flechette warhead contained 2,200 steel nails with fins on one end, resembling tiny darts. Additionally, each AH-64 carried 1,200 rounds for the 30mm M230 chain gun under the aircraft's nose.

The task force was divided into two teams, Red and White, each with four Apaches and two Pave Lows. The aircraft were located at Al Jouf, Saudi Arabia, days prior to the operation and departed from that outpost early on January 17, 1991. The attacks occurred at 2:38 a.m. The army aircraft fired 29 Hellfire missiles, with 22 hits, 3 duds, and 4 misses. Approximately 100 flechette rockets were also fired, along with some 4,000 rounds of 30mm ammunition. Their mission accomplished, both teams returned to base without loss, dodging at least two heat-seeking SA-7 surface-to-air missiles (SAMs) and small-arms fire en route.

At a subsequent press conference, coalition commander U.S. general H. Norman Schwarzkopf announced that "Army AH-64 Apaches plucked the eyes of the Iraqi air defenses." The successful destruction of the radar sites opened a 20-mile-wide corridor for U.S. Air Force and coalition air craft to commence the air campaign and enabled them to fly undetected to targets deep inside Iraq, including the capital city of Baghdad, a mere 22 minutes after the destruction of the radar sites.

JOHN R. DABROWSKI

### See also
Persian Gulf War, Air Campaign; Persian Gulf War, Overview; Schwarzkopf, H. Norman, Jr.

### References
Hallion, Richard P. *Storm over Iraq: Air Power and the Gulf War.* Washington, DC: Smithsonian Institution Press, 1997.

Mackenzie, Richard. "Apache Attack." *Air Force Magazine* 74 (1991): 54–60.

Naylor, Sean D. "Flight of Eagles: 101st Airborne Division's Raids into Iraq." *Army Times* (1991): 8–12, 15.

Schwarzkopf, H. Norman, with Peter Petre. *It Doesn't Take a Hero: General H. Norman Schwarzkopf, the Autobiography.* New York: Bantam Books, 1993.

## Tehran Treaty (November 25, 1814)

Treaty of alliance between Persia and Britain that remained the basis for relations between these two states until 1856. Also known as the Definitive Treaty of Friendship and Alliance between Great Britain and Persia and signed on November 25, 1814, in the Persian capital city of Tehran, the treaty sought to revise the Definitive Treaty of 1812 because during the Russo-Persian War of 1804–1813 Britain found itself in the difficult position of having to assist Persia against Russia with which Britain was allied against Napoleonic France.

The Tehran Treaty repeated most of the provisions of the Treaty of 1812, with the shah promising to resist any encroachment upon his country by European armies hostile to Britain and to use his influence with the rulers of "Karezan, Taturistan, Bokhara, Samarkan or other routes" to stop any invasion aimed at India through these territories. The treaty revised provisions dealing with British support of Iran. It specified that the purpose of the alliance was strictly defensive and provided that British military assistance or an annual war subsidy along with weapons would be implemented should Persia be attacked by a foreign state. Article 6 specified that should any European state at peace with Britain attack Persia, Britain pledged "to use its best endeavors" to mediate peace between the two sides. This provision was a disappointment to Persian leaders, as Persia had just lost a war to Russia and was forced to surrender vast territories in Caucasia.

The Treaty of Tehran seriously undermined Anglo-Persian relations during the Russo-Persian War of 1826–1828, when Britain failed to support Iran. Eventually, Britain bought its way entirely out of the entangling clauses of the Treaty of Tehran by paying an indemnity to Persia in an effort to mollify the terms of the Treaty of Turkmanchai (1828) that ended the Russo-Persian War.

ALEXANDER MIKABERIDZE

### See also
Definitive Treaty; Russo-Persian Wars

### References
Aitchison, C. U., ed. *A Collection of Treaties, Engagements, and Sanads Relating to India and Neighbouring Countries,* Vol. 10. Calcutta: Office of the Superintendent of Government Printing, 1892.

Daniel, Elton L. *The History of Iran.* Westport, CT: Greenwood, 2001.

# Tel el-Kebir, Battle of (September 13, 1882)

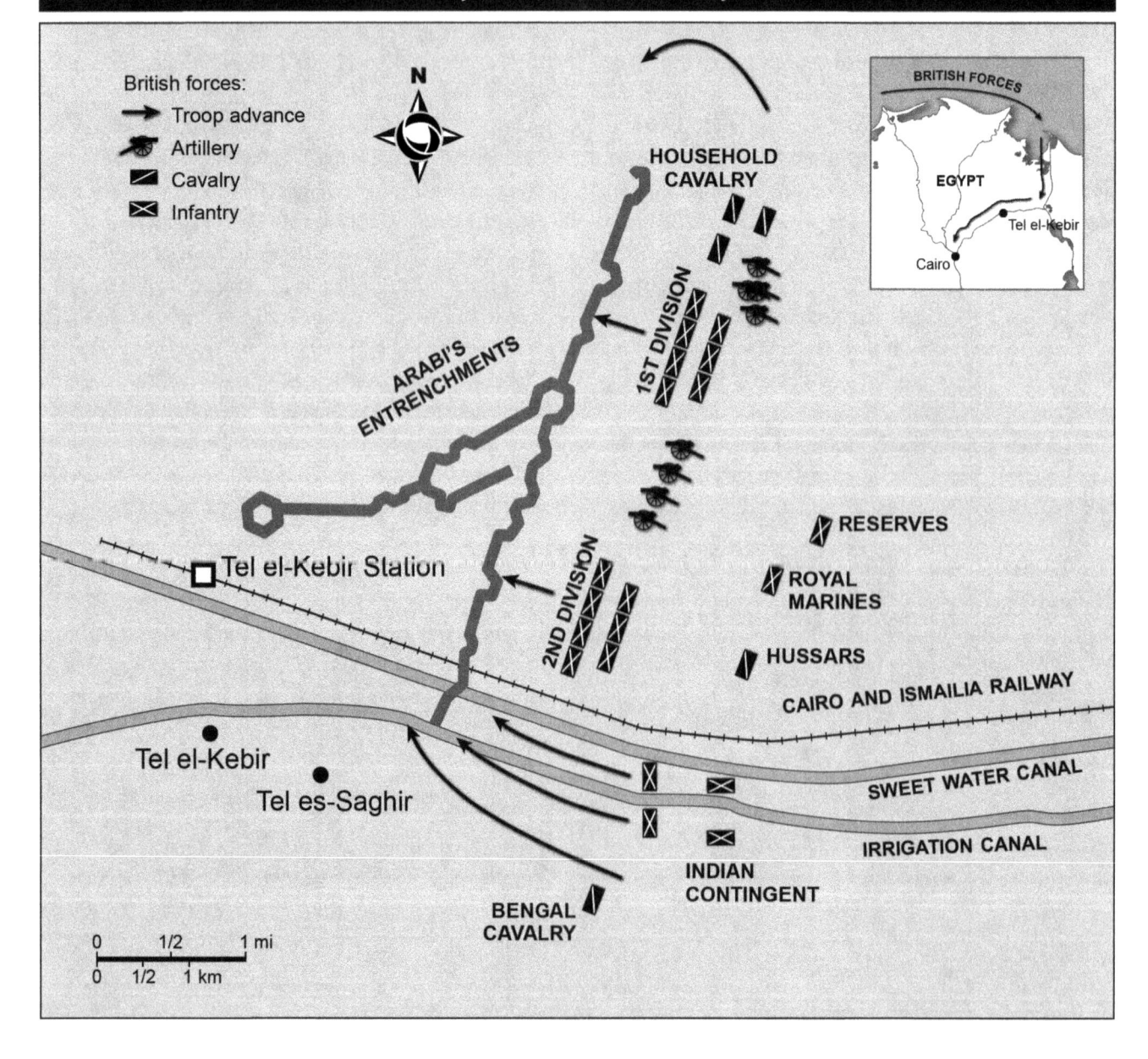

Decisive battle of the Anglo-Egyptian War of 1882. After their naval bombardment and occupation of Alexandria on July 11, 1882, the British assembled an expeditionary force of 24,000 men at Malta and Cyprus and 7,000 Indian Army troops at Aden. Lieutenant General Garnet Wolseley had overall command. Wolseley let it be known that he intended to land at Aboukir Bay but then proceeded instead to Ismailia, at the mouth of the Suez Canal, on August 20.

Although Egyptian revolutionary leader Ahmet Arabi (Urabi) had some 60,000 men at his disposal, he was forced to disperse them to defend different possible British axes of advance. Arabi established a defensive position of some 22,000–25,000 men equidistant between Cairo and the Suez Canal along a rail line connecting the two.

British advance forces drove the Egyptians back into a strong defensive position some four miles in length along a ridge line at Tel el-Kebir. The terrain in front of the ridge was flat, with excellent fields of fire for Arabi's 60 artillery pieces. In front of their defensive line, the Egyptians dug a long trench some six feet wide and four feet deep.

Impressed with the Egyptian defensive preparations, Wolseley spent four days in place planning his attack. Learning that the Egyptians were not manning their advanced posts at night, he decided to position his forces then. The

British advance began the night of September 12–13. Wolseley allowed the men five hours to cover the five and a half miles to the Egyptian lines.

By dawn on September 13 the British were in position only 300 yards from the Egyptian lines, with the sun at their backs. Wolsley had in line, from right to left, the 1st Division of English and Irish troops and the 2nd Division of Scottish Highlanders. He positioned his cavalry on both flanks. In all, Wolseley has available 17,400 men.

When the Egyptians discovered the British troops, they immediately opened fire. The British infantry divisions then assaulted and broke through the Egyptian lines. The flanking cavalry enveloped the Egyptian lines and turned the Egyptian retreat into a rout. The battle was over in about two hours, although British forces pursued the Egyptians the 50 miles to Cairo. The Egyptians lost some 2,000 men killed and 500 wounded. The British also captured all the Egyptian artillery. British casualties were 58 killed, 379 wounded, and 22 missing. The British entered Cairo on September 15, almost without opposition. Arabi surrendered, and the revolt quickly collapsed.

Spencer C. Tucker

See also
Anglo-Egyptian War

**References**
Farwell, Byron. *Queen Victoria's Little Wars*. New York: Norton, 1972.
Featherstone, Donald. *Tel el Kebir 1882: Wolseley's Conquest of Egypt*. London: Osprey, 1993.
Pakenham, Edward. *The Scramble for Africa, 1876–1912*. New York: Random House, 1991.

# Ten Thousand, March of the (401–399 BCE)

One of the most extraordinary military marches in history, the March of the Ten Thousand was a campaign during 401–399 BCE in Persia and then the return to Greece of an army of mercenaries, mainly Greek, employed by Cyrus the Younger for his attempt in 401 to overthrow his older brother and ruler of the Persian Empire, Artaxerxes II. The march to and battle at Cunaxa and the return to Greece were recorded by the Greek general and one the march leaders Xenophon in his work titled *The Anabasis*.

The mercenary force consisted at the maximum of 9,600 hoplites, 500 Greek light troops, 500 Greek peltasts, 800 Thracian peltasts, and 200 Cretan archers, a total of 11,900 men. Cyrus, supreme Persian commander in Asia Minor, increased his own force of Greek mercenaries and paid for others raised by trusted friends in the Greek world. In this he had the tacit cooperation of Sparta, whose keen ally he had been in the last phase of the Second Peloponnesian war.

In the early summer of 401 Cyrus assembled all available Greek mercenaries and his Asiatic forces, totaling some 100,000 men, at Celaenae in western Asia Minor. He then marched eastward, saying that his object was to stop raiding by the hill tribes of Pisidia. As he moved beyond Pisidia toward the Cilician Gates, the only route through the Taurus range into Cilicia, the Greek troops became increasingly uneasy. When they reached Tarsus they mutinied, but Cyrus reassured them by promising extra pay and saying that he was campaigning against Abrocomas, the satrap of Syria.

Cyrus had entered Cilicia with the connivance of its ruler Syennesis. At Issus, Cyrus was joined by his own fleet and also 35v triremes from Sparta, bringing 700 more hoplites under Cheirisophus. Cyrus had called upon Sparta for this open support. He intended to use his naval forces to turn the Syrian Gates, the pass leading from Cilicia to Syria, if Abrocomas resisted. However, Abrocomas withdrew, and Cyrus marched unopposed to the crossing of the Euphrates River at Thapasacus. It was now plain what Cyrus intended, and the Greek mercenaries again mutinied. They were won over by speeches from Cyrus's chief mercenary commander, the Spartan exile Clearchus, and Cyrus himself, accompanied by the promise of even higher pay and lavish rewards.

Cyrus marched southward down the left bank of the Euphrates as Artaxerxes's forces fell back. Finally, in about September at Cunaxa some 45 miles north of Babylon, Cyrus made contact with Artaxerxes's army. Artaxerxes had been following a defensive strategy but now had to defend the important city of Babylon.

Artaxerxes employed Asiatic infantry against Cyrus's Greek mercenaries. On Cyrus's left wing in the battle, these cleared away the Asiatic infantry opposite them. The rest of the battle went against Cyrus, who lost his life in a desperate attack on the Persian center.

At Cyrus's death his Asiatic troops fled or deserted to the other side. The Greeks were able to return to their camp unmolested by the Persian cavalry. The next day they refused a demand that they surrender. Cyrus's Persian friends were preoccupied with coming to terms with Artaxerxes, and the Greeks were left to make their own arrangements.

Tissaphernes was entrusted with dealing with the Greeks, whom Artaxerxes regarded as enemies deserving of vengeance. The Greeks were forced to rely on Tissaphernes's promises. They could not return on the same route they had come by. They were without supplies and in any case would have been exposed to attack by Tissaphernes's cavalry. Tissaphernes wanted to lure the Greeks out of the area round Babylon, which was crisscrossed by irrigation canals, and, by promising safe-conduct and supplies, led them south of Babylon to a crossing of the Tigris River at Sittace. They then marched north to the Zab River. There the Greeks' growing suspicions of Tissaphernes led Clearchus to attempt negotiations. With his chief officers and 20 other senior commanders, he was induced to attend a banquet at Tissaphernes's headquarters. There the Greeks were all treacherously seized and sent to Artaxerxes for execution.

In the crisis that followed, the Greeks decided to elect new officers, including the Spartan Cheirisophus as chief and Xenophon, a young Athenian. The army continued its march north in a hollow square, harassed by Tissaphernes's cavalry and slingers. In response, the Greeks improvised some cavalry and slingers of their own but did not even try forcing a crossing of the Tigris River at Jezirah.

At this point the Greeks' only way out was to strike northward through the mountains of Kurdistan in the hope of reaching the coast of the Black Sea, where there were Greek colonies that might help them get back to Greece. This route prevented any further attacks by Persian cavalry but required that the Greeks fight their way through hostile tribes. At the same time, the army had to keep up the march though increasing winter cold and heavy snowfalls. These mercenary hoplites showed the highest resilience and resourcefulness in flanking attacks and feints to force their way through strongly held positions. March discipline was maintained by example and exhortation of the officers, who did everything to keep the army moving.

Finally, in about February 400 BCE, the vanguard of the army caught sight of the Black Sea. Now reduced to about 8,600 in number, the Greeks still had to find their way home. The Greek cities on their route did not have sufficient numbers of ships to transport them by sea, however, and they were themselves justifiably anxious at the sudden arrival of such a large and hungry mercenary army.

The army now held more frequent meetings to decide on their movement, but dissensions became common, and separate groups went off on pillaging missions of their own, at times disastrously. By a combination of land marches and sea transport, the remainder finally reached Byzantium in late autumn. The local Spartan commanders had long been unhelpful or hostile to the army. Many mercenaries deserted as winter came on, and some 6,000 under Xenophon resorted to service with the Thracian king Seuthes in a winter campaign against rebellious subjects. Seuthes did not keep his promises of pay, and in the spring of 399 what was left of the army willingly took service under Thibron to fight in Sparta's war against Persia in Asia Minor. Some of these mercenaries, including Xenophon, were still in Spartan service at the Battle of Coronea in 394.

Xenophon's *Anabasis* is a graphic account of the march and is richly informative on the behavior and the thinking of Greek mercenaries. Xenophon did not underplay his own part as a leader. The spectacular successes of the "Ten Thousand" confirmed the belief among both Greek and Persian commanders in the superiority of Greek infantry to those of Asia. The successes also stimulated the idea that Greek military conquests in the Persian Empire were possible.

Douglas Kelly

**See also**
Achaemenid Empire; Cunaxa, Battle of; Cyrus the Younger; Xenophon

**References**
Anderson, John, K. *Xenophon*. London: Duckworth, 1974.
Fox, Robin Lane, ed. *The Long March: Xenophon and the Ten Thousand*. New Haven, CT: Yale University Press, 2004.
Prevas, John. *Xenophon's March into the Lair of the Persian Lion*. Cambridge, MA: Da Capo, 2002.
Waterfield, Robin. *Xenophon's Retreat: Greece, Persia and the End of the Golden Age*. Cambridge, MA: Belknap Press of Harvard University Press, 2006.
Xenophon. *The March Up Country: A Translation of Xenophon's Anabasis*. Translated by W. H. D. Rouse. Ann Arbor: University of Michigan Press, 1958.

# Terrorism

There is no settled definition of the word "terrorism." Most scholars and defense analysts believe that terrorism is a tactic rather than a philosophy or set ideology. History has shown that groups may employ terrorism at some times and not at others. There is an active debate about whether terrorism is the appropriate term solely for violence by nonstate entities or whether state terrorism must also be included. Some consider terrorism to be acts or threats of violence, directed against noncombatants, to shock or achieve a change in a political status quo by indirect means. However, others label some actions against military or governmental personnel to be terrorist in nature when they do not comply with international law. Still others write about terrorism as a pathology wherein violence is the motivating force and not merely a means to an end. This approach is problematic, as it could apply to individual pathological acts of violence as in recent cases of school shootings in Western countries. Terrorism may be employed for a wide variety of ideological, religious, or economic reasons.

Terrorism is also a tool in asymmetric conflict and a force magnifier. The impact of a small number of individuals committing terrorist actions can be huge, and even a large paramilitary or military force may seem ineffective in combating it, particularly if success is measured by the complete eradication of such incidents.

Numerous academic and governmental experts recognize the arguments regarding what constitutes terrorism and thus do not employ the term. Certainly there has been reaction to the U.S. government's application of the term in the global war on terror. "Violent extremism" has been used for many years in place of "Islamic terrorism" in the Muslim world and has begun to be used in the West in the last few years. Here, the focus is on the use, or relinquishment, of violence rather than the movement employing it.

Some analysts date modern terrorism to the Russian anarchist organization Narodnaya Volya (People's Will) of the 19th century, which attempted, through assassinations, to overthrow the tsarist regime. Their methods were adopted by anarchists throughout the world, and the decades leading up to World War I were marked by frequent assassinations. The assassinations of Austrian archduke Franz Ferdinand and his wife Sophie in Sarajevo in June 1914 sparked the outbreak of World War I.

Terrorist activities occurred in the Middle East prior to World War I, but in most cases the groups responsible were state-controlled forces that claimed to be acting in the interests of state security or to be engaged in war or militias or forces fighting against a state or another organization. Examples include the genocide perpetrated by Ottoman authorities against the Armenians and subsequent actions in recent years by Kurds against Turks in Turkey. Yet atrocities committed by Israeli forces in 1948 against Palestinians have often been excused in some quarters as legitimate acts of war.

Terrorism by both Arabs and Jews against each other and by Jewish forces against the British mandate power occurred in Palestine in the 1930s. Following Israeli independence in 1948, Palestinian groups, some supported by neighboring Arab governments, began to launch military attacks against Israel. After Israel's victory in the 1967 Six-Day War, Palestinian groups organized a wave of terrorist activities during 1969–1973. The political leadership of the movement then determined that these tactics brought too heavy an Israeli response and were detrimental to their cause, although they had served a purpose in focusing world attention on the plight of the Palestinians. In these same years, radical left-wing organizations in the United States such as the Weathermen and the Red Army in Europe and beyond (Japan) also engaged in acts of terrorism. Terrorism continued to be a major aspect of the Israeli-Palestinian confrontation and the inability to conclude an Arab-Israeli peace treaty but also as a response to Israeli military actions employing collective punishment against Palestinians or Palestinian communities.

Terrorist actions also appeared in Saudi Arabia. After the 1991 Persian Gulf War, extremists began preaching against U.S. military forces in Saudi Arabia, claiming that it was unconscionable for the Saudi government to allow Christian forces in the kingdom where the holy cities of Mecca and Medina are located. Saudi Arabia has long been home to a large expatriate community in its oil industry, and some extremists objected to their presence on Saudi soil as well.

On November 13, 1993, the Office of the Program Manager/Saudi Arabian National Guard was badly damaged by a car bomb. Four Saudi nationals confessed and were subsequently executed. They were veterans of jihads in Afghanistan, Bosnia, and Chechnya. They claimed that the Saudi rulers were apostates and that they were inspired by Islamic law to commit the attacks.

One month later, the Khobar Towers in Dhahran, Saudi Arabia, were destroyed by a truck bomb, killing 19 U.S. servicemen in a plot carried out by Saudi Hezbollah. In 1996 and again in 1998, Al Qaeda leader Osama bin Laden announced a fatwa declaring that Muslims should attack U.S. personnel and interests around the world, drive U.S. forces from Saudi Arabia, remove the Saudi royal family and other apostate Arab regimes from power, and liberate Palestine. Of these goals, the most vital, and yet most unattainable, for bin Ladin was the removal of the Saudi royal family, and in fact his campaign against the United States was based on his analysis of U.S. government support for the Saudi royal family's hold on power. Bin Laden moved to various locations—Pakistan, Afghanistan, the Sudan, and then back again to Afghanistan—to plan his campaign.

At Qaeda's devastating terrorist attack on the United States against New York City and Washington, D.C., on September 11, 2001, led to what U.S. officials styled the war on terror. It commenced with Operation ENDURING FREEDOM in Afghanistan a month later. Objectives of the operation included removing the Taliban from power, destroying Al Qaeda's training camps, and killing or capturing its operatives. In 2002, the Taliban was partially defeated, but many

Al Qaeda and Taliban members escaped, and new recruits soon appeared, drawn from Afghanistan and the religiously conservative northwest region of Pakistan. These groups continue to attack North Atlantic Treaty Organization (NATO) troops, Afghan government officials, and civilians. Suicide bombings, not before utilized in Afghanistan, became a regular occurrence, as Taliban and Al Qaeda operatives operated with relative freedom in the northwest reaches of Pakistan and could easily slip back across the border into Afghanistan. Terror attacks, often against civilians, continued in Afghanistan. At the same time, Al Qaeda was reasserting itself, and there were reports that the extremist Islamic State of Iraq and Syria (ISIS) was attempting to establish a foothold in the country.

Alleged ties between Iraqi president Saddam Hussein and Al Qaeda was one of the justifications for the U.S.-led invasion of Iraq (Operation IRAQI FREEDOM) in 2003. Although Saddam Hussein and his regime were swept from power, many groups of Sunni Muslims as well some Shiite militias opposed the occupation of Iraq and began to attack coalition forces. These included such groups as Al Qaeda in Mesopotamia, Ansar al-Islam, and others. They engaged in regular fighting but also used terrorist attacks, chiefly suicide bombings, against U.S., coalition, and Iraqi forces and civilians in attempts to destabilize the country so that they might drive the United States and its allies from Iraq and take power.

Between 2003 and 2005, more than 500 suicide car bombings and vest attacks occurred. Targets included refineries, electrical stations, police stations, open-air markets, and even mosques. The insurgents' intent was to undermine the public's confidence that the government would ever be able to provide essential services and security. However, in 2006, Sunni sheikhs, with strong financial incentives from both Saudi Arabia and the coalition, formed alliances to fight against Al Qaeda in Mesopotamia and other violent Islamist groups. This strategy was accompanied by a coalition troop surge that began in early 2007. Yet acts of terrorism increased in the spring of 2009 and targeted the sheikhs who had cooperated with the coalition forces.

After the last U.S. and coalition troops exited Iraq in December 2011, Iraq witnessed a steady increase in sectarian and Islamic extremist violence. By 2014, Al Qaeda in Iraq had given birth to the Islamic State of Iraq and Syria (ISIS), which began seizing large swaths of territory in Iraq and Syria. At the same time, the radical Sunni group was perpetrating horrific terror activities in both nations that included suicide bombings, car and truck bombings, beheadings, crucifixions, mass killings, and sexual enslavement. By early 2016, many international organizations and nations—including the United States—had declared ISIS guilty of committing genocide. The rise of ISIS and the violence it sponsored led the United States and other nations to renew military operations in Iraq, which soon spread to Syria. By late 2017, a multinational air coalition had been hammering ISIS targets for more than three years. At the same time, the United States had redeployed some 5,000 ground troops to Iraq and had sent several hundred others to Syria. By early 2018, the Iraqi and Syrian governments had both declared victory over ISIS, although there remained small pockets of ISIS insurgents in both countries into the summer of 2018. Meanwhile, ISIS elements were reportedly continuing to operate in Afghanistan and Pakistan.

In recent years, ISIS and Al Qaeda have sponsored or encouraged major terror attacks in areas well beyond the Middle East. Some of these include attacks in Boston, Massachusetts (April 2013); Paris (January and November 2015); San Bernardino, California (December 2015); Belgium (March 2016); Istanbul, Turkey (June 2016); Nice, France (July 2016); New Jersey and New York City (September 2016); Kabul, Afghanistan (February 2017); London (March 2017); Alexandria, Egypt (April 2017); Manchester, England (May 2017); Tehran, Iran (June 2017); Barcelona, Spain (August 2017); New York City (October 2017); Baghdad, Iraq (January 2018); Tripoli, Libya (May 2018); and Mastung and Bannu, Pakistan (July 2018). The diffusion of terrorism throughout large portions of the globe has made the ongoing global war on terror ever more difficult to wage. Since 2016, as ISIS suffered more losses on the battlefields of Iraq and Syria, the group increasingly turned toward terrorist attacks as an asymmetrical response to the war being waged against it.

At the same time, ISIS and Al Qaeda have attempted—with some success—to export their extremist ideology and terror tactics to such far-flung places as Africa and South Asia. In 2010, al-Shabaab pledged allegiance to Al Qaeda. That group operates chiefly in Somalia but has exported its operations to places such as Kenya, where it perpetrated a major terrorist attack that killed 63 people in a Nairobi shopping mall in September 2013. Since then there is ample evidence to suggest that al-Shabaab is attempting to spread its influence farther into East Africa. Boko Haram, a radical Islamist group based in Nigeria, has also been heavily influenced by Al Qaeda and ISIS, and in the spring of 2015 Boko Haram's leadership agreed to ally itself with ISIS. Boko Haram has perpetrated atrocities and terror attacks in several nations in Central and West-Central Africa, including a January 2015 massacre at Baga, Nigeria, in which at least

2,000 civilians were slaughtered. In March 2016, Al Qaeda in the Islamic Maghreb (AQIM) operatives struck an Ivory Coast resort, killing 16 people. It was believed that AQIM's attack had been inspired by ISIS.

The diffusion of terrorist ideology and attacks has flummoxed many world leaders, particularly those in the West who generally preside over multiethnic, multireligious nations. Many of these countries have porous or relatively open borders through which terrorists may come and go often without being detected. Stopping such activity might well impinge on freedom of movement for all. National leaders also fret about "home-grown" or "lone wolf" terrorists, who are even harder to detect and may have been radicalized online by terrorist groups such as Al Qaeda and ISIS. Indeed, the Internet has become a primary tool with which to indoctrinate and recruit would be terrorists around the world. Stopping such activity would be all but impossible without impinging on peoples' basic civil or constitutional rights.

Donald Redmond Dunne and Elliot Paul Chodoff

### See also
Al Qaeda; Hamas; Hezbollah; Iraq; Iraq War; Islamic State of Iraq and Syria; Israel

### References
Gettleman, Marvin, and Stuart Schaar, eds. *The Middle East and Islamic World Reader.* New York: Grove, 2003.

Gunaratna, Rohan. *Inside Al Qaeda: Global Network of Terror.* New York: Berkley Publishing Group, 2003.

Harel, Amos, and Avi Issacharoff. *34 Days: Israel, Hezbollah and the War in Lebanon.* New York: Palgrave Macmillan, 2008.

Hoffman, Bruce. *Inside Terrorism.* New York: Columbia University Press, 2006.

Wright, Lawrence. *The Terror Years: From Al Qaeda to the Islamic State.* New York: Knopf, 2016.

## Thani, Khalifa bin Hamad al- (1932–2016)

Emir of Qatar from 1972 to 1995 and a member of the ruling family of Al Thani. Born on September 17, 1932, Rayyan, Qatar, Sheikh Khalifa bin Hamad Al Thani was the fourth son of Hamad bin Ali al-Thani of the ruling Al Thani dynasty. His grandfather, Ali bin Abdullah Al Thani, was emir from 1913–1949, during Britain's rule of Qatar, and his father was heir apparent before his death in 1947. Sheikh Khalifa received a traditional Islamic education from private tutors.

In the 1950s, Khalifa held government posts in the ministries of security and education. In 1960, he assumed the role of minister of finance and petroleum affairs and was largely responsible for planning his country's economic development and modernization process. Officially recognized as deputy ruler and heir apparent to the throne of Qatar that same year, in 1960 Khalifa was responsible for government planning, policy, and implementation.

In 1968, three years before Qatar gained independence from Britain, Khalifa served as the first prime minister of the Provisional Federal Council, the forerunner of the United Arab Emirates (UAE). As such, he was influential in the establishment of the UAE, although Qatar became independent in September 1971.

Five months after Qatar became a sovereign nation, Khalifa deposed his cousin, Ahmad bin Ali Al Thani, and assumed power on February 22, 1972. In addition to assuming the title of emir, Khalifa retained his post as prime minister and immediately reorganized the government. In so doing he oversaw enormous economic growth, supported by massive revenues from oil sales and other natural resources.

On April 19, 1972, Khalifa amended the provisional constitution of Qatar and enlarged the Advisory Council. In addition, he cut the ruling family's allowance and increased spending on social services. Finally, after the price of oil increased dramatically beginning in 1973, Khalifa initiated a wave of industrial development in areas such as fertilizer production, steel making, and petrochemicals. In 1976, he fully nationalized Qatar's oil industry.

Qatar fought as a part of the United Nations–mandated coalition during the 1991 Persian Gulf War. In the Battle of Khafji, Qatari troops were among the first to engage Iraqi ground forces. However, Khalifa's involvement in the war was somewhat limited; his son Sheikh Hamad bin Khalifa, who wielded considerable power, essentially led Qatar during the war crisis. Hamad was also behind the 1992 bilateral Defense Cooperation Agreement that allowed the United States access to Qatari naval and air facilities. In 1995 Hamad, who had been the de facto ruler of Qatar for a number of years, deposed his father Khalifa in a bloodless coup d'état. This ended the 23-year reign of the emir.

The United States and other Western states quickly recognized Hamad as the new leader of Qatar. Khalifa meanwhile toured Arab capitals, where locals greeted him with open arms. Yet his dreams of returning to power were short-lived after his son gained a court order to freeze Khalifa's bank accounts. Khalifa bin Hamad lived in exile in France before returning to Qatar in 2004.

Khalifa died in Doha, Qatar, on October 23, 2016. He was succeeded by his son, Hamad bin Khalifa Al Thani.

Kirsty Anne Montgomery

**See also**
Persian Gulf War, Overview; Qatar; United Arab Emirates

**References**
Cordesman, Anthony H. *Bahrain, Oman, Qatar, and the UAE: Challenges of Security.* Boulder, CO: Westview, 1997.
Metz, Helen Chapin. *Persian Gulf States: Country Studies.* 3rd ed. Washington, DC: Federal Research Division, Library of Congress, 1994.
Zahlan, Rosemarie Said. *The Making of the Modern Gulf States: Kuwait, Bahrain, Qatar, the United Arab Emirates and Oman.* London: Unwin Hyman, 1989.

## Theodore I Laskaris (ca. 1174–1221)

Despot and first emperor of Nicaea (1204–1222) after the overthrow of the Byzantine Empire by the Fourth Crusade (1202–1204). Born around 1174 in Constantinople, while still a member of the Byzantine aristocracy Theodore married Anna, the second daughter of Emperor Alexios III Angelos (1199).

Theodore distinguished himself in the defense of Constantinople against the Latins, but with the latter having penetrated the city, in 1204 he fled with his wife and children to Nicaea (modern-day Iznik, Turkey), where he was acknowledged by the locals as their ruler as early as the fall of 1204. First using the title of despot, he was crowned emperor of the Romans in 1208 shortly after the election of the first patriarch of Constantinople in exile.

Theodore was unsuccessful in most of his military encounters with the Franks of the newly established Latin Empire of Constantinople and with the Venetians, but in 1211 in the Battle of Antioch on the Meander his Nicaeans successfully defeated an invasion by Sultan Kaykhusraw I of Rum at the instigation of deposed Byzantine emperor Alexios III, Theodore killing the sultan in combat.

Despite this victory Henry of Flanders, emperor of the Latin Empire, defeated Theodore's forces later that same year in the Battle of the Rhyndacus River (October 15), establishing his control over the southern shores of the Sea of Marmara. Nonetheless, Theodore was able to take advantage of the death of David Megas Komnenos, brother of Emperor Alexios I Megas Komnenos of Trebizond, in 1212 to extend his own control over Paphlagonia. Alexios I (r. 1204–1222) was, with his brother David, founder of the Empire of Trebizond. The two brothers were the only male descendants of Byzantine emperor Andronikos I, who had been dethroned and killed in 1185, and thus claimed to be the legitimate ruler of the Byzantine Empire following the conquest of Constantinople in 1204.

Theodore seems to have shown an interest in the negotiations between representatives of the Greek Orthodox and Latin Churches, and in 1214 he took an active role in the talks that took place in the Nicaean Empire. In 1214 Theodore concluded a peace treaty with the Latin Empire at Nymphaion, and in 1219 he married Marie de Courtenay, niece of the now deceased emperor Henry and daughter of the current regent, Yolanda of Flanders. In spite of predominantly peaceful relations, Theodore attacked the Latin Empire in 1220, but peace was restored. Theodore died in November 1221 without a male heir and was succeeded by his son-in-law, John III Doukas Vatatzes.

At the end of his reign Theodore ruled over a territory roughly coterminous with the old Roman provinces of Asia and Bithynia. Thanks to his courage and military skill, Theodore kept the Greek Byzantine nation alive and beat back the challenge posed by the Latins.

APHRODITE PAPAYIANNI AND SPENCER C. TUCKER

**See also**
Alexios III Angelos; Byzantine Empire

**References**
Brezeanu, Stelian. "Le premier traité économique entre Venise et Nicée." *Revue des études sud-est européennes* 12 (1974): 143–146.
Harris, Jonathan. *Byzantium and the Crusades.* New York: Palgrave Macmillan, 2003.
Savvides, Alexios G. C. "Constantine XI Lascaris, Uncrowned and Ephemeral 'Basileus of the Rhomaoi' after the Fall of Constantinople to the Fourth Crusade." *Byzantiaka* 7 (1987): 141–174.

## Thutmose III, Pharaoh (ca. 1504–1425 BCE)

Pharaoh (ruler) of Egypt. Dates vary widely, but Thutmose III (Thutmosis, full name Menkheperre' Thutmose) was born around 1504 BCE near Thebes, the second son of a concubine of Thutmose. Crowned pharaoh at age 7 with his stepmother and future mother-in-law, Hatshepsut, Thutmose was junior coregent for 22 years. During this time Egypt's hold on the Levant and Nubia weakened. On Hatshepsut's death in 1479, Thutmose assumed direct rule. He was immediately faced by a revolt against Egypt by some 300 cities in the Levant led by Kadesh and Megiddo.

Thutmose III was anxious to assert his power and restore Egyptian authority. After ordering the removal of

Hatshepsut's name from all public buildings, Thutmose rebuilt the Egyptian Army, which had been largely dormant for decades. Much is known of his military campaigns thanks to the royal scribe and army commander Thanuny, who wrote about Thutmose's campaigns. Indeed, Thutmose's Battle of Megiddo is said to have been the first in history of which there is record by an eyewitness.

In his second year as ruler, Thutmose marched the army into Palestine. Estimates of the size of his force range from 10,000 to 30,000 men. It is believed to have consisted largely of infantry, with some chariots. The infantrymen were armed with swords and axes and carried shields. The nobility fought from the chariots, probably as archers. Thutmose's adversaries were similarly armed.

The king of Kadesh had assembled a large force at the fortified city of Megiddo (Armageddon in Hebrew), north of Mount Carmel. Disregarding the advice of his generals, who feared an ambush, Thutmose chose the most direct route north to Megiddo, through a narrow pass. Apparently the king of Kadesh believed that the Egyptians would consider this route too risky, for he had deployed the bulk of his forces along another road to the east. Leading in person in a chariot, Thutmose pushed through Megiddo Pass, scattering its few defenders, then consolidated his forces while the king of Kadesh withdrew his covering troops back on Megiddo.

Preparing for what would probably be the largest battle of his many campaigns, Thutmose drew up his army in a concave formation of three main groups southwest of Megiddo and athwart the small Kina River. Both flanks were on high ground, with the left flank extending to the northwest of Megiddo to cut off any enemy escape along a road from the city. The rebel force was drawn up on high ground near Megiddo.

While the southern wing of his army held his adversary in place, Thutmose personally led the northern wing in an attack that sliced between the rebel left flank and Megiddo itself, enveloping the enemy and winning the battle. (Although the month and day are set as a lunar date, May 21, the years vary, with 1457, 1469, and 1479 often given.) The surviving enemy soldiers fled, saved by the fact that the Egyptian soldiers halted their pursuit to loot the enemy camp, something that greatly displeased Thutmose.

Thutmose then subjected Megiddo to a siege, lasting as long as eight months. On its surrender, Thutmose took most of the rebel kings prisoner, although the king of Kadesh escaped. Thutmose did capture the king's son and

Statue of Thutmose III at Amon Temple, Karnak, Egypt. Thutmose lived during ca. 1504–1425 BCE and was the sixth pharaoh of the 18th Dynasty of the New Kingdom. A great warrior and capable ruler, Thutmose mounted campaigns almost yearly that brought Egyptian control to the Euphrates River and the empire to its greatest extent. (Corel)

took him back to Egypt as a hostage, along with the sons of other captured kings. Among the spoils of war were more than 900 chariots and 2,200 horses as well as 200 suits of armor. Reportedly, in the campaign Thutmose acquired 426 pounds of gold and silver. The Assyrian, Babylonian, and Hittite kings all sent him gifts, which the Egyptians interpreted as tribute.

During the next two decades, Thutmose mounted as many as 16 additional campaigns. His 2nd and 3rd campaigns appear to have been little more than tours of Canaan and Syria to exact tribute. There is no record of his 4th campaign. The 5th, 6th, and 7th campaigns were all against Phoenician cities in Syria and Kadesh on the Orontes (Asi) River. The 8th campaign was against the state of Mitanni on the other side of the Euphrates, which Thutmose and his men crossed in boats, taking the Mitannians by surprise. His

9th campaign was a new invasion of Syria, probably more a raid than anything else.

The 10th campaign, against the king of Mitanni, involved considerably more fighting. The two sides came together near Aleppo, with Thutmose again victorious. Details regarding Thutmose's 11th and 12th campaigns are unknown but probably involved Qatna and Nukhashshe. He returned to the latter for his 13th campaign, while his 14th was against the Shasus, possibly in present-day Lebanon or across the Jordan River. His 15th campaign is obscure, but his 16th was sparked by a revolt led by Mitanni and involving major cities of Syria with significant fighting. Although Thutmose defeated the opposing armies, he failed to take Kadesh. His last campaign occurred late in his life and apparently in his 50th regnal year and was up the Nile southward into Nubia but only as far as the Fourth Cataract.

Thutmose fully understood the value of sea power, and one of his accomplishments was the creation of a fleet that controlled the eastern Mediterranean. Thutmose apparently was never defeated in battle and established an empire that extended to the Euphrates River and included the subjugation of Palestine and Syria as well as part of the Hittite Empire in Asia Minor (modern-day Turkey).

Thutmose ensured the peace of his empire by taking to Egypt the children of the conquered kings as hostages. They were educated to respect the pharaoh and then installed as governors in their fathers' cities. Thutmose proved to be a capable and effective administrator. He used the tribute and captives of his wars to rebuild the cities and temples of Egypt. According to the scribes, his reign lasted 54 years. He probably died in 1425 BCE near Thebes.

Thutmose III is widely regarded as one of the greatest, if not the greatest, of Egyptian pharaohs. His campaigns brought the Egyptian Empire to its greatest extent, into present-day southern Turkey, central Syria, and up the Nile into Nubia. He created a new vision for Egyptians of their place and role in the world, and the imperial system he created lasted well into the Twentieth Dynasty (1189–1077 BCE).

Spencer C. Tucker

**See also**
Egypt; Megiddo, Ancient Battle of; Thutmose III, Pharaoh

**References**
Cline, Eric H., and David O'Connor, ed. *Thutmose III: A New Biography.* Ann Arbor: University of Michigan Press, 2006.
Gardiner, Alan. *Egypt of the Pharaohs.* Oxford: Oxford University Press, 1964.
Nicolle, David. *The Mongol Warlords: Genghis Khan, Kublai Khan, Hulegu, Tamerlane.* London: Brookhampton Press, 1998.
Redford, Donald B. *The Wars in Syria and Lebanon of Thutmose III.* Leiden: Brill Academic Publishers, 2003.
Sokol. Edward D. *Tamerlane.* Lawrence, KS: Coronado, 1977.
Steindorff, George, and Keith C. Seele. *When Egypt Ruled the East.* Chicago: University of Chicago Press, 1963.

## Thymbra, Battle of (546 BCE)

In 612 BCE a coalition of Medes, Babylonians, and Scythians destroyed the city of Nineveh, ending the Assyrian Empire. The Babylonians took over the southern part of the empire, while the Medes ruled the north. Media was then the area of present-day northwestern Iran south of the Caspian Sea and into Armenia. The Medes also extended their control west to the borders of Asia Minor and east to Afghanistan.

Around 553 BCE Cyrus, son of Median king Astyages, took up arms against his father. Cyrus was supported by powerful members of the aristocracy who resented Astyages's tyrannical policies. The ensuing civil war went on for four years, but in 550 Cyrus won the Battle of Pasargadai in which he captured the Persian capital. He went on to take the Median capital of Ecbatana in 550–549 and then spent several years consolidating his authority, winning over many former enemies by giving them positions of authority in the army and government. Ruling as Cyrus II and known as Cyrus the Great, he became one of the most important of Persian rulers.

The increasing Persian power alarmed King Croesus of Lydia in Asia Minor, who appealed for assistance to Egypt, Babylon, and Sparta. Lydia was known for its excellent cavalry, which Cyrus rightly considered a threat to his own position. In 547 Croesus sent his troops across the Halys River into Media, and Cyrus gathered an army to meet them. His army moved west along the frontier between Media and Babylonia, crossing the Tigris River at Arbela. Gathering reinforcements in Armenia and Kurdistan, Cyrus gained the Cappadocian plain of Media in late 547.

The two sides fought an inconclusive winter battle near Pteria. Because his forces had already stripped Cappadocia of much of its food, Croesus decided to withdraw for the winter to his capital of Sardis in western Anatolia. Here he dismissed his Greek mercenaries and sent messages to his allies informing them what forces he would require for a spring campaign. Cyrus's advisers urged him to return home with his army as well and resume combat in the spring. Cyrus rejected what seemed to be wise counsel, though, and decided to fight while Croesus was bereft of the mercenaries. Cyrus also knew that Croesus's allies would not be able to reinforce him for at least several months.

After allowing sufficient time for Croesus to return to Sardis and dismiss the bulk of his forces, Cyrus followed, marching across Anatolia. Although Croesus received reports of the Persian advance, he dismissed them as untrue. Not until Cyrus had arrived with his army before Sardis did Croesus realize what had happened. Croesus still had reason for optimism, however. His forces were significantly larger than those of Cyrus, which numbered perhaps 20,000 to 50,000 men.

In early 546 the two armies came together on the Plain of Thymbra just outside of Sardis. Cyrus deployed his army in a large square, holding back his chariots and cavalry on the flanks, while Croesus deployed his forces in the traditional long ranks. Croesus opened the battle by sending his cavalry to envelop the Persian square. This created gaps in the Lydian line, and Cyrus sent against them cavalrymen mounted on camels. One of his generals had noted that at Pteria the Lydian horses were terrified of the camels the Persians used for supply purposes, and Cyrus now sought to take advantage of this. At the scent of the approaching camels, the Lydian horses bolted. Although the Lydian cavalrymen dismounted, they could not fight effectively on foot with their heavy lances.

Meanwhile, archers in the great Persian square launched volleys of arrows at the Lydian line, further breaking it apart. Cyrus then ordered his cavalry and infantry on the flanks to charge through the gaps in the opposing line, routing it. The remnants of the Lydian army withdrew into Sardis, which Cyrus promptly besieged.

After 14 days, the Persians took advantage of a weak point in the city wall where it joined a cliff. Cyrus dispatched a force to secure the high ground there and capture a portion of the wall as well as Croesus. Sardis surrendered the next day.

Cyrus's victory at Thymbra gave him the great resources of Lydia (Croesus's very name was synonymous with wealth). This cut off Babylonia from an important military ally and thus helped Cyrus to defeat the Neo-Babylonian Empire in 539 and establish the great Persian Empire.

SPENCER C. TUCKER

### See also
Babylonian Empire, Neo-; Cyrus II the Great

### References
Cook, J. M. *The Persian Empire*. New York: Schocken Books, 1983.
Lamb, Harold. *Cyrus the Great*. Garden City, NY: Doubleday, 1960.
Xenophon. *Cyropaedia*. Trans. Walter Miller. Cambridge, MA: Harvard University Press, 1979.

## Tiglath-Pileser I (?–1077 BCE)

Assyrian king and one of the greatest of Assyrian rulers. Tiglath-Pileser's birth date is unknown. The son of King Ashur-resh-ishi I, he became king of Assyria around 1116 BCE.

In 1112 Tiglath-Pileser went to war against the Moschi (Mushku), who had occupied portions of Assyrian territory along the upper Euphrates. He then conquered Commagene (the territory between the Toros Daglari and the Euphrates in modern-day southeastern Turkey). Next he invaded and drove the Hittites from Cappadocia (central Turkey). He then raided the Kurdish mountain areas to the north. Next he attacked Comana in Cappadocia. Later he campaigned in northern Syria against the Aramaeans and three times advanced as far as the sources of the Tigris River. His conquests ensured Assyria control of the trade routes from Persia and western Anatolia to the Mediterranean Sea. A great builder, Tiglith-Pileser restored a number of temples, including that of the gods Ashur and Hadad in the Assyrian capital city of Ashur. Tiglath-Pileser I died around 1077 BCE.

During Tiglath-Pileser's rule Assyria became the most powerful nation of the Middle East, a status it retained for the next 500 years.

SPENCER C. TUCKER

### See also
Assyrian Empire

### References
Olmstead, Albert T. E. *History of Assyria*. 1923, reprint, Chicago: University of Chicago Press, 1960.
Smith, Sidney. *Early History of Assyria to 1000 B.C.* London: Chatto & Windus, 1928.

## Tiglath-Pileser III (?–727 BCE)

King of Assyria. Tilglath-Pileser (Tukultī-Apil-Ešarra) became king as Tiglath-Pileser III. His birth date and place are unknown. He may have been a younger son of King Adad-mirari III but more probably was a military commander who seized the throne following a protracted period of unrest and decline. Shortly after becoming king in 745

BCE, Tiglath-Pileser III embarked on the first of many military campaigns. A major military reformer, he discarded the former militia system of military service in favor of a strong standing army based on spearmen, horse archers, and chariots. He also centralized authority, transferring powers formerly vested in the provincial governors to the monarch.

Tiglath-Pileser III first subdued the peoples of Syria who had become restless under Assyrian rule. He then established firm control over Media (central Iran). Next he turned north and defeated forces under King Sardur of Urartu in the region of present-day Armenia, who had extended his control into northern Mesopotamia and Syria. Tiglath-Pileser then invaded and overran Uratru itself, taking Arpad (near Aziz) after a prolonged three-year-long siege. When Arpad subsequently revolted against Assyrian rule, he recaptured it in 740 BCE.

Moving west, Tiglath-Pileser next campaigned against and defeated Azariah (Uzziah), king of Judah in 739. Tiglath-Pileser then turned north again, retaking Media (737) and Uratu (735). He next conquered Phoenicia and Philistia along the Mediterranean coast and took Damascus (734–733), going on to occupy most of the territory of present-day Israel. Tyre also became an Assyrian tributary state in 732. He then invaded Babylonia in 731 and, following two years of campaigning, captured the city of Babylon itself (729) and established Assyrian control, taking the title of king of Babylon under the name of Pulu.

Typically for Assyrian kings, Tiglath-Pileser spent virtually his entire reign campaigning. Assyrian rule was so harsh and arbitrary that the territories of the empire rebelled periodically and had to be reconquered. Prisoners were usually beheaded or impaled, and the conquered peoples were uprooted and transported to another part of the empire.

Having established the second Assyrian Empire, Tiglath-Pileser built a grand palace at Nineveh, where he died in 727. He was succeeded by his son Ulylaya, who took the throne under the name Shalmaneser V.

Tiglath-Pileser III's rule saw a considerable expansion of Assyrian power in the Near East. A highly effective general and indefatigable ruler, he created the Second Assyrian Empire and brought it to its greatest territorial extent.

SPENCER C. TUCKER

**See also**
Assyrian Empire

**References**
Astour, Michael. *The Arena of Tiglath-Pileser III's Campaign against Sarduri II (743 B.C.)*. Malibu, CA: Undena, 1979.

Tadmor, Hayim. *The Inscriptions of Tiglath-Pileser III, King of Assyria*. Jerusalem: Israel Academy of Science and Humanities, 1994.

# Tigris and Euphrates Valley

An area of the Fertile Crescent largely occupied by present-day Iraq and referred to in English as the "cradle of civilization" because it was the birthplace of the world's earliest cultures. It is known in Arabic as *al-bilad al-rafhidhayn* (land of the two rivers, referring to Mesopotamia). From the times of the Sumerians and Babylonians to the present, both the Tigris River and the Euphrates River have been dammed to control flooding and harnessed for irrigation and hydroelectric power. For more than six millennia, they have been essential to the environmental, economic, and political makeup of the Persian Gulf region. As the crossroads for trade between Egypt, India, and China, the Tigris-Euphrates River Valley has distinct geographical and political implications. The region has been subject to numerous invasions and controversies over the use of its waterways.

The valley's ecosystem of marshlands formed over thousands of years, but after Iraqi dictator Saddam Hussein's rise to power in the late 1970s, the ecology of the Tigris-Euphrates river system and salt marshes suffered greatly. It is estimated that up to 90 percent of the marshes and 60 percent of the wetlands were destroyed by Iraqi government policies. In the 1990s, the Hussein government's water-control projects drained the marsh areas to gain military access to the region and to drive out the rebellious native Marsh Arabs, leaving only about 10,000 people. Dikes and dams were built that diverted the waters of the Tigris and Euphrates around the marshes, causing the vegetation and water that fed the surrounding soil and many of the native wildlife and their habitats to disappear. The drainage policy was reversed by the new Iraqi government following the 2003 Anglo-American–led invasion of Iraq, and roughly half of the marshes have now been restored, but whether they will fully recover is uncertain.

Controversy over water rights and use of the rivers remains. Since 1990, Turkey's Southeastern Anatolia Development Project has built 22 dams and 19 power plants. The Turkish government hopes that by the end of its development on the two rivers nearly 2 million hectares of land will be irrigated. Syria in 1993 completed the Tabaqah (Euphrates) Dam to form a reservoir for irrigating cotton, but it and other dams have diverted much-needed water to Iraq.

Building dams was not a priority during Hussein's regime, but Iraq now has 7 dams in operation. Iraq is now concerned that construction of huge hydroelectric plants and dams along the two rivers by both Turkey and Syria will affect the social and economic stability of the region.

GARY LEE KERLEY

**See also**

Euphrates River; Marsh Arabs; Shatt al-Arab Waterway; Tigris River

**References**

Maxwell, Gavin. *People of the Reeds*. New York: Harper, 1957.

Metz, Helen Chapin, ed. *Iraq: A Country Study*. Washington, DC: Headquarters, Department of the Army, 1990.

Nicholson, Emma, and Peter Clark. *The Iraqi Marshlands: A Human and Environmental Study*. London: Politico's Publishing, 2002.

Thesiger, Wilfred. *The Marsh Arabs*. 2nd rev. ed. London: Harper.

# Tigris River

The Tigris River is one of the two great rivers of Mesopotamia, the other being the Euphrates. Located east of the Euphrates, the Tigris originates in eastern Turkey and flows southward for some 1,500 miles until it joins the Shatt al-Arab. Some 120 miles in length, the Shaat al-Arab connects both the Euphrates and the Tigris with the Persian Gulf.

The Tigris River has figured prominently in the history of the Middle East. Long an important transport route, the river can accommodate shallow-draft vessels as far as Baghdad, although rafts were necessary for transport upstream to Mosul. By 1861 steamers were plying the river, and the British employed steam gunboats in the Tigris against Ottoman forces during World War I. With the construction of the Basra-Baghdad-Mosul railway and highways, however, river transport declined in importance.

The Tigris is heavily dammed in Iraq and Turkey to provide water for irrigation in what is a semiarid climate. Damming was also necessary to prevent floods in Iraq following spring snow melt in the Turkish mountains. Recent Turkish dams on the Tigris (and on the Euphrates) have brought controversy for both the environmental effects within Turkey and the attendant reduction in the flow of water downstream. In 2014 representatives of the governments of Iraq and Turkey reached agreement in Geneva on standards pertaining to Tigris River flow.

Mosul Dam, located on the Tigris 45 miles north of Mosul and completed in 1985, is the largest dam in Iraq and the fourth largest in the Middle East. In 2014 fighters of the Islamic State of Iraq and Syria (ISIS) briefly took control of the dam, raising fears that this Islamic extremist group might blow up the dam in an effort to flood Mosul, Baghdad, and other Iraqi cities downstream. Indeed, the dam is in such poor repair that in 2016 U.S. embassy officials in Baghdad warned that should it give way, the ensuing release of water could drown as many as 1.5 million people. Although the Iraqi government is taking steps to remedy the situation, experts worry about the speed of the effort.

SPENCER C. TUCKER

**See also**

Euphrates River; Iraq; Islamic State of Iraq and Syria; Shatt al-Arab Waterway; Syria; Turkey

**References**

Hillel, Daniel. *Rivers of Eden: The Struggle for Water and the Quest for Peace in the Middle East*. New York: Oxford University Press, 1994.

Kliot, Nurit. *Water Resources and Conflict in the Middle East*. New York: Routledge, 1994.

Shapland, Greg. *Rivers of Discord: International Water Disputes in the Middle East*. New York: Palgrave Macmillan, 1997.

# Tiran Strait

*See* Strait of Tiran Crisis

# Titus, Emperor (39–81)

Titus Flavius Vespasianus was the second of the Flavian emperors and enjoyed a popular but short reign during 79–81. Born in 39 (Suetonius claims 41), he was the oldest son of Vespasian and was brought up in the imperial palace with Britannicus, the son of Claudius.

Titus began his military career in Germany and Britain, where he served with distinction. He was subsequently promoted to legionary legate in Judaea, assisting his father who commanded the suppression of the Jewish revolt during 67–70.

At the same time, Julius Vindex revolted in Gaul, and Servius Sulpicius Galba revolted in Spain. Emperor Nero, losing all support, committed suicide in 68. Galba then became emperor. Vespasian dispatched Titus to congratulate Galba on his accession, but Titus prudently avoided the ensuing struggle over the succession—the War of the Four Emperors in 69—and returned to Jerusalem.

Titus remained in Jerusalem when Vespasian was proclaimed emperor in Alexandria on July 1, 69. While his father was preoccupied with planning for civil war, Titus was in complete control of military operations in Judaea and completed the suppression of the revolt, destroying Jerusalem and the Jewish Temple in 70. Titus's troops acclaimed him as emperor, but out of modesty and loyalty to his father Titus refused the imperial role. The Jewish Flavius Josephus, the subsequent author of the *Jewish War* and *Jewish Antiquities,* was a client and friend of Vespasian and Titus and prophesied Vespasian's accession as emperor. Vespasian celebrated a triumph, depicted on the Arch of Titus at Rome.

Titus was his father's loyal subordinate and presumed successor. Returning to Rome in 71, Titus was accorded a triumph that included the execution of Simon bar Giora, one of the Jewish leaders of the Siege of Jerusalem. The triumphal Arch of Titus, located at one entrance to the Forum in Rome, memorializes Titus's victory. Titus was granted tribunician powers (an attribute of the emperor, often conferred on potential successors) in July 71 and later held the office of censor with his father. Titus and his younger brother Domitian both held consulships (now honorific offices only). The existence of Titus and Domitian guaranteed the survival of the Flavian dynasty.

Vespasian further distinguished Titus by conferring the praetorian prefecture on him in 71. The holder of this position was not merely commander of the Praetorian Guard but rather the emperor's deputy in civil administration.

On the death of Vespasian on June 23, 79, Titus became emperor. Like his father, Titus proved to be a capable emperor. He is famous for completion of the Coliseum in Rome, begun by his father.

Titus died on September 13, 81, from natural causes and not through any foul play, despite rumors at the time that Domitian had assassinated him. Titus married twice, but having no sons, he was succeeded as emperor by Domitian.

JAVIER LOPEZ

### See also
Jerusalem, Roman Siege of; Jewish-Roman War, First; Vespasian, Emperor

### References
Jones, Brian W. *The Emperor Titus.* New York: St. Martin's, 1984.
Levick, Barbara. *Vespasian.* London: Routledge, 1999.

## Townshend, Sir Charles Vere Ferrers (1861–1924)

British Army general. Born on February 21, 1861, in London, Charles Vere Ferrers Townshend was educated at a public school at Cranleigh (Surrey) and at Dartmouth Naval College. He joined the Royal Marines in 1881 and saw action in the Sudan. Having transferred to the Indian Army in 1886, Townshend withstood a protracted siege along the northwest frontier at Chitral in 1895. He led a Sudanese regiment with distinction in the Battle of Omdurman (September 8, 1898) and served in a staff position during the South African War (Second Boer War) of 1899–1902. Townshend was promoted to brigadier general in 1908 and to major general in 1911. Although he was recognized as an excellent officer who was courageous in battle, Townshend often alienated his superiors by vigorously promoting his own career and frequently applying for transfers.

Much to his despair, Townshend spent the first nine months of World War I on garrison duty in India before arriving in April 1915 in Mesopotamia to command the 6th Indian Division. Theater commander General Sir John Nixon ordered Townshend to proceed up the Tigris River to Baghdad. The campaign began with the capture of Ottoman defensive positions at Qurna on the Tigris in a large-scale amphibious operation on May 31, 1915.

With Ottoman forces apparently on the run, Townshend steamed up the Tigris in his river fleet to Amara in advance of his main body of troops, bluffing several towns and Ottoman garrisons into surrender, a progress that became known as "Townshend's Regatta." Following a brief sick leave, Townshend advanced farther up the Tigris and on September 27 turned two Ottoman divisions out of strong defensive positions at Kut al-Amara. Flushed with these victories, Nixon ordered him to move on Baghdad with what Townshend rightly considered to be insufficient force.

Townshend's Anglo-Indian force of 12,000 men was defeated with crippling losses south of Baghdad in the Battle of Ctesiphon on November 22. Townshend then withdrew to Kut, where on December 8 his men were invested by superior Turkish forces under Ottoman general Nureddin and German field marshal Colmar von der Goltz. The Turks repulsed three British relief attempts, and Townshend, who had remained passive and failed to attack in cooperation with the relief force, surrendered his remaining 10,000 men to Ottoman Sixth Army commander Halil Bey on April 29, 1916, after a siege of 147 days. It was the largest surrender of British troops until Singapore in 1942. While half of his men did not survive captivity, Townshend was held as an "honorable guest" on Prinkipo Island near Istanbul (Constantinople).

Townshend returned to Britain in October 1918, but his army career was terminated in 1920. Defeat at Kut and the apparent disregard for the fate of his men cast a pall of disgrace from which he never recovered. Townshend died in Paris, France, on May 18, 1924.

Dierk Walter

**See also**
Ctesiphon, 1915 Battle of; Goltz, Wilhelm Leopold Colmar von der; Kut al-Amara, Siege of; Mesopotamian Theater, World War I; Nixon, Sir John Eccles; Persian Front, World War I; Qurna, Battle of

**References**
Barker, A. J. *The Bastard War: The Mesopotamian Campaign of 1914–1918.* New York: Dial, 1967.
Barker, A. J. *Townshend of Kut: A Biography of Major-General Sir Charles Townshend K.C.B., D.S.O.* London: Cassell, 1967.
Erickson, Edward J. *Ordered to Die: A History of the Ottoman Army in the First World War.* Westport, CT: Greenwood, 2000.
Millar, Ronald William. *Death of an Army: The Siege of Kut, 1915–1916.* Boston: Houghton Mifflin, 1970.
Moberly, F. J. *The Campaign in Mesopotamia, 1914–1918.* 3 vols. Nashville: Battery, 1997–1998.
Townshend, Charles. *Desert Hell: The British Invasion of Mesopotamia.* Cambridge, MA: Belknap Press of Harvard University Press, 2011.
Townshend, Sir Charles V. F. *My Campaign in Mesopotamia.* London: Thornton Butterworth, 1920.

## Trajan (53–117)

Roman emperor. Born at Italica in Hispania Baetica (near present-day Seville, Spain) on September 18, 53, Marcus Ulpius Traianus carried the name of this father, a prominent Roman senator and general. Joining the Roman Army, young Trajan saw extensive service along the frontier. During 76–77 his father became governor of Syria, where Trajan became a tribune during 78–88. Taking command of a legion in Spain, he was ordered by Emperor Domitian to join him with his legion in Germany, where Trajan campaigned with success against Antonious Saturninus (88–89) and was rewarded by being named a consul in 91. Emperor Nerva (96–98), himself unpopular, won army approval by appointing the career soldier Trajan as governor of Upper Germany (96), then naming him his adoptive son and successor (October 97). Nerva thus began the adoptive process for emperors, leading to the so-called Five Good Emperors.

Trajan became emperor on the death of Nerva in 98 and immediately began an extensive inspection tour of the northern frontier. Although reportedly a man who drank to excess and a pederast, Trajan was an extraordinarily effective ruler. He kept a close watch on the army and maintained it at maximum efficiency. He also established good relations with the Senate and the power structure of Rome, freeing many citizens who had been unjustly imprisoned under Domitian and continuing the process begun under Nerva of returning private property to those from whom it had been confiscated.

A highly effective field commander, Trajan experienced his first major war as emperor against Dacia (101–102), located on the other side of the Daunbe River in present-day Romania. King Decabulus had broken the terms of a truce of 89, and Trajan invaded Dacia and defeated him. Decabulus, however, invaded Roman territory in 105, and Trajan again took to the field against him. After constructing a great bridge over the Danube, Trajan conquered all Dacia and destroyed its capital of Sarmizegetusa in 106. Decabulus committed suicide, and Trajan sent Romans to settle the area and annexed Dacia to the empire in 107, benefiting financially from the income provided by the area's gold mines. Trajan's Column survives today from the complex he built in Rome to celebrate his victory. A great builder, Trajan caused the construction of many arches and rebuilt many major roads.

Trajan also sent forces into the East. In the process he secured what became known as Arabia Petraea (today the Sinai Peninsula, the Negev desert, and southern Jordan).

The Parthian War (112–117) was prompted by the decision of the Parthians to place a ruler unacceptable to Rome on the throne of Armenia. Rome and Parthia had exercised joint hegemony over Armenia. Trajan led forces to Armenia, deposing its ruler and adding the country to the empire in 113. He then turned south and invaded Parthia, taking its major cities of Babylon, Seleucia, and finally the capital of Ctesiphon (115). Sailing down the Tigris River to the Persian Gulf, he annexed all Mesopotamia. He then captured the city of Susa and deposed Parthian king Ocroes I, placing his own candidate on the throne in what would be the farthest eastern projection of Roman power.

The fortress of Hatra in the Roman rear continued to resist a protracted siege, however. Trajan was also forced to deal with a Jewish revolt and a rebellion by the people of Mesopotamia against Roman rule. He put these down (117), but becoming ill, he departed for Rome. Trajan died en route from edema at Selinus, Cilicia, on August 8, 117. He was succeeded by Hadrian, believed to have been adopted by Trajan on his deathbed.

One of Rome's most capable emperors, Trajan was both a highly effective field commander and an efficient administrator.

Spencer C. Tucker

**See also**
Roman-Parthian Wars

**References**
Bennett, J. *Trajan: Optimus Princeps.* 2nd ed. New York: Routledge, 2001.
Campbell, J. B. *The Emperor and the Roman Army.* Oxford, UK: Clarendon, 1984.
Lepper, F. A. *Trajan's Parthian War.* London: Oxford University Press, 1948.

---

## Transjordan Campaign (1918)

World War I Middle Eastern campaign. By early 1918 British lieutenant general Sir Edmund Allenby's Egyptian Expeditionary Force (EEF) had secured southern Palestine and was poised to commence operations to the north. However, whereas the Dead Sea had previously protected his army's right flank, any further advance up the Palestinian coastal plain would take British forces past the Jordan River Valley. Farther east the Hejaz railway ran parallel to the Transjordan, and troops of the Ottoman Fourth Army could be quickly moved to threaten the right flank of any new British advance. Yet there were only two principal entry points connecting the Hejaz railway to the Transjordan: Samakh at the northern end of the valley, via the main junction at Daraa, and Amman, lying toward the southern end of the ranges that marked the eastern boundary of the Jordan Valley. A main road wound its way through these steep hills and cliffs from Amman to the village of Es Salt and then down to the valley floor and on to Jericho.

Allenby was quick to recognize the importance of Amman. Not only would its capture be crucial to any attempt to secure the Transjordan against Ottoman attacks on his right flank, but this would also cut the Hejaz railway, thereby isolating all remaining Ottoman garrisons between Amman and Medina to the south. British control of Amman would also allow the establishment of direct contact between the British forces and Emir Faisal's National Arab Army and would probably encourage more Arab tribes to join the revolt against their Ottoman masters. Finally, by taking Amman, the British, in conjunction with the Arabs, would be able to attack Daraa itself. The capture of Daraa would isolate the Jordan Valley and avoid the need for further operations there while at the same time cutting the direct link between the Hejaz railway and the Ottoman Seventh and Eighth Armies in Palestine.

In short, there were sound military and strategic reasons for Allenby and his army to try to capture Amman. Allenby had originally intended that any such attempt be made as a preliminary to a major offensive against the Seventh and Eighth Ottoman Armies in Palestine. These plans were formed on the basis of the promise of reinforcements from India and Mesopotamia to bring the units of the EEF to full strength and increase its number of infantry divisions from seven to nine.

The Ludendorff Offensives on the Western Front in France beginning on March 21, 1918, rendered Allenby's plans moot. Within two days of the German attack, Allenby received orders from London to prepare one of his British infantry divisions for embarkation to France. During the course of the next three months the EEF sent 60,000 men, including 54 infantry battalions, to the Western Front. Two Indian divisions and other units arrived to maintain a strength of seven infantry divisions, but these units lacked much of the supporting arms and equipment as well as experience of the British formations they replaced.

Because of the strains this placed on his command, Allenby postponed his planned offensive in Palestine. Nevertheless, he went ahead and launched two raids against Amman. The first (March 21–30, 1918) was carried out amid appalling weather, and while it seized Es Salt, the road from it to Amman turned into a quagmire. Forced to leave their artillery behind, the British attacked Amman for four consecutive days but could not break through its defenses. The second raid (April 30–May 4) again captured Es Salt but this time failed even to reach Amman in the face of stubborn Ottoman resistance along the road and vigorous counterattacks from the north and east. On both occasions Ottoman forces had been forewarned of the attacks due to poor security at Allenby's headquarters. In a related development, lack of support from the local Arab tribes supposedly sympathetic to Faisal had failed to materialize.

While the weather and the lack of Arab support may have been out of Allenby's hands, the root cause of the failure of the Transjordan raids appears to have been an episode of uncharacteristically poor judgment on his part. Allenby's failed gamble not only cost his army 3,000 casualties but also boosted the morale of Ottoman troops throughout Palestine and deterred local Arab tribes from declaring their support for Faisal and the Arab Revolt.

Even if the raids had succeeded, given the demands to transfer troops to the Western Front, the EEF would have struggled to defend the resulting extended line, let alone exploit such a victory as far as Daraa. Certainly by the time of the second raid Allenby could not doubt that his disrupted and weakened command was incapable of following up any victory at Amman. While it was true that the British government had pressured Allenby earlier in the year to remain on the offensive, this seems to have had little bearing on his decision to launch the raids. In fact, he was ordered on March 26 to go over to the defensive in view of the crisis in France.

Quite simply, Allenby seems to have overestimated the capabilities of his own troops while underestimating those of his opponent. With only a minimum of troops to spare for the enterprise (two divisions and a brigade in the first instance and three divisions in the second), Allenby was clearly attempting a coup de main and banking on an ineffective Ottoman response. The majority of both raiding parties consisted of Australian and New Zealand mounted troops, and while they had achieved some stunning successes against entrenched Ottoman positions in the past (including the recent victory at Beersheba), on this occasion they failed. The mountainous terrain, lack of artillery support, and an Ottoman Fourth Army alert to both the danger to and the importance of Amman combined to defeat the lightly equipped horsemen.

With the failure of the second raid, the Desert Mounted Corps retired to the Jordan Valley for the summer, and no further operations were attempted. In July a local offensive against the Abu Tulul salient by German and Ottoman troops was rebuffed, but apart from this foray, the Ottoman Fourth Army contented itself with improving its defenses. Amman and the Hejaz railway remained firmly in Ottoman hands until the Battle of Megiddo (September 19–25) later that year.

DAMIEN FENTON

**See also**
Allenby, Sir Edmund Henry Hynman; Amman Campaign; Arab Revolt in Palestine; Faisal I, King of Iraq; Megiddo, Battle of; Palestine and Syria Campaign, World War I

**References**
Braddon, Russell. *The Siege*. New York: Viking, 1970.
Bruce, Anthony P. C. *The Last Crusade: The Palestine Campaign in the First World War*. London: John Murray, 2002.
Bullock, David L. *Allenby's War: The Palestinian-Arabian Campaigns, 1916–1918*. London: Blandford, 1988.
Falls, Cyril. *Official History of the Great War: Military Operations; Egypt and Palestine: From June 1917 to the End of the War*. Vol 2. London: HMSO, 1930.
Hughes, Matthew. *Allenby and British Strategy in the Middle East, 1917–1919*. London: Frank Cass, 1999.
Wavell, Archibald P. *The Palestine Campaigns*. London: Constable, 1931.

# Trebizond, Empire of (1204–1461)

One of three Greek successor states of the Byzantine Empire that emerged with the conquest of Constantinople by the Fourth Crusade (1202–1204) in April 1204, the others being the despotate of Epiros in northern Greece and the empire of Nicaea in northwestern and northern Anatolia. Trebizond was located in northeastern Anatolia on the southern coast of the Black Sea and in the southern Crimea. It was named for its capital city of Trebizond (modern-day Trabzon, Turkey) and was in existence from 1204 until 1461. Although its foundation was not a direct consequence of the capture of Constantinople (modern-day Istanbul, Turkey) in 1204 by the Fourth Crusade (1202–1204), as was the case with the empire of Nicaea and the despotate of Epiros, it is generally considered to be one of the three Greek successor states. The empire was founded when two grandsons of the last Komnenian emperor of Byzantium, Andronikos I (d. 1185), namely the Megalokomnenoi (Great Komnenoi) Alexios I (1204–1222) and David (d. 1212/1213), seized Trebizond from its Byzantine duke, Nikephoros Palaiologos, with the help of their aunt Tamar, queen of Georgia, in March or early April 1204.

For most of its history the new state was cut off from the main Byzantine centers at Nicaea (modern-day Iznik, Turkey) and Constantinople and was restricted to a narrow strip of land along the southeast Pontic littoral. Its main coastal centers were Kerasous (modern-day Giresun, Turkey), Oinaion (modern-day Ünye), Amisos (modern-day Samsun), and Sinope (modern-day Sinop). Its chief inland centers were Bayberdon (modern-day Bayburt), Neocaesarea (modern-day Niksar), Amaseia (modern-day Amasya), and Payrae (modern-day Bafra).

Although not directly involved in the crusades, the empire holds a particular place in Anatolian affairs in the late Middle Ages, with its 21 rulers claiming the imperial Byzantine title until 1280/1282 and thereafter the title of *basileus* and *autokrator* (both reflecting Byzantine imperial usage) of all the East, the Iberians (i.e., Georgians), and Perateia.

The empire's early years were consumed in fratricidal strife with the rival empire of Nicaea and in attempts to ward off attacks from the Seljuks of Rum, who took Sinope in 1214 but failed twice before Trebizond itself (1205–1206 and 1222–1223). For much of the remainder of the century, the empire was in a state of vassalage to the Rum Sultanate and from 1243 to the Ilkhanids. However, with the decline of the sultanate, the empire was frequently attacked by Turkomans, especially the Ak-Koyunlu (White Sheep) confederacy, from the 1340s onward, and in the late 14th and early 15th centuries the Grand Komnenoi pursued a consistent policy of marriage alliances with Georgian and Turkoman dynasties. Alexios II (r. 1297–1330), Michael (r. 1344–1349), and Alexios III (r. 1349–1390) were also forced to grant commercial privileges to the Genoese and Venetians. However, the most menacing adversary was the Ottoman sultanate. John IV Kaloioannes (1429–1458/1460) was forced to acknowledge Ottoman suzerainty in 1456, and after a long Ottoman siege by land and sea the last Trebizondine ruler, David I (r. 1459–1461), was forced to capitulate on August 15, 1461, and surrender his capital to Sultan Mehmed II. The execution of David and his male descendants in 1463 shattered any future attempts to restore the Grand Komnenian Empire.

ALEXIOS G. C. SAVVIDES

### See also
Mehmed II, Sultan; Nicaea, Empire of; Ottoman Empire; Rum, Sultanate of

### References
Bryer, Anthony. *The Empire of Trebizond and the Pontos.* London: Variorum, 1980.
Bryer, Anthony, and David Winfield. *The Byzantine Monuments and Topography of the Pontos.* 2 vols. Washington, DC: Dumbarton Oaks Research Library and Collection, 1985.
Janssens, Emile. *Trébizonde en Colchide.* Bruxelles: Presses Universitaires de Bruxelles, 1969.
Karpov, Sergei. *L'Impero di Trebisonda, Venezia, Genoa e Roma, 1204–1461: Rapporti politici, diplomatici e commerciali.* Roma: Il Veltro, 1986.

## Trench, Battle of the
*See* Khandaq, Battle of

## Tripartite Declaration (May 25, 1950)

The Tripartite Declaration was a joint statement issued by the governments of the United Kingdom, France, and the United States on May 25, 1950, with the intention of controlling arms shipments to the Middle East, solidifying current territorial borders, and ensuring a measure of stability in the region. The declaration, formally known as the Tripartite Declaration Regarding the Armistice Borders, was issued after a meeting in London of the foreign ministers of Britain, France, and the United States. The conference undertook a review of security and stability in the Middle East. Concerned about access to oil in the Middle East as well as the continuing threat of Soviet encroachment, the three governments agreed to regulate arms sales and preserve the territorial status quo in the region. They hoped that by neutralizing the simmering Arab-Israeli conflict, they would be able to create a regional buffer against the potential expansion of Soviet Union influence in the Middle East.

The declaration recognized the need for the Arab states and Israel to maintain their armed forces at certain levels for internal security and legitimate self-defense. But it also stipulated that all future arms purchases in the Middle East would be carefully scrutinized. The governments of the United Kingdom, France, and the United States agreed that all future requests for arms and military equipment would be considered within the context of several principles.

First, the signatories mutually recognized their opposition to the development of an arms race between Israel and neighboring Arab states. Second, the three governments agreed that they would seek to gain assurances from any state supplying arms to Middle Eastern nations that the states requesting arms would not undertake hostile or aggressive actions against another state. Third, the signatories declared their opposition to the use of force or the threat of the use of force between states in the region. Finally, it was mutually agreed that should any government attempt to violate established frontiers or the 1949 armistice borders in the region, the signatories would take action to prevent such violations, within or outside of the United Nations (UN).

A broader aim of the Tripartite Declaration was to create a lasting status quo in the Middle East. The declaration can also be seen as one of the earliest attempts at arms control and limiting arms proliferation in the Middle East. Unfortunately, the declaration was largely ineffective at stopping the proliferation of arms in the region. The clause requiring that governments sell arms only with the assurance of the purchasing state that it would not use them for acts of aggression against other states proved entirely unenforceable. In addition, the Tripartite Declaration had no effect at all on arms purchases arranged between nonsignatories and Middle Eastern nations. Indeed, there was nothing to stop the Soviet Union and other nations in the communist bloc from supplying weaponry to the Middle East. In fact, within a few years of the Tripartite Declaration, Egypt turned to the Soviets for significant military support after the advent of the Gamal Abdel Nasser regime there. Iraq would follow suit after 1958, and Syria would begin purchasing large amounts of armaments from the Soviets beginning in the early 1960s. By that time the declaration was essentially null and void, as the Middle East became yet another region caught up in the superpower Cold War rivalry.

KEITH A. LEITICH

**See also**
Egypt; Iraq; Israel; Nasser, Gamal Abdel; Syria

**References**
Podeh, Elie. "The Desire to Belong Syndrome: Israel and Middle-Eastern Defense, 1948–1954." *Israel Studies* 4, no. 2 (Fall 1999): 121–144.
Reich, Bernard. *Arab-Israeli Conflict and Conciliation: A Documentary History*. Westport, CT: Greenwood, 1995.
Shlaim, Avi. "Israel between East and West, 1948–1956." *International Journal of Middle East Studies* 36 (July 2004): 657–673.

## Tripoli, County of

The fourth and last of the Frankish states founded in Outremer by the First Crusade (1096–1099). The county of Tripoli survived to the late 13th century.

The county of Tripoli came into existence when Raymond of Saint-Gilles, count of Toulouse, having seized Tortosa (modern-day Tartus, Lebanon) in 1102, attempted to conquer the surrounding country with his southern French followers, with the city of Tripoli as his principal objective. Raymond attacked Homs (1103), occupied Raphanea (modern-day Rafanyah, Syria) and Gibelet (modern-day Jubail, Lebanon) in 1104, and invested Tripoli (modern-day Trâblous, Lebanon) by constructing the castle of Mont-Pèlerin (Mount Pilgrim) outside the city.

On the death of Raymond in 1105, his cousin William-Jordan, count of Cerdagne, took possession of his conquests, while Raymond's younger son, Alphonse-Jordan, was sent back to Toulouse. William-Jordan had taken Arqah (1108 or 1109) when Raymond's elder son, Bertrand, arrived in Tortosa to claim his father's inheritance. King Baldwin I of Jerusalem imposed a settlement dividing the county between the two cousins, but William-Jordan died, whereupon Bertrand seized Arqah, and Tancred of Antioch, who had supported William-Jordan, occupied the rest of his share. Meanwhile, Bertrand had captured the city of Tripoli (1109) and pushed the frontier as far as the mountains that dominated the upper Orontes Valley. After Bertrand's death, his son Pons placed himself under the protection of Tancred, who ceded to him Tortosa, Chastel Blanc (Safitha), and Krak des Chevaliers (Isn al-Akrad). Thus, by 1113 the unity of the county was established.

Bertrand was succeeded by his descendants Pons (1112–1137), Raymond II (1137–1152), and Raymond III (1152–1187) without incident other than the unexpected arrival (1148) of the count of Toulouse, Alphonse-Jordan. The latter may have envisaged claiming the county for his own illegitimate son Bertrand but soon died in a manner regarded as suspicious; Bertrand seized the castle of Arima, and Raymond II was obliged to appeal to Nur al-Din, who recaptured the castle. The childless Raymond III intended that the county should pass to his godson Raymond, son of Bohemund III of Antioch, although he reserved the rights of the counts of Toulouse. Nevertheless, Bohemund III appointed his second son Bohemund (IV) as heir in Tripoli. After a war against his nephew Raymond-Rupen, Bohemund of Tripoli gained control of Antioch (1219), and thereafter Tripoli was ruled by successive princes of Antioch, who, however, maintained the separate character of the county, notably with regard to its legal customs, the usages of its chancery, and the appointment of its chief officers.

The political status of the county was a complex issue. Raymond of Saint-Gilles had benefited from the support of the Byzantine emperor, and Bertrand also received Byzantine subsidies and supplies and apparently agreed to support the emperor when he tried to establish a coalition against Tancred, but Pons did not continue such policies. In 1137 Raymond II went to Antioch to do homage to Emperor John II Komnenos, but by this time the county's ties with Byzantium had become much looser. Raymond III even led a punitive expedition against Cyprus when Manuel I Komnenos broke a promise of marriage made to his sister Melisende. Pons had done homage to the prince of Antioch when he received the north of the county from him, but this vassalage does not seem to have had further consequences. By contrast, Bertrand had done homage to the king of Jerusalem at the time of the capture of the city of Tripoli; he and his successors often took part in the military operations of the kings of Jerusalem, and King Amalric governed the county during the captivity of Raymond III (1164–1174), although it was always stipulated that Tripoli was not part of the kingdom.

At first the county expanded swiftly at the expense of its Muslim neighbors. The early counts apparently even intended to conquer Homs and Hama, and sometimes these towns did pay tribute. Yet it took a considerable effort to conquer Raphanea, which was taken only in 1126 by Pons after he had built the castle of Montferrand to control it, and both places were lost by 1137. Other castles (such as Tuban) dominated the plain of Homs, known to the Franks as the Bouquée (Arabic Buqaia). Raymond II even claimed fishing rights in the Lake of Homs. A series of defeats, however, demonstrated the limits of the counts' power: a Damascene raid reached Mont-Pèlerin in 1137 (the same year that Montferrand capitulated to Zangi), and Nur al-Din seized Tortosa in 1152 and in 1167 exploited the captivity of Raymond III to take Arima, Chastel Blanc, and Gibelcar (Jebel Akkar), albeit only temporarily. Thereafter the counts increasingly turned to the military orders to rebuild and garrison castles. In 1144 the Hospitallers received Krak des Chevaliers, Felis, and Lak (Tell Kalakh), which guarded the approaches to the valley of the Nahr al-Kabir; they received Chastel-Rouge in 1177, Tuban in 1180, and Eixserc in 1183. The Templars were given Tortosa in 1152 and Chastel Blanc in 1167. From that time, it was the orders who held the frontier facing Homs, Hama, and the mountain massif where the Nizaris, a sect of the Ismaili branch of Shiite Islam (better known as the Assassins) had built up a domain bristling with fortresses, of which at least one, La Coïble (al-Khawabi), had been captured from the Franks. The knights of the orders feared assassination by these fanatics much less than the secular rulers did: the Assassins' victims included Bohemund IV's eldest son Raymond (1213), but the orders were able to exact a tribute from the Ismailis.

The fall of the Kingdom of Jerusalem in 1187 occurred at a time when Count Raymond III's relations with the king, Guy of Lusignan, were strained. Although present at the crusader defeat in the Battle of Hattin (July 4, 1187), Raymond managed to return to his county, where he died not long afterward. In 1188 Saladin's army invaded the county but failed to take Krak des Chevaliers, Chastel Blanc, or Arima and made only a demonstration at the city of Tripoli, which was protected by a fleet sent by the king of Sicily. A complete collapse of Frankish positions in the county was thus prevented.

Hostilities with the Ayyubid rulers remained sporadic and primarily involved the military orders. Yet some Frankish raids went deep into Muslim territory, and Mamluk sultan Baybars I used one such as a pretext to punish the Christian inhabitants of Qara, supposedly for collusion with Frankish raiders from Gibelcar. The situation changed with the arrival of the Mongols in Syria and their alliance with Bohemund VI of Antioch-Tripoli. In 1261 Baybars invaded the county, capturing Tuban, Arqah, Halba, and Coliath and thus reaching the coastal plain. The Mamluks also seized Krak des Chevaliers, Chastel Blanc, and Gibelcar, and they forced the counts to share the revenues of the plain of Tripoli.

A treaty concluded in 1281 delimited the size of the count's domain, which included Tripoli, Nephin, Botron, Gibelet, Arqah, and 51 villages, and established a condominium in the mountains. Bohemund V married Luciana of Segni, a relative of Pope Innocent IV. Her brother Paul of Conti became bishop of Tripoli and attracted a number of "Roman" clerics and laymen who became members of the count's entourage. During the reign of Bohemund VI, a conflict broke out between the count and the lord of Gibelet, who had fought against him during the War of St. Sabas. In the course of hostilities, Bohemund was wounded by Bertrand of Gibelet, who was subsequently killed by peasants. Eventually a settlement was imposed by the master of the Temple, who set up a commission to mediate between the count and the barons (1258). Another conflict broke out between the count and the Gibelet family on the occasion of the marriage of a brother of the lord of Gibelet to the heiress of a rich lord whom Bohemund VI had intended for another suitor. The ensuing struggle pitted the Templars and Paul of Conti against the count and his vassals: the Templars' house in Tripoli and the cathedral were besieged, and many "Romans" were massacred, while the Templars attacked the count at Botron and inflicted two defeats upon him (1278–1279). When eventually it seemed that peace might be restored, the master of the Temple and Guy of Gibelet tried to take Tripoli by surprise. Guy was obliged to submit and was imprisoned and left to die of starvation. His heir placed himself under the sultan's protection.

On the death of Count Bohemund VII (1287), a fresh conflict erupted because of his mother's decision to confer the regency on Bartholomew Mansel, bishop of Tortosa. The count's vassals rejected this choice and refused to accept Bohemund's sister Lucy as countess unless she removed the cause of their grievances. A commune was established at Tripoli under the leadership of Bartholomew Embriaco, lord of Gibelet, and sought an alliance with Genoa. Lucy, who had found refuge at Nephin under the protection of the Hospitallers, was installed as countess after accepting the terms of the Genoese, but enemies of the republic provoked an intervention by Sultan Qalawun, who seized Tripoli by surprise on April 26, 1289, massacring its inhabitants. The lordship of Gibelet was permitted to survive as an *iqa'* (a grant of revenue in payment for military services) belonging to Qalawun's empire. Only in 1303, after the withdrawal of the Mongols from Syria, did the last of the Embriaci set fire to his castle and abandon the lordship.

Jean Richard

**See also**
Amalric of Jerusalem; Assassins; Baldwin I of Jerusalem; Baybars I; Bohemund VI of Antioch-Tripoli; Bohemund VII of Antioch-Tripoli; Crusades in the Holy Land, Christian; Hattin, Battle of; Manuel I Komnenos, Emperor; Nur al-Din; Qalawun; Saladin; Tancred

**References**

Deschamps, Paul. *La défense du comté de Tripoli et de la principauté d'Antioche.* Paris: Geuthner, 1973.

Deschamps, Paul. *Le comté de Tripoli sous la dynastie toulousaine (1102–1187).* 2nd ed. Paris: Geuthner, 2000.

Deschamps, Paul. *Le Crac des Chevaliers.* Paris: Geuthner, 1934.

Irwin, Robert. "The Mamlūk Conquest of the County of Tripoli." In *Crusade and Settlement: Papers Read at the First Conference of the Society for the Study of the Crusades and the Latin East,* ed. Peter W. Edbury, 246–250. Cardiff, UK: University College Cardiff Press, 1985.

Riley-Smith, Jonathan S. C. "The Templars and the Castle of Tortosa." *English Historical Review* 84 (1969): 278–288.

# Troop Surge, U.S., Iraq War

The term "troop surge" refers to the early January 2007 decision by the George W. Bush administration to deploy approximately 20,000–30,000 additional American troops to Iraq to arrest insurgent-inspired violence. Those insurgents included both Al Qaeda terrorists and rival Sunni and Shiite sectarian militias. U.S. Army general David Petraeus, commander of U.S. forces in Iraq, is credited with the surge strategy. The impetus for the troop surge was the November 2006 U.S. midterm election in which the Republican Party lost control of both houses of Congress largely because of growing public opposition to the Iraq War and dismay with the level of casualties among U.S. soldiers.

With the Democrats having made opposition to the Iraq War the central issue of the 2006 election and calling for a withdrawal of U.S. troops from Iraq, Bush announced a change in strategy to reduce violence and improve security in Iraq. This followed the resignation of Secretary of Defense Donald Rumsfeld, a key architect of the Iraq War, in December 2006. Referring to a "new way forward" in a televised national speech on January 10, 2007, the president announced a plan to secure the capital city, Baghdad, from both Al Qaeda and sectarian militias and rid Anbar Province (stretching west from Baghdad to the Syrian and Jordanian borders) of Al Qaeda fighters. Approximately 16,000 additional U.S. troops were deployed to secure Baghdad, and another 4,000 troops were sent to Anbar Province.

By June 15, 2007, with these additional troops in place, the surge began in earnest. Instead of simply launching raids against Al Qaeda and sectarian militias, U.S. and Iraqi forces in Baghdad established posts within neighborhoods controlled by these groups. In Anbar Province because of public outrage sparked by Al Qaeda's murdering of hundreds of Iraqi Muslims, Sunni tribes severed their ties with Al Qaeda and aligned themselves with the Iraqi government and the U.S. military. In so doing, these tribes formed militias ("Sons of Iraq") comprising some 103,000 men, many of them former insurgents and terrorists, armed and paid by the United States to defend their communities against Al Qaeda. Although this proved effective in rooting out Al Qaeda insurgents in the short term, in the long run these militias will have to be reintegrated into the Iraqi military or police forces or find gainful employment elsewhere in order for them to remain loyal to the Iraqi government.

The surge strategy emerged from the belated recognition that Iraqi security forces were as yet unable to provide security without significant American assistance and support and that the number of U.S. troops had to be increased to effectively stamp out the insurgency. It was also recognized that to defeat an insurgency, military forces must take up residence and maintain a physical presence within the areas infested by insurgents, because in the words of General Petraeus, "you can't commute to this fight; you must live among the people." Accordingly, the surge increased U.S. troop strength in Baghdad and Anbar Province, the two most violent regions of Iraq, not only to clear but also to hold territory, thus reinforcing Iraqi military and police presence. U.S. troops were also to assist Iraqi forces as they established security. The downside of this strategy was that it prolonged the foreign military presence in the country, which is what had provoked the insurgents and thus gave them cause to continue resistance.

Since early 2007 with continued American military assistance, particularly in the form of logistics and air support, Iraqi forces have demonstrated increasing competence and skill in battling insurgents and providing security. In addition, Iraqi prime minister Nuri al-Maliki, a leader of the Islamic Dawa Party, showed a willingness to confront militias, including Shia militias, as evinced by Iraqi military operations in the cities of Basra, Baghdad, and Ninawa. Also, Muqtada al-Sadr, the leader of the powerful Shiite Mahdi Army, agreed not to confront the Iraqi government and U.S. military and has maintained that promise since mid-June 2007. In both Baghdad and Anbar Province Al Qaeda was seriously weakened, but unfortunately its signature tactic of inflicting mass casualties through car bombs targeting Shiites, including Shiite mosques, had resumed again in 2009. Coalition efforts in these two areas forced the group to flee to the northern city of Mosul and the surrounding province of Nineveh as well as to the religiously mixed province of Diyala. Iraqi and U.S. forces then battled Al Qaeda in these

Soldiers with the latest Stryker brigade to arrive in Iraq as part of the U.S. troop "surge" seen here on patrol in Taji, May 15, 2007. (U.S. Department of Defense)

new areas. Nonetheless, the situation remained volatile, with Al Qaeda still a dangerous threat and the possibility that any one of the factors that had contributed to the military gains under the surge could be reversed and produce an increase in violence.

The results of the troop surge could be seen in the statistical decline in both Iraqi and U.S. casualties. According to a June 2008 Pentagon report, violence in Iraq dropped between 40 and 80 percent from presurge levels, while the number of violent incidents fell to their lowest point in more than four years. In addition, fewer U.S. troops were killed in May 2008, when 19 died (compared to 126 in May 2007), than in any other month since the invasion of Iraq in March 2003; 29 U.S. troops were killed in June 2008 compared to 101 in June 2007. The Iraqi Body Count, a group that keeps a tally of Iraqi casualties from media reports, noted that 712 Iraqi civilian deaths occurred in June 2008, less than a third of the average during the summer of 2007.

Expanding revenues from the export of Iraqi oil and continued growth in the Iraqi economy (4 percent in 2007) also contributed to a decline in violence in the country as unemployment dropped. The June 2008 Pentagon report, however, warned that security gains could not be preserved without continued progress in economic development and reconstruction; increasing government services, such as electricity (currently available for a national daily average of only 14.9 hours, including just 13 hours in Baghdad); health care; water and sewage treatment; and national political reconciliation among Iraq's rival religious and political groups. An important step in political reconciliation was taken with the passage of the long-awaited and long-needed Amnesty Law on February 26, 2008, for Iraqis accused or convicted of crimes of terrorism. In addition, Iraq's largest Sunni Arab bloc, the Iraqi Accord Front, prepared to rejoin Prime Minister Maliki's cabinet after a yearlong boycott protesting the government's alleged policies of excluding and marginalizing Sunnis. The inclusion of Sunnis into Iraq's government was cited by both the United States and Iraq as a major factor in bringing about national unity. Sunni Arabs had a great deal of power during Saddam Hussein's regime but became marginalized after he was toppled in 2003. Since then, the Iraqi government has been dominated by Shiites and Kurds.

Despite these developments, it was acknowledged that the Iraqi government remained corrupt and inefficient and that it lacked sufficiently qualified personnel to effectively govern and execute policy and programs.

The surge also entered presidential politics in the United States. In the summer of 2008, Republican candidate John McCain made much of his advocacy of and support for the surge. He sought to make the troop surge a major issue in the campaign, attacking his Democratic opponent Barack Obama for his opposition to it. Obama pointed out that it was not just the increase in troop strength but also the reconciliation of the Sunni tribes that had contributed to the decrease in violence. He also noted that McCain had supported the earlier Bush policies that had not worked, whereas he (Obama) had opposed the war from the beginning.

In sum, the surge proved to be successful, but as Petraeus remarked, "we can't kill ourselves out of this endeavor." Ultimately, it is only the Iraqi government that can build a stable, secure, prosperous, and united nation.

STEFAN BROOKS

### See also
Al Qaeda in Iraq; Anbar Awakening Movement; Iraq Insurgency; Iraq War; Maliki, Nuri Muhammed Kamil al-; Petraeus, David Howell; Sadr, Muqtada al-

### References
Engel, Richard. *War Journal: My Five Years in Iraq.* New York: Simon and Schuster, 2008.

Galbraith, Peter. *The End of Iraq: How American Incompetence Created a War without End.* New York: Simon and Schuster, 2007.

Isikoff, Michael, and David Corn. *Hubris: The Inside Story of Spin, Scandal, and the Selling of the Iraq War.* New York: Three Rivers/Random House, 2007.

## Troy, Siege of (1194–1184 BCE)

The chief source on the Siege of Troy is Homer's great epic, the *Iliad*. Its 24 chapters treat the last year of the siege; however, it was composed two or three centuries after the siege. Modern archaeological excavations have revealed a series of strata identifying a number of different cities built on the site. The one associated with the siege is the seventh stratum (from the bottom); it bears traces of a fire, and according to Homer, a great fire ended the siege. Scientific experts agree that the fire in the seventh stratum occurred in 1184 BCE. Homer tells us that the siege of Troy by the Mycenaeans (the mainland Greeks) went on for 10 years, hence the starting date of 1194 BCE.

The siege was undoubtedly motivated by economics. Located at the southern entrance to the Hellespont (the Dardanelles today), Troy controlled the important trade between East and West—that is, from the Black Sea to the Mediterranean. Along this route flowed such commodities as grain, precious metals, and timber to construct ships. Troy was allied with a number of other neighboring city-states, and the Mycenaeans saw this as a threat to their position in the Mediterranean. Homer tells us that the cause of the conflict was the rape of Helen, wife of Menelaus, king of Sparta, by Paris, the son of Piram, king of Troy. Helen fled to Troy with Paris, possibly taking part of Menelaus's treasure. Another account has the Trojans turning an official visit to Sparta into a raid of revenge for something done to them by the Greeks.

In any case, according to Homer, the city-states of Greece were outraged and provided both contingents of troops and 1,200 ships, which then came under the command of Agamemnon, king of Mycenae and the brother of Menelaus. Homer tells us that on the Greek side the greatest heroes of the fighting were Achilles, king of the Myrmidons of Thessaly, and Ulysses, king of Ithaca. On the Trojan side there were Hector, son of Piram, and Aeneas, son of Venus and Anchises.

Following an unsuccessful effort to take Troy by assault, the Greeks settled in for a siege, which apparently was not complete. The Trojans were able to communicate by land to the interior most of the time. Homer indicates that the ships were brought up on land, where they were protected by entrenchments. Quarreling between Agamemnon and Achilles served to divide the Greeks, allowing Hector and the Trojans to attack and destroy a number of the beached Greek ships. Following the deaths of a number of prominent figures on each side (including Hector and Achilles), the Greeks found themselves in desperate straits. Both sides, however, were exhausted by the long siege.

At this point, Ulysses came up with the ruse of an enormous wooden horse. Left on the field, it contained Ulysses and a number of other Greek warriors. The remaining Greeks got in their ships and sailed away. The Trojans, believing that the Greeks had given up, thought that the trophy had religious significance and brought it inside the city. At night Ulysses and his warriors climbed down out of the horse, signaled to the fleet offshore, and opened the city gates. The Trojans were taken by surprise, and the city was burned.

Some have suggested that the "Trojan horse" that ended the siege was rather a great moveable siege tower of wood, covered by horse hides for the protection of those working it, that the Greeks set against the western—and weakest—part of the great wall that protected the fortress. Others believe that the wooden horse refers to some type of battering ram or to the image of a horse painted on one of the gates of the city, which was opened by a Trojan traitor. In any case, as a consequence of their victory, the Greeks secured control of the important trade through the Dardanelles and the Black Sea.

SPENCER C. TUCKER

**See also**
Dardanelles Campaign

**References**
*The Iliad of Homer.* Translated by Alexander Pope. New York: Heritage Press, 1943.
Melegari, Vezio. *The Great Military Sieges.* New York: Thomas Y. Crowell, 1972.

## Turaba, Battle of (May 21, 1919)
*See* Saudi-Hashemite War

## Turan Shah (?–1250)

Al-Malik al-Muazzam Ghayath al-Din Turan Shah, known simply as Turan Shah (Turanshah), was the last Ayyubid sultan of Egypt in a brief reign of November 22, 1249, to May 2, 1250. Born in Syria (date unknown), Turan Shah was one of four sons of Sultan As-Salih Ayyub and acted as his father's deputy at Hisn Kayfa and other dominions of Diyar Bakr until the latter's death. As-Salih Ayyub had rejected advice to recall Turan Shah to the court in Egypt; neither did he nominate Turan Shah (or anyone else) as successor during his final illness, even though the Christian crusaders of the Seventh Crusade (1248–1254) in the Holy Land, led by King Louis IX of France, had occupied the eastern part of the Nile Delta.

When As-Salih Ayyub died on November 22, 1249, his widow Shajar al-Durr, with the help of prominent Egyptian military commanders, concealed his death from both the army and the local citizenry, fearing a collapse in morale in the struggle against the crusaders. Shajar al-Durr then dispatched an embassy to Hisn Kayfa to summon Turan Shah to Cairo to assume the sultanate.

Turan Shah arrived with a small military force in Egypt via Damascus and formally assumed power in early March 1250 with the full support of his father's widow and the military commanders. In April 1250 the Egyptians defeated the crusaders under King Louis IX in the delta, although Turan Shah made little personal contribution to the Ayyubid victory. Indeed, he showed ingratitude toward his father's commanders, replacing some of them with his Iraqi companions. He further alienated many of those close to the throne and isolated himself by threatening and even killing some of his key subordinates while drunk. Encouraged by Shajar al-Durr, a number of commanders led by Baybars and Aqtay assassinated Turan Shah in brutal fashion on May 2, 1250.

This coup d'état marked the inception of the Mamluk Sultanate in Egypt. King Louis was allowed to depart Egypt for Palestine the same month.

TAEF EL-AZHARI

**See also**
Baybars I; Crusades in the Holy Land, Christian; Egypt; Louis IX, King of France

**References**
Ayalon, David. *Eunuchs, Caliphs and Sultans: A Study of Power Relationships.* Jerusalem: Hebrew University Pres, 1999.
Humphreys, R. Stephen. *From Saladin to the Mongols: The Ayyubids of Damascus 1193–1260.* Albany: New York University Press, 1977

## Turcopoles

Turcopoles or Turcoples (Greek, Tourkopouloi; Latin, Turcopoli or Turcopolieri) were Christianized mercenaries of Turkish origin in the service of Byzantine and Frankish armies in the Balkans and the Near and Middle East in the period of the crusades, especially from the late 11th century onward.

Turcopoles were found fighting for the Franks of Outremer against the Muslims (12th–13th centuries), for Byzantium against the Catalan invaders in Greece, on the latter's side against the Eastern Empire (14th century), and in Cyprus and Rhodes in the course of the Latin dominations there (late 12th to early 16th centuries). Western sources such as Raymond of Aguilers and Albert of Aachen present them mainly as offspring of mixed marriages between Turkish (either Seljuk or Turkoman) fathers (archaically referred to as Persians by the Byzantines) and Christian (Anatolian Greek) mothers.

Initially encountered in late 11th-century Byzantine sources as Tourkopouloi, the Turcopoles were active in imperial service chiefly in the 13th and 14th centuries, according to the Byzantine historians Pachymeres and Gregoras. Turcopoles played a significant role in the Byzantine-Frankish War of 1263–1264 in the Peloponnese, while in the late 13th century the Turcopole descendants of Kay-Kawus II, Seljuk sultan of Rum (r. 1246–1257), were installed in imperial lands in central and northwest Macedonia in the area of the Axios (Vardar) River. In the early 14th century, several of them were settled in western Thrace following their participation in Catalan raids against Byzantium.

In Frankish states of Outremer, Cyprus, and Greece, Turcopoles were employed in imitation of the Byzantine Tourkopouloi. Several 12th- and 13th-century Western sources mention them as troops in the service of various Frankish rulers or of the military orders. After 1204 the Latin Empire of Constantinople received Turcopole reinforcements against the Bulgarian Asenids. In Cyprus, from 1192 the Lusignan rulers distributed fiefs among Turcopole mounted troops under the command of an officer known as the Grand Turcopolier, and from that time Latin sources refer to them mainly as light-armed archers who served in the capacity of police forces. The Hospitaller Knights effected the conquest of Rhodes (1306–1309/1310) with the help of light-armed horsemen called Turcopolieri or Turcupelleri, who were then used extensively by the order to patrol the island's coasts.

ALEXIOS G. C. SAVVIDES

**See also**
Constantinople, Latin Empire of; Seljuk Dynasty

**References**
Moravcsik, Gyula. *Byzantinoturcica*. 2nd ed., 2 vols. Leiden: Brill, 1983.
Richard, Jean. "Les turcoples au service des royaumes de Jérusalem et de Chypre: Musulmans convertis ou chrétiens orientaux?" *Revue des études islamiques* 54 (1986): 259–270.
Savvides, Alexios G. C. "Late Byzantine and Western Historiographers on Turkish Mercenaries in Greek and Latin Armies: The Turcoples/Tourkopouloi." In *The Making of Byzantine History: Studies Dedicated to D. M. Nicol*, ed. Roderick Beaton and Charlotte Roueché, 122–136. Aldershot, UK: Variorum, 1993.
Savvides, Alexios G. C. "Morea and Islam, 8th–15th Centuries: A Survey." *Journal of Oriental and African Studies* 2 (1990): 47–75.

## Turkey

The Republic of Turkey is a Eurasian nation covering 300,948 square miles. Bordering eight countries, Turkey is strategically located in both Europe and Asia Minor and includes the important Turkish Straits (the Dardanelles, the Sea of Marmara, and the Bosporus) connecting the Black Sea with the Mediterranean and separating Thrace from Anatolia. Eastern Thrace is the small geographical area of European Turkey. It is bordered by Greece to the west and Bulgaria to the northwest. The Aegean Sea is to the east, and the Mediterranean is to the south. Most of Turkey lies in Asia Minor, in Anatolia. In Asia Minor, Turkey shares common borders with Georgia to the northwest; Armenia, Iran, and the Azerbaijani enclave of Nakhchivan to the east; and Syria and Iraq to the south. The Black Sea is to the north.

Turkey is a democratic, secular, unitary, constitutional republic. A president, elected by popular vote, is head of state. There is also a prime minister, elected by parliament. In 2018 Turkey had a population of some 82 million. Its capital city is Ankara. Ethnic Turks constitute some 70–75 percent of the population, while Kurds make up perhaps 18 percent. Muslims are said to make up between 96.4 and 99.8 percent of the population. Three-quarters of these are Sunni Muslims. There are perhaps 200,000 Christians and 26,000 Jews.

An important regional power, Turkey has a strong military. Its 411,000 active-duty personnel and 186,000 personnel in the active reserve give Turkey the second-largest military establishment of the North Atlantic Treaty Organization (NATO). One source ranks Turkey's military as the world's eighth strongest. Turkey, which is a member of the United Nations (UN), NATO, the Council of Europe, and the G-20, became an associate member of the European Economic Commission in 1963, joined the European Union Customs Union in 1995, and started full membership negotiations with the European Union (EU) in 2005.

Turkey was home to many ancient civilizations, including those of the Greeks, Thracians, Armenians, and Assyrians. It then formed the western reaches of the Persian Empire, which was conquered by King Alexander III (the Great) of Macedon in 334 BCE and Hellenized. Although Turkey was subsequently part of the Roman Empire, Greek language and culture predominated.

In 324 CE, Emperor Constantine I designated Byzantium on the Bosporus as the new capital of the Roman Empire. In 395 the empire was permanently divided, and Byzantium, popularly known as Constantinople, became the capital of the Eastern Roman Empire, later designated the Byzantine Empire. Between the third and seventh centuries the Byzantine Empire engaged in frequent warfare with the Sassanid Empire to the east, with the result that both were weakened to the extent that they fell prey to Muslim conquest. The Seljuk Turks became a threat in the 11th century and defeated the Byzantines in the important Battle of Manzikert in 1071.

Osman I established the Ottoman Empire in 1299. Constantinople (now Istanbul) fell in 1453, and the empire subsequently included a considerable swath of the Mediterranean

# Turkey

Basin, including much of Southeastern Europe, Western Asia, North Africa, and the Middle East. The empire reached the peak of its power and influence from the 15th to 17th centuries, especially under Sultan Suleiman the Magnificent (r. 1520–1566). After the failure of a second Ottoman siege of Vienna in 1683 and the end of the Great Turkish War in 1699, the Ottoman Empire underwent steady decline and came to be known as "the Sick Man of Europe."

Russian efforts to secure control of the Bosporus and gain access to the Mediterranean brought the Crimean War of 1853–1856. Britain and France supported the Ottomans. Most of the fighting occurred in the Crimean Peninsula, with the major military operation being the siege of the Russian Black Sea port and the naval base of Sevastopol (October 17, 1854–September 9, 1855). The allies, joined by the Kingdom of Sardinia (Sardinia-Piedmont), at last secured Sevastopol and victory in the war.

Nonetheless, Russia persisted. It formed a coalition with the Ottoman principalities of Romania, Bulgaria, Serbia, and Montenegro and then in the Russo-Turkish War of 1877–1878 secured Kars and Batumi in the Caucasus and annexed the Budjak region. Romania, Serbia, and Montenegro were all formally recognized as independent, and Bulgaria was recognized as a principality. The subsequent Congress of Berlin also allowed Austria-Hungary to occupy Bosnia and Herzegovina and allowed Great Britain to secure Cyprus, ceded by the Ottomans in return for British protection against Russia.

Ottoman weakness brought increasing demands from within the empire for reform. Turkish nationalism was also on the rise. In 1908 the Committee of Union and Progress (CUP), part of the Young Turk movement, convinced Sultan Abdulhamid (Abdul Hamid) II (r. 1876–1909) to restore the parliament. Following an attempted counterrevolution later that year the CUP deposed the sultan and then on April 27, 1909, replaced him with his younger brother, Mehmed V.

Italy also sought to take advantage to secure Tripoli (present-day Libya). Italy declared war on September 29, 1911. Although Italian forces quickly occupied the city of Tripoli and outnumbered the scattered Ottoman garrisons, Italian forces were largely confined to coastal beachheads well into 1912. The war was brought to an end only when the Italians expanded the conflict to the eastern Mediterranean. In the Treaty of Lausanne of October 18, 1912, Italy secured sovereignty over Libya.

As many observers had predicted, Italy's success encouraged the Balkan states to try to take the remaining Ottoman territory in Europe. Montenegro declared war on October 8, 1912, followed by Bulgaria, Serbia, and Greece. During the next eight months, the larger and better-armed military establishments of the Balkan powers overcame the numerically inferior and strategically disadvantaged Ottoman armies. During October 28–November 3, the Bulgarians won a major victory over the Ottomans at Lulé Burgas. They then advanced to the last Ottoman defenses before Istanbul, although the Russians then warned the Bulgarians not to attempt to occupy the city. On November 16–18 the Serbs defeated the badly outnumbered Ottomans in the Battle of Monastir (Bitola), giving the Serbs control of southwestern Macedonia.

An acute international crisis ensued on November 24 when the Austro-Hungarian government announced its opposition to Serbian access to the Adriatic and insisted on the creation of an independent Albania. Italy supported the Austrians, while Russia backed Serbia. With both Austria and Russia mobilizing and with Austria allied to Germany and Russia allied to France, a general European war threatened. The crisis receded when Russia—clearly unready for war—withdrew its support from Serbia. On December 3 the Ottomans concluded an armistice with Bulgaria and Serbia, and a peace conference opened in London, only to collapse when the Ottomans refused to surrender Adrianople, the Aegean Islands, and Crete.

On January 23, 1913, a day after the major powers convinced the Ottoman government to yield Adrianople, a coup d'état occurred in Istanbul. The empire's steady stream of military defeats greatly discredited Mehmed V, and the CUP Young Turks seized power. A triumvirate now dominated Ottoman affairs: Ismail Enver Pasha as minister of war, Mehmed Talât Pasha as minister of the interior, and Ahmed Djemal Pasha as naval minister.

On February 3 the war resumed. The Bulgarians secured Adrianople on March 26. On April 16 the Ottomans concluded an armistice with Bulgaria, and the other warring Balkan powers soon followed suit. Tensions remained high over Albania, however, with both Montenegro and Serbia opposing its independence and occupying territory assigned to it and only yielding it under threat of war with Austria-Hungary. Talks in London resumed, and the Balkan states accepted the settlement developed by the Great Powers. In the Treaty of London of May 30 the Ottoman Empire ceded to the Balkan states the vast majority of its territory in Europe.

The victorious Balkan states now fell to quarreling among themselves regarding the spoils. Bulgaria had been the big winner territorially, but there were sharp differences between it and Serbia and Greece over Macedonia. Greece and Serbia resolved their own differences, and on June 1, 1913, they concluded a treaty of alliance against Bulgaria. With Greece and Serbia now planning war, on June 29 Bulgarian commander General Michael Savov opted for a preemptive strike without informing his government. Although the Bulgarian government subsequently disavowed Savov's action, the Serbs and Greeks, joined by Romania and even Ottoman forces, attacked Bulgaria in the Second Balkan War. By July 30, Bulgaria had been defeated. Under the terms of the Treaty of Bucharest of August 10, Bulgaria was left with only a small portion of Macedonia. On September 29 in a treaty between the Ottoman Empire and Bulgaria, the Ottomans recovered Adrianople in Europe and territory up to the Maritza River.

The Balkans were now largely a tinderbox. The rival European big power alliance systems of the Dual Alliance of Germany and Austria-Hungary and the Triple Entente of Russia, France, and Great Britain courted the Ottoman Empire, for in 1914 it still controlled all of Anatolia, Mesopotamia, Syria, and Palestine. Germany won the struggle for influence, and in December 1913 a military mission led by Lieutenant General Otto Liman von Sanders arrived in Istanbul to help reorganize the Ottoman Army.

Following the assassination of Archduke Franz Ferdinand in Sarajevo on June 28, 1914, the Austrian government actively sought war with Serbia, seeing the opportunity to end the threat to its own existence posed by Slavic nationalism. On July 28 Austrian forces invaded Serbia, beginning the Third Balkan War, which a few days later became World War I when Russia mobilized and Germany declared war on it. On August 2, Ottoman leaders signed a secret alliance with Germany promising joint action if Russia intervened militarily in the conflict between Austria-Hungary and Serbia. The next day the Ottoman Empire mobilized its military.

The Entente rejected Enver Pasha's offer of neutrality in return for a large loan and modification of the financial concessions enjoyed by the European powers in the Ottoman Empire. The British government had sequestered two Ottoman dreadnoughts under construction in British yards. As the ships had been paid for by public subscription, this action rallied Ottoman public opinion against the Entente. Enver also accepted a gift of the German battle cruiser *Goeben* and light cruiser *Breslau*, both of which had eluded French and British warships in the Mediterranean and escaped into the straits and then to Istanbul.

On September 8 the Ottoman Empire abolished the financial capitulations. And on October 28 the *Goeben* and *Breslau* (given Turkish names but still under German command) attacked Russian ports and shipping in the Black Sea. Russia declared war on November 4, followed by Britain and France the next day. On November 14 Mehmed V proclaimed jihad (holy war) against the Entente.

The Ottoman Empire's entry into World War I had immense consequences. Closure of the Dardanelles isolated Russia from its allies and severely weakened its ability to wage war. Great Britain was also forced to shift major resources to protect the Suez Canal. Soon Ottoman forces were fighting in Caucasia, Egypt, and Mesopotamia as well as in Europe at the Dardanelles.

At home the CUP leadership instituted numerous administrative and bureaucratic reforms and also worked to improve infrastructure. The government also challenged the power of the influential Islamic clerics by bringing Islam more under its own control. Prior to the war, the government had subordinated the Islamic courts to its secular system. During the war, the government secularized the religious courts and schools. The government also carried out major reforms in the emancipation of women, equalizing their legal rights in marriage and inheritance and enhancing educational and employment opportunities for girls and women.

The Ottoman leaders believed that the war would be short and thus failed to institute planning to secure sufficient food and civilian supplies for an extended conflict. By 1915, there was a grain shortage in Istanbul and many other cities. Famine became widespread because of the lack of agricultural laborers (many had been conscripted into the military), a prolonged drought, and the monopolization of railroads by the military. War refugees fleeing to the cities brought instability and a further drain on resources. Inflation skyrocketed, reaching perhaps 400 percent in the first year of the war alone.

While the potentially most dangerous front for the Ottomans was Thrace, where the frontier was less than 180 miles from the national capital, the major Ottoman military effort came in Caucasia. Enver hoped to catch the Russians off guard, regain territory lost to the Russians earlier, and stimulate revolts among Muslims in southern Russia.

The Ottoman Army was, however, unready for war. Ignoring this, the weather, mountainous terrain, and supply problems, Enver launched his Third Army from Armenia on December 17, 1914. Following some initial success, the Ottomans were badly mauled by the Russians in the Battle of Sarikamish (December 22, 1914–January 17, 1915). Rebuilt in the spring of 1915, the Third Army was almost destroyed in the Russian Erzurum Offensive early in 1916. Later in the same year, the Second Army was nearly destroyed in an offensive farther south in the Caucasus. After that, the war in the east ground to a halt. In 1918, after the November 1917 Bolshevik Revolution brought a Russian military withdrawal from Caucasia, the Third Army went over to the offensive and penetrated deep into Armenia and Azerbaijan.

In the European portions of the empire, the First and Fifth Armies under Liman von Sanders turned back and inflicted heavy losses on the Entente's Gallipoli landing of April 1915. But when the Allies broke out from Salonika in 1918, there was nothing left to prevent them from entering Istanbul.

The British easily rebuffed Ottoman efforts to seize the Suez Canal from Palestine in 1915 and 1916. Afterward, the Sinai-Palestinian front evolved into a state of protracted, indecisive warfare, aggravated by the rising Arab Revolt. During 1916–1917 the British built up their resources, and in 1918 the German-Ottoman army group finally collapsed under repeated attacks, and British forces seized Jerusalem and Damascus.

In Mesopotamia, an Anglo-Indian thrust toward Baghdad ended in a Turkish triumph on April 29, 1916, when an entire division surrendered to the Ottoman Sixth Army at Kut. Thereafter this theater remained more or less quiet until the British renewed their advance in 1918. Several Turkish invasions of Persia proved to be insignificant.

The war badly weakened the empire's internal stability. Two groups in particular rebelled against rule from Istanbul: the Armenian Christians in eastern Anatolia and the Arabs in the Hejaz. The Armenians, who sought independence, forced the Ottomans to divert troops there from major campaigns elsewhere. In an effort to stabilize the situation, the government forcibly relocated the Armenian population to the Syrian Desert, an area remote from potential collusion with the Russians. Inadequate water, food, clothing, and medical supplies brought the deaths of as many as 1.5 million Armenians in the forced desert march and other government operations both during and after World War I. This episode in Turkish history has been called the Armenian Massacre and, controversially, the Armenian Genocide.

The other major source of revolt was the Arab community of the Hejaz. Its push for independence began in June 1916 under the leadership of Sharif Hussein ibn Ali. His third son, Prince Faisal, and British lieutenant colonel T. E. Lawrence played key roles in this, supporting the British military campaign in Palestine and Syria in 1917 and 1918. The Arab insurgents forced the Ottomans to divert troops and attention from the main British advances.

An armistice ending Ottoman participation in the war was signed on October 30, 1918, aboard the British battleship *Agamemnon* off the island of Mudros. Allied troops then occupied much of the empire. According to recent estimates, in the war the Ottomans suffered some 770,000 dead and 760,000 wounded, each about 27 percent of the manpower mobilized; some 145,000 were taken prisoner.

The government at Istanbul meanwhile disintegrated, and its leaders fled. The Ottoman Empire unofficially ended on November 15 when Sultan Mehmed VI, who had succeeded to the throne only in October on the death of Mehmed V, established a new government under the control of Greek and British troops. The British, French, and Italians then established a tripartite administration of Istanbul, garrisoned the Alexandretta-Smyrna-Constantinople railway, and encouraged the creation of independent Georgian and Armenian armies. A buildup of British, Italian, French, and Greek forces also occurred.

Turkish nationalist resistance to these moves developed first in eastern Anatolia, particularly under General Mustafa Kemal in Samsun and General Kazım Karabekir in Erzurum. The nationalists turned to the Bolsheviks of Russia for military aid, concluding an agreement the following spring. Contact with the Bolsheviks also provided a bargaining chip with the anticommunist British.

On May 15, 1919, a large Greek force occupied Smyrna (Izmir). The Turkish War of Independence (1919–1923) can be said to have begun on May 19 with clashes between Greek and Turkish nationalist forces. The Greco-Turkish War is known to the Turks as the Western Front. Fighting in the east was largely between the Turks and Armenians. During September 4–11, an assembly of Turkish nationalist representatives from all the Anatolia provinces met in the city of Sivas in east-central Turkey.

On March 16, 1920, British troops seized government buildings in Istanbul and set up a pro-Allied cabinet, preparatory to forcing the Ottoman government to sign the punitive Treaty of Sèvres (August 10, 1920). In it, Ottoman control would be largely restricted to Anatolia, with the economy controlled by the Entente. The treaty made the Kingdom of Hejaz independent, gave Smyrna and many Aegean islands to Greece, ceded the Dodecanese Islands to Italy, internationalized the Turkish Straits, and granted Armenia independence. In addition, Syria, Palestine, and Mesopotamia were established as independent states under French and British mandates. The latter two powers also signed the San Remo oil agreement, delimiting their oil interests in Persia, Mesopotamia, and the Caucasus. These demands were presented to the sultan and the pro-Allied cabinet on June 10, 1920. Twelve days later, about 60,000 Greek troops advanced from Smyrna.

The Turkish forces were unprepared for the Greek military advance, and the Greek columns soon seized major cities in western Anatolia and Adrianople in Thrace. In the east an Armenian attack collapsed near Erzurum, and a Turkish counterattack forced the Armenians to sue for peace. The ensuing peace treaty reduced Armenia to the province of Erivan. On March 16, 1921, the Turkish nationalists signed a treaty with Soviet Russia delimiting the border in the east and securing additional military assistance.

On March 23, 1921, the Greeks opened a new offensive toward Ankara. It soon stalled, but the Greeks regrouped and advanced again in July. The Turks withdrew across the Sakarya River and stood on the defensive. During August 23–September 13, they fought a successful series of meeting engagements known as the Battle of the Sakarya across a 120-mile front. At this point the French (as with the Italians earlier in the summer) agreed to withdraw from Anatolia in return for economic concessions.

During the winter, the British attempted to negotiate an end to the war through a partial revision of the Treaty of Sèvres. The nationalists in Ankara refused, and the Turks took the offensive on August 18, 1922. Superior Turkish cavalry forced the Greeks back; the retreat then turned into a rout, and the Greeks fled to the coast.

In response to the Turkish advance toward Istanbul, a British force landed to protect the straits. Armistice negotiations began shortly thereafter. The Greeks agreed to an armistice on October 11, 1922. The opposing sides opened negotiations in November and signed the Treaty of Lausanne on July 24, 1923. Although the Turks agreed to relinquish all prewar non-Turkish territory in the Middle East and lost almost all the offshore islands in the Aegean and the Mediterranean, the Greeks departed Anatolia, the Turks avoided any reparations, and no legal restrictions remained on their government.

The war had seen widespread atrocities committed by Greeks against Turks and by Turks against Greeks and Armenians, and an ensuing population exchange treaty concluded by the two governments saw Greek orthodox citizens of Turkey and Turkish and Greek Muslim citizens residing in Greece subjected to a forced exchange. Some 1.5 million Orthodox Christians from Turkey and 500,000 Turks and Greek Muslims from Greece were uprooted from their homelands.

The last British troops evacuated Istanbul on October 2, and the Republic of Turkey was formally established under the presidency of Kemal on October 29, 1923. Determined to see his country a modern, secular nation, Kemal (known as Ataturk and regarded as the father of modern-day Turkey) immediately embarked on an ambitious reform program. Expanding education was a major priority, with primary education made free and compulsory. Women were accorded equal civil and political rights, and taxation was reformed. Ataturk also pushed a policy of Turkification and sharply limited the influence of Islam. The new Turkey, although much more homogeneous than before, was also far smaller, and its foreign policy centered on preserving the status quo.

Ataturk died in 1938, and Premier Ismet Inönü, his closest associate, took over the leadership of the nation and its one political party, the People's Party. Inönü was reelected president in 1943.

During World War II, Turkey resisted pressure from both sides to join the war. With the consequences of World War I still fresh, Turkish leaders were understandably reluctant to embark on a new conflict, especially as their military was obsolete. Turkey did keep its large army mobilized throughout the conflict, however, worried by the ambitions not only of Germany and the Soviet Union but also those of Italy. Once the Germans controlled the Balkans, Ankara signed the Treaty of Territorial Integrity and Friendship with Berlin on June 18, 1941. The treaty extended economic concessions to Germany. Inönü strongly resisted pressure by the Germans to enter the war on the Axis side, however.

When the tide of war turned against the Axis, Turkey resumed its general pro-West position, although it also resisted pressure from the United States and Britain to enter the war on their side. Although Turkey declared war on Germany on February 23, 1945, this was to ensure membership in the UN.

Following the war, the Soviet Union applied tremendous pressure on Turkey to secure the two northeastern Turkish provinces of Kars and Ardahan, both of which had long been in contention between the two countries. Moscow also demanded a share of control over defense of the Turkish Straits. This Soviet pressure on Turkey and the simultaneous communist threat to Greece led to the 1947 U.S. Truman Doctrine and to Turkish membership in NATO in 1952. During the Cold War, Turkey was firmly in the Western camp and sent troops to fight on the UN side in the Korean War (1950–1953).

The Turkish single-party period ended in 1945. During the next decades Turkey experienced a tumultuous transition to multiparty democracy marked by a fragmented party system and unstable governments. With increasing domestic strife, the Turkish military, which regarded itself as the principal defender of the ideals of Ataturk and a secular state, mounted coup d'états in 1960, 1971, and 1980. To their credit, however, each time the army leaders restored the democratic process.

In foreign affairs, ongoing tensions between Turkey and Greece regarding Cyprus almost brought war between the two NATO states. Following a decade of violence in Cyprus and a coup on July 15, 1974, by the Greek EOKA B paramilitary organization that sought enosis (union with Greece), five days later Turkish forces invaded the island. The Turks took additional territory in northern Cyprus, encouraged Turks to migrate there, and set up the Turkish Republic of Northern Cyprus. The standoff regarding Cyprus continues, with the Turkish-installed republic recognized only by Turkey itself.

Turkey was a member of the international coalition that expelled Iraqi forces from Kuwait in the 1991 Persian Gulf War. Although Turkey provided no ground troops, it dispatched two frigates to the Persian Gulf and was heavily involved in basing coalition forces, including air assets. Ankara also allowed overflights of its airspace when the air war began in January. Rigid enforcement of the international economic blockade against Iraq cost Turkey an estimated $3 billion in revenues, chiefly from shutting down an oil pipeline through the country.

Generally speaking, aside from strong opposition to the creation of a Kurdish state, Turkey maintained a policy of alleged noninvolvement in Middle Eastern affairs for fear of being dragged into one of the region's internecine conflicts, especially the Arab-Israeli conflict. Turkey generally enjoyed cordial diplomatic relations with both Israel and its Arab neighbors. Turkey's involvement in the 1955 Baghdad Pact, pushed by the United States and scorned by Muslim states except for Iraq and Iran, did alienate it from much of the Middle East, especially Egypt. In the early 1960s, Turkey sought a more evenhanded Middle East policy that meant less cooperation with the United States and greater rapprochement with the Arab states.

An entente developed between Turkey and Israel in the 1990s. Both were Western-oriented states with close ties to the United States, and both sought closer ties with Europe. Leaders in both countries worried about the threats to this posed by terrorism, Islamic radicalism, and perceived hostile regimes in Syria and Iran. Cooperation included trade and tourism but also military cooperation, with Israeli upgrades of Turkish military equipment and the sharing of intelligence. Inhibiting this cooperation was strong public sympathy in Turkey toward the Palestinians.

Turkish-Israeli relations plummeted on May 31, 2010, when Israeli commandos mounted a raid in international waters of the Mediterranean against a flotilla of six ships, carrying humanitarian assistance to Gaza, that had originated in Turkey. Violence flared, and the Israeli commandos killed 10 people in one of the ships. Condemnation of Israel was especially strong in Turkey, which recalled its ambassador from Israel. The 2014 Israel-Gaza War also saw Turkish president Recep Tayyip Erdoğan strongly condemn Israel's policies, characterizing them as more "barbaric" than those of Adolf Hitler.

Following the terrorist attacks on the United States of September 11, 2001, Ankara immediately offered its full support. It extended airspace and refueling rights as the U.S.-led coalition began operations against Afghanistan's Taliban regime in October 2001, and the next year Turkey dispatched troops to join the International Security Assistance Force in Afghanistan. The deployment numbered some 1,700 personnel in 2009, but the troops were not engaged in combat operations, and Erdoğan, then Turkish prime minister, resisted pressure from Washington to offer more combat troops in large part because Turkish public opinion was ambivalent about the mission in Afghanistan. Erdoğan also initially opposed any NATO military intervention in the 2011 Libyan Civil War, and when Turkey did go along with the operation, its military remained largely on the sidelines. Erdoğan also angered Washington when he engaged the Russians in a series of bilateral commercial and energy agreements to include a major pipeline deal in December 2014. He was also largely silent regarding the Russian seizure of Crimea and its intervention in eastern Ukraine.

In recent years, three political parties have vied for power in Turkey. The largest by far is the Justice and Development Party (AKP), followed in order of magnitude by the Republican People's Party (CHP) and the far-right Nationalist Movement Party (MHP). Erdoğan's AKP won a surprise landslide victory in the November 2002 legislative elections, and the charismatic Erdoğan became prime minister in 2003. He held that post until 2014, when he was elected president. Concerns were raised about the AKP's Islamic-based ideology, but Erdoğan initially focused on economic reform and securing Turkey's entrance into the EU.

Erdoğan did move against the Turkish military, long regarded as the guardian of the secular state, and dramatically purged its leadership. In July 2011, the nation's top 4 military commanders abruptly resigned to protest the detention of hundreds of military officers on charges of conspiring against the government in 2009. In September 2012, a Turkish court convicted 330 military officers, including the top former commanders of the army, navy, and air force, of the plot and sentenced them to as much as 20 years in prison. In August 2013, there were additional sentences. Former chief of staff of the army General Ilker Basbug received a life sentence; 3 former members of the Turkish parliament also received prison terms, as did 20 journalists. This purge brought international condemnation regarding judicial fairness and was seen by many as a move to stifle dissent.

Erdoğan also secured constitutional changes in 2010 that served to strengthen his authority. While the Turkish economy has registered solid gains, Erdoğan's Islamic stance and his authoritarianism remain concerns for many secular Turks as well as Western governments.

Erdoğan has also taken a hard line regarding the Kurds. The Kurds live in the mountainous region known as Kurdistan, encompassing southeastern Turkey, eastern Syria, northern Iraq, and western Iran. Kurdistan includes the oil fields in Iraq around Kirkuk and is rich in other natural resources. Most Kurds are Sunni Muslims.

Turkey is home to 15 million Kurds, representing nearly half of the world's Kurdish population of 30 million, the world's largest ethnic group without a state. (Some 7 million Kurds live in Iran, 6 million live in Iraq, and 2 million live in Syria.) Statehood appeared on the verge of realization following World War I. Indeed, the 1920 Treaty of Sèvres promised the Kurds autonomy leading to statehood after a plebiscite, but the Treaty of Lausanne of 1923 recognized Turkish sovereignty over northern Kurdistan, while the remainder of Kurdish territory fell in Iran and the new states of Iraq and Syria.

Kurdish rebellions occurred in the 1960s and 1970s in Iraq, while Kurds revolted in Iran during the Iranian Revolution of 1979. In 1988, Iraqi president Saddam Hussein ordered military force against the Iraqi Kurds. Conventional attacks and chemical warfare destroyed some 2,000 villages and killed upwards of 180,000 Kurds. The Iraqi Army crushed other Kurdish revolts following the Persian Gulf War in 1991 and also in 1995.

Turkey's Kurds have long claimed discrimination and attempts by the government to eradicate their culture. On November 27, 1978, Abdullah Öcalan established the Partiya Karkerên Kurdistan (Kurdistan Workers' Party, PKK), initially composed largely of students. In addition to stressing Kurdish nationalism, the PKK initially espoused a Marxist ideology.

Almost immediately the PKK was locked in combat with right-wing parties in Turkey and with those Kurdish leaders it accused of collaboration with the government. Beginning in 1984 the PKK commenced an insurgency in southern Turkey, home to most Turkish Kurds. This took the form of attacks and bombings against government institutions and military installations. In the mid-1990s the PKK initiated suicide bombings, the majority of which were carried out by women.

In March 1995 the Turkish Army responded with Operation STEEL, sending 35,000 troops into the Kurdish zone of northern Iraq in an effort to trap several thousand guerrillas and halt PKK cross-border raids. In the late 1990s, Turkey increased pressure on the PKK when an undeclared war between Turkey and Syria ended open Syrian support for the PKK.

In February 1999 Turkish commandos, assisted by U.S. intelligence, seized Öcalan in Kenya. Brought before a Turkish court, he was condemned to death, but this was commuted to life imprisonment as part of negotiations for Turkish membership in the EU. That same month the Turkish Army again invaded northern Iraq to wipe out PKK bases there.

Meanwhile, the Turkish government sought to allay international criticism of its actions by somewhat relaxing legislation directed against the Kurds, including bans on broadcasting and publishing in the Kurdish language. At the same time, the PKK found itself blacklisted in a number of states. Both the United States and the EU characterized it as a terrorist organization.

No reliable casualty figures exist, but the Turkish Army has set the numbers of killed through 1984 at 6,482 Turkish military personnel, 32,000 PKK troops, and 5,560 civilians. The army also claims 14,000 PKK troops taken prisoner. The PKK claims that the Turkish armed forces destroyed some 8,000 Kurdish communities and displaced 3 million to 4 million people.

Kurdish hopes for at least autonomy received a boost from the 2003–2011 Iraq War, when Kurds in northern Iraq all but established their own state, a development long opposed by Ankara, which long feared that if Iraq were to break into separate states, this would mean an independent Kurdish nation that could lay claim to Turkish territory. This possibility was a major factor in Ankara's decision to refuse support for the U.S.-led invasion, despite strong financial incentives offered by Washington. This decision by Ankara denied a secure northern base of operations for the U.S. Army's 4th Infantry Division and forced a recasting of the coalition's military plans, severely straining relations between the United States and Turkey. The war also saw Ankara accusing Washington of failing to wipe out PKK bases in northern Iraq.

In February 2008, Turkish military forces launched an incursion into northern Iraq again against the PKK. This brief eight-day incursion was preceded by Turkish air strikes against PKK targets beginning in December 2007. Perhaps 550 PPK fighters died in the fighting. Both the Iraqi and U.S. governments voiced their displeasure at the Turkish action.

Talks between the Turkish government and the PKK between 2009 and 2011 in Oslo failed, and in January 2013 the Erdoğan government entered into peace talks with Öcalan, who signaled an immense shift in PKK policy by calling for a cease-fire. A shaky cease-fire ensued in April, and despite isolated attacks thereafter, there was cautious optimism about resolving the conflict. The government demanded disarmament and withdrawal of PKK forces, while the Kurds sought more language and cultural rights within Turkey as well as a degree of autonomy.

On October 13, 2014, however, the Kurds were angered when Turkish aircraft, rather than coming to the relief of Kurds under attack by the Islamic extremist Islamic State of Iraq and Syria (ISIS) at Kobanî just across the Turkish border with Syria, attacked PKK positions in southeastern Turkey even though the PKK was aligned with the Kurds fighting ISIS in Syria. Then on July 20, 2015, an ISIS suicide bombing killed more than 30 Kurdish activists in the southern Turkish town of Suruc. The PKK blamed the government for not preventing the attack and declared the cease-fire at an end, although Öcalan had not issued such a statement. On July 22, a PKK-linked car bombing killed 2 Turkish soldiers. In retaliation, Turkey launched air strikes against PKK camps in northern Iraq and ISIS militants in Syria and also rounded up alleged supporters from both groups. On July 28, Erdoğan announced an end to the peace process. This occurred just as the liberal Kurdish-based People's Democratic Party (HDP) was becoming a rising force in Turkey's politics.

On February 17, 2016, a bomb-laden vehicle exploded near the Turkish parliament building in Ankara, targeting military vehicles stopped in traffic. The blast killed 28 people and injured 61 others. The next day Turkish prime minister Ahmet Davutoglu identified the assailant as having links to the People's Protection Units, the military wing of the Kurdish Democratic Union Party, a PKK offshoot. The Turkish military retaliated with air strikes in northern Iraq targeting the PKK.

Another blast occurred in Ankara in a busy square on March 13, 2016, killing 37 people and wounding 125. Turkish aircraft then mounted air strikes on what were described as PKK bases in northern Iraq, although subsequently the Kurdistan Freedom Falcons (Hawks, TAK), another PKK offshoot, claimed responsibility. A March 2017 UN report charged that from the summer of 2015 through 2016, Turkish forces had employed summary executions, torture, and rape and had illegally killed hundreds of people, including women and children, as well as having displaced hundreds of thousands more. Despite this, Turkey imported oil from the Kurdish region of northern Iraq.

Erdoğan now found himself engaged on three separate fronts, not only against the militant Kurds and ISIS but also the Syrian regime of president of Bashar al-Assad. Washington and Ankara were often at odds on policy decisions regarding Syria, however. Thus, Erdoğan extended aid to antigovernment rebels in the Syrian Civil War that began in 2011 without coordinating with Washington, which failed to support his calls for the imposition of a no-fly zone over portions of Syria. In 2012 Turkey joined Saudi Arabia and Qatar in establishing a center in Adana in southeastern Turkey to assist the rebel Free Syrian Army in its fight with Syrian government forces. In 2013, 2014, and 2015, Turkey shot down Syrian military aircraft that it claimed had violated its airspace.

In the early fall of 2014, Washington sought permission to use Turkey's Incirlik Air Base as a staging area for its aircraft attacking ISIS targets in Iraq and Syria. Erdoğan said that he would accede to the request only after Assad had been removed from power, a stance that angered Washington and may have cost Turkey a seat on the UN Security Council. On October 12, 2014, however, Erdoğan relented and permitted U.S. and other coalition forces some basing rights. On February 19, 2015, Turkey and the United States signed an agreement to train and arm Syrian rebels at a base in Kirsehir, Turkey.

Although the Turkish government had long been reluctant to attack ISIS, a day after ISIS militants fired on a Turkish border outpost, Turkish aircraft on August 24, 2015, struck ISIS targets in Syria. Ankara also announced that it would allow U.S.-led coalition forces to base manned and unmanned aircraft at its air bases for operations against ISIS and that Turkey's military would take part in the operations. This meant far shorter distances for U.S. aircraft to travel in order to strike ISIS targets. On August 28, the Turkish Air Force carried out its first air strikes as part of the anti-ISIS coalition.

On the morning of October 10 two powerful bombs exploded near the main train station in Ankara, targeting a peace rally. In this deadliest terrorist attack in modern Turkish history, 103 people were killed and some 400 others were injured. The explosions occurred during a gathering of some 14,000 people for a peace march at noon. The demonstrators included members of the Kurdish-based HDP, with the demonstrators calling for an end to the renewed conflict between the government and the PKK.

In national elections, held only three weeks later on November 1, 2015, Erdoğan's AKP won a landslide victory in the parliamentary elections, regaining the parliamentary majority it had lost five months earlier in the June 2015 general election. The results of this snap election called in August came as a surprise, with critics charging that government attacks on independent media and journalists by AKP supporters all but silenced the opposition. The election took place amid security concerns following the collapse of ceasefire negotiations with the PKK in July, resulting in a renewal of the Kurdish separatist conflict in which nearly 150 security personnel had lost their lives. Critics accused the government of deliberately sparking the conflict with the Kurds in order to win back votes it had lost to the MHP in June and decrease the turnout in the areas of the rising Kurdish HDP.

On November 24, 2015, Turkish aircraft shot down a Russian Sukhoi Su-24 bomber. The Turks claimed that it had violated their airspace and that the Russian pilot had been warned. The Russians denied this. Washington supported Ankara's version. Russian president Vladimir Putin said the shoot-down would have "serious consequences." Russia then deployed S-400 antiaircraft missiles to its Khmeimim air base in Syria. These missiles have a range of some 155 miles, and the Turkish border is less than 30 miles distant. Putin also imposed economic sanctions on Turkey, including a ban on tourist travel there. Still, Turkey strongly opposed plans by the new Donald Trump administration in Washington announced in February 2017 to increase U.S. military assistance to the Syrian opposition forces, including the 27,000-strong People's Protection Units, a mostly Kurdish militia formation in Syria.

Terrorism continued in Turkey. Seeking to answer complaints by foreign governments that it was not doing enough to prevent ISIS access to its territory and the transit of recruits from Turkey to Syria, Turkey began a crackdown on ISIS. On January 12, 2016, an explosion rocked Sultanahmet Square in Istanbul, killing at least 10 people (8 of them Germans) and wounding 15 others. ISIS claimed responsibility. Then on March 19 a suicide bomber, reportedly also linked to ISIS, killed 4 people and wounded at least 36 others in a busy Istanbul shopping district. The dead included 2 Israelis and 2 Americans. Many Turks resented the phobia expressed by many Americans and West Europeans toward their country's Muslim identity and what they perceived as a lack of support for Ankara's efforts to stamp out the Kurdish threat.

In May 2016 Erdoğan forced out his handpicked premier, Davutoglu, reportedly because he was upset over the international attention Davutoglu had received in negotiating a pact regarding the numerous refugees from Syria and other Middle Eastern trouble spots making their way through Turkey to other European nations.

In late June, Turkey reestablished diplomatic relations with both the Soviet Union and Israel. Then on June 29, three suicide bombers armed with automatic weapons and wearing suicide vests attacked Ataturk International Airport, Europe's third-busiest airport, in Istanbul, killing 42 people and wounding 239. The government blamed ISIS, which had called for such attacks during the Muslim holy month of Ramadan.

On July 15, 2016, an attempted coup d'état occurred in Turkey, headed by a faction of junior officers within the Turkish Armed Forces known as the Peace at Home Council. The council justified its action in an erosion of secularism and democratic rule, the regime's disregard of human rights, and Turkey's loss of credibility internationally. The coup leaders sought to seize control of several key locations, principally in Ankara and Istanbul. The coup attempt was badly organized and in any case encountered forces loyal to the state. Erdoğan also called on the people to take to the streets and demonstrate their support for the government, and large numbers did so. All the major political parties, including that of the Kurds, rallied to the regime.

Although the coup was easily put down, more than 300 people had been killed and more than 2,100 injured. There was also some damage to government buildings, including the Turkish parliament and the Presidential Palace, which were attacked from the air. The government proclaimed a state of emergency, mass arrests followed, and firings began almost immediately. Within a week, a mass purge saw more than 45,000 members of the Turkish military (including 163 generals and admirals, constituting 45 percent of the armed forces' total), police officers, judges, governors, and civil servants arrested or suspended. This included 2,700 judges, 15,000 teachers, and every university dean in the country. The licenses of 21,000 teachers working at private institutions were also revoked. By the spring of 2017 some 47,000 people had been jailed (including some 120 journalists, more than in any other nation in the world) and 120,000 others had been fired or suspended from their jobs in what can only be described as a naked power grab by Erdoğan.

The government accused those purged of connection with Fethullah Gülen, a Turkish businessman and cleric and prominent critic of Erdoğan who had been granted asylum in the United States. Gülen denied any involvement in the coup attempt, which appeared borne out by independent international investigations, and charged that it was in fact carried out by Erdoğan himself to consolidate his grip on power. Certainly Erdoğan had used it for such, and there was considerable international criticism of the Turkish president for what many saw as a naked power grab. Erdoğan demanded that the U.S. government extradite Gülen, which the Barack Obama administration rejected out of hand.

On December 10, 2016, about 11:00 p.m., a remote-controlled device detonated a car bomb outside Besiktas Vodafone Arena in Istanbul following a heavily attended soccer game. Shortly afterward, less than a mile distant a suicide bomber caused a second explosion at Macka Park. The two blasts killed 38 people, most of them police officers, and injured another 155. The radical Kurdish group TAK assumed responsibility.

Erdoğan continued his efforts to concentrate power in his own hands and to crack down on press freedoms and critics of his government. He also used the coup attempt to support his push for a new constitution that would give the president ultimate authority, an executive presidency having been a long-standing proposal of Erdoğan and the AKP. In October 2016 the MHP announced its cooperation in producing draft proposals, and this combined parliamentary strength brought a national referendum on April 18, 2017, regarding 18 amendments to the Turkish Constitution. If approved, Turkey's existing parliamentary government would be replaced by a presidential system with greatly expanded powers.

Those supporting the changes claimed they were necessary for a strong and stable Turkey, ending the unstable coalition governments that had dominated Turkish politics from the 1960s until 2002. Those in opposition, most notably supporters of the CHP, claimed that it would give Erdoğan too much power, effectively ending the separation of powers and taking legislative authority away from Parliament.

Twenty-five million Turks, including those overseas, took part, the voting occurring under the state of emergency, which was still in place from the July 2016 attempted coup. The government trumpeted a 51.5–48.5 percent favorable vote, and on April 27 the Supreme Electoral Council declared that the referendum had passed. In so doing it had validated as many as 1.5 million nonstamped ballots, something decried as illegal by the main opposition parties. Large-scale prodemocracy protests erupted following the results to no avail.

Erdoğan extended his far-reaching autocratic rule with an announcement on May 22 that the state of emergency introduced as a temporary measure following the 2016 coup attempt would be extended indefinitely, until the country achieved "welfare and peace." The state of emergency allows Erdoğan to issue sweeping decrees without parliamentary oversight or review by the constitutional court. Thus, in late April a presidential decree blocked Turks from access to Wikipedia. Erdoğan strengthened his grip on power during the June 2018 general elections, and his governing coalition garnered 52.6 percent of the vote. Because of changes made to the Turkish Constitution in 2017, Erdoğan now serves as head of state as well as head of government.

By the summer of 2018 it was obvious that the Turkish government was moving closer to Russia, cooperating with it in efforts to work out a solution to the long civil war in Syria. Meanwhile, in September 2017 there was a clear sign of the Turkish pivot toward Russia and away from the West and NATO when Ankara announced that it was purchasing the S-400 Russian surface-to-air missile defense system for a reported $2.5 billion. The S-400 cannot be integrated into the NATO defense system.

During 2018, Erdoğan's government was facing a major currency and debt crisis. By the summer of that year, Turkey's currency was in a near freefall while government debt continued to pile up. Clearly, Erdoğan's spending policies, driven largely by his military adventures in the region and a sprawling national security apparatus, had badly distorted Turkey's economy. Erdoğan's highly unorthodox manipulation of Turkish interest rates has also been blamed for the economic maelstrom. On August 10, 2018, the Turkish lira hit an all-time low of 6.24 per U.S. dollar. To make matters worse, the Trump administration doubled U.S. tariffs on Turkey's steel and aluminum imports, chiefly over a dispute concerning a U.S. pastor who had been detained in Turkey since 2016. Erdoğan's government insisted that he had been involved in a terror campaign against the Turkish regime. Since early 2017, the Trump administration had steadily increased pressure on Ankara to release the clergyman. In retaliation for the new U.S. tariffs, on August 15, 2018, Turkey imposed tariffs on a variety of U.S. products, including automobiles.

The cost of Erdoğan's policies has been high, with Turkey perhaps approaching a point of no return in its relations with Western Europe, the United States, and NATO. Would Turkey then abandon its longtime quest to join the EU in favor of closer ties with Russia? In early 2019 this was by no means clear, with the situation further clouded by rocky relations with the United States as well as the Kurds, Syria, and Iraq. Because of its important geographical position, large population, and potent military establishment, Turkey continues to be the source of much watchful international concern.

TIMOTHY L. FRANCIS, LAURA J. HILTON, SEDAT CEM KARADELI, KEITH A. LEITICH, PAUL G. PIERPAOLI JR., AND SPENCER C. TUCKER

**See also**
Abdulhamid II; Alexander III the Great; Arab Revolt in Palestine; Assad, Bashar al-; Ataturk, Mustafa Kemal; Balkan Wars; Byzantine Empire; Constantine I; Constantinople, Latin Empire of; Constantinople, Ottoman Siege of; Cyprus; Cyprus, Ottoman Conquest of; Dardanelles Campaign; Djemal Pasha, Ahmed; Enver Pasha; Erdoğan, Recep Tayyip; Erzurum Offensive; Greco-Turkish War; Hussein, Saddam; Hussein ibn Ali ibn Mohammed; Hussein ibn Talal, King of Jordan; Iraq War; Islamic State of Iraq and Syria; Italo-Ottoman War; Kurds; Kut al-Amara, Siege of; Lausanne, Second Treaty of; Lawrence, Thomas Edward; London, 1913 Treaty of; Mahmud II, Sultan; Manzikert, Battle of; Mehmed II, Sultan; Montenegrin-Ottoman Wars; Osman I; Ottoman Empire; Ottoman Empire, Entry into World War I; Ottoman Empire, Post–World War I Revolution in; Ottoman-Habsburg Wars; Ottoman-Hungarian Wars; Ottoman-Persian Wars of the 18th and 19th Centuries; Ottoman-Polish Wars of the 17th Century; Ottoman-Safavid Wars; Persian Gulf War, Overview; Russo-Ottoman Wars; Sakarya, Battle of the; San Stefano, Treaty of; Sarikamish, Battle of; Sassanid Empire; Seljuk Dynasty; Sèvres, Treaty of; Suleiman I; Syrian Civil War; Taalat Pasha, Mehmed

**References**
Barkey, Henri J., ed. *Reluctant Neighbor: Turkey's Role in the Middle East.* Washington, DC: U.S. Institute of Peace, 1996.
Butler, Daniel Allen. *Shadow of the Sultan's Realm: The Destruction of the Ottoman Empire and the Creation of the Modern Middle East.* Dulles, VA: Potomac Books, 2011.
Carkoglu, Ali, and William Hale, eds. *The Politics of Modern Turkey.* London: Taylor and Francis, 2008.
Deringil, Selim. *Turkish Foreign Policy during the Second World War.* New York: Cambridge University Press, 1989.
Finkel, Caroline. *Osman's Dream: The History of the Ottoman Empire.* New York: Basic Books, 2007.
Fromkin, David. *A Peace to End All Peace: The Fall of the Ottoman Empire and the Creation of the Modern Middle East.* Lakewood, WA: Owl Books, 2001.
Howard, Douglas Arthur. *The History of Turkey.* Westport, CT: Greenwood, 2001.
Karpat, H. Kemal. *Turkey's Foreign Policy in Transition, 1950–1974.* Leiden: E. J. Brill, 1975.

Lewis, Bernard. *The Emergence of Modern Turkey.* 3rd ed. New York: Oxford University Press, 2002.
Macfie, A. L. *The End of the Ottoman Empire, 1918–1923.* London: Longman, 1998.
Mango, Andrew. *Ataturk: The Biography of the Founder of Modern Turkey.* New York: Penguin, 2002.
Makovsky, Alan, ed. *Turkey's New World: Changing Dynamics in Turkish Foreign Policy.* Washington, DC: Washington Institute for Near East Policy, 2000.
McCarthy, Justin. *The Ottoman Turks.* London: Longman, 1997.
Metz, Helen Chapin. *Turkey: A Country Study.* Washington, DC: Federal Research Division, Library of Congress, U.S. Government Printing Office, 1996.
Millman, Brock. *The Ill-Made Alliance: Anglo-Turkish Relations, 1934–1940.* Montreal: McGill-Queen's University Press, 1998.
Natali, Denise. *The Kurds and the State.* Syracuse, NY: Syracuse University Press, 2005.
Palmer, Alan. *The Decline and Fall of the Ottoman Empire.* London: Murray, 1992.
Robins, Philip. *Turkey and the Middle East.* New York: Council on Foreign Relations Press, 1991.
Shaw, Stanford J., and Ezel Kural Shaw. *History of the Ottoman Empire and Modern Turkey.* 2 vols. Cambridge: Cambridge University Press, 1977.
Tahiri, Hussein. *The Structure of Kurdish Society and the Struggle for a Kurdish State.* Costa Mesa, CA: Mazda Publications, 2007.
Turfan, M. Naim. *The Rise of the Young Turks: Politics, the Military and Ottoman Collapse.* New York: I. B. Tauris, 2000.
Weisband, Edward. *Turkish Foreign Policy, 1943–1945: Small State Diplomacy and Great Power Politics.* Princeton, NJ: Princeton University Press, 1973.

## Turki ibn Abdullah, Campaigns of (1823–1833)

The first Saudi state, established by Muhammad ibn Saud in 1744, came to an end in 1818 following the invasion of Mehmed Ali's Egyptian forces. The Saudis soon regrouped, and during 1823–1824 Turki ibn Abdullah established the second Saudi state in central Arabia with his capital in Riyadh. His authority bolstered by the support of al-Wahhab's descendants, Turki conducted vigorous campaigns to reassert his authority throughout central Arabia, controlling al-Arid, al-Kharj, al-Hawta, Mahmal, Sudair, al-Aflaj, and Washm by 1925. In 1926–1928, he raided various tribes that refused to recognize his authority and forced the sheikhs of the Subai, Suhul, Ajman, Qajtan, and Mutair tribes to pledge their allegiances to him. By late 1820s, the Saudi detachments appeared in Hejaz as well. They raided Medina, Mecca, and al-Taif in late 1827 but were unable to secure control of the region.

Turki was more successful in eastern Arabia, where he was concerned about the al-Arayar tribesmen led by sheikhs Muhammad and Majid in the al-Hasa region. In 1830, the al-Arayar sheikhs organized an alliance of local Bedouin Arabs and invaded the Saudi lands in Nejd. In a decisive battle, Turki defeated Majid (who was killed in the fighting) and drove Muhammad back into al-Hasa, where he sacked Hufuf and captured the fortress of Qut. This victory allowed Turki to place eastern Arabia under his control and spread the Wahhabi teachings.

In late 1830 the Saudi leader turned his attention to southeastern Arabia, forcing the rulers of Bahrain to pay heavy tribute to him. In 1832 he raided Oman, whose sultan agreed to pay tribute to the Saudi. Thus, by 1833 Turki controlled the whole coast of the Persian Gulf and most of central Arabia, although many Bedouin tribes continued to defy his authority.

In 1834 Abdallah ibn Ahmad al-Khalifa, the ruler of Bahrain, attacked the Saudi coastal towns in al-Hasa. Before Turki was able to mobilize his army to counter this threat, he was killed by assassins sent by his rival Mishari ibn Abd al-Rahman on May 9, 1834. Turki's death marked a turning point in the history of the Saudi state and launched almost a decade of internecine wars and unrest in central Arabia.

ALEXANDER MIKABERIDZE

**See also**
Ibn Saud, King; Saudi-Hashemite War; Saudi-Rashidi Wars

**References**
Bowen, Wayne. *The History of Saudi Arabia.* Westport, CT: Greenwood, 2008.
Vassiliev, Alexei. *The History of Saudi Arabia.* London: Saqi Books, 1998.

## Turkish-Armenian War (1920)

Conflict between the Turkish National Movement (successor to the Ottoman Empire) and the Democratic Republic of Armenia (DRA), fought for control of eastern Asia Minor (present-day northeastern Turkey).

By the end of World War I, the Ottoman and Russian Empires had collapsed. In 1918, Armenia declared its independence and sought to reclaim Armenian lands that had been under Ottoman control for the past several centuries. The situation was particularly grave in Western Armenia following the Russian army's withdrawal. In 1917–1918 the Western Armenian Bureau, an executive body of the umbrella union of Armenian political groups, established a defense council to organize Armenian military units in Western Armenia. This brought regular skirmishes between Armenians and Turks.

In March 1918, Bolshevik Russia had agreed to the punitive Treaty of Brest-Litovsk with the Central Powers (then ascendant in Would War I). In Article 4 of the treaty, the Bolsheviks had agreed to cede the Russian provinces of Eastern Anatolia to the Ottoman Empire. During March–April 1918 Ottoman forces had successfully entered parts of Western Armenia, occupying Erzinjan, Erzerum, Van, Khnus, Alashkert, and Kars. In May at the conference in Batum, the Ottoman representative Halil Bey put forth additional territorial demands, calling for Ottoman occupation of Batum, Alexandropol, Akhalkalaki, Shirak, and Echmiadzin. However, Ottoman defeat in World War I put an end to such territorial claims and revived Armenian hopes for recovering some of the land.

The Treaty of Sèvres in August 1920 between the victorious Allies and the Ottoman Empire played into Armenian hands since it called for the transfer of substantial Ottoman territory—Erzurum, Bitlis, and Van Provinces as well as parts of Erzurum and Trapesund Provinces—to Armenia. Although the Ottoman sultan accepted the treaty, Turkish nationalist leaders in Ankara rejected it and prepared to defend Ottoman territory by force. In early September 1920, skirmishes erupted between the Turkish and Armenian forces in the Oltu district and quickly escalated into a war.

Armenia proved to be unprepared for the ensuing Turkish attack. Led by General Kazim Karabekir, the Turks defeated the Armenians at Sarikamish on September 28–29 and captured Kaghizman and Merdenik. In October, Karabekir pushed toward Kars, which the Armenians abandoned on October 30, and Alexandropol (Gyumri), which the Turks secured a week later. By mid-November, Karabekir's forces were preparing to attack the Armenian capital of Yerevan. With more than half of its territory occupied by the Turks and unable to secure military assistance from the Western powers, the DRA was forced to sue for peace on November 18, 1920, and sign the Treaty of Alexandropol on December 2, 1920. Armenia renounced the provisions of the Treaty of Sèvres, accepted the territorial division outlined in the Treaty of Brest-Litovsk, and agreed to dramatic restrictions on its military forces (fewer than 2,000 troops, 8 artillery pieces, etc.). Just days after the treaty was signed, a Bolshevik army invaded the rump Armenian state and established a soviet republic there. In 1921, Turkey and the Soviet Union signed the Treaties of Moscow and Kars that resulted in territorial exchanges establishing the present borders between Turkey and Armenia.

ALEXANDER MIKABERIDZE

**See also**
Sèvres, Treaty of

**References**
Hovannisian, Richard G. "The Republic of Armenia." In *Armenian People from Ancient to Modern Times*, Vol. 2, ed. R. G. Hovannisian, 303–347. New York: Palgrave Macmillan, 2004.

Payaslian, Simon. *The History of Armenia.* New York: Macmillan, 2007.

## Tutush I (1066–1095)

Tutush I ibn Alp Arslan was the Seljuk emir of Damascus during 1078–1092, ruling under the overlordship of his brother, the Great Seljuk sultan Malik Shah I (r. 1072–1092). Tutush was then sultan during 1092–1095. Tutush was a son of Sultan Alp Arslan, whose armies conquered Syria from the Fatimids of Egypt during 1070–1075. Tutush's appointment as ruler in Syria came about after the defeat of Atsiz ibn Uwaq, the Seljuk commander of southern Syria and Palestine, by the Fatimids at Cairo in February 1077 and the ensuing rebellions against Seljuk rule in Palestine. At this time Malik Shah I was busy crushing a civil war in Persia, but he wanted to ensure continued Seljuk rule of Syria and Palestine and ultimately a successful invasion of Egypt and the ending of the Fatimid Shiite caliphate.

Tutush came to Syria in 1078. He executed Atsiz ibn Uwaq and took control of Damascus and most of Palestine, including Jerusalem and the important coastal cities of Jaffa (modern-day Tel Aviv–Yafo) and Sidon (modern-day Saïda, Lebanon). In governing Syria the young king depended on several Turkoman officers, notably his faithful commander Zahir al-Din Tughtigin, who acted as his deputy. Tutush did not gain control of all of inland Syria until May 1094, when he finally captured Aleppo. He established a modus vivendi with the ruling dynasties of Tyre, the Banu 'Uqail, and of Tripoli (modern-day Trâblous, Lebanon), the Banu Ammār. In 1081 Tutush seized Tortosa (modern-day Tartu, Syria) from the Fatimids, further weakening the Fatimid naval presence in Syria.

With most of the Palestinian coast under Tutush's control, the Fatimids allied with the Uqailids of Aleppo, who refused to submit to Tutush's authority. In June 1083 Damascus came under siege from the Aleppo army, which Tutush defeated. The Fatimid-Aleppo alliance caused Tutush to change his strategy by seeking good relations with the Fatimids, although his diplomatic initiatives proved fruitless. In 1086 Sultan Malik Shah arrived in northern Syria and appointed some of his commanders governors in key cities there: Yaghi Siyan at Antioch (modern-day Antakya, Turkey) and Aq Sunqur at Aleppo. As they answered to Malik Shah in Persia, Tutush's authority and ambition in Syria were restricted. The Fatimids continued to press Tutush in Palestine, capturing Sidon, Tyre, and Acre (modern-day Akko, Israel).

On the death of Malik Shah in December 1092, Tutush decided to claim the sultanate, challenging the designated heir, the dead sultan's sons Mamud and Barkiyaruq. Tutush secured the support of all the Turkish leaders of Syria (including Aq Sunqur) and was about to confront his nephew Barkiyaruq in battle at al-Rayy in the summer of 1093 when Aq Sunqur and another commander, Buzān, shifted their loyalties to Barkiyaruq, forcing Tutush to retire to Damascus.

Tutush spent the winter of 1093–1094 in Damascus. In the spring of 1094 he attacked Aleppo, having arranged a marriage between his son Riwan and a daughter of Yaghi Siyan of Antioch. In May 1094 Tutush defeated the Aleppo army and had Aq Sunqur executed. By January 1095 Tutush had gained recognition as sultan from the Abbasid caliph. Tutush now controlled most of Syria, Anatolia, Iraq, and western Persia. However, on February 26, 1095, Barkiyaruq defeated him in battle at the village of Dashlu, south of the Caspian Sea, and Tutush was killed. He left five sons; two of them, Duqaq and Riwan, started a civil war in Syria that continued up to the arrival of the First Crusade (1096–1099).

TAEF EL-AZHARI

### See also
Alp Arslan; Malik Shah I

### References
Bosworth, C. E. "The Political and Dynastic History of the Iranian World (A.D. 1000–1217)." In *The Cambridge History of Iran*, Vol. 5, *The Saljuq and Mongol Periods*, ed. R. N. Frye, 1–202. Cambridge: Cambridge University Press, 1968.

El-Azhari, Taef. *The Saljūqs of Syria during the Crusades, 463–549 A.H./1070–1154 A.D.* Berlin: Schwarz, 1997.

Mouton, Jean-Michel. *Damas et sa principauté sous les Saljoukides et les Bourides, 1076–1154*. Cairo: Institut Français d'Archéologie Orientale, 1994.

## Tuwaitha Nuclear Facility

Iraqi nuclear site and, prior to the 1991 Persian Gulf War, the centerpiece of Iraq's nuclear ambitions. Tuwaitha was part of the Baghdad Nuclear Research Facility located about 12 miles southeast of Baghdad. Tuwaitha was home to the Osiraq (Tammuz 1) nuclear reactor, which the Israeli Air Force bombed and destroyed in 1981. It is believed that the Iraqis had achieved up to 95 percent uranium enrichment at Tuwaitha, higher than at any of their other nuclear sites. During Operation DESERT STORM, many facilities at Tuwaitha sustained heavy damage from coalition air strikes. Tuwaitha, which encompasses 23,000 acres and was surrounded by a four-mile-long earthen berm nearly 160 feet high, was also home to the Iraqi Nuclear Commission.

As the most important of Iraq's nuclear facilities, Tuwaitha was a sprawling facility that contained research-grade nuclear reactors, plutonium-separation and waste-processing facilities, uranium research and metallurgy labs, neutron-initiator development facilities, and other nuclear-related research laboratories. Significant amounts of industrial and nuclear waste were also stored in and around Tuwaitha, including a waste site of several thousand acres. Just outside the Tuwaitha complex, the Iraqis had built a manufacturing plant where insulators and magnetic coils were produced to aid in their nuclear programs. The Iraqis had also built a biological weapons laboratory at Tuwaitha.

It is estimated that coalition bombing in 1991 destroyed only about 20 percent of Iraq's nuclear development facilities. Although damage at Tuwaitha was fairly extensive, it was largely limited to facilities run by the Iraqi Nuclear Power Commission and administrative offices. Damage to the reactors was not complete, and the main reactor, built after the Osiraq bombing, had been shut down before the war began. The Iraqis reported mild nuclear contamination after the air strikes on Tuwaitha, although it was closed for only a few days before reopening.

As part of the cease-fire agreement and United Nations Security Council Resolution 687 following DESERT STORM, Iraq was obliged to open Tuwaitha and other nuclear facilities to international inspections to be conducted by the International Atomic Energy Agency (IAEA). The IAEA conducted numerous inspections and in the process removed all known stores of highly enriched uranium and plutonium located at Tuwaitha. By 2002, the inspections had quarantined Iraq's low-grade enriched uranium and natural and depleted uranium in locked storage facilities on site.

During the Iraq War, which began in March 2003, there was some controversy surrounding the IAEA's attempts to keep the Tuwaitha facility from contributing to further nuclear weapons development. Specifically, fault was found with the decision to store any nuclear materials there instead of shipping them out of the country to ensure that they did not fall into the wrong hands. Tuwaitha, like many parts of Iraq, in particular areas in and around Baghdad, were subject to widespread looting in the immediate aftermath of the coalition invasion. Unprepared and not expecting such problems, coalition forces were ill-equipped to handle this. Apparently, looters infiltrated the Tuwaitha nuclear facilities and made off with much material, although it is not known for sure what exactly was taken. In April 2003 U.S. marines, who were attempting to secure Tuwaitha, claimed that they had discovered a secret cache of nuclear material and related facilities. The IAEA denied the claims, alleging that it had checked every inch of Tuwaitha and could not have overlooked such a thing. The media claimed that the facilities were in fact not new or were previously undiscovered. Instead, it seemed probable that looters had broken seals placed on the material by the IAEA, which made it appear as if the goods had never been inventoried. If this was indeed the case, then it cannot be known what potentially dangerous materials may have been carted off.

U.S. forces quickly took control of Tuwaitha after the looting and began to decontaminate it, with the assistance of U.S. civilian contractors. After extensive cleanup efforts, coalition forces turned over control of Tuwaitha to the Iraqi Ministerial Guard on October 7, 2003. It was the first change of command to take place in the aftermath of the invasion. By 2004, the Iraqis had outlined an ambitious plan to use the facilities at Tuwaitha for scientific—but not nuclear—purposes, including water, agriculture, and petrochemical endeavors. The rebuilding at Tuwaitha was not being funded by coalition authorities but rather by the Development Fund for Iraq, established by the United Nations. The reconstruction efforts have been estimated to cost as much as $30 billion.

Paul G. Pierpaoli Jr.

**See also**
Iraq; Iraq War; Persian Gulf War, Overview

**References**
Khadduri, Imad. *Iraq's Nuclear Mirage: Memoirs and Delusions.* Toronto: Springhead Publishers, 2003.

U.S. Congress. *Iraq's Nuclear Weapons Capability and IAEA Inspections in Iraq: Joint Hearing before the Subcommittees on Europe and the Middle East and International Security, International Organizations, and Human Rights.* Committee on Foreign Affairs, U.S. House of Representatives. Washington, DC: U.S. Government Printing Office, 1993.

# Tyre and Gaza, Sieges of (332 BCE)

Alexander the Great's sieges of Tyre and Gaza in 332 BCE are two of history's great military operations. In the summer of 334, Alexander III (353–326), ruler of Macedon and master of all Greece, led some 35,000 men across the Hellespont in an invasion of Asia Minor. Alexander defeated the Persian army on the Granicus River and conquered much of Asia Minor. In 333 he defeated Persian king Darius III at Issus, then turned south to conquer Egypt. This move would secure his southern flank prior to resuming his eastward march to the extremities of the Persian Empire. Securing the Phoenician coastal city-states of Syria would also open those ports for his own triremes and deny them to the Persian fleet, preventing a Persian naval descent on Greece.

Tyre was the most important of the Phoenician coastal city-states. Ruled by King Azemilk and located in present-day Lebanon, Tyre was actually two cities. Old Tyre was located on an island about three miles in circumference, separated from the mainland city by half a mile of water. The channel between the island and the mainland was more than 20 feet deep. The island citadel was protected by massive walls up to 150 feet high on the land side and reputedly impregnable. Alexander wanted to bypass Tyre but had to reduce it before he could move against Egypt, lest it be used as a base for Darius's fleet. Alexander predicted that once Tyre fell the Phoenician ships, deprived of their bases, would desert to the winning side.

Determined to hold out, the Tyrians rejected Alexander's overtures. They were confident in their defenses and believed that a protracted siege would purchase time for Darius to mobilize a new army and campaign in Asia Minor. Alexander had second thoughts about the task ahead and sent heralds to the Tyrians to urge a peaceful resolution. The Tyrian leaders, however, saw this as a sign of weakness; they killed the heralds and threw their bodies over the walls. This foolish act cemented Alexander's resolve and won him solid support for his plans from his generals.

Alexander took mainland Old Tyre without difficulty and initiated siege operations against the island in January 332. He ordered Dyadis the Thessalian, head of the Macedonian Army's corps of engineers, to construct a great mole, about 200 feet wide, out from the land and reach the island and then bring up siege engines. The Macedonians secured wood from the forests of Lebanon for the piles of the mole, while the structures of mainland Tyre were demolished for the fill. Alexander reportedly worked alongside his men on the project.

The Tyrians sent ships from the island filled with archers to attack the Macedonians working on the mole. To counter such forays, Alexander ordered his men to construct two great siege towers 150 feet in height. As the mole advanced, the towers moved with it. One night with a favorable wind, the Tyrians sent an old horse transport rigged as a fireship and laden with combustibles against the towers and the causeway. The towers caught fire and were destroyed. At the same time, a flotilla of smaller Tyrian craft arrived; men from them attacked Alexander's men on the mole and destroyed other siege equipment that had escaped destruction in the fire. They then withdrew.

Alexander responded by ordering the construction of two more towers. Leaving operations at Tyre in the hands of trusted lieutenants, he then traveled to Sidon to secure ships to operate against the island and protect those working on the mole. Soon he had gathered 223 ships from Sidon, Cyprus, Rhodes, and other eastern Mediterranean city-states. Alexander placed in them some 4,000 hoplites recruited from the Peloponnese by Cleander. This flotilla then sailed for Tyre. Alexander commanded its right wing and Pinitagoras its left.

The Tyrians learned of Alexander's activities and planned to give battle at sea, but noting the size of the approaching fleet, the Tyrian admiral changed his mind; he chose instead to protect the two narrow entrances to the island's harbor. A number of ships sunk side-by-side were sufficient to block both. Alexander concentrated offensive actions against the smaller of these entrances, known as Sidonian Harbor, which was about 200 feet wide, but he was unsuccessful. Subsequently the Tyrians substituted heavy iron chains for their block ships.

Thanks to the presence of Alexander's flotilla, it was no longer possible for the Tyrians to attack the mole with their ships. Instead, they employed catapults against both it and the Macedonian siege towers as the latter came within range. Alexander's catapults replied. Although the Macedonians suffered setbacks, the mole gradually advanced and ultimately reached the island. Under the protection of the towers, the Macedonians employed battering rams against the citadel's walls, but the Tyrian defenses stood firm.

Alexander had also ordered construction of naval battering rams. Each was mounted on a large platform lashed between two barges. Other barges carried catapults. Finally, this naval assault opened a breach in the walls; unfortunately, a gale then arose. Some of Alexander's vessels were sunk, and others were badly damaged.

During this respite, the Tyrians demolished a number of buildings and dropped the masonry over the walls to keep Alexander's naval rams at a distance. They also devised drop-beams, which could be swung out against the ships by derricks, and, at the end of lines, grappling irons or barbed hooks known as "crows" that could be dropped on the Macedonians, hooking and hoisting them up to a tortured death in front of their colleagues.

Alexander's men now had to remove the debris in the water around the walls, allowing the assault craft to close on the island. The Tyrians replied by tipping on the attackers bowls of red-hot sand. Finally, Alexander's naval rams broke down a section of the wall; infantry were sent into the breach on boarding ramps, as the defenders continued their resistance in the city center.

Tyre fell at the end of July. Frustration regarding the length and ferocity of the siege gave way to rage, and the Macedonian troops extended no quarter to the inhabitants. Reportedly 8,000 Tyrians died during the siege; the Macedonians slew another 7,000 afterward, as the city became one large abattoir. Another 30,000 inhabitants, including women and children, were sold into slavery.

With Tyre destroyed, the Macedonian Army set out on foot in July or early August for Egypt. Some 160 miles from Tyre, the army encountered the fortress city of Gaza, situated on a rocky hill on the sole route between Egypt and Syri. The city's governor, Batis, rejected calls for surrender. Macedonian siege operations here were quite difficult, as the siege engines sank in the sand. On occasion, the defenders sallied to destroy the Macedonian siege equipment. On one such foray, Alexander was badly wounded in the shoulder by an arrow.

Alexander again called on Dyadis, this time to build an earth rampart around the city. In two months the Macedonians had constructed an earthen rampart topped by a wooden platform encircling Gaza—a mammoth undertaking. Finally a breach was made in the walls, and Macedonian troops entered the city. The Macedonians had also carried out mining operations, and another group went in by a tunnel.

After heavy fighting, the city fell. Reportedly, the Macedonians slew 10,000 defenders, and the women and children were all sold as slaves. Batis was among the captured. Alexander ordered him lashed by his ankles behind a chariot and dragged around the city walls until he was dead.

Although it was fortunate for Alexander that during these operations Darius III did not move against the Macedonian lines of communication, the successful sieges of both Tyre and Gaza thoroughly demonstrated Alexander's mastery of this type of warfare and greatly added to his mystique of invincibility.

SPENCER C. TUCKER

**See also**
Alexander III the Great; Darius III

**References**
Green, Peter. *Alexander of Macedon, 356–323 B.C.: A Historical Biography.* Berkeley: University of California Press, 1991.
Kern, Paul Bentley. *Ancient Siege Warfare.* Bloomington: Indiana University Press, 1999.
Sekunda, Nick, and John Warry. *Alexander the Great: His Armies and Campaigns, 332–323 B.C.* London: Osprey, 1988.

## Umayyad Caliphate (661–750)

The Umayyad dynasty was in power from 661 to 750, a relatively short but formative period as the Umayyads' consolidated Islamic control of conquered lands and adapted the classical Roman, Greek, and Persian heritages to Islamic civilization. The Umayyad dynasty chose Damascus as its capital and established its presence there with the construction of the great mosque out of the Christian cathedral that had previously been a temple to Jupiter. The Umayyads laid the foundations for classical Islamic civilization yet along with the Greek Byzantines and Frankish Carolingians were also inheritors of the Roman Empire that had preceded them. The Umayyads maintained much of the Late Antiquity Byzantine administrative system. They transformed the caliphate from an elected leader based on consensus to a hereditary monarch relying on a trained bureaucracy.

The first Umayyad caliph, Muawiyah (r. 661–680), came to power by defeating Ali, the son-in-law of Prophet Muhammad, in the First Muslim Civil War. Muawiyah established his capital in Damascus in Syria, since the earlier capital of Medina had seemed to contribute to instability. Medina was in the midst of the factionalized tribes of the Hejaz, and the wealth and power center had shifted to Syria. Muawiyah divided his empire into a few large provinces ruled by his closest associates and family members. For local government, he relied on provincial scribes and elites. Through marriage and cooperation, he managed to keep factions and warring tribes at peace. He designated his son, Yazid (r. 680–683), as his successor.

After Yazid's death, civil war erupted again. Marwan I (r. 684–685) was elected by the leading tribe, the Qudaa, and he succeeded in maintaining the Umayyad power base of Syria and Egypt. Ibn-Zubayr, linked to the family of Prophet Muhammad, led the revolt and was recognized as caliph by the rebels. However, the opponents to Umayyad rule, although initially successful, were not united. Ibn Zubayr was killed in the siege of Mecca by al-Hadjdjadj, who had been sent by Abd al-Malik (r. 685–705), son and successor to Marwan. Abd al-Malik managed to finish the civil war and reconquer Iraq (and to build the Dome of the Rock around 692).

Abd al-Malik then presided over a period of peace and prosperity. He reformed and formalized the Umayyad administration and taxation, and he also made Arabic the official language of the government. In 744 the caliph al-Walid II was assassinated after being on the throne for only one year. His assassination unleashed a civil war that was not ended until 750, when the Abbasids came to power and moved the capital to Baghdad. However, Abd al-Rahman ibn Muawiyah, an Umayyad prince, escaped to Spain and set up the Umayyad caliphate of Cordoba, which presided over a great cultural flowering in Islamic Spain. The last Umayyad caliph in Spain ruled until 976.

The Umayyads conquered a vast territory. Immediately after the end of the First Muslim Civil War, Muawiyah continued his assault through North Africa. By 711 the Muslims had conquered Spain, and by 751 they had reached Central Asia and India. Although these conquering armies were initially the great nomadic warriors of the Arabian Peninsula, by the later Umayyad period the caliphs employed professional armies of mixed ethnicities.

The Umayyads were great patrons of the arts. Their transformation of the cathedral of Damascus into a mosque (709–715) symbolized their synthesis of the classical pre-Islamic Roman and Byzantine heritage with the new religion of Islam. Like the Dome of the Rock in Jerusalem (692), the construction of the mosque relied on Byzantine artisans and utilized Byzantine mosaics and architectural techniques. Early Umayyad caliphs also built numerous desert retreats near Damascus. Many of these pleasure palaces and complexes were masterpieces of early Islamic art, but by the reign of Yazid III (744) such expenditures had depleted the treasury, and he was forced to reside in Damascus.

Although the Abbasids maligned the Umayyads as impious, the foundations of Islamic civilization were laid in the Umayyad period as Islam came into its own as an organized religion. The *ulema* (Islamic scholars) debated and discussed every aspect of Islamic law and life. The *hadith* (sayings of the prophet) were collected and authenticated. It was also in the later Umayyad period that the major sects of Islam arose, most notably the division between the Shias and the Sunnis.

By the end of the Umayyad period, Islamic civilization had developed and advanced far beyond its tribal, militaristic roots. Soldiers, tribesmen, and free people were all subjects of a central government. The Muslims were not an occupying army but were now part of a new culture that had arisen from the collapse and transformation of Late Antiquity culture.

BENJAMIN DELEE

### See also
Abbasid Caliphate; Abbasid Revolution; Islamic Civil War, First; Islamic Civil War, Second; Muawiyah I; Religious Sites in the Middle East, Muslim

### References
Dixon, Abd al-Ameer Abd. *The Umayyad Caliphate, 65–86/684–705.* London: Luzac, 1971.

Hawting, Gerald R. *The First Dynasty of Islam: The Umayyad Caliphate, AD 661–750.* London: Croom Helm, 1986.

Kennedy, Hugh. *The Prophet and the Age of the Caliphates.* 2nd ed. London: Pearson-Longman, 2004.

# Umm Qasr, Battle of (March 21–23, 2003)

First military engagement of the 2003 Iraq War (Operation IRAQI FREEDOM). The Battle of Umm Qasr unfolded in and around the Iraqi port city of Umm Qasr, located in the southern part of the country on the Faw (Fao) peninsula, on March 21–25, 2003. The port at Umm Qasr, which is Iraq's only deepwater port, is very close to Kuwait; indeed, only a small inlet separates the two nations.

Taking control of Umm Qasr was one of the coalition's first military objectives during the opening days of Operation IRAQI FREEDOM. American and British commanders knew that seizing the city and port would deny the Iraqis any way of challenging the naval blockade. More importantly, they also hoped to secure the port as the base for a large humanitarian mission whereby tons of food, medicine, clothing, and other supplies would be moved into Iraq once Iraqi president Saddam Hussein's regime had been toppled.

The Umm Qasr offensive, which involved the 15th U.S. Marine Expeditionary Unit, British Royal Marines, and integrated units from Poland's Operational Mobile Reaction Group (GROM), moved toward Umm Qasr overland from Kuwait and through the very southern edge of Iraq. The operation began on March 21, 2003. Coalition forces were confident that the port and surrounding city could be taken quickly and with little resistance. As a convoy of about 20 coalition vehicles lumbered toward Umm Qasr, the Iraqis peppered it with small-arms fire. They then opened up with mortar fire, taking the allies by surprise. The Americans called in British artillery support from northern Kuwait not far from the border. While some shells hit Iraqi positions, others fell perilously close to U.S. marine units, who were forced into a hasty withdrawal. After regrouping, the coalition forces called for M1-Abrams tanks, which then punched through Iraqi defensive positions.

Many of the Iraqi defenders were members of Hussein's elite Republican Guard, who resorted to guerrilla-style tactics to keep coalition forces off balance. Some were disguised in civilian clothing and would hold up white flags. When coalition forces approached, they would scurry into foxholes and bunkers and open fire. The Iraqi resistance at Umm Qasr was unexpectedly stout, and some critics have claimed that coalition forces took the Iraqi threat too lightly and were thus ill-prepared for a protracted fight there.

After more determined fighting on the part of the Iraqis, coalition forces made use of Bradley Fighting Vehicles and had intended on calling in Cobra attack helicopters to help root out resistance in and near the port. The Bradleys arrived, but the Cobras did not, as there had been insufficient time to organize a mission. On March 25 the port was declared free of Iraqi opposition, but sporadic and pitched fighting continued to occur in the old city of Umm Qasr.

Not until the first few days in April had all of Umm Qasr been pacified. Meanwhile, coalition minesweepers, U.S. Navy SEALS, and even trained dolphins began the laborious task of clearing the port waters and approaches of mines. Navy personnel made an unsettling discovery when they found a number of Iraqi civilian boats rigged with mines and explosive devices, making the minesweeping operation all the more difficult. The first ship to make it into port was the British RFA *Sir Gallahad*.

The Battle of Umm Qasr gave pause to many coalition commanders and strategists who had believed that securing the port city would be a quick and easy affair. Fortunately, subsequent operations went more or less according to plan, but the battle proved that no operation, however well planned, can proceed successfully without proper intelligence and preparation.

PAUL G. PIERPAOLI JR.

**See also**
Umm Qasr, Battle of

**Reference**
Gordon, Michael R., and General Bernard E. Trainor. *Cobra II: The Inside Story of the Invasion and Occupation of Iraq.* New York: Pantheon Books, 2006.

# United Arab Emirates

The United Arab Emirates (UAE) is located on the Persian Gulf along the southeastern end of the Arabian Peninsula. The UAE is bordered by the Persian Gulf to the north, Oman and the Gulf of Oman to the east, and Saudi Arabia to the west and south. Known as the Trucial States until 1971, the UAE is a federation of seven emirates: Abu Dhabi, Ajman, Fujayrah, Sharjah, Dubai, Ras Khaymah, and Umm Qaiwain. The UAE comprises 32,278 square miles in area, just slightly larger than the U.S. state of South Carolina.

In 2018 the UAE had a population of some 9.5 million. Dubai is the most populous city of the emirates, which accounts for nearly 36 percent of the total population. About 50 percent of the UAE population is South Asian in ethnicity (including many Pakistanis, Indians, and Sri Lankans), while 42 percent are Amirati Arabs and Iranians, and 8 percent are others. Islam is the official religion and is practiced by some 96 percent of the population; the remaining 4 percent practice Hinduism, Buddhism, and varying denominations of Christianity. Owing to its considerable oil reserves, the UAE is a prosperous and relatively wealthy nation, making it a significant draw for foreigners from other parts of the region.

Politics in the UAE are tightly controlled by the ruling sheikhs, and there are no political parties. The presidency and the post of prime minister are both hereditary positions, and members of the Supreme Council and the Council of Ministers are chosen by the leaders of the seven emirates.

Islam was established as the religion of the region in 630 CE. The Persian Gulf was a major trade route with India and China and attracted the Portuguese, then the Dutch and the British. Extensive piratical activity with attacks on merchant trade with India brought British military intervention in 1809 and again in 1819. In 1820 Britain and a number of local rulers signed a treaty to combat piracy. Known as the General Treaty of Peace and the General Maritime Treaty, it and later agreements led to the term of "Trucial States," which defined the status of the coastal emirates. Another treaty with the British was signed in 1843.

Beginning in 1853, Great Britain forced the separate emirates of the area to sign treaties to prevent conflicts between them, reduce piracy in the Persian Gulf, and eliminate participation in the slave trade. During March 6–8, 1892, the British and the emirates signed another treaty that tightened the bonds between the two. As with treaties entered into by the British with other Persian Gulf principalities, the sheikhs agreed not to cede territory to any other nation or enter into commercial arrangements or other venues of exchange with foreign governments without the consent of the British government. In return, the British pledged to protect the emirates from outside aggression.

In 1952, the sheikhs formed the Trucial States Council. The tribal nature of society and the lack of drawn borders produced frequent territorial disputes, which were settled either through mediation or on occasion by force. To keep the peace, the British established a military formation known first as the Trucial Oman Levies, then the Trucial Oman Scouts.

Oil was discovered in drilling off Abu Dhabi in 1958, and oil exports began four years later. Subsequent oil revenues led Abu Dhabi ruler Zayed bin Sultan Al Nahyan to undertake a massive public works program. When Dubai's oil exports commenced in 1969, its ruler, Sheikh Rashid bin Saeed Al Maktoum, began the construction of modern-day Dubai.

The independence of India and Pakistan in 1947 greatly reduced British interest in controlling the Persian Gulf region. Britain also could no longer afford the expense. On January 24, 1968, British prime minister Harold Wilson

# United Arab Emirates

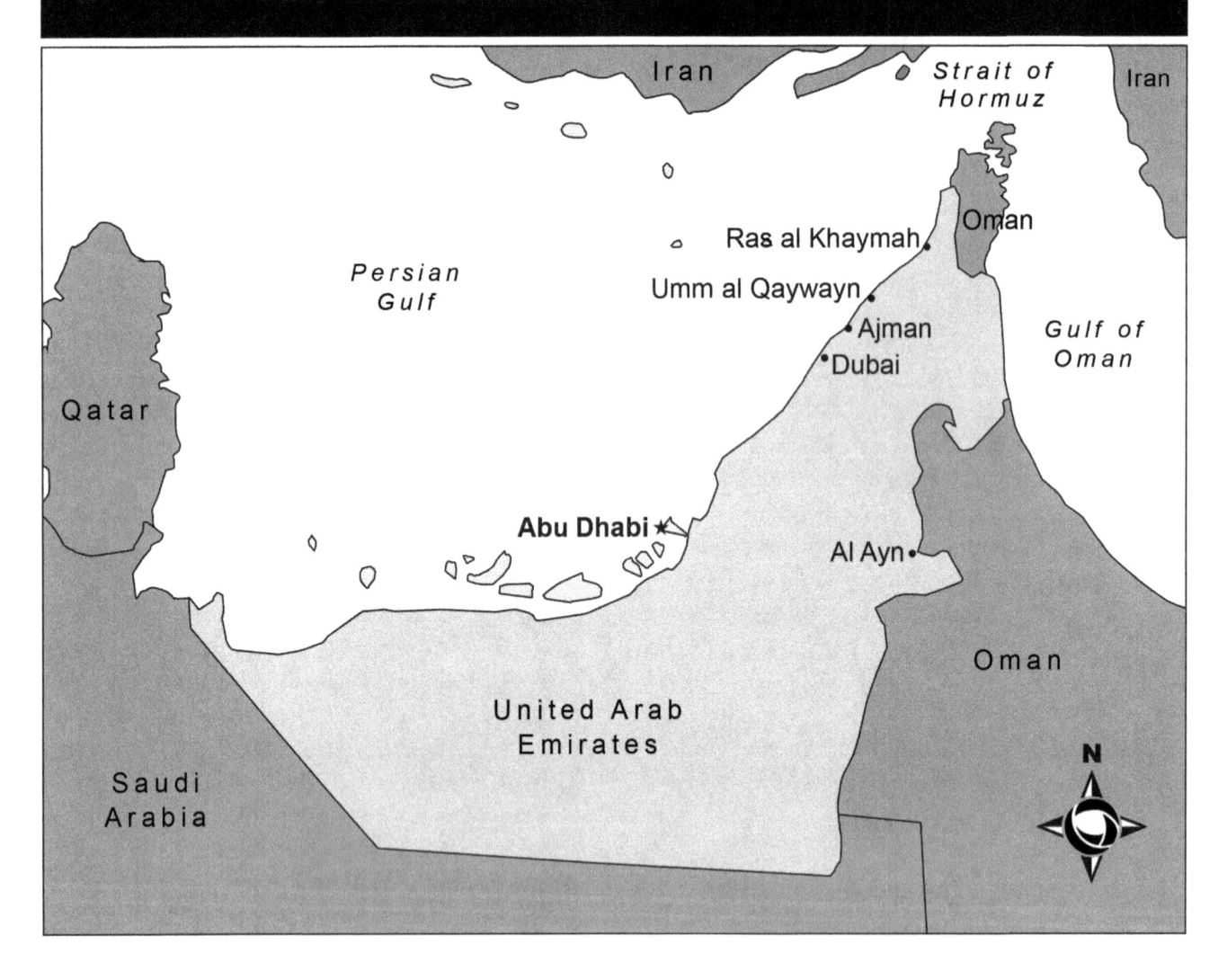

announced his government's decision to let the treaties with the emirates lapse in three years. This was reaffirmed in March 1971 by Prime Minister Edward Heath. Sufficiently worried about the ensuing threat from more powerful neighboring states, Abu Dhabi ruler Sheikh Zayed bin Sultan Al Nahyan offered to pay the full costs of keeping the British armed forces in the emirates if London would reconsider, but the Labor government refused. That the threat to the emirates was real was apparent when Iran seized by force the Tunb Islands and Saudi Arabia claimed territory in Abu Dhabi. In July 1971, six of the emirates rulers met in Dubai and there agreed to establish a union. In September, however, Qatar reversed course and declined to join.

With the expiration of the British treaty, the emirates became fully independent on December 1, 1971. The rulers of Abu Dhabi and Dubai formed a union of their two emirates, then drafted a constitution and called for the rulers of the other emirates to join. On December 2, 1971, four other emirates agreed to form the UAE. Bahrain and Qatar declined, while Ras al-Khaimah joined in early 1972. Meanwhile, the Trucial Oman Scouts became the Union Defence Force (UDF) upon formation of the UAE.

In February 1972 the a Federal National Council (FNC) was created, a 40-member consultative body appointed by the seven rulers. The UAE joined the Arab League in 1971. In May 1981, the UAE was a founding member of the Gulf Cooperation Council (GCC). In January 1982, prompted by the perceived threats of the Islamic Republic of Iran, the ongoing Iran-Iraq War (1980–1988), and the Soviet-Afghan War (1979–1989), the UAE joined Saudi Arabia, Bahrain, Kuwait, Oman, and Qatar in establishing a joint military command structure and integrated air defense system.

During the Iran-Iraq War the UAE staked out a studiously ambivalent position toward the conflict. This was partly because its government sought to eschew entanglements with foreign powers, but it was also because the nation profited handsomely from the war. UAE oil revenues rose dramatically as those of Iran and Iraq flagged. In late July 1990, however, when Iraqi forces were threatening to move against Kuwait, the UAE was among the first nations to recommend joint military action to deter Iraqi aggression. Indeed, the week prior to the August 2, 1990, Iraqi invasion of Iraq, the air forces of the United States and the UAE engaged in a joint air-refueling exercise meant as a warning to Iraqi president Saddam Hussein.

Since its formation in 1971, the UAE has maintained generally good relations with the West and in particular with the United States. The UAE contributed several hundred troops to the coalition effort in the 1991 Persian Gulf War and also provided air support and permitted U.S. military aircraft flying from its airfields to bomb Iraqi positions. By mid-1991 the UAE had given or pledged as much as $6 billion to foreign nations that had waged the war against Iraq. Six UAE soldiers were killed during the Persian Gulf War.

The UAE was one of only three nations to recognize the Taliban government of Afghanistan, the others being Pakistan and Saudi Arabia. The UAE has eyed Iran with trepidation since the 1979 revolution there brought a fundamentalist Islamic republic to power. Relations between the two nations have remained tense, abetted by disputes over control of several islands in the Persian Gulf. In the hopes of securing these islands, the UAE joined Kuwait and Saudi Arabia in providing considerable financial support to Iraq during the Iran-Iraq War. With Iran repeatedly threatening Israel and Western nations with the prospect of closing the strait at the mouth of the Persian Gulf, in July 2012 the UAE opened an overland oil pipeline bypassing the Strait of Hormuz.

Following the September 11, 2001, terrorist attacks against the United States, the UAE sharply condemned such violence and has been a steady and reliable partner in the global war on terror. In the immediate aftermath of the attacks, the UAE promptly severed diplomatic ties with the ruling Taliban government in Afghanistan.

UAE armed forces, although still small in number, are equipped with some of the most modern weapon systems available. The United States, France, and Great Britain are the principal suppliers. In contrast to most other Arab states, the UAE permitted U.S. and coalition troops access to its military facilities to prosecute the Iraq War beginning in 2003. The UAE also contributed as many as 20,000 troops to protect Kuwait in the event Iraqi forces moved against that country at the beginning of the war. However, as the war dragged on, UAE support for it waned, and the government condemned the conflict.

In March 2011, the UAE agreed to join the North Atlantic Treaty Organization's enforcement of a no-fly zone over Libya with a contribution of a dozen aircraft. The UAE and Egypt are close allies and military partners, with both opposing political Islam. In late August 2014 UAE and Egyptian aircraft carried out air strikes against Islamist-allied militias battling for control of Tripoli, Libya.

A member of the coalition formed to eradicate the radical Islamic State of Iraq and Syria (ISIS), the UAE in late September sent aircraft to join those of Saudi Arabia and the United States in attacking ISIS targets in Iraq and Syria. The UAE aircraft were led by Major Mariam Al Mansouri, the first female UAE fighter pilot.

In 2015, UAE force joined the Saudi Arabian–led military coalition that intervened in Yemen largely through air strikes against the Iran-backed Houthi rebels. On September 4, 2015, at least 50 soldiers from the UAE and Bahrain were killed in the Marib area of central Yemen. As of early 2019, UAE military forces continued to be engaged in the Saudi-led Yemen intervention.

Wyndham E. Whynot and Spencer C. Tucker

**See also**
General Treaty of Peace; Houthis; Iran-Iraq War; Iraq War; Persian Gulf War, Overview; Saudi Arabia; Yemen; Yemen Civil War

**References**
Abd Allah, Muhammad Mursi, and Muhammad Morsy Abdullah. *The United Arab Emirates: A Modern History*. New York: Barnes & Noble, 1978.
Congressional Quarterly. *The Middle East*. 10th ed. Washington, DC: CQ Press, 2005.
Davidson, Christopher M. *The United Arab Emirates: A Study in Survival*. Boulder, CO: Lynne Rienner, 2005.
Morton, Michael Quentin. *Keepers of the Golden Shore: A History of the United Arab Emirates*. London: Reaktion Books, 2016.
Ochsenwald, William, and Sydney Nettleton Fisher. *The Middle East: A History*. 6th ed. New York: McGraw-Hill, 2004.
Zahlan, Rosemarie Said. *The Origins of the United Arab Emirates: A Political and Social History of the Trucial States*. London: Routledge, 2016.

# United Arab Republic (1958–1961)

The union between Egypt and Syria. By late 1957 there was considerable interest in Arab unity. In the case of Syria and Egypt, the motivation was chiefly ideological—with ruling elites in both countries dedicated to Arab unity, social revolution, and neutralism in foreign affairs—and secondarily political. Egyptian president Gamal Abdel Nasser had supported Arab unity ever since a well-known speech in which he declared that the "Arab nation is one nation." On November 18, 1957, in Damascus, the Syrian parliament, dominated by the Baath Party, met jointly with a visiting Egyptian delegation and called for a Syrian-Egyptian federation. The Baathists were apparently prompted by the growing influence of a different political faction within their own party in Syria. Baathist leaders believed that Syria would benefit from the union, which would also destabilize various elements within the military and in the bourgeoisie in Syria.

Nasser was at first reluctant for a variety of reasons, including the sharp contrast in the two countries and their political and social configurations. Egypt's authoritarian military government differed sharply from Syria's multiparty parliamentary system and free press. Nasser responded to the Syrian overture by insisting that any union would have to be a unitary rather than a federal state and that Syria would have to dissolve its political parties. The ruling Baathists accepted Nasser's conditions including the elimination of all political parties, which he regarded as symbols of internal division and a potential political threat.

The union was formally approved by resolutions in both national parliaments and became official on February 1, 1958. The new unitary state was known as the United Arab Republic (UAR). In the new state, the president held the bulk of the power. He had executive authority, assisted by executive councils in the Egyptian and Syrian regions. Between these and the president there would be four vice presidents, two from each region. Legislative authority would be in the hands of an assembly appointed by the president. At least half of the assembly members were to be selected from the existing Syrian and Egyptian parliaments. At an unspecified future date a new constitution would be adopted, confirmed by a plebiscite.

On February 21, 1958, both the Egyptian and Syrian regions voted nearly unanimously for the union and for Nasser as its president. On March 5, Nasser proclaimed the provisional constitution in effect. Society would be organized along the lines of social solidarity and a planned economy according to principles of social justice. Political parties were abolished. In their place was a National Union, the principles behind which the president would define. Nasser then appointed the first UAR cabinet and the two regional executive councils.

On March 8, Yemen entered into a formal arrangement with the UAR, with the new entity to be known as the United Arab States. Although there was a Supreme Council

Egyptian president Gamal Abdel Nasser (left) and Syrian president Shukri al-Quwatli clasp hands to symbolize the merger of their two countries into the United Arab Republic on al-Quwatli's arrival in Cairo with members of his cabinet, March 2, 1958. (Bettmann/Getty Images)

of the heads of the member states—in sharp contrast to the UAR—in the United Arab States, each state retained its own form of government and, in most cases, maintained separate diplomatic representation abroad. In effect, the United Arab States was a very loose-knit organization, with Yemen largely going its own way. No doubt prompted by these developments, only weeks after the establishment of the UAR Iraq and Jordan announced the formation of their own federation.

In foreign affairs and in his regional radio communications, Nasser claimed that the Arab peoples supported the doctrine of Arab solidarity and that it was their governments that were preventing Arab unity. Tensions immediately developed between the UAR and a number of Arab states with which there were already strains, such as Saudi Arabia, and where the governments feared Nasserists among their own population, as in Tunisia and Lebanon. Then, in the late spring of 1958 Camille Chamoun, who was anti-Nasserist, began a political struggle in Lebanon. His foes protested, and he complained to the United States that Nasserists were threatening to take over the country. This came on the heels of a coup attempt against Jordan's King Hussein, who had other enemies as well. This possibility was stymied by the arrival in Jordan of British paratroopers, which widened the chasm between Pan-Arabists and pro-Westerners.

In internal developments, the UAR never worked out as Nasser had hoped. By the time of the union, Nasser had firmly consolidated his rule in Egypt, so the pressure was on Syria to conform to the Egyptian model. There were, however, strong elements, especially among the established political figures and the bourgeoisie in Syria, that resented the union with Egypt and also among the growing numbers of Communist Party members in Syria, as Nasser had outlawed their party both in Egypt and in Syria.

To his credit, Nasser recognized the areas of Syrian reluctance regarding the UAR and at first pursued a deliberate, slow approach. For example, Syria was allowed complete economic autonomy in the first two years of the union. After about a year, however, Nasser did begin to eliminate certain Baath Party members from positions of leadership. In place of the multiparty system, he established the same National Union that existed in Egypt.

Two years after the UAR was established, Nasser did finally move, with fateful results, in the economic sphere in an effort to bring Syria in line with Egypt as far as its economic policies were concerned. In a number of speeches, he stated that the UAR meant a commitment to the goals of Arab socialism. In November 1958 he introduced agrarian reform in Syria. Opposition to such change from among the Syrian landholding classes, nostalgia for the former multiparty system, a stifling educational atmosphere in the schools and universities, and the desire to maintain a free enterprise economy all translated into opposition to the UAR itself. Syrians also resented certain heavy-handed Egyptian officials in the government. At the same time, as Nasser sought to play an increasingly active role on the world stage, he involved the UAR in a host of matters that had no direct bearing on the people of either region.

In July 1961 Nasser met this growing Syrian discontent with a number of wide-sweeping decrees that virtually socialized the entire Syrian economy. Among the decrees were the nationalization of banks, insurance companies, and hundreds of large businesses and economic enterprises; controlling government stock interest in large corporations; new income taxes that ranged up to 90 percent for the highest incomes; and new real estate taxes. These decrees took Egyptians as well as Syrians by surprise. The crowning blows came, however, when Nasser abolished the three-cabinet system in favor of a single cabinet for the UAR, sweeping aside the last vestiges of local autonomy, and introduced a common currency for both regions.

Then on September 28, 1961, the Syrian military seized power in Damascus in a coup carried out without great bloodshed. The new leaders immediately announced the separation of Syria from Egypt. Although the new government's leaders expressed their support for Arab unity, they also insisted that this be based on equality rather than the dominance of one party over another. They also claimed that they sought socialism.

On learning of the coup Nasser at first ordered Egyptian paratroopers into action, but within hours he countermanded this and insisted that the Egyptian military in Syria surrender. According to journalist Muhammad Haykal, Nasser's longtime friend, Nasser intuitively knew that it was pointless to force an unwanted union, as it would undermine his desire to represent popular will. In public pronouncements, Nasser blamed the coup on "reactionaries" and "agents of imperialism."

The breakup of the UAR was greeted with great relief not only by Syria but also by the other Arab states of the region, especially Jordan. Jordan, Turkey, and Iran immediately recognized the new Syrian government.

SPENCER C. TUCKER

### See also
Arab League; Egypt; Nasser, Gamal Abdel; Pan-Arabism and Pan-Arabist Thought; Syria

### References
Dawisha, A. I. *Egypt in the Arab World.* New York: Wiley, 1976.
Jankowski, James P. *Nasser's Egypt, Arab Nationalism, and the United Arab Republic.* Boulder, CO: Lynne Rienner, 2001.
Lenczowski, George. *The Middle East in World Affairs.* 4th ed. Ithaca, NY: Cornell University Press, 1980.
Podeh, Elie. *The Decline of Arab Unity: The Rise and Fall of the United Arab Republic.* New York: Sussex Academic, 1999.
Waterbury, John. *The Egypt of Nasser and Sadat: Political Economy of Two Regimes.* Princeton, NJ: Princeton University Press, 1983.

## United Nations Palestine Partition Plan (November 29, 1947)

Proposed plan for the division of Palestine into Jewish and Arab states. On February 18, 1947, British foreign secretary Ernest Bevin announced to the House of Commons that Britain no longer held out hope of reaching agreement with the Arabs and Jews of Palestine and would turn the future of the mandate over to the United Nations (UN) for resolution. On April 2 the British UN delegation requested a special session of the General Assembly to establish a committee to study the matter and then to report its findings to the regular General Assembly fall session.

The General Assembly special session met on April 27. The five Arab states immediately demanded consideration of a new agenda item, to wit an immediate end to the British mandate and its independence. This was overwhelmingly defeated. On the other hand, the General Assembly heard from Arab spokesmen but refused to receive a Jewish representative, despite the fact that the American Section of the Jewish Agency had requested that it be heard as "a matter of simple fairness." The rejection was on the basis that the agency was a nongovernmental body. Subsequently, the General Assembly voted 44 to 7 with 3 abstentions to instruct the committee to grant a hearing to the Jewish Agency as the sole spokesman for the Jewish people.

Three prominent members of the Jewish Agency—David Ben-Gurion, Abba Hillel Silver, and Moshe Shertok—all addressed the First Committee (Political and Security Committee) and presented the Jewish case. This was a precedent, the first time that Jewish representatives had been able to address the community of nations.

The first debate was over the composition of the investigating committee itself. Ultimately, it consisted of representatives from 11 member nations. None of the big powers or Arab states was represented. Debate also occurred on the issue of whether the committee should visit the displaced persons (DP) camps in Europe, which the Jewish Agency sought. The Arab states claimed that this had nothing to do with the situation in Palestine, while the Jewish Agency claimed that it went to the very heart of the matter. The instructions to the committee gave it the "widest powers to ascertain all questions and issues relative to the problem of Palestine."

During the next three months the UN Special Commission on Palestine (UNSCOP) gathered information in Europe and in Palestine, where it met with representatives of both the Jewish Agency and the Arabs, hearing 34 witnesses and holding 13 public meetings and 18 closed sessions. It also toured Palestine. The Arab High Committee decided to boycott the hearings, so most of the testimony came from the Jewish Agency and Palestinian government officials. At the same time, militant Arab groups staged anti-Zionist demonstrations in the cities. UNSCOP then went to Beirut, Lebanon, where it met with representatives of the Arab governments. Then a subcommittee visited certain DP camps in Austria and Germany.

UNSCOP spent most of August debating alternative solutions. Its final report was signed in Geneva on August 31, 1947. The committee could not reach unanimous opinion, and both majority and minority reports were presented. A majority of the representatives (Canada, Czechoslovakia, Guatemala, the Netherlands, Peru, Sweden, and Uruguay) voted for the partition of Palestine into two separate states, one Arab and the other Jewish, to be joined in an economic union. Following a transition period of two years, both states were to be completely independent, provided they had adopted a constitution, guaranteed minority and religious rights, and made provision for the protection of holy places. Jerusalem would be placed under a UN trusteeship.

Three of the representatives (India, Iran, and Yugoslavia) objected to the majority report and produced a minority report. It called for a brief transition period and then the creation of a federal state of Palestine. It would have both a Jewish and Arab state within it and two federal legislative bodies, one on the basis of proportionate representation and the other with equal representation from both Arabs and Jews. The Australian delegate refused to endorse either plan.

On September 23, 1947, at its regular fall session, the UN General Assembly referred the reports of the committee to the Special Committee on the Question of Palestine, which had representatives of all member states. It was before this committee that Silver, speaking on behalf of the Jewish Agency, stated that while the partition plan presented by the majority report would impose hardship on the Jewish people, the Jewish Agency was prepared to accept it. On October 11 the U.S. delegate stated his government's support for the partition plan. Two days later, the Soviet Union followed suit.

Nonetheless, the committee continued its deliberations. It divided into two subcommittees. Subcommittee No. 2 worked on the minority report, and Subcommittee No. 1 worked on the majority report. The major stumbling block in the latter was over the territorial arrangements for partition. The investigating committee had come up with a map of three Jewish and three Arab sections and additional enclaves. The Jewish Agency pressed for an additional 200,000 acres for the Jewish state for future settlement and defensible borders. On the other hand, the United States initially sought a reduction in the area allocated to the Jewish state, and it was because of this that the port and city of Jaffa became an Arab enclave and that most of western Galilee was assigned to the proposed Arab state.

Jewish hopes were dealt another blow in the planned internationalization of Jerusalem. On the other hand, the Jewish state was awarded the Bet Ntofa Valley and Lydda

(Lod) Airport as well as gains in Lower Galilee, the Beit She'an Valley, and the Gilboa area of the Jezreel Valley. Also, thanks to a last-minute visit by Chaim Weizmann with President Harry S. Truman, Israel was awarded the thinly populated but large Negev region, which the Jews hoped to use for future settlement. The plan also included the Arab-Jewish economic union. Thus, of the some 10,000 square miles of Mandate Palestine, the final report awarded the Jewish state 5,579 square miles. This area also contained an estimated Arab population of 397,000 people, or 46.5 percent of the total there.

On November 25, 1947, the committee voted on the two reports. The minority report from Subcommittee No. 2 was rejected by 29 to 12 votes with 16 abstentions. The majority report of Subcommittee No. 1 was accepted in a vote of 25 to 13 with 17 abstentions and 2 members absent. This was 1 vote short of the two-thirds vote that would be required in the final vote to be taken by the General Assembly.

The General Assembly voted on November 29, 1947. There were 33 votes for partition, 13 opposed, 10 abstentions, and 1 absent (Siam). Those voting no were Afghanistan, Cuba, Egypt, Greece, India, Iran, Iraq, Lebanon, Pakistan, Saudi Arabia, Syria, Turkey, and Yemen. States abstaining included the United Kingdom, China, and a number of Latin American countries.

While the Jewish Agency accepted the vote, the Arabs did not. Immediately on learning of the UN decision, Arabs in Palestine began attacking Jewish settlements in Palestine. This marked the beginning of the Arab-Jewish Communal War (November 30, 1947–May 14, 1948).

SPENCER C. TUCKER

**See also**
Arab-Jewish Communal War; Ben-Gurion, David; Palestine, British Mandate for; Palestine, Partition of

**References**
Sachar, Howard M. *A History of Israel: From the Rise of Zionism to Our Time.* 3rd ed. New York: Knopf, 2007.
Shepherd, Naomi. *Ploughing Sand: British Rule in Palestine, 1917–1948.* New Brunswick, NJ: Rutgers University Press, 1999.

## United Nations Special Commission on Palestine (May 13–August 31, 1947)

The United Nations Special Commission on Palestine (UNSCOP) was the United Nations (UN) committee that on August 31, 1947, recommended the partitioning of Palestine into a Jewish state and an Arab state, with Jerusalem and Bethlehem remaining neutral areas. UNSCOP was formed on May 15, 1947, to study the so-called Palestine problem after the British government had informed the UN on February 18, 1947, that it would no longer administer the British Mandate for Palestine as directed by the League of Nations on September 29, 1923. UNSCOP's 11 member states (Australia, Canada, Czechoslovakia, Guatemala, India, Iran, the Netherlands, Peru, Sweden, Uruguay, and Yugoslavia) voted unanimously to terminate British administration. Seven of the 11 members issued the report eventually accepted by the UN General Assembly on November 29, 1947, that divided Palestine into independent Jewish and Arab states with well-defined borders. A minority report recommended a federal state uniting the two factions. No member recommended the Arab state proposal favored by the Arab Higher Committee.

World War II had left the United Kingdom unwilling and unable to bare the expense of its empire. The British were also facing a rising tide of violence in Palestine, where 80,000 British soldiers continued to be garrisoned. The Zionists, comprising just over a third of the population of Palestine, saw the British as pro-Arab and orchestrated legal and illegal immigration to Palestine in an attempt to bolster their numbers for what both they and the Arabs saw as an eventual war for Palestine. Other more radical Zionists, some of whom had fought with the British in World War II, attacked British facilities in Palestine. Both the Jews and the Arabs fought one another, and the British seemed incapable of quelling the violence. The British held a conference in London on February 7, 1947, seeking to resolve the issues between the Jews and the Arabs, but this proved impossible and led to the decision to cede the problem to the UN. The British government offered its recommendations on the future of Palestine when it detailed its administration of the mandate on April 2, 1947.

UNSCOP began its study in Palestine on June 15, 1947. The Jewish Agency cooperated with UNSCOP, but the Arab Higher Committee boycotted all the meetings and hearings and demanded the immediate creation of an independent Arab state. UNSCOP held two hearings, receiving reports and testimonies from the Jewish Agency and the Arab government of Palestine before touring Jerusalem and Arab and Jewish settlements and cities throughout the mandate on July 4–17.

UNSCOP departed Palestine on July 20 and traveled to Lebanon, a visit that included an informal side trip to Damascus, Syria, on July 21. Hamid Franjiyya (Frangie) communicated the views of the Arab states to UNSCOP at a meeting in Beirut on July 22. UNSCOP's study included 13 public hearings and 4 private hearings involving testimony by representatives of 6 Arab states as well as 31 Jews and 17 Jewish organizations.

The committee divided itself into four subcommittees and three working groups. One of these subcommittees visited King Abdullah I of Transjordan on July 25. During August 8–14 a subcommittee or its members met with Austrian, American, and British officials dealing with displaced persons (DPs) in Europe and visited a hospital and camps in Germany and Austria servicing more than 26,000 adult and child DPs. More than 100 DPs were interviewed. The drama of the 1947 *Exodus* transport ship incident with 4,515 DP passengers (all Jewish, some orphaned children) occurred during the UNSCOP visit to Palestine. Two UNSCOP members were at the port of Haifa when the *Exodus* was towed there and the passengers deported on ships to Toulon, France. The *Exodus* deportees rejected disembarkation in France and began a 24-day hunger strike. UNSCOP members testified later that the plight of the DPs, the *Exodus* deportees in particular, helped shape their recommendations.

The whole committee held 39 private meetings. Additional meetings of its subcommittees and working groups were also held before UNSCOP began writing its report in Geneva on July 28. UNSCOP'S report began with a preface and was followed by four chapters of factual information and analysis. As part of this analysis, the report asserted that the League of Nations had committed itself to the creation of a Jewish state in Palestine and had not fulfilled that promise. UNSCOP also asserted that British policies had unfairly restricted Jewish immigration and land purchases to less than 6 percent of the land. Chapters 5–7 contained UNSCOP'S recommendations and proposals. The final chapter listed reservations voiced by some UNSCOP members and then in the appendix detailed those reservations and some observations.

UNSCOP'S August 31 partition plan allotted 56 percent of the land remaining in the mandate to the Jewish state. Although Palestine and Transjordan remained a single administrative unit until 1946, Transjordan was removed, over Zionist protests, on September 11, 1922, by the League of Nations from the geographical area to which the 1917 Balfour Declaration applied. Transjordan comprised 77 percent of the original mandate, leaving only 23 percent to be divided in UNSCOP'S partition. Jerusalem and its environs comprised 2 percent of the partition, leaving 42 percent of the non-Transjordan land for an Arab state. The land allotted to the Jewish state was 75 percent desert and 61 percent Jewish in population. The population of the Arab partition was just over 2 percent Jewish, and the Jerusalem trusteeship was almost equal in Arab, Christian, Muslim, and Jewish inhabitants. UNSCOP's partition plan was rejected by the Arab Higher Committee on September 29, 1947, but was accepted by the Jewish Agency on October 2.

In early November UNSCOP determined May 14 as the recommended date for the dissolution of the British Mandate for Palestine and its partition. The UN General Assembly adopted Resolution 181, UNSCOP recommendations with minor revisions, with a two-thirds majority (33 to 13 and 9 others abstaining) on November 29, 1947. On March 12, 1948, UNSCOP informed the UN that it believed that dissolution would bring chaos and war to the region and on March 18 recommended that the UN attempt to maintain order and peace by assuming temporary trusteeship over Palestine. The UN responded by creating the Truce Commission for Palestine on April 23, 1948, to assist the UN Security Council in bringing peace and order to Palestine per UN Resolution 46.

The British Mandate for Palestine was dissolved, the partition was enacted, and the independent Jewish State of Israel was created at midnight Palestine time on May 14, 1948. Egypt, Syria, Jordan, Lebanon, and Iraq attacked Israel on May 15. The UN dissolved UNSCOP on May 20 believing that appointed mediator Count Folke Bernadotte, working with the Truce Commission, had a better chance at bringing peace to the region.

RICHARD M. EDWARDS

**See also**
Abdullah I; *Exodus* Incident; Palestine, British Mandate for; Palestine, Partition of; United Nations Palestine Partition Plan

**References**
Berry, Mike, and Greg Philo. *Israel and Palestine: Competing Histories.* London: Pluto, 2006.
Gelvin, James L. *The Israel-Palestine Conflict: One Hundred Years of War.* New York: Cambridge University Press, 2005.
Harms, Gregory, and Todd Ferry. *The Palestine-Israel Conflict: A Basic Introduction.* London: Pluto, 2005.
Pappe, Ilan. *A History of Modern Palestine: One Land, Two Peoples.* Cambridge: Cambridge University Press, 2003.

## Uzun Hasan (1425–1478)

Ruler of the Turkoman dynasty of the Aq-Qoyunlu who carved a vast empire out of Iraq, Persia, and southern Caucasia. Born Abu al-Nasr Hasan Bahadur in Amida (Diyarbakir) in 1425, Uzun Hasan was a member of the ruling dynasty of the Aq-Qoyunlu state. After the death of Kara

Osman, who founded the Aq-Qoyunlu dynasty, in 1435 a successionist struggle ensued, but in the late 1450s Uzun Hasan emerged victorious. The situation was then nonetheless quite threatening to Uzun Hasan's fledgling state. In the west, the Ottoman Turks just destroyed the last vestiges of the Byzantine Empire, securing control of Anatolia, while in the east a much larger and hostile Kara Koyunlu dynasty ruled western Persia and parts of Iraq.

Uzun Hasan quickly demonstrated his political and military acumen. He successfully dealt with internal opposition and then concluded alliances to protect his state, strengthening diplomatic ties with the empire of Trebizond as well as with Venice, Muscovy, Burgundy, Poland, and Egypt. Uzun Hasan also vastly expanded his territorial holdings. His first campaigns in the late 1450s were directed against his rival Qara Qoyunlu, whose army, led by Jahan Shah, was routed on the banks of the Tigris River in May 1457.

During 1458–1463 Uzun Hasan conducted several *ghaza* campaigns against the Christian Kingdom of Georgia, where he secured immense booty that helped fund his subsequent wars. He also won the accolade of "sultan of the ghazis," which gained him support among the Turkmen tribes. In 1461 he clashed for the first time with the Ottomans but after several inconclusive skirmishes chose to avoid a prolonged conflict and stood by while the Ottomans destroyed his ally, the Empire of Trebizond. In 1464–1466 he successfully campaigned in northern Iraq and eastern Anatolia, where he captured the fortress of Harput.

In 1467, Uzun Hasan's rival Jahan Shah of the Qara-Qoyunlu invaded Aq-Qoyunlu territory but suffered defeat near Sanjaq (Chapakchur region) on November 10. Uzun Hasan was able to exploit poor weather and his enemy's tactical mistake to attack the Qara-Qoyunlu camp at dawn. Jahan Shah and his sons were among those slain. With Jahan Shah's death, the Qara-Qoyunlu state was thrown into turmoil, allowing Uzun Hasan to proceed rapidly with its conquest.

Uzun Hasan captured Mosul and besieged Baghdad for 40 days before Jahan Shah's successor, Hasan Ali, counterattacked, supported by Timurid sultan Abu Said (Timur's great-grandson), who also marched with a separate army from Khurasan in the spring of 1468. Nevertheless, Uzun Hasan managed to incite division among his opponents and then defeated Hasan Ali's weakened army near Marand in August 1468. Uzun Hasan exploited this success to conquer Karabagh, where he faced the approach of Abu Said's army. The Timurid advance proved to be disastrous, however. Wintering on the Mughan steppe, Abu Said surrounded his camp with a ditch and wagons chained together. Uzun Hasan avoided attacking the Timurid wagon laager, however, and instead cut off the Timurid supplies and isolated the sultan diplomatically. After several weeks the Timurid troops wavered in their loyalties, with many deserting or going over to the Turkmens. On January 29, 1469, Sultan Abu Said himself tried to escape but was captured and executed a week later.

The death of Sultan Abu Said opened doors to the Aq-Qoyunlu expansion eastward. Uzun Hasan's forces spread throughout Persia, campaigning in Kirman, Fars, Luristan, Khuzistan, and Kurdistan. The remaining Qara-Qoyunlu forces were destroyed at Hamadan in 1468, while later the same year Uzun Hasan captured Baghdad. Thus, by 1469 Uzun Hasan emerged as a ruler of a vast state that included much of Iraq and Persia and was the only polity in Western Asia capable of dealing with the Ottoman. He demolished the Qara-Qoyunlu and reduced the once mighty Timurid Empire to a few local kingdoms in Central Asia.

The rise of Uzun Hasan did not go unnoticed in Europe, where the Ottoman destruction of the Byzantine Empire had caused alarm. The Republic of Venice was the first to establish diplomatic contacts with Uzun Hasan. Negotiations began as early as 1458, and a formal alliance was concluded in 1464. During the Ottoman-Venetian War of 1463–1479, the Venetians were concerned about the Turkish conquest of Euboea during 1469–1470 and urged Uzun Hasan to take action against the Ottomans. In the summer of 1472, the Aq-Qoyunlu ruler responded by organizing an invasion of Anatolia and Syria. His troops sacked Tokat and invaded Karaman, seizing several fortresses. That fall Uzun Hasan turned to the Mamluk provinces in Syria, penetrating deep into Mamluk territory to the outskirts of Aleppo.

Upset by these attacks as well as Uzun Hasan's insolent letters, Ottoman sultan Mehmed II counterattacked in the spring of 1473 with an army of some 100,000 men, driving the Turkomans out of the Kireli region west of Konya and sacking Kemakh. By late July, Uzun Hasan gathered his army (no more than 40,000 men) near Erzinjan, where on August 4 he defeated part of the Ottoman army under Hass Murad Pasha as it was trying to cross the Euphrates River. Just a week later Uzun Hasan encountered the main Ottoman army, under Sultan Mehmed, near the village of Bashkent on the Otlukbeli River, where a decisive battle occurred on August 11, 1473.

Unlike the traditional cavalry-dominated army of Uzun Hasan, Mehmed's troops incorporated firearms and artillery. Deployed behind a barrier of wagons, the Ottomans exploited their superiority in firearms to inflict heavy losses on the Aq-Qoyunlu. The battle ended with a complete rout of

Uzun Hasan's army and opened eastern Anatolia to Ottoman expansion. Although Uzun Hasan suffered no immediate appreciable territorial losses, the damage to his reputation and prestige was grave indeed.

Despite this setback, Uzun Hasan rallied his remaining forces and spent five years suppressing rebellions that erupted following the news of his defeat in the Battle of Otlukbeli. In 1476–1477 he launched a new campaign against Georgia, most probably to refurbish his image and gain much-needed plunder. However, the winter campaign in Georgia had a detrimental effect on his health. Uzun Hasan died on January 5, 1478, in Tabriz. He left behind a vast Turkmen empire but had made no provision for the succession.

ALEXANDER MIKABERIDZE

**See also**

Byzantine-Ottoman Wars; Mehmed II, Sultan; Otlukbeli, Battle of; Venetian-Ottoman Wars

**Referencess**

Jackson, Peter, and Lawrence Lockhart, eds. *The Cambridge History of Iran: The Timurid and Safavid Periods,* Vol. 6. Cambridge: Cambridge University Press, 1986.

Woods, John E. *The Aqquyunlu: Clan, Confederation, Empire.* Salt Lake: University of Utah Press, 1999.

## Valens, Emperor (ca. 328–378)

Emperor of the Eastern Roman Empire during March 28, 364–August 9, 378. Flavius Valens was born at Cibalae in Pannonia in 328, the son of General Gratianus and brother to Emperor Valentinian I (r. 364–375). Valens's pre-imperial career was undistinguished. He served as a low-ranking army officer and was only named emperor after the army forced his brother Valentinian to choose an imperial colleague. Valentinian's choice of Valens was not a popular one, and in 365 Julian's relative Procopius revolted, challenging Valens's rule. Procopius enjoyed early success and attracted some army units to his cause. However, in 366 he was defeated by Valens's forces and subsequently executed. This event left Valens increasingly fearful of betrayal, and in 371–372 he executed some high-ranking officials whom he believed were engaged in magical practices designed to remove him from power.

Valens was an able administrator who kept taxation under control and fought against entrenched patrimonial corruption among public officials, albeit with limited success. Some Christian writers state that he was an aggressive supporter of the Arian cause, but whatever religious impact he had was limited. Valens was active on the empire's frontiers. In the east he forcefully intervened in the internal politics of Armenia in an effort to counter Persian claims on the kingdom. He was only dissuaded from launching a full-scale invasion owing to troubles with the Goths on the Danubian frontier, which had been problematic throughout his reign.

During 367–369 Valens had campaigned against the Goths, but only limited success obliged him to negotiate for peace. In 376 he allowed Gothic tribes to settle in Thrace in return for providing military recruits. However, when local officials mistreated the Goths, they attacked Roman forces and heavily defeated them. Because he was then at Antioch preparing a campaign against the Persians, Valens was not able to move immediately to meet the Gothic threat and only personally moved into Thrace in 378. On August 9, having ignored advice to wait for military assistance from Gratian, he engaged the Gothic army at Adrianople. In the course of the battle the Roman army was annihilated, and Valens himself was among those slain. He was succeeded by Theodosius I (r. 379–395).

Mark Hebblewhite

### See also
Adrianople, Battle of; Roman-Sassanid Wars

### References
Curran, John. "From Jovian to Theodosius," In *Cambridge Ancient History*, 13:80–101. Cambridge: Cambridge University Press, 1998.

Errington, R. M. *Roman Imperial Policy from Julian to Theodosius*. Chapel Hill: University of North Carolina Press, 2006.

Lenski, Noel. *Failure of Empire: Valens and the Roman State in the 4th Century A.D.* Berkeley: University of California Press, 2002.

Potter, David S. *The Roman Empire at Bay: AD 180–395*. London: Routledge, 2004.

## Valerian, Emperor (ca. 193–260/264)

Roman emperor. Publius Licinius Valerianus, born around 193 CE, was a senator from an old and distinguished Roman family. In 253, he became emperor as Valerian I. His rule marks one of the most disastrous and volatile periods in the crisis that was the third century for Rome. At least five usurpers claimed the throne in various parts of the empire during Valerian's reign. Plague was rampant. The Roman frontiers were under attack from a multitude of enemies, including the Goths in Greece and Asia, the Franks and Alamanni in Gaul, the Saxons on the North Sea, the Persians in Syria, and the Quadi and the Marcomanni in Pannonia.

Valerian sent his son and coemperor Gallienus to take care of the military threats in the West, while he himself went to the East, where by 257 CE he had recovered Antioch from the Persians. At this point he faced the Gothic invasion of Asia Minor in 258, then in 259 moved to Edessa to address a renewed Persian attack. Many of his soldiers died of the plague, and in 260 he became the first Roman emperor to become the prisoner of a foreign power when he was taken prisoner during negotiations by Shapur I of Persia. Roman sources claim that the Persians subjected Valerian to humiliation thereafter. In any case, he remained a prisoner of the Sassanids for the rest of his life.

KATHRYN H. MILNE

**See also**
Sassanid Empire; Shapur I the Great

**References**
Potter, David S. *The Roman Empire at Bay: AD 180–395*. New York: Routledge, 2004.
Southern, Pat. *The Roman Empire from Severus to Constantine*. London: Routledge, 2001.

## Valley of Tears, Battle of the (October 6–9, 1973)

When Syria launched its surprise attack at 2:05 p.m. on October 6, 1973, to open the northern front of the Yom Kippur War (Ramadan War), Israel had only 177 tanks and 11 batteries of artillery on the Golan Heights. The Syrian attack force had some 900 tanks and 140 batteries of artillery, with another 600 tanks in reserve. Most of the Israeli tanks were British Centurions and American M-48s, and both types had been upgraded by the Israelis. Each of the three attacking Syrian infantry divisions had an armored brigade with Soviet T54/55 tanks. The two follow-on armored divisions and the brigade-size Assad Republican Guard operated Soviet T-62s. The Syrian tanks were equipped with the most current night sights. The Israeli tanks had no such equipment.

Only days prior to the attack, Israeli armored presence on the Golan Heights had been even less. The entire front had been held by the 188th Armored Brigade, also known as the Barak Brigade, commanded by Colonel Yitzhak Ben Shoham. On September 26 the 77th Armored Battalion, known as Oz 77, was detached from the 7th Armored Brigade and deployed to the Golan Heights as a counterattack force in support of the Barak Brigade. On October 4–5, the remainder of the 7th Armored Brigade, commanded by Colonel Avigdor Ben Gal, also deployed to the Golan Heights.

When the Syrian attack occurred, the 74th Armored Battalion, commanded by Lieutenant Colonel Yair Nafsi, was occupying preestablished firing positions on high ground that ran from Tel Hermonit about three miles south to a strongpoint that the Israelis called Booster and the Arabs referred to as Tall al-Mehafi. The valley floor below the Israeli positions was covered by minefields and antitank barriers. In the first wave of the Syrian attack, Nafsi's tanks destroyed some 60 tanks of the Syrian 7th Infantry Division, commanded by Brigadier General Omar Abrash.

Late on October 6, Israeli northern front commander Major General Yitzhak Hofi ordered the 7th Armored Brigade to assume responsibility for the Golan Heights line from Quneitra north, with the Barak Brigade covering the southern sector. The 36th Armored Division, under Brigadier General Rafael Eitan, was the headquarters for the two brigades. Since the sector assigned to the 7th Armored Brigade also included the Booster position, the 74th Armored Battalion was detached from the Barak Brigade and reassigned to the 7th Armored Brigade.

Israeli tactics centered on long-range precision engagement and first-round hits. During the day, with the sun to their backs, the Israelis held the advantage. But after dark, the Israelis could no longer engage at the longer ranges. The Syrians, with their advanced night sights, then held the advantage. The Israelis also counted on their airpower to counter any enemy's numerical advantages in tanks, but from the very start it became clear that the Syrian air defenses rendered Israeli air attacks near suicidal. The opening phases of the fight for the Golan Heights became an almost pure tank-on-tank battle.

As the Syrians attacked throughout the night, the engagement ranges closed to as little as 100 yards. By dawn on October 7, more than 100 knocked-out Syrian tanks littered the valley floor in front of the Israeli positions. Later that morning the Syrian 78th Armored Brigade renewed the

Israeli Centurion tanks breaking through the Syrian lines on the Golan Heights, October 9, 1973, during the Yom Kippur War (Ramadan War). (Israeli Government Press Office)

attack, as Ben Gal constantly shifted his battalions to meet the threat. Later that afternoon the 77th Armored Battalion, under Lieutenant Colonel Avigdor Kahalani, moved to the Booster positions. At 10:00 p.m. the Syrians attacked again, this time augmented by the 81st Armored Brigade of the 3rd Armored Division, commanded by Brigadier General Mustafa Sharba. The Israelis had 40 tanks against 500. Using the darkness, the Syrian tanks got to within 50 yards, while Syrian infantrymen armed with rocket-propelled grenades attempted to infiltrate the Israeli positions.

About 1:00 a.m. on October 8, the Syrians broke off the attack and attempted to recover knocked-out vehicles. The Israelis called in artillery fire and rearmed and refueled their surviving tanks. The Syrians attacked again at 4:00 a.m., with Abrash withdrawing his decimated first echelon and committing his second. The battle waxed and waned throughout the day. Abrash planned another all-out assault for that night, but he was killed just at dusk when his command tank took a direct hit. Resumption of the Syrian attack was postponed.

Early on October 9, the Syrians hit the Israeli positions with a massive barrage of accurate artillery and rocket fire.

Ben Gal ordered Kahalani to pull his battalion back 500 yards and then rush back into position as soon as the fire lifted. The Syrians, however, moved too fast and seized the Booster crest before the 77th Armored Battalion could reach it. Charging headlong into the smoke and dust and firing at point blank range, Kahalani's command tank knocked out four Syrian T-62s within a minute and a half. In short order Oz 77 decimated two battalions of the Assad Republican Guard.

Other elements of the Republican Guard had managed to break through in the north and were driving toward El Rom, west of Tel Hermonit. General Eitan ordered the 71st Armored Battalion under Lieutenant Colonel Menachem Ratess to block the thrust, but Ratess was killed almost immediately. Ben Gal then ordered Kahalani to absorb the remnants of the 71st Armored Battalion and stop the Republican Guard. With only 15 tanks, Kahalani attacked.

As the fighting on October 9 ground on, the 7th Armored Brigade was down to only 7 of the 105 tanks with which it had started the battle. Each tank had only about four rounds remaining. The remnants of the 7th Armored Brigade were completely surrounded and fighting at 360 degrees. Just as

Ben Gal was about to order his surviving units to break contact and escape and evade, a relief force under Lieutenant Colonel Yosi Ben Hannan arrived on the battlefield. By scrounging tanks from the rear-area repair depots and pulling together pick-up crews of replacements and the lightly wounded, Ben Hannan had managed to assemble a force of 13 tanks.

Crashing into the Syrian left flank, Ben Hannan's tiny force knocked out 30 Syrian tanks in short order. The unexpected attack stunned the Syrians, who assumed that Ben Hannan's force was the point element of a large Israeli reserve that had finally reached the battlefield after mobilization. Just on the verge of punching through into northern Galilee, the Syrians broke contact and started to withdraw along the line. Behind them they left 260 tanks and 500 antipersonnel carriers and other vehicles littering the low ground beneath the Booster–to–Tel Hermonit ridge, a place that would become known as the Valley of Tears. The surviving members of the 7th Armored Brigade had been in combat for more than 50 straight hours. Kahalani was later awarded the Medal of Valor, Israeli's highest combat decoration.

David T. Zabecki

**See also**
Golan Heights; Yom Kippur War

**References**
Dunstan, Simon. *The Yom Kippur War, 1973*. 2 vols. Westport, CT: Praeger, 2005.
Herzog, Chaim. *The War of Atonement: The Inside Story of the Yom Kippur War*. London: Greenhill, 2003.
Kahalani, Avigdor. *The Heights of Courage: A Tank Leader's War on the Golan*. Westport, CT: Praeger, 1992.

# Varna Crusade (1444)

The last great Christian land-based crusade against the Ottoman Empire, which ended in the defeat of a Balkan Christian coalition by Ottoman forces near the city of Varna (in modern-day Bulgaria).

The Varna Crusade came about in response to Ottoman advances in the Balkans, notably the occupation of Serbia (1439) and the siege of Belgrade (1440). In 1443 for the first time after the disastrous Nikopolis Crusade (1396), Hungary initiated an ambitious offensive campaign against the Ottoman Empire, encouraged by Pope Eugenius IV and Cardinal Giuliano Cesarini, sent as papal legate to Hungary. A Hungarian army of some 35,000 men, led by General John Hunyadi (Hunyadi János), was accompanied by Cesarini, Serbian despot George Brankovic, and King Vladislav I (king of Poland as Władysław III), who had been elected as king of Hungary, all in expectation of significant Polish support against the Turks.

The Christian forces departed Buda on July 22, 1443, and then crossed the Serbian border by mid-October and occupied Sofia by December. Having gained some other minor victories and after learning that Sultan Murad II had crossed the Bosporus, they returned home in January and celebrated with a triumphal review in Buda.

Faced with a revolt by the Karamanids in Anatolia in the spring of 1444, Murad II was unwilling to face war on two fronts, and he therefore offered favorable peace conditions to Hungary: peace for 10 years, the surrender of Serbia and Bosnia, the liberation of the sons of Brankovic, and payment of 100,000 gold florins. These extravagant terms confused the political parties in Hungary. Before the sultan's offer in April, the Hungarian Diet had voted for war, and the king had taken a solemn oath to carry it out. The war was also supported by Cardinal Cesarini, who envisaged the union of the Roman Catholic and Greek Orthodox churches and the relief of Constantinople, and by the Polish court party in Buda, though it was rejected by Warsaw.

The period between April and September is confusing. Despot Brankovic accepted the sultan's conditions and offered John Hunyadi his own immense possessions in Hungary in exchange for his support of a future peace treaty. Hunyadi seems to have accepted Brankovic's offer, which meant that Hungary was preparing for war and negotiating peace terms at the same time.

A tentative peace treaty was concluded by the Hungarians at Adrianople (modern-day Edirne, Turkey) on June 15, and the sultan left Europe on July 12 to lead his troops against his adversaries in Anatolia. In this situation, the Hungarians tried to win both peace and war. On August 4 at Szeged, King Vladislav, with Cesarini's approval, declared invalid any former or future treaties made with the infidels. Meanwhile, the Hungarian-Ottoman peace treaty was ratified on August 15 in Várad (modern-day Oradea, Romania), only a few miles from the forward outposts of the royal army, by the king, John Hunyadi, and Brankovic.

Meanwhile, a papal-Venetian fleet sailed to blockade the Dardanelles, but the Hungarian-Ottoman diplomatic activity disturbed the European Christian coalition and the efficacy of the blockade, causing delay and depriving the campaign of surprise. Coalition unity was now in tatters. Despot Brankovic was satisfied to have at least regained northern Serbia together with its capital (August 22); he not only failed to join the coming war but even tried to hinder it.

The Christian coalition army numbered some 20,000 men, considerably fewer than the previous year. It consisted mostly of Hungarians, along with Polish and Bohemian mercenaries and some 2,000–3,000 Walacian light cavalry led by Vlad Dracul; the absence of any Serbian and Albanian auxiliary troops should have been a warning signal.

The army departed Orflova on September 20, intending to strike at Adrianople. The Christians marched along the Danube route via Vidin (September 26) and Nikopolis (October 26), then turned southeast via Novi Pazar and Shumen, capturing and plundering all these cities. Owing to poor reconnaissance, they did not know that Ottoman forces under Murad had already crossed the Bosporus and were perhaps twice the size of their own army.

The Christians met the Ottomans at the city of Varna on November 9, 1444, on terrain unfavorable for them, between the Devna Lake and the seacoast. Despite John Hunyadi's proven military talent, the Christians were defeated as a result of poor cooperation among the multinational coalition forces. Hunyadi initially gained the upper hand on both wings, thanks to an overwhelming attack by his heavy cavalry. The sultan considered a retreat, but then Polish troops under King Vladislav attacked the elite Ottoman janissary. This upset Hunyadi's tactical plans and resulted in the deaths of both the king and the papal legate. The Christian force broke, and their cavalry departed the field in panic-stricken flight, Hunyadi among them. Hunyadi escaped to Walacia. Both sides suffered heavy losses in the battle, above all among the Christian infantry units that attempted to defend their camp behind a laager of wagons.

The Hungarian and papal war parties had been correct in their assessment that 1444 presented the best opportunity in a long time to wear down Ottoman power by force of arms. The Varna Crusade, however, proved to be the last spectacular failure of the traditional crusading strategy. Sweeping the Ottomans out of Europe in a single campaign proved impossible given the absence of political unity among the fragmented Christian forces involved. Much more could have been achieved by accepting the peace terms than by launching a campaign into an unstable region.

As had been the case with King Sigismund after the defeat of the Nikopolis Crusade in 1396, the Hungarian kings again adopted a deliberate defensive strategy (particularly under King Matthias Corvinus, son of John Hunyadi) up to the final collapse of the Hungarian defense system in 1521 and of the medieval kingdom of Hungary itself in 1526.

LÁSZLÓ VESZPRÉMY

**See also**
Murad II, Sultan; Nikopolis, Crusade in; Ottoman-Hungarian Wars

**References**
Engel, Pál. "János Hunyadi: The Decisive Years of His Career, 1440–1444." In *From Hunyadi to Rákoczi: War and Society in Medieval and Early Modern Hungary,* ed. János M. Bak and Béla K. Király, 103–123. Boulder, CO: Atlantic, 1982.
Engel, Pál. "János Hunyadi and the Peace of Szeged." *Acta Orientalia Academiae Scientiarum Hungaricae* 47 (1994): 241–257.
Halecki, Oscar. *The Crusade of Varna: A Discussion of Controversial Problems.* New York: Polish Institute of Arts and Sciences in America, 1943.
Imber, Colin. *The Crusade of Varna, 1443–45.* Aldershot, UK: Ashgate, 2006.

## Vasvár, Treaty of (August 10, 1664)

Treaty between the Ottoman Empire and the Habsburgs signed on August 10, 1664, at Vasvár in Hungary that concluded the Ottoman-Habsburg War of (1663–1664). Under the leadership of Grand Vizier Köprülü Fazil Ahmed Pasha, the Ottomans sought to counter Habsburg interference in Transylvania. In 1663 following the Habsburg rejection of the Ottoman demands to evacuate Transylvania, Fazil Ahmed led some 100,000 Ottoman troops into Hungary. After capturing the key fortress of Nove Zamky (Neuhausel), the Ottomans returned to Serbia to winter there.

In the spring of 1664 Fazil Ahmed resumed his campaign, and the Habsburgs agreed in late July to commence negotiations for a peace treaty. These occurred at Vasvár, Hungary. Under the terms agreed to, the Habsburgs were to surrender a number of border fortresses (Neuhausel and Grosswardein), recognize Ottoman control of Transylvania, and agree to pay the sultan an annual "gift" of some 200,000 florins. In return, the Ottomans agreed to make a suitable gift to the emperor, maintain a 20-year truce with the empire, and allow the Habsburgs to build a new fortress on the Waag River.

However, while the treaty's text was on its way to Vienna, the imperial and Ottoman armies clashed on August 1, 1664, at St. Gotthard, fought near Mogersdorf, Burgenland, with the Ottomans suffering a major defeat. In spite of the victory, Holy Roman emperor Leopold was well aware of the weakness of his forces and chose to confirm the terms of the treaty. The Treaty of Vasvár held until 1683, when border skirmishing escalated to a full-scale war and culminated in the Ottoman siege of Vienna that same year.

ALEXANDER MIKABERIDZE

**See also**

Köprülü Fazil Ahmed Pasha

**Reference**

Carsten, Francis Ludwig, ed. *The New Cambridge Modern History: The Ascendancy of France, 1648–88,* Vol. 5. Cambridge: Cambridge University Press, 1961.

# Venetian-Ottoman Wars (1416–1718)

A series of military conflicts between the Republic of Venice and the Ottoman Empire regarding hegemony in the eastern Mediterranean Sea and the Balkan Peninsula. Ottoman expansion into the Balkans in the 14th century was initially welcomed by Venice. In fact, Venetians sent two ambassadors to congratulate Murad I (r.1362–89) for his conquest of Adrianople (Edirne) in 1365. In 1384 the Ottoman envoys arrived at Venice to discuss an alliance against Genoa. Although an alliance against Genoa never materialized, Venice and the Porte did conclude several agreements in 1403, 1408, and 1411. Yet as the Ottoman westward expansion continued, the Venetian attitudes changed. In June 1416 following the Ottoman incursions into the Aegean Sea, the Venetian fleet under Pietro Loredan attacked and destroyed the Ottoman Navy in a battle off Gallipoli. Building on this success, the Venetians secured control of the Dalmatian coastline and established outposts in southern Greece.

The Second Venetian-Ottoman war was fought between 1425 and 1430 when Sultan Murad II (1403–51) targeted Venetian settlements along the Albanian coast and at Epirus in western Greece. The two powers fought for control of Salonika, which the Venetians had bought from the Byzantines in 1423 and where they had a large garrison. In 1430, the Ottomans besieged and captured the city, forcing Venice to sue for peace.

In 1443, Venice gave help to the crusader army that marched against the Ottoman Empire but was routed at Varna in 1444. During the Third Venetian-Ottoman War, Venetians contributed warships to the defense of Constantinople against the Ottomans. Their efforts, however, proved futile, as the Byzantine capital fell to the Ottomans in May 1453.

During the Fourth Venetian-Ottoman War, Sultan Mehmed II "the Conqueror" (1432–1481) raided Venetian settlements along the Dalmatian coast, capturing the Venetian fortresses of Lepanto (the Italian name for Nafpaktos) in 1462 and Argos in 1463. Venice officially declared war in July 1463 and concluded an alliance with Hungary, the Papal States, and Burgundy, promising to divide the Balkans among the allies in case of victory over the Ottomans. In 1463–1466, a Venetian army under Alvise Loredan landed in the Morea (Peloponessus) while the Hungarian forces under King Matthias Corvinus campaigned in Bosnia. Both the Venetians and the Hungarians achieved considerable success and captured a number of Ottoman cities and locations. To confront this threat, Sultan Mehmed II ordered the establishment of the new shipyard in Istanbul (Constantinople), which was to produce warships to neutralize the Venetian fleet. He then dispatched Grand Vizier Mahmud Pasha Angelovic against the Venetian land forces, which were defeated and driven into the Morea. Sultan Mehmed II led another army into Bosnia, where he became embroiled in a prolonged conflict with Corvinus.

In 1464 Venice sent one of its ablest commanders, Sigismondo Malatesta, to take command of its forces in the Morea, but Malatesta failed to produce any decisive result. The Venetian fleet, under Orsato Giustinian, tried to capture Mytilene, the capital city of Lesbos island, but was driven back by the Ottoman navy led by Mahmud Pasha. Simultaneously, the Venetians became embroiled in a new conflict with the Knights Hospitaller of Rhoes, which diverted their manpower and resources. In 1466–1467 the new Venetian naval commander, Vettore Cappello, reinvigorated Venetian naval operations in the Aegean Sea, where he captured several Ottoman-held islands, but he was defeated in his attempt to take Athens. At the same time, Mehmed II conducted operations in Albania, where he faced ongoing Arbanian resistance under the leadership of Skenderberg.

In 1470, the Ottomans captured Negroponte (Chalcis), the Venetian port on Euboea. Venice responded by negotiating an alliance with the Aq-Qoyunlu Turkmen and supporting Sultan Uzun Hasan's invasion of the Ottoman realm; yet, in the battles at Erzinjan (Erzincan) on the upper Euphrates and at Otlukbeli in August 1473, Mehmed decisively defeated Uzun Hasan, depriving Venice of a powerful ally. In the next six years, the Ottomans overran much of central Greece and Albania, threatening the outskirts of Venice. By the Treaty of Constantinople in 1479, the Venetians recognized the loss of their territorial possession in the Aegean, paid a 100,000-ducat indemnity, and agreed to pay annual tributes to the Ottomans in return for trading rights. The two states also agreed on the creation of common borders, which they marked by heaps of stones or other devices in Albania and the Morea.

In 1499, the Fifth Venetian-Ottoman War began over continued territorial claims between two states. Venice received help from France, Aragon, and Portugal, but the tide of war soon turned against Venice. In August 1499 Kemal Reis, leading a massive Ottoman fleet, inflicted a devastating defeat on the Venetian fleet under Antonio Grimani at the Battle of Zonchio (also known as the Battle of Sapienza and the First Battle of Lepanto). This is touted as the first naval battle that featured warships with cannon. After repelling a Venetian attack on Lepanto in December 1499, Kemal Reis bombarded the Venetian ports on the island of Corfu, and in August 1500 he routed the Venetian fleet at the Battle of Modon (also known as the Second Battle of Lepanto). Later that year the Ottoman fleet raided Modon, Coron, Sapientza (Sapienza), Voiussa, and the Island of Lefkada before returning to Istanbul in November. The Venetians fared better on the lands as their army, commanded by Gonzalo de Córdoba and supported by the Spanish, captured Kefalonia. However, the Ottoman raids continued and in 1501–1502 reached as far as Vicenza, forcing Venice to sue for peace in 1503. Under the terms of the peace treaty, the Ottomans took control of parts of Morea and islands in the Aegean and Adriatic seas but lost Cephalonia, the largest of the Ionian islands.

After 1503, Venice was sidelined in the continued struggle for the Mediterranean as France, Spain, and the Ottoman Empire clashed over regional hegemony. Over three decades passed before the Sixth Venetian-Ottoman War began. In the meantime, the Ottomans' offensives into Austrian territory brought them to the gates of Vienna, which was besieged in 1529. Seven years later Süleyman I the Magnificent concluded an alliance with France against the Habsburgs and extended commercial privileges, known as capitulations, to French merchants. He then sent an envoy to Venice proposing that it enter the Ottoman-French alliance. However, his offer was rejected, since the Habsburgs could present a more immediate threat to Venetia than the Ottomans. The leader of the republic then signed an alliance with Emperor Charles V of the Holy Roman Empire.

The war began in 1537 with Süleyman marching an army to Vlore on the Adriatic coast. He intended to launch a two-pronged invasion of Italy but first had to besiege the Venetian island of Corfu. The siege had to be abandoned following the arrival of a strong imperial-Venetian fleet commanded by Andrea Doria. The Ottoman fleet under Hayreddin (Khair ad-Din) Barbarossa meanwhile laid waste to the Aegean and Adriatic coastlines. The two fleets finally met at Preveza, an Ionian coastal town south of Corfu, on September 27, 1538, and Barbarossa gained a decisive victory over Doria. By 1540, Venice had ceded to the Ottomans virtually all of its Aegean islands and outposts in Morea, including Nauplia and Monemvasia.

The next three decades produced a relative lull in Venetian-Ottoman hostilities, and despite some frictions in 1564–1565 when the Ottomans attacked Malta, the peace treaty was renewed in 1567. By then, Venice retained only two major colonies in the eastern Mediterranean, the islands of Cyprus and Crete, which nonetheless allowed it to control the lucrative Levantine trade; nevertheless, the republic had to pay an annual tribute to the Egyptian Mamluks until 1517 and then to the Ottomans. However, Cyprus's location, near the Ottoman heartland and on the trade routes to and from Levant, turned it into a target for Ottoman expansion. The Venetian refusal to cede Cyprus to Sultan Selim II led to the Seventh Venetian-Ottoman War.

Selim II organized a major expeditionary force to seize the island, with Lala Mustafa Pasha commanding the land forces and Müezzinzade Ali Pasha leading the navy. In the summer of 1570, some 5,000 Venetian soldiers at Nicosia fought off a besieging 60,000-man Ottoman army until they succumbed on September 9. The entire Venetian garrison and much of the population were put to the sword. The Ottomans then blockaded Venetian-held Famagusta, but it held out for almost a year before surrendering in mid-May 1571.

In the meantime, Venice sought allies to face the Ottoman onslaught. Unable to recruit the leaders of the Holy Roman Empire and France, Venice turned to Spain, the status of which in the Mediterranean was threatened by the Ottomans. On May 15, 1571, Venice, Spain, Naples, the Papal States, and the Italian states established the Holy League to fight the Porte. The Holy League's fleet of some 200 galleys, commanded by Don Juan of Austria, assembled at Messina in August 1571 and in a battle off Lepanto on October 7, 1571, inflicted a decisive defeat on the Ottoman fleet commanded by Müezzinzade Ali Pasha. Although the battle ended Ottoman naval dominance in eastern Mediterranean, Venice was unable to recover Cyprus and suffered territorial losses in Dalmatia.

The Ottomans soon replenished their naval forces, which were now led by Kılıç Ali Pasha, and resumed naval operations. In 1573 Venice left the Holy League and signed a peace treaty (March 7, 1573) with the Porte, ceding Cyprus and possessions in Albania and Epirus and paying a large indemnity. Cyprus remained under Ottoman rule until 1878.

The peace established in 1573 proved to be lasting and was only broken in 1645 when Venice and the Ottoman Empire clashed (for the eighth time) over the island of Crete. Known as the Cretan or Candian War, this conflict was caused when the Knights of Malta attacked an Ottoman convoy and landed with their loot at Candia (Crete) in 1644.

In response, Sultan Ibrahim I accused the Venetians of collusion with the knights and sent Yussuf Pasha with some 50,000 troops to capture the Venetian colony in 1645; Silahdar Yusuf Pasha, the sultan's son-in-law, commanded the naval forces. Although the Ottomans conquered most of the island in the first three years of the war, the fortress of Candia (modern-day Heraklion) withstood one of the longest sieges in history, lasting from 1648 to 1669.

After 1659 Venice received active support from France, an expeditionary force of which fought the Ottomans until 1669. The French withdrawal, however, proved to be a turning point in the Candia defense, and the Venetian captain general Francesco Morosini accepted the terms of surrender from Great Vizier Ahmed Köprülü on September 27, 1669. The subsequent peace treaty left Crete in Ottomans hands, ending some 400 years of Venetian presence there. Crete would remain under Ottoman control until 1913.

The Cretan War was not, however, limited to the siege of Candia. Although the Venetian Navy could not directly take on the Ottoman fleet at Crete, it directed its efforts to providing supplies to the besieged garrison and blockading the Dardanelles. Ottoman attempts to break through the blockade were largely unsuccessful. In May 1649 the Venetians, under Giacomo da Riva, scored a major victory over the Ottoman fleet led by Voinok Ahmed, and two years later Alvise Mocenigo defeated another Ottoman fleet commanded by Hosambegzade Ali Pasha south of Naxos on July 8–10, 1651. The Ottomans responded by increasing production of warships and concentrating their naval forces in the eastern Mediterranean. Starting in May 1654, the Ottoman and Venetian Navies fought a series of naval battles in the mouth of the Dardanelles Straits. While the Ottomans scored an initial victory, the Venetians under Lazaro Mocenigo inflicted a series of defeats on them between 1655 and 1668, but nonetheless Venice was unable to turn the tide of war.

The third theater of war was in Dalmatia. It saw significant action in the early stages of the war. The Ottomans initially made major gains in capturing the islands of Veglia, Pag, and Cres and the fortress of Novigrad in 1646. Supported by the local population, the Venetians turned the tide the following year as their counterattack drove the Ottoman forces back and enabled them to reclaim their territories. By 1669, Venice almost tripled its territorial holdings in Dalmatia and ensured its control of the Adriatic. Still, the war had a profound effect on Venice, as its treasury was exhausted, its most prosperous colony was lost, and its trading position in the Mediterranean was diminished.

The Ninth Venetian-Ottoman War began in 1684 as part of the wider conflict known as the Great Turkish War, waged between the Ottomans and an alliance of the Holy Roman Empire, Hungary, Russia, Spain, and Poland-Lithuania. Although the war saw military operations conducted in the Habsburg lands, Hungary, Serbia, and Ukraine, the Venetian efforts were directed toward the conquest of the Morea (Peloponnese) Peninsula in southern Greece. In 1684 the Venetians secured the Ionian Islands, while Francesco Morosini seized parts of Dalmatia and the Morea between 1685 and 1687. In September 1687, the Venetians captured Athens (in the process destroying much of the famed Parthenon when they shelled it and Ottoman ammunition stored there blew up), but they were later forced to abandon the city. In 1688–1689 the Ottomans successfully repelled Venetian attacks on Negroponte and Monemvasia, marking the end of the Venetian ascendancy. In 1689, the Ottomans raided Messolonghi and swept through central Greece and the Peloponnese.

The Venetian capture of Chios in 1694 led to a major naval battle near the Oinousses Islands in February 1695 that resulted in a decisive victory of the Ottoman fleet led by Mezzo Morto Hüseyin Pasha. The Ottomans reclaimed Chios and held it until the First Balkan War in 1912. The war was concluded with the Treaty of Karlowitz (January 1699). It confirmed the Venetian possession of the island of Kephalonia, the Morea, and most of Dalmatia.

The Tenth, and last, Venetian-Ottoman War began in 1714. In response to Venetian incitement of an uprising in Montenegro in 1714, the Porte declared war on Venice and sent land and sea forces to capture Venetian islands and fortresses in the Aegean. The campaign unfolded rather swiftly as the Ottoman army under Grand Vizier Silahdar Damat Ali Pasha swept through the entire Morea while naval forces under Canum Hoca drove the Venetians from the Aegean islands. In 1716, an Ottoman assault on Corfu was repulsed by the Venetians with help from Spain, Portugal, and several Italian states. Nevertheless, Venice was exhausted by the war and was saved from further defeats by the intervention of Austria in 1716. Austrian success eventually led to the Treaty of Passarowitz (July 1718). Venice gave up the Peloponnesus but acquired a few Albanian and Dalmatian outposts.

ALEXANDER MIKABERIDZE

**See also**
Hayreddin Barbarossa; Karlowitz, Treaty of; Köprülü Fazil Ahmed Pasha; Mehmed II, Sultan; Murad II, Sultan; Otlukbeli, Battle of; Passarowitz, Treaty of; Suleiman I; Uzun Hasan; Varna Crusade

### References

Fabris, Antonio. "From Adrianople to Constantinople: Venetian-Ottoman Diplomatic Missions, 1360–1453." *Mediterranean Historical Review* 7, no. 2 (December 1992): 154–200.

Faroqhi, Suraiya. "The Venetian Presence in the Ottoman Empire (1600–1630)." *Journal of European Economic History* 15, no. 2 (1986): 345–384.

Fleet, Kate, Suraiya Faroqhi, and Reşat Kasaba. *The Cambridge History of Turkey: The Later Ottoman Empire, 1603–1839.* Cambridge: Cambridge University Press, 2006.

Lane, Frederic Chapin. *Venice, a Maritime Republic.* Baltimore: John Hopkins University Press, 1973.

Murphey, Rhoads. *Ottoman Warfare, 1500–1700.* New York: Routledge, 1999.

Pedani, Maria Pia. "The Ottoman Venetian Frontier." In *The Great Ottoman-Turkish Civilization,* 1:171–177. Ankara: Yeni Türkiye, 2000.

Shaw, Stanford Jay. *History of the Ottoman Empire and Modern Turkey.* Cambridge: Cambridge University Press, 1976.

## Vespasian, Emperor (9–79)

Roman emperor who ruled during 69–79. Titus Flavius Vespasianus was born on November 17, 9 CE, near Reate in Sabine Italy and raised by his paternal grandmother Tertulla. Vespasian served as legionary tribune in Thrace, as quaestor to the provinces of Crete and Cyrene, as aedile, and as praetor.

Under Emperor Claudius (r. 41–54), Vespasian commanded a legion in Germany and then moved to Britain. He enjoyed some success in subduing parts of Britain, earning him triumphal decorations, the highest honor accorded to senators in this period; he was also rewarded with two priesthoods. He then held a governorship in Roman Africa, where he was unpopular.

During Nero's reign (54–68), Vespasian accompanied the emperor on his tour of Greece in 66. Late that year, Nero appointed Vespasian to subdue the Jewish rebellion in Judaea. Nero allegedly wanted to send away competent potential rivals for the imperial power, though Vespasian's small-town origins made him a low risk. Another reason for the selection of Vespasian was his proven military ability.

During 67–68, Vespasian subdued the rebellion for the most part except for Jerusalem. While still in Judaea with his son Titus, Vespasian was declared emperor by the legions at Alexandria on July 1, 69. Two days later Vespasian's troops in Judaea followed suit. Vespasian's allies, Syrian governor Licinius Mucianus and Antonius Primus in the Balkan provinces, led armies into Italy to fight the Vitellians. Primus defeated the Vitellians at Cremona in October 69 and besieged Rome. After the downfall of Vitellius in December 69, the Senate declared Vespasian emperor on December 22.

The rebellion in Judaea was left for Titus to subdue as Vespasian headed for Rome to quell any remaining disharmony left by the civil wars. A successful usurper, Vespasian desired legitimacy and the reputation of a traditional emperor, along the lines established by Augustus. Vespasian's relationship with his son Titus was very close, as Titus was clearly his designated successor and assistant. Vespasian even conferred the praetorian prefecture on Titus. This, however, angered certain senators who disapproved of dynastic rule. A more serious plot to overthrow Vespasian was discovered and defeated by Titus in 79 near the end of Vespasian's reign.

Vespasian carried out architectural restorations and new construction in Rome, including beginning work on the Colosseum. This extensive building required more efficient taxation and exploitation of unoccupied public land. Vespasian became notorious throughout the empire for his imposition of financial austerity, both imperial and senatorial. In 73 CE, Vespasian became censor with his son Titus. Vespasian conferred honors on highly distinguished Italians and provincials by elevating them to the Senate, refilling its ranks that had thinned because of the civil wars. Through such patronage, he obtained the loyalty and favor of the new senators. Vespasian also gave Latin rights to all of the towns of Spain and founded many provinces throughout his reign. The focus of strategy shifted to securing the frontiers while keeping the number of legions at 28. Wales was completely brought under Roman rule, which advanced as far as Scotland. In the West, the Germanic frontier was enhanced by creating new roads and forts between the Upper Rhine and the Danube.

Vespasian died on June 23, 79, of illness; his alleged last words were "Alas, I'm becoming a god!" He was deified by his son and successor, Titus. Vespasian's legacy was the Jewish War and the subsequent peace, advertised on his coinage. With his sons Titus and Domitian, the Flavian dynasty created a legacy of imperial stability.

Javier Lopez

**See also**
Jewish-Roman War, First; Titus, Emperor

### References
Levick, Barbara. *Vespasian.* London: Routledge, 1999.
Wellesley, Kenneth. *The Year of the Four Emperors.* London: Routledge, 2000.

## VIGILANT WARRIOR, Operation (October 8, 1994–December 8, 1994)

Military operation led by the United States to deter a potential Iraqi military action against Kuwait. Initiated on October 8, 1994, Operation VIGILANT WARRIOR ended on December 8.

In the aftermath of the 1991 Persian Gulf War, coalition armed forces responded to a series of provocations by Iraqi president Saddam Hussein's regime by increasing troop levels in the region as a deterrent to further aggression. Through 1993, however, U.S. forces in the region declined as President William J. Clinton's administration sought to reduce military deployments and use United Nations sanctions and weapons inspections, along with enforcement of the northern and southern no-fly zones, to contain Hussein's regime.

In September 1994, Iraqi forces were detected moving toward the Kuwaiti border. By October 8, two Iraqi Republican Guard armored divisions were south of the 32nd parallel (the southern no-fly zone began at the 32nd parallel). This increased the number of Iraqi military forces near Kuwait from 50,000 to 71,000 men. One of these units, the elite Hammurabi Division moved to within 12.5 miles of the Kuwaiti border and deployed its artillery in that direction.

Hussein had endeavored to rebuild his military in the aftermath of Iraq's defeat in the Persian Gulf War, and the deployment was a means of assessing their capabilities. Also, Hussein sought to test the Clinton administration, increasingly preoccupied with the crisis in Bosnia and the potential for military action there. The deployment was also seen as a warning to anti-Baathist elements in the southern areas of the country, especially among the predominantly Shiite population there. It was also a warning to regional powers that the Iraqi military remained a potent force. In addition, the deployment was seen as an effort to test the will of the international community in maintaining economic sanctions.

During the previous year Hussein had undertaken only limited cooperation with the UN weapons inspections regime engaged while having failed to remove UN economic and military sanctions, which were crippling his nation. He had, however, gained some support from China, France, and Russia to end the sanctions. The Iraqi leader apparently believed that a show of strength would prompt the international community to revise the sanctions regime rather than face the prospect of escalation and another war.

In response, the Clinton administration reacted quickly, both militarily and diplomatically. Operation VIGILANT WARRIOR was initiated on October 8, 1994. Army and marine units, including the I Marine Expeditionary Force (MEF), were put on alert, and air and naval units were ordered to the region. More than 1,800 additional U.S. troops were in Kuwait within five days of the Iraqi troop movement. In total, more than 156,000 U.S. troops were put on alert for possible deployment to Kuwait. Headquarters units, including that of U.S. Central Command (CENTCOM), were deployed to the Persian Gulf for the first time since the 1991 war. Meanwhile, Washington worked to secure passage of a UN resolution calling for the withdrawal of Iraqi forces from the Kuwaiti border.

On October 15, the UN Security Council passed Resolution 949. This called on the Iraqi regime to withdraw its forces to their positions as of September 20, 1994; forbade any additional Iraqi military buildup in the southern areas of the country; and condemned any aggressive or hostile acts toward Kuwait or other neighboring countries. The resolution also called upon Iraq to expand its cooperation with ongoing UN weapons inspections. The Clinton administration was thus able to convince China, France, and Russia of the necessity of continued containment of Iraq.

The buildup of U.S. forces in the region continued through October. An aircraft carrier battle group, centered on the *George Washington,* steamed to the region, as did an amphibious ready group. In all, 20 additional U.S. naval vessels sailed to the Persian Gulf. Two brigades of the U.S. Army's 24th Mechanized Infantry Division were dispatched to Kuwait, as were elements of the 101st Airborne Division, and special operations forces. Finally, the U.S. Air Force sent 275 additional aircraft to the area. In all, more than 28,000 additional personnel, including 2,000 marines, were deployed. The deployment of forces occurred rapidly, surprising the Iraqis who were preparing to move an additional division to the south.

Operation VIGILANT WARRIOR took advantage of lessons learned form the Persian Gulf War and prepositioned equipment and facilities at Camp Doha, Kuwait. More than 2,000 strategic lift sorties were flown during the course of a single month, bringing in 21,000 troops and more than 9,000 tons of weapons and supplies. In addition to the 58 M-1 Abrams main battle tanks and 122 Bradley Fighting Vehicles sent as part of the 24th Division, there were 116 Abrams and 122 Bradleys prepositioned in Kuwait, awaiting only crews and minor maintenance to make them combat ready. These and other weapons were left in Kuwait and maintained so that a brigade could be deployed to Kuwait, which would immediately be able to use the weapons and equipment.

Although the forces deployed were substantially fewer than for the 1991 war, the coalition soldiers were in defensive positions and enjoyed both air and naval superiority. In

A command-and-control vehicle rolls off the USS *Cape Decision* at a port in the Arabian Gulf, October 19, 1994. The Ready Reserve Force ship and the equipment being unloaded were part of Operation VIGILANT WARRIOR, the U.S. response to a threatened Iraqi military action against Kuwait. (U.S. Department of Defense)

addition, had combat commenced, the United States could have rapidly increased its forces.

As the troops came into Kuwait, the United States launched a series of military exercises that included both U.S. and select coalition forces. The missions included air, land, and sea activities and were designed to test the ability of incoming troops to be quickly acclimated and ready for combat operations. The exercises were also meant to deter the Iraqis by demonstrating the capabilities and resources of the allied forces. Finally, the training efforts provided the coalition forces opportunities to practice joint and combined operations. VIGILANT WARRIOR confirmed that the U.S. military had achieved significant improvements in strategic airlift and interservice communications.

One challenge that emerged from the operation was the strain that it placed on the available strategic lift. Reserves were not activated, and only limited assets were brought in from outside of the theater. Planners realized that current operational plans were designed for a major deployment, similar to DESERT SHIELD/DESERT STORM. Pentagon plans had not envisioned a small- or medium-size deployment and had to be revised to address possible future contingencies.

During the operation, the United States had minor support from other coalition partners. The United Kingdom dispatched a destroyer and a frigate and sent six additional fighter aircraft and an airborne refueling tanker to the region. The British also more than doubled their ground forces to 1,000 men with the deployment of an additional battalion along the Kuwaiti border. France sent a destroyer. In addition to the American, British, and French troops, the United Arab Emirates provided a mechanized infantry battalion, and Kuwait had available two armored brigades, one mechanized infantry, and one motorized cavalry. Six members of the Gulf Cooperation Council—Bahrain, Kuwait, Oman, Qatar, Saudi Arabia, and the United Arab Emirates—granted the United States overflight permissions and offered the use of facilities in the event of war.

Even as U.S. and allied troops were being deployed, Hussein announced his intention to withdraw the additional forces he had sent south. However, there was little or no movement, and Clinton publicly repudiated the Iraqi assertions that they had begun to pull back. It was not until October 18 that the Republican Guard divisions began their withdrawal. On October 20, the United States and the United Kingdom each issued separate but similar warnings to Iraq that they would enforce Resolution 949, including the use of military force if necessary.

By the end of October, the Iraqi divisions had been withdrawn north of the 32nd parallel. U.S. redeployments began simultaneously. U.S. troops were taken off alert, and the bulk of forces that had been deployed were returned home by the end of November. Operation VIGILANT WARRIOR officially ended on December 8, 1994.

In an effort to deter future ploys by Iraq, the Clinton administration decided to increase its deployments in the region and maintain 5,000 ground troops and at least 120 aircraft in theater. As a result of VIGILANT WARRIOR, the U.S. military increased its predeployment resources in the area so that the army had equipment for eight battalions prepositioned in Kuwait. The United States also increased its exercises in the region so that there were at least two operations per year in Kuwait. Nonetheless, in August 1995 Hussein again moved forces toward Kuwait, leading to Operation VIGILANT SENTINEL, a much smaller-scale version of VIGILANT WARRIOR that ended with the same results. In response to the continued provocations, the southern no-fly zone was later extended northward to the 33rd parallel.

TOM LANSFORD

**See also**
Hussein, Saddam; Iraq No-Fly Zones; Persian Gulf War, Overview; Republican Guard, Iraq; SOUTHERN WATCH, Operation

**References**
Davis, John, ed. *Presidential Policies and the Road to the Second Iraq War: From Forty One to Forty Three.* Aldershot, UK: Ashgate, 2006.
Knights, Michael Andrew. *Cradle of Conflict: Iraq and the Birth of Modern U.S. Military Power.* Annapolis, MD: Naval Institute Press, 2005.
Mahajan, Rahul. *Full Spectrum Dominance: U.S. Power in Iraq and Beyond.* New York: Seven Stories, 2003.
Woods, Kevin M. *The Mother of All Battles: Saddam Hussein's Strategic Plan for the Gulf War.* Annapolis, MD: Naval Institute Press, 2008.

## VIKING HAMMER, Operation (March 28–30, 2003)

Part of the 2003 Anglo-American–led invasion of Iraq (Operation IRAQI FREEDOM), Operation VIKING HAMMER was an offensive during March 28–30, 2003, carried out in northern Iraq by anti–Saddam Hussein Kurds assisted by coalition special operations forces against the Islamic terrorist group Ansar al-Islam.

Planning for the invasion of Iraq had called for a coalition invasion of northern Iraq from Turkey, but when Ankara denied coalition forces the use of its territory, planners had to shift their strategy. Instead, they hoped to utilize pro-American militias of the Kurdish Regional Government. The latter was dominated by two groups, the Patriotic Union of Kurdistan (PUK), led by Jalal Talabani, and the Kurdistan Democratic Party (KDP), led by Masoud Barzani. The PUK's Peshmerga militias were the largest and best trained of the Kurdish forces.

In the months preceding the invasion, the United States had inserted special operations forces to train and coordinate with the Kurds. Coalition planners believed that a Kurdish military campaign would keep Iraqi units tied down in the northern regions of the country, rendering them unavailable to fight the two main prongs of the forces moving from the south. To support the Kurds, the coalition planned to deploy additional special operations forces. Later, airborne units would be dropped in to fight alongside the Peshmerga and KDP fighters in attacks on Iraqi targets, including the important cities of Mosul and Kirkuk.

VIKING HAMMER was designed essentially to neutralize the threat to the Kurdish heartland. VIKING HAMMER and subsequent offensives were also an effort by the United States to demonstrate the country's commitment to the Kurds and ensure support from the Kurdish Regional Government in a postwar Iraq. However, the United States was concurrently trying to avoid further straining relations with Turkey, which faced an ongoing Kurdish separatist insurgency. Consequently, the United States chose not to supply the Peshmerga with extensive weaponry for fear that some might be used against Turkish forces.

The plan was a bold endeavor, as it asked a small number of special operations forces, airborne troops, and Kurdish fighters to accomplish the same goals as 60,000 U.S. ground troops in order to tie down 13 Iraqi divisions. The Kurds were apprehensive that if they deployed their forces southward, they would be vulnerable to attacks by Islamic terrorist groups located along the border with Iran.

Before the Peshmerga could engage the Iraqi forces, they had to first secure their own territory and suppress Ansar al-Islam, the Kurdish Sunni Islamist group. Ansar al-Islam had been formed in 2001 by Islamist Kurdish factions. The group was dominated by Kurds who had fought against the Soviets in Afghanistan. Led by Mullah Krekar, Ansar al-Islam sought to impose a strict version of Islamic law (sharia) on towns near the border with Iran, including Halabja, Biyara, and Tawela. It also worked with other smaller Islamist groups against the Kurdish Regional Government and was blamed for a number of terrorist attacks against rival Kurdish groups. Ansar al-Islam had some 500–600 fighters and controlled more than 100 square miles of territory. Its allies in the other small Islamist groups provided an additional 100–300 fighters. U.S. defense officials were especially concerned about Ansar al-Islam because of intelligence that it was harboring senior Al Qaeda figures, although this proved unfounded.

The Peshmerga and KDP militias in VIKING HAMMER numbered approximately 7,000 troops of varying quality with an assortment of mainly Soviet-era weaponry, including mortars, some artillery, and a limited number of armored vehicles. Most Peshmerga were armed with AK-47 assault rifles and had about 150–200 rounds apiece. Many lacked uniforms, boots, and helmets and instead wore tennis shoes and identified themselves with red scarves. However, the Kurds were highly motivated, and U.S. special operations forces provided additional firepower in the form of mortars, grenade launchers, and machine guns. U.S. personnel also had charge of communications between units and, most important, were able to coordinate ground support from coalition aircraft and cruise missiles.

There were approximately 600 U.S. soldiers from the 10th Special Forces Group with the PUK and the KDP, organized into 12-member teams. U.S. colonel Charlie Cleveland was the operational commander of the covert U.S. troops. The special operations forces had previously staged in Romania and been given the code name Task Force Viking (which led in turn to the offensive's title, VIKING HAMMER).

U.S. special forces' participation in VIKING HAMMER was led by 40 members of the 3rd Battalion of the 10th Special Forces Group commanded by Lieutenant Colonel Ken Tovo. Tovo divided his men into split teams; each 6 member group worked with a Kurdish unit of 150–800 troops.

Ansar al-Islam and its allies had constructed a series of complexes on mountains and hilltops overlooking the surrounding valleys near Halabja, Iraq. The Kurds were apprehensive that any attack would leave them vulnerable to mortar and machine-gun fire from the heights, but U.S. personnel scouted the positions and pretargeted them for air strikes.

On March 21, 2003, 64 cruise missiles hit Ansar al-Islam bunkers in a three-hour period. The procoalition Kurds were impressed by both the precision and the power of the attack. Some 100 members of the radical Islamic Group of Kurdistan, an ally of Ansar al-Islam, were killed in the initial strikes, and the remainder of the group surrendered the following morning. Another small Islamic group also surrendered before the main offensive commenced.

The Kurds assisted by the U.S. forces began their attack at 6:00 a.m. on March 28. The attackers were split into four groups, each led by a special forces team. The Ansar al-Islam fighters proved to be a tough and experienced foe, for they had the routes into the mountains covered with mortars and would fire a limited number of rounds and then move in an effort to avoid being targeted by U.S. spotters. Peshmerga artillery and mortars provided the opening fire support for the coalition forces.

When the advance encountered its first organized resistance, air strikes were called in. By 9:00 a.m. the Kurds had captured Gulp, the first significant village. There coalition forces recovered various weapons, including explosive suicide vests and bomb-making materials. The four teams had to assault and capture a series of bunkers and complexes under mortar fire and Katyusha rockets. By the afternoon the attacking forces had taken the strategic town of Sagrat, which had served as the headquarters of the senior Ansar al-Islam leaders.

During the next two days, U.S.-Kurdish forces continued their advance. Much of the fighting involved attacks on cave complexes. The coalition forces endeavored unsuccessfully to use tear gas to force the fighters from the caves. When that tactic failed, grenades and antitank missiles were employed to destroy the cave bunkers.

The Peshmerga did not possess night-fighting equipment, which limited their ability to pursue the Ansar al-Islam fighters. Nonetheless, after the first day of combat, an increasing number of the Islamic fighters had fled across the border into Iran, where they were disarmed but not detained, although some were forcibly returned across the border.

U.S. forces were able to collect a considerable amount of intelligence on Ansar al-Islam and its links with Al Qaeda. In addition, coalition forces discovered that almost half of the fighters killed or captured were foreign born and had come to Iraq to train for terrorist missions. On March 29, a U.S. team explored a suspected chemical weapons manufacturing and training facility in Sagrat. They also found chemical protection suits and traces of the highly toxic ricin.

Sporadic fighting continued until March 30, the day VIKING HAMMER officially ended. During the operation, 3 Peshmerga soldiers were killed and 23 were wounded. No U.S. personnel were killed or seriously wounded. Approximately

150–250 Ansar al-Islam fighters were killed, in addition to the 100 killed among the Islamic Group of Kurdistan. After VIKING HAMMER, the Kurdish forces moved south as part of the broader coalition northern offensive against the regular Iraqi Army. Ansar al-Islam reemerged, however, after the fall of Iraqi president Saddam Hussein as one of the numerous groups in the anticoalition insurgency.

TOM LANSFORD

**See also**
Al Qaeda in Iraq; Ansar al-Islam; Hussein, Saddam; Iraq Insurgency; Iraq War; Kurds; Peshmerga

**References**
Gunter, Michael M. *The Kurds Ascending: The Evolving Solution to the Kurdish Problem in Iraq and Turkey.* New York: Palgrave Macmillan, 2008.
McKiernan, Kevin. *The Kurds: A People in Search of Their Homeland.* New York: St. Martin's, 2006.
O'Leary, Brendan, John McGarry, and Khaled Salih, eds. *The Future of Kurdistan in Iraq.* Philadelphia: University of Pennsylvania Press, 2005.
Tucker, Mike. *Among Warriors in Iraq.* New York: Lyons, 2005.
Yildiz, Kerim. *The Kurds in Iraq: The Past, Present and Future.* London: Pluto, 2007.

## Wadi al-Batin, Battle of (February 26, 1991)

Wadi al-Batin was essentially a tank battle fought during the Persian Gulf War between units of the U.S. VII Corps and the Iraqi Republican Guard Tawakalnah Mechanized Division on February 26, 1991. A gulch that originates near the town of Hafar al-Batin in Saudi Arabia and runs in a northeasterly direction for about 200 miles, the Wadi al-Batin delineates most of Kuwait's western border with Iraq. The gulch passes through the triborder area where Kuwait, Saudi Arabia, and Iraq intersect and is also a natural invasion route into Kuwait and therefore played an important role in coalition planning for the liberation of Kuwait.

Reconnaissance of Iraqi positions confirmed that Iraqi forces were deployed to fight off coalition attacks via the Wadi al-Batin as well as attacks in southern Kuwait and from the sea off Kuwait. In fact, coalition commander U.S. Army general H. Norman Schwarzkopf planned that the main coalition attack would come to the west of the gulch in the form of a giant left hook around Iraqi positions in Kuwait. The Iraqis failed to understand that Global Positioning System (GPS) technology nullified the need for topographical landmarks in maneuver. They also underestimated the ability of the Americans to provide adequate logistical support for a major armor advance through the difficult desert terrain. Consequently, the principal Iraqi defenses did not extend much more than 100 miles beyond Wadi al-Batin, leaving a major gap farther to the west for coalition armies to exploit.

Coalition planners, however, sought to divert Iraqi attention from the western desert and keep them focused on Kuwait and the Wadi al-Batin. On February 16, 1991, U.S. 1st Cavalry Division artillery fired at Iraqi artillery positions in the Wadi al-Batin. Helicopter attacks on Iraqi artillery here followed, and on February 19 units from the 1st Cavalry conducted a reconnaissance in force that ran into heavy resistance from the Iraqi 27th Division defending the gulch. All of this diverted Iraqi attention away from the buildup of the U.S. VII Corps, massing to the west for the main attack.

On February 24, the first day of the ground war, 1st Cavalry units launched a feint into the Wadi al-Batin. When these withdrew, the Iraqis concluded that they had repulsed the main coalition attack. Soon, however, the Iraqis realized the danger they faced from the coalition left hook and began repositioning Republican Guard divisions to meet that threat. The Tawakalnah Mechanized Division was deployed just west of the Wadi al-Batin to stop the American VII Corps and allow Iraqi troops to escape from Kuwait.

The Battle of Wadi al-Batin was fought in the afternoon and evening of February 26 between the U.S. Army 3rd Armored Division and the Iraqi Republican Guard Tawakalnah Division. The Iraqis could muster only some 200 tanks against more than 1,000 American tanks. The VII Corps also enjoyed the advantage of complete air supremacy. Although the men of the Tawakalnah Division fought with great determination and tenacity, their T-72 tanks were completely outclassed by the American M1A1 Abrams tanks, which could destroy the T-72s at a range of two and a half miles, far beyond the effective range of the T-72s.

In the battle, the Tawakalnah Division lost 177 tanks and 107 armored personnel carriers and was destroyed as a fighting unit. Four U.S. M1A1 tanks and a number of Bradley armored fighting vehicles were rendered hors de combat, however, a feat unmatched by any other Iraqi division in the war.

Paul William Doerr

**See also**
Persian Gulf War, Overview; Republican Guard, Iraq

**References**
Bourque, Stephen A. *Jayhawk! The VII Corps in the Persian Gulf War.* Washington, DC: United States Army, Center of Military History, 2002.
Gordon, Michael R., and General Bernard E. Trainor. *The Generals' War: The Inside Story of the Conflict in the Gulf.* New York: Little, Brown, 1995.
Pollack, Kenneth M. *Arabs at War: Military Effectiveness, 1948–1991.* Lincoln: University of Nebraska Press, 2002.

# Wahhabism

Western term for the beliefs of the *muwahhidun*, the followers of Muhammad ibn Abd al-Wahhab (1702–1792). They constituted a political and religious movement that appeared in central Arabia in the 1740s. Wahhabism has its greatest influence in Saudi Arabia, where it is associated with the Saudi dynasty, and in the other Persian Gulf states.

Abd al-Wahhab's followers sought a return to the practices of the first three generations of Islamic history and also sought to cleanse Islamic practice of illicit innovations (*bid'a*). Abd al-Wahhab's followers rejected Ottoman political as well as religious authority, accusing the Ottomans of corrupting Islam and Islamic society; indeed, they went further, choosing to regard the Ottomans as unbelievers and therefore legitimate targets for warfare. This process of labeling other Muslims as unbelievers is known as *takfir*. The Saudi government today, however, officially rejects *takfir* as employed by violent Islamic extremists.

The early Wahhabis attacked others who carried out practices they deemed innovative, syncretic, or polytheistic, such as visits to and veneration of Islamic holy figures' graves, including even the prophet's burial place. They also opposed and fought Shia Muslim groups and attacked their holy places in connection with their battles against the Ottomans. Because the followers of Abd al-Wahhab united with the expanding Saudi tribe, they are associated with all stages of the Saudi state's development.

Today in Saudi Arabia, the Hanbali *madhhab* (legal school) influenced by the followers of Abd al-Wahhab is the dominant—although not sole—doctrine in Islamic courts and education. The followers of Abd al-Wahhab do not believe in absolute strict adherence to any legal school; however, because the Hanbali school was the first established, it is prevalent. When it comes to Saudi foreign policy, such as the Arab-Israeli conflict, Wahhabism is subordinate to government calculations of the national interest.

Sheikh Muhammad ibn Abd al-Wahhab was a religious scholar from a small town near the present-day Saudi capital of Riyadh. In 1740 he composed a theological essay condemning common Muslim religious practices. For example, many Muslims went to holy men to seek their blessings. Other Muslims visited the tombs of holy men to ask that they intercede with God on their behalf. Sheikh Abd al-Wahhab considered such actions to be idolatrous because they violated Islam's central belief in worshipping God alone without any intermediaries. Because Abd al-Wahhab's followers branded other Muslims as unbelievers, their views were initially challenged.

Abd al-Wahhab was expelled from two Arabian towns before he formed an alliance with Muhammad ibn Saud in 1744. Sheikh Muhammad Abd al-Wahhab gave religious legitimacy to Saudi military expeditions in the guise of Muslim holy war against unbelievers in return for Saudi political support.

By 1800, Saudi-Wahhabi forces had conquered much of Arabia. The major Muslim power of the time, the Ottoman Empire, responded to the Saudi conquest of the holy city of Mecca with a military campaign to crush the first Saudi state. That war lasted from 1811 to 1818 and ended in an Ottoman victory. However, the Saudis staged a comeback in the early 1820s to rule over a smaller Arabian realm. The second Saudi state refrained from aggression against Ottoman territories. Because the Saudis were unwilling to wage jihad, Wahhabi leaders urged their loyal followers to avoid all contact with outsiders, such as Egyptian and Iraqi Muslims, on the grounds that if these were truly unbelievers, their company would threaten the purity of true Muslims' belief. The second Saudi state fell to a rival Arabian power in 1891.

The present Kingdom of Saudi Arabia began to emerge when Saudi prince Abd al-Aziz ibn Saud, also known as Ibn Saud, seized Riyadh in 1902. During the next 30 years, he

The Wahhabism Amiriya Madrasa. One of the largest monuments in Yemen, it was commissioned by Sultan Amir bin abd al-Wahab of the Tahirid Dynasty in 1504 and is in Rada, some 168 miles southeast of the Yemeni capital of Sana'a. (Khaled Fazaa/AFP/Getty Images)

conquered the territories that presently comprise the Kingdom of Saudi Arabia. A major element in those conquests was a new wave of the Wahhabi movement called Ikhwan (Brethren). The Ikhwans became fierce warriors for Ibn Saud and gained a fearsome reputation for their savage treatment of defeated enemies. They provided the shock troops for Ibn Saud's military campaigns, but he eventually had to restrain them from pursuing holy war against tribes in Iraq and Transjordan. At the time, those two countries were governed by British-appointed monarchs. Consequently, Ikhwan raids threatened to embroil Ibn Saud in a confrontation with Great Britain. When he ordered the Ikhwans to cease their raids, they rose up in rebellion, but he was able to crush them by 1930.

Three years later, Ibn Saud granted American oil companies the right to explore for petroleum. Wahhabi clerics were unhappy to see Americans permitted into the kingdom, but Ibn Saud and the oil companies minimized contact between Saudis and foreign workers by creating special self contained residential compounds for non-Saudis.

Throughout the Cold War, Saudi Arabia joined forces with the United States to combat the spread of Nasserism and populism in the Muslim world and, like the United States, opposed communism. Saudi efforts included exporting of their own religious doctrine, which is firmly anticommunist. It is also firmly anti-Jewish because of its attachment to historical religious texts emphasizing early clashes between Prophet Muhammad and Jewish clans in Arabia. When it comes to setting foreign policy, however, Saudi rulers take a practical approach and only consult Wahhabi leaders when seeking their approval for sensitive initiatives. Hence, Saudi Arabia supported the Madrid peace process of the 1990s and announced a peace initiative in March 2002 for a comprehensive settlement of the Arab-Israeli conflict, and King Abdullah has called for interfaith dialogue.

Before and during the 1991 Persian Gulf War, Saudi leaders had to walk a fine line when they allowed the buildup of hundreds of thousands of troops to occur on Saudi soil, lest they incur the wrath of religious leaders. Nevertheless, many Saudis opposed the presence of foreigners in their nation, and the Saudi government refused to garrison troops on its soil for the 2003 Iraq War.

Neo-Wahhabism has produced a current of opposition to the Saudi state, even though the vast majority of devout Wahhabis in Saudi Arabia support the government.

DAVID COMMINS

**See also**
Jihad; Saudi Arabia; Shia Islam; Sunni Islam

**References**
Bronson, Rachel. *Thicker Than Oil: America's Uneasy Partnership with Saudi Arabia.* New York: Oxford University Press, 2006.
Commins, David. *The Wahhabi Mission and Saudi Arabia.* London: Tauris, 2006.
Kostiner, Joseph. "Coping with Regional Challenges: A Case Study of Crown Prince Abdullah's Peace Initiative." In *Saudi Arabia in the Balance,* ed. Paul Aarts and Gerd Nonneman, 352–371. London: Hurst, 2005.
Piscatori, James. "Islamic Values and National Interest: The Foreign Policy of Saudi Arabia." In *Islam in Foreign Policy,* ed. Adeed Dawisha, 33–53. Cambridge: Cambridge University Press, 1983.

## War of Atonement

*See* Yom Kippur War

## War of Attrition (July 1969–August 1970)

A long series of low-level protracted clashes between the Israelis and the Arabs from July 1967 to August 1970. Israel had emerged victorious from the Six-Day War of June 1967, more than doubling the territory under its control. This included the Sinai Peninsula. The most important function of the Sinai for the Israelis was as a buffer against any Egyptian attack. As the conflict ensued, both sides deployed new equipment and developed new tactics. The Suez Canal Zone and the Jordanian border were the two principal areas of the fighting, with additional clashes taking place on the Golan Heights.

The Soviets put pressure on the Egyptians to maintain an aggressive posture against the Israelis along the Suez Canal, and within three weeks of the end of the Six-Day War the first major clash occurred. On July 1, 1967, Egyptian troops crossed the canal and attempted to ambush Israeli forces on the eastern bank. The main engagement took place 10 miles south of Port Said. The Israelis responded by committing a mechanized infantry company to counterattack the Egyptians. Despite supporting artillery fire from the Egyptian side of the canal, the attacking forces were driven back. The Israelis suffered 1 killed and 13 wounded.

The next major incident occurred on July 11. The Israeli government maintained that the 1967 cease-fire line ran down the middle of the Suez Canal and resolved to test its position by launching a number of small boats into the canal. When the Israeli force drew fire from the Egyptians, both sides opened fire from tanks dug into defensive positions on either side of the canal. Both sides also launched air sorties in support of the ground action. The Israeli Air Force (IAF) downed seven Egyptian aircraft during the fight. Israeli ground force casualties were 9 killed and 55 wounded.

On the night of July 11 the Israeli destroyer *Eilat,* accompanied by two torpedo boats, encountered and sank two Egyptian torpedo boats off the Rumani coast. The conflict then settled down into a routine of running low-level clashes.

Egyptian president Gamal Abdel Nasser made it clear that it was only a matter of time before Egypt attempted to recapture the Sinai. He also made no secret of his attrition strategy. Given Egypt's vast population advantage over Israel, Egypt could afford to absorb lopsided casualty ratios almost indefinitely.

A second major round of fighting began in September 1967 when Egyptian forces on Green Island, a man-made island fortress in the northern section of the Gulf of Suez, engaged Israeli shipping. This brought widespread artillery exchanges along the Suez Canal during which the cities of Kantara, Ismailia, and Suez were hit. Many Egyptians fled to escape the danger, with an estimated 700,000 becoming internal refugees.

The naval war escalated on October 21, 1967, when the *Eilat* approached Egyptian territorial waters near Port Said and came under attack from two Egyptian missile boats firing Soviet-supplied Styx missiles. The Egyptians fired four missiles at the *Eilat,* sinking it. Of the ship's 190-man crew, 47 were killed or missing, and another 90 were wounded. It was the first time a warship had been sunk by guided missiles.

The Israelis responded to the Egyptian attack on October 25 with an artillery barrage against Egyptian oil refineries in Suez. The shelling claimed more than $100 million worth of oil and petrochemical products and killed or wounded 103 people.

No major incidents occurred during the next 11 months, but in the intervening period the Egyptian armed forces received a wide array of new equipment from the Soviet bloc, including large numbers of modern artillery pieces. The Soviets also sent 1,500 military advisers.

In June 1968 the Egyptians began sporadic artillery bombardments against the leading Israeli positions on the eastern bank of the Suez Canal. On September 8, 1968, the Egyptians resumed large-scale hostilities with a coordinated artillery barrage along a 65-mile front of the canal. This lasted three weeks, with Israeli losses totaling 28 killed or wounded. The Israelis retaliated on the night of October 30 with a heliborne commando raid against two Egyptian bridges and an electricity substation on the Nile just north of Aswan. Egyptian attacks along the Suez Canal then declined for a period.

In the meantime, the Israeli General Staff decided to strengthen defenses along the Suez Canal. The resulting Bar-Lev Line of fortifications, named for chief of staff Lieutenant General Chaim Bar-Lev, was based on 35 small strongpoints located every seven miles between which Israel Defense Force (IDF) patrols maintained constant observation of Egyptian forces on the other side. Armored formations in assembly areas some distance from the canal were positioned to counterattack any Egyptian attempt to cross.

The Bar-Lev fortifications were completed in March 1969, and on March 8 the Egyptians commenced a massive artillery barrage against the line. During the IDF's counterbarrage on March 20, Egyptian chief of staff General Abd al-Muneim Riadh and several other senior Egyptian officers were killed at an observation post close to Ismailia.

Another short lull followed, but the conflict resumed with a vengeance on April 10, 1969. Fighting escalated significantly on May 1 when Nasser declared the termination of the cease-fire that had been in existence since 1967. The Egyptian high command hoped that their continuous artillery exchanges across the Suez Canal would eventually wear down the Israelis and give Egyptian forces an opening to cross the canal.

The investment made by the Israelis in the Bar-Lev Line proved its worth, as the Egyptian artillery inflicted only moderate damage. The Israelis strengthened their canal defenses by constructing an earthen berm close to the bank. Its chief purpose was to prevent Egyptian artillery from having direct line-of-sight observation of Israeli forces. The Israelis also continued to launch commando raids across the canal. Targets included electrical installations, which were relatively easy to damage. The attendant electricity disruptions had a direct impact on the Egyptian civilian sector.

On July 19, 1969, the Israelis conducted one of their most successful commando operations against Green Island. The position was heavily fortified, and the Egyptian garrison there numbered about 200 troops. The Israeli commandos took the island at a cost of only 16 casualties (killed or wounded), then blew up most of the installation and withdrew.

During that same month the IAF increased the number of its offensive missions, resulting in the downing of five Egyptian aircraft. The main IAF target was the new Egyptian surface-to-air missiles (SAMs), acquired from the Soviet Union. During the next two months, Israeli aircraft flew more than 1,000 combat sorties.

On September 8, 1969, the Israelis launched a large-scale offensive. Israeli divers sank two Egyptian torpedo boats in the port of Ras-a-Sadat in the northern part of the Gulf of Suez, 16 miles north of the planned Israeli landing site. Their objective was to reduce the risk of Egyptian interception of the Israeli landing craft. The following day an Israeli task force, including armor, landed at A-Dir at dawn and struck southward down the Gulf of Suez toward the intended objective, the Egyptian Army base at Ras Abu Daraj. The attack was supported by Israeli helicopters and aircraft.

The Egyptians were slow to respond to the assault on Ras Abu Daraj, and the Israelis were thus able to destroy 12 positions, including 2 radar stations, and inflict more than 100 casualties before disengaging with only minimal losses of their own. The most vexing thing for the Egyptians was the fact that the IDF had operated for more than 10 hours on Egyptian soil without being significantly challenged by Egyptian forces. The poor response was mainly the result of inadequate communications and the rigid Egyptian command structure based on the Soviet model, which allowed little room for individual initiative. Many Egyptian commanders were afraid to move their forces unless they received explicit orders from their superiors, something hard to achieve in any fluid engagement. Nasser reacted by dismissing the senior commanders responsible for the defense of that area.

Three days later on September 11, 1969, the Egyptians suffered another reverse, losing 11 aircraft while shooting down only a single Israeli plane. On October 25, the Israelis scored another significant victory when they successfully attacked a radar station at Ras-Arab on the Gulf of Suez. The Egyptians had newly installed Soviet P-12 radar equipment at the site. The attack force flew to the objective in 2 helicopters. The Egyptian garrison was quickly overcome, and then the Israeli forces worked diligently to remove the radar, housed in two trailers partially dug into the ground. The Israelis dug out the trailers and then sling-loaded them beneath the helicopters. Despite the helicopters being dangerously overloaded, they were able to return to the Israeli side of the gulf. The Israelis subsequently made information exploited from the equipment available to Western intelligence agencies.

The Israelis launched 23 raids across the Suez Canal and the Gulf of Suez from October 1969 to July 1970. The Egyptian high command was greatly concerned that their considerable investment in Soviet SAM systems had produced little degradation in IAF assets. In December 1969 several Soviet generals arrived in Cairo to evaluate the situation. The next month, Nasser traveled to Moscow. The Soviets then deployed more of their own personnel to Egypt to man new SAM-3 Goa systems.

The SAM-3, designed specifically to engage low-flying aircraft, was more effective than the larger and longer-range SAM-2. The SAM-3 system also could be deployed on a three-missile mobile-launch platform, increasing the flexibility of the Egyptian coverage. Soviet personnel manned most of the SAM-3s. The Soviets now had almost 4,000 military advisers in Egypt, including pilots who flew frontline aircraft. This, of course, increased the chances of a direct confrontation between Soviet and Israeli forces.

The strengthening of the Egyptian air defense umbrella had relatively little impact on the effectiveness of the IAF, however. The IAF did, however, change its mission-attack profiles. Instead of attacking facilities close to the Suez Canal and the Gulf of Suez, the Israelis now flew missions to strike positions as close as 25 miles from Cairo. Many of these were against Egyptian Army reserve units, further degrading the overall morale of the Egyptian armed forces. The attacks also made clear the relative impotence of the Egyptian Air Force.

Between February and March 1970, the Egyptian Air Force lost 20 aircraft to the Israelis. On April 8, 1970, an IAF strike killed 47 Egyptian children at a school inside a military compound, which brought the Israeli air offensive to a halt. That same month the Soviet air elements in Egypt assumed a much more aggressive posture, taking over direct responsibility for the defense of Egyptian air space. This freed the Egyptian Air Force to focus its operations in the Sinai in support of army operations along the Suez Canal, which included reconstructing SAM batteries in more forward positions. The renewed Egyptian offensive resulted in relatively high Israeli casualties between April and May 1969, with 64 Israeli soldiers killed and 149 wounded.

By June 1969 there were almost 12,000 Soviet advisers, including more than 100 pilots, in Egypt. That same month the Soviets again intervened to reorganize the Egyptian air defenses. Instead of defending the entire (approximate 100-mile) length of the Suez Canal, the Soviets decided that the vast majority of the SAMs should be located in a box, 25 miles wide and 45 miles long, covering the central and southern sectors of the canal. The SAM systems were positioned in packs whereby a small number of launchers could be protected by conventional short-range antiaircraft guns. Such a configuration allowed the defenders to engage an enemy aircraft with multiple missiles, increasing the kill probability. Nevertheless, the Israelis managed to destroy five SAM sites in July.

Since April, Soviet-piloted MiGs had been approaching IAF aircraft, but the Israeli pilots had standing orders to break off such contacts. It was only a matter of time, however, before the Soviets and Israelis would clash head-on. On June 25, two Soviet-piloted MiG-21s fired on and hit an Israeli A-4 Skyhawk, which made a forced landing at a base in the Sinai. A series of running dogfights during the next few days resulted in no losses for either side. On July 30 a patrol of Israeli aircraft engaged eight Soviet-piloted aircraft, with the Israelis downing four and losing none. A fifth MiG was hit and later crashed on its way back to its base. Three of the Soviet pilots were killed, and another two were wounded. Neither side issued a communiqué about the engagement, but the Soviets were greatly shaken by the results. That same day, Moscow dispatched senior air force commanders to Egypt to investigate.

Although the major area of conflict in the War of Attrition was along the Suez Canal, clashes also occurred in other areas, principally along the border with Jordan. Between 1968 and 1969, the majority of the fighting took place in the Beyt Shean Valley.

Following the Six-Day War, the Palestine Liberation Organization (PLO) had tried to retain a foothold in the West Bank. Because of the IDF's very effective system of patrolling and the relatively poor local support, the PLO was forced to withdraw entirely to the East Bank of the Jordan. From there the PLO launched a series of attacks, and the Jordanian Army and units of the Iraqi Army stationed in Jordan often fired artillery on Israeli positions across the border.

Many of the PLO attacks were aimed at civilian targets. Following an attack on an Israeli school bus on March 18, 1968, in which a doctor and a teacher were killed, the IDF launched a major attack on the PLO base at Karameh, located just south of the Dead Sea within eight miles of Jericho. The PLO previously had moved the original population away, and many of its fighting elements were located there and had established fortified positions, including at least 11 firing positions for artillery.

The Israeli attack began at dawn on March 21, 1968. The Israelis planned to launch three armored thrusts across the Jordan River to seal off Karameh. The village itself would be assaulted by paratroopers. Although they came under fire from the Jordanian Army, the Israeli armored elements crossed the Jordan at the Damya Bridge in the north and the Allenby Bridge in the south. The IDF paratroopers came under heavy fire from PLO fighters hiding in caves to the west of the village. The assault faltered, and the paratroopers became bogged down in house-to-house combat. After a few hours of fighting, the Israelis had killed some 120 PLO fighters and taken a large number of prisoners.

That same day the Israelis also attacked the village of Safi, held by the Jordanian Army, south of the Dead Sea. Israeli losses during that operation were 28 killed and 69 wounded, with half a dozen armored vehicles destroyed. The Jordanian Army lost 40 soldiers killed, while the PLO lost more than 200. Both sides claimed victory.

For the Israelis, the day's fighting forced the Jordanian Army and the PLO to pull back farther to the east, thus making it harder for them to hit Israeli positions with artillery fire. This was the last major encounter of the War of Attrition along the Jordanian border. From that point on, the fighting largely took the form of terrorist actions by the PLO and intermittent artillery fire from Jordanian positions.

The War of Attrition officially ended on July 31, 1970, when the Israeli government accepted the terms of a cease-fire that went into effect on August 8. The cease-fire resulted from negotiations that began in October 1969 and eventually produced a plan put forth by U.S. secretary of state William P. Rogers. The agreement required a three-month freeze on military activity during which neither side was allowed to make any military changes or improvements in the zone that ran 31 miles on either side of the Suez Canal. Almost the same day that the cease-fire went into effect, however, the Egyptians started moving new SAM batteries into the Canal Zone. By October they had some 100 SAM sites in place, and those batteries would prove to be a critical factor at the start of the Yom Kippur War (Ramadan War) in October 1973.

During the War of Attrition, Israeli casualties were 367 soldiers killed and more than 3,000 soldiers and civilians wounded. Egypt sustained losses of 8,000–10,000 men and several thousand civilians. The IAF lost 14 aircraft in combat while shooting down 98 Egyptian planes. Jordan lost approximately 130 soldiers. The PLO suffered at least 250 fighters killed. The Soviets lost 3 pilots and perhaps another 50 or more advisers on the ground.

Ralph Martin Baker and David T. Zabecki

See also
Bar-Lev Line; Egypt; *Eilat,* Sinking of; Israel; Jordan; Karameh, Battle of; Nasser, Gamal Abdel; Palestine Liberation Organization; Six-Day War; Suez Canal; Yom Kippur War

References
Bar-Siman-Tov, Yaacov. *The Israel-Egyptian War of Attrition, 1969–1970: A Case-Study of Limited Local War.* New York: Columbia University Press, 1980.
Heikal, Mohamad. *Autumn of Fury.* New York: Random House, 1983.
Herzog, Chaim. *The Arab-Israeli Wars: War and Peace in the Middle East from the War of Independence to Lebanon.* Westminster, MD: Random House, 1984.
Korn, David A. *Stalemate: The War of Attrition and Great Power Diplomacy in the Middle East, 1967–1970.* Boulder CO: Westview, 1992.
Nordeen, Lon. *Fighters over Israel.* London: Greenhill, 1991.
Roth, Stephen J. *The Impact of the Six-Day War: A Twenty-Year Assessment.* London: Palgrave Macmillan, 1988.

# Wauchope, Sir Arthur Grenfell (1874–1947)

British Army general and high commissioner of the British Mandate for Palestine (1931–1938). Born in Edinburgh on March 1, 1874, Arthur Grenfell Wauchope fought in the South African (Boer) War of 1899–1902 and was severely wounded. He was stationed in India during 1903–1912. During World War I he served on the Western Front in France until 1916, when he was transferred to the Mesopotamia front and was again wounded. In 1923 he was a member of the overseas settlement delegation to Australia and New Zealand. During 1924–1927 he was chief of the British section of the Inter-Allied Military Commission of Control (IMCC) in Berlin. During 1927–1929 he served in Northern Ireland.

In 1931 Wauchope was appointed British high commissioner for Palestine, a post he held until 1938. He chose to interpret British immigration regulations liberally, and during his administration the Jewish population in Palestine expanded rapidly, including many German, Austrian, and Czech Jews. Wauchope endeavored to meet growing Arab opposition to the increased Jewish immigration by establishing the Legislative Council.

Wauchope received considerable criticism as a consequence of the Arab Revolt that began in April 1936. At first his administration took firm steps to end the rioting. Wauchope, however, continued his liberal immigration policy but at the same time did not move to arrest Arab leaders inciting the riots. A temporary halt in the violence occurred during the visit of the fact-finding Peel Commission to Palestine in 1938, but the violence resumed after the commission's departure. This time Wauchope moved against the Arab leaders. Following the assassination of acting district commissioner Louis Y. Andrews in the Galilee district, Wauchope declared the Arab Higher Committee and other Arab nationalist groups to be illegal associations. British authorities deported half a dozen Arab leaders, and Haj Amin al-Husseini, mufti of Jerusalem, was removed from office. In November 1937 Wauchope authorized the emergency establishment of military courts.

Wauchope's relief from his post and departure from Palestine in March 1938 signaled the beginning of a much harsher British policy toward Jewish immigration and land sales as well as a more pro-Arab policy in the mandate, carried out under his successor Sir Harold MacMichael. Wauchope retained his interest in Palestine following his retirement. He died in London on September 14, 1947.

SPENCER C. TUCKER

### See also
Arab Revolt in Palestine; Husseini, Haj Amin al-; MacMichael, Sir Harold; Palestine, British Mandate for; Peel Commission

### References
Sachar, Howard M. *A History of Israel: From the Rise of Zionism to Our Time*. 3rd ed. New York: Knopf, 2007.

Shepherd, Naomi. *Ploughing Sand: British Rule in Palestine, 1917–1948*. New Brunswick, NJ: Rutgers University Press, 1999.

## West Bank

The West Bank is the common name for the territory that lies west of the Jordan River and south of the Sea of Galilee. It was earlier known as Cisjordan (for "this side of the Jordan River") and by its biblical names of Judaea in the south and Samaria in the north. Today about 40 percent of the area and 98 percent of the population are under the jurisdiction of the Palestinian Authority (PA), although Israel, which has occupied the territory since the 1967 Six-Day War, controls, has settlements in, and maintains forces in much of the remainder. East Jerusalem, although located in the West Bank, was annexed by Israel in the same war (a step not recognized by the international community) and is usually treated as a separate issue in peace negotiations. However, East Jerusalem is contiguous to the West Bank.

Until the end of World War I, the West Bank was part of the territory of the Ottoman Empire, after which it was part of the League of Nations British Mandate for Palestine. The West Bank was captured by Jordanian forces in the Israeli War of Independence (1948–1949) despite the fact that it had been designated as part of a proposed Palestinian state by the United Nations (UN) in 1947. Following that war, the boundary separating Israel and Jordan and Jordanian occupied territory became known as the Green Line. Palestinian Arab refugees from Israel flooded into the area. Jordan annexed the West Bank in 1950, although the move was not recognized by any country except the United Kingdom.

Despite Israel's effort to persuade Jordan to remain neutral in the 1967 Six-Day War, Israeli forces moved into and occupied the West Bank after Jordan entered the conflict. UN Security Council Resolution 242 of 1967 called for the withdrawal of Israeli forces from all the territories occupied in the Six-Day War, which included East Jerusalem, the West Bank, the Gaza Strip, the Golan Heights, and the Sinai Peninsula. Israel refused to comply with the resolution and throughout the 1970s established Jewish settlements in all the occupied territories, with the most being in the West Bank.

After almost 20 years of Israeli occupation and the expanding encroachment of Palestinian land by the settlements, the First Intifada started in 1987. The following year Jordan's King Hussein relinquished all claims to the West Bank, partly to support Palestinian claims and partly to reinforce Jordanian national identity.

The Palestine Liberation Organization (PLO) proclaimed the West Bank independent in 1988, although Israel did not recognize either the area's independence or the PLO as a legitimate governing body. The promise of a breakthrough came with the 1993 Oslo Accords, when Israel and the Palestinians agreed to a conditional withdrawal of Israeli troops from some West Bank areas. The Oslo Accords, however, stipulated that the status of the territory would not be determined finally until both sides entered into a permanent agreement.

Frustrated by the torturously slow peace process and the ever-encroaching Israeli settlements, Palestinian patience finally ran out. And when Ariel Sharon enraged the Palestinian public by visiting the al-Aqsa Mosque area of the Haram al-Sharif with Israeli security forces, the Second (al-Aqsa) Intifada erupted in 2000. Far more violent than the First Intifada, the Palestinian attacks and suicide bombings of the Second Intifada initially led Israel to send large military and security forces back into the West Bank.

Convinced that they had no reliable negotiating partner on the Palestinian side who could make agreements and deliver on them, the Israelis finally initiated steps that were intended to lead to a unilateral disengagement between the two peoples. In 2001 the Israelis obtained Israeli Jewish signatures on petitions supporting the construction of a security wall, and in 2002, despite strong Palestinian protests against the project, the Israelis began constructing the controversial security barrier around the West Bank. But rather than conforming to the boundary of the pre-1967 Green Line, the planned line of the Israeli Security Fence cut deep into the West Bank in various sectors to encompass Israeli settlements established since 1967. The Palestinians, along with much of the rest of the world, have condemned the Israeli move as nothing short of a blatant land grab.

In 2004 Sharon began the process of unilaterally withdrawing all Israeli settlements from the Gaza Strip as well as four smaller settlements in the West Bank. Meanwhile, the Israelis have continued to expand some of their larger settlements in the West Bank, resettling some of those Israelis evicted from the Gaza settlements.

By 2018 the Palestinian population in the West Bank totaled some 2.9 million. About 30 percent of these are refugees or their descendants from the 1948 war. Among the more populous Palestinian cities of the West Bank are East Jerusalem, Nablus, Ramallah, Bethlehem (home to a large number of Palestinian Christians), Hebron, Tulkarem, and Qlaquilla. The total population of all Jewish settlements in the West Bank and East Jerusalem numbers some 800,000, or 13 percent of Israel's total population. Half of those individuals reside in the West Bank.

David T. Zabecki

### See also
Expellees and Refugees, Palestinian; Hussein ibn Talal, King of Jordan; Intifada, Second; Israeli Security Fence; Oslo Accords; Palestine Liberation Organization; Palestinian National Authority; Sharon, Ariel; Six-Day War

### References
Oren, Michael B. *Six Days of War: June 1967 and the Making of the Modern Middle East.* Novato, CA: Presidio, 2003.

Said, Edward W. *The End of the Peace Process: Oslo and After.* New York: Vintage Books, 2001.

Smith, Charles D. *Palestine and the Arab-Israeli Conflict: A History with Documents.* 6th ed. New York: Bedford/St. Martin's, 2006.

## White Paper of 1922 (June 3, 1922)

British government position paper on Palestine issued on June 3, 1922. The white paper of 1922 was prompted by increasing Arab resistance to Jewish immigration and land purchases in the British Mandate for Palestine. The paper also closely followed establishment of Transjordan, constituting the land of Palestine east of the Jordan River that was part of Britain's League of Nations Palestine mandate. In 1921 the British government recognized Abdullah ibn Hussein as de facto king of Transjordan, which was nonetheless still considered part of the British mandate. Abdullah would reign rather than rule. The British government merely promised to confer independence at some future date.

Zionists were slow to realize the implications of the creation of Transjordan, which in effect excluded land east of the Jordan River as falling under the provisions of the Balfour Declaration. The Arabs' position was quite clear. They wanted a complete repudiation of the Balfour Declaration and an end to Jewish immigration. They also claimed that the land being settled by Jews had been specifically promised to the Arabs in letters exchanged during World War I between British high commissioner for Egypt Sir A. Henry McMahon and Hussein ibn Ali, emir of the Arabian Hejaz and sharif of Mecca.

The white paper of 1922 was commonly known as the Churchill White Paper because it was issued under the authority of Colonial Secretary Winston Churchill. It was based on correspondence among Churchill, the Arab Palestine delegation, and the World Zionist Organization (WZO). The paper was prompted by the return to London in May 1922 of British high commissioner for Palestine Sir Herbert Samuel, who impressed upon Churchill the need to issue some statement to allay growing Arab concerns over the future of Palestine. The high commissioner is generally assumed to have had a major hand in the preparation of the declaration, which was intended to be a definitive statement on the Balfour Declaration and British intentions regarding Palestine.

In his official response on June 3, Churchill denied that the McMahon-Hussein correspondence had promised Palestine to the Arabs. While Churchill reaffirmed British support for a Jewish national home in Palestine, he also denied that the British government had at any time contemplated "that Palestine as a whole should be converted into a Jewish National Home." He noted that there were then some 80,000 Jews in Palestine, a great many of them working in agricultural pursuits and 25,000 of them having arrived under the mandate. He identified the national home as "not the imposition of a Jewish nationality" on all Palestine but the further development of the existing Jewish community so that it might become a center "in which the Jewish people as a whole may take, on grounds of religion and race, an interest and a pride." Toward that end, the British government supported additional immigration into Palestine but only enough so as to not exceed the economic capacity of Palestine to receive them. He also specified that the immigration should not deprive from employment "any section of the present population." Churchill called for the establishment of a special committee in Palestine, drawn entirely from the newly elected Legislative Council, to confer on immigration matters and then report any concerns to the British government for decision.

Zionist leaders denounced the white paper as a dilution of the Balfour Declaration and as a British government attempt to restrict Jewish immigration. Nonetheless, the WZO, fearful of losing British support altogether, reluctantly accepted the declaration. The Arab delegation rejected it altogether, however. In testimony before the Peel Commission in 1936, Churchill maintained that the white paper of 1922 did not preclude the establishment of a Jewish state in Palestine.

SPENCER C. TUCKER

**See also**
Abdullah I; Balfour Declaration; Jordan; McMahon-Hussein Correspondence

**References**
Sachar, Howard M. *A History of Israel: From the Rise of Zionism to Our Time.* 3rd ed. New York: Knopf, 2007.
Shepherd, Naomi. *Ploughing Sand: British Rule in Palestine, 1917–1948.* New Brunswick, NJ: Rutgers University Press, 1999.

## White Paper of 1930 (October 31, 1930)

British policy statement on Palestine issued by the London government on October 31, 1930, under the authority of Colonial Secretary Sidney Webb, Lord Passfield. Prompted by the Arab Uprising in Palestine of 1929–1930, the white paper incorporated the recommendations of both the Shaw Commission and the Hope-Simpson Report. The latter had recommended that the London government issue a declaration that would clarify its position regarding the future of the British Mandate for Palestine.

The Passfield White Paper was clearly pro-Arab and anti-Zionist in its approach and was an effort to reinterpret the 1917 Balfour Declaration so as to placate the Arab population of Palestine by arresting the movement toward a Jewish state. While it committed Britain to the development of a Jewish national homeland in Palestine, it also said that this was not considered central to the mandate. The white paper stressed that Britain had an equal obligation to both Jews and Arabs in Palestine and that the British authorities had the task of reconciling any differences that arose between them.

Based on the Hope-Simpson findings and alleged shortages of arable land, the Passfield White Paper held that there was no land available in Palestine for agricultural use by new immigrants. The white paper stated that the Palestine government did not hold any land that it might be able to assign to immigrants, and even if it did have such land available, it would have to be assigned to landless Arab farmers. The paper noted that the Arab population had sharply increased in numbers, while at the same time the amount of land available for Arab farmers had decreased because of land sales to Jews.

The white paper was also critical of a number of Jewish organizations, including the Jewish Agency and the Histadrut (General Federation of Labor). The paper accused these groups of stipulating the employment of Jewish labor only on holdings owned by them or under their auspices. Although Jews who had purchased land would be able to continue to develop it, in the future Jews would be required to secure approval from the British authorities for any land purchases. In considering such requests, the authorities would take into consideration the ability of the land to absorb the population as well as the unemployment rates of both Arabs and Jews. This implied future restraints on Jewish immigration, for it held that if economic conditions would not allow, it was the duty of the mandatory power to suspend immigration.

The Passfield White Paper caused an outcry among Zionists and Zionist organizations worldwide, which in turn prompted a debate in Parliament on it during November 17, 1930, in which there was considerable criticism of the government position. Chaim Weizmann and other leading members of the Jewish Agency resigned in protest. As a consequence, British prime minister Ramsay MacDonald wrote a conciliatory letter to Weizmann on February 12, 1931. Made public the next day, this letter somewhat eased the offensive language in the report. MacDonald also said that he would encourage further Jewish settlement in Palestine while at the same time working to safeguard the interests of all groups in the country.

SPENCER C. TUCKER

**See also**
Balfour Declaration; Palestine, British Mandate for; Shaw Commission

**References**
Sachar, Howard M. *A History of Israel: From the Rise of Zionism to Our Time.* 3rd ed. New York: Knopf, 2007.

Shepherd, Naomi. *Ploughing Sand: British Rule in Palestine, 1917–1948.* New Brunswick, NJ: Rutgers University Press, 1999.

## White Paper of 1939 (May 17, 1939)

A British government policy statement that sought to mollify mounting Arab anger over increasing Jewish immigration into Palestine. British efforts to formulate a partition plan for Palestine met staunch opposition from both Arab leaders, who were adamantly opposed to partition, and Zionist leaders, who objected to the small area assigned to the proposed Jewish state. During February 7–March 17, 1939, the British government hosted a conference in London in the hopes of reaching some solution to the Palestinian problem. This London Round Table Conference (also known as the St. James Palace Conference) was a failure, and two months later on May 17, 1939, the British government issued a white paper spelling out its Palestine policy. Colonial Secretary Malcolm MacDonald had already revealed its basic provisions to the Jewish delegation at the end of the London talks.

In the white paper, the British government stated that 450,000 Jews had settled in Palestine and that the British government had, in consequence, fulfilled its pledges under the Balfour Declaration of 1917 to establish a Jewish national home in Palestine. It called for the establishment of an independent Palestine state within 10 years to be governed jointly by Arabs and Jews. The British government held that it was not the intention of the Balfour Declaration that Palestine be converted into a Jewish state against the will of its Arab population and that London had an obligation to the Arabs to prevent that from happening.

The white paper sharply restricted Jewish immigration to 75,000 people over the next five years, with immigration thereafter to be entirely contingent on Arab agreement. The white paper also noted that land sales by Arabs to Jews risked sharply reducing the Arab standard of living, and the document therefore invested the British high commissioner in Palestine with full authority to prohibit and regulate transfers of land.

The House of Commons approved the white paper in a vote of 208 to 179. The white paper represented a clear tilt to the Arab position. Jews in Palestine bitterly resented the white paper, regarding it as a severe check to their hopes of a Jewish state. The immigration restrictions were particularly onerous, given the persecution of Jews in Germany and in Poland. Arabs also opposed the white paper, however. The Arab Higher Committee, representing the Palestinian Arabs, opposed any new immigration of Jews to Palestine and the establishment of a state there in which the Jews would have a joint governing role. The Arab side sought a complete repudiation of the principle of a Jewish national home in Palestine.

Implementation of the white paper proceeded slowly, and when the government fell in May 1940 and Winston Churchill became prime minister, it was dropped. Nonetheless, the British government was anxious to maintain Arab support during World War II and worked to prevent widescale Jewish immigration to Palestine, turning away Jews there even after full knowledge of the Holocaust. On May 15, 1948, however, the new government of Israel officially abolished the provisions of the white paper.

Spencer C. Tucker

**See also**
Balfour Declaration; Holocaust; London Round Table Conference

**References**
Bethell, Nicholas. *The Palestine Triangle: The Struggle for the Holy Land, 1935–48.* New York: Putnam, 1979.
Hurewitz, J. C. *The Struggle for Palestine.* New York: Schocken, 1976.
Sachar, Howard M. *A History of Israel: From the Rise of Zionism to Our Time.* 3rd ed. New York: Knopf, 2007.

## Wingate, Orde Charles (1903–1944)

British Army general. Orde Wingate was born to a military family in Naini Tal, India, on February 23, 1903. He attended Charterhouse Public School and then the Royal Military Academy at Woolwich, from which he graduated in 1923 with a commission in the Royal Artillery. From 1928 to 1933 he served with the Sudan Defense Force, where he learned Arabic and honed his skills in small-unit leadership by conducting patrols and ambushes along the Ethiopian border.

Wingate was assigned to the British Mandate for Palestine as an intelligence officer in 1936, just after the start of the Arab Revolt. Although most British officers and official British government policy were openly pro-Arab, Wingate became fervently pro-Jewish. His mother had come from a missionary family affiliated with the Plymouth Brethren, and Wingate grew up imbued with Christian Zionist ideals. He soon set about learning Hebrew, although he never really mastered it.

Wingate first convinced resistant British commanders to permit him to arm and train Jewish volunteers to counter the increasing Arab raids and guerrilla attacks, and then he overcame the skepticism of the leaders of the Jewish Agency and Haganah. In 1938 Wingate formed, trained, and commanded the Special Night Squads (SNS) composed of Haganah volunteers and a cadre of British regulars. The SNS mission was to defend Jewish settlements that were completely surrounded by Arab territory.

Up until that point, Haganah had relied almost exclusively on passive defensive tactics, waiting until a settlement was attacked and then defending from inside the perimeter. Wingate taught the Jews to take the battle to the Arabs, mounting active defenses of the settlements in the form of night patrols and ambushes near the exits to Arab villages to stop the attackers even before they could get started. Stressing leadership from the front, Wingate taught the importance of speed, surprise, imagination, and psychological leverage. A soldier's most important weapon was his mind.

Wingate's extreme views helped bring about his transfer back to Britain in May 1939. He subsequently gained fame as one of the most aggressive and innovative special operations commanders of World War II. Sent to the Sudan to drive the Italians from Ethiopia (Abyssinia), he commanded the Gideon Force during the East African Campaign of 1941 and was awarded the Distinguished Service Order. Exhausted and ill, he attempted suicide in Cairo in June 1941. In early 1942 he went to the China-Burma-India theater and formed the Chindits, a long-range penetration group designed for operations against the Japanese in Burma. Although his large-scale raids had only mixed military results, they raised Allied morale in a theater in which the Japanese had heretofore enjoyed only success. On March 24, 1944, Major General Wingate was returning to India from a Chindit base in Burma when the American B-25 bomber in which he was a passenger crashed into a jungle-covered mountain, killing all on board.

Wingate was a dynamic small-unit leader and a brilliant tactician. He was also a man with huge personal eccentricities and some would also say psychological problems. Nonetheless, he completely changed Haganah's thinking about military operations, and his influence can be clearly seen in the Israel Defense Force (IDF) approach to war fighting to this day. Two of his protégés in the SNS, Yigal Yadin and Moshe Dayan, would become two of the most important leaders in the IDF. Israel's National Center for Physical Education and Sport is known as the Wingate Institute.

DAVID T. ZABECKI

**See also**
Arab Revolt in Palestine; Dayan, Moshe; Haganah

**References**
Bierman, John, and Colin Smith. *Fire in the Night: Wingate of Burma, Ethiopia, and Zion.* New York: Random House, 1999.
Royle, Trevor. *Orde Wingate: Irregular Soldier.* London: Weidenfeld and Nicolson, 1995.
Sykes, Christopher. *Orde Wingate.* London: Collins, 1959.

## Woodhead Report (November 9, 1938)

British government report of November 9, 1938, designed to address the partition of the British Mandate for Palestine in light of the Peel Commission findings of July 1937. Faced with mounting Arab violence in Palestine, the British government appointed yet another commission to study the Palestine situation. The government hoped that the commission might reassure the Arabs and reduce Arab violence.

The commission was charged with making recommendations to Parliament regarding the partition of the mandate into separate Arab and Jewish states as called for by the Peel Commission and providing specific delineation of the borders of the two proposed states. Sir John Woodhead, a former official in the British administration in India, headed the four-man commission. The members of the commission traveled to Palestine in April 1938. Arab leaders there, who were resolutely opposed to partition, refused to meet with the commission, and as a result it met almost exclusively with British officials and representatives of the Jewish community.

The Woodhead Commission remained in Palestine until August. The members then discussed their findings and duly delivered a report to Parliament on November 9, 1958. This 310-page document held that no plan would win the support of both Arabs and Jews. It also stated that while a Jewish state might be viable economically, this was unlikely to be the case for an Arab state without the Jewish hinterland. Indeed, the commission itself was in sharp disagreement on any specific recommendations. The report rejected the Peel Commission plan (Plan A) and proposed two alternatives. Plan B would reduce the size of the proposed Jewish state by the addition of Galilee to the permanently mandated area and the addition of the southern part of the region south of Jaffa to the Arab state. Plan C would limit the Jewish state to the coastal plain between Zikhron Yaagov and Rehovoth, while northern Palestine and all of southern Palestine would be under a separate mandate. Two commission members favored Plan C, one favored Plan B, and one declared that no partition plan was possible.

Upon publication of the Woodhouse Report, the British government issued a statement to the effect that the report proved that partition was impracticable. At the same time, however, the government suggested that some sort of accommodation might yet be possible between Arabs and Jews. This hope led to the futile London Round Table talks (St. James Palace Conference) of February–March 1939.

Spencer C. Tucker

**See also**
Balfour Declaration; Peel Commission; White Paper of 1939

**References**
Bethell, Nicholas. *The Palestine Triangle: The Struggle for the Holy Land, 1935–48.* New York: Putnam, 1979.
Hurewitz, J. C. *The Struggle for Palestine.* New York: Schocken, 1976.
Sachar, Howard M. *A History of Israel. From the Rise of Zionism to Our Time.* 3rd ed. New York: Knopf, 2007.

# World War I, Impact on the Middle East

World War I (1914–1918) was the most important event in the evolution of the modern Middle East. The issues that fuel the current Arab-Israeli dispute and the unsettled conditions in the present-day Persian Gulf and Middle East originated during World War and its immediate aftermath. The war had three notable effects on the development of what would become an ongoing war between Arabs and Zionists in Palestine. The first was the destruction of the Ottoman Empire and its division into a number of smaller political units that ultimately became independent states in the modern Middle East. The second was the assumption of direct administrative responsibility for the territories in and around Palestine by Britain and France, two of the victors in that war. The third was the British declaration of support for the central goal of the Zionist movement, a Jewish homeland in Palestine. This was accomplished with the 1917 Balfour Declaration.

World War I had larger consequences not only in Palestine but also in the region that stretched from the Dardanelles through North Africa as a whole. The conflict stimulated nationalism among the area's indigenous peoples, through the Allied-supported revolt among the Bedouin tribes on the Arabian Peninsula and through the many British military reversals at the hands of the Ottoman Empire forces, notably in the Gallipoli Campaign and Kut in 1915 and 1916, which demonstrated that the West was not invincible and boosted pride among indigenous peoples of the region. Nationalism was also stoked by Arab resentment at Allied intrigues to divide the region among themselves.

Moreover, the declaration of jihad (holy war) by Ottoman sultan Mehmed V (r. 1909–1918) on November 11, 1914, marked the first time that a Muslim leader had ever taken such a step against any of the Great Powers. The proclamation caused concern among the Allies, particularly the British, about the potential effects on the empire's Muslim subjects. Political and economic developments in Egypt and French North Africa also stimulated Arab nationalism and resentment of Western rule.

The war accelerated political and social trends that had been eroding the strength of the Ottoman Empire for the preceding century and a half. Meanwhile, the Great Powers of Europe had been steadily expanding their influence in Ottoman-controlled areas. Britain's worldwide influence and its strategic presence in the Middle East had grown considerably since the construction of the Suez Canal in 1869. Indeed, safeguarding the route to India was a cornerstone of British policy in the Middle East. As such, the British sought to dominate the territories near Suez and the Persian Gulf—Egypt, Palestine, and Iraq—in order to keep their passage to India and the Far East secure. France, for its part, sought to control Syria and Lebanon to safeguard the Maronite Christian population and give France a presence in the eastern Mediterranean. France also controlled French Morocco, Algeria, and Tunisia in Northwest Africa. Italy, having wrested Tripolitania from the Ottoman Empire during the Italo-Ottoman War of 1911–1912, sought to consolidate and expand its control over the remainder of Libya. Tsarist Russia sought an opening through the Dardanelles and the protection of Orthodox Christian sites in Jerusalem. Germany wanted to influence the region and tap its resources through the construction of the so-called Berlin-Baghdad railway.

In addition to the growing encroachment of the European powers, the Ottoman Empire faced growing ethnic unrest among its minority populations. This was particularly the case among the Armenians, the growing Jewish population in Palestine (most of whom were fleeing persecution in Russia), and the Bedouin Arab tribes in the Arabian Peninsula.

The outbreak of war in August 1914 and the Ottoman Empire's entry into the conflict on the German side in September along with wartime developments greatly accelerated the process of Ottoman disintegration. Wartime privations and Ottoman repression (manifested in the Armenian massacres of 1915 and in intensified persecution of Jews in Palestine) triggered nationalist feelings and hatred of Ottoman rule among these minorities. The British, hoping to take advantage of this, encouraged unrest among Arabs throughout the Ottoman Empire by promising them support for independence. At the same time, however, the British were negotiating postwar spheres of influence in the Middle East with the French. This was effected through the 1916 Sykes-Picot Agreement, which recognized France's sphere of influence in the future Syria and Lebanon and British predominance in Palestine, Jordan, and Iraq. Later, Italy and Russia would also become parties to these clandestine machinations.

The idea of instigating a revolt against the Ottomans among the Arabs originated with the British high commissioner in Egypt, Sir Henry MacMahon, in November 1914 and gained momentum with British military defeats at Gallipoli and Kut in 1915 and early 1916. With the Ottomans still threatening Suez and the British unable to make any headway in Sinai, the British command in Cairo needed to find some way to tie Ottoman forces down. The British also hoped to undermine the sultan's holy war proclamation.

In July 1915 Emir Abdullah Hussein, the sharif of Mecca, notified MacMahon of his willingness to initiate an Arab revolt if Britain would support an independent Arab state under Hussein after the war. MacMahon agreed, although he avoided any explicit promises about the exact borders of any such future state. Hussein hesitated to call for open revolt. The Ottomans' decision to reinforce their Medina garrison in June 1916 and the unrest that increase caused finally convinced Hussein to proceed.

Hussein and his oldest son, Emir Faisal, moved to attack the Hejaz railway and isolate Medina. In October, the British appointed as liaison to the Arabs an officer in the Arab Bureau in Cairo who spoke fluent Arabic and had a reputation for intense pro-Arab sympathies, Thomas Edward Lawrence, who would become immortalized as "Lawrence of Arabia." Lawrence formed a close relationship with Faisal, whom he viewed as the most promising of the Arab leaders. The relationship eventually led to Faisal attending the 1919 Paris Peace Conference as spokesman for the Arab cause and Lawrence accompanying him as his adviser.

The importance of the Arab Revolt in British Middle East strategy grew after the failure of the drive to take Gaza in March 1917. The British provided arms and naval transport across the Red Sea to further the Arab uprising. Faisal and Lawrence provided leadership, with both men proving adept at guerrilla warfare. The Arabs cut rail lines, tied down thousands of Ottoman troops in the Hejaz, and made a renewed British offensive across the Sinai and into Palestine possible. The most dramatic moment of the uprising occurred in August 1917 when Lawrence led a force of 2,000 Arabs across some of the worst desert in the Arabian Peninsula and seized the vital port of Aqaba by surprising the Ottoman garrison with an attack from the landward side. Aqaba's capture secured the flank of the British forces in Palestine and opened the way for an offensive by the British and their Arab allies into Jordan and Syria.

Lawrence then made an equally dramatic journey across the Sinai to Cairo to report to the British command on the capture of Aqaba and the success of the Arab uprising. With Aqaba under Allied control, British forces, now commanded by Lieutenant General Sir Edmund Allenby, launched a new offensive against the Ottomans in Gaza and Palestine that resulted in the capture of Jerusalem on December 11, 1917. The British were now in a position to attack into Jordan and Syria. At the same time, a renewed British drive in Mesopotamia succeeded in capturing Baghdad.

While in Cairo, Lawrence learned of the Sykes-Picot Agreement, which threatened the prospects for Arab independence. On returning to the Hejaz, he urged Faisal—whose Arab forces were to support Allenby's upcoming attack into Jordan and Syria by protecting the British right flank—to push into Syria and Jordan, hoping that Britain and France would not be able to deny them Arab land they already controlled. Just before the end of the war, in October 1918 the Arab army, with Faisal and Lawrence in the lead, captured Damascus, further muddying an already confused political situation.

Anglo-French imperial ambitions had thus run head-on into growing Arab and Jewish nationalism. The fall of the Ottoman Empire destroyed the state that had united Ottomans, Arabs, Armenians, and Jews within a single political and social framework for more than four centuries. Its disappearance brought the emergence of a variety of competing nationalist movements that offered their citizens alternate approaches of constructing their political identities and their cultural communities. Many times, one movement's goals were diametrically opposed to those of another. British pledges to the Arabs and their support for uprisings on the Arabian Peninsula fueled Arab nationalism that was to translate into resentment of Allied duplicity and a sense of betrayal when Britain and France established League of Nations mandates in Iraq, Syria, Lebanon, and Palestine after the war.

Britain's postwar difficulties with Palestinian Arabs were greatly compounded by the Balfour Declaration. Of all the wartime promises made by the British, the Balfour Declaration would have the most far-reaching consequences. In

July 1917, British foreign secretary Arthur Balfour placed a notice in the *Times of London* promising British support for a Jewish homeland in Palestine. Based on a draft written by Baron Edmund de Rothschild (although Balfour modified it considerably before publication), it stated that the British government viewed favorably the establishment of a Jewish national home in Palestine. The declaration avoided any mention of a Jewish state and stated clearly that there was to be no impingement on the civil and religious rights of indigenous non-Jewish populations.

Why the British chose to support Zionist ambitions in 1917 has been the subject of considerable controversy among scholars and analysts of British wartime Middle Eastern policies. Clearly, a number of factors were involved. Some observers have emphasized the strategic benefits that the British government believed Britain would derive from Jewish settlement in Palestine. Many British policy makers believed that a Jewish national homeland in Palestine, surrounded by a large Arab population and dependent on Britain for support and security, would provide an ideal safeguard for the Suez Canal and the route to India. Others argue that the British had one eye on influential Jews in the United States, particularly prominent Zionists such as Louis D. Brandeis and Felix Frankfurter who were close to the Woodrow Wilson administration. In this view, the British government was influenced by a patrician form of anti-Semitism that overestimated Jewish influence in the United States. Other viewpoints emphasize intense lobbying efforts by Zionist leaders, particularly Chaim Weizmann; fears that Germany might take over the Zionist movement; or efforts by Allied policy makers to reach out to the leaders of the Russian Revolution, many of whom were Jewish. No doubt all of these played a role.

Whatever the reasons behind Balfour's action and however careful the declaration's wording, the declaration ultimately poisoned Arab-Jewish relations in Palestine and undermined Britain's credibility in both communities. The leadership of the Zionist movement and the Jewish community in Palestine took the declaration as a British commitment to a Jewish state in the long run and, in the short run, as support for unlimited Jewish immigration to Palestine.

The Palestine, Mesopotamian, and Arabian campaigns of 1917–1918 were significant military victories for Britain. The many promises that British officials made to so many conflicting groups, however, put them in a precarious political position. Arabs, both in Palestine and in the wider Middle East, saw both the Balfour Declaration and the Sykes-Picot Agreement as great betrayals and evidence of Britain's lack of good faith. Arab nationalism now took on an intensely anti-British and anti-Western bent that could not be contained by the fragmented postwar order of protectorates dominated by the British and the French. The administrators of the British Mandate for Palestine were plagued by intensifying communal violence between the growing number of Jewish settlers and the indigenous Arab population. Nationalistic feelings in both Arab and Jewish camps—intensified by the persecution and suffering during World War I and, in the case of the Jews, fueled by persecution in Europe—simply could not be reconciled. British and French wartime measures taken to aid the Allied war effort against the Ottoman Empire opened a Pandora's box that has not been closed.

The war also had long-term effects on the future of Iran, Turkey, and North Africa west of Suez, although political unrest took differing forms and revolved around different issues. In the years before the war, Muslim leaders in French North Africa had pursued legal equality in assimilation into metropolitan French society. During the war years, Muslim leaders stepped up their agitation for legal equality. This was true in North Africa as elsewhere; however, the French opposed nationalist agitation in Algeria, Morocco, and Tunisia (the so-called Maghreb) especially. For the most part, Arabs in French North Africa remained loyal to France. Efforts by German agents to foster Bedouin uprisings in the Maghreb early in the war largely failed, and by the end of the war the same was true in Persia where, with the defeat of the Germans and the Russian Civil War, the British secured a dominant place.

WALTER F. BELL

**See also**
Allenby, Sir Edmund Henry Hynman; Aqaba, Capture of; Arab Nationalism; Armenians and the Armenian Genocide; Balfour Declaration; Bedouins; Damascus, Allied Capture of; Egypt; Faisal I, King of Iraq; Gallipoli Campaign; Iran; Iraq; Italo-Ottoman War; Jerusalem, Capture of; Jordan; Kut al-Amara, Siege of; Lawrence, Thomas Edward; Lebanon; Mandates, League of Nations; Ottoman Empire, Entry into World War I; Suez Canal; Sykes-Picot Agreement; Syria; World War II, Impact on the Middle East

**References**
Albertini, Rudolf von. "The Impact of Two World Wars on the Decline of Colonialism." *Journal of Contemporary History* 4, no. 1 (January 1969): 17–35.
Fromkin, David. *A Peace to End All Peace: The Fall of the Ottoman Empire and the Creation of the Modern Middle East.* New York: Avon, 1989.
Gelvin, James L. *The Israel-Palestine Conflict: One Hundred Years of War.* New York: Cambridge University Press, 2005.

Morris, Benny. *Righteous Victims: A History of the Zionist-Arab Conflict, 1881–2001.* New York: Vintage Books, 2001.

Morrow, John H., Jr. *The Great War: An Imperial History.* New York: Routledge, 2005.

## World War I Caucasian Front

*See* Caucasus Front, World War I

## World War I Mesopotamian Front

*See* Mesopotamian Theater, World War I

## World War I Palestine and Syria Campaign

*See* Palestine and Syria Campaign, World War I

## World War I Persian Front

*See* Persian Front, World War I

## World War II, Impact on the Middle East

World War II directly affected the Middle East in the considerable fighting in the region but even more so indirectly in terms of decolonization, the spread of Arab nationalism, the enhanced importance of the region's oil resources, and the impact of Great Power rivalries that sprang from the conflict. For good or ill, the United States and the Soviet Union became the major players in the region. Nothing is more emblematic of the change in importance of the region than photographs of King Abdul Aziz bin Abdul Rahman Al Saud (Ibn Saud) of Saudi Arabia meeting as an equal with U.S. president Franklin D. Roosevelt aboard the U.S. Navy cruiser *Quincy* in Egypt's Great Bitter Lake on February 14, 1945.

North Africa was a major theater of war, particularly from 1940 to 1943, and combat there involved Egypt, Libya, Tunisia, Morocco, and Algeria. Fighting also occurred in the Horn of Africa, and there was limited combat in Syria and Iraq. The war brought decolonization, which most keenly affected Great Britain and France. Not only had much of each power's empire been cut off from the mother country during the conflict, but at least in the case of France, portions of the empire had kept the war alive in its name. Clearly, the peoples of the French and British Empires expected to be rewarded for their loyalty during the war. Free French leader General Charles de Gaulle recognized the necessity of a changed relationship between France and its empire during a meeting at Brazzaville in January 1944, which resulted in a declaration heralding the need for political, social, and economic reforms. Independence did not come all at once, of course, nor did Britain and France intend it for all. Thus, France considered Algeria, with its large European population, to be an integral part of France as three French departments, even as the Muslim majority there did not enjoy equal rights.

Opposition to European rule brought some violence at the end of the war, as in Syria. There also was a bloody uprising in Sétif in May 1945 in Algeria that may have claimed as many as 10,000 dead, and in Madagascar a major uprising against French rule claimed between 11,000 and 80,000 lives. It was impossible not to recognize how the war had shattered myths of European military invincibility. The French had been forced to give in to Japanese demands in Indochina, and the British were humiliated in Malaya. The Japanese victory in the Battle of Singapore has been called one of the greatest military disasters in British history. After the war, the peoples of the British and French Empires sensed their masters' weakness and were far less likely to be satisfied with slow, evolutionary change. Of course, declarations of basic human rights by such organizations at the United Nations gave cachet to their aspirations.

Many in Britain and France were loath to give up their empires. This was most pronounced in France. It is said that it is hard for the weak to be generous, and France in 1945 was very weak indeed. It had suffered a humiliating defeat and occupation at the hands of Germany, and only with its empire could it still be counted as a major power after the war. This and the fact that Indochina was France's wealthiest colony help to explain the determination of the French to hold on to their Southeast Asian empire, even if it meant war. The same might be said of the British in Burma (today Myanmar). The British were also slow to yield some imperial privileges. Although they were forced to acknowledge the reality of Egyptian independence, it was not until 1956 that they were forced to cede their remaining bases in Egypt.

During the war Soviet forces had entered northern Iran, and British and American forces moved into the south, their presence justified by the need to establish a secure logistical route to the Soviet Union, then desperately fighting for survival against the bulk of the German military. A crisis soon developed at the end of the war, with Moscow reluctant to withdraw its forces from northern Iran and indeed encouraging secessionist movements. One of the first challenges for the new United Nations, this crisis was defused in a reluctant Soviet departure, but the British were also reluctant to give up their control of the Iranian oil industry, which subsequently triggered an Iranian government crisis.

Turkey was little affected by the war, having remained neutral during it until the very end. Indeed, during World War II the German-Turkish Non-Aggression Pact was signed on June 18, 1941, only a few days before the German invasion of the Soviet Union. Turkey maintained diplomatic relations with Germany until August 1944, when Ankara severed its diplomatic and commercial relations with Germany. Despite pleas from the Allied side, Turkey did not declare war on Germany and Japan until February 23, 1945, and then largely to secure membership in the United Nations. After the war the Soviet Union put tremendous pressure on Turkey, and this situation helped bring about the Truman Doctrine in March 1947.

The most difficult problem in the Middle East became that of resolving the conflict between Arabs and Jews. In September 1939, the political situation in Palestine was at best troubled. British authorities had largely tamped down the Palestinian Arab Revolt of 1936–1939, but there was still considerable unrest. The British did try to win some Arab support by clamping down on Jewish immigration, and this brought acts of terrorism by Jewish extremists against British authorities. Indeed, a three-way struggle ensued as Jews and Arab fought the British occupier and each other. Toward the end of the war the British actually diverted warships to keep Jews out of Palestine, and yet pressures grew afterward, especially from the United States, with the world's largest Jewish population, for the British to admit the survivors of the Holocaust. Some 6 million European Jews had died in the Nazi-inspired genocide, and there was worldwide support for resettling the few survivors in Palestine and also to permit establishment of some sort of Jewish state that might protect the interests of Jews in the future.

Arab nationalism remained relatively dormant during World War II, the British having made some concessions in Egypt and elsewhere. There was fighting between British forces and the Iraqi Army in Iraq and between British, British Empire, and Free French forces with Vichy France forces in Syria; both of these conflicts were prompted largely by fears of spreading German influence in the region and the threat this might pose to the supply of oil.

The war left Britain and France financially and militarily exhausted. Prime Minister Clement Attlee in Britain, whose Labour Party came to power in Britain as a consequence of its stunning surprise victory in the July 1945 elections, was determined to reduce its imperial commitments, particularly those that seemed to be especially volatile. The haste to divest certain colonial holdings brought great bloodshed in both the Empire of India and in Palestine. In the case of the latter, when Britain was unable to arrange a partition agreement between Jewish and Arab leaders, it simply walked away from its guardianship responsibilities. The British government set a deadline of May 15, 1948, for the departure of its troops and the end of the mandate. Anticipated by all, on May 14 Jewish leaders in Palestine proclaimed the establishment of the new State of Israel, and the first Arab-Israeli war immediately began.

As a newcomer to the Middle East, the United States sought during the war to secure regional stability to ensure the flow of oil and war supplies to and through the region, including Lend-Lease assistance, to the Soviet Union. To help expedite Lend-Lease aid, during the war Soviet forces occupied northern Iran, while the British had moved into the south. Little thought was given in Washington to the tensions that would surface at the end of the war. The focus was always on ending the war as quickly and at as little cost in American lives as possible. Thus, Roosevelt assured Ibn Saud that the United States did not support the Zionist aspiration of a Jewish state in Palestine, and his administration acquiesced in British efforts to restrict immigration into Palestine, even with proof positive of the Holocaust. American public opinion helped force a change in policy after the war, prompted by the all too horrible revelations of Jewish wartime suffering. In 1948, the United States was the first nation to recognize the new State of Israel (closely followed as it turned out by the Soviet Union).

In time, American policy shifted from a hands-off approach to stalwart support of Israel, while still claiming to be even-handed as far as the Arabs were concerned. U.S. support for the new Jewish state included arms shipments that made Israel by far the most powerful regional military power. The Soviet Union meanwhile largely reversed course to oppose Israel and to arm the Arab states against it. The theme was thus struck on which the Cold War in the Middle East would be played out and would make the region one of the most volatile in the world.

WALTER F. BELL AND SPENCER C. TUCKER

**See also**
Arab Nationalism; Egypt; Ibn Saud, King; Iran; Iraq; Israel; Palestine, British Mandate for; Saudi Arabia; Syria; Syria and Lebanon Campaign; Turkey; World War I, Impact on the Middle East

**References**
Albertini, Rudolf von. "The Impact of Two World Wars on the Decline of Colonialism." *Journal of Contemporary History* 4, no. 1 (January 1969): 17–35.
Bauer, Yehuda. *From Diplomacy to Resistance: A History of Jewish Palestine, 1930–1945.* Translated by Alton M. Winters. Philadelphia: Jewish Publication Society of America, 1970.
Gelvin, James L. *The Israel-Palestine Conflict: One Hundred Years of War.* New York: Cambridge University Press, 2005.
Hahn, Peter L. *Crisis and Cross-Fire: The United States in the Middle East.* Dulles, VA; Potomac Books, 2005.
Morris, Benny. *Righteous Victims: A History of the Zionist-Arab Conflict, 1881–2001.* New York: Vintage Books, 2001.
Oren, Michael B. *Power, Faith, and Fantasy: America in the Middle East, 1776 to the Present.* New York: Norton, 2007.
Segev, Tom. *The Seventh Million: The Israelis and the Holocaust.* Translated by Haim Watzman. New York: Hill and Wang, 1993.

# Wye River Agreement (October 23, 1998)

Concluded on October 23, 1998, the Wye River Agreement was between Israel and the Palestinians. For the first time, the United States took a direct role in guaranteeing the implementation of the terms of the agreement. Under the terms of the agreement, Israel was to pull out of additional territories in the West Bank, while the Palestinians made concessions toward Israel's security. The strict timetable for implementing the agreements was not met, however.

On September 28, 1995, Israel and the Palestine Liberation Organization (PLO) signed an interim agreement in regard to the West Bank and the Gaza Strip following secret negotiations in Oslo, Norway. Moderates on both sides hoped that this treaty was the first step in a peace process for the Middle East. Instead, Prime Minister Yitzhak Rabin was assassinated by a right-wing Israeli fanatic. Continued terrorist attacks by Muslims on Israeli targets helped bring about the election of Benjamin Netanyahu, a hard-liner. Netanyahu suspended the withdrawal of Israeli troops from occupied sections of the West Bank to permit new Israeli settlements in the area. A focal point for both sides was the creation of a Jewish settlement named Har Homa near Jerusalem.

In an effort to get the peace process started again, U.S. president Bill Clinton arranged for Israeli and Palestinian representatives to meet in the United States. Beginning on October 14, 1998, the two sides got together under U.S. sponsorship at the Wye River Conference Center in Maryland. For nine days, tough negotiations continued before an agreement was hammered out. On October 23, the agreement was signed by Netanyahu and PLO leader Yasser Arafat. King Hussein of Jordan attended the ceremony as well. The treaty was criticized by many on both sides, but it marked the first time that the United States offered to take an active role in guaranteeing the security and implementation of an agreement between Israel and its neighbors.

Most of the provisions of the Wye River Agreement had to do with security and the turnover of certain areas to the control of the Palestinian Authority (PA). The first step was a withdrawal of Israeli forces from an additional 13 percent of the West Bank. The Israelis originally refused to accept that figure, requested by the United States. A compromise was reached in which the PA under Arafat would occupy 10 percent of the land, while the remaining 3 percent would be turned into nature preserves.

The second part of the agreement had to do with improving Israel's security. Arafat agreed to take measures to halt terrorist attacks launched from the West Bank and Gaza against Israeli targets. Specific individuals accused of terrorist activities were to be apprehended by Palestinian police and prosecuted. A joint U.S.-Palestinian committee was to be formed to review Palestinian plans to reduce terrorism. Representatives of the U.S. Central Intelligence Agency (CIA) were to be appointed to provide expertise and evaluation of Palestinian efforts. Another joint committee would review the prosecution of individuals accused of terrorism. The PA undertook the task of collecting illegal weapons from individuals in areas under its control and preventing the importation or manufacture of additional weapons. The United States agreed to assist in collecting the illegal weapons and in preventing the smuggling of additional weapons. To reduce incidents of terrorism, the Palestinian authorities were required to prohibit all forms of incitement to violence.

Other provisions of the Wye River Agreement included a reduction in the number of Palestinian policemen from 36,000 to 30,000. Arafat also confirmed that he would have the Palestinian Central Council amend the Palestinian Charter

Israeli prime minister Benjamin Netanyahu, U.S. president Bill Clinton, and Palestinian Authority chairman Yasser Arafat signing the Wye River Agreement at the White House in Washington, D.C., on October 23, 1998. (Israeli Government Press Office)

to remove references to the destruction of Israel as a goal. In return for their concessions, the Palestinians were to receive free passage from the Gaza Strip to the West Bank. Also approved was the Palestinian National Airport, which opened in Gaza on November 24, 1998. Palestinian prisoners held by the Israelis were to be released soon after the treaty was signed. A strict timeline was included in the agreement for the two sides to meet their commitments and to get the peace process back on track.

The United States made several secret agreements with both sides to help the process along. In one, Washington agreed to overlook the Israeli settlement at Har Homa. The United States also arranged for Israel to agree to restrict building in West Bank settlements, with the exception of natural growth. Finally, the U.S. government promised both sides financial assistance to remove settlements and build infrastructure. The United States also promised Israel that it would meet any attack on that country by weapons of mass destruction (WMD) with counterweapons.

Optimism regarding the Wye River Agreement evaporated soon after its signing. Netanyahu refused to implement the treaty until it was approved by his cabinet and the Knesset. Several of the terms of the agreement were modified by the cabinet. Also, Israel refused to release any prisoner accused of causing Israeli bloodshed. On December 20, Netanyahu suspended implementation of the treaty. In the May 1999 elections Ehud Barak was voted in as prime minister of Israel, and he opposed the Wye River Agreement.

In an effort to restart the process, the United States sponsored further negotiations. An agreement was signed at the Egyptian resort of Sharm El Sheikh on September 5, 1999. Also known as Wye River Two, the Sharm El Sheikh agreement committed Israel to withdrawal from another 11 percent of the West Bank and the release of 350 Palestinian political prisoners. Although a promising beginning was made to implement Wye River Two, the agreement ground to a halt by the end of 1999. Further negotiations at Camp David in July 2000 brought no results. The election of George W. Bush to the presidency at the end of 2000 further halted direct guarantees by the United States for implementing the Wye River Agreement.

TIM J. WATTS

**See also**

Arafat, Yasser; Barak, Ehud; Gaza Strip; Hussein ibn Talal, King of Jordan; Netanyahu, Benjamin; Oslo Accords; Palestinian National Authority; Rabin, Yitzhak; Settlements, Israeli; Sharm El Sheikh

**References**

Enderlin, Charles. *Shattered Dreams: The Failure of the Peace Process in the Middle East, 1995–2002.* New York: Other Press, 2003.

Kimmerling, Baruch, and Joel S. Migdal. *The Palestinian People: A History.* Cambridge, MA: Harvard University Press, 2003.

Ojeda, Auriana. *The Middle East.* San Diego, CA: Greenhaven, 2003.

Ross, Dennis. *The Missing Peace: The Inside Story of the Fight for Middle East Peace.* New York: Farrar, Straus, and Giroux, 2004.

Rubenberg, Cheryl. *The Palestinians: In Search of a Just Peace.* Boulder, CO: Lynne Rienner, 2003.

## Xenophon (ca. 431–ca. 354 BCE)

Greek general and mercenary commander who campaigned in Persia. Born the son of Gryllus, an upper-class Athenian, around 431 BCE, Xenophon grew up during the Peloponnesian War (431–404) and no doubt fought in the Athenian Army in its latter stages. He had sufficient economic means to be able to maintain a horse and serve in the cavalry. Xenophon also became acquainted with and much admired the philosopher Socrates.

Xenophon may have become disillusioned by the trial of Athenian admirals after the defeat at Arginusae (406 BCE). In any case, he left Greece after the Peloponnesian War to become one of 10,000–12,000 Greek mercenaries in the service of Cyrus the Younger against his older brother King Artaxerxes II of Persia. Cyrus was defeated and killed in the Battle of Cunaxa (401), although the Greek mercenary force remained largely intact. When its commander, Clearchus of Sparta, was invited to a peace conference at which he was treacherously executed, the Greeks found themselves bereft of leadership deep in hostile territory in Mesopotamia. The mercenaries, known as the Ten Thousand, then elected new leadership, which included Xenophon, and began an extraordinary journey home. They were obliged to fight their way through Persians, Armenians, and Kurds to reach Trapezus on the Black Sea, where they proceeded by ship back to Greece.

Xenophon's record of that extraordinary five-month journey (401–400), the *Anabasis* (Expedition or March Upcountry), has him playing a key role in the survival of the force. It also discusses military leadership traits. Xenophon also wrote, among other works, the earliest extant cavalry manuals *Hipparchikos* (On the Cavalry General), which treats the duties of a cavalry commander, and *Peri hippikēs* (The Art of Riding). Another notable work is his *Hellenica* (A History of My Times).

Returning to Greece, Xenophon eventually became the commander of all forces under King Seuthes II of Thrace in fighting against Persia during 400–399 BCE. Xenophon then joined the Spartans and fought with them in Asia in 399–394. Later he was awarded an estate at Spartan state expense for his services. The exact circumstances are unclear, but in Athens Xenophon was declared a traitor, probably because he fought for Spartan king Agesilaus against Athens in the Battle of Coronea (394) or perhaps because of his activities in the service of Cyrus, and was banished in absentia. Although the banishment was removed in 371, Xenophon chose to live in Corinth. Some sources suggest that he may have returned to Athens in 365. He died in Corinth or in Athens around 354 BCE.

A general of considerable ability and a keen judge of what constitutes effective military leadership, Xenophon was a prolific writer who is today admired for his style and diction. He is less reliable as a historian. No democrat, Xenophon much admired Sparta and its constitution.

SPENCER C. TUCKER

**See also**
Achaemenid Empire; Artaxerxes II

## References

Anderson, J. K. *Xenophon*. New York: Scribner, 1974.
Hutchinson, Godfrey. *Xenophon and the Art of Command*. Mechanicsburg, PA: Stackpole, 2000.
Strauss, Leo. *Xenophon's Socrates*. Ithaca, NY: Cornell University Press, 1972.
Xenophon. *A History of My Times (Hellenica)*. London: Penguin, 1979.

---

# Xerxes I (519–465 BCE)

King of Persia. Xerxes, also known as Xerxes the Great, was the fourth king of kings of the Achaemenid Empire. Born in 519 BCE, Xerxes was the son of Darius I (Darius the Great) and Atosa, daughter of King Cyrus the Great. Revolt in Egypt in 486 BCE led Darius to plan a military campaign there. Persian law required that the ruler designate a successor before setting out on campaign, and Darius designated Xerxes. Before he could set out, however, Darius fell ill and died in late 486. Xerxes was then proclaimed ruler. He was not the eldest son of Darius, who by tradition should have inherited the crown, but he was the eldest son by Atosa and thus a descendant of Cyrus with perhaps superior claim. In any case, there was no challenge to Xerxes's assumption of the crown.

Xerxes soon campaigned in Egypt and Babylon, crushing the revolts, but in 484 BCE he greatly angered Babylonians by melting down the golden statue of their deity Marduk. This led to fresh revolts that year and in 482. Having quelled these, Xerxes then turned to deal with Greece.

In 499 BCE the rich Greek city-states of Asia Minor had rebelled against Darius I. Aided by some of the city-states of Greece, notably Athens, they had burned the Persian city of Sardis. Darius I had put down the Ionian Revolt in 494 but then set out to punish Greece for its interference in Persian affairs. His expedition had ended in humiliating defeat in the Battle of Marathon (490 BCE). Darius then began assembling another army to invade Greece. Indeed, it was his raising of taxes to finance this expedition that had prompted the revolt in Egypt. Xerxes was determined to complete the task begun by his father.

The size of the Persian expeditionary force of 481 BCE has been much debated. The Greek historian Herodotus, known as the Father of History, calculated it at more than 1 million men, but modern reckoning puts it at perhaps 600 ships and three army corps of 60,000 men each, still a Persian advantage over the Greeks of some three to one. In the spring of 480, this host reached the Dardanelles (Hellespont) where Egyptian and Phoenician engineers had constructed a bridge of boats across the straits that was among the most admired mechanical achievements of antiquity. The Persian army then quickly occupied Thrace and Macedonia, and the northern Greek city-states surrendered and allowed their troops to be added to those of the invaders. Only Plataea and Thespiae in the north prepared to fight. Sparta furnished the main contingent of land forces sent north under King Leonidas to hold the Persians long enough for the Athenian fleet to meet and destroy the Persian fleet.

Themistocles commanded 271 Athenian and allied warships. The Persian force of more than 650 ships had been reduced by storms to perhaps 500 serviceable warships, but this was still a comfortable advantage in numbers. The ensuing Battle of Artemisum off the northern coast of Euboea (mid-August 480 BCE) was inconclusive, although the Greeks managed to capture some 30 Persian vessels. Meanwhile, some 4,000 Greeks under Leonidas had taken up position at the narrow Pass of Thermopylae. The Greeks held for several days against overwhelming odds, but a Greek traitor led the Persians to flank the Greek position. Seven hundred Thespians and 300 Thebans refused the order to withdraw and remained with 300 Spartans. All were killed.

Themistocles withdrew southward with his ships, and Xerxes occupied Athens. Themistocles, now with some 310 ships, induced Xerxes, with 500, to order an attack, and the Persians were defeated in the Battle of Salamis (ca. September 20, 480 BCE). This prevented Xerxes from moving to conquer the Peloponnese.

Unrest in Babylon caused Xerxes to send a large part of his army back to Persia. The Greeks defeated the remaining Persian forces the next year at Plataea (August 479 BCE) and shortly thereafter attacked and burned the remaining Persian ships anchored at Mycale and inflicted heavy casualties on the Persian forces ashore (ca. August 29). The Persians then withdrew entirely.

Xerxes returned to his capital of Persepolis and indulged his taste in monumental construction projects. He died in August 465 BCE, assassinated by Artabanus, commander of the royal bodyguard.

A capable ruler who did much to strengthen Persia and campaigned widely, Xerxes is nonetheless largely remembered today for his defeat at the hands of the Greeks.

SPENCER C. TUCKER

**See also**
Achaemenid Empire; Darius I; Greco-Persian Wars

## References

Boardman, John, et al. *The Cambridge Ancient History,* Vol. 4, *Persia, Greece and the Western Mediterranean c. 525 to 479 B.C.* Cambridge: Cambridge University Press, 1988.

Burn, A. R. *Persia and the Greeks: The Defence of the West, c. 546–478 BC.* Stanford, CA: Stanford University Press, 1984.

Dandamaev, M. A. *A Political History of the Achaemenid Empire.* New York: E. J. Brill, 1989.

Fisher, William Bayne, et al. *The Cambridge History of Iran,* Vol. 2. Cambridge: Cambridge University Press, 1985.

Frye, Richard N. *The Heritage of Persia.* London: Weidenfeld and Nicolson, 1963.

Green, Peter. *The Greco-Persian Wars.* Berkeley: University of California Press, 1996.

## Yarmouk River, Battle of (August 15–20, 636)

The Battle of the Yarmouk (Yarmük, Yarmuk) River was fought between Arab forces of the Rashidun caliphate, led by Abu Ubaidah ibn al-Jarrah and Khalid ibn al-Walid, and Byzantine Empire forces under Mahan of Armenia. The battle took place in Palestine over the course of six days during August 15–29, 636, next to the Yarmouk River, the largest tributary of the Jordan River. The battle marked the beginning of the first great wave of Islamic military conquests.

In 634 Caliph Abu Bakr ordered Muslim forces to invade Syria, long a Byzantine Empire preserve. The Arab army captured Damascus and took most of Palestine. Faced with these developments, Byzantine emperor Heraclius assembled a large force at Antioch. Organized as five separate armies, it included native Byzantines as well as Slavs, Franks, Armenians, Georgians, and Christian Arabs. Heraclius sought to take advantage of the fact that the Arab forces were separated into four main armies: at Palestine, in Jordan, at Caesarea, and at Emesa (Homs) in Syria. The emperor planned to concentrate his own forces and defeat the Arabs in detail. In June 636 he sent reinforcements under his son Constantine to Caesarea, hoping to tie down Arab forces there, while sending his remaining four armies on converging axes toward Damascus and Emesa.

The Arabs learned the broad outlines of the Byzantine plan from prisoners, and in a council of war Jarrah accepted the advice of his subordinate, Walid, to withdraw from northern and central Syria and concentrate on the plain of Yarmouk, which was more suitable for cavalry operations. Close to the Rashidun stronghold of Nejd, this location also offered an escape route.

The Byzantine army camped just north of the Wadi Raqqad. The two sides conducted protracted negotiations, but these soon collapsed. Muslim accounts place the Byzantine force at 200,000–250,000 men and their own army at only 24,000–40,000. Modern estimates are something on the order of 50,000–100,000 for the Byzantines and only 7,500–25,000 for the Arabs. Whatever the numbers, all accounts agree that the Arabs were heavily outnumbered.

Byzantine commander Mahan formed his four armies in a line of battle some 12 miles wide. He distributed the cavalry equally among the armies, situating it in the rear to act as a reserve. He deployed his Arab Christian forces in front. Mounted on camels and horses, they acted as a light screening force and skirmish line.

On the Muslim side, Khalid offered to assume command of the army for the battle; Jarrah, who lacked the experience of his subordinate, accepted. Khalid divided the army into 36 infantry and 4 cavalry units, holding a total front of about 10 miles, with the Muslim left anchored on the Yarmouk River. The cavalry constituted about a quarter of the Muslim strength, and Khalid distributed much of it to his flanks as a reserve to arrest any Byzantine breakthrough there. The remainder he held as a mobile reserve under his personal command in the center. The army thus consisted of

4 subgroups of 9 infantry formations each. Each was organized on the basis of clan or tribe.

The battle opened on August 15, with the two armies less than a mile apart. The Byzantines began with an advance by all four armies in line. The initial assault was not strong, however, as Mahan tried to locate weak points in the Muslim line.

On the second day Mahan attacked at dawn, launching two armies against the Muslim center to fix the Muslim forces in place but with the main thrusts coming on the flanks. The Byzantines made considerable headway in each of their flanking attacks and came close to achieving victory. However, Khalid's cavalry reserve was the difference; it shored up first the Muslim right and then its left.

On the third day the Byzantines attacked again, this time trying to break through where the Muslim right flank joined the center. Again the Muslim mobile reserve averted disaster and pushed the Byzantines back to their original position.

On the fourth day the Byzantines again came close to victory. Believing that the previous day's assault had severely weakened the Muslim right wing, Mahan resumed the attack there. The Armenian portion of the Byzantine army broke completely through the Muslim line and drove on their camp. Once again Khalid's cavalry reserve averted disaster. Khalid split it into two main bodies in order to attack the Armenians on each flank. Facing Muslim forces on three sides, the Armenians were forced to withdraw, and the original line was restored. There were significant losses on each side.

Early on the fifth day Mahan dispatched an emissary to the Muslims, who asked for a truce of several days to negotiate. Jarrah was willing to accept the proposal, but Khalid was opposed. The battle continued, although there was no major fighting that day.

To this point the Muslims had remained on the defensive. On the sixth day, assuming correctly that Byzantine morale was low, Khalid ordered an attack. He planned to use his cavalry to defeat that of the Byzantines, leaving their infantry without cavalry support and open to attacks from the flanks and rear. He also planned a major simultaneous flanking attack on the Byzantine left that would roll up their line against the river ravine to the west. While Mahan was attempting to organize his cavalry, the Muslim cavalry struck in force, causing the Byzantine horsemen to withdraw to the north and abandon the infantry. Khalid then directed his cavalry to attack the rear of the Armenian infantry on the Byzantine left. Under the pressure of a three-pronged attack of Muslim cavalry the Armenians broke, carrying the rest of the Byzantine army with them. Pinned against the steep ravines of the Yarmouk so closely that they were hardly able to use their weapons, the Byzantines were slaughtered in large numbers. Many others were killed or maimed by falling into the ravines.

The Battle of Yarmouk secured Syria and Palestine for the Muslims. Khalid then recaptured both Damascus and Emesa. Emperor Heraclius returned to Constantinople to consolidate his forces against a Muslim drive in Egypt.

Spencer C. Tucker

**See also**
Bakr, Ahmad Hassan al-; Heraclius; Khalid ibn al-Walid

**References**
Akram, A. I. *The Sword of Allah, Khalid bin al-Waleed: His Life and Campaigns.* Rawalpindi, Pakistan: National Publishing House, 1970.
Donner, Fred. *The Early Islamic Conquests.* Princeton, NJ: Princeton University Press, 1981.
Gil, Moshe, and Ethel Broido. *A History of Palestine, 634–1099.* Cambridge: Cambridge University Press, 1997.
Kaegi, Walter E. *Byzantium and the Early Islamic Conquests.* New York: Cambridge University Press, 1992.
McGraw, Donner F. *The Early Islamic Conquests.* Princeton, NJ: Princeton University Press, 1981.
Nicolle, David. *Yarmuk 636 A.D.: The Muslim Conquest of Syria.* Osprey Campaign Series #31. London: Osprey, 1994.

# Yazidis

Yazidis are an ethnic and religious minority people residing chiefly in northern Iraq. Although they have a cultural affinity with the Kurds, they are not related to them ethnically (indeed, their ethnic origin is obscure). The Yazidis generally speak Kurdish, but they practice a unique religion that combines elements of a number of different religions, including Zoroastrianism (the religion of ancient Persia), Sufism, and Mithraism. They are, however, monotheistic. Worldwide, the Yazidi population is estimated to be about 600,000, with 400,000 to 500,000 living in northern Iraq (primarily in Nineveh Province). Since the 1990s a number of Yazidis have fled persecution in Iraq, settling in Western Europe (mainly Germany).

Socially, the Yazidis organize themselves in a strictly hierarchical fashion. Their secular leader is a hereditary emir, Prince Tahseen Said. The Yazidis' religious leader, known as the Baba Sheikh, is Khurto Hajji Ismail. The Yazidis are divided into three castes: murids, sheikhs, and pirs. Within each caste are clans, and Yazidis are obliged to marry within their own clan. Marriage outside one's caste is considered a grave sin. The Yazidis do not permit non-Yazidi people to live among them, and their religion does not permit conversion from other religions.

Because of their stand-alone religion, the Yazidis have been habitually subjected to discrimination, segregation, and persecution, particularly during the rule of Iraqi president Saddam Hussein. In more recent years, they have suffered persecution at the hands of Muslim extremists in Iraq. In 2007 during the Iraq War, a bombing perpetrated by a group associated with Al Qaeda—and quite possibly the forerunner of the Islamic State of Iraq and Syria (ISIS)—killed at least 500 Yazidi civilians in the worst such attack since the start of the war in 2003. In 2009, suicide bombers killed 20 Yazidi civilians and injured another 30 in an attack in Sinjar, a largely Yazidi town west of Mosul.

The Yazidis were then subjected to a campaign of virtual genocide by ISIS, which viewed the Yazidis as devil worshippers. The campaign against the Yazidis was part of a larger effort by ISIS to rid Iraq and neighboring Syria of all non-Muslim people and to establish a fundamentalist caliphate under sharia law. Iraqi Christians have also been similarly threatened.

ISIS forced Kurdish Peshmerga troops to retreat and then captured Sinjar in early August 2014, forcing that city's majority Yazidi population to flee for their lives. With few places to go, many took refuge in the nearby mountains, particularly Mount Sinjar. This created a potential humanitarian catastrophe as some 50,000 Yazidi peoples, most of them women and children, were trapped in the mountains with no way to secure food, water, or other necessities. Meanwhile, ISIS rebels mounted attacks against the Yazidis and slaughtered anyone who attempted to escape Mount Sinjar. With the United Nations (UN) warning of genocide against the Yazidis, the United States and other Western nations decided to act.

Humanitarian aid from the United States, Britain, France, and several other countries began on August 7 as planes dropped tons of food, water, and other supplies to help the Yazidis. Soon thereafter, U.S. air strikes against ISIS targets permitted Syrian Kurds and Peshmerga soldiers to rescue 20,000–30,000 Yazidis from the mountains, escorting them to Iraqi Kurdistan via Syria. Meanwhile, the rescue operations continued, as there were still thousands of people still trapped in the mountains. By mid-August U.S. air strikes continued, and many Western nations vowed to arm the Peshmerga fighters with better weaponry to fight ISIS and protect the Yazidis. The UN proposed creating a humanitarian corridor that would be opened and protected by Western air assets through which other Yazidis could be rescued and resettled in Kurdish areas in Iraq. On August 14, American officials announced that the ISIS siege of Mount Sinjar had been broken.

In October 2014 UN officials reported that ISIS had murdered more than 5,000 Yazidis and had abducted some 5,000–7,000 others, most of them women and children. ISIS has claimed religious justification for enslaving Yazidi women. Yazidi women have taken up arms against ISIS and are said to constitute about one-third of Kurd-Yazidi coalition forces. During 2015 and 2016 much of the international community, including the U.S. government in 2016, officially declared the ISIS campaign against the Yazidis a genocide.

During 2017 as ISIS was being defeated in Iraq and Syria, some Yazidis began returning to their ancestral lands in Iraq. But Kurds were also trying to reclaim the area, which set up potential conflict between the two peoples. By the summer of 2018, only about 15 percent of Yazidis had returned to Sinjar. What they returned to, however, was heartbreaking. Many of Sinjar's buildings had been badly damaged or destroyed, roads were impassable, and the area was strewn with improvised explosive devices (IEDs) previously deployed by ISIS insurgents.

Paul G. Pierpaoli Jr.

**See also**
Islamic State of Iraq and Syria; Peshmerga

**References**
Acikyildiz, Birgul. *The Yazidis: The History of a Community, Culture and Religion*. London: I. B. Tauris, 2014.
BBC World News. "Thousands of Yazidis 'still trapped' on Iraq Mountain." BBC, August 12, 2014, http://www.bbc.com/news/world-middle-east-28756544.
Commins, David Dean. *Historical Dictionary of Syria*. Lanham, MD: Scarecrow, 1996.

# Yemen

Yemen, officially known as the Republic of Yemen, is located in Western Asia in the southern part of the Arabian Peninsula. Yemen comprises 203,850 square miles and is thus halfway in size between the U.S. states of California and Texas. Yemeni territory includes some 200 islands. Yemen itself is bordered by Saudi Arabia to the north, Oman to the east, the Arabian Sea and the Gulf of Aden to the south, and the Red Sea to the west. Yemen's coastline stretches for about 1,200 miles. Not far off the western and southern coasts of the country lie the East African nations of Eritrea, Djibouti, and Somalia.

Yemen is the poorest country in the Arab world and has been identified by the international community as both a developing country and a failed state. The country's

# YEMEN

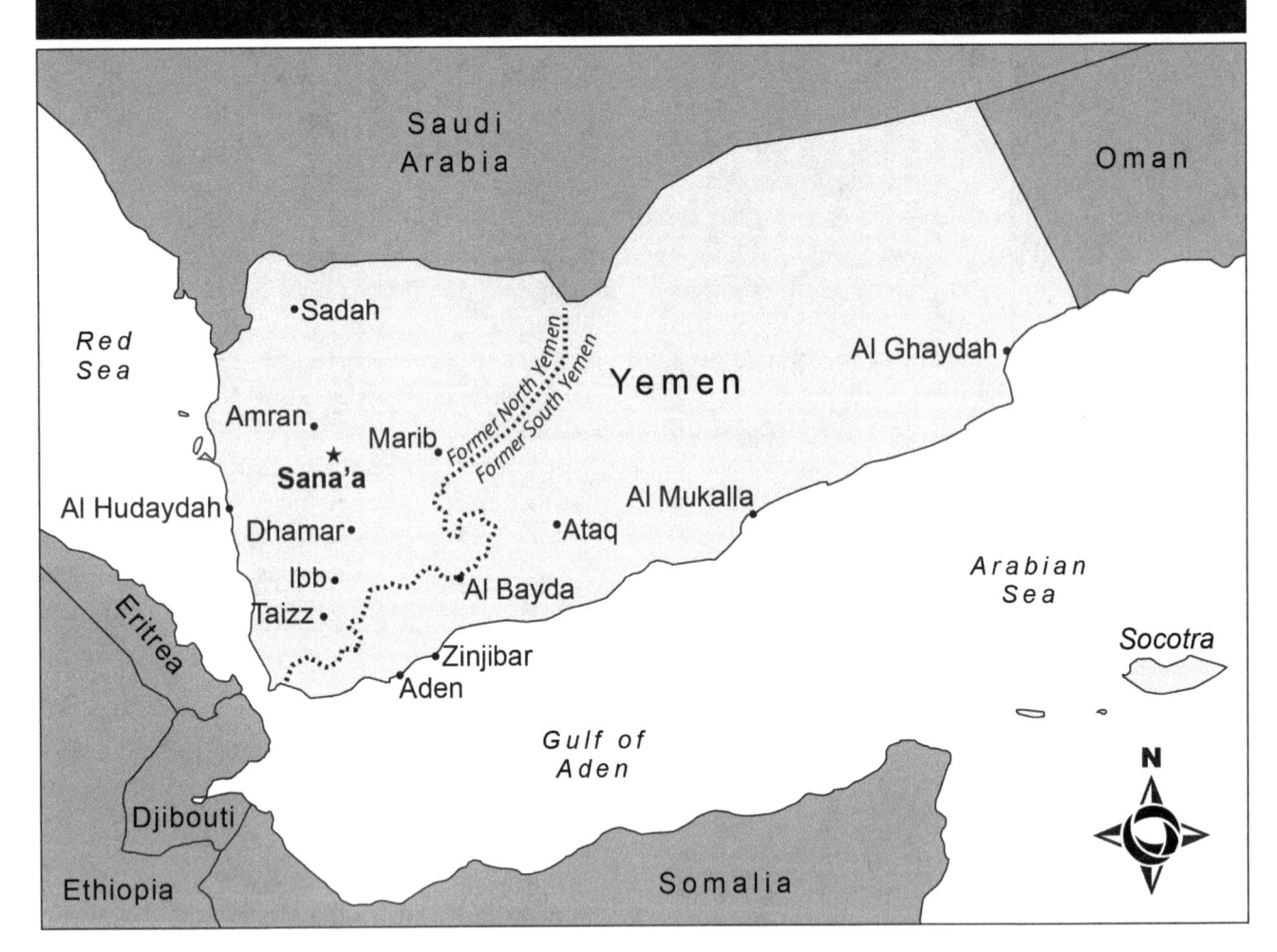

population in 2018 was some 28.9 million. Yemen's normal capital and largest city is Sana'a, but with the civil war now in progress the capital of the internationally recognized government has been temporarily relocated to the port city of Aden.

Yemen is of Arab ethnicity and is overwhelmingly Muslim. There is a sharp religious divide. About 52 percent of the nation's Muslims are Sunnis, while 48 percent are Shiites. The Sunnis live principally in south and southeastern Yemen, while the Shiites are in the north. Yemen has one of the world's highest birthrates; indeed, some 46 percent are age 14 and younger, and fewer than 3 percent are older than 65. The median age is 16. Yemen's legal system is a mix of Islamic law, Turkish law (a holdover from Ottoman Empire rule), English common law, and local tribal dictates. Nevertheless, Islamic law almost always takes precedence.

Recorded human habitation in the region can be traced as far back as the ninth century BCE. Yemen's location on the Red Sea and the Gulf of Aden has made it an important crossroads and center for East-West trade as well as that from Asia to Africa. Christianity arrived in the fourth century CE, but in the seventh century Muslim caliphs began to exert their influence across the region. They gradually gave way to dynastic imams who retained the caliph's theocratic government until the modern era. Egyptian caliphs also held sway in Yemen. The Ottoman Empire controlled some or most of Yemen sporadically between the 1500s and 1918, when that empire collapsed with its defeat in World War I. Ottoman influence was the most pronounced in northern Yemen; in the south, imams tended to be in control, although they were usually overseen to some extent by authorities in Istanbul (Constantinople).

The British came to be influential in south Yemen. They were anxious to secure a coal depot in the southern Arabian Peninsula to service their steamers plying the route to India. After a British merchant ship went down off the coast of Aden and was subsequently plundered, the British

East India Company sent a warship commanded by Captain Stafford Haines to demand compensation. When this was rejected, Haines bombarded the port of Aden and on January 19, 1839, sent men ashore to take possession. The British then reached agreement with the sultan of Lahej for an annual payment for the port. That November some 5,000 tribesmen tried to retake Aden but were repulsed, and perhaps 200 of them were slain.

To secure their position, the British concluded treaties with the tribes surrounding Aden that guaranteed their independence in return for a pledge that they would not conclude any treaties with another foreign government. Aden soon became a major entrepôt. Known as the Aden Settlement until 1937 when it was detached from administration by India, Aden and its harbor was the only area under full British sovereignty. Together with some offshore islands, it was known as Aden Province (1932–1937), the Crown Colony of Aden (1937–1963), and the State of Aden (1963–1967).

As noted, North Yemen secured its independence in 1918 as a consequence of World War I. The new state was known as the Mutawakkilite Kingdom of Yemen from 1918 to 1962, the Yemen Arab Republic during 1962–1990, while the south was known as the People's Republic of Southern Yemen during 1967–1970. The two Yemeni states united in 1990 to form the Republic of Yemen.

Before 1962, the ruling imams in the Kingdom of Yemen pursued an isolationist foreign policy, although it did have commercial and cultural ties with Saudi Arabia. In the late 1950s the Chinese and Soviets attempted to lure the Kingdom of Yemen into their orbit with technological missions, and by the early 1960s North Yemen had become dependent on Egypt for financial and technical support.

Civil War broke out in the Kingdom of Yemen in 1962. The immediate catalyst was the death of Ahmad bin Yahya Hamidaddin in September 1962. Ahmad had been the ruling imam in the region since 1948 and had established there a thoroughly repressive regime. Although he harbored visions of uniting all of Yemen under his rule, Ahmad was unable to garner sufficient support to end British rule in the south. In 1955 Ahmad had fended off a coup attempt instigated by two of his brothers and disgruntled army officers.

To bolster his position, in April 1956 Ahmad entered into a formal military pact with Egypt and Saudi Arabia that placed Yemeni military forces under a unified command structure. That same year Ahmad also named his son, Muhammad al-Badr, as crown prince and heir apparent and established formal ties with the Soviet Union. In 1960, Ahmad left North Yemen to seek medical treatment. In his absence, al-Badr began to carry out several reform measures that his father had promised to implement but had gone unfulfilled. Outraged by this, Ahmad promptly reversed the measures when he returned home. This hardly endeared him to his subjects, and several weeks of civil unrest ensued, which the government crushed with a heavy hand.

Ahmad died on September 19, 1962, and al-Badr became imam. One of his first official acts was to grant a blanket amnesty to all political prisoners. This step did not long stave off discord. Indeed, on September 27 in the capital city of Sana'a, Abdullah as-Sallal, commander of the royal guard who had just been appointed to that post by al-Badr, launched a coup supported by half a dozen tanks and some artillery and declared himself president of the "Free Yemen Republic."

The rebels easily seized key locations in Sana'a, including the radio station and armory. They also moved against the Al-Bashaer Palace. The Imamate Guard refused to surrender, and fighting occurred, with the defenders surrendering the next day. The coup, however, brought on full-blown civil war. Meanwhile, an insurgency was in progress in South Yemen.

Al-Badr escaped to the northern reaches of the kingdom, where he received support from royalist tribes. He also secured support from the conservative monarchy of Saudi Arabia that bordered Yemen on the north. Al-Sallal received military assistance from Egypt. As early as October 5 an Egyptian battalion had been deployed to act as a personal guard for him. Egyptian president Gamal Abdel Nasser, reeling from the breakup of the United Arab Republic of Egypt and Syria, hoped to recoup his prestige as well as deliver a rebuff to Egypt's rival, Saudi Arabia. In undertaking this step, Nasser ignored repeated warnings by Ahmed Abu-Zeid, former Egyptian ambassador to the Kingdom of Yemen, that the country lacked a sense of nationhood, that no combat troops should be sent there, and that any aid should be limited to equipment and financial support. Nasser also failed to appreciate the depth of anger in Saudi Arabia regarding any Egyptian intervention, which the Saudi royal family saw as a direct challenge to their hegemony over Yemen and the other Persian Gulf states.

Nasser soon discovered that many more troops would be required than initially thought. Egyptian numbers steadily increased to a maximum of 55,000 men in late 1965. By the mid-1960s, the royalists had also secured assistance from Iraq, Jordan, Pakistan, Iran, and Britain as well as covert assistance from Israel, while the Soviet Union and several other communist bloc nations joined Egypt in supporting the Republican side. The conflict developed along Cold War lines, with the United States and other Western powers tending to support the royalists. On several occasions the United Nations attempted to mediate an end to the bloodshed, but the regional and international dynamics of the struggle worked against this.

Egyptian forces initially performed poorly. A paucity of maps, unfamiliarity with the terrain, and lack of knowledge of local conditions all impeded effectiveness. The Saudis did not have this problem, as they and the northern Yemeni tribes were closely related. In January 1964, royalist forces laid siege to Sana'a.

Egyptian air strikes within Saudi territory on Najran and Jizan—staging areas for the royalist forces—almost led to war between Egypt and Saudi Arabia. U.S. president John F. Kennedy then supplied air defense systems and U.S. aircraft to help defend the kingdom if need be.

Although Egyptian tactics gradually improved, including the extensive use of aircraft in a ground support role, the war became a stalemated low-intensity conflict and a great drain on the Egyptian treasury and military. Indeed, the presence in Yemen of so many well-trained Egyptian troops and much equipment was keenly felt in the June 1967 Six-Day War. Egypt's ignominious defeat in that conflict forced Nasser to begin withdrawing his troops from Yemen. That same year the British withdrew from South Yemen.

The withdrawal of all foreign troops led to an agreement on April 14, 1970, whereby Saudi Arabia recognized the republican government of Yemen in return for the inclusion of royalists in several key government posts. There was, however, no role for al-Badr, for the agreement stipulated that he and his family leave the country. Al-Badr lived in Britain until his death in 1996. The eight-year-long conflict had claimed some 100,000–150,000 lives and had an immense adverse economic effect.

Meanwhile, fighting had broken out in South Yemen on October 14, 1963. Known in Britain as the Aden Emergency, it pitted the British and local sheikhs against two leftist nationalist groups: the Front for the Liberation of Occupied South Yemen (FLOSY) and the National Liberation Front (NLF). The British government announced in July 1964 its decision to grant independence to the Federation of South Arabia with the intention of maintaining its military base at Aden, but the ongoing insurgency and additional British military retrenchment led London to announce on November 2, 1967, that it was withdrawing all military forces from east of Suez. The British opened talks in Geneva with the NLF and signed with it an independence agreement, in effect abandoning the local sheikhdoms and emirates of the Federation of South Arabia with which Britain had protection agreements.

Southern Yemen became independent as the People's Republic of Southern Yemen on November 30, 1967, and the NLF gradually secured control. Following several unsuccessful coups in 1968, on June 22, 1969, a radical Marxist wing of the NLF seized power, and on December 1, 1970, Yemen became the People's Democratic Republic of Yemen (PDRY). All political parties were forced into the NLF, which was then renamed the Yemeni Socialist Party (YSP), the only legal political party.

The PDRY soon established close ties with the Soviet Union, the People's Republic of China, and other communist states as well as the Palestine Liberation Organization. In addition, the PDRY acquired arms and training for its military from the communist bloc countries, while the Soviet Union secured access to PDRY naval facilities. The PDRY also aided rebels in Dhofar fighting the government of Oman and engaged in hostilities with Saudi Arabia when, during November 26–December 5, 1969, there was fierce fighting between Yemeni and Saudi Arabian forces over the disputed Al Wadeiah oasis that ended with the Saudis in firm control.

During the transition, several hundred thousand Yemenis from the south fled to North Yemen, overwhelming that nation's inadequate resources. Animosity between the two Yemeni states ebbed and flowed but led to sporadic fighting that would endure for two decades.

Heavy fighting also occurred in 1972. It ended in a cease-fire and negotiations under the auspices of the Arab League and a decision that the two Yemeni states would eventually be joined. On October 11, 1977, Yemen Arab Republic president Ibrahim al-Hamdi and his brother, Vice President Colonel Abdullah Mohammed al-Hamdi, were assassinated, probably to prevent talks with South Yemen regarding union. The new president, Ahmad al-Ghasmi, lasted only eight months. On June 24, 1978, he was killed by a bomb planted in the briefcase of the South Yemen ambassador, who also died in the blast. A three-man military council briefly assumed power. Then on June 25 in South Yemen, PDRY president Salem Rubaya Ali, suspected of wanting to reduce ties with the Soviet Union and improve relations with Saudi Arabia and the United States, was overthrown and later executed.

On July 18, 1978, Ali Abdallah Saleh became president of the Yemen Arab Republic. The next year fighting resumed between the two states, bringing renewed efforts for unification. During February 24–26, 1979, and May 1–June 1, 1980, there was more fighting.

Much more bloodshed occurred in the two-week-long South Yemen Civil War of January 1986. On January 13, gunmen loyal to President Ali Nasir Muhammad killed several of his political rivals before a YSF Politburo meeting in Aden. Fighting immediately began in Aden between Ali Nasir's supporters and those loyal to former president Abdul Fattah Ismail. Thousands died, among them Ismail, killed later that day. Ali Nasser was ousted on January 25. Some 60,000 people, including Ali Nasser and his supporters, fled into North Yemen, and much of the city of Aden was in ruins when the fighting ended on January 24.

Finally, in 1990 the governments of the two Yemeni states reached agreement and on May 22 established the Republic of Yemen. The constitution of the new state called for a popularly elected president and a prime minister appointed by the president. The executive branch was to share power with a bicameral legislature. Saleh became the first president, with the vice president being Ali Salem al-Beidh, the secretary-general of the YSP in South Yemen.

The new government opposed non-Arab military intervention in the region. After Iraq invaded and annexed Kuwait in August 1990, Yemen, then a member of the UN Security Council, abstained from a number of votes condemning Iraq and voted against the resolution authorizing use of force. The government of Saudi Arabia was especially upset at this stance and expelled some 800,000 Yemenis, creating staggering unemployment and an economic crisis in Yemen.

Following food riots in major towns in 1992, a new coalition government was formed. In August 1993, however, al-Beidh returned to Aden, declaring his refusal to participate in the government until "marginalization" of the south was addressed. Negotiations occurred, and on February 20, 1994, an accord was signed in Amman, Jordan. It, however, failed to resolve differences, and the armed forces of both north and south, having never been integrated, mobilized for war. The brief Yemeni Civil War of May–June 1994 saw the defeat of the southern forces backing secession and the flight abroad of many YSP leaders and other southern secessionists.

As the Yemeni government struggled with high inflation, excessive spending, and corruption on a vast scale, a new threat arose in Islamic militants. Indeed, at least three different types of Islamic militants have waged a persistent low-level insurgency, which the government has been unable to curtail. The kidnapping of foreigners remained an intractable problem.

On December 29, 1992, terrorists associated with the Al Qaeda Islamic terrorist organization carried out what many consider to be the first Al Qaeda attack on the United States, detonating bombs at two different tourist hotels in an apparent effort to kill U.S. marines staying there. The United States had been using Aden as a base to support its operations in Somalia. The blast killed two and wounded seven, but none of these were Americans. Shortly thereafter, however, Washington ordered U.S. military personnel from Yemen, and Al Qaeda claimed this a victory.

A more devastating attack occurred on October 12, 2000, again reportedly planned by Al Qaeda, when two suicide bombers detonated a large explosive device aboard a small coastal craft next to the U.S. Navy destroyer *Cole* while it rode at anchor in Aden Harbor. The blast killed 17 U.S. sailors, wounded 39, and badly damaged their ship. It also strained U.S.-Yemeni relations for several years.

On September 17, 2008, a least 16 people were killed in an attack on the heavily fortified U.S. embassy compound in Sana'a by terrorists wearing uniforms identifying them as Yemeni security personnel and riding in cars painted to resemble police vehicles but filled with explosives. The attackers failed to penetrate the gate, and an intense short gun battle followed the blasts. The 16 dead included 6 guards, 4 civilians, and 6 terrorists. Islamic Jihad of Yemen claimed responsibility.

In August 2009, Houthi rebels in northwestern Yemen broke a yearlong cease-fire to renew warfare against the Yemeni government. The minority Houthis (officially known as Ansar Allah) are a revivalist Zaydi (Shia) Islamist sect. They had commenced warfare in 2004. On September 27, the Yemeni Army turned back a rebel offensive on the northern city of Sa'dah near the border with Saudi Arabia, and in early November Saudi Arabian forces retook control of the strategic mountain area known as the Jebel Dukhan on the Saudi-Yemeni border that had been seized by Houthi rebels a week earlier. The fighting raised the threat of a proxy war between Iran, supporting its coreligionist Houthis, and Saudi Arabia, supporting the Sunni-dominated Yemeni government. The Houthis are also strongly anti-American and anti–Saudi Arabian.

At the same time, Al Qaeda in the Arab Peninsula (AQAP) began activities in Yemen. Established in 2009, AQAP soon demonstrated why it is widely recognized as the most dangerous of the Al Qaeda–affiliated organizations. AQAP launched a number of terrorist plots directed against the United States, including a December 25, 2009, attempt by a Nigerian, Umar Farouk Abdulmultallab, to blow up a Detroit-bound U.S. airliner. The United States responded with a series of drone strikes that killed a number of AQAP senior members.

On February 11, 2010, the Yemeni government agreed to a cease-fire with Houthi rebels, but the country was plunged into a new crisis in January 2011 during the so-called Arab Spring that swept much of the Arab world. Demonstrations began in Independence Square of the capital city protesting endemic poverty, high unemployment, and pervasive corruption (Saleh's presidency was widely characterized as a kleptocracy). Critics also condemned Saleh's plan to amend the constitution so as to eliminate the presidential term limit, in effect making him president for life. Saleh was also clearly grooming his eldest son Ahmed Saleh, commander of the Republican Guard, to succeed him. Saleh announced on February 1 that he would not run for reelection when his term ended in 2013, but opposition leaders called this insufficient and called for protests to continue. By mid-February there were clashes with security forces. Having secured the support of at least 11 tribal sheikhs, Saleh on February 27 vowed to remain in power and to resist with "every drop of his blood." On March 19, he instituted a government crackdown in Sana'a resulting in the destruction of the demonstrators' makeshift encampments and the deaths of 46 people and the injuring of hundreds. Meanwhile, protestors had seized control of Dar Saad and Taiz in southern Yemen in what was easily the greatest challenge to Saleh's 32-year rule.

On March 21, three prominent Yemeni Army commanders defected and called for an end to Saleh's rule. Massive demonstrations occurred in Sana'a, despite Saleh's declared state of emergency. Saleh's forceful actions led Washington to end its support for its longtime ally. On June 3, Saleh was badly injured in a rocket attack on a mosque in his compound in Sana'a and two days later flew to Saudi Arabia for medical treatment.

Saleh returned to Yemen on September 23. This brought fighting and the risk of all-out civil war, but on November 23 in an arrangement worked out by the United States and the Gulf Cooperation Council, Saleh agreed to resign. Under the terms of the agreement he was to step aside within 30 days, handing over power to Vice President Abd Rabbuh Mansur Hadi. Presidential elections would then follow. The deal also gave Saleh immunity from prosecution. Saleh departed as arranged, and on February 24 in a one-person race Hadi was elected president.

On March 18, 2012, the National Dialogue Conference began meeting to try to resolve the major issues dividing Yemen. AQAP remained active, and on May 12 an AQAP suicide bomber in Sana'a killed at least 90 soldiers and wounded 222 as the men were rehearsing for a parade.

Iran also upped its support for the Houthi rebels. On January 28, 2013, Yemeni authorities, acting on information provided by the United States, intercepted a 130-foot dhow that was transporting weapons to Yemen. These included 10 heat-seeking antiaircraft missiles of Chinese manufacture, explosives, shells, rocket-propelled grenades, and equipment for making bombs. The Yemeni government claimed that the weapons had been shipped from Iran and were intended for the Houthi rebels.

In January 2014, the National Dialogue Conference extended Hadi's term for another year. U.S. aid increased, and on April 21, 2014, the Yemeni government announced that it had killed at least 65 AQAP members in a joint operation with the United States. According to one report, U.S. drone strikes in Yemen between 2011 and mid-2018 numbered nearly 300 and had killed as many as 2,000 people, of whom the large majority were militants, but at least 100 or more had been identified as civilians. U.S. drone and air strikes increased threefold during 2017 after the Donald Trump administration vowed to turn up the heat against AQAP and other insurgents operating in Iraq. Trump's intensification of the strikes was also no doubt tied to his administration's hostility toward Iran and its eagerness to lend more support to the Saudi government. Meanwhile Saleh, now in exile, allied with the Houthis.

On September 21, 2014, the Houthis seized control of Sana'a, and Hadi fled. The Houthis then organized a "unity government" of various factions. Hadi, his prime minister, and his cabinet all resigned on January 22, 2015. This came only one day after an apparent power-sharing arrangement with the Houthis, who had nonetheless stripped Hadi of his powers. The UN, the United States, and the Persian Gulf states, however, refused to recognize the new regime and characterized its seizure of power as a coup d'état. The UN Security Council voted unanimously to demand that Shiite rebels immediately relinquish control of Yemen's government. A number of Arab countries now pressed for military intervention to reverse what they characterized as an illegitimate seizure of power. On February 21, meanwhile, Hadi took back his resignation and from Aden declared that he was still the legitimate president. With Sana'a still under rebel control, Hadi proclaimed Aden to be Yemen's "temporary capital."

On March 20, 2015, two suicide bombers attacked two mosques in Aden, killing 137 people and wounding 357 in the deadliest assault yet targeting Shiites. An affiliate of the Sunni extremist Islamic State of Iraq and Syria (ISIS) claimed responsibility.

Saudi officials regarded the Yemeni situation as a major security threat, given their long border with Yemen and being home to some 1 million people of Yemeni descent. Saudi Arabia has also found itself locked in an intense geopolitical struggle with Iran. On March 26, Saudi Arabia and its regional allies openly entered the Yemeni Civil War, launching air strikes against the Houthis now besieging Aden. The coalition included Saudi Arabia, the United Arab Emirates (UAE), Bahrain, Kuwait, Qatar, Jordan, Morocco, and Sudan. The U.S. government announced its support and has provided "logistical and intelligence support."

A widened Yemen conflict posed risks for global oil supplies. Tankers from Arab producers such as Saudi Arabia, the UAE, Kuwait, and Iraq pass Yemen's coastlines via the narrow 25-mile-wide strait between Yemen and Djibouti and the Strait of Hormuz between Saudi Arabia and Iran in the Gulf of Aden in order to transit the Red Sea and the Suez Canal to Europe. Thus, crude oil prices shot up nearly 6 percent on news of the operation.

Despite the Saudi intervention and a week of intense air strikes, on April 1, with Hadi safely in Saud Arabia, Houthi rebels and their allies supported by tanks pushed into central Aden. Heavy coalition bombing continued, and this apparently turned many Yemenis against the Saudis and the United States for having furnished the weaponry and munitions.

On April 14, the UN Security Council voted to impose an arms embargo on the Houthis. The resolution passed 14 to 0, with Russia abstaining. The Russians had been pressing for a ban on air strikes to let in humanitarian assistance, but the Persian Gulf states had opposed this. On April 20, Washington ordered the U.S. Navy aircraft carrier *Theodore Roosevelt* to join other American warships off Yemen to intercept Iranian vessels that might be transporting weapons to the Houthis. U.S. drone strikes against AQAP also continued. These did not deter AQAP, however. On December 1, 2015, hundreds of AQAP fighters took control of the major cities of Zinjbare and Jaaar.

Additional proof that Iran was supplying the Houthis was provided in the March 5, 2016, seizure by an Australian Navy ship of a small stateless fishing vessel well off the coast of Oman, identified as having sailed from Iran with arms destined for Yemen by way of Somalia. The seized weapons included nearly 2,000 AK-47 assault rifles and 100 rocket-propelled grenades.

Ground combat continued, and on April 25, 2016, Yemeni government forces scored a significant victory. Supported by Saudi and Emirati special forces, they secured control of AQAP's main stronghold of the port city of Al Mukalla and the surrounding coastal area, which AQAP had held for a year. Saudi Arabia claimed that more than 800 AQAP militants had been killed, although journalists on the spot disputed that number and claimed that AQAP fighters had merely withdrawn.

U.S. special forces have also been active in Yemen operating against AQAP. In late January 2017, elite SEAL Team 6 carried out a raid. The first such operation authorized by President Donald Trump, it was not successful owing to a communications intercept and ended in the death of a SEAL team member and the wounding of 3 others as well as the deliberate destruction of a $75 million aircraft; as many as 25 civilians were also killed. On May 12, 2017, however, SEAL Team 6 members carried out a successful raid, killing 7 militants in an AQAP compound in central Yemen.

On December 4, 2017, there was yet another turn in the Yemeni political drama. Only days before, Saleh had ended the alliance between his own followers and the Houthis and denounced the latter. The Houthis then struck back and killed Saleh in Sana'a. Violence in the city then soared. This further political fracturing complicated the possibilities of securing a deal that would end the fighting in Yemen that had placed some 7 million of its people at risk of death from starvation. Only the month before, UN officials had warned that the country was on the brink of "the largest famine the world has seen for many decades."

During 2018, the fighting in Yemen continued unabated. In January, the UN announced that at least 50,000 Yemeni children had died from starvation and malnutrition during 2017 alone. In February the Southern Transitional Council, a secessionist group backed by the UAE, seized control of Aden. That development only further complicated the internecine civil war, even though the council had denounced the Houthis and was nominally supportive of Hadi's government. During the spring of 2018, a series of Saudi air strikes killed or wounded scores of civilians, which elicited strong protests from the international community. In May, Yemeni rebels fired missiles at Saudi Arabia's Jizan Airport. There were no casualties, but it was also not the first time insurgents in Yemen had targeted Saudi soil. In June, Yemeni rebel forces shot down a Saudi helicopter gunship, killing all on board. Meanwhile, as 2018 progressed and U.S.-Iranian relations plummeted, the likelihood that Iran would facilitate an end to the carnage seemed increasingly remote. During the summer of 2018, there were reports of Israeli warplanes operating in Yemeni airspace. That development potentially threatened a wider regional conflict. At the same time, the Saudis were being lambasted in much of the international community because of their killing of Yemeni civilians and their blockade of Yemen, the latter of which has been largely blamed for the building famine in Yemen.

Yemen has been devastated by the war. Its economy is reeling, with the important agricultural sector hard hit by periodic droughts. Coffee production, once a mainstay of northern Yemeni crops, has fallen off dramatically. Yemen does have significant oil deposits, but these are not of the same quality as Persian Gulf oil and so have not brought in substantial profit. Yemen possesses major natural gas reserves, but these remains underdeveloped. Even if the civil war were to end tomorrow, future development would be very difficult.

PAUL G. PIERPAOLI JR. AND SPENCER C. TUCKER

**See also**
Aden Emergency; Al Qaeda; *Cole*, USS, Attack on; Houthis; Nasser, Gamal Abdel; South Yemen Civil War; Yemen, Civil War in the North; Yemen, Civil War in the South; Yemen Civil War; Yemen Hotel Bombings

**References**
Clark, Victoria. *Yemen: Dancing on the Heads of Snakes.* New Haven, CT: Yale University Press, 2010.
Day, Stephen W. *Regionalism and Rebellion in Yemen.* Cambridge: Cambridge University Press, 2012.
Dresch, Paul. *A History of Modern Yemen.* New York: Cambridge University Press, 2001.
Fraihat, Ibrahim. *Unfinished Revolutions: Yemen, Libya, and Tunisia after the Arab Spring.* New Haven, CT: Yale University Press, 2016.
Johnson, Gregory D. *The Last Refuge: Yemen, al-Qaeda, and America's War in Arabia.* New York: Norton, 2014.
Jones, Clive. *Britain and the Yemen Civil War.* London: Sussex Academic, 2004.
Mackintosh-Smith, Tim. *Yemen: The Unknown Arabia.* New York: Overlook, 2014.
Pridham, Brian. *Contemporary Yemen: Politics and Historical Background.* London: Palgrave Macmillan, 1984.
Rabi, Uzi. *Yemen: Revolution, Civil War and Unification.* London: I. B. Tauris, 2014.
Walker, Jonathan. *Aden Insurgency: The Savage War in Yemen, 1962–67.* Barnsley, UK: Pen and Sword, Military, 2014.

# Yemen, Civil War in the North (1962–1970)

Civil conflict in North Yemen (Yemen Arab Republic) that lasted from 1962 until 1970. The conflict arose from a 20-year-long opposition movement in Yemen to the authority of the descendants of Imam Yahya, who had ruled Yemen from its independence from the Ottoman Empire. The most important office in Zaydi Islam is that of imam, and in Yemen it is both a religious and political position that can only be held by one of the *sada'* (sayyids), individuals descended from Prophet Muhammad. In recent centuries, the imams came from only certain families of the *sada',* such as Bayt al-Qasim, Bayt Sharaf al-Din, Bayt al-Wazir, and Bayt Hamid al-Din (the family of Imam Yahya).

On October 30, 1918, following the collapse of the Ottoman Empire in World War I, Imam Yahya Muhammad declared Yemen to be independent. In 1926, he declared himself king of the Mutawakkilite Kingdom of Yemen. Among his goals was the imposition of sharia (Islamic law) over all of Yemen, a difficult task because the tribes usually relied on *'urf* (tribal law). To cement his authority and retain power, Yahya also sought to weaken the tribes politically and militarily. This would also serve to diminish the threat posed to the Hamid al-Dins from the other great families. Imam Yahya also wanted to secure for his kingdom parts of historic Yemen that had been taken by the British, such as Aden and Asir. There was considerable opposition to Yahya regarding his domestic policies, and the opposition factions to him united and assassinated him in 1948.

A usurper held power for several months, but Yahya's son, Ahmad bin Yahya, secured power. His reign saw growing repression as well as tension with Britain over the continued efforts to create a Greater Yemen by expansion to the south. In March 1955 Ahmad was briefly deposed in a coup led by army officers and two of his brothers, but it was soon reversed.

To bolster his position, Ahmad entered into a formal military pact with Egypt in 1956 that placed Yemeni military forces under a unified command structure. That same year Ahmad named his son, Sayf al-Islam Mohammed al-Badr (known as Muhammad al-Badr), as crown prince and heir apparent. Ahmad also established formal ties with the Soviet Union.

In 1960 Ahmad left North Yemen to seek medical treatment. In his absence Crown Prince al-Badr began to implement several reform measures that his father had promised to implement but had as yet gone unfulfilled. Outraged that his son made such moves without his knowledge or assent, Ahmad promptly reversed the measures when he returned home.

Yemeni royalist forces man a recoilless rifle on the crest of Algenat Alout in 1964 during the 1962–1970 civil war. The fighting erupted after army officers successfully staged a coup against Yemeni leader Muhammad al-Badr. Egyptian leader Gamal Abdel Nasser eventually sent 75,000 troops to support the coup against Saudi-sponsored royalists. (Hulton Archive/Getty Images)

This action did not, of course, endear Ahmad to his subjects, and several weeks of civil unrest ensued, which the government quashed with a heavy hand. The 1955 coup attempt and growing resentment toward Ahmad rendered the last years of his rule both paranoid and reactionary.

Ahmad died on September 19, 1962, and was followed by Crown Prince Muhammad al-Badr as both imam and king. One of his first official acts was to grant a blanket amnesty to all political prisoners who had been imprisoned during his father's reign. He did so in hopes of maintaining power and keeping the kingdom's detractors at bay. But al-Badr's tactics did not stave off discord. Indeed, just a week later on September 27, Abdullah al-Sallal, commander of the royal guard who had just been appointed to that post by al-Badr, launched a coup in the capital city of Sana'a.

The rebels, supported by half a dozen tanks and several artillery pieces, proclaimed the establishment of the Free Yemen Republic. They seized key locations in Sana'a, including the radio station and armory. They also moved against Dar al-Bashair Palace in the capital of Sana'a. The Imamate Guard there rejected demands that it surrender, and fighting began, with the defenders surrendering the next day. This coup, however, brought on a full-blown civil war. Meanwhile, an insurgency continued against the British in southern Yemen.

Despite a radio announcement by the new government that al-Badr had been killed in the shelling by the rebels of the palace, he in fact escaped to the northern reaches of Yemen, where he received the support of tribes allied to his family and loyal to him as imam. Al-Badr also was supported by the conservative Kingdom of Saudi Arabia, which bordered Yemen on the north. At the same time, al-Sallal received military assistance from Egypt. Indeed, Egyptian General Ali abd al-Hamid arrived in Sana'a on September 29 to assess the needs of the new revolutionary government. As early as October 5 an Egyptian battalion was in place to act as a personal guard for Colonel al-Sallal. Apparently, Egyptian president Gamal Abdel Nasser, reeling from the breakup of the United Arab Republic with Syria, hoped that Egyptian support for a republican victory in Yemen would recoup his prestige in the Arab world as well as deliver a rebuff to Egypt's rival Saudi Arabia.

Nasser soon discovered that many more troops would be required than initially thought. The numbers of Egyptian forces in Yemen steadily increased, growing to some 55,000 men in late 1965. In so doing, Cairo ignored repeated warnings by Ahmed Abu-Zayd, Egyptian ambassador to royalist Yemen during 1957–1961, that the Yemenis lacked a sense of nationhood, that no Egyptian combat troops should be sent there, and that any aid should be limited to equipment and financial support. As well as underestimating the situation on the ground, Nasser failed to understand the depth of anger in Saudi Arabia regarding the Egyptian intervention, which the Saudi royal family saw as a direct threat to its domination of Yemen and the other Persian Gulf states.

By the mid-1960s, the imamate's supporters had also secured the help of Iraq, Jordan, Pakistan, Iran, and Britain as well as covert assistance from Israel, while the Soviet Union and several other communist bloc nations supported the republican side. The conflict also became politicized along Cold War lines, with the United States, Great Britain, and many other Western powers siding with the royalists. On several occasions, the United Nations attempted to mediate an end to the bloodshed, but the regional and international dynamics of the struggle made this an almost impossible task.

Egyptian forces initially performed poorly in Yemen. The paucity of maps, an unfamiliarity with the terrain, lack of knowledge of local conditions, and the fact that they were foreigners all impeded their effectiveness. The Saudis did not have this problem, as they and the northern Yemeni tribes were closely related. In January 1964, royalist forces even laid siege to Sana'a.

Egyptian air strikes on Najran and Jizan within Saudi Arabia, staging areas for the Yemeni royalist forces, threatened a direct shooting war between Egypt and Saudi Arabia. In these circumstances, U.S. president John F. Kennedy responded to appeals by supplying air defense systems to the Saudis. He also dispatched U.S. aircraft to Dhahran Airbase in the kingdom, demonstrating an American commitment to defend Saudi Arabia against an Egyptian attack.

Although Egyptian tactics gradually improved, to include the extensive use of airpower in a ground support role, the war settled in to a protracted stalemate and became a huge drain on the Egyptian treasury and military. Indeed, the presence in Yemen of so many well-trained troops and much equipment was greatly felt in the June 1967 Six-Day War with Israel. Nasser desperately wanted a mutual withdrawal of Egyptian and Saudi forces, and his excuse came with Egypt's ignominious defeat in the Six-Day War.

The two Yemeni sides then decided to strike a compromise, in part because they wished to rid themselves of their foreign supporters. By 1969, both sides had agreed that the first step to ending the war would be the withdrawal of all foreign troops. This formed the basis for a subsequent agreement on April 14, 1970. It specified a republican form of government but one that would include some royalists. The Zaydi imam, Muhammad al-Badr, agreed to go into exile; he lived in Britain until his death in 1996. Discussion continued about creating a constitutional imamate.

As part of the peace settlement, Nasser was compelled to begin troop withdrawals from Yemen. That same year, the British withdrew from southern Yemen. This was an extremely significant time for Yemen that brought to the fore a number of intra-Yemeni conflicts, with south Yemen greatly impacted by socialist doctrine.

The Yemen Civil War left deep scars on that country's society and politics that were a long time in healing. It is estimated that the eight years of war claimed the lives of 100,000–150,000 people. Border clashes continued between the two Yemeni states, however. Finally, on May 22, 1990, following protracted and difficult negotiations, the two Yemeni states united as the Republic of Yemen.

In the unification, the heavily socialist South had to come to terms with the tribally dominated North. Tensions continued as a result of past policies. For example, support from Saudi Arabia strengthened the tribes who supported Salafism, and the Yemeni government employed these tribes against its other enemies, especially the Shiite al-Houthi rebellion also supported by tribal elements. Another brief civil war occurred in 1994. There was also considerable support in Yemen for the al-Qa'ida fi jazirat al-'arabiyya (Al Qaeda in the Arabian Peninsula) movement. There were also border clashes with Saudi Arabia that, however, have resulted in the construction of barriers between the two countries. A new civil war began in 2015.

PAUL G. PIERPAOLI JR., SPENCER C. TUCKER,
AND SHERIFA ZUHUR

### See also
Egypt; Houthi, Hussein Badr al-Din al-; Nasser, Gamal Abdel; Saudi Arabia; Shia Islam; Six-Day War; Yemen

### References
Dresch, Paul. *A History of Modern Yemen.* New York: Cambridge University Press, 2001.

Jones, Clive. *Britain and the Yemen Civil War.* London: Sussex Academic Press, 2004.

Pridham, Brian. *Contemporary Yemen: Politics and Historical Background.* London: Palgrave Macmillan, 1984.

Wenner, Manfred W. *Yemen Arab Republic.* Boulder, CO: Westview, 1991.

## Yemen, Civil War in the South (May 4–July 7, 1994)

Following a long civil war between 1962 and 1970 and a brief war in 1979, the leaders of North and South Yemen agreed to the union of their states. In January 1990 the two countries opened their borders and officially united in May, when Ali Abdullah Saleh was chosen as the leader of the new Republic of Yemen. However, the country's first free elections, held in April 1993, proved to be highly contentious, and although Saleh's General People's Congress, representing conservative northern interests, secured the most seats, its political authority was challenged by the Yemen Socialist Party, led by Ali Saleh al-Beidh, which claimed support in former South Yemen. As political tensions escalated, civil strife erupted in April 1994, and in May al-Baidh announced South Yemen's secession from the union.

The conflict began on May 4, 1994, and lasted nine weeks, until July 7, when the southern forces had been decisively defeated and their capital of Aden surrendered. Still, the civil war jeopardized regional stability and caused a stern response from Saudi Arabia, which denounced the former North Yemen. After the war, in October 1994 Saleh was reelected president, keeping the Republic of Yemen intact but dominated by the north. Although peace and stability were largely restored in the country, Yemen still suffered occasional flare-ups of violence. The clashes in the Saada region (North Yemen), where the Shiite Houthi tribesmen complained of economic and religious discrimination, had seen increasing levels of fighting since 2004. In 2009, the fighting between the rebels and the government became so intensive that neighboring Saudi Arabia became involved in the conflict as well. In July 2010 the Saada region saw skirmishes and clashes that claimed some 34 lives. Then in March 2015, a new civil war began.

Alexander Mikaberidze

### See also
South Yemen Civil War; Yemen; Yemen, Civil War in the North; Yemen Civil War; Yemenite War

### References
Day, Stephen W. *Regionalism and Rebellion in Yemen.* Cambridge: Cambridge University Press, 2012.

Dresch, Paul. *A History of Modern Yemen.* New York: Cambridge University Press, 2001.

Fraihat, Ibrahim. *Unfinished Revolutions: Yemen, Libya, and Tunisia after the Arab Spring.* New Haven, CT: Yale University Press, 2016.

## Yemen Civil War (2015–Present)

Since March 2015, Yemen has been devastated by civil war. The conflict is being fought between forces loyal to the internationally recognized government of President Abdrabbuh Mansour Hadi and the Houthi rebels and their allies. Yemen, already the poorest country in the Middle East, has been hard hit by the fighting and the naval blockade imposed by the coalition to prevent military assistance from Iran reaching the Houthis.

In August 2009, Houthi rebels in northwestern Yemen broke a yearlong cease-fire to renew warfare against the Yemeni government. The minority Houthis (officially known as Ansar Allah) are a revivalist Zaydi (Shia) Islamist sect that had first begun warfare in 2004. Houthi raids along the Saudi Arabian border soon brought in the Saudis, and this raised the threat of a proxy war between Iran, supporting its coreligionist Shiite Muslim Houthis, and Saudi Arabia, supporting the Sunni-dominated Yemeni government. The Houthis are strongly anti-American and anti–Saudi Arabian.

At the same time, Al Qaeda in the Arab Peninsula (Ansar al-Sharia, AQAP) began activities in Yemen. Established in 2009, it soon demonstrated why it is widely recognized as the most dangerous of the Al Qaeda–affiliated organizations. AQAP carried out a number of terrorist plots directed against the United States, leading to U.S. drone strikes that killed a number of AQAP senior members.

On February 11, 2010, the Yemeni government agreed to a cease-fire with the Houthi rebels, but the country was plunged into a new crisis in January 2011 during the so-called Arab Spring and demands for an end to corruption and for democratic change that swept much of the Arab world. Demonstrations began in the Yemeni capital city of Sana'a calling for the resignation of longtime Yemeni strongman president Ali Abdullah Saleh. This led to a government crackdown and increasing violence. Iran also upped its support of the Houthi rebels with weapons deliveries by sea.

Finally, after repeated delays and a failed assassination attempt that nonetheless badly wounded him, Saleh agreed to step aside in favor of Vice President Hadi. In February 2012 Hadi assumed the presidency, but he faced seemingly intractable problems including a number of army officers who remained loyal to former president Saleh, the Houthi separatist threat and that posed by AQAP, a faltering economy, high unemployment, and an agricultural crisis.

The Houthis took advantage of Hadi's weak position by taking control of their northern heartland of Saada Province and neighboring areas. Then on September 21, 2014, in a surprise move the Houthis seized control of the capital city of Sana'a, and President Hadi fled. Many non-Houthi Yemenis, disillusioned with the lack of progress under the Hadi administration, supported the revels. The Houthis then organized a "unity government" of various factions. Hadi, his prime minister, and his cabinet all resigned on January 22, 2015. This came only one day after an apparent power-sharing arrangement with the Houthis, who had nonetheless stripped Hadi of his powers. The United Nations (UN), the United States, and the Persian Gulf states, however, refused to recognize the new regime and characterized the Houthi seizure of power as a coup d'état. The UN Security Council also voted unanimously to demand that Shiite rebels immediately relinquish control of Yemen's government. Headed by Saudi Arabia, a number of Arab countries now pressed for military intervention to reverse what they characterized as an illegitimate seizure of power.

On February 21 meanwhile, Hadi took back his resignation and from the Yemeni port city of Aden declared that he was still the legitimate president. With Sana'a still under rebel control, Hadi proclaimed Aden to be Yemen's temporary capital.

On March 20, 2015, two suicide bombers attacked two mosques in Aden, killing 137 people and wounding 357 in the deadliest assault yet targeting Shiites. An affiliate of the Sunni extremist Islamic State of Iraq and Syria (ISIS) claimed responsibility.

On March 21, the Houthi-led Supreme Revolutionary Committee declared a general mobilization with the aim of overthrowing Hadi and securing control of the southern provinces. The Houthi offensive began the next day, now in alliance with forces loyal to former president Saleh.

The Saudi government saw the Yemeni situation as a major security threat, given Saudi Arabia's long border with Yemen and as home to some 1 million people of Yemeni descent. Sunni Saudi Arabia also found itself locked in an intense geopolitical struggle with Shiite Iran. On March 26 Saudi Arabia and its regional allies openly entered the Yemeni Civil War, launching air strikes against the Houthis who had laid siege to Aden. The anti-Houthi coalition included Saudi Arabia, the United Arab Emirates (UAE), Bahrain, Kuwait, Qatar, Jordan, Morocco, and Sudan. The U.S. government announced its support and agreed to provide the coalition with logistical and intelligence support. The United Kingdom and France also announced their support for the coalition air offensive.

Despite the Saudi intervention and intense air strikes, on April 1, with Hadi then safely in Saudi Arabia, Houthi rebels and their allies supported by tanks pushed into central Aden. Heavy coalition bombing continued, with these apparently turning many Yemenis against both the Saudis for the strikes and the United States for having furnished the weaponry and munitions.

On April 14, the UN Security Council voted to impose an arms embargo on the Houthis. The resolution passed 14 to 0, with Russia abstaining. The Russians had been pressing for a ban on air strikes to let in humanitarian assistance, but the Persian Gulf states opposed this. On April 20, Washington ordered the U.S. Navy aircraft carrier *Theodore Roosevelt* to join other American warships off Yemen to aid in intercepting Iranian vessels that might be transporting weapons to the Houthis.

A five-day cease-fire proposed by Saudi Arabia in May and accepted by the Houthis, which was designed to allow the distribution of humanitarian assistance throughout Yemen, went into effect on May 12 but collapsed after only four days amid renewed fighting.

At the same time Oman, which shares a common border with Yemen and was the only Middle Eastern monarchy not taking part in the coalition against the Houthis, presented a seven-point peace plan to both Iran and Saudi Arabia. Oman had played an important role in the negotiations between the Iranian government and the West to freeze the Iranian nuclear program, and there were hopes that it might be successful in Yemen. Among its major provisions, the plan called for the withdrawal of the Houthis and forces loyal to former president Saleh from all Yemeni cities and the return of military hardware and munitions seized from the Yemeni Army, the restoration of president Hadi and his government, the right of Ansar Allah (the Houthis) to form a political party, early parliamentary and presidential elections, an international aid conference, and the right of Yemen to join the Gulf Cooperation Council. Nothing came of the proposal, however.

Additional proof that Iran was supplying the Houthis was provided in the March 5, 2016, seizure by an Australian Navy warship of a small stateless fishing vessel well off the coast of Oman, identified as having sailed from Iran and carrying arms destined for Yemen by way of Somalia. The seized weapons included nearly 2,000 AK-47 assault rifles and 100 rocket-propelled grenades.

Ground combat continued. On April 25, 2016, Yemeni government forces scored a significant victory. Supported by Saudi and Emirati special forces, they secured control of AQAP's main stronghold of the port city of Al Mukalla and the surrounding coastal area, which AQAP had held for a year. Saudi Arabia claimed that more than 800 AQAP militants had been killed, although journalists on the spot disputed that number and claimed that AQAP fighters had merely withdrawn.

At the same time progovernment forces, including members of the Yemeni armed forces loyal to Hadi and predominantly Sunni southern tribesmen, were able to drive the rebels from Aden but only after a four-month-long battle that saw heavy fighting. Some coalition ground forces came ashore at Aden in August. These forces assisted in driving the Houthis and their allies from much of the south during the course of the next two months. Hadi and senior members of his government also returned to Yemen from exile at the same time and established themselves for what they hoped would be a temporary residence in Aden.

U.S. drone strikes against AQAP and ISIS also continued. These did not deter AQAP, however. On December 1, 2015, hundreds of AQAP fighters took control of the major cities of Zinjbare and Jaaar.

In February 2016, Loyalist forces managed to enter Sana'a by capturing its Nihm district. Nonetheless, despite the coalition air campaign and naval blockade continuing unabated, progovernment forces have been unable to dislodge the rebels from their northern strongholds, including most of Sana'a and its surrounding province. The Houthis were also able to maintain a siege of the southern city of Taiz and to continue firing missiles and mortars across the border into Saudi Arabia.

In December 2016 the administration of U.S. president Barack Obama, alarmed by what have been characterized as indiscriminate Saudi and coalition air strikes including attacks on hospitals and schools, with attendant mounting civilian casualties, imposed a freeze on the transfer of certain munitions to Saudi Arabia, putting U.S.-Saudi relations in a deep freeze. This policy was, however, promptly reversed by the new Donald Trump administration, which gave the Saudis and their coalition partners a virtual free hand.

U.S. special forces have continued their operations against AQAP. In late January 2017, elite SEAL Team 6 carried out a raid. The first such operation authorized by Trump, it was not successful owing to a communications intercept and ended in the death of a SEAL team member and the wounding of 3 others as well as the deliberate destruction of a $75 million aircraft; as many as 25 civilians were also killed. On May 12, however, SEAL Team 6 members carried out a successful raid, killing 7 militants in an AQAP compound in central Yemen. Certainly AQAP was having no problem gathering recruits with anger growing among desperate Yemenis.

Iran meanwhile has supplied the Houthis with more powerful weapons. These reportedly included antiship missiles and sea mines as well as explosive-laden boats with which to attack shipping in the Red Sea and Saudi territory. In consequence of this, the United States supported the Yemeni government and allied forces in retaking some coastal areas that had been held by the Houthis in order to lessen the possible threat to international shipping.

The alliance between Saleh and the Houthis broke down in late 2017, with armed clashes between Saleh's followers and the Houthis occurring in Sana'a from November 28. Violence in Sana'a soared on December 2 when Saleh announced the split in a televised statement. He called on his supporters to take back the country and expressed his willingness to meet with representatives of the Saudi-led coalition. On December 4 the Houthis killed Saleh in Sana'a, reportedly as he was trying to make his way to Saudi-held territory.

By the end of 2017 Yemen was in dire straits, with humanitarian aid groups begging Riyadh to lift the embargo. Reportedly some 7 million Yemenis were at risk of death from starvation. Only the month before, UN officials had warned that the country was on the brink of "the largest famine the world has seen for many decades." During March 2015–July 2017 alone, more than 7,600 people had been killed and 42,000 injured, the majority in coalition air strikes. Yemen was also in the throes of the world's worst recent outbreak of cholera, which had killed more than 2,000 people with some 1 million affected by the end of 2017.

During 2018, the civil war in Yemen continued unabated. In February the Southern Transitional Council, a separatist group backed by the United Arab Emirates, seized control of Aden. That development only further complicated the internecine war, even though the council denounced the Houthis and is nominally supportive of Hadi. During the spring of 2018, a series of Saudi air strikes killed or wounded scores of civilians, which elicited strong protests by the international community. In May, Yemeni rebels fired missiles at Saudi Arabia's Jizan Airport. There were no casualties, but it was also not the first time insurgents in Yemen had targeted Saudi soil. In June, Yemeni rebel forces shot down a Saudi helicopter gunship, killing all on board. Meanwhile, as 2018 progressed and U.S.-Iranian relations plummeted, the likelihood that Iran would work to end the conflict seemed increasingly remote. During the summer of 2018, there were reports of Israeli warplanes operating in Yemeni airspace. If true, that development threatened a potentially wider regional conflict. At the same time, the Saudis were being severely criticized by many in the international community because of their killing of Yemeni civilians and their blockade of Yemen. The latter has been largely blamed for the building famine in Yemen.

Into early 2019, there seemed little chance of ending the conflict anytime soon. Three rounds of UN-sponsored peace talks had not produced a breakthrough, and the United States was strongly assisting the Saudis, with U.S. operatives directly assisting the Saudis in targeting Houthi rebels. Indeed, during his visit to Riyadh in May 2017, Trump praised the Saudis for their efforts against the Houthis while offering them another $110 billion in weaponry. The British government has also sold the Saudis more than $1 billion in arms. With no pressure on them to change, the Saudis are likely to continue the embargo and the bombings. Even with the end of the conflict, restoring Yemen to anything approaching normalcy will be exceedingly difficult.

SPENCER C. TUCKER

### See also
Al Qaeda in the Arabian Peninsula; Gulf Cooperation Council; Houthis; Oman; Saleh, Ali Abdullah; Saudi Arabia; Yemen

### References
Clark, Victoria. *Yemen: Dancing on the Heads of Snakes.* New Haven, CT: Yale University Press, 2010.

Day, Stephen W. *Regionalism and Rebellion in Yemen.* Cambridge: Cambridge University Press, 2012.

Dresch, Paul. *A History of Modern Yemen.* New York: Cambridge University Press, 2001.

Fraihat, Ibrahim. *Unfinished Revolutions: Yemen, Libya, and Tunisia after the Arab Spring.* New Haven, CT: Yale University Press, 2016.

Johnson, Gregory D. *The Last Refuge: Yemen, al-Qaeda, and America's War in Arabia.* New York: Norton, 2014.

Schmitt, Eric. "United States Ramps Up Airstrikes against Al Qaeda in Yemen." *New York Times,* March 3, 2017.

Schmitt, Eric, and David E. Sanger. "Raid in Yemen: Risky from the Start and Costly in the End." *New York Times,* February 1, 2017.

## Yemen Hotel Bombings (December 29, 1992)

The bombing of two hotels in Aden, Yemen, on December 29, 1992, attributed to the terrorist organization Al Qaeda in Yemen. Long before the events of September 11, 2001, the Al Qaeda group centered in Afghanistan and Pakistan was well known to intelligence experts. It carried out or was linked to a number of attacks on Western interests, including the bombings of the World Trade Center in New York City in February 1993, the U.S. embassies in East Africa in August 1998, and USS *Cole* at Aden in October 2000. Al Qaeda in Yemen, a separate organization, has also been active within that country. One of its earliest and least known plots unfolded in December 1992, aimed at Western hotels in Yemen.

The hotel bombings came at the end of a year that had witnessed considerable terrorist activity in the country. In April, the Yemeni justice minister was seriously wounded by a gunman while driving in the capital city of Sana'a. In June, the brother of Yemeni prime minister Haydar Abu Bakr al-Attas was assassinated in the city of al-Mukalla. In a separate incident the same month, an adviser to the minister of defense was killed by unknown assailants. Throughout the spring and summer of 1992, several top officers in the Yemeni military were also assassinated or mysteriously killed. That August and September, bombs went off at homes and offices of leading Yemeni government officials.

Westerners were also targeted. In September and again in November 1992, small bombs were detonated near the U.S. embassy, while another exploded just outside the German embassy in October. Yemeni officials released little information on the incidents to the world press, just as other countries such as Egypt and Saudi Arabia had not readily admitted opposition activity. Members of the Yemeni Islamic Jihad were eventually arrested for some of the attacks.

The larger attacks came on December 29, 1992, when bombs went off at two major hotels in the city of Aden. One exploded at the Gold Mohur Hotel, frequented by foreigners. A second blast occurred in the parking lot of the Aden

Movenpick Hotel, adjacent to where U.S. military personnel were staying en route to assist with relief operations in Somalia. It is believed that the attacks were in protest of American soldiers being billeted in Yemen and the perceived Westernization of Aden, a major international port and the economic capital of the country.

Two people—an Austrian tourist and a Yemeni hotel worker—died in the first attack. Several dozen others were wounded, including two suspected terrorists involved in the second attack. They turned out to be Yemenis trained in Afghanistan, where Al Qaeda had camps for an international network of operatives. There were no casualties from the second bombing. In response to the incidents, U.S. forces stationed in Aden were withdrawn by December 31.

Six men were eventually arrested in connection with the bombings, but all managed to escape from jail in July 1993. This development led to allegations that Yemeni government officials had connections to the terrorists and had aided in their escape. Two of the terrorist bombers involved in the hotel bombings later took part in other terrorist plots, including the attack on USS *Cole* on October 12, 2000, that killed 17 U.S. sailors.

ARNE KISLENKO

**See also**
Al Qaeda; Bin Laden, Osama; *Cole*, USS, Attack on; Terrorism; Yemen

**References**
Rotberg, Robert I. *Battling Terrorism in the Horn of Africa*. Washington, DC: Brookings Institution Press, 2005.
Shai, Shaul. *The Red Sea Terror Triangle: Sudan, Somalia, Yemen, and Islamic Terror*. New Brunswick, NJ: Transactions Publishers, 2005.
West, Deborah L. *Combating Terrorism in the Horn of Africa and Yemen*. Cambridge, MA: World Peace Foundation, 2005.

## Yemenite War (February 24–March 19, 1979)

A brief conflict in 1979 between the pro-Western Yemen Arab Republic (North Yemen) and the Soviet-backed People's Democratic Republic of Yemen (South Yemen). The two states had been involved in a prolonged conflict during 1962–1970 that left deep scars on both society and politics. North Yemen experienced considerable political turbulence during the next seven years as its pro-Saudi ruler Colonel Ibrahim al-Hamadi, who seized power in 1974, was assassinated three years later. His successor as a president, Colonel Ahmed ibn Hussein al-Ghashmi, survived for only four years before being killed by the explosion of a suitcase bomb carried by a South Yemeni envoy on June 24, 1978.

In the aftermath of Ghashmi's death, South Yemen president Rubayi Ali was deposed and executed. As accusations flew back and forth between the two states, tensions led to open hostilities on February 24, 1979, when troops on both sides of the border fired on each other. Each side blamed the other for having started it.

North Yemenite forces then attacked across the border and raided several villages in South Yemen. Supported by the Soviet Union, Cuba, and East Germany, South Yemen responded by attacking North Yemenite territory. Concerned about the escalating fighting, the government of Saudi Arabia called an emergency meeting of the League of Arab States (Arab League), while the United States began providing arms to North Yemen and dispatched a naval task force to the Arabian Sea. The Arab League negotiated several armistices, but these were routinely violated until a cease-fire was accepted by both sides on March 19, 1979.

The two Yemenite armies returned to status quo ante bellum, while Arab League forces were deployed on the border to maintain peace. Despite talks between the two sides immediately after the cease-fire went into effect and subsequent agreement on unification of the two Yemens, this did not occur.

ALEXANDER MIKABERIDZE

**See also**
Yemen; Yemen, Civil War in the North; Yemen, Civil War in the South

**References**
Dresch, Paul. *A History of Modern Yemen*. New York: Cambridge University Press, 2001.
Pridham, Brian. *Contemporary Yemen: Politics and Historical Background*. London: Palgrave Macmillan, 1984.

## Yom Kippur War (October 6–25, 1973)

The Yom Kippur War of October 6–25, 1973, also known as the Ramadan War, the October War, and the 1973 Arab-Israeli War, was a major conflict between Israel and its Arab neighbors that had a profound effect on the Middle East. Egyptian president Gamal Abdel Nasser died in September 1970. His successor, Anwar Sadat, was determined to change the status quo regarding Israel. He called for a gradual peace settlement that would lead to Israeli withdrawal from the

Sinai but without a formal general peace agreement. Sadat expelled the Soviet advisers brought in by Nasser and resumed negotiations with the United States that Nasser had ended in 1955.

The failure of his diplomatic efforts in 1971, however, led Sadat to begin planning a military operation that would break the political stalemate along the Israeli-Egyptian front. Sadat believed that even a minor Egyptian military success would change the military equilibrium and force a political settlement. Israel's strength was in its air force and armored divisions, which were well trained in maneuver warfare. Egyptian strengths lay in the ability to build a strong defense line and in new Soviet-supplied surface-to-air missiles (SAMs) deployed in batteries along the canal and deep within Egypt. Sadat hoped to paralyze the Israeli Air Force by the SAMs and counter the Israelis' advantage in maneuver warfare by forcing them to attack well-fortified and well-defended Egyptian strongholds.

In an attempt to dilute the Israeli military forces on the Sinai front, Sadat brought in Syria. A coordinated surprise attack by both states would place maximum stress on the Israel Defense Force (IDF). Above anything else, the key to the plan's success was secrecy. Were Israel to suspect that an attack was imminent, it would undoubtedly launch a preventive attack, as in 1967. That part of Sadat's plan, at least, was successful.

A combination of effective Egyptian deceptive measures and Israeli arrogance contributed to Israel's failure to comprehend what was happening. One deception consisted of repeated Egyptian drills along the Suez Canal, simulating a possible crossing. The Israelis thus became accustomed to large Egyptian troop concentrations at the canal and interpreted Egyptian preparations for the actual crossings as just another drill. Even the Egyptian soldiers were told that it was simply a drill. Only when the actual crossing was under way were they informed of its true nature. Even with the actual attack, however, the real intent of Egyptian and Syrian forces remained unclear to the Israelis, and they initially refrained from offensive action.

On the Israeli-Egyptian front, Egypt amassed nearly 800,000 soldiers, 2,200 tanks, 2,300 artillery pieces, 150 SAM batteries, and 550 aircraft. Along the canal Egypt deployed

Israeli Army long-range 175mm artillery in action on the Syrian front, on October 11, during the Yom Kippur War (Ramadan War) of October 6–25, 1973. (Israeli Government Press Office)

five infantry divisions with accompanying armored elements, supported by additional infantry and armored independent brigades. This force was backed by three mechanized divisions and two armored divisions. Opposing this impressive Egyptian force on the eastern bank of the Suez Canal, Israel had only a single division, supported by 280 tanks.

On October 4–5, 1973, Sadat expelled some 15,000 Soviet advisers and all their dependents. Not until the early morning hours of October 6 did Israeli military intelligence conclude that an Egyptian attack was imminent. Brigadier General Eliahu Zeira, Israeli director of intelligence, warned IDF chief of staff Lieutenant General David Elazar of this, but Prime Minister Golda Meir decided against a preemptive strike.

### Operations on the Sinai Front

At 2:00 p.m. on October 6, Egypt launched a massive air strike against Israeli artillery and command positions. At the same time, Egyptian artillery shelled the Israeli Bar-Lev Line fortifications along the Suez Canal. Egyptian commandos crossed the canal followed by engineers, who quickly constructed bridges, allowing the Egyptians to get sizable numbers of infantry and armor across. By October 8, the Egyptians had established a three- to five-mile-deep penetration on the east bank with some 500 tanks. They then fortified this zone with more troops. Two Egyptian divisions held the seized area, which was also defended by SAM batteries.

The Israelis meanwhile mobilized two armored divisions under Major Generals Ariel Sharon and Abraham (Bren) Adan and on October 8 launched a quick counteroffensive in an attempt to repel the Egyptian troops. The undermanned and underequipped Israeli troops, however, came up against the far larger well-organized and well-equipped Egyptian force protected by highly effective handheld antitank missiles. The Egyptians crushed the Israeli counteroffensive. In the fighting, Israeli ground support aircraft also suffered heavy losses against Egyptian antiaircraft defenses, especially from the SAMs. Following this setback, the Israeli General Staff decided to halt offensive actions on the Suez Front and give priority to the fighting in the north against Syria.

Sadat now overruled his ground commander, Field Marshal Ahmed Ismail Ali, and, following Syrian pleas for assistance, ordered a resumption of the Sinai offensive on October 11. This, however, took Egyptian forces out of their prepared defensive positions and removed them from the effective SAM cover on the other side of the canal, which was to Israeli advantage. On October 14 the Israelis threw back the Egyptians, inflicting heavy losses, especially in tanks.

On October 15–16 the Israelis located a gap between the two Egyptian divisions defending the occupied area that had gone unnoticed by the Egyptian command. Sharon's division then drove through that gap, and part of the division crossed the canal. An Israeli paratroop brigade established a bridgehead on the west bank. The Israeli high command now had two goals: establishing a SAM-free zone over which Israeli aircraft could maneuver free from the threat of missile attack and cutting off Egyptian troops east of the canal from their bases west of it.

The Egyptian Second Army then closed behind Sharon, isolating his division on both sides of the canal. Adan's division, however, broke through, bringing a bridge forward to the crossing point. The Egyptian Second Army, assisted by units of the Third Army, was unable to close the Israeli supply corner and cut off the Israelis at the canal.

Fighting during October 14–18 was known as the Battle of the Chinese Farm. It took its name from a former Japanese experimental agricultural station there, which the Israelis assumed to have been Chinese. The Egyptians suffered heavy losses, especially in tanks, and on the night of October 17–18 Adan's division crossed the canal.

Adan's division then pushed westward, rolling up Egyptian base camps and capturing antiaircraft positions and SAM sites, which greatly facilitated Israeli aircraft support. On October 19, however, Sharon was unsuccessful in seizing Ismailia. During October 20–22 he continued his attacks on Ismailia but encountered heavy resistance from the Egyptian Second and Third Armies. Adan enjoyed more success, cutting the Suez-Cairo road northeast of Suez.

On October 22 Egypt and Israel agreed to a cease-fire, to take effect that evening, but this was soon broken. The Israeli high command then dispatched strong reinforcements across the canal, while Adan was ordered to continue his drive southward to the Gulf of Suez. Another Israeli division, commanded by Major General Kalman Magen, followed after Adan, reaching Adabiya on the Gulf of Suez.

The Egyptians turned back an Israeli effort to take Suez during October 23–24. A second cease-fire then went into effect at 7:00 a.m. on October 24. Despite some military activity thereafter, it eventually took hold.

### Operations on the Syrian Front

Syrian president Hafez al-Assad's chief motivation in joining Sadat in the war was to regain the 480 square miles of the Golan Heights along the 45-mile Syrian-Israeli border. Israeli forces had captured the Golan Heights from Syria in the 1967 Six-Day War, thereby gaining security for Israel's northern settlements from sporadic Syrian bombardment. Unlike Sadat, Assad had no diplomatic goals and no intention of using the war as leverage for a settlement with Israel.

At 2:00 p.m. on October 6 simultaneous with the Egyptian air strikes to the south, Syria launched a massive air strike accompanied by a heavy artillery bombardment against Israeli positions on the Golan Heights. Syrian ground forces then advanced in an effort to recapture this area and drive on Jerusalem from the north. Syrian Army major general Yousef Chakour commanded the attacking force of some 60,000 men in two armored divisions (600 tanks) and two infantry divisions (another 300 tanks). The Syrians also had some 140 artillery batteries, including long-range 130mm and 154mm guns. Opposing them, Israeli major general Yitzhak Hofi's Northern Command numbered only some 12,000 troops, 177 tanks, and 11 artillery batteries.

With the exception of one important outpost, however, Israeli forces were not taken by surprise. Israeli intelligence had accurately detected the massive Syrian buildup, and Israeli forces on this front were on full alert. The tanks were in hull-down positions behind earthen barricades, with the infantry in their fighting positions.

The one exception was Mount Hermon. At the very start of the war on the northern front, helicopters carried Syrian commandos to the back of the fortified Israeli observation post on Mount Hermon that provided an excellent view of the Golan Heights and the Damascus Plateau. The two-platoon Israeli garrison there was taken completely by surprise and wiped out.

The main Syrian attack by the four divisions occurred in three axes against two Israeli brigades in defensive positions. Israel mobilization was excellent, and reservists were soon on the scene, but it took time to ready their equipment and tanks for action and bring them forward. Nonetheless, within a day the Israeli 7th Armored Brigade halted the northernmost thrust by the Syrian 7th Infantry Division, destroying most of the Syrian tanks. The Israelis also repulsed an attack by the Syrian 3rd Tank Division, which was to pass through the 7th Infantry Division.

The two Syrian thrusts in the south nearly entered the Jordan River Valley, however. At Rafid during October 6–7, the Syrian 5th Mechanized Division broke through and virtually destroyed the Israeli 188th Armored Brigade. Reinforced by the Syrian 1st Tank Division, the 5th Mechanized Division pushed to the western escarpment of the Golan Heights, where it halted as much for logistical reasons as from the actions of Israeli reserve units, which were now entering the fighting. If the Syrians could push beyond the escarpment, they could cross the Jordan River and Galilee, cutting Israel in two. If the Israeli troops failed here, the Syrians would spill into the valleys that contained the defenders' family homes.

Israeli aircraft went into action immediately following the first Syrian attacks, targeting the clusters of many Syrian tanks, armored personnel carriers, and artillery pieces. Some 1,500 tanks of the two sides were now crammed into a relatively small space. The Golan Heights quickly became one vast graveyard of armored vehicles and abandoned guns, but many of the Israeli jets also fell prey to Syrian SAMs and mobile antiaircraft guns. And many of the Israeli tanks were also knocked out. Only the Israeli close air support, rapid arrival of Israeli reserves, and unimaginative Syrian attacks prevented the Syrians from overrunning the Israeli positions and retaking the southern Golan Heights on the second day of fighting.

During October 8–9 the Israelis counterattacked in the south, assisted by the 7th Armored Brigade brought down from the northern Golan Heights. On October 9 the Israeli 7th Brigade halted a Syrian thrust north of Quneitra (Kuneitra), and the next day the Israelis mounted a major counteroffensive north of the Quneitra-Damascus road. Three divisions pushed the Syrian 5th Mechanized and 1st Tank Divisions back to and beyond the prewar Israeli-Syrian border.

Beginning on October 12, the Israelis began to withdraw some units south to fight on the Sinai front. Nonetheless, by October 14 the Israelis had opened up a salient inside Syria some 10 miles deep and 30 miles wide and only 25 miles from Damascus. The Israelis held here during October 15–19 against fierce Syrian and Iraqi counterattacks, Iraq and Jordan having now entered the war. On October 15 the Israelis repulsed the Iraqi 3rd Armored Division, and on October 19 they halted another Arab counterattack against the salient, this one spearheaded by Jordanian units. The Israelis maintained these positions until the cease-fire of October 24.

On October 22 following two failed assaults on October 8 and 21 and just before a cease-fire went into effect, Israeli helicopter-borne paratroopers recaptured the Syrian observation post on Mount Hermon, above the original Israeli position, while Israeli infantry retook the original Israeli observation post. The cease-fire on the Golan front went into effect at 6:52 p.m.

The constrained area of the Golan Heights and the large forces involved ensured fierce fighting and heavy losses on both sides. Israel lost nearly 800 dead and 250 tanks put out of action, along with a number of ground support aircraft shot down. Certainly a key factor in the Israelis' success was their ability to quickly return disabled tanks to battle. Syrian losses were significantly greater: perhaps 8,000 men killed, 1,150 tanks destroyed, and 118 aircraft lost.

### The Air War

Israeli ground support aircraft first arrived over the Sinai and Golan fronts on October 6 some 40 minutes after the commencement of the Arab attack but immediately encountered heavy Arab antiaircraft fire and SAMs. The Israelis lost more than 30 aircraft, and for the first few days of the war Israeli air support was ineffective. Beginning on October 8 with the employment of electronic countermeasures and chaff, Israeli aircraft were able to provide far greater assistance to the troops on the ground. They also destroyed some Egyptian bridges over the Suez Canal and attacked Arab airfields.

Beginning on October 9, using the excuse of Syrian surface-to-surface missile attacks against the Hula Valley, Israel launched a major aerial campaign against Syria. Israeli aircraft struck deep within Syria, hitting the Ministry of Defense in Damascus as well as seaports, industrial sites, and fuel storage areas. These attacks profoundly affected the Syrian economy and continued until October 21.

Meanwhile, the Israelis won control of the air over the Suez front. The success of Adan's armor division in capturing Egyptian antiaircraft units and SAM sites on the western bank of the Suez Canal greatly aided the Israeli Air Force in its highly effective support of the Battle of the Chinese Farm and the Israeli army breakout to the south.

### The War at Sea

On the start of the war, the Egyptians imposed a naval blockade of Israel's coasts to disrupt its Mediterranean trade, while Egyptian destroyers and submarines at the Strait of Bab al-Mandab halted seaborne traffic to Eilat.

On the first night of the war, however, Israeli missile boats attacked the chief Syrian Mediterranean port of Latakia (Ladhaqiyya). Syrian missile boats engaged the attackers, and in the first naval battle in history between missile-firing ships, the Israelis defeated the incoming Syrian fire-and-forget Styx missiles while using their own radar-guided Gabriel ship-to-ship missiles to destroy three missile boats and a minesweeper. No Israeli vessels were lost. The Syrian Navy then remained in port for the rest of the war. The Battle of Latakia brought new prestige for the Israeli Navy, previously regarded as only a poor relation of its highly regarded army and air force. Israeli electronic countermeasure techniques employed in the battle set a new standard for subsequent naval engagements employing missiles.

A second Israeli strike at Latakia on the night of October 7–8 was inconclusive, as were engagements that same night between Israeli and Egyptian naval units in the Mediterranean and Red Seas. On October 8–9 in a naval action off the Egyptian port of Damietta, Egyptian missile boats sortied to engage an Israeli missile boat task force, which sank four of them. There were no Israeli losses. In an action the next night off Egyptian Port Said, another Egyptian missile boat was sunk. The remaining Egyptian missile boats were then withdrawn to Damietta and Alexandria.

During the nights of October 9–10 and 12–13, Israeli missile boats struck the Syrian ports of Latakia, Tartus, and Banias. No Syrian missile boats challenged them. In the second raid, the Israelis again struck Latakia and Tartus. This time Syrian missile boats sought to engage the Israelis but without success.

During October 15–16 Israeli missile boats attacked the Nile Delta and sank a number of Egyptian landing craft. Finally, on October 21–22, the Israelis attacked Abu Kir (Aboukir) Bay and Alexandria and there sank two Egyptian patrol boats.

### Conclusion

Both the United States, supporting Israel, and the Soviet Union, supporting the Arab states, were caught off guard by the war, although the Soviets probably learned of the Egyptian and Syrian plans several days in advance of the actual attacks. Both sides in the war were soon in need of resupply. On October 8 Israel sent aircraft to the United States to procure supplies, and the next day the Soviet Union commenced an airlift of supplies to Syria and Egypt through Hungary and Yugoslavia. On October 13 the United States augmented the Israeli airlifts by sending American transport planes to Israel by way of the Azores. Between October 14 and 21 the United States airlifted some 20,000 tons of supplies to Israel, as opposed to some 15,000 tons supplied by the Soviet Union to the Arab states.

On October 24 the Soviet Union had threatened intervention in announcing that it was placing seven airborne divisions on alert, presumably to be sent to Egypt if necessary to break the Israeli stranglehold on the Egyptian Third Army east of the Suez Canal. The next day, U.S. secretary of state Henry Kissinger announced that the United States had placed its armed forces—including its nuclear assets—on precautionary alert, based on the possibility of Soviet intervention. Any possibility of a Soviet–U.S. armed clash over the Middle East ended with a United Nations (UN) Security Council resolution—with both the Soviet and U.S. representatives voting in the affirmative—to establish a 7,000-man UN emergency force to be sent to the Middle East to enforce the cease-fires in the Sinai Peninsula and the Golan Heights.

Casualty figures for the war vary depending on the source and especially for Egypt and Syria, which did not release any official figures. Israel suffered 2,521–2,800 killed in action and 7,250–8,800 wounded; 293 were captured. Some 400 Israeli tanks were destroyed; another 600 were disabled but returned to service. The Israeli Air Force lost 102 airplanes and 2 helicopters. There were no navy losses.

Arab casualties were much higher. Most estimates fall in the range of 5,000–15,000 Egyptians and 3,000–3,500 Syrians killed; the number of wounded is unknown. Iraq lost 278 killed and 898 wounded, while Jordan suffered 23 killed and 77 wounded. A total of 8,372 Egyptians, 392 Syrians, 13 Iraqis, and 6 Moroccans were taken prisoner. The Arab states lost 2,250–2,300 tanks, 400 of which were taken by the Israelis in good working order and added to their inventory. Arab aircraft losses are estimated at 450–512. Nineteen Arab naval vessels, including 10 missile boats, were sunk.

The war revealed the vulnerability of tanks, aircraft, and ships to the new missile weapons. In the end, however, the outcome of the war secured Israel's borders. Nonetheless, the war shocked Israel. The early losses and hard fighting of the 1973 Yom Kippur War brought new respect for the Egyptian and Syrian armed forces. Yet there was anger over the surprise of the Arab attack. An investigatory agency, the Agranat Commission, fixed blame on several military officers and recommended that they be dismissed, including General Elazar. The commission did not assess the responsibility of the civilian leadership, but Meir resigned in April 1974, as did defense minister Moshe Dayan.

Although the Arab states lost the war, the conflict certainly erased the trauma of their rapid defeat in the Six-Day War of 1967 and allowed them to negotiate as equals with Israel. Yet the Yom Kippur War had seen Israel secure additional Arab territory, and this may have helped convince many in the Arab world that Israel could not be defeated militarily. The war brought the removal of a number of Arab military commanders.

Talks between Egyptian and Israeli military representatives on the west bank of the canal on October 28, 1973, led to an agreement that Egypt might send noncombatant supplies to its Third Army trapped east of the Suez Canal. Nonmilitary supplies were also allowed to pass, and prisoners of war were to be exchanged.

In December 1973 a summit conference, recognized by UN Security Council Resolution 344 calling for a "just and durable peace," opened in Geneva. All parties to the war were invited, but the talks adjourned on January 9, 1974, after Syria refused to participate. Kissinger commenced shuttle diplomacy ending in the initial military disengagement agreement, signed by Israel and Egypt on January 18, 1974, known as Sinai I. Israel agreed to pull back its forces from west of the Suez Canal and also from the length of the front to create security zones for Egypt, UN observers, and Israel, although Israel still held nearly all of Sinai. Another agreement, of September 4, 1975, known as Sinai II saw Israel withdrawing another 20–40 kilometers, with UN observer forces taking over that area. Still, Israel held more than two-thirds of Sinai.

A peace agreement between Israel and Egypt known as the Camp David Accords was finally reached on September 17, 1978, following negotiations hosted by President Jimmy Carter. In accordance with the treaty, Israeli forces withdrew gradually from Sinai, with the last troops exiting on April 26, 1982. There is still no formal peace agreement between Israel and Syria. On October 6, 1981, while attending a military review commemorating the ninth anniversary of the start of the war, Sadat was assassinated by Islamist Egyptian Army members outraged at his negotiations with Israel.

On the Syrian front, from February to May 1974 Syria engaged Israel in a war of attrition along the Golan Heights consisting of artillery fire along the cease-fire line between Quneitra and Damascus. The Syrians hoped thereby to force Israel to agree to withdraw its troops from the Golan Heights. On May 31 following 32 days of shuttle diplomacy by U.S. secretary of state Kissinger, the two sides agreed to disengage. An exchange of prisoners occurred, and Israel relinquished all territory taken from Syria in the October 1973 war, two small strips taken in 1967, and the town of Quneitra. A cease-fire line was established between the two states, to be patrolled by troops of the UN Disengagement Observer Force.

Finally, the Yom Kippur War brought a major world economic shock. On October 17, 1973, in response to U.S. support of Israel, the Arab members of the Organization of Oil Exporting Countries, led by Saudi Arabia, decided to reduce oil production by 5 percent per month. When on October 19 U.S. president Richard Nixon authorized a major allocation of arms supplies and $2.2 billion in appropriations for Israel, Saudi Arabia declared an embargo against the United States, later joined by other oil exporters and extended against other states as well. Unlike the ineffective embargo of the 1967

Six-Day War, this resulted in a full-blown energy crisis in much of the West and great havoc for the Western economies. The embargo lasted five months, until March 18, 1974.

SPENCER C. TUCKER

**See also**

Adan, Avraham "Bren"; Assad, Hafez al-; Elazar, David; Meir, Golda Mabovitch; Sadat, Anwar; Sharon, Ariel

**References**

Adan, Avraham. *On the Banks of the Suez: An Israeli General's Personal Account of the Yom Kippur War.* Novato, CA: Presidio, 1980.

Dunstan, Simon. *The Yom Kippur War 1973.* 2 vols. Oxford, UK: Osprey, 2003.

El-Gamasy, Mohamed Abdul Ghani. *The October War: Memoirs of Field Marshal El-Gamasy of Egypt.* Translated by Gillian Potter, Nadra Morcos, and Rosette Frances. Cairo: American University in Cairo Press, 1993.

Gawrych, George W. *The 1973 Arab-Israeli War: The Albatross of Decisive Victory.* Leavenworth Papers No. 21. Fort Leavenworth, KS: Combat Studies Institute, 1996.

Heikal, Mohammed Hasanyn. *The Road to Ramadan.* New York: Quadrangle/New York Times Book Company, 1975.

Kahana, Ephraim. "Early Warning versus Concept: The Case of the Yom Kippur War, 1973." *Intelligence and National Security* 17 (Summer 2002): 81–104.

Rabinovich, Abraham. *The Yom Kippur War: An Epic Encounter That Transformed the Middle East.* New York: Schocken Books, 2004.

Shazli, Saad al. *The Crossing of the Suez.* San Francisco: Mideast Research, 1980.

# Young Turks

A coalition of groups that brought about the fall of Ottoman sultan Abdulhamid II in 1909. Initially welcomed for their democratic aspirations and modernizing goals for the Ottoman Empire, the Young Turks did not fare well in the destructive geopolitics of World War I and indeed presided over the disintegration of the Ottoman state and rise of Turkish nationalism.

In the 19th century, the Ottoman Empire was in the process of disintegration because of the failure of the ruling sultans to stem the tide of decay and because of the rise of ethnic nationalism inside their nation. The stronger Western powers responded to Ottoman weakness by creating new states and annexing Ottoman territory into their own empires. The so-called Tanzimat reforms instituted by Ottoman sultans in the mid-19th century were designed to reverse the process of decline and resulted in the modernization of many parts of the government of the empire.

Under the Tanzimat reforms, many government officials were trained in Western methods and concepts. A number became dissatisfied with the pace of reform, however. They came to believe that the Tanzimat reformers were not interested in real change but rather in accumulating power in their own hands. Some of these disaffected individuals established the Young Ottoman organization. The Young Ottomans promoted constitutionalism and parliamentary government. Many worked in such agencies as the Bureau of Translation and the Ministry of Foreign Affairs, where they had constant contact with Western institutions and publications.

When Abdulhamid II became ruler in 1876, he first approved and then suspended a new constitution. In response to his authoritarian rule after 1876, the Young Ottomans became involved in plots to reform the government. Although the authorities discovered a number of these and arrested those involved, in 1889 a group of medical students formed the Committee of Union and Progress (CUP). This led to the League of Private Initiative and Decentralization around 1902. (The CUP was the first to adopt the name Young Turks, after the name of a journal produced by one of its members. Later the name became loosely identified with other factions advocating the overthrow of Abdulhamid II.)

Both the CUP and the league called for military and moral strengthening of the Ottoman Empire, equal rights for all ethnic and religious groups, and the restoration of the Constitution of 1876 that Abdulhamid had set aside. The CUP favored a strong central government, however, while the league preferred a more decentralized government and European assistance.

Spurred on by the revolutionary publications of the exiles, the CUP steadily gained adherents. They included teachers and students but also bureaucrats, army officers, and even members of the Muslim clergy. Chapters were formed in the major cities of Romania, Bulgaria, and Albania. An attempt in 1885 to overthrow the Ottoman government failed, however. Abdulhamid endeavored to disperse the revolutionaries to such remote parts of the empire as Macedonia, believing that the revolutionary spirit would fade. However, this move only increased their revolutionary fervor. Abdulhamid then offered amnesty and high positions to exiles to get them to return and work with the government.

Still, the CUP continued to add followers. The new secular schools instituted under the Tanzimat reforms produced thousands of educated bureaucrats, officers, and intellectuals who came from the lower classes and resented restrictions placed on them. Many were strong patriots who believed that if the sultan's corrupt regime were swept away, they could build a stronger country. The growing strength of reformers and the increasing attacks of nationalistic minorities caused the government to become more and more repressive. By the beginning of the 20th century, CUP members were increasingly convinced that only radical change would save the empire.

The initiative for revolution came from military officers, especially those of the III Corps in Macedonia. Led by Senior Captain Mustafa Kemal, they formed the Ottoman Liberty Society in 1906. In 1907 the group merged with the CUP, a key development. Events in 1908 spurred the reformers to action. Bosnia and Herzegovina was annexed by the Austro-Hungarian Empire, while Bulgaria and Crete declared their independence from Ottoman rule. On July 3, the III Corps launched a revolt that quickly spread to other military units throughout the empire. Unable to rely on his troops, Abdulhamid restored the Constitution of 1876 and reconvened the parliament, hoping to undercut the rebellion, but his rule lasted only another year. He was forced to abdicate on April 27, 1909.

The Young Turks then took charge of the government and began to introduce numerous and diverse reform programs, though by 1911 the CUP's political agenda was contested by liberal, conservative, and nationalistic forces internally. In 1913 the CUP gained effective control, thanks in part to rigged elections and in part to the chaos of two Balkan Wars that brought further territorial losses in Europe for the empire. By the time the Young Turks had consolidated their power, the empire had lost territory in the Balkans and therefore most of the empire's Christians, and the ideals of a multinational Ottomanism had faded, replaced by a preference for congressional representatives who were ethnic Turks and members of the CUP.

The new CUP leadership included Ismail Enver Pasha as war minister, Ahmad Djemal Pasha as naval minister, and Mehmed Taalat Pasha as interior minister. Those men carried out many reforms of the provincial administrations, which led to greater centralization. They also secularized the legal system and established an improved system of elementary school education, especially for girls. The Young Turks are hailed for those modernizing programs. The CUP government also made Turkish the language of administration and instruction, however, which alienated the large number of Arabs in the empire.

With the onslaught of World War I, the Young Turks chose to ally with Germany. They also embarked on an effort to reconquer Egypt from the British and the Caucasus from Russia. The Young Turks began to fear that the Armenians (Christians living in eastern Anatolia) were supporting the Russians, though they had shown no sign of disloyalty to the Ottoman government since the overthrow of Abdulhamid II. The Young Turk leadership then ordered the relocation of the Armenian population, with the result being the Armenian Genocide.

Their genocidal persecution of the Armenians did not endear the Young Turks to the Arabs. Though theoretically united by Islam, many Arabs were suspicious of the way the Young Turks combined religion with nationalism. More damage was done, however, by former naval minister Djemal Pasha as he and his troops were in Syria during 1915 to reorganize for an attack on the British and the Suez Canal. Djemal's treatment of the Syrians was so cruel and arbitrary that he inspired them to join in the British-sponsored Arab Uprising, led by the Hussein clan from Mecca. That revolt beginning in 1916 forced Jemal to withdraw from Syria, ceding control of the entire region south of Anatolia to the French and the British.

By late 1918 with military defeat imminent, the CUP leaders resigned from the government in October, just before the Armistice of Mudros ended the war. In spite of their misfortunes and their mistakes, however, the Young Turks are today regarded by the Turkish people as having led an important phase in the regeneration of their nation. Their transformation from Ottoman to Turkish nationalism and their ideas about Islam allowed for subsequent leaders to make more rapid national progress. Arguing that religion should be a matter of conscience and that the legal aspects of Islam should be surrendered to secular legislation, they called for a separation between Islam and the state. That idea became the foundation for the policy of secularization later adopted by the Turkish republic under Mustafa Kemal Ataturk.

ALEXANDER MIKABERIDZE

**See also**
Arab Revolt of World War I; Armenians and the Armenian Genocide; Ataturk, Mustafa Kemal; Balkan Wars; Djemal Pasha, Ahmed; Enver Pasha; Ottoman Empire, Entry into World War I; Taalat Pasha, Mehmed

**References**
Ahmad, Feroz. *The Young Turks*. Oxford, UK: Clarendon, 1969.
Berkes, Niyazi. *The Development of Secularism in Turkey*. Montreal: McGill University Press, 1964.
Hanioglu, M. Sukru. *The Young Turks in Opposition*. New York: Oxford University Press, 1995.
Kinross, Lord. *The Ottoman Centuries: The Rise and Fall of the Turkish Empire*. New York: Oxford University Press, 1977.

Ramsaur, Ernest Edmondson, Jr. *The Young Turks: Prelude to the Revolution of 1908*. Princeton, NJ: Princeton University Press, 1957.

Shaw, Stanford J., and Ezel Kural Shaw. *History of the Ottoman Empire and Modern Turkey*. Cambridge: Cambridge University Press, 1977.

# Yudenich, Nikolai Nikolaevich (1862–1933)

Russian Army general who fought against Ottoman Empire forces in World War I. Born to a noble family in Minsk Province on July 30, 1862, Nikolai Nikolaevich Yudenich graduated from the Aleksandrovsky Military College in 1881. He completed the General Staff Academy in 1887. During 1889–1890 he served in the Life Guards Regiment in Lithuania. Transferred to the Turkestan Military District in 1892, he was promoted to lieutenant colonel that April and to colonel in 1896. During 1900–1902 Yudenich was assigned to the staff of the 1st Turkestan Rifle Brigade.

In 1902 Yudenich assumed command of the 18th Infantry Regiment, which he commanded during the 1904–1905 Russo-Japanese War. He was wounded in the battles at Sandepu and Mukden. Promoted to major general in 1905, Yudenich was posted to the Caucasus, where he was deputy chief of staff of the Caucasus Army in 1907. Assigned as chief of staff there by 1912, he was serving in that capacity on the beginning of World War I.

Many Caucasus Army units were being relocated to other fronts at the beginning of the war when the Ottoman Third Army invaded. Yudenich resisted orders from Caucasus Army commander General Viktor Myshlaevsky that Russian forces withdraw. Instead Yudenich defeated the Ottomans under Enver Pasha in the Battle of Sarikamish (Sarıkamış, December 22, 1914–January 17, 1915). In this significant Russian victory, he inflicted far heavier casualties on the Ottomans than his forces received and forced the Ottomans into a costly retreat.

In January 1915 Yudenich was advanced to lieutenant general and took command of the Caucasus Army. Known as a daring, resourceful commander, he defeated another Ottoman offensive, this one in the summer of 1915. The next year he mounted a series of spoiling attacks that captured Erzurum, Trebizond, and Erzincan.

In March 1917 Yudenich replaced Grand Duke Nikolai Nikolaevich as supreme civil and military commander of the Caucasian Front. Yudenich himself was then recalled. He remained in Petrograd until the Bolshevik seizure of power that November, when he went into hiding.

In 1919 Yudenich joined anti-Bolshevik White forces near Petrograd, and in October he became the commander of the Northwestern Front. That same month his small White force of only some 14,000 men attacked from northeast Estonia and reached the outskirts of Petrograd but, short of supplies and equipment, was driven back and forced to retire into Estonia. Yudenich went into exile in 1920. He died at Nice, France, on October 5, 1933.

CLAUDE R. SASSO AND SPENCER C. TUCKER

**See also**
Erzurum Offensive; Sarikamish, Battle of

**References**

Allen, W. E. D., and Paul Muratoff. *Caucasian Battlefields: A History of the Wars on the Turco-Caucasian Border, 1828–1921*. Cambridge: Cambridge University Press, 1953.

Rutherford, Ward. *The Russian Army in World War I*. London: Cremonesi, 1975.

Wildman, Allan K. *The End of the Russian Imperial Army*. 2 vols. Princeton, NJ: Princeton University Press, 1980–1987.

# Z

## Zab, Battle of (February 26, 750)

Decisive battle between the Umayyad Army and the forces of the rising Abbasid faction. In 747 the Abbasids, descendants of Prophet Muhammad's uncle Abbas, exploited the rising public discontent at the Umayyad government to launch a revolt in Khurasan (northern Persia). After capturing the town of Merv in February 748 the Abbasid forces advanced westward, taking control of central Persia by the end of the year. In 749 they captured most of Iraq, and the head of the movement, Abu al-Abbas, was declared caliph at Kufa.

Umayyad caliph Marwan led a largely Syrian army against the rebels. The sides met on the banks of the Zab River, a tributary of the Tigris, in early 750. Marwan made the mistake of building a bridge and crossing the river, which placed his army in a disadvantaged position. Estimates of the size of the Abbasid forces, led by Abdallah ibn Ali, range between 10,000 and 30,000 men, while the Umayyad army is said to have had some 120,000 men, which is certainly an exaggeration.

The battle was fought on February 26, 750, and was a very close-run thing. The Abbasid commanders chose a defensive tactic, deploying their troops in closed formations with their spears pointed forward to protect them against the veteran Syrian cavalry. The Syrian cavalry charges failed to break through the enemy formation, and the cavalry suffered in heavy losses and shattered morale. Marwan, seemingly losing his nerve, ordered a retreat but then destroyed the bridge before all his men had crossed, stranding many of them on the other side.

The battle was a decisive Abbasid victory. Marwan fled to the Levant, pursued by the Abbasid forces who rapidly took over Syria as well. Unable to find shelter in Syria and Palestine, the caliph fled to Egypt, where he was killed in a skirmish near the village of Busir in early August 750. The victory on the Zab River thus signaled the end of the Umayyad Caliphate and the rise of the Abbasid dynasty, which would remain in power until the 13th century.

ALEXANDER MIKABERIDZE

### See also
Abbasid Caliphate; Abbasid Revolution; Abu Muslim Khorasani; Umayyad Caliphate

### References
Kennedy, Hugh. *The Early Abbasid Caliphate: A Political History.* London: Taylor & Francis, 1986.

Lassner, Jacob. *The Shaping of 'Abbāsid Rule.* Princeton, NJ: Princeton University Press, 1980.

Shaban, M. A. *The Abbasid Revolution.* Cambridge: Cambridge University Press, 1970.

## Zaidan, Muhammad
*See* Abbas, Abu

# Zangi, Imad ad-Din (1084/1085–1146)

Ottoman *atabeg* and ruler of Mosul, Aleppo, Hama, and Edessa who was also the founder of the Zangid dynasty. Imad ad-Din Zangi (Zengi, Zenki, and Zanki) was born in 1084/1085. His father, Aq Sunqur al-Hajib, the governor of Aleppo, was beheaded in 1094 for treason, and Zangi was brought up by Kerbogha, the governor of Mosul.

Zangi became *atabeg* of Mosul in 1127. He then took other territories in Iraq and upper Mesopotamia, including Nisbis (modern-day Nusaybin, Turkey). When the governor of Aleppo became unpopular with his people, who besieged him in its citadel, Zangi proceeded there in June 1128, taking with him the remains of his father, who had been a popular ruler. Zangi then added Aleppo to his holdings. To solidify his position there, he married the daughter of one of the former rulers.

With the death in 1128 of Toghtekin, *atabeg* of Damascus, it appeared that the Christian crusaders might take advantage of the situation. In 1130 Zangi formed an alliance against the crusaders with Taj al-Mulk Buri, ruler of Damascus, but this was only a power grab, for Zangi took prisoner Buri's son, Baha' al-Din Sawinj, the ruler of Hama, Syria, and thereby gained possession of Hama itself. Zangi also attempted to take Homs, but its inhabitants resisted. That same year Zangi raided the Frankish fortress of Atharib.

Zangi then involved himself in Artuqid affairs. In 1134 he made war on the Artuqid ruler of Hisn Kayfa, defeating his forces near Amida (modern-day Diyarbakir, Turkey) but failing to take the latter. Meanwhile, Zangi had been invited to intervene in Damascus by Shams al-Muluk Ismail, the son of Buri, who had succeeded his father but feared for his safety from his people. When Zangi arrived at Damascus with his army in February 1135, he found that Ismail had been murdered and replaced by his brother Shihab al-Din Mamud. After a number of inconclusive skirmishes with Damascene troops, a message arrived from the Abbasid caliph in Baghdad ordering Zangi to return to Mosul. He was thus able to withdraw honorably.

Zangi then campaigned against the Franks, taking Atharib, Zerdana, Tell A'di, and Ma'arrat al-Nu'man and repelling an attack by Bertrand, count of Tripoli. Zangi also besieged Homs but was forced to withdraw on learning of instability in Iraq.

In December 1135 fearing a renewed assault from Zangi, the ruler of Homs handed it over to the rulers of Damascus. In May 1137 Zangi took troops from Mosul and Aleppo and besieged Homs. In July hearing that the Franks had moved on Hama, Zangi was forced to make peace. The Franks entrenched themselves at Montferrand (modern-day Barin, Syria), a stronghold west of Hama and Homs. Zangi besieged Montferrand, while his troops took Kafartab and Ma'arrat al-Nu'man from the Franks. Learning of the approach of Christian reinforcements from Jerusalem and Tripoli, Zangi accepted the capitulation of Montferrand, which he had previously rejected, in August 1137.

Another factor affecting Zangi's decision to accept the capitulation of Montferrand was the arrival at Antioch of Byzantine emperor John II Komnenos. John had wanted to bring Antioch under his control, but in 1138 he made an alliance with Prince Raymond of Antioch. In April 1138 John took Buza'ah and, reinforced by troops from Tripoli, then besieged Aleppo. In order to isolate the city, Frankish troops reoccupied Atharib, Ma'arrat al-Nu'man, and Kafartab, while the emperor besieged Shaizar (modern-day Shayzar, Syria). Owing to harassment by Zangi's troops and disagreements with the Franks, Emperor John allowed himself to be bought off by the inhabitants of Shaizar and withdrew in May. By the end of October Kafartab, Buza'ah, and Atharib had been retaken, removing the threat to Aleppo. Meanwhile, in August 1138 Zangi finally took possession of Homs when he married Buri's widow, Safwat al-Mulk, who brought him the city as her dowry.

In June 1139 Shihab al-Din Mamud of Damascus was assassinated and replaced by his brother Jamal al-Din Muhammad. Zangi, then campaigning against the Artuqid Timurtash, was incited by afwat al-Mulk to avenge her son's assassination and proceed against Damascus. Before doing so he attacked and took Baalbek in October. Zangi then advanced on Damascus, besieging it in October and November 1139.

Jamal al-Din died in March 1140 and was succeeded by his son Mujir al-Din, who was a minor. Acting on his behalf was Mu'in al-Din Unur, an old opponent of Zangi. Unur sought aid from the Franks, promising them the border town of Banyas (modern-day Baniyas, Syria) along with hostages and payment for their expedition. Hearing of this Zangi withdrew and then reinforced the defenses of Baalbek, which he left in the hands of Najm al-Din Ayyub, the father of Saladin.

In June 1140 Zangi returned to Damascus but then was forced to withdraw following a sortie by its forces. He was able to secure an agreement, however, whereby Damascus recognized his sovereignty. Zangi then returned to Mosul. He spent the next three years subduing rebellions and rivals to the north and east. This, however, brought friction with Seljuk sultan Masud (r. 1143–1144), but Zangi avoided major conflict by agreeing to pay an indemnity.

In the late spring of 1144 following both the instructions of the sultan and the interests of Mosul, Zangi set out toward Edessa (modern-day Sanliurfa in southeastern Turkey), taking several towns en route. He was operating against the Artuqids in the Diyar Bakr region when he heard that Count Joscelin II of Edessa, responding to a request for help from the Artuqid Qara Arslan, had left Edessa with a strong force. Seizing the opportunity, Zangi besieged Edessa and took it by storm on December 24, 1144. Edessa was thus the first of the capitals of the Frankish states of Outremer to be retaken by the Muslims.

Building on this success, in January 1143 Zangi took Saruj (modern-day Suruç, Turkey). In March he besieged Bira (modern-day Birecik, Turkey) but was forced to abandon operations in May on learning that his deputy in Mosul had been assassinated.

After dealing with plots against him in Mosul and Edessa, Zangi set out on campaign again in the spring of 1146. He subdued Timurtash and then besieged Qal'at Ja'bar on the Euphrates, where on September 14, 1146, Zangi was assassinated by a Frankish slave. Zangi was succeeded at Mosul by his eldest son, Sayf al-Din Ghazi, and at Aleppo by his second son, Nur al-Din Mamud.

NIALL CHRISTIE

**See also**
Crusades in the Holy Land, Christian; Malik Shah I

**References**
Elisséeff, Nikita. *Nur ad-Din: Un grand prince musulman de Syrie au temps des croisades.* 3 vols. Damascus, Syria: Institut Français de Damas, 1967.
Hillenbrand, Carole. "'Abominable Acts': The Career of Zengi." In *The Second Crusade: Scope and Consequences,* ed. Jonathan Phillips and Martin Hoch, 111–132. Manchester, UK: Manchester University Press, 2001.
Hillenbrand, Carole. *The Crusades: Islamic Perspectives.* Edinburgh, UK: Edinburgh University Press, 1999.
Holt, Peter M. *The Age of the Crusades.* London: Longman, 1986.
Sivan, Emmanuel. *L'Islam et la Croisade.* Paris: Maisonneuve, 1968.

---

# Zanj Slave Revolts

A series of uprisings of slaves of African descent in the Islamic world, including the vast revolt of 869–883 that was one of the longest and most destructive slave revolts in history.

By the seventh century, Western Asia had a history of commercial ties with the East African littoral that included the slave trade. The rise of Islam strengthened these ties because of its prohibition of the enslavement of Muslims but allowance of slavery in general. Thus, sub-Saharan Africa became a major source of slaves for the Islamic world. These slaves were distinguished by their origin, with the Bantu-speaking peoples of East Africa being called the Zanj as opposed to *al-aswad* (blacks from south of the Sahara). The African slaves were employed in various capacities, but most of the Zanj slaves were committed to hard labor projects in lower Mesopotamia, where they dried marshes and worked in the fields.

Subject to inhumane treatment and conditions, the Zanj slaves rebelled in 689 but were quickly subdued. In 694 a slave named Riyah organized a more successful revolt that quickly grew in size, defeated local government forces, and devastated the Euphrates region before major Abbasid Army forces suppressed it. During the span of the next two centuries the Abbasids faced several Zanj revolts throughout Mesopotamia, but the Abbasids managed to suppress all of them.

The most serious of these revolts was that of 869 initiated by Ali ibn Muhammad. An Arab who preached social and political egalitarianism, Ali pointed out the injustice of the slaves' social position and promised them equality and freedom. The slaves were supported by the lowly classed Muslims of the Basra area who embraced Ali's sociopolitical ideas. The rebels, whose numbers grew rapidly in size and power, defeated Abbasid forces and established their capital, al-Mukhtarah (the Chosen), in an inaccessible region in the salt flats of southern Mesopotamia. They then sacked the prosperous port towns of al-Ubullah and Abbadan.

The caliphal army, led by al-Muwaffaq, the brother of Caliph al-Mutamid (r. 870–892), could not cope with the rebels, who captured Basra in September 871 and routed the caliphal army in battle in April 872. Exploiting the Abbasid preoccupation with a revolt in Persia, the Zanj conquered Wasit (877), Nummaniya (878), and Djardjaraya (just 70 miles south of Baghdad), in effect creating a vast Zanj state.

In 879 Caliph al-Mutamid organized a new offensive against the black slaves, who were gradually driven into lower Mesopotamia. In 880 the Abbasids reclaimed Khuzistan, and in 881 they laid siege to al-Mukhtarah, which was captured after a two-year siege in 883.

The consequences of the slave revolt were profound. The importing of Zanj slaves was restricted, and Muslims became more averse to Africans in general, which led to a widespread diffusion of negative and unfavorable images of blacks in the Islamic world. The revolt also distracted the Abbasid caliphate from other regions, for example, allowing Ahmad ibn Tulun to establish the Tulunid dynasty in Egypt.

ALEXANDER MIKABERIDZE

**See also**

Abbasid Caliphate

**References**

Popovic, A. *La revolte des esclaves en Iraq au IIIe/IXe siecle.* Paris: Geuthner, 1976.

Sertima van, I., ed. *African Presence in Early Asia.* New Brunswick, NJ: Transaction Books, 1985.

Talhami, Ghada Hashem. "The Zanj Rebellion Reconsidered." *International Journal of African Historical Studies* 10, no. 3 (1977): 443–461.

## Zarqawi, Abu Musab al- (1966–2006)

Leader of Al Qaeda in Iraq and one of the world's most wanted terrorists until his death in June 2006. Abu Musab al-Zarqawi, whose given name may have been Ahmad Fadeel al-Nazal al-Khalayleh, was born on October 20, 1966, in Zarqa, Jordan (Zarqawi means "man from Zarqa"). Although very little is known about his childhood, he was believed to have left school when he was 17. After serving a short time in prison for petty crimes, he traveled to Afghanistan in 1989. He remained there only briefly, but it is suspected that during this time he became acquainted with Osama bin Laden.

Zarqawi returned to Jordan, where in 1992 he was imprisoned for plotting to replace its monarchy with an Islamic regime. After his release in 1999, he again traveled from his homeland, spending time in Europe in addition to the Middle East and South Asia. Zarqawi reportedly raised funds and gathered members for a new organization—the Jama'at al-Tawhid wal-Jihad (Organization of Monotheism and Jihad)—aimed at establishing an Islamic caliphate in Jordan. Although some reports indicate that he may have received $200,000 from bin Laden in support of the group, captured members reportedly told German government officials that the organization was designed for militants who were looking for an alternative to Al Qaeda. It was at this time that Zarqawi was charged in absentia in Jordan for his role in a plot to use explosives at the Radisson Hotel, a popular site for U.S. and Israeli tourists in the Jordanian capital of Amman. The judge hearing the charges sentenced Zarqawi to death in absentia.

Back in Afghanistan, Zarqawi is believed to have established a militant training camp near the Iranian border and may have reconnected with bin Laden. Following the September 11, 2001, terrorist attacks on the United States and subsequent U.S. attacks on Afghanistan, Zarqawi may have fled to Iraq following a missile strike on the camp. Once in Iraq he joined with a militant Kurdish group in the northern part of the country, where he reportedly continued to mastermind attacks in his Jordanian homeland in addition to plotting violence in Morocco, Turkey, and Iraq. The U.S. government attributed the October 2002 assassination of Laurence Foley, a U.S. Agency for International Development official who worked in Amman, to Zarqawi. Again Zarqawi was charged in absentia in Jordan, and again he was sentenced to death.

Zarqawi attained notoriety in the United States in February 2003 when U.S. secretary of state Colin Powell claimed that Zarqawi's presence (and possible medical treatment for injuries sustained in the missile attack in Afghanistan) in Iraq was evidence of Saddam Hussein's connection to Al Qaeda. This Iraq–Al Qaeda connection—since disproved—was considered by some to be a substantial justification for the U.S. invasion of Iraq and the subsequent Iraq War (2003–2011).

After the Iraq War began, Zarqawi instigated a variety of attacks on U.S. targets and was the first proponent of widespread sectarian conflict in the country. By the time of his death in June 2006, Shiite civilians in Iraq were his Sunni supporters' primary target. U.S. officials accused him of more than 700 killings, and the U.S. State Department named him as the person primarily responsible for the bombing of a United Nations hotel in August 2003, while the U.S. Central Intelligence Agency claimed that he was the man who beheaded American communications worker Nicholas Berg in a videotape released in May 2004. Indicative of the contradictory accounts that surrounded Zarqawi, many reports had claimed that he lost a leg in the 2001 Afghan missile attack, although the videotape proved this claim to be false. Although Zarqawi was accused of planning a series of bombings in November 2005 that killed 70 people in Amman, a Shiite cleric in Iraq went so far as to claim that Zarqawi himself was fictitious and possibly a creation of U.S. propagandists.

Although possibly captured by Iraqi forces in 2004 and released because Iraqi officials' failed to recognize him, Zarqawi remained on the loose. Despite an April 2006 report that he had resigned as the leader of a coalition of Iraqi militant groups, it was believed that he still led Al Qaeda in Iraq, which was established in 2004 when his Organization of Monotheism and Jihad merged with bin Laden's Al Qaeda.

Zarqawi was considered the number two man in Al Qaeda, and the U.S. offer of $25 million for information leading to his capture was the same amount that the U.S. government offered for bin Laden. Zarqawi was killed on June 7, 2006, when a U.S. warplane bombed a safe house north of Baghdad while he was attending a meeting there.

JESSICA BRITT

**See also**
Al Qaeda; Al Qaeda in Iraq; Bin Laden, Osama; Iraq Insurgency; Iraq War

**References**
Brisard, Jean-Charles, and Damien Martinez. *Zarqawi: The New Face of Al-Qaeda.* New York: Other Press, 2005.
Filkins, Dexter, and John F. Burns. "At Site of Attack on Zarqawi, All That's Left Are Questions." *New York Times,* June 11, 2006.
Napoleoni, Loretta, *Insurgent Iraq: Al-Zarqawi and the New Generation.* New York: Seven Stories, 2014.

# Zayed bin Sultan Al Nahyan (1918–2004)

President of the United Arab Emirates (UAE) from 1971 to 2004 and emir of Abu Dhabi from 1966 to 2004. Sheikh Zayed bin Sultan Al Nahyan (al-Nuhayyan) was born on May 6, 1918, in the Ain region of Abu Dhabi. He was the youngest of four sons of Sheikh Sultan bin Zayed bin Khalifa Al Nahyan, who ruled Abu Dhabi from 1922 until his assassination in 1926. Zayed received no formal education other than basic instruction in Islam. He lived among the Bedouins, getting to know the people and experiencing firsthand the difficulties of their existence.

Turnover in rulers proved frequent. Zayed's eldest brother, Sheikh Shakhbut bin Sultan Al Nahyan, became ruler of Abu Dhabi in 1928 upon the assassination of their uncle, Saqr bin Zayed Al Nahyan. Under his brother's rule, Sheikh Zayed served as governor of Abu Dhabi's agricultural Eastern Province from 1946 to 1966. In 1966 he deposed his brother, Sheikh Shakbut Al Nahyan, to become emir of Abu Dhabi.

As emir, Sheikh Zayed was the principal architect behind the formation of the Trucial States, a group of Arab states or sheikhdoms that included Abu Dhabi. In December 1971 Zayed became president of the Trucial States (soon renamed the United Arab Emirates). In 1973 he reorganized the UAE's political structure, bringing most of Abu Dhabi's ministries under central control. Under the direction of Zayed, the UAE's provisional constitution (a document that essentially defined the federation of the seven states) was ratified on July 18, 1971, but did not become permanent until 1996.

In Zayed's second term as president of the UAE, which began in 1976, he promulgated more political reforms, including the centralization of the government, integration of defense forces, and increased financial contributions from member states. One of his primary goals as emir of Abu Dhabi and president of the UAE was to use oil revenues to raise the standard of living in the region. To meet this goal, Zayed shared Abu Dhabi's oil wealth with the poorer sheikhdoms, thereby reflecting his traditional tribal values. As such, it was no surprise that Zayed was reelected president of the UAE in 1981, 1986, 1991, 1996, and 2001. Under his rule, the country became a prosperous nation and a leading financial center and adopted measures to advance women's rights.

Zayed is also credited for his involvement in the creation of the Cooperation Council for the Arab States of the Gulf, also known as the Gulf Cooperation Council (GCC). In terms of foreign relations, particularly with the West, Zayed proved to be an able diplomat. During the 1991 Persian Gulf War, the UAE joined the United Nations (UN) coalition to force Iraq from Kuwait. Furthermore, in 1992 heightened tensions with Iran induced the emir to expand the UAE's military cooperation with the United States. In June 2001 after facing increased international criticism of the UAE's poor record on human rights, Zayed ordered the release on humanitarian grounds of more than 6,000 prisoners.

Zayed supported the 2001 U.S.-led invasion of Afghanistan to topple the Taliban regime and also supported the 2003 Anglo-American–led invasion of Iraq. Indeed, U.S. and allied forces have used UAE facilities as staging areas for these conflicts. Sheikh Zayed died on November 2, 2004, in Abu Dhabi. His son, Sheikh Khalifa bin Zayid al-Nahyan, who had played an increasing role in government affairs since the 1990s, succeeded his father as emir.

Kirsty Anne Montgomery

**See also**
Gulf Cooperation Council; Iraq War; United Arab Emirates

**References**
Countrywatch. *United Arab Emirates: 2003 Country Review.* Houston, TX: Countrywatch, 2003.
Davidson, Christopher M. *The United Arab Emirates: A Study in Survival.* Boulder, CO: Lynne Rienner, 2005.
Metz, Helen Chapin. *Persian Gulf States: Country Studies.* 3rd ed. Washington, DC: Federal Research Division, Library of Congress, 1994.
Zahlan, Rosemarie Said. *The Making of the Modern Gulf States: Kuwait, Bahrain, Qatar, the United Arab Emirates, and Oman.* London: Unwin Hyman, 1989.

# Zenobia (240–274?)

Queen of Palmyra in Roman Syria who led a revolt against Rome. Zenobia was of Arab ancestry; her name in Aramaic was Bat-Zabbai. Arab writers know her as al-Zabbā, but her Roman name was Julia Aurelia Zenobia. Born in Palmyra in 240, Zenobia was reportedly a member of the Amlaqui tribe. Her father, whose Roman name was Julius Aurelius Zenobius, was killed by members of a rival tribe, and Zenobia then became head of the Amlaquis. Classical and Arab sources and tradition describe her as of dark complexion and possibly of Egyptian origin but more beautiful than Cleopatra; well educated and fluent in Greek, Aramaic, and Egyptian, with some knowledge of Lain; interested in the arts; and carrying herself as a man in riding and hunting.

By 258 Zenobia was married to king of Palmyra Septimus Odaenathus. She was his second wife, with Odaenathus having had a son, Hairan, from his first marriage. Around 266 Odaenathus and Zenobia also had a son, Vaballathus.

Meanwhile, warfare resumed between Rome and Persia. Reinforced by troops sent by Roman emperor Gallienus (r. 253–268), in 262 Odaenathus and a small army invaded the former Roman provinces east of the Euphrates River that had been taken by Persia. Driving off a Persian army besieging Edessa, Odaenathus retook Nisibis and Carrhae. During the next two years in raids deep into Mesopotamia, Odaenathus consistently defeated Persian ruler Shapur I (r. 240/242–270/272) and his generals and twice captured Ctesiphon. Reportedly, Zenobia accompanied him in the campaign. Odaenathus's successes led Shapur to sue for peace in 264.

In 266 Odaenathus campaigned against the Goths, who had been ravaging Asia Minor. Although successful, he and his son Hairan were assassinated. Vaballathus then succeeded to the throne, but because he was only an infant, Zenobia was the effective ruler of Palmyra.

Uncertain of Zenobia's loyalty, in 267 Emperor Gallienus sent an army to the East to reassert Roman control there. Zenobia and her general Zobdas defeated the Romans. Zenobia then went on to confirm the independence of Palmyra by conquering Egypt in 269. Zenobia reportedly accompanied the army in battle and walked with the men. Her actions led to her being known as the "Warrior Queen."

Zenobia now controlled most of the former Roman eastern dominions including Egypt, Syria, Mesopotamia, and much of Anatolia. In 271, however, Roman emperor Aurelian (r. 270–275) marched east with an army and in the hard-fought Battle of Immae near Antioch defeated Zenobia and her general Zobdas, who were reported as entering Antioch that day with a man resembling Aurelian in chains but then fleeing the city that night.

Aurelian pursued and in 272 defeated Zenobia and Zobdas decisively at Emesa (modern-day Homs, Syria). Zenobia was unable to remove its treasury before Aurelian entered the city. Zenobia then sought refuge in her desert capital of Palmyra, but Aurelian followed and laid siege to it. Despite harassment of his supply lines by guerrillas, Aurelian was able to continue the siege, forcing Zenobia to surrender. Aurelian spared her and left her in control of Palmyra.

On Aurelian's departure, however, Zenobia again declared independence. Aurelian returned in 273, again laid siege to Palmyra, and, when it surrendered, sacked the city. Zenobia and Vaballathus were captured trying to flee and were taken by Aurelian to Rome, Vaballathus reportedly dying en route. At Rome, Zenobia was exhibited in chains in Aurelian's triumph in 274. Her fate is uncertain. She is variously said to have been beheaded, to have died in a hunger strike, or to have succumbed to illness, although one account has her freed by Aurelian and then marrying a Roman senator.

SPENCER C. TUCKER

**See also**
Aurelian, Emperor

**References**
Ball, Warwick. *Rome in the East: The Transformation of an Empire.* New York: Routledge, 2001.
Heriot, Angus. *Zenobia.* London: Secker & Warburg, 1958.
Naum, Gellu. *Zenobia.* Evanston, IL: Northwestern University Press, 1995.
Stoneman, Richard. *Palmyra and Its Empire: Zenobia's Revolt against Rome.* Ann Arbor: University of Michigan Press, 1995.
Winsbury, Rex. *Zenobia of Palmyra: History, Myth and the Neo-Classical Imagination.* London: Duckworth, 2010.

## Zionism

Zionism holds that Jews constitute a people and a nation. As a political movement, it supports the creation of a homeland for the Jewish people. Zionism began in the late 19th century, arising out of the general movement of nationalism and increased anti-Semitism. It soon became a well-organized and well-funded settlement movement focused on Palestine, which many Jews believe was the ancient homeland granted them by God. Zionism eventually contributed directly to the formation of the State of Israel and continued to influence the politics of Israeli Jews for the rest of the 20th century.

The word "Zionism" derives from Mount Zion, the high ground in Jerusalem just south of the Temple Mount and the traditional burial place of King David. The term was first used in 1890 by Austrian Jew Nathan Birnbaum. Zionists found justification for their movement in the Hebrew Bible (and Christian Old Testament) account of God giving the land of Israel to the Israelites in perpetuity and from the long-standing belief of diaspora Jews that they would one day return to the Holy Land. Zionism also grew out of the rise of nationalism in the 19th century, as various European nations developed national identities and political systems. Many Jews at that time had a secular view of their Judaism. They abandoned their religious practices but embraced the concept of Jews as a people and a nation that deserved a national homeland. Other ideas, such as socialism and rationalism, also influenced early Zionists. Zionism was fueled by the persecution of Jews in many places in Europe, most notably the Russian Empire. Jews came to believe, with some justification, that only a Jewish state could protect them.

Although other locations were suggested, Palestine seemed to be the obvious choice for the establishment of a Jewish nation. It had biblical connotations, and many Jews believed that it was their historical homeland. In 1862 Moses Hess wrote *Rome and Jerusalem,* which urged Jews to settle in Palestine in an agrarian socialist state. Hess and other writers, such as Ber Borochov and Nahum Syrkin, believed that Jews had become weak and downtrodden as a result of their centuries of working as merchants and pawnbrokers and that they needed to redeem themselves with healthful outdoor labor and socialism. Zionism and socialism often went hand in hand in the late 1800s and early 1900s. Many Jews looked on the creation of a Jewish state as an opportunity for them to build an ideal society, a religious community founded on the principles of socialism. This belief coalesced in a movement known as Labor Zionism, which held that the creation of a Jewish state must necessarily be part of a class struggle in which Jews would become agriculturists, living on collective socialist farms known as kibbutzim.

From the late 1870s through 1882 some Russian Jews went to Palestine, then a part of the Ottoman Empire, there to establish small farms in a movement that became known as the First Aliya. Beginning in 1882 thousands of Russian Jews immigrated to Palestine, fleeing from pogroms and Tsar Alexander III's 1882 anti-Semitic May Laws. These settlers called themselves Biluim, after a verse from the Book of Isaiah. Their goal was to establish a Jewish national homeland in the land they called Israel. These first settlers nearly starved during their attempt to support themselves on land without adequate freshwater, and many of them left. Baron Edmond de Rothschild provided the remaining settlers with money to establish a winery, which soon became successful. The settlers also used his money to found the town of Zichron Yaakov.

In 1894 the Dreyfus Affair in France, which triggered an explosion of anti-Semitism in that country, persuaded many European Jews that anti-Semitism was a growing problem even in supposedly enlightened Western Europe. Theodor Herzl, a Jewish-Austrian journalist who covered the trial, became a staunch supporter of Zionism in the course of the Dreyfus Affair. In 1896 Herzl wrote *Der Judenstaat* (The Jewish State) in which he called for the Jews to create their own homeland in either Palestine or Argentina.

In 1897 Herzl organized the First Zionist Congress in Switzerland. It created the Zionist Organization (ZO), the goal of which was to raise money and buy land in Palestine so that Jews could settle there. Herzl was the group's first president. The group spent the next 52 years purchasing land and creating governmental procedures for the new Israeli state. The ZO was later renamed the World Zionist Organization (WZO).

All Jews were allowed to join the ZO. People from countries all over the world came to the group's congresses, which were held every two years between 1897 and 1946. Members assembled in delegations according to ideology instead of geographic origin. Some Zionists were ardent socialists or communists. Many were vehemently secular or even atheist. Others had more religious leanings.

The ZO organized the Jewish Colonial Trust to handle financial matters. The Jewish National Fund, created in 1901, took responsibility for purchasing land. The Anglo-Palestine Bank, established in 1903, provided financial services for settlers. Gradually the group created an infrastructure for the Jewish homeland that made the process of settling in Palestine easier than it had been in the 1800s.

In the early years of the 20th century, Zionists debated whether Palestine was the ideal location for the Jewish homeland. In 1903 the British government proposed a Jewish homeland in Kenya. This plan was known as the British Uganda Program. Herzl suggested this to the Sixth Zionist Congress as a temporary safe haven for Russian Jews, but the Russian Jews themselves disliked the idea, and the Seventh Zionist Congress abandoned the idea in 1905. The Jewish Territorialist Organization wanted to create a Jewish homeland wherever it could but disbanded in 1917. In the 1930s the Soviet Union created the Jewish Autonomous Republic in the Far Eastern Federal District, but few Jews wanted to move there. For the most part, Palestine remained the sole focus of the Zionist movement.

During the early 1900s, many small groups of settlers went to Palestine. A number arrived there following the

1905 Revolution in Russia. Leaders such as Joseph Baratz and other settlers pooled their money, added to it contributions from Jews all over the world, and founded kibbutzim on plots of land that they lived on and farmed collectively. By 1914 there were kibbutzim throughout Palestine. Residents shared all work and all profits and governed themselves democratically.

Cultural Zionists looked on the settlement movement as an opportunity to create a unique Jewish culture. Many Jews were quite critical of Jewish culture in the late 19th century, which they saw as downtrodden and weak after centuries of diaspora. Some Zionist thinkers such as Asher Ginsberg and Eliezer Ben Yehudah thought that Palestine would be the ideal place to revive Hebrew language and culture, allowing Jews to replace their Germanic Yiddish language and speak to one another in a uniquely Jewish language that would unite diverse groups of Jews. Herzl wanted German to be the official language of Palestine, but most settlers and Zionists supported the use of Hebrew. Tel Aviv, founded in 1909, was the first city to make Hebrew its official language.

The United Kingdom was an important ally in the creation of the Jewish state. Jews were generally made welcome in Britain in the early 20th century, and many British people appreciated Jewish culture. During World War I the British government sought to mobilize the support of Jews for the war effort, and in 1917 British foreign secretary Arthur Balfour issued a statement (known as the Balfour Declaration) in which the British government expressed its support for the establishment of a Jewish homeland (not a state) in Palestine.

In Balfour's declaration, he said that a Jewish homeland should not harm the civil rights of non-Jewish people already living in Palestine. Zionists realized that the Muslim Arabs already living in Palestine would become a source of conflict, but many of them chose to ignore the issue or to suggest that Jewish immigration could only benefit the current residents. Zionist leaders such as Israel Zangwill concocted slogans such as "A land without a people, for a people without a land," which deliberately glossed over the presence of the Arab population in the land in question.

In the early days of settlement (the 1880s and earlier) Arabs did not object to the incursion of Jews. The first Jewish settlers had been unable to farm successfully, so they ended up hiring Arab laborers to work their farms. In the 1890s, however, as Arabs began to realize what the Zionists intended, they grew concerned about losing their farmland and water. The socialist agrarian settlers of the early 1900s did not employ Arabs because their whole raison d'être was to encourage Jews to work the land themselves. The Balfour Declaration, the partitioning of Palestine in 1918, and their increasing landless status and poverty all prompted Palestinian Arabs to agitate for a state of their own. Also around this time, some Zionists suggested that Palestinian Arabs should be expelled from the country or should be made to accept the Jewish presence through armed force.

In the early 1920s the ZO, having reached the conclusion that socialism was the only way to distribute available economic resources among a rapidly growing group of Jewish immigrants, decided that Jewish settlement in Palestine should be socialist. During the 1920s David Ben-Gurion, a leader of Histadrut, the Jewish Labor Zionist trade union that dominated Jewish Palestine, officially opposed the use of force against Arabs, claiming that it would be unnecessary because Arabs would soon decide that Zionism was good for them. In private, however, he said that conflict was inevitable because Arabs would never accept Zionist settlement. In the late 1930s Ben-Gurion and the Labor Zionists supported the idea of a Jewish state with no Arabs in it, the existing Arabs having been removed forcibly.

Zionism became somewhat more popular after the creation of the British Mandate for Palestine in 1922. Increasing numbers of Jews moved to Palestine, as the ZO and other Zionist organizations raised money and lobbied the British government not to allow the Palestinian Arabs to create their own state. Palestinian nationalism also increased during this time, as the Muslims saw their land and livelihood increasingly threatened by Jewish newcomers.

Zionism was made up of many different streams. "General Zionism" is the term used to describe the general or transcending beliefs held in common by all Zionists exemplified by the goals of the ZO. General Zionism sought unity by placing the importance of the Jewish homeland above class, party, political, social, religious, or personal interests. Political Zionism centered on the creation of a legal and political entity in Palestine, the existence and sovereignty of which would be sanctioned by the great world powers.

Socialist Zionism asserted that the fusion of Zionist and socialist ideals in Palestine would create a labor-based communal society (socialism) that would transform Palestine and become an attractive haven for the downtrodden of world Jewry. Socialist Zionism eventually evolved into the Labor Zionism of Ben-Gurion. Although the Socialist Zionists and the Labor Zionists were more ethnic Jews than religious Jews, both respected Jewish religious traditions as part of their national heritage.

Labor Zionism held that the best foundation for a Jewish state was a strong economy and shared economic opportunity that benefited all of the society's members, such as collective settlements (*kibbutzim*). Labor Zionism generally believed that Arabs in Palestine should and could be encouraged to transfer out of Palestine.

Practical Zionism asserted that the best way to achieve the Zionist goal was through a massive immigration movement (*aliya*). The aliya would be oriented toward settling both rural and urban areas and the creation of industries, educational institutions, and social services.

Messianic Zionism effectively ignored the practical and simply asserted that the Jewish state would come to be and would last because it was part of the original divine decree given to Abraham, a promise on which those settling in Palestine could depend. Religious Zionism asserted that the formation of an ethnic Jewish state with no religious heart would be temporary. Religious Zionism argued that the only Jewish state that would survive and attract other Jews would be one that wove a conservative Torah-based Jewish religion into its political and social fabric. In other words, the state should be based on the commandments and laws of the Torah. Spiritual Zionism agreed with Religious Zionism but asserted further that the then-prevalent form of Judaism in the Zionist movement, the more liberal and intellectual Ashkenazic Judaism, had lost its guiding spirit. Spiritual Zionism believed that Palestine could not practically hold all of world Jewry, and even if it could, a Jewish state would not elevate the social and economic status of Jews, nor would it end persecution. Spiritual Zionism advocated a modest settlement plan and the formation of a national spiritual center in Palestine instead of a Jewish political state. Chaim Weizmann's Synthetic Zionism combined political, social, practical, and ethno-religious Judaism into a single entity that tried to incorporate all of the different ideals into a Jewish state reflecting all of the concerns of the Zionist spectrum.

Revisionist Zionism argued that the British Mandate for Palestine should be revised to create a sovereign Jewish state encompassing both sides of the Jordan River. Revisionist Zionists also held that Zionism should shift its emphasis from social and economic development in Palestine to the immediate creation of a Jewish state aligned with Great Britain.

Not all Jews supported the Zionist movement, of course. Some socialist Jews disliked the idea of a state because it smacked of unsocialistic nationalism. Communist Jews in Russia also rejected the idea of a Jewish state in Palestine. Many Jews believed that there was no need for a Jewish homeland because Jews could live perfectly well in other nations, such as the United States. American Jews argued that the United States was the Jewish homeland.

All of these arguments changed after Adolf Hitler came to power in Germany in 1933. The United States, formerly so welcoming to Jews, closed its doors to Jewish immigration. Jews became refugees in the Europe that they had formerly considered a perfectly adequate home. Increasing numbers of Jews moved to Palestine in the 1930s, but this angered Palestinian Arabs. After riots broke out, in 1939 the British government restricted Jewish immigration to Palestine. Jews living in Palestine armed themselves and began fighting the Arabs and launching attacks on British targets.

After World War II, Zionism experienced a huge upsurge of popularity and support thanks to the horrific events of the Holocaust, Hitler's attempt to exterminate the Jews in Europe. The United States was one of the strongest backers of the formation of a Jewish state in Palestine. Jews themselves were almost unanimous in their support for the creation of Israel. Following the failure of British partition efforts, in 1947 the United Nations (UN) voted to create two states within Palestine, one Arab and one Jewish, with Jerusalem as a shared possession. The Jews accepted the plan, but the Palestinian Arabs rejected it. With the British withdrawal, Jewish leaders in Palestine declared the independent State of Israel on May 14, 1948.

Once the Jewish homeland was established, Israeli leaders turned their attention to expelling Arab agitators, welcoming a new influx of Jewish settlers, and organizing the Israel Defense Force (IDF). International Zionist organizations continued their support for Israel, raising money and sponsoring immigration and development. In 1960 the ZO became the WZO, dedicated to making Israel the center of Jewish life, preserving Jewish identity, and protecting the rights of Jews around the world.

AMY HACKNEY BLACKWELL

### See also
Balfour Declaration; Ben-Gurion, David; Israel; Palestine, British Mandate for

### References
Hertzberg, Arthur, ed. *The Zionist Idea: A Historical Analysis and Reader*. Philadelphia: Jewish Publication Society, 1997.
Herzl, Theodor. *The Jewish State*. Mineola, NY: Dover, 1989.
Laqueur, Walter. *A History of Zionism: From the French Revolution to the Establishment of the State of Israel*. Reprint ed. New York: Schocken, 2003.

Pappe, Ilan. *A History of Modern Palestine: One Land, Two Peoples.* Cambridge: Cambridge University Press, 2003.
Rose, John. *The Myths of Zionism.* London: Pluto, 2004.

# Zoroastrianism

Influential religion combining elements of dualism and monotheism to form its complicated cosmology. Zoroastrianism developed in ancient Persia. Although undergoing a great decline during the course of centuries, it retains fervent adherents today.

Zoroastrianism takes its name from sixth-century BCE founder and prophet Zoroaster. Although initially a priest in the ancient polytheistic religion of the Persians, Zoroaster began to preach against that tradition. According to Zoroaster, Ahura Mazda, the primary god of the Persian pantheon, had revealed himself to be the only deity worthy of worship. On receiving those revelations, Zoroaster began to compose the Gathas, which was part of the canon of sacred scriptures called the Avesta.

The Gathas consists of 17 hymns laying out Zoroaster's ideas about the nature of the universe. Ahura Mazda is portrayed as the sole creator of all, including Heaven and Earth. Ahura Mazda, who created morality, nature, light, and dark, also created the Amesha Spentas, or "beneficial immortals," who worked to do his bidding. As angelic reflections of Ahura Mazda, the Amesha Spentas included Spenta Mainyu, the holy spirit; Vohu Manah, the righteous spirit; Apenta Armaiti, devotion; Haurvatat, wholeness; Asha Vahishta, truth and justice; Ameretat, immortality; and Khshathra Vairya, desirable dominion. The attributes of those beings are considered to be the moral compass for Zoroastrian believers. By achieving their behaviors, Zoroastrians believe that they are closer to Ahura Mazda himself and to realizing the desirable dominion reflected in Khshathra Vairya.

By framing Ahura Mazda as the sole creator of the universe, Zoroastrianism moved away from the polytheism of the ancient Persians. However, there is a strong dualism in Zoroastrian theology that is reflected in the story of the origin of the universe and cosmology. According to the Gathas, at the beginning of time Ahura Mazda gave birth to two diametrically opposed spirits, Ohrmazd and Ahriman. (Some traditions contend that Ahura Mazda and Ohrmazd are the same being, with the latter name being a corruption of the former.) Ohrmazd chose to follow the path of good and light, while Ahriman chose to support that which was evil in the universe. The two forces are thus pitted against each other in a battle between supreme good and supreme evil. Through their ethical and moral decisions and actions, humans participate in this struggle; those who fight for all that is good are members of a kingdom of justice and truth, while those who promote the cause of evil are members of the kingdom of the lie.

Upon death every human soul passes over a bridge that leads to Ahura Mazda, who will judge persons according to their position taken during life. Those who fought for good will spend the afterlife in bliss, while those who sided with evil Ahriman will be tortured.

Zoroastrian scriptures explain that when the battle between Ohrmazd and Ahriman reaches its conclusion and the evil forces are destroyed forever, the world as it previously existed will be purged. In its place a renewed world will emerge, and evil will no longer exist. Then, the souls of those who sided with Ohrmazd will be reunited with their restored bodies in a form of resurrection. Humans will live in a timeless earthly splendor without the fears of evil that had plagued them before the end of time.

One of the notable aspects of Zoroastrian ritual was a strong reverence for the four elements of earth, air, water, and fire. Life was to avoid corrupting those elements, viewed as sacred creations of Ahura Mazda. For example, Zoroastrians were careful not to bury or cremate the dead so as to avoid contaminating the earth and polluting the fire, respectively.

Of all of the natural elements, fire was crucial to Persian religious rituals even before Zoroastrianism and Zoroaster revered fire. Fire represented Asha, the light of all that is good in the universe. As such, sacred fires burning in Zoroastrian temples were tended by the Magi, the ritual priests of Zoroastrianism. Fire is revered for its symbolic value as the spark of animation as well as the power of goodness. Indeed, fire became a central focus for Zoroastrian ritual in the centuries after the death of Zoroaster.

During Zoroaster's life, his new religion spread through parts of northern Persia and into the territory of modern-day Afghanistan. Zoroastrianism was the official religion of the Sassanid Persian Empire from around 600 BCE to 650 CE. However, following their conquests of Persia during 633–654, the Muslim rulers suppressed Zoroastrianism. There are today perhaps no more than 190,000 adherents, most of them in India and Iran.

Despite its small number of believers, Zoroastrianism is recognized by many scholars and theologians as an extremely influential force on the monotheistic faiths of

Judaism, Christianity, and Islam. Its insistence on one creator god and its highly ethical theological framework echo the ethical monotheism of the traditions of Abraham. Its belief in the ultimate triumph of good over evil and in resurrection of the good are other points of interest for those looking for links between Zoroastrianism and other monotheistic traditions.

NANCY L. STOCKDALE

**See also**
Sassanid Empire

**References**
Boyce, Mary. *Zoroastrians: Their Religious Beliefs and Practices.* London: Routledge, 1979.
Clark, Peter. *Zoroastrianism: An Introduction to an Ancient Faith.* Brighton, UK: Sussex Academic Press, 1998.
Dhalla, Maneckji Nusservanji. *History of Zoroastrianism.* New York: Oxford University Press, 1938.

# Zsitvatorok, Peace of (November 11, 1606)

Peace treaty that ended the Thirteen Years' War (1593–1606) between the Ottoman Empire and the Habsburg monarchy. Signed on November 11, 1606, at Zsitvatorok, Hungary, the treaty marked the first major check of the Ottoman advance into Habsburg territory and stabilized the Habsburg-Ottoman frontier for half a century. In the Thirteen Years' War the Ottomans had failed to break the resistance of the Habsburgs, while the Imperial troops behaved with such callousness toward the Protestants in Transylvania and Hungary that István Bocskay, a Transylvanian lord and a Habsburg supporter, rebelled and drove the Habsburgs out of Transylvania altogether. In June 1606 Bocskay signed the Peace of Vienna with the Habsburgs, which recognized him as ruler of an enlarged Transylvania and guaranteed the rights of Protestants in Royal Hungary. Bocskay then mediated the Peace of Zsitvatorok between Habsburg emperor Rudolf II and Sultan Ahmed I.

The treaty is noteworthy for the sultan's acknowledgment of the emperor as an equal. Since the time of Suleiman I the Magnificent the Habsburgs had been compelled to yield tribute to the Ottoman rulers, who considered the emperors as their vassals. The Peace of Zsitvatorok, however, specified that the sultan would accord the emperor his full rank and titles, therefore accepting him as an equal. The annual tribute that Habsburgs had hitherto paid to the sultans was ceased in exchange for a single lump payment of 200,000 gulden and a triennial exchange of voluntary gifts through ambassadors. Each side retained the territories then under its control, with the Ottomans gaining only two fortresses, Erlau and Kanizsa. Both sides agreed to maintain the treaty for 20 years, although in reality it lasted for half a century.

ALEXANDER MIKABERIDZE

**See also**
Ottoman-Habsburg Wars

**Reference**
Parry, Vernon J., and M. A. Cook. *History of the Ottoman Empire to 1730.* Cambridge: Cambridge University Press, 1976.

# Zuhab, Treaty of (May 17, 1639)

Peace treaty signed between Safavid Persia and the Ottoman Empire, also known as the Treaty of Qasr-e-Shirin. The treaty, concluded on May 17, 1639, between Ottoman sultan Murad IV and Shah Safi of Safavid Persia, ended a 15-year-long war between the two states. During the last conflict, which began in 1623, the Safavids under Shah Abbas gained substantial success and occupied Iraq for 15 years before the Ottoman counterattack recaptured it in 1638. The following year the peace treaty of Zuhab established the boundary between the two empires.

The treaty was referred to as a *sulh* (truce), not as a *silm* (peace). It permanently divided the Caucasus between the two states. The Safavid Empire secured possession of eastern Armenia, eastern Georgia, Dagestan, and Azerbaijan. The Ottomans took possession of western Georgia and most of western Armenia. The Persians also recognized Ottoman sovereignty over all of Mesopotamia (including Baghdad and the Shatt al-Arab).

Although border disputes continued and there would be some 18 different future treaties dealing with these, the Treaty of Zuhab essentially set the border that remained virtually unchanged into modern times. Ottoman sovereignty in Iraq, however, continued to be disturbed by Arab and Kurdish tribal unrest.

ALEXANDER MIKABERIDZE

**See also**
Abbas I the Great; Ottoman-Safavid Wars

**Reference**
Fisher, William Bayne, Peter Jackson, and Laurence Lockhart, eds. *The Cambridge History of Iran,* Vol. 6, *The Timurid and Safavid Periods.* Cambridge: Cambridge University Press, 1986.

## Zuravno, Treaty of (October 16, 1676)

Peace treaty between Poland and the Ottoman Empire concluded on October 16, 1676, at Zuravno (Zorawno), Ukraine. The treaty ended the ongoing conflict between the two states and revised the previous treaty of Buczacz of 1672, which Poles found unfavorable for them. The Porte recognized Polish control over western Ukraine and agreed to relinquish its claim to an annual tribute to be paid to the Ottoman sultan. The Ottomans retained control over southern Ukraine.

Alexander Mikaberidze

**See also**
Ottoman-Polish Wars of the 17th Century

**Reference**
Davies, Norman. *God's Playground: A History of Poland.* New York: Columbia University Press, 1981.

# Chronology

| | | | |
|---|---|---|---|
| 10,000 BCE | Earliest neolithic sanctuaries at Göbekli Tepe in southern Turkey. | 2334–2154 | Period of the Akkadian Empire. |
| 8400–8100 | First settlements at Nevalı Cori in Turkey. | 2055–1650 | Middle Kingdom in Egypt. |
| 8000 | Human settlements at Sagalassos in southwest Turkey. | 2025–1378 | Old Assyrian Empire. |
| | | 2004 | Elamites destroy Ur. |
| 7000 | Jarmo, one of the oldest agricultural communities, in northern Iraq. | 2004–1763 | Rise of the Amorites, who establish several city-states in Mesopotamia. |
| 6000 | First systematic irrigation and flood control in Mesopotamia and Egypt. | 1894–911 | Old Babylonian Empire. |
| | | 1650–1550 | Rule of the Hyksos in Egypt. Known as the "Shepherd Kings," they introduce the horse and wheeled chariot into Egypt. |
| 5500 | First large-scale agriculture by the Sumerians and Egyptians in the Nile Valley. | | |
| 4500 | Civilizations of Susa and Kish in Mesopotamia. | 1595 | Hittites attack and sack Babylon. |
| | | 1595–1155 | Kassites control Babylonia. |
| 4000–3100 | The Urkuk period, named for the Sumerian city of Ur that sees the emergence of urban life in Mesopotamia. | 1550–1069 | New Kingdom of Egypt. |
| | | 1457 | Battle of Megiddo., the first in history recorded by eyewitnesses. |
| | | 1392–934 | Middle Assyrian Empire. |
| 3600 | First world civilization in the form of the city-state of Sumer in modern-day southern Iraq. | 1370–1200 | Hittite Empire. |
| | | 1274 | Battle of Kadesh. |
| | | 1234? | Babylon is taken by the Assyrians. |
| 3500 | First cities in Egypt. | 1200–884 | The Sea Peoples—groups of seafaring raiders—invade Anatolia, Syria, Canaan, Cyprus, and Egypt. |
| 3500–3000 | First appearances of wheeled vehicles in Mesopotamia. | | |
| 3100–2686 | First Dynasty of Egypt (the Archaic period). | 1200–546 | Lydian Empire. |
| | | 1194–1184 | Siege and fall of Troy. |
| 3000 | First examples of Sumerian writing in Mesopotamia, in the form of cuneiform in Uruk and Susa. | 1180–700 | Neo-Hittite kingdoms. |
| | | 1157 | Babylon is taken and sacked by the Elamites. |
| 2686–2181 | Old Kingdom of Egypt. | 1100–539 | Neo-Elamite period. |
| 2334–2279 | Reign of King Sargon of Akkad, founder of the Akkad dynasty. | 1087 | Babylon is destroyed by Assyrians. |
| | | 1050–931 | Kingdom of Israel. |

| Date | Event |
|---|---|
| 1000 | King David captures the Jebusite city of Jerusalem and makes it the Israelite capital. |
| 883–612 | Neo-Assyrian Empire. |
| 689 | Assyrian king Sennacherib 689 Seenacherib again takes Babylon and this time slaughters its inhabitants and utterly destroys the city. |
| 678–549 | Median Empire. |
| 626–539 | The Neo-Babylonian or Chaldean Empire. |
| 612 | A coalition of Babylonians, Medes, Persians, Chaldeans, Scythians, and Cimmerians brings the capture of the Assyrian capital of Nineveh and the end of the Neo-Assyrian Empire. |
| 597 | Babylonian king Nebuchadnezzar II captures Jerusalem. |
| 587 | Babylonian king Nebuchadnezzar II again takes Jerusalem following a prolonged siege. He destroys Solomon's Temple and removes much of the city population to Babylon. |
| 550–330 | Achaemenid Empire (First Persian Empire). |
| 546 | Battle of Thymbra. |
| 539–538 | King Cyrus II the Great of Persia conquers Babylonia. |
| 525 | Persians conquer Egypt. Battle of Pelusium. |
| 499–493 | Ionian Revolt. |
| 499–479 | Greco-Persian Wars. |
| 494 | Siege of Miletus. |
| 479 | Battle of Mycale. |
| 450–449 | Athenian expedition against Cyprus. |
| 411–410 | Hellespont Campaign. |
| 401–399 | March of the Ten Thousand. |
| 334 | King Alexander III of Macedon the Great conquers the Persian Empire. |
| 333 | Battle of Issus. |
| 332 | Sieges of Tyre and Gaza. |
| 331 | Battle of Gaugamela (Arbela). |
| 323–275 | Wars of the Diadochi. |
| 323–31 | Hellenistic period with widespread Greek influence. |
| 317 | Battle of Paraetacene. |
| 312–63 | Seleucid Empire. |
| 305–304 | Siege of Rhodes. |
| 305–30 | Ptolemaic Kingdom. |
| 301 | Battle of Ipsus. |
| 274–168 | Syrian-Egyptian Wars. |
| 247 BCE–224 CE | Parthian Persian Empire. |
| 217 | Battle of Raphia. |
| 192–188 | Roman-Seleucid War (Syrian-Roman War). |
| 190 | Battle of Magnesia. |
| 167–160 | Maccabean Revolt. |
| 89–63 | Mithridatic Wars. |
| 53 BCE–215 CE | Roman-Parthian Wars. |
| 48–47 | Julius Caesar's campaign in Egypt. |
| 31 | Battle of Actium. |
| 66 CE | Battle of Beth-Horon. |
| 66–73 | First Jewish-Roman War. |
| 70 | Siege of Jerusalem. |
| 72–73 | Siege of Masada. |
| 132–135 | Bar Kochba Revolt. |
| 217 | Battle of Nisibis. |
| 224–651 | Sassanid Empire of Persia. |
| 232–440 | Roman-Sassanid Wars. |
| 330–1453 | Byzantine Empire. |
| 378 | Battle of Adrianople (Edirne). |
| 532 | Nika Uprising. |
| 602–628 | Byzantine-Sassanid War. |
| 622–632 | Campaigns of Prophet Muhammad. |
| 623–732 | Muslim Wars of Expansion. |
| 624 | Battle of Badr. |
| 627 | Battle of Nineveh. Battle of Khandaq (Battle of the Trench). |
| 629–1035 | Byzantine-Muslim Wars. |
| 632 | Death of Muhammad; Abu Bakr is chosen as caliph. |
| 632–633 | Ridda Wars. |
| 632–661 | Rashidun Caliphate. |
| 634–641 | Muslim conquest of the Levant. |
| 636 | Battle of Qadisiyya. Battle of Yarmouk River (Yarmuk). |
| 640–642 | Muslim conquest of Egypt. |
| 642–671 | Muslim conquest of Persia. |
| 656 | Battle of Bassorah. |
| 656–661 | First Islamic Civil War (First Fitna). |
| 657 | Battle of Siffin. |
| 661–750 | Umayyad Caliphate. |
| 680 | Battle of Karbala. |
| 680–692 | Second Islamic Civil War (Second Fitna). |
| 717–718 | Siege of Constantinople. |
| 747–751 | Abbasid Revolution. |
| 750 | Battle of Zab. |
| 750–1258 | Abbasid Caliphate. |
| 869–883 | Zangu (Zanj) Slave Revolt. |
| 969–1171 | Fatimid dynasty of Egypt. |
| 1016–1153 | Seljuk Turk dynasty. |
| 1048–1308 | Byzantine-Seljuk Wars. |

| | | | | |
|---|---|---|---|---|
| 1071 | Battle of Manzikert. | | 1485–1491 | Mamluk-Ottoman War. |
| 1080–1307 | Rum Sultanate. | | 1501–1736 | Safavid dynasty of Persia. |
| 1092–1105 | Seljuk War of Succession. | | 1514 | Battle of Chaldiran. |
| 1096–1291 | Christian crusades in the Holy Land. | | 1516 | Battle of Marj Dabiq (Marj Dabik). |
| 1099 | Siege of Jerusalem. | | 1516–1517 | Mamluk-Ottoman War. |
| 1101 | First Battle of Ramla. | | 1522 | Siege of Rhodes. |
| 1101–1408 | Artuqid dynasty. | | 1526–1639 | Ottoman-Safavid Wars. |
| 1102 | Second Battle of Ramla. | | 1529–1791 | Ottoman-Habsburg Wars. |
| 1104 | Battle of Harran. | | 1570–1571 | Ottomans take possession of Cyprus. |
| 1105 | Third Battle of Ramla. | | 1570–1573 | Ottoman-Venetian War. |
| 1113 | Battle of al-Sannabra. | | 1571 | Battle of Lepanto. |
| 1119 | Battle of Ager Sanguinis. | | 1606 | Peace of Zsitvatorok. |
| 1149 | Battle of Inab. | | 1612 | Treaty of Nasuh Pasha. |
| 1164 | Battle of Harim. | | 1622–1623 | Mughal-Safavid War. |
| 1171–1260 | Ayyubid dynasty. | | 1633–1699 | Polish-Ottoman Wars. |
| 1176 | Battle of Myriokephalon. | | 1639 | Treaty of Zuhab. |
| 1177 | Battle of Mount Giscard. | | 1648–1653 | Mughal-Safavid War. |
| 1187 | Battle of Hattin. | | 1664 | Treaty of Vasvar. |
| 1192 | Battle of Jaffa. | | 1676 | Treaty of Zuravno. |
| 1204 | Siege of Constantinople. | | 1676–1911 | Russo-Ottoman Wars. |
| 1204–1461 | Empire of Trebizond. | | 1699 | Treaty of Karlowitz. |
| 1230 | Battle of Erzican. | | 1711 | Treaty of Pruth. |
| 1239 | Battle of Gaza. | | 1722 | Siege of Isfahan. |
| 1241–1244 | Mongol invasions of Anatolia. | | 1722–1911 | Russo-Persian Wars. |
| 1243 | Battle of Köse Dag (Kosedagh). | | 1730 | Patrona Halil Revolt. |
| 1250 | Battle of Mansurah. | | 1730–1823 | Ottoman-Persian Wars. |
| 1250–1517 | Mamluk Sultanate. | | 1732 | Treaty of Resht. |
| 1256–1270 | War of St. Sabas. | | 1733 | Battle of Leilan. |
| 1256–1280 | Mongol invasions of the Middle East. | | 1739 | Treaty of Nissa. |
| 1258 | Mongol forces capture and sack Baghdad. | | 1745 | Battle of Kars. |
| 1260 | Battle of Ayn Jalut. | | 1772 | Battle of Gulnabad. |
| | First Battle of Homs. | | 1774 | Treaty of Kuchuk Kainardji. |
| 1260–1323 | Mamluk-Ilkhanid Wars. | | 1792 | Treaty of Jassy. |
| 1261–1353 | Ilkhan dynasty. | | 1798–1801 | French invasion and occupation of Egypt, led by Napoleon Bonaparte. |
| 1261–1517 | Mamluk Sultanate of Cairo. | | | |
| | Abbasid Caliphate. | | 1807–1809 | Anglo-Ottoman War. |
| 1280–1479 | Byzantine-Ottoman Wars. | | 1811–1818 | Ottoman-Wahhabi War. |
| 1281 | Second Battle of Homs. | | 1811–1840 | Egyptian-Arab Wars. |
| 1299 | Third Battle of Homs. | | 1814 | Tehran Treaty. |
| 1299–1922 | Ottoman Empire. | | 1823–1833 | Campaigns of Turki ibn Abdullah. |
| 1329 | Battle of Pelekanon. | | 1831–1833 | Egyptian-Ottoman War. |
| 1341–1447 | Byzantine Empire Civil War. | | 1832 | Battle of Konya. |
| 1344–1348 | Smyrna Crusade. | | 1839 | Battle of Nizip. |
| 1396 | Nikopolis Crusade. | | 1838–1841 | Egyptian-Ottoman War. |
| 1402 | Battle of Ankara. | | 1852–1913 | Montenegrin-Ottoman Wars. |
| 1353–1718 | Venetian-Ottoman Wars. | | 1853 | Battle of Sinope. |
| 1426 | Battle of Khirokitia. | | 1853–1856 | Crimean War. |
| 1437–1526 | Ottoman-Hungarian Wars. | | 1856–1857 | Anglo-Persian War. |
| 1444 | Varna Crusade. | | 1860 | Mount Lebanon Civil War. |
| 1453 | Siege and fall of Constantinople. | | 1869 | Completion of the Suez Canal. |
| 1473 | Battle of Otlukbeli. | | 1876 | Serbian-Ottoman War. |

| Year | Event |
|---|---|
| 1878 | Treaty of San Stefano. |
| 1882 | Anglo-Egyptian War. |
| 1887–1921 | Saudi-Rashidi Wars. |
| 1911–1912 | Italo-Ottoman War. |
| 1911–1913 | Saudi-Ottoman War. |
| 1912–1913 | Two wars in the Balkans. |
| 1914–1915 | Battle of Sarikamish. |
| 1914–1918 | World War I. |
| 1915–1916 | Dardanelles and Gallipoli Campaigns. |
| 1915–1917 | Armenian Genocide. |
| 1915–1918 | Palestine and Syria Campaign. |
| 1916 | Sykes-Picot Agreement. |
| | Erzurum Offensive. |
| | Siege of Kut al-Amara. |
| 1916–1918 | Arab Revolt. |
| 1916–1920 | Siege of Medina. |
| 1917 | Balfour Declaration, announcing British government support for a Jewish "national home" in Palestine. |
| | First, Second, and Third Battles of Gaza. |
| | Sinai Campaign. |
| 1918 | Battle of Megiddo. |
| | Transjordan Campaign. |
| | Armistice of Mudros. |
| | Britain and France occupy former Ottoman Empire lands in what will be Palestine, Lebanon, Jordan, Syria, and Iraq. |
| 1919 | Battle of Turaba. |
| 1919–1921 | Franco-Syrian War. |
| 1919–1922 | Greco-Turkish War. |
| 1919–1925 | Saudi-Hashemite War. |
| 1920 | Turkish-Armenian War. |
| | Franco-Turkish War (Cilicia War). |
| | Battle of Maysalun. |
| | Franco-Syrian War. |
| | Treaty of Sèvres. |
| | San Remo Conference. |
| 1920–1922 | Operation NEMESIS. |
| 1921 | Battle of Sakarya. |
| 1921–1922 | Saudi-Kuwaiti War. |
| 1922–1948 | British Mandate for Palestine. |
| 1923 | Treaty of Lausanne. |
| 1925 | Siege of Jeddah. |
| 1929 | Hebron Massacre. |
| 1932 | Kingdom of Saudi Arabia declared with the unification of the Nejd and Hejaz. |
| 1934 | Saudi-Yemeni War. |
| 1935 | Persia officially becomes Iran. |
| 1936 | Anglo-Egyptian Treaty. |
| 1936–1939 | Arab Revolt in Palestine. |
| 1937 | Pan Arab Congress. |
| | Peel Commission. |
| 1939 | London Round Table Talks regarding Palestine. |
| | British white paper regarding Palestine. |
| 1939–1945 | World War II. |
| 1941 | Syria and Lebanon campaigns. |
| 1941–1945 | Holocaust. |
| 1942 | First and Second Battles of Mursa Matruh. |
| | First and Second Battles of El Alamein. |
| 1946 | The Emirate of Transjordan becomes the Kingdom of Jordan (named Transjordan until 1948). |
| 1947 | United Nations Palestine Partition Plan. |
| 1947–1948 | Arab-Jewish Communal War. |
| 1948–1949 | Israeli War of Independence. |
| 1949–1956 | Israel's Border Wars. |
| 1950 | Tripartite Declaration. |
| 1951–1953 | Anglo-Egyptian Oil Crisis. |
| 1952 | Revolution in Egypt ending the monarchy. |
| 1953 | Coup d'état in Iran. |
| | Qibya Massacre. |
| 1955 | Creation of the Central Treaty Organization (Baghdad Pact). |
| 1955 | Egyptian-Soviet arms deal. |
| 1956 | Kafr Qasim Massacre. |
| | Suez Crisis. |
| | Sinai Campaign. |
| 1956–1967 | Strait of Tiran Crisis. |
| 1958 | U.S. intervention in Lebanon. |
| 1958–1961 | United Arab Republic of Egypt and Syria. |
| 1962–1970 | Yemen Civil War. |
| 1962–1976 | Dhofar (Dhofur) Rebellion. |
| 1963 | Coup d'état in Iraq. |
| 1963–1967 | Aden Emergency. |
| 1966 | Samu Raid. |
| 1967 | Six-Day War. |
| | Khartoum Resolution. |
| 1968 | Military coup in Iraq. |
| | Battle of Karameh. |
| 1969–1970 | War of Attrition. |
| 1970–1971 | Black September. |
| 1972–1973 | Samita Incident. |
| 1973 | Yom Kippur War (Ramadan War). |
| 1973–1974 | Arab oil embargo. |
| 1974 | Turkish invasion of Cyprus. |
| | Rabat Summit. |
| | Sinai I and Sinai II Agreements. |
| 1975–1990 | Lebanese Civil War. |
| 1977 | Libyan-Egyptian War. |

| | |
|---|---|
| 1978 | Camp David Accords. |
| | Israeli invasion of Lebanon (Operation LITANI). |
| 1978–1979 | Iranian Islamic Revolution. |
| 1979 | Egypt-Israel Peace Treaty. |
| | Yemenite War. |
| 1979–1981 | Iran Hostage Crisis. |
| 1980–1988 | Iran-Iraq War. |
| 1981 | Osiraq Raid. |
| 1982 | Lebanon-Israeli War. |
| | Hama Massacre. |
| | Sabra and Shatila Massacre. |
| 1982–1984 | U.S. intervention in Lebanon. |
| 1986 | South Yemen Civil War. |
| 1987 | Operation NIMBLE ARCHER. |
| | USS *Stark* incident. |
| 1987–1988 | Al-Anfal Campaign. |
| 1987–1993 | First Palestinian Intifada. |
| 1988 | Downing of Iran Air Flight 655. |
| 1989 | Taif Accords. |
| 1990 | Iraqi invasion and occupation of Kuwait. |
| 1991 | The Persian Gulf War and liberation of Kuwait. |
| | Madrid Conference. |
| 1992 | Yemen hotel bombings. |
| 1992–2003 | Operation SOUTHERN WATCH. |
| 1993 | Oslo Accords. |
| 1994 | Yemen Civil War. |
| | Israel-Jordan Peace Treaty. |
| 1996 | Khobar Towers bombing. |
| 1997–2003 | Operation NORTHERN WATCH. |
| 1998 | Wye River Agreement. |
| 2000–2004 | Second Palestinian Intifada (Al-Aqsa Intifada). |
| 2001 | September 11 attacks on the United States. |
| 2002 | Battle of Jenin. |
| 2003 | Geneva Accord. |
| | Battle of Samawah. |
| 2003–2011 | Iraq War. |
| 2005 | Israeli disengagement from the Gaza Strip. |
| | Battle of Haditha. |
| | Operation STEEL CURTAIN. |
| 2006 | Gaza War. |
| | Israeli operations against Lebanon. |
| 2007 | Battles of Haifa Street and Najaf. |
| | Siege of Nahr Al Barad Refugee Camp. |
| 2008 | Battle of Sadr City. |
| 2008–2009 | Gaza War. |
| 2010–2012 | Arab Spring. |
| 2011 | Egyptian Revolution. |
| 2011–present | Syrian Civil War. |
| 2012 | Gaza War. |
| 2012–2016 | Battle for Aleppo. |
| 2014 | Gaza War. |
| 2014–2015 | Battle of Kobanî. |
| 2014–present | Operation INHERENT RESOLVE. |
| 2015 | Iran Nuclear Deal. |
| 2015–present | Yemen Civil War. |
| 2016 | Third Battle of Fallujah. |
| 2016–2017 | Battle of Mosul. |
| | Battle of Raqqa. |
| 2017 | ISIS is defeated in Iraq. |
| | ISIS is defeated in Syria. |
| | Kurdish Independence Declaration, Iraq. |
| 2018 | The United States exits the Iran Nuclear Deal. |
| | Syrian government forces take Eastern Ghouta. |
| | U.S.-Iranian relations plummet. |
| | The U.S. government reimposes sanctions on Iran. |
| | U.S.-Turkish relations plummet. |

# Glossary

| | |
|---|---|
| **Akinci** | Turkmen volunteers in the Ottoman Army who received in return most of the disposal booty from campaigns. They were usually light cavalry engaged in raiding. |
| **Al-Rum** | Arabic term for the Byzantine Empire. |
| **amir** | Arabic term for prince or military commander. |
| ***atabeg*** (also ***atabek, atabey***) | A hereditary title of nobility of Iranian and Turkic origin, indicating a governor of a nation or province subordinate to a monarch and charged with raising the crown prince. |
| **ayatollah** | Honorific title for most important Shiite religious authorities. |
| **Bedouins** | Nomadic tribes originally in the Arabian desert, but following the expansion of Islam they are found across North Africa and southern Iraq. |
| **bey** | A Turkic term for a chief or ruler in Central Asia and in the early and later Ottoman Empire. The term also refers to a general or military commander. |
| **Beylik** | An Ottoman province under the jurisdiction of a bey. |
| **caliph** | "Successor of the Prophet of God." The title used by the Muslim rulers to indicate their connection with Mohammad's leadership of Muslims. |
| **caliphate** | The jurisdiction of a caliph. |
| **derya bey** | Commanders in the Ottoman Navy. |
| **emir** | Ruler in Arabia, the governor of a province, and later a member of the ruling Al Saud house. |
| **fatwa** | A legal opinion issued by a mufti or other recognized Islamic scholar. |
| *ghazi* | A Muslim fighter against non-Muslims. |
| **Ilkhans** | Mongol rulers of Iran. |
| **imam** | In Sunni tradition, a legal scholar or prayer leader in a mosque; in certain cases, it may be the head of a Muslim state. Among Shia Muslims it refers to the infallible guide to the community, descended from the Prophet Mohammad. |
| **intifada** | "Shaking off." The Palestinian uprisings against Israeli rule of the West Bank and Gaza. |
| **jihad** | Muslim term for the inner struggle for purification; also holy war. |
| **kapitan pasha** | Ottoman term for admiral. |
| **Levant** | Geographical term referring to a large area in the eastern Mediterranean region. It originates from the Italian *levante,* meaning "rising" from the rising of the sun in the east. In its widest historical sense, the Levant included all of the eastern |

| | | | |
|---|---|---|---|
| | Mediterranean with its islands, from Greece to Cyrenaica. Eventually the term was restricted to the Muslim countries of Syria-Palestine and Egypt. | *sabkha* | Marsh. |
| | | Salafiyyah | A philosophical and political movement that began in 19th-century Egypt and sought to reconcile Islam with secular materialism and modernization. |
| **Levant States** | Term for the French mandate over Syria and Lebanon following World War I. | | |
| **mufti** | Islamic scholar who is empowered to give authoritative rulings on religious matters. | **Saracens** | An indiscriminate term for Muslims during the era of the Christian crusades in the Holy Land. |
| **Outremer** | French for "overseas" and a general name applied to the Christian crusader states of the county of Edessa, the principality of Antioch, the county of Tripoli, and the Kingdom of Jerusalem. During the Renaissance, the term often equated to the area of the Levant. | **shah** | Term of the kings of Iran. |
| | | *shahanshah* | "King of kings." One of the titles employed by the kings of Iran. |
| | | *shamal* | Wind from the north. |
| | | **sharif** | Arabic title restricted to those of the Hashemite clan and referring to the direct descendants of the Prophet Mohammad's uncle al-Abbas and Abi Talib and the latter's son Ali by Mohammad's daughter Fatima. |
| **pasha (*pasa*)** | A nonhereditary official title conferred upon wealthy landowners, government administrators, and senior military officers in the Ottoman Empire (1299–1918). | | |
| **Porte (Sublime Porte)** | Term used by Western diplomats for the government of the Ottoman Empire. The term has its origins in the high gate (*porte* in French) to the court of the grand vizier in Topkap Palace in Istanbul, where royal decrees were announced and diplomats were received. | **Sipahi** | Arabic cavalry. |
| | | **Sultan** | According to the Quran, this denotes Muslim religious or political authority but in effect denoted political or governmental power. |

SPENCER C. TUCKER

# Selective Bibliography

Abrahamian, Ervand. *A History of Modern Iran.* 2nd ed. New York: Cambridge University Press, 2018.

Aburish, Said K. *Arafat: From Defender to Dictator.* New York: Bloomsbury, 1998.

Adas, Michael, ed. *Islamic and European Expansion: The Forging of a Global Order.* Philadelphia: Temple University Press, 1993.

Adnan, Abu-Odeh. *Jordanians, Palestinians, and the Hashemite Kingdom in the Middle East Peace Process.* Washington, DC: United States Institute of Peace Press, 1999.

Agresto, John. *Mugged by Reality: The Liberation of Iraq and the Failure of Good Intentions.* New York: Encounter Books, 2007.

Ajami, Fouad. *The Arab Predicament.* 2nd ed. New York: Cambridge University Press, 1992.

Ajami, Fouad. *The Foreigner's Gift: The Americans, the Arabs, and the Iraqis in Iraq.* New York: Free Press, 2008.

Allawi, Ali A. *The Occupation of Iraq: Winning the War, Losing the Peace.* New Haven, CT: Yale University Press, 2007.

Amos, Deborah. *Lines in the Sand: Desert Storm and the Remaking of the Arab World.* New York: Simon and Schuster, 1992.

Anderson, Jon Lee. *The Fall of Baghdad.* New York: Penguin, 2004.

Armajani, Yahya and Thomas Ricks. *Middle East Past and Present.* Englewood Cliffs, NJ: Prentice Hall, 1986.

Armstrong, Karen. *Islam: A Short History.* New York: Modern Library, 2002.

Asbridge, Thomas. *The Crusades: The Authoritative History of the War for the Holy Land.* New York: Ecco, 2010.

Asbridge, Thomas. *The First Crusade: A New History; The Roots of Conflict between Christianity and Islam.* New York: Oxford University Press, 2005.

Asher, Jerry. *Duel for the Golan: The 100 Hour Battle That Saved Israel.* New York: William Morrow, 1987.

Atkinson, Rick. *Crusade: The Untold Story of the Gulf War.* New York: Houghton Mifflin, 1993.

Atkinson, Rick. *In the Company of Soldiers: A Chronicle of Combat.* New York: Henry Holt, 2004.

Avi-Yonah, Michael. *The Jews of Palestine: A Political History of Palestine from the Bar Kokhba War to the Arab Conquest.* New York: Schocken, 1984.

Barkey, Henri J., and Graham E. Fuller. *Turkey's Kurdish Question.* Lanham, MD: Rowman and Littlefield, 1998.

Bin, Alberto, Richard Hill, and Archer Jones. *Desert Storm: A Forgotten War.* Westport, CT: Praeger, 1998.

Bosworth, Albert B. *Alexander and the East: The Tragedy of Triumph.* Oxford: Oxford University Press, 2001.

Bourque, Stephen A. *Jayhawk! The VII Corps in the Persian Gulf War.* Washington, DC: U.S. Army Center of Military History, 2002.

Bowden, Mark. *Guests of the Ayatollah: The First Battle in America's War with Militant Islam.* New York: Atlantic Monthly, 2007.

Bowen, Jeremy. *Six Days: How the 1967 War Shaped the Middle East.* New York: Thomas Dunne Books, 2005.

Bowie, Robert. *Suez 1956: International Crisis and the Rule of Law.* New York: Oxford University Press, 1974.

Boyne, Walter J. *Operation Iraqi Freedom: What Went Right, What went Wrong, and Why.* New York: Forge, 2003.

Brands, H. W. *Into the Labyrinth: The United States and the Middle East, 1945–1993.* New York: McGraw-Hill, 1994.

Bremer, L. Paul, III. *My Year in Iraq: The Struggle to Build a Future of Hope.* New York: Simon and Schuster, 2006.

Browning, Robert. *The Byzantine Empire.* London: Weidenfeld and Nicolson, 1980.

Bryce, Trevor. *The Routledge Handbook of the Peoples and Places of Ancient Western Asia: The Near East from the Early Bronze Age to the Fall of the Persian Empire.* London: Routledge, 2009.

Bullard, Reader. *Britain and the Middle East: From Earliest Times to 1963.* London: Hutchinson University Library, 1964.

Bulloch, John, and Harvey Morris. *Saddam's War: The Origins of the Kuwait Conflict and the International Response.* London: Faber and Faber, 1991.

Bush, George, and Brent Scowcroft. *A World Transformed.* New York: Knopf, 1998.

Cassidy, Robert. *Counterinsurgency and the Global War on Terror: Military Culture and Irregular War.* Palo Alto, CA: Stanford University Press, 2008.

Cavaleri, David. *Easier Said Than Done: Making the Transition between Combat Operations and Stability Operations.* Ft. Leavenworth, KS: Combat Studies Institute Press, 2005.

Charpin, Dominique. *Hammurabi of Babylon.* London: I. B. Tauris, 2012.

Chehab, Zaki. *Iraq Ablaze: Inside the insurgency.* New York: I. B. Tauris, 2006.

Claire, Rodger William. *Raid on the Sun: Inside Israel's Secret Campaign That Denied Saddam the Bomb.* New York: Broadway Books, 2004.

Clark, Bruce. *Twice a Stranger: The Mass Expulsions That Forged Modern Greece and Turkey.* Cambridge, MA: Harvard University Press, 2006.

Cleveland, William, and Martin P. Bunton. *A History of the Modern Middle East.* 6th ed. Boulder, CO: Westview, 2017.

Cockburn, Patrick. *The Occupation: War and Resistance in Iraq.* New York: Verso, 2007.

Cohen, Raymond. *Culture and Conflict in Egyptian-Israel Relations: A Dialogue of the Deaf.* Bloomfield: Indiana University Press, 1990.

Cohen, Roger, and Claudio Gatti. *In the Eye of the Storm: The Life of General H. Norman Schwarzkopf.* New York: Farrar, Straus & Giroux, 1991.

Coogan, Michael D., ed. *The Oxford History of the Biblical World.* New York: Oxford University Press, 2001.

Cook, David. *Understanding Jihad.* Berkeley: University of California Press, 2005.

Cook, J. M. *The Persian Empire.* London: Dent, 1983.

Cooley, John K. *Payback: America's Long War in the Middle East.* Washington, DC: Brassey's, 1991.

Cordesman, Anthony H. *The Iraq War: Strategy, Tactics, and Military Lessons.* Washington, DC: CSIS, 2003.

Curtis, John, ed. *Forgotten Empire: The World of Ancient Persia.* Berkeley: University of California Press, 2005.

Darraj, Susan Muaddi. *Bashar Al-Assad.* New York: Chelsea House, 2005.

Darraj, Susan Muaddi. *Hosni Mubarak.* New York: Chelsea House, 2007.

Dawood, N. J., trans. *The Koran.* New York: Penguin, 1999.

Dayan. Moshe. *Moshe Dayan: Story of My Life.* New York: William Morrow, 1976.

Diamond, Larry. *Squandered Victory: The American Occupation and the Bungled Effort to Bring Democracy to Iraq.* New York: Times Books, 2005.

Dickinson, William. *Defense for a New Era: Lessons of the Gulf War.* Washington, DC: Brassey's, 1992.

Dreyfus, Robert. *Devil's Game: How the United States Helped Unleash Fundamentalist Islam.* New York: Metropolitan Books, 2005.

Drogin, Bob. *Curveball: Spies, Lies, and the Con Man Who Caused a War.* New York: Random House, 2007.

Dudley, William, ed. *The Attack on America, September 11, 2001.* San Diego: Greenhaven, 2002.

Edwards, I. E. S., C. J. Gadd, N. G. L. Hammond, et al. *The Cambridge Ancient History.* 14 vols. in 19 pts. Cambridge: Cambridge University Press, 1970–2005.

Esposito, John L. *The Islamic Threat: Myth or Reality?* 3rd ed. New York: Oxford University Press, 1999.

Feldman, Noah. *The Fall and Rise of the Islamic State.* Rev. ed. Princeton, NJ: Princeton University Press, 2012.

Findley, Carter Vaughan. *The Turks in World History.* New York: Oxford University Press, 2005.

Fisher, Sydney N., and William Ochsenwald. *The Middle East: A History.* 2 vols. 7th ed. New York: McGraw-Hill, 2010.

Fisk, Robert. *The Great War for Civilization: The Conquest of the Middle East.* New York: Knopf, 2005.

Foster, Benjamin R. *The Age of Akkad: Inventing Empire in Ancient Mesopotamia.* London: Routledge, 2016.

Franks, Tommy, with Malcolm McConnell. *American Soldier.* New York: Regan Books, 2004.

Fregosi, Paul. *Jihad in the West: Muslim Conquests from the 7th to the 21st Centuries.* Amherst, NY: Prometheus, 1998.

Friedman, Norman. *Desert Victory: The War for Kuwait.* Annapolis, MD: Naval Institute Press, 1991.

Friedman, Thomas L. *From Beirut to Jerusalem.* New York: Random House, 1990.

Fromkin, David. *A Peace to End All Peace: The Fall of the Ottoman Empire and the Creation of the Modern Middle East.* New York: Avon Books, 1989.

Fuller, Graham E. *The New Turkish Republic: Turkey as a Pivotal State in the Muslim World.* Washington, DC: U.S. Institute of Peace, 2007.

Galbraith, Peter. *The End of Iraq: How American Incompetence Created a War without End.* New York: Simon & Schuster, 2006.

Gale, General Sir Richard. *Great Battles of Biblical History.* New York: John Day, 1970.

Gerges, Fawaz A. *The Far Enemy: Why Jihad Went Global.* New York: Cambridge University Press, 2005.

Glubb, John Bagot. *Glubb Pasha: A Soldier with the Arabs.* London: Hodder and Stoughton, 1957.

Glubb, John Bagot. *The Great Arab Conquests.* London: Quarter Books, 1963.

Goldschmidt, Arthur, Jr., and Ibrahim Al-Marashi. *A Concise History of the Middle East.* 12th ed. New York: Routledge, 2018.

Gordon, Matthew. *Hafez Al-Assad.* New York: Chelsea House, 1989.

Gordon, Michael R., and Bernard R. Trainor. *Cobra II: The Inside Story of the Invasion and Occupation of Iraq.* New York: Pantheon Books, 2006.

Gordon, Michael R., and Bernard R. Trainor. *The Generals' War: The Inside Story of the Conflict in the Gulf.* Boston: Little, Brown, 1995.

Green, Peter. *Alexander of Macedon, 356–323 B.C.: A Historical Biography.* Berkeley: University of California Press, 1991.

Gunaratna, Rohan. *Inside Al Qaeda: Global Network of Terror.* New York: Columbia University Press, 2002.

Gunning, Jeroen. *Hamas in Politics: Democracy, Religion, and Violence.* New York: Columbia University Press, 2008.

Haass, Richard. *War of Necessity, War of Choice: A Memoir of Two Iraq Wars.* New York: Simon and Schuster, 2009.

Hackett, John. *Warfare in the Ancient World.* New York: Facts on File, 1989.

Haddad, George M. *Revolutions and Military Rule in the Middle East.* 3 vols. New York: Robert Speller & Sons, 1965–1973.

Hafez, Mohammed. *Suicide Bombers in Iraq: The Strategy and Ideology of Martyrdom.* Washington, DC: United States Institute of Peace Press, 2007.

Hajjar, Sami G. *Hezbollah: Terrorism, National Liberation, or Menace?* Carlisle Barracks, PA: Strategic Studies Institute, 2002.

Hall, John G., and Adam Wong. *Palestinian Authority: Creation of the Modern Middle East.* 2nd ed. Langhorne, PA: Chelsea House, 2008.

Hallion, Richard P. *Storm over Iraq: Air Power and the Gulf War.* Washington, DC: Smithsonian Institution, 1992.

Harris, Jonathan. *Byzantium and the Crusades.* 2nd ed. London: Bloomsbury, 2014.

Hatina, Meir. *Islam and Salvation in Palestine: The Islamic Jihad Movement.* Syracuse, NY: Syracuse University Press, 2001.

Herzog, Chaim. *The Arab-Israeli Wars.* New York: Random House, 1982.

Herzog, Chaim. *The War of Atonement: The Inside Story of the Yom Kippur War.* Philadelphia: Casemate, 2009.

Herzog, Chaim, and Mordechai Gichon. *Battles of the Bible.* 2nd ed. New York: Barnes and Noble, 2006.

Hindley, Geoffrey. *The Crusades: Islam and Christianity in the Struggle for World Supremacy.* New York: Carroll and Graf, 2004.

Hindley, Geoffrey. *Saladin: Hero of Islam.* Barnsley, South Yorkshire, UK: Pen and Sword Military, 2007.

Hitti, Philip K. *History of the Arabs: From the Earliest Times to the Present.* 10th ed. New York: Palgrave Macmillan, 2002.

Hourani, Albert, and Malise Ruthven. *A History of the Arab Peoples.* 2nd ed. Cambridge, MA: Belknap, 2010.

Isikoff, Michael, and David Corn. *Hubris: The Inside Story of Spin, Scandal, and the Selling of the Iraq War.* New York: Crown Publishers, 2006.

Jaber, Hala. *Hezbollah: Born with a Vengeance.* New York: Columbia University Press, 1997.

Karsh, Efraim. *The Iran-Iraq War, 1980–1988.* Oxford, UK: Osprey, 2002.

Karsh, Efraim. *Islamic Imperialism: A History.* 2nd ed. New Haven, CT: Yale University Press, 2013.

Karsh, Efraim, and Inari Karsh. *Empires of the Sand: The Struggle for Mastery of the Middle East, 1789–1923.* Cambridge, MA: Harvard University Press, 1999.

Karsh, Efraim, and Inari Rautsi. *Saddam Hussein: A Political Biography.* New York: Grove/Atlantic, 2002.

Katouzian, Homa. *The Persians: Ancient, Medieval, and Modern Iran.* New Haven, CT: Yale University Press, 2010.

Kiernan, Thomas. *Arafat: The Man and the Myth.* New York: Norton, 1976.

Kinzer, Stephen. *All the Shah's Men: An American Coup and the Roots of the Middle Eastern Terror.* 2nd ed. Hoboken, NJ: Wiley, 2008.

Kostiner, Joseph. *The Making of Saudi Arabia, 1916–1936.* New York: Oxford University Press, 1993.

Kramer, S. Noah. *The Sumerians: Their History, Culture and Character.* Chicago: University of Chicago Press, 2008.

Kriwaczek, Paul. *Babylon: Mesopotamia and the Birth of Civilization.* New York: St. Martin's Griffin, 2012.

Kurzman, Dan. *Ben-Gurion: Prophet of Fire.* New York: Simon and Schuster, 1983.

Laqueur, Walter. *A History of Zionism.* New York: Holt, Rinehart & Winston, 1972.

Lenczowski, George. *The Middle East in World Affairs.* 4th ed. Ithaca, NY: Cornell University Press, 1980.

Lesser Ian O. *Oil, the Persian Gulf, and Grand Strategy: Contemporary Issues in Historical Perspective.* Santa Monica, CA: Rand, 1991.

Lewis, Bernard. *Cultures in Conflict: Christians, Muslims, and Jews in the Age of Discovery.* New York: Oxford University Press, 1995.

Lewis, Bernard. *Islam and the West.* New York: Oxford University Press, 1993.

Lewis, Bernard. *The Middle East: A Brief History of the Last 2,000 Years.* New York: Scribner, 1995.

Lilie, Ralph-Johannes. *Byzantium and the Crusader States (1096–1204).* Oxford, UK: Clarendon, 1993.

Lorch, Netanel. *The Edge of the Sword: Israel's War of Independence, 1947–1949.* New York: Putnam, 1961.

Mango, Andrew. *Atatürk: The Founder of Modern Turkey.* Woodstock, NY: Overlook, 2000.

Mango, Cyril, ed. *The Oxford History of Byzantium.* New York: Oxford University Press, 2002.

Mansfield, Peter. *The Arab World: A Comprehensive History.* New York: Thomas Crowell, 1976.

Mansfield, Peter, and Nicolas Pelham. *A History of the Middle East.* 4th ed. New York: Penguin, 2013.

Mayer, Hans Eberhard. *The Crusades.* 2nd ed. Oxford: Oxford University Press, 1988.

Murray, Williamson, and Robert H. Scales Jr. *The Iraq War.* Cambridge, MA: Belknap Press/Harvard University, 2003.

Murray, Williamson, and Kevin M. Woods. *The Iran-Iraq War: A Military and Strategic History.* Cambridge: Cambridge University Press, 2014.

Nakash, Yitzhak. *Reaching for Power: The Shi'a in the Modern Arab World.* Princeton, NJ: Princeton University Press, 2006.

Nardo, Don. *The Assyrian Empire.* Farmington Hills, MI: Greenhaven, 1998.

Norton, Augustus Richard. *Hezbollah: A Short History.* 2nd ed. Princeton, NJ: Princeton University Press, 2014.

Nusse, Andrea. *Muslim Palestine: The Ideology of Hamas.* London: Routledge, 1999.

O'Ballance, Edgar. *Civil War in Lebanon, 1975–92.* New York: Palgrave Macmillan, 2002.

O'Ballance, Edgar. *The Kurdish Struggle, 1920–94.* New York: Palgrave Macmillan, 1996.

O'Ballance, Edgar. *No Victor, No Vanquished: The Yom Kippur War.* San Rafael, CA: Presidio, 1978.

O'Ballance, Edgar. *War in the Yemen.* Hamden, CT: Archon Books, 1971.

Oppenheim, A. Leo. *Ancient Mesopotamia: Portrait of a Dead Civilization.* Chicago: University of Chicago Press, 2013.

Oren, Michael B. *Power, Faith, and Fantasy: America in the Middle East, 1776 to the Present.* New York: Norton, 2007.

Ostrogorsky, Georg. *History of the Byzantine State.* Oxford, UK: Blackwell, 1984.

Ovendale, Ritchie. *The Longman Companion to the Middle East since 1914.* 2nd ed. London: Longman, 1998.

Palmer, Michael A. *Guardians of the Gulf: A History of America's Expanding Role in the Persian Gulf, 1833–1992.* New York: Free Press, 1992.

Pappe, Ilan. *A History of Modern Palestine: One Land, Two Peoples.* 2nd ed. Cambridge: Cambridge University Press, 2006.

Perlmutter, Amos. *The Life and Times of Menachem Begin.* New York: Doubleday, 1987.

Peters, F. E. *Muhammad and the Origins of Islam.* Albany, NY: SUNY Press, 1994.

Polk, William R. *Understanding Iraq: The Whole Sweep of Iraqi History, from Genghis Khan's Mongols to the Ottoman Turks to the British Mandate to the American Occupation.* New York: HarperCollins, 2005.

Pollack, Kenneth M. *Arabs at War: Military Effectiveness, 1948–1991.* Lincoln: University of Nebraska Press, 2002.

Rabil, Robert G. *Embattled Neighbors: Syria, Israel and Lebanon.* Boulder, CO: Lynne Rienner, 2003.

Rabin, Yitzhak. *The Rabin Memoirs.* Boston: Little, Brown, 1979.

Rabinovitch, Itamar. *The Road Not Taken: Early Arab-Israeli Negotiations.* New York: Oxford University Press, 1991.

Rhoads, Murphey. *Ottoman Warfare, 1500–1700.* New Brunswick, NJ: Rutgers University Press, 1999.

Riley-Smith, Jonathan, ed. *The Oxford History of the Crusades.* New York: Oxford University Press, 2002.

Robinson, Linda. *Tell Me How This Ends: General David Petraeus and the Search for a Way Out of Iraq.* New York: PublicAffairs, 2007.

Ross, Dennis. *The Missing Peace: The Inside Story of the Fight for Middle East Peace.* New York: Farrar, Straus & Giroux, 2004.

Roth, S. J. *The Impact of the Six-Day War: A Twenty-Year Assessment.* Basingstoke, UK: Macmillan in association with the Institute of Jewish Affairs, 1988.

Rougier, Bernard. *Everyday Jihad: The Rise of Militant Islam among Palestinians in Lebanon.* Cambridge, MA: Harvard University Press, 2007.

Roux, Georges. *Ancient Iraq.* 3rd ed. London: Penguin, 1992.

Sachar, Howard. *The Emergence of the Middle East, 1914–1924.* London: Allen Lane, 1970.

Sachar, Howard. *A History of Israel: From The Rise of Zionism to Our Time.* 3rd ed. New York: Knopf, 2007.

Saggs, H. W. F. *The Greatness That Was Babylon: A Survey of the Ancient Civilization of the Tigris-Euphrates Valley.* London: Sidgwick & Jackson, 1988.

Scales, Robert H., Jr. *Certain Victory: The U.S. Army in the Gulf War.* Washington, DC: Office of the Chief of Staff, U.S. Army, 1993.

Segev, Tom. *1967: Israel, the War, and the Year That Transformed the Middle East.* New York: Metropolitan Books, 2007.

Sharon, Ariel, with David Chanoff. *Warrior: The Autobiography of Ariel Sharon.* New York: Simon and Schuster, 1989.

Shaw, Ian, ed. *The Oxford History of Ancient Egypt.* Oxford: Oxford University Press, 2003.

Shimoni, Yaacov. *Biographical Dictionary of the Middle East.* New York: Facts on File, 1991.

Smith, Dan. *The Penguin State of the Middle East: An Atlas of Conflict and Resolution.* 3rd ed. Berkeley: University of California Press, 2015.

Stephens, Robert. *Nasser: A Political Biography.* New York: Simon and Schuster, 1971.

Sultan, Khaled bin, with Patrick Seale. *Desert Warrior: A Personal View of the Gulf War by the Joint Forces Commander.* New York: HarperCollins, 1995.

Sykes, Percy M. *History of Persia.* New York: Routledge, 2003.

Thomas, Hugh. *Suez.* New York: Harper & Row, 1967.

Tyldesley, Joyce A. *Ramesses: Egypt's Greatest Pharaoh.* Harmondsworth, UK: Penguin, 2001.

Van de Mieroop, Marc. *A History of the Ancient Near East: Ca. 3000–323 BC.* Chichester, West Sussex, UK: Wiley, 2015.

Vatikiotis, P. J. *The History of Egypt: From Muhammad Ali to Mubarak.* 4th ed. Baltimore: Johns Hopkins University Press, 1991.

Viorst, Milton. *Storm from the East: The Struggle between the Arab World and the Christian West.* New York: Modern Library, 2006.

Warraq, Ibn, ed. *The Quest for the Historical Muhammad.* Amherst, NY: Prometheus, 2000.

Weinberger, Naomi. *Syrian Intervention in Lebanon.* New York: Oxford University Press, 1986.

Westwood, J. N. *The History of the Middle East Wars.* London: Bison Books, 1991.

Willet, Edward C. *The Iran-Iraq War.* New York: Rosen Publishing Group, 2004.

Wise, Terrence. *Ancient Armies of the Middle East.* Oxford, UK: Osprey, 1984.

Yapp, M. E. *The Near East since the First World War: A History to 1995.* 2nd ed. London: Routledge, 2016.

# Editors and Contributors

**Volume Editor**
Dr. Spencer C. Tucker
Senior Fellow
Military History, ABC-CLIO, LLC

**Editor, Documents Volume**
Dr. Priscilla Roberts
Associate Professor of Business
Codirector, Asia-Pacific Business
  Research Centre
City University of Macau
Taipa, Macao Special Administrative
  Region of China

**Contributors**
Dr. Rebecca Adelman
Assistant Professor
University of Maryland–Baltimore
  County

Dr. Adam Ali
Lecturer
University of Toronto

Dr. Reuven Amitai
Faculty of Humanities
The Hebrew University of Jerusalem
Israel

Dr. Elena Andreeva
Department of History
Virginia Military Institute

Christopher Paul Anzalone
Independent Scholar

James Arnold
Independent Scholar

Ralph Martin Baker
Independent Scholar

Dr. Michael B. Barrett
Department of History
The Citadel

Colin F. Baxter
Professor
Department of History
East Tennessee State University

Michael K. Beauchamp
Texas A&M University

Walter F. Bell
Information Services Librarian
Aurora University

Dr. Bestami S. Bilgiç
Canakkale Onsekiz Mart University &
  Turkish Historical Society
Turkey

Dr. Tuba Ünlü Bilgiç
Associate Professor
Middle East Technical University
Turkey

Dr. Jessalynn Bird
Independent Scholar

Amy Hackney Blackwell
Independent Scholar

Dr. Uta-Renate Blumenthal
Professor
Department of History
The Catholic University of America

Dr. Stephen A. Bourque
Professor
U.S. Army Command and General Staff
  College

Walter J. Boyne
Independent Scholar

# Editors and Contributors

Dr. Michael Brett
University of London
United Kingdom

Jessica Britt
Independent Scholar

Dr. Stefan Brooks
Assistant Professor of Political Science
Lindsey Wilson College

Brad Brown
Independent Scholar

Dr. Robert M. Brown
Assistant Professor
U.S. Army Command & General Staff
    College

Dr. Dino E. Buenviaje
Visiting Assistant Professor
Riverside Community College

Dr. Jochen Burgtorf
Professor of Medieval World History
California State University, Fullerton

Tamar Burris
Independent Scholar

Dr. James M. Burns
Professor and Department Chair
Clemson University

Dr. Paul J. Burton
Lecturer
Australian National University

Russell Buzby
Executive Officer
Australian National University

Dr. Stanley D. M. Carpenter
Professor of Strategy and Policy
United States Naval War College

Dr. Sergio Catignani
Senior Lecturer in Security and Strategic
    Studies
Strategy and Security Institute
University of Exeter

Dr. Mark W. Chavalas
Professor of Ancient History
University of Wisconsin–La Crosse

Elliot Paul Chodoff
University of Haifa
Israel

Dr. Niall Christie
History Coordinator
Langara College
Vancouver, Canada

Dr. Paul H. Collier
Independent Scholar

Dr. David Commins
Professor of History
Dickinson College

Dr. Sherwood Cordier
Emeritus Professor of History
University of Western Michigan

Alex Correll
Virginia Military Institute

Dr. Nicholas J. Cull
Professor
University of Southern California

John R. Dabrowski
Independent Scholar

Dr. Farhad Daftary
Head of the Department of Academic
    Research and Publications
The Institute of Ismaili Studies
United Kingdom

Dr. Caillan Davenport
Lecturer in Roman History
Macquarie University
Australia

Abigail Dawson
Subject Coordinator for Classical Studies
Taylors College
New Zealand

Dr. Benedict Edward Dedominicis
Associate Professor of Political Science
American University in Bulgaria

Dr. Benjamin DeLee
Assistant Professor
State University of New York, Cortland

Marcel A. Derosier
Independent Scholar

Lieutenant Colonel Louis A. DiMarco
    (Retired)
Associate Professor
U.S. Army Command and Staff College

Dr. Paul William Doerr
Associate Professor
Acadia University
Canada

Michael Doidge
Independent Scholar

Dr. Michael E. Donoghue
Assistant Professor
Marquette University

Dr. Timothy Doran
Assistant Professor of History
California State University, Los Angeles

Dr. Charlotte M. R. Dunn
Professional Practice Fellow
University of Otago
New Zealand

John P. Dunn
Professor of History
Valdosta State University

Colonel Donald Redmond Dunne
U.S. Army

Dr. Susan B. Edgington
Teaching and Research Fellow
University of London

Dr. Richard M. Edwards
Senior Lecturer
University of Wisconsin Colleges

Editors and Contributors 1399

Dr. Taef El-Azhari
Qatar University, Doha
Qatar

Mary J. Elias
ITT Technical Institute

Dr. Michael R. Evans
Independent Scholar

Dr. Chuck Fahrer
Professor of Geography
Georgia College

Damien Fenton
Independent Scholar

Dr. Shawn Fisher
Assistant Professor
History and Social Sciences
Harding University

Dr. Kate Fleet
Director
Skilliter Centre for Ottoman Studies
University of Cambridge
United Kingdom

Dr. Jean Flori
Professor
Center of Higher Studies of Medieval
    Civilization of Poitiers
France

Major Benjamin D. Forest
Instructor
Air Command and Staff College
Maxwell Air Force Base, Alabama

William E. Fork
Independent Scholar

Dr. John France
Professor
University of Swansea
United Kingdom

Dr. Timothy L. Francis
Naval Historical Center (N09B)
Department of the Navy

Dr. Elun Gabriel
Associate Professor of History
St. Lawrence University

Dr. Richard A. Gabriel
Distinguished Professor
Department of History and War Studies
Royal Military College of Canada

Brent Geary
Independent Scholar

Dr. Ioannis Georganas
Academic Director and Lecturer
Hellenic International Studies in the Arts
Greece

Dr. Deborah Gerish
Associate Professor of History
Emporia State University

Dr. John Gillingham
Emeritus Professor of Medieval History
London School of Economics and Politi-
    cal Science

Dr. Linda Goldsmith
Guildford County School
United Kingdom

Dr. Aryeh Grabois
Professor
Department of History
University of Haifa
Israel

Ryan Hackney
Harvard Center for Hellenic Studies

Dr. Michael R. Hall
Professor of History
Armstrong Atlantic State University

Dr. Richard C. Hall
Professor of History
Georgia Southwestern State University

Dr. Bernard Hamilton
Professor
University of Nottingham

Neil Hamilton
Independent Scholar

Dr. Jonathan Harris
Professor
Royal Holloway
University of London

David Harthen
Independent Scholar

Dr. William P. Head
Historian/Chief, WR-ALC Office of History
U.S. Air Force

Mark Hebblewhite
Macquarie University
Australia

Dr. Benjamin Hendrickx
Professor and Lecturer
Department of Greek and Latin Studies
University of Johannesburg
South Africa

Dr. Carole Hillenbrand
Professor
Islamic and Middle Eastern Studies
University of Edinburgh
United Kingdom

Dr. Laura J. Hilton
Professor
Department of History
Muskingum College

Dr. Charles Francis Howlett
Associate Professor of Education
Molloy College

Dr. Timothy D. Hoyt
Professor of Strategy and Policy
U.S. Naval War College

Dr. Harry Raymond Hueston II
Professor of Criminal Justice
West Texas A&M University

Robert Irwin
Historian
University of London

Dr. Donna R. Jackson
Research Fellow
Wolfson College, Cambridge
United Kingdom

Dr. Peter Jackson
Professor of Medieval History
Keele University
United Kingdom

Dr. Janus Møller Jensen
Østfyns Museer, Nyborg Slot
Denmark

Jack Vahram Kalpakian
Associate Professor of International Studies
Al Akhawayn University
Morocco

Dr. Robert B. Kane
Adjunct Professor of History
Troy University

Dr. Sedat Cem Karadeli
Assistant Professor
Cankaya University
Turkey

Jonas Kauffeldt
Associate Professor of History
University of North Georgia

Dr. Katharine Keats-Rohan
Researcher
Linacre College
University of Oxford
United Kingdom

Dr. Douglas Kelly
Department of Ancient History
Macquarie University
Australia

Dr. Gary Lee Kerley
Independent Scholar

Dr. Carool Kersten
Department of Theology & Religious Studies
King's College London

Chen Kertcher
School of History
Tel Aviv University

Dr. Mehrdad Kia
Professor of History
University of Montana

Dr. Deborah Kidwell
Command Historian
U.S. Army Command and General Staff College
Fort Leavenworth

Robert S. Kiely
Independent Scholar

Dr. Arne Kislenko
Associate Professor of History
Ryerson University
Canada

Rana Kobeissi
Katholieke Universiteit Leuven
Belgium

Stacy Kowtko
Professor
Spokane Community College

Matthew J. Krogman
Independent Scholar

Dr. John T. Kuehn
Professor of Military History
U.S. Army Command and General Staff College
Fort Leavenworth

Daniel W. Kuthy
Assistant Professor of Political Science
Brescia University

Dr. Peter Lacovara
Part-Time Instructor of Art History
Syracuse University

Dr. Andrew Lambert
Laughton Professor of Naval History
King's College London

Dr. Jeffrey LaMonica
Assistant Professor of History
Delaware County Community College

Dr. Tom Lansford
Professor of Political Science
University Southern Mississippi

Dr. John Lavalle
Professor of History
Western New Mexico University

Keith A. Leitich
Independent Scholar

Dr. LaVonne Jackson Leslie
Howard University

Dr. Lucian N. Leustean
Senior Lecturer
Aston University
United Kingdom

Dr. Yaacov Lev
Professor
Department of Middle Eastern Studies
Bar-Ilan University
Israel

Shawn Livingston
Public Service Librarian
University of Kentucky

Dr. Peter Londey
Lecturer
Centre for Classical Studies
Australian National University, Canberra

Javier Lopez
Independent Scholar

Dr. Graham A. Loud
Professor
University of Leeds
United Kingdom

Adam B. Lowther
Independent Scholar

Sebastian Lukasik
Assistant Professor
Department of Leadership and Strategy
U.S. Air Force Air Command and Staff College

Britton W. MacDonald
Independent Scholar

Dr. Christopher MacEvitt
Associate Professor of Religion
Dartmouth College

Dr. Thomas F. Madden
Professor of History
Director of the Center for Medieval and Renaissance Studies
Saint Louis University

Dr. Paul J. Magnarella
Director of Peace and Justice Studies
Warren Wilson College

Dr. Shamiran Mako
Assistant Professor of International Relations
Pardee School of Global Studies
Boston University

Robert W. Malick
Adjunct Professor of History
Harrisburg Area Community College

Julie Manning
Graduate Student
Georgetown University

Dr. Antoinette Mannion
Honorary Fellow
University of Reading
United Kingdom

J. David Markham
President
International Napoleonic Society

Dr. Bruce Marshall
Honorary Senior Research Fellow
Department of Ancient History
Macquarie University
Australia

Dr. Jerome V. Martin
Command Historian
U.S. Strategic Command

Dr. Timothy May
Professor
Department of History, Anthropology and Philosophy
University of North Georgia

Dr. Jack E. McCallum
Adjunct Professor of History
Texas Christian University

James McDonald
Independent Scholar

Dr. James B. McNabb
Professor
Department of Social Science
American University of Iraq, Sulaimani

Karen Mead
Independent Scholar

Abraham O. Mendoza
Independent Scholar

Larissa Mihalisko
Political Officer, Afghanistan
U.S. State Department

Dr. Alexander Mikaberidze
Sybil T. and J. Frederick Patten Professor of History
Louisiana State University (Shreveport)

Brett Mills
Virginia Military Institute

Dr. Kathryn H. Milne
Assistant Professor of Ancient History
Wofford College

Dr. Patit Mishra
Professor
Sambalpur University
India

Kirsty Anne Montgomery
Independent Scholar

Dennis Moran
Independent Scholar

Gregory Wayne Morgan
Independent Scholar

Dr. Rosemary Morris
Department of History
University of York
United Kingdom

Alec Mulinder
The National Archives
United Kingdom

Dr. B. Keith Murphy
Associate Dean
Fort Valley State University

Dr. Alan V. Murray
Senior Lecturer in Medieval Studies
University of Leeds
United Kingdom

Dr. Nicholas Murray
Associate Professor
U.S. Naval War College

Dr. Michael S. Neiberg
Chair of War Studies
Department of National Security and Strategy
United States Army War College

Dr. Helen J. Nicholson
Professor
Cardiff University
United Kingdom

Dr. David Nicolle
Honorary Research Fellow
Nottingham University
United Kingdom

Dr. Peter S. Noble
Professor
University of Reading
United Kingdom

Dr. Peter Overlack
Independent Scholar

Dr. Nikolaus Leo Overtoom
Visiting Lecturer of Ancient History
University of New Mexico

Dr. Johannes Pahlitzsch
Professor
Johannes Gutenberg–Universität Mainz
Germany

Dr. Aphrodite Papayianni
Lecturer
University of London
United Kingdom

Brian Parkinson
Independent Scholar

Jacques Paviot
Department of History
University Paris–Est Créteil
France

Dr. Sara E. Phang
Librarian
The Foundation Schools

Dr. Paul G. Pierpaoli Jr.
Fellow
Military History, ABC-CLIO, Inc.

Evan M. Pitt
University Associate
University of Tasmania

Dr. Markus Pöhlmann
Historian
German Armed Forces Military History Research Office
Potsdam, Germany

John Poirot
Tulane University

Dr. Denys Pringle
Professor of Archaeology
Cardiff University
United Kingdom

Dr. Harold E. Raugh Jr.
Command Historian
U.S. Army V Corps
Heidelberg, Germany

Dr. John David Rausch Jr.
Teel Bivins Professor of Political Science
West Texas A&M University

Dr. Jean Richard
Professor
University of Burgundy, Dijon
France

Annette Richardson
Independent Scholar

Christopher J. Richman
Virginia Military Institute

Adam Rinkleff
University of North Texas

Dr. Priscilla Roberts
Associate Professor of Business
Codirector, Asia-Pacific Business Research Centre
City University of Macau
Taipa, Macao Special Administrative Region of China

Russell G. Rodgers
Command Historian
U.S. Army

Dr. Margaret D. Sankey
Director of Research and Electives
Air War College
Maxwell Air Force Base

Dr. Claude R. Sasso
William Jewell College

Richard Sauers
Independent Scholar

Dr. Alexios G. C. Savvides
Professor of Medieval and Byzantine History
Peloponnesos University (Kalamata)
Greece

Anthony J. Schmaus
Virginia Military Institute

Nathan Schumer
Columbia University

Captain Carl Otis Schuster, MA
U.S. Navy (retired)

Larry Schweikart
Independent Scholar

Jeff Seiken
Independent Scholar

Simone Selva
Independent Scholar

Dr. Rami Y. Siklawi
University of Exeter
United Kingdom

Vadim Konstantine Simakhov
Virginia Military Institute

Dr. George L. Simpson Jr.
Professor of History
High Point University

Dr. Cathy Skidmore-Hess
Associate Professor
Georgia Southern University

Dr. Daniel Skidmore-Hess
Professor
Armstrong Atlantic State University

Dr. Daniel E. Spector
Independent Scholar

Dr. Iain Spence
School of Classics, History and Religion
University of New England
Australia

Dr. Paul J. Springer
Professor of Comparative Military Studies
Chair of the Department of Research and Publications
Air Command and Staff College
Maxwell Air Force Base

Dirk Steffen
Independent Scholar

Dr. Stephen K. Stein
Associate Professor
Department of History
University of Memphis

Dr. Christopher H. Sterling
Emeritus Professor of Media and Public Affairs
School of Media and Public Affairs
George Washington University

Dr. Gaius Stern
Professor of Classical History, Classics, and Archaeology
University of California, Berkeley

Dr. Nancy L. Stockdale
Associate Professor of History
University of North Texas

Dr. Douglas E. Streusand
Professor
Marine Corps Command & Staff College

Dr. Heather J. Tanner
Associate Professor of History
Ohio State University

Randy Jack Taylor
Librarian
Howard Payne University

Moshe Terdiman
Independent Scholar

Dr. W. Andrew Terrill
General Douglas MacArthur Research Professor of National Security Affairs
U.S. Army War College

Dr. Andrew Theobald
Queen's University

Dr. Haruo Tohmatsu
Associate Professor
Tamagawa University
Japan

John Tolan
Professor of History
Université de Nantes
France

Bradley P. Tolppanen
History Librarian
Eastern Illinois University

Dr. Spencer C. Tucker
Senior Fellow
Military History, ABC-CLIO, Inc.

Dr. Christopher Tuplin
Professor
University of Liverpool

Brian Ulrich
Assistant Professor of History
Shippensburg University

Dallace W. Unger Jr.
Independent Scholar

Dr. Mesut Uyar
Associate Professor
New South Wales, Canberra
Australia

Dr. Bruce Vandervort
Professor of History
Virginia Military Institute

Dr. Richard B. Verrone
Instructor
Texas Tech University

Dr. László Veszprémy
Director
Institute of Military History
Hungary

Dr. Thomas D. Veve
Professor of History
Dalton State College

Roderick Vosburgh
Independent Scholar

Dr. James Wald
Associate Professor of History
Hampshire College

Dr. Dierk Walter
Lecturer
Hamburger Institut für Sozialforschung
Germany

Dr. Andrew J. Waskey
Professor of Social Science
Dalton State College

Tim J. Watts
Subject Librarian
Kansas State University

Thomas J. Weiler
Associate Professor
Universities of Bonn and Trier
Germany

Dr. Kurt Werthmuller
Senior Analyst
CyberPoint International

Colin White
Independent Scholar

Dr. Wyndham E. Whynot
Assistant Professor of History
Livingstone College

Dr. James H. Willbanks
Director, Department of Military History
U.S. Army Command and General Staff College,
Fort Leavenworth

Dr. Harold Wise
Adjunct Professor of History
Elizabeth City State University

# Editors and Contributors

Dr. Graham Wrightson
Assistant Professor of History
South Dakota State University

Yuanyuan Ding
Independent Scholar

Dr. David T. Zabecki
Major General
Army of the United States, Retired

Dr. David Zierler
Historian
U.S. Department of State

Dr. Sherifa Zuhur
Visiting Professor of National Security Affairs
Regional Strategy and Planning Department
Strategic Studies Institute
U.S. Army War College

Dr. Stephen Zunes
Professor
University of San Francisco